New Era of Management

Eleventh Edition

New Era of Management

Eleventh Edition

Richard L. Daft

Vanderbilt University

SOUTH-WESTERN
CENGAGE Learning·

Australia • Brazil • Japan • Korea • Mexico • Singapore • Spain • United Kingdom • United States

SOUTH-WESTERN
CENGAGE Learning

New Era of Management, **Eleventh International Edition**

Richard L. Daft, with the assistance of Patricia G. Lane

Senior Vice President, LRS/Acquisitions & Solutions Planning: Jack W. Calhoun

Editorial Director, Business & Economics: Erin Joyner

Executive Editor: Scott Person

Managing Developmental Editor: Jennifer King

Editorial Assistant: Tamara Grega

Sr Content Project Managers: Cliff Kallemeyn

Media Editor: Rob Ellington

Manufacturing Planner: Ron Montgomery

Brand Manager: Robin LeFevre

Market Development Manager: Jonathan Monahan

Executive Marketing Communications Manager: Jason LaChapelle

Production Service: MPS Limited

Sr. Art Director: Stacy Jenkins Shirley

Internal Designer: cmiller design

Cover Photo Credit:
  b/w image: JoLin/iStockphoto
  color image: Shutterstock/ANP

Rights Acquisitions Specialist: Amber Hosea

Library of Congress Control Number: 2012956484

International Edition:

ISBN-13: 978-1-285-06877-0

ISBN-10: 1-285-06877-7

Cengage Learning International Offices

Asia
www.cengageasia.com
tel: (65) 6410 1200

Australia/New Zealand
www.cengage.com.au
tel: (61) 3 9685 4111

Brazil
www.cengage.com.br
tel: (55) 11 3665 9900

India
www.cengage.co.in
tel: (91) 11 4364 1111

Latin America
www.cengage.com.mx
tel: (52) 55 1500 6000

UK/Europe/Middle East/Africa
www.cengage.co.uk
tel: (44) 0 1264 332 424

Represented in Canada by Nelson Education, Ltd.
tel: (416) 752 9100 / (800) 668 0671
www.nelson.com

Cengage Learning is a leading provider of customized learning solutions with office locations around the globe, including Singapore, the United Kingdom, Australia, Mexico, Brazil, and Japan. Locate your local office at: **www.cengage.com/global**

For product information: **www.cengage.com/international**

Visit your local office: **www.cengage.com/global**

Visit our corporate website: **www.cengage.com**

Printed in Canada
1 2 3 4 5 6 7 17 16 15 14 13

With deep appreciation to Dorothy,
the playwright and partner in my life,
and to my parents, who started my life
toward outcomes that I could not understand at the time.

About the Author

About the Author

Courtesy of the Author

Richard L. Daft, Ph.D., is the Brownlee O. Currey, Jr., Professor of Management in the Owen Graduate School of Management at Vanderbilt University. Professor Daft specializes in the study of organization theory and leadership. Dr. Daft is a fellow of the Academy of Management and has served on the editorial boards of the *Academy of Management Journal, Administrative Science Quarterly,* and *Journal of Management Education.* He was the associate editor-in-chief of *Organization Science* and served for three years as associate editor of *Administrative Science Quarterly.*

Professor Daft has authored or co-authored 14 books, including *Building Management Skills: An Action-First Approach* (with Dorothy Marcic, South-Western, 2014), *The Executive and the Elephant: A Leader's Guide for Building Inner Excellence* (Jossey-Bass, 2010), *Organization Theory and Design* (South-Western, 2013), *The Leadership Experience* (South-Western, 2011), and *Fusion Leadership: Unlocking the Subtle Forces That Change People and Organizations* (Berrett-Koehler, 2000, with Robert Lengel). He has also written dozens of scholarly articles, papers, and chapters in other books. His work has been published in *Administrative Science Quarterly, Academy of Management Journal, Academy of Management Review, Strategic Management Journal, Journal of Management, Accounting Organizations and Society, Management Science, MIS Quarterly, California Management Review,* and *Organizational Behavior Teaching Review.* Professor Daft is also an active teacher and consultant. He has taught management, leadership, organizational change, organizational theory, and organizational behavior.

In addition, Professor Daft has served as associate dean, produced for-profit theatrical productions, and helped manage a start-up enterprise. He has been involved in management development and consulting for many companies and government organizations, including the American Banking Association, Bridgestone, Bell Canada, the National Transportation Research Board, Nortel, the Tennessee Valley Authority (TVA), Pratt & Whitney, State Farm Insurance, Tenneco, the U.S. Air Force, the U.S. Army, J. C. Bradford & Co., Central Parking System, Entergy Sales and Service, Bristol-Myers Squibb, First American National Bank, and the Vanderbilt University Medical Center.

Brief Contents

Contents

part 3   Planning   206

part 5 Leading 452

16 Motivation  524

17 Communication 556

18 Teamwork 586

part 6   Controlling   628

19 Quality and Performance 628

Preface

Innovative Management for a Changing World

Today's managers and organizations are being buffeted by massive and far-reaching social, technological, and economic changes. Any manager who believed in the myth of stability was rocked out of complacency when, one after another, large financial institutions in the United States began to fail, automakers filed for bankruptcy, the housing market collapsed, European economies faced financial challenges, and a global economic recession took hold and wouldn't let go. Business schools, as well as managers and businesses, are still scrambling to cope with the aftermath, keep up with fast-changing events, and evaluate the impact that this volatile period of history will have on organizations in the future. This edition of *New Era of Management* addresses themes and issues that are directly relevant to the current, fast-shifting business environment.

I revised *New Era of Management*, 11th edition, with a goal of helping current and future managers find innovative solutions to the problems that plague today's organizations—whether they are everyday challenges or once-in-a-lifetime crises. The world in which most students will work as managers is undergoing a tremendous upheaval. Ethical turmoil, the need for crisis management skills, e-business, economic recession and rampant unemployment, rapidly changing technologies, globalization, outsourcing, increasing government regulation, social media, global supply chains, the Wall Street meltdown, and other challenges place demands on managers that go beyond the techniques and ideas traditionally taught in management courses. Managing today requires the full breadth of management skills and capabilities. This text provides comprehensive coverage of both traditional management skills and the new competencies needed in a turbulent environment characterized by economic turmoil, political confusion, and general uncertainty.

In the traditional world of work, management's job was to control and limit people, enforce rules and regulations, seek stability and efficiency, design a top-down hierarchy, and achieve bottom-line results. To spur innovation and achieve high performance, however, managers need different skills, particularly in today's tough economy that has caused suffering for many employees. Managers have to find ways to engage workers' hearts and minds, as well as take advantage of their physical labor. The new workplace asks that managers focus on building trust, inspiring commitment, leading change, harnessing people's creativity and enthusiasm, finding shared visions and values, and sharing information and power. Teamwork, collaboration, participation, and learning are guiding principles that help managers and employees maneuver the difficult terrain of today's turbulent business environment. Rather than controlling their employees, managers focus on training them to adapt to new technologies and extraordinary environmental shifts, and thus achieve high performance and total corporate effectiveness.

My vision for this edition of *New Era of Management* is to present the newest management ideas for turbulent times in a way that is interesting and valuable to students, while retaining the best of traditional management thinking. To achieve this vision, I have included the most recent management concepts and research and have shown the contemporary application of management ideas in organizations. A questionnaire at the beginning of each chapter draws students personally into the topic and gives them some insight into their own management skills. A chapter feature for new managers, called the New Manager Self-Test, gives students personal feedback about what will be expected when they become managers. At the end of each major chapter section, I have added a Remember This feature that provides a quick review of the salient concepts and terms students should remember. Within each chapter, a new feature called Green Power highlights how various organizations are responding to the growing demand for socially and environmentally responsible ways of doing business. Thoughtful or inspiring quotes within each chapter—some from business leaders, others from novelists, philosophers, and everyday people—help students expand their thinking about management issues. The combination of established scholarship, new ideas, and real-life applications gives students a taste of the energy, challenge, and adventure inherent in the dynamic field of management. The South-Western/Cengage Learning staff and I have worked together to provide a textbook that is better than any other at capturing the excitement of organizational management.

I revised *New Era of Management* to provide a book of utmost quality that will create in students both respect for the changing field of management and confidence that they can understand and master it. The textual portion of this book has been enhanced through the engaging, easy-to-understand writing style and the many new in-text examples, boxed items, and short exercises that make the concepts come alive for students. The graphic component has been enhanced with several new and revised exhibits and updated photo essays that illustrate specific management concepts. The well-chosen photographs provide vivid illustrations and intimate glimpses of management scenes, events, and people. The photos are combined with brief essays that explain how a specific management concept looks and feels. Both the textual and graphic portions of the textbook help students grasp the often abstract and distant world of management.

FOCUS ON INNOVATION: NEW TO THE 11TH EDITION

A primary focus for revising the 11th edition has been to relate management concepts and theories to events in today's turbulent environment by bringing in present-day issues that real-life managers face. Sections that are particularly relevant to fast-shifting current events are marked with a "Hot Topic" icon.

LEARNING OPPORTUNITIES

The 11th edition includes several innovative pedagogical features to help students understand their own management capabilities and learn what it is like to manage in an organization today. Each chapter begins with an opening questionnaire that directly relates to the topic of the chapter and enables students to see how they respond to situations and challenges typically faced by real-life managers. A New Manager Self-Test in each chapter provides further opportunity for students to understand their management abilities. These short feedback questionnaires, which are all new for this edition, give students insight into how they would function in the real world of management. The Remember This bullet-point summaries at the end of each major chapter section give students a snapshot of the key points and concepts covered in that section. The end-of-chapter questions have been carefully revised to encourage critical thinking and application of chapter concepts, and Small Group Breakout exercises give students the opportunity to apply concepts while building teamwork skills. Ethical dilemmas (found at the end of each part) and all-new end-of-chapter cases help students sharpen their diagnostic skills for management problem solving.

CHAPTER CONTENT

Within each chapter, many topics have been added or expanded to address the current issues that managers face. Chapter text has been tightened and sharpened to provide greater focus on the key topics that count for management today. The essential elements concerning operations and information technology, subject matter that is frequently covered in other courses, have been combined into an appendix for students who want more information about these topics.

Chapter 1 includes a discussion of some of the high-impact events and changes that have made innovative management so critical to the success of organizations today and into the future. This introductory chapter also talks about making the leap from being an individual contributor in the organization to becoming a new manager and getting work done primarily through the efforts of others. It introduces the skills and competencies needed to manage organizations effectively, including issues such as managing one's time, maintaining appropriate control, and building trust and credibility.

Chapter 2 provides solid coverage of the historical development of management and organizations. It includes an expanded discussion of the positive and negative aspects of bureaucracy and an updated discussion of the use of the management science approach in recent years. The chapter also examines contemporary management tools for turbulent times. The final part of the chapter looks at managing the technology-driven workplace, including social media programs, customer relationship management, and supply chain management.

Chapter 3 contains an updated view of current issues related to the environment and corporate culture, including a new discussion of organizational ecosystems, the growing importance of the international environment, and trends in the sociocultural environment, including a growing minority population and today's technologically connected consumer. The chapter includes a new discussion of the concept of strategic issues and also describes how managers shape a high-performance culture as an innovative response to a shifting environment.

Chapter 4 takes a thoroughly updated look at the shifting international landscape, including the Arab Spring and the growing clout of China, India, and Brazil, as well as what these changes mean for managers around the world. The chapter includes a new discussion of the importance of a global mindset and an updated review of the globalization backlash. The chapter also discusses the bottom-of-the-pyramid concept, economic interdependence, and recent challenges brought about by economic difficulties in European Union countries.

Chapter 5 makes the business case for incorporating ethical values in the organization and looks at the role that managers play in creating an ethical organization. The chapter includes an updated discussion of the state of ethical management today, the pressures that can contribute to unethical behavior in organizations, and criteria that managers can use for resolving ethical dilemmas. The chapter considers corporate social responsibility issues as well, including new discussions of challenges in the global supply chain, the concept of a triple bottom line, and stakeholder mapping.

Chapter 6 has been thoroughly revised and updated to include the most current thinking on entrepreneurship and small business management. The chapter describes the impact of entrepreneurial companies both in the United States and internationally, examines the state of minority- and women-owned small businesses, and looks at some of the typical characteristics of entrepreneurs. It also describes the process of launching an entrepreneurial start-up and managing a growing company, including a new discussion of using tools and techniques such as social media and crowdfunding. The chapter includes a section on social entrepreneurship.

Chapter 7 provides a discussion of the overall planning and goal-setting process, including the use of strategy maps for aligning goals. A new section describes the socially constructed nature of goals and how managers decide which goals to pursue. The chapter also outlines the benefits and limitations of planning and goal setting, includes a new discussion of management by means (MBM), and takes a close look at crisis planning and how to use scenarios. The final section describes innovative approaches to planning, including the use of intelligence teams and business performance dashboards to help managers plan in a fast-changing environment.

Chapter 8 continues its focus on the basics of formulating and implementing strategy, including the elements of strategy and Porter's competitive strategies. It includes a new section on identifying the target customer as one of the components of competitive advantage. In addition, the chapter explains global strategies, the Boston Consulting Group (BCG) matrix, and diversification strategy, looking at how managers use unrelated diversification, related diversification, or vertical integration as strategic approaches in shifting environments. The final section of the chapter provides an updated discussion of how managers effectively execute strategy.

Chapter 9 gives an overview of managerial decision making, including decision making models, personal decision styles, and an updated discussion of biases that can cloud managers' judgment and lead to bad decisions. The final section looks at innovative group decision making and includes new discussions of evidence-based decision making and the use of after-action reviews.

Chapter 10 discusses basic principles of organizing and describes both traditional and contemporary organizational structures in detail. The chapter includes a discussion of the strengths and weaknesses associated with each structural approach. It also offers a new discussion of relational coordination as a way to enhance horizontal collaboration and coordination and describes contingency factors that shape structure, including strategy and technology.

Chapter 11 focuses on the critical role of managing change and innovation. The chapter includes new discussions of the bottom-up approach to innovation and the use of innovation contests, as well as an expanded discussion of the horizontal linkage model for new product development. It also describes disruptive innovation and reverse (trickle-up) innovation, open innovation, and crowdsourcing. This chapter provides information about product and technology changes, as well as about changing people and culture, and it discusses techniques for implementing change effectively.

Chapter 12 has been revised thoroughly to reflect the shifting role of human resource management (HRM) in today's turbulent economic environment. The chapter includes an updated discussion of the strategic role of HRM in building human capital, a new discussion of employer branding, and expanded sections on the trends toward contingent employment and flexible scheduling. There are also new sections on using social media and internships for recruiting, online checking of job candidates, and a brief discussion of extreme interviewing. The section on training and development has been updated and includes a new discussion of social learning.

Chapter 13 has been revised to reflect the most recent thinking on organizational diversity issues. The chapter includes a thoroughly updated discussion of demographic changes occurring in the domestic and global workforce and how organizations are responding. It also includes a new section on the importance of a diversity of perspective within organizations, a revised section on the glass ceiling and the "bamboo ceiling," and a new section offering tips for aspiring female and minority managers.

Chapter 14 continues its solid coverage of the basics of understanding individual behavior, including personality, attitudes, perception, and emotions. In addition, the chapter includes a new section on the value and difficulty of self-awareness, techniques for enhancing self-awareness, a new discussion of self-management, and a step-by-step guide to time management. The section on stress management has been enhanced by a new discussion of challenge stress versus threat stress and new sections describing ways both individuals and organizations can combat the harmful effects of too much stress.

Chapter 15 examines contemporary approaches to leadership, including Level 5 leadership, authentic leadership, and servant leadership. The chapter also discusses charismatic and transformational leadership, task versus relationship leadership behaviors, gender differences in leadership, the importance of leaders discovering and honing their strengths, and the role of followers. The section on leadership power has been revised to include the concept of *hard* versus *soft* power.

Chapter 16 covers the foundations of motivation and incorporates a new section on positive versus negative approaches to motivating employees. The chapter also includes new sections on building a thriving workforce and the importance of making progress as a factor contributing to high employee motivation. The sections on empowerment and employee engagement have been updated as well.

Chapter 17 explores the basics of good communication and includes new discussions of asking questions and communicating with candor, a revised section on creating an open communication climate, and an expanded and enriched discussion of communicating to influence and persuade. A new section discusses using social media to enhance communication within the organization and with stakeholders.

Chapter 18 takes a fresh look at the contributions that teams make in organizations. It also acknowledges that work teams are sometimes ineffective and explores the reasons for this, including such problems as free riders and lack of trust. The chapter covers the types of teams and includes a look at using technology effectively in virtual teams. It also discusses how factors such as team diversity, member roles, norms, and team cohesiveness influence effectiveness. There is a revised section on negotiation and managing conflict, including an explanation of task versus relationship conflict.

Chapter 19 provides an overview of financial and quality control, including the feedback control model, Six Sigma, International Organization for Standards (ISO) certification, and use of the balanced scorecard. The chapter includes a new section on zero-based budgeting, a new discussion of quality partnering, and a new step-by-step benchmarking process. The chapter also addresses current concerns about corporate governance, including new government regulations and requirements.

In addition to the topics listed previously, this text integrates coverage of the Internet, social media, and new technology into the various topics covered in each and every chapter.

ORGANIZATION

The chapter sequence in *New Era of Management* is organized around the management functions of planning, organizing, leading, and controlling. These four functions effectively encompass both management research and the characteristics of the manager's job.

Part One introduces the world of management, including the nature of management, issues related to today's chaotic environment, historical perspectives on management, and the technology-driven workplace.

Part Two examines the environments of management and organizations. This section includes material on the business environment and corporate culture, the global environment, ethics and social responsibility, and the environment of small business and entrepreneurship.

Part Three presents three chapters on planning, including organizational goal setting and planning, strategy formulation and execution, and the decision-making process.

Part Four focuses on organizing processes. These chapters describe dimensions of structural design, the design alternatives that managers can use to achieve strategic objectives, structural designs for promoting innovation and change, the design and use of the human resource function, and how the approach to managing diverse employees is significant to the organizing function.

Part Five is devoted to leadership. The section begins with a chapter on understanding individual behavior, including self-awareness and self-understanding. This foundation paves the way for subsequent discussions of leadership, motivation of employees, communication, and team management.

Part Six describes the controlling function of management, including basic principles of total quality management (TQM), the design of control systems, and the difference between hierarchical and decentralized control.

INNOVATIVE FEATURES

A major goal of this book is to offer better ways of using the textbook medium to convey management knowledge to the reader. To this end, the book includes several innovative features that draw students in and help them contemplate, absorb, and comprehend management concepts. South-Western has brought together a team of experts to create and coordinate color photographs, video cases, beautiful artwork, and supplemental materials for the best management textbook and package on the market.

Chapter Outline and Objectives. Each chapter begins with a clear statement of its learning objectives and an outline of its contents. These devices provide an overview of what is to come and also can be used by students to guide their study and test their understanding and retention of important points.

Opening Questionnaire. The text grabs student attention immediately by giving the student a chance to participate in the chapter content actively by completing a short questionnaire related to the topic.

Take a Moment. At strategic places within the chapter, students are invited to Take a Moment to complete a New Manager Self-Test or end of chapter activity that relates to the concepts being discussed.

New Manager Self-Test. A New Manager Self-Test in each chapter provides opportunities for self-assessment as a way for students to experience management issues in a personal way. The change from individual performer to new manager is dramatic, and these self-tests, which are all new for the 11th edition, provide insight into what to expect and how students might perform in the world of the new manager.

Green Power. A new feature for this edition is a Green Power box in each chapter that highlights how managers in a specific company are innovatively addressing issues of sustainability and environmental responsibility. Examples of companies spotlighted in the Green Power boxes include Deutsche Post DHL Group, Nike, Acciona, BMW, Waste Management, Inc., Bean and Body, PepsiCo, Fujitsu, The Honest Company, SAP, and Royal DSM.

Concept Connection Photo Essays. A key feature of the book is the use of photographs accompanied by detailed photo essay captions that enhance learning. Each caption highlights and illustrates one or more specific concepts from the text to reinforce student understanding of the concepts. Although the photos are beautiful to look at, they also convey the vividness, immediacy, and concreteness of management events in today's business world.

Contemporary Examples. Every chapter of this book contains several written examples of management incidents. They are placed at strategic points in the chapter and are designed to illustrate the application of concepts to specific companies. These in-text examples—indicated by the title "Innovative Way"—include well-known U.S. and international organizations, including Apple, Four Seasons, Lenovo, Amazon, Nokia, the Central Intelligence Agency (CIA), and Semco, as well as lesser-known companies and not-for-profit organizations including Godrej & Boyce, Strand Brewing Company, Trader Joe's, Hilcorp Energy, Johnson Storage and Moving, and IGN. The 11th edition includes 47 new and 9 updated Innovative Way examples that put students in touch with the real world of organizations so that they can appreciate the value of management concepts.

Manager's Shoptalk. A Manager's Shoptalk box in each chapter addresses a specific topic straight from the field of management that is of special interest to students. These boxes, most of which are new for the 11th edition, may describe a contemporary topic or problem that is relevant to chapter content, or they may contain a diagnostic questionnaire or a special example of how managers handle a problem. The boxes heighten student interest in the subject matter and provide an auxiliary view of management issues not typically available in textbooks.

Video Cases. At the end of each part, there is a video case for each chapter that illustrates the concepts presented in the text. These 19 "On the Job" videos (one per chapter) enhance the classroom experience by giving students the chance to hear from real-world business leaders so they can see the direct application of the management theories they have learned. Companies discussed include Holden Outerware, Living Social Escapes, Camp Bow Wow, and Theo Chocolate. Each video case explores the issues covered in the video, allowing students to synthesize material they've just viewed. The video cases culminate with several questions that can be used to launch classroom discussion or can be assigned as homework. Suggested answers are provided in the Instructor's Manual.

Exhibits. Several exhibits have been added or revised in this edition to enhance student understanding. Many aspects of management are research based, and some concepts tend to be abstract and theoretical. The many exhibits throughout this book enhance students' awareness and understanding of these concepts. These exhibits consolidate key points, indicate relationships among concepts, and visually illustrate concepts. They also make effective use of color to enhance their imagery and appeal.

Remember This. At the end of each major section of a chapter is a Remember This bullet-point summary of the key concepts, ideas, and terms discussed in that section. The Remember This feature gives students an easy way to review the salient points covered in the chapter.

Glossaries. Learning the management vocabulary is essential to understanding contemporary management. This process is facilitated in three ways. First, key concepts are bold-faced and completely defined where they first appear in the text. Second, brief definitions are set out at the end of each major section in the Remember This bullet points for easy review and follow-up. Third, a glossary summarizing all key terms and definitions appears at the end of the book for handy reference.

Discussion Questions. Each chapter closes with discussion questions that will enable students to check their understanding of key issues, to think beyond basic concepts, and to determine areas that require further study.

Apply Your Skills Exercises. End-of-chapter exercises called "Apply Your Skills: Experiential Exercise" and end-of-part exercises called "Apply Your Skills: Ethical Dilemma" provide a self-test for students and an opportunity to experience management issues in a personal way. These exercises take the form of questionnaires, scenarios, and activities. The exercises are tied into the chapter through the Take a Moment feature that refers students to the end-of-chapter and end-of-part exercises at the appropriate point in the chapter content.

Small Group Breakout Exercises. Small Group Breakout exercises at the end of each chapter give students a chance to develop both team and analytical skills. Completing the small-group activities will help students learn to use the resources provided by others in the group, to pool information, and to develop a successful outcome together. The Small Group Breakouts provide experiential learning that leads to deeper understanding and application of chapter concepts.

Case for Critical Analysis. At the end of each part is a brief but substantive case for each chapter that offers an opportunity for student analysis and class discussion. These cases are based on real management problems and dilemmas, but the identities of companies and managers have been disguised. These cases, which are all new for the 11th edition, allow students to sharpen their diagnostic skills for management problem solving.

Integrative Cases. Located at the end of each part, the six Integrative Cases provide additional real-world insights into how managers deal with planning, leading, organizing, controlling, and other managerial issues. The six interrelated cases also reinforce the "green" theme, as they all reference aspects of the emerging natural gas fuel industry.

Instructor's Companion Website. Key instructor ancillaries (Instructor's Manual, Test Bank, ExamView, and Microsoft PowerPoint slides) are provided on the Instructor's Companion Web site, giving instructors the ultimate tool for customizing lectures and presentations and assessing students' progress.

Instructor's Manual. Designed to provide support for instructors new to the course, as well as innovative materials for experienced professors, the Instructor's Manual includes Chapter Outlines, annotated learning objectives, Lecture Notes, and sample Lecture Outlines. In addition, the Instructor's Manual includes answers and teaching notes to end-of-chapter materials and the video cases and integrative cases.

Test Bank. Scrutinized for accuracy, the Test Bank includes more than 3,000 multiple-choice, true/false, completion, short-answer, and essay questions. Each question is identified by difficulty level, Bloom's taxonomy level, and other useful reference points and outcomes.

ExamView. Available only on the Instructor's Companion Web site, ExamView contains all the questions in the Test Bank. This program is easy-to-use test creation software that is compatible with Microsoft Windows or the Mac operating system. Instructors can add or edit questions, instructions, and answers, and select questions (randomly or numerically) by previewing them on the screen.

PowerPoint Lecture Presentation. Available on the companion Web site, the Power-Point Lecture Presentation enables instructors to customize their own multimedia classroom presentation. Containing an average of 27 slides per chapter, the package includes figures and tables from the text, as well as outside materials to supplement chapter concepts. The material is organized by chapter and can be modified or expanded for individual classroom use.

Reel to Real Video Package. Put management in action with this edition's new video package. The "On the Job" videos illustrate management concepts at work within familiar companies, large and small, giving students an insider's perspective.

To access the following additional course materials and companion resources, please visit www.cengagebrain.com. At the CengageBrain.com home page, search for the ISBN of your title (from the back cover of your book) using the search box at the top of the page. This will take you to the product page, where free companion resources can be found. Students can purchase access to these resources for additional fees; please contact your Cengage sales representative for more information.

Management CourseMate. Engaging, trackable, and affordable, the new MANAGE-MENT CourseMate Web site offers a dynamic way to bring course concepts to life with interactive learning, study, and exam preparation tools that support this printed edition of the text. Watch student comprehension soar with all-new flashcards and engaging crossword puzzles, video-based media quizzes, test-prep quizzes, and more in this textbook-specific Web site. A complete e-book provides you with the choice of an entire online learning experience. MANAGEMENT CourseMate goes beyond the book to deliver what you need!

CengageNOW. This robust, online course management system gives you more control in less time and delivers better student outcomes—NOW. CengageNOW for *New Era of Management*, 11th edition, includes teaching and learning resources organized around lecturing, creating assignments, grading, quizzing, and tracking student progress and performance. Flexible assignments, automatic grading, and a gradebook option provide more control while saving you valuable time. A Personalized Study diagnostic tool empowers students to master concepts, prepare for exams, and become more involved in class.

Aplia. Engage, prepare and educate your students with this ideal online learning solution. Aplia's™ management solution ensures that students stay on top of their coursework with regularly scheduled homework assignments and automatic grading with detailed, immediate feedback on every question. Interactive teaching tools and content further increase engagement and understanding. Aplia™ assignments match the language, style, and structure of *New Era of Management*, 11th edition, allowing your students to apply what they've learned in this book directly to their homework.

Acknowledgments

A gratifying experience for me was working with the team of dedicated professionals at South-Western, who all were committed to the vision of producing the best management text ever. I am grateful to Scott Person, executive editor, whose interest, creative ideas, and assistance kept this book's spirit alive. Jennifer King, managing developmental editor, provided encouragement, superb project coordination, and excellent ideas that helped the team meet a demanding and sometimes arduous schedule. Scott Dillon and Emily Nesheim, senior content project managers, expertly managed the production phase and ensured that everyone working on the production process adhered to high standards of quality. Stacy Jenkins Shirley, art director, contributed her graphic arts skills to create a visually dynamic design. Tamara Grega, editorial assistant, and Robin LeFevre, marketing brand manager, skillfully pitched in to help keep the project on track. Joe Devine deserves a special thank-you for his layout expertise and commitment to producing an attractive, high-quality textbook. In addition, BJ Parker, Copyshop, USA, contributed the solid and well-researched Integrative Cases. Thanks also to media editors Rob Ellington and Sally Nieman, manufacturing planner Ron Montgomery, and rights acquisition specialist Amber Hosea.

Here at Vanderbilt, I want to extend special appreciation to my assistant, Barbara Haselton. Barbara provided excellent support and assistance on a variety of projects that gave me time to write. I also want to acknowledge an intellectual debt to my colleagues, Bruce Barry, Rich Oliver, David Owens, Ty Park, Ranga Ramanujam, Bart Victor, and Tim Vogus. Thanks also to Deans Jim Bradford and Ray Friedman, who have supported my writing projects and maintained a positive scholarly atmosphere in the school. Another group of people who made a major contribution to this textbook are the management experts who provided advice, reviews, answers to questions, and suggestions for changes, insertions, and clarifications. I want to thank each of these colleagues for their valuable feedback and suggestions on the 11th edition:

Andy Bertsch
Minot State University

Kathy Hastings
Greenville Technical College

Frank Bosco
Marshall University

Donna LaGanga
Tunxis Community College

Peggy Cerrito
Augsburg College

Joan McBee
Southern Oregon University

Camille Chapman
Greenville Technical College

Barbara Stasek
Pasco Hernando Community College

V. J. Daviero
Pasco Hernando Community College

Kevin Wayne
Rivier College

Alexandra Giesler
Augsburg College

I would also like to continue to acknowledge those reviewers who have contributed comments, suggestions, and feedback on previous editions:

David C. Adams
Manhattanville College

Deb Buerkley
Southwest Minnesota State University

David Alexander
Christian Brothers University

Thomas Butte
Humboldt State University

Erin M. Alexander
University of Houston–Clear Lake

Peter Bycio
Xavier University, Ohio

David Arseneau
Eastern Illinois University

Diane Caggiano
Fitchburg State College

Reginald L Audibert
California State University—Long Beach

Douglas E. Cathon
St. Augustine's College

Hal Babson
Columbus State Community College

Peggy Cerrito
Augsburg College

Reuel Barksdale
Columbus State Community College

Bruce Charnov
Hofstra University

Gloria Bemben
Finger Lakes Community College

Jim Ciminskie
Bay de Noc Community College

Pat Bernson
County College of Morris

Gloria Cockerell
Collin College

Art Bethke
Northeast Louisiana University

Dan Connaughton
University of Florida

Burrell A. Brown
California University of Pennsylvania

Bruce Conwers
Kaskaskia College

Paula Buchanan
Jacksonville State University

Jack Cox
Amberton University

Byron L. David
City College of New York

H. Kristl Davison
University of Mississippi

Richard De Luca
William Paterson University

Robert DeDominic
Montana Tech

Mark DeHainaut
California University of Pennsylvania

Joe J. Eassa, Jr.
Palm Beach Atlantic University

John C. Edwards
East Carolina University

Mary Ann Edwards
College of Mount St. Joseph

Paul Ewell
Bridgewater College

Mary M. Fanning
College of Notre Dame of Maryland

Janice M. Feldbauer
Austin Community College

Merideth Ferguson
Baylor University

Daryl Fortin
Upper Iowa University

Karen Fritz
Bridgewater College

Michael P. Gagnon
New Hampshire Community Technical College

Richard H. Gayor
Antelope Valley College

Dan Geeding
Xavier University, Ohio

James Genseal
Joliet Junior College

Peter Gibson
Becker College

Yezdi H. Godiwalla
University of Wisconsin—Whitewater

Carol R. Graham
Western Kentucky University

Gary Greene
Manatee Community College

James Halloran
Wesleyan College

Ken Harris
Indiana University Southeast

Paul Hayes
Coastal Carolina Community College

Dennis Heaton
Maharishi University of Management, Iowa

Stephen R. Hiatt
Catawba College

Jeffrey D. Hines
Davenport College

Bob Hoerber
Westminster College

Betty Hoge
Bridgewater College

James N. Holly
University of Wisconsin–Green Bay

Genelle Jacobson
Ridgewater College

Jody Jones
Oklahoma Christian University

C. Joy Jones
Ohio Valley College

Kathleen Jones
University of North Dakota

Sheryl Kae
Lynchburg College

Jordan J. Kaplan
Long Island University

J. Michael Keenan
Western Michigan University

Jerry Kinard
Western Carolina University

Renee Nelms King
Eastern Illinois University

Gloria Komer
Stark State College

Paula C. Kougl
Western Oregon University

Cynthia Krom
Mount St. Mary College

Sal Kukalis
California State University–Long Beach

Mukta Kulkarni
University of Texas–San Antonio

William B. Lamb
Millsaps College

Ruth D. Lapsley
Lewis-Clark State College

Robert E. Ledman
Morehouse College

George Lehma
Bluffton College

Joyce LeMay
Bethel University

Cynthia Lengnick-Hall
University of Texas–San Antonio

Janet C. Luke
Georgia Baptist College of Nursing

Jenna Lundburg
Ithaca College

Walter J. MacMillan
Oral Roberts University

Iraj Mahdavi
National University

Myrna P. Mandell
California State University, Northridge

Daniel B. Marin
Louisiana State University

Michael Market
Jacksonville State University

Wade McCutcheon
East Texas Baptist College

James C. McElroy
Iowa State University

Tom D. McFarland
Tusculum College

Dennis W. Meyers
Texas State Technical College

Alan N. Miller
University of Nevada–Las Vegas

Irene A. Miller
Southern Illinois University

Tom Miller
Concordia University

W J Mitchell
Bladen Community College

James L. Moseley
Wayne State University

Micah Mukabi
Essex County College

David W. Murphy
Madisonville Community College

Nora Nurre
Upper Iowa University

Ross O'Brien
Dallas Baptist University

Tomas J. Ogazon
St. Thomas University

Allen Oghenejbo
Mills College

John Okpara
Bloomsburg University

Linda Overstreet
Hillsborough Community College

Ken Peterson
Metropolitan State University

Lori A. Peterson
Augsburg College

Clifton D. Petty
Drury College

James I. Phillips
Northeastern State University

Michael Provitera
Barry University

Linda Putchinski
University of Central Florida

Abe Qastin
Lakeland College

Kenneth Radig
Medaille College

Gerald D. Ramsey
Indiana University Southeast

Holly Caldwell Ratwani
Bridgewater College

Barbara Redmond
Briar Cliff College

William Reisel
St. John's University–New York

Terry L. Riddle
Central Virginia Community College

Walter F. Rohrs
Wagner College

Meir Russ
University of Wisconsin–Green Bay

Marcy Satterwhite
Lake Land College

Don Schreiber
Baylor University

Kilmon Shin
Ferris State University

Daniel G. Spencer
University of Kansas

Gary Spokes
Pace University

M. Sprencz
David N. Meyers College

Shanths Srinivas
*California State Polytechnic University,
Pomona*

Jeffrey Stauffer
Ventura College

William A. Stower
Seton Hall University

Mary Studer
Southwestern Michigan College

James Swenson
Moorhead State University, Minnesota

Thomas Sy
California State University–Long Beach

Irwin Talbot
St. Peter's College

Andrew Timothy
Lourdes College

Frank G. Titlow
St. Petersburg Junior College

John Todd
University of Arkansas

Kevin A. Van Dewark
Humphreys College

Linn Van Dyne
Michigan State University

Philip Varca
University of Wyoming

Dennis L. Varin
Southern Oregon University

Gina Vega
Merrimack College

George S. Vozikis
University of Tulsa

Noemy Wachtel
Kean University

Peter Wachtel
Kean University

Bruce C. Walker
Northeast Louisiana University

Mark Weber
University of Minnesota

Emilia S. Westney
Texas Tech University

Stan Williamson
Northeast Louisiana University

Alla L. Wilson
University of Wisconsin–Green Bay

Ignatius Yacomb
Loma Linda University

Imad Jim Zbib
Ramapo College of New Jersey

Vic Zimmerman
Pima Community College

I'd like to pay special tribute to my longtime editorial associate, Pat Lane. I can't imagine how I would ever complete such a comprehensive revision on my own. Pat provided truly outstanding help throughout every step of writing this edition of *New Era of Management*. She skillfully drafted materials for a wide range of chapter topics, boxes, and cases; researched topics when new sources were lacking; and did an absolutely superb job with the copyedited manuscript and page proofs. Her commitment to this text enabled us to achieve our dream for its excellence. In addition, I want to thank Mary Hillebrand Emmons, who stepped in to help with the research and revision of the eleventh edition. We could not have completed this revision without Mary's excellent assistance. I also express my gratitude to DeeGee Lester for drafting material for the Green Power boxes that are new to this edition. DeeGee shared my dream for concise, useful information to share with students about what managers in forward-thinking companies are doing in the area of sustainability.

Finally, I want to acknowledge the love and contributions of my wife, Dorothy Marcic. Dorothy has been very supportive during this revision as we share our lives together. I also want to acknowledge the love and support from my five daughters—Danielle, Amy, Roxanne, Solange, and Elizabeth—who make my life special during our precious time together. Thanks also to B. J. and Kaitlyn and Kaci and Matthew for their warmth and smiles that brighten my life, especially during our time together visiting interesting places.

Richard L. Daft
Nashville, Tennessee

New Era of Management

Eleventh Edition

Managing in Turbulent Times

Timothy Hearsum/Jupiter Images

Chapter Outline

Learning Outcomes

After studying this chapter, you should be able to:

1. Describe the four management functions and the type of management activity associated with each.

2. Explain the difference between efficiency and effectiveness and their importance for organizational performance.

3. Describe conceptual, human, and technical skills and their relevance for managers.

4. Describe management types and the horizontal and vertical differences between them.

5. Define ten roles that managers perform in organizations.

6. Appreciate the manager's role in small businesses and nonprofit organizations.

7. Understand the personal challenges involved in becoming a new manager.

8. Discuss the innovative competencies needed to be an effective manager in today's environment.

1 INTRODUCTION

2 ENVIRONMENT

3 PLANNING

4 ORGANIZING

5 LEADING

6 CONTROLLING

Are You Ready to Be a Manager?[1]

Welcome to the world of management. Are you ready for it? This questionnaire will help you see whether your priorities align with the demands placed on today's managers.

INSTRUCTIONS: Rate each of the following items based on what you think is the appropriate emphasis for that task to your success as a new manager of a department. Your task is to rate the top four priority items as "High-Priority" and the other four as "Low-Priority."

	High-Priority	Low-Priority
1. Spend 50 percent or more of your time in the care and feeding of people.	_____	_____
2. Make sure that people understand you are in control of the department.	_____	_____
3. Use lunches to meet and network with peers in other departments.	_____	_____
4. Implement the changes that you believe will improve department performance.	_____	_____
5. Spend as much time as possible talking with and listening to subordinates.	_____	_____
6. Make sure that jobs get out on time.	_____	_____
7. Reach out to your boss to discuss his or her expectations for you and your department.	_____	_____
8. Make sure that you set clear expectations and policies for your department.	_____	_____

SCORING AND INTERPRETATION: All eight items in the list may be important, but the odd-numbered items are considered more important than the even-numbered items for long-term success as a manager. If you checked three or four of the odd-numbered items, consider yourself ready for a management position. A successful new manager discovers that a lot of time has to be spent in the care and feeding of people, including subordinates and colleagues. People who fail in new management jobs often do so because they have poor working relationships or they misjudge management philosophy or cultural values. Developing good relationships in all directions is typically more important than holding on to old work skills or emphasizing control and task outcomes. Successful outcomes typically will occur when relationships are solid. After a year or so in a managerial role, successful people learn that more than half their time is spent networking and building relationships.

When Steve Jobs died in October 2011, Apple, the company he cofounded in 1976, was the most valuable company in the world in terms of market capitalization. Millions of people are devoted to Apple's innovative products, such as the iPhone and iPad. After Jobs's death, magazines, newspapers, scholarly journals, and Web sites rushed to publish articles about the legendary CEO's legacy and his management style. In his 600-plus-page biography of Jobs, Walter Isaacson calls him "the greatest business executive of our era," and managers around the world began reading the book to tap into the power of Jobs's management ideas.[2] It seems hard to believe that 26 years earlier, after founding Apple, Jobs had been fired from his own company at the age of 30. During his first 10 years with Apple, Jobs was clearly visionary and innovative, characteristics that he continued to display throughout his lifetime. But he didn't know or care much for the "management" side of the business, and that led to a humiliating and humbling fall and a chance to learn some management lessons that eventually took Jobs back to Apple and produced one of the greatest corporate success stories of all time.

HOT TOPIC

Take a Moment

What makes a good manager? Go to the Small Group Breakout on page 30 that pertains to the qualities and characteristics of effective and ineffective managers.

For most people, being a manager doesn't come naturally. Steve Jobs had both positive and negative qualities as a manager, but over the course of his career, he learned how to coordinate and lead people effectively to accomplish amazing results. One surprise for many people when they first step into a management role is that they are much less in control of things than they expected to be. The nature of management is to motivate and coordinate others to cope with diverse and far-reaching challenges. Many new managers expect to have power, to be in control, and to be personally responsible for departmental outcomes. However, managers depend on subordinates more than the reverse, and they are evaluated on the work of other people rather than on their own achievements. Managers set up the systems and conditions that help other people perform well.

In the past, many managers did exercise tight control over employees. But the field of management is undergoing a revolution that asks managers to do more with less, to engage employees' hearts and minds as well as their physical energy, to see change rather than stability as natural, and to inspire vision and cultural values that allow people to create a truly collaborative and productive workplace. This textbook introduces and explains the process of management and the changing ways of thinking about the world that are critical for managers. By reviewing the actions of some successful and not-so-successful managers, you will learn the fundamentals of management. By the end of this chapter, you will already recognize some of the skills that managers use to keep organizations on track, and you will begin to understand how managers can achieve astonishing results through people. By the end of this book, you will understand the fundamental management skills for planning, organizing, leading, and controlling a department or an entire organization.

Concept Connection ◀◀◀

Visions of America, LLC/Alamy Limited

In Kenya, an emerging economy, Safaricom is one of several new companies providing affordable mobile telephone service to the region. The company's **innovative managers** search for better ways to serve customers and expand the business. In 2012, Safaricom was awarded a Global Mobile Award for developing a mobile app that allows its customers to use their cell phones to purchase clean drinking water.

Why Innovative Management Matters

"By inventing Twitter, Jack may have well brought down dictators in North Africa and the Middle East," said Virgin Group CEO Richard Branson.[3] He was talking about Jack Dorsey, one of the cofounders of the microblogging service Twitter, which had more than 140 million active users and 340 million "tweets" a day in early 2012. As Branson's comment reflects, tweeting isn't just about gossiping or showing off. It's used for all sorts of activities, from organizing protests and spreading the word about political turbulence or natural disasters to marketing products and gathering customer feedback.[4] Jack Dorsey's other company, Square, founded in 2010, may eventually have even greater impact and influence. Square started with one product—a simple credit card reader that can be plugged into an iPhone and allow anyone to accept credit card payments. Today, more than a million small businesses and individuals use Square to process credit cards, and Dorsey's team is looking for how to expand into Latin America, Asia, and Europe. Square is also creating a variety of other products and services and is growing rapidly.[5]

Much of the success of Twitter and Square can be attributed to managers' effectiveness at innovation. Dorsey refers to new initiatives at Square as "resets" because they aim to be so groundbreaking that they reset the nature of the financial world. "Everything we do is about getting people to be more open, more creative, more courageous," says Dorsey. Square quickly zoomed to No. 5 on *Fast Company*'s list of the world's most innovative companies.[6]

Why does innovative management matter? Innovations in products, services, management systems, production processes, corporate values, and other aspects of the organization are what keep companies growing, changing, and thriving. Without innovation, no company can survive over the long run. Industries, technologies, economies, governments, and societies are in constant flux, and managers are responsible for helping their organizations navigate through the unpredictable with flexibility and innovation.[7] Events such as tumultuous global economies; the meltdown of the housing and finance industries in the United States; volatile oil prices and a devastating oil spill on the Gulf Coast; sweeping government changes; disasters such as an earthquake and tsunami in Japan and the resulting accidents at the Fukushima Daiichi nuclear power plant; continuing threats of terrorism; and global health scares have confirmed for managers the folly of managing for stability. The growing clout and expertise of companies in developing countries, particularly China and India, also have many Western managers worried. In such a turbulent and hypercompetitive global environment, managers must help their companies innovate more—and more quickly—than ever.

People can learn to manage innovatively. Interestingly, some hard-nosed business executives have turned to a study of a surprising example—the Grateful Dead rock band—for a lesson or two.

Innovative Way

The Grateful Dead

Who said, "[in an information economy] the best way to raise demand for your product is to give it away"? Perhaps Mark Zuckerberg, founder of Facebook? Maybe Sergey Brin or Larry Page, cofounders of Google?

Actually, those words were written by Grateful Dead lyricist John Perry Barlow in a 1994 issue of *Wired* magazine, long before most people were even thinking about "Internet business models." The Dead were famous for allowing fans to tape their shows, giving up a major source of revenue in potential record sales but dramatically widening their fan base in the process—and those fans spent plenty of money on concert tickets, merchandise, and so forth, not to mention records.

Far from being lackadaisical about their job, Dead members always treated it as a business, incorporating early on and establishing a board of directors that included people from all levels of the organization. They pioneered numerous ideas and practices that were later embraced by corporations. One example was their decision to focus intensely on their most loyal fan base and find ways to create and deliver superior customer value. Even more interesting is how, in a pre-Facebook world, the band found innovative ways to stay in touch with fans and foster a "community of interest" that defied distance. Decades before the Internet and social networking sites, intense bonds of friendship and loyalty often developed among Deadheads living thousands of miles apart.

Barry Barnes, a business professor who lectures to business leaders about the Grateful Dead, says the band's ability to think and behave innovatively at all times is a lesson for today's managers. The band thrived for decades, through bad times as well as good. "If you're going to survive this economic downturn," Barnes says, "you better be able to turn on a dime. The Dead were exemplars."[8]

Innovation has become the new imperative, despite the need for companies to control costs in today's economy. In a recent survey of corporate executives in Asia, North America, Europe, and Latin America, 80 percent agreed that "innovation is more important than cost-reduction for long-term success."[9] Throughout this text, we will spotlight various companies that reflect managers' ability to think and act innovatively, as the Grateful Dead did. In addition, Chapter 11 discusses innovation and change in detail. First, let's begin our adventure in the world of management by learning some basics about what it means to be a manager.

The Definition of Management

Every day, managers solve difficult problems, turn organizations around, and achieve astonishing performances. To be successful, every organization needs good managers.

What do managers actually do? The late famed management theorist Peter Drucker, often credited with creating the modern study of management, summed up the job of the manager by specifying five tasks, as outlined in Exhibit 1.1.[10] In essence, managers set goals, organize activities, motivate and communicate, measure performance, and develop people. These five manager activities apply not only to top executives such as Mark Zuckerberg at Facebook, Alan Mulally at Ford Motor Company, and Ursula Burns at Xerox, but also to the manager of a restaurant in your hometown, the leader of an airport security team, a supervisor at a Web hosting service, or the director of sales and marketing for a local business.

The activities outlined in Exhibit 1.1 fall into four core management functions: planning (setting goals and deciding activities), organizing (organizing activities and people), leading (motivating, communicating with, and developing people), and controlling (establishing targets and measuring performance). Depending on their job situation, managers perform numerous and varied tasks, but they all can be categorized under these four primary functions. Thus, our definition of management is as follows:

Management is the attainment of organizational goals in an effective and efficient manner through planning, organizing, leading, and controlling organizational resources. This definition includes two important ideas: (1) the four functions of planning, organizing,

> "*Management means, in the last analysis, the substitution of thought for brawn and muscle, of knowledge for folklore and superstition, and of cooperation for force. . . .*"
>
> — PETER DRUCKER, MANAGEMENT EXPERT

EXHIBIT 1.1

What Do Managers Do?

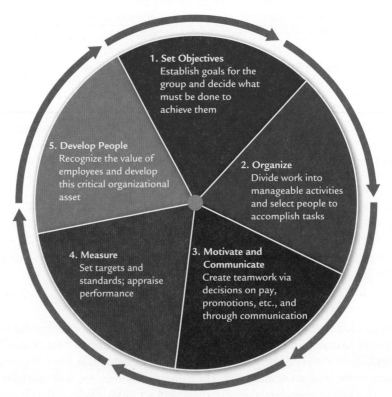

1. **Set Objectives** Establish goals for the group and decide what must be done to achieve them

2. **Organize** Divide work into manageable activities and select people to accomplish tasks

3. **Motivate and Communicate** Create teamwork via decisions on pay, promotions, etc., and through communication

4. **Measure** Set targets and standards; appraise performance

5. **Develop People** Recognize the value of employees and develop this critical organizational asset

SOURCE: Based on "What Do Managers Do?" *The Wall Street Journal Online*, http://guides.wsj.com/management/developinga-leadership-style/what-do-managers-do/ (accessed August 11, 2010), article adapted from Alan Murray, *The Wall Street Journal Essential Guide to Management* (New York: Harper Business, 2010).

leading, and controlling, and (2) the attainment of organizational goals in an effective and efficient manner. Let's first look at the four primary management functions. Later in this chapter, we'll discuss organizational effectiveness and efficiency, as well as the multitude of skills that managers use to perform their jobs successfully.

Remember This

- Managers get things done by coordinating and motivating other people.
- Management often is a different experience from what people expect.
- Innovative management is critical in today's turbulent world.

- The success of Twitter and Square can be attributed to the effectiveness of its innovative managers.
- **Management** is defined as the attainment of organizational goals in an effective and efficient manner through planning, organizing, leading, and controlling organizational resources.

The Four Management Functions

Exhibit 1.2 illustrates the process of how managers use resources to attain organizational goals through the functions of planning, organizing, leading, and controlling. Chapters of this book are devoted to the multiple activities and skills associated with each function, as well as to the environment, global competitiveness, and ethics that influence how managers perform these functions.

PLANNING

Planning means identifying goals for future organizational performance and deciding on the tasks and use of resources needed to attain them. In other words, managerial planning defines where the organization wants to be in the future and how to get there. A good example of planning comes from General Electric (GE), where managers have sold divisions such as plastics, insurance, and media to focus company resources on four key business areas: energy, aircraft engines, health care, and financial services. GE used to relocate senior executives every few years to different divisions so that they developed broad,

EXHIBIT 1.2 The Process of Management

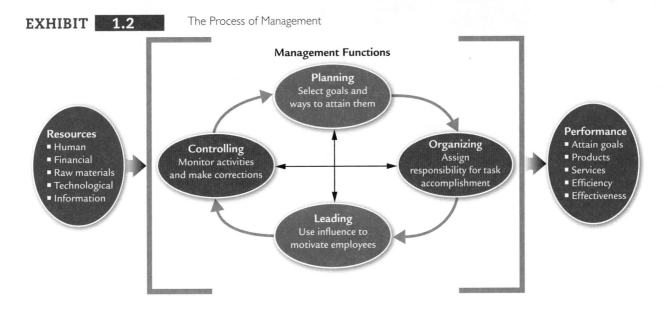

general expertise. In line with the strategic refocusing, the company now will keep people in their business units longer so they gain a deeper understanding of products and customers within each of the four core businesses.[11]

ORGANIZING

Organizing typically follows planning and reflects how the organization tries to accomplish the plan. **Organizing** involves assigning tasks, grouping tasks into departments, delegating authority, and allocating resources across the organization. In recent years, organizations as diverse as IBM, the Catholic Church, Estée Lauder, and the Federal Bureau of Investigation (FBI) have undergone structural reorganization to accommodate their changing plans. Organizing is a key task for Oprah Winfrey as she strives to turn around her struggling start-up cable network, OWN. She took over as CEO of the company, repositioned some executives and hired new ones, and cut jobs to reduce costs and streamline the company. She is hoping the structural changes will bring a lean, entrepreneurial approach that will get OWN on solid ground. Winfrey said "I prided myself on leanness," referring to the early days of her TV talk show. "The opposite was done here."[12]

LEADING

Leading is the use of influence to motivate employees to achieve organizational goals. Leading means creating a shared culture and values, communicating goals to people throughout the organization, and infusing employees with the desire to perform at a high level. As CEO of Chrysler Group, Sergio Marchionne spends about two weeks a month in Michigan meeting with executive teams from sales, marketing, and industrial operations to talk about his plans and motivate people to accomplish ambitious goals. Marchionne, who spends half his time in Italy running Fiat, rejected the 15th-floor executive suite at Chrysler headquarters so he could provide more hands-on leadership from an office close to the engineering center.[13] One doesn't have to be a top manager of a big corporation to be an exceptional leader. Many managers working quietly in both large and small organizations around the world provide strong leadership within departments, teams, nonprofit organizations, and small businesses.

Concept Connection ◀◀◀

John Arundel/Local Kicks

Warren Brown, a lawyer turned entrepreneur, finds that as the owner of CakeLove, a specialty bakery chain in the Washington, D.C., area, his job involves all four management functions. Once he's charted the course for the operation (**planning**) and put all the necessary policies, procedures, and structural mechanisms in place (**organizing**), he supports and encourages his employees (**leading**) and makes sure that nothing falls through the cracks (**controlling**). "After doing the leadership, kind of being the locomotive, I stand back and then I'm the caboose," says Brown.

CONTROLLING

Controlling is the fourth function in the management process. **Controlling** means monitoring employees' activities, determining whether the organization is moving toward its goals, and making corrections as necessary. One trend in recent years is for companies to place less emphasis on top-down control and more emphasis on training employees to monitor and correct themselves. However, the ultimate responsibility for control still rests with managers.

The U.S. Secret Service agency recently became embroiled in a public relations nightmare, partly due to a breakdown of managerial control. When news broke that members of the security team sent to prepare for President Barack Obama's visit to Cartagena, Colombia, engaged in a night of heavy drinking, visited strip clubs, and brought prostitutes to their hotel rooms, there was a public and legislative uproar. Several agents were fired, and director Mark Sullivan and other managers were called before a

Senate subcommittee to explain the breakdown in control. The widespread investigation has brought other allegations of agent misconduct and "morally repugnant behavior" to light. One response from managers has been to create stricter rules of conduct, rules that apply even when agents are off duty.[14]

Remember This

- Managers perform a wide variety of activities that fall within four primary management functions.
- **Planning** is the management function concerned with defining goals for future performance and how to attain them.
- **Organizing** involves assigning tasks, grouping tasks into departments, and allocating resources.

- **Leading** means using influence to motivate employees to achieve the organization's goals.
- **Controlling** is concerned with monitoring employees' activities, keeping the organization on track toward meeting its goals and making corrections as necessary.
- The U.S. Secret Service agency prostitution scandal can be traced partly to a breakdown of management control.

Organizational Performance

The second part of our definition of management is the attainment of organizational goals in an efficient and effective manner. Management is so important because organizations are so important. In an industrialized society where complex technologies dominate, organizations bring together knowledge, people, and raw materials to perform tasks that no individual could do alone. Without organizations, how could technology be provided that enables us to share information around the world in an instant; electricity be produced from huge dams and nuclear power plants; and millions of songs, videos, and games be available for our entertainment at any time and place? Organizations pervade our society, and managers are responsible for seeing that resources are used wisely to attain organizational goals.

Our formal definition of an **organization** is a social entity that is goal directed and deliberately structured. *Social entity* means being made up of two or more people. *Goal directed* means designed to achieve some outcome, such as make a profit (Walmart), win

Local Impact

Logistics giant **Deutsche Post DHL Group** planned for corporate social responsibility with sustainability at the *local* level. Deutsche Post DHL Group's commitment to social responsibility is reflected in its three pillars: *Go Green* (climate protection), *Go Help* (disaster relief), and *Go Teach* (education). Each pillar in this corporate plan is indicative of broad goals—such as a 30 percent reduction in CO_2 emissions by 2020—that are customized to fit local needs and cultures.

For example, DHL has 38 locations in Thailand, where Buddhist teachings about caring for one another lend themselves to helping and teaching the local population. By pinpointing local needs and issues, DHL planned site-specific strategies, such as efficient lighting and the reduction of air conditioner demand in Thailand's hot climate, and the installation of global positioning satellite (GPS) systems to minimize fuel consumption. In addition, DHL Thailand asks potential business partners to buy into the company's Go Green philosophy, reflecting a giant leap in sustainability at the local level.

Source: David Ferguson, "CSR in Asian Logistics: Operationalisation within DHL (Thailand)," *Journal of Management Development* 30, no. 10 (2011): 985–999.

pay increases for members (AFL-CIO), meet spiritual needs (United Methodist Church), or provide social satisfaction (a college sorority). *Deliberately structured* means that tasks are divided, and responsibility for their performance is assigned to organization members. This definition applies to all organizations, including both profit and nonprofit. Small, offbeat, and nonprofit organizations are more numerous than large, visible corporations—and just as important to society.

Based on our definition of management, the manager's responsibility is to coordinate resources in an effective and efficient manner to accomplish the organization's goals. Organizational **effectiveness** is the degree to which the organization achieves a *stated goal*, or succeeds in accomplishing what it tries to do. Organizational effectiveness means providing a product or service that customers value. Organizational **efficiency** refers to the amount of resources used to achieve an organizational goal. It is based on how much raw material, money, and people are necessary for producing a given volume of output. Efficiency can be calculated as the amount of resources used to produce a product or service. Efficiency and effectiveness can both be high in the same organization. Managers at Illumination Entertainment, the film production company behind *Dr. Seuss' The Lorax*, continually look for ways to increase efficiency while also meeting the company's goal of producing creative and successful animated films.

Innovative Way

Illumination Entertainment

You can't quite make a blockbuster movie on a dime, but Christopher Meledandri is out to prove that strict cost controls and hit animated films aren't mutually exclusive. Most computer-generated animated films cost at least $100 million, with some budgets pushing $150 million. In contrast, Illumination Entertainment made the hit film *Despicable Me* for only $69 million. The budget for *Hop* came in at a mere $63 million. And the company produced its third blockbuster, *Dr. Seuss' The Lorax*, for $70 million—less than the movie brought in at the box office on its opening weekend.

Managers at the company use many approaches to increase efficiency. For example, when making *Despicable Me*, they decided to eliminate details such as animal fur, which the audience couldn't see on the screen. Other details that were extremely costly to render in computer graphics but that weren't central to the story were also cut, saving the detail work for sets that were used repeatedly. The company paid big bucks for the voice of Steve Carell, but it hired other vocal talent with less star power, a practice that managers follow for all their films. They also seek out first-time directors and young, enthusiastic, less-experienced animators, who often cost less than half what a more experienced artist commands. Organizational details also contribute to efficiency—Meledandri keeps layers of the hierarchy to a minimum so that decisions can be made fast and movies don't languish for years in development, eating up money. Offices are in a low-rent area behind a cement plant rather than being housed in sumptuous surroundings.

Illumination Entertainment is quickly becoming the envy of Hollywood. Moviegoing in general is down, but animated family films are hot. And Illumination has had some of the hottest ones going. Peter Chernin, former president of News Corporation, said of Meledandri: "It is rare to find people whose business sense is as strong as their creative sense." Meledandri and his management team are using their business sense to run an efficient operation, and their creative instincts to put money in the right places to produce popular, often critically acclaimed animated films.[15]

So far, Illumination Entertainment has managed to adhere to its efficient, low-cost model as well as be highly effective in meeting its goals. Meledandri is committed to keeping things "lean and mean" so that costs don't creep up over time and require harsh cost slashing measures later on. All managers have to pay attention to costs, but severe cost cutting to improve efficiency can sometimes hurt organizational effectiveness. The ultimate responsibility of managers is to achieve high **performance**, which is the attainment of organizational goals by using resources in an efficient *and* effective manner. Consider what happened at music company EMI. Weak sales led managers to focus on financial efficiency, which successfully trimmed waste and boosted operating income. However, the efficiencies damaged the company's ability to recruit new artists, which are vital to record companies, and also led to internal turmoil that caused some longtime acts like the Rolling Stones to leave the label. Thus, the company's overall performance suffered. Managers are struggling to find the right balance between efficiency and effectiveness to get EMI back on the right track.[16]

Remember This

- An **organization** is a social entity that is goal directed and deliberately structured.
- Good management is important because organizations contribute so much to society.
- **Efficiency** pertains to the amount of resources—raw materials, money, and people—used to produce a desired volume of output.
- **Effectiveness** refers to the degree to which the organization achieves a stated goal.

- **Performance** is defined as the organization's ability to attain its goals by using resources in an efficient and effective manner.
- Managers at Illumination Entertainment are concerned both with keeping costs low (efficiency) and producing animated films such as *The Lorax* that are critically and financially successful (effectiveness).

Management Skills

A manager's job requires a range of skills. Although some management theorists propose a long list of skills, the necessary skills for managing a department or an organization can be placed in three categories: conceptual, human, and technical.[17] As illustrated in Exhibit 1.3, the application of these skills changes dramatically when a person is promoted to management. Although the degree of each skill that is required at different levels of an organization may vary, all managers must possess some skill in each of these important areas to perform effectively.

CONCEPTUAL SKILLS

Conceptual skill is the cognitive ability to see the organization as a whole system and the relationships among its parts. Conceptual skill involves knowing where one's team fits into the total organization and how the organization fits into the industry, the community, and

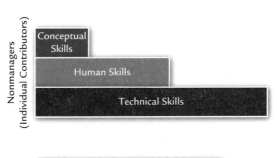

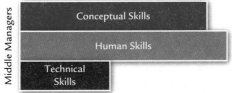

EXHIBIT 1.3

Relationship of Conceptual, Human, and Technical Skills to Management

Concept Connection ◀◀◀

Holding degrees in both physics and economics, entrepreneur Elon Musk certainly possesses his share of **technical skills**. He designed and created the first viable electric car—the Tesla roadster—as well as the Web-based payment service PayPal and a spacecraft that will enable private citizens to travel to outer space. But it is his stellar **conceptual skills** that allow him to lead the innovative companies that are making these products and services available to people worldwide.

the broader business and social environment. It means the ability to *think strategically*—to take the broad, long-term view—and to identify, evaluate, and solve complex problems.[18]

Conceptual skills are needed by all managers, but especially for managers at the top. Many of the responsibilities of top managers, such as decision making, resource allocation, and innovation, require a broad view. For example, Ursula Burns, who in 2009 became the first African American woman to lead a major U.S. corporation, needs superb conceptual skills to steer Xerox through the tough economy and the rapidly changing technology industry. Sales of copiers and printers have remained flat, prices have declined, and Xerox is battling stronger competitors in a consolidating industry. To keep the company thriving, Burns needs a strong understanding not only of the company, but also of shifts in the industry and the larger environment.[19]

HUMAN SKILLS

Human skill is the manager's ability to work with and through other people and to work effectively as a group member. Human skill is demonstrated in the way a manager relates to other people, including the ability to motivate, facilitate, coordinate, lead, communicate, and resolve conflicts. Human skills are essential for frontline managers who work with employees directly on a daily basis.[20] However, human skills are increasingly important for managers at all levels and in all types of organizations.[21]

Even at a company such as Google that depends on technical expertise, human skills are considered essential for managers. Google analyzed performance reviews and feedback surveys to find out what makes a good manager of technical people and found that technical expertise ranked dead last among a list of eight desired manager qualities, as shown in Exhibit 1.4. The exhibit lists eight effective behaviors of good managers. Notice that almost all of them relate to human skills, such as communication, coaching, and teamwork. People want managers who listen to them, build positive relationships, and show an interest in their lives and careers.[22] A recent survey comparing the importance of managerial skills today with those from the late 1980s found a decided increase in the role of skills for building relationships with others.[23]

EXHIBIT 1.4

Google's Rules: Eight Good Behaviors for Managers

To know how to build better managers, Google executives studied performance reviews, feedback surveys, and award nominations to see what qualities made a good manager. Here are the "Eight Good Behaviors" they found, in order of importance:

1. Be a good coach.
2. Empower your team and don't micromanage.
3. Express interest in team members' success and personal well-being.
4. Don't be a sissy: Be productive and results-oriented.
5. Be a good communicator and listen to your team.
6. Help your employees with career development.
7. Have a clear vision and strategy for the team.
8. Have key technical skills so you can help advise the team.

SOURCE: Google's Quest to Build a Better Boss, by Adam Bryant, published March 12, 2011 in the *New York Times*. Courtesy of Google, Inc.

Technical Skills

Technical skill is the understanding of and proficiency in the performance of specific tasks. Technical skill includes mastery of the methods, techniques, and equipment involved in specific functions such as engineering, manufacturing, or finance. Technical skill also includes specialized knowledge, analytical ability, and the competent use of tools and techniques to solve problems in that specific discipline. Technical skills are particularly important at lower organizational levels. Many managers get promoted to their first management jobs by having excellent technical skills. However, technical skills become less important than human and conceptual skills as managers move up the hierarchy. Top managers with strong technical skills sometimes have to learn to step back so others can do their jobs effectively. David Sacks, founder and CEO of Yammer, designed the first version of the product himself, but now the company has 200 employees and a dozen or so product managers and design teams. Sacks used to "walk around and look over the designers' shoulders to see what they were doing," but says that habit prevented some people from doing their best work.[24]

> **Take a Moment**
>
> Complete the Experiential Exercise on pages 29–30 that pertains to management skills. Reflect on the strength of your preferences among the three types of skills and the implications for you as a manager.

When Skills Fail

Everyone has flaws and weaknesses, and these shortcomings become most apparent under conditions of rapid change, uncertainty, or crisis.[25] Consider how Tony Hayward, a geologist by training, handled the BP Deepwater Horizon crisis in the Gulf of Mexico that ended his career as CEO and further damaged BP's reputation. Until the spring of 2010, Hayward had been praised for leading a successful turnaround at the oil giant. Yet, after an oil rig drilling a well for BP exploded in April, killing 11 workers and sending hundreds of millions of gallons of oil spewing into the Gulf of Mexico, Hayward faltered in his role as a crisis leader. His ill-advised comment that he wanted the crisis over as much as anyone because he "wanted his life back" showed an insensitivity and lack of diplomacy that roiled the public. Hayward's poor handling of the crisis eventually led to calls for his ouster, and he resigned in July 2010.[26]

During turbulent times, managers really have to stay on their toes and apply all their skills and competencies in a way that benefits the organization and its stakeholders—employees, customers, investors, the community, and so forth. In recent years, numerous highly publicized examples have shown what happens when managers fail to apply their skills effectively to meet the demands of an uncertain, rapidly changing world. Ethical and financial scandals have left people cynical about business managers and even less willing to overlook mistakes.

Crises and examples of corporate deceit and greed grab the headlines, but many more companies falter or fail less spectacularly. Managers fail to listen to customers, are unable to motivate employees, or can't build a cohesive team. For example, the reputation of Netflix went from "beloved icon of innovation to just another big, bad company ripping off customers" because managers didn't listen. Reed Hastings and other top executives couldn't help but hear the angry complaints from customers when they decided to increase prices and split the company's mail-order and streaming businesses at the same time, causing users to have to manage their accounts in two places. However, managers clearly weren't listening, as the company pushed forward with its plans despite growing customer frustration and resentment.[27]

Exhibit 1.5 shows the top ten factors that cause managers to fail to achieve desired results, based on a survey of managers in U.S. organizations operating in rapidly changing business environments.[28] Notice that many of these factors are due to poor human skills, such as the inability to develop good work relationships, a failure to clarify

EXHIBIT   1.5

Top Causes of Manager
Failure

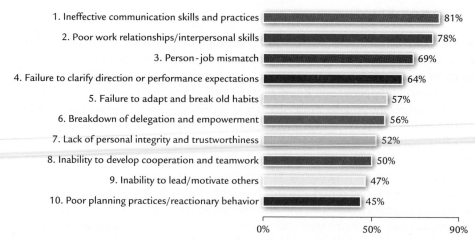

SOURCE: Adapted from Clinton O. Longenecker, Mitchell J. Neubert, and Laurence S. Fink, "Causes and Consequences of Managerial Failure in Rapidly Changing Organizations," *Business Horizons* 50 (2007): 145–155, Table 1, with permission from Elsevier.

direction and performance expectations, or an inability to create cooperation and team-work. The number one reason for manager failure is ineffective communication skills and practices, cited by 81 percent of managers surveyed. Especially in times of uncertainty or crisis, if managers do not communicate effectively, including listening to employees and customers and showing genuine care and concern, organizational performance and reputation suffer.

Remember This

- Managers have complex jobs that require a range of abilities and skills.
- **Conceptual skill** is the cognitive ability to see the organization as a whole and the relationship among its parts.
- **Human skill** refers to a manager's ability to work with and through other people and to work effectively as part of a group.
- **Technical skill** is the understanding of and proficiency in the performance of specific tasks.
- The two major reasons that managers fail are poor communication and poor interpersonal skills.
- A manager's weaknesses become more apparent during stressful times of uncertainty, change, or crisis.

Management Types

Managers use conceptual, human, and technical skills to perform the four management functions of planning, organizing, leading, and controlling in all organizations—large and small, manufacturing and service, profit and nonprofit, traditional and Internet-based. But not all managers' jobs are the same. Managers are responsible for different departments, work at different levels in the hierarchy, and meet different requirements for achieving high performance. Twenty-five-year-old Daniel Wheeler is a first-line supervisor in his first management job at Del Monte Foods, where he is directly involved in promoting products, approving packaging sleeves, and organizing people to host sampling events.[29] Kevin Kurtz is a middle manager at Lucasfilm, where he works with employees to develop marketing campaigns for some of the entertainment company's hottest films.[30] And Domenic Antonellis is CEO of the New England Confectionary Co. (Necco), the company that makes those tiny pastel candy hearts stamped with phrases such as "Be Mine" and "Kiss Me."[31] All three are managers and must contribute to planning, organizing, leading, and controlling their organizations—but in different amounts and ways.

VERTICAL DIFFERENCES

An important determinant of the manager's job is the hierarchical level. Exhibit 1.6 illustrates the three levels in the hierarchy. A study of more than 1,400 managers examined how the manager's job differs across these three hierarchical levels and found that the primary focus changes at different levels.[32] For first-level managers, the main concern is facilitating individual employee performance. Middle managers, though, are concerned less with individual performance and more with linking groups of people, such as allocating resources, coordinating teams, or putting top management plans into action across the organization. For top-level managers, the primary focus is monitoring the external environment and determining the best strategy to be competitive.

Let's look in more detail at differences across hierarchical levels. **Top managers** are at the top of the hierarchy and are responsible for the entire organization. They have titles such as president, chairperson, executive director, CEO, and executive vice president. Top managers are responsible for setting organizational goals, defining strategies for achieving them, monitoring and interpreting the external environment, and making decisions that affect the entire organization. They look to the long-term future and concern themselves with general environmental trends and the organization's overall success. Top managers are also responsible for communicating a shared vision for the organization, shaping corporate culture, and nurturing an entrepreneurial spirit that can help the company innovate and keep pace with rapid change.[33]

Middle managers work at middle levels of the organization and are responsible for business units and major departments. Examples of middle managers are department head, division head, manager of quality control, and director of the research lab. Middle managers typically have two or more management levels beneath them. They are responsible for implementing the overall strategies and policies defined by top managers. Middle managers generally are concerned with the near future, rather than with long-range planning.

The middle manager's job has changed dramatically over the past two decades. Many organizations improved efficiency by laying off middle managers and slashing middle

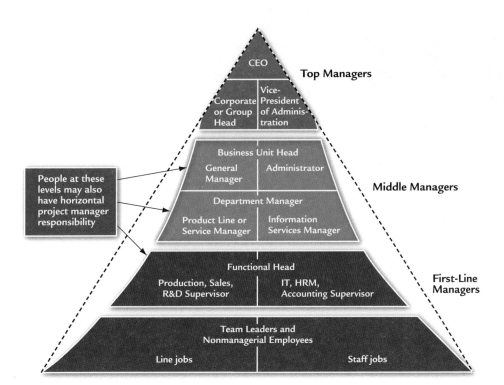

EXHIBIT 1.6

Management Levels in the Organizational Hierarchy

SOURCE: Adapted from Thomas V. Bonoma and Joseph C. Lawler, "Chutes and Ladders: Growing the General Manager," *Sloan Management Review* (Spring 1989): 27–37.

management levels. Traditional pyramidal organization charts were flattened to allow information to flow quickly from top to bottom and decisions to be made with greater speed. In addition, technology has taken over many tasks once performed by middle managers, such as monitoring performance and creating reports.[34] Exhibit 1.6 illustrates the shrinking middle management.

Yet even as middle management levels have been reduced, the middle manager's job has taken on a new vitality. Research shows that middle managers play a crucial role in driving innovation and enabling organizations to respond to rapid shifts in the environment.[35] As Ralph Stayer, CEO of Johnsonville Sausage, said, "Leaders can design wonderful strategies, but the success of the organization resides in the execution of those strategies. The people in the middle are the ones who make it work."[36] A study by Nicholas Bloom and John Van Reenen seems to support Stayer's observation. In an experiment with textile factories in India, improved middle management practices were introduced into 20 factories in India, and the results were compared to factories that did not improve management procedures. After just four months of training in better management methods, the 20 factories cut defects by 50 percent, boosted productivity and output, and improved profits by $200,000 a year.[37]

Middle managers' status also has escalated because of the growing use of teams and projects. A **project manager** is responsible for a temporary work project that involves the participation of people from various functions and levels of the organization, and perhaps from outside the company as well. Many of today's middle managers work with a variety of projects and teams at the same time, some of which cross geographical and cultural boundaries as well as functional ones.

First-line managers are directly responsible for the production of goods and services. They are the first or second level of management and have such titles as supervisor, line manager, section chief, and office manager. They are responsible for teams and non-management employees. Their primary concern is the application of rules and procedures to achieve efficient production, provide technical assistance, and motivate subordinates. The time horizon at this level is short, with the emphasis on accomplishing day-to-day goals. For example, Alistair Boot manages the menswear department for a John Lewis department store in Cheadle, England.[38] Boot's duties include monitoring and supervising shop floor employees to make sure that sales procedures, safety rules, and customer service policies are followed. This type of managerial job might also involve motivating and guiding young, often inexperienced workers; providing assistance as needed; and ensuring adherence to company policies.

Concept Connection ◄◄◄

Father and son Don (left) and Donnie (right) Nelson have both held the position of **general manager** for the Dallas Mavericks of the NBA. In 1997, when Don Nelson took over as general manager and head coach of the Mavericks, the basketball team was in a freefall. Donnie joined his father the next year as assistant coach to help build the team. They were rewarded for their efforts in 2003 when the team broke through with a dynamic defense. Donnie moved into the general manager position in 2005 when his father stepped down and has enjoyed overseeing the Mavericks as they won the NBA Championship in 2011, as well as their division titles in both 2007 and 2010.

HORIZONTAL DIFFERENCES

The other major difference in management jobs occurs horizontally across the organization. **Functional managers** are responsible for departments that perform a single functional task and have employees with similar training and skills. Functional departments include advertising, sales, finance, human resources, manufacturing, and accounting. *Line managers* are responsible for the manufacturing and marketing departments that make or sell the product or service. *Staff managers* are in charge of departments, such as finance and human resources, that support line departments.

General managers are responsible for several departments that perform different functions. A general manager is responsible for a self-contained division, such as a Nordstrom department store or a Honda assembly plant, and for all the functional departments within it. Project managers also have general management responsibility because they coordinate people across several departments to accomplish a specific project.

Remember This

- There are many types of managers, based on their purpose and location in an organization.
- A **top manager** is one who is at the apex of the organizational hierarchy and is responsible for the entire organization.
- **Middle managers** work at the middle level of the organization and are responsible for major divisions or departments.
- A **project manager** is a manager who is responsible for a temporary work project that involves people from various functions and levels of the organization.

- Most new managers are **first-line managers**— managers who are at the first or second level of the hierarchy and are directly responsible for overseeing groups of production employees.
- A **functional manager** is responsible for a department that performs a single functional task, such as finance or marketing.
- **General managers** are responsible for several departments that perform different functions, such as the manager of a Macy's department store or a Ford automobile factory.

What Is It Like to Be a Manager?

"Despite a proliferation of management gurus, management consultants, and management schools, it remains murky to many of us what managers actually do and why we need them in the first place," wrote Ray Fisman, a Columbia Business School professor.[39] Unless someone has actually performed managerial work, it is hard to understand exactly what managers do on an hour-by-hour, day-to-day basis. One answer to the question of what managers actually do to plan, organize, lead, and control was provided by Henry Mintzberg, who followed managers around and recorded all their activities.[40] He developed a description of managerial work that included three general characteristics and ten roles. These characteristics and roles, discussed in detail later in this section, have been supported by other research.[41]

Researchers also have looked at what managers *like* to do. Both male and female managers across five different countries report that they most enjoy activities such as leading others, networking, and leading innovation. Activities managers like least include controlling subordinates, handling paperwork, and managing time pressures.[42] Many new managers in particular find the intense time pressures of management, the load of administrative paperwork, and the challenge of directing others to be quite stressful as they adjust to their new roles and responsibilities. Indeed, the initial leap into management can be one of the scariest moments in a person's career.

MAKING THE LEAP: BECOMING A NEW MANAGER

Many people who are promoted into a manager position have little idea what the job actually entails and receive little training about how to handle their new role. It's no wonder that, among managers, first-line supervisors tend to experience the most job burnout and attrition.[43]

Making the shift from individual contributor to manager is often tricky. Mark Zuckerberg, whose company, Facebook, went public a week before he turned 28 years old, provides an example. In a sense, the public has been able to watch as Zuckerberg "grows up" as a manager. He was a strong individual performer in creating the social media platform and forming the company, but he fumbled with day-to-day management, such as interactions with employees and communicating with people both inside and outside

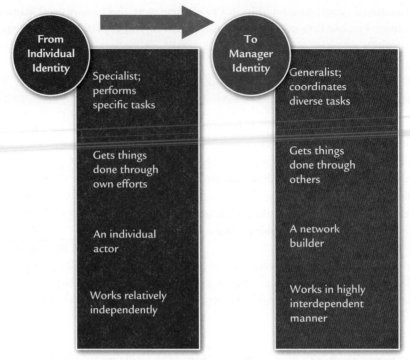

From Individual Identity → To Manager Identity

From Individual Identity	To Manager Identity
Specialist; performs specific tasks	Generalist; coordinates diverse tasks
Gets things done through own efforts	Gets things done through others
An individual actor	A network builder
Works relatively independently	Works in highly interdependent manner

SOURCE: Based on Exhibit 1.1, "Transformation of Identity," in Linda A. Hill, *Becoming a Manager: Mastery of a New Identity*, 2d ed. (Boston, MA: Harvard Business School Press, 2003), p. 6.

Facebook. Zuckerberg was smart enough to hire seasoned managers, including former Google executive Sheryl Sandberg, and cultivate advisors and mentors who have coached him in areas where he is weak. He also shadowed David Graham at the offices of The Post Company (publisher of *The Washington Post*) for four days to try to learn what it is like to manage a large organization. Now that Facebook is a public company, Zuckerberg will be watched more closely than ever to see if he has what it takes to be a manager of a big public corporation.[44]

Harvard professor Linda Hill followed a group of 19 managers over the first year of their managerial careers and found that one key to success is to recognize that becoming a manager involves more than learning a new set of skills. Rather, becoming a manager means a profound transformation in the way people think of themselves, called *personal identity*, which includes letting go of deeply held attitudes and habits and learning new ways of thinking.[45] Exhibit 1.7 outlines the transformation from individual performer to manager. Recall our earlier discussion of the role of manager as the person who builds systems rather than doing specific tasks. The individual performer is a specialist and a "doer." His or her mind is conditioned to think in terms of performing specific tasks and activities as expertly as possible. The manager, on the other hand, has to be a generalist and learn to coordinate a broad range of activities. Whereas the individual performer strongly identifies with his or her specific tasks, the manager has to identify with the broader organization and industry.

In addition, the individual performer gets things done mostly through his or her own efforts and develops the habit of relying on self rather than others. The manager, though, gets things done through other people. Indeed, one of the most common mistakes that new managers make is wanting to do all the work themselves, rather than delegating to others and developing others' abilities.[46] Hill offers a reminder that, as a manager, you must "be an instrument to get things done in the organization by working with and through others, rather than being the one doing the work."[47]

Another problem for many new managers is that they expect to have greater freedom to do what they think is best for the organization. In reality, though, managers

Take a Moment

Can you make a personal transformation from individual performer to manager, accomplishing work by engaging and coordinating other people? Look back at your results on the questionnaire at the beginning of this chapter to see how your priorities align with the demands placed on a manager.

find themselves hemmed in by interdependencies. Being a successful manager means thinking in terms of building teams and networks and becoming a motivator and organizer within a highly interdependent system of people and work. Although the distinctions may sound simple in the abstract, they are anything but. In essence, becoming a manager means becoming a new person and viewing oneself in a completely new way.

Many new managers have to make the transformation in a "trial by fire," learning on the job as they go, but organizations are beginning to be more responsive to the need for new manager training. The cost to organizations of losing good employees who can't make the transition is greater than the cost of providing training to help new managers cope, learn, and grow. In addition, some organizations use great care in selecting people for managerial positions, including ensuring that each candidate understands what management involves and really wants to be a manager.

MANAGER ACTIVITIES

Most new managers are unprepared for the variety of activities that managers routinely perform. One of the most interesting findings about managerial activities is how busy managers are and how hectic the average workday can be.

Adventures in Multitasking

Managerial activity is characterized by variety, fragmentation, and brevity.[48] The widespread and voluminous nature of a manager's tasks leaves little time for quiet reflection. A recent study by a team from the London School of Economics and Harvard Business School found that the time CEOs spend working alone averages a mere six hours a week. The rest of their time is spent in meetings, on the phone, traveling, and talking with others inside and outside the organization.[49]

Managers shift gears quickly. In his study, Mintzberg found that the average time a top executive spends on any one activity is less than nine minutes, and another survey indicates that some first-line supervisors average one activity every 48 seconds![50] Significant crises are interspersed with trivial events in no predictable sequence. Every manager's job is similar in its diversity and fragmentation to what *Workforce Management* described as a typical day in the life of human resources (HR) manager Kathy Davis:[51]

- 6:55 A.M.—Arrives at work early to begin investigating a complaint of sexual harassment at one of the factories, but as she's walking to her office, she bumps into someone carrying a picket sign that reads "Unfair Hiring! Who Needs HR?" Spends a few minutes talking with the young man, who is a temp that she had let go due to sloppy work.

- 7:10 A.M.—Finds the factory shift supervisor and a security staff member already waiting outside her door to discuss the sexual harassment complaint.

- 7:55 A.M.—Sue, a member of Kathy's team who has just arrived and is unaware of the meeting, interrupts to let Kathy know there is someone picketing in the hallway outside her office and the CEO wants to know what's going on.

- 8:00 A.M.—Alone at last, Kathy calls the CEO and explains the picketing situation, and then she begins her morning routine. Checking voice mail, she finds three messages that she must respond to immediately, and she passes four others to members of her team. She begins checking e-mail but is interrupted again by Sue, who reminds her they have to review the recent HR audit so that the company can respond promptly and avoid penalties.

- 9:15 A.M.—As she is reviewing the audit, Kathy gets a call from manager Pete Channing, asking if she's sent the offer letter to a prospective hire. "Don't send it," Pete said, "I've changed my mind." Weeks of interviewing and background checks, and now Pete wants to start over!

Take a Moment

How will you make the transition to a new manager's position and effectively manage your time to keep up with the hectic pace? Complete the New Manager Self-Test on page 20 to see how good you are at time management.

New Manager  Self-Test

Managing Your Time

Instructions: Think about how you normally handle tasks during a typical day at work or school. Read each item and check whether it is Mostly True or Mostly False for you.

	Mostly True	Mostly False
1. I frequently take on too many tasks.	_____	_____
2. I spend too much time on enjoyable but unimportant activities.	_____	_____
3. I feel that I am in excellent control of my time.	_____	_____
4. Frequently during the day, I am not sure what to do next.	_____	_____
5. There is little room for improvement in the way I manage my time.	_____	_____
6. I keep a schedule for events, meetings, and deadlines.	_____	_____
7. My workspace and paperwork are well organized.	_____	_____
8. I am good at record keeping.	_____	_____
9. I make good use of waiting time.	_____	_____
10. I am always looking for ways to increase task efficiency.	_____	_____

Scoring and Interpretation: For questions 3 and 5–10, give yourself one point for each Mostly True answer. For questions 1, 2, and 4, give yourself one point for each Mostly False answer. Your total score pertains to the overall way you use time. Items 1–5 relate to taking mental control over how you spend your time. Items 6–10 pertain to some mechanics of good time management. Good mental and physical habits make effective time management much easier. Busy managers have to learn to control their time. If you scored 8 or higher, your time-management ability is good. If your score is 4 or lower, you may want to reevaluate your time-management practices if you aspire to be a manager. How important is good time management to you? Read the Manager's Shoptalk box on page 22 for ideas to improve your time management skills.

- 11:20 A.M.—Kathy is getting to the end of her critical e-mail list when she hears a commotion outside her door and finds Linda and Sue arguing. "This report IT did for us is full of errors," Linda says, "but Sue says we should let it go." Kathy agrees to take a look at the IT department's report and discovers that there are only a few errors, but they have critical implications.

- 12:25 P.M.—As she's nearing the end of the IT report, Kathy's e-mail pings an "urgent" message from a supervisor informing her that one of his employees will be absent from work for a few weeks "while a felony morals charge is worked out." This is the first she's heard about it, so she picks up the phone to call the supervisor.

- 1:20 P.M.—Time for lunch—finally. She grabs a sandwich at a local supermarket and brings one back for the picketer, who thanks her and continues his march.

- 2:00 P.M.— Meets with CEO Henry Luker to review the audit and IT reports, discuss changes to the company's 401(k) plan, and talk about ideas for reducing turnover.

- 3:00 P.M.— Rushes back to her office to grab her keys so that she can drive to a meeting with the manufacturing facilities manager, who has asked Kathy to "shadow" him and share ideas about training and skills development.

- 3:15 P.M.—As she gets out of her car at the facility, Kathy runs into a man who had attended a supervision training course a few months earlier. He tells her that the class really helped him—there are fewer misunderstandings, and the staff seems to respect him more.

- 3:30 P.M.—Arrives right on time and spends the next couple of hours observing and asking questions, talking to employees to learn about the problems and obstacles they face.

- 5:40 P.M.—All is quiet back in the HR department, but there's a message from Sue that Kathy has an appointment first thing tomorrow morning with two women who had gotten into a fight in the elevator. Sighing, Kathy returns to her investigation of the sexual harassment complaint that she had begun at 7:00 that morning.

Life on Speed Dial

The manager performs a great deal of work at an unrelenting pace.[52] Managers' work is fast paced and requires great energy. Most top executives routinely work at least 12 hours a day and spend 50 percent or more of their time traveling.[53] Calendars are often booked months in advance, but unexpected disturbances erupt every day. Mintzberg found that the majority of executives' meetings and other contacts are ad hoc, and even scheduled meetings are typically surrounded by other events such as quick phone calls, scanning of e-mail, or spontaneous encounters. During time away from the office, executives catch up on work-related reading, paperwork, phone calls, and e-mail. Technology, such as e-mail, text messaging, cell phones, and laptops, intensifies the pace. Brett Yormark, the National Basketball Association (NBA)'s youngest CEO (of the New Jersey Nets), typically responds to about 60 messages before he even shaves and dresses for the day, and employees are accustomed to getting messages that Yormark has zapped to them in the wee hours of the morning.[54]

The fast pace of a manager's job is illustrated by Heather Coin, manager of the Sherman Oaks, California, branch of The Cheesecake Factory. Coin arrives at work about 9:30 A.M. and checks the financials for how the restaurant performed the day before. Next comes a staff meeting and various personnel duties. Before and during the lunch shift, she's pitching in with whatever needs to be done—making salads in the kitchen, expediting the food, busing the tables, or talking with guests. After lunch, from 3:00 to 4:30 P.M., Heather takes care of administrative duties, paperwork, or meetings with upper management, media, or community organizations. At 4:30, she holds a shift-change meeting to ensure a smooth transition from the day crew to the night crew. Throughout the day, Heather also mentors staff members, which she considers the most rewarding part of her job. After the evening rush, she usually heads for home about 10 P.M., the end of another 12½-hour day.[55]

Where Does a Manager Find the Time?

With so many responsibilities and so many competing demands on their time, how do managers cope? *The Wall Street Journal*'s "Lessons in Leadership" video series asked CEOs of big companies how they managed their time and found that many of them carve out time just to think about how to manage their time.[56] Time is a manager's most valuable resource, and one characteristic that identifies successful managers is that they know how to use time effectively to accomplish the important things first and the less important things later.[57] **Time management** refers to using techniques that enable you to get more done in less time and with better results, be more relaxed, and have more time to enjoy your work and your life. New managers in particular often struggle with the increased workload, the endless paperwork, the incessant meetings, and the constant interruptions that come with a management job. Learning to manage their time effectively is one of the greatest challenges that new managers face. This chapter's Manager's Shoptalk box offers some tips for time management.

Manager's *Shoptalk*

Time Management Tips for New Managers

Becoming a manager is considered by most people to be a positive, forward-looking career move and, indeed, life as a manager offers appealing aspects. However, it also holds many challenges, not the least of which is the increased workload and the difficulty of finding the time to accomplish everything on one's expanded list of duties and responsibilities. The following classic time management techniques can help you eliminate major time-wasters in your daily routines.

- **Keep a To-Do List.** If you don't use any other system for keeping track of your responsibilities and commitments, at the very least you should maintain a "To Do" list that identifies all the things you need to do during the day. Although the nature of management means that new responsibilities and shifting priorities occur frequently, it's a fact that people accomplish more with a list than without one.

- **Remember Your ABCs.** This is a highly effective system for prioritizing tasks or activities on your To Do list:

  - An "A" item is something highly important. It *must* be done, or you'll face serious consequences.

  - A "B" item is a *should do*, but consequences will be minor if you don't get it done.

  - "C" items are things that would be nice to get done, but there are no consequences at all if you don't accomplish them.

  - "D" items are tasks that you can delegate to someone else.

- **Do a Daily Review and Look-Ahead.** Spend 10–15 minutes each evening reviewing the day and then thinking ahead to the next day. Reviewing what worked well and what didn't will increase your awareness of your behavior and reduce your bad habits the next day. Then, look ahead and plan what you want to accomplish the next day. Some experts propose that every minute spent in planning saves 10 minutes in execution.

- **Do One Thing at a Time.** Multitasking has become the motto of the early twenty-first century, but too much multitasking is a time waster. Research has shown that multitasking *reduces* rather than enhances productivity. The authors of one study suggest that an inability to focus on one thing at a time could reduce efficiency by 20 to 40 percent. Even for those whose job requires numerous brief activities, the ability to concentrate fully on each one (sometimes called *spotlighting*) saves time. Give each task your full attention, and you'll get more done and get it done better, too.

Sources: Based on information in Pamela Dodd and Doug Sundheim, *The 25 Best Time Management Tools & Techniques* (Ann Arbor, MI: Peak Performance Press, Inc., 2005); Brian Tracy, *Eat That Frog: 21 Great Ways to Stop Procrastinating and Get More Done in Less Time* (San Francisco: Berrett-Koehler, 2002); Joshua S. Rubinstein, David E. Meyer, and Jeffrey E. Evans, "Executive Control of Cognitive Processes in Task Switching," *Journal of Experimental Psychology: Human Perception and Performance* 27, no. 4 (August 2001): 763–797; and Sue Shellenbarger, "Multitasking Makes You Stupid: Studies Show Pitfalls of Doing Too Much at Once," *The Wall Street Journal* (February 27, 2003): D1.

MANAGER ROLES

Mintzberg's observations and subsequent research indicate that diverse manager activities can be organized into ten roles.[58] A **role** is a set of expectations for a manager's behavior. Exhibit 1.8 describes activities associated with each of the roles. These roles are divided into three conceptual categories: informational (managing by information), interpersonal (managing through people), and decisional (managing through action). Each role represents activities that managers undertake to ultimately accomplish the functions of planning, organizing, leading, and controlling. Although it is necessary to separate the components of the manager's job to understand the different roles and activities of a manager, it is important to remember that the real job of management isn't practiced as a set of independent parts; all the roles interact in the real world of management.

EXHIBIT 1.8   Ten Manager Roles

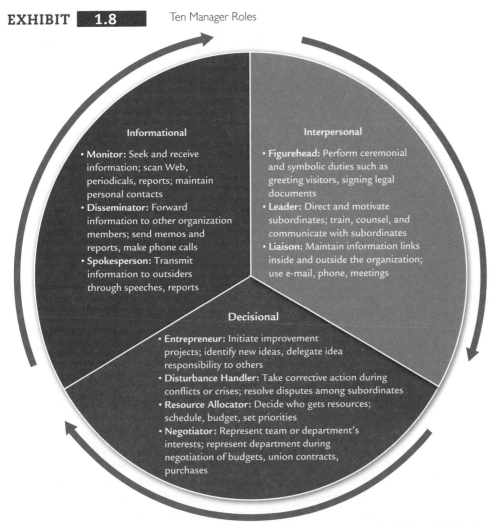

Informational

- **Monitor:** Seek and receive information; scan Web, periodicals, reports; maintain personal contacts
- **Disseminator:** Forward information to other organization members; send memos and reports, make phone calls
- **Spokesperson:** Transmit information to outsiders through speeches, reports

Interpersonal

- **Figurehead:** Perform ceremonial and symbolic duties such as greeting visitors, signing legal documents
- **Leader:** Direct and motivate subordinates; train, counsel, and communicate with subordinates
- **Liaison:** Maintain information links inside and outside the organization; use e-mail, phone, meetings

Decisional

- **Entrepreneur:** Initiate improvement projects; identify new ideas, delegate idea responsibility to others
- **Disturbance Handler:** Take corrective action during conflicts or crises; resolve disputes among subordinates
- **Resource Allocator:** Decide who gets resources; schedule, budget, set priorities
- **Negotiator:** Represent team or department's interests; represent department during negotiation of budgets, union contracts, purchases

SOURCE: Adapted from Henry Mintzberg, *The Nature of Managerial Work* (New York: Harper & Row, 1973), pp. 92–93; and Henry Mintzberg, "Managerial Work: Analysis from Observation," *Management Science* 18 (1971), B97–B110.

Informational Roles

Informational roles describe the activities used to maintain and develop an information network. General managers spend about 75 percent of their time communicating with other people. The *monitor* role involves seeking current information from many sources. The manager acquires information from others and scans written materials to stay well informed. The *disseminator* and *spokesperson* roles are just the opposite: The manager transmits current information to others, both inside and outside the organization, who can use it. Steve Jobs of Apple was a master of the spokesperson role when introducing new Apple products to the public, and employees and the media have been watching to see if new CEO Tim Cook can match his predecessor's proficiency. Cook has a distinctly different style from Jobs, less passionate and more controlled, but the comments about his first appearance as spokesperson for Apple at the 2012 "D: All Things Digital" conference were generally positive.[59]

Interpersonal Roles

Interpersonal roles pertain to relationships with others and are related to the human skills described earlier. The *figurehead* role involves handling ceremonial and symbolic activities for the department or organization. The manager represents the organization in his or her formal managerial capacity as the head of the unit. The presentation of employee awards by a branch manager for Commerce Bank is an example of the figurehead role. The *leader* role encompasses relationships with subordinates, including motivation, communication, and influence. The *liaison* role pertains to the development of information sources both inside and outside the organization. Consider the challenge of the leader and liaison roles for managers at National Foods, Pakistan's largest maker of spices and pickles. Managers in companies throughout Pakistan struggle with growing political instability, frequent power outages, government corruption and inefficiency, and increasing threats of terrorism, all of which makes the leader role even more challenging. "In the morning, I assess my workers," says Sajjad Farooqi, a supervisor at National Foods. If Farooqi finds people who are too stressed out or haven't slept the night before, he changes their shift or gives them easier work. Farooqi also pays a lot of attention to incentives because people are under so much pressure. As for the liaison role, managers have to develop information sources not only related to the business, but related to safety and security concerns.[60]

Decisional Roles

Decisional roles pertain to those events about which the manager must make a choice and take action. These roles often require conceptual as well as human skills. The *entrepreneur* role involves the initiation of change. Managers are constantly thinking about the future and how to get there.[61] The *disturbance handler* role involves resolving conflicts among subordinates or between the manager's department and other departments. The *resource allocator* role pertains to decisions about how to assign people, time, equipment, money, and other resources to attain desired outcomes. The manager must decide which projects receive budget allocations, which of several customer complaints receive priority, and even how to spend his or her own time. The founders and co-CEOs of Research in Motion (RIM), Mike Lazaridis and Jim Balsillie, were not very effective in fulfilling their decisional roles in the several years before the two resigned under pressure from angry shareholders and frustrated board members in early 2012. Rather than pushing for innovative new products and change at RIM, they kept pouring more resources into the BlackBerry, even as the iPhone and Android models devastated market share.[62]

Concept Connection ◄◄◄

COURTESY OF SBTV.COM

Small business owners often assume multiple management roles. Here, Susan Solovic (right), founder and CEO of sbtv.com, an Internet news and information site for small business, functions as a **spokesperson** in an interview with Phoenix anchor Tess Rafols of KTVK. When Solovic develops new ideas for sbtv.com, she functions as an **entrepreneur**, while she fills the **monitor** role when she keeps an eye on current trends that might benefit her evolving company and the small businesses her channel serves.

The relative emphasis that a manager puts on these ten roles depends on a number of factors, such as the manager's position in the hierarchy, natural skills and abilities, type of organization, or departmental goals to be achieved. For example, Exhibit 1.9 illustrates the varying importance of the leader and liaison roles as reported in a survey of top-, middle-, and lower-level managers. Note that the importance of the leader role typically declines, while the importance of the liaison role increases, as a manager moves up the organizational hierarchy.

Other factors, such as changing environmental conditions, also may determine which roles are more important for a manager at any given time. Robert Dudley, who took over as CEO of troubled oil giant BP after Tony Hayward was forced out due to mishandling the Deepwater Horizon crisis, has found informational roles and decisional roles at the top of his list as he has personally worked to repair relationships with U.S. government officials, mend fences with local communities, carve a path toward restoring the company's reputation, and take steps to prevent such a disastrous event from ever happening again.[63] Managers stay alert to needs both within and outside the organization to determine which roles are most critical at various times. A top manager may regularly put more emphasis on the roles of spokesperson, figurehead, and negotiator, but the emergence of new competitors may

EXHIBIT 1.9   Hierarchical Levels and Importance of Leader and Liaison Roles

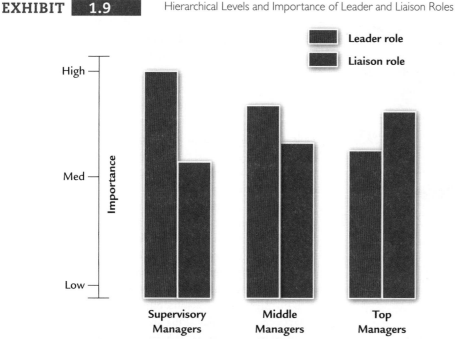

- Leader role
- Liaison role

SOURCE: Based on information from A. I. Kraut, P. R. Pedigo, D. D. McKenna, and M. D. Dunnette, "The Role of the Manager: What's Really Important in Different Management Jobs," *Academy of Management Executive* 3 (1989), 286–293.

require more attention to the monitor role, or a severe decline in employee morale and direction may mean that the CEO has to put more emphasis on the leader role. A marketing manager may focus on interpersonal roles because of the importance of personal contacts in the marketing process, whereas a financial manager may be more likely to emphasize decisional roles such as resource allocator and negotiator. Despite these differences, all managers carry out informational, interpersonal, and decisional roles to meet the needs of the organization.

Remember This

- Becoming a new manager requires a shift in thinking from being an individual performer to playing an interdependent role of coordinating and developing others.
- Because of the interdependent nature of management, new managers often have less freedom and control than they expect to have.
- The job of a manager is highly diverse and fast-paced, so managers need good time management skills.

- A **role** is a set of expectations for one's behavior.
- Managers at every level perform ten roles, which are grouped into informational roles, interpersonal roles, and decisional roles.
- After the death of Steve Jobs, Tim Cook has taken over the role of *spokesperson* for introducing new products at Apple.

Managing in Small Businesses and Nonprofit Organizations

Small businesses are growing in importance. Hundreds of small businesses open every month, but the environment for small business today is highly complicated. Chapter 6 provides detailed information about managing in small businesses and entrepreneurial startups.

One interesting finding is that managers in small businesses tend to emphasize roles different from those of managers in large corporations. Managers in small companies often

Concept Connection ◄◄◄

Despite having launched and sold several successful start-ups already, San Francisco-based **small business** owner Loic Le Meur is still a hands-on kind of manager. His daily blog about the blogosphere and the web in general is read by hundreds of thousands of people worldwide, and he is the chief organizer behind Europe's largest annual tech conference, LeWeb.

see their most important role as that of spokesperson because they must promote the small, growing company to the outside world. The entrepreneur role is also critical in small businesses because managers have to be innovative and help their organizations develop new ideas to remain competitive. At LivingSocial, for example, founder and CEO Tim O'Shaughnessy spends a lot of his time promoting the rapidly growing daily-deal site and talking with department heads about potential new products and services.[64] Small-business managers tend to rate lower on the leader role and on information-processing roles, compared with their counterparts in large corporations.

Nonprofit organizations also represent a major application of management talent.[65] Organizations such as the Salvation Army, Nature Conservancy, Greater Chicago Food Depository, Girl Scouts, and Cleveland Orchestra all require excellent management. The functions of planning, organizing, leading, and controlling apply to nonprofits just as they do to business organizations, and managers in nonprofit organizations use similar skills and perform similar activities. The primary difference is that managers in businesses direct their activities toward earning money for the company, whereas managers in nonprofits direct their efforts toward generating some kind of social impact. The characteristics and needs of nonprofit organizations created by this distinction present unique challenges for managers.[66]

Financial resources for nonprofit organizations typically come from government appropriations, grants, and donations rather than from the sale of products or services to customers. In businesses, managers focus on improving the organization's products and services to increase sales revenues. In nonprofits, however, services are typically provided to nonpaying clients, and a major problem for many organizations is securing a steady stream of funds to continue operating. Nonprofit managers, committed to serving clients with limited resources, must focus on keeping organizational costs as low as possible.[67] Donors generally want their money to go directly to helping clients rather than for overhead costs. If nonprofit managers can't demonstrate a highly efficient use of resources, they might have a hard time securing additional donations or government appropriations. Although the Sarbanes-Oxley Act (the 2002 corporate governance reform law) doesn't apply to nonprofits, for example, many are adopting its guidelines, striving for greater transparency and accountability to boost credibility with constituents and be more competitive when seeking funding.[68]

In addition, because nonprofit organizations do not have a conventional *bottom line*, managers often struggle with the question of what constitutes results and effectiveness. It is easy to measure dollars and cents, but the metrics of success in nonprofits are much more ambiguous. Managers have to measure intangibles such as "improve public health," "make a difference in the lives of the disenfranchised," or "increase appreciation for the arts." This intangible nature also makes it more difficult to gauge the performance of employees and managers. An added complication is that managers often depend on volunteers and donors who cannot be supervised and controlled in the same way that a business manager deals with employees. Many people who move from the corporate world to a nonprofit are surprised to find that the work hours are often longer and the stress greater than in their previous management jobs.[69]

The roles defined by Mintzberg also apply to nonprofit managers, but these may differ somewhat. We might expect managers in nonprofit organizations to place more emphasis on the roles of spokesperson (to "sell" the organization to donors and the public), leader (to build a mission-driven community of employees and volunteers), and resource allocator (to distribute government resources or grant funds that are often assigned top-down).

Managers in all organizations—large corporations, small businesses, and nonprofit organizations—carefully integrate and adjust the management functions and roles to meet challenges within their own circumstances and keep their organizations healthy.

Remember This

- Good management is just as important for small businesses and nonprofit organizations as it is for large corporations.
- Managers in these organizations adjust and integrate the various management functions, activities, and roles to meet the unique challenges they face.
- Managers in small businesses often see their most important roles as being a *spokesperson* for the business and acting as an *entrepreneur*.

- Managers in nonprofit organizations direct their efforts toward generating some kind of social impact rather than toward making money for the organization.
- Nonprofit organizations don't have a conventional bottom line, so managers often struggle with what constitutes effectiveness.

State-of-the-Art Management Competencies

In recent years, rapid environmental shifts have caused a fundamental transformation in what is required of effective managers. Technological advances and the rise of virtual work, global market forces, and shifting employee and customer expectations have led to a decline in organizational hierarchies and more empowered workers, which calls for a new approach to management that may be quite different from managing in the past.[70] Exhibit 1.10 shows the shift from the traditional management approach to the new management competencies that are effective in today's environment.

Instead of being a *controller*, today's effective manager is an *enabler* who helps people do and be their best. Managers help people get what they need, remove obstacles, provide learning opportunities, and offer

> "I was once a command-and-control guy, but the environment's different today. I think now it's a question of making people feel they're making a contribution."
>
> — JOSEPH J. PLUMERI, CHAIRMAN AND CEO OF WILLIS GROUP HOLDINGS

EXHIBIT 1.10

State-of-the-Art Management Competencies for Today's World

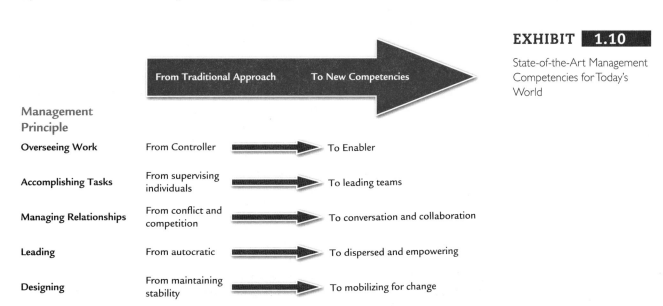

Management Principle	From Traditional Approach	To New Competencies
Overseeing Work	From Controller	To Enabler
Accomplishing Tasks	From supervising individuals	To leading teams
Managing Relationships	From conflict and competition	To conversation and collaboration
Leading	From autocratic	To dispersed and empowering
Designing	From maintaining stability	To mobilizing for change

Take a Moment

Read the Ethical Dilemma for Chapter 1 on page 62 that pertains to managing in the new workplace. Think about what you would do and why to begin understanding how you will solve thorny management problems.

feedback, coaching, and career guidance. Instead of "management by keeping tabs," they employ an empowering leadership style. Much work is done in teams rather than by individuals, so team leadership skills are crucial. People in many organizations work at scattered locations, so managers can't monitor behavior continually. In addition, managers sometimes are coordinating the work of people who aren't under their direct control, such as those in partner organizations, sometimes even working with competitors. Managing relationships based on authentic conversation and collaboration is essential for successful outcomes. In addition, today's best managers are "future-facing." That is, they design the organization and culture for creativity, adaptation, and innovation rather than maintaining the status quo. Today's world is constantly changing, and success depends on innovation and continuous improvement.

One manager who exemplifies the new management competencies is Vineet Nayar, CEO of India's HCL, with 80,000 employees and operations in more than 25 countries. When he took over as CEO, HCL was a traditional, hierarchical, command-and-control workplace, but Nayar shifted the mindset to treat employees like customers. He is always on the lookout to upgrade management competencies to serve employees and help them do their jobs better. When HCL needed to cut expenses by $100 million due to the global recession, managers asked the employees to come up with ideas for cutting costs without issuing massive layoffs.[71] The shift to a new way of managing isn't easy for traditional managers who are accustomed to being "in charge," making all the decisions, and knowing where their subordinates are and what they're doing at every moment.

Even more changes and challenges are on the horizon for organizations and managers. This is an exciting and challenging time to be entering the field of management. Throughout this book, you will learn much more about the new workplace, about the new and dynamic roles managers are playing in the twenty-first century, and about how you can be an effective manager in a complex, ever-changing world.

Remember This

- Turbulent environmental forces have caused a significant shift in the competencies required for effective managers.
- Traditional management competencies could include a command-and-control leadership style, a focus on individual tasks, and standardizing procedures to maintain stability.

- New management competencies include the ability to be an enabler rather than a controller, using an empowering leadership style, encouraging collaboration, leading teams, and mobilizing for change and innovation.
- Vineet Nayar, CEO of India's HCL, illustrates many of the new management competencies.

ch1: Discussion Questions

1. How do you feel about having management responsibilities in today's world, characterized by uncertainty, ambiguity, and sudden changes or threats from the environment? Describe some skills and qualities that are important to managers working in these conditions.

2. Assume that you are a project manager at a biotechnology company, working with managers from research, production, and marketing on a major product modification. You notice that every memo you receive from the marketing manager has been copied to senior management. At every company function, she spends time talking to the big shots. You are also aware that sometimes when you and the other project members

are slaving away over the project, she is playing golf with senior managers. What is your evaluation of her behavior? As project manager, what do you do?

3. Jeff Immelt of GE said that the most valuable thing he learned in business school was that "there are 24 hours in a day, and you can use all of them." Do you agree or disagree? What are some of the advantages to this approach to being a manager? What are some of the drawbacks?

4. Why do some organizations seem to have a new CEO every year or two, whereas others have top leaders who stay with the company for many years (e.g., Jack Welch's 20 years as CEO at GE)? What factors about the manager or about the company might account for this difference?

5. Think about Toyota's highly publicized safety problems. One observer said that a goal of efficiency had taken precedent over a goal of quality within Toyota. Do you think managers can improve both efficiency and effectiveness simultaneously? Discuss. How do you think Toyota's leaders should respond to the safety situation?

6. You are a bright, hard-working, entry-level manager who fully intends to rise up through the ranks. Your performance evaluation gives you high marks for your technical skills, but low marks when it comes to people skills. Do you think people skills can be learned, or do you need to rethink your career path? If people skills can be learned, how would you go about doing it?

7. If managerial work is characterized by variety, fragmentation, and brevity, how do managers perform basic management functions such as planning, which would seem to require reflection and analysis?

8. A college professor told her students, "The purpose of a management course is to teach students about management, not to teach them to be managers." Do you agree or disagree with this statement? Discuss.

9. Discuss some of the ways that organizations and jobs have changed over the past ten years. What changes do you anticipate over the next ten years? How might these changes affect the manager's job and the skills that a manager needs to be successful?

10. How might the teaching of a management course be designed to help people make the transition from individual performer to manager in order to prepare them for the challenges they will face as new managers?

ch1: Apply Your Skills: Experiential Exercise

Management Aptitude Questionnaire

Rate each of the following questions according to the following scale:

① I am never like this.
② I am rarely like this.
③ I am sometimes like this.
④ I am often like this.
⑤ I am always like this.

1. When I have a number of tasks or homework to do, I set priorities and organize the work around deadlines.
   1 2 3 4 5

2. Most people would describe me as a good listener.
   1 2 3 4 5

3. When I am deciding on a particular course of action for myself (such as hobbies to pursue, languages to study, which job to take, special projects to be involved in), I typically consider the long-term (three years or more) implications of what I would choose to do.
   1 2 3 4 5

4. I prefer technical or quantitative courses rather than those involving literature, psychology, or sociology.
   1 2 3 4 5

5. When I have a serious disagreement with someone, I hang in there and talk it out until it is completely resolved.
   1 2 3 4 5

6. When I have a project or assignment, I really get into the details rather than the "big picture" issues.
   1 2 3 4 5

7. I would rather sit in front of my computer than spend a lot of time with people.
   1 2 3 4 5

8. I try to include others in activities or discussions.
   1 2 3 4 5

9. When I take a course, I relate what I am learning to other courses I took or concepts I learned elsewhere.
   1 2 3 4 5

10. When somebody makes a mistake, I want to correct the person and let her or him know the proper answer or approach.
    1 2 3 4 5

11. I think it is better to be efficient with my time when talking with someone, rather than worry about the other person's needs, so that I can get on with my real work.
    1 2 3 4 5

12. I have a long-term vision of career, family, and other activities and have thought it over carefully.
    1 2 3 4 5

13. When solving problems, I would much rather analyze some data or statistics than meet with a group of people.
    1 2 3 4 5

14. When I am working on a group project and someone doesn't pull a fair share of the load, I am more likely to complain to my friends rather than confront the slacker.
    1 2 3 4 5

15. Talking about ideas or concepts can get me really enthusiastic or excited.
    1 2 3 4 5

16. The type of management course for which this book is used is really a waste of time.
    1 2 3 4 5

17. I think it is better to be polite and not hurt people's feelings.
    1 2 3 4 5

18. Data and things interest me more than people.
    1 2 3 4 5

Scoring and Interpretation

Subtract your scores for questions 6, 10, 14, and 17 from the number 6, and then add the total points for the following sections:

1, 3, 6, 9, 12, 15 Conceptual skills total score _____

2, 5, 8, 10, 14, 17 Human skills total score _____

4, 7, 11, 13, 16, 18 Technical skills total score _____

These skills are three of the skills needed to be a good manager. Ideally, a manager should be strong (though not necessarily equal) in all three. Anyone noticeably weaker in any of these skills should take courses and read to build up that skill. For further background on the three skills, please refer to the explanation on page 13.

ch1: Apply Your Skills: Small Group Breakout

Your Best and Worst Managers

Step 1. On your own, think of two managers that you have had—the best and the worst. The managers could be anyone who served as an authority figure over you, including an instructor, a boss at work, a manager of a student organization, a leader of a student group, a coach, a volunteer committee in a nonprofit organization, and so on. Think carefully about the specific behaviors that made each manager the best or the worst and write down what that manager did.

The best manager I ever had did the following:

_____

_____

_____

_____

The worst manager I ever had did the following:

_____

_____

_____

_____

Step 2. Divide into groups of four to six members. Each person should share his or her experiences, one at a time. Write on a sheet or whiteboard separate lists of best manager and worst manager behaviors.

Step 3. Analyze the two lists. What themes or patterns characterize "best" and "worst" manager behaviors? What are the key differences between the two sets of behaviors?

Step 4. What lessons does your group learn from its analysis? What advice or "words of wisdom" would you give managers to help them be more effective?

ch1: Endnotes

1. This questionnaire is adapted from research findings reported in Linda A. Hill, *Becoming a Manager: How New Managers Master the Challenges of Leadership*, 2d ed. (Boston, MA: Harvard Business School Press, 2003); and John J. Gabarro, *The Dynamics of Taking Charge* (Boston, MA: Harvard Business School Press, 1987).

2. This example is based on Jon Katzenbach, "The Steve Jobs Way," *Strategy + Business* (Summer 2012), www .strategy-business.com/article/00109?gko=d331b (accessed June 11, 2012); Leslie Kwoh and Emma Silverman, "Bio as Bible: Managers Imitate Steve Jobs," *The Wall Street Journal* (March 31, 2012), B1; and Joel Siegel, "When Steve Jobs Got Fired by Apple," *ABC News* (October 6, 2011), http://abcnews.go.com/Technology/ steve-jobs-fire-company/story?id=14683754 (accessed June 11, 2012).

3. Quoted in Ellen McGirt. "05: Square, For Making Magic Out of the Mercantile," *Fast Company* (March

2012), 82–85, 146–147 (part of the section, "The World's 50 Most Innovative Companies").

4. Will Self, "Twitter Is Just a New Home for Old Bores," *New Statesman* (March 26, 2012): 53; "Could Tunisia Be the Next Twitter Revolution?" *The Atlantic* (January 13, 2011), www.theatlantic.com/daily-dish/archive/2011/01/ could-tunisia-be-the-next-twitter-revolution/177302/ (accessed June 11, 2012); Alexander Mills et al., "Web 2.0 Emergency Applications: How Useful Can Twitter Be For Emergency Response? *Twitter for Emergency Management and Mitigation*, 2009, http://denman-mills.net/web_ documents/jips_mills.etal._2009.07.22_finalsubmission .pdf (accessed June 11, 2012); and McGirt, "05: Square, For Making Magic Out of the Mercantile."

5. McGirt, "05: Square, For Making Magic."

6. *Ibid.*

7. See Joshua Cooper Ramo, *The Age of the Unthinkable: Why the New World Disorder Constantly Surprises*

Us and What We Can Do About It (New York: Little Brown, 2009); and Richard Florida, *The Great Reset: How New Ways of Living and Working Drive Post-Crash Prosperity* (New York: Harper Collins, 2010).

8. Joshua Green, "Management Secrets of the Grateful Dead," *The Atlantic* (March 2010): 64–67; Jordan Timm, "Jerry Bears, Doobage, and the Invention of Social Networking," *Canadian Business* (September 2010): 74–75; David Meerman Scott and Brian Halligan, *Marketing Lessons from the Grateful Dead: What Every Business Can Learn from the Most Iconic Band in History* (New York: John Wiley & Sons, 2010); and Barry Barnes, *Everything I Know About Business I Learned from the Grateful Dead* (New York: Business Plus, 2011).

9. Darrell Rigby and Barbara Bilodeau, "Management Tools and Trends 2011," Bain and Company, Inc., www.bain.com/publications/articles/Management-tools-trends-2011.aspx (accessed June 22, 2012).

10. "What Do Managers Do?" *The Wall Street Journal Online*, http://guides.wsj.com/management/developing-a-leadership-style/what-do-managers-do/ (accessed August 11, 2010); article adapted from Alan Murray, *The Wall Street Journal Essential Guide to Management* (New York: Harper Business, 2010).

11. Kate Linebaugh, "The New GE Way: Go Deep, Not Wide," *The Wall Street Journal* (March 7, 2012), B1.

12. Christopher S. Stewart, "Oprah Struggles to Build Her Network," *The Wall Street Journal* (May 7, 2012), A1.

13. Jeff Bennett and Neal E. Boudette, "Boss Sweats Details of Chrysler Revival," *The Wall Street Journal* (January 31, 2011), A1.

14. Ed O'Keefe, "Lieberman Calls for Wider Inquiry into Secret Service Scandal," *The Washington Post* (April 23, 2012), A3; Laurie Kellman and Alicia A. Caldwell, "Inquiry Hears of Wider Secret Service Misbehavior," *The Salt Lake Tribune* (May 25, 2012); and "Secret Service Toughens Agent Conduct Rules after Prostitution Scandal: Political Notebook," *The Boston Globe* (April 28, 2012), A8.

15. Based on Lauren A. E. Schuker, "Movie Budget Lesson #1: Skip the Fur," *The Wall Street Journal* (July 15, 2010), B1; Brooks Barnes, "Animation Meets Economic Reality," *The New York Times* (April 4, 2011), B1; and Allison Corneau, "*The Lorax* Tops Weekend Box Office," *US Weekly* (March 4, 2012), www.usmagazine.com/entertainment/news/the-lorax-tops-weekend-box-office-201243 (accessed June 12, 2012).

16. Aaron O. Patrick, "EMI Deal Hits a Sour Note," *The Wall Street Journal*, August 15, 2009.

17. Robert L. Katz, "Skills of an Effective Administrator," *Harvard Business Review* 52 (September–October 1974): 90–102.

18. Troy V. Mumford, Michael A. Campion, and Frederick P. Morgeson, "The Leadership Skills Stratiplex: Leadership Skills Requirements Across Organizational Levels," *The Leadership Quarterly* 18 (2007): 154–166.

19. Nanette Byrnes and Roger O. Crockett, "An Historic Succession at Xerox," *BusinessWeek* (June 8, 2009): 18–22.

20. Sue Shellenbarger, "From Our Readers: The Bosses That Drove Me to Quit My Job," *The Wall Street Journal*, February 7, 2000.

21. Boris Groysberg, L. Kevin Kelly, and Bryan MacDonald, "The New Path to the C-Suite," *Harvard Business Review* (March 2011): 60–68; Jeanne C. Meister and Karie Willyerd, "Leadership 2020: Start Preparing People Now," *Leadership Excellence* (July 2010): 5; Neena Sinha, N. K. Kakkar, and Vikas Gupta, "Uncovering the Secrets of the Twenty-First-Century Organization," *Global Business and Organizational Excellence* (January–February 2012): 49–63; and Rowena Crosbie, "Learning the Soft Skills of Leadership," *Industrial and Commercial Training*, 37, no. 1 (2005).

22. Adam Bryant, "The Quest to Build a Better Boss," *The New York Times* (March 13, 2011), BU1.

23. William A. Gentry, Lauren S. Harris, Becca A. Baker, and Jean Brittain Leslie, "Managerial Skills: What Has Changed Since the Late 1980s?" *Leadership and Organization Development Journal* 29, no. 2 (2008): 167–181.

24. David Sacks, "The Way I Work: Yammer," *Inc.* (November 2011): 122–124.

25. Clinton O. Longenecker, Mitchell J. Neubert, and Laurence S. Fink, "Causes and Consequences of Managerial Failure in Rapidly Changing Organizations," *Business Horizons* 50 (2007): 145–155.

26. Paul Sonne, "The Gulf Oil Spill: Hayward Fell Short of Modern CEO Demands," *The Wall Street Journal*, July 26, 2010.

27. Sydney Finkelstein, "The Worst C.E.O.s of 2011," *The New York Times*, December 27, 2011; and Ethan Smith, "Netflix CEO Unbowed: Ignoring Customers' Anger, Company Says Separating DVD Business Is Essential," *The Wall Street Journal*, September 20, 2011.

28. Longenecker, Neubert, and Fink, "Causes and Consequences of Managerial Failure in Rapidly Changing Organizations."

29. Eileen Sheridan, "Rise: Best Day, Worst Day," *The Guardian*, September 14, 2002.

30. Heath Row, "Force Play" (Company of Friends column), *Fast Company* (March 2001): 46.

31. Charles Fishman, "Sweet Company," *Fast Company* (February 2001): 136–145.

32. A. I. Kraut, P. R. Pedigo, D. D. McKenna, and M. D. Dunnette, "The Role of the Manager: What's Really Important in Different Management Jobs," *Academy of Management Executive* 19, no. 4 (2005): 122–129.

33. Christopher A. Bartlett and Sumantra Ghoshal, "Changing the Role of Top Management: Beyond Systems to People," *Harvard Business Review* (May–June 1995): 132–142; and Sumantra Ghoshal and Christopher A. Bartlett, "Changing the Role of Top Management: Beyond Structure to Processes," *Harvard Business Review* (January–February 1995): 86–96.

34. Lynda Gratton, "The End of the Middle Manager," *Harvard Business Review* (January–February 2011): 36.

35. Paul Osterman, "Recognizing the Value of Middle Management," *Ivey Business Journal* (November–December 2009), http:// www.iveybusinessjournal.com /article.asp?intArticle_id=866; Quy Nguyen Huy, "In Praise of Middle Managers," *Harvard Business Review* (September 2003): 72–79; Rosabeth Moss Kanter, *On the Frontiers of Management* (Boston: Harvard Business School Press, 2003).

36. Quoted in Lisa Haneberg, "Reinventing Middle Management," *Leader to Leader* (Fall 2005): 13–18.

37. Reported in Ray Fisman, "In Defense of Middle Management," *The Washington Post*, October 16, 2010, www.washingtonpost.com/wp-dyn/content/ article/2010/10/16/AR2010101604266_pf.html (accessed June 13, 2012).

38. Miles Brignall, "Rise; Launch Pad: The Retailer; Alistair Boot, an Assistant Manager at the John Lewis Store in Cheadle, Talks to Miles Brignall," *The Guardian*, October 4, 2003.

39. Fisman, "In Defense of Middle Management."

40. Henry Mintzberg, *Managing* (San Francisco: Berrett-Kohler Publishers, 2009); Mintzberg, *The Nature of Managerial Work* (New York: Harper & Row, 1973); and Mintzberg, "Rounding Out the Manager's Job," *Sloan Management Review* (Fall 1994): 11–26.

41. Robert E. Kaplan, "Trade Routes: The Manager's Network of Relationships," *Organizational Dynamics* (Spring 1984): 37–52; Rosemary Stewart, "The Nature of Management: A Problem for Management Education," *Journal of Management Studies* 21 (1984): 323–330; John P. Kotter, "What Effective General Managers Really Do," *Harvard Business Review* (November–December 1982): 156–167; and Morgan W. McCall, Jr., Ann M. Morrison, and Robert L. Hannan, "Studies of Managerial Work: Results and Methods," Technical Report No. 9, Center for Creative Leadership, Greensboro, NC, 1978.

42. Alison M. Konrad, Roger Kashlak, Izumi Yoshioka, Robert Waryszak, and Nina Toren, "What Do Managers *Like* to Do? A Five-Country Study," *Group and Organizational Management* 26, no. 4 (December 2001): 401–433.

43. For a review of the problems faced by first-time managers, see Linda A. Hill, "Becoming the Boss," *Harvard Business Review* (January 2007): 49–56; Loren B. Belker and Gary S. Topchik, *The First-Time Manager: A Practical Guide to the Management of People*, 5th ed. (New York: AMACOM, 2005); J. W. Lorsch and P. F. Mathias, "When Professionals Have to Manage," *Harvard Business Review* (July–August 1987): 78–83; R. A. Webber, *Becoming a Courageous Manager: Overcoming Career Problems of New Managers* (Englewood Cliffs, NJ: Prentice Hall, 1991); D. E. Dougherty, *From Technical Professional to Corporate Manager: A Guide to Career Transition* (New York: Wiley, 1984); J. Falvey, "The Making of a Manager," *Sales and Marketing Management* (March 1989): 42–83; M. K. Badawy, *Developing Managerial Skills in Engineers and Scientists: Succeeding as a Technical Manager* (New York: Van Nostrand Reinhold, 1982); and M. London, *Developing Managers: A Guide to Motivating and Preparing People for Successful Managerial Careers* (San Francisco, CA: Jossey-Bass, 1985).

44. Based on Evelyn Rusli, Nicole Perlroth, and Nick Bilton, "The Hoodie amid the Pinstripes: As Facebook IPO Nears, Is Its Chief up to Running a Public Company?" *International Herald Tribune*, May 14, 2012, 17.

45. This discussion is based on Linda A. Hill, *Becoming a Manager: How New Managers Master the Challenges of Leadership*, 2d ed. (Boston, MA: Harvard Business School Press, 2003), 6–8; and Hill, "Becoming the Boss."

46. See also the "Boss's First Steps" sidebar in White, "Learning to Be the Boss"; and Belker and Topchik, *The First-Time Manager.*

47. Quoted in Eileen Zimmerman, "Are You Cut Out for Management?" (Career Couch column), *The New York Times*, January 15 2011, www.nytimes.com/2011/ 01/16/jobs/16career.html (accessed June 14, 2012).

48. Henry Mintzberg, *Managing*, 17–41.

49. Study reported in Rachel Emma Silverman, "Where's The Boss? Trapped in a Meeting," *The Wall Street Journal*, February 14, 2012, http://online.wsj.com/article/ SB10001424052970204642604577215013504567548 .html (accessed June 14, 2012).

50. *Ibid.*

51. Based on Allan Halcrow, "A Day in the Life of Kathy Davis: Just Another Day in HR," *Workforce Management* 77, no. 6 (June 1998): 56–62.

52. Mintzberg, *Managing*, 17–41.

53. Carol Hymowitz, "Packed Calendars Rule," *The Asian Wall Street Journal*, June 16, 2009; and "The 18-Hour Day," *The Conference Board Review* (March–April 2008): 20.

54. Adam Shell, "CEO Profile: Casting a Giant (New Jersey) Net," *USA Today*, August 25, 2008; Matthew Boyle and Jia Lynn Yang, "All in a Day's Work," *Fortune* (March 20, 2006): 97–104.

55. Susan Spielberg, "The Cheesecake Factory: Heather Coin," *Nation's Restaurant* (January 26, 2004): 38–39.

56. "Four CEOs' Tips on Managing Your Time," *The Wall Street Journal*, February 14, 2012, http://online.wsj.com/ article/SB10001424052970204883304577221551714 492724.html (accessed June 14, 2012).

57. A. Garrett, "Buying Time to Do the Things That Really Matter," *Management Today* (July 2000): 75; and Robert S. Kaplan, "What to Ask the Person in the Mirror," *Harvard Business Review* (January 2007): 86–95.

58. Mintzberg, *Managing*; Lance B. Kurke and Howard E. Aldrich, "Mintzberg Was Right! A Replication and Extension of *The Nature of Managerial Work,*"

Management Science 29 (1983): 975–984; Cynthia M. Pavett and Alan W. Lau, "Managerial Work: The Influence of Hierarchical Level and Functional Specialty," *Academy of Management Journal* 26 (1983): 170–177; and Colin P. Hales, "What Do Managers Do? A Critical Review of the Evidence," *Journal of Management Studies* 23 (1986): 88–115.

59. Jessica E. Vascellaro, "Apple Chief Executive Cook to Climb on a New Stage," *The Wall Street Journal*, May 29, 2012, B2; Walt Mossberg and Kara Swisher, "All Things Digital (A Special Report) – Apple After Jobs," *The Wall Street Journal*, June 4, 2012, R3; and Troy Wolverton, "Apple CEO Tim Cook Isn't Trying to Be the Next Steve Jobs," *Oakland Tribune*, May 29, 2012.

60. Naween Mangi, "Convoys and Patdowns: A Day at the Office in Pakistan," *Bloomberg Businessweek* (July 25–July 31, 2011): 11–13.

61. Harry S. Jonas III, Ronald E. Fry, and Suresh Srivastva, "The Office of the CEO: Understanding the Executive Experience," *Academy of Management Executive* 4 (August 1990): 36–48.

62. Will Connors and Chip Cummins, "RIM CEOs Give up Top Posts in Shuffle," *The Wall Street Journal Online*, January 23, 2012, http://online.wsj.com/article/SB100 01424052970204624204577177184275959856.html (accessed July 9, 2012); and Finkelstein, "The Worst C.E.O.s of 2011."

63. Guy Chazan and Monica Langley, "Dudley Faces Daunting To-Do List," *The Wall Street Journal Europe*, July 27, 2010.

64. Tim O'Shaughnessy, "The Way I Work: LivingSocial," *Inc.* (March 2012): 104–108.

65. Jean Crawford, "Profiling the Non-Profit Leader of Tomorrow," *Ivey Business Journal* (May–June 2010), www.iveybusinessjournal.com/topics/leadership/profiling-the-non-profit-leader-of-tomorrow (accessed June 14, 2012).

66. The following discussion is based on Peter F. Drucker, *Managing the Non-Profit Organization: Principles and Practices* (New York: HarperBusiness, 1992); and Thomas Wolf, *Managing a Nonprofit Organization* (New York: Fireside/Simon & Schuster, 1990).

67. Christine W. Letts, William P. Ryan, and Allen Grossman, *High Performance Nonprofit Organizations* (New York: Wiley & Sons, 1999), pp. 30–35.

68. Carol Hymowitz, "In Sarbanes-Oxley Era, Running a Nonprofit Is Only Getting Harder," *The Wall Street Journal*, June 21, 2005; and Bill Birchard, "Nonprofits by the Numbers," *CFO* (June 2005): 50–55.

69. Eilene Zimmerman, "Your True Calling Could Suit a Nonprofit" (interview, Career Couch column), *The New York Times*, April 6, 2008.

70. This discussion is based on ideas in Stephen Denning, "Masterclass: The Reinvention of Management," *Strategy & Leadership* 39, no. 2 (2011): 9–17; Julian Birkinshaw and Jules Goddard, "What Is Your Management Model?" *MIT Sloan Management Review* (Winter 2009): 81–90; Paul McDonald, "It's Time for Management Version 2.0: Six Forces Redefining the Future of Modern Management," *Futures* (October 2011): 797ff; Jeanne C. Meister and Karie Willyerd, "Leadership 2020: Start Preparing People Now," *Leadership Excellence* (July 2010): 5.

71. Described in Birkinshaw and Goddard, "What Is Your Management Model?"; Denning, "The Reinvention of Management"; and Traci L. Fenton, "Inspiring Democracy in the Workplace: From Fear-Based to Freedom-Centered Organizations," *Leader to Leader* (Spring 2012): 57–63.

The Evolution of Management Thinking

Timothy Hearsum/Jupiter Images

Learning Outcomes

After studying this chapter, you should be able to:

1. Understand how historical forces influence the practice of management.

2. Identify and explain major developments in the history of management thought.

3. Describe the major components of the classical and humanistic management perspectives.

4. Discuss the management science approach and its current use in organizations.

5. Explain the major concepts of systems thinking, the contingency view, and total quality management.

6. Name contemporary management tools and some reasons that management trends change over time.

7. Describe the management changes brought about by a technology-driven workplace, including the role of social media programs, customer relationship management (CRM), and supply chain management.

1 INTRODUCTION
2 ENVIRONMENT
3 PLANNING
4 ORGANIZING
5 LEADING
6 CONTROLLING

Are You a New-Style or an Old-Style Manager?[1]

http: See It Online www.

INSTRUCTIONS: The following are various behaviors in which a manager may engage when relating to subordinates. Read each statement carefully and rate each one Mostly True or Mostly False, to reflect the extent to which you would use that behavior.

	Mostly True	Mostly False
1. Supervise my subordinates closely to get better work from them.	_____	_____
2. Set the goals and objectives for my subordinates and sell them on the merits of my plans.	_____	_____
3. Set up controls to ensure that my subordinates are getting the job done.	_____	_____
4. Make sure that my subordinates' work is planned out for them.	_____	_____
5. Check with my subordinates daily to see if they need any help.	_____	_____
6. Step in as soon as reports indicate that progress on a job is slipping.	_____	_____
7. Push my people if necessary in order to meet schedules.	_____	_____
8. Have frequent meetings to learn from others what is going on.	_____	_____

SCORING AND INTERPRETATION: Add the total number of Mostly True answers and mark your score on the scale below. Theory X tends to be "old-style" management, and Theory Y "new-style," because the styles are based on different assumptions about people. To learn more about these assumptions, you can refer to Exhibit 2.4 and review the assumptions related to Theory X and Theory Y. Strong Theory X assumptions are typically considered inappropriate for today's workplace. Where do you fit on the X-Y scale? Does your score reflect your perception of yourself as a current or future manager?

X-Y Scale

Theory X ←—— 10 .... 5 .... 0 ——→ Theory Y

W hat do managers at India's Tata Group, U.S.-based General Electric (GE), and Africa's M-Pesa mobile money transfer service have in common with eighteenth-century inventor and statesman Benjamin Franklin? The authors of a recent book on innovation say they have all applied a concept called *jugaad* (pronounced joo-gaardh). *Jugaad* is a Hindi word that basically refers to creating something of benefit from limited resources. Benjamin Franklin, the authors say, is a great historical example because he faced scarcity firsthand, but he improvised to create inventions that were for the benefit of the masses.[2]

Management—like most disciplines—loves buzzwords, and *jugaad* is one of the most recent to appear on the radar. *Jugaad* basically refers to an innovation mindset, used widely by Indian companies, that strives to meet customers' immediate needs quickly and inexpensively. With research and development budgets strained in today's economy, U.S. and other Western managers have quickly picked up on the approach, sometimes calling it *frugal engineering*.[3] Will this be a buzzword that quickly fades from managers' vocabularies, or will it become as ubiquitous in management circles as terms such as total quality or *kaizen*?

Managers are always on the lookout for fresh ideas, innovative management approaches, and new tools and techniques. Management philosophies and organizational forms change over time to meet new needs. The questionnaire at the beginning of this chapter describes two differing philosophies about how people should be managed, and you will learn more about these ideas in this chapter.

If management is always changing, why does history matter to managers? The workplace of today is different from what it was 50 years ago—indeed, from what it was even 10 years ago—yet historical concepts form the backbone of management education.[4] One reason is that a historical perspective provides managers with a broader way of thinking, a way of searching for patterns and determining whether they recur across time periods. It is a way of learning from others' mistakes so as not to repeat them; learning from others' successes so as to repeat them in the appropriate situation; and most of all, learning to understand why things happen to improve organizations in the future. Certain management practices that seem modern, such as open-book management or employee stock ownership, have actually been around for a long time. These techniques have repeatedly gained and lost popularity since the early twentieth century because of shifting historical forces.[5]

This chapter provides a historical overview of the ideas, theories, and management philosophies that have contributed to making the workplace what it is today. The final section of the chapter looks at some recent trends and current approaches that build on this foundation of management understanding. This foundation illustrates that the value of studying management lies not in learning current facts and research, but in developing a perspective that will facilitate the broad, long-term view needed for management success.

Management and Organization

Take a Moment

Go to the Small Group Breakout on page 58 that pertains to how historical events and forces shape the lives of individuals.

Studying history doesn't mean merely arranging events in chronological order; it means developing an understanding of the impact of societal forces on organizations. Studying history is a way to achieve strategic thinking, see the big picture, and improve conceptual skills. Let's begin by examining how social, political, and economic forces have influenced organizations and the practice of management.[6]

Social forces refer to those aspects of a culture that guide and influence relationships among people. What do people value? What do people need? What are the standards of behavior among people? These forces shape what is known as the *social*

Drop Back and Punt

Glenn Rink's great product—popcorn-like sponges for absorbing oil spills—received a cool reception in the 1990s. Corporate skeptics said that traditional skimming of oil off water remained the preferred choice for disaster cleanup. Blocked by resistance to his product, Rink, founder of **Abtech Industries,** followed the historic and time-honored tradition of football teams, which sometimes need to drop back and punt before they can go on offense again.

Rink decided to focus on smaller-scale disasters instead. For more than a decade, Abtech Industries built a reputation for offering low-cost alternatives to address the cleanup needs of cities struggling with a variety of water pollution problems. The strategy paid off. In 2011, a revitalized Abtech, maker of the Smart Sponge Plus, partnered with the huge company Waste Management Inc. as the exclusive North American distributor to cities, and oil cleanup orders began pouring in. To date, Smart Sponge Plus has been used in more than 15,000 spill locations worldwide.

Source: "Innovation #71: Glenn Rink, Founder of Abtech Industries," *Fast Company* (June 2012): 136 (part of "The 100 Most Creative People in Business 2012," pp. 78–156).

contract, which refers to the unwritten, common rules and perceptions about relationships among people and between employees and management.

One social force is the changing attitudes, ideas, and values of Generation Y employees (sometimes called Millennials).[7] These young workers, the most educated generation in the history of the United States, grew up technologically adept and globally conscious. Unlike many workers of the past, they typically are not hesitant to question their superiors and challenge the status quo. They want a flexible, collaborative work environment that is challenging and supportive, with access to cutting-edge technology, opportunities to learn and further their careers and personal goals, and the power to make substantive decisions and changes in the workplace.

Political forces refer to the influence of political and legal institutions on people and organizations. One significant political force is the increased role of government in business after the collapse of companies in the financial services sector and major problems in the auto industry. Some managers expect increasing government regulation in the coming years.[8] Political forces also include basic assumptions underlying the political system, such as the desirability of self-government, property rights, contract rights, the definition of justice, and the determination of innocence or guilt of a crime.

Economic forces pertain to the availability, production, and distribution of resources in a society. Governments, military agencies, churches, schools, and business organizations in every society need resources to achieve their goals, and economic forces influence the allocation of scarce resources. Companies in every industry have been affected by the recent financial crisis, which is the worst since the Great Depression of the 1930s. Reduced consumer spending and tighter access to credit have curtailed growth and left companies scrambling to meet goals with limited resources. Although liquidity for large corporations has increased, smaller companies continued to struggle to find funding.[9] Another economic trend that affects managers worldwide is the growing economic power of countries such as China, India, and Brazil.[10]

Management practices and perspectives vary in response to these social, political, and economic forces in the larger society. Exhibit 2.1 illustrates the evolution of significant management perspectives over time. The timeline reflects the dominant time period for each approach, but elements of each are still used in today's organizations.[11]

EXHIBIT 2.1 Management Perspectives Over Time

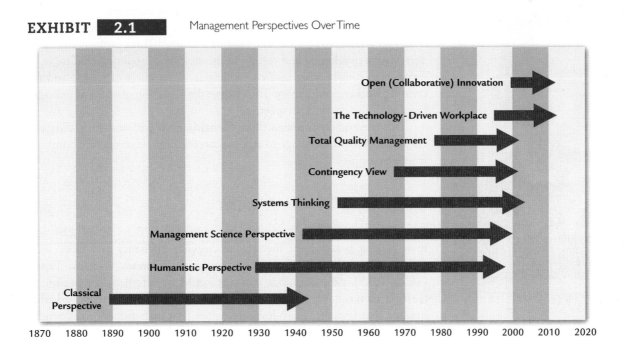

Classical Perspective

The practice of management can be traced to 3000 B.C., to the first government organizations developed by the Sumerians and Egyptians, but the formal study of management is relatively recent.[12] The early study of management as we know it today began with what is now called the **classical perspective**.

The classical perspective on management emerged during the nineteenth and early twentieth centuries. The factory system that began to appear in the 1800s posed challenges that earlier organizations had not encountered. Problems arose in tooling the plants, organizing managerial structure, training employees (many of them non-English-speaking immigrants), scheduling complex manufacturing operations, and dealing with increased labor dissatisfaction and resulting strikes.

These myriad new problems and the development of large, complex organizations demanded a new approach to coordination and control, and a "new sub-species of economic man—the salaried manager"[13]—was born. Between 1880 and 1920, the number of professional managers in the United States grew from 161,000 to more than 1 million.[14] These professional managers began developing and testing solutions to the mounting challenges of organizing, coordinating, and controlling large numbers of people and increasing worker productivity. Thus began the evolution of modern management with the classical perspective.

This perspective contains three subfields, each with a slightly different emphasis: scientific management, bureaucratic organizations, and administrative principles.[15]

SCIENTIFIC MANAGEMENT

Scientific management emphasizes scientifically determined jobs and management practices as the way to improve efficiency and labor productivity. In the late 1800s, a young engineer, Frederick Winslow Taylor (1856–1915), proposed that workers "could be retooled like machines, their physical and mental gears recalibrated for better productivity."[16] Taylor insisted that improving productivity meant that management itself would have to change and, further, that the manner of change could be determined only by scientific study; hence, the label *scientific management* emerged.

Concept Connection ◀◀◀

Frederick Winslow Taylor (1856–1915).
Taylor's theory that labor productivity could be improved by scientifically determined management practices earned him the title of "father of scientific management."

The Granger Collection, New York

Taylor suggested that decisions based on rules of thumb and tradition be replaced with precise procedures developed after careful study of individual situations.[17]

The scientific management approach is illustrated by the unloading of iron from rail cars and reloading finished steel for the Bethlehem Steel plant in 1898. Taylor calculated that with the correct movements, tools, and sequencing, each man was capable of loading 47.5 tons per day instead of the typical 12.5 tons. He also worked out an incentive system that paid each man $1.85 a day for meeting the new standard, an increase from the previous rate of $1.15. Productivity at Bethlehem Steel shot up overnight.

Although known as the *father of scientific management*, Taylor was not alone in this area. Henry Gantt, an associate of Taylor's, developed the *Gantt chart*, a bar graph that measures planned and completed work along each stage of production by time elapsed. Two other important pioneers in this area were the husband-and-wife team of Frank B. and Lillian M. Gilbreth. Frank B. Gilbreth (1868–1924) pioneered *time and motion study* and arrived at many of his management techniques independent of Taylor. He stressed efficiency and was known for his quest for the one best way to do work. Although Gilbreth is known for his early work with bricklayers, his work had great impact on medical surgery by drastically reducing the time that patients spent on the operating table. Surgeons were able to save countless lives through the application of time and motion study. Lillian M. Gilbreth (1878–1972) was more interested in the human aspect of work. When her husband died at the age of 56, she had 12 children ages 2 to 19. The undaunted "first lady of management" went right on with her work. She presented a paper in place of her late husband, continued their seminars and consulting, lectured, and eventually became a professor at Purdue University.[18] She pioneered in the field of industrial psychology and made substantial contributions to human resource management.

Exhibit 2.2 shows the basic ideas of scientific management. To use this approach, managers should develop standard methods for doing each job, select workers with the appropriate abilities, train workers in the standard methods, support workers and eliminate interruptions, and provide wage incentives.

▶ ▶ ▶ **Concept Connection**

Rue des Archives/The Granger Collection, New York

Automaker Henry Ford made extensive use of Frederick Taylor's **scientific management** techniques, as illustrated by this assembly of an automobile at a Ford plant circa 1930. Ford replaced workers with machines for heavy lifting and moving autos from one worker to the next. This reduced worker hours and improved efficiency and productivity. Under this system, a Ford car rolled off the assembly line every 10 seconds.

EXHIBIT 2.2

Characteristics of Scientific Management

General Approach
- Developed standard method for performing each job
- Selected workers with appropriate abilities for each job
- Trained workers in standard methods
- Supported workers by planning their work and eliminating interruptions
- Provided wage incentives to workers for increased output

Contributions
- Demonstrated the importance of compensation for performance
- Initiated the careful study of tasks and jobs
- Demonstrated the importance of personnel selection and training

Criticisms
- Did not appreciate the social context of work and higher needs of workers
- Did not acknowledge variance among individuals
- Tended to regard workers as uninformed and ignored their ideas and suggestions

The ideas of scientific management that began with Taylor dramatically increased productivity across all industries, and they are still important today. Indeed, the idea of engineering work for greater productivity has enjoyed a renaissance in the retail industry. Supermarket chains such as Meijer Inc. and Hannaford, for example, use computerized labor waste elimination systems based on scientific management principles. The system breaks down tasks such as greeting a customer, working the register, scanning items, and so forth, into quantifiable units and devises standard times to complete each task. Executives say the computerized system has allowed them to staff stores more efficiently because people are routinely monitored by computer and are expected to meet strict standards.[19]

A *Harvard Business Review* article discussing innovations that shaped modern management puts scientific management at the top of its list of 12 influential innovations. Indeed, the ideas of creating a system for maximum efficiency and organizing work for maximum productivity are deeply embedded in our organizations.[20] However, because scientific management ignores the social context and workers' needs, it can lead to increased conflict and clashes between managers and employees. The United Food and Commercial Workers Union, for instance, filed a grievance against Meijer in connection with its cashier-performance system. Under such performance management systems, workers often feel exploited—a sharp contrast from the harmony and cooperation that Taylor and his followers had envisioned.

BUREAUCRATIC ORGANIZATIONS

A systematic approach developed in Europe that looked at the organization as a whole is the **bureaucratic organizations approach**, a subfield within the classical perspective. Max Weber (1864–1920), a German theorist, introduced most of the concepts on bureaucratic organizations.[21]

During the late 1800s, many European organizations were managed on a personal, familylike basis. Employees were loyal to a single individual rather than to the organization or its mission. The dysfunctional consequence of this management practice was that resources were used to realize individual desires rather than organizational goals. Employees in effect owned the organization and used resources for their own gain rather than to serve customers. Weber envisioned organizations that would be managed on an impersonal, rational basis. This form of organization was called a *bureaucracy*. Exhibit 2.3 summarizes the six characteristics of bureaucracy as specified by Weber.

Weber believed that an organization based on rational authority would be more efficient and adaptable to change because continuity is related to formal structure and positions rather than to a particular person, who may leave or die. To Weber, rationality in organizations meant employee selection and advancement based not on whom you know, but rather on competence and technical qualifications, which are assessed by examination or according to specific training and experience. The organization relies on rules and written records for continuity. In addition, rules and procedures are impersonal and applied uniformly to all employees. A clear division of labor arises from distinct definitions of authority and responsibility, legitimized as official duties. Positions are organized in a hierarchy, with each position under the authority of a higher one. The manager gives orders successfully not on the basis of his or her personality, but on the legal power invested in the managerial position.

The term *bureaucracy* has taken on a negative meaning in today's organizations and is associated with endless rules and red tape. We have all been frustrated by waiting in long lines or following seemingly silly procedures. However, the value of bureaucratic principles is still evident in many organizations, such as United Parcel Service (UPS), sometimes nicknamed *Big Brown*.

> "Students would be more likely to have a positive impact on the future of management if they were more engaged with the history and traditions of management—particularly that of a German sociologist [Weber] who died nearly 100 years ago."
>
> —STEPHEN CUMMINGS AND TODD BRIDGMAN, VICTORIA UNIVERSITY OF WELLINGTON, NEW ZEALAND

EXHIBIT 2.3   Characteristics of Weberian Bureaucracy

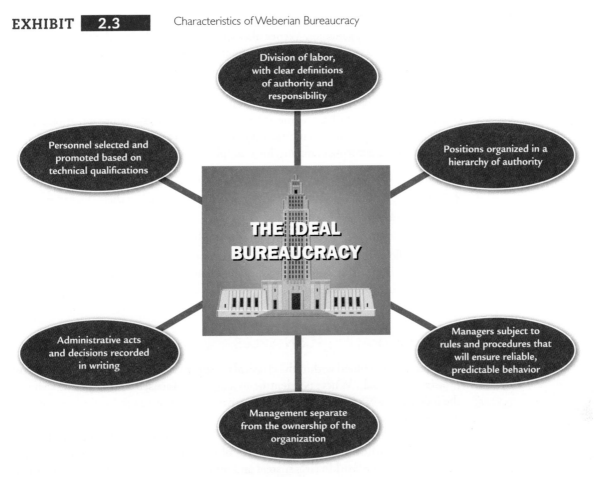

SOURCE: Adapted from Max Weber, *The Theory of Social and Economic Organizations,* ed. and trans. A. M. Henderson and Talcott Parsons (New York: Free Press, 1947), pp. 328–337.

Innovative Way

UPS

UPS is the largest package delivery company in the world and a leading global provider of specialized transportation and logistics services. The company operates in more than 200 countries and territories worldwide.

Why has UPS been so successful? One important factor is the concept of bureaucracy. UPS operates according to strict rules and regulations. It teaches drivers an astounding 340 steps for how to deliver a package correctly, such as how to load the truck, how to fasten their seat belts, how to walk, and how to carry their keys. Specific safety rules apply to drivers, loaders, clerks, and managers. Strict dress codes are enforced—clean uniforms (called *browns*), every day, black or brown polished shoes with nonslip soles, no beards, no hair below the collar, no tattoos visible during deliveries, and so on. Before each shift, drivers conduct a "Z-scan," a Z-shaped inspection of the sides and front of their vehicles. Employees are asked to clean off their desks at the end of each day so they can start fresh the next morning. Managers are given copies of policy books with the expectation that they will use them regularly, and memos on various policies and rules circulate by the hundreds every day.

UPS has a well-defined division of labor. Each plant consists of specialized drivers, loaders, clerks, washers, sorters, and maintenance personnel. UPS thrives on written records, and it has been a leader in using new technology to enhance reliability and efficiency. All drivers have daily worksheets that specify performance goals and work output. Technical qualification is the criterion for hiring and promotion. The UPS policy book says the leader is expected to have the knowledge and capacity to justify the position of leadership. Favoritism is forbidden. The bureaucratic model works just fine at UPS, "the tightest ship in the shipping business."[22]

Take ⓐ Moment

Read the Ethical Dilemma for Chapter 2 on pages 63–64 that pertains to problems with bureaucracy.

As this example shows, there are positive as well as negative aspects associated with bureaucratic principles. Weber also struggled with the good and bad sides of bureaucracy.[23] Although he perceived bureaucracy as a threat to basic personal liberties, he recognized it as the most efficient and rational form of organizing. Rules and other bureaucratic procedures provide a standard way of dealing with employees. Everyone gets equal treatment, and everyone knows what the rules are. Almost every organization needs to have some rules, and rules multiply as organizations grow larger and more complex. Some examples of rules governing employee behavior in a furniture manufacturing company, for example, might include:[24]

- Employees must wear protective eye and ear equipment when using machines.
- Employees must carry out any reasonable duty assigned to them, including shop maintenance.
- Employees must maintain an accurate time sheet, showing job and activity.
- The following will be considered causes for dismissal: excessive tardiness or absenteeism; willful damage to equipment; continual careless or unsafe behavior; theft; being under the influence of alcohol or illegal drugs while at work.

Take ⓐ Moment

What would it be like for you to be a manager in a bureaucratic organization? Complete the Experiential Exercise on pages 57–58 to find out if you would thrive in that type of environment.

ADMINISTRATIVE PRINCIPLES

Another major subfield within the classical perspective is known as the *administrative principles* approach. Whereas scientific management focused on the productivity of the individual worker, the **administrative principles approach** focused on the total organization. The major contributor to this approach was Henri Fayol (1841–1925), a French mining engineer who worked his way up to become head of a large mining group known as Comambault. Pieces of Comambault survive today as part of ArcelorMittal, the world's largest steel and mining company. In his later years, Fayol wrote down his concepts on administration, based largely on his own management experiences.[25]

In his most significant work, *General and Industrial Management*, Fayol discussed 14 general principles of management, several of which are part of management philosophy today. For example:

- *Unity of command.* Each subordinate receives orders from one—and only one—superior.
- *Division of work.* Managerial work and technical work are amenable to specialization to produce more and better work with the same amount of effort.
- *Unity of direction.* Similar activities in an organization should be grouped together under one manager.
- *Scalar chain.* A chain of authority extends from the top to the bottom of the organization and should include every employee.

Fayol felt that these principles could be applied in any organizational setting. He also identified five basic functions or elements of management: *planning, organizing, commanding, coordinating,* and *controlling.* These functions underlie much of the general approach to today's management theory.

The overall classical perspective as an approach to management was very powerful and gave companies fundamental new skills for establishing high productivity and effective treatment of employees. Indeed, the United States surged ahead of the world in management techniques, and other countries, especially Japan, borrowed heavily from American ideas.

Remember This

- The study of modern management began in the late nineteenth century with the **classical perspective**, which took a rational, scientific approach to management and sought to turn organizations into efficient operating machines.
- **Scientific management** is a subfield of the classical perspective that emphasizes scientifically determined changes in management practices as the solution to improving labor productivity.
- Frederick Winslow Taylor is known as "the father of scientific management."
- Scientific management is considered one of the most significant innovations influencing modern management.
- Some supermarket chains are using computerized systems based on scientific management principles to schedule employees for maximum efficiency.

- Another subfield of the classical perspective is the **bureaucratic organizations approach**, which emphasizes management on an impersonal, rational basis through elements such as clearly defined authority and responsibility, formal recordkeeping, and separation of management and ownership.
- Max Weber introduced most of the concepts about bureaucratic organizations.
- The **administrative principles approach** is a subfield of the classical perspective that focuses on the total organization rather than the individual worker and delineates the management functions of planning, organizing, commanding, coordinating, and controlling.
- Henri Fayol, a major contributor to the administrative principles approach, outlined 14 general principles of management, several of which are a part of management philosophy today.

Humanistic Perspective

▶ ▶ ▶ Concept Connection

The **humanistic perspective** on management emphasized the importance of understanding human behaviors, needs, and attitudes in the workplace, as well as social interactions and group processes.[26] There are three primary subfields based on the humanistic perspective: the human relations movement, the human resources perspective, and the behavioral sciences approach.

EARLY ADVOCATES

Two early advocates of a more humanistic approach were Mary Parker Follett and Chester Barnard. Mary Parker Follett (1868–1933) was trained in philosophy and political science, but she applied herself in many fields, including social psychology and management. She wrote of the importance of common superordinate goals for reducing conflict in organizations.[27] Her work was popular with businesspeople of her day but was often overlooked by management scholars.[28] Follett's ideas served as a contrast to scientific management and are re-emerging as applicable for modern managers dealing with rapid changes in today's global environment. Her approach to leadership stressed the importance of people rather than engineering techniques. She offered the pithy admonition, "Don't hug your blueprints," and analyzed the dynamics of management-organization interactions. Follett addressed issues that are timely today, such as ethics, power, and leading in a way that encourages employees to give their best. The concepts of *empowerment*, facilitating rather than controlling employees, and allowing employees to act depending on the authority of the situation opened new areas for theoretical study by Chester Barnard and others.[29]

Mary Parker Follette Foundation and Reading University, UK

Mary Parker Follett (1868–1933). Follett was an early advocate of the **humanistic perspective** on management. Her emphasis on worker participation and shared goals among managers was embraced by many businesspeople of the day and has been recently "rediscovered" by corporate America.

Concept Connection ◀◀◀

This 1914 photograph shows the initiation of a new arrival at a Nebraska planting camp. This initiation was not part of the formal rules and illustrates the significance of the **informal organization** described by Barnard. Social values and behaviors were powerful forces that could help or hurt the planting organization, depending on how they were managed.

Take a Moment

Before reading on, take the New Manager Self-Test on page 46. This test will give you feedback about your personal approach to getting things done through others.

Chester I. Barnard (1886–1961) studied economics at Harvard but failed to receive a degree because he did not take a course in laboratory science. He went to work in the statistical department of AT&T, and in 1927, he became president of New Jersey Bell. One of Barnard's significant contributions was the concept of the informal organization. The *informal organization* occurs in all formal organizations and includes cliques, informal networks, and naturally occurring social groupings. Barnard argued that organizations are not machines and stressed that informal relationships are powerful forces that can help the organization if properly managed. Another significant contribution was the *acceptance theory of authority*, which states that people have free will and can choose whether to follow management orders. People typically follow orders because they perceive positive benefit to themselves, but they do have a choice. Managers should treat employees properly because their acceptance of authority may be critical to organization success in important situations.[30]

HUMAN RELATIONS MOVEMENT

The **human relations movement** was based on the idea that truly effective control comes from within the individual worker rather than from strict, authoritarian control.[31] This school of thought recognized and directly responded to social pressures for enlightened treatment of employees. The early work on industrial psychology and personnel selection received little attention because of the prominence of scientific management. Then a series of studies at a Chicago electric company, which came to be known as the **Hawthorne studies**, changed all that.

Beginning about 1895, a struggle developed between manufacturers of gas and electric lighting fixtures for control of the residential and industrial market.[32] By 1909, electric lighting had begun to win, but the increasingly efficient electric fixtures used less total power, which was less profitable for the electric companies. The electric companies began a campaign to convince industrial users that they needed more light to get more productivity. When advertising did not work, the industry began using experimental tests to demonstrate their argument. Managers were skeptical about the results, so the Committee on Industrial Lighting (CIL) was set up to run the tests. To further add to the tests' credibility, Thomas Edison was made honorary chairman of the CIL. In one test location—the Hawthorne plant of the Western Electric Company—some interesting events occurred.

The major part of this work involved four experimental and three control groups. In all, five different tests were conducted. These pointed to the importance of factors *other* than illumination in affecting productivity. To examine these factors more carefully, numerous other experiments were conducted.[33] The results of the most famous study, the first Relay Assembly Test Room (RATR) experiment, were extremely controversial. Under the guidance of two Harvard professors, Elton Mayo and Fritz Roethlisberger, the RATR studies lasted nearly six years (May 10, 1927 to May 4, 1933) and involved 24 separate experimental periods. So many factors were changed and so many unforeseen factors uncontrolled that scholars disagree on the factors that truly contributed to the general increase in performance over that time period. Most early interpretations, however, agreed on one point: Money was not the cause of the increased output.[34] It was believed that the factor that best explained increased output was *human relations*. Employees performed better when managers treated them in a positive manner. Recent re-analyses of the experiments have revealed that a number of factors were different for the workers involved, and some suggest that money may well have been the single most important factor.[35] An interview with one of the original participants revealed that just getting into the experimental group meant a huge increase in income.[36]

These new data clearly show that money mattered a great deal at Hawthorne. In addition, worker productivity increased partly as a result of the increased feelings of importance and group pride that employees felt by virtue of being selected for this important project.[37] One unintended contribution of the experiments was a rethinking of field research practices. Researchers and scholars realized that the researcher can influence the outcome of an experiment by being too closely involved with research subjects. This phenomenon has come to be known as the *Hawthorne effect* in research methodology. Subjects behaved differently because of the active participation of researchers in the Hawthorne experiments.[38]

From a historical perspective, whether the studies were academically sound is less important than the fact that they stimulated an increased interest in looking at employees as more than extensions of production machinery. The interpretation that employees' output increased when managers treated them in a positive manner started a revolution in worker treatment for improving organizational productivity. Despite flawed methodology or inaccurate conclusions, the findings provided the impetus for the human relations movement. This approach shaped management theory and practice for well over a quarter-century, and the belief that human relations is the best area of focus for increasing productivity persists today.

▶ ▶ ▶ **Concept Connection**

Western Electric Photographic Services

This is the Relay Room of the Western Electric Hawthorne, Illinois, plant in 1927. Six women worked in this relay assembly test room during the controversial experiments on employee productivity. Professors Mayo and Roethlisberger evaluated conditions such as rest breaks and workday length, physical health, amount of sleep, and diet. Experimental changes were fully discussed with the women and were abandoned if they disapproved. Gradually the researchers began to realize they had created a change in supervisory style and **human relations**, which they believed was the true cause of the increased productivity.

HUMAN RESOURCES PERSPECTIVE

The human relations movement initially espoused a *dairy farm* view of management—just as contented cows give more milk, satisfied workers will produce more work. Gradually, views with deeper content began to emerge. The **human resources perspective** maintained an interest in worker participation and considerate leadership but shifted the emphasis to consider the daily tasks that people perform. The human resources perspective combines prescriptions for design of job tasks with theories of motivation.[39] In the human resources view, jobs should be designed so that tasks are not perceived as dehumanizing or demeaning but instead allow workers to use their full potential. Two of the best-known contributors to the human resources perspective were Abraham Maslow and Douglas McGregor.

Abraham Maslow (1908–1970), a practicing psychologist, observed that his patients' problems usually stemmed from an inability to satisfy their needs. Thus, he generalized his work and suggested a hierarchy of needs. Maslow's hierarchy started with physiological needs and progressed to safety, belongingness, esteem, and, finally, self-actualization needs. Chapter 16 discusses his ideas in more detail.

Douglas McGregor (1906–1964) had become frustrated with the early simplistic human relations notions while president of Antioch College in Ohio. He challenged both the classical perspective and the early human relations assumptions about human behavior. Based on his experiences as a manager and consultant, his training as a psychologist, and the work of Maslow, McGregor formulated Theory X and Theory Y, which are explained in Exhibit 2.4.[40] McGregor believed that the classical perspective was based on Theory X assumptions about workers. He also felt that a slightly modified version of

New Manager  Self-Test

What's Your Mach?

Instructions: Managers differ in how they view human nature and the tactics that they use to get things done through others. Answer the questions below based on how you view others. Think carefully about each question and be honest about what you feel inside. Please answer whether each item below is Mostly False or Mostly True for you.

	Mostly True	Mostly False
1. Overall, it is better to be humble and honest than to be successful and dishonest.		
2. If you trust someone completely, you are asking for trouble.		
3. A leader should take action only when it is morally right.		
4. A good way to handle people is to tell them what they like to hear.		
5. There is no excuse for telling a white lie to someone.		
6. It makes sense to flatter important people.		
7. Most people who get ahead as leaders have led very moral lives.		
8. It is better not to tell people the real reason you did something unless it benefits you to do so.		

9. The vast majority of people are brave, good, and kind. _____ _____

10. It is hard to get to the top without sometimes cutting corners. _____ _____

Scoring and Interpretation: To compute your Mach score, give yourself one point for each Mostly False answer to items 1, 3, 5, 7, and 9, and one point for each Mostly True answer to items 2, 4, 6, 8, and 10. These items were drawn from the works of Niccoló Machiavelli, an Italian political philosopher who wrote *The Prince* in 1513 to describe how a prince can retain control of his kingdom. Successful management intrigue at the time of Machiavelli was believed to require behaviors that today would be considered ego-centered and manipulative, which is almost the opposite of more enlightened management that arose from the human relations movement. A score of 8–10 points suggests that you have a high Mach score. From 4–7 points indicates a moderate score, and 0–3 points would indicate a low Mach score. Having a high Mach score does not mean that the individual is a sinister or vicious person, but it probably means that he or she has a cool detachment, sees life as a game, and is not personally engaged with other people. Discuss your results with other students, and talk about whether you think politicians and top executives would have a high or a low Mach score.

Source: Adapted from R. Christie and F. L. Geis, *Studies in Machiavellianism* (New York: Academic Press, 1970).

Theory X fit early human relations ideas. In other words, human relations ideas did not go far enough. McGregor proposed Theory Y as a more realistic view of workers for guiding management thinking.

The point of Theory Y is that organizations can take advantage of the imagination and intellect of all their employees. Employees will exercise self-control and will contribute to organizational goals when given the opportunity. A few companies today still use Theory X management, but many are using Theory Y techniques. Consider how Semco applies Theory Y assumptions to tap into employee creativity and mind power.

EXHIBIT 2.4   Theory X and Theory Y

Assumptions of Theory X

- The average human being has an inherent dislike of work and will avoid it if possible.
- Because of the human characteristic of dislike for work, most people must be coerced, controlled, directed, or threatened with punishment to get them to put forth adequate effort toward the achievement of organizational objectives.
- The average human being prefers to be directed, wishes to avoid responsibility, has relatively little ambition, and wants security above all.

Assumptions of Theory Y

- The expenditure of physical and mental effort in work is as natural as play or rest. The average human being does not inherently dislike work.
- External control and the threat of punishment are not the only means for bringing about effort toward organizational objectives. A person will exercise self-direction and self-control in the service of objectives to which he or she is committed.
- The average human being learns, under proper conditions, not only to accept but to seek responsibility.
- The capacity to exercise a relatively high degree of imagination, ingenuity, and creativity in the solution of organizational problems is widely, not narrowly, distributed in the population.
- Under the conditions of modern industrial life, the intellectual potentialities of the average human being are only partially utilized.

SOURCE: Douglas McGregor, *The Human Side of Enterprise* (New York: McGraw-Hill, 1960), pp. 33–48. (c) McGraw-Hill Companies, Inc. Reprinted by permission.

Innovative Way

Semco

The Brazil-based company Semco's fundamental operating principle is to harness the wisdom of all its employees. It does so by letting people control their work hours, location, and even pay plans. Employees also participate in all organizational decisions, including what businesses Semco should pursue.

Semco leaders believe that economic success requires creating an atmosphere that puts power and control directly in the hands of employees. People can veto any new product idea or business venture. They choose their own leaders and manage themselves to accomplish goals. Information is openly and broadly shared so that everyone knows where they and the company stand. Instead of dictating Semco's identity and strategy, leaders allow it to be shaped by individual interests and efforts. People are encouraged to seek challenges, explore new ideas and business opportunities, and question the ideas of anyone in the company.

This high level of trust in employees has helped Semco achieve decades of high profitability and growth despite fluctuations in the economy and shifting markets. "At Semco, we don't play by the rules," says Ricardo Semler. Semler, whose father started the company in the 1950s, says it doesn't unnerve him to "step back and see nothing on the company's horizon." He is happy to watch the company and its employees "ramble through their days, running on instinct and opportunity. . . ."[41]

For managers like Ricardo Semler, command and control is a thing of the past, with the future belonging to those companies that build leadership throughout the organization. The Theory Y approach has helped Semco succeed in a tough environment. Although few go as far as Semco, other companies are also using Theory Y principles that are more in line with today's emphasis on employee empowerment and involvement.

BEHAVIORAL SCIENCES APPROACH

The **behavioral sciences approach** uses scientific methods and draws from sociology, psychology, anthropology, economics, and other disciplines to develop theories

Take a Moment

Look back at your scores on the questionnaire at the beginning of this chapter related to Theory X and Theory Y. How will your management assumptions about people fit into an organization today?

about human behavior and interaction in an organizational setting. This approach can be seen in practically every organization. When a company such as Zappos.com conducts research to determine the best set of tests, interviews, and employee profiles to use when selecting new employees, it is using behavioral science techniques. When Best Buy electronics stores train new managers in the techniques of employee motivation, most of the theories and findings are rooted in behavioral science research.

One specific set of management techniques based in the behavioral sciences approach is *organization development* (OD). In the 1970s, OD evolved as a separate field that applied the behavioral sciences to improve the organization's health and effectiveness through its ability to cope with change, improve internal relationships, and increase problem-solving capabilities.[42] The techniques and concepts of OD have since been broadened and expanded to address the increasing complexity of organizations and the environment, and OD is still a vital approach for managers. OD will be discussed in detail in Chapter 11. Other concepts that grew out of the behavioral sciences approach include matrix organizations, self-managed teams, ideas about corporate culture, and management by wandering around. Indeed, the behavioral sciences approach has influenced the majority of tools, techniques, and approaches that managers have applied to organizations since the 1970s.

All the remaining chapters of this book contain research findings and management applications that can be attributed to the behavioral sciences approach.

Remember This

- The **humanistic perspective** emphasized understanding human behavior, needs, and attitudes in the workplace.
- Mary Parker Follett and Chester Barnard were early advocates of a more humanistic approach to management.
- Follett emphasized worker participation and empowerment, shared goals, and facilitating rather than controlling employees. Barnard's contributions include the acceptance theory of authority.
- The **human relations movement** stresses the satisfaction of employees' basic needs as the key to increased productivity.

- The **Hawthorne studies** were important in shaping ideas concerning how managers should treat workers.
- The **human resources perspective** suggests that jobs should be designed to meet people's higher-level needs by allowing employees to use their full potential.
- The **behavioral sciences approach** draws from psychology, sociology, and other social sciences to develop theories about human behavior and interaction in an organizational setting.
- Many current management ideas and practices can be traced to the behavioral sciences approach.

Management Science

World War II caused many management changes. The massive and complicated problems associated with modern global warfare presented managerial decision makers with the need for more sophisticated tools than ever before. **Management science**, also referred to as the *quantitative perspective*, provided a way to address those problems. This view is distinguished for its application of mathematics, statistics, and other quantitative techniques to management decision making and problem solving. During World War II, groups of mathematicians, physicists, and other scientists were formed to solve military problems that frequently involved moving massive amounts of materials and large numbers of people quickly and efficiently. Managers soon saw how quantitative techniques could be applied to large-scale business firms.[43]

Management scholar Peter Drucker's 1946 book *Concept of the Corporation* sparked a dramatic increase in the academic study of business and management. Picking up on techniques developed for the military, scholars began cranking out numerous mathematical tools for corporate managers, such as the application of linear programming for optimizing operations, statistical process control for quality management, and the capital asset pricing model.[44]

These efforts were enhanced with the development and perfection of the computer. Coupled with the growing body of statistical techniques, computers made it possible for managers to collect, store, and process large volumes of data for quantitative decision making, and the quantitative approach is widely used today by managers in a variety of industries. The Walt Disney Company used **quantitative techniques** to develop FASTPASS, a sophisticated computerized system that spares parents the ordeal of standing in long lines for the most popular rides. Disney theme parks have machines that issue coupons with a return time that's been calculated based on the number of people standing in the actual line, the number who have already obtained passes, and each ride's capacity. The next generation of technology, xPass, will let visitors book times for rides before they even leave home.[45] Let's look at three subsets of management science.

Operations research grew directly out of the World War II military groups (called *operational research teams* in Great Britain and *operations research teams* in the United States).[46] It consists of mathematical model building and other applications of quantitative techniques to managerial problems.

Operations management refers to the field of management that specializes in the physical production of goods or services. Operations management specialists use management science to solve manufacturing problems. Some commonly used methods are forecasting, inventory modeling, linear and nonlinear programming, queuing theory, scheduling, simulation, and break-even analysis.

Information technology (IT) is the most recent subfield of management science, which is often reflected in management information systems designed to provide relevant information to managers in a timely and cost-efficient manner. IT has evolved to include intranets and extranets, as well as various software programs that help managers estimate costs, plan and track production, manage projects, allocate resources, or schedule employees. Most of today's organizations have IT specialists who use quantitative techniques to solve complex organizational problems.

However, as events in the mortgage and finance industries show, relying too heavily on quantitative techniques can cause problems for managers. Mortgage companies used quantitative models that showed their investments in subprime mortgages would be okay even if default rates hit historically high proportions. However, the models didn't take into account that no one before in history had thought it made sense to give $500,000 loans to people making minimum wage![47] "Quants" also came to dominate organizational decisions in other financial firms. The term **quants** refers to financial managers and others who base their decisions on complex quantitative analysis, under the assumption that using advanced mathematics and sophisticated computer technology can accurately predict how the market works and help them reap huge profits. The virtually exclusive use of these quantitative models led aggressive traders and managers to take enormous risks. When the market began to go haywire as doubts about subprime mortgages grew, the models went haywire as well. Stocks predicted to go up went down, and vice versa. Events that were predicted to happen only once every 10,000 years happened three days in a row in the market madness. Scott Patterson, a *Wall Street Journal* reporter and author of *The Quants: How a New Breed of Math Whizzes Conquered Wall Street and Nearly Destroyed It*, suggests that the financial crisis that began in 2008 is partly due to the quants' failure to observe market fundamentals, pay attention to human factors, and heed their own intuition.[48]

Remember This

- Management science became popular based on its successful application in solving military problems during World War II.
- **Management science**, also called the *quantitative perspective*, uses mathematics, statistical techniques, and computer technology to facilitate management decision making, particularly for complex problems.
- The Walt Disney Company uses management science to solve the problem of long lines for popular rides and attractions at its theme parks.

- Three subsets of management science are operations research, operations management, and information technology.
- **Quants** have come to dominate decision making in financial firms, and the Wall Street meltdown in 2007–2008 shows the danger of relying too heavily on a quantitative approach.
- Management scholar Peter Drucker's classic 1946 book *Concept of the Corporation* sparked a dramatic increase in the academic study of business and management.

Recent Historical Trends

Despite recent heavy use of management science techniques by some managers, among the approaches that we've discussed so far the humanistic perspective has remained most prevalent from the 1950s until today. The post–World War II period saw the rise of new concepts, along with a continued strong interest in the human aspect of managing, such as team and group dynamics and other ideas that relate to the humanistic perspective. Three new concepts that appeared were systems thinking, the contingency view, and total quality management.

SYSTEMS THINKING

Systems thinking is the ability to see both the distinct elements of a system or situation and the complex and changing interaction among those elements. A **system** is a set of interrelated parts that function as a whole to achieve a common purpose.[49] **Subsystems** are parts of a system, such as an organization, that depend on one another. Changes in one part of the system (the organization) affect other parts. Managers need to understand the synergy of the whole organization, rather than just the separate elements, and to learn to reinforce or change whole system patterns.[50] **Synergy** means that the whole is greater than the sum of its parts. The organization must be managed as a coordinated whole. Managers who understand subsystem interdependence and synergy are reluctant to make changes that do not recognize subsystem impact on the organization as a whole.

Many people have been trained to solve problems by breaking a complex system, such as an organization, into discrete parts and working to make each part perform as well as possible. However, the success of each piece does not add up to the success of the whole. In fact, sometimes changing one part to make it better actually makes the whole system function less effectively. For example, a small city embarked on a road-building program to solve traffic congestion without whole-systems thinking. With new roads available, more people began moving to the suburbs. Rather than reduce congestion, the solution actually increased traffic congestion, delays, and pollution by enabling suburban sprawl.[51]

It is the *relationship* among the parts that form a whole system—whether a community, an automobile, a nonprofit agency, a human being, or a business organization—that matters. Systems thinking enables managers to look for patterns of movement over time and focus on the qualities of rhythm, flow, direction, shape, and networks of relationships that accomplish the performance of the whole. When managers can see the structures that underlie complex situations, they can facilitate improvement. But doing that requires a focus on the big picture.

An important element of systems thinking is to discern circles of causality. Peter Senge, author of *The Fifth Discipline*, argues that reality is made up of circles rather than straight

EXHIBIT 2.5 Systems Thinking and Circles of Causality

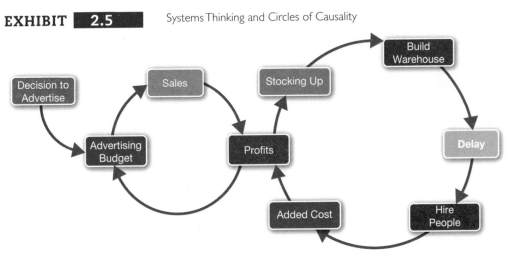

SOURCE: Based on concepts presented in Peter M. Senge, *The Fifth Discipline: The Art and Practice of the Learning Organization* (New York: Doubleday/Currency, 1990).

lines. For example, Exhibit 2.5 shows circles of influence for increasing a retail firm's profits. The events in the circle on the left are caused by the decision to increase advertising; hence the retail firm adds to the advertising budget to aggressively promote its products. The advertising promotions increase sales, which increase profits, which provide money to further increase the advertising budget.

But another circle of causality is being influenced as well. The decision by marketing managers will have consequences for the operations department. As sales and profits increase, operations will be forced to stock up with greater inventory. Additional inventory will create a need for additional warehouse space. Building a new warehouse will cause a delay in stocking up. After the warehouse is built, new people will be hired, all of which adds to company costs, which will have a negative impact on profits. Thus, understanding all the consequences of their decisions via circles of causality enables company leaders to plan and allocate resources to warehousing as well as to advertising to ensure stable increases in sales and profits. Without understanding system causality, top managers would fail to understand why increasing advertising budgets could cause inventory delays and temporarily reduce profits.

CONTINGENCY VIEW

A second recent extension to management thinking is the **contingency view**. The classical perspective assumed a *universalist* view. Management concepts were thought to be universal; that is, whatever worked in terms of management style, bureaucratic structure, and so on in one organization would work in any other one. In business education, however, an alternative view exists. In this *case* view, each situation is believed to be unique. Principles are not universal, and one learns about management by experiencing a large number of case problem situations. Managers face the task of determining what methods will work in every new situation.

To integrate these views, the contingency view emerged, as illustrated in Exhibit 2.6.[52] Here, neither of the other views is seen as entirely correct. Instead, certain contingencies, or variables, exist for helping managers identify and understand situations. The contingency view tells us that what works in one setting might not work in another. Contingency means that one thing depends on other things and a manager's response to a situation depends on identifying key contingencies in an organizational situation.

One important contingency, for example, is the industry in which the organization operates. The organizational structure that is effective for an Internet company, such as Google, would not be successful for a large auto manufacturer, such as Ford. A

EXHIBIT 2.6   Contingency View of Management

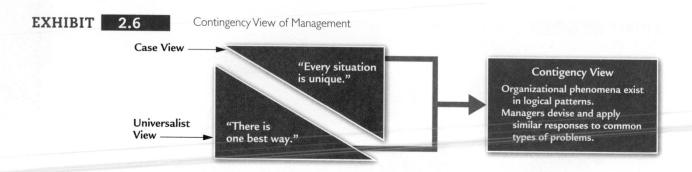

Case View → "Every situation is unique."

Universalist View → "There is one best way."

Contigency View
Organizational phenomena exist in logical patterns.
Managers devise and apply similar responses to common types of problems.

management-by-objectives (MBO) system that works well in a manufacturing firm, in turn, might not be right for a school system. When managers learn to identify important patterns and characteristics of their organizations, they can fit solutions to those characteristics.

Concept Connection ◀◀◀

Hyundai

Hyundai Motor Company's rise from 1 percent of the U.S. market in 1999 to about 9 percent of the U.S. market in 2011 shows how commitment to **total quality management** can improve a company's products and market position. First, managers increased the quality team from 100 to 865 people and held quality seminars to train employees. Then they **benchmarked** products, using vehicle lifts and high-intensity spotlights to compare against competing brands. Today, Hyundai earns quality ratings comparable to its main competitors, Honda and Toyota.

TOTAL QUALITY MANAGEMENT

The theme of quality is another concept that permeates current management thinking. The quality movement is strongly associated with Japanese companies, but these ideas emerged partly as a result of American influence after World War II. The ideas of W. Edwards Deming, known as the "father of the quality movement," were initially scoffed at in the United States, but the Japanese embraced his theories and modified them to help rebuild their industries into world powers.[53] Japanese companies achieved a significant departure from the American model by gradually shifting from an inspection-oriented approach to quality control toward an approach that emphasized employee involvement in the prevention of quality problems.[54]

During the 1980s and into the 1990s, **total quality management (TQM)**, which focuses on managing the total organization to deliver better quality to customers, moved to the forefront in helping U.S. managers deal with global competition. The approach infuses high-quality values throughout every activity within a company, with frontline workers intimately involved in the process. Four significant elements of quality management are employee involvement, focus on the customer, benchmarking, and continuous improvement, often referred to as *kaizen*.

Employee involvement means that achieving better quality requires companywide participation in quality control. All employees are *focused on the customer*; companies find out what customers want and try to meet their needs and expectations. *Benchmarking* refers to a process whereby companies find out how others do something better than they do and then try to imitate or improve on it. *Continuous improvement* is the implementation of small, incremental improvements in all areas of the organization on an ongoing basis. TQM is not a quick fix, but companies such as GE, Texas Instruments, Procter & Gamble, and DuPont achieved astonishing results in efficiency, quality, and customer satisfaction through total quality management.[55] TQM is still an important part of today's organizations, and managers consider benchmarking in particular a highly effective and satisfying management technique.[56]

Some of today's companies pursue highly ambitious quality goals to demonstrate their commitment to improving quality. For example, *Six Sigma*, popularized by Motorola and GE, specifies a goal of no more than 3.4 defects per million parts. However, the term also refers to a broad quality control approach that emphasizes a disciplined and relentless pursuit of higher quality and lower costs. TQM will be discussed in detail in Chapter 19.

Remember This

- A **system** is a set of interrelated parts that function as a whole to achieve a common purpose. An organization is a system.
- **Systems thinking** means looking not just at discrete parts of an organizational situation, but also at the continually changing interactions among the parts.
- When managers think systemically and understand subsystem interdependence and synergy, they can get a better handle on managing in a complex environment.
- **Subsystems** are parts of a system that depend on one another for their functioning.
- The concept of **synergy** says that the whole is greater than the sum of its parts. The organization must be managed as a whole.

- The **contingency view** tells managers that what works in one organizational situation might not work in others. Managers can identify important *contingencies* that help guide their decisions regarding the organization.
- The quality movement is associated with Japanese companies, but it emerged partly as a result of American influence after World War II.
- W. Edwards Deming is known as the "father of the quality movement."
- **Total quality management** focuses on managing the total organization to deliver quality to customers.
- Four significant elements of TQM are employee involvement, focus on the customer, benchmarking, and continuous improvement.

Innovative Management Thinking for a Changing World

All of the ideas and approaches discussed so far in this chapter go into the mix that makes up modern management. Dozens of ideas and techniques in current use can trace their roots to these historical perspectives.[57] In addition, innovative concepts continue to emerge to address new management challenges. Smart managers heed the past but know that they and their organizations have to change with the times. General Motors (GM) was the "ideal" organizational model in a post–World War II environment, but by 2009, it had collapsed into bankruptcy and sought billions of dollars in government aid because managers failed to pay attention as the world changed around them.[58] GM managers assumed that the preeminence of their company would shelter it from change, and they stuck far too long with a strategy, culture, and management approach that were out of tune with the shifting environment.

CONTEMPORARY MANAGEMENT TOOLS

Recall from the beginning of this chapter our discussion of *jugaad*, an approach to innovation management used in India that many U.S. managers are trying. Management fads and fashions come and go, but managers are always looking for new techniques and approaches that more adequately respond to customer needs and the demands of the environment. A recent survey of European managers reflects that managers pay attention to currently fashionable management concepts. The following table lists the percentage of managers reporting that they were aware of these selected management trends that have been popular over the past decade.[59]

Concept	Awareness Percentage
E-business	99.41
Decentralization	99.12
Customer Relationship Management	97.50
Virtual Organization	91.19
Empowerment	83.41
Reengineering	76.65

Managers especially tend to look for fresh ideas to help them cope during difficult times. For instance, recent challenges such as the tough economy and volatile stock market, environmental and organizational crises, lingering anxieties over war and terrorism, and public suspicion and skepticism resulting from the crisis on Wall Street have left today's executives searching for any management tool—new or old—that can help them get the most out of limited resources. The Manager's Shoptalk lists a wide variety of ideas and techniques used by today's managers. Management idea life cycles have been growing shorter as the pace of change has increased. A study by professors at the University of Louisiana at Lafayette found that, from the 1950s to the 1970s, it typically took more than a decade for interest in a popular management idea to peak. Now, the interval has shrunk to fewer than three years, and some trends come and go even faster.[60]

MANAGING THE TECHNOLOGY-DRIVEN WORKPLACE

Two popular contemporary tools that have shown some staying power (as reflected in the Shoptalk Box) are customer relationship management and supply chain management. These techniques are related to the shift to a technology-driven workplace. A more recent tool in the technology-driven workplace, social media, is also growing in use and importance.

Social Media Programs

Companies use social media programs to interact electronically with employees, customers, partners, and other stakeholders. Although only 29 percent of managers surveyed by Bain & Company said their companies used social media programs in 2010, more than half said they planned to use them in 2011.[61] **Social media programs** include company online community pages, social media sites such as Facebook or LinkedIn, microblogging platforms such as Twitter and China's Weibo, and company online forums. One frequent, and controversial, use of social media has been to look into the backgrounds and activities of job candidates. A survey by CareerBuilder found that 37 percent of hiring managers said they had used social media sites to see if job applicants present themselves professionally, to learn more about an applicant's qualifications, or to see if the candidate would be a good fit with the organizational culture.[62] Other uses of social media programs include generating awareness about the company's products and services, sharing ideas and seeking feedback from customers and partners, strengthening relationships among employees, and selling products. One concern for many managers is how to measure the effectiveness of the use of social media programs.

Concept Connection ◄◄◄

The success and popularity of **social media** tools continues to drive innovation on the Web. In 2012, after an initial launch in France, Muxi went international. Muxi's creators describe it as a combination of the professional networking power of LinkedIn and the truly social aspects of Facebook.

Blend_Images/iStockphoto.com

Manager's *Shoptalk*

Management Tools and Trends

Over the history of management, many fashions and fads have appeared. Critics argue that new techniques may not represent permanent solutions. Others feel that managers must adopt new techniques for continuous improvement in a fast-changing world.

In 1993, Bain and Company started a large research project to interview and survey thousands of corporate executives about the 25 most popular management tools and techniques. The most recent list and usage rates for 2010–2011 are shown below. How many of the tools do you know? For more information on specific tools, see Bain's *Management Tools 2011: An Executive's Guide* at www.bain.com/publications/articles/management-tools-2011-executives-guide.aspx.

Popularity. In the 2010–2011 survey, benchmarking held onto the top spot as the most popular tool, reflecting managers' concern with efficiency and cost-cutting in a difficult economy. Mergers and acquisitions have decreased in popularity, with only 35 percent of managers using this technique. Three tools that ranked high in both use and satisfaction were *strategic planning, mission and vision statements*, and *customer segmentation*, tools that can guide managers' thinking on strategic issues during times of rapid change.

Global Trends. For the first time, firms in emerging markets reported using more tools than those in developed markets. More than half of emerging market executives reported using the *balanced scorecard*. North American managers decreased their use of *outsourcing* and were the largest users of *social media programs*. Managers in Latin American companies used more tools than any other region, but they were the lightest users of *downsizing* and *customer relationship management (CRM)*. Asian companies were the greatest users of *knowledge management*. Benchmarking and *change management programs* were top tools for managers in Europe, where acute economic uncertainty continues.

Source: Darrell Rigby and Barbara Bilodeau, "Management Tools and Trends 2011," Copyright © 2011, Bain and Company, Inc., http://www.bain.com/publications/articles/Management-tools-trends-2011.aspx. Reprinted by permission.

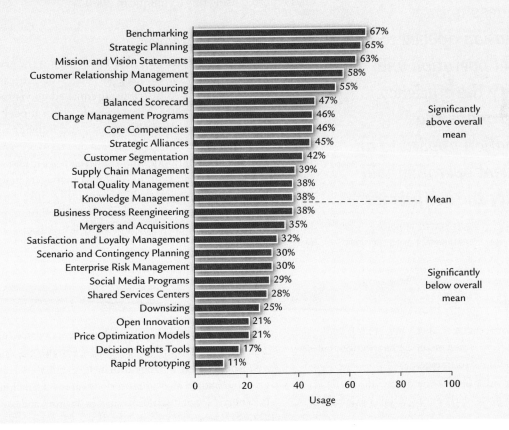

EXHIBIT 2.7   Supply Chain for a Retail Organization

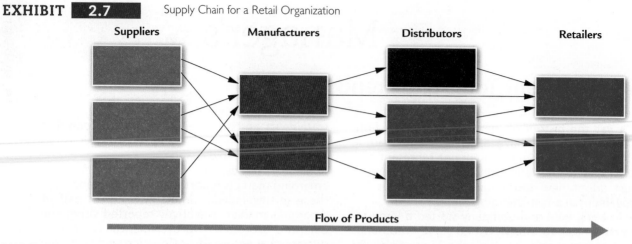

SOURCE: Adapted from an exhibit from the Global Supply Chain Games Project, Delft University and the University of Maryland, R. H. Smith School of Business, www.gscg.org:8080/opencms/export/sites/default/gscg/images/supplychain_simple.gif (accessed February 6, 2008).

Customer Relationship Management

Unlike social media, many managers have become quite comfortable and adept at using technology for **customer relationship management (CRM)**. CRM systems use the latest information technology to keep in close touch with customers and to collect and manage large amounts of customer data. These systems can help managers be more accurate in their sales forecasts, coordinate sales and service staff more easily, improve product design and marketing, and act quickly to respond to shifting customer needs and desires. There has been an explosion of interest in CRM. In the Manager's Shoptalk, 58 percent of surveyed managers reported their companies used CRM in 2010, whereas only 35 percent of companies reported using this technique in 2000.

Supply Chain Management

Supply chain management refers to managing the sequence of suppliers and purchasers, covering all stages of processing from obtaining raw materials to distributing finished goods to consumers.[63] Exhibit 2.7 illustrates a basic supply chain model. A *supply chain* is a network of multiple businesses and individuals that are connected through the flow of products or services.[64] Many organizations manage the supply chain with sophisticated electronic technology. In India, for example, Walmart managers have invested in an efficient supply chain that electronically links farmers and small manufacturers directly to the stores, maximizing value for both ends.[65] Supply chain management will be discussed in detail in the Appendix.

> "The first rule of any technology used in a business is that automation applied to an efficient operation will magnify the efficiency. The second is that automation applied to an inefficient operation will magnify the inefficiency."
>
> — BILL GATES, FOUNDER AND CHAIRMAN OF MICROSOFT

Remember This

- Modern management is a lively mix of ideas and techniques from varied historical perspectives, but new concepts continue to emerge.
- Managers tend to look for innovative ideas and approaches particularly during turbulent times.

- Many of today's popular techniques are related to the transition to a technology-driven workplace.
- **Social media programs** include online community pages, social media sites such as Facebook and LinkedIn, microblogging platforms such as Twitter, and company

(Continued)

online forums that enable managers to interact electronically with employees, customers, partners, and other stakeholders.

- **Customer relationship management (CRM)** systems use information technology to keep in close touch with customers, collect and manage large amounts of customer data, and provide superior customer value.

- **Supply chain management** refers to managing the sequence of suppliers and purchasers, covering all stages of processing from obtaining raw materials to distributing finished goods to consumers.

- These new approaches require managers to think in fresh ways about managing their relationships with employees, customers, and business partners.

ch2: Discussion Questions

1. How do you think management practices might change in response to increasing government regulation in the banking and health care industries? What other recent political, social, or economic forces can you identify that might affect your job as a manager?

2. The 2010–2011 Bain survey of management tools and trends found that the use of social media programs is growing, but as a tool, social media also has one of the lowest satisfaction ratings. How would you explain this?

3. Can you think of potential drawbacks to retailers using labor-waste elimination systems based on scientific management principals, as described in the text? Despite their being about 100 years old, do you believe scientific management characteristics will ever cease to be a part of organizational life? Discuss.

4. A management professor once said that for successful management, studying the present was most important, studying the past was next, and studying the future was least important. Do you agree? Why?

5. As organizations become more technology-driven, which do you think will become more important—the management of the human element of the organization or the management of technology? Discuss.

6. Why do you think Mary Parker Follett's ideas tended to be popular with businesspeople of her day but were ignored by management scholars? Why are her ideas appreciated more today?

7. Explain the basic idea underlying the contingency view. How would you go about identifying key contingencies facing an organization?

8. Why can an event such as the Hawthorne studies be a major turning point in the history of management, even if the results of the studies are later shown to be in error? Discuss.

9. How would you apply systems thinking to a problem such as poor performance in your current academic studies? To a problem with a romantic partner or family member? Try to identify all the elements and their interdependencies.

10. Do you think management theory will ever be as precise as theories in the fields of finance, accounting, or experimental psychology? Why or why not?

ch2: Apply Your Skills: Experiential Exercise

Security or Autonomy[66]

Respond to each statement below based on whether you Mostly Agree or Mostly Disagree with it.

	Mostly Disagree	Mostly Agree
1. I value stability in my job.	_____	_____
2. Rules, policies, and procedures generally frustrate me.	_____	_____
3. I enjoy working for a firm that promotes employees based heavily on seniority.	_____	_____
4. I'd prefer some kind of freelance job to working for the government.	_____	_____
5. I'd be proud to work for the largest and most successful company in its field.	_____	_____
6. Given a choice, I'd rather make $90,000 a year as a VP in a small company then $100,000 a year as a middle manager in a large company.	_____	_____
7. I'd rather work directly for a single manager than on a team with shared responsibilities.	_____	_____
8. I generally prefer to multitask and be involved in multiple projects.	_____	_____
9. Good employee benefits are important to me.	_____	_____
10. Rules are made to be broken.	_____	_____

Scoring

Give yourself one point for each answer of Mostly Agree to the odd-numbered questions and one point for each Mostly Disagree to the even-numbered questions.

Interpretation

Your answers determine whether your preferences would fit better with a bureaucratic organization. If your score is 8–10, a large, formal company would be compatible with your style and wishes. A score of 4–7 suggests that you would receive modest satisfaction from working within a bureaucratic organization. A score of 1–3 suggests that you would likely be frustrated by working in a large bureaucracy.

A large, bureaucratic organization provides security, benefits, and certainty compared to smaller or entrepreneurial firms, where freedom and autonomy are greater. Do you want to optimize security or autonomy in your career? Would you be more satisfied in a large formal organization or in an organization that emphasizes a human resources perspective? Compare your scores with other students' scores and discuss any differences.

ch2: Apply Your Skills: Small Group Breakout

Turning Points on the Road to Management

Step 1. Interview a manager you know at your university or place of employment, or a parent or friend who is a manager, and ask the following question: "What was a turning point in your life that led you to become the person, and manager, that you are today?" (A turning point could be an *event*, such as a divorce, birth of a child, business failure, loss of job; or a *decision*, such as to quit college and start a business, go back to school, get married, and so on.) Collect information on a second turning point if the interviewee has one to describe. Your goal is to learn the specifics about how each turning point led to the person's current position in life.

Step 2. Divide into groups of four to six members. One person at a time, share what you learned about a manager's career turning points. What themes or patterns characterize the turning points among the managers interviewed?

Step 3. Have you personally experienced any turning points in your life? Each group member should describe your personal turning point to the group. With the additional turning points, analyze again for themes and patterns across all the turning points.

Step 4. What lessons does your group learn from its analysis? How does history (events, decisions) play a role in the lives and careers of the managers interviewed, and in the lives of your group members?

ch2: Endnotes

1. This questionnaire is from William Pfeiffer and John E. Jones, eds., "Supervisory Attitudes: The X-Y Scale," in *The 1972 Annual Handbook for Group Facilitators* (New York: John Wiley & Sons, 1972), pp. 65–68. This material is used by permission of John Wiley & Sons, Inc. The X-Y scale was adapted from an instrument developed by Robert N. Ford of AT&T for in-house manager training.

2. "Q&A: Why the West Needs 'Jugaad' Creativity" (an interview with Navi Radjou, Jaideep Prabhu, and Simone Ahuja), *The Wall Street Journal India Online*, June 6, 2012, http://blogs.wsj.com /indiarealtime/2012/06/06/qa-why-the-west-needs-jugaad-creativity/ (accessed June 19, 2012); and Navi Radjou, Jaideep Prabhu, and Simone Ahuja, *Jugaad Innovation: Think Frugal, Be Flexible, Generate Breakthrough Growth* (San Francisco: Jossey-Bass, 2012).

3. Devita Saraf, "India's Indigenous Genius: Jugaad," *The Wall Street Journal Online*, July 13, 2009, http://online .wsj.com/article/SB124745880685131765.html (accessed June 19, 2012); Nirmalya Kumar and Phanish Puranam, "Frugal Engineering: An Emerging Innovation Paradigm," *Ivey Business Journal* (March–April 2012) www.iveybusinessjournal.com/topics/innovation /frugal-engineering-an-emerging-innovation-paradigm (accessed June 19, 2012).

4. M. S. S. el Namaki, "Does the Thinking of Yesterday's Management Gurus Imperil Today's Companies?" *Ivey Business Journal* (March–April 2012), www .iveybusinessjournal.com/topics/strategy/does-the-thinking-of-yesterdays-management-gurus-imperil-todays-companies (accessed June 19, 2012).

5. Eric Abrahamson, "Management Fashion," *Academy of Management Review* 21, no. 1 (January 1996): 254–285. Also see "75 Years of Management Ideas and Practice," a supplement to the *Harvard Business Review* (September–October 1997), for a broad overview of historical trends in management thinking.

6. The following discussion is based on Daniel A. Wren, *The Evolution of Management Thought*, 4th ed. (New York: Wiley, 1994).

7. Based on Todd Henneman, "Talkin' About Their Generations: The Workforce of the '50s and Today," *Workforce* (April 2, 2012), www.workforce.com/article/20120402/ WORKFORCE90/120319965/talkin-about-their-

generations-the-workforce-of-the-50s-and-today (accessed June 19, 2012); and Stephanie Armour, "Generation Y: They've Arrived at Work with a New Attitude," *USA Today*, November 6, 2005, www.usatoday.com/money/workplace/ 2005-11-06-gen-y_x.htm (accessed November 10, 2005).

8. Jena McGregor, "'There Is No More Normal,'" *Business-Week* (March 23 and 30, 2009): 30–34.

9. Michael Aneiro, "Credit Market Springs to Life," *The Wall Street Journal*, March 11, 2010.

10. Aziz Hannifa, "India, China Growth Dominates World Bank Meet," *India Abroad* (New York edition), November 2, 2007.

11. Robert Tell and Brian Kleiner, "Organizational Change Can Rescue Industry," *Industrial Management* (March–April 2009): 20–24.

12. Daniel A. Wren, "Management History: Issues and Ideas for Teaching and Research," *Journal of Management* 13 (1987): 339–350.

13. Business historian Alfred D. Chandler, Jr., quoted in Jerry Useem, "Entrepreneur of the Century," *Inc.* (20th Anniversary Issue, 1999): 159–174.

14. Useem, "Entrepreneur of the Century."

15. The following is based on Wren, *Evolution of Management Thought*, Chapters 4 and 5; and Claude S. George, Jr., *The History of Management Thought* (Englewood Cliffs, NJ: Prentice-Hall, 1968), Chapter 4.

16. Cynthia Crossen, "Early Industry Expert Soon Realized a Staff Has Its Own Efficiency," *The Wall Street Journal*, November 6, 2006.

17. Alan Farnham, "The Man Who Changed Work Forever," *Fortune* (July 21, 1997): 114; Charles D. Wrege and Ann Marie Stoka, "Cooke Creates a Classic: The Story Behind F. W. Taylor's Principles of Scientific Management," *Academy of Management Review* (October 1978): 736–749; Robert Kanigel, *The One Best Way: Frederick Winslow Taylor and the Enigma of Efficiency* (New York: Viking, 1997); and "The X and Y Factors: What Goes Around Comes Around," special section in "The New Organisation: A Survey of the Company," *The Economist* (January 21–27, 2006): 17–18.

18. Wren, *Evolution of Management Thought*, 171; and George, *History of Management Thought*, 103–104.

19. Vanessa O'Connell, "Stores Count Seconds to Trim Labor Costs," *The Wall Street Journal*, November 17, 2008; and Vanessa O'Connell, "Retailers Reprogram Workers in Efficiency Push," *The Wall Street Journal*, September 10, 2008.

20. Gary Hamel, "The Why, What, and How of Management Innovation," *Harvard Business Review* (February 2006): 72–84; Peter Coy, "Cog or CoWorker?" *BusinessWeek* (August 20 and 27, 2007): 58–60.

21. Max Weber, *General Economic History*, trans. Frank H. Knight (London: Allen & Unwin, 1927); Max Weber, *The Protestant Ethic and the Spirit of Capitalism*, trans. Talcott Parsons (New York: Scribner, 1930); and Max

Weber, *The Theory of Social and Economic Organizations*, ed. and trans. A. M. Henderson and Talcott Parsons (New York: Free Press, 1947).

22. Nadira A. Hira, "The Making of a UPS Driver," *Fortune* (November 12, 2007), 118–129; David J. Lynch, "Thanks to Its CEO, UPS Doesn't Just Deliver," *USA Today*, July 24, 2006, www.usatoday.com/money/companies/management/2006-07-23-ups_x .htm?tab1=t2 (accessed July 24, 2006); Kelly Barron, "Logistics in Brown," *Forbes* (January 10, 2000): 78–83; Scott Kirsner, "Venture Vérité: United Parcel Service," *Wired* (September 1999): 83–96; "UPS," *The Atlanta Journal and Constitution*, April 26, 1992; Kathy Goode, Betty Hahn, and Cindy Seibert, "United Parcel Service: The Brown Giant" (unpublished manuscript, Texas A&M University, 1981); and "About UPS," UPS corporate Web site, www.ups.com/content/us/en/about/index.html (accessed June 19, 2012).

23. Stephen Cummings and Todd Bridgman, "The Relevant Past: Why the History of Management Should Be Critical to Our Future," *Academy of Management Learning & Education* 10, no. 1 (2011): 77–93.

24. These are based on Paul Downs, "How I Fire People," You're the Boss blog, *The New York Times*, June 4, 2012, http://boss.blogs.nytimes.com/2012/06/04/how-i-fire-people/ (accessed June 20, 2012).

25. Henri Fayol, *Industrial and General Administration*, trans. J. A. Coubrough (Geneva: International Management Institute, 1930); Henri Fayol, *General and Industrial Management*, trans. Constance Storrs (London: Pitman and Sons, 1949); and W. J. Arnold et al., *Business-Week, Milestones in Management* (New York: McGraw-Hill, vol. I, 1965; vol. II, 1966).

26. Gregory M. Bounds, Gregory H. Dobbins, and Oscar S. Fowler, *Management: A Total Quality Perspective* (Cincinnati, OH: South-Western Publishing, 1995), pp. 52–53.

27. Mary Parker Follett, *The New State: Group Organization: The Solution of Popular Government* (London: Longmans, Green, 1918); and Mary Parker Follett, *Creative Experience* (London: Longmans, Green, 1924).

28. Henry C. Metcalf and Lyndall Urwick, eds., *Dynamic Administration: The Collected Papers of Mary Parker Follett* (New York: Harper & Row, 1940); Arnold, *Business-Week, Milestones in Management*.

29. Follett, *The New State*; Metcalf and Urwick, *Dynamic Administration* (London: Sir Isaac Pitman, 1941).

30. William B. Wolf, *How to Understand Management: An Introduction to Chester I. Barnard* (Los Angeles: Lucas Brothers, 1968); and David D. Van Fleet, "The Need-Hierarchy and Theories of Authority," *Human Relations* 9 (Spring 1982): 111–118.

31. Curt Tausky, *Work Organizations: Major Theoretical Perspectives* (Itasca, IL: F. E. Peacock, 1978), p. 42.

32. Charles D. Wrege, "Solving Mayo's Mystery: The First Complete Account of the Origin of the Hawthorne

Studies—The Forgotten Contributions of Charles E. Snow and Homer Hibarger," paper presented to the Management History Division of the Academy of Management (August 1976).

33. Ronald G. Greenwood, Alfred A. Bolton, and Regina A. Greenwood, "Hawthorne a Half Century Later: Relay Assembly Participants Remember," *Journal of Management* 9 (Fall/Winter 1983): 217–231.

34. F. J. Roethlisberger, W. J. Dickson, and H. A. Wright, *Management and the Worker* (Cambridge, MA: Harvard University Press, 1939).

35. H. M. Parson, "What Happened at Hawthorne?" *Science* 183 (1974): 922–932; John G. Adair, "The Hawthorne Effect: A Reconsideration of the Methodological Artifact," *Journal of Applied Psychology* 69, no. 2 (1984): 334–345; and Gordon Diaper, "The Hawthorne Effect: A Fresh Examination," *Educational Studies* 16, no. 3 (1990): 261–268.

36. R. G. Greenwood, A. A. Bolton, and R. A. Greenwood, "Hawthorne a Half Century Later," 219–221.

37. F. J. Roethlisberger and W. J. Dickson, *Management and the Worker*.

38. Ramon J. Aldag and Timothy M. Stearns, *Management*, 2d ed. (Cincinnati, OH: South-Western Publishing, 1991), pp. 47–48.

39. Tausky, *Work Organizations: Major Theoretical Perspectives*, p. 55.

40. Douglas McGregor, *The Human Side of Enterprise* (New York: McGraw-Hill, 1960), pp. 16–18; Robert A. Cunningham, "Douglas McGregor: A Lasting Impression," *Ivey Business Journal* (October 2011): 5–7.

41. Ricardo Semler, "Out of This World: Doing Things the Semco Way," *Global Business and Organizational Excellence* (July–August 2007): 13–21.

42. Wendell L. French and Cecil H. Bell Jr., "A History of Organizational Development," in Wendell L. French, Cecil H. Bell Jr., and Robert A. Zawacki, *Organization Development and Transformation: Managing Effective Change* (Burr Ridge, IL: Irwin McGraw-Hill, 2000), pp. 20–42.

43. Mansel G. Blackford and K. Austin Kerr, *Business Enterprise in American History* (Boston: Houghton Mifflin, 1986), Chapters 10 and 11; and Alex Groner and the editors of *American Heritage* and *Business Week*, *The American Heritage History of American Business and Industry* (New York: American Heritage Publishing, 1972), Chapter 9.

44. Geoffrey Colvin, "How Alfred P. Sloan, Michael Porter, and Peter Drucker Taught Us All the Art of Management," *Fortune* (March 21, 2005): 83–86.

45. Brooks Barnes, "Disney Technology Tackles a Theme-Park Headache: Lines," *The New York Times*, December 28, 2010, B1; and "Disney Cracks Down on FastPass Enforcement," *Tampa Bay Times*, March 9, 2012, B2.

46. Larry M. Austin and James R. Burns, *Management Science* (New York: Macmillan, 1985).

47. Dan Heath and Chip Heath, "In Defense of Feelings: Why Your Gut Is More Ethical Than Your Brain," *Fast Company* (July–August 2009): 58–59.

48. Scott Patterson, *The Quants: How a New Breed of Math Whizzes Conquered Wall Street and Nearly Destroyed It* (New York: Crown Business, 2010); and Harry Hurt III, "In Practice, Stock Formulas Weren't Perfect," *The New York Times*, February 21, 2010.

49. Ludwig von Bertalanffy et al., "General Systems Theory: A New Approach to Unity of Science," *Human Biology* 23 (December 1951): 302–361; and Kenneth E. Boulding, "General Systems Theory—The Skeleton of Science," *Management Science* 2 (April 1956): 197–208.

50. This section is based on Peter M. Senge, *The Fifth Discipline: The Art and Practice of the Learning Organization* (New York: Doubleday, 1990); John D. Sterman, "Systems Dynamics Modeling: Tools for Learning in a Complex World," *California Management Review* 43, no. 4 (Summer 2001): 8–25; Andrea Gabor, "Seeing Your Company as a System," *Strategy + Business* (Summer 2010), www.strategy-business.com/article/10210?gko=20cca (accessed June 20, 2012); and Ron Zemke, "Systems Thinking," *Training* (February 2001): 40–46.

51. This example is cited in Sterman, "Systems Dynamics Modeling."

52. Fred Luthans, "The Contingency Theory of Management: A Path Out of the Jungle," *Business Horizons* 16 (June 1973): 62–72; and Fremont E. Kast and James E. Rosenzweig, *Contingency Views of Organization and Management* (Chicago: Science Research Associates, 1973).

53. Samuel Greengard, "25 Visionaries Who Shaped Today's Workplace," *Workforce* (January 1997): 50–59; and Ann Harrington, "The Big Ideas," Fortune (November 22, 1999): 152–154.

54. Mauro F. Guillen, "The Age of Eclecticism: Current Organizational Trends and the Evolution of Managerial Models," *Sloan Management Review* (Fall 1994): 75–86.

55. Jeremy Main, "How to Steal the Best Ideas Around," *Fortune* (October 19, 1992): 102–106.

56. Darrell Rigby and Barbara Bilodeau, "Management Tools and Trends 2009," Bain & Company Inc., 2009, www.bain.com /management_tools/home.asp (accessed March 10, 2010).

57. Thomas H. Davenport and Laurence Prusak, with Jim Wilson, *What's the Big Idea? Creating and Capitalizing on the Best Management Thinking* (Boston, MA: Harvard Business School Press, 2003); Theodore Kinni, "Have We Run out of Big Ideas?" *Across the Board* (March–April 2003): 16–21, Hamel, "The Why, What, and How of Management Innovation"; and Joyce Thompson Heames and Michael Harvey, "The Evolution of the Concept of the Executive from the 20th-Century Manager to the 21st-Century Global Leader," *Journal of Leadership and Organizational Studies* 13, no. 2 (2006): 29–41.

58. David Hurst, "The New Ecology of Leadership: Revisiting the Foundations of Management," *Ivey Business Journal* (May–June 2012): 1–5; Michael Murphy, "The Race to Failure" (a review of *Crash Course* by Paul Ingrassia, Random House 2010), *The Wall Street Journal*, January 29, 2010, A13.

59. Annick Van Rossem and Kees Van Veen, "Managers' Awareness of Fashionable Management Concepts: An Empirical Study," *European Management Journal* 29 (2011): 206–216.

60. Study reported in Phred Dvorak, "Why Management Trends Quickly Fade Away" (Theory and Practice column), *The Wall Street Journal*, June 26, 2006.

61. Darrell Rigby and Barbara Bilodeau, "Management Tools and Trends 2011," Bain and Company, Inc., www.bain.com/publications/articles/Management-tools-trends-2011.aspx (accessed June 22, 2012).

62. "Survey: 37% Use Social Media to Check Candidates," *Workforce* (April 18, 2012), www.workforce.com/article/20120418/NEWS01/120419964 (accessed June 22, 2012).

63. Definition based on Steven A. Melnyk and David R. Denzler, *Operations Management: A Value-Driven Approach* (Burr Ridge, IL: Richard D. Irwin, 1996): p. 613.

64. The Global Supply Chain Games project, www.gscg.org (accessed July 16, 2008).

65. Eric Bellman and Cecilie Rohwedder, "Western Grocer Modernizes Passage to India's Markets," *The Wall Street Journal*, November 28, 2007.

66. Adapted from Don Hellriegel, Susan E. Jackson, and John W. Slocum Jr., *Managing: A Competency-Based Approach* (Mason, OH: Cengage South-Western, 2008), p. 73.

ch1: Apply Your Skills: Ethical Dilemma

Can Management Afford to Look the Other Way?*

Harry Rull had been with Shellington Pharmaceuticals for 30 years. After a tour of duty in the various plants and seven years overseas, Harry was back at headquarters, looking forward to his new role as vice president of U.S. marketing.

Two weeks into his new job, Harry received some unsettling news about one of the managers that he supervises. During a casual lunch conversation, Sally Barton, the director of human resources, mentioned that Harry should expect a phone call about Roger Jacobs, manager of new product development. Jacobs had a history of being "pretty horrible" to his subordinates, she said, and one disgruntled employee asked to speak to someone in senior management. After lunch, Harry did some follow-up work. Jacobs's performance reviews have been stellar, but his personnel file also contains a large number of notes documenting charges of Jacobs's mistreatment of subordinates. The complaints ranged from "inappropriate and derogatory remarks" to charges of sexual harassment (which were subsequently dropped). What was more disturbing was the fact that the number and the severity of the complaints have increased with each of Jacobs's ten years with Shellington.

When Harry questioned the company president about the issue, he was told, "Yeah, he's had some problems, but

you can't just replace someone with an eye for new products. You're a bottom-line guy; you understand why we let these things slide." Not sure how to handle the situation, Harry met briefly with Jacobs and reminded him to "keep the team's morale up." Just after the meeting, Barton called to let him know that the problem that she'd mentioned over lunch had been worked out. However, she warned, another employee has now come forward, demanding that her complaints be addressed by senior management.

What Would You Do?

1. Ignore the problem. Jacobs's contributions to new product development are too valuable to risk losing him, and the problems over the past ten years have always worked themselves out anyway. There's no sense starting something that could make you look bad.

2. Launch a full-scale investigation of employee complaints about Jacobs and make Jacobs aware that his documented history over the past ten years has put him on thin ice.

3. Meet with Jacobs and the employee to try to resolve the current issue, and then start working with Barton and other senior managers to develop stronger policies regarding sexual harassment and treatment of employees, including clear-cut procedures for handling complaints.

*Based on Doug Wallace, "A Talent for Mismanagement: What Would You Do?" *Business Ethics* 2 (November–December 1992): 3–4.

ch1: Apply Your Skills: Case for Critical Analysis

SmartStyle Salons

Jamika Westbrook takes pride in her position as salon manager for SmartStyle Salon, one of six local hair salons associated with a large retail store chain located in the Southeast and one of five chain store groups under the Gold Group umbrella. She oversees a staff of 30, including hairdressers, a nail technician, receptionists, shampoo assistants, and a custodian. She enjoys a reputation as a manager who works very hard and takes care of her people. Hairdressers want to work for her.

Following the salon's new-hire policy, Jamika began as a shampoo assistant and quickly became a top hairdresser in the company through a combination of skill, a large and loyal client base, and long hours at work. In 2007, retiring manager Carla Weems hand-picked Jamika as her successor, and the board quickly approved.

Initially, the salon, located in a suburban mall, managed a strong, steady increase, holding its position as one of the corporate's top performers. But economic woes hit the area hard, with increases in unemployment, mortgage woes, and foreclosures among current and potential customers. As families sought ways to save, the luxury of regular visits to

the hair salon was among the first logical budget cuts. The past year has reflected this economic reality, and Jamika's salon saw a sharp decrease in profits.

Jamika's stomach is in knots as she arrives at the salon on Monday. Scheduled to fly to Atlanta the next morning for a meeting at corporate, she fears potential staffing cuts, but more important, she fears the loss of opportunity to secure her dream job, replacing the retiring manager at Riverwood Mall, the top-performing salon located in an upscale area of the city.

Distracted, Jamika walks past the receptionist, Marianne, who is busily answering the phones. Hanging up the phone, Marianne tells Jamika that Holly and Carol Jean, two popular hairdressers, called in sick, and Jamika now has to reschedule their clients. Jamika had denied their earlier request to travel out of town to attend a concert, and her irritation is obvious. She orders Marianne to call both women and instruct them that, when they return to work, they are to bring a doctor's statement and a copy of any prescriptions that they were given. "They had better be sick!" Jamika shouts as she enters her office, slamming the door more forcefully than she intended. Startled employees and early-morning customers heard the outburst, and, after a momentary pause, they resumed their activities and quiet conversation, surprised by the show of managerial anger. Jamika knows she has let Holly and Carol Jean get away with unwarranted absences before and worries that she will do it again. She needs every head of hair they can style to help the salon's profit.

Jamika takes a deep breath and sits at her desk, turning on the computer and checking e-mails, including one from the group manager reminding her to send the salon's status report in advance of tomorrow's meeting. She buzzes Marianne on the intercom to request final figures for the report on her desk by 1:00 P.M.

Picking up the phone, she calls Sharon, a manager at another SmartStyle salon. "I really lost my cool in front of everyone, but I'm not apologizing," Jamika admits, adding that she wished she had the guts to fire both stylists. "But this is not the day for that drama. I've got that report hanging over my head. I have no idea how to make things look better than they are, but I have to come up with something. Things look pretty dismal."

Sharon assures her that she did the best she could dealing with two "irresponsible" employees. "What will you do if they show up tomorrow with no doctor's statement?"

"I don't know. I hope I scared them enough so that they'll come in with something."

"I know you're worried about the report and the effect it might have on the Riverwood job," Sharon says. "But everyone knows you can't control the economy and its effect on the business. Just focus on the positive. You'll be fine."

At 10:30, as Jamika struggles to put the best possible spin on the report, she is paged to the receptionist desk to speak to an angry customer. "Another interruption," Jamika fumes to herself. Just then, the door opens and top stylist/

assistant manager Victoria Boone sticks her head into the office.

"I know you're busy with the report. I'll handle this," she says enthusiastically.

"Thanks," Jamika replies.

No sooner had she handed off the irate client to Victoria than she second-guessed the decision. In addition to her talents as a hairdresser, Victoria had experience as the manager of a successful salon in another city before moving to the area. Recognizing her organizational and people skills, Jamika promoted Victoria to assistant manager soon after her arrival. Now each "I'll handle this" remark by Victoria convinces Jamika that her assistant manager is positioning herself as a potential rival for the Riverwood job. Jamika appreciates her enthusiastic attitude, but she's also trying to limit her opportunities to lead or appear too competent before staff, customers, and company officials. Jamika finds herself wanting to hide Victoria's competence, and she has condescendingly reminded management that Victoria is a "great help to me."

Now, thinking of Victoria's cheerful "I'll handle this," Jamika rises from her desk and marches to the door. *No, Jamika thinks, I'll take care of this personally.*

Questions

1. What positive and negative managerial characteristics does Jamika possess?
2. How do these traits help or hinder her potential to get the top position at the Riverwood Mall salon?
3. How do you think Jamika should have handled each of the incidents with Marianne? Holly and Carol Jean? Victoria?

ch1: On the Job Video Cases

On the Job: Camp Bow Wow: Innovative Management for a Changing World

Questions

1. List the three broad management skill categories and explain which skills are needed most for each of the Camp Bow Wow leaders highlighted in the video.

2. Which activities at Camp Bow Wow require high efficiency? Which activities require high effectiveness?

3. List two activities that leaders at Camp Bow Wow perform daily, and identify which of the ten managerial roles discussed in the chapter figure prominently for each.

ch2: Apply Your Skills: Ethical Dilemma

The New Test*

The Civil Service Board in a midsize city in Indiana decided that a written exam should be given to all candidates for promotion to supervisor. A written test would assess mental skills and would open access to all personnel

who wanted to apply for the position. The board believed a written exam for promotion would be completely fair and objective because it eliminated subjective judgments and personal favoritism regarding a candidate's qualifications.

Maxine Othman, manager of a social service agency, loved to see her employees learn and grow to their full potential. When a rare opening for a supervising clerk occurred, Maxine quickly decided to give Sheryl Hines a shot at the job. Sheryl had been with the agency for 17 years and had shown herself to be a true leader. Sheryl worked hard at becoming a good supervisor, just as she had always worked hard at being a top-notch clerk. She paid attention to the human aspects of employee problems and introduced modern management techniques that strengthened the entire agency. Because of the board's new ruling, Sheryl would have to complete the exam in an open competition—anyone could sign up and take it, even a new employee. The board wanted the candidate with the highest score to get the job but allowed Maxine, as manager of the agency, to have the final say.

Because Sheryl had accepted the provisional opening and proved herself on the job, Maxine was upset that the entire clerical force was deemed qualified to take the test. When the results came back, she was devastated. Sheryl placed twelfth in the field of candidates, while one of her newly hired clerks placed first. The Civil Service Board,

impressed by the high score, urged Maxine to give the new clerk the permanent supervisory job; however, it was still Maxine's choice. Maxine wonders whether it is fair to base her decision only on the results of a written test. The board was pushing her to honor the objective written test, but could the test really assess fairly who was the right person for the job?

What Would You Do?

1. Ignore the test. Sheryl has proved herself via work experience and deserves the job.

2. Give the job to the candidate with the highest score. You don't need to make enemies on the Civil Service Board, and, although it is a bureaucratic procedure, the test is an objective way to select a permanent placement.

3. Press the board to devise a more comprehensive set of selection criteria—including test results as well as supervisory experience, ability to motivate employees, and knowledge of agency procedures—that can be explained and justified to the board and to employees.

*Based on Betty Harrigan, "Career Advice," *Working Woman* (July 1986): 22–24.

ch2: Apply Your Skills: Case for Critical Analysis

More Hassle from HR?

In their three years at Vreeland Pharmaceuticals, Vitorio Nuños and Gary Shaw had rarely crossed paths, and they had exchanged no more than a dozen sentences. But here they were, seatmates on a plane headed to company headquarters in Kansas City, Missouri. And suddenly, they had a lot to say to each other.

"What I'd like to know is why we're wasting a trip to Kansas City to thrash out some new policies about leader competencies," Vitorio said.

"Because Connie Wyland *is* HR at Vreeland, and you and I both know that policies and models and all of that touchy-feely people stuff is the lifeblood of HR," Gary replied. "I also think a lot of this is the result of panic on the heels of the scandals in sales last year."

"I don't think there's cause for panic. The company fired the guys, apologized, and then you just move on," said Vitorio.

Gary laughed sarcastically. "No, you fire them, you apologize, and then you analyze the whole thing *ad nauseam*, and *then* you hamstring your management team with endless rules and bureaucratic standards just to make sure it doesn't happen again."

"So we all pay for *their* mistakes," replied Vitorio.

"We pay because HR feels guilty that those guys moved up so high in the system," Gary replied. "So now Connie and her staff have devised the ultimate solution to the problem. I don't know why we all have to go in to discuss it; she's already decided what she's going to do and she's positive this is the cure-all to prevent any further embarrassment to the company."

"Let's look at the document," Vitorio said. He reached under the seat, retrieved and unpacked his tablet, placed it on the tray table, and turned it on.

"Too much glare," Gary said, peeking over. Vitorio pulled down the window shade.

"Is that better?"

Gary nodded. The two men read through the document.

"I resent the term 'rogue leaders,'" Gary remarked, pointing to the phrase.

Vitorio shrugged. "It's a rough draft. They'll clean up the language . . . I think."

"It's really just a rehash of the mission statement and all of the things we learned in training. This is stuff we all learned in business school. I feel like I'm being lectured."

"Yeah." Vitorio scrolled up and down the document. "Any business student could have written this."

"I hear the HR crew put in lots of overtime," said Gary.

Vitorio smirked. "For this? I'll tell you . . . and this is just between you and me, but I really resent this and we're some of the newer members of management. I would love to hear what the older managers are saying."

"I know Connie," Gary said. "She and her staff are going to come in tomorrow all gung-ho on this." He turned the tablet in order to see it easier. "We already *know* what's expected of us." He scrolled down, stopping at key phrases. "Look at this . . . 'critical values' . . . 'core behaviors' . . . 'fostering conflict resolution' . . . and here's one—'implementing employee involvement strategies.' How does she think we got these jobs in the first place?" Gary paused. "What really makes me angry is that I heard Connie is going to start manager training sessions where she will teach us the behaviors associated with each value! Can you believe that? She will have us role-playing and stuff. I will fight this if it goes beyond general value statements that we can follow in our own way."

"I can't wait to hear what Vreeland says," Vitorio remarked.

"Are you kidding? He'll go along with it. He'll spend 10 to 15 minutes telling us how great we all are and insinuating that we don't really need this, and then he'll back Connie all the way. Face it, this is the way it's going to be, and he really doesn't *need* our input or approval. It just looks good," commented Gary.

Vitorio turned off and closed the tablet. "I just feel that imposing something like this on management is a slap at every one of us. We know what's expected. We don't need training. We also know our people and we have to have some flexibility within a broad set of boundaries. This sort of thing just hamstrings us. Connie wants the Stepford Wives."

"I just hope a couple of senior managers speak up at this meeting and voice some concerns. Maybe it will be toned down a little," Gary said. "You and I are middle management and we haven't been with the company long enough. All we can do at this meeting is sit and nod."

Questions

1. Are Connie and her staff on the right track to avoid manager mishaps by defining a new set of leader rules and core values and imposing it by fiat from the top down?

2. Do you think a more participative and open culture can be imposed on managers with value statements and training sessions? Why?

3. Why do you think Vitorio and Gary are on the defensive? Might the emphasis on core leadership behaviors be handled in a different way? What do you suggest?

ch2: On the Job Video Cases

On the Job: Barcelona Restaurant Group: The Evolution of Management Thinking

Questions

1. In what ways is Barcelona's management approach consistent with modern developments in management thinking?

2. In what ways does Barcelona's management approach run counter to contemporary developments in management thinking?

3. What aspects of restaurant work are especially challenging to wait staff, and how does Barcelona's approach to management help employees overcome the downsides of the job?

pt1: Integrative Case

The Clean-Energy Future Is Now

As *Green Car Journal* prepared to publish its much-anticipated "Green Car of the Year" edition for 2012, audiences might have expected a tribute to the Toyota Prius, Nissan Leaf, or another innovation in electric motoring. Instead, the panel of environmental and automotive experts assembled by the magazine made a surprising choice—one that signaled a sea change in green energy. The judges selected the 2012 Honda Civic Natural Gas, an alternative-fuel, partial-zero emissions vehicle that operates solely on compressed natural gas. As the journal noted, not only is the Civic's sticker price of $26,155 more affordable than electric vehicles, and not only does the model possess a driving range and horsepower on par with conventional compacts, but the Civic's alternative fuel costs

approximately half the price of gasoline and is sourced almost entirely from abundant reserves in the United States.

Against a backdrop of ubiquitous marketing for electric cars and hybrids, the choice of a natural gas vehicle for Green Car of the Year was an unmistakable nod to a development in green energy that is so immense that it promises to transform the U.S. energy grid and end North American dependence on foreign oil. That development is the discovery of the Marcellus Shale. Located throughout the Appalachian Basin of the eastern United States, the Marcellus Shale is a massive sedimentary rock formation deep beneath the Earth's surface that contains one of the largest methane deposits anywhere in the world. Once thought to possess a modest 1.9 trillion cubic feet of natural gas, this 600-mile-wide black shale formation below Pennsylvania, Ohio, New York, and West Virginia was explored by geologists in 2004 and was found to contain between 168 trillion and 516 trillion cubic feet of natural gas. Combined with other U.S. shale plays, including the Barnett Shale in Texas, the discovery of the Marcellus led the International Energy Agency (IEA) to rank the United States the new number one natural gas producer in the world, edging out resource-rich Russia. In addition, the Marcellus has triggered a green-energy boom known as the Great Shale Gas Rush, which is creating thousands of green jobs, revitalizing the nation's economy, and pointing the way to a clean-energy future.

The breakthrough couldn't have come at a better time. In a highly turbulent business environment shaken by a global recession and new government restrictions on traditional energy, today's business managers struggle to know which energy alternatives are viable, or even affordable. The unexpected bankruptcy of well-funded green-energy darlings Solyndra and Beacon Power further underscore the uncertainty of the alternative energy marketplace. To gain stability for their organizations, managers need solutions that are reliable now, not decades into the future.

Thanks to an abundant supply of affordable natural gas, the green energy future has arrived. According to the U.S. Environmental Protection Agency (EPA) profile on clean energy, natural gas is a clean-burning fuel that generates roughly half the carbon emissions of coal and oil while releasing zero sulfur dioxide or mercury emissions. Given its low price relative to other energy sources, natural gas has game-changing implications for trucking fleets, consumer autos, electric power generation, and commercial heating—not to mention natural gas ovens, clothes dryers, water heaters, and other appliances.

While shale gas is a win-win for business and the environment, its impact on green jobs and the economy is equally important. According to a 2011 IHS Global Insight study, shale gas production—currently 34 percent of all natural gas production in the United States—supported more than 600,000 green jobs in 2010, a number that will increase to 870,000 jobs by 2015. As for the national economy, shale gas contributed $76.9 billion to the U.S. gross domestic product (GDP) in 2010 and is projected to contribute $118.2 billion by 2015. Over the next 25 years, shale gas will raise more than $933 billion in tax revenue for local, state, and federal governments. The news about natural gas is good for average consumers as well. In 2011, property owners in the Marcellus region received $400 million in natural gas royalties—a number that will

climb even higher in the next decade. Additionally, individual U.S. consumers can expect $926 in new disposable income per year from cost savings related to natural gas. Combined, this economic activity equates to much-needed relief in hard times.

What does the switch to natural gas mean for industry-leading companies? For automakers like Honda and Volvo, natural gas vehicles have begun making their way into regular assembly-line production. Transport businesses such as UPS are converting fleets from diesel to natural gas as part of the White House's National Clean Fleets Partnership. Transit leaders like Navistar and Clean Energy Fuels have launched strategic partnerships to build America's Natural Gas Highway. Manufacturers such as Westport Innovations have made organizational changes to become leading producers of liquefied and compressed natural gas engines. Utility companies like Dominion are replacing coal-based electricity with gas-fired electric generation. And drillers like Range Resources are finding new ways to improve the quality and safety of natural gas exploration while controlling costs.

There are no limits to the possibilities of the Great Shale Gas Rush. However, it will take visionary leadership and skillful management to deliver on the promise of a truly sustainable clean-energy future.

Integrative Case Questions

1. What turbulent forces are causing business leaders to rethink their use of energy?

2. Which managers—top managers, middle managers, or first-line managers—would make companywide decisions about energy use? How might *the new workplace* enable all managers to capitalize on the Great Shale Gas Rush?

3. Which historical management perspectives have particular relevance to the exploration and extraction of natural gas? Explain.

Sources: Based on "Honda Civic Natural Gas Is 2012 Green Car of the Year," *Green Car Journal*, November 17, 2011, www.greencar.com/articles/honda-civic-natural-gas-2012-green-car-year.php (accessed June 7, 2012); Elwin Green, "Natural gas Locked in the Marcellus Shale Has Companies Rushing to Cash in on Possibilities," *Pittsburgh Post-Gazette*, March 16, 2012, www.post-gazette.com/stories/business/news/natural-gas-locked-in-the-marcellus-shale-has-companies-rushing-to-cash-in-on-possibilities-370058/(accessed June 7, 2012); Kevin Begos, "Gas Drillers Generate About $3.5 Billion in Revenues From Marcellus Shale," Associated Press, May 5, 2012, www.timesunion.com/business/article/AP-Pa-gas-drilling-brought-3-5-billion-in-2011-3536873.php (accessed June 8, 2012); Timothy J. Considine, Robert Watson, and Seth Blumsack, *The Pennsylvania Marcellus Natural Gas Industry: Status, Economic Impacts, and Future Potential*, John and Willie Leone Family Department of Energy and Mineral Engineering, Penn State University, July 20, 2011, http://marcelluscoalition.org/wp-content/uploads/2011/07/Final-2011-PA-Marcellus-Economic-Impacts.pdf (accessed June 8, 2012); IHS, "Shale Gas Supports More than 600,000 American Jobs Today; by 2015, Shale

Gas Predicted to Support Nearly 870,000 Jobs and Contribute $118.2 Billion to GDP," press release, December 6, 2011, http://press.ihs.com/press-release/energy-power/shale-gas-supports-more-600000-american-jobs-today-2015-shale-gas-predict (accessed June 8, 2012); "IEA: U.S. to Overtake Russia as Top Gas Producer, Reuters, Jun 5, 2012, http://af.reuters.com/article/energyOilNews/idAFL3E8H45WZ20120605 (accessed June 8, 2012); Environmental Protection Agency, "Clean Energy: Air Emissions," www.epa.gov/cleanenergy/energy-and-you/affect/air-emissions.html (accessed June 8, 2012); Clifford Krauss, "There's Gas in Those Hills, *The New York Times*, April 8, 2008, www.nytimes.com/2008/04/08/business/08gas.html (accessed June 8, 2012).

Corporate Culture and the Environment

Christian Mueller/Shutterstock.com

Learning Outcomes

After studying this chapter, you should be able to:

1. Define an organizational ecosystem and how the general and task environments affect an organization's ability to thrive.

2. Explain the strategies that managers use to help organizations adapt to an uncertain or turbulent environment.

3. Define corporate culture and give organizational examples.

4. Explain organizational symbols, stories, heroes, slogans, and ceremonies and their relationship to corporate culture.

5. Describe four types of cultures and how corporate culture relates to the environment.

6. Define a cultural leader and explain the tools that a cultural leader uses to create a high-performance culture.

Are You Fit for Managerial Uncertainty?[1]

INSTRUCTIONS: Do you approach uncertainty with an open mind? Think back to how you thought or behaved during a time of uncertainty when you were in a formal or informal leadership position. Please answer whether each of the following items was Mostly True or Mostly False in that circumstance.

	Mostly True	Mostly False
1. Enjoyed hearing about new ideas even when trying to meet a deadline.	_____	_____
2. Welcomed unusual viewpoints of others, even if we were working under pressure.	_____	_____
3. Made it a point to attend industry trade shows and company events.	_____	_____
4. Specifically encouraged others to express opposing ideas and arguments.	_____	_____
5. Asked "dumb" questions.	_____	_____
6. Always offered comments on the meaning of data or issues.	_____	_____
7. Expressed a controversial opinion to bosses and peers.	_____	_____
8. Suggested ways of improving my and others' ways of doing things.	_____	_____

SCORING AND INTERPRETATION: Give yourself one point for each item that you marked as Mostly True. If you scored less than 5, you might want to start your career as a manager in a stable rather than an unstable environment. A score of 5 or above suggests a higher level of mindfulness and a better fit for a new manager in an organization with an uncertain environment.

In an organization in a highly uncertain environment, everything seems to be changing. In that case, an important quality for a new manager is "mindfulness," which includes the qualities of being open-minded and an independent thinker. In a stable environment, a manager with a closed mind may perform okay because much work can be done in the same old way. In an uncertain environment, even a new manager needs to facilitate new thinking, new ideas, and new ways of working. A high score on the preceding items suggests higher mindfulness and a better fit with an uncertain environment.

M ost managers don't pop on a crash helmet and fire-resistant Nomex suit to guide an organization through tumultuous change. But when Toyota Motor Corporation's president, Akio Toyoda, faced a series of calamities during his first few years as president, he tapped into his skills as a certified test car driver—high endurance, precise steering, and strong mental focus—to lead Toyota to a surprising rebound. In 2011, Toyota toppled from its number one position as the world's largest automaker to third, behind General Motors and Volkswagen, after suffering the effects of a global recession, the recall of 8 million vehicles, and a deadly tsunami in Japan. Within the organization, storms were also brewing. Toyota's tortuous bureaucracy slowed decision-making and response times. Plus, Toyota had lost touch with its customers. Toyota's growth had been underpinned by "quality, dependability, and reliability," but customers also wanted style and design, and they were flocking to Hyundai, which had seized design leadership.[2]

These environmental factors—both external and internal—served as wake-up calls for a company that had grown complacent. Akio Toyoda's response was to upend the corporate culture and create a more responsive organization—one that could navigate with ease through even subtle environmental shifts. This chapter explores in detail components of

1 INTRODUCTION

2 ENVIRONMENT

3 PLANNING

4 ORGANIZING

5 LEADING

6 CONTROLLING

the external environment and how they affect the organization. The chapter also examines a major part of the organization's internal environment—corporate culture. Corporate culture is both shaped by the external environment and shapes how managers respond to changes in the external environment.

The External Environment

The environmental changes that shook Toyota's leadership position in the auto industry—a global recession, natural disasters, and changing customer needs—were part of its external organizational environment, The external **organizational environment** includes all elements existing outside the boundary of the organization that have the potential to affect the organization.[3] The environment includes competitors, resources, technology, and economic conditions that influence the organization. It does not include those events so far removed from the organization that their impact is not perceived.

The organization's external environment can be conceptualized further as having two components: general and task environments, as illustrated in Exhibit 3.1.[4] The **general environment** affects organizations indirectly. It includes social, economic, legal-political, international, natural, and technological factors that influence all organizations about equally. Changes in federal regulations or an economic recession are part of the organization's general environment. These events do not directly change day-to-day operations, but they do affect all organizations eventually. The **task environment** is closer to the organization and includes the sectors that conduct day-to-day transactions with the organization and directly influence its basic operations and performance. It is generally considered to include competitors, suppliers, customers, and the labor market.

A new view of the environment argues that organizations are now evolving into business ecosystems. An **organizational ecosystem** is a system formed by the interaction among a community of organizations in the environment. An ecosystem includes organizations in all the sectors of the task and general environments that provide the resource and information transactions, flows, and linkages necessary for an organization to thrive.[5] For example, Apple's ecosystem includes hundreds of suppliers and millions of customers for the products that it produces across several industries, including consumer electronics, Internet services, mobile phones, personal computers, and entertainment.[6]

The organization also has an **internal environment**, which includes the elements within the organization's boundaries. The internal environment is composed of current employees, management, and especially corporate culture, which defines employee behavior in the internal environment and how well the organization will adapt to the external environment.

> "It is not the strongest of the species that survives, nor the most intelligent that survives. It is the one that is the most adaptable to change."
>
> — CHARLES DARWIN (1809–1882), NATURALIST

EXHIBIT 3.1

Dimensions of the Organization's General, Task, and Internal Environments

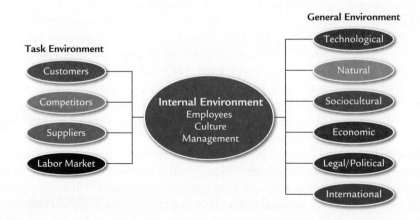

Exhibit 3.1 illustrates the relationship among the general, task, and internal environments. As an open system, the organization draws resources from the external environment and releases goods and services back to it. We will now discuss the two components of the external environment in more detail. Then we will discuss corporate culture, the key element in the internal environment. Other aspects of the internal environment, such as structure and technology, will be covered in later chapters of this book.

GENERAL ENVIRONMENT

The dimensions of the general environment include international, technological, sociocultural, economic, legal-political, and natural.

International

In his book *The World Is Flat*, Thomas Friedman challenges managers to view global markets as a level playing field where geographical divisions are irrelevant.[7] A flat world, Friedman argues, creates opportunities for companies to expand into global markets and build a global supply chain. As managers plan for expansion into global markets, they have to consider the **international dimension** of the external environment, which includes events originating in foreign countries, as well as new opportunities for U.S. companies in other countries. The international environment provides new competitors, customers, and suppliers and shapes social, technological, and economic trends as well.

Consider the mixed results Starbucks experienced as it expanded into European markets. Starbucks fans packed stores in Germany and the United Kingdom, for example, but sales and profits in the company's French stores were disappointing. In fact, after eight years operating 63 stores, Starbucks never turned a profit in France. What international factors could be hindering the company's success in France? First, a sluggish economy and Europe's debt crisis hurt sales. Plus, Starbucks faced high rent and labor costs in France, which eroded profits. The company was also slow to tailor the Starbucks experience to the French café culture. Whereas a New Yorker might grab a paper cup of coffee to go, the French prefer to linger over a large, ceramic mug of coffee with friends in a café-style environment. To respond to these challenges, Starbucks launched a multimillion-dollar campaign in France that includes an upscale makeover of stores, with more seating and customized beverages and blends that appeal to local tastes.[8]

As geographic boundaries dissolve and opportunities in developing economies like China increase, more companies are finding advantages in the global marketplace. For example, Coca-Cola's CEO Muhtar Kent predicts that the China division will double its sales of Coke products, helping meet Kent's goal of doubling Coke's overall business by 2020. "China will be Coke's largest market," Kent promises. "I can't give you a time, but it will happen."[9] With more companies establishing a competitive presence in China, managers working in that country recognize that their competitive success begins with their ability to build personal relationships and emotional bonds with their Chinese contacts. The Manager's Shoptalk offer tips for creating successful business relationships in China.

Technological

The **technological dimension** of the general environment includes scientific and technological advancements in a specific industry, as well as in society at large.

▶ ▶ ▶ **Concept Connection**

ROB KIM/Landov

Changes in the **technological dimension** of the environment have enabled H&R Block to expand its services, as well as its marketing practices, on the Web. Because managers discovered customers were uncomfortable with spelling out their tax problems on Facebook and Twitter, H&R Block uses those sites to direct customers to a Q&A Web page, where people can find answers to common questions or reach specially trained employees who field unique questions.

Manager's *Shoptalk*

Creating *Guanxi* in China

With its low labor costs and huge potential market, China is luring thousands of U.S. companies in search of growth opportunities. Yet University of New Haven's Usha C. V. Haley recently found that only one-third of multinationals doing business in China have actually turned a profit. One reason many Western businesses fall short of expectations, experts agree, is that they fail to grasp the centuries-old concept of *guanxi* that lies at the heart of Chinese culture.

At its simplest level, *guanxi* is a supportive, mutually beneficial connection between two people. Eventually, those personal relationships are linked together into a network, and it is through networks like this that business gets done. Anyone considering doing business in China should keep in mind the following basic rules:

- **Business is always personal.** It is impossible to translate "Don't take it so personally—it's only business" into Chinese. Western managers tend to believe that if they conclude a successful transaction, a good business relationship will follow. The development of a personal relationship is an added bonus, but it is not really necessary when it comes to getting things done. In the Chinese business world, however, a personal relationship must be in place before managers even consider entering a business transaction. Western managers doing business in China should cultivate personal relationships—both during and outside business hours. Accept any and all social invitations—for drinks, a meal, or even a potentially embarrassing visit to a karaoke bar, which some Chinese businessmen consider an important part of solidifying good business relationships.

- **Don't skip the small talk.** Getting right down to business and bypassing the small talk during a meeting might feel like an efficient use of time to an American manager. To the Chinese, however, this approach neglects the all-important work of forging an emotional bond. Be aware that the real purpose of your initial meetings with potential business partners is to begin building a relationship, so keep your patience if the deal that you are planning to discuss never even comes up—there's always tomorrow.

- **Remember that relationships are not short-term.** The work of establishing and nurturing *guanxi* relationships in China is never done. Western managers must put aside their usual focus on short-term results and recognize that it takes a long time for foreigners to be accepted into a *guanxi* network. Often, foreign companies must prove their trustworthiness and reliability over time. For example, firms that weathered the political instability that culminated in the 1989 student protests in Tiananmen Square found it much easier to do business afterward.

- **Make contact frequently.** Some experts recommend hiring ethnic Chinese staff members and then letting them do the heavy lifting of relationship building. Others emphasize that Westerners themselves should put plenty of time and energy into forging links with Chinese contacts; those efforts will pay off because the contacts can smooth the way by tapping into their own *guanxi* networks. Whatever the strategy, contact should be frequent and personal. In addition, be sure to keep careful track of the contacts that you make. In China, any and all relationships are bound to be important at some point in time.

Sources: Michelle Dammon Loyalka, "Before You Set Up Shop in China," part of the "Doing Business in China" special report, *BusinessWeek Online*, January 4, 2006, www.businessweek.com/smallbiz/content/jan2006/sb20060104_466114.htm (accessed January 6, 2006); Los Angeles Chinese Learning Center, "Chinese Business Culture," http://chinese-school.netfirms.com/guanxi.html; Beijing British Embassy, "Golden Hints for Doing Business in China," http://chinese-school.netfirms.com/goldenhints.html; and Emily Flitter, "Faux Pas: With Karaoke, a Deal in China for a Song," *The Wall Street Journal Online*, June 9, 2008, http://online.wsj.com/article/SB121268021240548769.html (accessed September 24, 2012).

In recent years, as the economic recovery in the United States sputtered forward, managers began buying equipment and software that could enable them to accomplish more work with fewer employees. Motivated by temporary tax breaks and historically low interest rates, companies boosted spending on machines and software but were slow to put employees back on the payroll, leading to a "jobless recovery." Instead of hiring more workers, for example, companies such as Cincinnati-based Sunny Delight Beverages Company invested in technology to make operations faster and more productive. In fact, since the

U.S. economy began growing again in 2009, spending on equipment and software has surged 31 percent. On the other hand, private-sector jobs have grown just 1.4 percent over the same span.[10]

Advances in technology drive competition and help innovative companies gain market share. They also have the potential to transform consumer expectations of an entire industry. Driven by the popularity of e-readers, Barnes & Noble is reinventing its traditional bookstore image with a new digital strategy that managers hope will help it compete with rivals Amazon, Apple, and Google on the digital book front. With its renewed focus as a seller of downloads, reading devices, and apps, and a market share of 27 percent of the e-book market, Barnes & Noble is using its brick-and-mortar bookstores to introduce customers to its Nook e-readers and build e-book audiences.[11]

Sociocultural

The **sociocultural dimension** of the general environment represents the demographic characteristics as well as the norms, customs, and values of the general population. Important sociocultural characteristics are geographical distribution and population density, age, and education levels. Today's demographic profiles are the foundation of tomorrow's workforce and consumers. By understanding these profiles and addressing them in the organization's business plans, managers prepare their organizations for long-term success. Smart managers may want to consider how the following sociocultural trends are changing the consumer and business landscape:

1. A new generation of technologically-savvy consumers, often called the *Connected Generation* or *Generation C*, has intimately woven technology into every aspect of their lives. Their primary digital devices (PDDs) shape the way they communicate, shop, travel, and earn college credits. Generation C (typically defined as people born after 1990) will make up 40 percent of the population in the United States and Europe by 2020 and will constitute the largest cohort of consumers worldwide.[12]

2. As the U.S. population continues to age, organizations are rushing to create senior-friendly products and services. Currently, the U.S. population includes 78 million baby boomers, and roughly one-third will be 62 years old or older by 2013.[13] Organizations realize that it makes good business sense to create products and services for this aging population.

3. The most recent U.S. census data show that more than half of all babies born in 2011 were members of minority groups, the first time that has happened in U.S. history. Hispanics, African Americans, Asians, and other minorities in 2011 represented 50.4 percent of births. The nation's growing diversity has huge implications for business. "Children are in the vanguard of this transition," says Kenneth Johnson, a demographer at the University of New Hampshire's Carsey Institute.[14]

Economic

The **economic dimension** represents the general economic health of the country or region in which the organization operates. Consumer purchasing power, the unemployment rate,

▶▶▶ **Concept Connection**

Jay Clendenin/Aurora Photos

Shrewd home builders are responding to shifts in the **sociocultural dimension.** Aging baby boomers have been a mainstay of the housing market during the economic downturn, and what they want are smaller houses designed with features to help them stay in their own homes as long as possible. For example, this award-winning Green Lake Residence in Seattle, Washington, designed by Emory Baldwin of ZAI, Inc., offers an efficient, adaptable plan that includes no-step entries and closets stacked on top of each other that can be converted into an elevator shaft if necessary.

ENVIRONMENT 2

and interest rates are part of an organization's economic environment. Because organizations today are operating in a global environment, the economic dimension has become exceedingly complex and creates enormous uncertainty for managers. The global economic environment will be discussed in more detail in the next chapter.

In the United States, many industries, such as banking, are finding it difficult to make a comeback despite the slowly rebounding economy. Consider KeyCorp, one of the nation's largest banking-based financial services organizations. As the economy struggles forward, KeyCorp reports an uneven turnaround, with a mix of both good and bad news. While KeyCorp faces a reduction in total assets, a drop in revenue, and a decline in the profit margin in the lending business, it also reports fewer delinquent loans and strong demand from corporate customers for new loans. With banks stretching from Alaska to Maine, Key-Corp has benefited from geographic diversity because some regions of the United States rebounded faster than others. "As we are in economic recovery . . . our business model, our size, our geographic diversity is an advantage," said Beth Mooney, KeyCorp's CEO. "Conventional wisdom five years ago would have said differently."[15]

Legal-Political

The **legal-political dimension** includes government regulations at the local, state, and federal levels, as well as political activities designed to influence company behavior. The U.S. political system encourages capitalism, and the government tries not to over-regulate business. However, government laws do specify rules of the game. The federal government influences organizations through the Occupational Safety and Health Administration (OSHA), Environmental Protection Agency (EPA), fair trade practices, libel statutes allowing lawsuits against business, consumer protection and privacy legislation, product safety requirements, import and export restrictions, and information and labeling requirements.

Many companies work closely with national lawmakers, educating them about products and services and legislation's impact on their business strategies. Long before its NASDAQ debut in May 2012, Facebook had been quietly befriending the nation's top lawmakers. Facebook hired former political aides with access to top leaders in both parties and had them lead training sessions on using Facebook to communicate with voters. In

Reaching Mythical Proportions

In Greek mythology, Nike was the winged goddess of victory. With headquarters in Portland, Oregon— considered one of the world's "greenest" cities— **Nike Inc.** has a corporate culture centered around a commitment to victory, both on the athletic field and as one of the top 100 most sustainable corporations. Some companies give a nod to sustainability by reducing toxins, but Nike goes further. The company's predictive tool, the Considered Design Index, monitors the total environmental impact of the running shoe production cycle, scoring everything from fabric to reducing waste.

Victory in sustainability also means influencing other companies. Nike CSR staff spearheaded GreenX-change, which brought together companies to explore opportunities, share information, and keep abreast of trends and issues. As Nike's sustainability influence grows, its cultural mantra reflects the winged deity: "There is no finish line for environmental efforts—we can always go further."

Sources: Marc J. Epstein, Adriana Rejc Buhovac, and Kristi Yuthas, "Why Nike Kicks Butt in Sustainability," *Organizational Dynamics* 39 (2010): 353–356; and "Sustainable Business at Nike, Inc.," Nike corporate Web site, http://nikeinc.com/pages/responsibility (accessed July 24, 2012).

addition, Facebook stepped up its lobbying efforts and set up a political action committee. "It's smart advocacy 101," said Rey Ramsey, CEO of TechNet, an industry group that includes Facebook. "It starts with giving people an education. Then you start explaining more of your business model. What you ultimately want is for a legislator to understand the consequences of their actions."[16]

Natural

In response to pressure from environmental advocates, organizations have become increasingly sensitive to the Earth's diminishing natural resources and the environmental impact of their products and business practices. As a result, the natural dimension of the external environment is growing in importance. The **natural dimension** includes all elements that occur naturally on Earth, including plants, animals, rocks, and resources such as air, water, and climate. Protection of the natural environment is emerging as a critical policy focus around the world. Governments are increasingly under pressure to explain their performance on pollution control and natural resource management. Nations with the best environmental performance, along with some comparison countries, are listed in Exhibit 3.2. Note that the top performer is Switzerland, which gets most of its power from renewable sources—hydropower and geothermal energy.

The natural dimension is different from other sectors of the general environment because it has no voice of its own. Influence on managers to meet needs in the natural

Rank	Country	Score
1	Switzerland	76.69
2	Latvia	70.37
3	Norway	69.92
4	Luxembourg	69.2
5	Costa Rica	69.03
6	France	69
7	Austria	68.92
8	Italy	68.9
9	Sweden	68.82
10	United Kingdom	68.82
11	Germany	66.91
12	Slovakia	66.62
13	Iceland	66.28
14	New Zealand	66.05
15	Albania	65.85
37	Canada	58.41
49	United States	56.59
116	China	42.24
125	India	36.23
132	Iraq	25.32

EXHIBIT 3.2

2012 Environmental Performance Index

SOURCE: 2012 Environmental Performance Index, Yale Center for Environmental Law and Policy, Yale University, http://epi.yale.edu/epi2012/rankings; and Center for International Earth Science Information Network, Columbia University.

Note: The scores for each country are based on 25 performance indicators covering both environmental public health and ecosystem vitality, such as air pollution and greenhouse gas emissions.

ENVIRONMENT 2

Concept Connection ◀◀◀

Whether they are motivated by a desire to preserve natural resources, to impress their customers with their social responsibility, or to comply with new legislation, many companies are looking for ways to treat the **natural environment** better. Some are doing it by switching to renewable energy sources, while others are trying to reduce pollution. Promoting the use of cloth carrying bags like these is just one example of how retailers can help minimize the amount of trash going into the world's landfills.

Andy Shaw/Bloomberg/Getty Images

HOT TOPIC

environment may come from other sectors, such as government regulation, consumer concerns, the media, competitors' actions, or even employees.[17] For example, environmental groups advocate various action and policy goals that include reduction and cleanup of pollution, development of renewable energy resources, reduction of greenhouse gases such as carbon dioxide, and sustainable use of scarce resources such as water, land, and air. The oil spill in the Gulf of Mexico in 2010 brought environmental issues to the forefront. Months after a BP-Transocean rig at the Deepwater Horizon oil well exploded, hundreds of thousands of gallons of oil were still flowing into open water each day, adding to the millions of gallons already contaminating the water and beaches along the coast in Louisiana, Mississippi, Alabama, and Florida, and threatening the region's fish, birds, turtles, and vegetation. "One of the last pristine, most biologically diverse coastal habitats in the country is about to get wiped out," said Felicia Coleman, who directs the Florida State University Coastal and Marine Laboratory. "And there's not much we can do about it." The effects of the devastating spill are likely to continue for dozens of years.[18]

Remember This

- The **organizational environment**, consisting of both general and task environments, includes all elements existing outside the boundary of the organization that have the potential to affect the organization.
- An **organizational ecosystem** includes organizations in all the sectors of the task and general environments that provide the resource and information transactions, flows, and linkages necessary for an organization to thrive.
- The **general environment** indirectly influences all organizations within an industry and includes five dimensions.
- The **task environment** includes the sectors that conduct day-to-day transactions with the organization and directly influence its basic operations and performance.
- The **international dimension** of the external environment represents events originating in foreign countries, as well as opportunities for U.S. companies in other countries.

- The **technological dimension** of the general environment includes scientific and technological advances in society.
- The **sociocultural dimension** includes demographic characteristics, norms, customs, and values of a population within which the organization operates.
- The **economic dimension** represents the general economic health of the country or region in which the organization operates.
- The **legal-political dimension** includes government regulations at the local, state, and federal levels, as well as political activities designed to influence company behavior.
- The **internal environment** includes elements within the organization's boundaries, such as employees, management, and corporate culture.
- The **natural dimension** includes all elements that occur naturally on Earth, including plants, animals, rocks, and natural resources such as air, water, and climate.

TASK ENVIRONMENT

As described earlier, the task environment includes those sectors that have a direct working relationship with the organization, among them customers, competitors, suppliers, and the labor market.

Customers

Those people and organizations in the environment that acquire goods or services from the organization are **customers**. As recipients of the organization's output, customers are important because they determine the organization's success. Organizations have to be responsive to marketplace changes. The Hershey Company, which practically invented modern candy with its popular Hershey's bars and Hershey's Kisses, experienced serious losses in profits, market share, and stakeholder confidence after failing to understand customers' tastes. Hershey assumed that customers would embrace its dizzying array of Hershey's Kisses featuring different types of chocolate (milk, dark, and white), different fillings (caramel, peanut butter, and truffle), different flavors (orange, mint, and cherry), and with or without nuts. Instead, people saw a confusing tangle of flavors, and retailers were unhappy trying to find shelf space for all these varieties. With sales and profits sagging, Hershey refocused its efforts to understand its customers' desires, needs, and tastes better. Hershey then aligned its management teams in a strategic focus to meet those needs. The resulting turnabout and focus on customer needs have rescued the company and restored its luster.[19]

Competitors

Organizations in the same industry or type of business that provide goods or services to the same set of customers are referred to as **competitors**. Competitors are constantly battling for loyalty from the same group of customers. For example, managers at Target realized customers were scoping out merchandise in Target stores and later buying it at lower prices from Amazon. This procedure, known as "showrooming," means that customers check out products in stores and then buy them cheaper online, which hurts the bottom lines of traditional retailers such as Target. In response to this new trend, Target managers immediately began pushing suppliers to offer products that were exclusively available at Target, as well as expanding the number of items available at Target.com. Walmart also felt the pinch of showrooming and started promoting the convenience of in-store pickups for online orders—many available the same day they are purchased.[20]

Suppliers

Suppliers provide the raw materials that the organization uses to produce its output. A candy manufacturer, for example, may use suppliers from around the globe for ingredients such as cocoa beans, sugar, and cream. A *supply chain* is a network of multiple businesses and individuals that are connected through the flow of products or services. For Toyota, the supply chain includes over 500 global parts suppliers organized by a production strategy called *just-in-time (JIT)*.[21] JIT improves an organization's return on investment, quality, and efficiency because much less money in invested in idle inventory. In the 1970s, the Japanese taught U.S. companies how to boost profit by keeping inventories lean through JIT. "Instead of months' worth of inventory, there are now days and even hours of inventory," says Jim Lawton, head of supply management solutions at consultant Dun & Bradstreet. Lawton points out that there is a downside, however—one that became dramatically clear after a March 2011 earthquake in Japan: "If supply is disrupted, as in this situation, there's nowhere to get product."[22]

The recent crisis in Japan revealed the fragility of today's JIT supply chains. A powerful earthquake triggered massive tsunami waves and caused the second-worst nuclear disaster in history, at the Fukushima power plant along the Pacific coastline. Japanese parts suppliers for the global auto industry were shut down, disrupting production at auto factories around the world. "Even a missing $5 part can stop an assembly line," said a Morgan Stanley representative.[23] Because of this natural disaster, Toyota's production was down 800,000 vehicles—10 percent of its annual output. Most organizations aren't willing to boost inventory to minimize risks of supply-chain disruptions. Boosting inventory even slightly to provide a cushion against disruptions can cost big companies millions of dollars. "I don't see any of us moving away from a very disciplined supply-chain management," says Ford Motor Co. finance chief Lewis Booth.[24]

Labor Market

The **labor market** represents people in the environment who can be hired to work for the organization. Every organization needs a supply of trained, qualified personnel. Unions, employee associations, and the availability of certain classes of employees can influence the organization's labor market. Labor market forces affecting organizations right now include (1) the growing need for computer-literate knowledge workers; (2) the necessity for continuous investment in human resources through recruitment, education, and training to meet the competitive demands of the borderless world; and (3) the effects of international trading blocs, automation, outsourcing, and shifting facility locations on labor dislocations, creating unused labor pools in some areas and labor shortages in others.

Changes in these various sectors of the general and task environments can create tremendous challenges, especially for organizations operating in complex, rapidly changing industries. Costco Wholesale Corporation, with warehouses throughout the world, is an example of an organization operating in a highly complex environment.

Innovative Way

Costco Wholesale Corporation

Costco Wholesale Corporation, a no-frills, self-service warehouse club, operates an international chain of membership warehouses offering a limited selection of products at reduced prices. Costco's business model focuses on maintaining its image as a pricing authority, consistently providing the most competitive prices. "Everything we do is to provide goods and services to the customer at a lower price," said Jim Sinegal, CEO and founder. Costco warehouses are designed to operate efficiently and to communicate value to members. The warehouse decor—high ceilings, metal roofs, exposed trusses—keeps costs low and contributes to the perception that Costco is for serious shoppers seeking serious bargains. Other strategies for keeping prices low include offering only 3,600 unique products at a time (Walmart offers over 100,000) and negotiating low prices with suppliers. Only about a quarter of sales come from outside the United States, but same store sales in overseas markets have been growing about four times faster than those in the United States. Costco plans to expand its customer base by delving further into the Asian markets, where consumer spending and growth is higher than mature U.S. and European markets. Costco's complex environment is illustrated in Exhibit 3.3.

Costco's biggest competitive advantage is its workforce. "Costco compensates employees very well, well above the industry in terms of wages and benefits," says R. J. Hottovey, a retail analyst at Morningstar. "When retailers are cutting health benefits, Costco employees don't have to worry about that," he says. The happiness and morale of employees is often overlooked in the retail industry, but not at Costco. Thanks to its good treatment of workers, Costco has one of the lowest turnovers in the retail industry (only 6 percent), and it earns $530,000 of revenue per employee.[25]

Remember This

- **Customers** are part of the task environment and include people and organizations that acquire goods or services from the organization.
- **Competitors** are organizations within the same industry or type of business that vie for the same set of customers.

- Traditional stores such as Target and Walmart are competing with online retailers such as Amazon and Zappos.
- **Suppliers** provide the raw materials the organization uses to produce its output.
- The **labor market** represents the people available for hire by the organization.

EXHIBIT ▮ **3.3**

The External Environment
of Costco Wholesale
Corporation

General Environment

2

ENVIRONMENT

Task Environment

Technological
- Costco.com offers opportunities to reach a wider audience
- Applies technology to manage store and corporate operations

Customers
- 66.5 million members
- 30% are small business owners
- Appeals to customers seeking high-volume and low price
- 89% membership renewal

Natural
- Greenhouse inventories to track emission trends
- Energy-efficient building design
- Committed to aggressive environmental protection in the gasoline business

Competitors
- Vigorous and widespread
- Sam's Club, BJ's Wholesale Club, Kroger, Walmart, Walgreens, Kohl's, Home Depot, Lowe's

Costco Wholesale Corporation

Sociocultural
- Focuses on bulk needs of families in suburban communities
- Targets wide range of customers
- Average customer income is $57,000

Economic
- Negatively affected by economic slowdown
- Susceptible to fluctuating currency exchange rates
- Value pricing drives customer traffic

Suppliers
- Brand-name vendors, such as P&G, Kraft, and Whirlpool
- Builds close supplier relationships to keep prices low
- Supplier Diversity Program for minority- and women-owned businesses

Legal/Political
- Offers government-required health insurance for employees
- Government-mandated minimum wage
- Supports privatization of liquor sales (license states)

Labor Market
- 160,000 loyal, highly productive employees
- Considers employees a competitive advantage
- Lean and stable executive ranks
- Labor & benefits comprise 70% of operating costs

International
- Strong growth expected in Asian markets
- 27% of sales from countries outside of U.S.

SOURCES: Costco Wholesale Corporation Website, www.costco.com (accessed July 10, 2012); "Costco Wholesale Corporation," *Marketline* (April 30, 2012): 3–9; Alaric DeArment, "Costco's Lobbying Changes WA's Liquor Laws: Who Is Next?" DrugstoreNews.com, December 12, 2011, p. 12 (www.drugstorenews .com/article/costco%E2%80%99s-lobbying-changes-%E2%80%A9wa%E2%80%99s-liquor-laws-who-next); and Sharon Edelson, "Costco Keeps Formula As It Expands," *Women's Wear Daily* (January 30, 2012): 1.

The Organization–Environment Relationship

Why do organizations care so much about factors in the external environment? The reason is that the environment creates uncertainty for organization managers, and they must respond by designing the organization to adapt to the environment.

ENVIRONMENTAL UNCERTAINTY

Uncertainty means that managers do not have sufficient information about environmental factors to understand and predict environmental needs and changes.[26] As indicated in Exhibit 3.4, environmental characteristics that influence uncertainty are the number of factors that affect the organization and the extent to which those factors change. Managers at a large multinational like Costco must deal with thousands of factors in the external environment that create uncertainty. When external factors change rapidly, the organization experiences high uncertainty; examples are telecommunications and aerospace firms, computer and electronics companies, and Internet organizations. When MySpace's audience plummeted 27 percent in 2010, managers struggled to identify the factors that were upending this fledgling social media service. One factor included the changing tastes of fickle social media customers, which are difficult to predict. When Facebook provided a better customer experience and a simple Google-like interface, customers left MySpace in droves. In fact, MySpace lost 9 million customers between 2009 and 2010. "MySpace was like a big party, and then the party moved on," said Michael J. Wolf, the former president of Viacom's MTV Networks and managing partner at media consulting firm Activate.[27]

When an organization deals with only a few external factors and these factors are relatively stable, such as those affecting soft-drink bottlers or food processors, managers experience low uncertainty and can devote less attention to external issues.

ADAPTING TO THE ENVIRONMENT

Environmental changes may evolve unexpectedly, such as shifting customer tastes for social media sites, or they may occur violently, such as the devastating Japanese earthquake and tsunami. The level of turbulence created by an environmental shift will determine the type

Take a Moment

Refer to your score on the opening questionnaire to see how well you might adapt as a new manager in an uncertain environment.

EXHIBIT 3.4

The External Environment and Uncertainty

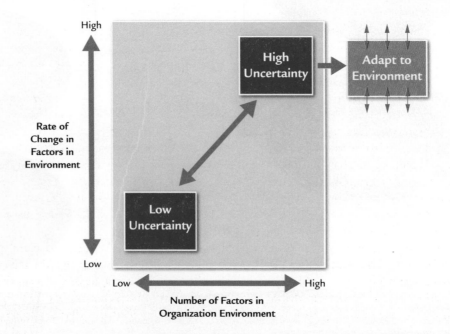

of response that managers must make in order for the organization to survive. Managers continuously scan the business horizon for both subtle and dramatic environmental changes, also called *strategic issues*, and identify those that require strategic responses. **Strategic issues** are "events or forces either inside or outside an organization that are likely to alter its ability to achieve its objectives." As environmental turbulence increases, strategic issues emerge more frequently.[28] Managers use several strategies to adapt to these strategic issues, including boundary-spanning roles, interorganizational partnerships, and mergers or joint ventures.

Boundary-Spanning Roles

Boundary-spanning roles link to and coordinate the organization with key elements in the external environment. Boundary spanners serve two purposes for the organization: They detect and process information about changes in the environment, and they represent the organization's interests to the environment.[29] As an example of boundary-spanning, General Electric spends $39.3 million on political lobbying to influence government officials to take actions that positively affect the company's business performance. GE's political lobbyists serve to span the boundary between the organization and the government, a critical aspect of the external environment.[30]

Another approach to boundary spanning is the use of *business intelligence*, which results from using sophisticated software to search through large amounts of internal and external data to spot patterns, trends, and relationships that might be significant. For example, Verizon uses business intelligence software to monitor customer interactions and fix problems almost immediately.[31] Business intelligence is related to the growing area of boundary spanning known as *competitive intelligence (CI)*, which refers to activities to get as much information as possible about one's rivals.[32] Visa has an employee who searches the Web for two hours each day for insights on MasterCard and other competitors. Harley-Davidson hires an outside research firm to search through massive amounts of data and reveal patterns that help decipher and predict competitors' actions.[33]

Boundary spanning is an increasingly important task in organizations because environmental shifts can happen quickly in today's world. Managers need good information about their competitors, customers, and other elements of the environment to make good decisions. Thus, the most successful companies involve everyone in boundary-spanning activities.

Interorganizational Partnerships

With tough global competition, constantly changing technology, and shifting government regulations, few companies can compete effectively unless they join with other firms in various partnerships. Organizations around the world are embedded in complex networks of confusing relationships—collaborating in some markets, competing fiercely in others. The number of corporate alliances has been increasing at a rate of 25 percent annually, and many of those have been between competitors.[34] For example, in the auto industry, Ford and General Motors (GM) compete fiercely, but the two joined together to develop a six-speed transmission. Hyundai, Chrysler, and Mitsubishi jointly run the Global Engine Manufacturing Alliance to build four-cylinder engines. Volvo is now owned by Zhejiang Geely Holding Group of China, but it maintains an alliance with its previous owner, Ford, to supply engines and certain other components.[35] In a partnership, each organization both supports and depends on the others for success, and perhaps for survival, but that doesn't mean they don't still compete fiercely in certain areas.[36]

Managers in partnering organizations shift from an adversarial orientation to a partnership orientation. The new paradigm, shown in Exhibit 3.5, is based on trust and the ability of partners to work out equitable solutions to conflicts so that everyone profits from the relationship. Managers work to reduce costs and add value to both sides, rather than trying to get all the benefits for their own company. The new model is also characterized by

Take a Moment

Read the Ethical Dilemma for Chapter 3 on page 196 that pertains to competitive intelligence (CI). Do you have the courage to risk your job by challenging the boss's inappropriate use of confidential information?

2

ENVIRONMENT

EXHIBIT 3.5

The Shift to a Partnership Paradigm

From Adversarial Orientation ⟶	To Partnership Orientation
• Suspicion, competition, arm's length	• Trust, value added to both sides
• Price, efficiency, own profits	• Equity, fair dealing, everyone profits
• Information and feedback limited	• E-business links to share information and conduct digital transactions
• Lawsuits to resolve conflict	• Close coordination; virtual teams and people onsite
• Minimal involvement and up-front investment	• Involvement in partner's product design and production
• Short-term contracts	• Long-term contracts
• Contracts limit the relationship	• Business assistance goes beyond the contract

a high level of information sharing, including e-business links for automatic ordering, payments, and other transactions. In addition, person-to-person interaction provides corrective feedback and solves problems. People from other companies may be on site, or they may participate in virtual teams to enable close coordination. Partners are frequently involved in one another's product design and production, and they are committed for the long term. It is not unusual for business partners to help one another, even outside of what is specified in the contract.[37]

Mergers and Joint Ventures

A step beyond strategic partnerships is for companies to become involved in mergers or joint ventures to reduce environmental uncertainty. A frenzy of merger and acquisition activity both in the United States and internationally in recent years is an attempt by organizations to cope with the tremendous volatility of the environment.[38] A **merger** occurs when two or more organizations combine to become one. When managers saw sales of Corn Flakes

Concept Connection ◀◀◀

Already the largest drugstore chain in the United States, Walgreens decided to expand its business through a major acquisition in 2011. The company paid nearly $400 million to purchase the online health and beauty care product retailer Drugstore.com. Mergers and acquisitions are one way organizations **adapt to an uncertain environment**.

Michael Loccisano/Getty Images Entertainment/Getty Images

and Rice Krispies fall flat as price-conscious consumers chose generic, private-label cereals instead, Kellogg bought Pringles from Procter & Gamble (P&G) in May 2012 to bolster its foreign snacks divisions. Growth for Kellogg, as well as for rivals PepsiCo and Frito-Lay, is in snack foods in foreign markets. "We're not happy with our performance the last couple of years," says Kellogg CEO John A. Bryant. "We have to keep bringing new foods to consumers and delighting them, because if we stand still, people catch up." With the merger, Kellogg gains not only a snack that is already hugely popular internationally, but also a group of P&G merchandisers that understand global markets.[39]

A **joint venture** involves a strategic alliance or program by two or more organizations. A joint venture typically occurs when a project is too complex, expensive, or uncertain for one firm to handle alone. Sikorsky Aircraft and Lockheed Martin, for example, teamed up to bid on a new contract for a fleet of Marine One helicopters. The joint venture would have Sikorsky building the helicopters and Lockheed Martin providing the vast array of specialized systems that each one uses. Although the two companies have previously competed to build presidential helicopters, they joined together to be more competitive against rivals such as Boeing, Bell Helicopters, and Finmeccanica SpA's Agusta Westland.[40] Joint ventures are on the rise as companies strive to keep pace with rapid technological change and compete in the global economy.

Remember This

- When external factors change rapidly, the organization experiences high uncertainty.
- **Strategic issues** are events and forces that alter an organization's ability to achieve its goals. As environmental turbulence increases, strategic issues emerge more frequently.
- **Boundary-spanning roles** link to and coordinate the organization with key elements in the external environment.

- **Interorganizational partnerships** reduce boundaries and increase collaboration with other organizations.
- A **merger** occurs when two or more organizations combine to become one.
- A **joint venture** is a strategic alliance or program by two or more organizations.
- Sikorsky Aircraft and Lockheed Martin teamed up to bid on a new contract for Marine One helicopters.

The Internal Environment: Corporate Culture

The internal environment within which managers work includes corporate culture, production technology, organization structure, and physical facilities. Of these, corporate culture surfaces as extremely important to competitive advantage. The internal culture must fit the needs of the external environment and company strategy. When this fit occurs, highly committed employees create a high-performance organization that is tough to beat.[41]

Most people don't think about culture; it's just "how we do things around here" or "the way things are here." However, managers have to think about culture because it typically plays a significant role in organizational success. Organizational culture has been defined and studied in many and varied ways. For the purposes of this chapter, we define **culture** as the set of key values, beliefs, understandings, and norms shared by members of an organization.[42] The concept of culture helps managers understand the hidden, complex aspects of organizational life. Culture is a pattern of shared values and assumptions about how things are done within the organization. This pattern is learned by members as they cope with external and internal problems and taught to new members as the correct way to perceive, think, and feel.

EXHIBIT 3.6

Levels of Corporate Culture

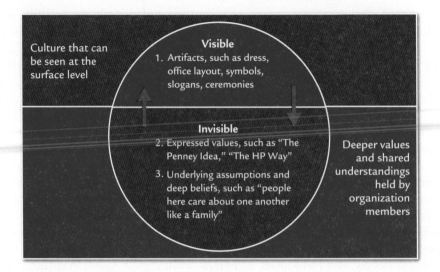

Take a Moment

Complete the Small Group Breakout on pages 95–96 that deals with identifying cultural norms.

HOT TOPIC

Although strong corporate cultures are important, they can also sometimes promote negative values and behaviors. When the actions of top leaders are unethical, for instance, the entire culture can become contaminated. Consider what happened at News Corporation, a corporate giant with a lucrative string of media properties all over the world. Rupert Murdoch, chairman and CEO, has been accused of frequently applying unethical, sometimes seedy tactics in his business dealings. In addition, Murdoch has allegedly used "blunt force" spending to cover up unscrupulous tactics and silence critics with multimillion dollar payoffs. "Bury your mistakes," Murdoch was fond of saying.[43] But he couldn't bury the scandal that rocked the organization after journalists working for News Corporation newspapers allegedly hacked private voice-mail messages and offered bribes to police in the pursuit of hot scoops. Journalists went so far as to hack the voice mail of a murdered 13-year-old girl, Milly Dowler, while she was still listed as missing.[44] As this example illustrates, the values and behaviors of top leaders have the potential to shape significantly the decisions made by employees throughout the organization. Mark Lewis, the lawyer for the family of the murdered girl, pointed out: "This is not just about one individual, but about the culture of an organization."[45]

Culture can be analyzed at two levels, as illustrated in Exhibit 3.6.[46] At the surface level are visible artifacts, which include things such as manner of dress, patterns of behavior, physical symbols, organizational ceremonies, and office layout. Visible artifacts are all the things one can see, hear, and observe by watching members of the organization. At a deeper, less obvious level are values and beliefs, which are not observable but can be discerned from how people explain and justify what they do. Members of the organization hold some values at a conscious level. These values can be interpreted from the stories, language, and symbols that organization members use to represent them.

Some values become so deeply embedded in a culture that members are no longer consciously aware of them. These basic, underlying assumptions and beliefs are the essence of culture and subconsciously guide behavior and decisions. In some organizations, a basic assumption might be that people are essentially lazy and will shirk their duties whenever possible; thus, employees are closely supervised and given little freedom and colleagues are frequently suspicious of one another. More enlightened organizations operate on the basic assumption that people want to do a good job; in these organizations, employees are given more freedom and responsibility and colleagues trust one another and work cooperatively. At the Zappos Family of companies, a culture of well-being and happiness has been instrumental in the growth of this successful online retailer.

Innovative Way

Zappos Family

2

ENVIRONMENT

Zappos.com, an online retail site best known for its wide selection of shoes and its free shipping, boldly proclaims its unique culture in an offbeat set of ten core values. CEO Tony Hsieh believes that these values illustrate the company's innovative culture and demonstrate its ultimate business goal—*cultivating happiness*. Hsieh's management theory goes like this: If you create a work culture that fosters well-being, good practices and (eventually) good profits will naturally flow out of the operation. So far, his theory is producing outstanding business results. Zappos.com, Inc. is raking in $1 billion worth of annual gross sales, and employees widely report that their work is exciting and challenging. "We really buy into the idea that the better we treat each other, the better we'll all be able to treat our customers," says Rebecca Ratner, director of human resources.

Hsieh knows firsthand how important a strong, positive culture is when it comes to employee and customer happiness. Before Zappos, he had experienced the joyless grind of working in a job that had no meaning, where technical skill was all that mattered. Hsieh decided to write the book *Delivering Happiness* to document his journey from "chasing profits to chasing passion," the life lessons he has learned, and how those lessons have been applied at Zappos. Here are some key points for business leaders:

- *Get the right values.* Zappos has a set of 10 core values that include "Create fun and a little weirdness"; "Deliver WOW through service"; "Embrace and drive change"; "Be adventurous, creative, and open-minded"; "Pursue growth and learning"; and "Be humble." But Hsieh didn't dictate the values from on high. He sent an e-mail to all employees asking them what values should guide the company. The responses were discussed, condensed, and combined to come up with the final list.

- *Get the right people.* Zappos does two sets of interviews when hiring new employees. The first focuses on relevant experience, professional and technical skills, and the ability to work with the team. The second focuses purely on culture fit. There are questions for each of the core values, such as "How weird are you?" People are carefully selected to fit the Zappos culture, even if that means rejecting people with stronger technical skills.

- *Make culture a top priority.* All employees attend a four-week training session and commit the core values to memory. At the end of training, they're offered $2,000 to resign if they believe that they aren't a good fit with the culture. Every year, Zappos puts out a *Culture Book*, in which employees share their own stories about what the Zappos culture means to them.[47]

The Zappos Family of companies has created a unique culture that is reflected in its core values. Fundamental values are demonstrated in organizations through symbols, stories, heroes, slogans, and ceremonies.

SYMBOLS

A **symbol** is an object, act, or event that conveys meaning to others. Symbols can be considered a rich, nonverbal language that vibrantly conveys the organization's important values concerning how people relate to one another and interact with the environment.[48] Mindy Grossman, CEO of HSN Inc., found that something as simple as an office chair can be symbolic. When Grossman became HSN's eighth CEO in ten years, she inherited a downtrodden workforce. During her first few months, Grossman learned as much about the business as possible. "As I grew to understand the business, it became clear that it was fundamentally broken. To fix it, I needed to dramatically alter the company's culture," she said. Part of the cultural transformation included improving the work environment, which had dirty offices full of broken-down office furniture and clutter. "I looked around and realized we had 40 different kinds of office chairs. So I bought several thousand Herman Miller Aeron chairs," said Grossman. She received over 100 e-mails expressing appreciation on the day they were delivered.[49] For Grossman, the new office chairs were an important symbol of a new company value of caring for employees.

Concept Connection ◄◄◄

REUTERS/JP Moczulski

Toyota's handling of its 2010 recall crisis drove some observers to characterize Toyota's **corporate culture** as parochial. Critics attributed the company's reticence to go public with its quality problems to its deep roots in Japanese culture, in which airing dirty linen in public is impolite. However, the Toyota culture has also been historically linked with a powerful commitment to quality, which enabled the company, under the leadership of president and CEO Akio Toyoda (pictured here painting an eye on a traditional Japanese doll), to return to its previous strong market position within a couple of years.

STORIES

A **story** is a narrative based on true events and is repeated frequently and shared among organizational employees. Stories paint pictures that help symbolize the firm's vision and values and help employees personalize and absorb them.[50] A frequently told story at UPS concerns an employee who, without authorization, ordered an extra Boeing 737 to ensure timely delivery of a load of Christmas packages that had been left behind in the holiday rush. As the story goes, rather than punishing the worker, UPS rewarded his initiative. By telling this story, UPS workers communicate that the company stands behind its commitment to worker autonomy and customer service.[51]

HEROES

A **hero** is a figure who exemplifies the deeds, character, and attributes of a strong culture. Heroes are role models for employees to follow. Heroes with strong legacies may continue to influence a culture even after they are gone. Many people have wondered if the culture that Steve Jobs created at Apple would be sustained after his death in 2011. Jobs exemplified the creativity, innovation, risk-taking, and boundary-breaking thinking that made the company famous.[52] When Jobs's health began to fail, Apple's board began considering replacements who could sustain the fertile culture that Jobs created. They chose Tim Cook, who long had served as second-in-command. Cook now cultivates a culture that reflects the values and behaviors of Apple's hero, Steve Jobs. "Apple has a culture of excellence that is, I think, so unique and so special. I'm not going to witness or permit the change of it," he said.[53]

SLOGANS

A **slogan** is a phrase or sentence that succinctly expresses a key corporate value. Many companies use a slogan or saying to convey special meaning to employees. For example, Disney uses the slogan "The happiest place on earth." The Ritz-Carlton adopted the slogan, "Ladies and gentlemen taking care of ladies and gentlemen" to demonstrate its cultural commitment to take care of both employees and customers. "We're in the service business, and service comes only from people. Our promise is to take care of them, and provide a happy place for them to work," said general manager Mark DeCocinis, who manages the Portman Hotel in Shanghai, recipient of the "Best Employer in Asia" award for three consecutive years.[54] Cultural values can also be discerned in written public statements, such as corporate mission statements or other formal statements that express the core values of the organization. The mission statement for Hallmark Cards, for example, emphasizes values of excellence, ethical and moral conduct in all relationships, business innovation, and corporate social responsibility.[55]

CEREMONIES

A **ceremony** is a planned activity at a special event that is conducted for the benefit of an audience. Managers hold ceremonies to provide dramatic examples of company values. Ceremonies are special occasions that reinforce valued accomplishments, create a bond among people by allowing them to share an important event, and anoint and celebrate heroes.[56] In a ceremony to mark its 20th anniversary, Southwest Airlines rolled out a specialty plane called the "Lone Star One," which had the Texas state flag painted on it to signify the company's start in Texas. Later, when the National Basketball Association (NBA) chose Southwest Airlines as the league's official airline, Southwest launched another specialty plane, the "Slam Dunk One," colored blue and orange with a large basketball painted on the nose of the plane. Today, ten specialty planes celebrate significant milestones in Southwest's history and demonstrate key cultural values.[57]

Remember This

- Organizational **culture** is the set of key values, beliefs, understandings, and norms shared by members of an organization.
- A **symbol** is an object, act, or event that conveys meaning to others.
- A **story** is a narrative based on true events and is repeated frequently and shared among organizational employees.
- A **hero** is a figure who exemplifies the deeds, character, and attributes of a strong culture.

- Steve Jobs is a hero at Apple, representing the creativity, risk taking, and striving for excellence that define the company's culture.
- A **slogan**, such as Disney's "The happiest place on earth," succinctly expresses a key corporate value.
- Managers hold **ceremonies**, planned activities at special events, to reinforce company values.

Types of Culture

A big influence on internal corporate culture is the external environment. Cultures can vary widely across organizations; however, organizations within the same industry often reveal similar cultural characteristics because they are operating in similar environments.[58] The internal culture should embody what it takes to succeed in the environment. If the external environment requires extraordinary customer service, the culture should encourage good service; if it calls for careful technical decision making, cultural values should reinforce managerial decision making.

In considering what cultural values are important for the organization, managers consider the external environment, as well as the company's strategy and goals. Studies suggest that the right fit between culture, strategy, and the environment is associated with four categories or types of culture, as illustrated in Exhibit 3.7. These categories are based on two dimensions: (1) the extent to which the external environment requires flexibility or stability, and (2) the extent to which a company's strategic focus is internal or external. The four categories associated with these differences are adaptability, achievement, involvement, and consistency.[59]

ADAPTABILITY CULTURE

The **adaptability culture** emerges in an environment that requires fast response and high-risk decision making. Managers encourage values that support the company's ability to rapidly detect, interpret, and translate signals from the environment into new behaviors.

EXHIBIT   3.7

Four Types of Corporate
Culture

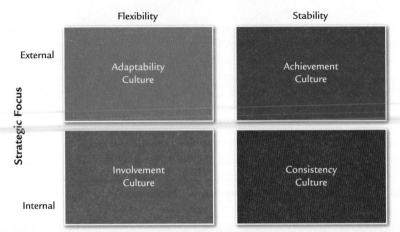

SOURCES: Based on D. R. Denison and A. K. Mishra, "Toward a Theory of Organizational Culture and Effectiveness," *Organization Science* 6, no. 2 (March–April 1995): 204–223; R. Hooijberg and F. Petrock, "On Cultural Change: Using the Competing Values Framework to Help Leaders Execute a Transformational Strategy," *Human Resource Management* 32, no. 1 (1993): 29–50; and R. E. Quinn, *Beyond Rational Management: Mastering the Paradoxes and Competing Demands of High Performance* (San Francisco: Jossey-Bass, 1988).

Employees have the autonomy to make decisions and act freely to meet new needs, and responsiveness to customers is highly valued. Managers also actively create change by encouraging and rewarding creativity, experimentation, and risk taking. Lush Cosmetics, a fast-growing maker of shampoos, lotions, and bath products made from fresh ingredients such as mangoes and avocados, provides a good example of an adaptability culture. A guiding motto at the company is "We reserve the right to make mistakes." Founder and CEO Mark Constantine is passionately devoted to change and encourages employees to break boundaries, experiment, and take risks. The company kills off one-third of its product line every year to offer new and offbeat products.[60] Other companies in the cosmetics industry, as well as those involved in electronics, e-commerce, and fashion, often use an adaptability culture because they must move quickly to respond to rapid changes in the environment.

ACHIEVEMENT CULTURE

The **achievement culture** is suited to organizations concerned with serving specific customers in the external environment, but without the intense need for flexibility and rapid change. This results-oriented culture values competitiveness, aggressiveness, personal initiative, cost cutting, and willingness to work long and hard to achieve results. An emphasis on winning and achieving specific ambitious goals is the glue that holds the organization together.[61] Brewing giant InBev provides an example. When InBev bought Anheuser-Busch, it replaced lavish perks and generous spending with a no-frills culture focused intently on cost cutting and meeting strict profit goals. Managers also created an incentive-based compensation system to reflect "an increased focus on meritocracy." The system handsomely rewards high performers rather than spreading dollars more evenly among employees. "We always say, the leaner the business, the more money we'll have at the end of the year to share," said Carlos Brito, InBev's CEO.[62]

INVOLVEMENT CULTURE

The **involvement culture** emphasizes an internal focus on the involvement and participation of employees to adapt rapidly to changing needs from the environment. This culture places high value on meeting the needs of employees, and the organization may be characterized by a caring, family-like atmosphere. Managers emphasize values such as cooperation, consideration of both employees and customers, and avoiding status differences. Consider the Four Seasons hotel chain, where the culture embodies a commitment to the company's greatest asset—its employees.

Four Seasons is considered by many people to be the world's premier hospitality company, offering a worldwide chain of luxury hotels and resorts. One reason is that it consistently inspires employees to provide exceptional, customized, 24-hour service and strive for the goal of creating "the world's best hospitality experience." The company has been named one of the "100 Best Companies to Work For" by *Fortune* magazine every year since the survey's inception in 1998, ranking number 85 in 2012. With 86 luxury properties in 35 countries, Four Seasons has nurtured a corporate culture that values employees above all other assets. This relentless commitment to employees has sustained Four Seasons during an economic recession that battered many companies in the hospitality industry. With most of the industry in shambles as vacationers and business travelers canceled travel plans, how did Four Seasons stay on track and position itself for future success?

Managers created a unified culture whose employees rally behind an inspiring purpose. The purpose of Four Seasons—to create the world's best hospitality experience—is a deeply instilled belief that each employee takes personally. "We have 34,000 employees who get up every morning thinking about how to serve our guests even better than the day before," said CEO Katie Taylor. "So while all of this trouble is swirling around us, our brand promise of providing the most exceptional guest experience wherever and whenever you visit us is instilled in the hearts and minds of our dedicated employees. They are the ones who fulfill that promise day in and day out."

Four Seasons also clarified its corporate vision by ensuring that it could be personalized by employees and provide stability through an unpredictable recession. The new vision includes (1) achieving a first-choice ranking among guests, (2) being the best employer, and (3) being the industry's number one builder of sustainable value. These clear and meaningful statements provide a compelling and aspirational vision that motivates employees to do their best. The results? Bookings have gone up dramatically, and employee engagement scores are higher than ever.[63]

CONSISTENCY CULTURE

The final category of culture, the **consistency culture**, uses an internal focus and a consistency orientation for a stable environment. Following the rules and being thrifty are valued, and the culture supports and rewards a methodical, rational, orderly way of doing things. In today's fast-changing world, few companies operate in a stable environment, and most managers are shifting toward cultures that are more flexible and in tune with changes in the environment. However, Pacific Edge Software (now part of Serena Software), successfully implemented elements of a consistency culture to ensure that all its projects stayed on time and under budget. The husband-and-wife team of Lisa Hjorten and Scott Fuller implanted a culture of order, discipline, and control from the moment they founded the company. The emphasis on order and focus meant employees could generally go home by 6:00 P.M. rather than working all night to finish an important project. Although sometimes being careful means being slow, Pacific Edge managed to keep pace with the demands of the external environment.[64]

Each of these four categories of culture can be successful. In addition, organizations usually have values that fall into more than one category. The relative emphasis on various cultural values depends on the needs of the environment and the organization's focus. Managers are responsible for instilling the cultural values the organization needs to be successful in its environment.

New Manager 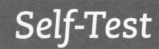 Self-Test

Culture Preference

Instructions: The fit between a new manager and organizational culture can determine success and satisfaction. To understand your culture preference, rank the items below from 1 to 8 based on the strength of your preference (1 = strongest preference).

1. The organization is very personal, much like an extended family.

2. The organization is dynamic and changing, where people take risks.

3. The organization is achievement oriented, with the focus on competition and getting jobs done.

4. The organization is stable and structured, with clarity and established procedures.

5. Management style is characterized by teamwork and participation.

6. Management style is characterized by innovation and risk taking.

7. Management style is characterized by high performance demands and achievement.

8. Management style is characterized by security and predictability.

Scoring and Interpretation: Each question pertains to one of the four types of culture in Exhibit 3.7. To compute your preference for each type of culture, add together the scores for each set of two questions as follows:

Involvement culture—total for questions 1, 5: _____

Adaptability culture—total for questions 2, 6: _____

Achievement culture—total for questions 3, 7: _____

Consistency culture—total for questions 4, 8: _____

A lower score means a stronger culture preference. You will likely be more comfortable and more effective as a new manager in a corporate culture that is compatible with your personal preferences. A higher score means the culture would not fit your expectations, and you would have to change your style and preference to be comfortable. Review the text discussion of the four culture types. Do your cultural preference scores seem correct to you? Can you think of companies that fit your culture preference?

Source: Adapted from Kim S. Cameron and Robert D. Quinn, *Diagnosing and Changing Organizational Culture* (Reading, MA: Addison-Wesley, 1999).

Remember This

- For an organization to be effective, corporate culture should be aligned with organizational strategy and the needs of the external environment.
- Organizations within the same industry often reveal similar cultural characteristics because they are operating in similar environments.
- The **adaptability culture** is characterized by values that support the company's ability to interpret and translate signals from the environment into new behavior responses.

- An **achievement culture** is a results-oriented culture that values competitiveness, personal initiative, and achievement.
- A culture that places high value on meeting the needs of employees and values cooperation and equality is an **involvement culture**.
- A **consistency culture** values and rewards a methodical, rational, orderly way of doing things.

Shaping Corporate Culture for Innovative Response

Research conducted by a Stanford University professor indicates that the one factor that increases a company's value the most is people and how they are treated.[65] In addition, surveys show that CEOs often cite organizational culture as their most important mechanism for attracting, motivating, and retaining talented employees, a capability considered the single best predictor of overall organizational excellence.[66] In a survey of Canadian senior executives, fully 82 percent believe a direct correlation exists between culture and financial performance.[67] Consider how an "employees first" corporate culture drives stellar financial performance at Southwest Airlines. Profitable for 38 consecutive years and touting the lowest ratio of complaints per passengers in the industry, Southwest offers industry-leading salaries and benefits, intense career development programs, and a commitment to diversity among its workforce. In addition, Southwest promotes a strong collaborative culture and fosters good relationships with organized labor.[68] At Southwest, a positive culture that reflects an intense commitment to employees results in a competitive advantage.

Corporate culture plays a key role in creating an organizational climate that enables learning and innovative responses to threats from the external environment, challenging new opportunities, or organizational crises. However, managers realize they can't focus all their effort on values; they also need a commitment to solid business performance.

MANAGING THE HIGH-PERFORMANCE CULTURE

Companies that succeed in a turbulent world are those that pay careful attention to both cultural values *and* business performance. Cultural values can energize and motivate employees by appealing to higher ideals and unifying people around shared goals. In addition, values boost performance by shaping and guiding employee behavior, so that everyone's actions are aligned with strategic priorities.[69] Exhibit 3.8 illustrates four organizational outcomes based on the relative attention managers pay to cultural values and business performance.[70] For example, a company in Quadrant C pays little attention to either values or business results and is unlikely to survive for long. Managers in Quadrant D organizations are highly focused on creating a strong cohesive culture, but they don't tie organizational values directly to goals and desired business results.

When cultural values aren't connected to business performance, they aren't likely to benefit the organization during hard times. The corporate culture at the LEGO Group, with headquarters in Billund, Denmark, nearly doomed the toymaker in the 1990s when sales plummeted as children turned from traditional toys to video games. At that time, LEGO reflected the characteristics found in Quadrant D of Exhibit 3.8. Imagination and creativity, not business performance, were what guided the company. The attitude among employees was, "We're doing great stuff for kids—don't bother us with financial goals." A new CEO, Jørgen Vig Knudstorp, upended the corporate culture with a new employee motto: "I am here to make money for the company." The shift to bottom-line results had a profound impact, and LEGO has become one of the most successful companies in the toy industry.[71]

Quadrant A represents organizations that are focused primarily on bottom-line results and pay little attention to organizational values. This approach may be profitable in the short run, but the success is difficult to sustain over the long term because the "glue" that holds the organization

"If you see your job not as chief strategy officer and the guy who has all the ideas, but rather as the guy who is obsessed with enabling employees to create value, I think you will succeed."

— VINEET NAYAR, CEO OF HCL TECHNOLOGIES

EXHIBIT **3.8**

Combining Culture and
Performance

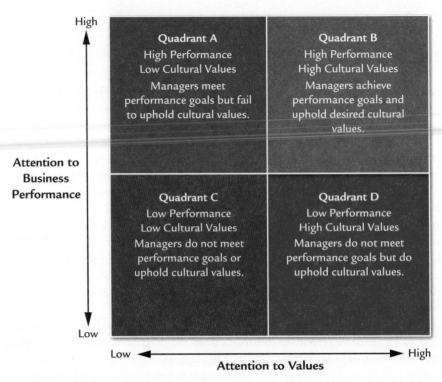

High

Quadrant A
High Performance
Low Cultural Values
Managers meet
performance goals but fail
to uphold cultural values.

Quadrant B
High Performance
High Cultural Values
Managers achieve
performance goals and
uphold desired cultural
values.

**Attention to
Business
Performance**

Quadrant C
Low Performance
Low Cultural Values
Managers do not meet
performance goals or
uphold cultural values.

Quadrant D
Low Performance
High Cultural Values
Managers do not meet
performance goals but do
uphold cultural values.

Low

Low ◀─────────────▶ High
Attention to Values

SOURCES: Adapted from Jeff Rosenthal and Mary Ann Masarech, "High-Performance Cultures: How Values Can Drive Business Results," *Journal of Organizational Excellence* (Spring 2003): 3–18; and Dave Ulrich, Steve Kerr, and Ron Ashkenas, Figure 11-2, GE Leadership Decision Matrix, *The GE Work-Out: How to Implement GE's Revolutionary Method for Busting Bureaucracy and Attacking Organizational Problems—Fast!* (New York: McGraw-Hill, 2002), p. 230.

Concept Connection ◀◀◀

Furthering Target's partnerships with unique designer brands, the idea to create the new Shops at Target in-store boutiques was born in Target's **high-performance culture**. Target has quarterly Big Idea internal contests, in which departments compete for additional budget allocations awarded for innovative ideas. The fun, creative competition encourages a sense of employee ownership and reinforces shared values. Tapping into employee talent helps Target meet its mission of providing customers with more for less.

AP Photo/Bebeto Matthews

together—that is, shared cultural values—is missing. Consider how a bottom-line focus at Zynga, the Web's largest social games company, is damaging the organization. Zynga, founded in July 2007 and led by CEO Mark Pincus, recorded a phenomenal $828 million in revenue in the first nine months of 2011, more than double the amount earned a year earlier. Zynga also met ambitious profitability goals, rare among Internet start-ups. With this type of financial performance, one might assume working for Zynga would be all fun and games. Instead, autonomous teams for each game, like FarmVille and CityVille, work under aggressive deadlines and are continuously challenged to meet lofty performance goals. Managers emphasize performance reports, relentlessly aggregating data, and using the data to demote or fire weak employees. Little attention is paid to cultural values that bind people into a unified whole.

The relentless focus on financial performance began to take a toll when employees started voicing their frustration, complaining about long hours and aggressive deadlines. Former employees describe emotionally charged encounters, including loud outbursts from Pincus, threats from top managers, and moments when colleagues broke down in tears. The company's success likely cannot be sustained without an increased focus on building a more positive culture. Already, valued employees are being lured away by competitors in an industry where talent is scarce.[72]

Finally, companies in Quadrant B put high emphasis on both culture and solid business performance as drivers of organizational success. Managers in these organizations align values with the company's day-to-day operations—hiring practices, performance management, budgeting, criteria for promotions and rewards, and so forth. Consider the approach that General Electric (GE) took to accountability and performance management. When he was CEO, Jack Welch helped GE become one of the world's most successful and admired companies. He achieved this by creating a culture in which risk was rewarded and accountability and measurable goals were keys to individual success and company profitability.[73] The company's traditional approach had achieved stellar financial results, but managers motivated people to perform primarily through control, intimidation, and reliance on a small circle of staff. Welch was interested in more than just financial results—he wanted managers to exhibit the following cultural values in addition to "making their numbers":[74]

- Have a passion for excellence and hate bureaucracy.
- Be open to ideas from anywhere.
- "Live" quality, and drive cost and speed for competitive advantage.

Welch knew that for the company to succeed in a rapidly changing world, managers needed to pay careful attention to both cultural values and business performance. Quadrant D organizations represent the **high-performance culture**, a culture that (1) is based on a solid organizational mission or purpose, (2) embodies shared adaptive values that guide decisions and business practices, and (3) encourages individual employee ownership of both bottom-line results and the organization's cultural backbone.[75]

One of the most important things managers do is create and influence organizational culture to meet strategic goals because culture has a significant impact on performance. In *Corporate Culture and Performance*, John Kotter and James Heskett provided evidence that companies that intentionally managed cultural values outperformed similar companies that did not. Recent research validates that elements of corporate culture are positively correlated with higher financial performance.[76]

CULTURAL LEADERSHIP

A primary way in which managers shape cultural norms and values to build a high-performance culture is through *cultural leadership*. Managers must *overcommunicate* to ensure that employees understand the new culture values, and they signal these values in actions as well as words.

A **cultural leader** defines and uses signals and symbols to influence corporate culture. Cultural leaders influence culture in two key areas:

1. *The cultural leader articulates a vision for the organizational culture that employees can believe in.* The leader defines and communicates central values that employees believe in and will rally around. Values are tied to a clear and compelling mission, or core purpose.

2. *The cultural leader heeds the day-to-day activities that reinforce the cultural vision.* The leader makes sure that work procedures and reward systems match and reinforce the values. Actions speak louder than words, so cultural leaders "walk their talk."[77]

Managers widely communicate the cultural values through words and actions. Values statements that aren't reinforced by management behavior are meaningless, or even harmful, for employees and the organization. Whole Foods founder and CEO John Mackey wants his managers to place more value on creating "a better person, company, and world" than on pursuing personal financial gain. To demonstrate his personal commitment to this belief, he asked the board of directors to donate all his future stock options to the company's two foundations, the Animal Compassion Foundation and the Whole Planet Foundation.[78]

Cultural leaders also uphold their commitment to values during difficult times or crises. Upholding the cultural values helps organizations weather a crisis and come out stronger on the other side. Creating and maintaining a high-performance culture is not easy in today's turbulent environment and changing workplace, but through their words—and particularly their actions—cultural leaders let everyone in the organization know what really counts.

Remember This

- Managers emphasize both values and business results to create a **high-performance culture**.
- Culture enables solid business performance through the alignment of motivated employees with the mission and goals of the company.

- Managers create and sustain adaptive high-performance cultures through cultural leadership.
- **Cultural leaders** define and articulate important values that are tied to a clear and compelling mission, which they communicate widely and uphold through their actions.

ch3: Discussion Questions

1. What are the characteristics of a *flat world*, a term used by Thomas Friedman to describe today's business environment? What challenges do they pose? How can you prepare to manage in a flat world?

2. Would the task environment for a cellular phone provider contain the same elements as that for a government welfare agency? Discuss.

3. What strategic issues have the potential to create environmental uncertainty in the following four industries: (a) automobile; (b) social media; (c) newspaper; and (d) medical services?

4. Contemporary best-selling management books often argue that customers are the most important element in the external environment. Do you agree? In what company situations might this statement be untrue?

5. Why do you think many managers are surprised by environmental changes and hence are less able to help their organizations adapt?

6. Why are interorganizational partnerships so important for today's companies? What elements in the current environment might contribute to either an increase or a decrease in interorganizational collaboration? Discuss.

7. Consider the factors that influence environmental uncertainty (rate of change in factors and number of factors in the environment) that are presented in

Exhibit 3.4. Classify each of the following organizations as operating in either (a) a low-uncertainty environment or (b) a high-uncertainty environment: Hyundai, Facebook, a local Subway franchise, FedEx, a cattle ranch in Oklahoma, and McDonald's. Explain your reasoning.

8. Cultural symbols are usually noticed through sight, sound, touch, and smell. For example, Costco displays a limited amount of low-priced merchandise in a no-frills, self-service warehouse with concrete floors. What do these elements communicate as symbols about its corporate culture?

9. Both China and India are rising economic powers. How might your approach to doing business with China, a communist country, be different from your approach to doing business with India, the world's most populous democracy? In which country would you expect to encounter the most rules? The most bureaucracy?

10. As described in this chapter, Zynga CEO Mark Pincus is obsessed with high performance, and demanding deadlines define the corporate culture. Describe how this culture may be good for the short term but ultimately could hurt the organization's long-term sustainability.

ch3: Apply Your Skills: Experiential Exercise

Working in an Adaptability Culture[79]

Think of a specific full-time job that you have held. Please answer the following questions according to your perception of the *managers above you* in that job. Circle a number on the 1–5 scale based on the extent to which you agree with each statement about the managers above you:

⑤ Strongly agree

④ Agree

③ Neither agree nor disagree

② Disagree

① Strongly disagree

1. Good ideas got serious consideration from management above me.
    1   2   3   4   5

2. Management above me was interested in ideas and suggestions from people at my level in the organization.
    1   2   3   4   5

3. When suggestions were made to management above me, they received a fair evaluation.
    1   2   3   4   5

4. Management did not expect me to challenge or change the status quo.
    1   2   3   4   5

5. Management specifically encouraged me to bring about improvements in my workplace.
    1   2   3   4   5

6. Management above me took action on recommendations made from people at my level.
    1   2   3   4   5

7. Management rewarded me for correcting problems.
    1   2   3   4   5

8. Management clearly expected me to improve work unit procedures and practices.
    1   2   3   4   5

9. I felt free to make recommendations to management above me to change existing practices.
    1   2   3   4   5

10. Good ideas did not get communicated upward because management above me was not very approachable.
    1   2   3   4   5

Scoring and Interpretation

To compute your score: Subtract each of your scores for questions 4 and 10 from 6. Using your adjusted scores, add the numbers for all 10 questions to give you the total score. Divide that number by 10 to get your average score: _____.

An adaptability culture is shaped by the values and actions of top and middle managers. When managers actively encourage and welcome change initiatives from below, the organization will be infused with values for change. These ten questions measure your management's openness to change. A typical average score for management openness to change is about 3. If your average score was 4 or higher, you worked in an organization that expressed strong cultural values of adaptation. If your average score was 2 or below, the company probably did not have an adaptability culture.

Think about this job. Was the level of management openness to change correct for the organization? Why? Compare your scores to those of another student, and take turns describing what it was like working for the managers above you in your jobs. Do you sense a relationship between job satisfaction and your management's openness to change? What specific management characteristics and corporate values explain the openness scores in the two jobs?

ch3: Apply Your Skills: Small Group Breakout

Organizational Culture in the Classroom and Beyond

Step 1. Write down the norms that you believe to be operating in the following places: (1) in most of your courses, (2) in formal social groups such as fraternities and sororities, and (3) in student clubs or school-sponsored organizations. Use your personal experience in each place and consider the norms. Some norms are implicit, so you may have to think carefully to identify them. Other norms may be explicit.

Step 2. After you have developed your lists, divide into groups of four to six students to discuss norms. Each student should share with the group the norms identified for each of the assigned places. Make a list of norms for each place and brainstorm with fellow group members to come up with additional norms.

Step 3. Try to group the norms by common themes, and give each group of norms a title. Decide as a group which norms are most important for regulating student behavior in each location.

Step 4. As a group, analyze the source or origin of each of the more important norms. Does the norm originate in the environment, from a leader, or elsewhere? Can you find any examples of norms that are expressed but not followed, which means that people do not "walk the talk" of the norms?

ENVIRONMENT 2

Step 5. What did you learn about cultural norms that exist in organizations and social groups? How is it helpful to make explicit those aspects of organization culture that are typically implicit? Who should be responsible for setting norms in your courses or in student social groups and organizations?

ch3: Endnotes

1. These questions are based on ideas from R. L. Daft and R. M. Lengel, *Fusion Leadership* (San Francisco: Berrett Koehler, 2000): Chapter 4; B. Bass and B. Avolio, *Multifactor Leadership Questionnaire*, 2d ed. (Menlo Park, CA: Mind Garden, Inc., 2004); and Karl E. Weick and Kathleen M. Sutcliffe, *Managing the Unexpected: Assuring High Performance in an Age of Complexity* (San Francisco: Jossey-Bass, 2001).

2. Geoff Colvin, "How It Works," *Fortune* (February 27, 2012): 72–79.

3. This section is based on Richard L. Daft, *Organization Theory and Design*, 10th ed. (Cincinnati, OH: South-Western, 2010), pp. 140–143.

4. L. J. Bourgeois, "Strategy and Environment: A Conceptual Integration," *Academy of Management Review 5* (1980): 25–39.

5. James Moore, *The Death of Competition: Leadership and Strategy in the Age of Business Ecosystems* (New York: HarperCollins, 1996).

6. David J. Teece, "Dynamic Capabilities: A Guide for Managers," *Ivey Business Journal* (March/April, 2011), www.iveybusinessjournal.com/topics/strategy/dynamic-capabilities-a-guide-for-managers (accessed June 12, 2012).

7. Thomas L. Friedman, *The World Is Flat: A Brief History of the Twenty-First Century* (New York: Farrar, Straus and Giroux, 2005), pp. 3–23.

8. Liz Alderman, "In Europe, Starbucks Adjusts to a Café Culture," *The New York Times*, March 30, 2012.

9. Patricia Sellers, "The New Coke," *Fortune* (May 21, 2012): 140.

10. Timothy Aeppel, "Man vs. Machine, A Jobless Recovery," *The Wall Street Journal Online* (January 17, 2012), http://online.wsj.com/article/SB10001424052970204468004577164710231081398.html (accessed June 12, 2012).

11. Jeffrey A. Trachtenberg, "Barnes & Noble Focuses on E-Books," *The Wall Street Journal Online* (July 20, 2011), http://allthingsd.com/20110720/barnes-noble-focuses-on-e-books/ (accessed June 12, 2012).

12. Roman Friedrich, Michael Peterson, and Alex Koster, "The Rise of Generation C," *Strategy + Business*, Issue 62 (Spring 2011), www.strategy-business.com/article/11110?gko=64e54 (accessed June 25, 2012).

13. Sara Lin, "Designing for the Senior Surge," *The Wall Street Journal*, April 25, 2008.

14. Dennis Cauchon and Paul Overberg, "Census Data Shows Minorities Now a Majority of U.S. Births," *USA TODAY* (May 17, 2012), www.usatoday.com/news/nation/story/2012-05-17/minority-births-census/55029100/1 (accessed June 12, 2012).

15. Matthias Rieker, "Uneven Economy Hits Banks," *The Wall Street Journal Online* (January 25, 2012), http://online.wsj.com/article/SB10001424052970203718504577180672516174122.html (accessed June 22, 2012).

16. Somini Sengupta, "Facebook Builds Network of Friends in Washington," *The New York Times Online* (May 18, 2012), www.nytimes.com/2012/05/19/technology/facebook-builds-network-of-friends-in-washington.html?_r=1&emc=eta1 (accessed June 12, 2012).

17. Dror Etzion, "Research on Organizations and the Natural Environment," *Journal of Management* 33 (August 2007): 637–654.

18. Elizabeth Weise and Doyle Rice, "Even the 'Best' Outcome Won't Be Good; The Oil Spill's Potential Toll Is Becoming Clear," *USA Today*, June 9, 2010.

19. Rick Kash, "The Hershey Company: Aligning Inside to Win on the Outside," *Ivey Business Journal* (March–April 2012), www.iveybusinessjournal.com/topics/strategy/the-hershey-company-aligning-inside-to-win-on-the-outside-2 (accessed June 12, 2012).

20. Ann Zimmerman, "Can Retailers Halt Showrooming?" *The Wall Street Journal Online* (April 11, 2012), http://online.wsj.com/article/SB10001424052702304587704577334370670243032.html (accessed June 13, 2012).

21. Geoff Colvin, "Toyota's Comeback Kid," *Fortune* (February 2, 2012): 73.

22. "Downsides of Just-in-Time Inventory," *Bloomberg Businessweek* (March 28–April 3, 2011): 17–18.

23. Peter Valdes-Dapena, "Japan Earthquake Impact Hits U.S. Auto Plants," *CNNMoney* (March 30, 2011), http://money.cnn.com/2011/03/28/autos/japan_earthquake_autos_outlook/index.htm# (accessed June 13, 2012).

24. Maxwell Murphy, "Reinforcing the Supply Chain," *The Wall Street Journal*, January 11, 2012, B6.

25. Sharon Edelson, "Costco Keeps Formula as It Expands," *Women's Wear Daily*, Issue 19 (January 30, 2012): 1; Andria Cheng, "Costco Cracks Taiwan Market," *The Wall Street Journal*, April 2, 2010, B5; and "Form 10-K for Costo Wholesale Corporation," Item 7—Management's Discussion and Analysis of Financial Conditions and Results of Operations, *Costco Annual Report*, www.sec.gov/Archives/edgar

/data/909832/000119312511271844/d203874d10k.
htm#toc203874_9 (accessed July 10, 2012).

26. Robert B. Duncan, "Characteristics of Organizational Environment and Perceived Environmental Uncertainty," *Administrative Science Quarterly* 17 (1972): 313–327; and Daft, *Organization Theory and Design*, pp. 144–148.

27. Tim Arango, "Hot Social Networking Site Cools as Facebook Grows," *The New York Times Online* (January 11, 2011), www.nytimes.com/2011/01/12/technology/internet/12myspace.html?pagewanted=all (accessed June 14, 2012).

28. Bruce E. Perrott, "Strategic Issue Management as Change Catalyst," *Strategy & Leadership* 39, no. 5 (2011): 20–29.

29. David B. Jemison, "The Importance of Boundary Spanning Roles in Strategic Decision-Making," *Journal of Management Studies* 21 (1984): 131–152; and Marc J. Dollinger, "Environmental Boundary Spanning and Information Processing Effects on Organizational Performance," *Academy of Management Journal* 27 (1984): 351–368.

30. Sean Lux, T. Russell Crook, and Terry Leap, "Corporate Political Activity: The Good, the Bad, and the Ugly," *Business Horizons* 55, no. 3 (May–June 2012): 307–312.

31. Tom Duffy, "Spying the Holy Grail," *Microsoft Executive Circle* (Winter 2004): 38–39.

32. Alexander Garrett, "Crash Course in Competitive Intelligence," *Management Today* (May 1, 2011): 18.

33. Kim Girard, "Snooping on a Shoestring," *Business 2.0* (May 2003): 64–66.

34. Jonathan Hughes and Jeff Weiss, "Simple Rules for Making Alliances Work," *Harvard Business Review* (November 2007): 122–131; Howard Muson, "Friend? Foe? Both? The Confusing World of Corporate Alliances," *Across the Board* (March–April 2002): 19–25; and Devi R. Gnyawali and Ravindranath Madhavan, "Cooperative Networks and Competitive Dynamics: A Structural Embeddedness Perspective," *Academy of Management Review* 26, no. 3 (2001): 431–445.

35. Katie Merx, "Automakers Interconnected Around World," *Edmonton Journal* April 6, 2007, H14; and Keith Bradsher, "Ford Agrees to Sell Volvo to a Fast-Rising Chinese Company," *The New York Times Online* (March 28, 2010), www.nytimes.com/2010/03/29/business/global/29auto.html (accessed August 1, 2011).

36. Thomas Petzinger, Jr., *The New Pioneers: The Men and Women Who Are Transforming the Workplace and Marketplace* (New York: Simon & Schuster, 1999), pp. 53–54.

37. Stephan M. Wagner and Roman Boutellier, "Capabilities for Managing a Portfolio of Supplier Relationships," *Business Horizons* (November–December 2002): 79–88; Peter Smith Ring and Andrew H. Van de Ven, "Developmental Processes of Corporate Interorganizational Relationships," *Academy of Management Review* 19 (1994): 90–118; Myron Magnet, "The New Golden Rule of Business," *Fortune* (February 21, 1994): 60–64; and Peter Grittner, "Four Elements of Successful Sourcing Strategies," *Management Review* (October 1996): 41–45.

38. Richard L. Daft, "After the Deal: The Art of Fusing Diverse Corporate Cultures into One," paper presented at the Conference on International Corporate Restructuring, Institute of Business Research and Education, Korea University, Seoul, Korea (June 16, 1998).

39. David Segal, "When a Sugar High Isn't Enough," *The New York Times Online* (April 21, 2012), www.nytimes.com/2012/04/22/business/kellogg-takes-aim-at-snack-foods.html?pagewanted=all (accessed June 15, 2012).

40. Peter Sanders, "Sikorsky's Business Heads Up," *The Wall Street Journal Online* (April 19, 2010), http://online.wsj.com/article/SB10001424052702304180804575188821353177134.html (accessed April 19, 2010).

41. Yoash Wiener, "Forms of Value Systems: A Focus on Organizational Effectiveness and Culture Change and Maintenance," *Academy of Management Review* 13 (1988): 534–545; V. Lynne Meek, "Organizational Culture: Origins and Weaknesses," *Organization Studies* 9 (1988): 453–473; John J. Sherwood, "Creating Work Cultures with Competitive Advantage," *Organizational Dynamics* (Winter 1988): 5–27; and Andrew D. Brown and Ken Starkey, "The Effect of Organizational Culture on Communication and Information," *Journal of Management Studies* 31, no. 6 (November 1994): 807–828.

42. Joanne Martin, *Organizational Culture: Mapping the Terrain* (Thousand Oaks, CA: Sage Publications, 2002); Ralph H. Kilmann, Mary J. Saxton, and Roy Serpa, "Issues in Understanding and Changing Culture," *California Management Review* 28 (Winter 1986): 87–94; and Linda Smircich, "Concepts of Culture and Organizational Analysis," *Administrative Science Quarterly* 28 (1983): 339–358.

43. David Carr, "Troubles That Money Can't Dispel," *The New York Times Online* (July 17, 2011), www.nytimes.com/2011/07/18/business/media/for-news-corporation-troubles-that-money-cant-dispel.html?pagewanted=all (accessed June 13, 2012).

44. John F. Burns and Jeremy W. Peters, "Two Top Deputies Resign as Crisis Isolates Murdoch," *The New York Times Online* (July 16, 2011), www.hongkong-mart.com/forum/viewtopic.php?f=2&t=367 (accessed June 13, 2012).

45. Carr, "Troubles That Money Can't Dispel."

46. Based on Edgar H. Schein, *Organizational Culture and Leadership*, 2d ed. (San Francisco: Jossey-Bass, 1992): 3–27.

47. Carlin Flora, "Paid to Smile," *Psychology Today* (September–October 2009): 59–59; and Tony Hsieh,

Delivering Happiness: A Path to Profits, Passion, and Purpose (New York: Business Plus 2012).

48. Michael G. Pratt and Anat Rafaeli, "Symbols as a Language of Organizational Relationships," *Research in Organizational Behavior* 23 (2001): 93–132.

49. Mindy Grossman, "HSN's CEO on Fixing the Shopping Network's Culture," *Harvard Business Review* (December 2011): 43–46.

50. Chip Jarnagin and John W. Slocum, Jr., "Creating Corporate Cultures through Mythopoetic Leadership," *Organizational Dynamics* 36, no. 3 (2007): 288–302.

51. Robert E. Quinn and Gretchen M. Spreitzer, "The Road to Empowerment: Seven Questions Every Leader Should Consider," *Organizational Dynamics* (Autumn 1997): 37–49.

52. Yukari Iwatani Kane and Jessica E. Vascellaro, "Successor Faces Tough Job at Apple," *The Wall Street Journal Online* (August 26, 2011), http://allthingsd.com/20110826/successor-faces-tough-job-at-apple/ (accessed June 13, 2012).

53. Based on an interview with Tim Cook conducted by *Wall Street Journal's* Walt Mossberg and Kara Swisher (June 4, 2012), http://online.wsj.com/article/SB10001424052702303552104577436952829794614.html?KEYWORDS=steve+jobs+apple+culture (accessed June 16, 2012).

54. Arthur Yeung, "Setting People up for Success: How the Portman Ritz-Carlton Hotel Gets the Best from Its People," *Human Resource Management* 45, no. 2 (Summer 2006): 267–275.

55. Patricia Jones and Larry Kahaner, *Say It and Live It: 50 Corporate Mission Statements That Hit the Mark* (New York: Currency Doubleday, 1995).

56. Harrison M. Trice and Janice M. Beyer, "Studying Organizational Cultures Through Rites and Ceremonials," *Academy of Management Review* 9 (1984): 653–669.

57. PRWeb, "Southwest Airlines Launches New NBA-Themed Specialty Airplane; Slam Dunk One Marks First Southwest Specialty Plane with a Partner in 17 Years," November 3, 2005, www.prweb.com/releases/2005/11/prweb306461.php (accessed February 7, 2008).

58. Jennifer A. Chatman and Karen A. Jehn, "Assessing the Relationship Between Industry Characteristics and Organizational Culture: How Different Can You Be?" *Academy of Management Journal* 37, no. 3 (1994): 522–553.

59. This discussion is based on Paul McDonald and Jeffrey Gandz, "Getting Value from Shared Values," *Organizational Dynamics* 21, no. 3 (Winter 1992): 64–76; Daniel R. Denison and Aneil K. Mishra, "Toward a Theory of Organizational Culture and Effectiveness," *Organization Science* 6, no. 2 (March–April 1995): 204–223; and Richard L. Daft, *The Leadership Experience*, 3d ed. (Cincinnati, OH: South-Western, 2005), pp. 570–573.

60. Lucas Conley, "Rinse and Repeat," *Fast Company* (July 2005): 76–77.

61. Robert Hooijberg and Frank Petrock, "On Cultural Change: Using the Competing Values Framework to Help Leaders Execute a Transformational Strategy," *Human Resource Management* 32, no. 1 (1993): 29–50.

62. David Kesmodel and Suzanne Vranica, "Unease Brewing at Anheuser as New Owners Slash Costs," *The Wall Street Journal Online*, April 23, 2009, http://online.wsj.com/article/SB124096182942565947.html (accessed June 22, 2012).

63. Based on *Fortune's* survey results, "100 Best Companies to Work For," http://money.cnn.com/magazines/fortune/best-companies/2012/full_list/ (accessed September 25, 2012); and Douglas A. Ready and Emily Truelove, "The Power of Collective Ambition," *Harvard Business Review* (December 2011): 94–102.

64. Rekha Balu, "Pacific Edge Projects Itself," *Fast Company* (October 2000): 371–381.

65. Jeffrey Pfeffer, *The Human Equation: Building Profits by Putting People First* (Boston, MA: Harvard Business School Press, 1998).

66. Jeremy Kahn, "What Makes a Company Great?" *Fortune* (October 26, 1998): 218; James C. Collins and Jerry I. Porras, *Built to Last: Successful Habits of Visionary Companies* (New York: HarperCollins, 1994); and James C. Collins, "Change Is Good—But First Know What Should Never Change," *Fortune* (May 29, 1995): 141.

67. Andrew Wahl, "Culture Shock," *Canadian Business* (October 10–23, 2005): 115–116.

68. Based on information in Alison Beard and Richard Hornik, "It's Hard to Be Good," *Harvard Business Review* (November, 2011): 88–96.

69. Jennifer A. Chatman and Sandra Eunyoung Cha, "Leading by Leveraging Culture," *California Management Review* 45, no. 4 (Summer 2003): 20–34.

70. This section is based on Jeff Rosenthal and Mary Ann Masarech, "High-Performance Cultures: How Values Can Drive Business Results," *Journal of Organizational Excellence* (Spring 2003): 3–18.

71. Nelson D. Schwartz, "One Brick at a Time," *Fortune* (June 12, 2006): 45–46; and Nelson D. Schwartz, "Lego's Rebuilds Legacy," *International Herald Tribune* (September 5, 2009).

72. Evelyn M. Ruslie, "Zynga's Tough Culture Risks a Talent Drain," *The New York Times Online* (November 27, 2011), http://dealbook.nytimes.com/2011/11/27/zyngas-tough-culture-risks-a-talent-drain/ (accessed June 18, 2012).

73. This example is based on Dave Ulrich, Steve Kerr, and Ron Ashkenas, *The GE Work-Out* (New York: McGraw-Hill, 2002), pp. 238–230.

74. From Ulrich et al., "GE Values," in *The GE Work-Out*, Figure 11-2.

75. Rosenthal and Masarech, "High-Performance Cultures."

76. John P. Kotter and James L. Heskett, *Corporate Culture and Performance* (New York: The Free Press, 1992); Eric Flamholtz and Rangapriya Kannan-Narasimhan, "Differential Impact of Cultural Elements on Financial Performance," *European Management Journal* 23, no. 1 (2005): 50–64. Also see J. M. Kouzes and B. Z. Posner, *The Leadership Challenge: How to Keep Getting Extraordinary Things Done in Organizations*, 3d ed. (San Francisco: Jossey-Bass, 2002).

77. Rosenthal and Masarech, "High-Performance Cultures"; Patrick Lencioni, "Make Your Values Mean Something,"

Harvard Business Review (July 2002): 113–117; and Thomas J. Peters and Robert H. Waterman, Jr., *In Search of Excellence* (New York: Warner, 1988).

78. Jarnagin and Slocum, "Creating Corporate Cultures through Mythopoetic Leadership."

79. Based on S. J. Ashford et al., "Out on a Limb: The Role of Context and Impression Management in Issue Selling," *Administrative Science Quarterly* 43 (1998): 23–57; and E. W. Morrison and C. C. Phelps, "Taking Charge at Work: Extrarole Efforts to Initiate Workplace Change," *Academy of Management Journal* 42 (1999): 403–419.

ENVIRONMENT 2

Managing in a Global Environment

Christian Mueller/Shutterstock.com

Learning Outcomes

After studying this chapter, you should be able to:

1. Define globalization and explain how it is creating a borderless world for today's managers.

2. Describe a global mindset and why it has become imperative for companies operating internationally.

3. Describe the characteristics of a multinational corporation and explain the "bottom of the pyramid" concept.

4. Define international management and explain how it differs from the management of domestic business operations.

5. Indicate how dissimilarities in the economic, sociocultural, and legal-political environments throughout the world can affect business operations.

6. Discuss how the international landscape is changing, including the growing power of China, India, and Brazil.

7. Describe how regional trading alliances are reshaping the international business environment.

Are You Ready to Work Internationally?[1]

http:
See It
Online
www.

INSTRUCTIONS: Are you ready to negotiate a sales contract with someone from another country? Companies large and small deal on a global basis. To what extent are you guilty of the behaviors below? Please answer each item as Mostly True or Mostly False for you.

Are You Typically:	Mostly True	Mostly False
1. Impatient? Do you have a short attention span? Do you want to keep moving to the next topic?	_____	_____
2. A poor listener? Are you uncomfortable with silence? Does your mind think about what you want to say next?	_____	_____
3. Argumentative? Do you enjoy arguing for its own sake?	_____	_____
4. Unfamiliar with cultural specifics in other countries? Do you have limited experience in other countries?	_____	_____
5. Short-term-oriented? Do you place more emphasis on the short term than on the long term in your thinking and planning?	_____	_____
6. "All business"? Do you think that it is a waste of time getting to know someone personally before discussing business?	_____	_____
7. Legalistic to win your point? Do you hold others to an agreement regardless of changing circumstances?	_____	_____
8. Thinking "win/lose" when negotiating? Do you usually try to win a negotiation at the other's expense?	_____	_____

SCORING AND INTERPRETATION: American managers often display cross-cultural ignorance during business negotiations compared to counterparts in other countries. American habits can be disturbing, such as emphasizing areas of disagreement over agreement, spending little time understanding the views and interests of the other side, and adopting an adversarial attitude. Americans often like to leave a negotiation thinking that they won, which can be embarrassing to the other side. For this quiz, a low score shows better international presence. If you answered "Mostly True" to three or fewer questions, then consider yourself ready to assist with an international negotiation. If you scored six or more "Mostly True" responses, it is time to learn more about other national cultures before participating in international business deals. Try to develop a greater focus on other people's needs and an appreciation for different viewpoints. Be open to compromise and develop empathy for people who are different from you.

Japan's Nissan has headquarters in Yokohama, but the chief executive of its luxury Infiniti division has his office in Hong Kong. The skin, cosmetics, and personal care business of Procter & Gamble (P&G) is based in Singapore. And the entire senior management team for Starwood, a hotel company based in Stamford, Connecticut, relocated to Shanghai for a month so managers could immerse themselves in the local culture and gain a better understanding of how the Chinese market differs from that in the United States.[2] The trend toward moving executives and divisions to Asia is both practical and symbolic. Hong Kong is considered a gateway to mainland China, while Singapore is a springboard into Southeast Asia and India. In addition, locating in the region "is a visible demonstration of your commitment," said Michael Andrew, global chairman of KPMG International, who is based in Hong Kong.[3]

1 INTRODUCTION

2 ENVIRONMENT

3 PLANNING

4 ORGANIZING

5 LEADING

6 CONTROLLING

Managers around the world are eager to make a commitment to China and India, where the potential for growth is huge. Brazil, Russia, India, and China (often referred to as BRIC), as well as other emerging economies, are growing rapidly as providers of both products and services to the United States, Canada, Europe, and other developed nations. At the same time, these regions are becoming major markets for the products and services of North American firms. Finding managers with the mindset needed to succeed in these countries is proving difficult for multinational firms. China, India, and Brazil are expected to see the greatest shortage of executive talent for the next few years.[4]

Every manager today needs to think globally because the whole world is a source of business threats and opportunities. Even managers who spend their entire careers working in their hometowns have to be aware of the international environment and probably interact with people from other cultures. The international dimension is an increasingly important part of the external environment discussed in Chapter 3. This chapter introduces basic concepts about the global environment and international management. First, we provide an overview of today's borderless world and the global mindset needed to be effective. Next, we discuss multinational corporations, consider the globalization backlash, and describe the "bottom of the pyramid" concept. We then touch on various strategies and techniques for entering the global arena and take a look at the economic, legal-political, and sociocultural challenges that companies encounter within the global business environment. The chapter also describes how emerging markets and regional trade agreements are reshaping the international business landscape.

A Borderless World

The reality facing most managers is that isolation from international forces is no longer possible. Organizations in all fields are being reordered around the goal of addressing needs and desires that transcend national boundaries. Consider that the Federal Bureau of Investigation (FBI) now ranks international cybercrime as one of its top priorities because electronic boundaries between countries are virtually nonexistent.[5] "The whole boundary mindset has been obliterated," says John Hering, the 26-year-old CEO of Lookout Mobile Security. Hering's company has customers in 170 countries using 400 mobile networks around the world. "For many people, this is the only computer they have," he says. "The thought of something bad happening to your phone is untenable."[6]

Concept Connection ◄◄◄

Munshi Ahmed

Today's companies compete in a **borderless world**. Procter & Gamble's sales in Southeast Asia make up a rapidly growing percentage of the company's worldwide sales. These shoppers are purchasing P&G's Pampers diapers in Malaysia.

GLOBALIZATION

Business, just like crime, has become a unified, global field. **Globalization** refers to the extent to which trade and investments, information, social and cultural ideas, and political cooperation flow between countries. One result is that countries, businesses, and people become increasingly interdependent. India-based Tata Consultancy Services gets more than half of its revenue from North America, while the U.S. firm IBM gets 65 percent of its tech services revenue from overseas, with sales in India growing 41 percent in one recent quarter.[7] And while Japan's Honda gets 65 percent of its parts for the Accord from the United States or Canada and assembles the vehicle in Ohio, U.S.-based General Motors (GM) makes the Chevrolet HHR in Mexico with parts that come from all over the world.[8]

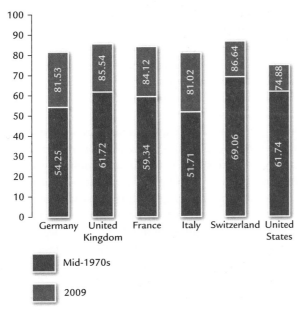

SOURCE: Based on "2012 KOF Index of Globalization," KOF Swiss Economic Institute, www.kof.ethz.ch/static_media/filer/2012/03/15/rankings_2012.pdf (accessed June 26, 2012) and "KOF Index of Globalization 2010," Press Release (January 22, 2010), http://globalization.kof.ethz.ch/ (accessed January 22, 2010). Note: The 2012 KOF analysis of globalization dimensions is based on the year 2009.

EXHIBIT **4.1**

Ranking of Six Countries on the Globalization Index

ENVIRONMENT 2

Globalization has been on the rise since the 1970s, and most industrialized nations show a high degree of globalization today.[9] The KOF Swiss Economic Institute measures economic, political, and social aspects of globalization and ranks countries on a globalization index. Not surprisingly, the pace of economic globalization slowed in the most recent survey, reflecting the impact of the global financial and economic crisis, but social and political globalization continued its upward trend. Exhibit 4.1 shows how selected countries ranked on the 2012 KOF Index of Globalization (based on the year 2009) compared to their degree of globalization in the mid-1970s. Note that the United States is the least globalized of the countries shown in the exhibit. Among the 187 countries on the KOF Index, the United States ranks number 35, down from number 27 on the 2011 index. The 10 most globalized countries, according to the KOF Index, are Belgium, Ireland, the Netherlands, Austria, Singapore, Sweden, Denmark, Hungary, Portugal, and Switzerland.[10]

DEVELOPING A GLOBAL MINDSET

Succeeding on a global level requires more than a desire to go global and a new set of skills and techniques; it requires that managers develop a *global mindset*. As more managers find themselves working in foreign countries or working with foreign firms within their own country, they need a mindset that enables them to navigate through ambiguities and complexities that far exceed anything they encounter within their traditional management responsibilities.[11] A **global mindset** can be defined as the ability of managers to appreciate and influence individuals, groups, organizations, and systems that represent different social, cultural, political, institutional, intellectual, and psychological characteristics.[12] A manager with a global mindset can perceive and respond to many different perspectives at the same time rather than being stuck in a domestic mindset that sees everything from one's own perspective. Reliance Industries, the largest private sector company in India, specifically lists "global mindset" as one of the core competencies for its managers.[13]

People who have had exposure to different cultures develop a global mindset more easily. For example, the Dutch have to learn English, German, and French, as well as Dutch, to interact and trade with their economically dominant neighbors. English Canadians

Take a Moment

Complete the Experiential Exercise on page 128 that pertains to your global management potential. How well do your knowledge and preferences reflect a global mindset?

Take a Moment

Go to the Small Group Breakout on page 129 that pertains to exposure to different cultures and ideas.

must not only be well versed in American culture and politics, but they also have to consider the views and ideas of French Canadians, who, in turn, must learn to think like North Americans, members of a global French community, Canadians, and Quebecois.[14] People in the United States who have grown up with this kind of language and cultural diversity typically have more difficulties with foreign assignments, but willing managers from any country can learn to open their minds and appreciate other viewpoints.

Developing a global mindset requires managers who are genuinely curious and inquisitive about other people and cultures, are open-minded and nonjudgmental, and can deal with ambiguity and complexity without becoming overwhelmed or frustrated. One of the best ways managers develop a global mindset is by engaging with people from different cultures. In the past, many managers who were sent on overseas assignments lived an insular lifestyle that kept them from truly becoming immersed in the foreign culture. "You can lead a true-blue German lifestyle in China," says Siegfried Russwurm, former head of human resources at Siemens (now running the company's industrial sector). "You can live in a gated community with German neighbors. They will tell you where you can find a German baker and butcher."[15] Today, though, the goal for managers who want to succeed is to globalize their thinking. John Rice, vice chairman of General Electric (GE) and president and chief executive of global growth and operations for the company, recently moved with his wife to Hong Kong. "Being outside the United States makes you smarter about global issues," Rice said. "It lets you see the world through a different lens."[16]

> "Global managers are made, not born. This is not a natural process."
> — PERCY BARNEVIK, FORMER CEO OF ABB

Remember This

- Today's companies and managers operate in a borderless world that provides both risks and opportunities.
- **Globalization** refers to the extent to which trade and investments, information, ideas, and political cooperation flow between countries.
- The most globalized countries according to one ranking are Belgium, Ireland, Austria, the Netherlands, and Singapore.
- To succeed on a global level requires managers at all levels to have a **global mindset**, which is the ability to appreciate and influence individuals, groups, organizations, and systems that represent different social, cultural, political, institutional, intellectual, and psychological characteristics.

Multinational Corporations

The size and volume of international businesses are so large that they are hard to comprehend. For example, if revenues were valued at the equivalent of a country's gross domestic product (GDP), the revenue of ExxonMobil is comparable in size to the GDP of Egypt. The revenue of Walmart is comparable to Greece's GDP, that of Toyota to Algeria's GDP, and that of GE to the GDP of Kazakhstan.[17]

A large volume of international business is being carried out by large international businesses that can be thought of as *global corporations*, *stateless corporations*, or *transnational corporations*. In the business world, these large international firms typically are called *multinational corporations (MNCs)*, which have been the subject of enormous attention. MNCs can move a wealth of assets from country to country and influence national economies, politics, and cultures.

Although the term has no precise definition, a **multinational corporation (MNC)** typically receives more than 25 percent of its total sales revenues from operations outside the parent's home country. During the recent economic slump, the percentage of revenue from foreign operations increased for many multinationals because of stronger sales in developing markets such as China and India. In the third quarter of 2010, revenues for Yum! Brands (including restaurants such as KFC and Pizza Hut) in China surpassed those in the United States for the first time, and the company's China business may be twice as large as that in the United States by 2015.[18] MNCs also have the following distinctive managerial characteristics:

1. An MNC is managed as an integrated worldwide business system in which foreign affiliates act in close alliance and cooperation with one another. Capital, technology, and people are transferred among country affiliates. The MNC can acquire materials and manufacture parts wherever in the world it is most advantageous to do so.

2. An MNC is ultimately controlled by a single management authority that makes key strategic decisions relating to the parent and all affiliates. Although some headquarters are *binational*, such as the Royal Dutch/Shell Group, some centralization of management is required to maintain worldwide integration and profit maximization for the enterprise as a whole.

3. MNC top managers are presumed to exercise a global perspective. They regard the entire world as one market for strategic decisions, resource acquisition, and location of production, advertising, and marketing efficiency.

In a few cases, the MNC management philosophy may differ from that just described. For example, some researchers have distinguished among *ethnocentric companies*, which place emphasis on their home countries; *polycentric companies*, which are oriented toward the markets of individual foreign host countries; and *geocentric companies*, which are truly world oriented and favor no specific country.[19] The truly global companies that transcend national boundaries are growing in number. These companies no longer see themselves as American, Chinese, or German; they operate globally and serve a global market. Nestlé SA provides a good example. The company gets most of its sales from outside the "home" country of Switzerland, and its 280,000 employees are spread all over the world. CEO Paul Bulcke is Belgian, chairman Peter Brabeck-Letmathe was born in Austria, and more than half of the company's managers are non-Swiss. Nestlé has hundreds of brands and has production facilities or other operations in almost every country in the world.[20]

▶▶▶ **Concept Connection**

The Maharaja Mac and Vegetable Burger served at this McDonald's in New Delhi, India, represent how this **multinational corporation** changed its business model by decentralizing its operations. When McDonald's initiated international units, it copied what it did and sold in the United States. Today, though, the fast-food giant seeks local managers who understand the culture and laws of each country. Country managers have the freedom to use different furnishings and develop new products to suit local tastes.

A GLOBALIZATION BACKLASH

The size and power of multinationals, combined with the growth of free trade agreements, which we will discuss later in this chapter, has sparked a backlash over globalization. In a *Fortune* magazine poll, 68 percent of Americans say other countries benefit the most from free trade, and a survey by *The Wall Street Journal* and NBC News found that 53 percent of Americans surveyed said free trade has actually hurt the United States. That figure is up from 46 percent in 2007 and 32 percent in 1999. The sentiment is reflected in other countries such as Germany, France, and even India. "For some reason, everyone thinks they are the loser," said former U.S. trade representative Mickey Kantor.[21]

In the United States, the primary concern has been the loss of jobs as companies expanded their offshoring activities by exporting more and more work overseas. The transfer of jobs such as making shoes, clothing, and toys began decades ago, and in recent years, services and knowledge work have also been outsourced to developing countries. Many American shoppers say they'd be willing to pay higher prices for U.S.-made products to keep jobs from going overseas.[22]

Business leaders, meanwhile, insist that economic benefits of globalization flow back to the U.S. economy in the form of lower prices, expanded markets, and increased profits that can fund innovation.[23] However, another troubling issue for some people in the United States is how overseas contractors and suppliers treat their employees. In the first few months of 2010, ten employees at Foxconn Technologies, a Chinese contract manufacturer that makes electronic products for Apple, Dell, and other U.S. companies, committed suicide. After a coalition of advocacy groups sent an open letter to Apple calling for an investigation to ensure safe and decent working conditions at all its suppliers, managers asked the Fair Labor Association to investigate Foxconn. The group found widespread problems, including excessively long work hours, low pay, and unsafe working conditions. In a symbolic gesture to emphasize the company's commitment, Apple's new CEO, Tim Cook, visited Foxconn's manufacturing plant where the iPhone is made and met with both company and government leaders in China.[24]

With concerns over jobs and labor practices, the anti-globalization fervor is just getting hotter—and is not likely to dissipate anytime soon. In the end, it is not whether globalization is good or bad, but how business and government managers can work together to ensure that the advantages of a global world are fully and fairly shared.

SERVING THE BOTTOM OF THE PYRAMID

Although large multinational organizations are accused of many negative contributions to society, they also have the resources needed to do good things in the world. One approach that combines business with social responsibility is referred to as *serving the bottom of the pyramid*.

Concept Connection ◀◀◀

Having dominated almost every market in the world, Coca-Cola has turned its sights on Africa in recent years. The beverage giant sees tremendous potential in countries across the continent, many of whose inhabitants would be considered to be part of the **bottom of the pyramid (BOP)**. The company is working closely with distributors and small business owners to promote its products by offering plenty of incentives and rewards, as well as marketing support.

Joao Silva/The New York Times/Redux

The **bottom of the pyramid (BOP) concept** proposes that corporations can alleviate poverty and other social ills, as well as make significant profits, by selling to the world's poorest people. The term *bottom of the pyramid* refers to the more than 4 billion people who make up the lowest level of the world's economic "pyramid" as defined by per-capita income. These people earn less than US$1,500 a year, with about one-fourth of them earning less than a dollar a day.[25] Traditionally, these people haven't been served by most large businesses because products and services are too expensive, inaccessible, and not suited to their needs; therefore, in many countries, the poor end up paying significantly more that their wealthier counterparts for some basic needs.

A number of leading companies are changing that by adopting BOP business models geared to serving the poorest of the world's consumers. Consider this example from India's Godrej & Boyce.

Innovative Way

Godrej & Boyce

By one estimate, a third of India's food is lost to spoilage, but in 2007, refrigerator market penetration was just 18 percent. Many lower-income people couldn't afford even a basic refrigerator. Another problem for poor people, particularly in rural areas, was that electric service was usually unreliable. Godrej & Boyce managers decided it was time to do something about this.

"As a company that made refrigerators for more than 50 years, we asked ourselves why it was that refrigerator penetration was just 18 percent," said G. Sunderraman, vice president of corporate development. The first major insight was that many people not only couldn't afford a refrigerator but didn't *need* a large refrigerator that took up too much space in a small house and used a lot of electricity. What they needed was the ChotuKool ("The Little Cool"), an innovative appliance introduced by Godrej & Boyce in 2010. The ChotuKool, a mini-fridge designed to cool five or six bottles of water and store a few pounds of food, was portable, ran on batteries, and sold for about 3,250 rupees (US$69), about 35 percent less than the cheapest refrigerator on the market.

To sell the new product, Godrej & Boyce trained rural villagers as salespeople. The villagers earn a commission of about US$3 for each refrigerator sold, and the system reduces Godrej's distribution costs. When asked how many ChotuKools the company expected to sell, George Menezes, COO of Godrej Appliances, said, "In three years, probably millions." Godrej & Boyce managers spend a lot of time working directly with consumers and are now testing ideas for other low-cost products aimed at rural markets. "Currently, the rural market accounts for only 10 percent, but it is all set to expand in a huge way," said Menenez.[26]

U. S. companies are getting in on the BOP act too. P&G researchers are visiting homes in China, Brazil, India, and other developing countries to see how the company can come up with entirely new products and services for consumers living at the bottom of the pyramid. However, P&G is late getting into marketing to the poor. Rival Unilever, for instance, introduced Lifebuoy soap to India more than a century ago, promoting it as the enemy of dirt and disease.[27] Unilever gets more than 50 percent of its sales from developing markets. "P&G is still very U.S.-centric," says Unilever's CEO Paul Polman. "Emerging markets are in the DNA of our company." To try to catch up, P&G's top executive, Robert McDonald, is focusing employees on the mission of "touching and improving more lives, in more parts of the world, more completely." When people feel they are changing lives, "it's almost like you don't have to pay us to do this," said one R&D scientist.[28] Proponents of BOP thinking believe multinational firms can contribute to positive lasting change when the profit motive goes hand in hand with the desire to make a contribution to humankind.

Remember This

- A **multinational corporation (MNC)** is an organization that receives more than 25 percent of its total sales revenues from operations outside the parent company's home country and has a number of distinctive managerial characteristics.
- Nestlé SA is a good example of a multinational corporation.
- Some researchers distinguish among *ethnocentric companies,* which place emphasis on their home countries, *polycentric companies,* which are oriented toward the markets of individual host countries, and *geocentric companies,* which are truly world oriented.

- The increasing size and power of MNCs has sparked a globalization backlash.
- Multinational corporations have the resources to reach and serve the world's poorest people who cannot afford the typical products and services offered by big companies.
- The **bottom of the pyramid (BOP) concept** proposes that corporations can alleviate poverty and other social ills, as well as make significant profits, by selling to the world's poor.
- Godrej & Boyce created an innovative battery-powered refrigerator called the ChotuKool for rural markets in India.

EXHIBIT 4.2   Strategies for Entering the International Arena

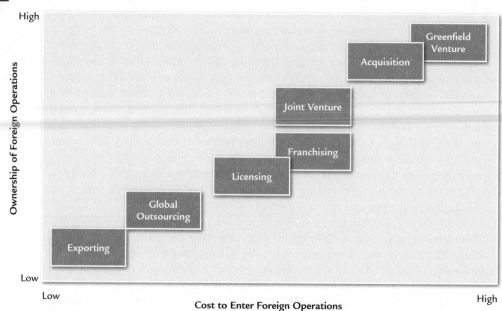

Getting Started Internationally

Organizations have a couple of ways to become involved internationally. One is to seek cheaper resources such as materials or labor offshore, which is called *offshoring* or *global outsourcing*. Another is to develop markets for finished products or services outside their home countries, which may include exporting, licensing, and direct investing. Exporting, licensing, and direct investing are called **market entry strategies** because they represent alternative ways to sell products and services in foreign markets. Exhibit 4.2 shows the strategies that companies can use to engage in the international arena, either to acquire resources or to enter new markets.

Concept Connection ◀◀◀

Christopher Norman Chocolates found that perfection-obsessed Japanese customers appreciate the difference between their New York company's hand-painted chocolates and French and Belgian chocolates. Joe Guiliano (left) and John Down (right), partners in the high-end specialty chocolate company, first **exported** the chocolates through a Japanese distributor with experience in this niche market. Later, they moved to a **licensing** agreement, with the distributor making the confections in a facility near Tokyo.

Roger Hagadone

EXPORTING

With **exporting**, the company maintains its production facilities within the home nation and transfers its products for sale in foreign countries.[29] Exporting enables a company to market its products in other countries at modest resource cost and with limited risk. Exporting does entail numerous problems based on physical distances, government regulations, foreign currencies, and cultural differences, but it is less expensive than committing the firm's own capital to build plants in host countries. For example, Skooba Designs, a Rochester, New York, manufacturer of carrying cases for laptops, iPads, and other tools, exports to more than 30 countries. Service companies can also export. Netflix is exporting its movie streaming service to customers in Latin America, the United Kingdom, and Ireland, as well as exploring other countries to move into.[30] Hollywood movie studios have long exported films to foreign countries, but they're taking a different approach than in the past.

Hollywood films have long been quintessentially American products, and years ago, audiences in Japan or Brazil or South Korea would faithfully go watch movies that were written for and marketed primarily to American audiences. No longer. Local films are giving Hollywood a run for its money. At the same time, audiences are declining in the United States but growing overseas. Hollywood movies now get about 70 percent of their revenue from abroad. Today, a few Hollywood studios have gone as far as making movies specifically for certain foreign markets, and almost all of them are reframing their films to suit foreign tastes. Here are some examples of tactics they are using:

- **Use foreign actors.** For Paramount's *G.I. Joe,* Byung-hun Lee, a major Korean movie star, was placed in a title role, and a South African actor played another key character.

- **Set the movie in a growing market—or in no man's land.** Several recent films, such as *Rio* and *Fast Five*, have been set in Brazil, which is a rapidly growing market for Hollywood movies. Others, like *Avatar* and *The Lord of the Rings* films, are set in fantasy worlds that are home to no one nationality.

- **Stuff the film with foreign brands.** In the latest *Transformers* movie, DreamWorks Studios had a character gulping Shuhua low-lactase milk from China's Yili dairy company.

- **Shoot in foreign cities.** Pixar's *Cars* didn't do well abroad, so the studio set the sequel in Paris, London, Tokyo, and on the Italian Riviera.

These and other techniques represent a whole new approach to making movies. Rather than trying to lure audiences to their films, studios are targeting their films to the audiences. In addition, managers are increasingly looking for films with global appeal. "I can tell you that no studio is going to make a big expensive movie that costs $150 million or $200 million unless it has worldwide appeal," said Mark Zoradi, former president of Walt Disney Company's Motion Pictures Group.[31]

OUTSOURCING

Global outsourcing, also called *offshoring,* means engaging in the international division of labor so that work activities can be done in countries with the cheapest sources of labor and supplies. Millions of low-level jobs such as textile manufacturing, call center operations, and credit card processing have been outsourced to low-wage countries in recent years. The Internet and plunging telecommunications costs have enabled companies to outsource more and higher-level work as well, such as software development, accounting, or medical services. A patient might have a magnetic resonance imaging (MRI) test performed in Minneapolis and have it read by doctors in India. After the Sarbanes-Oxley Act went into effect requiring extensive new financial reporting procedures and enhanced oversight, Unisys had a hard time finding enough internal auditors in the United States, so managers outsourced their core auditing practice to China. Large pharmaceutical companies farm out much of their early-stage chemistry research to cheaper labs in China and India.[32]

LICENSING

With **licensing,** a corporation (the licensor) in one country makes certain resources available to companies in another country (the licensee). These resources include technology, managerial skills, and patent or trademark rights. They enable the licensee to produce and market a product or service similar to what the licensor has been producing. Heineken, which has been called the world's first truly global brand of beer, usually begins by exporting to help boost familiarity with its products; if the market looks enticing enough, Heineken then licenses its brands to a local brewer. Licensing offers a business firm relatively easy access to international markets at low cost, but it limits the company's participation in and control over the development of those markets.

One special form of licensing is **franchising**, which occurs when a franchisee buys a complete package of materials and services, including equipment, products, product ingredients, trademark and trade name rights, managerial advice, and a standardized operating system. Whereas with licensing, a licensee generally keeps its own company name, autonomy, and operating systems, a franchise takes the name and systems of the franchisor. The fast-food chains are some of the best-known franchisors. The story is often told of the Japanese child visiting Los Angeles who excitedly pointed out to his parents, "They have McDonald's in America."

DIRECT INVESTING

A higher level of involvement in international trade is direct investment in facilities in a foreign country. **Direct investing** means that the company is involved in managing the productive assets, which distinguishes it from other entry strategies that permit less managerial control.

Currently, the most popular type of direct investment is to engage in strategic alliances and partnerships. In a **joint venture**, a company shares costs and risks with another firm, typically in the host country, to develop new products, build a manufacturing facility, or set up a sales and distribution network.[33] A partnership is often the fastest, cheapest, and least risky way to get into the global game. For example, Abbott Laboratories has teamed up with an Indian drug firm, Biocon Ltd., to develop nutritional supplements and generic drugs tailored to the local market.[34] A Chinese firm has formed a joint venture with an American partner to refurbish New York City's Alexander Hamilton Bridge and work on other construction projects in the United States.[35] In addition to joint ventures, the complexity of today's global business environment is causing managers at many companies to develop alliance networks, which are collections of partnerships with various other firms, often across international boundaries.[36]

The other choice is to have a **wholly owned foreign affiliate**, over which the company has complete control. Direct *acquisition* of an affiliate may provide cost savings over exporting by shortening distribution channels and reducing storage and transportation costs. Local managers also have a better understanding of economic, cultural, and political conditions. Kraft Foods bought Cadbury PLC in large part because the firm had established local contacts and distribution networks in emerging markets. Home Depot purchased Home Mart, the number two home-improvement retailer in Mexico, Philip Morris acquired Indonesia's third-largest cigarette maker to tap into the lucrative Asian cigarette market, and Walmart is buying Africa's Massmart.[37] The most costly and risky direct investment is called a **greenfield venture**, which means a company builds a subsidiary from scratch in a foreign country. The advantage is that the subsidiary is exactly what the company wants and has the potential to be highly profitable. For example, in 2012, Airbus announced plans to build jetliners in its first assembly plant in the United States. By building a huge plant in Alabama and employing American workers, Airbus managers expect to become part of U.S. culture, thereby reducing political opposition to the purchase of the company's airplanes.[38] The disadvantage is that the company has to acquire all market knowledge, materials, people, and know-how in a different culture, and mistakes are possible. Another example of a greenfield venture is the Nissan plant in Canton, Mississippi. The plant represents the first auto factory ever built in Mississippi, where the Japanese company had to rely on an untested and largely inexperienced workforce. The logistical and cultural hurdles were so enormous and the risks so high that one Nissan executive later said, "We did what nobody thought was possible."[39]

Remember This

- Two major alternatives for engaging in the international arena are to seek cheaper resources via outsourcing and to develop markets outside the home country.
- **Global outsourcing**, sometimes called *offshoring*, means engaging in the international division of labor so as to obtain the cheapest sources of labor and supplies, regardless of country.
- **Market entry strategies** are various tactics that managers use to enter foreign markets.
- **Exporting** is a market entry strategy in which a company maintains production facilities within its home country and transfers products for sale in foreign countries.
- With a market entry strategy of **licensing**, a company in one country makes certain resources available to companies in other countries to participate in the production and sale of its products abroad.
- **Franchising** is a form of licensing in which a company provides its foreign franchisees with a complete package of materials and services.

- McDonald's and other U.S. fast food companies have franchises all over the world.
- **Direct investing** is a market entry strategy in which the organization is directly involved in managing its production facilities in a foreign country.
- Alternatives for direct investing include engaging in joint ventures, acquiring foreign affiliates, and initiating a greenfield venture.
- With a **joint venture**, an organization shares costs and risks with another firm in a foreign country to build a facility, develop new products, or set up a sales and distribution network.
- A **wholly owned foreign affiliate** is a foreign subsidiary over which an organization has complete control.
- Home Depot purchased the chain Home Mart in Mexico as a wholly owned foreign affiliate.
- The most risky type of direct investment is the **greenfield venture**, in which a company builds a subsidiary from scratch in a foreign country.

The International Business Environment

International management is the management of business operations conducted in more than one country. The fundamental tasks of business management—including the financing, production, and distribution of products and services—do not change in any substantive way when a firm is transacting business across international borders. The basic management functions of planning, organizing, leading, and controlling are the same whether a company operates domestically or internationally. However, managers will experience greater difficulties and risks when performing these management functions on an international scale. Consider the following blunders:

- It took McDonald's more than a year to figure out that Hindus in India do not eat beef because they consider the cow sacred. The company's sales took off only after McDonald's started making burgers sold in India out of lamb.[40]
- When IKEA launched a superstore in Bangkok, managers learned that some of its Swedish product names sound like crude terms for sex when pronounced in Thai.[41]
- In Africa, the labels on bottles show pictures of what is inside so illiterate shoppers can know what they're buying. When a baby-food company showed a picture of an infant on its label, the product didn't sell very well.[42]
- United Airlines discovered that even colors can doom a product. The airline handed out white carnations when it started flying from Hong Kong, only to discover that, to many Asians, such flowers represent death and bad luck.[43]

Some of these examples might seem humorous, but there's nothing funny about them to managers trying to operate in a highly competitive global environment. What should managers of emerging global companies look for to avoid making obvious international

EXHIBIT 4.3

Key Factors in the
International Environment

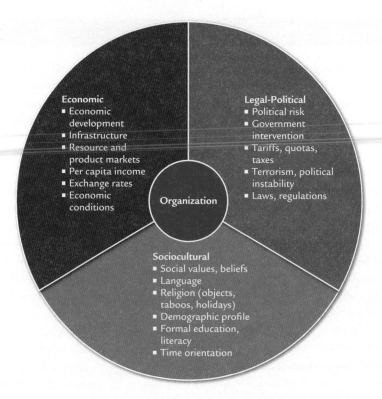

mistakes? When they are comparing one country with another, the economic, legal-political, and sociocultural sectors present the greatest difficulties. Key factors to understand in the international environment are summarized in Exhibit 4.3.[44]

Remember This

- The basic management functions are the same in either a domestic or an international subsidiary, but managers will experience greater difficulties and risks when performing these functions internationally.
- **International management** means managing business operations in more than one country.

- When operating on an international basis, it is important for managers to give considerable thought to economic, legal-political, and sociocultural factors.

The Economic Environment

The economic environment represents the economic conditions in the country where the international organization operates. This part of the environment includes factors such as economic development and resource and product markets. In addition, factors such as inflation, interest rates, and economic growth are also part of the international economic environment.

ECONOMIC DEVELOPMENT

Economic development differs widely among the countries and regions of the world. Countries can be categorized as either *developing* or *developed*. Developing countries are referred to as *less-developed countries* (LDCs). The criterion traditionally used to classify countries as developed or developing is *per-capita income*, which is the income

Take a Moment

Read the Ethical Dilemma for Chapter 4 on pages 197–198 that pertains to conducting business in less-developed countries.

generated by the nation's production of goods and services divided by total population. The developing countries have low per-capita incomes. LDCs generally are located in Asia, Africa, and South America. Developed countries are generally located in North America, Europe, and Japan. Most international business firms are headquartered in the wealthier, economically advanced countries, but smart managers are investing heavily in Asia, Eastern Europe, Latin America, and Africa.[45] These companies face risks and challenges today, but they stand to reap huge benefits in the future.

Each year, the World Economic Forum analyzes data to gauge how companies are doing in the economic development race and releases its Global Competitiveness Report, which tallies numerous factors that contribute to an economy's competitiveness.[46] The report considers both hard data and perceptions of business leaders around the world and considers government policies, institutions, market size, the sophistication of financial markets, and other factors that drive productivity and thus enable sustained economic growth. Exhibit 4.4 shows the top ten countries in the overall

▶ ▶ ▶ **Concept Connection**

While working as a New York investment banker, Bangladesh native Iqbal Quadir realized that connectivity equals productivity. He also knew his impoverished homeland was one of the least connected places on Earth. That prompted him to collaborate with countryman Muhammad Yunus, Grameen Bank founder and 2006 Nobel Peace Prize winner, to create Village Phone. Entrepreneurs, mostly women, use Grameen Bank microloans to purchase cell phones. "Telephone ladies," such as Monwara Begum pictured here, then earn the money to repay the debt by providing phone service to fellow villagers. Village Phone has resulted in thousands of new small businesses, as well as an improved communication **infrastructure**, that makes **economic development** possible.

EXHIBIT 4.4   Country Competitiveness Comparison

Country	World Economic Forum Competitiveness Ranking	Gross Domestic Product	Number of People in Labor Force
Switzerland	1	$ 344,200,000,000	4,899,000
Singapore	2	$ 318,900,000,000	3,237,000
Sweden	3	$ 386,600,000,000	5,018,000
Finland	4	$ 198,200,000,000	2,682,000
United States	5	$ 15,290,000,000,000	153,600,000
Germany	6	$ 3,139,000,000,000	43,670,000
Netherlands	7	$ 713,100,000,000	7,809,000
Denmark	8	$ 209,200,000,000	2,851,000
Japan	9	$ 4,497,000,000,000	65,910,000
United Kingdom	10	$ 2,290,000,000,000	31,720,000
Canada	12	$ 1,414,000,000,000	18,700,000
Saudi Arabia	17	$ 691,500,000,000	7,630,000
China	26	$ 11,440,000,000,000	795,500,000
Kuwait	34	$ 155,500,000,000	2,227,000
South Africa	50	$ 562,200,000,000	17,660,000
Brazil	53	$ 2,324,000,000,000	104,700,000
India	56	$ 4,515,000,000,000	487,600,000

SOURCE: Based on "The Global Competitiveness Report 2011–2012," World Economic Forum, www3.weforum.org/docs/WEF_GCR_Report_2011-12.pdf (accessed June 27, 2012); CIA World Factbook 2011, www.cia.gov/library/publications/the-world-factbook (accessed November 15, 2012).

ranking for 2011–2012, along with several other countries for comparison. The United States has steadily fallen to fifth place, from first place in 2008–2009. Note that highly developed countries typically rank higher in the competitiveness index. One important factor in gauging competitiveness is the country's **infrastructure**, that is, the physical facilities such as highways, airports, utilities, and telephone lines that support economic activities.

ECONOMIC INTERDEPENDENCE

One thing the recent global financial crisis has made abundantly clear is how economically interconnected the world is. Although the recent crisis might seem atypical, savvy international managers realize that their companies will probably be buffeted by similar crises fairly regularly. For example, most students are probably familiar with the bursting of the dot-com bubble in the early part of this century, which caused a severe drop in the stock market and affected companies around the globe. The Asian financial crisis of 1997–1998 similarly affected firms in North America, Europe, and other parts of the world. More recently, Greece's inability to make payments on its debt sparked a panic that devalued the euro and threatened the stability of financial markets worldwide.[47]

Recent financial woes have left a number of countries reeling, as reflected in a "misery index" created by a Moody's economist and illustrated in Exhibit 4.5. The misery index adds together a country's unemployment rate and the budget deficit as a percentage of gross domestic product (GDP). The 2010 figures suggest significantly greater misery for almost every country compared to the beginning of this century. Iceland and Ireland, two countries hit particularly hard by the recent economic crisis, had a negative misery index in 2000 but registered high scores for misery in 2010. The United States went from a misery score of less than 5 in 2000 to about 21 in 2010.[48]

Another reflection of economic interdependence is the fact that parts and supplies for many companies come from around the world, which presents managers with new complexities. For example, a recent challenge for Honda and Toyota auto plants in the United States, Canada, and Asia was getting the electronics and other parts they needed from suppliers in Thailand, where flooding swamped huge industrial sections of the country. Walmart, the world's largest retailer, with stores around the world, has been under

EXHIBIT 4.5

How Countries Are Bearing the Economic Crisis: Misery Index, 2010 Compared to 2000

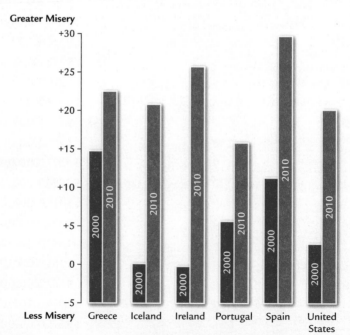

SOURCE: Based on "A New Definition of Misery," *The New York Times* (December 18, 2009), based on data from Moody's; www.nytimes.com/imagepages/2009/12/18/business/economy/20091219_CHARTS_GRAPHIC.html (accessed on December 19, 2009).

pressure to evaluate and disclose how suppliers treat workers. At a recent shareholder meeting, a Bangladeshi labor organizer complained that many factories that produce goods for the giant U.S.-based chain mistreat workers, and he presented a proposal that the company require suppliers to describe working conditions in detail.[49]

Remember This

- Countries vary widely in terms of **economic development** and are classified as either developed countries or less-developed countries (LDCs).
- **Infrastructure** refers to a country's physical facilities, such as highways, utilities, and airports, that support economic activities.
- The United States has fallen from first to fifth place on a ranking of global competitiveness.

- As recent financial crises in the United States and Europe show, countries are economically interconnected, and financial problems in one area of the world can spread rapidly around the globe.
- International business managers can expect their companies to be affected periodically by economic problems that cross geographical boundaries.

The Legal-Political Environment

Differing laws and regulations make doing business a challenge for international firms. Host governments have myriad laws concerning libel statutes, consumer protection, information and labeling, employment and safety, and wages. International managers must learn these rules and regulations and abide by them. In addition, managers must deal with unfamiliar political systems when they go international, as well as with more government supervision and regulation. Government officials and the general public often view foreign companies as outsiders (or even intruders) and are suspicious of their impact on economic independence and political sovereignty.

Political risk is defined as the risk of loss of assets, earning power, or managerial control due to politically based events or actions by host governments. Although many developing countries today welcome and support foreign firms, political risk is a major concern for international companies, which face a broader and more complex array of threats than ever.[50] For example, National Security Agency (NSA) investigators say they traced a series of online attacks on Google and dozens of other U.S. corporations to two Chinese educational institutions with ties to the Chinese military. The attacks were aimed at stealing trade secrets and tapping into the e-mail of suspected Chinese human rights activists.[51] Political risk also includes government takeovers of property and acts of violence directed against a firm's properties or employees.

Another frequently cited problem for international companies is **political instability**, which includes riots, revolutions, civil disorders, and frequent changes in government. The Arab Spring, for instance, a revolutionary wave of protests in the Arab world that began in late 2010, has created a tumultuous environment for businesses operating in

▶ ▶ ▶ **Concept Connection**

GOH CHAI HIN/AFP/Getty Images

Amway, the U.S.-based network marketing company, spent years patiently negotiating China's **legal-political environment**. In 1998, the Chinese government closed down Amway operations in China because it suspected the company was either an illegal pyramid scheme or a sinister cult. Amway survived by cultivating relationships with government officials and by departing from its business model. For example, it opened more than 200 retail stores like this one to demonstrate its commitment. In 2006, the Chinese government once again allowed Amway to sell directly to consumers, and the company now earns billions in annual revenue in China.

the region (including Tunisia, Egypt, Libya, Syria, Yemen, and Bahrain). "No president, no government, no police," said Jalilia Mezni, owner of Société d'Articles Hygiéniques in Tunisia. "Only complete disorder."[52] Political risk and political instability remain elevated throughout the Arab world, causing problems for both local and foreign organizations. Zaid Qadoumi, the CEO of Canada's BroadGrain, which has been delivering agricultural commodities to emerging markets and political hot spots since the company was founded, offered extra pay for a crew to deliver a load of wheat to Libya, but advised workers to "cut the ropes and leave" if they believed the situation was too dangerous.[53]

Remember This

- Complicated legal and political forces can create huge risks for international managers and organizations.
- **Political risk** refers to a company's risk of loss of assets, earning power, or managerial control due to politically based events or actions by host governments.
- **Political instability** includes events such as riots, revolutions, or government upheavals that can affect the operations of an international company.

- A revolutionary wave of protests in the Arab world that began in late 2010, known as the *Arab Spring*, has created a tumultuous environment for businesses operating in the region.
- Managers must understand and follow the differing laws and regulations in the various countries where they do business.

The Sociocultural Environment

A nation's culture includes the shared knowledge, beliefs, and values, as well as the common modes of behavior and ways of thinking among members of a society. Cultural factors sometimes can be more perplexing than political and economic factors when working or living in a foreign country.

SOCIAL VALUES

Many managers fail to realize that the values and behaviors that typically govern how business is done in their own country don't always translate to the rest of the world. American managers in particular are regularly accused of an ethnocentric attitude that assumes their way is the best way. This chapter's Shoptalk looks further at how American managers sometimes are perceived by people in other countries. **Ethnocentrism** refers to a natural tendency of people to regard their own culture as superior and to downgrade or dismiss other cultural values. Ethnocentrism can be found in all countries, and strong ethnocentric attitudes within a country make it difficult for foreign firms to operate there.

One way that managers can fight their own ethnocentric tendencies is to understand and appreciate differences in social values.

Hofstede's Value Dimensions

In research that included 116,000 IBM employees in 40 countries, Dutch scientist Geert Hofstede identified four dimensions of national value systems that influence organizational and employee working relationships.[54] Examples of how countries rate on the four dimensions are shown in Exhibit 4.6.

1. *Power distance.* High **power distance** means that people accept inequality in power among institutions, organizations, and people. Low power distance means that people expect equality in power. Countries that value high power distance are Malaysia, India, and the Philippines. Countries that value low power distance are Denmark, Israel, and New Zealand.

Manager's *Shoptalk*

Are You an Ugly American?

Americans have been accused of a tendency to think everyone does things the way they are done in the United States and to believe "the American way is the best way." Those attitudes hurt U.S. firms in the global business environment.

How People in Developing Countries View Corporate America

PepsiCo conducted a perception study to see how corporate America is viewed in developing countries. One finding is that U.S. companies are rarely perceived as being multinational; rather, they are perceived as U.S. companies doing business internationally. Here are a few other perceptions:

- American managers are "traveling salesmen" who come in fast, give a quick presentation, make promises, and then disappear.

- When things go wrong, American managers don't fix them; they dump them and move on.

- American managers take a mercenary approach and do not build or value consistency and stability.

Americans as Global Managers

One expert on business etiquette says inexperienced American managers commit blunders more than 70 percent of the time when doing business abroad. Here are a few cultural mistakes American managers working overseas or with people from foreign countries frequently make:

- American managers often come across as cold or insensitive. In relationship-oriented societies such as Latin America, Asia, and Mexico, for example, managers are expected to use a warm, personal approach and show interest and concern for the personal lives of subordinates as well as colleagues.

- American managers demonstrate a take-charge attitude that is considered impolite or offensive in some countries. Cultural values in China, for example, emphasize that the leader is much more modest, less visible, and accomplishes things behind the scenes. In India, a take-charge attitude in the workplace may be considered disrespectful.

- American managers are typically informal and refer to everyone by their first names, which can be insulting to people in areas such as Mexico and some Asian and Latin American countries, where business is conducted much more formally.

Sources: Based on information in Carlos Sanchez-Runde, Luciara Nardon, and Richard M. Steers, "Looking Beyond Western Leadership Models: Implications for Global Managers," *Organizational Dynamics* 40 (2011): 207–213; Christine Uber Grosse, "Global Managers' Perceptions of Cultural Competence," *Business Horizons* 54 (2011): 307–314; Sarah Salas, "Business Etiquette in Latin America," BellaOnline Website, www.bellaonline.com/articles/art40307.asp (accessed June 29, 2012); "PepsiCo's Perception Study," in *Managing Diversity for Sustained Competitiveness: A Conference Report* (New York: The Conference Board, 1997), p. 16.

ENVIRONMENT 2

2. *Uncertainty avoidance.* High **uncertainty avoidance** means that members of a society feel uncomfortable with uncertainty and ambiguity and thus support beliefs that promise certainty and conformity. Low uncertainty avoidance means that people have high tolerance for the unstructured, the unclear, and the unpredictable. High uncertainty avoidance countries include Greece, Portugal, and Uruguay. Countries with low uncertainty avoidance values are Sweden, Singapore, and Jamaica.

3. *Individualism and collectivism.* **Individualism** reflects a value for a loosely knit social framework in which individuals are expected to take care of themselves. **Collectivism** means a preference for a tightly knit social framework in which individuals look after one another and organizations protect their members' interests. Countries with individualist values include the United States, Canada, and Great Britain. Countries with collectivist values are China, Mexico, and Brazil.

4. *Masculinity/femininity.* **Masculinity** stands for preference for achievement, heroism, assertiveness, work centrality (with resultant high stress), and material success. **Femininity**

EXHIBIT 4.6   Rank Orderings of Ten Countries Along Four Dimensions of National Value Systems

Country	Power Distance[a]	Uncertainty Avoidance[b]	Individualism[c]	Masculinity[d]
Australia	7	7	2	5
Costa Rica	8 (tie)	2 (tie)	10	9
France	3	2 (tie)	4	7
West Germany	8 (tie)	5	5	3
India	2	9	6	6
Japan	5	1	7	1
Mexico	1	4	8	2
Sweden	10	10	3	10
Thailand	4	6	9	8
United States	6	8	1	4

a. 1 = Highest power distance   b. 1 = Highest uncertainty avoidance
    10 = Lowest power distance   10 = Lowest uncertainty avoidance
c. 1 = Highest individualism   d. 1 = Highest masculinity
    10 = Lowest individualism   10 = Lowest masculinity

SOURCES: Dorothy Marcic, *Organizational Behavior and Cases*, 4th ed. (St. Paul, MN: West, 1995). Based on two books by Geert Hofstede: *Culture's Consequences* (London: Sage Publications, 1984) and *Cultures and Organizations: Software of the Mind* (New York: McGraw-Hill, 1991).

reflects the values of relationships, cooperation, group decision making, and quality of life. Societies with strong masculine values are Japan, Germany, Italy, and Mexico. Countries with feminine values are Sweden, Costa Rica, Norway, and France. Both men and women subscribe to the dominant value in masculine and feminine cultures.

Hofstede and his colleagues later identified a fifth dimension, long-term orientation versus short-term orientation. The **long-term orientation**, found in China and other Asian countries, includes a greater concern for the future and highly values thrift and perseverance. A **short-term orientation**, found in Russia and West Africa, is more concerned with the past and the present and places a high value on tradition and meeting social obligations.[55] Researchers continue to explore and expand on Hofstede's findings.[56] For example, in the last 30 years, more than 1,400 articles and numerous books were published on individualism and collectivism alone.[57]

GLOBE Project Value Dimensions

Recent research by the Global Leadership and Organizational Behavior Effectiveness (GLOBE) Project extends Hofstede's assessment and offers a broader understanding for today's managers. The GLOBE Project used data collected from 18,000 managers in 62 countries to identify nine dimensions that explain cultural differences. In addition to the ones identified by Hofstede, the GLOBE project identifies the following characteristics:[58]

Take a Moment

Answer the questions in the New Manager Self-Test on page 120 to see how you rate on some of the value dimensions described by Hofstede and the GLOBE project.

1. *Assertiveness.* A high value on assertiveness means a society encourages toughness, assertiveness, and competitiveness. Low assertiveness means that people value tenderness and concern for others over being competitive.

2. *Future orientation.* Similar to Hofstede's time orientation, this dimension refers to the extent to which a society encourages and rewards planning for the future over short-term results and quick gratification.

3. *Gender differentiation.* This dimension refers to the extent to which a society maximizes gender role differences. In countries with low gender differentiation, such as Denmark, women typically have a higher status and play a stronger role in decision making. Countries with high gender differentiation accord men higher social, political, and economic status.

4. *Performance orientation.* A society with a high performance orientation places high emphasis on performance and rewards people for performance improvements and excellence. A low performance orientation means people pay less attention to performance and more attention to loyalty, belonging, and background.

5. *Humane orientation.* The final dimension refers to the degree to which a society encourages and rewards people for being fair, altruistic, generous, and caring. A country high on humane orientation places a great value on helping others and being kind. A country low on this orientation expects people to take care of themselves. Self-enhancement and gratification are of high importance.

Exhibit 4.7 gives examples of how some countries rank on these GLOBE dimensions. These dimensions give managers an added tool for identifying and managing cultural differences. Social values greatly influence organizational functioning and management styles. Consider the difficulty that Emerson Electric managers had when Emerson opened a new manufacturing facility in Suzhou, China. One area in which the American view and the Chinese view differed widely was in terms of time orientation. The American managers favored a short time horizon and quick results, and they viewed their assignments as stepping stones to future career advancement. The Chinese managers, on the other hand, favored a long-term approach, building a system and setting a proper course of action to enable long-term success.[59] Other companies have encountered similar cultural differences. Consider the American concept of self-directed teams, which emphasizes shared power and authority, with team members working on a variety of problems without formal guidelines, rules, and structure. Managers trying to implement teams have had trouble in areas where cultural values support high power distance and a low tolerance for uncertainty, such as Mexico. Many workers in Mexico, as well as in France and Mediterranean countries, expect organizations to be hierarchical. In Russia, people are good at working in groups and like competing as a team rather than on an individual basis. Organizations in Germany and other central European countries typically strive to be impersonal, well-oiled machines. Effective management styles differ in each country, depending on cultural characteristics.[60]

> *"Because management deals with the integration of people in a common venture, it is deeply embedded in culture. What managers do in Germany, in the United Kingdom, in the United States, in Japan, or in Brazil is exactly the same. How they do it may be quite different."*
>
> — PETER DRUCKER, MANAGEMENT EXPERT

EXHIBIT **4.7**

Examples of Country Rankings on Selected GLOBE Value Dimensions

Dimension	Low	Medium	High
Assertiveness	Sweden Switzerland Japan	Egypt Iceland France	Spain United States Germany (former East)
Future Orientation	Russia Italy Kuwait	Slovenia Australia India	Denmark Canada Singapore
Gender Differentiation	Sweden Denmark Poland	Italy Brazil Netherlands	South Korea Egypt China
Performance Orientation	Russia Greece Venezuela	Israel England Japan	United States Taiwan Hong Kong
Humane Orientation	Germany France Singapore	New Zealand Sweden United States	Indonesia Egypt Iceland

SOURCE: Mansour Javidan and Robert J. House, "Cultural Acumen for the Global Manager: Lessons from Project GLOBE," *Organizational Dynamics* 29, no. 4 (2001): 289–305, with permission from Elsevier.

New Manager 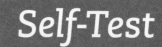 Self-Test

What Are Your Social Values?

Instructions: Respond to each of the following statements based on your beliefs, indicating whether the statement is Mostly True or Mostly False for you.

	Mostly True	Mostly False
1. Achieving one's personal goals is more important than achieving team or organization goals.	_____	_____
2. Children should take great pride in the individual accomplishments of their parents and vice versa.	_____	_____
3. Pay and bonus systems should be designed to maximize individual interests over mutual interests.	_____	_____
4. I believe that orderliness and consistency should be stressed in society, even at the expense of experimentation and innovation.	_____	_____
5. Organizations work better when people do not break rules.	_____	_____
6. Organizations should spell out job requirements in detail so employees know what they are supposed to do.	_____	_____
7. I want to compete for high-level jobs and high earnings.	_____	_____
8. People should be encouraged to be assertive rather than nonassertive.	_____	_____
9. In an organization, people should be encouraged to be tough more than tender.	_____	_____
10. As a manager, I would want an egalitarian working relationship with my direct reports rather than maintaining distance from them.	_____	_____
11. Organizations should encourage subordinates to question their leaders.	_____	_____
12. Authority should be based on one's ability and contribution rather than on one's position in the hierarchy.	_____	_____
13. People in society will be happier if they accept the status quo rather than try to change things for the days ahead.	_____	_____
14. I prefer a norm of taking life events as they occur rather than constantly planning ahead.	_____	_____
15. I believe in focusing on current problems rather than trying to make things happen for the future	_____	_____

Scoring and Interpretation: These questions represent a measure of five cultural values as described by Geert Hofstete and the GLOBE Project, as described in the chapter. Give yourself one point for each answer marked Mostly True. Questions 1–3 are for *individualism-collectivism.* A higher score of 2–3 represents a belief toward individualism; a lower score of 0–1 means a belief more toward collectivism. Questions 4–6 are about *uncertainty avoidance.* A higher score of 2–3 means a value for low uncertainty in life; a lower score of 0–1 means a value for higher uncertainty. Questions 7–9 represent *assertiveness.* A higher score of 2–3 represents a value for people being assertive; a lower score of 0–1 means a value for people being nonassertive. Questions 10–12 represent *power distance.* A higher score of 2–3 means a value for low power distance; a lower score of 0–1 means a value for high power distance. Questions 13–15 represent *time orientation*. A higher score of 2–3 means an orientation toward the present; a lower score of 0–1 represents a future orientation.

Your scores have both individual and societal meaning. Compare your scores to other students to understand your perception of the different values in your colleague group. On which of the five values would you personally like to score higher? Lower? These five values also differ widely across national cultures. Go to the website www.geert-hofstede .com/hofstede_dimensions.php and compare your country's scores on the five values to the scores of people from other countries. At this site, the term *masculinity* is used instead of *assertiveness*. What surprises you about the differences across countries?

Sources: Adapted from Robert J. House et al. (eds.), *Culture, Leadership, and Organizations: The GLOBE Study of 62 Societies* (Thousand Oaks, CA: Sage Publications, 2004); Geert Hofstede, *Culture's Consequences* (London: Sage Publications, 1984); and D. Matsumoto et al., "Context-Specific Measurement of Individualism-Collectivism on the Individual Level: The Individualism-Collectivism Interpersonal Assessment Inventory," *Journal of Cross-Cultural Psychology* 28, no. 6 (1997): 743–767.

ENVIRONMENT 2

Remember This

- Managers working internationally should guard against **ethnocentrism**, which is the natural tendency among people to regard their own culture as superior to others.
- Hofstede's sociocultural value dimensions measure power distance, uncertainty avoidance, individualism-collectivism, and masculinity-femininity.
- **Power distance** is the degree to which people accept inequality in power among institutions, organizations, and people.
- **Uncertainty avoidance** is characterized by people's intolerance for uncertainty and ambiguity and resulting support for beliefs that promise certainty and conformity.
- **Individualism** refers to a preference for a loosely knit social framework in which individuals are expected to take care of themselves.
- **Collectivism** refers to a preference for a tightly knit social framework in which individuals look after one

another and organizations protect their members' interests.
- **Masculinity** is a cultural preference for achievement, heroism, assertiveness, work centrality, and material success.
- **Femininity** is a cultural preference for relationships, cooperation, group decision making, and quality of life.
- Hofstede later identified another dimension: **long-term orientation**, which reflects a greater concern for the future and a high value on thrift and perseverance, versus **short-term orientation**, which reflects a concern with the past and present and a high value on meeting current obligations.
- Additional value dimensions recently identified by Project GLOBE are assertiveness, future orientation, gender differentiation, performance orientation, and humane orientation.

COMMUNICATION DIFFERENCES

People from some cultures tend to pay more attention to the social context (social setting, nonverbal behavior, social status, etc.) of their verbal communication than Americans do. For example, American managers working in China have discovered that social context is considerably more important in that culture, and they need to learn to suppress their impatience and devote the time necessary to establish personal and social relationships.

Exhibit 4.8 indicates how the emphasis on social context varies among countries. In a **high-context culture**, people are sensitive to circumstances surrounding social exchanges. People use communication primarily to build personal social relationships; meaning is derived from context—setting, status, and nonverbal behavior—more than from explicit words; relationships and trust are more important than business; and the welfare and harmony of the group are valued. In a **low-context culture**, people use communication primarily to exchange facts and information; meaning is derived primarily from words;

EXHIBIT   4.8

High-Context and Low-
Context Cultures

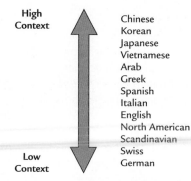

High
Context

Chinese
Korean
Japanese
Vietnamese
Arab
Greek
Spanish
Italian
English
North American
Scandinavian
Swiss
German

Low
Context

SOURCES: Edward T. Hall, *Beyond Culture* (Garden City, NY: Anchor Press/Doubleday, 1976); and J. Kennedy and A. Everest, "Put Diversity in Context," *Personnel Journal* (September 1991): 50–54.

Take a Moment

Refer to your score on the questionnaire at the beginning of this chapter, which will give you some insight into whether you lean toward low-context or high-context communications. A higher score indicates low-context behavior, which would clash when trying to do business in a high-context culture.

business transactions are more important than building relationships and trust; and individual welfare and achievement are more important than the group.[61]

To understand how differences in cultural context affect communications, consider the American expression, "The squeaky wheel gets the grease." It means that the loudest person will get the most attention, and attention is assumed to be favorable. Equivalent sayings in China and Japan are "Quacking ducks get shot," and "The nail that sticks up gets hammered down," respectively. In these latter two cultures, standing out as an individual merits unfavorable attention. Consider the culture gap when China's Lenovo Group acquired IBM's PC business. In meetings and conference calls, Western executives were frustrated by their Chinese counterparts' reluctance to speak up, while the Chinese managers were irritated by the Americans' propensity to "just talk and talk," as one vice president of human resources put it.[62]

High-context cultures include Asian and Arab countries. Low-context cultures tend to be American and Northern European. Even within North America, cultural subgroups vary in the extent to which context counts, explaining why differences among groups can hinder successful communication. White females, Native Americans, and African Americans all tend to prefer higher context communication than do white males. A high-context interaction requires more time because a relationship has to be developed, and trust and friendship must be established. Furthermore,

Concept Connection ◄◄◄

Pictured at a traditional Japanese ceremony is Hiroshi Mikitani (second from right), Rakuten, Inc.'s founder and CEO. Tokyo-based Rakuten is an Internet group that includes Rakuten Marketplace, a flourishing e-commerce site. In keeping with Rakuten's ambitious global expansion plans, Mikitari holds all board meetings, strategy discussions, and weekly employee gatherings in English, the most commonly used language in international business. As Rakuten expands, managers from Japan's **high-context culture**, where communication is used to build relationships, must not only become proficient in a foreign language, but also learn to communicate effectively with managers from **low-context cultures**, where communication is used primarily to conduct business.

Kiyoshi Ota/Getty Images

most male managers and most people doing the hiring in organizations are from low-context cultures, which conflicts with people entering the organization from a background in a higher-context culture.

Remember This

- A **high-context culture** is one in which people use communication to build personal relationships.
- In a **low-context culture**, people use communication primarily to exchange facts and information.

- The United States is a low-context culture. China is an example of a high-context culture.

The Changing International Landscape

Many companies today are going straight to China or India as a first step into international business, either through outsourcing or by using various market entry strategies. China and India have been the world's fastest growing economies in recent years. In addition, Brazil is coming on strong as a major player in the international business landscape.

CHINA, INC.

For the past several years, foreign companies have invested more in business in China than they spent anywhere else in the world. A market that was of little interest a decade ago has become the one place nearly every manager is thinking about. China is German car maker BMW's biggest market for its largest and most profitable sedans.[63] The U.S.-based company Apple has two stores in Shanghai, and they are so busy that the company is opening a third, along with dozens of other stores throughout China. Apple's four stores in Beijing and Shanghai are the company's most heavily used—as well as the most profitable.[64] Apple had to jump through all sorts of legal and regulatory hurdles to sell in China, but it was worth it to get the iPhone into the largest mobile phone market in the world.[65] Although outsourcing has been the most widespread approach to involvement in China, the country is rapidly moving toward a consumer-driven economy, with the fastest-growing middle

Green Power

When Bentonville Met Beijing

Establishing his business in Bentonville, Arkansas, in 1962, all-American entrepreneur Sam Walton could not have imagined eventual expansion to over 350 stores and 20,000 suppliers in China. In 2008, Walmart CEO Lee Scott publicly addressed environmental concerns in China and put Walmart's vast resources behind his pledge to make sustainability a priority in the Chinese market. To address waste and pollution, Walmart trained and monitored workers across the Chinese supply chain, from factory and transport to retail stores, and then set environmental standards as a *requirement* for other companies to do business

with Walmart. The company also joined forces with China's Institute of Public and Environmental Affairs to map water pollution and wastewater management. The efforts resulted in dramatic drops in water use at many supplier factories. To address mounting food safety concerns among the Chinese, Walmart established the Direct Farm Program, offering local farmers higher incomes for providing safe supplies of fresh food to consumers through the giant retailer.

Source: Orville Schell, "How Walmart Is Changing China—and Vice Versa," *The Atlantic* (December 2011): 80–98.

class in history. China is the largest or second-largest market for a variety of products and services, including mobile phones, automobiles, consumer electronics, luxury goods, and Internet use.[66]

Yet, doing business in China has never been smooth, and it appears to be getting even tougher. New regulations and government policies are making life hard for foreign companies in all industries. For Internet companies such as Facebook, Twitter, eBay, and Google, China has been more a source of trouble and frustration than of new customers.[67] Google closed its Chinese site, Google.cn, in early 2010 because of government restrictions and censorship, although the company later renewed its license to provide limited services in China. Some multinational firms doing business with Chinese organizations, particularly big state-owned companies, have also had problems getting payments on their contracts. "A contract is not an unchangeable bible for Chinese companies," said Beijing-based lawyer Jingzhou Tao. Chinese managers frequently withhold payments as a tactic in price negotiations. Part of the reason is that these organizations are not just companies but also political entities. But another reason is because of cultural differences. "Chinese culture will build a relationship before the contract," said Arthur Bowring, managing director of the Hong Kong Shipowners Association. "The relationship is always something that can be talked about. The contract is just a set of papers that you keep in your bottom drawer."[68]

Despite the problems, China is a market that foreign managers can't afford to ignore. However, competition from domestic companies in China is growing fast. In some industries, local companies have already become market leaders, such as Midea in consumer appliances and 7 Days Inn in budget hotels.[69] One Chinese company that is rapidly becoming a global leader is Lenovo.

Innovative Way

Lenovo

The fastest-growing company in the PC industry is one that most people outside of China hadn't even heard of a few years ago, even after it bought IBM's ThinkPad brand in 2005. Lenovo is now the No. 2 seller of computers in the world (behind Hewlett-Packard) and is innovating in new product categories such as tablets, smartphones, and smart TVs. Lenovo's CEO, Yang Yuanqing, who started as a salesman and once delivered computers by bicycle, is now China's highest-paid executive.

With its emphasis on quality (its machines rank tops for reliability), Lenovo is redefining the perception of the phrase "made in China." Moreover, it is redefining the meaning of a Chinese company, blending the best of Eastern philosophy and culture with the best of Western business and management thinking. The company has headquarters in Beijing, but Yang spends a third of his time at Lenovo's offices in Raleigh, North Carolina. Lenovo's top managers, once almost all Chinese with no international experience, now come from 14 different nations. Most members of the top leadership team speak two or more languages. They live and work in six different cities on three continents. Dan Stone, who was born in Israel, has his office in the United States, while Gerry Smith, born in the United States, works out of Singapore.

Lenovo's top executives know that appreciating and merging Chinese and non-Chinese perspectives is crucial to success. It's an idea that U. S. managers need to be paying attention to. "Chinese people know Americans or the United States more than vice versa," says Lenovo's founder and chairman, Liu Chuanzhi. "Much more."[70]

INDIA, THE SERVICE GIANT

India, second only to China in population, has taken a different path toward economic development. Whereas China is strong in manufacturing, India is a rising power in software design, services, and precision engineering. Numerous companies see India as a major source of technological and scientific brainpower, and the country's large English-speaking population makes it a natural for U.S. companies wanting to outsource services. One index lists more than 900 business services companies in India, which employ around 575,000 people.[71]

One of the fastest-growing industries in India is pharmaceuticals, medical devices, and diagnostics. The country has a large number of highly trained scientists, doctors, and researchers, and U.S. firms Abbott Laboratories and Covidien have both opened research and development centers there. India is also a growing manufacturer of pharmaceuticals and is the world's largest exporter of generic drugs. By 2020, India's pharmaceuticals industry will likely be a global leader, according to a report by PricewaterhouseCoopers.[72]

BRAZIL'S GROWING CLOUT

Brazil is another country that is increasingly gaining managers' attention. Although Brazil's economic growth slowed in 2011, it is still one of the fastest-growing emerging economies in the world, with large and growing agricultural, mining, manufacturing, and service sectors.[73] The country's economy, already the seventh-largest in the world, is projected to move into fourth place by 2050. The choice of Rio de Janeiro to host the 2016 Summer Olympics is also an indication of Brazil's growing clout in the international arena.

Brazil has a young, vibrant population, the largest in Latin America, and a rapidly growing middle class eager to experience the finer things in life. Consumer spending represents about 60 percent of Brazil's economy. The Brazilian government has initiated major investments in the development of infrastructure such as highways, ports, and electricity projects, which is creating jobs as well as spurring the development of other businesses. In addition, in 2010, Brazil announced a $22 billion investment in science and technology innovation.

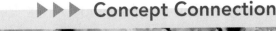

Companies such as Bug Agentes Biologicos, located in Piracicaba, Brazil, reflect the **changing international landscape**. One of *Forbes* magazine's top 50 most innovative companies worldwide, Bug Agentes Biologicos supplies the agriculture industry with predatory insect eggs and parasitoids, which are a natural alternative to harmful agricultural pesticides. Bug sells its products throughout the three largest agricultural producers—the United States, the European Union (EU), and Brazil—and far beyond.

Jefferson Bernardes/Getty Images News/Getty Images

ENVIRONMENT 2

Remember This

- Many companies are going straight to China or India as a first step into international business.
- Outsourcing is the most widespread involvement by foreign firms in these two countries.
- China is strong in manufacturing, whereas India is a major provider of services.
- The Chinese company Lenovo is emerging as the country's first global corporation, with managers coming from 14 different nations, living and working in six cities on three continents.
- Brazil, with its rapidly growing consumer market, is becoming a major player in the shifting international landscape.
- Managers also look to China, India, and Brazil as sources of lower-cost technological and scientific brainpower.

International Trade Alliances

Another highly visible change in the international business environment in recent years has been the development of regional trading alliances and international trade agreements.

GATT AND THE WTO

The General Agreement on Tariffs and Trade (GATT), signed by 23 nations in 1947, started as a set of rules to ensure nondiscrimination, clear procedures, the negotiation of disputes, and the participation of lesser-developed countries in international trade.[74] GATT sponsored eight rounds of international trade negotiations aimed at reducing trade restrictions. The 1986 to 1994 Uruguay Round (the first to be named for a developing country) involved 125 countries and cut more tariffs than ever before. In addition to lowering tariffs 30 percent from the previous level, it boldly moved the world closer to global free trade by calling for the establishment of the World Trade Organization (WTO) in 1995.

The WTO represents the maturation of GATT into a permanent global institution that can monitor international trade and has legal authority to arbitrate disputes on some 400 trade issues. As of July 2008, 153 countries, including China, Vietnam, and Ukraine, were members of the organization. As a permanent membership organization, the WTO is bringing greater trade liberalization in goods, information, technological developments, and services; stronger enforcement of rules and regulations; and greater power to resolve disputes among trading partners.

EUROPEAN UNION

An alliance begun in 1957 to improve economic and social conditions among its members, the European Economic Community has evolved into the 27-nation European Union (EU) illustrated in Exhibit 4.9. The biggest expansion came in 2004, when the EU welcomed 10 new members from central and eastern Europe.[75]

The goal of the EU is to create a powerful single-market system for Europe's millions of consumers, allowing people, goods, and services to move freely. The increased competition

EXHIBIT 4.9

The Nations of the European Union

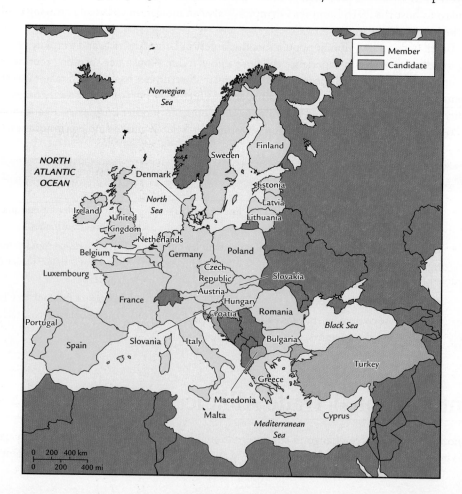

and economies of scale within Europe enable companies to grow large and efficient, becoming more competitive in the United States and other world markets. Another aspect of European unification is the introduction of the euro. Several member states of the EU have adopted the **euro**, a single European currency that replaced national currencies in Austria, Belgium, Cyprus, Finland, France, Germany, Greece, Ireland, Italy, Luxembourg, Malta, the Netherlands, Portugal, Slovakia, Slovenia, and Spain.[76]

However, not all has gone smoothly for the integration, particularly since the global recession began. As economic stability varied from country to country, pitting winners against losers, the economic crisis revived national loyalties and cross-border resentments, slowing the move toward a unified and cohesive "European identity."[77] Spain, Ireland, and particularly Greece have all had trouble paying their debts, putting the entire eurozone at risk and leading to a possible breakup of the euro system. As EU officials scrambled to dispel the fears that Greece would exit the euro, multinational firms doing business in EU countries were bracing for the worst and taking steps to protect themselves. Managers at companies such as Heineken NV and GlaxoSmithKline PLC, for instance, moved all cash reserves out of the eurozone and into currencies such as the U.S. dollar or British pound. Some analysts think that a broad breakup of the eurozone is unlikely, but the uncertainty has smart managers rethinking what they would do in the event that a return to national currencies required a rethinking of everything from how to expand operations to how to pick suppliers and pay employees.[78]

NORTH AMERICAN FREE TRADE AGREEMENT (NAFTA)

The North American Free Trade Agreement (NAFTA), which went into effect on January 1, 1994, merged the United States, Canada, and Mexico into a single market. Intended to spur growth and investment, increase exports, and expand jobs in all three nations, NAFTA broke down tariffs and trade restrictions over a 15-year period in a number of key areas. Thus, by 2008, virtually all U.S. industrial exports into Canada and Mexico were duty-free.

Over the first decade of NAFTA, U.S. trade with Mexico increased more than threefold, while trade with Canada also rose dramatically.[79] Significantly, NAFTA spurred the entry of small businesses into the global arena. Jeff Victor, general manager of Treatment Products, Ltd., which makes car cleaners and waxes, credits NAFTA for his surging export volume. Prior to the pact, Mexican tariffs as high as 20 percent made it impossible for the Chicago-based company to expand its presence south of the border.[80]

However, opinions over the benefits of NAFTA appear to be as divided as they were when talks began, with some people calling it a spectacular success and others referring to it as a dismal failure.[81] In Bain & Company's 2011 survey of managers, only 53 percent of North American managers surveyed said they thought reducing trade barriers and increasing free trade was a positive thing, down from 74 percent in 2003.[82] Although NAFTA has not lived up to its grand expectations, experts stress that it increased trade, investment, and income and continues to enable companies in all three countries to compete more effectively with rival Asian and European firms.[83]

Remember This

- Regional trading alliances and international trade agreements are reshaping global business.
- The World Trade Organization (WTO) is a permanent membership organization that monitors trade and has authority to arbitrate disputes among 153 member countries.
- Two important, yet sometimes controversial, regional alliances are the European Union (EU) and the North American Free Trade Agreement (NAFTA).
- The **euro** is a single European currency that has replaced the currencies of 16 EU member nations.

ch4: Discussion Questions

1. What specifically would the experience of living and working in another country contribute to your skills and effectiveness as a manager in your own country?

2. Do you think it is realistic that BOP business practices can have a positive effect on poverty and other social problems in developing countries? Discuss.

3. Somnio, a start-up running shoe company in California, decided to start selling its products around the world from the very beginning. In general terms, name some of the challenges a start-up company such as Somnio might face internationally.

4. Do you think it's possible for someone to develop a global mindset if they never live outside their native country? How might they do that?

5. Compare the advantages associated with the market entry strategies of exporting, licensing, and wholly owned subsidiaries. What information would you need to collect and what factors would you consider when selecting a strategy?

6. Should a multinational organization operate as a tightly integrated, worldwide business system, or would it be more effective to let each national subsidiary operate autonomously?

7. Why do you think many people are so frightened by globalization? Based on what is occurring in the world today, do you expect the globalization backlash to grow stronger or weaker over the next decade?

8. Two U.S. companies are competing to take over a large factory in the Czech Republic. One delegation tours the facility and asks questions about how the plant might be run more efficiently. The other delegation focuses on ways to improve working conditions and produce a better product. Which delegation do you think is more likely to succeed with the plant? Why? What information would you want to collect to decide whether to acquire the plant for your company?

9. Which style of communicating do you think would be most beneficial to the long-term success of a U.S. company operating internationally—high-context or low-context communications? Why?

10. How might the social value of low versus high power distance influence how you would lead and motivate employees? What about the value of low versus high performance orientation?

ch4: Apply Your Skills: Experiential Exercise

Rate Your Global Management Potential[84]

A global environment requires that managers learn to deal effectively with people and ideas from a variety of cultures. How well prepared are you to be a global manager? Read the following statements and circle the number on the response scale that most closely reflects how well the statement describes you.

Good Description 10 9 8 7 6 5 4 3 2 1 Poor Description

1. I reach out to people from different cultures.
   10   9   8   7   6   5   4   3   2   1

2. I frequently attend seminars and lectures about other cultures or international topics.
   10   9   8   7   6   5   4   3   2   1

3. I believe female expatriates can be equally as effective as male expatriates.
   10   9   8   7   6   5   4   3   2   1

4. I have a basic knowledge about several countries in addition to my native country.
   10   9   8   7   6   5   4   3   2   1

5. I have good listening and empathy skills.
   10   9   8   7   6   5   4   3   2   1

6. I have spent more than two weeks traveling or working in another country.
   10   9   8   7   6   5   4   3   2   1

7. I easily adapt to the different work ethics of students from other cultures when we are involved in a team project.
   10   9   8   7   6   5   4   3   2   1

8. I can speak at least one foreign language.
   10   9   8   7   6   5   4   3   2   1

9. I know which countries tend to cluster into similar sociocultural and economic groupings.
   10   9   8   7   6   5   4   3   2   1

10. I feel capable of assessing different cultures on the basis of power distance, uncertainty avoidance, individualism, and masculinity.
    10   9   8   7   6   5   4   3   2   1

Total Score: _____

Scoring and Interpretation

Add up the total points for the ten questions. If you scored 81–100 points, you have a great capacity for developing good global management skills. A score of 61–80 points indicates that you have potential but may lack skills in certain areas, such as language or foreign experience. A score of 60 or less means you need to do some serious work to improve your potential for global management. Regardless of your total score, go back over each item and make a plan of action to increase scores of less than 5 on any question.

ch4: Apply Your Skills: Small Group Breakout

Where Have You Been?[85]

Step 1. Make a list of the names of the countries that you have visited outside your home country.

Step 2. Go to "List of Countries by Population" on Wikipedia and write down the population of each country you have visited.

Step 3. The world population is approximately 6,800,000,000. Compute the percentage of world population for each country you have visited. Also compute the percentage of world population for all countries you have visited.

Step 4. Estimate the grand total of number of countries and percentage of world population visited by your group.

Step 5. Discuss in your group: What is the reason for the variability among group members? What are the implications of high exposure versus low exposure to people in other countries for a career in management? What can you do to increase your international exposure?

Step 6. Present your group's results to the entire class if called upon to do so.

ch4: Endnotes

1. Adapted from Cynthia Barnum and Natasha Wolniansky, "Why Americans Fail at Overseas Negotiations," *Management Review* (October 1989): 54–57.

2. Bettina Wassener, "Living in Asia Appeals to More Company Leaders," *The New York Times*, June 21, 2012, B3; and Emily Glazer, "P&G Unit Bids Goodbye to Cincinnati, Hello to Asia," *The Wall Street Journal*, May 10, 2012, B1.

3. Quoted in Wassener, "Living in Asia Appeals to More Company Leaders."

4. Joann S. Lublin, "Hunt Is on for Fresh Executive Talent—Cultural Flexibility in Demand," *The Wall Street Journal*, April 11, 2011, B1.

5. Lolita C. Baldor, "FBI Sends More Agents Abroad to Shield U.S. from Cybercrime; Foreign Hackers Stepping up Their Attacks," *South Florida Sun-Sentinel*, December 10, 2009; and Cassell Bryan-Low, "Criminal Network: To Catch Crooks in Cyberspace, FBI Goes Global," *The Wall Street Journal*, November 21, 2006.

6. Ryan Underwood, "Going Global," *Inc.* (March 2011): 96–98.

7. Steve Hamm, "IBM vs. Tata: Which Is More American?" *BusinessWeek* (May 5, 2008): 28.

8. Chris Woodyard, "The American Car," *USA Today*, February 17, 2009.

9. "KOF Index of Globalization 2012," press release, KOF Swiss Economic Institute (March 26, 2012), www.kof.ethz.ch/static_media/filer/2012/03/16/kof_index_of_globalization_2012_1.pdf (accessed June 26, 2012).

10. "2012 KOF Index of Globalization," www.kof.ethz.ch/static_media/filer/2012/03/15/rankings_2012.pdf (accessed June 26, 2012). Note: The 2012 KOF analysis of globalization dimensions is based on the year 2009.

11. This section is based on Schon Beechler and Dennis Baltzley, "Creating a Global Mindset," *Chief Learning Officer* (May 29, 2008), http://clomedia.com/articles/view/creating_a_global_mindset/1 (accessed June 26, 2012); Joana S. P. Story and John E. Barbuto, Jr., "Global Mindset: A Construct Clarification and Framework," *Journal of Leadership and Organizational Studies* 18, no. 3 (2011): 377–384; and Stephen L. Cohen, "Effective Global Leadership Requires a Global Mindset," *Industrial and Commercial Training* 42, no. 1 (2010): 3–10.

12. Definition based on Mansour Javidan and Mary B. Teagarden, "Conceptualizing and Measuring Global Mindset," *Advances in Global Leadership* 6 (2011): 13–39; and Beechler and Baltzley, "Creating a Global Mindset."

13. Amol Titus, "Competency of Intercultural Management," *The Jakarta Post*, March 11, 2009, www.thejakartapost.com/news/2009/03/11/competency-intercultural-management.html (accessed June 30, 2012).

14. Karl Moore, "Great Global Managers," *Across the Board* (May–June 2003): 40–43.

15. Siegfried Russwurm et al., "Developing Your Global Know-How," *Harvard Business Review* (March 2011): 70–75.

16. Quoted in Wassener, "Living in Asia Appeals to More Company Leaders."

17. "Count: *Really* Big Business," *Fast Company* (December 2008–January 2009): 46.

18. David E. Bell and Mary L. Shelman, "KFC's Radical Approach to China," *Harvard Business Review* (November 2011): 137–142.

19. Howard V. Perlmutter, "The Tortuous Evolution of the Multinational Corporation," *Columbia Journal of World Business* (January–February 1969): 9–18; and Youram Wind, Susan P. Douglas, and Howard V. Perlmutter, "Guidelines for Developing International Marketing Strategies," *Journal of Marketing* (April 1973): 14–23.

20. Deborah Ball, "Boss Talk: Nestlé Focuses on Long Term," *The Wall Street Journal*, November 2, 2009; Transnationale Web site, www.transnationale.org/companies/nestle.php (accessed March 17, 2010); Company Analytics Web site, www.company-analytics.org/company/nestle.php (accessed March 17, 2010); and Nestlé SA Web site, www.nestle.com (accessed March 17, 2010).

21. Sara Murray and Douglas Belkin, "Americans Sour on Trade: Majority Say Free-Trade Pacts Have Hurt U.S.," *The Wall Street Journal*, October 4, 2010; and Nina Easton, "Make the World Go Away," *Fortune* (February 4, 2008): 105–108.

22. Easton, "Make the World Go Away."

23. Michael Schroeder and Timothy Aeppel, "Skilled Workers Sway Politicians with Fervor Against Free Trade," *The Wall Street Journal*, December 10, 2003.

24. Stephanie Wong, John Liu, and Tim Culpan, "Life and Death at the iPad Factory," *Bloomberg Businessweek* (June 7–June 13, 2010): 35–36; Charles Duhigg and Steven Greenhouse, "Apple Supplier in China Pledges Big Labor Changes," *The New York Times*, March 29, 2012, www.nytimes.com/2012/03/30/business/apple-supplier-in-china-pledges-changes-in-working-conditions.html?pagewanted=all (accessed June 30, 2012); and Kevin Drew, "Apple's Chief Visits iPhone Factory in China," *The New York Times*, March 29, 2012, www.nytimes.com/2012/03/30/technology/apples-chief-timothy-cook-visits-foxconn-factory.html (accessed June 30, 2012).

25. C. K. Prahalad, "The Fortune at the Bottom of the Pyramid," *Fast Company* (April 13, 2011), www.fastcompany.com/1746818/fortune-at-the-bottom-of-the-pyramid-ck-prahalad (accessed June 30, 2012); C. K. Prahalad and S. L. Hart, "The Fortune at the Bottom of the Pyramid," *Strategy + Business* 26 (2002): 54–67; and Scott Johnson, "SC Johnson Builds Business at the Base of the Pyramid," *Global Business and Organizational Excellence* (September–October, 2007): 6–17.

26. Bala Chakravarthy and Sophie Coughlan, "Emerging Market Strategy: Innovating Both Products and Delivery Systems," *Strategy & Leadership* 40, no. 1 (2012): 27–32; T. V. Mahalingam, "Godrej's Rediscovery of India: They Say They Touch More Consumers than Any Other Indian Company," *Business Today* (July 25, 2010): 58–64; and "Godrej Eyes Youth to Expand Portfolio," *Mail Today*, July 12, 2009.

27. Rob Walker, "Cleaning Up," *New York Times Magazine* (June 10, 2007): 20.

28. Jennifer Reingold, "Can P&G Make Money in Places Where People Earn $2 a Day?" *Fortune* (January 17, 2011): 86–91.

29. Jean Kerr, "Export Strategies," *Small Business Reports* (May 1989): 20–25.

30. Mark Sweney, "Netflix Non-US Losses Hit $100m But Subscribers Increase," *The Guardian*, April 24, 2012, www.guardian.co.uk/media/2012/apr/24/netflix-losses-100m-subscribers-increase (accessed June 27, 2012).

31. Lauren A. E. Schuker, "Plot Change: Foreign Forces Transform Hollywood Films," *The Wall Street Journal*, July 31, 2010, A1; and Nicole Allan, "How to Make a Hollywood Hit," *The Atlantic* (May 2012): 70–71.

32. Alison Stein Wellner, "Turning the Tables," *Inc.* (May 2006): 55–59.

33. Kathryn Rudie Harrigan, "Managing Joint Ventures," *Management Review* (February 1987): 24–41; and Therese R. Revesz and Mimi Cauley de Da La Sierra, "Competitive Alliances: Forging Ties Abroad," *Management Review* (March 1987): 57–59.

34. Christopher Weaver, "Abbott Looks to Consumer for Growth," *The Wall Street Journal*, May 2, 2012, http://online.wsj.com/article/SB10001424052702303990604577367760661436198.html (accessed June 28, 2012).

35. James T. Areddy, "European Project Trips China Builder," *The Wall Street Journal*, June 4, 2012, A1; and Kirk Semple, "Bridge Repairs by a Company Tied to Beijing," *The New York Times*, August 10, 2011, www.nytimes.com/2011/08/11/nyregion/china-construction-co-involved-in-new-yorks-public-works.html (accessed June 27, 2012).

36. Anthony Goerzen, "Managing Alliance Networks: Emerging Practices of Multinational Corporations," *Academy of Management Executive* 19, no. 2 (2005): 94–107.

37. Anjali Cordeiro, "Tang in India and Other Kraft Synergies," *The Wall Street Journal Online*, April 19, 2010, http://online.wsj.com/article/SB1000142405270230334850457518410310638886.html (accessed June 28, 2012); Lorrie Grant, "An 'Infinite' Opportunity for Growth: CEO Bob Nardelli Sees Expansion in Home Depot's Future," *USA Today*, July 28, 2005; Donald Greenlees, "Philip Morris to Buy Indonesian Cigarette Maker," *The New York Times*, March 14, 2005; and Tiisetso Motsoeneng and Wendell Roelf, "Wal-Mart Wins Final Go-Ahead for Massmart Deal," Reuters.com, March 9, 2012, www.reuters.com/article/2012/03/09/us-massmart-walmart-idUSBRE8280KH20120309 (accessed June 27, 2012).

38. Daniel Michaels, Jon Ostrower, and David Pearson, "Airbus's New Push: Made in the U.S.A.," *The Wall Street Journal*, July 2, 2012.

39. G. Pascal Zachary, "Dream Factory," *Business 2.0* (June 2005): 96–102.

40. Jim Holt, "Gone Global?" *Management Review* (March 2000): 13.

41. James Hookway, "IKEA's Products Make Shoppers Blush in Thailand," *The Wall Street Journal*, June 5, 2012, A1.

42. Holt, "Gone Global?"

43. "Slogans Often Lose Something in Translation," *The New Mexican*, July 3, 1994.

44. For a recent overview of various environmental factors influencing firms that operate internationally, see David Conklin, "The Global Environment of Business: New Paradigms for International Management," *Ivey Business Journal* (July–August 2011), www.iveybusinessjournal.com/topics/global-business/the-global-environment-of-business-new-paradigms-for-international-management (accessed June 27, 2012).

45. Louis S. Richman, "Global Growth Is on a Tear," in *International Business 97/98, Annual Editions*, ed. Fred Maidment (Guilford, CT: Dushkin Publishing Group, 1997), pp. 6–11.

46. "The Global Competitiveness Report 2011–2012," World Economic Forum, www3.weforum.org/docs/WEF_GCR_Report_2011-12.pdf (accessed June 27, 2012).

47. M. Walker, C. Forelle, and D. Gauthier-Villars, "Europe Bailout Lifts Gloom," *The Wall Street Journal*, May 11, 2010; and G. Bowley and C. Hauser, "Stocks Plunge on Fears of a Spreading European Crisis," *The New York Times*, May 21, 2010.

48. "A New Definition of Misery," *The New York Times*, December 18, 2009 (based on data from *Moody's*), www.nytimes.com/imagepages/2009/12/18/business/economy/20091219_CHARTS_GRAPHIC.html (accessed September 27, 2012).

49. Mike Ramsey and Yoshio Takahashi, "Car Wreck: Honda and Toyota," *The Wall Street Journal Online*, November 1, 2011, http://online.wsj.com/article/SB1000142405297020452820457700904417078765 0.html (accessed June 29, 2012); Stephanie Clifford, "Rattling Wal-Mart's Supply Chain," *International Herald Tribune*, June 1, 2011, 17.

50. Ian Bremmer, "Managing Risk in an Unstable World," *Harvard Business Review* (June 2005): 51–60; Mark Fitzpatrick, "The Definition and Assessment of Political Risk in International Business: A Review of the Literature," *Academy of Management Review* 8 (1983): 249–254; and Jo Jakobsen, "Old Problems Remain, New Ones Crop Up: Political Risk in the 21st Century," *Business Horizons* 53 (2010): 481–490.

51. John Markoff and David Barboza, "Inquiry Is Said to Link Attack on Google to Chinese Schools," *The New York Times*, February 19, 2010.

52. Peter Wonacott, "An Entrepreneur Weathers a Tumultuous Arab Spring," *The Wall Street Journal*, January 17, 2012, http://online.wsj.com/article/SB10001424052970203436904577150690233235850.html (accessed June 27, 2012).

53. Mary Gooderham, "Companies That Go Where Others Fear to Tread," *The Globe and Mail*, June 21, 2012, B7.

54. Geert Hofstede, *Culture's Consequences: International Differences in Work-Related Values* (Beverly Hills, CA: Sage, 1980); G. Hofstede, "The Interaction Between National and Organizational Value Systems," *Journal of Management Studies* 22 (1985): 347–357; and G. Hofstede, *Cultures and Organizations: Software of the Mind* (revised and expanded 2d ed.) (New York: McGraw-Hill, 2005).

55. Geert Hofstede, "Cultural Constraints in Management Theory," *Academy of Management Executive* 7 (1993): 81–94; and G. Hofstede and M. H. Bond, "The Confucian Connection: From Cultural Roots to Economic Growth," *Organizational Dynamics* 16 (1988): 4–21.

56. Vas Taras, Piers Steel, and Bradley L. Kirkman, "Three Decades of Research on National Culture in the Workplace: Do the Differences Still Make a Difference?" *Organizational Dynamics* 40 (2011): 189–198.

57. For an overview of the research and publications related to Hofstede's dimensions, see "Retrospective: *Culture's Consequences*," a collection of articles focusing on Hofstede's work, in *The Academy of Management Executive* 18, no. 1 (February 2004): 72–93. See also Michele J. Gelfand et al., "Individualism and Collectivism," in *Culture, Leadership and Organizations: The Globe Study of 62 Societies*, ed. R. J. House et al. (Thousand Oaks, CA: Sage, 2004).

58. Mansour Javidan et al., "In the Eye of the Beholder: Cross-Cultural Lessons from Project GLOBE," *Academy of Management Perspectives* (February 2006): 67–90; Robert J. House et al., eds., *Culture, Leadership, and Organizations: The GLOBE Study of 62 Societies* (Thousand Oaks, CA: Sage Publications, 2004); M. Javidan and R. J. House, "Cultural Acumen for the Global Manager: Lessons from Project GLOBE," *Organizational Dynamics* 29, no. 4 (2001): 289–305; and R. J. House et al., "Understanding Cultures and Implicit Leadership Theories Across the Globe: An Introduction to Project GLOBE," *Journal of World Business* 37 (2002): 3–10.

59. Carlos Sanchez-Runde et al., "Looking Beyond Western Leadership Models: Implications for Global Managers," *Organizational Dynamics* 40 (2011): 207–213.

60. Chantell E. Nicholls, Henry W. Lane, and Mauricio Brehm Brechu, "Taking Self-Managed Teams to Mexico," *Academy of Management Executive* 13, no. 2 (1999): 15–27; Carl F. Fey and Daniel R. Denison, "Organizational Culture and Effectiveness: Can American Theory Be Applied in Russia?" *Organization Science* 14, no. 6 (November–December 2003): 686–706; Ellen F. Jackofsky, John W. Slocum, Jr., and Sara J. McQuaid, "Cultural Values and the CEO: Alluring Companions?" *Academy of Management Executive* 2 (1988): 39–49.

61. J. Kennedy and A. Everest, "Put Diversity in Context," *Personnel Journal* (September 1991): 50–54.

62. Jane Spencer, "Lenovo Goes Global, But Not Without Strife," *The Wall Street Journal*, November 4, 2008.

63. Bob Davis, "As Global Economy Shifts, Companies Rethink, Retool," *The Wall Street Journal*, November 7,

2010, http://online.wsj.com/article/SB10001424052
74870404990457555429093215312.html (accessed
June 29, 2012).

64. David Barboza, "Apple Cracks the Code for Success in
China," *International Herald Tribune*, July 26, 2011, 15.

65. Loretta Chao, Lorraine Luk, and Aaron Back, "Sales of
iPhone in China Set Under 3-Year Accord," *The Wall
Street Journal*, August 31, 2009; and Loretta Chao,
Juliet Ye, and Yukari Iwatani Kane, "Apple, Facing
Competition, Readies iPhone for Launch in Giant
China Market," *The Wall Street Journal*, August 28,
2009.

66. George Stalk and David Michael, "What the West
Doesn't Get About China," *Harvard Business Review*
(June 2011): 25–27; Zoe McKay, "Consumer Spending
in China: To Buy or Not to Buy," *Forbes.com*, June 15,
2012, www.forbes.com/sites/insead/2012/06/15
/consumer-spending-in-china-to-buy-or-not-to-buy/
(accessed June 29, 2012); and Adam Davidson, "Come
On, China, Buy Our Stuff!" *The New York Times*,
January 25, 2012, www.nytimes.com/2012/01/29/
magazine/come-on-china-buy-our-stuff.html?
pagewanted=all (accessed June 29, 2012).

67. David Barboza and Brad Stone, "A Nation That Trips
up Many," *The New York Times*, January 16, 2010.

68. Andrew Galbraith and Jason Dean, "In China, Some
Firms Defy Business Norms," *The Wall Street Journal
Online*, September 6, 2011, http://online.wsj.com
/article/SB1000142405311190389590457654638151
2015722.html (accessed June 29, 2012).

69. Stalk and Michael, "What the West Doesn't Get About
China."

70. Chuck Salter, "Lenovo: Protect and Attack," *Fast
Company* (December 2011–January 2012): 116–121,
154–155.

71. W. Michael Cox and Richard Alm, "China and India:
Two Paths to Economic Power," *Economic Letter*,
Federal Reserve Bank of Dallas, August 2008, www
.dallasfed.org /research/eclett/2008/el0808.html
(accessed July 14, 2010).

72. "Pharmaceuticals," India Brand Equity Foundation, IBEF
.org, May 2012, www.ibef.org/industry/pharmaceuticals
.aspx (accessed June 29, 2012); and Sushmi Dey,
"Indian Pharma Eyes US Generic Gold Rush," *Business
Standard*, June 27, 2012, www.business-standard.com
/india/news/indian-pharma-eyes-us-generic-gold-
rush/478593/ (accessed June 29, 2012).

73. This section is based on "Brazil GDP Growth Rate,"
Trading Economics Website, www.tradingeconomics.
com/brazil/gdp-growth (accessed June 29, 2012);
"Brazil," The World Factbook, Central Intelligence
Agency Website, https://www.cia.gov/library/
publications/the-world-factbook/geos/br.html#top
(accessed June 29, 2012); Paulo Prada, "For Brazil, It's
Finally Tomorrow," *The Wall Street Journal*, March 29,

2010; Melanie Eversley, "Brazil's Olympian Growth,"
USA Today, October 5, 2009; and Liam Denning, "Are
Cracks Forming in the BRICs?" *The Wall Street Journal*,
February 16, 2010.

74. This discussion is based on "For Richer, for Poorer," *The
Economist* (December 1993): 66; Richard Harmsen,
"The Uruguay Round: A Boon for the World Economy,"
Finance & Development (March 1995): 24–26; Salil S.
Pitroda, "From GATT to WTO: The Institutionaliza-
tion of World Trade," *Harvard International Review*
(Spring 1995): 46–47, 66–67; and World Trade
Organization Web site, www.wto.org (accessed February
11, 2008).

75. EUROPA Web site, "The History of the European
Union," http://europa .eu/about-eu/eu-history/
index_en.htm (accessed July 14, 2010).

76. European Commission Economic and Financial Affairs
Web site, http://ec.europa.eu/economy_finance/euro
/index_en.htm (accessed March 18, 2010).

77. Clive Crook, "Opening Remarks: Who Lost the Euro?"
part of a "Special Euro Crisis" section, *Bloomberg
Businessweek* (May 28–June 3, 2012): 10–12; and
Howard Schneider, "In Greece, The Money Flowed
Freely, Until It Didn't," *The Washington Post*, June 14,
2012, www.washingtonpost.com/business/economy
/in-greece-the-money-flowed-freely-until-it-didnt
/2012/06/14/gJQA7Z4YcV_story.html (accessed
June 30, 2012).

78. Vanessa Fuhrmans and Dana Cimilluca, "Business Braces for Europe's Worst—Multinationals
Scramble to Protect Cash, Revise Contracts, Tighten
Payment Terms," *The Wall Street Journal*, June 1,
2012, B1.

79. Tapan Munroe, "NAFTA Still a Work in Progress,"
Knight Ridder/Tribune News Service, January 9, 2004;
and J. S. McClenahan, "NAFTA Works," *IW*
(January 10, 2000): 5–6.

80. Amy Barrett, "It's a Small (Business) World," *Business-
Week* (April 17, 1995): 96–101.

81. Eric Alterman, "A Spectacular Success?" *The Nation*
(February 2, 2004): 10; Jeff Faux, "NAFTA at 10:
Where Do We Go from Here?" *The Nation* (Febru-
ary 2, 2004): 11; Geri Smith and Cristina Lindblad,
"Mexico: Was NAFTA Worth It? A Tale of What
Free Trade Can and Cannot Do," *BusinessWeek*
(December 22, 2003): 66; Jeffrey Sparshott, "NAFTA
Gets Mixed Reviews," *The Washington Times*, Decem-
ber 18, 2003; and Munroe, "NAFTA Still a Work in
Progress."

82. Darrell Rigby and Barbara Bilodeau, "Management
Tools and Trends 2011," Bain & Company, Inc.,
www.bain.com/publications/articles/Management-
tools-trends-2011.aspx (accessed June 22, 2012).

83. Munroe, "NAFTA Still a Work in Progress"; Sparshott,
"NAFTA Gets Mixed Reviews"; and Amy Borrus, "A

Free-Trade Milestone, with Many More Miles to Go," *Business Week* (August 24, 1992): 30–31.

84. Based in part on "How Well Do You Exhibit Good Inter-cultural Management Skills?" in John W. Newstrom and Keith Davis, *Organizational Behavior: Human Behavior at Work* (Boston, MA: McGraw-Hill Irwin, 2002), pp. 415–416.

85. Based on Paul Beamish, "Where Have You Been? An Exercise to Assess Your Exposure to the Rest of the World's Peoples," August 25, 2008, Richard Ivey School of Business, the University of Western Ontario, available for purchase at Ivey Publishing, https://www.iveycases.com/ProductView.aspx?id=52899.

2

ENVIRONMENT

Ethics and Social Responsibility

Christian Mueller/Shutterstock.com

Learning Outcomes

After studying this chapter, you should be able to:

1. Define ethics and explain how ethical behavior relates to behavior governed by law and free choice.

2. Discuss why ethics is important for managers and identify recent events that call for a renewed commitment to ethical management.

3. Explain the utilitarian, individualism, moral rights, justice, and practical approaches for making ethical decisions.

4. Describe the factors that shape a manager's ethical decision making, including levels of moral development.

5. Identify important stakeholders for an organization and discuss how managers balance the interests of various stakeholders.

6. Explain the philosophy of sustainability and why organizations are embracing it.

7. Describe what is meant by "the triple bottom line."

8. Define corporate social responsibility and how to evaluate it along economic, legal, ethical, and discretionary criteria.

9. Discuss how ethical organizations are created through ethical leadership and organizational structures and systems.

1 INTRODUCTION
2 ENVIRONMENT
3 PLANNING
4 ORGANIZING
5 LEADING
6 CONTROLLING

Will You Be a Courageous Manager?

http: See It Online www.

INSTRUCTIONS: It probably won't happen right away, but soon enough in your duties as a new manager, you will be confronted with a situation that will test the strength of your moral beliefs or your sense of justice. Are you ready? To find out, think about times when you were part of a student or work group. To what extent does each of the following statements characterize your behavior? Please answer each of the following items as Mostly True or Mostly False for you.

	Mostly True	Mostly False
1. I risked substantial personal loss to achieve a vision.	_____	_____
2. I took personal risks to defend my beliefs.	_____	_____
3. I would say no to inappropriate things, even if I had a lot to lose.	_____	_____
4. My significant actions were linked to higher values.	_____	_____
5. I easily acted against the opinions and approval of others.	_____	_____
6. I quickly told people the truth as I saw it, even when it was negative.	_____	_____
7. I spoke out against group or organizational injustice.	_____	_____
8. I acted according to my conscience, even if I could lose stature.	_____	_____

SCORING AND INTERPRETATION: Each of these questions pertains to some aspect of displaying courage in a group situation, which often reflects a person's level of moral development. Count the number of checks for Mostly True. If you scored 5 or more, congratulations! That behavior would enable you to become a courageous manager about moral issues. A score below 4 indicates that you may avoid difficult issues or have not been in situations that challenged your moral courage.

Study the specific questions for which you scored Mostly True and Mostly False to learn more about your specific strengths and weaknesses. Think about what influences your moral behavior and decisions, such as need for success or approval. Study the behavior of others whom you consider to be moral individuals. How might you increase your courage as a new manager?

W hat does courage have to do with a chapter on ethics? If you read articles about the U.S. Secret Service prostitution scandal, the subprime mortgage mess in the United States, the implosion of financial icons such as Lehman Brothers and Bear Stearns, or the child sexual abuse case against former Pennsylvania State University defensive coordinator Jerry Sandusky, it soon becomes apparent. These organizations not only had managers behaving unethically, but they also had plenty of managers who thought the behavior was wrong but lacked the courage to challenge their superiors or call attention to the misdeeds.

Unfortunately, many managers slide into unethical or even illegal behavior simply because they don't have the courage to stand up and do the right thing. Lack of courage isn't the only problem, of course. Managers and organizations engage in unethical behavior for any number of reasons, such as personal ego, greed, or pressures to increase profits or appear successful. Mark Hurd was fired as CEO of Hewlett-Packard after an investigation revealed that he submitted inaccurate expense reports in an attempt to cover up an inappropriate relationship with a female contractor.[1] Interviews with people in the mortgage wholesale industry reveal that many wholesalers (who work for banks and buy loan applications from independent mortgage brokers) operated from pure greed.

HOT TOPIC

They frequently altered documents, coached brokers on how to skirt the rules, and even offered bribes and sexual favors to generate more loans—and thus more profits. And the CEO of Yahoo!, Scott Thompson, resigned under pressure after only four months on the job because reports revealed he had inaccurately claimed on his resume that he had a degree in computer science. Moreover, Thompson initially tried to blame the inaccuracy on the executive search firm that had placed him in an earlier job at PayPal. "The cover-up became worse than the crime," said one person familiar with the fiasco.[2]

This chapter expands on the ideas about environment, corporate culture, and the international environment discussed in Chapters 3 and 4. We first focus on the topic of ethical values, which builds on the idea of corporate culture. We look at the current ethical climate in corporate America, examine fundamental approaches that can help managers think through difficult ethical issues, and consider various factors that influence how managers make ethical choices. Understanding these ideas will help you build a solid foundation on which to base future decision making. We also examine organizational relationships to the external environment as reflected in corporate social responsibility. The final section of the chapter describes how managers build an ethical organization using codes of ethics and other organizational policies, structures, and systems.

What Is Managerial Ethics?

Ethics is difficult to define in a precise way. In a general sense, **ethics** is the code of moral principles and values that governs the behaviors of a person or group with respect to what is right or wrong. Ethics sets standards as to what is good or bad in conduct and decision making.[3] An ethical issue is present in a situation when the actions of a person or organization may harm or benefit others.[4] Yet ethical issues sometimes can be exceedingly complex. People may hold widely divergent views about the most ethically appropriate or inappropriate actions related to a situation.[5]

Consider the issue of competitive intelligence. Companies are increasingly using social media sites to learn more about their competition, some even going so far as to "friend" customers or employees of rivals and post seemingly innocuous questions to gather information that can provide them with a competitive advantage.[6] The laws regarding information gathering aren't clear-cut, and neither are opinions regarding the ethics of such tactics. What do you think? Whereas some people think any form of corporate spying is wrong, others think it is an acceptable way of learning about the competition.[7] Managers frequently face situations in which it is difficult to determine what is right. In addition, they might be torn between their misgivings and their sense of duty to their bosses and the organization.

Ethics can be more clearly understood when compared with behaviors governed by law and by free choice. Exhibit 5.1 illustrates that human behavior falls into three categories. The first is codified law, in which values and standards are written into the legal system and enforceable in the courts. In this area, lawmakers set rules that people and corporations

EXHIBIT   **5.1**

Three Domains of Human Action

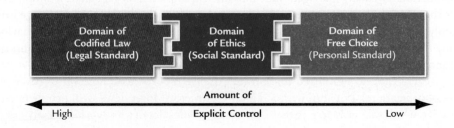

must follow in a certain way, such as obtaining licenses for cars, paying corporate taxes, or following other local, state, and national laws. For example, former vice chairman of Walmart, Thomas Coughlin, pleaded guilty to fraud and tax evasion charges. Coughlin resigned in 2005 amid allegations that he defrauded the giant retailer out of hundreds of thousands of dollars, and the investigation was turned over to federal prosecutors.[8] Behaviors such as fraud and tax evasion are clearly against the law. The domain of free choice is at the opposite end of the scale and pertains to behavior about which the law has no say and for which an individual or organization enjoys complete freedom. An example is a manager's choice of where to buy a new suit, or an organization's choice of which of two well-qualified candidates to hire for an open position.

Between these domains lies the area of ethics. This domain has no specific laws, yet it does have standards of conduct based on shared principles and values about moral conduct that guide an individual or company. For example, it is not

▶ ▶ ▶ **Concept Connection**

Goldman Sachs CEO Lloyd Blankfein (center) was on the hot seat as he defended the firm's role in creating Abacus, a mortgage-backed investment fund allegedly designed to fail. While Goldman bet against the fund as a way to hedge against a weakening housing market, its trading side facilitated sales of Abacus to institutional customers. The maneuver helped Goldman weather the financial crisis but raised serious questions about its **managerial ethics**. Blankfein said that the firm's trading side is simply "a machine that lets people buy and sell what they want to buy and sell." Despite this defense, Goldman agreed in 2010 to pay $550 million to settle federal claims that it misled investors.

illegal for a manager like Harry Stonecipher, former CEO of Boeing, to have an extramarital affair with a female executive, but his behavior violated Boeing's code of ethical conduct, and Stonecipher was replaced. However, a manager who commits sexual harassment is not just being unethical but is breaking U.S. laws. Steven J. Heyer was fired as CEO of Starwood Hotels & Resorts Worldwide Inc. after the board received an anonymous letter that accused Heyer of inappropriately touching female employees and creating a hostile work environment.[9]

Many companies and individuals get into trouble with the simplified view that decisions are governed by either law or free choice. This view leads people to mistakenly assume that if it's not illegal, it must be ethical, as if there were no third domain.[10] A better option is to recognize the domain of ethics and accept moral values as a powerful force for good that can regulate behaviors both inside and outside organizations.

Remember This

- Managers face many pressures that can sometimes tempt them to engage in unethical behavior.
- **Ethics** is the code of moral principles and values that governs the behaviors of a person or group with respect to what is right or wrong.
- Just because managers aren't breaking the law doesn't necessarily mean they are being ethical.

- An ethical issue is present in any situation when the actions of an individual or organization may harm or benefit others.
- Managers sometimes need courage to stand up and do the right thing.

Ethical Management Today

Every decade seems to experience its share of scoundrels, but the pervasiveness of ethical lapses during the first decade or so of this century has been astounding. In Gallup's 2010 poll regarding the perception of business leaders, just 15 percent of respondents rated leaders' honesty and ethical standards as "high" or "very high."[11] Although public confidence in business managers in particular is at an all-time low, politics, sports, and nonprofit organizations also have been affected. Cycling star Lance Armstrong was stripped of his seven Tour de France championship titles after an investigation showed that he used performance-enhancing drugs and gave them to teammates. At the nonprofit Wyckoff Heights Medical Center, located in one of the poorest neighborhoods in Brooklyn, an investigation revealed a pattern of insider dealing that lavishly benefited top managers, board members, and local politicians, while damaging the organization to the point that it might be closed, further limiting health care options for the poor.[12] And the Catholic Church, already reeling from two decades of clergy sexual abuse scandals, was further tarnished when Pope Benedict XVI's butler, Paolo Gabriele, was arrested and charged with leaking the pope's confidential correspondence that revealed internal conflicts and accusations of cronyism and corruption.[13]

In the business world, the names of once-revered corporations have become synonymous with greed, deceit, irresponsibility, and lack of moral conscience: AIG, Lehman Brothers, Enron, Bear Stearns, Countrywide, WorldCom. No wonder a poll found that 76 percent of people surveyed say corporate America's moral compass is "pointing in the wrong direction"; 69 percent say executives rarely consider the public good in making decisions; and a whopping 94 percent say executives make decisions based primarily on advancing their own careers.[14]

Managers carry a tremendous responsibility for setting the ethical climate in an organization and can act as role models for others.[15] Managers are responsible for seeing that resources are used to serve the interests of stakeholders, including shareholders, employees, customers, and society. Exhibit 5.2 details various ways that organizations sometimes behave unethically toward customers, employees, and other stakeholders.[16] Unfortunately, in today's environment, an overemphasis on pleasing shareholders may cause some managers to behave unethically toward customers, employees, and the broader society. Managers are under enormous pressure to meet short-term earnings goals, and some even use accounting gimmicks or other techniques to show returns that meet market expectations rather than ones that reflect true performance. Moreover, most executive compensation plans include hefty stock-based incentives, a practice that encourages managers to do whatever will increase the share price, even if it hurts the company in the long run. When managers "fall prey to the siren call of shareholder value," all other stakeholders may suffer.[17]

Executive compensation has become a hot-button issue.[18] In 2011, the average pay of CEOs at large U.S. corporations was 380 times what the average employee was paid. A study by the Economic Policy Institute found that between 1978 and 2011, the average worker's annual pay grew 5.7 percent, while average CEO pay increased a whopping 726.7 percent.[19] The question of whether it is ethical for managers to rake in huge sums of money compared to other employees is of growing concern, and in general, the widespread ethical lapses of the past decade have put managers under increasing scrutiny.

Take a Moment

Review your responses to the questions at the beginning of this chapter, which will give you some insight into your own level of manager courage. A high level of courage can help managers make ethical choices in the face of opposition or pressure from others.

> "The bottom line is that when shareholder value capitalism is paramount, the rest of us suffer. CEOs will readily dupe customers, sack employees, and spoil the environment to meet expectations."
>
> — ROGER MARTIN, DEAN AND PROFESSOR AT THE ROTMAN SCHOOL OF MANAGEMENT, TORONTO

HOT TOPIC

EXHIBIT | **5.2** | Examples of Unethical and Illegal Organizational Behavior

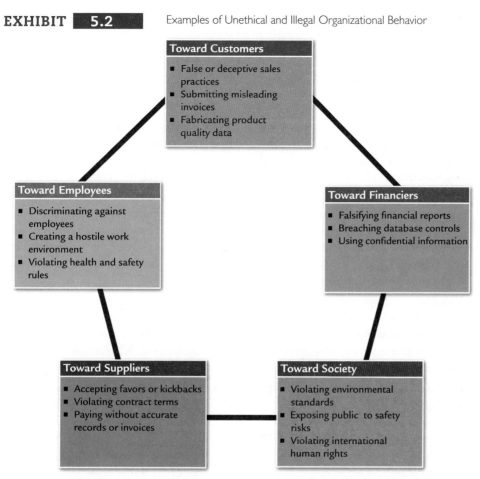

Toward Customers
- False or deceptive sales practices
- Submitting misleading invoices
- Fabricating product quality data

Toward Employees
- Discriminating against employees
- Creating a hostile work environment
- Violating health and safety rules

Toward Financiers
- Falsifying financial reports
- Breaching database controls
- Using confidential information

Toward Suppliers
- Accepting favors or kickbacks
- Violating contract terms
- Paying without accurate records or invoices

Toward Society
- Violating environmental standards
- Exposing public to safety risks
- Violating international human rights

SOURCE: Based on Muel Kaptein, "Developing a Measure of Unethical Behavior in the Workplace: A Stakeholder Perspective," *Journal of Management* 34, no. 5 (October 2008): 978–1008.

Remember This

- Managers are ethically responsible for seeing that organizational resources are used to serve the interests of stakeholders, including shareholders, employees, customers, and the broader society.
- Unethical managers seek to serve their own needs and interests at the expense of stakeholders.

- Confidence in business managers and leaders in all walks of life is at an all-time low.
- One hot-button ethical issue concerns excessive executive compensation.

Ethical Dilemmas: What Would You Do?

Being ethical is always about making decisions, and some issues are difficult to resolve. Although most companies have codes of ethics that specify expected behavior, disagreements and dilemmas about what is appropriate often occur. An **ethical dilemma** arises in a situation concerning right or wrong when values are in conflict.[20] Right and wrong cannot be clearly identified.

The individual who must make an ethical choice in an organization is the *moral agent*.[21] Here are some dilemmas that a manager in an organization might face. Think about how you would handle them:

1. Your small company has clear procedures for providing supplies to employees who choose to work from home, as well as a strict code of conduct specifying that any employee caught taking supplies without authorization will be fired. At the end of a long hard day, you notice Sarah, one of your best employees, putting printer paper, highlighters, and notepads in her laptop bag. According to company policy, you are required to report her immediately to your superior, who is the only one who can authorize employees taking supplies. But your boss is gone for the day, and you know Sarah often works from home.[22]

2. As a sales manager for a major pharmaceuticals company, you've been asked to promote a new drug that costs $2,500 per dose. You've read the reports saying the drug is only 1 percent more effective than an alternative drug that costs less than $625 per dose. The vice president of sales wants you to promote the $2,500-per-dose drug aggressively. He reminds you that if you don't, lives could be lost that might have been saved with that 1 percent increase in the drug's effectiveness.

3. You work at a large corporation that requires a terrorist watch list screening for all new customers, which takes approximately 24 hours from the time an order is placed. You can close a lucrative deal with a potential long-term customer if you agree to ship the products overnight, even though that means the required watch list screening will have to be done after the fact.[23]

4. On the train ride from your home in Ipswich to your office in London, your peaceful morning routine is disturbed by neighboring passengers carrying on a loud mobile business meeting. After trying to quiet them with cold stares, you eventually decide to just listen in. Within minutes, you realize they are discussing a client that your own firm has been courting. Furthermore, you soon have the time, phone number, and passcode for a conference call the consultants are having with the client later that day. It isn't your fault that they gave out that information in a public place, but you wonder what you should do with it.[24]

These kinds of dilemmas and issues fall squarely in the domain of ethics. How would you handle each of the above situations? Now consider the following hypothetical dilemma, which scientists are using to study human morality:[25]

- A runaway trolley is heading down the tracks toward five unsuspecting people. You're standing near a switch that will divert the trolley onto a siding, but there is a single workman on the siding who cannot be warned in time to escape and almost certainly will be killed. Would you throw the switch?

- Now, what if the workman is standing on a bridge over the tracks and you have to push him off the bridge to stop the trolley with his body in order to save the five unsuspecting people? (Assume that his body is large enough to stop the trolley, and yours is not.) Would you push the man, even though he almost certainly will be killed?

These dilemmas show how complex questions of ethics and morality can sometimes be. In *Time* magazine's readers' poll, 97 percent of respondents said they could throw the switch (which would almost certainly lead to the death of the workman), but only 42 percent said they could actually push the man to his death.[26]

Remember This

- Ethics is about making choices.
- Most managers encounter ethical dilemmas that are tough to resolve.

- An **ethical dilemma** is a situation in which all alternative choices or behaviors have potentially negative consequences. Right and wrong cannot be clearly distinguished.

Criteria for Ethical Decision Making

Most ethical dilemmas involve a conflict between the needs of the part and the whole—the individual versus the organization or the organization versus society as a whole. For example, should a company scrutinize job candidates' or employees' social media postings, which might benefit the organization as a whole but reduce the individual freedom of employees? Or should products that fail to meet tough Food and Drug Administration (FDA) standards be exported to other countries where government standards are lower, benefiting the company but potentially harming world citizens? Sometimes ethical decisions entail a conflict between two groups. For example, should the potential for local health problems resulting from a company's effluents take precedence over the jobs it creates as the town's leading employer?

Managers faced with these kinds of tough ethical choices often benefit from a normative strategy—one based on norms and values—to guide their decision making. Normative ethics uses several approaches to describe values for guiding ethical decision making. Five approaches that are relevant to managers are the utilitarian approach, individualism approach, moral-rights approach, justice approach, and practical approach.[27]

Utilitarian Approach

The **utilitarian approach**, espoused by the nineteenth-century philosophers Jeremy Bentham and John Stuart Mill, holds that moral behavior produces the greatest good for the greatest number. Under this approach, a decision maker is expected to consider the effect of each decision alternative on all parties and select the one that optimizes the benefits for the greatest number of people. In the trolley dilemma earlier in this chapter, for instance, the utilitarian approach would hold that it would be moral to push one person to his death in order to save five. The utilitarian ethic is cited as the basis for the recent trend among companies to monitor employee use of the Internet and police personal habits such as alcohol and tobacco consumption, because such behavior affects the entire workplace.[28]

Individualism Approach

The **individualism approach** contends that acts are moral when they promote the individual's best long-term interests.[29] In theory, with everyone pursuing self-direction, the greater good is ultimately served because people learn to accommodate each other in their own long-term interest. Individualism is believed to lead to honesty and integrity because that works best in the long run. Lying and cheating for immediate self-interest just causes business associates to lie and cheat in return. Thus, proponents say, individualism ultimately leads to behavior toward others that fits standards of behavior that people want toward themselves.[30] However, because individualism is easily misinterpreted to support immediate self-gain, it is not popular in the highly organized and group-oriented society of today.

Moral-Rights Approach

The **moral-rights approach** asserts that human beings have fundamental rights and liberties that cannot be taken away by an individual's decision. Thus, an ethically correct

▶▶▶ **Concept Connection**

Protective Life Corporation

Protective Life Corporation shows its commitment to ethics through its corporate strategy: "Offer great products at highly competitive prices and provide the kind of attentive service we'd hope to get from others." Treating others the way you want to be treated is one approach to making ethically responsible decisions and handling **ethical dilemmas**. However, insurance companies often have to rely on a **utilitarian approach** to ethical decision making that considers how to provide the greatest good to the greatest number of policyholders.

decision is one that best maintains the rights of those affected by it. To make ethical decisions, managers need to avoid interfering with the fundamental rights of others, such as the right to privacy, the right of free consent, or the right to freedom of speech. Performing experimental treatments on unconscious trauma patients, for example, might be construed to violate the right to free consent. A decision to monitor employees' nonwork activities violates the right to privacy. The right of free speech would support whistle-blowers who call attention to illegal or inappropriate actions within a company.

Justice Approach

The **justice approach** holds that moral decisions must be based on standards of equity, fairness, and impartiality. Three types of justice are of concern to managers. **Distributive justice** requires that different treatment of people not be based on arbitrary characteristics. For example, men and women should not receive different salaries if they have the same qualifications and are performing the same job. **Procedural justice** requires that rules be administered fairly. Rules should be clearly stated and consistently and impartially enforced. **Compensatory justice** argues that individuals should be compensated for the cost of their injuries by the party responsible. The justice approach is closest to the thinking underlying the domain of law in Exhibit 5.1 because it assumes that justice is applied through rules and regulations. Managers are expected to define attributes on which different treatment of employees is acceptable.

Practical Approach

The approaches discussed so far presume to determine what is "right" or good in a moral sense. However, as has been mentioned, ethical issues are frequently not clear-cut and there are disagreements over what is the ethical choice. The **practical approach** sidesteps debates about what is right, good, or just and bases decisions on prevailing standards of the profession and the larger society, taking the interests of all stakeholders into account.[31] The decision of Paula Reid, the manager who set the U.S. Secret Service prostitution scandal in motion by reporting the misconduct of agents in Cartagena, Colombia, was based largely on the practical approach.

Innovative Way

Paula Reid, U.S. Secret Service

Put aside the issue of whether it is morally wrong to hire a prostitute, particularly in a country where prostitution is legal in certain areas. The bottom line for Paula Reid is that visits to strip clubs, heavy drinking, and payments to prostitutes are not acceptable behavior for Secret Service agents charged with protecting the president of the United States.

"If every boss was Paula Reid," said a former agent, "the Secret Service would never have a problem. It would be a lot more boring, but never a problem." Reid, the new supervising manager for the Miami office, a prestigious division that oversees the South American region, acted swiftly when she received a report of a disturbance at the hotel where agents preparing for President Barack Obama's visit to Cartagena were staying. Based on information from the hotel manager, Reid swiftly rounded up a dozen agents, ordered them out of the country, and notified her superiors that she had found evidence of "egregious misconduct." She acted in spite of a potential internal backlash because she believed the actions of the agents had both hurt the agency's reputation and damaged its ability to fulfill its protective and investigative missions.

The resulting scandal threw the Secret Service into turmoil and put Director Mark Sullivan and other managers on the hot seat. Four of the agents dismissed for engaging in inappropriate conduct have since challenged their dismissals, saying they are being made scapegoats for behavior that the agency has long tolerated so long as there is no breach of operational security. Yet, for Reid and others, the "boys will be boys" mentality is not acceptable in today's world. According to former director Ralph Basham, there are many former and current agents who are "deeply ashamed of what these people did."[32]

With the practical approach, a decision would be considered ethical if it is one that would be considered acceptable by the professional community, one that the manager would not hesitate to publicize on the evening news, and one that a person would typically feel comfortable explaining to family and friends. One Secret Service agency director offered this practical advice to his staff in a recent memo: "You should always assume you are being watched when on an official assignment. Do not put yourself in a situation in your personal or professional life that would cause embarrassment to you, your family, or the Secret Service."[33] Using the practical approach, managers may combine elements of the utilitarian, moral rights, and justice approaches in their thinking and decision making. For example, one expert on business ethics suggests managers can ask themselves the following five questions to help resolve ethical dilemmas.[34] Note that these questions cover a variety of the approaches discussed above.

1. What's in it for me?
2. What decision would lead to the greatest good for the greatest number?
3. What rules, policies, or social norms apply?
4. What are my obligations to others?
5. What will be the long term impact for myself and important stakeholders?

Remember This

- Most ethical dilemmas involve a conflict between the interests of different groups or between the needs of the individual versus the needs of the organization.
- Managers can use various approaches based on norms and values to help them make ethical decisions.
- The **utilitarian approach** to ethical decision making says that the ethical choice is the one that produces the greatest good for the greatest number.
- The **individualism approach** suggests that actions are ethical when they promote the individual's best long-term interests, because with everyone pursuing self-interest, the greater good is ultimately served.
- The individualism approach is not considered appropriate today because it is easily misused to support one's personal gain at the expense of others.
- Some managers rely on a **moral-rights approach**, which holds that ethical decisions are those that best maintain the fundamental rights of the people affected by them.
- The **justice approach** says that ethical decisions must be based on standards of equity, fairness, and impartiality.
- **Distributive justice** requires that different treatment of individuals not be based on arbitrary characteristics.
- **Procedural justice** holds that rules should be clearly stated and consistently and impartially enforced.
- **Compensatory justice** argues that individuals should be compensated for the cost of their injuries by the party responsible, and individuals should not be held responsible for matters over which they have no control.
- Many managers also use the **practical approach**, which sidesteps debates about what is right, good, or just, and bases decisions on prevailing standards of the profession and the larger society, taking the interests of all stakeholders into account.

The Individual Manager and Ethical Choices

A number of factors influence a manager's ability to make ethical decisions. Individuals bring specific personality and behavioral traits to the job. Personal needs, family influence, and religious background all shape a manager's value system. In addition, the corporate culture and pressures from superiors and colleagues can also influence an individual's ethical choices. A recent study found that organizational pressures can indeed induce employees to behave unethically. Moreover, when people experience organizational pressure to go against their sense of what is right, they typically become frustrated and emotionally exhausted.[35] Clearly, unethical behavior inhibits a person's ability to do his or her best for the company, as well

EXHIBIT 5.3 Three Levels of Personal Moral Development

Level 1 Preconventional	Level 2 Conventional	Level 3 Postconventional
Follows rules to avoid punishment. Acts in own interest. Obedience for its own sake.	Lives up to expectations of others. Fulfills duties and obligations of social system. Upholds laws.	Follows self-chosen principles of justice and right. Aware that people hold different values and seeks creative solutions to ethical dilemmas. Balances concern for individual with concern for common good.
← Self-Interest	Societal Expectations	Internal Values →

Leader Style:	Autocratic/coercive	Guiding/encouraging, team oriented	Transforming, or servant leadership
Employee Behavior:	Task accomplishment	Work group collaboration	Empowered employees, full participation

SOURCE: Based on L. Kohlberg, "Moral Stages and Moralization: The Cognitive-Developmental Approach," in *Moral Development and Behavior: Theory, Research, and Social Issues*, ed. T. Lickona (New York: Holt, Rinehart, and Winston, 1976), pp. 31–53; and Jill W. Graham, "Leadership, Moral Development, and Citizenship Behavior," *Business Ethics Quarterly* 5, no. 1 (January 1995): 43–54.

as hindering the individual's personal and professional well-being. Specific personality characteristics, such as ego strength, self-confidence, and a strong sense of independence, may enable managers to make more-ethical choices despite outside pressures and personal risks.

One important personal trait is the stage of moral development.[36] A simplified version of one model of personal moral development is shown in Exhibit 5.3.

At the *preconventional level*, individuals are concerned with external rewards and punishments and obey authority to avoid detrimental personal consequences. In an organizational context, this level may be associated with managers who use an autocratic or coercive leadership style, with employees oriented toward dependable accomplishment of specific tasks.

At level two, called the *conventional level*, people learn to conform to the expectations of good behavior as defined by colleagues, family, friends, and society. Meeting social and interpersonal obligations is important. Work-group collaboration is the preferred manner of accomplishing organizational goals, and managers use a leadership style that encourages interpersonal relationships and cooperation.

At the *postconventional*, or *principled* level, individuals are guided by an internal set of values based on universal principles of justice and right and will even disobey rules or laws that violate these principles. Internal values become more important than the expectations of significant others. One recent example of the postconventional or principled approach was the lifeguard in Hallandale Beach, Florida, who was fired for leaving his assigned zone to help a drowning man. Tomas Lopez rushed

Concept Connection ◄◄◄

In many cases, the people of Africa have relatively few natural resources to use in creating goods to sell. Fortunately, some business leaders, functioning at the **postconventional level of moral development**, have been inspired to help African entrepreneurs create opportunities for themselves, either through microfinancing or through nonprofit organizations. The Africa InKNITiative is just one example. The organization provides Ugandan widows and refugees with raw materials for knitting scarves out of old T-shirts. The scarves are then shipped to the United States, where they're sold, and the proceeds go back to the women in Uganda.

Courtesy of African inKNITiative

to offer assistance when he saw a man struggling, even though his supervisor ordered him not to leave his zone and to call 911 instead. "What he did was his own decision," said manager Susan Ellis. "He knew the rules." The company cited liability issues as the reason for the rules, and later offered Lopez his job back (he refused).[37] When managers operate from this highest level of development, they use transformative or servant leadership, focusing on the needs of followers and encouraging others to think for themselves and to engage in higher levels of moral reasoning. Employees are empowered and given opportunities for constructive participation in governance of the organization.

The great majority of managers operate at level two, meaning their ethical thought and behavior is greatly influenced by their superiors, colleagues, and other significant people in the organization or industry. A few have not advanced beyond level one. Only about 20 percent of American adults reach the level-three postconventional stage of moral development. People at level three are able to act in an independent, ethical manner regardless of expectations from others inside or outside the organization. Managers at level three of moral development will make ethical decisions whatever the organizational consequences are for them.

Take a Moment

Complete the New Manager Self-Test below to assess your capacity for servant leadership, which is related to a high level of moral development.

ENVIRONMENT 2

New Manager Self-Test

Servant Leadership

Managers differ in how they view other people and the tactics they use to get things done. Respond to the items below based on how you view yourself and others. Please answer whether each item is Mostly True or Mostly False for you.

	Mostly True	Mostly False
1. My actions meet the needs of others before my own needs.		
2. I am always offering a helping hand to those around me.		
3. I give away credit and recognition to others.		
4. I tend to feel competitive with my coworkers.		
5. I often interrupt someone to make my point.		
6. I encourage the growth of others, expecting nothing in return.		
7. I like to be of service to others.		
8. Giving makes me happier than receiving.		
9. I reach out to orient new people even though it is not required.		

Scoring and Interpretation: Sum questions 1–3 and 6–9 with one point for each Mostly True, and sum questions 4–5 with one point for each Mostly False. Your score pertains to a concept that was introduced by Robert Greenleaf in his book, *Servant Leadership*. Servant leadership means that managers try to place service to others before self-interest, listen as a way to care about others, and nourish others to help them become whole. This approach to management was based on Greenleaf's Quaker beliefs. A score of 7–9 would be considered high on servant leadership, and 0–3 low, with a score of 4–6 in the middle range. How do you feel about your score? Are you attracted to the qualities of servant leadership, or would you prefer a different approach to managing others?

Source: Based on Robert Greenleaf, *Servant Leadership: A Journey into the Nature of Legitimate Power and Greatness*, 25th anniversary ed. (New York: Paulist Press, 2002).

Remember This

- Organizational pressures can influence people to go against their own sense of right or wrong, and the resulting stress can lead to mental exhaustion and burnout.
- Personality characteristics, family influence, religious background, and other factors influence a manager's ability to make ethical choices.

- One important factor is whether a manager is at a preconventional, conventional, or postconventional level of moral development.
- Most managers operate at a *conventional level*, conforming to standards of behavior expected by society.
- Only about 20 percent of adults reach the *postconventional level* and are able to act in an independent, ethical manner regardless of the expectations of others.

What Is Corporate Social Responsibility?

Now let's turn to the issue of corporate social responsibility. In one sense, the concept of social responsibility, like ethics, is easy to understand: It means distinguishing right from wrong and doing right. It means being a good corporate citizen. The formal definition of **corporate social responsibility (CSR)** is management's obligation to make choices and take actions that will contribute to the welfare and interests of society, not just the organization.[38]

As straightforward as this definition seems, CSR can be a difficult concept to grasp because different people have different beliefs as to which actions improve society's welfare.[39] To make matters worse, social responsibility covers a range of issues, many of which are ambiguous with respect to right or wrong. If a bank deposits the money from a trust fund into a low-interest account for 90 days, from which it makes a substantial profit, is it being a responsible corporate citizen? How about two companies engaging in intense competition? Is it socially responsible for the stronger corporation to drive the weaker one out of business or into a forced merger? Or consider General Motors (GM), Kmart, Lehman Brothers, and the numerous other companies that have declared bankruptcy in recent years—which is perfectly legal—and thus avoided having to meet their mounting financial obligations to suppliers, labor unions, or competitors. These examples contain moral, legal, and economic complexities that make socially responsible behavior hard to define.

ORGANIZATIONAL STAKEHOLDERS

One reason for the difficulty of understanding and applying CSR is that managers must confront the question, "Responsibility to whom?" Recall from Chapter 3 that the organization's environment consists of several sectors in both the task and the general environment. From a social responsibility perspective, enlightened organizations view the internal and external environment as a variety of stakeholders.

A **stakeholder** is any group or person within or outside the organization that has some type of investment or interest in the organization's performance and is affected by the organization's actions (employees, customers, shareholders, and so forth). Each stakeholder has a different criterion of responsiveness because it has a different interest in the organization.[40] There is growing interest in a technique called **stakeholder mapping**, which basically provides a systematic way to identify the expectations, needs, importance, and relative power of various stakeholders, which may change over time.[41] Stakeholder mapping helps managers identify or prioritize the key stakeholders related to a specific issue or project. For instance, Gap Inc., struggling to cope with the turmoil created after the company was targeted by protesters for using contractors that polluted the environment and engaged in child labor practices, decided to use mapping to identify key stakeholders with which the firm could develop deeper, transparent relationships.

Innovative Way

Gap Inc.

ENVIRONMENT **2**

When reports surfaced in 2009 that a contractor in Lesotho, Africa, making clothing for Gap Inc. and other U.S. companies was dumping toxic materials into local landfills and discharging chemicals into the Caledon River, Gap managers swung into action. A similar crisis related to child labor and unsafe conditions ten years earlier had resulted in global protests that raged for months and tarnished Gap's reputation, damaged employee morale, and devastated the firm's performance. In contrast, the 2009 Lesotho story died down quickly and Gap came out stronger on the other side.

What happened in those ten years to make a difference? It's certainly not that the public was less outraged by the stories of poor children being harmed by dangerous chemicals while playing near the river or scavenging through refuse. The result was different this time because Gap managers had carefully cultivated open relationships with labor groups, human rights organizations, trade unions, nongovernmental organizations, and other stakeholders that enabled them to swing into action immediately and take specific steps to solve the problem. In the past, managers' approach would have been to deny responsibility and blame the subcontractor. With the Lesotho incident, though, Gap's top leaders immediately stepped forward to declare the company's commitment to fair and safe conditions and outline the steps it would take. The company later joined Levi Strauss, which also had clothing made by this contractor, to issue a statement detailing actions that had been taken or were in progress. Because of the relationships Gap had developed with numerous stakeholder groups, the company had the support of labor and human rights organizations, which praised managers' commitment and actions.

Gap embarked on the process of engaging with key stakeholders because even though the company had made a strong commitment to social and environmental responsibility since 1992, the previous approach wasn't working. Multimillion-dollar efforts at solving ethical problems in the supply chain had failed. So, managers started by drawing a stakeholder map that listed as many stakeholders as possible, then ranked them by their importance. Starting with mapping gave managers a way to focus their efforts and join with the most influential stakeholders to improve labor practices. It was a long and difficult journey, but the results have been well worth it. The company has received awards and public recognition as a leader in ethics and social responsibility.[42]

The global supply chain is a source of ongoing challenges for managers today. As Dan Rees, former director of the Ethical Trading Initiative (ETI) said, "It is not a crime to find child labor in your supply chain. What is important is what you do about it when you find out." By using stakeholder mapping and cultivating open, trust-based relationships with key stakeholders, Gap has ensured that managers are able to do the right thing swiftly, sometimes even turning crises into opportunities.[43]

Exhibit 5.4 illustrates important stakeholders for a large organization such as Gap. Most organizations are influenced by a similar variety of stakeholder groups. Investors and shareholders, employees, customers, and suppliers are considered primary stakeholders, without whom the organization cannot survive. Investors, shareholders, and suppliers' interests are served by managerial efficiency—that is, use of resources to achieve profits. Employees expect work satisfaction, pay, and good supervision. Customers are concerned with decisions about the quality, safety, and availability of goods and services. When any primary stakeholder group becomes seriously dissatisfied, the organization's viability is threatened.[44]

Other important stakeholders are the government and the community, which have become increasingly important in recent years. Most corporations exist only under the proper

EXHIBIT 5.4 Major Stakeholders Relevant to Gap Inc.

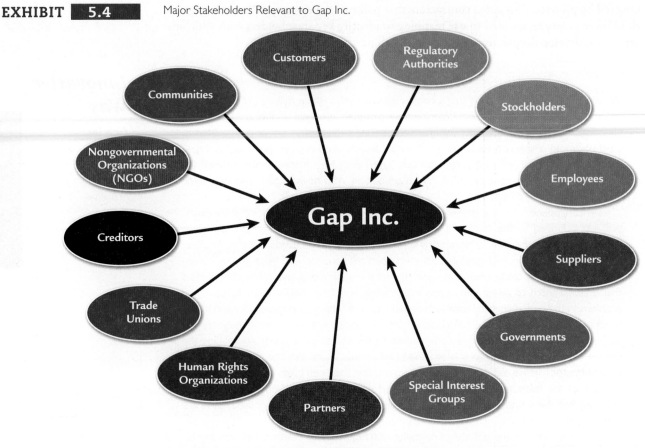

SOURCE: Based on information in D. Wheeler, B. Colbert, and R. E. Freeman, "Focusing on Value: Reconciling Corporate Social Responsibility, Sustainability, and a Stakeholder Approach in a Networked World," *Journal of General Management* 28, no. 3 (Spring 2003): 1–28; J. E. Post, L. E. Preston, and S. Sachs, "Managing the Extended Enterprise: The New Stakeholder View," *California Management Review* 45, no. 1 (Fall 2002): 6–28; and N. Craig Smith, Sean Ansett, and Lior Erex, "How Gap Inc. Engaged with Its Stakeholders," *MIT Sloan Management Review* 52, no. 4 (Summer 2011): 69–76.

charter and licenses and operate within the limits of safety laws, environmental protection requirements, antitrust regulations, antibribery legislation, and other laws and regulations in the government sector. Government regulations affecting business are increasing because of recent events. The community includes local governments, the natural environment, and the quality of life provided for residents. For many companies such as Gap, trade unions and human rights organizations are highly important stakeholders. Special interest groups may include trade associations, political action committees, professional associations, and consumerists. One special interest group of particular importance today is the green movement.

THE GREEN MOVEMENT

The year was 2004, and Jeffrey Immelt, CEO of General Electric (GE), had just presented a plan for a "green" business initiative to 35 top GE executives. They voted it down. But Immelt, in a rare move, overruled them, and Ecomagination was born. Today, GE's Ecomagination is one of the world's most widely recognized corporate green programs. It has not only cut GE's greenhouse gas emissions by 30 percent but also added innovative products that are generating billions in annual revenue.[45]

Going green has become a new business imperative, driven by shifting social attitudes, new governmental policies, climate changes, and information technology (IT) that quickly spreads any news of a corporation's negative impact on the environment. A recent survey

Ecomagination

The question hovering on the horizon for enlightened CEOs such as **General Electric's** Jeff Immelt: *How do we apply technology and sustainability to addressing the economics of scarcity?* Immelt had only to tap into the historical precedent of innovation and imagination set by the creative genius of GE founder Thomas Edison. The result was GE's major commitment to social responsibility through a green technology movement.

GE became a CSR pioneer by initiating *The Ecomagination Campaign,* a plan that packs a punch. Immelt doubled R&D funding to establish new labs and load them with Ph.D.s undertaking innovative sustainability research. The company also created an Ecomagination Advisory Council fueled by "dreaming sessions" that allowed customers and stakeholders to envision the future and the products and services that can improve those futures while providing an innovative business opportunity for GE. Founder Edison must be smiling.

Source: Philip Mirvis, Bradley Googins, and Sylvia Kinnicutt, "Vision, Mission, Values: Guideposts to Sustainability," *Organizational Dynamics* 39 (2010): 316–324.

ENVIRONMENT 2

found that 90 percent of Americans agree that there are important "green" issues and problems, and 82 percent think that businesses should implement environmentally friendly practices.[46] Each chapter of this text contains a Green Power example that highlights what companies are doing to improve their environmental performance.

Energy is an area of ongoing concern for the green movement, as reflected in the conflict associated with the proposed building of the Keystone XL pipeline that would add a link running from the oil sands of Alberta, Canada, to refineries on the Texas coast of the Gulf of Mexico. Nearly six in ten Americans polled are in favor of the U.S. government approving the project, believing that it will create jobs without causing significant environmental damage. But green groups are up in arms, targeting Keystone and the entire oil sands industry, which releases 30 million tons of carbon dioxide a year into the atmosphere and will release more as the industry grows. Opponents point

out that the "well-to-gas tank" emissions of Canadian oil sands are about twice as high as the average barrel of U.S. imported crude oil. Supporters insist it is better to tap the oil sands of Canada than to continue helping oil-rich countries that may abuse both people and the environment.[47]

SUSTAINABILITY AND THE TRIPLE BOTTOM LINE

Some corporations are embracing an idea called *sustainability* or *sustainable development.* **Sustainability** refers to economic development that generates wealth and meets the needs of the current generation while preserving the environment and society so future generations can meet their needs as well.[48] With a philosophy of sustainability, managers weave environmental and social concerns into every strategic decision so that financial goals are achieved in a way that is socially and

▶▶▶ **Concept Connection**

Zuma/Zuma Wire Service/Alamy Limited

As early proponents of the **green movement**, Ahmed and Reem Rahim founded Numi Tea in Oakland, California, with a vision to honor the planet and its people. They use nothing but organically grown teas and work only with fair-trade vendors. The company's packaging and all other aspects of its production operations are designed to reduce Numi's impact on the environment.

environmentally responsible. Managers in organizations that embrace sustainability measure their success in terms of a triple bottom line. The term **triple bottom line** refers to measuring an organization's social performance, its environmental performance, and its financial performance. This is sometimes called the three Ps: People, Planet, and Profit.[49]

The People part of the triple bottom line looks at how socially responsible the organization is in terms of fair labor practices, diversity, supplier relationships, treatment of employees, contributions to the community, and so forth. The Planet aspect measures the organization's commitment to environmental sustainability. The third P, of course, looks at the organization's profit, the financial bottom line. Based on the principle that what you measure is what you strive for and achieve, using a triple bottom line approach to measuring performance ensures that managers take social and environmental factors into account, rather than blindly pursuing profit no matter the cost to society and the natural environment.

Remember This

- **Corporate social responsibility** refers to the obligation of organizational managers to make choices and take actions that will enhance the welfare and interests of society, as well as the organization.

- Different stakeholders have different interests in the organization and thus different criteria for social responsiveness.

- The term **stakeholder** refers to any group or person within or outside the organization that has some type of investment or interest in the organization's performance.

- Shareholders, employees, customers, and suppliers are considered primary stakeholders, without whom the organization could not survive.

- Government, the community, and special interest groups are also important stakeholders.

- **Stakeholder mapping** provides a systematic way to identify the expectations, needs, importance, and relative power of various stakeholders.

- The *green movement* is a special interest group of particular importance today.

- **Sustainability** refers to economic development that generates wealth and meets the needs of the current population while preserving society and the environment for the needs of future generations.

- Companies that embrace sustainability measure performance in terms of financial performance, social performance, and environmental performance, referred to as the **triple bottom line**.

- A survey found that 90 percent of Americans agree that there are important "green" issues and problems, and 82 percent think that businesses should implement environmentally friendly practices.

Evaluating Corporate Social Responsibility

A model for evaluating corporate social performance is presented in Exhibit 5.5. The model indicates that total corporate social responsibility can be divided into four primary criteria: economic, legal, ethical, and discretionary responsibilities.[50] These four criteria fit together to form the whole of a company's social responsiveness.

The first criterion of social responsibility is *economic responsibility*. The business institution is, above all, the basic economic unit of society. Its responsibility is to produce the goods and services that society wants and to maximize profits for its owners and shareholders. Economic responsibility, carried to the extreme, is called the *profit-maximizing view*, advocated by Nobel economist Milton Friedman. This view argues that the corporation should be operated on a profit-oriented basis, with its sole mission to increase its profits so long as it stays within the rules of the game.[51] The purely profit-maximizing view is no longer considered an adequate criterion of

> "For a long time, people believed that the only purpose of industry was to make a profit. They are wrong. Its purpose is to serve the general welfare."
>
> — HENRY FORD, SR. (1863–1947), AMERICAN INDUSTRIALIST

EXHIBIT **5.5**

Criteria of Corporate Social Performance

SOURCE: Based on Archie B. Carroll, "A Three-Dimensional Conceptual Model of Corporate Performance," *Academy of Management Review* 4 (1979): 499; A. B. Carroll, "The Pyramid of Corporate Social Responsibility: Toward the Moral Management of Corporate Stakeholders," *Business Horizons* 34 (July–August 1991): 42; and Mark S. Schwartz and Archie B. Carroll, "Corporate Social Responsibility: A Three-Domain Approach," *Business Ethics Quarterly* 13, no. 4 (2003): 503–530.

social performance in Canada, the United States, and Europe. This approach means that economic gain is the only responsibility and can lead companies into trouble, as recent events in the mortgage and finance industries have clearly shown.

Legal responsibility defines what society deems as important with respect to appropriate corporate behavior.[52] That is, businesses are expected to fulfill their economic goals within the framework of legal requirements imposed by local town councils, state legislators, and federal regulatory agencies. Examples of illegal acts by corporations include corporate fraud, intentionally selling defective goods, performing unnecessary repairs or procedures, deliberately misleading consumers, and billing clients for work not done. Organizations that knowingly break the law are poor performers in this category. Walmart, for example, is currently embroiled in a bribery scandal amid allegations that the company's largest foreign subsidiary, Walmart de Mexico, paid bribes to local officials and covered up the wrongdoing to corner every edge of the market in that country. Investigators found "reasonable suspicion" that Walmart managers had violated U.S. and Mexican laws and called for a broader inquiry into the allegations.[53]

Ethical responsibility includes behaviors that are not necessarily codified into law and may not serve the corporation's direct economic interests. As described earlier in this chapter, to be *ethical*, organization decision makers should act with

▶ ▶ ▶ **Concept Connection**

In the United States, employers have a **legal responsibility** to comply with laws designed to protect workers, such as the health and safety laws enforced by the Occupational Safety and Health Administration (OSHA). For example, companies that run manufacturing plants like this one are required to provide employees with safety goggles, earplugs, hard hats, and other protective gear as needed for various jobs.

equity, fairness, and impartiality, respect the rights of individuals, and provide different treatment of individuals only when relevant to the organization's goals and tasks.[54] *Unethical* behavior occurs when decisions enable an individual or company to gain at the expense of other people or society as a whole. Managers at Merck & Company, for example, seriously damaged the company's reputation by continuing to market the arthritis medication Vioxx aggressively even after they had information suggesting that there were heart attack and stroke risks associated with the drug. Merck was facing stiff competition from Pfizer's Celebrex and chose to pursue profits, even at the risk of harming patients.

Discretionary responsibility is purely voluntary and is guided by a company's desire to make social contributions not mandated by economics, law, or ethics. Discretionary activities include generous philanthropic contributions that offer no payback to the company and are not expected. For example, Royal DSM, a Netherlands-based company that produces nutritional supplements, pharmaceutical ingredients, and energy-efficient building products, partners with the World Food Programme to give vitamins, supplements, and fortified food products to malnourished people in Nepal, Kenya, Bangladesh, and Afghanistan; offers free medical services to poor villagers in India; and has donated building supplies to construct schools in poor countries. "We don't really put a value on it. . . . ," said Fokko Wientjes, DSM's director of sustainability. "But shareholders haven't ever called me up and said, 'Please stop'."[55] Gap Inc., described earlier, donates 50 percent of profits on a particular line of "Red"-branded Gap products to lead U2 singer Bono's Red campaign against HIV/AIDS.[56] As another example, a week after a massive earthquake and tsunami devastated Japan, corporations had pledged about $151 million in cash and in-kind donations for disaster relief.[57] Discretionary responsibility is the highest criterion of social responsibility because it goes beyond societal expectations to contribute to the community's welfare.

Take a Moment

Read the Ethical Dilemma for Chapter 5 on pages 199–200 that pertains to legal and ethical responsibilities.

Remember This

- The model for evaluating a company's social performance uses four criteria: economic, legal, ethical, and discretionary.
- Companies may get into trouble when they use economic criteria as their only measure of responsibility, sometimes called the *profit-maximizing* view.
- **Discretionary responsibility** is purely voluntary and is guided by the organization's desire to make social contributions not mandated by economics, laws, or ethics.
- Corporations that sent generous donations to Japan following the devastating earthquake and tsunami were practicing discretionary responsibility.

Managing Company Ethics and Social Responsibility

An expert on the topic of ethics said, "Management is responsible for creating and sustaining conditions in which people are likely to behave themselves."[58] Exhibit 5.6 illustrates ways in which managers create and support an ethical organization. One of the most important steps managers can take is to practice ethical leadership. *Ethical leadership* means that managers are honest and trustworthy, fair in their dealings with employees and customers, and behave ethically in both their personal and professional lives. In response to recent ethical violations and critics of management education saying MBA stands for "Me Before Anyone,"[59] some business schools and students are taking a fresh look at how future managers are trained.

EXHIBIT 5.6 Building an Ethical Organization

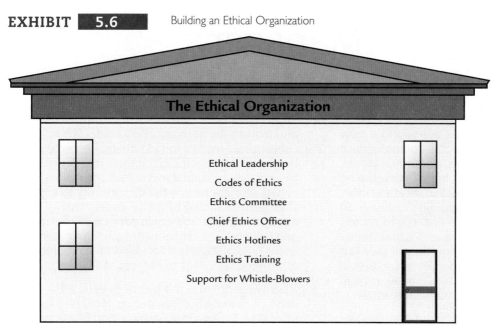

The Ethical Organization

Ethical Leadership
Codes of Ethics
Ethics Committee
Chief Ethics Officer
Ethics Hotlines
Ethics Training
Support for Whistle-Blowers

SOURCE: Adapted from Linda Klebe Treviño, Laura Pincus Hartman, and Michael Brown, "Moral Person and Moral Manager," *California Management Review* 42, no. 4 (Summer 2000): 128–142.

ENVIRONMENT 2

Innovative Way

Harvard Business School, Columbia Business School, Yale School of Management

Some members of a recent graduating class of Harvard Business School did something unusual. They signed a voluntary student-led pledge saying that the goal of a business manager is to "serve the greater good" and promising that they will act responsibly and ethically and refrain from advancing their "own narrow ambitions" at the expense of others.

At Harvard and other business schools, there has been an explosion of interest in ethics classes and activities that focus on personal and corporate responsibility. Many students, as well as educators, are recognizing a need to give future managers a deeper understanding of how to practice ethical leadership rather than just how to make money. At Columbia Business School, which requires an ethics course, students formed a popular Leadership and Ethics Board that sponsors lectures and other activities. Yale School of Management developed sessions in its core curriculum related to the recent ethical crisis in the mortgage and finance industries and worked with the Aspen Institute to create a curriculum aimed at teaching business students how to act on their values at work. About 55 business schools are using all or part of the curriculum in pilot programs. "There is a feeling that we want our lives to mean something more and to run organizations for the greater good," said Max Anderson, one of the organizers of Harvard's pledge. "No one wants to have their future criticized as a place filled with unethical behaviors."[60]

Changing how future managers are trained could be one key to solving the ethics deficit pervading organizations. Managers and first-line supervisors are important role models for ethical behavior, and they strongly influence the ethical climate in the organization by adhering to high ethical standards in their own behavior and decisions. Moreover, managers are proactive in influencing employees to embody and reflect ethical values.[61] This chapter's Shoptalk describes an approach that some leading companies are taking to strengthen managers' ethical and socially responsible underpinning.

Managers can also implement organizational mechanisms to help employees and the company stay on an ethical footing. Some of the primary ones are codes of ethics, ethical structures, and measures to protect whistle-blowers.

Manager's *Shoptalk*

Cultivating a Service Mindset

Some of today's best companies are taking a new approach to developing managers—global service programs that place employees with nonprofit organizations or small businesses, often in developing countries, to provide free or low-cost technical and managerial assistance. In line with the growing emphasis on sustainability and the triple bottom line, organizations want managers who have a service and sustainability mindset rather than an attitude of getting all they can for themselves. In one survey, 88 percent of top executives said it was important that future managers have the mindset and skills to address sustainability issues.

- **Global service programs benefit everyone.** Global service programs have been described as a "win-win-win." It might seem obvious that the nonprofit organizations served by these programs benefit, but the companies investing in them and the employees participating in them gain just as much. IBM credits its program with generating about $5 billion in new business. Companies gain greater knowledge of emerging markets, develop social capital and goodwill, and get more well-rounded managers with the service and sustainability mindset needed in today's world. Participants benefit in numerous ways, including increased self-awareness, new skills, and greater cross-cultural understanding.

- **Many managers view these opportunities as plum assignments.** Laura Benetti of Dow Corning spent four weeks working nine-hour-days with rural women in India, helping them learn how to price

and market the garments they made. She and nine colleagues slept in a lodge with limited access to hot water and electricity. "It gives more meaning to your career," said Benetti. Participants in global service also appreciate the opportunity to expand their understanding of global issues. "We all *know* about things like poverty in Africa and corruption and bribery . . .," said one IBM participant who spent time in Nigeria. "This kind of experience really brings . . . things to life, you really feel it."

- **How widespread is the trend?** In early 2012, at least 27 *Fortune* 500 companies, including PepsiCo, IBM, FedEx, Dow Corning, and Pfizer, had some type of global service program, up from only 6 in 2006. Since 2008, IBM has sent more than 1,400 employees to work with projects such as reforming Kenya's postal system or developing ecotourism in Tanzania. Pfizer's program lends employees to nongovernmental organizations (NGOs) to address health care needs in Asia and Africa. The Accenture Development Partnership has been involved in more than 200 projects in 55 countries, where Accenture's professionals work at 50 percent pay for up to six months with organizations such as UNICEF and Freedom from Hunger.

Sources: Based on Philip Mirvis, Kevin Thompson, and John Gohring, "Toward Next-Generation Leadership: Global Service," *Leader to Leader* (Spring 2012): 20–26; Matthew Gitsham, "Experiential Learning for Leadership and Sustainability at IBM and HSBC," *Journal of Management Development* 31, no, 3 (2012): 298–307; and Anne Tergesen, "Doing Good to Do Well," *The Wall Street Journal*, January 9, 2012, B7.

CODE OF ETHICS

A **code of ethics** is a formal statement of the company's values concerning ethics and social issues; it communicates to employees what the company stands for. Codes of ethics tend to exist in two types: principle-based statements and policy-based statements. *Principle-based statements* are designed to affect corporate culture; they define fundamental values and contain general language about company responsibilities, quality of products, and treatment of employees. *Policy-based statements* generally outline the procedures to be used in specific ethical situations. These situations include marketing practices, conflicts of interest, observance of laws, proprietary information, political gifts, and equal opportunities.

General statements of principle are often called *corporate credos*. One good example is Johnson & Johnson's "The Credo." Available in 36 languages, The Credo has guided Johnson & Johnson's managers for more than 60 years in making decisions that honor the company's responsibilities to employees, customers, the community, and stockholders. Another example is Google's *Code of Conduct*. Portions of the Google code are shown in the following example.

Google is one of the best-known companies in the world, and managers take seriously its reputation for both technological superiority and a commitment to ethics and social responsibility. Google's Code of Conduct starts with these words: "'Don't be evil.' Googlers generally apply those words to how we serve our users. But 'Don't be evil' is much more than that."

Google uses a well-designed Code of Conduct to put the motto "Don't be evil" into practice. The code is divided into seven sections, with each subdivided into sections that describe specific values, policies, and expectations. The code also clearly states that employees will be protected if they call attention to ethical violations or misconduct. Here are some excerpts from Google's code:

Serve Our Users
Our users value Google not only because we deliver great products and services, but because we hold ourselves to a higher standard in how we treat users and operate more generally.

Respect Each Other
We are committed to a supportive work environment, where employees have the opportunity to reach their fullest potential. Each Googler is expected to do his or her utmost to create a respectful workplace culture that is free of harassment, intimidation, bias and unlawful discrimination of any kind.

Preserve Confidentiality
We get a lot of press attention around our innovations and our culture, and that's usually fine. However, company information that leaks prematurely into the press or to competitors can hurt our product launches, eliminate our competitive advantage and prove costly in other ways.

Ensure Financial Integrity and Responsibility
Financial integrity and fiscal responsibility are core aspects of corporate professionalism. . . . The money we spend on behalf of Google is not ours; it's the company's and, ultimately, our shareholders'.

Obey the Law
Google takes its responsibilities to comply with laws and regulations very seriously and each of us is expected to comply with applicable legal requirements and prohibitions.

Conclusion
Google aspires to be a different kind of company. It's impossible to spell out every possible ethical scenario we might face. Instead, we rely on one another's good judgment to uphold a high standard of integrity for ourselves and our company.

And remember . . . don't be evil, and if you see something that you think isn't right—speak up![62]

Having a strong code of conduct or code of ethics doesn't guarantee that companies won't get into ethical trouble or be challenged by stakeholders on ethical issues. Codes of ethics in and of themselves do little to influence and ensure ethical behavior among employees and managers.[63] However, they are one key element of the organization's ethical framework. Codes of ethics state the values or behaviors expected and those that will not be tolerated. When top management supports and enforces these codes, including rewards for compliance and discipline for violation, ethics codes can boost a company's ethical climate.[64]

ETHICAL STRUCTURES

Ethical structures represent the various systems, positions, and programs that a company can undertake to encourage and support ethical behavior.[65] An **ethics committee** is a group of executives (and sometimes lower-level employees as well) appointed to oversee company ethics. The committee provides rulings on questionable ethical issues and assumes responsibility for disciplining wrongdoers. Motorola's Ethics Compliance Committee, for instance, is charged with interpreting, clarifying, and communicating the company's code of ethics and with adjudicating suspected code violations.

Many companies set up ethics offices with full-time staff to ensure that ethical standards are an integral part of company operations. These offices are headed by a **chief ethics officer**, sometimes called a *chief ethics and compliance officer*, a company executive who oversees all aspects of ethics and legal compliance, including establishing and broadly communicating standards, ethics training, dealing with exceptions or problems, and advising senior managers in the ethical and compliance aspects of decisions.[66] The title *chief ethics officer* was almost unheard of a decade ago, but highly publicized ethical and legal problems in recent years have sparked a growing demand for these ethics specialists. The Ethics and Compliance Officer Association, a trade group, reports that membership soared 70 percent, to more than 1,260 companies, in the five years following the collapse of Enron due to financial wrongdoing.[67] Most ethics offices also work as counseling centers to help employees resolve difficult ethical issues. A toll-free confidential *ethics hotline* allows employees to report questionable behavior, as well as seek guidance concerning ethical dilemmas.

Take a Moment

Complete the Experiential Exercise on page 159 that pertains to ethical work environments.

WHISTLE-BLOWING

Employee disclosure of illegal, unethical, or illegitimate practices on the employer's part is called **whistle-blowing**.[68] No organization can rely exclusively on codes of conduct and ethical structures to prevent all unethical behavior. Holding organizations accountable depends to some degree on individuals who are willing to speak up if they detect illegal, dangerous, or unethical activities. Whistle-blowers often report wrongdoing to outsiders, such as regulatory agencies, senators, or newspaper reporters. Some firms have instituted innovative programs and confidential hotlines to encourage and support internal whistle-blowing. For this practice to be an effective ethical safeguard, however, companies must view whistle-blowing as a benefit to the company and make dedicated efforts to encourage and protect whistle-blowers.[69]

For instance, in 2001, Mike McQueary, at the time a graduate assistant in the football program at Pennsylvania State University, reported to head football coach Joe Paterno, athletic director Tim Curley, and others that he saw defensive coordinator Jerry Sandusky sexually abusing a young boy in the locker room. But allegedly, no one took the next step to stop the immoral (and illegal) behavior, and Sandusky went on to molest more boys before one of his victims brought the abuse to light. In the summer of 2012, more than ten years after McQueary's initial report, Sandusky was convicted on 45 counts of child sexual abuse. The courts and the public were astonished to learn how many people knew about Sandusky's behavior and apparently did nothing beyond talking with Sandusky and urging him to get professional help. The fact is that most managers have a natural inclination to protect their colleagues and the organization.[70]

For people throughout an organization to be willing to "blow the whistle" on unethical or illegal behavior, managers have to *revere* whistle-blowing and make heroes of those who come forward. At Penn State, the opposite seemed to happen. In fact, Vicky Triponey, vice president of student affairs at Penn State from 2003 to 2007, says she was fired after trying to punish football players for acts of wrongdoing ranging from brutal fights to sexual assault. According to Triponey, Penn State president Graham Spanier told her she wasn't fitting in with "the Penn State way." Triponey says there was a "blind sense of loyalty—not just at the top, but at all levels. I think people, in order to keep their jobs, have had to turn a blind eye."[71] Indeed, managers want employee loyalty in their organization, and it can be difficult to set aside when unethical activities are discovered.

Penn State managers aren't alone in trying to protect the organization, even at the risk of allowing unethical behavior to continue. The U.S. Office of Special Counsel recently found three Air Force officials guilty of retaliating against civilian employees who reported the mishandling of the remains of deceased soldiers at Dover Air Force Base, for example. A former executive at Countrywide Financial Corporation says he was bullied and eventually fired after he questioned the company's use of so-called "Ninja loans" (no income, no job, no assets) at the height of the subprime mortgage craze. And Matthew Lee, a former senior vice president in Lehman Brothers' accounting division, lost his job just weeks after he raised concerns about how the firm was masking risks by temporarily "parking" $50 billion in risky loan assets off its balance sheet.[72]

Unfortunately, many managers still look on whistle-blowers as disgruntled employees who aren't good team players. Yet to maintain high ethical standards, organizations need people who are willing to point out wrongdoing. Managers can be trained to view whistle-blowing as a benefit rather than a threat, and systems can be set up to protect employees who report illegal or unethical activities.

The Business Case for Ethics and Social Responsibility

Most managers now realize that paying attention to ethics and social responsibility is as important a business issue as paying attention to costs, profits, and growth. For one thing, in today's information age, bad behavior is increasingly hard to hide, and "outbehaving the competition" can provide a real competitive advantage.[73]

Naturally, the relationship of a corporation's ethics and social responsibility to its financial performance concerns both managers and management scholars and has generated a lively debate.[74] One concern of managers is whether good citizenship will hurt performance—after all, ethics programs and social responsibility cost money. A commitment to sustainability means that things often have to be done in a more costly way. Hundreds of studies have been undertaken to determine whether heightened ethical and social responsiveness increases or decreases a company's financial performance. Studies have provided varying results, but they have generally found a positive relationship between ethical and socially responsible behavior and firm financial performance.[75] For example, a recent study of the top 100 sustainable global companies found that they had significantly higher sales growth, return on assets, profits, and cash flow from operations in at least some areas of business.[76] Another review of the financial performance of large U.S. corporations considered "best corporate citizens" found that they enjoy both superior reputations and superior financial performance.[77] Similarly, Governance Metrics International, an independent corporate governance ratings agency in New York, reports that the stocks of companies run on more selfless principles perform better than those run in a self-serving manner.[78] Although results from these studies are not proof, they do provide an indication that using resources for ethics and social responsibility does not hurt companies.[79]

▶▶▶ **Concept Connection**

Gen-Yers throughout the world expect a serious **commitment to sustainability** from their employers. In fact, one study found that more than 95 percent of Gen-Y respondents wanted to work for an organization that goes beyond merely complying with existing environmental legislation. That's why Cleveland-based Eaton Corporation, a diversified power management company, prominently features its commitment to sustainability on its career Web page and at career fairs, such as the one pictured here. "It's actually helped us in acquiring top talent at a lot of top universities," says Joel Wolfsberger, Eaton vice president for environment, health, and safety.

Companies are also making an effort to measure the nonfinancial factors that create value. Researchers find, for example, that people prefer to work for sustainable companies or companies that demonstrate a high level of ethics and social responsibility; thus, these organizations can attract and retain high-quality employees.[80] Customers pay attention too. A study by Walker Research indicates that, price and quality being equal, two-thirds of customers say they would switch brands to do business with a company that is ethical and socially responsible.[81] Another series of experiments by Remi Trudel and June Cotte of the University of Western Ontario's Ivey School of Business found that consumers were willing to pay slightly more for products they were told had been made using high ethical standards.[82]

Enlightened managers realize that integrity and trust are essential elements in sustaining successful and profitable business relationships with an increasingly connected and well-informed web of employees, customers, suppliers, and partners. Although doing the right thing might not always be profitable in the short run, many managers believe that it can provide a competitive advantage by developing a level of trust that money can't buy.

Remember This

- Managers are role models. One of the most important ways that managers create ethical and socially responsible organizations is by practicing ethical leadership.
- Some students at Harvard Business School sign a pledge promising to act responsibly and ethically as managers.
- A **code of ethics** is a formal statement of the organization's values regarding ethics and social issues.
- An **ethics committee** is a group of executives (and sometimes lower-level employees as well) charged with overseeing company ethics by ruling on questionable issues and disciplining violators.
- Some organizations have ethics offices headed by a **chief ethics officer**, a manager who oversees all aspects of ethics and legal compliance.

- Managers who want ethical organizations support **whistle-blowing**, the disclosure by employees of unethical, illegitimate, or illegal practices by the organization.
- Companies that are ethical and socially responsible perform as well as—often even better than—those that are not socially responsible.
- One study found that sustainable companies have significantly higher sales growth, return on assets, and profits than companies that are not run on a philosophy of sustainability.

ch5: Discussion Questions

1. Is it reasonable to expect that managers can measure their social and environmental performance on the same level as they measure financial performance with a triple bottom line? Discuss.

2. What various stakeholder groups did oil giant BP have to respond to concerning the massive 2010 oil spill in the Gulf of Mexico? From what you know about the BP oil spill, how would you evaluate BP executives' behavior in terms of corporate social responsibility?

3. Imagine yourself in a situation of being encouraged by colleagues to inflate your expense account. What factors do you think would influence your decision? Explain.

4. Is it socially responsible for organizations to undertake political activity or join with others in a trade association to influence the government? Discuss.

5. Managers at some banks and mortgage companies have argued that providing subprime mortgages was based on their desire to give poor people a chance to participate in the American dream of home ownership. What is your opinion of this explanation in terms of ethics and social responsibility?

6. A noted business executive said, "A company's first obligation is to be profitable. Unprofitable enterprises can't afford to be socially responsible." Discuss why you agree or disagree with this statement.

7. Do you believe that it is ethical for organizational managers to try to get access to and scrutinize the Facebook pages of employees or job applicants? Discuss.

8. Which do you think would be more effective for shaping long-term ethical behavior in an organization: a written code of ethics combined with ethics training,

or strong ethical leadership? Which would have more impact on you? Why?

9. The technique of stakeholder mapping lets managers classify which stakeholders they will consider more important and will invest more time to satisfy. Is it appropriate for management to define some stakeholders as more important than others? Should all stakeholders be considered equal?

10. According to a survey, many people think cheating is more common today than it was a decade ago. Do you think cheating is really more common, or does it just seem so? Why?

ch5: Apply Your Skills: Experiential Exercise

Ethical Work Climates[83]

Think of an organization for which you were employed. Answer the following questions twice: The first time, circle the number that best describes the way things actually were. The second time, answer the questions based on your beliefs about the ideal level that would meet the needs of both individuals and the organization.

Disagree   (1) (2) (3) (4) (5)   Agree

1. What was best for everyone in the company was the major consideration there.
   1   2   3   4   5

2. Our major concern was always what was best for the other person.
   1   2   3   4   5

3. People were expected to comply with the law and professional standards over and above other considerations.
   1   2   3   4   5

4. In the company, the first consideration was whether a decision violated any law.
   1   2   3   4   5

5. It was very important to follow the company's rules and procedures there.
   1   2   3   4   5

6. People in the company strictly obeyed the company policies.
   1   2   3   4   5

7. In the company, people were mostly out for themselves.
   1   2   3   4   5

8. People were expected to do anything to further the company's interests, regardless of the consequences.
   1   2   3   4   5

9. In the company, people were guided by their own personal ethics.
   1   2   3   4   5

10. Each person in the company decided for himself or herself what was right and wrong.
    1   2   3   4   5

Scoring and Interpretation

Subtract each of your scores for questions 7 and 8 from the number 6. Then, add up your score for all ten questions: Actual = _____. Ideal = _____. These questions measure the dimensions of an organization's ethical climate. Questions 1 and 2 measure caring for people; questions 3 and 4 measure lawfulness; questions 5 and 6 measure adherence to rules; questions 7 and 8 measure emphasis on financial and company performance; and questions 9 and 10 measure individual independence. A total score above 40 indicates a highly positive ethical climate. A score from 30 to 40 indicates above-average ethical climate. A score from 20 to 30 indicates a below-average ethical climate, and a score below 20 indicates a poor ethical climate. How far from your ideal score was the actual score for your organization? What does that difference mean to you?

Go back over the questions and think about changes that you could have made to improve the ethical climate in the organization. Discuss with other students what you could do as a manager to improve ethics in future companies for which you work.

ch5: Apply Your Skills: Small Group Breakout

Current Events of an Unethical Type[84]

Step 1. Prior to meeting as a group, each person find two newspaper or magazine articles from the past several months relating to someone violating business ethics or potentially breaking the law regarding business practices.

Step 2. Summarize the key points of the articles you found.

Step 3. Meet as a group. Each person in turn shares key points from articles with group members.

Step 4. Identify similar themes across the unethical incidents reported in the articles. What was the source or underlying cause of the unethical behavior? What was the hoped-for outcome? Was an individual or a group involved? Can you identify similar conditions of any kind across incidents? Did the accused seem repentant or defensive? Write the common themes in a list on a sheet of paper or whiteboard.

Step 5. What could you do as a manager to prevent such unethical behavior in your organization? What could you do to fix this kind of problem after it occurred in your organization?

Step 6. Report your findings to the class if asked to do so by your instructor.

ch5: Endnotes

1. Ben Worthen and Joann S. Lublin, "Mark Hurd Neglected to Follow H-P Code," *The Wall Street Journal*, August 9, 2010, B1.

2. Mara Der Hovanesian, "Sex, Lies, and Mortgage Deals," *BusinessWeek* (November 24, 2009): 71–74; Amir Efrati and Joann S. Lublin, "Yahoo CEO's Downfall," *The Wall Street Journal Online*, May 15, 2012, http://online.wsj.com/article/SB1000142405270230419270457740453099458956.html (accessed July 2, 2012).

3. Gordon F. Shea, *Practical Ethics* (New York: American Management Association, 1988); and Linda K. Treviño, "Ethical Decision Making in Organizations: A Person-Situation Interactionist Model," *Academy of Management Review* 11 (1986): 601–617.

4. Thomas M. Jones, "Ethical Decision Making by Individuals in Organizations: An Issue-Contingent Model," *Academy of Management Review* 16 (1991): 366–395.

5. Shelby D. Hunt and Jared M. Hansen, "Understanding Ethical Diversity in Organizations," *Organizational Dynamics* 36, no 2 (2007): 202–216.

6. "Socialising for Intelligence," *Computer News Middle East*, November 2, 2011.

7. Justin Scheck, "Accusations of Snooping in Ink-Cartridge Dispute," *The Wall Street Journal Online*, August 11, 2009, http://online.wsj.com/article /SB124995836273921661.html ?KEYWORDS=%22Accusations +of+Snooping +in+Ink-Cartridge +Dispute%22 (accessed August 14, 2009).

8. Marcus Kabel, "Former Walmart Executive to Plead Guilty to Fraud," *USAToday*, January 27, 2006, www.usatoday.com/money/industries/retail/2006-01-27-retail-fraud_x.htm (accessed July 2, 2012); and Ashby Jones and Nathan Koppel, "Ethical Lapses Felled Long List of Company Executives," *The Wall Street Journal*, August 7, 2010, http://online.wsj.com/article/SB10001424052748703309704575413842089375632.html (accessed July 2, 2012).

9. These examples are from Jones and Koppel, "Ethical Lapses Felled Long List of Company Executives."

10. Rushworth M. Kidder, "The Three Great Domains of Human Action," *Christian Science Monitor*, January 30, 1990.

11. Gallup Survey results reported in Roger Martin, "The CEO's Ethical Dilemma in the Era of Earnings Management," *Strategy & Leadership* 39, no. 6 (2011): 43–47.

12. John Revill and Vanessa O'Connell, "Armstrong Is Stripped of Titles in Cycling," *The Wall Street Journal*, October 23, 2012, A4; and Anemona Hartocollis, "At Ailing Brooklyn Hospital, Insider Deals and Lavish Perks," *The New York Times*, March 26, 2012, A1.

13. Elizabeth Povoledo, "Vatican Allows That Butler Scandal Is Hurting Trust," *The New York Times*, May 28, 2012, www.nytimes.com/2012/05/29/world/europe/vatican-says-scandal-involving-popes-butler-erodes-trust.html (accessed July 2, 2012).

14. Marist College Institute for Public Opinion and Knights of Columbus survey, results reported in Kevin Turner, "Corporate Execs: Nobody Trusts Us; U.S. Lacks Confidence in Business Ethics, Poll Says," *Florida Times Union*, February 27, 2009.

15. Gary R. Weaver, Linda Klebe Treviño, and Bradley Agle, "'Somebody I Look Up To:' Ethical Role Models in Organizations," *Organizational Dynamics* 34, no. 4 (2005): 313–330.

16. These measures of unethical behavior are from Muel Kaptein, "Developing a Measure of Unethical Behavior in the Workplace: A Stakeholder Perspective," *Journal of Management* 34, no. 5 (October 2008): 978–1008.

17. Roger Martin, "The CEO's Ethical Dilemma in the Era of Earnings Management," *Strategy & Leadership* 39, no. 6 (2011): 43–47.

18. Nicholas D. Kristof, "Lehman CEO Fuld Takes the Prize; Need a Job?: $17,000 an Hour; No Success Required," *The Gazette*, September 19, 2008; Paul Goodsell, "Are CEOs Worth Their Salt?" *Omaha World-Herald*, October 5, 2008; Jackie Calmes and Louise Story, "AIG Bonus Outcry Builds: Troubled Insurance Giant Gave out More Millions Last Week," *Pittsburgh Post Gazette*, March 18, 2009; Graham Bowley, "Wall Street '09 Bonuses Increase 17% to $20 Billion," *The New York Times*, February 24, 2010; and Adam Shell, "Despite Recession, Average Wall Street Bonus Leaps 25%; About $20.3 Billion Distributed in 2009," *USA Today*, February 24, 2010.

19. Jennifer Liberto, "CEO Pay Is 380 Times Average Worker's—AFL-CIO," *CNNMoney*, April 19, 2012, http://money.cnn.com/2012/04/19/news/economy /ceo-pay/index.htm (accessed July 3, 2012); and Jena McGregor, "Crazy Data Point of the Day: How Much CEO Pay vs. Worker Pay Has Grown," Post Leadership Blog, *WashingtonPost.com*, May 11, 2012, www.washingtonpost.com/blogs/post-leadership/post/crazy-data-point-of-the-day-how-much-ceo-vs-worker-pay-has-grown/2012/05/11/gIQArUISIU_blog.html (accessed July 3, 2012).

20. Linda K. Treviño and Katherine A. Nelson, *Managing Business Ethics: Straight Talk About How to Do It Right* (New York: John Wiley & Sons, Inc. 1995), p. 4.

21. Jones, "Ethical Decision Making by Individuals in Organizations."

22. This example is from Francis J. Flynn and Scott S. Wiltermuth, "Who's with Me? False Consensus, Brokerage, and Ethical Decision Making in Organizations," *Academy of Management Journal* 53, no. 5 (2010): 1074–1089.

23. Based on a question from a General Electric (GE) employee ethics guide, reported in Kathryn Kranhold, "U.S. Firms Raise Ethics Focus," *The Wall Street Journal*, November 28, 2005.

24. D. Wallis, "Loose Lips Can Sink Trips," *The New York Times*, May 3, 2012, F1.

25. From Jeffrey Kluger, "What Makes Us Moral?" *Time* (December 3, 2007): 54–60.

26. "The Morality Quiz," *Time*, www.time.com/morality (accessed February 19, 2008).

27. This discussion is based on Gerald F. Cavanagh, Dennis J. Moberg, and Manuel Velasquez, "The Ethics of Organizational Politics," *Academy of Management Review* 6 (1981): 363–374; Justin G. Longenecker, Joseph A. McKinney, and Carlos W. Moore, "Egoism and Independence: Entrepreneurial Ethics," *Organizational Dynamics* (Winter 1988): 64–72; Carolyn Wiley, "The ABCs of Business Ethics: Definitions, Philosophies, and Implementation," *IM* (February 1995): 22–27; and Mark Mallinger, "Decisive Decision Making: An Exercise Using Ethical Frameworks," *Journal of Management Education* (August 1997): 411–417.

28. Michael J. McCarthy, "Now the Boss Knows Where You're Clicking," and "Virtual Morality: A New Workplace Quandary," *The Wall Street Journal*, October 21, 1999; and Jeffrey L. Seglin, "Who's Snooping on You?" *Business 2.0* (August 8, 2000): 202–203.

29. John Kekes, "Self-Direction: The Core of Ethical Individualism," in *Organizations and Ethical Individualism*, ed. Konstanian Kolenda (New York: Praeger, 1988), pp. 1–18.

30. Tad Tulega, *Beyond the Bottom Line* (New York: Penguin Books, 1987).

31. Bill Lynn, "*Ethics,*" Practical Ethics Web site, www.practicalethics.net/ethics.html (accessed March 23, 2010); Richard E. Thompson, "So, Greed's Not Good After All," *Trustee* (January 2003): 28; and Dennis F. Thompson, "*What Is Practical Ethics?*" Harvard University Edmond J. Safra Foundation Center for Ethics Web site, www.ethics.harvard.edu/the-center/what-is-practical-ethics (accessed March 23, 2010).

32. Carol D. Leonnig and David Nakamura, "Official Quickly Corralled Agents," *The Washington Post*, April 22, 2012, A1; David Nakamura, "Out of Public Eye, a Disgusted Secret Service Director," *The Washington Post*, April 26, 2012, A1; and Carol D. Leonnig and David Nakamura, "Four in Secret Service Fight Back," *The Washington Post*, May 23, 2012, A1.

33. Anonymous official quoted in Leonnig and Nakamura, "Four in Secret Service Fight Back."

34. Gerard L. Rossy, "Five Questions for Addressing Ethical Dilemmas," *Strategy & Leadership* 39, no. 6 (2011): 35–42.

35. John D. Kammeyer-Mueller, Lauren S. Simon, and Bruce L. Rich, "The Psychic Cost of Doing Wrong: Ethical Conflict, Divestiture Socialization, and Emotional Exhaustion," *Journal of Management* 38, no. 3 (May 2012): 784–808.

36. L. Kohlberg, "Moral Stages and Moralization: The Cognitive-Developmental Approach," in *Moral Development and Behavior: Theory, Research, and Social Issues*, ed. T. Lickona (New York: Holt, Rinehart and Winston, 1976), pp. 31–83; L. Kohlberg, "Stage and Sequence: The Cognitive-Developmental Approach to Socialization," in *Handbook of Socialization Theory and Research*, ed. D. A. Goslin (Chicago: Rand McNally, 1969); Linda K. Treviño, Gary R. Weaver, and Scott J. Reynolds, "Behavioral Ethics in Organizations: A Review," *Journal of Management* 32, no 6 (December 2006): 951–990; and Jill W. Graham, "Leadership, Moral Development, and Citizenship Behavior," *Business Ethics Quarterly* 5, no. 1 (January 1995): 43–54.

37. Ihosvani Rodriguez, "Hallandale Beach Lifeguard Fired After Participating in Beach Rescue," *Sun Sentinel*, July 3, 2012, http://articles.sun-sentinel.com/2012-07-03/news/fl-hallandale-beach-lifeguards-20120703_1_lifeguard-services-jeff-ellis-beach-rescue (accessed July 9, 2012); and Gilma Avalos and Ari Odzer, "Hallandale Beach Lifeguard Fired for Leaving His Zone to Rescue Drowning Man," *NBCMiami.com*, July 5, 2012, www.nbcmiami.com/news/local/Hallandale-Beach-Lifeguard-Fired-For-Leaving-His-Zone-For-Rescue-161372785.html (accessed July 9, 2012).

38. Eugene W. Szwajkowski, "The Myths and Realities of Research on Organizational Misconduct," in *Research in Corporate Social Performance and Policy*, ed. James E. Post (Greenwich, CT: JAI Press, 1986), 9: 103–122; and Keith Davis, William C. Frederick, and Robert L. Blostrom, *Business and Society: Concepts and Policy Issues* (New York: McGraw-Hill, 1979).

39. Douglas S. Sherwin, "The Ethical Roots of the Business System," *Harvard Business Review* 61 (November–December 1983): 183–192.

40. Nancy C. Roberts and Paula J. King, "The Stakeholder Audit Goes Public," *Organizational Dynamics* (Winter 1989): 63–79; Thomas Donaldson and Lee E. Preston, "The Stakeholder Theory of the Corporation: Concepts, Evidence, and Implications," *Academy of Management Review* 20, no. 1 (1995): 65–91; and Jeffrey S. Harrison and Caron H. St. John, "Managing and Partnering with External Stakeholders," *Academy of Management Executive* 10, no. 2 (1996): 46–60.

41. R. Mitchell, B. Agle, and D. J. Wood, "Toward a Theory of Stakeholder Identification and Salience: Defining the Principle of Who or What Really Counts," *Academy of Management* Review 22 (1997): 853–886; Virginie Vial, "Taking a Stakeholders' Approach to Corporate Social Responsibility," *Global Business and Organizational Excellence* (September–October 2011): 37–47; and Martijn Poel, Linda Kool, and Annelieke van der Giessen, "How to Decide on the Priorities and Coordination of Information Society Policy? Analytical Framework and Three Case Studies," *Info: The Journal of Policy, Regulation and Strategy for Telecommunications, Information, and Media* 12, no. 6 (2010): 21–39.

42. N. Craig Smith, Sean Ansett, and Lior Erex, "How Gap Inc. Engaged with Its Stakeholders," *MIT Sloan Management Review* 52, no. 4 (Summer 2011): 69–76.

43. *Ibid.*

44. Max B. E. Clarkson, "A Stakeholder Framework for Analyzing and Evaluating Corporate Social Performance," *Academy of Management Review* 20, no. 1 (1995): 92–117.

45. Rich Kauffeld, Abhishek Malhotra, and Susan Higgins, "Green Is a Strategy," *Strategy + Business* (December 21, 2009).

46. Reported in Dung K. Nguyen and Stanley F. Slater, "Hitting the Sustainability Sweet Spot: Having It All," *Journal of Business Strategy* 31, no. 3 (2010): 5–11.

47. Steven Mufson, "Keystone XL Pipeline Expansion Driven by Oil-Rich Tar Sands in Alberta," *The Washington Post*, June 30, 2012, www.washingtonpost .com/business/economy/keystone-xl-pipeline-expansion-driven-by-oil-rich-tar-sands-in-alberta/2012/06/30/gJQAVe4ZEW_story.html?wpisrc (accessed July 4, 2012).

48. This definition is based on Marc J. Epstein and Marie-Josée Roy, "Improving Sustainability Performance: Specifying, Implementing and Measuring Key Principles," *Journal of General Management* 29, no. 1 (Autumn 2003): 15–31; World Commission on Economic Development, *Our Common Future* (Oxford, U.K.: Oxford University Press, 1987); and A. W. Savitz and K. Weber, *The Triple Bottom Line: How Today's Best-Run Companies Are Achieving Economic, Social, and Environmental Success* (San Francisco: Jossey-Bass, 2006).

49. This discussion is based on Nguyen and Slater, "Hitting the Sustainability Sweet Spot"; Savitz and Weber, *The Triple Bottom Line*; and "Triple Bottom Line," an article adapted from *The Economist Guide to Management Ideas and Gurus*, by Tim Hindle (London: Profile Books, 2008), *The Economist* (November 17, 2009), www.economist.com/node/14301663 (accessed July 5, 2012). The "people, planet, profit" phase was first coined in 1994 by John Elkington, founder of a British consulting firm called SustainAbility.

50. Mark S. Schwartz and Archie B. Carroll, "Corporate Social Responsibility: A Three-Domain Approach," *Business Ethics Quarterly* 13, no. 4 (2003): 503–530; and Archie B. Carroll, "A Three-Dimensional Conceptual Model of Corporate Performance," *Academy of Management Review* 4 (1979): 497–505. For a discussion of various models for evaluating corporate social performance, also see Diane L. Swanson, "Addressing a Theoretical Problem by Reorienting the Corporate Social Performance Model," *Academy of Management Review* 20, no. 1 (1995): 43–64.

51. Milton Friedman, *Capitalism and Freedom* (Chicago: University of Chicago Press, 1962), p. 133; and Milton Friedman and Rose Friedman, *Free to Choose* (New York: Harcourt Brace Jovanovich, 1979).

52. Eugene W. Szwajkowski, "Organizational Illegality: Theoretical Integration and Illustrative Application," *Academy of Management Review* 10 (1985): 558–567.

53. David Barstow, "Vast Mexico Bribery Case Hushed up by Walmart After Top-Level Struggle," *The New York Times*, April 21, 2012, www.nytimes.com/2012/04/22/business/at-walmart-in-mexico-a-bribe-inquiry-silenced.html?pagewanted=all (accessed July 6, 2012).

54. David J. Fritzsche and Helmut Becker, "Linking Management Behavior to Ethical Philosophy—An Empirical Investigation," *Academy of Management Journal* 27 (1984): 165–175.

55. "Royal DSM," segment in Alison Beard and Richard Hornik, "Spotlight on the Good Company: It's Hard to Be Good," *Harvard Business Review* (November 2011): 88–94.

56. Smith, Ansett, and Erex, "How Gap Inc. Engaged with Its Stakeholders."

57. Jessica Dickler, "Donations to Japan Lag Far Behind Haiti or Katrina," *CNNMoney.com*, March 18, 2011, http://money.cnn.com/2011/03/18/pf/japan_earthquake_aid/index.htm (accessed July 6, 2012).

58. Saul W. Gellerman, "Managing Ethics from the Top Down," *Sloan Management Review* (Winter 1989): 73–79.

59. Attributed to Philip Delves Broughton in David A. Kaplan, "MBAs Get Schooled in Ethics," *Fortune* (October 26, 2009): 27–28.

60. Leslie Wayne, "A Promise to Be Ethical in an Era of Temptation," *The New York Times*, May 30, 2009; and Kelley Holland, "Is It Time to Retrain B-Schools?" *The New York Times*, March 15, 2009.

61. Michael E. Brown and Linda K. Treviño, "Ethical Leadership: A Review and Future Directions," *The Leadership Quarterly* 17 (2006): 595–616; Weaver, Treviño, and Agle, "'Somebody I Look Up To'"; and L. K. Treviño et al., "Managing Ethics and Legal Compliance: What Works and What Hurts?" *California Management Review* 41, no. 2 (Winter 1999): 131–151.

62. "Code of Conduct," Google Investor Relations, April 25, 2012, http://investor.google.com/corporate/code-of-conduct.html (accessed September 28, 2012).

63. M. A. Cleek and S. L. Leonard, "Can Corporate Codes of Ethics Influence Behavior?" *Journal of Business Ethics* 17, no. 6 (1998): 619–630.

64. K. Matthew Gilley, Chris Robertson, and Tim Mazur, "The Bottom-Line Benefits of Ethics Code Commitment," *Business Horizons* 53 (January–February 2010): 31–37; Joseph L. Badaracco and Allen P. Webb, "Business Ethics: A View from the Trenches," *California Management Review* 37, no. 2 (Winter 1995): 8–28; and Ronald B. Morgan, "Self- and Co-Worker Perceptions of Ethics and Their Relationships to Leadership and Salary," *Academy of Management Journal* 36, no. 1 (February 1993): 200–214.

65. Cheryl Rosen, "A Measure of Success? Ethics After Enron," *Business Ethics* (Summer 2006): 22–26.

66. Alan Yuspeh, "Do the Right Thing," *CIO* (August 1, 2000): 56–58.

67. Reported in Rosen, "A Measure of Success? Ethics After Enron."

68. Marcia P. Miceli and Janet P. Near, "The Relationship Among Beliefs, Organizational Positions, and Whistle-Blowing Status: A Discriminant Analysis," *Academy of Management Journal* 27 (1984): 687–705; and Michael T. Rehg et al., "Antecedents and Outcomes of Retaliation Against Whistleblowers: Gender Differences and Power Relationships," *Organization Science* 19, no. 2 (March–April 2008): 221–240.

69. Eugene Garaventa, "*An Enemy of the People* by Henrik Ibsen: The Politics of Whistle-Blowing," *Journal of Management Inquiry* 3, no. 4 (December 1994): 369–374; Marcia P. Miceli and Janet P. Near, "Whistleblowing: Reaping the Benefits," *Academy of Management Executive* 8, no. 3 (1994): 65–74.

70. Jeremy Roebuck and Amy Worden, "McQueary Affirms Report to Officials: Says He Told of Seeing 'Severe Sexual Acts' in the Showers," *Philadelphia Inquirer*, December 17, 2011, A1; Jo Becker, "E-Mails Suggest Paterno Role in Silence on Sandusky," *The New York Times*, July 1, 2012, www.nytimes.com/2012/07/01/sports/ncaafootball/paterno-may-have-influenced-decision-not-to-report-sandusky-e-mails-indicate.html?_r=1&emc=eta1 (accessed July 9, 2012); Drew Sharp, "At Penn State, Football Bigger Than Principle," *Pittsburgh Post-Gazette*, June 25, 2012, A8; and Alina Tugent, "Doing the Ethical Thing May Be Right, But It Isn't Automatic," *The New York Times*, November 18, 2011.

71. Jessica Bennett, "Meet Penn State's New Whistleblower, Vicky Triponey," *The Daily Beast*, November 23, 2011, www.thedailybeast.com/articles/2011/11/23/meet-penn-state-s-new-whistleblower-vicky-triponey.html (accessed July 9, 2012).

72. Nicole Gaudiano, "Report: Air Force Whistle-Blowers Targeted," *USA Today*, February 1, 2012, 3A; Gretchen Morgenson, "How a Whistle-Blower Conquered Countrywide," *The New York Times*, February 20, 2011, BU1; and Christine Seib and Alexandra Frean, "Lehman Whistleblower Lost Job Month After Speaking Out," *The Times*, March 17, 2010, 43.

73. Richard McGill Murphy, "Why Doing Good Is Good For Business," *Fortune* (February 8, 2010): 90–95.

74. Homer H. Johnson, "Does It Pay to Be Good? Social Responsibility and Financial Performance," *Business Horizons* (November–December 2003): 34–40; Jennifer J. Griffin and John F. Mahon, "The Corporate Social Performance and Corporate Financial Performance Debate: Twenty-Five Years of Incomparable Research," *Business and Society* 36, no. 1 (March 1997): 5–31; Bernadette M. Ruf et al., "An Empirical Investigation of the Relationship Between Change in Corporate Social Performance and Financial Performance: A Stakeholder Theory Perspective," *Journal of Business Ethics* 32, no. 2 (July 2001): 143ff; Philip L. Cochran

and Robert A. Wood, "Corporate Social Responsibility and Financial Performance," *Academy of Management Journal* 27 (1984): 42–56.

75. Heli Wang, Jaepil Choi, and Jiatao Li, "Too Little or Too Much? Untangling the Relationship Between Corporate Philanthropy and Firm Financial Performance," *Organization Science* 19, no. 1 (January–February 2008): 143–159; Philip L. Cochran, "The Evolution of Corporate Social Responsibility," *Business Horizons* 50 (2007): 449–454; Paul C. Godfrey, "The Relationship Between Corporate Philanthropy and Shareholder Wealth: A Risk Management Perspective," *Academy of Management Review* 30, no. 4 (2005): 777–798; Oliver Falck and Stephan Heblich, "Corporate Social Responsibility: Doing Well by Doing Good," *Business Horizons* 50 (2007): 247–254; J. A. Pearce II and J. P. Doh, "The High Impact of Collaborative Social Initiatives," *MIT Sloan Management Review* (Spring 2005): 31–39; Curtis C. Verschoor and Elizabeth A. Murphy, "The Financial Performance of Large U.S. Firms and Those with Global Prominence: How Do the Best Corporate Citizens Rate?" *Business and Society Review* 107, no. 3 (Fall 2002): 371–381; Johnson, "Does It Pay to Be Good?"; Dale Kurschner, "5 Ways Ethical Business Creates Fatter Profits," *Business Ethics* (March–April 1996): 20–23.

76. Rashid Ameer and Radiah Othman, "Sustainability Practices and Corporate Financial Performance: A Study Based on the Top Global Corporations," *Journal of Business Ethics* 108, no. 1 (June 2012): 61–79.

77. Verschoor and Murphy, "The Financial Performance of Large U.S. Firms."

78. Phred Dvorak, "Finding the Best Measure of 'Corporate Citizenship,'" *The Wall Street Journal*, July 2, 2007.

79. Jean B. McGuire, Alison Sundgren, and Thomas Schneeweis, "Corporate Social Responsibility and Firm Financial Performance," *Academy of Management Journal* 31 (1988): 854–872; and Falck and Heblich, "Corporate Social Responsibility: Doing Well by Doing Good."

80. Daniel W. Greening and Daniel B. Turban, "Corporate Social Performance as a Competitive Advantage in Attracting a Quality Workforce," *Business and Society* 39, no. 3 (September 2000): 254; and Kate O'Sullivan, "Virtue Rewarded," *CFO* (October 2006): 47–52.

81. "The Socially Correct Corporate Business," in Leslie Holstrom and Simon Brady, "The Changing Face of Global Business," a special advertising section, *Fortune* (July 24, 2000): S1–S38.

82. Remi Trudel and June Cotte, "Does Being Ethical Pay?" *The Wall Street Journal*, May 12, 2008.

83. Based on Bart Victor and John B. Cullen, "The Organizational Bases of Ethical Work Climates," *Administrative Science Quarterly* 33 (1988): 101–125.

84. Adapted from Richard L. Daft and Dorothy Marcic, *Understanding Management* (Mason, OH: South-Western, 2008), 134.

Small Business Start-Ups

Christian Mueller/Shutterstock.com

Learning Outcomes

After studying this chapter, you should be able to:

1. Define entrepreneurship and the four classifications of entrepreneurs.

2. Describe the importance of entrepreneurship to the global and U.S. economies.

3. Appreciate the impact of minority- and women-owned businesses.

4. Define the personality characteristics of a typical entrepreneur.

5. Explain social entrepreneurship as a vital part of today's small business environment.

6. Outline the planning necessary to launch an entrepreneurial start-up.

7. Describe the five stages of growth for an entrepreneurial company.

8. Explain how the management activities of planning, organizing, decision making, and controlling apply to a growing entrepreneurial company.

Do You Think Like an Entrepreneur?[1]

INSTRUCTIONS: An entrepreneur faces many demands. Do you have the proclivity to start and build your own business? To find out, consider the extent to which each of the following statements characterizes your behavior. Please answer each of the following items as Mostly True or Mostly False for you.

	Mostly True	Mostly False
1. Give me a little information and I can come up with a lot of ideas.	_____	_____
2. I like pressure in order to focus.	_____	_____
3. I don't easily get frustrated when things don't go my way.	_____	_____
4. I identify how resources can be recombined to produce novel outcomes.	_____	_____
5. I enjoy competing against the clock to meet deadlines.	_____	_____
6. People in my life have to accept that nothing is more important than the achievement of my school, my sport, or my career goals.	_____	_____
7. I serve as a role model for creativity.	_____	_____
8. I think "on my feet" when carrying out tasks.	_____	_____
9. I am determined and action-oriented.	_____	_____

SCORING AND INTERPRETATION: Each question pertains to some aspect of improvisation, which is a correlate of entrepreneurial intentions. Entrepreneurial improvisation consists of three elements. Questions 1, 4, and 7 pertain to creativity and ingenuity, the ability to produce novel solutions under constrained conditions. Questions 2, 5, and 8 pertain to working under pressure and stress, the ability to excel in pressure-filled circumstances. Questions 3, 6, and 9 pertain to action and persistence, the determination to achieve goals and solve problems in the moment. If you answered "Mostly True" to at least two of three questions for each subscale, or six of all the nine questions, then consider yourself an entrepreneur in the making, with the potential to manage your own business. If you scored one or fewer "Mostly True" on each subscale or three or fewer for all nine questions, you might want to consider becoming a manager by working for someone else.

S cott Adams, the writer of the satirical *Dilbert* comic strip, was a budding entrepreneur during his college years at Hartwick College in New York. An economics major who aspired to be a banker, Adams grew to see the world through an entrepreneur's eyes during a variety of small-business ventures. First, he convinced his accounting professor to hire him as "Minister of Finance" at the campus coffeehouse, where he created and oversaw an accounting system. The system replaced a previous one that Adams described as "seven students trying to remember where all the money went." Adams's next venture was a plan to become student manager of his dormitory and get paid to do it. "For the next two years, my friends and I each had a private room at no cost, a base salary, and the experience of managing the dorm. On some nights, I also got paid to do overnight security, while also getting paid to clean the laundry room," Adams said.

After college, Adams started his career in banking, but it didn't work out as he'd hoped, so he left to pursue a career in writing. He is convinced his experiences during his entrepreneurial stints in college paid off. "Every good thing that has happened to me as an adult can be traced back to that training," he says. What is Scott Adams's advice to up-and-coming entrepreneurs? First, he says, take risks and try to get paid while you're doing the failing,

1 INTRODUCTION

2 ENVIRONMENT

3 PLANNING

4 ORGANIZING

5 LEADING

6 CONTROLLING

and learn new skills that will be useful later. Second, replace fear and shyness with enthusiasm and learn to enjoy speaking to a crowd. Third, learn how to persuade. "Students of entrepreneurship should learn the art of persuasion in all its forms, including psychology, sales, marketing, negotiating, statistics, and even design," says Adams.[2]

Starting and growing your own business requires a combination of many skills to be successful. Adams, a highly successful entrepreneur, combined business smarts, creativity, and passion when he left the corporate world for a writing career. His passion is shared by many other courageous self-starters, who take the leap and start a sole proprietorship, one of the fastest-growing segments of small business in both the United States and Canada. Approximately 600,000 new businesses are launched in the U.S each year by self-starting entrepreneurs.[3]

What Is Entrepreneurship?

Entrepreneurship is the process of initiating a business venture, organizing the necessary resources, and assuming the associated risks and rewards.[4] An **entrepreneur** is someone who engages in entrepreneurship. An entrepreneur recognizes a viable idea for a business product or service and carries it out by finding and assembling the necessary resources—money, people, machinery, location—to undertake the business venture. Entrepreneurs also assume the risks and reap the rewards of the business. They assume the financial and legal risks of ownership and receive the business's profits.

Matt Maloney and Mike Evans are good examples of entrepreneurs. Working late on a snowy Chicago night, these two software engineers flipped through a stack of to-go menus to find a restaurant. As they searched for a restaurant that would deliver to their downtown office, they became intrigued by the idea of an online solution to their dilemma. Maloney and Evans combined their programming expertise with an unbridled entrepreneurial energy and started GrubHub, which organizes neighborhood restaurants at one Web site where diners can place carryout orders. Participating restaurants pay an average of 15.5 percent commission on each order. Maloney, who serves as CEO, admits the early days were rough. "We never doubted our vision. But there were frustrating times early on—a bug in the Web site or something that temporarily stumped us. Right now, we list over 13,000 restaurants on our site. Within three months, we'll list over 80,000, with all menus keyed in completely," he said.[5] Maloney and Evans were willing to take the risks, and they are now reaping the rewards of entrepreneurship.

Successful entrepreneurs have many different motivations, and they measure rewards in different ways. One study classified small business owners into five different categories, as illustrated in Exhibit 6.1. Some people are *idealists*, who like the idea of working on something that is new, creative, or personally meaningful. *Optimizers* are rewarded by the personal satisfaction of being business owners. Entrepreneurs in the *sustainer* category like the chance to balance work and personal life and often don't want the business to grow too large, while *hard*

Concept Connection ◀◀◀

Environmentalist Laurie Brown, pictured here, is an **idealist entrepreneur** who translated her love for nature into Minneapolis-based Restore Products Company, a producer of nontoxic cleaning products. What sets Restore apart is the patented Restore Refilling Station. The store kiosk reads the product's bar code, refills the plastic bottle with a highly concentrated mixture, and then rewards the consumer with a discount coupon. Environmental benefits include reducing the number of plastic bottles that get trucked to landfills, substantially eliminating packaging, and saving water. According to Brown, at least 45 percent of her product is sold in refill form.

Neal St. Anthony/ZUMA Press/Newscom

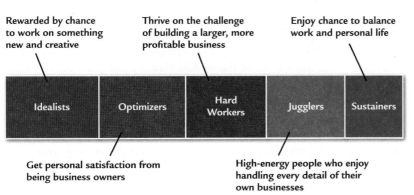

EXHIBIT 6.1

Five Types of Small Business Owners

SOURCE: Based on a study conducted by Yankelovich Partners for Pitney Bowes in Mark Henricks, "Type-Cast," *Entrepreneur* (March 2000): 14–16.

workers enjoy putting in the long hours and dedication to build a larger, more profitable business. The *juggler* category includes entrepreneurs who like the chance that a small business gives them to handle everything themselves. These high-energy people thrive on the pressure of paying bills, meeting deadlines, and making payroll.[6]

Compare the motivation of Susan Polis Schutz, the owner of Blue Mountain Arts, to that of Jeff Bezos, founder of Amazon.com. Schutz has always written poetry about love and nature. On a whim, her husband illustrated one of her poems and created 12 posters to sell at a local bookstore. The posters sold quickly, and the bookstore placed another order. That was the start of Blue Mountain Arts. With her husband working as illustrator and her mother working as sales manager, Schutz was content with a life that blended work and family. When the company exploded to more than 300 employees, this perfect balance was jeopardized. To give herself more family time, Schutz hired a business manager to take over daily operations. "I still love connecting to people's emotions on love, nature, friendship, and family in my work, but my favorite thing these days is doting on my grandson, who is five years old," said Schutz.[7] In contrast, Jeff Bezos launched Amazon in 1994 with a vision to build "an important and lasting company." Bezos was in no hurry, then or now, to boost profits. Instead, he focuses on revenue growth and customer service. Leading this closely watched, high-growth business is demanding and requires that Bezos continuously seek out new ideas and products. Jeff Bezos reflects the motivation of a *hard worker*, whereas Susan Polis Schutz's motivation is more that of a *sustainer*.

Remember This

- **Entrepreneurship** is the process of initiating a business, organizing the necessary resources, and assuming the associated risks and rewards.
- One of the fastest-growing segments of small business is in one-owner operations, called *sole proprietorships*.
- An **entrepreneur** recognizes a viable idea for a business product or service and carries it out by finding and assembling the necessary resources to start the business.
- Scott Adams, creator of *Dilbert*, started his first entrepreneurial ventures while still in college.
- Entrepreneurs may be classified as *idealists*, *optimizers*, *sustainers*, *hard workers*, or *jugglers*.

Impact of Entrepreneurial Companies

Small businesses have been hit particularly hard by the global economic crisis and weak consumer demand. But rejuvenation in the economy is underway, and small businesses and entrepreneurs are the engine behind the rebound that's occurring in many markets.

2

ENVIRONMENT

ENTREPRENEURSHIP INTERNATIONALLY

Globally, entrepreneurship has experienced a tremendous boost due to huge advances in technology and the rapid expansion of the middle class in countries such as China and India. Consider one of India's most successful entrepreneurs, Narayana Murthy. He and several co-founders launched Infosys and sparked an outsourcing revolution that has brought billions of dollars into the Indian economy. Infosys offers business consulting, technology, engineering, and outsourcing services and has been ranked Number 1 on the list of India's most admired companies in the *Wall Street Journal Asia 200* survey every year since 2000. Murthy started the organization from scratch and, typical of most start-ups, endured years of hardship. "It is all about sacrifice, hard work, lots of frustration, being away from your family, in the hope that someday you will get adequate returns from that," explains Murthy.[8]

Entrepreneurship in other countries is also booming. The list of entrepreneurial countries around the world, shown in Exhibit 6.2, is intriguing. A project monitoring entrepreneurial activity reports that an estimated 24 percent of adults age 18 to 64 in China are either starting or managing new enterprises. The percentage in Chile is 24 percent; in Peru, 23 percent. Argentina, Brazil, and Jamaica also show higher rates of entrepreneurial activity than the U.S. rate of 12 percent.[9]

ENTREPRENEURSHIP IN THE UNITED STATES

The impact of entrepreneurial companies on the U.S. economy is astonishing. In the United States, small businesses—including outsourcing firms in Chicago and high-tech start-ups in California—create two out of every three new jobs. The 28 million small firms

EXHIBIT 6.2

Entrepreneurial Activity Around the World

Country	Percentage of Individuals Age 18 to 64 Active in Starting or Managing a New Business, 2011
China	24
Chile	24
Peru	23
Argentina	22
Brazil	15
Jamaica	13
Turkey	12
United States	12
Mexico	9
Poland	8
Greece	8
Portugal	8
Germany	6
Belgium	6
Japan	5

Note: Total early-stage Entrepreneurial Activity (TEA): % of 18-64 population who are either a "nascent entrepreneur" or owner-manager of a "new business." A "nascent entrepreneur" is defined as someone actively involved in setting up a business they will own or co-own; this business has not paid salaries, wages, or any other payments to the owners for more than three months. A "new business" is defined as a running business that has paid salaries, wages, or any other payments to the owners for more than three months, but not more than 42 months.

SOURCE: From Donna J. Kelley, Slavica Singer, and Mike Herrington, *Global Entrepreneurship Monitor 2011 Executive Report.* Permission to reproduce a figure from the GEM 2011 Global Report, which appears here, has been kindly granted by the copyright holders. The Global Entrepreneurship Monitor (GEM) is an international consortium, and this report was produced from data collected in, and received from, 54 countries in 2011. Our thanks go to the authors, national teams, researchers, funding bodies and other contributors who have made this possible.

in the United States employ 60 million Americans, about half of the private sector work-force.[10] According to the Small Business Administration (SBA), small businesses represent 98 percent of all businesses in the United States.[11] In addition, small businesses represent 97 percent of America's exporters and produce 30.2 percent of all export value.[12]

Not surprisingly, online businesses are forming at record rates. Powerful technology, such as Google's application engine, Amazon's Web services, and Facebook's authentication technology, is readily available and inexpensive. These building blocks make it easier for tech start-ups to create products and services within a year of being founded. A decade ago, it was pricey to start a company. But in the past few years, with each new breakthrough in Internet and mobile technology, entrepreneurs "can start a company for little money and run it almost anywhere," says Joe Beninato, CEO of Tello, a free customer-service rating application on the iPhone and iPad. "It used to take the first $5 million to set up the infra-structure," he says. "Now you can pull out your credit card and spend $5,000 on Amazon Web services."[13]

In the United States, entrepreneurship and small business are the engines behind job creation and innovation:

- **Job creation.** Researchers disagree over what percentage of new jobs is created by small business. Research indicates that the *age* of a company, more than its size, determines the number of jobs it creates. That is, virtually *all* new jobs in recent years have come from new companies, which include not only small companies, but also new branches of huge, multinational organizations.[14] However, small companies still are thought to create a large percentage of new jobs in the United States. Jobs created by small businesses give the United States an economic vitality that no other country can claim.

- **Innovation.** Small business owners typically gain an intimate understanding of their customers, which places them in an ideal position to innovate. According to research by entrepreneurship expert David Birch that traced the employment and sales records of some 9 million companies, new and smaller firms have been responsible for 55 percent of the innovations in 362 different industries and 95 percent of all radical innovations. In addition, fast-growing businesses, which Birch calls *gazelles*, produce twice as many product innovations per employee as do larger firms. Small firms that file for patents typically produce 13 times more patents per employee than large patenting firms.[15]

Remember This

- Entrepreneurship and small business are essential parts of the U.S. economy, representing 98 percent of all firms and employing about half of all private sector employees.

- Entrepreneurial activity is booming in other countries, with some of the highest rates in developing nations.

- Entrepreneurship and small business in the United States is an engine for job creation and innovation.

Who Are Entrepreneurs?

The heroes of American business—Henry Ford, Mary Kay Ash, Sam Walton, Oprah Winfrey, Steve Jobs—are almost always entrepreneurs. Entrepreneurs start with a vision. Often they are unhappy with their current jobs and see an opportunity to bring together the resources needed for a new venture. However, the image of entrepreneurs as bold pioneers probably is overly romantic. A survey of the CEOs of the nation's fastest-growing small firms found that these entrepreneurs could be best characterized as hardworking and practical, with great familiarity with their market and industry.[16]

MINORITY-OWNED BUSINESSES

As the minority population of the United States has grown, so has the number of minority-owned businesses. "The rise in minorities is a reflection of demographic changes," said Matthew Haller of the International Franchising Association. "As more minorities establish themselves in the U.S., they are looking to control their destiny through business ownership."[17] Consider former veterinarian Salvador Guzman, who moved from Mexico to become a busboy in a friend's Mexican restaurant in Nashville, Tennessee. Energized by the opportunities to succeed in the United States as an entrepreneur, Guzman started his own restaurant with three partners and a savings of $18,000, joining more than 2.4 million self-employed immigrants in the United States. Now he owns 14 restaurants and two Spanish-language radio stations in Tennessee.[18]

The number of minority-owned businesses increased by 45.6 percent between 2002 and 2007, to 5.8 million firms, according to the most recent data available. That's more than twice the national rate of all U.S. businesses. These new firms generated $1.0 trillion in revenues and employed 5.9 million people. Increases in the number of minority-owned businesses range from 60.5 percent for black-owned businesses to 17.9 percent for Native American– and Alaska Native–owned businesses. Hispanic-owned businesses increased by 43.6 percent.[19] Exhibit 6.3 summarizes the racial and ethnic composition of business owners in the United States.

The types of businesses launched by minority entrepreneurs are also increasingly sophisticated. The traditional minority-owned mom-and-pop retail store or restaurant is being replaced by firms in industries such as financial services, insurance, and online businesses. Several successful Silicon Valley companies have been founded or co-founded by minority entrepreneurs, including textbook-rental start-up Chegg, online dating service Zoosk, and online craft marketplace Etsy.

WOMEN-OWNED BUSINESSES

Women are also embracing entrepreneurial opportunities in greater numbers. Women own nearly 8 million firms, or 28 percent of all businesses, according to the Center for Women's Business Research. Sales of these businesses generated $1.9 million as of 2008 and provided 16 percent of all jobs in a range of industries like business services, personal services, retail, health care, and communication. While these numbers are impressive,

EXHIBIT 6.3

Racial and Ethnic Composition of Small Business Owners

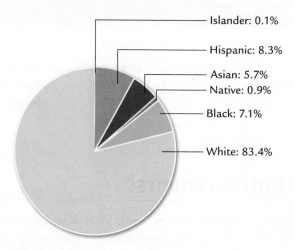

- Islander: 0.1%
- Hispanic: 8.3%
- Asian: 5.7%
- Native: 0.9%
- Black: 7.1%
- White: 83.4%

Note: The survey permitted multiple counts (for example, an owner might be counted as both Hispanic and Black) so figures add up to more than 100 percent.

SOURCE: Summary of Findings, "Preliminary Estimates of Business Ownership by Gender, Ethnicity, Race, and Veteran Status: 2007," Survey of Business Owners (SBO), U.S. Census Bureau, www.census.gov/econ/sbo/#nhpi (accessed August 23, 2010).

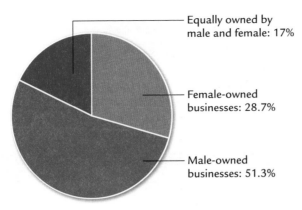

Equally owned by male and female: 17%

Female-owned businesses: 28.7%

Male-owned businesses: 51.3%

SOURCE: "Summary Statistics for All U.S. Firms by Gender: 2007," *Survey of Business Owners—Women-Owned Firms*, U.S. Census Bureau, www.census.gov/econ/sbo/get07sof.html?12# (accessed August 9, 2012).

EXHIBIT 6.4

Gender Composition of Small Business Owners

ENVIRONMENT 2

the results could be much better. Only 20 percent of women-owned businesses have employees, an area of great growth and opportunity. "The reason most businesses don't grow is [women] try to do everything themselves," claims Nell Merlino, who created the Take Our Daughters to Work campaign. "The most important thing to do is hire people. With 10 million out of work," she added, "there is an extraordinary labor pool."[20] Another challenge faced by women is the stark imbalance of the sexes in high-tech fields. Statistics show that women create only 8 percent of the venture-backed technology start-ups.[21] Exhibit 6.4 displays the gender composition of business owners in the United States.

As the cost of launching an online business falls, more women are taking a gamble in this competitive market. When Apple introduced the iPhone in 2007, the market for smartphone applications skyrocketed. Today, over 350,000 apps are available, and the market is crowded with developers trying to create apps that mobile consumers will use loyally. Reg Stettinius decided to invest $100,000 of her own money and develop a new app to solve a recurring problem. Stettinius was frustrated that she couldn't quickly find a restaurant in Washington, D.C., to entertain out-of-town guests. So she set out to build Venga, an app created for restaurants and bars to alert customers to happy-hour specials, live music, and featured entrees. Restaurants pay a monthly fee for a profile on Venga, where they can promote daily specials or regular events. Patrons can download the app for free and share it on social networks or book a table on the restaurant's Web site. One of the challenges Stettinius and her co-founders faced was finding a balance between what restaurants wanted and what consumers would use. "Not only do they need to get to restaurants," said Elana Fine, director of venture investments at the University of Maryland's Dingman Center for Entrepreneurship, "but now they need to get to users. And that's where they have to compete with all the noise that's around."[22]

TRAITS OF ENTREPRENEURS

A number of studies have investigated the characteristics of entrepreneurs and how they differ from successful managers in established organizations.

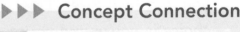

▶▶▶ **Concept Connection**

Paul Bradbury/OJO Images/Jupiter Images

Many people are motivated to start their own businesses by a desire for **autonomy**—meaning the freedom to work the way they want to work under the conditions they choose for themselves—or by a desire for **power** or **influence**. But in order for an entrepreneur to be successful, he or she needs to have a number of other important personal traits, such as unflagging enthusiasm, commitment, and confidence. Entrepreneurs are also typically comfortable with risk and ambiguity.

EXHIBIT **6.5**

Characteristics of
Entrepreneurs

SOURCE: Adapted from Leigh Buchanan, "The Motivation Matrix," *Inc.*, March 2012, www.inc.com/magazine/201203/
motivation-matrix.html (accessed August 20, 2012); and Charles R. Kuehl and Peggy A. Lambing, *Small Business: Planning and
Management* (Ft. Worth, TX: The Dryden Press, 1994), p. 45.

> "When you reach an obstacle, turn it into an opportunity. You have the choice. You can overcome and be a winner, or you can allow it to overcome you and be a loser. The choice is yours and yours alone."
>
> — MARY KAY ASH, AMERICAN BUSINESSWOMAN AND FOUNDER OF MARY KAY COSMETICS

Some suggest that entrepreneurs in general want something different from life than do traditional managers. Entrepreneurs seem to place high importance on being free to achieve and maximize their potential. Some 40 traits are identified as being associated with entrepreneurship, but seven have special importance.[23] These characteristics are illustrated in Exhibit 6.5.

Autonomy

In a survey of 2,000 entrepreneurs, the desire for autonomy was the primary motivator for pursuing an entrepreneurial life. Entrepreneurs driven by the desire for autonomy cherish the freedom of making their own decisions about their business. Because of this desire for independent planning and decision making, these entrepreneurs may consider flying solo, without partners or significant investors. But flying solo has drawbacks. It may limit a firm's growth and result in a smaller-scale business.[24] For start-ups to succeed in the long run, a founder may have to forego autonomy and allow someone else with a different set of managerial skills to lead the company into the next phase of growth. "When you're facing that tradeoff, you have to strike a stark balance. You're going to have to give up something dear to you in order to get something that is even more dear to you," said Noam Wasserman, author of *The Founder's Dilemmas: Anticipating and Avoiding the Pitfalls That Can Sink a Startup*.[25] Sometimes, this means giving up the autonomy that motivated an entrepreneur to start a business in the first place.

Entrepreneurial Struggle

Another common trait among entrepreneurs is the ability to persevere and stay positive after long periods of struggle. Consider Justin Carden, a 29-year-old software engineer, who shares cramped, communal housing with other aspiring tech entrepreneurs near Silicon Valley. He and other hopeful entrepreneurs toil for long hours in tiny living spaces working to develop ideas for new apps and Web sites. These "hacker hostels" often house ten or more people, crammed into two bedrooms. People try out their sales talks on one another before pitching them to investors. "We work so hard and we don't care about where we're staying," said Ethan Mollick, a former graduate student at the Massachusetts Institute of Technology (MIT) and assistant professor at the Wharton School of the University of Pennsylvania. "People always complain that academic study of computer science doesn't do a lot for you as a programmer. What does [work] are these sorts of environments," he said.[26] In another example of entrepreneurial struggle, two surfing buddies endured years of financial struggle as they built a new microbrewery, described in the following example.

2

ENVIRONMENT

Innovative Way

Strand Brewing Company

Joel Elliott and Rich Marcello, two surfing buddies, jumped at the idea of starting a microbrewery called Strand Brewing Company in Southern California, where rising demand for craft beers was creating opportunity. With no money or business experience, the two borrowed money from relatives and friends and maxed out their own credit cards. They built their brewery in a small, 1,000-foot warehouse and used the only fermenters they could afford—small ones, each capable of producing seven 31-gallon barrels. Marcello worked another job from 5 A.M. to 1 P.M., which freed up his afternoons, nights, and weekends for Strand. Money was so tight that they delivered kegs in Marcello's '98 Chrysler van to avoid the expense of bottling or canning. When they ran out of money, Elliott's uncle gave him his retirement funds. The two friends worked grueling hours: 100-hour work weeks for three years, without vacation or pay.

Elliott and Marcello persevered under pressure and ultimately reaped rewards for their years of struggle. As their customer base grew, the small fermenters couldn't produce enough beer for the brewery to survive. In 2010, they went back to friends and relatives and asked for more money to expand. With it, they bought three 15-barrel fermenters for about $12,000 each. It was a smart purchase: by the middle of 2011, the number of accounts exceeded 100 and the brewery was nearing capacity again. Strand raised another $300,000 for a second expansion. Today, the partners are drawing salaries, and Elliott predicts that they will repay all loans within 14 months. These entrepreneurs devoted long hours and incurred mounting debt during the start-up phase of Strand Brewing Company, but are now enjoying the taste of success.[27]

Power and Influence

Some entrepreneurs are driven by the desire for power and influence. Sam Walton, founder of Walmart, was the most successful retailer in U.S. history, partly because he was way ahead of his competitors in bringing efficiency to the supply chain and selling goods at the lowest possible prices. Walton was able to exert significant pressure on manufacturers to improve their efficiency and bring down costs. As Walmart's influence grew, so did Walton's power to dictate price, volume, delivery, packaging, and quality of many of its suppliers' products. Walton was a man who was driven by power and influence and will long be recognized as the entrepreneur who flipped the supplier-retailer relationship upside down.[28]

High Energy

A business start-up requires great effort. A survey of small business owners by Staples found that 43 percent of small business owners work more than a regular 40-hour week, 31 percent report working during holidays, and 13 percent say they regularly work more than 80 hours a week.[29] High levels of passion also help entrepreneurs overcome inevitable obstacles and traumas.[30] You can recognize entrepreneurial passion in people by their unwavering belief in a dream, intense focus, and unconventional risk taking. "To succeed, you have to believe in something with such a passion that it becomes a reality," said Anita Roddick of the Body Shop."[31]

Take a Moment

Are you an entrepreneur in the making? Do you have the persistence to endure setbacks and disappointments? Review your responses in the opening questionnaire to assess your potential to start and manage your own business.

Long before "going green" was popular, Roddick created a business that was socially and environmentally responsible. By 2007, she had an empire of more than 2,000 Body Shop stores in 50 countries.[32]

Need to Achieve

Another characteristic closely linked to entrepreneurship is the **need to achieve**, which means that people are motivated to excel and pick situations in which success is likely.[33] People who have high achievement needs like to set their own goals, which are moderately difficult. Easy goals present no challenge; unrealistically difficult goals cannot be achieved. Intermediate goals are challenging and provide great satisfaction when achieved. High achievers also like to pursue goals for which they can obtain feedback about their success. "I was very low and I had to achieve something," recalls *Harry Potter* creator and billionaire author J. K. Rowling. "Without the challenge, I would have gone stark raving mad." [34]

Self-Confidence

People who start and run a business must act decisively. They need confidence about their ability to master the day-to-day tasks of the business. They must feel sure about their ability to win customers, handle the technical details, and keep the business moving. Entrepreneurs also have a general feeling of confidence that they can deal with anything in the future; complex, unanticipated problems can be handled as they arise.

Tolerance for Ambiguity

Many people need work situations characterized by clear structure, specific instructions, and complete information. **Tolerance for ambiguity** is the psychological characteristic that allows a person to be untroubled by disorder and uncertainty. This trait is important for entrepreneurs because few situations present more uncertainty than starting a new business. Decisions are made without clear understanding of options or certainty about which option will succeed.

These traits and the demographic characteristics discussed earlier offer an insightful but imprecise picture of the entrepreneur. Successful entrepreneurs come in all ages, from all backgrounds, and may have a combination of personality traits and other characteristics. No one should be discouraged from starting a business because he or she doesn't fit a specific profile. One review of small business suggests that the three most important traits of successful entrepreneurs, particularly in a turbulent environment, are realism, flexibility, and passion. Even the most realistic entrepreneurs tend to underestimate the difficulties of building a business, so they need flexibility and a passion for their idea to survive the hurdles.[35]

Remember This

- Entrepreneurs often have backgrounds, demographic characteristics, and personalities that distinguish them from successful managers in established organizations.
- One survey suggests that the desire for autonomy is the primary motivator for people to pursue entrepreneurship.
- Characteristics common to entrepreneurs include the ability to persevere, a desire for power and influence, self confidence, a high energy level, a need to achieve, and a tolerance of ambiguity.
- The **need to achieve** means that entrepreneurs are motivated to excel and pick situations in which success is likely.
- **Tolerance for ambiguity** is the psychological characteristic that allows a person to be untroubled by disorder and uncertainty.

Social Entrepreneurship

Today's consumers have a growing expectation that organizations will operate in socially responsible ways. In response, a new breed of business is emerging that is motivated to help society solve all types of social problems, including environmental pollution, global hunger, and deaths from treatable diseases. In many ways, these businesses function like traditional businesses, but their primary focus is on providing social benefits, not maximizing financial returns. **Social entrepreneurship** focuses primarily on creating social value by providing solutions to social problems, with a secondary purpose of generating profit and returns.[36] A well-known social entrepreneur is Muhammad Yunus, who founded Grameen Bank. Yunus pioneered the concept of lending small amounts of money, called *microcredit*, to small businesses in poverty-stricken villages in India. By 2006, when Yunus won the Nobel Peace Prize, the Grameen Bank had outstanding loans to nearly 7 million poor people in 73,000 villages in Bangladesh. The Grameen model expanded into more than 100 countries and helped millions of people rise out of poverty.[37] As another example, Kathy Giusti unexpectedly became a social entrepreneur after a devastating medical diagnosis.

▶ ▶ ▶ **Concept Connection**

Social entrepreneurs Eric Schwartz and Ned Rimer created Citizen Schools to reach out to middle school students, pictured here, with after-school programs that include hands-on apprenticeships taught by volunteer professionals. The apprentices create actual products, ranging from solar cars to well-managed stock portfolios. The goal is to give students the skills and motivation to do well in their academic and personal lives. One reason the organization is so successful is that it is run on solid business principles, with a well-honed strategy and growth plan that includes concrete objectives and specific performance measures.

Citizen Schools

Green **Power**

Star Power

Jessica Alba is not the first movie beauty lured by a desire to find solutions to social problems, but she may be the first to start a company focused on a problem that many new mothers are concerned with: *How to have healthy baby products that also assure a healthy environment.*

While researching healthy-baby issues during her own pregnancy, Alba read Christopher Gavigan's book *Healthy Child, Healthy World.* Concerned by Gavigan's reports on toxin levels in baby products, Alba (in her own words) *hounded* the author, urging him to join forces with her in the creation of eco-friendly baby care products. The duo launched **The Honest Company** with a flagship product necessary to every new mom—the disposable diaper.

Independent testing demonstrated a 33 percent increase in diaper absorbency through a natural combination of wheat, corn, and wood fluff from sustainable forests, appealing to eco-conscious consumers. The new diapers are also 85 percent biodegradable, right down to the addition of "green tab" fasteners. Today, The Honest Company offers a variety of products aimed at helping children grow up in a world free of toxins and carcinogens.

Sources: "The 100 Most Creative People in Business 2012: #17 Jessica Alba," *Fast Company* (June 2012): 96–97; and "About Us: Health and Sustainability Standards," The Honest Company Web site, https://www.honest.com/about-us/health-and-sustainability (accessed October 2, 2012).

Innovative Way

The Reluctant Social Entrepreneur

Kathy Giusti never dreamed she would leave the corporate world to become an entrepreneur. She was on the fast track at the pharmaceutical company G. D. Searle and aspired to be one of the first women on the executive committee. At Searle, she was quickly identified as a "high-potential" employee. Alan Heller, who was Searle's co-president, described Giusti as "highly intelligent, highly analytical, and very driven." At Searle, she played an instrumental role in launching two successful drugs: Ambien and Daypro. An introvert by nature, she loved working for a big corporation and didn't consider herself a risk taker.

Then, Giusti received news that would change her life. She was diagnosed with multiple myeloma, a deadly blood cancer, and told that myeloma patients were living, on average, three or four years. She extensively researched treatments and was devastated by what she learned. The drugs used to fight the disease were from the 1960s, and no one was devoting research and development resources to it. Her next move was surprising. She resigned from Searle and started a nonprofit. She channeled her business smarts, passion for a cure, and high energy level to start two organizations for helping accelerate the development of treatments for the disease: the Multiple Myeloma Research Foundation and the Multiple Myeloma Research Consortium.

As a self-described "big-company person," Giusti had little respect for nonprofits because she thought most were not professionally managed. "I wanted people to see that I wasn't going to run some schlocky nonprofit. I was going to try to do this right," she says. Giusti requires the foundation and the consortium to use metrics, benchmarking, and scorecards so that all parties know their individual and collective performance and are consistently striving to do better. The leaders of a 24-person staff hold a strategy meeting every Monday and an operations meeting every Tuesday. To date, Giusti has raised more than $165 million for myeloma research, an extraordinary achievement given that the vast majority of U.S. nonprofits never surpass $1 million. "What Kathy brought to the table was an unwillingness to accept the norm," says Keith Stewart, dean for research at the Mayo Clinic in Arizona. "She's a demanding person. She knows what she wants, and she doesn't rest until she's found a solution to thorny problems."[38]

Remember This

- A **social entrepreneur** is an entrepreneurial leader who is committed to both good business and changing the world for the better.
- Social entrepreneurs are creating new business models that meet critical human needs and resolve important problems unsolved by current economic and social institutions.
- Social entrepreneurship combines the creativity, business smarts, passion, and work of the traditional entrepreneur with a social mission.

Launching an Entrepreneurial Start-Up

Whether one starts a nonprofit organization, a socially oriented business, or a traditional for-profit small company, the first step in pursuing an entrepreneurial dream is to come up with a viable idea and then plan like crazy. Once someone has a new idea in mind, a business plan must be drawn and decisions must be made about legal structure, financing, and basic tactics, such as whether to start the business from scratch and whether to pursue international opportunities from the start.

STARTING WITH AN IDEA

To some people, the idea for a new business is the easy part. They do not even consider entrepreneurship until they are inspired by an exciting idea. Other people decide they want to run their own business and set about looking for an idea or opportunity. Exhibit 6.6 shows the most important reasons that people start a new business and the source of

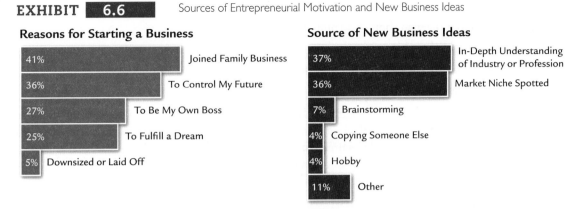

EXHIBIT 6.6 Sources of Entrepreneurial Motivation and New Business Ideas

Reasons for Starting a Business

- 41% Joined Family Business
- 36% To Control My Future
- 27% To Be My Own Boss
- 25% To Fulfill a Dream
- 5% Downsized or Laid Off

Source of New Business Ideas

- 37% In-Depth Understanding of Industry or Profession
- 36% Market Niche Spotted
- 7% Brainstorming
- 4% Copying Someone Else
- 4% Hobby
- 11% Other

SOURCE: John Case, "The Rewards," *Inc.* (May 15, 2001): 50–51; and Leslie Brokaw, "How to Start an Inc. 500 Company," *Inc.* (October 15, 1994): 51–65. Copyright 1994 and 2001 by Mansueto Ventures LLC. Reproduced with permission of Mansueto Ventures LLC.

new business ideas. Note that 37 percent of business founders got their idea from an in-depth understanding of the industry, primarily because of past job experience. Interestingly, almost as many—36 percent—spotted a market niche that wasn't being filled.[39] An example is Spanx founder Sara Blakely, who was eagerly looking for a new business idea while working full-time selling office equipment. "I had been thinking about a product I could come up with on my own," says Blakely. "I liked to sell and I was good at it. But I [wanted] to sell something that I was really passionate about." While trying to find some figure-flattering hosiery to wear under white pants, she came up with the idea for a new business. She created Spanx, a footless, body-shaping pantyhose that skyrocketed to success after Oprah Winfrey selected Spanx to be featured on the popular "favorite things" episode of her TV show. Today, Spanx has more than 100 employees and products that include swimwear, pants, skirts, and underwear.[40]

The trick for entrepreneurs is to blend their own skills and experience with a need in the marketplace. Acting strictly on one's own skills may produce something no one wants to buy. On the other hand, finding a market niche that one does not have the ability to fill doesn't work either. Both personal skill and market need typically must be present.

WRITING THE BUSINESS PLAN

Once an entrepreneur is inspired by a new business idea, careful planning is crucial. A **business plan** is a document specifying the business details prepared by an entrepreneur prior to opening a new business. Planning forces the entrepreneur to think carefully through the issues and problems associated with starting and developing the business. Most entrepreneurs have to borrow money, and a business plan is absolutely critical for persuading lenders and investors to participate in the business. Studies show that small businesses with a carefully thought-out, written business plan are much more likely to succeed than those without one.[41] To attract the interest of venture capitalists or other potential investors, the entrepreneur should keep the plan crisp and compelling.

The details of a business plan may vary, but successful business plans generally share several characteristics:[42]

- Demonstrate a clear, compelling vision that creates an air of excitement.
- Provide clear and realistic financial projections.
- Profile potential customers and the target market.
- Include detailed information about the industry and competitors.
- Provide evidence of an effective entrepreneurial management team.

2

ENVIRONMENT

- Pay attention to good formatting and clear writing.
- Keep the plan short—no more than 50 pages.
- Highlight critical risks that may threaten business success.
- Spell out the sources and uses of start-up funds and operating funds.
- Capture the reader's interest with a killer summary.

> "The first purpose of the business plan is to convince yourself that it's an idea you really want to do. If you're not convinced, you'll never be able to convince anyone else."
>
> — MAXINE CLARK, CHIEF EXECUTIVE, BUILD-A-BEAR WORKSHOP

Starting a business is a rewarding and complex process that starts with good planning, preparation, and insight. A well-crafted business plan summarizes the road map for success. As the business begins to grow, however, the entrepreneur should be prepared to handle common pitfalls, as described in this chapter's Manager's Shoptalk.

CHOOSING A LEGAL STRUCTURE

Before entrepreneurs begin a business, and perhaps again as it expands, they must choose an appropriate legal structure for the company. The three basic choices are proprietorship, partnership, or corporation.

Sole Proprietorship

A **sole proprietorship** is defined as an unincorporated business owned by an individual for profit. Proprietorships make up the majority of businesses in the United States. This form is popular because it is easy to start and has few legal requirements. A proprietor has total ownership and control of the company and can make all decisions without consulting anyone. However, this type of organization also has drawbacks. The owner has unlimited liability for the business, meaning that if someone sues, the owner's personal as well as business assets are at risk. Also, financing can be harder to obtain because business success rests on one person's shoulders.

Partnership

A **partnership** is an unincorporated business owned by two or more people. Partnerships, like proprietorships, are relatively easy to start. Two friends may reach an agreement to start a graphic arts company. To avoid misunderstandings and to make sure the business is well planned, it is wise to draw up and sign a formal partnership agreement with the help of an attorney. The agreement specifies how partners are to share responsibility and resources and how they will contribute their expertise. The disadvantages of partnerships are the unlimited liability of the partners and the disagreements that almost always occur among strong-minded people. A poll by *Inc.* magazine illustrated the volatility of partnerships. According to the poll, 59 percent of respondents considered partnerships a bad business move, citing reasons such as partner problems and conflicts. Partnerships often dissolve within five years. Respondents who liked partnerships pointed to the equality of partners (sharing of workload and emotional and financial burdens) as the key to a successful partnership.[43]

Corporation

A **corporation** is an artificial entity created by the state and existing apart from its owners. As a separate legal entity, the corporation is liable for its actions and must pay taxes on its income. Unlike other forms of ownership, the corporation has a legal life of its own; it continues to exist regardless of whether the owners live or die. And the corporation, not the owners, is liable in case the company gets sued. Thus, continuity and limits on owners' liability are two principal advantages of forming a corporation. For example, a physician can form a corporation so that liability for malpractice will not affect his or her personal assets. The major disadvantage of the corporation is that it is expensive and complex to do the paperwork required to incorporate the business and to keep the records required by law. When proprietorships and partnerships are successful and grow large, they often incorporate to limit liability and to raise funds through the sale of stock to investors.

Why Start-ups Fail

Small businesses face many challenges as they navigate through today's economy and confront issues that jeopardize their success: slow job growth, weak consumer confidence, and a slow housing recovery. It's no wonder that small business failure rates increased by 40 percent from 2007 to 2010. To keep a small business running successfully, an entrepreneur should know how to avoid potential land mines that can knock a business off course. While it is impossible to avoid all risks, a savvy entrepreneur will be alert to the most frequent reasons small business ventures fail.

- **Poor management.** Many small business owners lack the necessary business skills to manage all areas of their business, such as finance, purchasing, inventory, sales, production, and hiring. When Jay Bean founded sunglassesonly .com, he had no experience managing inventory. "Having inventory requires you to deal with a different set of complex issues, including theft control," he said. Bean's sales plummeted during the economic recession, and he closed the business in November 2010, selling the assets at a loss.

- **Overexpansion.** Some overzealous business owners confuse success with the need to expand. This may include moving into markets that are not as profitable or borrowing too much money in an attempt to keep growth at a particular rate. When the cofounders of Large Format Digital spent $1 million to build their own installation facility, they believed it would save them money in the long term. The business had been growing at about 60 percent each year since 2006. Within a month of building the facility in 2008, sales dropped 50 percent, and the company closed in March 2011.

- **Sloppy accounting.** Financial statements are the backbone of a small business, and owners need to understand the numbers to control the business. The income statement and balance sheet help diagnose potential problems before they become fatal. It's also important to understand the ratio of sales to expenses that will result in profitability. Managing cash flow is another important role of the small business owner. Businesses go through cycles and smart managers have a cash cushion that helps them recover from the inevitable bumps.

- **No Web site.** As the number of online customers increases, it's important for every business to have a professional, well-designed Web site. According to the U.S. Department of Commerce, e-commerce sales totaled $165.4 billion in 2010. The key to a successful Web site is to make it easy for users to navigate. Wesabe, a personal finance Web site, helped consumers budget their money and make smart buying decisions. With 150,000 members in the first year, the co-founders were ecstatic. A new competitor, Mint.com, launched a Web site with a better design and a more memorable name. Within three months, Mint had 300,000 users and $17 million in venture financing. Wesabe was unable to compete and closed its site soon after. Co-founder Marc Hedlund says the managers at Wesabe should have made the site easier to use. "We wanted to help people," he said, "but it was too much work to get that help."

- **Operational mediocrity.** An important role of the entrepreneur is to set high standards in essential areas such as quality control, customer service, and the company's public image. Most businesses depend on repeat and referral business, so it's important to create a positive first impression with customers. Franchisors often assist in providing high-quality products and services, reducing some of the stress entrepreneurs can face. Immigrant Lyudmila Khonomov pursued her American dream by opening a Subway restaurant in Brooklyn. "You don't have to prepare the foods from scratch," she said. Subway takes the guesswork out of preparing high-quality sandwiches in a consistent way.

- **Fear of firing.** Firing an employee is uncomfortable and difficult, but if business owners plan to outperform competitors, it's important to build and maintain an excellent staff. Unfortunately, it's very easy to keep mediocre employees around, especially those who are nice and loyal. However, it will hurt the business in the long run. Ask yourself, "Would I be relieved if anyone on my team quit tomorrow?" If the answer is yes, you may have a problem.

Sources: Patricia Schaefer, "The Seven Pitfalls of Business Failures and How to Avoid Them," *BusinessKnow-How.com*, April, 2011, www .businessknowhow.com/startup/business-failure.htm (accessed August 14, 2012); Jay Goltz, "You're the Boss: The Art of Running a Small Business," *The New York Times*, January 5, 2011, http://boss.blogs .nytimes.com/2011/01/05/top-10-reasons-small-businesses-fail/ (accessed August 14, 2012); Eilene Zimmerman, "How Six Companies Failed to Survive 2010," *The New York Times*, January 5, 2011, www .nytimes.com/2011/01/06/business/smallbusiness/06sbiz.html (accessed August 14, 2012); "The State of Small Businesses Post Great Recession: An Analysis of Small Businesses Between 2007 and 2011," Dun & Bradstreet, May 2011, www.dnbgov.com/pdf/DNB_SMB_ Report_May2011.pdf (accessed August 14, 2012); Adriana Gardella, "Advice From a Sticky Web Site on How to Make Yours the Same," *The New York Times*, April 13, 2011, www.nytimes.com/2011/04/14/ business/smallbusiness/14sbiz.html (accessed August 14, 2012).

ARRANGING FINANCING

Most entrepreneurs are particularly concerned with financing the business. A few types of businesses can still be started with a few thousand dollars, but starting a business usually requires coming up with a significant amount of initial funding. An investment is required to acquire labor and raw materials, and perhaps a building and equipment as well. High-tech businesses, for example, typically need from $50,000 to $500,000 just to get through the first six months, even with the founder drawing no salary.[44]

Many entrepreneurs rely on their own resources for initial funding, but they often have to mortgage their homes, depend on credit cards, borrow money from a bank, or give part of the business to a venture capitalist.[45] Exhibit 6.7 summarizes the most common sources of start-up capital for entrepreneurs. The financing decision initially involves two options—whether to obtain loans that must be repaid (debt financing) or whether to share ownership (equity financing).

Debt Financing

Borrowing money that has to be repaid at a later date to start a business is referred to as **debt financing**. One common source of debt financing for a start-up is to borrow from family and friends. Increasingly, entrepreneurs are using their personal credit cards as a form of debt financing. Another common source is a bank loan. Banks provide some 25 percent of all financing for small business. Sometimes entrepreneurs can obtain money from a finance company, wealthy individuals, or potential customers. A typical source of funds for businesses with high potential is through **angel financing**. Angels are wealthy individuals, typically with business experience and contacts, who believe in the idea for

Concept Connection ◄◄◄

Chipotle Mexican Grill founder, chairman, and CEO Steve Ells used both **debt** and **equity financing** when he launched his "quick gourmet" restaurant chain. An $85,000 loan from his father made the first Denver restaurant possible. Later, Ells borrowed more from his father, took out an SBA loan, and raised $1.8 million from friends and private investors. Eventually, the chain received equity financing: first from McDonald's, and later from the stock that Chipotle issued when it went public. Ironically, Ells's main reason for starting Chipotle was to generate cash to finance an upscale restaurant. With Chipotle's success, he no longer has any plans to open that fancy restaurant.

Jeff Kowalsky/Bloomberg/Getty Images

EXHIBIT 6.7

Sources of Start-up Capital for Entrepreneurs

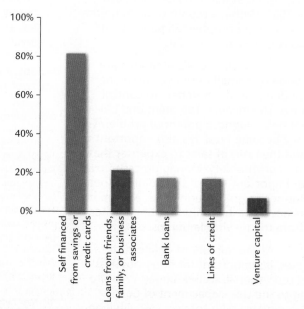

SOURCE: Jim Melloan, "The Inc. 5000," *Inc.* (September 1, 2006): 187. Copyright 2006 by Mansueto Ventures LLC. Reproduced with permission of Mansueto Ventures LLC.

New Manager Self-Test

Perceived Passion

Instructions: An entrepreneur starting a business often has to make presentations to investors in order to raise money. Respond to the following statements about how you would normally make a persuasive presentation to investors for a business you are starting. Answer whether each statement is Mostly True or Mostly False for you.

When making a formal presentation, I would:

	Mostly True	Mostly False
1. Use energetic body movements to act out the idea.	_____	_____
2. Show animated facial expressions.	_____	_____
3. Use a lot of gestures.	_____	_____
4. Talk with varied tone and pitch.	_____	_____
5. Dramatize my excitement.	_____	_____
6. Point out explicitly the relationship between the topic and its broader context.	_____	_____
7. Make sure my content has real substance.	_____	_____
8. Confirm that the presentation is coherent and logical.	_____	_____
9. Make certain the presentation is thoughtful and in-depth.	_____	_____
10. Cite facts and examples to support my points and arguments.	_____	_____

Scoring and Interpretation: This questionnaire was developed to measure the persuasiveness of presentations to venture capitalists by entrepreneurs in an effort to obtain investment money. Two aspects of presentation are measured above—passion and preparedness. Give yourself one point for each Mostly True answer.

Passion: Items 1–5 score _____.

Preparedness: Items 6–10 score _____.

The research showed consistently that preparedness, not passion, had the most positive impact on decisions to invest money with entrepreneurs. Thus, a higher score on preparedness is more important for an effective presentation to investors than is a high score on presentation passion. Compare your scores to other students. Why do you think preparedness has more impact than passion on potential investors?

Source: Based on Xiao-Ping Chen, Xin Yao, and Suresh Kotha, "Entrepreneur Passion and Preparedness in Business Plan Presentations: A Persuasion Analysis of Venture Capitalists' Funding Decisions," *Academy of Management Journal* 52, no. 1 (2009): 199–214.

the start-up and are willing to invest their personal funds to help the business get started. Significantly, angels also provide advice and assistance as the entrepreneur is developing the company. The entrepreneur wants angels who can make business contacts, help find talented employees, and serve as all-around advisors.

Another form of loan financing is provided by the Small Business Administration (SBA). Staples, which started with one office supply store in Brighton, Massachusetts, in 1986, got its start toward rapid growth with the assistance of SBA financing. Today, Staples is the world's largest office products company, with 90,000 employees, $29 billion in sales, and a presence in 26 countries.[46] SBA financing is especially helpful for people without substantial assets, providing an opportunity for single parents, minority group members, and others with a good idea but who might be considered

Take a Moment

How effective would you be at pitching a new business idea to potential investors? You can get an idea by completing the New Manager Self-Test above.

high-risk by a traditional bank. The percentage of SBA loans to women, Hispanics, African Americans, and Asian Americans has increased significantly in recent years.[47]

Equity Financing

Any money invested by owners or by those who purchase stock in a corporation is considered equity funds. **Equity financing** consists of funds that are invested in exchange for ownership in the company.

A **venture capital firm** is a group of companies or individuals that invests money in new or expanding businesses for ownership and potential profits. This is a potential source of capital for businesses with high earning and growth possibilities. Venture capitalists are particularly interested in high-tech businesses such as biotechnology, innovative online ventures, or telecommunications because they have the potential for high rates of return on investment.[48] Venture capitalist Andreessen Horowitz, a Facebook investor, contributed part of the $1 million seed money for an e-commerce start-up called the Dollar Shave Club, which hopes to claim a part of the razor market with home delivery and low prices. At the Dollar Shave Club, customers sign up for one of three plans that give them a razor and a supply of blades for $3 to $9 per month. Venture capitalists are hoping that the Dollar Shave Club totally upends the market for men's razors and blades, where competitor Gillette controls 66 percent of the market.[49]

A new option available to entrepreneurs is called **crowdfunding**, which is a way of raising capital by receiving small amounts of money from a large number of investors, usually through social media and the Internet. The Jumpstart Our Business Startups (JOBS) Act, signed into law by President Barack Obama in April 2012, opened the door for this type of fundraising from a wide pool of small investors who are not burdened with restrictions. The law allows businesses to raise money from investors in exchange for equity in the company and allows non-accredited investors (like relatives) to sink their own cash into start-ups.[50] Currently, the most successful crowdfunding Web site is Kickstarter, which began as a way for people to raise money for quirky projects like offbeat documentaries and pop-up wedding chapels. Kickstarter has expanded to include video game production and innovative new gadgets. It enables budding entrepreneurs to test new ideas and see if there's a market for them before they trade ownership of their company for money from venture capitalists. To date, Kickstarter has raised more than $200 million for 290,000 projects, or about 44 percent of those that sought financing on the site.[51]

Remember This

- The two most common sources of new business ideas come from a thorough understanding of an industry, often derived from past job experience, and identifying a market niche.
- Prior to opening a business, an entrepreneur should prepare a **business plan**, a document specifying the details of the business.
- Businesses with carefully written business plans are more likely to succeed than those without business plans.
- An unincorporated for-profit business owned by an individual is called a **sole proprietorship**.
- A **partnership** is formed when two or more people choose to own an unincorporated business.
- A **corporation** is an artificial entity created by the state and existing apart from its owners.

- **Debt financing** involves borrowing money, such as from friends, family, or a bank, that has to be repaid at a later date in order to start a business.
- **Angel financing** occurs when a wealthy individual who believes in the idea for a start-up provides personal funds and advice to help the business get started.
- **Equity financing** consists of funds that are invested in exchange for ownership in the company.
- A **venture capital firm** is a group of companies or individuals that invests money in new or expanding businesses for ownership and potential profits.
- **Crowdfunding** is a way of raising capital that involves getting small amounts of money from a large number of investors, usually using social media or the Internet.

TACTICS FOR BECOMING A BUSINESS OWNER

Aspiring entrepreneurs can become business owners in several different ways. They can start a new business from scratch, buy an existing business, or start a franchise. Another popular entrepreneurial tactic is to participate in a business incubator.

Start a New Business

One of the most common ways to become an entrepreneur is to start a new business from scratch. This approach is exciting because the entrepreneur sees a need for a product or service that has not been filled before and then sees the idea or dream become a reality. Sara and Warren Wilson, co-founders of the Snack Factory, built a $42 million business by coming up with new snack-sized versions of traditional foods. Together, they dreamed up the concept of bagel chips, which are flat, crunchy chips made from bagels. "We didn't just daydream ideas; we figured out a way to make them happen," said Warren Wilson. After selling Bagel Chips to Nabisco in 1992, the dream continued, and they went on to create pita chips and pretzel chips. "As with our two previous businesses, we built Pretzel Chips little by little and with great attention to detail and care," he said.[52]

The advantage of starting a business is the ability to develop and design the business in the entrepreneur's own way. The entrepreneur is solely responsible for its success. A potential disadvantage is the long time it can take to get the business off the ground and make it profitable. The uphill battle is caused by the lack of established clientele and the many mistakes made by someone new to the business. Moreover, no matter how much planning is done, a start-up is risky, with no guarantee that the new idea will work. Some entrepreneurs, especially in high-risk industries, develop partnerships with established companies that can help the new company get established and grow. Others use the technique of outsourcing—having some activities handled by outside contractors—to minimize the costs and risks of doing everything in-house.[53]

Buy an Existing Business

Because of the long start-up time and the inevitable mistakes, some entrepreneurs prefer to reduce risk by purchasing an existing business. This direction offers the advantage of a shorter time to get started and an existing track record. The entrepreneur may get a bargain price if the owner wishes to retire or has other family considerations. Moreover, a new business may overwhelm an entrepreneur with the amount of work to be done and procedures to be determined. An established business already has filing systems, a payroll tax system, and other operating procedures. Potential disadvantages are the need to pay for goodwill that the owner believes exists and the possible existence of ill will toward the business. In addition, the company may have bad habits and procedures or outdated technology, which may be why the business is for sale.

Buy a Franchise

Franchising is a business arrangement where a firm (franchisor) collects upfront and ongoing fees in exchange for other firms (franchisees) to offer products and services under its brand name and using its processes.[54] The franchisee invests his or her money and owns the business but does not have to develop a new product, create a new company, or test the market. According to the International Franchising Association, the 735,571 franchise outlets in the United States employed nearly 8 million people in 2011, a decline since 2007. Franchise growth has been stalled by weak consumer spending and tight credit standards, which limit small business owners from borrowing money. But after three years of decline, the number of franchises was expected to increase 1.9 percent in 2012.[55] Exhibit 6.8 lists some of the fastest-growing franchises, including the type of business, the number of outlets worldwide,

Take **a** Moment

How motivated are you to keep working toward a goal despite setbacks? The answer may reveal your entrepreneurial potential. For a better assessment, complete the Experiential Exercise on pages 191–192.

EXHIBIT 6.8

Some of Today's Fastest-
Growing Franchises

Franchise	Type of Business	Number of Outlets*	Franchise Fee
Subway	Submarine sandwiches	37,003	$15,000
Pizza Hut	Pizza, pasta, wings	13,432	$25,000
Jimmy John's Gourmet Sandwiches	Gourmet sandwiches	1,347	$35,000
Anytime Fitness	Fitness center	1,886	$18,000–$25,000
Dunkin' Donuts	Doughnuts, coffee, baked goods	8,924	$40,000–$80,000
McDonald's	Hamburgers, chicken, salads	33,427	$45,000
Great Clips	Hair salon	2,940	$20,000–$45,000
Liberty Tax Service	Tax preparation	4,183	$40,000
Hampton Hotels	Mid-priced hotel	1,868	$65,000

*Does not include company-owned outlets.

SOURCE: "2011 Fastest-Growing Franchise Rankings," *Entrepreneur*, www.entrepreneur.com/franchises/rankings/fastestgrowing-115162/2011,-1.html (accessed August 14, 2012).

and the initial franchise fee. Initial franchise fees don't include the other start-up costs that the entrepreneur will have to cover.

The powerful advantage of a franchise is that management help is provided by the owner. Franchisors provide an established name and national advertising to stimulate local demand for the product or service. For example, Dunkin' Donuts supports its franchisees with recipes, employee training, and ongoing marketing support in exchange for a franchising fee of between $40,000 to $80,000 and an ongoing royalty fee of 5.9 percent.[56] Potential disadvantages are the lack of control that occurs when franchisors want every business managed in exactly the same way. In some cases, franchisors dictate the prices of products or require franchisees to purchase expensive equipment to support new product offerings. Vince Eupierre, a 71-year-old immigrant from Cuba, owns 34 Burger King franchises in Southern California and employs 2,500 workers. His sales are down 25 percent from three years ago due to the economic recession. As part of his franchising agreement with Burger King, he was required to purchase $1.3 million in smoothie stations and new freezers when Burger King added smoothies and frappés to its menu. Facing declining sales, Eupierre is concerned about the future. "If you ask me, 'Will you buy another store today?' I'd say, Let's wait a little bit and see what happens in the next 60 to 90 days," he said.[57] In addition, franchises can be expensive, and the high start-up costs are followed with monthly payments to the franchisor that can run from 2 percent to 15 percent of gross sales.[58]

Entrepreneurs who are considering buying a franchise should investigate the company thoroughly. The prospective franchisee is legally entitled to a copy of franchisor disclosure statements, which include information on 20 topics, including litigation and bankruptcy history, identities of the directors and executive officers, financial information, identification of any products that the franchisee is required to buy, and from whom those purchases must be made. The entrepreneur also should talk with as many franchise owners as possible because they are among the best sources of information about how the company really operates.[59] Exhibit 6.9 lists some specific questions entrepreneurs should ask when considering buying a franchise. Answering such questions can reduce the risks and improve the chances of success.

Questions About the Franchisor	Questions About Financing
1. Does the franchisor provide support such as marketing and training?	1. Do I understand the risks associated with this business, and am I willing to assume them?
2. How long does it take the typical franchise owner to start making a profit?	2. Have I had a lawyer review the disclosure documents and franchise agreement?
3. How many franchisees are there and what is the failure rate?	3. What is the initial investment?
4. How do the products or services of the franchise differ from those of competitors?	4. How much working capital is required?
5. Does the company have a history of litigation?	5. Is an existing franchise a better purchase than opening a new one?
6. What is the background of top management?	6. Is the franchisor willing to negotiate the franchise agreement?

EXHIBIT 6.9

Sample Questions for Choosing a Franchise

2 ENVIRONMENT

SOURCE: Based on Kermit Pattison, "A Guide to Assessing Franchising Opportunities," *The New York Times*, (September 17, 2009); Thomas Love, "The Perfect Franchisee," *Nation's Business* (April 1998): 59–65; and Roberta Maynard, "Choosing a Franchise," *Nation's Business* (October 1996): 56–63.

Participate in a Business Incubator

An attractive option for entrepreneurs who want to start a business from scratch is to join a business incubator. A **business incubator** typically provides shared office space, management support services, and management and legal advice to entrepreneurs. Incubators also give entrepreneurs a chance to share information with one another about local business, financial aid, and market opportunities. A recent innovation is the *virtual incubator*, which does not require that people set up on-site. These virtual organizations connect entrepreneurs with a wide range of experts and mentors and offer lower overhead and cost savings for cash-strapped small business owners. Christie Stone, co-founder of Ticobeans, a coffee distributor in New Orleans, likes the virtual approach because it gives her access to top-notch advice while allowing her to keep her office near her inventory.[60]

Business incubators have become a significant segment of the small business economy, with approximately 1,400 in operation in North America and an estimated 7,000 worldwide.[61] The incubators that are thriving are primarily nonprofits and those that cater to niches or focus on helping women or minority entrepreneurs. These incubators include those run by government agencies and universities to boost the viability of small business and spur job creation. The great value of an incubator is the expertise of a mentor, who serves as advisor, role model, and cheerleader, and ready access to a team of lawyers, accountants, and other advisors. Incubators also give budding entrepreneurs a chance to network and learn from one another.[62] "The really cool thing about a business incubator is that when you get entrepreneurial people in one place, there's a synergistic effect," said Tracy Kitts, vice president and chief operating officer of the National Business Incubation Association. "Not only do they learn from staff, they learn tons from each other, and this really contributes to their successes."[63]

STARTING AN ONLINE BUSINESS

Many entrepreneurs are turning to the Internet to expand their small businesses or launch a new venture. Anyone with an idea, a computer, access to the Internet, and the tools to create a Web site can start an online business. These factors certainly fueled Ashley Qualls's motivation to create a Web site that has become a destination for millions of teenage girls. Starting at age 15, Ashley launched Whateverlife.com with a clever Web site, an $8 domain name, and a vision to provide free designs (hearts, flowers, celebrities) for social networking pages. Her hobby has exploded into a thriving business, with advertising revenue of more than $1 million so far.[64]

As Whateverlife.com illustrates, one incentive for starting an online business is that an entrepreneur can take a simple idea and turn it into a lucrative business. Another example comes from entrepreneurs Andrew Miller and Michael Zapolin. When they bought the generic domain name *chocolate.com*, Miller and Zapolin aspired to turn a simple domain name into an online emporium. "We knew nobody was doing a good job with chocolate in the online space," says Miller. In two years, the partners have built a business that is on track to clear $2 million in annual revenue. Always in pursuit of the next big online success story, Miller and Zapolin now own 17 domain names, including *software.com* and *relationship.com*.[65]

Entrepreneurs who aspire to start online businesses follow the usual steps required to start a traditional business: Identify a profitable market niche, develop an inspiring business plan, choose a legal structure, and determine financial backing. Beyond that, they need to be unusually nimble, persistent in marketing, savvy with technology, and skillful at building online relationships. Several steps required to start an online business are highlighted here.

- **Find a market niche.** To succeed in the competitive online market, the entrepreneur needs to identify a market niche that isn't being served by other companies. Online businesses succeed when they sell unique, customized, or narrowly focused products or services to a well-defined target audience.

- **Create a professional Web site.** Online shoppers have short attention spans, so a Web site should entice them to linger. In addition, Web sites should be easy to navigate and intuitive, and also offer menus that are easy to read and understand. Even "small-time" sites need "big-time" designs and should avoid common mistakes such as typos, excessively large files that are slow to load, too much information, and sensory overload.[66] FragranceNet.com competes with big-time competitors with a Web site that clearly communicates its value proposition (designer brands at discount prices), easy navigation, and superior customer service.[67]

- **Choose a domain name.** A domain name gives a company an address on the Web and a unique identity. Domain names should be chosen carefully and be easy to remember, pronounce, and spell. How is a domain name selected? The crux of Miller and Zapolin's business, described above, is the simplicity of their domain names. Chocolate.com, for example, gets thousands of visitors a day from anyone keying "chocolate" into the address line of their Web browser. There are many options for creating a domain name, including (1) using the company name (Dell.com); (2) creating a domain name that describes your product or service (1-800-Flowers.com); or (3) choosing a domain name that doesn't have a specific meaning and provides options for expanding (Google.com).[68]

- **Use social media.** Social media sites, such as Facebook, Twitter, and YouTube, have the potential to be powerful tools for small business owners. The benefits of using social media include gaining valuable feedback on products and services, building communities of loyal followers, and promoting special events and pricing. Under the best of circumstances, loyal customers view the business as a social activity itself, making recommendations that will stream on the Facebook news feeds of all their friends. Facebook won't reveal how many businesses combine its core features with commerce, but more than 7 million apps and Web sites are integrated with the popular social network.[69] For some start-ups, social media will help them grow. For others, such as Instagram, recently purchased by Facebook, it is the basis of the business.

Concept Connection ◄◄◄

Pink Sun Media/Alamy

Etsy.com is a textbook example of how to start an online company. Co-founder and CEO Rob Kalin identified a clear **market niche**: providing an online store where crafters and artisans can sell handmade items like these. He built an engaging, user-friendly **professional Web site** that includes a community section that nurtures **online relationships**. Finally, Etsy's **domain name** is intriguing. Kalin once said he came up with it after noticing that characters in Fellini movies kept saying *et si*, but others insist Etsy stands for "easy to sell yourself."

Innovative Way

Instagram

Crammed into a small ground-floor office in the South Park neighborhood of San Francisco, Kevin Systrom and Mike Krieger worked tirelessly to develop a mobile app that would let people share pictures with friends. Recognizing that consumers are increasingly mobile, the two Stanford graduates wanted to design a social network built around photography. Initially, they launched Burbn, which let people post photos and other updates. Burbn only attracted a few hundred users, but they uploaded thousands of photos. So Systrom and Krieger went back to work and released a sleeker version for the iPhone, calling it Instagram.

Instagram lets people add quirky effects to their smartphone snapshots and share them with friends on Facebook and Twitter. Instagram became an immediate, out-of-nowhere Internet success. Early users posted their pictures to Twitter, which then sparked greater interest when people saw links to the photos in their feeds.

Today, Instagram has nearly a billion users. "It's the Web fairy tale that all start-ups dream of," said Melissa Parrish, an analyst with Forrester Research, who added: "They took a simple behavior—sharing pictures with friends—and made it a utility that people want." In September 2012, Facebook bought Instagram for around $750 million in cash and stock. Buying Instagram helps Facebook with one if its most urgent needs—making its service more appealing on smartphones. "It's easier to update Facebook when you're on the go with a snapshot rather than with text," says Rebecca Lieb of the Altimeter Group.[70]

Remember This

- The most common way to become an entrepreneur is to create a new business based on a marketable idea.
- The advantage of building a business from scratch is that the entrepreneur is solely responsible for its success; a potential drawback is the time required to make the business profitable.
- An entrepreneur may also choose to buy an existing business, shortening the time required to get started.
- **Franchising** is an arrangement by which the owner of a product or service allows others to purchase the right to distribute the product or service with help from the owner.
- **Business incubators** help start-up companies by connecting them with a range of experts and mentors who nurture them, thus increasing their likelihood of success.
- The steps in starting an online business include finding a market niche, creating a professional Web site, choosing a domain name, and using social media.

Managing a Growing Business

Once an entrepreneurial business is up and running, how does the owner manage it? Often the traits of self-confidence, creativity, and internal locus of control lead to financial and personal grief as the enterprise grows. A hands-on entrepreneur who gave birth to the organization loves perfecting every detail. But after the start-up, continued growth requires a shift in management style. Those who fail to adjust to a growing business can be the cause of the problems rather than the solution.[71] In this section, we look at the stages through which entrepreneurial companies move and then consider how managers should carry out their planning, organizing, decision making, and controlling.

STAGES OF GROWTH

Entrepreneurial businesses go through distinct stages of growth, with each stage requiring different management skills. The five stages are illustrated in Exhibit 6.10.

1. *Start-up.* In this stage, the main challenges include funding the business and adjusting the product or service in response to market demands. For example, technology entrepreneurs may cycle through several ideas for a new business idea before ultimately

Concept Connection ◄◄◄

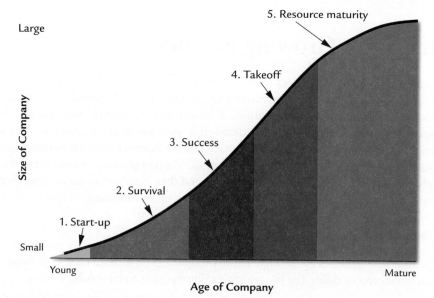

AP Photo/Lynn Hey

In 1999, Luis Brandwayn, Jochen Fischer, and Troy McConnell co-founded Batanga .com, a Hispanic online media company. McConnell is shown here in Batanga's original offices in the Nussbaum Center for Entrepreneurship **business incubator** in Greensboro, North Carolina. Initially, Batanga streamed audio and video online aimed at a Spanish-speaking audience. Its 2005 merger with Planeta Networks of Miami, a broadband platform supplier, propelled it into the **take-off stage of growth**. Now based in Coral Gables, Florida, it has continued its rapid growth by partnering with iTunes, raising $30 million in equity funding, and acquiring both LatCom Communications, a publishing and events company, and advertising network HispanoClick.

landing on the one that takes off. Because it's relatively cheap and easy to tinker with software and create new products, Internet businesses frequently **pivot**, which means to change the strategic direction of the business. "*Pivot* to me is not a four-letter word," says Tony Conrad, a partner in the early-stage venture capital firm True Ventures. "It represents some of the best methodology that the Valley has invented. Starting something, determining it's not working, and then leveraging aspects of that technology is extremely powerful."[72]

2. *Survival.* At this stage, the business demonstrates that it is a workable business entity. It produces a product or service and has sufficient customers. Concerns here involve finances—generating sufficient cash flow to run the business and making sure that revenues exceed expenses. The organization will grow in size and profitability during this period. At this critical stage, businesses must sustain their early momentum and chart a course for long-term success. Foursquare, a mobile app that lets people share their locations with friends, has nearly 1 million new users each month, yet has failed to generate income. To reach the next stage, Foursquare needs to continuously innovate, appeal to the ever-changing demands of the mobile consumer, and find ways to bring in revenues.[73]

3. *Success.* At this point, the company is solidly based and profitable. Systems and procedures are in place to allow the founder to slow down if desired. Another choice the

---

EXHIBIT 6.10

Five Stages of Growth for an Entrepreneurial Company

Size of Company

Large

Small

5. Resource maturity

4. Takeoff

3. Success

2. Survival

1. Start-up

Young   Mature

Age of Company

SOURCE: Based on Neil C. Churchill and Virginia L. Lewis, "The Five Stages of Small Business Growth," *Harvard Business Review* (May–June 1993): 30–50.

founder needs to make is whether to stay involved or turn the business over to professional managers. In making this decision, the founder who led the charge during the early years of development may confront "the paradox of entrepreneurial success." Although entrepreneurs possess the passion needed to build the business, they may have the wrong set of skills for the next stage of development. Research shows that for founders who hang onto the CEO position, their own personal equity stake is worth half as much as if they give up control to a new CEO with the skill set to grow the value of the business.[74]

4. *Takeoff.* Here the key problem is how to grow rapidly and finance that growth. The owner must learn to delegate, and the company must find sufficient capital to invest in major growth. This period is crucial in an entrepreneurial company's life. Properly managed, the company can become a big business.

5. *Resource maturity.* At this stage, the company's substantial financial gains may come at the cost of losing its advantages of small size, including flexibility and the entrepreneurial spirit. To keep that entrepreneurial spirit alive during the maturity stage, many companies fuel innovation through investments in research and development. Google, for example, has spent $11.8 billion on research and development in the past three years. Managing a massive organization while stimulating continuous innovation is often the most challenging stage for any company.[75]

PLANNING

In the early start-up stage, formal planning tends to be nonexistent except for the business plan described earlier in this chapter. The primary goal is simply to remain alive. As the organization grows, formal planning usually is not instituted until the success stage. Recall from Chapter 1 that planning means defining goals and deciding on the tasks and use of resources needed to attain them. Chapters 7, 8, and 9 describe how entrepreneurs can define goals and implement strategies and plans to meet them. It is important that entrepreneurs view their original business plan as a living document that evolves as the company grows, the market changes, or both.

One planning concern for today's small businesses is the need to plan and allocate resources for Internet operations from the beginning and grow those plans as the company grows. Of the small companies that have Web sites, more than half say that the site has broken even or paid for itself in greater efficiency, improved customer relationships, or increased business.[76]

ORGANIZING

In the first two stages of growth, the organization's structure is typically informal, with all employees reporting to the owner. At about stage 3—success—functional managers often are hired to take over duties performed by the owner. A functional organization structure will begin to evolve with managers in charge of finance, manufacturing, and marketing. Another organizational approach is to use outsourcing, as described earlier. Method, a company launched by two 20-something entrepreneurs to develop a line of nontoxic cleaning products in fresh scents and stylish packaging, contracted with an industrial designer for its unique dish soap bottle and uses contract manufacturers in every region of the country to rapidly make products and get them to stores.[77]

During the latter stages of entrepreneurial growth, managers must learn to delegate and decentralize authority. If the business has multiple product lines, the owner may consider creating teams or divisions responsible for each line. The organization must hire competent managers and have sufficient management talent to handle fast growth and eliminate problems caused by increasing size. As an organization grows, it might also be characterized by greater use of rules, procedures, and written job descriptions. Chapters 10 through 13 discuss organizing in detail.

DECISION MAKING

When managing a growing business, owners face a multitude of decisions that affect the organization's performance. These decisions may include determining inventory levels, hiring new employees, choosing a domain name for a Web site, or expanding into a new market. Every decision has the potential to alter the direction and success of the business. Paul Downs, who founded Paul Downs Cabinetmakers in 1986, confronts difficult decisions on a daily basis. With each decision, he considers alternatives, makes choices, and then follows up with necessary actions. Sometimes the decisions are easy to make. Others require careful consideration on how to best allocate limited resources. Consider the following examples of decisions that Downs has had to make:

- Should I buy a used sander that will decrease production time, or use that money to give my staff a 5 percent bonus?
- Do I purchase and move into a new building or renew my current lease that comes up next year?
- What are the risks of outsourcing work to Dubai, where I can hire ten workers for the price of one U.S. employee?
- How can I create a learning organization where workers are improving work processes constantly?
- Should I upgrade our database and customer files from an aging server and move everything to cloud computing?[78]

Several models that can help managers make better decisions will be discussed in Chapter 9.

CONTROLLING

Financial control is important in each stage of the entrepreneurial firm's growth. In the initial stages, control is exercised by simple accounting records and by personal supervision. By stage 3—success—operational budgets are in place, and the owner should start implementing more structured control systems. During the takeoff stage, the company will need to make greater use of budgets and standard cost systems and use computer systems to provide statistical reports. These control techniques will become more sophisticated during the resource maturity stage.

As Amazon.com grew and expanded internationally, for example, entrepreneur and CEO Jeff Bezos needed increasingly sophisticated control mechanisms. Bezos hired a computer systems expert to develop a system to track and control all the company's operations.[79] Control is discussed in Chapter 19 and the Appendix.

Remember This

- Small businesses generally proceed through five stages of growth: start-up, survival, success, takeoff, and resource maturity.
- In the start-up stage, Internet businesses frequently **pivot**, which means to change the strategic direction of the business.

- The management activities of planning, organizing, decision making, and controlling should be tailored to each stage of growth.

ch6: Discussion Questions

1. You are interested in being your own boss, and you have the chance to buy a franchise coffee and baked goods store that is for sale in your city. You will need outside investors to help pay the franchise fees and other start-up costs. How will you determine if this is a good entrepreneurial opportunity and make your decision about buying the store?

2. Over the past 20 years, entrepreneurship has been the fastest-growing course of study on campuses throughout the United States. Do you think it is possible to teach someone to be an entrepreneur? Why or why not?

3. Why would small business ownership have great appeal to immigrants, women, and minorities?

4. Consider the seven characteristics of entrepreneurs described in the chapter. Which two traits do you think are most like those of managers in large companies? Which two are least like those of managers in large companies?

5. How would you go about deciding whether you wanted to start a business from scratch, buy an existing business, or buy into a franchise? What information would you collect and analyze?

6. Many successful entrepreneurs say that they did little planning, perhaps scratching notes on a legal pad. How was it possible for them to do well, even so?

7. What personal skills do you need to keep your financial backers feeling confident in your new business? Which skills are most useful when you're dealing with more informal sources, such as family and friends, versus receiving funds from stockholders, a bank, or a venture capital firm? Would these considerations affect your financing strategy?

8. Many people who are successful at the start-up stage of a business are not the right people to carry the venture forward. How do you decide whether you're better suited to be a serial entrepreneur (start the business and then move on to start another), or whether you can guide the venture as it grows and matures?

9. How does starting an online business differ from starting a small business such as a local auto repair shop or delicatessen? Is it really possible for businesses that operate totally in cyberspace to build close customer relationships? Discuss.

10. Describe the benefits of using social media to help a start-up gain traction during the early stages of its life cycle. What are some possible disadvantages of using social media?

ch6: Apply Your Skills: Experiential Exercise

What's Your Entrepreneurial IQ?

Rate yourself on the following 15 behaviors and characteristics, according to the following scale.

1 = Strongly disagree   3 = Agree

2 = Disagree   4 = Strongly agree

1. I am able to translate ideas into concrete tasks and outcomes.

   1   2   3   4

2. When I am interested in a project, I tend to need less sleep.

   1   2   3   4

3. I am willing to make sacrifices to gain long-term rewards.

   1   2   3   4

4. Growing up, I was more of a risk-taker than a cautious child.

   1   2   3   4

5. I often see trends, connections, and patterns that are not obvious to others.

   1   2   3   4

6. I have always enjoyed spending much of my time alone.

   1   2   3   4

7. I have a reputation for being stubborn.

   1   2   3   4

8. I prefer working with a difficult but highly competent person to working with someone who is congenial but less competent.

   1   2   3   4

9. As a child, I had a paper route, lemonade stand, or other small enterprise.

   1   2   3   4

10. I usually keep New Year's resolutions.

    1   2   3   4

11. I'm not easily discouraged, and I persist when faced with major obstacles.

    1   2   3   4

12. I recover quickly from emotional setbacks.

    1   2   3   4

13. I would be willing to dip deeply into my "nest egg"— and possibly lose all I had saved—to go it alone.

    1   2   3   4

14. I get tired of the same routine day in and day out.
    1   2   3   4

15. When I want something, I keep the goal clearly in mind.
    1   2   3   4

Scoring and Interpretation

Total your score for the 15 items. If you tallied 50–60 points, you have a strong entrepreneurial IQ. A score of 30–50 indicates good entrepreneurial possibilities. Your chances of starting a successful entrepreneurial business are good if you have the desire and motivation. If you scored below 30, you probably do not have much entrepreneurial potential.

Go back over each question, thinking about changes you might make to become more or less entrepreneurial, depending on your career interests.

ch6: Apply Your Skills: Small Group Breakout

What Counts?[80]

Step 1. Listed below are several qualities that experts suggest are required to be a successful entrepreneur. Rank the items from 1–8 in order of what you personally think is most important to least important for successfully starting a business.

1. ____ Be motivated to the point of sacrificing your finances and lifestyle for several years.

2. ____ Enjoy all aspects of running a business, from accountant to receptionist.

3. ____ Have support from a mentor, business partner, or significant other who can supply a sympathetic ear or expertise you don't have.

4. ____ Be personally persuasive and well spoken.

5. ____ Have an idea or concept you are absolutely passionate about.

6. ____ Be a self-starter who can't wait to make things happen.

7. ____ Be comfortable making decisions on the fly without good data.

8. ____ Possess a track record of successful implementation of your own ideas.

Step 2. In groups of three to five students, each person shares his or her individual ranking and reasoning.

Step 3. Discuss rankings as a group and arrive at a single ranking for the group as a whole.

Step 4. Discuss the following questions in the group: What accounted for the differences in rankings by group members? Would the ranking differ depending on the type of business to be started? Does the ranking vary by gender? What would motivate you to start a business? Which quality on the above list would be your strongest?

ch6: Endnotes

1. Based on Keith M. Hmieleski and Andrew C. Corbett, "Proclivity for Improvisation as a Predictor of Entrepreneurial Intentions," *Journal of Small Business Management* 44, no. 1 (January 2006): 45–63; and "Do You Have an Entrepreneurial Mind?" *Inc.com*, October 19, 2005, www.inc.com (accessed October 19, 2005).

2. Scott Adams, "How to Get a Real Education," *The Wall Street Journal*, April 9–10, 2011, C1.

3. U.S. Small Business Administration, www.sba.gov/content/entrepreneurship-you-0 (accessed August 6, 2012).

4. Donald F. Kuratko and Richard M. Hodgetts, *Entrepreneurship: A Contemporary Approach*, 4th ed. (Fort Worth, TX: The Dryden Press, 1998), p. 30.

5. Megan Shank, "GrubHub Has a Full Menu," *The Washington Post*, February 26, 2011, www.washingtonpost.com/wp-dyn/content/article/2011/02/26/AR2011022603117.html (accessed August 6, 2012).

6. Study conducted by Yankelovich Partners, reported in Mark Henricks, "Type-Cast," *Entrepreneur* (March 2000): 14–16.

7. Susan Polis Schutz, "Poetry and a Pickup Truck," *The New York Times*, March 3, 2012, www.nytimes.com/2012/03/04/jobs/blue-mountain-arts-chief-on-how-the-business-began.html?_r=1&pagewanted=print (accessed August 6, 2012).

8. John A. Byrne, "The 12 Greatest Entrepreneurs of Our Time," *Fortune* (April 9, 2012): 67–86; "Asia 200: Infosys Tops India's Most Admired Companies," *The Wall Street Journal Asia Online*, November 2, 2010, http://online.wsj.com/article/SB10001424052702304173704575577683613256368.html (accessed October 2, 2012); and "Asia 200 Interactive," *The Wall Street Journal Online*, http://online.wsj.com/article/SB10001424052702304410504575559363431123480.html (accessed October 2, 2012).

9. Donna J. Kelley, Slavica Singer, and Mike Herrington, *Global Entrepreneurship Monitor 2011 Executive Report*,

July 26, 2012, http://www.gemconsortium.org/docs/2409/gem-2011-global-report (accessed October 9, 2012).

10. "Moving America's Small Businesses & Entrepreneurs Forward: Creating an Economy Built to Last," *National Economic Council* (May 2012), www.whitehouse.gov/sites/default/files/docs/small_business_report_05_16_12.pdf (accessed August 7, 2012).

11. Major L. Clark, III and Radwan N. Saade, Office of Advocacy U.S. Small Business Administration, September 2010, http://archive.sba.gov/advo/research/rs372tot.pdf (accessed August 6, 2012).

12. U.S. Small Business Administration, www.sba.gov/advo/stats/sbfaq.pdf (accessed August 7, 2012).

13. Jon Swartz, "Google, Amazon, Facebook Put Start-ups on Fast Track," *USA Today*, February 22, 2011, www.google.com/search?sourceid=navclient&aq=4&oq=google+amazon&ie=UTF-8&rlz=1T4ADRA_enUS426US427&q=google+amazon+facebook+put+startups+on+fast+track&gs_upl=0l0l0l5065llllllllllll0&aqi=g4s1&pbx=1 (accessed August 7, 2012).

14. Research and statistics reported in "The Job Factory," *Inc.* (May 29, 2001): 40–43.

15. Ian Mount, "The Return of the Lone Inventor," *Fortune Small Business* (March 2005): 18; Magnus Aronsson, "Education Matters—But Does Entrepreneurship Education? An Interview with David Birch," *Academy of Management Learning and Education* 3, no. 3 (2004): 289–292; Office of Advocacy, U.S. Small Business Administration, www.sba.gov/advo/stats/sbfaq.pdf (accessed August 19, 2010).

16. John Case, "The Origins of Entrepreneurship," *Inc.* (June 1989): 51–53.

17. Dinah Wisenberg Brin, "Franchises a Draw for Minority Entrepreneurs," *Entrepreneur*, December 22, 2011, www.entrepreneur.com/blog/222525 (accessed August 8, 2012).

18. "Small Business Ambassador," *Fortune Small Business* (February 2007): 28; and "Salvador Guzman Buys Second AM Radio Station," July 8, 2009, http://www.hispanicnashville.com/2009/07/salvador-guzman-buys-second-am-radio.html (accessed October 9, 2012).

19. U.S. Census Bureau, http://factfinder2.census.gov/faces/tableservices/jsf/pages/productview.xhtml?pid=SBO_2007_00CSA01&prodType=table (accessed August 8, 2012).

20. Mickey Meece, "One in Four Businesses Calls the Owner 'Ma'am,'" *The New York Times* (November 5, 2009), www.nytimes.com/2009/11/05/business/smallbusiness/05sbiz.html?scp=1&sq=one%20in%20four%20businesses%20calls%20the%20owner%20maam&st=Search (accessed November 4, 2009).

21. Claire Cain Miller, "Out of the Loop in the Silicon Valley," *The New York Times*, April 16, 2010, http://dealbook.blogs.nytimes.com/2010/04/19/out-of-the-loop-in-silicon-valley/?scp=1&sq= OUT%20OF%20THE%20LOOP%20IN%20SILICON%20VALLEY&st=Search (accessed June 1, 2010).

22. Steven Overly and Thomas Heath, "Venga Betting on an App Dream," *The Washington Post*, April 29, 2011, www.washingtonpost.com/business/venga-betting-on-an-app-dream/2011/04/26/AFL0nHFF_story.html (accessed August 9, 2012).

23. This discussion is based in part on Charles R. Kuehl and Peggy A. Lambing, *Small Business: Planning and Management*, 3d ed. (Ft. Worth, TX: The Dryden Press, 1994).

24. Leigh Buchanan, "The Motivation Matrix," *Inc.*, March 2012, www.inc.com/magazine/201203/motivation-matrix.html (accessed August 20, 2012).

25. Quoted in Jessica Bruder, "A Harvard Professor Analyzes Why Start-Ups Fail," *The New York Times*, May 25, 2012, http://boss.blogs.nytimes.com/2012/05/25/a-harvard-professor-analyzes-why-start-ups-fail/ (accessed August 9, 2012).

26. Brian X. Chen, "Crammed Into Cheap Bunks, Dreaming of Future Digital Glory," *The New York Times*, July 5, 2012, www.nytimes.com/2012/07/06/technology/at-hacker-hostels-living-on-the-cheap-and-dreaming-of-digital-glory.html?pagewanted=all (accessed August 9, 2012).

27. Drex Heikes, "Strand Brewing Is Tasting Success After Years of Struggle," *Los Angeles Times*, July 1, 2012, http://articles.latimes.com/2012/jul/01/business/la-fi-made-in-california-brewers-20120701 (accessed August 1, 2012).

28. Byrne, "The 12 Greatest Entrepreneurs of Our Time."

29. Reported in "Crunching the Numbers: Work-Life Balance," *Inc.* (July–August, 2011): 30.

30. Melissa S. Cardon et al., "The Nature and Experience of Entrepreneurial Passion," *Academy of Management Review* 34, no. 3 (2009): 511–532.

31. Quote from www.evancarmichael.com.

32. Byrne, "The 12 Greatest Entrepreneurs of Our Time."

33. David C. McClelland, *The Achieving Society* (New York: Van Nostrand, 1961).

34. Quote from www.evancarmichael.com.

35. Paulette Thomas, "Entrepreneurs' Biggest Problems—and How They Solve Them," *The Wall Street Journal*, March 17, 2003.

36. M. Tina Dacin, Peter A. Dacin, and Paul Tracey, "Social Entrepreneurship: A Critique and Future Directions," *Organization Science* 22, no. 5 (September–October 2011): 1203–1213.

37. Byrne, "The 12 Greatest Entrepreneurs of Our Time."

38. Steven Prokesch, "The Reluctant Social Entrepreneur," *Harvard Business Review* (June 2011): 124 – 126.

39. Leslie Brokaw, "How to Start an *Inc.* 500 Company," *Inc.* 500 (1994): 51–65.

40. Lottie L. Joiner, "How to Work Full-time While Launching a Business, Spanx," *USA Today*, June 25, 2011, www.usatoday.com/money/smallbusiness/2011-07-22-work-full-time-and-launch-small-business_n.htm (accessed August 13, 2012).

2

ENVIRONMENT

41. Paul Reynolds, "The Truth About Start-ups," *Inc.* (February 1995): 23; Brian O'Reilly, "The New Face of Small Businesses," *Fortune* (May 2, 1994): 82–88.

42. Based on Ellyn E. Spragins, "Venture Capital Express: How to Write a Business Plan That Will Get You in the Door," *Small Business Success*, November 1,1990, www.inc.com/magazine/19901101/5472.html (accessed August 18, 2010); Linda Elkins, "Tips for Preparing a Business Plan," *Nation's Business* (June 1996): 60R–61R; Carolyn M. Brown, "The Do's and Don'ts of Writing a Winning Business Plan," *Black Enterprise* (April 1996): 114–116; and Kuratko and Hodgetts, *Entrepreneurship*, pp. 295–397. For a clear, thorough, step-by-step guide to writing an effective business plan, see Linda Pinson and Jerry Jinnett, *Anatomy of a Business Plan*, 5th ed. (Virginia Beach, VA: Dearborn, 2001).

43. The INC. FAXPOLL, *Inc.* (February 1992): 24.

44. Duncan MacVicar, "Ten Steps to a High-Tech Start-up," *The Industrial Physicist* (October 1999): 27–31.

45. "Venture Capitalists' Criteria," *Management Review* (November 1985): 7–8.

46. "Staples Makes Big Business from Helping Small Businesses," *SBA Success Stories*, www.sba.gov/successstories.html (accessed March 12, 2004); and Staples Web site, www.staples.com/sbd/cre/marketing/about_us/index.html (accessed August 24, 2012).

47. Elizabeth Olson, "From One Business to 23 Million," *The New York Times*, March 7, 2004, http://query.nytimes.com/gst/fullpage.html?res=9C03E6D6113FF934A35750C0A9629C8B63 (accessed July 16, 2008).

48. "Where the Venture Money Is Going," *Business 2.0* (January–February 2004): 98.

49. Emily Glazer, "A David and Gillette Story," *The Wall Street Journal*, April 12, 2012, http://online.wsj.com/article/SB10001424052702303624004577338103789934144.html (accessed August 14, 2012).

50. Catherine Clifford, "Want to Raise Money With Crowdfunding? Consider These Tips," *Entrepreneur*, April 4, 2012, www.entrepreneur.com/article/223270 (accessed August 14, 2012).

51. Jenna Wortham, "Start-ups Look to the Crowd," *The New York Times*, April 29, 2012, www.nytimes.com/2012/04/30/technology/kickstarter-sets-off-financing-rush-for-a-watch-not-yet-made.html?pagewanted=all (accessed August 14, 2012).

52. Aviva Yael, "How We Did It," *Inc.* (September 2008): 143.

53. Wendy Lea, "Dancing with a Partner," *Fast Company* (March 2000): 159–161.

54. James G. Combs et al., "Antecedents and Consequences of Franchising: Past Accomplishments and Future Challenges," *Journal of Management* 37, no. 1 (January 2011): 99–126.

55. Data from "The Franchise Business Economic Outlook: 2012," Prepared by IHS Global Insight for the International Franchising Association, http://emarket.franchise.org/2012FranchiseBusinessOutlook.pdf (accessed August 15, 2012).

56. www.entrepreneur.com/franchises/dunkindonuts/282304-0.html.

57. Sarah E. Needleman and Angus Loten, "Fast-Food Franchises Bulking Up," *The Wall Street Journal*, April 12, 2012, http://online.wsj.com/article/SB10001424052702304587704577333443052487330.html (accessed August 15, 2012).

58. For a discussion of the risks and disadvantages of owning a franchise, see Anne Fisher, "Risk Reward," *Fortune Small Business* (December 2005–January 2006): 44.

59. Anne Field, "Your Ticket to a New Career? Franchising Can Put Your Skills to Work in Your Own Business," in *Business Week Investor: Small Business* section, *BusinessWeek* (May 12, 2003): 100; and Roberta Maynard, "Choosing a Franchise," *Nation's Business* (October 1996): 56–63.

60. Darren Dahl, "Getting Started: Percolating Profits," *Inc.* (February 2005): 38.

61. Statistics from the National Business Incubation Association, www.nbia.org/resource_library/faq/index.php#3 (accessed July 31, 2010).

62. Amy Oringel, "Sowing Success," *Working Woman* (May 2001): 72.

63. Laura Novak, "For Women, a Recipe to Create a Successful Business," *The New York Times*, June 23, 2007, www.nytimes.com/2007/06/23/business/smallbusiness/23cocina.html?_r=1&sq=Laura%20Novak,%20â€œFor%20Women,%20a%20Recipe%20to%20Create%20a%20Successful%20Business&st=cse&adxnnl=1&oref=slogin&scp=1&adxnnlx=1225894278-APkyZ4 kswGDrm3QtejIg6A (accessed June 23, 2007).

64. Chuck Salter, "Girl Power," *Fast Company* (September 2007): 104.

65. Aaron Pressman, "The Domains of the Day," *BusinessWeek* (June 25, 2007): 74.

66. Jason R. Rich, *Unofficial Guide to Starting a Business Online*, 2nd ed. (New York: Wiley Publishing, 2006), p. 116.

67. Ellen Reid Smith, *e-loyalty: How to Keep Customers Coming Back to Your Website* (New York: HarperBusiness, 2000), p. 19.

68. *Ibid*, p. 127.

69. Dennis Nishi, "Click 'Like' if This Tactic Makes Sense at Start-Ups," *The Wall Street Journal*, November 14, 2011, R6.

70. Jenna Wortham, "Facebook to Buy Photo-Sharing Service Instagram for $1 Billion," *The New York Times*, April 9, 2012, http://bits.blogs.nytimes.com/2012/04/09/facebook-acquires-photo-sharing-service-instagram/?pagewanted=print (accessed August 17, 2012); and Benny Evangelista, "Facebook's Instagram Purchase Final," *The San Francisco Chronicle*, September 6, 2012, www.sfgate.com/technology/article/Facebook-s-Instagram-purchase-final-3845127.php (accessed September 8, 2012).

71. Carrie Dolan, "Entrepreneurs Often Fail as Managers," *The Wall Street Journal*, May 15, 1989.

72. Lizette Chapman, "'Pivoting'" Pays Off for Tech Entrepreneurs, *The Wall Street Journal*, April 26, 2012, http://online.wsj.com/article/SB1000142405270230 3592404577364171598999252.html (accessed August 17, 2012).

73. Jenna Wortham, "Rather Than Share Your Location, Foursquare Wants to Suggest One," *The New York Times*, June 7, 2012, www.nytimes.com/2012/06/07/technology/in-app-overhaul-foursquare-shifts-focus-to-recommendations.html (accessed August 17, 2012).

74. Jessica Bruder, "A Harvard Professor Analyzes Why Start-Ups Fail," *The New York Times*, May 25, 2012, http://boss.blogs.nytimes.com/2012/05/25/a-harvard-professor-analyzes-why-start-ups-fail/ (accessed August 17, 2012).

75. Byrne, "The 12 Greatest Entrepreneurs of Our Time."

76. George Mannes, "Don't Give Up on the Web," *Fortune* (March 5, 2001): 184[B]–184[L].

77. Bridgett Finn, "Selling Cool in a Bottle," *Business 2.0*, December 1, 2003, http://money.cnn.com/ magazines/business2/business2 _archive/2003/12/01/354202/index.htm (accessed November 5, 2008).

78. Paul Downs, "My Business Problems This Week," *The New York Times*, March 11, 2011, http://boss.blogs.nytimes.com/2011/03/11/my-business-problems-this-week/ (accessed August 20, 2012).

79. Saul Hansell, "Listen Up! It's Time for a Profit: A Front-Row Seat as Amazon Gets Serious," *The New York Times*, May 20, 2001.

80. Based on Kelly K. Spors, "So, You Want to Be an Entrepreneur," *The Wall Street Journal*, February 23, 2009; and "So You Want to Be an Entrepreneur," *The Star-Phoenix*, January 23, 2010.

ENVIRONMENT 2

ch3:　Apply Your Skills: Ethical Dilemma

Competitive Intelligence Predicament*

Miquel Vasquez was proud of his job as a new product manager for a biotechnology start-up, and he loved the high stakes and tough decisions that went along with the job. But as he sat in his den after a long day, he was troubled, struggling over what had happened earlier that day and the information that he now possessed.

Just before lunch, Miquel's boss had handed him a stack of private strategic documents from their closest competitor. It was a competitive intelligence gold mine—product plans, pricing strategies, partnership agreements, and other documents, most of them clearly marked "proprietary and confidential." When Miquel asked where the documents came from, his boss told him with a touch of pride that he had taken them right off the competing firm's server. "I got into a private section of their intranet and downloaded everything that looked interesting," he said. Later, realizing Miquel was suspicious, the boss would say only that he had obtained "electronic access" via a colleague and had not personally broken any passwords. Maybe not, Miquel thought to himself, but this situation wouldn't pass the *60 Minutes* test. If word of this acquisition of a competitor's confidential data ever got out to the press, the company's reputation would be ruined.

Miquel didn't feel good about using these materials. He spent the afternoon searching for answers to his dilemma, but found no clear company policies or regulations that offered any guidance. His sense of fair play told him that using the information was unethical, if not downright illegal. What bothered him even more was the knowledge that this kind of thing might happen again. Using this confidential information would certainly give him and his company a competitive advantage, but Miquel wasn't sure that he wanted to work for a firm that would stoop to such tactics.

What Would You Do?

1. Go ahead and use the documents to the company's benefit, but make clear to your boss that you don't want him passing confidential information to you in the future. If he threatens to fire you, threaten to leak the news to the press.

2. Confront your boss privately and let him know you're uncomfortable with how the documents were obtained and what possession of them says about the company's culture. In addition to the question of the legality of using the information, point out that it is a public relations nightmare waiting to happen.

3. Talk to the company's legal counsel and contact the Society of Competitive Intelligence Professionals for guidance. Then, with their opinions and facts to back you up, go to your boss.

*Adapted from Kent Weber, "Gold Mine or Fool's Gold?" *Business Ethics* (January–February 2001): 18.

ch3:　Apply Your Skills: Case for Critical Analysis

Not Measuring Up

"I must admit, I'm completely baffled by these scoring results for Cam Leslie," Carole Wheeling said as she and company CEO Ronald Zeitland scrolled through the latest employee surveys for middle management.

For the second year, RTZ Corporation used Wheeling's consulting firm to survey and score managers. An increasingly younger workforce, changing consumer tastes, and technology changes in the industry had caused Zeitland to look more closely at culture and employee satisfaction. The goal of this process was to provide feedback in order to assure continuous improvement across a variety of criteria. The surveys could be used to highlight areas for improvement by showing manager and company strengths and weaknesses, anticipating potential problem areas, providing a barometer for individual job performance, and as a road map for transforming the culture as the company expanded.

From the outset, Zeitland insisted on employee honesty in scoring managers and providing additional comments for the surveys.

"We can't change what we don't know," Zeitland instructed employees in meetings two years ago. "This is your opportunity to speak up," Zeitland had told them. "We're not looking for gripe sessions. We're looking for constructive analysis and grading for what we do and how we do it. This method assures that everyone is heard. Every survey carries equal weight. Changes are coming to this organization. We want to make those changes as easy and equally beneficial as possible for everyone."

Now, two years into the process, the culture was showing signs of changing and improving.

"The results from last year to this year show overall improvement," Wheeling said. "But for the second year, Cam's survey results are disappointing. In fact, there appears to be a little slippage in some areas."

Zeitland leaned back in his chair, paused, and looked at the survey results on the screen.

"I don't really understand it," Wheeling remarked. "I've talked to Cam. He seems like a nice guy—a hard worker, intelligent, dedicated. He pushed his crew, but he's not a control freak."

"He actually implemented several of the suggestions from last year's survey," Zeitland said. "From all reports and my own observations, Cam has more presence in the department and has increased the number of meetings. He appears to have at least attempted to open up communications. I'm sure he will be as baffled as we are by these new results because he *has* put forth effort."

"Employees mentioned some of these improvements, but it's not altering the scores. Could it merely be a reflection of his personality?" Wheeling asked.

"Well, we have all kinds of personalities throughout management. He's very knowledgeable and very task-oriented. I admit he has a way of relating to people that can be a little standoffish, but I don't think it's always necessary to be slapping everyone on the back and buying them beers at the local pub in order to be liked and respected and. . ."

". . . in order to get high scores?" Wheeling finished his sentence. "Still, the low percentage of 'favorable' scores in relation to 'unfavorable' and even 'neutral'. . ." her voice trailed off momentarily. "That's the one that gets me. There are so many 'neutral' scores. That's really strange. Don't they have an opinion? I'd love to flesh that one out more. It seems that in a sea of vivid colors, he's beige."

"It's like he's not there," Zeitland said. "The response doesn't tell me that they dislike Cam; they just don't *see* him as their manager."

Wheeling laughed. "Maybe we can wrap him in gauze like the 'Invisible Man,'" she joked.

The joke appeared lost on Zeitland. "That invisibility leaves him disengaged. Look at the comments." He scrolled down. "Here's a follow-up comment: **Employee Engagement:** *Are you kidding?* And here's another: **Advocacy:** *I don't think and I don't believe anyone here thinks he would go to bat for us.*"

"I know," Wheeling said. "On the other hand, many of their remarks indicate they consider him fair in areas like distribution of workload, and they score him decently in the area of follow-through in achieving company goals. But overall satisfaction and morale levels are low."

"That's what I don't understand," Zeitland commented. "Morale and productivity are normally so strongly linked. Morale in this case is blah, blah, blah, and yet these guys manage to perform right up there with every other division in the company. So they're *doing* it. They just don't like it or find any sense of fulfillment."

"Does Cam?"

"Interesting question," Zeitland agreed.

"So, how do we help Cam improve these scores in the coming year?" Wheeling asked. "What positive steps can he take? I'd at least like to see an up-or-down vote—not all of this neutrality—on his management skills and job performance."

Questions

1. Do you think Zeitland's desire for changes in culture are related to changes in the external environment? Explain.

2. What additional investigation might Wheeling and Zeitland undertake before settling on a plan of action?

3. In which quadrant of Exhibit 3.8 would you place Cam? What are some steps you would recommend that Cam consider to better connect with the employees who report to him?

ch3: On the Job Video Cases

On the Job: Camp Bow Wow: The Environment and Corporate Culture

Questions

1. What aspects of Camp Bow Wow's corporate culture are visible and conscious? What aspects are invisible and unconscious?

2. Why did Camp Bow Wow have to change its culture when it became a national franchise?

3. What impact does Heidi Ganahl's story have on employees at Camp Bow Wow?

http: See It Online www.

ch4: Apply Your Skills: Ethical Dilemma

AH Biotech*

Dr. Abraham Hassan knew he couldn't put off the decision any longer. AH Biotech, the Bound Brook, New Jersey–based company started by this psychiatrist-turned-entrepreneur, had developed a novel drug that seemed to promise long-term relief from panic attacks. If it gained approval from the Food and Drug Administration (FDA), it would be the company's first product. It was now time for large-scale clinical trials. But where should AH Biotech conduct those tests?

David Berger, who headed up research and development, was certain he already knew the answer to that question: Albania. "Look, doing these trials in Albania will be quicker, easier, and a lot cheaper than doing them in the States," he pointed out. "What's not to like?"

Dr. Hassan had to concede that Berger's arguments were sound. If they did trials in the United States, AH Biotech would spend considerable time and money advertising for patients and then finding physicians who'd be willing to serve as clinical trial investigators. Rounding up U.S. doctors prepared to take on that job was getting increasingly difficult. They just didn't want to take time out of their busy practices to do the testing, not to mention all the recordkeeping that such a study entailed.

In Albania, it was an entirely different story. It was one of the poorest Eastern European countries—if not *the* poorest—with a just barely functioning health-care system. Albanian physicians and patients would practically line up at AH Biotech's doorstep begging to take part. Physicians there could earn much better money as clinical investigators for a U.S. company than they could actually practicing medicine, and patients saw signing up as test subjects as their best chance for receiving any treatment at all, let alone cutting-edge Western medicine. All these factors meant that the company could count on realizing at least a 25 percent savings (maybe even more) by running the tests overseas.

What's not to like? As the Egyptian-born CEO of a start-up biotech company with investors and employees hoping for its first marketable drug, there was absolutely nothing not to like. It was when he thought like a U.S.-trained physician that he felt qualms. If he used U.S. test subjects, he knew they'd likely continue to receive the drug until it was approved. At that point, most would have insurance that covered most of the cost of their prescriptions. But he already knew it wasn't going to make any sense to market the drug in a poor country like Albania, so when the study was over, he'd have to cut off treatment. Sure, he conceded, panic attacks weren't usually fatal. But he knew how debilitating these sudden bouts of feeling completely terrified

were—the pounding heart, chest pain, choking sensation, and nausea. The severity and unpredictability of these attacks often made a normal life all but impossible. How could he offer people dramatic relief and then snatch it away?

What Would You Do?

1. Do the clinical trials in Albania. You'll be able to bring the drug to market faster and cheaper, which will be good for AH Biotech's employees and investors and good for the millions of people who suffer from anxiety attacks.

2. Do the clinical trials in the United States. Even though it will certainly be more expensive and time-consuming, you'll feel as if you're living up to the part of the Hippocratic oath that instructed you to "prescribe regimens for the good of my patients according to my ability and my judgment and never do harm to anyone."

3. Do the clinical trials in Albania, and if the drug is approved, use part of the profits to set up a compassionate use program in Albania, even though setting up a distribution system and training doctors to administer the drug, monitor patients for adverse effects, and track results will entail considerable expense.

*Based on Gina Kolata, "Companies Facing Ethical Issue as Drugs Are Tested Overseas," *The New York Times*, March 5, 2004; and Julie Schmit, "Costs, Regulations Move More Drug Tests Outside USA," *USA Today*, June 16, 2005.

ch4: Apply Your Skills: Case for Critical Analysis

We Want More Guitars!

Adam Wainwright's early morning phone call from Valencia, Spain, initially startled his boss, Vincent Fletcher. Adam, a true slave to the latest techno-gadgetry, *never* called. Yet here he was at 8:00 A.M. Pacific time on the phone to the CEO of Fletcher Guitars in Los Angeles.

"What did they do—lose your luggage with all of your toys inside?" Fletcher joked. "Did the plant burn down?"

"No, I just decided to call you on this one. I've been here for a week, looking over operations. Forget the idea of getting any substantial increase in productivity. I don't think these guys are capable of upping production by *ten* guitars per year," Adam complained.

"Isn't that an exaggeration?" Fletcher asked.

There was a momentary silence on the other end of the line. "Adam, did I lose you?"

"No."

"Look, part of our reputation is based on the quality and craftsmanship of the acoustic guitars produced by Dominguez and his workers. This is all high-end stuff," Fletcher said in a voice that always reminded Adam of actor Jason Robards. "Now, with the tremendous rise in the popularity of Latin music, we want to encourage increased production. That's your task, Adam. I shouldn't have to tell you that your success with this assignment could lead to some great opportunities for you."

"I know." Adam paused, carefully weighing his next words. "Salvador and his people do a fabulous job. Just

walking through his operation, I have been blown away by the craftsmanship. But the slow pace of work is unbelievably frustrating. These guys act like they are birthing a baby. Everything is so precise, so touchy-feely with every guitar. I used my iPad to create some workflow specs for increased production. Salvador took one look, laughed, and said 'You Americans.'"

Poor Adam, Fletcher thought. *That had to be a major stab in his high-tech heart. Maybe I sent the wrong guy. Nope. He has great potential in management and he has to learn to work through this and deliver.* Fletcher's thoughts were interrupted by Adam's voice, flustered and increasing in volume.

"They go off to lunch and come wandering back in here hours later—hours, Fletcher."

"They're Spanish!" Fletcher replied. "So they take two-hour lunches. They work their schedule. It's just not *our* schedule. You may be a lot younger than I am, Adam. But you need to lighten up. Listen, talk to Salvador and see what works for them. They've increased output before and they can do it again. Get this done, Adam. And *e-mail* me."

The international rise in Latin music over the past decade, punctuated by the clear sound and dazzling rhythms of the acoustic guitar, created a sense of urgency for guitar makers around the globe to increase the availability of these classical instruments. Wanting to ride the crest of this musical trend, increase his product offerings, and tap into high-end market sales, Fletcher discovered master craftsman Salvador Dominguez and his Spanish company, Guitarra Dominguez, while attending the prestigious Frankfurt International Fair in 1980.

Salvador liked to tell that among the first sounds he heard following his birth were the words of his father's lullaby, accompanied by an acoustic guitar. As an adult, Salvador combined his lifelong passion for guitars with brilliant craftsmanship, staring his own company in 1976. Located in the Poligono Industrial Fuente del Jarro—Paterna, Valencia, Spain, the company now employed more than 30 craftsmen in the production of acoustic and Flamenco instruments. A thin, wiry bundle of energy with graying wavy hair and large eyes with that surprised "Salvador Dalí look," the guitar maker could grasp a piece of wood and, running his hand over the surface, be suddenly transformed into a patient, tender sculptor of sound. To watch this luthier work was almost mesmerizing. Salvador's total silence and habit of leaning his right ear close to the wood as he worked suggested that he was actually *hearing* the music of the instrument as he created it.

Following the phone call to Fletcher, Adam returned to the plant, determined that Salvador would now hear from him.

"Salvador, you do beautiful work. Latin music is one of the hottest trends in music, and musicians are clamoring for the instruments you make. But we can be doing so much more here. There's plenty of room for expansion in this place, and we could nearly double production within the next few years. I have visited companies all over the United States and analyzed their operations. If you will take time to look at the plan I've drawn up, you will clearly see the potential for cranking out more product and meeting the needs of more customers."

"Señor Wainwright. Here in Spain, we do not *crank out* product. We take pride in each creation, and it is important that our methods of craftsmanship remain the same. No two of these instruments are alike."

"Wait. Wait. I'm just saying that there are changes that can be made here that will make this operation more productive. In the States, I see a flow to their operations. Here, we have starts and stops. The Nato mahogany used in many of your acoustic guitar bodies provides a beautiful and unrestricted wood. But Carlos has been off in a corner most of the week, wearing protective gear and experimenting with his notions about the potential tonal qualities of Wenge in acoustic bodies. The bottom line is this: we simply must streamline this operation in order to increase your production."

"No, Señor. *My* bottom line is this: Guitarras Dominguez will not lower *our* standards of craftsmanship to meet *your* plan."

Questions

1. How accurate is Adam Wainwright's analysis of the situation at Guitarras Dominguez? Do you think craftsmanship is incompatible with increasing productivity in this company? Why?

2. What social values are present in Guitarras Dominguez that seem different from U.S. social values (Exhibit 4.6 and Exhibit 4.7)? Explain.

3. What do you recommend Adam do to increase production in a business setting that does not seem to value high production?

ch4: On the Job Video Cases

On the Job: Holden Outerware: Managing in a Global Environment

Questions

1. Identify Holden's primary approach to entering the international market. What are the benefits of this entry strategy?

2. Based on what you know of Holden from this video, do managers seem to have a global mindset? Discuss.

3. What are the challenges of international management for leaders at Holden?

ch5: Apply Your Skills: Ethical Dilemma

Should We Go Beyond the Law?*

Nathan Rosillo stared out his office window at the lazy curves and lush, green, flower-lined banks of the Dutch Valley River. He'd grown up near here, and he envisioned the day his children would enjoy the river as he had as a child. But now his own company might make that a risky proposition.

Nathan is a key product developer at Chem-Tech Corporation, an industry leader. Despite its competitive position, Chem-Tech experienced several quarters of dismal financial performance. Nathan and his team developed a

new lubricant product that the company sees as the turning point in its declining fortunes. Top executives are thrilled that they can produce the new product at a significant cost savings because of recent changes in environmental regulations. Regulatory agencies loosened requirements on reducing and recycling wastes, which means that Chem-Tech can now release waste directly into the Dutch Valley River.

Nathan is as eager as anyone to see Chem-Tech survive this economic downturn, but he doesn't think this route is the way to do it. He expressed his opposition regarding the waste dumping to both the plant manager and his direct supervisor, Martin Feldman. Martin has always supported Nathan, but this time was different. The plant manager, too, turned a deaf ear. "We're meeting government standards," he'd said. "It's up to them to protect the water. It's up to us to make a profit and stay in business."

Frustrated and confused, Nathan turned away from the window, his prime office view mocking his inability to protect the river he loved. He knew the manufacturing vice president was visiting the plant next week. Maybe if he talked with her, she would agree that the decision to dump waste materials in the river was ethically and socially irresponsible. But if she didn't, he would be skating on thin ice. His supervisor had already accused him of not being a team player. Maybe he should just be a passive bystander—after all, the company isn't breaking any laws.

*Adapted from Janet Q. Evans, "What Do You Do: What If Polluting Is Legal?" Business Ethics (Fall 2002): 20.

What Would You Do?

1. Talk to the manufacturing vice president and emphasize the responsibility that Chem-Tech has as an industry leader to set an example. Present her with a recommendation that Chem-Tech participate in voluntary pollution reduction as a marketing tool, positioning itself as the environmentally friendly choice.

2. Mind your own business and just do your job. The company isn't breaking any laws, and if Chem-Tech's economic situation doesn't improve, a lot of people will be thrown out of work.

3. Call the local environmental advocacy group and get them to stage a protest of the company.

ch5: Apply Your Skills: Case for Critical Analysis

Too Much Intelligence?

The rapid growth of Pace Technologies was due in no small part to sales manager Ken Bodine and to the skills of the savvy young sales staff he had assembled. Bodine prided himself on finding and hiring top grads from two major business schools in the area. In addition to the top salaries offered by Pace, the grads were attracted by Bodine's energy, innovative thinking, and can-do attitude. He was the embodiment of Pace culture—moving fast, ahead of the knowledge curve in high-tech. Pace's sales force consistently stunned the competition with their high performance level.

Among other things, Pace had the reputation for aggressive business intelligence. Competitors found both amusing and frustrating the company's ability to outmaneuver others and capture accounts. Bodine enjoyed the air of mystery surrounding the Pace organization. Awareness that some competitor sat on the verge of a big sale always stirred Bodine's passion for sales and ignited his desire to "one-up these guys" and grab the sale out from under them.

"If this was a poker game," one board member mused, "Pace would win every hand. It's like Bodine as well as his staff possess the uncanny ability to know the cards your company is holding. He keeps a straight face, a low profile throughout the game, and then suddenly he lays his cards on the table and you're sunk. Here at Pace, we all love it."

A former military intelligence officer, Bodine brought that "sneaky" air into the Pace culture, adding a bit of excitement to the day-to-day business of sales. "With a great product, great staff, and great business intelligence," Bodine was fond of saying, "you can dominate the market." He wanted everyone—customers, competitors, and the media—to see Pace everywhere. "Every time the competition holds a staff meeting," he said, "the first question should be, 'What's Pace doing?'"

The sales staff was a mirror image of Bodine—younger, but with the same air of invincibility, and very competitive with one another. This, too, Bodine encouraged. A chess player, he enjoyed observing and encouraging the competition within his own sales staff. And seeing the thrill it brought "the boss," ambitious salespeople worked vigorously to prove their competitive worth.

Bodine's latest competitive "match" pitted Cody Rudisell and Ali Sloan in an intellectual and strategic struggle for a coveted assignment to a potential major account with a company that had just expanded into the region. Bodine let it be known that Cody and Ali were being considered for the assignment and that each could submit a proposal to lure the account to Pace and away from its top rival, Raleigh-Tech.

Both Cody and Ali eagerly grabbed the opportunity to expand their influence within the company and to build their reputations. Putting together their presentations within a short time period meant working long days and late nights. On the evening before the presentations, Cody bounded into Ali's office and dropped a file on her desk. "Top that!" he said.

Ali began thumbing through the file, and as she looked up in startled amazement, Cody slammed the folder and jerked it from her desk.

"That's like a watershed of Raleigh-Tech's trade secrets," Ali said. "Where did you get that?"

"My secret, sweetie," Cody replied, taking a seat and noisily drumming his fingers on the folder. "With this information, R-T doesn't have a chance. And neither do you."

"You could get into all sorts of trouble," Ali said. "When you lay that on Bodine's . . ."

"Bodine's espionage side will love it," Cody interrupted. "This is classic Bodine, classic Pace. You can't tell me that with all of the brilliant moves he's made over the years, Bodine hasn't done the same thing. This is business, cutthroat business, and I may have just topped the master. See you tomorrow."

As he left, Ali sat in stunned silence. "Cutthroat, indeed," she whispered, reaching for the phone. She held the phone for a moment, wondering who she should call. *This is unethical, illegal,* she thought. She hung up the phone. *Should I let him hang himself tomorrow? What if Bodine really does love it? If I call some manager tonight, will everyone see me as a sore loser and a crybaby? Is this really what it takes to win in the big leagues? Is this really the culture of this organization?*

Questions

1. How has Ken Bodine shaped the sales culture at Pace Technologies? Do you consider this culture to be at

a preconventional, conventional, or postconventional level of ethical development? Why?

2. What should Ali Sloan do? What would you actually do if you were in her place? Explain.

3. How might Cody Rudisell's decision differ if he based it on the utilitarian approach vs. individualism approach vs. practical approach to ethical decision making? Which approach does he appear to be using?

ch5: On the Job Video Cases

On the Job: Theo Chocolate: Managing Ethics and Social Responsibility

Questions

1. What practices at Theo Chocolate reflect the concept of sustainability?

2. What does vice president Debra Music mean when she says that Theo is a "triple bottom line" company? How is this different from any other company?

3. What does the term *fair trade* mean to the leaders at Theo? What happens if fair trade goals conflict with a company's primary responsibility to be profitable?

ch6: Apply Your Skills: Ethical Dilemma

Closing the Deal*

As the new, heavily recruited CEO of a high-technology start-up backed by several of Silicon Valley's leading venture capitalists, Chuck Campbell is flying high—great job, good salary, stock options, and a chance to be in on the ground floor and build one of the truly great twenty-first-century organizations. Just a few days into the job, Chuck participated in a presentation to a new group of potential investors for funding that could help the company expand marketing, improve its services, and invest in growth. By the end of the meeting, the investors had verbally committed $16 million in funding.

But things turned sour pretty fast. As Chuck was leaving about 9 p.m., the corporate controller, Betty Mars, who just returned from an extended leave, cornered him. He was surprised to find her working so late, but before he could even open his mouth, Betty blurted out her problem: The numbers that Chuck had presented to the venture capitalists were flawed. "The assumptions behind the revenue growth plan are absolutely untenable," she said. "Not a chance of ever happening." Chuck was stunned. He told Betty to go home and he'd stay and take a look at the figures.

At 11 p.m., Chuck was still sitting in his office wondering what to do. His research showed that the numbers were indeed grossly exaggerated, but most of them were at least statistically possible (however remote that possibility was!). However, what really troubled him was that the renewal income figure was just flat-out false—and it was clear that

one member of the management team who participated in the presentation knew that it was incorrect all along. To make matters worse, it was the renewal income figure that ultimately made the investment so attractive to the venture capital firm. Chuck knew what was at stake—no less than the life or death of the company itself. If he told the truth about the deceptive numbers, the company's valuation would almost certainly be slashed and the $16 million possibly canceled. On the other hand, if he didn't come clean now, the numbers didn't pan out, and the investors found out later that he knew about the flawed numbers, the company could be ruined.

What Would You Do?

1. Say nothing about the false numbers. Of course, the company will miss the projections and have to come up with a good explanation, but, after all, isn't that par for the course among fledgling high-tech companies? Chances are, the whole thing will blow over without a problem.

2. Go ahead and close the deal, but come clean later. Explain that the controller had been on an extended leave of absence, and because you had been on the job only a few days, you had not had time to do an analysis of the numbers yourself.

3. Take swift action to notify the venture capitalists of the truth of the situation—and start cleaning house to get rid of people who would knowingly lie to close a deal.

*Adapted from Kent Weber, "The Truth Could Cost You $16 Million," *Business Ethics* (March–April 2001): 18.

ch6: Apply Your Skills: Case for Critical Analysis

Black-Jack Antiques

For 13 years, Jeremy Black and Kevin Jack worked in adjoining cubicles for the department of transportation in their state. Although Kevin was 8 years older than Jeremy, the two men developed a strong friendship. They grumbled about their humdrum jobs (decent pay, great benefits, no excitement or chance for advancement) and argued over the NBA (Cavs vs. Bulls) and the NFL (Browns vs. Bears). They discovered a mutual love for antique furniture—Jeremy for restoration and Kevin for collecting. Together with their wives, Jenny and Susan, they haunted estate sales and antique stores. At some point—neither remembered when—they began discussing the possibility of *someday* becoming partners and opening their own antique furniture sales and restoration business. Six years ago, talk became reality. They took the plunge, left their jobs with the state, and opened Black-Jack Antiques: Furniture and Restoration. They did not bother to write a business plan or a partnership agreement.

Kevin secured start-up loans for the business in his name because Jeremy's amount of personal debt and low credit score made it difficult for him to get a loan. Jeremy's construction skills and supply contacts saved the duo thousands of dollars in renovations to the building, and his reputation and client list, developed over years of restoring furniture, provided a solid base of customers and referrals. Both men considered it a win-win situation and spent no time trying to decide who had invested most in the business.

Black-Jack had its share of bumps along the way, but being aware of the high rate of failure among start-up businesses, the partners were pleased by the steady growth year after year. They agreed long ago on the division of labor. Kevin, a detail-oriented, business-savvy individual, would oversee the sales and business side, while Jeremy focused on the restoration of furniture. Each played to his strengths. When Kevin seemed to be losing his fire under the burden of mundane day-to-day activities, Jeremy suggested that Kevin and Susan build up antique sales with occasional buying trips. The suggestion reignited Kevin's excitement.

As Jeremy's young family grew, worries about his mounting personal debt led Kevin to offer financial help on two occasions. "He's my partner. We're in this thing together. Besides, he would do the same for me if the situation was reversed," he said. Kevin was impressed that, although Jeremy had considerable stress in his private life, he seldom brought it in to work. Focus on his work and on the clients remained strong. In recent months, Jeremy seemed particularly calm and more assured, and Kevin surmised that his partner was working through his financial woes.

The partners' wives also enjoyed a strong friendship and often met for lunch, shopping, and other activities. Recently, Jenny let slip to Susan that Jeremy might soon have a job with a nearby furniture design firm. It was a great opportunity for him to use his talents, and he thought perhaps he and Kevin could sell the store or Kevin could buy out his "share" of the business.

It was a great shock to Kevin. Hurt and angry, he could not bring himself to confront Jeremy right away. Instead, he took his fears and concerns to "Coach." Ed Morgan was his father-in-law, his old high school football coach, and a man of tremendous common sense. Coach's way was not to preach or to advise, but to let Kevin talk his way through a problem, with a few probing questions, until he discovered the solution for himself.

After explaining the situation to Coach, Kevin expressed his devotion to the friendship, as well as the partnership, and expressed concerns for Jeremy. "I'm worried that he is letting his dream die because of fear and that one day soon he will regret his decision," Kevin said. "I want to do the right thing for Jeremy, Jenny, and the kids, but if he leaves the business, he takes the restoration side away and I'm afraid the business will die. I don't know if the antique side can carry all the weight. If we sell, I made the major financial investment, so how do we split any profits from the sale? Jeremy has job prospects, but in today's job market, would I be able to find something else at my age? It is all overwhelming. I want to be fair, but . . ."

Coach leaned forward, placing his hands on his knees and looking at Kevin sitting on the nearby sofa. "I've been listening to you, Kevin, and your concerns sound legitimate to me. Remember you have a business partnership and a friendship. What should a friend and business partner do?"

Coach's question was a wake-up call. That night, Kevin and Susan discussed the options and ways to proceed, beginning with frank discussions between the partners. Kevin and Susan understood that the lack of a written agreement could cause a problem if Kevin and Jeremy couldn't work things out. On the friendship side, Kevin wanted to know what Jeremy was feeling that caused him to look for other work. On the business side, Kevin and Susan discussed the antiques side of the business, evaluating its strengths and potential separate from the restoration side. They also evaluated Kevin's strengths and options he might consider for the future. What has Kevin learned about himself? What options does Kevin have? What should be his next move?

Questions

1. If you were Kevin, how would you initiate a conversation with Jeremy? What would you want to learn? What would you say?

2. What does this case illustrate about the risks of starting a business with a partner? How might those risks be minimized? Explain.

3. Do you think Kevin could make a go of the business alone? Should he try? Discuss.

ch6: On the Job Video Cases

On the Job: Urban Escapes: Managing Small Business Start-Ups

Questions

1. Are Maia Josebachvili and Bram Levy entrepreneurs, social entrepreneurs, or both? Explain.

2. Describe the personality traits of the Urban Escapes founders.

3. How did the founders of Urban Escapes finance the company's growth, and what options did they have for additional funding?

pt2: Integrative Case

Brown Goes Green: UPS Embraces Natural Gas Trucking Fleet

Can 3 million commercial trucks consuming nearly 4 billion gallons of diesel fuel annually in the United States really "go green"? To find out, the White House in 2008 launched a National Clean Fleets Partnership aimed at helping businesses embrace vehicles that run on natural gas, electricity, hydrogen, and other alternative fuels. Since it was first announced, the public-private partnership has sparked close collaboration between the U.S. Department of Energy and top fleet operators like United Parcel Service (UPS; nicknamed "Brown").

UPS's participation in a national green highways initiative may seem counterintuitive to many—but it shouldn't. Brown's quest to attain cost savings through fuel-efficient motoring stretches back to the 1930s, when the parcel delivery service used 20-mph electric cars to deliver packages in New York City. In the 1980s, UPS introduced vehicles that ran on compressed natural gas. In 2006, the company partnered with the U.S. Environmental Protection Agency (EPA) to design and build the world's first hydraulic delivery vehicle—a truck propelled by hydraulic pumps that store and release energy captured during braking. Today, the Georgia-based delivery giant continues to test alternative-fuel technologies, seeking to transform 95,000 delivery vehicles into fuel-efficient green machines.

Although numerous alternative-fuel technologies are competing for dominance at UPS, liquefied natural gas (LNG) has gained significant momentum in recent years, especially for Brown's largest trucks. Like most eighteen-wheelers, UPS's 17,000 tractor-trailers run on diesel fuel. This is beginning to change, however. In the years since the 2004 discovery of massive shale gas fields in the Marcellus Shale region of the United States, natural gas supplies have skyrocketed, causing methane prices to drop to about half the price of diesel. This development has had a significant influence on business. In particular, transportation managers faced with an affordable supply of domestic clean energy have begun evaluating the efficiency and environmental impact of their fleets.

In 2011, UPS embraced the new natural gas boom by ordering 48 LNG-engine tractor-trailers—an investment that boosted the company's long-haul natural gas fleet total to 59. Brown was not alone; similar moves by Ryder Systems, Waste Management Inc., and AT&T led *Wall Street Journal* energy reporter Rebecca Smith to wonder if the entire trucking industry was about to "ditch diesel." As Smith noted, "Never before has the price gap between natural gas and diesel been so large, suddenly making natural-gas-powered trucks an alluring option for company fleets."

According to Mike Britt, the director of vehicle engineering at UPS, Brown has good reason to switch from diesel to LNG. "The added advantage of LNG," says Britt, "is it does not compromise the tractor's abilities, fuel economy, or drivability, and it significantly reduces greenhouse gases." The benefits of LNG are numerous indeed. While most alternative-fuel vehicles can drive only limited distances, LNG trucks have a 600-mile single-tank range, plus a reliable network of fueling stations. In addition, LNG-fueled trucks produce 25 percent less carbon emissions and consume 95 percent less diesel than conventional trucks. Most importantly, natural gas engines deliver full horsepower. Highlighting a stark contrast between LNG and electric-powered vehicles, Britt quips that a 450-horsepower eighteen-wheeler uses so much power that to haul two trailers through mountainous terrain, "the first trailer would have to be all batteries." The performance gap leads Britt to conclude: "LNG is the only suitable alternative to diesel for the really heavy long-haul tractor trailers you see on the highway."

At UPS, terms like "fleet efficiency" and "environmental impact" aren't mere buzzwords—they are increasingly part of Brown's corporate culture. In 2011, UPS created its first executive-level management position for green concerns: the chief sustainability officer (CSO). Scott Wicker, a longtime company veteran appointed to the new post, has been instrumental in defining what a CSO does. "The key thing I do in my job is try to keep UPS focused on the environmental impacts that we have as an organization—and we're constantly working to reduce those environmental impacts," Wicker states. "But it's not just the environment: sustainability is also about what we do as a company in terms of our people, our customers, and the communities in which we live and work." Under Wicker's leadership, sustainability has garnered significant attention at UPS, appearing prominently in the company's policy book, upside blog, and corporate Web site. In addition, Wicker and his management teams develop and roll out sustainability initiatives to UPS's 400,000 employees.

According to the new green chief, effective sustainability reinforces a company's economic responsibility. "Above all else, sustainability is about being able to maintain a balance between our impacts on the environment and society, but at the same time keep the company economically prosperous," Wicker says. Kurt Kuehn, UPS's chief financial officer (CFO), underscores this point, citing two key objectives of sustainability: "Doing what's right for the environment and society, and also being mindful of the bottom line so we're a healthy company financially."

Minding the bottom line is especially relevant to Brown's pursuit of alternative-fuel technologies. At $195,000 each, LNG tractor-trailers cost twice as much as conventional semi-trailers—a high premium for going green. However, Mike Britt says that UPS can offset that expense through a combination of government subsidies and natural-gas-related fuel savings. For Britt, added investment in LNG reaps added reward for companies and communities: "Liquefied natural gas is a cheaper, cleaner-burning fuel that is better for the environment and more sustainable than conventional diesel. It's also a fuel that's in abundant supply inside the United States—it doesn't have to be imported."

Questions

1. Explain how UPS's alternative-fuels fleet is a response to trends taking place in the company's general environment.

2. Describe how UPS is using *boundary-spanning roles* to adapt to energy-related uncertainty in its environment.

3. How does UPS's clean fleets initiative illustrate the concepts of *sustainability* and *corporate social responsibility*?

Sources: Based on White House Fact Sheet: "National Clean Fleets Partnership," press release, April 1, 2011, www.whitehouse.gov/the-press-office/2011/04/01/fact-sheet-national-clean-fleets-partnership (accessed June 14, 2012); Rebecca Smith, "Will Truckers Ditch Diesel?" *The Wall Street Journal*, May 23, 2012, http://online.wsj.com/article/SB10001424 052702304707604577422192910235090.html (accessed June 14, 2012); Matthew L. Wald, "UPS Finds a Substitute for Diesel: Natural Gas, at 260 Degrees Below Zero," *The New York Times*, February 22, 2011, http://green.blogs.nytimes.com/2011/02/22/u-p-s-finds-a-substitute-for-diesel-natural-gas-at-260-degrees-below-zero (accessed June 14, 2012); Jeffrey Ball, "Natural-Gas Trucks Face Long Haul," *The Wall Street Journal*, May 17, 2011, http://online.wsj.com/article/SB1000142405274 8704740604576301550341227910.html (accessed June 15, 2012); "UPS Adds to Its Natural Gas Truck Fleet." *Environmental Leader*, February 25, 2011, www.environmentalleader.com/2011/02/25/ups-adds-to-its-natural-gas-truck-fleet (accessed June 15, 2012); Scott Wicker (CSO, United Parcel Service), interview by Kevin Coffey, upside blog, April 13, 2012, http://blog.ups.com/2012/04/13/talkin-sustainable-logistics-fortune-brainstorm-green (accessed June 16, 2012); William Smith, "New Terminology, Same Priority: Sustainability Engrained at UPS," upside blog, April 30, 2012, http://blog.ups.com/ 2012/04/30/new-terminology-same-priority-sustainability-engrained-at-ups (accessed June 16, 2012); Jill Swiecichowski, "Brown's Legacy of Being Green," upside blog, July 21, 2010, http://blog.ups.com/ 2010/07/21/browns-legacy-of-being-green (accessed June 15, 2012); "UPS Replaces Diesel with Cleaner LNG Tractor Trucks," Environment News Service, February 22, 2011, www.ens-newswire.com/ens/ feb2011/2011-02-22-091.html (accessed June 14, 2012).

Planning and Goal Setting

Dennis Flaherty/Jupiter Images

Learning Outcomes

After studying this chapter, you should be able to:

1. Define goals and plans and explain the relationship between them.

2. Explain the concept of organizational mission and how it influences goal setting and planning.

3. Describe the types of goals an organization should have and how managers use strategy maps to align goals.

4. Define the characteristics of effective goals.

5. Describe the four essential steps in the management-by-objectives (MBO) process.

6. Explain the difference between single-use plans and standing plans.

7. Discuss the benefits and limitations of planning.

8. Describe and explain the importance of contingency planning, scenario building, and crisis planning for today's managers.

9. Identify innovative planning approaches that managers use in a fast-changing environment.

Does Goal Setting Fit Your Management Style?

© Alan Bailey/Sexto Sol/Getty Images

INSTRUCTIONS: Are you a good planner? Do you set goals and identify ways to accomplish them? This questionnaire will help you understand how your work habits fit with making plans and setting goals. Answer the following questions as they apply to your work or study habits. Please indicate whether each item is Mostly True or Mostly False for you.

	Mostly True	Mostly False
1. I have clear, specific goals in several areas of my life.	_____	_____
2. I have a definite outcome in life I want to achieve.	_____	_____
3. I prefer general to specific goals.	_____	_____
4. I work better without specific deadlines.	_____	_____
5. I set aside time each day or week to plan my work.	_____	_____
6. I am clear about the measures that indicate when I have achieved a goal.	_____	_____
7. I work better when I set more challenging goals for myself.	_____	_____
8. I help other people clarify and define their goals.	_____	_____

SCORING AND INTERPRETATION: Give yourself one point for each item you marked as Mostly True, except items 3 and 4. For items 3 and 4, give yourself one point for each one that you marked Mostly False. A score of 5 or higher suggests a positive level of goal-setting behavior and good preparation for a new manager role in an organization. If you scored 4 or less, you might want to evaluate and begin to change your goal-setting behavior. An important part of a new manager's job is setting goals, measuring results, and reviewing progress for the department and subordinates.

These questions indicate the extent to which you have already adopted the disciplined use of goals in your life and work. But if you scored low, don't despair. Goal setting can be learned. Most organizations have goal setting and review systems that managers use. Not everyone thrives under a disciplined goal-setting system, but as a new manager, setting goals and assessing results are tools that will enhance your influence. Research indicates that setting clear, specific, and challenging goals in key areas will produce better performance.

Walmart's new mission for its U.S. stores is to provide everyday low prices for America's working-class consumer. Sound familiar? It's the formula that made Walmart the world's largest retailer, but several years ago, in the midst of a U.S. sales slump, managers tried a new direction. Instead of sticking with goals of strict operational efficiency and everyday low prices, they decided to court upscale customers with remodeled, less cluttered stores, organic foods, and trendy merchandise. The store raised prices on many items and promoted price cuts on only select merchandise. Walmart succeeded in meeting its goal of attracting a more upscale clientele, but many of its core customers—people making less than $70,000 a year—decided they'd start shopping at other discount and dollar store chains. Longtime suppliers were alienated as well, because of the cuts Walmart made in its selection of merchandise. Walmart's sales took a sharp downturn. "I think we tried to stretch the brand a little too far," said William Simon, head of the U.S. division. Managers are now reformulating goals to try to recapture a winning formula. The company still wants to grow its customer base in the United States, but it plans to do so primarily by building smaller stores in urban areas. "'Every Day Low Prices' can happen in 15,000 square feet," said Simon.[1]

1 INTRODUCTION

2 ENVIRONMENT

3 PLANNING

4 ORGANIZING

5 LEADING

6 CONTROLLING

One of the primary responsibilities of managers is to set goals for where the organization or department should go in the future and plan how to get it there. Walmart managers are facing a struggle that executives in every organization encounter as they try to decide what goals to pursue and how to achieve them. Lack of planning or poor planning can seriously hurt an organization. For example, the nuclear accident at the Fukushima Daiichi nuclear power plant after the earthquake and tsunami in Japan in 2011 has been blamed partly on poor planning. Kiyoshi Kurokawa, the chairman of the Fukushima Nuclear Accident Independent Investigation Commission, said: "It was a profoundly manmade disaster—that could and should have been foreseen and prevented. And its effect could have been mitigated by a more effective human response."[2] Managers cannot see the future, nor can they prevent natural disasters such as earthquakes, but proper planning can enable them to respond swiftly and effectively to such unexpected events. At Fukushima, near-chaos reigned as communications broke down, the chain of command was confused, and no one seemed to know what to do to maintain safety or to follow up once the accident had occurred.

Of the four management functions—planning, organizing, leading, and controlling—described in Chapter 1, planning is considered the most fundamental. Everything else stems from planning. Yet planning is also the most controversial management function. How do managers plan for the future in a constantly changing environment? The economic, political, and social turmoil of recent years has sparked a renewed interest in organizational planning, particularly planning for crises and unexpected events, yet it also has some managers questioning whether planning is even worthwhile in a world that is in constant flux. Planning cannot read an uncertain future. Planning cannot tame a turbulent environment. A statement by General Colin Powell, former U.S. secretary of state, offers a warning for managers: "No battle plan survives contact with the enemy."[3] Does that mean it is useless for managers to make plans? Of course not. No plan can be perfect, but without plans and goals, organizations and employees flounder. However, good managers understand that plans should grow and change to meet shifting conditions.

In this chapter, we explore the process of planning and consider how managers develop effective plans. Special attention is given to goal setting, for that is where planning starts. Then, we discuss the various types of plans that managers use to help the organization achieve those goals. We also take a look at planning approaches that help managers deal with uncertainty, such as contingency planning, scenario building, and crisis planning. Finally, we examine new approaches to planning that emphasize the involvement of employees (and sometimes other stakeholders) in strategic thinking and execution. Chapter 8 will look at strategic planning in depth and examine a number of strategic options that managers can use in a competitive environment. In Chapter 9, we look at management decision making. Appropriate decision-making techniques are crucial to selecting the organization's goals, plans, and strategic options.

Goal Setting and Planning Overview

A **goal** is a desired future circumstance or condition that the organization attempts to realize.[4] Goals are important because organizations exist for a purpose, and goals define and state that purpose. A **plan** is a blueprint for goal achievement and specifies the necessary resource allocations, schedules, tasks, and other actions. Goals specify future ends; plans specify today's means. The concept of **planning** usually incorporates both ideas; it means determining the organization's goals and defining the means for achieving them.[5]

LEVELS OF GOALS AND PLANS

Exhibit 7.1 illustrates the levels of goals and plans in an organization. The planning process starts with a formal mission that defines the basic purpose of the organization, especially for external audiences. The mission is the basis for the strategic (company) level of goals and plans, which in turn shapes the tactical (divisional) level and the operational (departmental) level.[6] Top managers are typically responsible for establishing *strategic* goals and plans that reflect a commitment to both organizational efficiency and effectiveness, as described in Chapter 1. *Tactical* goals and plans are the responsibility of middle managers, such as the heads of major divisions or functional units. A division manager will formulate tactical plans that focus on the major actions the division must take to fulfill its part in the strategic plan set by top management. *Operational* plans identify the specific procedures or processes needed at lower levels of the organization, such as individual departments and employees. Frontline managers and supervisors develop operational plans that focus on specific tasks and processes and that help meet tactical and strategic goals. Planning at each level supports the other levels.

THE ORGANIZATIONAL PLANNING PROCESS

The overall planning process, illustrated in Exhibit 7.2, prevents managers from thinking merely in terms of day-to-day activities. The process begins when managers develop the overall plan for the organization by clearly defining mission and strategic (company-level) goals. Second, they translate the plan into action, which includes defining tactical objectives and plans, developing a strategy map to align goals, formulating contingency and scenario plans, and identifying intelligence teams to analyze major competitive issues. Third, managers lay out the operational factors needed to achieve goals. This involves devising operational goals and plans, selecting the measures and targets that will be used to determine if things are on track, and identifying stretch goals and crisis plans that might need to be put into action. Tools for executing the plan include management by objectives, performance dashboards, single-use plans, and decentralized responsibility. Finally, managers periodically review plans to learn from results and shift plans as needed, starting a new planning cycle.

▶ ▶ ▶ **Concept Connection**

From its beginning as a seven-cow farm in New England to its current status as a $300 million organic yogurt business, Stonyfield Farm has incorporated environmental responsibility into its **organizational planning**. Today, every operational plan encompasses Stonyfield's **goal** of carbon-neutral operations.

Mike Fuentes/Bloomberg/Getty Images

3

PLANNING

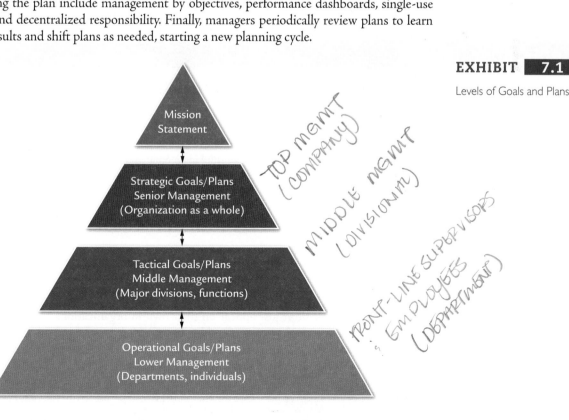

EXHIBIT   7.1

Levels of Goals and Plans

Mission Statement

Strategic Goals/Plans
Senior Management
(Organization as a whole)

Tactical Goals/Plans
Middle Management
(Major divisions, functions)

Operational Goals/Plans
Lower Management
(Departments, individuals)

(handwritten annotations:)
TOP MGMT (COMPANY)
MIDDLE MGMT (DIVISIONAL)
FRONT-LINE SUPERVISORS & EMPLOYEES (DEPARTMENT)

EXHIBIT 7.2   The Organizational Planning Process

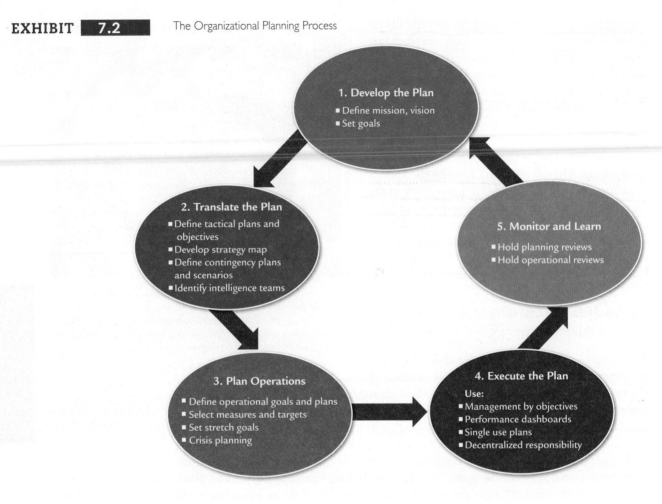

SOURCE: Based on Robert S. Kaplan and David P. Norton, "Mastering the Management System," *Harvard Business Review* (January 2008): 63–77.

Remember This

- Planning is the most fundamental of the four management functions.
- A **goal** is a desired future state that the organization wants to realize.
- **Planning** is the act of determining goals and defining the means of achieving them.

- A **plan** is a blueprint specifying the resource allocations, schedules, and other actions necessary for attaining goals.
- Planning helps managers think about the future rather than thinking merely in terms of day-to-day activities.

Goal Setting in Organizations

The overall planning process begins with a mission statement and goals for the organization as a whole. Goals don't just appear on their own in organizations. Goals are *socially constructed*, which means they are defined by an individual or group. Managers typically have different ideas about what goals should be, so they discuss and negotiate which goals to pursue. The Shoptalk describes the process of coalition building that often occurs during goal setting.

Manager's *Shoptalk*

Who Sets the Goals? Manager versus Coalition

Organizations perform many activities and pursue many goals simultaneously to accomplish an overall mission. But who decides what mission and goals to strive for? Pursuing some goals means that others have to be delayed or set aside, which means managers often disagree about priorities. After China's Zhejiang Geely Holding Group bought Volvo Car Corporation, for example, the Chinese and European managers disagreed strongly. The European managers wanted to continue pursuing goals of providing safe, reliable, family-friendly vehicles for a stable market. The new Chinese owners and managers, on the other hand, wanted to expand aggressively into the super-luxury car market. The goals of the two sides were mutually exclusive, so managers had to negotiate and come to some agreement on which direction the company would take.

Powerful, motivating goals that unite people are typically established not by a single manager, but by developing a coalition. *Coalitional management* involves building an alliance of people who support a manager's goals and can influence other people to accept and work toward them. Being an effective coalitional manager involves three key steps:

- **Talk to customers and other managers.** Building a coalition requires talking to many people both inside and outside the organization. Coalitional managers solicit the views of employees and key customers. They talk to other managers all across the organization to get a sense of what people care about and learn what challenges and opportunities they face. A manager can learn who believes in and supports a particular direction and goals, and who is opposed to them and the reasons for the opposition.

- **Address conflicts.** Good managers don't let conflicts over goals simmer and detract from goal accomplishment or hurt the organization. At Toyota, for example, the recent recall crisis exposed a longstanding internal conflict between managers who wanted to pursue goals of faster growth and higher profit margins and those who believed that rapid growth would strain the company's ability to ensure quality and reliability. Each side is blaming the other for the recent problems, but it is the failure of managers to unite toward a shared goal that is largely to blame.

- **Break down barriers and promote cross-silo cooperation.** A final step is to break down boundaries and get people to cooperate and collaborate across departments, divisions, and levels. When Colin Powell was chairman of the U.S. Joint Chiefs of Staff, he regularly brought together the heads of the Army, Air Force, Navy, and Marines so they could understand one another's viewpoints and come together around key goals. Cross-enterprise understanding and cooperation is essential so that the entire organization will be aligned toward accomplishing desired goals.

As a manager, remember that you will accomplish more and be more effective as part of a coalition than as an individual actor. When there are goals that are highly important to you, take steps to build a coalition to support them. Throw your support behind other managers when appropriate. And remember that building positive relationships, discussion, and negotiation are key skills for good management.

Sources: Stephen Friedman and James K. Sebenius, "Organization Transformation: The Quiet Role of Coalitional Leadership," *Ivey Business Journal* (January–February 2009), www.iveybusinessjournal .com/topics/leadership/organizational-transformation-the-quiet-role-of-coalitional-leadership (accessed January 27, 2012); Gerald R. Ferris et al., "Political Skill in Organizations," *Journal of Management* (June 2007): 290–320; Norihiko Shirouzu, "Chinese Begin Volvo Overhaul," *The Wall Street Journal*, June 7, 2011, B1; and Norihiko Shirouzu, "Inside Toyota, Executives Trade Blame Over Debacle," *The Wall Street Journal*, April 14, 2010, A1.

3

PLANNING

ORGANIZATIONAL MISSION

At the top of the goal hierarchy is the **mission**—the organization's reason for existence. The mission describes the organization's values, aspirations, and reason for being. A well-defined mission is the basis for development of all subsequent goals and plans. Without a clear mission, goals and plans may be developed haphazardly and not take the organization

EXHIBIT **7.3**

An Innovative Mission Statement: The Holstee Manifesto

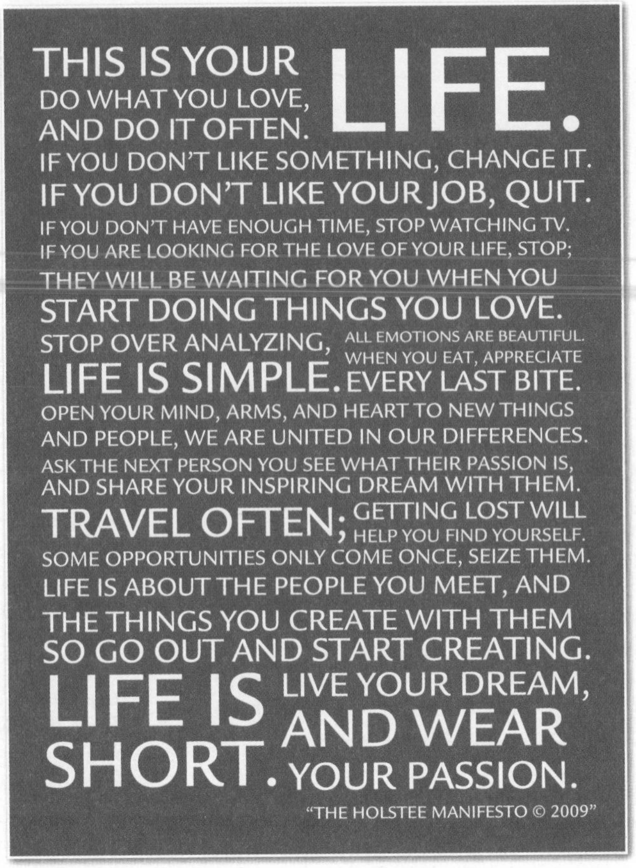

THIS IS YOUR **LIFE.**
DO WHAT YOU LOVE,
AND DO IT OFTEN.
IF YOU DON'T LIKE SOMETHING, CHANGE IT.
IF YOU DON'T LIKE YOUR JOB, QUIT.
IF YOU DON'T HAVE ENOUGH TIME, STOP WATCHING TV.
IF YOU ARE LOOKING FOR THE LOVE OF YOUR LIFE, STOP;
THEY WILL BE WAITING FOR YOU WHEN YOU
START DOING THINGS YOU LOVE.
STOP OVER ANALYZING, ALL EMOTIONS ARE BEAUTIFUL.
WHEN YOU EAT, APPRECIATE
LIFE IS SIMPLE. EVERY LAST BITE.
OPEN YOUR MIND, ARMS, AND HEART TO NEW THINGS
AND PEOPLE, WE ARE UNITED IN OUR DIFFERENCES.
ASK THE NEXT PERSON YOU SEE WHAT THEIR PASSION IS,
AND SHARE YOUR INSPIRING DREAM WITH THEM.
TRAVEL OFTEN; GETTING LOST WILL
HELP YOU FIND YOURSELF.
SOME OPPORTUNITIES ONLY COME ONCE, SEIZE THEM.
LIFE IS ABOUT THE PEOPLE YOU MEET, AND
THE THINGS YOU CREATE WITH THEM
SO GO OUT AND START CREATING.
LIFE IS LIVE YOUR DREAM,
AND WEAR
SHORT. YOUR PASSION.
"THE HOLSTEE MANIFESTO © 2009"

SOURCE: Holstee Web site, http://press.holstee.com/holstee-manifesto-poster © (accessed August 3, 2012).

in the direction it needs to go. One of the defining attributes of successful companies is that they have a clear mission that guides decisions and actions. When management actions and decisions go against the mission, organizations may get into trouble. Sam Walton, founder of Walmart, told his managers that the fledgling company was going to overtake Sears on the day he heard that Sears had reneged on its satisfaction guaranteed policy. At the time, Walmart had $20 billion less in sales than Sears, but Walton believed that stepping away from a core part of its mission would set Sears on a downhill path—and indeed, the company never recovered. Some people think Walmart made a similar blunder when it began trying to court upscale customers, as described in the opening example.[7]

The formal **mission statement** is a broadly stated definition of purpose that distinguishes the organization from others of a similar type. The founders of Holstee, a Brooklyn, New York–based company that sells eco-friendly clothing and accessories, created a mission statement for their company that has inspired people around the world. Holstee's innovative mission statement is shown in Exhibit 7.3. The Holstee mission was written to remind the founders and employees that there is nothing more important than pursuing your passion.

Although most corporate mission statements aren't as broad or quite as inspiring as Holstee's, a well-designed mission statement can enhance employee motivation and organizational performance.[8] The content of a mission statement often describes the company's basic business activities and purpose, as well as the values that guide the company. Some mission statements also describe company characteristics such as desired markets and customers, product quality,

"A real purpose can't just be words on paper. . . . If you get it right, people will feel great about what they're doing, clear about their goals, and excited to get to work every morning."

— ROY M. SPENCE JR., AUTHOR OF *IT'S NOT WHAT YOU SELL, IT'S WHAT YOU STAND FOR*

New Manager | Self-Test

My Personal Mission

Instructions: How much do you think about the positive outcomes you want in your future? Do you have a personal mission to guide your life? Indicate whether each item below is Mostly False or Mostly True for you.

	Mostly True	Mostly False
1. I can describe a compelling image of my future.	_____	_____
2. Life to me seems more exciting than routine.	_____	_____
3. I have created very clear life goals and aims.	_____	_____
4. I feel that my personal existence is very meaningful.	_____	_____
5. In my life, I see a reason for being here.	_____	_____
6. I have discovered a satisfying "calling" in life.	_____	_____
7. I feel that I have a unique life purpose to fulfill.	_____	_____
8. I will know when I have achieved my purpose.	_____	_____
9. I talk to people about my personal mission in life.	_____	_____
10. I know how to harness my creativity and use my talents.	_____	_____

Scoring and Interpretation: Add the number of Mostly True answers above for your score: _____. A score of 7 or above indicates that you are in great shape with respect to your life's personal mission. A score of 3 or below would suggest that you have not given much thought to a mission for your life. A score of 4–6 would be about average.

Creating or discovering a personal mission is difficult work for most people. It doesn't happen easily, or by accident. A personal mission is just like an organizational mission in that it requires focused thought and effort. Spend some time thinking about a mission for yourself and write it down.

Sources: The ideas for this questionnaire were drawn primarily from Chris Rogers, "Are You Deciding on Purpose?" *Fast Company* (February–March 1998): 114–117; and J. Crumbaugh, "Cross-Validation of a Purpose-in-Life Test Based on Frankl's Concepts," *Journal of Individual Psychology* 24 (1968): 74–81.

3

PLANNING

---

location of facilities, and attitude toward employees. An example of a short, straightforward mission statement comes from State Farm Insurance:

> State Farm's mission is to help people manage the risks of everyday life, recover from the unexpected, and realize their dreams.
>
> We are people who make it our business to be like a good neighbor; who built a premier company by selling and keeping promises through our marketing partnership; who bring diverse talents and experiences to our work of serving the State Farm customer.
>
> Our success is built on a foundation of shared values—quality service and relationships, mutual trust, integrity, and financial strength.[9]

Because of mission statements such as that of State Farm, employees as well as customers, suppliers, and stockholders know the company's stated purpose and values.

GOALS AND PLANS

Strategic goals, sometimes called *official goals*, are broad statements describing where the organization wants to be in the future. These goals pertain to the organization as a whole rather than to specific divisions or departments.

Take a Moment

As a new manager, you will need to understand what you want for your own future. Complete the New Manager Self-Test above to get some insight into whether you have a personal mission that guides your life.

Strategic plans define the action steps by which the company intends to attain strategic goals. The strategic plan is the blueprint that defines the organizational activities and resource allocations—in the form of cash, personnel, space, and facilities—required for meeting these targets. Strategic planning tends to be long term and may define organizational action steps from two to five years in the future. The purpose of strategic plans is to turn organizational goals into realities within that time period. Managers at Trader Joe's (TJ's) created a strategic goal of becoming a "nationwide chain of neighborhood specialty grocery stores."[10]

Innovative Way

Trader Joe's

In June 2012, residents of Lexington, Kentucky, finally got something that many of them had been hoping to get for years—a Trader Joe's (TJ's). The unusual grocery store chain was started in 1967 as a typical convenience store. Founder Joe Coulombe quickly modified TJ's into a novel business serving unique food and drink and expanded it to 17 stores in southern California. Today, there are 370 TJ's stores nationwide, and people are clamoring for more. But managers are very, very careful about how they expand.

Some years ago, managers set a strategic goal to grow in a controlled fashion that enabled TJ's to retain a "mom-and-pop store" vibe. TJ's doesn't carry any national brands; instead it offers innovative, high-quality, health-conscious food and beverage products at modest prices. About 80 percent of products carry TJ's private label, and the company is secretive about who makes products for them. Many TJ's stores carry only about 2,500 items, compared to a traditional supermarket that has more than 40,000, and the selection is constantly changing. What keeps people coming back is the novelty and sense of adventure—you never know what you're going to find—and the friendly service you might expect to get from the mom-and-pop shop around the corner.

TJ's mission is to provide value and dedicated service along with high-quality products. That means striving to develop a personal relationship with customers. If you want to know what something tastes like, an employee can probably tell you, but she might just open the bag so you can try it for yourself. Managers evaluate every decision with an eye to how it fits with the goal of maintaining a neighborhood-store feel. They resisted using checkout scanners for years, for instance, and finally adopted the technology only after carefully testing it in a few stores. A ringing bell rather than an intercom signals the need for more help at the checkouts. TJ's doesn't advertise in publications; it sends out a newsletter called The Fearless Flyer to describe new products.[11]

Concept Connection ◄◄◄

Walt Disney used to say, "I make movies for children and the child in all of us." DreamWorks, according to CEO Jeffrey Katzenberg, "makes movies for adults and the adult that exists in every child." That subtle difference in wording provides the key to the studio's sense of **mission** and the way it sets itself apart. Starting with *Shrek* in 2001, a film where the villain tortured the Gingerbread Man by dipping him into a glass of milk, DreamWorks has produced feature-length animated films aimed at appealing equally to adults and children by being irreverent and a little subversive.

AP Photo/Rob Griffith

Trader Joe's has achieved its strategic goal of becoming a nationwide chain of neighborhood grocery stores, but goals and plans for further expansion are testing the company's ability to retain its cozy feel. "In the early days, we never tried to be the neighborhood store," said one former employee. Now, with a bigger organization that requires more rules and procedures, it doesn't just come naturally.[12]

After strategic goals are formulated, the next step is to define **tactical goals**, which are the results that major divisions and departments within the organization intend to achieve. These goals apply to middle management and describe what major subunits must do for the organization to achieve its overall goals.

Tactical plans are designed to help execute the major strategic plans and to accomplish a specific part of the company's strategy.[13] Tactical plans typically have a shorter time horizon than strategic plans—over the next year or so. The word *tactical* originally comes from the military. In a business or nonprofit organization, tactical plans define what major departments and organizational subunits will do to implement the organization's strategic plan. For example, a tactical goal for Trader Joe's location scouting division might be to identify three new locations a year that fit TJ's target market of educated, adventurous consumers and could support a TJ's store. Tactical goals and plans help top managers implement their overall strategic plan. Normally, it is the middle manager's job to take the broad strategic plan and identify specific tactical plans.

The results expected from departments, work groups, and individuals are the **operational goals**. They are precise and measurable. "Process 150 sales applications each week," "Achieve 90 percent of deliveries on time," "Reduce overtime by 10 percent next month," and "Develop two new online courses in accounting" are examples of operational goals. An operational goal for Trader Joe's product development department is to identify ten new and intriguing items a week to phase into stores. In the human resources department, an operational goal might be to keep turnover to less than 5 percent a year so that there are longtime employees who have close relationships with customers.

Operational plans are developed at the lower levels of the organization to specify action steps toward achieving operational goals and to support tactical plans. The operational plan is the department manager's tool for daily and weekly operations. Goals are stated in quantitative terms, and the department plan describes how goals will be achieved. Operational planning specifies plans for department managers, supervisors, and individual employees. Schedules are an important component of operational planning. Schedules define precise time frames for the completion of each operational goal required for the organization's tactical and strategic goals. Operational planning also must be coordinated with the budget because resources must be allocated for desired activities.

ALIGN GOALS USING A STRATEGY MAP

Effectively designed organizational goals are aligned; that is, they are consistent and mutually supportive so that the achievement of goals at low levels permits the attainment of high-level goals. Organizational performance is an outcome of how well these interdependent elements are aligned, so that individuals, teams, and departments are working in concert to attain specific goals that ultimately help the organization achieve high performance and fulfill its mission.[14]

An increasingly popular technique for aligning goals into a hierarchy is the strategy map. A **strategy map** is a visual representation of the key drivers of an organization's success. Because the strategy map shows how specific goals and plans in each area are linked, it provides a powerful way for managers to see the cause-and-effect relationships among goals and plans.[15] The simplified strategy map in Exhibit 7.4 illustrates four key areas that contribute to a firm's long-term success—learning and growth, internal processes, customer service, and financial performance—and how the various goals and plans in each area link to the other areas. The idea is that learning and growth goals serve as a foundation to help achieve goals for excellent internal business processes. Meeting business process goals, in turn, enables the organization to meet goals for customer service and satisfaction, which helps the organization achieve its financial goals and optimize its value to all stakeholders.

In the strategy map shown in Exhibit 7.4, the organization has learning and growth goals that include developing employees, enabling continuous learning and knowledge sharing, and building a culture of innovation. Achieving these will help the organization build internal business processes that promote good relationships with suppliers and partners, improve the quality and flexibility of operations, and excel at developing innovative products and services. Accomplishing internal process goals, in turn, enables the organization to maintain strong relationships with customers, be a leader in quality and reliability, and provide innovative solutions to emerging customer needs. At the top of the strategy map, the accomplishment of these lower-level goals helps the organization increase revenues in existing markets, increase productivity and efficiency, and grow through selling new products and services and serving new market segments.

In a real-life organization, the strategy map would typically be more complex and would state concrete, specific goals relevant to the particular business. However, the generic map

Take a Moment

Go to the Experiential Exercise on page 230 that pertains to developing action plans for accomplishing strategic goals.

3

PLANNING

EXHIBIT 7.4   A Strategy Map for Aligning Goals

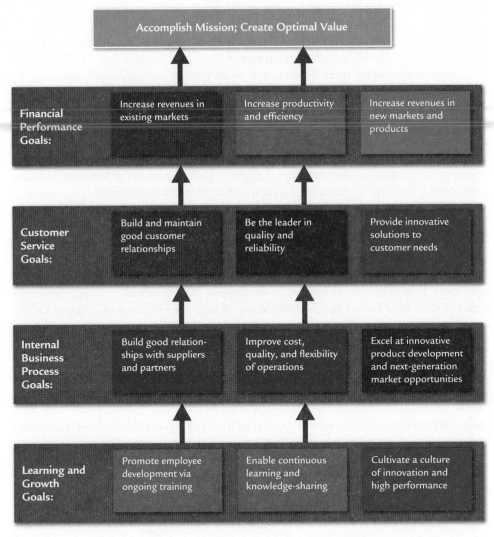

SOURCES: Based on Robert S. Kaplan and David P. Norton, "Mastering the Management System," *Harvard Business Review* (January 2008): 63–77; and R. S. Kaplan and D. P. Norton, "Having Trouble with Your Strategy? Then Map It," *Harvard Business Review* (September–October 2000): 167–176.

in Exhibit 7.4 gives an idea of how managers can map goals and plans so that they are mutually supportive. The strategy map is also a good way to communicate goals because all employees can see what part they play in helping the organization accomplish its mission.

Remember This

- Planning starts with the organization's purpose or reason for existence, which is called its **mission.**
- A **mission statement** is a broadly stated definition of the organization's basic business scope and operations that distinguishes it from similar types of organizations.
- Goals begin with broad strategic goals, followed by more specific tactical goals and then operational goals.

- Plans are defined similarly, with strategic, tactical, and operational plans used to achieve the goals.
- **Strategic goals** are broad statements of where the organization wants to be in the future and pertain to the organization as a whole rather than to specific divisions or departments.
- **Strategic plans** are the action steps by which an organization intends to attain strategic goals.

(Continued)

- The outcomes that major divisions and departments must achieve for the organization to reach its overall goals are called **tactical goals**.
- **Tactical plans** are designed to help execute major strategic plans and to accomplish a specific part of the company's strategy.
- **Operational goals** are specific, measurable results that are expected from departments, work groups, and individuals.

- **Operational plans** specify the action steps toward achieving operational goals and support tactical activities.
- Managers at Trader Joe's set a strategic goal to become "a nationwide chain of neighborhood grocery stores."
- Goals and plans need to be in alignment so that they are consistent and mutually supportive.
- A **strategy map** is a visual representation of the key drivers of an organization's success, showing the cause-and-effect relationship among goals and plans.

Operational Planning

Managers use operational goals to direct employees and resources toward achieving specific outcomes that enable the organization to perform efficiently and effectively. One consideration is how to establish effective goals. Then managers use a number of planning approaches, including management-by-objectives (MBO), single-use plans, and standing plans.

CRITERIA FOR EFFECTIVE GOALS

Research has identified certain factors, shown in Exhibit 7.5, that characterize effective goals. First and foremost, goals need to be *specific and measurable*. When possible, operational goals should be expressed in quantitative terms, such as increasing profits by 2 percent, having zero incomplete sales order forms, or increasing average teacher effectiveness ratings from 3.5 to 3.7. Not all goals can be expressed in numerical terms, but vague goals have little motivating power for employees. By necessity, goals are qualitative as well as quantitative. The important point is that the goals be precisely defined and allow for measurable progress. Effective goals also have a *defined time period* that specifies the date on which goal attainment

The Bees Buzz

Moving sustainability beyond fashionable "buzzwords" is a focus of North Carolina–based **Burt's Bees**—makers of personal care products made from natural substances (including, but not limited to, beeswax). Employees at Burt's Bees get down and dirty with the annual companywide Dumpster Dive, sorting through accumulated trash that reached monthly totals of up to 40 tons in one recent year. Employees recommitted to a zero-waste goal, which the company achieved in 2009. With 100 percent employee engagement, Burt's Bees has now focused on achieving a loftier "zero-waste, zero-carbon" goal by 2020.

Sustainability planning and goal-setting at Burt's Bees engages employees in activities such as reducing water use by "steam-cleaning" containers (resulting in a 90 percent water reduction) or extending the paper label on lip balm to eliminate shrink-wrapping (eliminating 900 miles of film). Managerial goals also extend to consumer education through the "Natural Vs." campaign (aimed at clarifying industry terms, such as *natural*). Through all its efforts, Burt's Bees works toward a goal of helping take the "sting" out of environmental problems.

Source: Christopher Marquis and Bobbi Thomason, "Leadership and the First and Last Mile of Sustainability," *Ivey Business Journal*, September–October 2010, www.iveybusinessjournal.com/topics/leadership/leadership-and-the-first-and-last-mile-of-sustainability (accessed August 2, 2012).

EXHIBIT 7.5

Characteristics of Effective
Goals

will be measured. For instance, school administrators might set a deadline for improving teacher effectiveness ratings by the end of the 2013 school term. When a goal involves a two- to three-year time horizon, setting specific dates for achieving parts of it is a good way to keep people on track toward the goal.

Goals should *cover key result areas.* Goals cannot be set for every aspect of employee behavior or organizational performance; if they were, their sheer number would render them meaningless. Instead, managers establish goals based on the idea of *choice and clarity.* A few carefully chosen, clear, and direct goals can focus organizational attention, energy, and resources more powerfully.[16] Managers should set goals that are *challenging but realistic.* When goals are unrealistic, they set employees up for failure and lead to a decrease in employee morale. However, if goals are too easy, employees may not feel motivated. Goals should also be *linked to rewards.* The ultimate impact of goals depends on the extent to which salary increases, promotions, and awards are based on goal achievement. Employees pay attention to what gets noticed and rewarded in the organization.[17]

MANAGEMENT BY OBJECTIVES (MBO)

Described by famed management scholar Peter Drucker in his 1954 book, *The Practice of Management,* management-by-objectives has remained a popular and compelling method for defining goals and monitoring progress toward achieving them. **Management-by-objectives (MBO)** is a system whereby managers and employees define goals for every department, project, and person and use them to monitor subsequent performance.[18] A model of the essential steps of the MBO system is presented in Exhibit 7.6. Four major activities make MBO successful:[19]

1. *Set goals.* Setting goals involves employees at all levels and looks beyond day-to-day activities to answer the question, "What are we trying to accomplish?" Managers heed the criteria of effective goals described in the previous section and make sure to assign responsibility for goal accomplishment. However, goals should be derived jointly. Mutual agreement between employee and supervisor creates the strongest commitment to achieving goals. In the case of teams, all team members may participate in setting goals.

2. *Develop action plans.* An *action plan* defines the course of action needed to achieve the stated goals. Action plans are made for both individuals and departments.

3. *Review progress.* A periodic progress review is important to ensure that action plans are working. These reviews can occur informally between managers and subordinates,

EXHIBIT **7.6** Model of the MBO Process

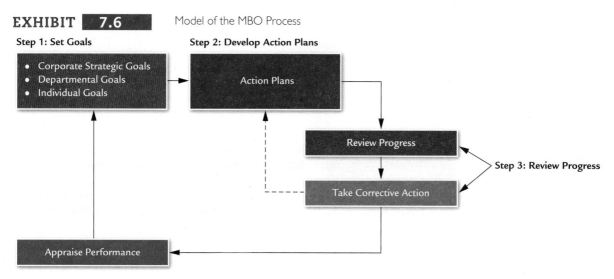

Step 1: Set Goals

Step 2: Develop Action Plans

Step 3: Review Progress

Step 4: Appraise Overall Performance

where the organization may wish to conduct three-, six-, or nine-month reviews during the year. This periodic checkup allows managers and employees to see whether they are on target or whether corrective action is needed. Managers and employees should not be locked into predefined behavior and must be willing to take whatever steps are necessary to produce meaningful results. The point of MBO is to achieve goals. The action plan can be changed whenever goals are not being met.

4. **Appraise overall performance.** The final step in MBO is to evaluate whether annual goals have been achieved for both individuals and departments. Success or failure to achieve goals can become part of the performance appraisal system and the designation of salary increases and other rewards. The appraisal of departmental and overall corporate performance shapes goals for the next year. The MBO cycle repeats itself annually.

Many companies, including Intel, Tenneco, Black & Decker, and DuPont, have used MBO, and most managers think that it is an effective management tool.[20] Tim O'Shaughnessy, founder and CEO of LivingSocial, a daily deal Web site with more than 5,000 employees and 46 million members in 25 countries, uses the principles of MBO to keep the fast-growing business on track. O'Shaughnessy meets regularly with the heads of every department to set goals for items such as sales and membership growth and develop action plans for how to achieve them. Then, he is obsessive about tracking metrics to see whether things are on target toward meeting the numbers. Each week, O'Shaughnessy meets with department heads to talk about their key metrics and review their progress. "The more data you gather, the more likely you'll be successful in the long term," he says.[21] Most managers, like Tim O'Shaughnessy, believe they are better oriented toward goal achievement when MBO is used.

MBO can provide a number of benefits, which are summarized in Exhibit 7.7. Corporate goals are more likely to be achieved when they focus manager and employee efforts. Using a performance measurement system such as MBO helps employees see how their jobs and performance contribute to the business, giving them a sense of ownership and commitment.[22] Performance is improved when employees are committed to attaining the goal, are motivated because they help decide what is expected, and are free to be resourceful. Goals at lower levels are aligned with and enable the attainment of goals at top management levels.

However, like any system, MBO can cause problems when used improperly. For example, an overemphasis on "meeting the goals" can obscure the means that people

3

PLANNING

Take a Moment

You can practice setting goals and developing action plans by completing the Small Group Breakout on page 230.

EXHIBIT **7.7**   MBO Benefits

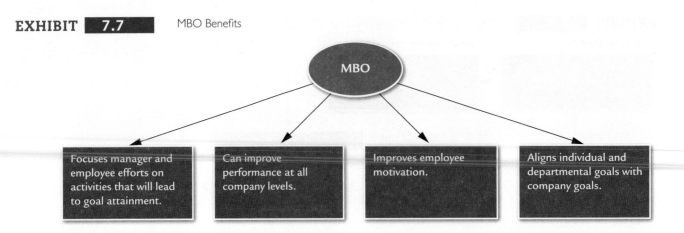

use to get there. People may cut corners, ignore potential problems, or behave unethically just to meet the targets. In addition, MBO cannot stand alone; it is only a part of effectively managing people to achieve goals. MBO is "like training wheels on a bicycle." [23] It gets you started, but it isn't all you need. In the United States, for example, the implementation of rigorous MBO-type systems in urban police departments and school systems has led to cheating on the numbers, with people lying about their work performance in order to score well on the metrics. The means for achieving goals is just as important as the outcomes. A new systematic approach that has recently emerged is called **management by means (MBM)**, which focuses attention on the methods and processes used to achieve goals. A term coined by H. Thomas Johnson and his co-authors in the book *Profit Beyond Measures*, MBM is based on the idea that when managers pursue their activities in the right way, positive outcomes will result. MBM focuses people on considering the means rather than just on reaching the goals. [24]

At Toyota, the "sticky accelerator" problem has been blamed in part on a breakdown between goals and the methods used to achieve them. Years of aggressive growth goals eventually strained managers' ability to control the means by which the goals were achieved. People had to be hired quickly, with little time for adequate training and development. Therefore, the limited number of highly trained managers and engineers had to do more to keep pace toward the goals. Since the crisis, Toyota has refocused on improving the abilities of managers and employees to use the right means of achieving ambitious goals. [25]

SINGLE-USE AND STANDING PLANS

Single-use plans are developed to achieve a set of goals that are not likely to be repeated in the future. **Standing plans** are ongoing plans that provide guidance for tasks or situations that occur repeatedly within the organization. Exhibit 7.8 outlines the major types of single-use and standing plans. Single-use plans typically include both programs and projects. The primary standing plans are organizational policies, rules, and procedures. Standing plans generally pertain to matters such as employee illness, absences, smoking, discipline, hiring, and dismissal. Many companies are discovering a need to develop standing plans regarding the use of social media. According to the Society for Human Resource Management, 40 percent of organizations surveyed have a formal social media policy, and more than half of them include a statement about the company's right to monitor social media usage. Good social media policies are clear, simple, and specific. They define appropriate behavior, clearly specify what is off-limits, let employees know the company can monitor their online activities, and explain the consequences for breaking the rules. [26]

Single-Use Plans	Standing Plans
Program • Plans for attaining a one-time organizational goal • Major undertaking that may take several years to complete • Large in scope; may be associated with several projects **Examples:** Building a new headquarters Converting all paper files to digital **Project** • Also a set of plans for attaining a one-time goal • Smaller in scope and complexity than a program; shorter in horizon • Often one part of a larger program **Examples:** Renovating the office Setting up a company intranet	**Policy** • Broad in scope—general guide to action • Based on organization's overall goals/strategic plan • Defines boundaries within which to make decisions **Examples:** Sexual harassment policies Internet and social media policies **Rule** • Narrow in scope • Describes how a specific action is to be performed • May apply to specific setting **Example:** No eating rule in areas of company where employees are visible to the public **Procedure** • Sometimes called a standard operating procedure • Defines a precise series of steps to attain certain goals **Examples:** Procedures for issuing refunds Procedures for handling employee grievances

EXHIBIT 7.8

Major Types of Single-Use and Standing Plans

3

PLANNING

Remember This

- Managers formulate goals that are specific and measurable, cover key result areas, are challenging but realistic, have a defined time period, and are linked to rewards.
- Types of operational planning include management by objectives, single-use plans, and standing plans.
- **Management by objectives (MBO)** is a method whereby managers and employees define goals for every department, project, and person and use them to monitor subsequent performance.
- MBO includes the steps of setting goals, developing action plans, reviewing progress, and appraising performance.

- A recent approach that focuses people on the methods and processes used to attain results, rather than on the results themselves, is called **management by means (MBM).**
- **Single-use plans** are plans that are developed to achieve a set of goals that are unlikely to be repeated in the future.
- **Standing plans** are ongoing plans that are used to provide guidance for tasks that occur repeatedly in the organization.
- One example of a standing plan is a social media policy.

Benefits and Limitations of Planning

Some managers believe planning ahead is necessary to accomplish anything, whereas others think planning limits personal and organizational performance. Both opinions have merit, because planning can have both advantages and disadvantages.

Research indicates that planning generally positively affects a company's performance.[27] Here are some reasons why:[28]

- *Goals and plans provide a source of motivation and commitment.* Planning can reduce uncertainty for employees and clarify what they should accomplish. The lack of a clear goal hampers motivation because people don't understand what they're working toward.

- **Goals and plans guide resource allocation.** Planning helps managers decide where they need to allocate resources, such as employees, money, and equipment. At Netflix, for example, a goal of having more video offerings online rather than in DVD format means allocating more funds for Internet movie rights and spending more of managers' time developing alliances with other companies.[29]
- **Goals and plans are a guide to action.** Planning focuses attention on specific targets and directs employee efforts toward important outcomes. Planning helps managers and other employees know what actions they need to take to achieve the goal.
- **Goals and plans set a standard of performance.** Because planning and goal-setting define desired outcomes, they also establish performance criteria so managers can measure whether things are on- or off-track. Goals and plans provide a standard of assessment.

Despite these benefits, some researchers also think planning can hurt organizational performance in some ways.[30] Thus, managers should understand the limitations to planning, particularly when the organization is operating in a turbulent environment:

- **Goals and plans can create a false sense of certainty.** Having a plan can give managers a false sense that they know what the future will be like. However, all planning is based on assumptions, and managers can't know what the future holds for their industry or for their competitors, suppliers, and customers.
- **Goals and plans may cause rigidity in a turbulent environment.** A related problem is that planning can lock the organization into specific goals, plans, and time frames, which may no longer be appropriate. Managing under conditions of change and uncertainty requires a degree of flexibility. Managers who believe in "staying the course" will often stick with a faulty plan even when conditions change dramatically.

> "In preparing for battle, I have always found that plans are useless, but planning is indispensable."
> — DWIGHT D. EISENHOWER (1890–1969), U.S. PRESIDENT

- **Goals and plans can get in the way of intuition and creativity.** Success often comes from creativity and intuition, which can be hampered by too much routine planning. For example, during the process of setting goals in the MBO process described earlier, employees might play it safe to achieve objectives rather than offer creative ideas. Similarly, managers sometimes squelch creative ideas from employees that do not fit with predetermined action plans.[31]

Remember This

- Benefits of planning and goal setting include serving as a source of motivation, determining resource allocation, providing a guide to action, and setting a standard for performance measurement.
- Limitations of planning and goal setting include the potential to create a false sense of certainty, create rigidity that hinders response to a turbulent environment, and get in the way of creativity and intuition.

Planning for a Turbulent Environment

Considering the limitations to planning, what are managers to do? One way managers can gain benefits from planning and control its limitations is by using innovative planning approaches that are in tune with today's turbulent environment. Three approaches that help brace the organization for unexpected—even unimaginable—events are contingency planning, building scenarios, and crisis planning.

CONTINGENCY PLANNING

When organizations are operating in a highly uncertain environment or dealing with long time horizons, sometimes planning can seem like a waste of time. Indeed, inflexible plans may hinder rather than help an organization's performance in the face of rapid technological, social, economic, or other environmental change. In these cases, managers can develop multiple future alternatives to help them form more adaptive plans.

Contingency plans define company responses to be taken in the case of emergencies, setbacks, or unexpected conditions. To develop contingency plans, managers identify important factors in the environment, such as possible economic downturns, declining markets, increases in cost of supplies, new technological developments, or safety accidents. Managers then forecast a range of alternative responses to the most likely high-impact contingencies, focusing on the worst case.[32] For example, if sales fall 20 percent and prices drop 8 percent, what will the company do? Managers can develop contingency plans that might include layoffs, emergency budgets, new sales efforts, or new markets. A real-life example comes from the Oscars. What happens if writers or actors go on strike just before the annual Academy Awards show? The Academy of Motion Picture Arts and Sciences has to have contingency plans in place to put the show on using alternatives such as film clips, historical background, and other out-of-the-ordinary ideas. "We have an obligation to the art form to present the Oscars, so we have to deal with the possibility of not being able to do the show because of pickets or agreements not being concluded," said Sid Ganis of the academy.[33]

▶ ▶ ▶ **Concept Connection**

After several outbreaks of the H1N1 flu revealed the dangers of widespread diseases, Mike Claver, State Farm Insurance Company's emergency management superintendent, oversaw the development of a thorough **contingency plan** designed to protect State Farm employees during any potential outbreaks in the future. In addition to coordinating with area agencies and encouraging employees to get vaccines, Claver tested the company's ability to function should managers have to ask employees to work at home during an outbreak. More than 1,000 people, about 10 percent of the workforce at the Bloomington, Illinois, headquarters, logged into the company computer network from their homes one August day. Managers used the results of the dry run to fine-tune contingency plans.

BUILDING SCENARIOS

An extension of contingency planning is a forecasting technique known as *scenario building*.[34] **Scenario building** involves looking at current trends and discontinuities and visualizing future possibilities. Rather than looking only at history and thinking about what has been, managers think about what *could be*. The events that cause the most damage to companies are those that no one even conceived of. In today's tumultuous world, traditional planning can't help managers cope with the many shifting and complex variables that might affect their organizations.

Managers can't predict the future, but they can rehearse a framework within which future events can be managed. Some managers use published global scenarios, such as debt problems in Europe, a slowdown in Asia, or global warming to analyze patterns and driving forces that might affect their industry as a starting point for scenario building. This *abbreviated scenario thinking* can give managers a head start on asking "What if," leading to increased understanding even before any scenarios are written.[35] Then, a broad base of managers mentally rehearses different

Take a Moment

As a new manager, get in the mindset of scenario planning. Go to www.shell.com/home/content/future_energy/scenarios/, where Shell Oil publishes the outline of its annual scenario-planning exercise. You might also want to do an Internet search and type in "national intelligence agency scenarios" to find links to reports of global trends and scenario planning done by various organizations.

scenarios based on anticipating the varied changes that could affect the organization. Scenarios are like stories that offer alternative vivid pictures of what the future will be like and how managers will respond. Typically, two to five scenarios are developed for each set of factors, ranging from the most optimistic to the most pessimistic view. For example, after the United States became involved in a military operation in Libya in early 2011, leaders created four broad scenarios of what might happen—two that were positive for the United States and two that could have highly troublesome consequences—and developed plans for how to respond.[36] Similarly, in businesses and other organizations, scenario building forces managers to rehearse mentally what they would do if their best-laid plans collapse.

CRISIS PLANNING

Many firms also engage in *crisis planning* to enable them to cope with unexpected events that are so sudden and devastating that they have the potential to destroy the organization if managers aren't prepared with a quick and appropriate response. Because so many things can go wrong in their business, most airlines, such as JetBlue, have teams of people dedicated to crisis planning.

Innovative Way

JetBlue

Penny Neferis has been the "worrier in chief" at JetBlue Airways for more than 12 years. As director of care and emergency response, she leads a team that is always thinking about what could go wrong. Neferis's team develops JetBlue's emergency response plan and trains employees in handling a crisis, whether it be an accident, health scare, terrorist attack, or natural disaster.

Many organizations weren't prepared when the swine flu outbreak hit the United States in 2009, but JetBlue had procedures in place that could be adapted to the crisis. They quickly set up training to help employees recognize symptoms, provided hand sanitizer and gloves for planes, established reporting procedures, and created a plan for how to operate if staff or headquarters personnel were affected. Regardless of where a crisis occurs in the world, Neferis and her team swing into action. Following the earthquake in Haiti, for instance, Neferis immediately set up a task force that coordinated with the Haitian consulate and the Red Cross. The airport in Haiti was closed, but JetBlue, which flies to the Dominican Republic, was able to get supplies and people in.

Neferis has always known that anything can happen in the airline business, but that was never clearer than on September 11, 2001. Neferis says she "went on autopilot" during the emergency response at Kennedy Airport following the terrorist attacks. Because the airline had crisis plans in place, JetBlue was able to help passengers and ease some of the chaos. The team set up a passenger assistance center that took passengers from any carrier, not just JetBlue. "You've got to stay strong and grounded in a crisis," Neferis says, "but eventually you have to deal with what you've experienced." She adds, "You're also never done with planning. The minute you get comfortable, think you're ready for anything and become overconfident, it's an indication that you're not in the right field. You've got to stay humble."[37]

Airlines aren't the only organizations that have to be prepared for potentially devastating events. Crises have become integral features of the organizational environment. A few of the recent crises include Hurricane Sandy on the east coast, with massive destruction in New York and New Jersey; the earthquake, tsunami, and nuclear disaster in Japan; the mass shooting at an Aurora, Colorado, movie theater during the premiere of *The Dark Knight Rises*; the massive BP oil spill in the Gulf of Mexico; and the collapse of a stage at the Indiana State Fair that killed seven people and injured dozens more. In addition, consider that the Federal Emergency Management Agency (FEMA) issued 30 disaster declarations in the first quarter of 2010 alone. In 2009, there were a total of 59 FEMA disasters, and in 2008, the total was 75.[38]

EXHIBIT 7.9

Essential Stages of Crisis
Planning

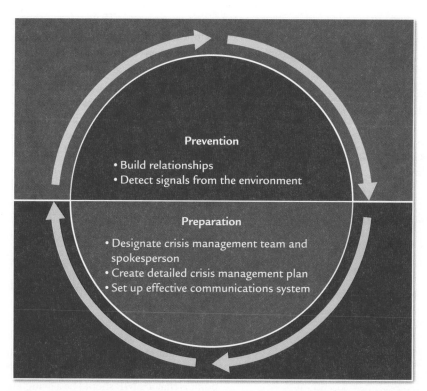

Prevention

• Build relationships
• Detect signals from the environment

Preparation

• Designate crisis management team and
  spokesperson
• Create detailed crisis management plan
• Set up effective communications system

SOURCE: Based on information in W. Timothy Coombs, *Ongoing Crisis Communication: Planning, Managing, and Responding*
(Thousand Oaks, CA: Sage Publications, 1999).

Although crises may vary, a carefully thought-out and coordinated plan can be used to respond to any disaster. In addition, crisis planning reduces the incidence of trouble, just as putting a good lock on a door reduces burglaries.[39] Indiana State Fair officials, for example, have been sharply criticized for a lack of planning that probably contributed to the 2011 stage collapse disaster. Because plans were so haphazard, no one seemed to know who had the authority to delay or cancel the show or what procedures should be followed in case of severe weather. In early 2012, the Indiana Department of Labor fined the state fair commission, as well as Mid-America Sound (which built the stage), and a stagehands union for faulty planning, insufficient inspections, and sloppy construction practices.[40]

Exhibit 7.9 outlines two essential stages of crisis planning.[41]

• **Crisis prevention.** The *crisis prevention* stage involves activities that managers undertake to try to prevent crises from occurring and to detect warning signs of potential crises. A critical part of the prevention stage is building open, trusting relationships with key stakeholders such as employees, customers, suppliers, governments, unions, and the community. By developing favorable relationships, managers can often prevent crises from happening and respond more effectively to those that cannot be avoided.[42]

  For example, organizations that have open, trusting relationships with employees and unions may avoid crippling labor strikes. At the software firm 37signals, managers prevented a crisis by responding quickly and openly when Campfire, a real-time chat tool for small businesses, kept turning off and on unexpectedly. Customers were furious because they used Campfire to run their organizations. Managers immediately began tweeting with customers and posting regular updates on the company's Web site to let people know what was going on and that they were working on the problem. If they didn't understand something, they admitted it. "We responded to every complaint and took the blame every time—even when people went overboard and launched into personal attacks," said Jason Fried of 37signals. Once the problem was fixed, they gave all customers a free month of service. Thanks to quick action, 37signals came out of the episode with stronger customer loyalty and goodwill than ever.[43]

Concept Connection ◀◀◀

Cheryl Casey/Shutterstock.com

After the Deepwater Horizon oil rig drilling a well for BP exploded in the Gulf of Mexico, U.S. congressman Henry Waxman (D-CA) observed that "a striking feature of the incident is the apparent lack of an adequate plan to contain the spreading environmental damage." BP's CEO at the time, Tony Hayward, admitted Waxman was right. Because BP saw a deepwater leak as highly unlikely and touted the Deepwater Horizon as one of the world's most technologically advanced drilling platforms, it had no specific **crisis plan** for an uncontrolled blowout. Since then, BP has committed up to $1 billion to cleaning up both the damage to the gulf and the damage to the BP brand.

- *Crisis preparation.* The *crisis preparation* stage includes all the detailed planning to handle a crisis when it occurs. Three steps in the preparation stage are (1) designating a crisis management team and spokesperson, (2) creating a detailed crisis management plan, and (3) setting up an effective communications system. The crisis management team, for example, is a cross-functional group of people who are designated to swing into action if a crisis occurs. The organization should also designate a spokesperson to be the voice of the company during the crisis.[44] The crisis management plan (CMP) is a detailed, written plan that specifies the steps to be taken, and by whom, if a crisis occurs. The CMP should include the steps for dealing with various types of crises, such as natural disasters like fires or earthquakes; normal accidents like economic crises, industrial accidents, or product and service failures; and abnormal events such as product tampering or acts of terrorism.[45] A key point is that a CMP should be a living, changing document that is regularly reviewed, practiced, and updated as needed.

Remember This

- Managers use innovative planning approaches to cope with today's turbulent environment.
- **Contingency planning** identifies important factors in the environment and defines a range of alternative responses to be taken in the case of emergencies, setbacks, or unexpected conditions.
- With **scenario building**, managers look at trends and discontinuities and imagine possible alternative futures to build a framework within which unexpected future events can be managed.

- Scenarios are alternative vivid pictures of what the future might be like.
- Many companies increased their use contingency and scenario planning because of the global financial crisis and volatile economic conditions.
- Crisis planning involves the two major stages of prevention and preparation.

Innovative Approaches to Planning

The process of planning changes over time, like other aspects of managing, to become more in tune with shifts in the environment and employee attitudes. A fresh approach to planning is to involve everyone in the organization, and sometimes outside stakeholders as well, in the planning process. The evolution to a new approach began with a shift to **decentralized planning**, which means that planning experts work with managers in major divisions or departments to develop their own goals and plans. Managers throughout the company come up with their own creative solutions to problems and become more committed to following through on the plans. As the environment became even more volatile, top executives saw the benefits of pushing decentralized planning even further by having planning experts work directly with line managers and frontline employees to develop dynamic plans that meet fast-changing needs.

In a complex and competitive business environment, strategic thinking and execution become the expectation of every employee.[46] Planning comes alive when employees are involved in setting goals and determining the means to reach them. The following sections provide some guidelines for innovative planning.

Take a Moment

Go to the Ethical Dilemma for Chapter 7 on page 297 that pertains to potential problems with innovative planning approaches.

SET STRETCH GOALS FOR EXCELLENCE

Stretch goals are reasonable yet highly ambitious goals that are so clear, compelling, and imaginative that they fire up employees and engender excellence. Stretch goals are typically so far beyond the current levels that people have to be innovative to find ways to reach them. Consider the following example from Amazon.com.

Innovative Way

Amazon

When Jeff Bezos, CEO of Amazon, first asked engineers in 2004 to create a lightweight, simple e-reader with built in cellular access, systems engineer Jateen Parekh said, "I thought it was insane. I really did." At the time, nothing like that had ever been tried. But Bezos believed that configuring devices to WiFi networks would be too complicated for many users, and he didn't want people to have to connect to a personal computer. Essentially, he didn't want people to even have to think about the wireless connection. The challenge eventually got Parekh and others fired up.

It took the development group several years, but in 2007, the Kindle was born. It proved to be such a hit that the first batch sold out in just a few hours. Amazon had to scramble to find a key part that had been discontinued by a supplier to get more on the market. "You look at the history of the Kindle, they developed some real skills around the creation of that product. They cut their teeth, so to speak," said Brian Blair, an analyst with Wedge Partners.

Building its own hardware—much less something that hadn't been done before—was an audacious, high-stakes bet for Amazon, but it paid off. Moreover, making four successive generations of the Kindle e-reader led down the path to the Kindle Fire, which is today the only serious competitor to Apple's iPad.[47]

Asking a group of engineers to create the first Kindle e-reader might be considered what James Collins and Jerry Porras have called a *big hairy audacious goal (BHAG).* This phrase was first proposed by Collins and Porras in their 1996 article entitled "Building Your Company's Vision."[48] Since then, it has evolved to a term used to describe any goal that is so big, inspiring, and outside the prevailing paradigm that it hits people in the gut and shifts their thinking. At the same time, however, goals must be seen as achievable or employees will be discouraged and demotivated, and some might resort to extreme or unethical measures to meet the targets.[49]

Stretch goals and BHAGs have become extremely important because things move fast. A company that focuses on gradual, incremental improvements in products, processes, or systems will be left behind. Managers can use

Dan Krauss/The New York Times/Redux Pictures

▶▶▶ **Concept Connection**

Back in 2005, Netflix CEO Reed Hastings announced a **stretch goal** of quadrupling the company's subscriber base to 20 million by 2012. "That's a bit aggressive," he said at the time, "but it's theoretically possible." Fast forward to 2012, and Netflix had not only met this goal but surpassed it, for a total of 30 million subscribers! With success like this, it's no surprise that Hastings has set a new stretch goal of 60 million to 90 million subscribers in the future.

3

PLANNING

these goals to compel employees to think in new ways that can lead to bold, innovative breakthroughs.[50]

USE PERFORMANCE DASHBOARDS

People need a way to see how plans are progressing and gauge their progress toward achieving goals. Companies began using *business performance dashboards* as a way for executives to keep track of key performance metrics, such as sales in relation to targets, number of products on back order, or percentage of customer service calls resolved within specified time periods. Dashboards have evolved into organizationwide systems that help align and track goals across the enterprise. Exhibit 7.10 shows an example of a business performance dashboard that can deliver real-time key performance metrics. The true power of dashboards comes from applying them throughout the company, even on the factory or sales floor, so that all employees can track progress toward goals, see when things are falling short, and find innovative ways to get back on course toward reaching the specified targets. At Emergency Medical Associates, a physician-owned medical group that manages emergency rooms for hospitals in New York and New Jersey, dashboards enable the staff to see when performance thresholds related to patient wait times, for example, aren't being met at various hospitals.[51] Some dashboard systems also incorporate software that lets users perform what-if scenarios to evaluate the impact of various alternatives for meeting goals.

DEPLOY INTELLIGENCE TEAMS

Anticipating and managing uncertainty and turbulence in the environment is a crucial part of planning, which means managers need good intelligence to make informed choices about goals and plans. A growing number of leading companies are using intelligence teams to manage this challenge. An **intelligence team** is a cross-functional group of managers and

EXHIBIT 7.10   A Performance Dashboard for Planning

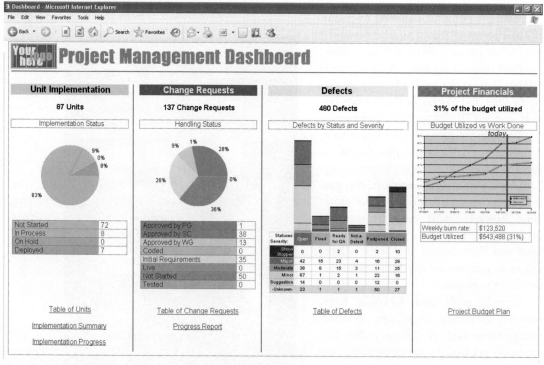

SOURCE: Sample Dashboard by Conflair, "Management Dashboards," Conflair.com, www.conflair.com/ConflairServices/41_ManagementDashboards.asp (accessed July 23, 2012).

employees, usually led by a competitive intelligence professional, who work together to gain a deep understanding of a specific business issue, with the aim of presenting insights, possibilities, and recommendations about goals and plans related to that issue.[52] Intelligence teams are useful when the organization confronts a major intelligence challenge. For example, consider a large financial services firm that learns that an even-larger rival is potentially moving to compete directly with one of its major profit-generating businesses. Top managers might form an intelligence team to identify when and how this might happen and how it might affect the organization. Intelligence teams can provide insights that enable managers to make more informed decisions about goals, as well as to devise contingency plans and scenarios related to major strategic issues.

Remember This

- Approaches to planning change with the times. In many companies today, planning is decentralized.
- **Decentralized planning** means that top executives or planning experts work with managers in major divisions or departments to develop their own goals and plans.
- **Stretch goals** are reasonable yet highly ambitious and compelling goals that energize people and inspire excellence.

- At Amazon, a stretch goal was to build the first Kindle e-reader with built-in cellular access so people didn't have to connect to a PC.
- Business performance dashboards can help managers oversee plans and measure progress toward goals.
- An **intelligence team** is a cross-functional group of people who work together to gain a deep understanding of a specific competitive issue and offer insight and recommendations for planning.

ch7: Discussion Questions

1. Write a brief mission statement for a local business with which you are familiar. How might having a clear, written mission statement benefit a small organization?

2. What strategic plans could the college or university at which you are taking this management course adopt to compete for students in the marketplace? Would these plans depend on the school's goals?

3. One of the benefits of a strategy map is that goals and how they are linked can be communicated clearly to everyone in the organization. Does a minimum-wage maintenance worker in a hospital really need to understand any goals beyond keeping the place clean? Discuss.

4. The MBO technique has been criticized for putting too much emphasis on achieving goals (ends) and not enough on the methods that people use to achieve them (means). Do you think this is a flaw in the technique, or in the way managers apply it? How would you place a balanced emphasis on ends and means?

5. A new business venture must develop a comprehensive business plan to borrow money to get started. Companies such as FedEx and Nike say they did not follow the original plan closely. Does that mean that developing the plan was a waste of time for these eventually successful companies?

6. How do you think planning in today's organizations compares to planning 25 years ago? Do you think planning becomes more important or less important in a world where everything is changing quickly and crises are a regular part of organizational life? Why?

7. Assume that Southern University decides to do two things: (1) raise its admission standards, and (2) initiate a business fair to which local townspeople will be invited. What types of plans might it use to carry out these two activities?

8. LivingSocial started with one "daily deal," a $25 voucher for $50 worth of food at a Washington, D.C., area restaurant. Since then, the company has grown at breakneck speed, has 46 million members in 25 countries, and has acquired a dozen companies that offer related deals and services. Why and how might a company such as LivingSocial want to use an intelligence team? Discuss.

9. Some people say an organization could never be "prepared" for a disaster such as the shooting at an Aurora, Colorado, movie theater, the Japan nuclear disaster, or the huge BP oil spill in the Gulf of Mexico. Discuss the potential value of crisis planning in situations like these, even if the situations are difficult to plan for.

10. Goals that are overly ambitious can discourage employees and decrease motivation, yet the idea of stretch goals is proposed as a way to get people fired up and motivated. As a manager, how might you decide where to draw the line between a "good" stretch goal and a "bad" one that is unrealistic?

3

PLANNING

ch7: Apply Your Skills: Experiential Exercise

Business School Ranking

The dean of the business school at a major university in your state has contacted students in your class to develop a plan for improving its national ranking among business schools. The school recently dropped ten places in the rankings, and the dean wants to restore the school's perceived luster. The dean provided the following list of variables on which the national ranking is based.

- Written assessment by deans from peer institutions, on a scale of 1 to 5
- Written assessment by recruiters, on a scale of 1 to 5
- Average grade point average (GPA) of incoming students
- Acceptance rate of student applications (a lower percentage is better)
- Average starting salary of the school's most recent graduates

- Percentage of graduates employed on the date of graduation
- Percentage of graduates employed three months after graduation
- Average Scholastic Aptitude Test (SAT; for the undergraduate program) and Graduate Management Admission Test (GMAT; for the MBA program) scores for entering students

The business school has a goal of improving its ranking by ten places in two years. Brainstorm ideas and develop a ten-point action plan that will list the steps the dean can take to achieve this goal. To develop the plan, think carefully about actions the school might take to improve its ranking on any or all of the measured variables listed above.

After writing down your ideas to develop a plan, meet with a partner to share ideas and discuss the most helpful action steps that will be part of the action plan recommended to the business school dean.

ch7: Apply Your Skills: Small Group Breakout

Course Goal Setting[53]

Step 1. Make your goals for yourself regarding desired outcomes for this course explicit. What is your goal for a grade? Your goal for learning specific knowledge or skills? Define at least two goals for this course.

Step 2. The next step is to break down each goal into "goal behaviors." These are the specific behaviors that will allow you to achieve each goal in Step 1. Examples of goal behaviors might include 100 percent attendance, taking good class notes every day, reading assigned chapters before class, outlining chapters, writing definitions of new words, participating in class discussions, setting specific study times for exams, answering end-of-chapter questions, or completing "Workbook" assignments. Define a minimum

of four goal behaviors that will lead to the achievement of each goal in Step 1.

Step 3. In groups of three to five students, compare your goals and goal behaviors. Students should take turns sharing goals and behaviors with the group.

Step 4. What did you learn from hearing the goals and goal behaviors of group members? How different were the goals and behaviors of group members? Which combination of goal and goal behaviors seems most likely to be successful?

Step 5. On the last day of class, meet again as a group. Each student should report on the degree of success following goal behaviors and achieving goals. Share what you learned from this experience. Your instructor may ask your group members to report their findings to the class.

ch7: Endnotes

1. Miguel Bustillo, "Corporate News—Boss Talk: Wal-Mart's U.S. Chief Aims for Turnaround," *The Asian Wall Street Journal*, March 22, 2011, 22; and Miguel Bustillo, "Wal-Mart Tries to Recapture Mr. Sam's Winning Formula," *The Wall Street Journal Online*, February 22, 2011, http://online.wsj.com/article/SB10001424052748703803904576152753111788930.html (accessed July 17, 2012).

2. Hiroko Tabuchi, "Inquiry Declares Fukushima Crisis a Man-Made Disaster," *The New York Times*, July 5, 2012, www.nytimes.com/2012/07/06/world/asia/fukushima-nuclear-crisis-a-man-made-disaster-report-says.html (accessed July 19, 2012).

3. Quoted in Oren Harari, "Good/Bad News About Strategy," *Management Review* (July 1995): 29–31.

4. Amitai Etzioni, *Modern Organizations* (Englewood Cliffs, NJ: Prentice Hall, 1984), p. 6.

5. *Ibid.*

6. Max D. Richards, *Setting Strategic Goals and Objectives*, 2d ed. (St. Paul, MN: West, 1986).

7. Reported in Matthew Budman, "Why Are We In Business? Ad Man Roy Spence Wants to Know What Your

Purpose Is," The Conference Board Review (March–April 2009): 35–41.

8. Mary Klemm, Stuart Sanderson, and George Luffman, "Mission Statements: Selling Corporate Values to Employees," *Long-Range Planning* 24, no. 3 (1991): 73–78; John A. Pearce II and Fred David, "Corporate Mission Statements: The Bottom Line," *Academy of Management Executive* (1987): 109–116; Jerome H. Want, "Corporate Mission: The Intangible Contributor to Performance," *Management Review* (August 1986): 46–50; and Forest R. David and Fred R. David, "It's Time to Redraft Your Mission Statement," *Journal of Business Strategy* (January–February 2003): 11–14.

9. "Tennessee News and Notes from State Farm," State Farm Mutual Automobile Insurance Company, 2004.

10. The quote is from Mark Mallinger, a Pepperdine University management professor who has studied TJ's for years; quoted in Shan Li, "Can Trader Joe's Stay 'Homey' as It Grows? Grocer Tries to Retain Neighborly Vibe as It Opens Larger Stores," *Los Angeles Times*, October 27, 2011, B1.

11. Scott Sloan, "Lexington's Trader Joe's Opens Friday," *Kentucky.com* (June 28, 2012), www.kentucky.com /2012/06/28/2241801/lexingtons-trader-joes-opens-friday.html (accessed July 17, 2012); Mark Mallinger, "The Trader Joe's Experience: The Impact of Corporate Culture on Business Strategy," *Graziadio Business Review*, Graziadio School of Business and Management, Pepperdine University, Vol. 10, Issue 2 (2007), www.gbr .pepperdine.edu/2010/08/the-trader-joes-experience/ (accessed July 17, 2012); Shan Li, "Can Trader Joe's Stay 'Homey' as It Grows?"; and Beth Kowitt, "Inside Trader Joe's," *Fortune* (September 6, 2010), 86ff.

12. Kowitt, "Inside Trader Joe's."

13. Paul Meising and Joseph Wolfe, "The Art and Science of Planning at the Business Unit Level," *Management Science* 31 (1985): 773–781.

14. Geary A. Rummler and Kimberly Morrill, "The Results Chain," *TD* (February 2005): 27–35; and John C. Crotts, Duncan R. Dickson, and Robert C. Ford, "Aligning Organizational Processes with Mission: The Case of Service Excellence," *Academy of Management Executive* 19, no. 3 (August 2005): 54–68.

15. This discussion is based on Robert S. Kaplan and David P. Norton, "Mastering the Management System," *Harvard Business Review* (January 2008): 63–77; and Robert S. Kaplan and David P. Norton, "Having Trouble with Your Strategy? Then Map It," *Harvard Business Review* (September–October 2000): 167–176.

16. Sayan Chatterjee, "Core Objectives: Clarity in Designing Strategy," *California Management Review* 47, no. 2 (Winter 2005): 33–49.

17. Edwin A. Locke, Gary P. Latham, and Miriam Erez, "The Determinants of Goal Commitment," *Academy of Management Review* 13 (1988): 23–39.

18. Peter F. Drucker, *The Practice of Management* (New York: Harper & Row, 1954); George S. Odiorne, "MBO: A Backward Glance," *Business Horizons* 21 (October 1978): 14–24; and William F. Roth, "Is Management by Objectives Obsolete?" *Global Business and Organizational Excellence* (May–June 2009): 36–43.

19. Jan P. Muczyk and Bernard C. Reimann, "MBO as a Complement to Effective Leadership," *The Academy of Management Executive* 3 (1989): 131–138; and W. Giegold, *Objective Setting and the MBO Process*, vol. 2 (New York: McGraw-Hill, 1978).

20. John Ivancevich et al., "Goal Setting: The Tenneco Approach to Personnel Development and Management Effectiveness," *Organizational Dynamics* (Winter 1978): 48–80.

21. Tim O'Shaughnessy, as told to Liz Welch, "The Way I Work: Tim O'Shaughnessy, LivingSocial," *Inc.* (March 2012): 104–108.

22. Eileen M. Van Aken and Garry D. Coleman, "Building Better Measurement," *Industrial Management* (July–August 2002): 28–33.

23. This analogy is from Jeffrey K. Liker and Timothy N. Ogden, "The Toyota Recall: Missing the Forest for the Trees," *Ivey Business Journal* (November–December 2011), www.iveybusinessjournal.com/topics/marketing/ the-toyota-recall-missing-the-forest-for-the-trees (accessed July 19, 2012).

24. Reylito A. H. Elbo, "MBM: Management by Means, Not Results," *The Manila Times*, June 11, 2012, www.manilatimes.net/index.php/business/business-columnist/24633-mbm-management-by-means-not-results (accessed August 8, 2012); and Liker and Ogden, "The Toyota Recall."

25. Liker and Ogden, "The Toyota Recall."

26. Sarah Fister Gale, "Big Brother Is Watching: Why Social Media Policies Make Good Business Sense," *Workforce*, June 21, 2012, www.workforce .com/article/20120621/NEWS02/120629994/ big-brother-is-watching-why-social-media-policies-make-good-business-sense# (accessed July 18, 2012); and Sarah Fister Gale, "Five Things Every Social Media Policy Should Do," *Workforce*, June 21 2012, www.workforce.com/article/20120621/NEWS02/ 120629995 (accessed July 18, 2012).

27. C. Chet Miller and Laura B. Cardinal, "Strategic Planning and Firm Performance: A Synthesis of More than Two Decades of Research," *Academy of Management Journal* 37, no. 6 (1994): 1649–1685.

28. These are based on E. A. Locke and G. P. Latham, *A Theory of Goal Setting & Task Performance* (Englewood Cliffs, N.J.: Prentice Hall, 1990); Richard L. Daft and Richard M. Steers, *Organizations: A Micro/Macro Approach* (Glenview, IL: Scott, Foresman, 1986), pp. 319–321; Herbert A. Simon, "On the Concept of Organizational Goals," *Administrative Science Quarterly* 9 (1964): 1–22; and Charles B. Saunders and Francis

3

PLANNING

D. Tuggel, "Corporate Goals," *Journal of General Management* 5 (1980): 3–13.

29. Nick Wingfield, "Netflix Boss Plots Life After the DVD," *The Wall Street Journal*, June 23, 2009.

30. These are based on Henry Mintzberg, *The Rise and Fall of Strategic Planning* (New York: The Free Press, 1994); H. Mintzberg, "Rethinking Strategic Planning, Part I: Pitfalls and Fallacies," *Long Range Planning* 27 (1994): 12–21; and H. Mintzberg, "The Pitfalls of Strategic Planning," *California Management Review* 36 (1993): 32–47.

31. Roth, "Is Management by Objectives Obsolete?"

32. Curtis W. Roney, "Planning for Strategic Contingencies," *Business Horizons* (March–April 2003): 35–42; and "Corporate Planning: Drafting a Blueprint for Success," *Small Business Report* (August 1987): 40–44.

33. Sandy Cohen, "Oscars Contingency Plan," *USAToday*, January 30, 2008, www.usatoday.com/life/music/2008-01-30-1092823826_x.htm (accessed July 20, 2012).

34. This section is based on Steven Schnaars and Paschalina Ziamou, "The Essentials of Scenario Writing," *Business Horizons* (July–August 2001): 25–31; Peter Cornelius, Alexander Van de Putte, and Mattia Romani, "Three Decades of Scenario Planning in Shell," *California Management Review* 48, no. 1 (Fall 2005): 92–109; Audrey Schriefer and Michael Sales, "Creating Strategic Advantage with Dynamic Scenarios," *Strategy & Leadership* 34, no. 3 (2006): 31–42; William J. Worthington, Jamie D. Collins, and Michael A. Hitt, "Beyond Risk Mitigation: Enhancing Corporate Innovation with Scenario Planning," *Business Horizons* 52 (2009): 441–450; and Gill Ringland, "Innovation: Scenarios of Alternative Futures Can Discover New Opportunities for Creativity," *Strategy & Leadership* 36, no. 5 (2008): 22–27.

35. Kathleen Wilburn and Ralph Wilburn, "Abbreviated Scenario Thinking," *Business Horizons* 54 (2011): 541–550.

36. Gerald F. Seib, "Four Scenarios for Libya—Some Good and Some Bad," *The Wall Street Journal*, March 29, 2011, http://online.wsj.com/article/SB10001424052 748703739204576228620384027448.html (accessed July 20, 2012).

37. Penny Neferis, as told to Patricia R. Olsen, "Call Her the Worrier in Chief," *The New York Times*, April 30, 2011, www.nytimes.com/2011/05/01/jobs/01pre.html (accessed July 20, 2012).

38. Reported in W. Jack Duncan et al., "Surviving Organizational Disasters," *Business Horizons* 54 (2011): 135–142.

39. Ian Mitroff with Gus Anagnos, *Managing Crises Before They Happen* (New York: AMACOM, 2001); Ian

Mitroff and Murat C. Alpaslan, "Preparing for Evil," *Harvard Business Review* (April 2003): 109–115.

40. Jack Nicas, "Faulty Planning, Stage Cited in Fair Collapse," *The Wall Street Journal*, April 12, 2012, http://online.wsj.com/article/SB2000142405270230 4356604577339923897959492.html (accessed July 20, 2012).

41. The following discussion is based largely on W. Timothy Coombs, *Ongoing Crisis Communication: Planning, Managing, and Responding* (Thousand Oaks, CA: Sage Publications, 1999).

42. Ian I. Mitroff, "Crisis Leadership," *Executive Excellence* (August 2001): 19; Andy Bowen, "Crisis Procedures that Stand the Test of Time," *Public Relations Tactics* (August 2001): 16.

43. Jason Fried, "How to Ride a Storm," *Inc.* (February 2011): 37–39.

44. Christine Pearson, "A Blueprint for Crisis Management," *Ivey Business Journal* (January–February 2002): 69–73.

45. See Mitroff and Alpaslan, "Preparing for Evil," for a discussion of the "wheel of crises" outlining the many different kinds of crises that organizations may face.

46. Harari, "Good/Bad News About Strategy."

47. Brad Stone, "The Omnivore," *Bloomberg Businessweek* (October 3–October 9, 2011): 58–65.

48. James C. Collins and Jerry I. Porras, "Building Your Company's Vision," *Harvard Business Review* (September–October 1996): 65–77.

49. Steven Kerr and Steffan Landauer, "Using Stretch Goals to Promote Organizational Effectiveness and Personal Growth: General Electric and Goldman Sachs," *Academy of Management Executive* 18, no. 4 (November 2004): 134–138; and Lisa D. Ordóñez et al., "Goals Gone Wild: The Systematic Side Effects of Overprescribing Goal Setting," *Academy of Management Perspectives* (February 2009): 6–16.

50. See Kenneth R. Thompson, Wayne A. Hockwarter, and Nicholas J. Mathys, "Stretch Targets: What Makes Them Effective?" *Academy of Management Executive* 11, no. 3 (August 1997): 48.

51. Doug Bartholomew, "Gauging Success," *CFO-IT* (Summer 2005): 17–19.

52. This section is based on Liam Fahey and Jan Herring, "Intelligence Teams," *Strategy & Leadership* 35, no. 1 (2007): 13–20.

53. Adapted by Dorothy Marcic from Nancy C. Morey, "Applying Goal Setting in the Classroom," *The Organizational Behavior Teaching Review*, 11 (4) (1986–1987): 53–59.

Strategy Formulation and Implementation

Dennis Flaherty/Jupiter Images

Learning Outcomes

After studying this chapter, you should be able to:

1. Define the components of strategic management and discuss the levels of strategy.

2. Describe the strategic management process and SWOT analysis for evaluating the company's strengths, weaknesses, opportunities, and threats.

3. Define corporate-level strategies and explain the Boston Consulting Group (BCG) matrix, portfolio, and diversification approaches.

4. Describe Michael Porter's competitive strategies.

5. Discuss organizational dimensions that managers use to execute strategy.

What Is Your Strategy Strength?[1]

INSTRUCTIONS: As a new manager, what are your strengths concerning strategy formulation and implementation? To find out, think about *how you handle challenges and issues* in your school or job. Then mark (a) or (b) for each of the following items, depending on which is more descriptive of your behavior. There is no right or wrong answer to these questions. Respond to each item as it best describes how you respond to work situations.

1. When keeping records, I tend to:
   _____ a. Be careful about documentation.
   _____ b. Be haphazard about documentation.

2. If I run a group or a project, I:
   _____ a. Have the general idea and let others figure out how to do the tasks.
   _____ b. Try to figure out specific goals, timelines, and expected outcomes.

3. My thinking style could be more accurately described as:
   _____ a. Linear thinker, going from A to B to C.
   _____ b. Thinking like a grasshopper, hopping from one idea to another.

4. In my office or home, things are:
   _____ a. Here and there, in various piles.
   _____ b. Laid out neatly, or at least in reasonable order.

5. I take pride in developing:
   _____ a. Ways to overcome a barrier to a solution.
   _____ b. New hypotheses about the underlying cause of a problem.

6. I can best help strategy by encouraging:
   _____ a. Openness to a wide range of assumptions and ideas.
   _____ b. Thoroughness when implementing new ideas.

7. One of my strengths is:
   _____ a. Commitment to making things work.
   _____ b. Commitment to a dream for the future.

8. I am most effective when I emphasize:
   _____ a. Inventing original solutions.
   _____ b. Making practical improvements.

SCORING AND INTERPRETATION: Managers have differing strengths and capabilities when it comes to formulating and implementing strategy. Here's how to determine yours. For *Strategic Formulator* strength, score 1 point for each (a) answer marked for questions 2, 4, 6, and 8, and for each (b) answer marked for questions 1, 3, 5, and 7. For *Strategic Implementer* strength, score 1 point for each (b) answer marked for questions 2, 4, 6, and 8, and for each (a) answer marked for questions 1, 3, 5, and 7. Which of your two scores is higher, and by how much? The higher score indicates your strategy strength.

New managers bring value to strategic management as formulators, implementers, or both. New managers with implementer strengths tend to work within the situation and improve it by making it more efficient and reliable. Managers with the formulator strength push toward out-of-the-box strategies and like to seek dramatic breakthroughs. Both styles are essential to strategic management. Strategic formulators often use their skills in creating whole new strategies and strategic implementers often work with strategic improvements and implementation.

If the difference between your two scores is 2 or less, you have a balanced formulator/implementer style and work well in both arenas. If the difference is 4 or 5 points, you have a moderately strong style and probably work best in the area of your strength. If the difference is 7 or 8 points, you have a distinctive strength and almost certainly would want to work in the area of your strength rather than in the opposite domain.

Best Buy was one of the hottest companies in the 1990s and early 2000s. Rapid growth was fueled by a strategy of selling a large selection of electronic and technology products, such as global positioning satellite (GPS) systems, computers,

1 INTRODUCTION

2 ENVIRONMENT

3 PLANNING

4 ORGANIZING

5 LEADING

6 CONTROLLING

televisions, DVDs, and digital cameras, in huge superstores. But rapid changes in the competitive environment, including greater use of the Internet for such purchases, the availability of streaming music and video, and new devices that incorporate what used to be stand-alone technology, have eaten away at Best Buy's competitive advantage. To cope, managers announced a strategy of opening smaller stores focused on sales and service for ever-smaller, more versatile technology products. Plans are to dramatically reduce overall square footage by closing some stores, negotiating smaller lease spaces, opening tiny "Best Buy Mobile" stores, and subleasing space in some of the company's big box stores to other retailers. Is it too little too late? Some analysts think so, expressing doubt that Best Buy's new strategy is an adequate response to the rapid shifts occurring in the retail and electronics environments.[2]

How important is strategic management? It largely determines which organizations succeed and which ones struggle. Differences in the strategies that managers chose and how effectively they executed them help explain why Amazon.com is thriving and Best Buy is floundering, how Facebook all but killed MySpace in social networking, and why Apple is beating Microsoft in the world of mobile computing.

Every company is concerned with strategy. In the fast food industry, managers revived Domino's by formulating and aggressively advertising a new pizza recipe that responded to changing consumer tastes. McDonald's has succeeded with a revamped strategy of adding the McCafe line of hot and iced coffee drinks, offering snacks and small dessert items throughout the day, and enhancing its line of products for health-conscious consumers. YUM Brands' KFC chain is thriving with an ambitious global strategy, rapidly expanding overseas, particularly in China.[3]

> **"It's hard to outrun the future if you don't see it coming."**
>
> — GARY HAMEL, MANAGEMENT
> SCHOLAR AND AUTHOR

Strategic blunders can hurt a company. For instance, Kodak still hasn't recovered from its managers' failure to plan for the rapid rise of digital photography. A recent article touting the success of a thriving, innovative, adaptive company referred to the firm as the "anti-Kodak." And remember when Liz Claiborne was one of the most popular clothing lines around? No, you probably don't. The company that pioneered career apparel for women has been in decline for years, with managers failing to latch onto a strategy that could keep the clothing line relevant as baby boomers retired and began spending less money on career outfits.[4]

Managers at Liz Claiborne, McDonald's, Kodak, Best Buy, and Facebook are all involved in strategic management. They look for ways to respond to competitors, cope with difficult environmental challenges, meet changing customer needs, and effectively use available resources. Strategic management has taken on greater importance in today's environment because managers are responsible for positioning their organizations for success in a world that is constantly changing.

Chapter 7 provided an overview of the types of goals and plans that organizations use. In this chapter, we explore strategic management, which is one specific type of planning. First, we define the components of strategic management and discuss the purposes and levels of strategy. Then, we examine several models of strategy formulation at the corporate, business, and functional levels. Finally, we discuss the tools that managers use to execute their strategic plans.

Thinking Strategically

What does it mean to think strategically? Strategic thinking means to take the long-term view and to see the big picture, including the organization and the competitive environment, and consider how they fit together. Strategic thinking is important for both businesses and nonprofit organizations. In for-profit firms, strategic planning typically pertains

New Manager | Self-Test

Systemic Thinking

Instructions: Respond to each of the following statements based on how you have *actually* approached a difficult problem at work. Please indicate whether each item is Mostly True or Mostly False for you.

	Mostly True	Mostly False
1. I tried to see the problem in its entirety and how it affected other people.	_____	_____
2. I started by acquiring and integrating information from different areas.	_____	_____
3. I enjoyed solving a complex rather than a simple problem.	_____	_____
4. I systematically talked to people who had diverse perspectives on the problem.	_____	_____
5. I attempted to link a solution to an overall strategy or plan.	_____	_____
6. I analyzed root causes of the problem to find leverage points for a solution.	_____	_____
7. My approach was to focus on one part of the problem at a time.	_____	_____
8. I took time to consider the situation from all angles.	_____	_____
9. I studied how different parts of the organization interacted to affect the problem.	_____	_____

Scoring and Interpretation: Systemic thinking represents a strategic approach to problem solving that seeks the big picture of how things fit together, rather than focusing on a specific part. Systemic thinking is considered strategic because it welcomes the challenge of system complexity and how all the parts interact. Analytical thinkers, for example, may break a problem down into individual parts, whereas a systemic thinker would strive to understand how the parts fit together in a larger context.

Give yourself 2 points for each Mostly True answer and 1 point for each Mostly False answer, except for question 7, which should be reverse-scored—2 points for Mostly False and 1 point for Mostly True. If your score is 14 or higher, you probably have a tendency toward systemic thinking. If your score is 6 or less, you probably approach problems by focusing on individual parts of a system, rather than on the interaction of the parts to create the whole system. A score of 7–13 implies that you use some elements of systemic thinking some of the time.

to competitive actions in the marketplace. In nonprofit organizations such as the American Red Cross or the Salvation Army, strategic planning pertains to events in the external environment.

Research has shown that strategic thinking and planning positively affect a firm's performance and financial success.[5] Most managers are aware of the importance of strategic planning, as evidenced by a *McKinsey Quarterly* survey. Of responding executives whose companies had no formal strategic planning process, 51 percent said they were dissatisfied with the company's development of strategy, compared to only 20 percent of those at companies that had a formal planning process.[6] CEOs at successful companies make strategic thinking and planning a top management priority. For an organization to succeed, the CEO must be actively involved in making the tough choices and trade-offs that define and support strategy.[7] However, senior

Take a Moment

Completing the New Manager Self-Test will give you an idea about your ability to see the big picture and how different aspects of the organization and its environment interact, which is an important part of strategic thinking.

executives at today's leading companies want middle- and lower-level managers to think strategically as well. Understanding the strategy concept and the levels of strategy is an important start toward strategic thinking.

Remember This

- To think strategically means to take the long-term view and see the big picture.

- Managers in all types of organizations, including businesses, nonprofit organizations, and government agencies, have to think about how the organization fits in the environment.

What Is Strategic Management?

Strategic management refers to the set of decisions and actions used to formulate and execute strategies that will provide a competitively superior fit between the organization and its environment so as to achieve organizational goals.[8] Managers ask questions such as the following: What changes and trends are occurring in the competitive environment? Who are our competitors, and what are their strengths and weaknesses? Who are our customers? What products or services should we offer and how can we offer them most efficiently? What does the future hold for our industry, and how can we change the rules of the game? Answers to these questions help managers make choices about how to position their organizations in the environment with respect to rival companies.[9] Superior organizational performance is not a matter of luck. It is determined by the choices that managers make.

PURPOSE OF STRATEGY

The first step in strategic management is to define an explicit **strategy**, which is the plan of action that describes resource allocation and activities for dealing with the environment, achieving a competitive advantage, and attaining the organization's goals. **Competitive advantage** refers to what sets the organization apart from others and provides it with a distinctive edge for meeting customer or client needs in the marketplace. The essence of formulating strategy is choosing how the organization will be different.[10] Managers make decisions about whether the company will perform different activities or will execute similar activities differently than its rivals do. Strategy necessarily changes over time to fit environmental conditions, but to achieve competitive advantage, companies develop strategies that incorporate the elements illustrated in Exhibit 8.1: target specific customers, focus on core competencies, provide synergy, and create value.

Take a Moment

Managers develop their ability to think strategically through both work experiences and formal study. See if your experiences have given you a good start toward strategic thinking by completing the Experiential Exercise on pages 259–260.

Target Customers

An effective strategy defines the customers and which of their needs are to be served by the company.[11] Managers can define a target market geographically, such as serving people in a certain part of the country; demographically, such as aiming toward people in a certain income bracket or targeting preteen girls; or by a variety of other means. Some firms target people who purchase primarily over the Internet, whereas others aim to serve people who like to shop in small stores with a limited selection of high-quality merchandise. When Southwest Airlines was founded, managers identified the target customer as regular bus travelers, people who wanted to get from one place to another in a convenient, lost-cost way.[12] Volvo's new owners and managers are shifting the company's strategy toward a new target customer. Rather than aiming for people who appreciate the brand's reputation for safe, reliable family vehicles, Li Shufu, the company's new Chinese owner, is aiming to expand aggressively into the luxury car market. Volvo is particularly courting the emerging class of rich

EXHIBIT   8.1

The Elements of Competitive Advantage

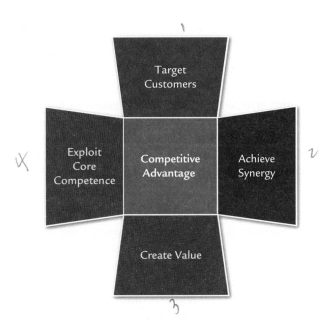

consumers in China and other overseas markets. Li wants Volvo to offer innovative, electrifying designs that turn heads and win new luxury-minded customers with flashy tastes. [13]

Exploit Core Competence

A company's **core competence** is something that the organization does especially well in comparison to its competitors. A core competence represents a competitive advantage because the company acquires expertise that competitors do not have. A core competence may be in the area of superior research and development, expert technological know-how, process efficiency, or exceptional customer service. [14] Managers at companies such as Family Dollar and Southwest Airlines, for example, focus on a core competence of operational efficiency that enables them to keep costs low. Gaylord Hotels, which has large hotel and conference centers in several states as well as the Opryland complex near Nashville, Tennessee, thrives based on a strategy of superior service for large group meetings. [15] Robinson Helicopter succeeds through superior technological know-how for building small, two-seater helicopters used for everything from police patrols in Los Angeles to herding cattle in Australia. [16] In each case, leaders identified what their company does especially well and built strategy around it.

Build Synergy

When organizational parts interact to produce a joint effect that is greater than the sum of the parts acting alone, **synergy** occurs. The organization may attain a special advantage with respect to cost, market power, technology, or management skill. When properly managed, synergy can create additional value with existing resources, providing a big boost to the bottom line. [17] Synergy was the motivation for Kraft to buy Cadbury, for instance, and for Oracle to buy Sun Microsystems. Kraft can use Cadbury's established distribution network in emerging markets to share trucks and store contacts and sell more Kraft products. Oracle's purchase of Sun gives the software company a giant hardware business, enabling Oracle to provide corporations with most of the technology they need in a single package. [18]

▶▶▶ **Concept Connection**

When the U.S. Marines needed rugged motorcycles, they looked to manufacturers of on- and off-road bikes. But most motorcycles run on gasoline, which is the wrong fuel for military purposes. Hayes Diversified Technologies had the competitive advantage. After 20 years of building adapted motorcycles for the Marines and the Army Special Forces, Hayes had developed a **core competence** in technology that addresses the fuel limitations faced by the military. Most military machines run on JB8 fuel, a formulation of diesel and kerosene. Hayes Diversified's HDT M1030M1 motorcycle is designed for diesel service, so Hayes readily won the contract.

Courtesy of Hayes Diversified Technologies

3

PLANNING

Synergy can also be obtained by good relationships between organizations. For example, Coinstar, the company behind Redbox movie rentals, uses partnerships to attain synergy. As rentals of physical videos decline, the Redbox division has partnered with Verizon Communications on a service that combines DVD rental and streaming video, benefiting both companies. In another partnership, Coinstar has joined with Starbucks to provide self-serve coffee vending machines that grind the beans and provide a cup of fresh coffee that is miles away from the vending machine coffee of the past. Just as there are now thousands of Redbox kiosks in Walmarts, drugstores, and other locations, the company plans to put coffee kiosks "where the consumer goes every day."[19]

Deliver Value

Delivering value to the customer is at the heart of strategy. *Value* can be defined as the combination of benefits received and costs paid. Managers help their companies create value by devising strategies that exploit core competencies and attain synergy. Starbucks introduced the Starbucks Card, which works like a typical retail gift card except that users get benefits like points for free coffee.[20] Cable companies such as Time Warner Cable and Comcast offer *value packages* that provide a combination of basic cable, digital premium channels, video-on-demand, high-speed Internet, and digital phone service for a reduced cost. Some movie theaters are trying to provide greater value by offering "dinner and a movie." In-theater dining provides a more time-efficient way for people to spend a night out, and costs are reasonable compared to eating in a restaurant before or after the film.[21]

Amazon.com is thriving with a strategy based on targeting customers, exploiting core competencies, building synergy, and providing value.

Innovative Way

Amazon

It's hard to believe Amazon was once a struggling online bookseller. Today, it is "an existential threat" to every retailer, as Fiona Dias, executive vice president of GSI Commerce, put it. Amazon targets customers who want to find good deals and purchase products conveniently over the Internet. Those customers can find just about anything they want on Amazon.com. They will often pay less for it than they would anywhere else. And if they belong to Amazon Prime, they get free two-day shipping.

Amazon wants to provide "premium products at nonpremium prices." To do that, it has developed an extensive network of third-party merchants—partners with whom it maintains close, mutually beneficial relationships, is constantly honing its operational efficiency, and has created one of the most finely tuned distribution systems around. As if all that wasn't enough, along came Prime. For $79 a year, customers get free two-day shipping, as well as free streaming video and other perks. Prime allows Amazon to capitalize on its core competencies of wide selection, cost efficiency, and slick distribution. When asked how they decided on the $79 price tag, a member of the Prime team said it "was never about the $79. It was really about changing people's mentality so they wouldn't shop anywhere else."

Prime was conceived as a way to further cement the loyalty of Amazon's best customers, and it has been more successful than even CEO Jeff Bezos imagined. Amazon Prime, said one recent business article "turns casual shoppers . . . into Amazon addicts." It provides value to customers, but it also increases sales for Amazon. According to some estimates, customers increase their purchases on the site by about 150 percent after joining Prime. It is credited for helping Amazon's sales zoom 30 percent during the recent recession while other retailers struggled to attract customers.[22]

LEVELS OF STRATEGY

Another aspect of strategic management concerns the organizational level to which strategic issues apply. Strategic managers normally think in terms of three levels of strategy, as illustrated in Exhibit 8.2.[23]

EXHIBIT   8.2   Three Levels of Strategy in Organizations

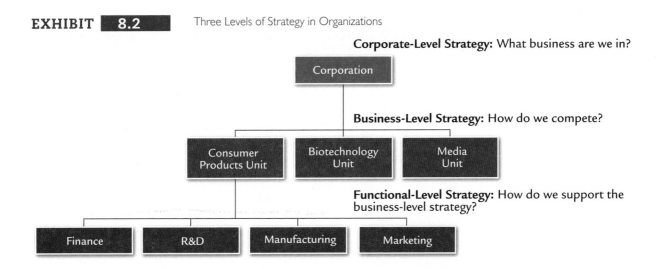

Corporate-Level Strategy: What business are we in?

Corporation

Business-Level Strategy: How do we compete?

Consumer Products Unit   Biotechnology Unit   Media Unit

Functional-Level Strategy: How do we support the business-level strategy?

Finance   R&D   Manufacturing   Marketing

- *What business are we in?* Managers ask this question when they consider corporate-level strategy. **Corporate-level strategy** pertains to the organization as a whole and the combination of business units and product lines that make up the corporate entity. Strategic actions at this level usually relate to the acquisition of new businesses; additions or divestments of business units, plants, or product lines; and joint ventures with other corporations in new areas. An example of corporate-level strategy is Garmin. Founded by Gary Burrell and Min Kao, Garmin is the company that first became known for stand-alone GPS products. Garmin has evolved into an international corporation that has a consumer products division, a division making dashboard-embedded GPS for the automotive market, a division that makes guidance and avionics systems for airplanes and marine vessels, a division that provides mobile weather solutions, and a division that focuses on personal monitoring technology such as foot pods and heart rate monitors for sports and fitness products. The company's growth has been fueled by acquisitions, including the purchase of UPS Aviation Technologies, Inc. (now Garmin AT) and Dynastream Innovations (personal monitoring products).[24]

- *How do we compete?* **Business-level strategy** pertains to each business unit or product line. Strategic decisions at this level concern amount of advertising, direction and extent of research and development, product changes, new-product development, equipment and facilities, and expansion or contraction of product and service lines. At Garmin, sales of GPS devices to consumers have been hurt because so many people use their smartphones to get directions or maps, so Garmin's consumer products division decided to create a phone of its own. The company partnered with computer maker Asus to develop a Garmin-branded smartphone with built-in GPS. In addition, Garmin's consumer division created its own app for the iPhone that lets users do everything from check for traffic jams to look up their destinations on Wikipedia.[25]

- *How do we support the business-level strategy?* **Functional-level strategy** pertains to the major functional departments within the business unit. Functional strategies involve all of the major functions, including finance, research and development, marketing, and manufacturing. One element of functional-level strategy for Gap's marketing department is to use mobile technology to offer targeted deals to customers. Gap created a mobile app that uses GPS technology, so that when a customer opens the app near a Gap store, it provides special sales offers exclusive to that location.[26]

Take a Moment

Go to the Ethical Dilemma for Chapter 8 on pages 298–299 that pertains to business-and functional-level strategy.

Remember This

- **Strategic management** refers to the set of decisions and actions used to formulate and implement strategies that will provide a competitively superior fit between the organization and its environment so as to achieve organizational goals.
- A **strategy** is the plan of action that describes resource allocation and activities for dealing with the environment, achieving a competitive advantage, and attaining goals.
- **Competitive advantage** refers to what sets the organization apart from others and provides it with a distinctive edge in the marketplace.
- Four elements of competitive advantage are the company's target customer, core competencies, synergy, and value.
- A **core competence** is something that the organization does particularly well in comparison to others.
- Amazon.com has core competencies of operational efficiency and a superb distribution system.

- **Synergy** exists when the organization's parts interact to produce a joint effect that is greater than the sum of the parts acting alone.
- Oracle bought Sun Microsystems to gain synergy by being able to provide customers with most of the technology that they need in a single package.
- The heart of strategy is to deliver value to customers.
- **Corporate-level strategy** pertains to the organization as a whole and the combination of business units and products that make it up.
- **Business-level strategy** pertains to each business unit or product line within the organization.
- **Functional-level strategy** pertains to the major functional departments within each business unit, such as manufacturing, marketing, and research and development.

The Strategic Management Process

The overall strategic management process is illustrated in Exhibit 8.3. It begins when executives evaluate their current position with respect to mission, goals, and strategies. They then scan the organization's internal and external environments and identify strategic issues that might require change. Managers at BP didn't have to look far to see a need for change after a giant drilling rig exploded and sank in April 2010, killing 11 crew members and spilling massive amounts of oil into the Gulf of Mexico. BP's strategy had been based on being a leader in pushing the frontiers of the oil industry, such as drilling

EXHIBIT 8.3   The Strategic Management Process

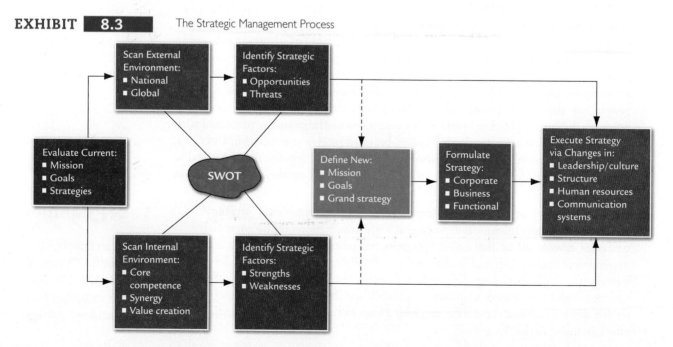

Manager's Shoptalk

Will Strategy Ever Be the Same?

"Strategy, as we knew it, is dead," said Walt Shill, head of management consulting in North America for Accenture Ltd. It might be an overstatement, but during the economic turmoil of the past few years many managers have discovered they need new approaches to strategy.

- **Managers build flexibility into strategic plans.** Management scholar and strategic thinker Gary Hamel uses the term *strategic decay* to describe the fact that the value of even the most brilliant strategy declines over time. Static long-range strategic plans can be a liability in a topsy-turvy world. What was a strength yesterday might be the beginnings of a weakness today. To overcome the natural tendency to depend on what has worked in the past, managers at organizations such as McKinsey & Company build a culture of inquiry, healthy debate, and constructive conflict.

- **Strategy is built actively and interactively.** Managers don't sit at their desks and dream up strategy. They get out and talk to employees, customers, suppliers, and other stakeholders. In the early days of Hewlett-Packard, for example, Dave Packard and Bill Hewlett were seldom at their desks. They were out talking to people and gaining a solid, realistic grounding for the creation of effective strategy.

- **Strategic partnerships are key components of strategy.** Collaboration with other organizations is an important part of how successful companies enter new areas of business. To find new ways to make money as e-books, which provide less revenue per unit than traditional hardcover books, become more popular, Random House is striking deals with videogame publishers to write original stories for games and offer advice to developers on their own storylines.

- **Strategy comes to life with creative execution.** Creative execution is the implementation of a strategy that is so well conceived, compelling, and embraced by everyone throughout the organization that it practically guarantees a successful outcome. For example, Google's strategy of focusing on search rather than content—on organizing existing information and making it accessible and useful—was so clear and compelling that employees rallied behind it. Managers use visionary leadership, open and honest communication, and bold action to drive strategy. Ignoring the seemingly impossible nature of the task, Google managers have inspired people with a strategic goal to digitize every book in the world's libraries.

Sources: Gary Hamel, "Outrunning Change—The CliffsNotes Version," Gary Hamel's Management 2.0, *WSJ Blogs*, October 21, 2009, http://blogs.wsj.com/management/2009/10/21/outrunning-change-the-cliffsnotes-version/ (accessed July 31, 2012); Eric Beaudan, "Creative Execution," *Ivey Business Journal* (March–April 2010), www.iveybusinessjournal.com/article.asp?intArticle_ID=891 (accessed March 26, 2010); Jeffrey A. Trachtenberg, "Random House Harnesses Skills to Venture into Videogame Action," *The Wall Street Journal*, March 1, 2010; and Don Tapscott, "Rethinking Strategy in a Networked World," *Strategy & Business* 24 (Third Quarter 2001): 34–41.

the world's deepest wells, scouting for oil in the Arctic, and other aggressive efforts. The strategy succeeded; BP steadily increased production and overtook Royal Dutch Shell PLC in market capitalization in January 2010.[27] A few months later, though, disaster struck, presenting a crisis that required a new approach to strategy for the oil giant. BP managers evaluated whether the company's strategy fit the environment and its own capabilities and shifted strategic goals to focus on safety and consistency.

For all organizations, internal or external events sometimes indicate a need to redefine the mission or goals or to formulate a new strategy at either the corporate, business, or functional level. Factors that alter a company's ability to achieve its goals are called *strategic issues*, as described in Chapter 3. In turbulent environments and fast-changing industries, managers have to stay alert to strategic issues that require a shift in strategy to stay in line with both internal and external changes.[28] The final stage in the strategic management process outlined in Exhibit 8.3 is execution of the new strategy. This chapter's Shoptalk discusses some recent trends in strategy formulation and execution.

Concept Connection ◄◄◄

State University of New York (SUNY) chancellor Nancy L. Zimpher toured all 64 SUNY campuses—including Herkimer County Community College, shown here—as she began overseeing the process of **formulating a new strategy** for the system. The effort was precipitated by the $450 million in state funding cuts SUNY experienced over a two-year period as New York tried to cope with a daunting budget deficit resulting from the recession. A key part of the new strategy involves finding ways to translate theoretical knowledge into tangible economic benefits, a point Zimpher hopes will convince legislators that any further budget cuts would only hurt the state's economy.

STRATEGY FORMULATION VERSUS EXECUTION

Strategy formulation includes the planning and decision making that lead to the establishment of the firm's goals and the development of a specific strategic plan.[29] **Strategy formulation** includes assessing the external environment and internal problems to identify strategic issues, then integrating the results into goals and strategy. This process is in contrast to **strategy execution**, which is the use of managerial and organizational tools to direct resources toward accomplishing strategic results.[30] Strategy execution is the administration and implementation of the strategic plan. Managers may use persuasion, new equipment, changes in organization structure, or a revised reward system to ensure that employees and resources are used to make a formulated strategy a reality.

SWOT ANALYSIS

Formulating strategy begins with understanding the circumstances, forces, events, and issues that shape the organization's competitive situation, which requires that managers conduct an audit of both internal and external factors that influence the company's ability to compete.[31] **SWOT analysis** includes a careful assessment of strengths, weaknesses, opportunities, and threats that affect organizational performance. Managers obtain external information about opportunities and threats from a variety of sources, including customers, government reports, professional journals, suppliers, bankers, friends in other organizations, consultants, or association meetings. Many firms contract with special scanning organizations to provide them with newspaper clippings, Internet research, and analyses of relevant domestic and global trends. Others hire competitive intelligence professionals to scope out competitors, as we discussed in Chapter 3, and use intelligence teams, as described in Chapter 7.

Executives acquire information about internal strengths and weaknesses from a variety of reports, including budgets, financial ratios, profit and loss statements, and surveys of employee attitudes and satisfaction. In addition, managers build an understanding of the company's internal strengths and weaknesses by talking with people at all levels of the hierarchy in frequent face-to-face discussions and meetings.

Internal Strengths and Weaknesses

Strengths are positive internal characteristics that the organization can exploit to achieve its strategic performance goals. *Weaknesses* are internal characteristics that might inhibit or restrict the organization's performance. Some examples of what managers evaluate to interpret strengths and weaknesses are shown in the audit checklist in Exhibit 8.4. Managers perform an internal audit of specific functions such as marketing, finance, production, and research and development. Internal analysis also assesses overall organization structure, management competence and quality, and human resource characteristics. Based on their understanding of these areas, managers can determine their strengths or weaknesses compared with other companies.

External Opportunities and Threats

Threats are characteristics of the external environment that may prevent the organization from achieving its strategic goals. One threat to Microsoft, for example, is the

Take a Moment

Go to the Small Group Breakout on page 260 that pertains to SWOT analysis. Before reading further, you might also want to review your strategic strengths as determined by your responses to the questionnaire at the beginning of this chapter.

AP Photo/Steve Jacobs

Management and Organization	Marketing	Human Resources
Management quality	Distribution channels	Employee experience,
Staff quality	Market share	education
Degree of centralization	Advertising efficiency	Union status
Organization charts	Customer satisfaction	Turnover, absenteeism
Planning, information,	Product quality	Work satisfaction
control systems	Service reputation	Grievances
	Sales force turnover	

Finance	Production	Research and Development
Profit margin	Location, resources	Basic applied research
Debt-equity ratio	Machinery obsolescence	Laboratory capabilities
Inventory ratio	Purchasing system	Research programs
Return on investment	Quality control	New-product innovations
Credit rating	Productivity/efficiency	Technology innovations

proliferation of cheap or free software available over the Internet.[32] *Opportunities* are characteristics of the external environment that have the potential to help the organization achieve or exceed its strategic goals. For example, U.S. auto manufacturers had an unprecedented opportunity to steal customers from Toyota because of the quality, safety, and public relations problems that Toyota recently experienced.[33] German retailer Aldi found an opportunity to expand in the United States because of heated opposition in urban areas to Walmart. Aldi has quietly been setting up small, drugstore-sized shops in cities around the United States, including New York City. "Wal-Mart has sort of become the bad guy that there's a concerted effort against," said Craig Johnson, president of consulting firm Customer Growth Partners. "There's no reason to oppose an Aldi." Because Aldi is a smaller format and has opened only a limited number of stores a year, it was able to slip in under the radar, obtaining space from small landlords while people were focused on fighting Walmart.[34]

Managers evaluate the external environment based on the ten sectors described in Chapter 3. The task environment sectors are the most relevant to strategic behavior and include the behavior of competitors, customers, suppliers, and the labor supply. The general environment contains those sectors that have an indirect influence on the organization but nevertheless must be understood and incorporated into strategic behavior. The general environment includes technological developments, the economy, legal-political and international events, the natural environment, and sociocultural changes. Additional areas that might reveal opportunities or threats include pressure groups, such as those opposing Walmart's expansion into urban areas, interest groups, creditors, and potentially competitive industries.

A good example of SWOT analysis comes from Dana Holding Corporation, a world leader in axles, driveshafts, transmissions, and other automotive products.

▶ ▶ ▶ **Concept Connection**

AFLO/Newscom

On March 11, 2011, the people of Japan experienced an astounding 9.0 magnitude earthquake and tsunami, which struck the east coast of the country's main island, Honshu. The devastating natural disaster took the lives of more than 15,000 people and destroyed well over 100 million homes and businesses. The recovery efforts took many months, and during that time, many Japanese businesses suffered under the **threat** of failure due to the lack of energy, resources, labor, and many other factors. And yet there were **opportunities** as well, especially in the reconstruction of the country's infrastructure and real estate development.

Innovative Way

Dana Holding Corporation

Dana Holding Corporation had its start in 1904, when a 29-year-old engineering student at Cornell designed the first practical universal joint to power an automobile and left school to start a business. Innovation and ingenuity still drive Dana's mission: "To anticipate and address customers' needs with innovative solutions." Dana Corporation is never standing still, and managers are continually evaluating the company's competitive situation and making strategic decisions based on looking at the company's strengths, weaknesses, opportunities, and threats.

Dana's *strengths* include technological know-how, an innovative culture, and a strong research and development department. The company has won global recognition as a technological innovator due to its cellular manufacturing methods, statistical process control techniques, and flexible production. It has a well-trained workforce and major manufacturing facilities in 26 countries. Diverse products enable Dana to serve customers across the light-duty, heavy-duty, and off-highway vehicle markets to improve sales and profits. A final strength comes from strong partnerships through alliances and joint ventures with other automotive component suppliers.

A primary *weakness* is that Dana is still dealing with fallout from a 2006 bankruptcy filing. The company emerged from bankruptcy in 2008, but customer and investor confidence has not fully recovered. In addition, operational costs remain high, contributing to lower profit margins.

The biggest *threats* to the company are a decline in demand for sport utility vehicles and pressures from auto manufacturing customers such as General Motors (GM), Chrysler, Ford, and Volkswagen for lower prices on components. *Opportunities* exist in the ongoing development of electric and hybrid systems, where Dana has strong expertise, and in growing consumer pressures for more environmentally friendly products.

What does SWOT analysis suggest for Dana Corporation? To reduce costs and improve profit margins, managers have been selling off noncore businesses and closing weak or underperforming facilities. They are investing heavily in the Power Technologies unit, which produces products that incorporate sealing and thermal management technologies that help reduce fuel and oil consumption, cut emissions, and improve vehicle durability. The investment seems to be paying off: Sales in the Power Technologies division exceeded $1 billion for the first time in 2011. The company is also working to expand its international business, with particular emphasis on emerging markets including Asia and South America, where demand for construction vehicle and industrial equipment products is growing.[35]

Remember This

- **Strategy formulation** is the stage of strategic management that includes the planning and decision making that lead to the establishment of the organization's goals and a specific strategic plan.

- Managers often start with a **SWOT analysis**, an audit or careful examination of *strengths, weaknesses, opportunities,* and *threats* that affect organizational performance.

- The proliferation of free software over the Internet is a *threat* to Microsoft. Opposition to the expansion of Walmart provided German retailer Aldi an *opportunity* to gain a foothold in urban areas.

- **Strategy execution** is the stage of strategic management that involves the use of managerial and organizational tools to direct resources toward achieving strategic outcomes.

Formulating Corporate-Level Strategy

Three approaches to understanding corporate-level strategy are portfolio strategy, the BCG matrix, and diversification.

PORTFOLIO STRATEGY

Individual investors often wish to diversify in an investment portfolio with some high-risk stocks, some low-risk stocks, some growth stocks, and perhaps a few income bonds. In much the same way, corporations like to have a balanced mix of business divisions called **strategic business units (SBUs)**. An SBU has a unique business mission, product line, competitors, and markets relative to other SBUs in the corporation.[36] Executives in charge of the entire corporation generally define an overall strategy and then bring together a portfolio of SBUs to carry it out. Managers don't like to become too dependent on one business. **Portfolio strategy** pertains to the mix of business units and product lines that fit together in a logical way to provide synergy and competitive advantage for the corporation. An interesting example of using portfolio strategy to attain synergy and competitive advantage comes from the health care industry.

Innovative Way

UnitedHealth Group

UnitedHealth Group used to be an insurance company. Today, it describes itself as a health care company with a mission of "helping people live healthier lives." That's because United-Health is now a portfolio of different companies—one subsidiary provides insurance, and others provide services such as information technology and data management for hospitals, drug delivery and clinical trial management, continuing medical education, and even physicians and other medical services. The company serves 75 million people worldwide and "touches nearly every aspect of health care," as stated on the UnitedHealth Web site.

UnitedHealth might be the largest insurer, but it isn't the only one that has begun buying doctor's groups or medical facilities to develop a portfolio of divisions. WellPoint, for example, bought CareMore, a group of 26 health care clinics in the Los Angeles area. Humana bought Concentra, a chain of urgent care centers. And Highmark, which runs BlueCross BlueShield plans in Pennsylvania and West Virginia, is trying to buy a Pittsburgh-based chain of six hospitals. The strategy is partly in response to increasing financial pressure on insurers brought about by the Patient Protection and Affordable Care Act in the United States, and pressure from customers tired of paying ever-higher insurance premiums. "It's just trying many different ways to see what appeals to the American public and what adds value," said Gail Wilensky, a United board member.[37]

It is too soon to tell if insurers' new portfolio strategy will provide value to customers or simply higher profits for insurers. Some consumer advocates are worried, while others believe the trend can be positive for patients as well as the organizations.

Green **Power**

Beyond the Dump

Houston-based **Waste Management Inc.** CEO David Steiner is leading a new "Think Green" strategy that is reaching consumers as well as employees. This new approach began with consultants hired to examine Waste Management's sustainability strengths and weaknesses and to assess future opportunities. What emerged was a strategy to move the company beyond trash pickup—beyond the dump. In alignment with the company's "Think Green" moniker, managers focus on extracting "value" from waste by allowing consumers to place all recyclables in one container, with the various items separated on site through forced air, magnets, and optical scanning. Waste Management also responded to the need for massive clean-up efforts created by frequent natural disasters. One popular new product is the Bagster Dumpster in a Bag, with the capacity to hold up to 3,300 pounds of debris and trash.

Source: Marc Gunther, "Waste Management's New Direction," *Fortune* (December 6, 2010): 103–108.

EXHIBIT 8.5

The BCG Matrix

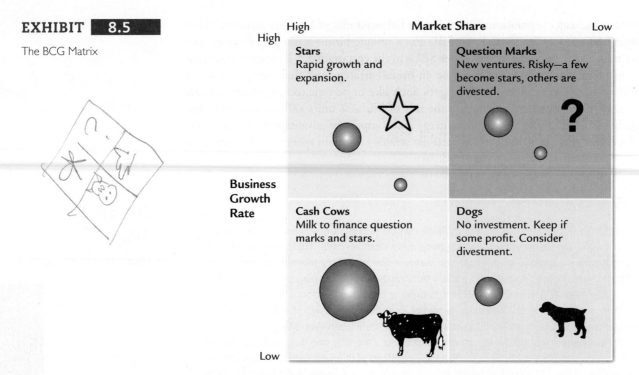

THE BCG MATRIX

One coherent way to think about portfolio strategy is the BCG matrix. The BCG matrix (named for the Boston Consulting Group, which developed it) is illustrated in Exhibit 8.5. The **BCG matrix** organizes businesses along two dimensions—business growth rate and market share.[38] *Business growth rate* pertains to how rapidly the entire industry is increasing. *Market share* defines whether a business unit has a larger or smaller share than competitors. The combinations of high and low market share and high and low business growth provide four categories for a corporate portfolio.

The *star* has a large market share in a rapidly growing industry. It is important because it has additional growth potential, and profits should be plowed into this business as investment for future growth and profits. The star is visible and attractive and will generate profits and a positive cash flow even as the industry matures and market growth slows.

The *cash cow* exists in a mature, slow-growth industry but is a dominant business in the industry, with a large market share. Because heavy investments in advertising and plant expansion are no longer required, the corporation earns a positive cash flow. It can milk the cash cow to invest in other, riskier businesses.

The *question mark* exists in a new, rapidly growing industry, but has only a small market share. The question mark business is risky: It could become a star, or it could fail. The corporation can invest the cash earned from cash cows in question marks with the goal of nurturing them into future stars.

The *dog* is a poor performer. It has only a small share of a slow-growth market. The dog provides little profit for the corporation and may be targeted for divestment or liquidation if turnaround is not possible.

The circles in Exhibit 8.5 represent the business portfolio for a hypothetical corporation. Circle size represents the relative size of each business in the company's portfolio. Most large organizations, such as General Electric (GE), have businesses in more than one quadrant, thereby representing different market shares and growth rates. The most famous cash cow in GE's portfolio, for example, is the appliance division. This business holds a large share of a stable market and accounts for a big portion of GE's sales and profits. The GE Healthcare and Aviation divisions have star status, and GE is pumping money into development of new products in these fast-growing areas, such as products for wind energy. GE's consumer finance division is a question mark. The division expanded too aggressively into areas such as real estate and took a big hit during the recent financial crisis. The media division has probably gained dog status because it doesn't fit well in the GE portfolio. A dog for GE might be a star for someone else, so GE executives recently sold a majority stake in NBC Universal to Comcast.[39]

DIVERSIFICATION STRATEGY

The strategy of moving into new lines of business, as UnitedHealth Group did by purchasing medical groups, or as search leader Google did by purchasing YouTube, is called **diversification**. Other examples of diversification include Apple's entry into the mobile phone business with the iPhone, Amazon.com's move into consumer electronics with the Kindle electronic reader, and Nestlé's entry into the pet food business with the purchase of Ralston.

The purpose of diversification is to expand the firm's business operations to produce new kinds of valuable products and services. When the new business is related to the company's existing business activities, the organization is implementing a strategy of **related diversification**. For example, UnitedHealth's move into medical services and Nestlé's move into pet foods are linked to these firms' existing health care and nutrition businesses. **Unrelated diversification** occurs when an organization expands into a totally new line of business, such as GE's entry into media or food company Sara Lee's move into the intimate apparel business. With unrelated diversification, the company's lines of business aren't logically associated with one another; therefore, it can be difficult to make the strategy successful. Most companies are giving up on unrelated diversification strategies, selling off unrelated businesses to focus on core areas.

A firm's managers may also pursue diversification opportunities to create value through a strategy of vertical integration. **Vertical integration** means that the company expands into businesses that either produce the supplies needed to make products and services or that distribute and sell those products and services to customers. In recent years, there has been a noticeable shift toward vertical integration, with large corporations getting into businesses that will give them more control over materials, manufacturing, and distribution.[40] To gain more control over raw materials, for instance, steelmaker Nucor acquired a major scrap-metal processor, and rival Arcelor bought mines in Brazil, Russia, and the United States. An example of diversifying to distribute products comes from PepsiCo, which began repurchasing bottling companies that it spun off in the late 1990s. PepsiCo controls marketing, manufacturing, and distribution in 80 percent of North America and is expected to buy the remaining independent bottlers over the next few years. Service companies can pursue vertical integration too. Ticketmaster, for example, merged with Live Nation Entertainment, which produces and promotes concerts.[41]

Remember This

- Frameworks for corporate-level strategy include portfolio strategy, the BCG matrix, and diversification strategy.
- **Portfolio strategy** pertains to the mix of SBUs and product lines that fit together in a logical way to provide synergy and competitive advantage.
- A **strategic business unit (SBU)** is a division of the organization that has a unique business, mission, product or service line, competitors, and markets relative to other units of the same organization.
- The **BCG matrix** is a concept developed by the Boston Consulting Group that evaluates SBUs with respect to two dimensions—business growth rate and market share—and classifies them as cash cows, stars, question marks, or dogs.

- The strategy of moving into new lines of business is called **diversification**.
- Apple diversified when it moved into the mobile phone business, and Nestlé diversified by purchasing the Ralston pet food business.
- **Related diversification** means moving into a new business that is related to the corporation's existing business activities.
- **Unrelated diversification** refers to expanding into totally new lines of business.
- Some managers pursue diversification through a strategy of **vertical integration**, which means expanding into businesses that either provide the supplies needed to make products or distribute and sell the company's products.

Formulating Business-Level Strategy

Now we turn to strategy formulation within the strategic business unit, in which the concern is how to compete. A popular and effective model for formulating strategy is Porter's competitive strategies. Michael E. Porter studied a number of business organizations and proposed that business-level strategies are the result of understanding competitive forces in the company's environment.[42]

THE COMPETITIVE ENVIRONMENT

The competitive environment is different for different kinds of businesses. Most large companies have separate business lines and do an industry analysis for each line of business or SBU. Mars, Inc., for example, operates in six business segments: chocolate (Snickers); pet care (Pedigree); gum and confections (Juicy Fruit); food (Uncle Ben's); drinks (Flavia); and symbioscience (veterinary care, plant care). The competitive environment for the chocolate division would be different from that for the symbioscience division, so managers would do a competitive analysis for each business segment, looking at factors such as competitors, customers, suppliers, the threat of substitute products or services, potential new markets, and so forth.

PORTER'S COMPETITIVE STRATEGIES

To find a competitive edge within the specific business environment, Porter suggests that a company can adopt one of three strategies: differentiation, cost leadership, or focus. The organizational characteristics typically associated with each strategy are summarized in Exhibit 8.6.

EXHIBIT 8.6

Organizational Characteristics of Porter's Competitive Strategies

Broad / Narrow — Strategic Target; Distinctiveness / Low Costs — Source of Advantage

Differentiation
- Acts in a flexible, loosely knit way; strong coordination among departments
- Strong capability in basic research
- Creative flair, thinks "out of the box"
- Strong marketing abilities
- Rewards employee innovation
- Corporate reputation for quality or technological leadership

Cost Leadership
- Strong central authority; tight cost controls
- Maintains standard operating procedures
- Easy-to-use manufacturing technologies
- Highly efficient procurement and distribution systems
- Close supervision; finite employee empowerment

Focused Differentiation
- Uses characteristics of differentiation strategy directed at particular target customer
- Values flexibility and customer intimacy
- Pushes empowerment to employees with customer contact

Focused Cost Leadership
- Uses characteristics of cost leadership strategy directed at particular target customer
- Frequent detailed control reports
- Measures cost of providing product or service and maintaining customer loyalty

SOURCES: Based on Michael E. Porter, *Competitive Strategy: Techniques for Analyzing Industries and Competitors* (New York: The Free Press, 1980); Michael Treacy and Fred Wiersema, "How Market Leaders Keep Their Edge," *Fortune* (February 6, 1995): 88–98; and Michael A. Hitt, R. Duane Ireland, and Robert E. Hoskisson, *Strategic Management* (St. Paul, MN: West, 1995), pp. 100–113.

- **Differentiation.** The **differentiation strategy** involves an attempt to distinguish the firm's products or services from others in the industry. The organization may use creative advertising, distinctive product features, exceptional service, or new technology to achieve a product perceived as unique. Examples of products that have benefited from a differentiation strategy include Harley-Davidson motorcycles, Apple computers and phones, and Gore-Tex fabrics, all of which are perceived as distinctive in their markets. Apple computers, the iPhone, and the iPad, for example, can command significantly higher prices because of their distinctiveness. Apple has never tried to compete on price and likes being perceived as an "elite" brand. Service companies such as Starbucks, Whole Foods Market, and IKEA also use a differentiation strategy.

  A differentiation strategy can reduce rivalry with competitors and fight off the threat of substitute products because customers are loyal to the company's brand. However, a differentiation strategy requires a number of costly activities, such as product research and design and extensive advertising. Companies need a robust marketing department and creative employees who are given the time and resources to seek innovation.

- **Cost leadership.** With a **cost leadership strategy**, the organization aggressively seeks efficient facilities, pursues cost reductions, and uses tight cost controls to produce products more efficiently than competitors. Although cost leadership doesn't always mean low prices, most cost leadership companies keep internal costs low so that they can provide products and services to customers at lower prices and still make a profit. A cost leadership position means that the company can undercut competitors' prices and still offer comparable quality and earn a reasonable profit. For example, Spirit Airlines, which has taken cut-rate fares to new extremes, is one of the most profitable companies in the airline industry, earning 40 percent more per plane than any other U.S. airline.[43]

  The cost leadership strategy is concerned with maintaining stability rather than pursuing innovation and growth. However, cost leadership can certainly lead to growth, as evidenced by Walmart, which became the world's largest retailer with a cost leadership strategy. Acer Inc. has grown to the world's second-largest computer maker with a cost leadership strategy. Acer has a bare-bones cost structure. Its overhead expenses are about 8 percent of sales, compared to around 14 to 15 percent for rival companies. Cost savings are passed on to consumers, with a high-quality ultrathin laptop selling for around $650, compared to $1,800 for a similar Hewlett-Packard (HP) model and $2,000 for Dell's ultrathin version. Acer has now moved into the smartphone market. With its cost leadership position, Acer can give consumers quality smartphones at lower prices and still see profit margins in the range of 15 percent to 20 percent.[44]

- **Focus.** With a **focus strategy**, the organization concentrates on a specific regional market or buyer group. The company will use either a differentiation or cost leadership approach, but only for a narrow target market. An example of a focused cost leadership strategy is Family Dollar. Family Dollar stores can offer prices on major brands such as Tide or Colgate that are 20 to 40 percent lower than those found in major supermarkets. The company locates its stores on inexpensive, unglamorous real estate such as strip malls and markets to people

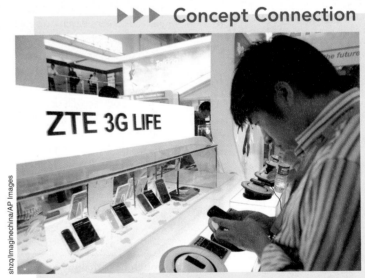

▶▶▶ **Concept Connection**

shzq/Imaginechina/AP Images

While Americans and Europeans enjoy snapping up the latest—and more expensive—smartphones that feature all kinds of bells and whistles, many cell phone users around the world look for simple, reliable cell phones at affordable prices. And China's ZTE is there to meet their needs. ZTE has employed a **cost leadership strategy**, using efficient production to keep prices low for many of its models. The approach has made the company one of the biggest mobile phone producers in the world.

3

PLANNING

making around $35,000 a year rather than trying to court a more upscale clientele.[45] Proamérica Bank succeeds with a focused differentiation strategy. Mexican-born Maria Contreras-Sweet founded the bank to concentrate on serving largely family-owned businesses in Los Angeles's Hispanic community. She believes the Latino-owned bank can differentiate itself from its larger commercial competitors, such as Bank of America, by establishing close personal relationships with customers.[46]

Managers should think carefully about which strategy will provide their company with a competitive advantage. Gibson Guitar Corporation, famous in the music world for its innovative, high-quality products, found that switching to a cost leadership strategy to compete against Japanese rivals such as Yamaha and Ibanez actually hurt the company. When managers realized that people wanted Gibson products because of their reputation, not their price, they went back to a differentiation strategy and invested in new technology and marketing.[47]

In his studies, Porter found that some businesses did not consciously adopt one of these three strategies and were stuck with no strategic advantage. Without a strategic advantage, businesses earned below-average profits compared with those that used differentiation, cost leadership, or focus strategies. Similarly, a five-year study of management practices in hundreds of businesses, referred to as the "Evergreen Project," found that a clear strategic direction was a key factor that distinguished winners from losers.[48] JCPenney is currently floundering through a transition because customers are confused by a strategy that seems to combine cost leadership and differentiation.

Innovative Way

JCPenney

Ron Johnson, the current CEO of JCPenney, is a former Apple executive who was largely responsible for creating Apple's innovative retail store concept. With that kind of success, can he transform the struggling JCPenney stores? Maybe, maybe not. Penney's has been under pressure for years, and at the time of his appointment, Johnson was hailed as just the right executive to get the retailer back on track at long last.

Johnson introduced a new strategy that did away with the company's hundreds of annual sales events (there were nearly 600 of them in 2011) in favor of an "everyday fair and square" price model. Prices were cut about 40 percent across the board. The strategy also included a new logo and a makeover of stores into distinctive vendor-branded and themed "boutiques." Regular customers haven't responded favorably, though. The retailer's sales have plummeted since the "fair and square" pricing model was introduced. Johnson says customers were initially confused by the change, and he believes the new model will pay off as they realize that store prices are low every day and they don't have to wait for sales.

The problem, though, say some analysts, is that JCPenney isn't Apple. The company doesn't have the brand recognition, distinctiveness, and customer loyalty that Apple enjoys. Apple's status-symbol products keep customer coming to the stores no matter what. JCPenney, on the other hand, needed those regular sales to bring people in—and to get them to buy once they were there. Everyday low pricing takes away the fun of searching for deals and getting a bargain. "A discount gives shoppers the incentive to buy today," said Kit Yarrow, consumer psychologist and author of *Gen BuY: How Tweens, Teens, and Twenty-Somethings Are Revolutionizing Retail*. "Without that, there's no sense of urgency for people to purchase things that, frankly, they probably don't need." Johnson might agree. He recently reintroduced the word *sale* into the company's lexicon.[49]

Although he is making adjustments, Johnson is sticking with his basic strategy to revolutionize JCPenney with across-the-board low prices, a boutique approach, and eventually, a checkout-free concept that uses WiFi and mobile technology to let customers pay without having to go through a checkout counter. Getting rid of cashiers, cash registers, and checkout stands could save millions of dollars that can be put toward lowering prices and providing superior customer service, Johnson says.[50] Will it work? Time will tell. Old-time customers might be alienated, but a new generation of customers might find it just the right approach.

Formulating Functional-Level Strategy

Functional-level strategies are the action plans used by major departments to support the execution of business-level strategy. Major organizational functions include marketing, production, finance, human resources, and research and development. Managers in these and other departments adopt strategies that are coordinated with business-level strategy to achieve the organization's strategic goals.

For example, consider a company that has adopted a differentiation strategy and is introducing new products that are expected to experience rapid growth. The human resources department should adopt a strategy appropriate for growth, which would mean recruiting additional personnel and training middle- and lower-level managers for new positions. The marketing department should undertake test marketing, aggressive advertising campaigns, and consumer product trials. The finance department should adopt plans to borrow money, handle large cash investments, and authorize construction of new facilities.

A company with mature products or a cost leadership strategy will have different functional-level strategies. The human resources department should develop strategies for retaining and developing a stable workforce. Marketing should stress brand loyalty and the development of established, reliable distribution channels. Production should use a strategy of long production runs, standard procedures, and cost reduction. Finance should focus on net cash flows and positive cash balances.

Remember This

- A popular model for formulating business-level strategy is Porter's competitive strategies.
- Managers analyze the competitive environment and adopt one of three types of strategy: differentiation, cost leadership, or focus.
- A **differentiation strategy** is a strategy with which managers seek to distinguish the organization's products and services from those of others in the industry.
- A **cost leadership strategy** is a strategy with which managers aggressively seek efficient facilities, cut costs, and use tight cost controls to be more efficient than others in the industry.

- With a **focus strategy**, managers use either a differentiation or a cost leadership approach, but they concentrate on a specific regional market or buyer group.
- Managers at Family Dollar stores use a focus strategy by concentrating on selling to people who make less than $35,000 a year.
- Once business-level strategies are formulated, managers in functional departments devise functional-level strategies to support them.

Global Strategy

Many organizations operate globally and pursue a distinct strategy as the focus of global business. Senior executives try to formulate coherent strategies to provide synergy among worldwide operations for the purpose of fulfilling common goals.

One consideration for managers is the strategic dilemma between the need for global standardization and national responsiveness. The various global strategies are shown in Exhibit 8.7. The first step toward a greater international presence is when companies begin exporting domestically produced products to selected countries. The *export strategy* is shown in the lower-left corner of the exhibit. Because the organization is domestically focused, with only a few exports, managers have little need to pay attention to issues of either local responsiveness or global standardization. Organizations that pursue further

EXHIBIT 8.7

Global Corporate Strategies

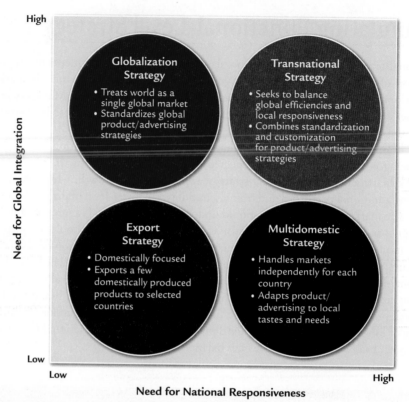

SOURCES: Based on Michael A. Hitt, R. Duane Ireland, and Robert E. Hoskisson, *Strategic Management: Competitiveness and Globalization* (St. Paul, MN; West, 1995), p. 239; and Thomas M. Begley and David P. Boyd, "The Need for a Corporate Global Mindset," *MIT Sloan Management Review* (Winter 2003): 25–32.

international expansion must decide whether they want each global affiliate to act autonomously or if activities should be standardized and centralized across countries. This choice leads managers to select a basic strategy alternative, such as globalization versus multidomestic strategy. Some corporations may seek to achieve a degree of both global standardization and national responsiveness by using a transnational strategy.

GLOBALIZATION STRATEGY

When an organization chooses a **globalization strategy**, it means that product design and advertising strategies are standardized throughout the world.[51] This approach is based on the assumption that a single global market exists for many consumer and industrial products. The theory is that people everywhere want to buy the same products and live the same way. The idea is that people everywhere want to eat McDonald's hamburgers and use iPhones.[52] A globalization strategy can help an organization reap efficiencies by standardizing product design and manufacturing, using common suppliers, introducing products around the world faster, coordinating prices, and eliminating overlapping facilities. For example, Gillette has large production facilities that use common suppliers and processes to manufacture razors and other products whose technical specifications are standardized around the world.[53]

Globalization enables marketing departments alone to save millions of dollars. One consumer products company reports that, for every country where the same commercial runs, the company saves $1 million to $2 million in production costs. More millions have been saved by standardizing the look and packaging of brands.[54] Domino's Pizza is using a globalization strategy as it expands into emerging markets such as India, China, Russia, and Brazil. Although local franchisees can modify ingredients to suit local tastes, Domino's managers say the strategy in emerging markets is "to go in there with a tried-and-true business model of delivery and carryout pizza that we deploy around the world." Domino's facilities, packaging, and marketing materials look essentially the same in Russia, India, or the United States.[55]

Multidomestic Strategy

When an organization chooses a **multidomestic strategy**, it means that competition in each country is handled independently of industry competition in other countries. Thus, a multinational company is present in many countries, but it encourages marketing, advertising, and product design to be modified and adapted to the specific needs of each country.[56] Many companies reject the idea of a single global market. They have found that the French do not drink orange juice for breakfast, that laundry detergent is used to wash dishes in parts of Mexico, and that people in the Middle East prefer toothpaste that tastes spicy. Kraft Foods Inc. has introduced new products, reformulated recipes, and redesigned packaging to suit local tastes in various countries. In China, for instance, Kraft cookie flavors include green tea, ice cream, and mango and mandarin orange; and Ritz crackers are offered in flavors such as "fantastic beef stew" and "very spicy chicken" and sold in portable cuplike packages that resemble ramen-noodle containers.[57] Service companies also have to consider their global strategy carefully. The 7-Eleven convenience store chain uses a multidomestic strategy because the product mix, advertising approach, and payment methods need to be tailored to the preferences, values, and government regulations in different parts of the world. For example, in Japan, customers like to use convenience stores to pay utility and other bills. 7-Eleven Japan responded by offering that as a service, as well as setting up a way for people to pick up and pay for purchases made over the Internet at their local 7-Eleven store.[58]

Transnational Strategy

A **transnational strategy** seeks to achieve both global standardization and national responsiveness.[59] A true transnational strategy is difficult to achieve, though, because one goal requires close global coordination while the other requires local flexibility. However, many industries are finding that, although increased competition means that they must achieve global efficiency, growing pressure to meet local needs demands national responsiveness.[60] One company that effectively achieves both aspects of a transnational strategy is Coca-Cola. The giant soft drink company can attain efficiencies by manufacturing, advertising, and distributing well-known brands such as Coke, Fanta, and Sprite on a global basis. However, CEO Muhtar Kent has pushed the company to expand beyond well-known brands and embrace local tastes. The company sells more than 400 different drinks globally. In Russia, for instance, Coca-Cola's version of the traditional *kvas* is the fastest-growing soft drink.[61]

Although most multinational companies want to achieve some degree of global standardization to hold costs down, even global

▶▶▶ **Concept Connection**

Since first going international in 1971, Dallas-based Mary Kay Inc. has expanded to more than 30 markets on five continents. The company uses a **multidomestic strategy** that handles competition independently in each country. In China, for example, Mary Kay has developed products that appeal to the unique tastes and preferences of Chinese women. Under the direction of Mary Kay China president Paul Mak (center), the company is building a $25 million distribution center in Hangzhou, the first such location outside the United States. Within the next several years, China is poised to become Mary Kay's biggest market, surpassing all others, including its home market.

3

PLANNING

products may require some customization to meet government regulations in various countries or some tailoring to fit consumer preferences. In addition, increased competition means many organizations need to take advantage of global opportunities as well as respond to the heterogeneity of the international marketplace.

Remember This

- When formulating a strategy as the focus for global operations, managers face a dilemma between the need for global standardization and the need for local responsiveness.
- With a **globalization strategy**, product design and advertising are standardized throughout the world.
- A **multidomestic strategy** means that competition in each country is handled independently; product design and advertising are modified to suit the specific needs of individual countries.

- Kraft has reformulated cookie and cracker recipes and redesigned packaging to suit tastes in China.
- A **transnational strategy** is a strategy that combines global coordination to attain efficiency with local flexibility to meet needs in different countries.
- Most large companies use a combination of global strategies to achieve global standardization and efficiency, as well as respond to local needs and preferences in various countries.

Strategy Execution

The final step in the strategic management process is strategy execution—how strategy is implemented or put into action. Many companies have file drawers full of winning strategies, but they still struggle to succeed. Why? Practicing managers remind us that "strategy is easy, but execution is hard."[62] Indeed, many strategy experts agree that execution is the most important, yet the most difficult, part of strategic management.[63]

No matter how brilliant the formulated strategy, the organization will not benefit if it is not skillfully executed. One key to effective strategy execution is *alignment*, so that all aspects of the organization are in congruence with the strategy and every department and individual's efforts are coordinated toward accomplishing strategic goals. Alignment basically means that everyone is moving in the same direction. Grand goals have to be translated into a clear blueprint for execution, so that everyone's actions are in line with managers' strategic intentions.[64] Recall our discussion of strategy maps from the previous chapter. Just as managers make sure goals are in alignment, they check that all aspects of the organization are coordinated to be supportive of the strategies designed to achieve those goals.

Exhibit 8.8 illustrates the primary tools that managers use to implement strategy effectively: visible leadership, clear roles and accountability, candid communication, and appropriate human resource practices.[65]

> "If you want to build a ship, don't drum up the men to gather wood, divide the work, and give orders. Instead, teach them to yearn for the vast and endless sea."
>
> — ANTOINE DE SAINT-EXUPÉRY (1900–1944), *CITADELLE (THE WISDOM OF THE SANDS)*

- *Visible leadership.* The primary key to successful strategy execution is good leadership. *Leadership* is the ability to influence people to adopt the new behaviors needed for putting the strategy into action. Leaders actively use persuasion, motivation techniques, and cultural values that support the new strategy. They might make speeches to employees, build coalitions of people who support the new strategic direction, and persuade middle managers to go along with their vision for the company. Most important, they lead by example.[66] Pixar, the animation studio, has a rule about leadership that supports its strategy of producing highly creative animated films: no studio executives.

EXHIBIT 8.8 Tools for Putting Strategy into Action

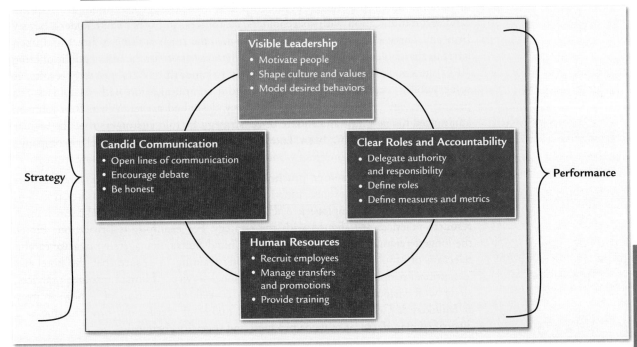

SOURCES: Based on Jay R. Galbraith and Robert K. Kazanjian. *Strategy Implementation: Structure, Systems, and Process,* 2d ed. (Cincinnati, OH: South-Western, Cengage Learning, 1986); Lawrence G. Hrebiniak, *Making Strategy Work: Leading Effective Execution and Change* (Upper Saddle River, NJ: Wharton School Publishing/Pearson Education Inc., 2005); and Eric Beaudan, "Creative Execution," *Ivey Business Journal* (March–April 2010), www.iveybusinessjournal.com/article.asp?intArticle_ID=891 (accessed March 26, 2010).

Pixar's leaders are the creative artists, an approach that maintains a "film school without the teachers" culture that gives people maximum freedom to develop and pursue unique, innovative ideas. At Pixar, everyone from janitors to auditors is encouraged to submit ideas for new films.[67]

- **Clear roles and accountability.** People need to understand how their individual actions can contribute to achieving the strategy. Trying to execute a strategy that conflicts with structural design, particularly in relation to managers' roles, authority, and accountability, is a top obstacle to putting strategy into action.[68] To execute strategy effectively, top executives clearly define roles and delegate authority to individuals and teams who are accountable for results. A lack of clear roles and accountability is partly to blame for the debacle at JPMorgan Chase, which announced a multibillion-dollar loss in May 2012. Why did implementation of the company's careful, low-risk trading strategy falter? Ina Drew, the senior banker who has been blamed for the problems, had won the complete trust of CEO Jamie Dimon after she steered the company through the 2008 financial crisis. However, Drew was out of the office a great deal of time due to illness beginning in 2010, and long-simmering conflicts and divisions over roles and responsibilities emerged. Drew's deputy in New York, Althea Duersten, disagreed with the risky, outsized bets being made by Achilles Macris, the deputy in London, but the London deputy used his stronger personality to shout down Duersten's objections and gain more power. "It felt like there was a land grab where no one was pushing back because Althea and Achilles both wanted more responsibility," a former trader said. Another trader underscored the lack of clear roles when he said he "didn't know who to listen to."[69]

- **Candid communication.** Managers openly and avidly promote their strategic ideas, but they also listen to others and encourage disagreement and debate. They create a culture

PLANNING 3

based on openness and honesty, which encourages teamwork and collaboration across hierarchical and departmental boundaries. Effective strategy execution also requires candid communication with shareholders, customers, and other stakeholders. Sergey Brin and Larry Page, the founders of Google, take turns writing a direct and open letter to shareholders each year. The original letter written for the initial public offering (IPO) makes clear that Google wouldn't try to "smooth out" its quarterly results, as some publicly traded companies do.[70] Candid communication with customers was part of strategy implementation at JCPenney, described earlier. When Ron Johnson announced his new "fair and square price" strategy, he told customers that the regular prices in stores have long been "fake and inflated." Johnson felt that the company's rejection of marketing gimmicks would win trust and support for the new strategy.[71]

- *Appropriate human resource practices.* The organization's *human resources* are its employees. The human resource function recruits, selects, trains, compensates, transfers, promotes, and lays off employees to achieve strategic goals. Managers make sure human resource practices are aligned with the strategy. For example, at Broadmoor Hotel, the longest-reigning five-star resort in the United States, managers emphasize careful selection of employees and extensive ongoing training to ensure that the hotel has "exceptional people" who will provide exceptional service.[72] Human resource practices, along with visionary leadership, were also crucial to execution of a new strategy at Milliken & Company, once a traditional maker of textiles but now thriving as a diversified manufacturer of niche products and specialty chemicals.

Innovative Way
Milliken & Company

"All of Milliken's traditional textile competitors are gone," says John Fly, a top executive at Milliken & Company in Spartanburg, South Carolina. "They're out of business. And Milliken is having the best economic performance it's ever had. It's clear we did something different."

What Milliken did differently was adopt a strategy of innovation and diversification. Traditional textile manufacturing began leaving the United States long ago to take advantage of lower labor costs overseas. Milliken's managers knew they had to change—and they had to change fast. Visible and visionary leadership was crucial to implementing a new strategy. Roger Milliken, who died at the age of 95 in 2010, was constantly "pounding the drum" for new ideas, new products, and new techniques. Ever wonder who makes the fabric that reinforces duct tape? How about the additives that make children's markers washable or that make combat gear protective? Those products, and hundreds of others that touch our lives every day, are made by Milliken. Milliken still makes textiles, but it isn't a textile company. "We're an innovation company," says CEO Joe Salley.

Getting the right people on board was essential to executing the strategy. Around 350 of Milliken's managers and supervisors have advanced degrees, a third of them Ph.Ds. Hiring scientists and researchers from top schools is a priority. The company is able to get them because when they come to Milliken, they know they'll have the opportunity to work seriously in the sciences. The Milliken Hall of Fame posts employee names alongside their patents (thousands of them). Researchers can use 15 percent of their time to work on anything they like, and proven innovators get a whopping 50 percent of their time to work on projects of their own choosing.[73]

Remember This

- Even the most creative strategies have no value if they cannot be translated into action.
- Execution is the most important, but also the most difficult, part of strategy.
- One key to effective execution is making sure that all parts of the organization are in alignment to support the strategy.
- Managers use visible leadership, clear roles and accountability, candid communication, and appropriate human resource practices to execute strategy effectively.
- Milliken & Company hires top scientists and researchers to implement its strategy of innovation and diversification.

ch8: Discussion Questions

1. Based on your knowledge of the following companies, how effective would you say any one of the following acquisitions were in terms of creating synergy:
   a) The purchase of MySpace by News Corporation (owner of Fox Broadcasting)?
   b) Google's purchase of YouTube?
   c) PepsiCo's purchase of Frito-Lay?
   d) Luby's purchase of Fuddruckers?
   e) InBev's acquisition of Budweiser?

2. How might a corporate management team go about determining whether the company should diversify? What factors should they consider? What kinds of information should they collect?

3. You are a middle manager helping to implement a new corporate cost-cutting strategy, and you're meeting skepticism, resistance, and in some cases, outright hostility from your subordinates. In what ways might you or the company have been able to avoid this situation? Where do you go from here?

4. Perform a SWOT analysis for the school or university you attend. Do you think university administrators consider the same factors when devising their strategy?

5. *Fortune* magazine and the Hay Group found that a clear, stable strategy is one of the defining characteristics of companies on the list of "The World's Most Admired Companies." Why might this be the case?

6. Using Porter's competitive strategies, how would you describe the strategies of Walmart, Macy's, and Target?

7. Walt Disney Company has four major strategic business units: movies (including Miramax and Touchstone), theme parks, consumer products, and television (the ABC TV network and the Disney Channel cable network). Place each of these SBUs on the BCG matrix based on your knowledge of them.

8. As an administrator for a medium-sized hospital, you and the board of directors have decided to change to a drug dependency hospital from a short-term, acute-care facility. How would you go about executing this strategy?

9. Game maker Electronic Arts (EA) was criticized as "trying to buy innovation" in its bid to acquire Take-Two Interactive, known primarily for the game "Grand Theft Auto." Does it make sense for EA to offer more than $2 billion to buy Take-Two when creating a new video game costs only $20 million? Why would EA ignore internal innovation to choose an acquisition strategy?

10. If you are the CEO of a global company, how might you determine whether a globalization, multidomestic, or transnational strategy would work best for your enterprise? What factors would influence your decision?

ch8: Apply Your Skills: Experiential Exercise

Strategic Thinking Blueprints[74]

Strategic thinking involves a mental blueprint that includes a desired future, ways to achieve that future, and specific actions needed to arrive at that future. The strategic thinking blueprint can apply to a company, a department, or an individual. Strategic thinking can be developed through work experiences in addition to formal study. Please mark Mostly True or Mostly False based on whether you have experienced each of the following work situations.

	Mostly True	Mostly False
1. Participated in organizational strategic planning	_____	_____
2. Started a major organizational project or initiative	_____	_____
3. Been responsible for periodically monitoring performance indicators	_____	_____
4. Been challenged by a colleague on my thinking or plan	_____	_____
5. Learned from colleagues about practices outside my organization	_____	_____
6. Been mentored on strategic thinking or planning	_____	_____
7. Handled a substantial threat to organizational (or work unit) survival	_____	_____
8. Served as a general manager (such as CEO) of an organization	_____	_____
9. Attended industry conferences	_____	_____
10. Read professional journals	_____	_____

Scoring and Interpretation

The first eight items above are listed in descending order of frequency of work experiences that contributed to the strategic thinking ability of 207 managers. (Item 1 was experienced most often, item 8 least often.) Items 8, 7, and 2 had the most impact on strategic thinking when experienced, and the other items were important, but somewhat less so. Items 9 and 10 were educational experiences that were considered valuable, but a little less important than the work experiences. If you checked Mostly True for four or more items above, you have a good start on strategic thinking. If you scored 8 or more, you should be a true strategic thinker. You can involve yourself in additional strategic work experiences to develop your mind's ability to develop and implement strategic blueprints.

Why do you think items 8, 7, and 2 have the most impact on developing strategic thinking? Why do you think direct experiences with strategic planning were more important than the educational experiences in items 9 and 10? Discuss your answers with other students as directed by your instructor.

ch8: Apply Your Skills: Small Group Breakout

SWOT Analysis[75]

Step 1. In a group of three to five students, select a local eating establishment for a SWOT analysis. This could be a restaurant, an ice cream store, or a bakery with which your group is familiar.

Step 2. Write a statement of what you perceive to be the business's current strategy.

Step 3. What do you perceive to be the key strengths and weaknesses of this business from a customer's perspective? Make one list for strengths and another list for weaknesses.

Step 4. What do you perceive to be potential opportunities and threats for this business? Make one list for opportunities and another for threats.

Step 5. If the store manager or owner is available, interview the person for his or her perception of strategy strengths, weaknesses, opportunities, and threats. Add new items to your lists.

Step 6. Use your SWOT analysis findings to set a goal of where this business could be in two years in terms of growth, size, new offerings, or expanded customer base. What steps do you recommend to achieve this goal?

Step 7. How did your SWOT analysis help you determine the goal and how to accomplish it during the next two years? What did you learn from this exercise?

ch8: Endnotes

1. This questionnaire is adapted from Dorothy Marcic and Joe Seltzer, *Organizational Behavior: Experiences and Cases* (Cincinnati, OH: SouthWestern, 1998), pp. 284–287, and William Miller, *Innovation Styles* (Global Creativity Corporation, 1997).

2. Miguel Bustillo, "Best Buy to Shrink 'Big Box' Store Strategy," *The Wall Street Journal Online*, April 15, 2011, http://online.wsj.com/article/SB1000142405274870 39831045762627730062546648.html (accessed July 23, 2012); and Miguel Bustillo and Joan E. Solsman, "Amid Loss, Best Buy Rethinks Stores," *The Wall Street Journal Europe*, March 30, 2012, 20.

3. Bruce Horovitz, "New Pizza Recipe Did Wonders for Domino's Sales," *USA Today*, May 5, 2010, B1; Julie Jargon, "How McDonald's Hit the Spot," *The Wall Street Journal*, December 13, 2011; Paul Lilley, "Weight Watchers Reveals New Partner: McDonald's," *Virginian-Pilot*, March 4, 2010; David E. Bell and Mary Shelman, "KFC's Radical Approach to China," *Harvard Business Review* (November 2011): 137–142.

4. John Bussey, "The Business: The Anti-Kodak: How a U.S. Firm Innovates," *The Wall Street Journal*, January 13, 2012, B1; Rachel Dodes, "Targeting Younger Buyers, Liz Claiborne Hits a Snag," *The Wall Street Journal*, August 16, 2010, A1.

5. Chet Miller and Laura B. Cardinal, "Strategic Planning and Firm Performance: A Synthesis of More than Two

Decades of Research," *Academy of Management Journal* 37, no. 6 (1994): 1649–1665.

6. Renée Dye and Olivier Sibony, "How to Improve Strategic Planning," *McKinsey Quarterly*, no. 3 (2007).

7. Keith H. Hammonds, "Michael Porter's Big Ideas," *Fast Company* (March 2001): 150–156.

8. John E. Prescott, "Environments as Moderators of the Relationship Between Strategy and Performance," *Academy of Management Journal* 29 (1986): 329–346; John A. Pearce II and Richard B. Robinson, Jr., *Strategic Management: Strategy, Formulation, and Implementation*, 2d ed. (Homewood, IL: Irwin, 1985); and David J. Teece, "Economic Analysis and Strategic Management," *California Management Review* 26 (Spring 1984): 87–110.

9. Jack Welch, "It's All in the Sauce," excerpt from his book, *Winning*, published in *Fortune* (April 18, 2005): 138–144; and Constantinos Markides, "Strategic Innovation," *Sloan Management Review* (Spring 1997): 9–23.

10. Michael E. Porter, "What Is Strategy?" *Harvard Business Review* (November–December 1996): 61–78.

11. This discussion is based on Ken Favaro with Kasturi Rangan and Evan Hirsh, "Strategy: An Executive's Definition," *Strategy + Business* (March 5, 2012), www.strategy-business.com/article/cs00002?gko=d59c2 (accessed July 24, 2012).

12. Example from Favaro et al., "Strategy: An Executive's Definition."

13. Norihiko Shirouzu, "Chinese Begin Volvo Overhaul," *The Wall Street Journal*, June 7, 2011, B1.

14. Arthur A. Thompson, Jr., and A. J. Strickland III, *Strategic Management: Concepts and Cases*, 6th ed. (Homewood, IL: Irwin, 1992); and Briance Mascarenhas, Alok Baveja, and Mamnoon Jamil, "Dynamics of Core Competencies in Leading Multinational Companies," *California Management Review* 40, no. 4 (Summer 1998): 117–132.

15. "Gaylord Says Hotels Prosper by Becoming Destinations," *The Tennessean*, July 24, 2005.

16. Chris Woodyard, "Big Dreams for Small Choppers Paid Off," *USA Today*, September 11, 2005.

17. Michael Goold and Andrew Campbell, "Desperately Seeking Synergy," *Harvard Business Review* (September–October 1998): 131–143.

18. Anjali Cordeiro "Boss Talk: Tang in India and Other Kraft Synergies," *The Wall Street Journal Online*, April 19, 2010, http://online.wsj.com/article/SB1000142405 27023033485045751841031063 88686.html (accessed October 8, 2012); and Ashlee Vance, "Oracle Elbows Its Way into a Crowded Fight; With Close of Sun Deal, It Hopes to Beat Out Rivals Offering One-Stop Shops," *International Herald Tribune*, January 28, 2010.

19. Nick Wingfield, "Thinking Outside the Redbox," *The New York Times*, February 18, 2012, B1.

20. John Jannarone, "Starbucks Sees New Growth on the Card," *The Wall Street Journal*, January 17, 2012, C10.

21. Lauren A. E. Schuker, "Double Feature: Dinner and a Movie—To Upgrade from Dirty Carpets and Tubs of Popcorn, Theater Chains Try Full Menus, Seat-Side Service," *The Wall Street Journal*, January 5, 2011, D1.

22. Brad Stone, "What's in the Box? Instant Gratification," *Bloomberg Businessweek* (November 29–December 5, 2010): 39–40; and S. Levy, "CEO of the Internet: Jeff Bezos Owns the Web in More Ways than You Think," *Wired* (December 2011), www.wired.com/magazine/2011/11/ff_bezos/ (accessed July 24, 2012).

23. Milton Leontiades, *Strategies for Diversification and Change* (Boston: Little, Brown, 1980), p. 63; and Dan E. Schendel and Charles W. Hofer, eds., *Strategic Management: A New View of Business Policy and Planning* (Boston: Little, Brown, 1979), pp. 11–14.

24. Erik Rhey, "A GPS Maker Shifts Gears," *Fortune* (March 19, 2012): 62; "Garmin International, Inc. Announces Completion of the Acquisition of UPS Aviation Technologies, Inc.," *PR Newswire*, August 22, 2003, www.prnewswire.com/news-releases/garmin-international-inc-announces-completion-of-the-acquisition-of-ups-aviation-technologies-inc-70979722.html (accessed July 25, 2012); and "Garmin Ltd. Acquires Dynastream Innovations, Inc." Garmin Press Release, December 1, 2006, Garmin Web site, www8.garmin.com/pressroom/corporate/120106.html (accessed July 25, 2012).

25. Rhey, "A GPS Maker Shifts Gears."

26. Example reported in Armen Ovanessoff and Mark Purdy, "Global Competition 2021: Key Capabilities for Emerging Opportunities," *Strategy & Leadership* 39, no. 5 (2011): 46–55.

27. Guy Chazan, "BP's Worsening Spill Crisis Undermines CEO's Reforms," *The Wall Street Journal*, May 3, 2010.

28. Bruce E. Perrott, "Strategic Issue Management as Change Catalyst," *Strategy & Leadership* 39, no. 5 (2011): 20–29.

29. Milton Leontiades, "The Confusing Words of Business Policy," *Academy of Management Review* 7 (1982): 45–48.

30. Lawrence G. Hrebiniak and William F. Joyce, *Implementing Strategy* (New York: Macmillan, 1984).

31. Christopher B. Bingham, Kathleen M. Eisenhardt, and Nathan R. Furr, "Which Strategy When?" *MIT Sloan Management Review* (Fall 2011): 71–78.

32. Peter Burrows, "Microsoft Defends Its Empire," *BusinessWeek* (July 6, 2009): 28–33.

33. David Welch, Keith Naughton, and Burt Helm, "Detroit's Big Chance," *Bloomberg BusinessWeek* (February 22, 2010): 38–44.

34. Stephanie Clifford, "Where Wal-Mart Failed, Aldi Succeeds," *The New York Times* (March 29, 2011), www.nytimes.com/2011/03/30/business/30aldi.html?pagewanted=all (accessed July 26, 2012).

35. "Company Overview and Quick Facts," Dana Holding Corporation Web site, www.dana.com/wps/wcm/connect/dext/Dana/Company/ (accessed July 26, 2012); "Dana History," www.dana.com/wps/wcm/connect/dext/Dana/Company/History/ (accessed July 26, 2012); "Dana: 2009 Company Profile Edition 1: SWOT Analysis," *Just-Auto* (February 2009): 14–16; "Dana: 2009 Company Profile Edition 2: Chapter 6 SWOT Analysis," *Just-Auto* (June 2009): 16–18; and Dana Holding Corporation 2012 Fact Sheet, www.dana.com/wps/wcm/connect/0642380 041f3cfb59a80be1c9e250a89/dext-2012DanaFact.pdf?MOD=AJPERES (accessed July 26, 2012).

36. Frederick W. Gluck, "A Fresh Look at Strategic Management," *Journal of Business Strategy* 6 (Fall 1985): 4–19.

37. Christopher Weaver, "Managed Care Enters the Exam Room as Insurers Buy Doctors Groups," *The Washington Post*, July 1, 2011, www.washingtonpost.com/insurers-quietly-gaining-control-of-doctors-covered-by-companies-plans/2011/06/29/AG5DNftH_story.html (accessed July 27, 2012); Anna Wilde Matthews, "Corporate News: UnitedHealth Buys California Group of 2,300 Doctors," *The Wall Street Journal*, September 1, 2011, B3; "About Us," UnitedHealth Group Web site, www.unitedhealthgroup.com/main/aboutus.aspx (accessed July 27, 2012).

38. Thompson and Strickland, *Strategic Management*; and William L. Shanklin and John K. Ryans, Jr., "Is the International Cash Cow Really a Prize Heifer?" *Business Horizons* 24 (1981): 10–16.

3

PLANNING

39. William E. Rothschild, "GE and Its Naysayers," *Chief Executive* (November–December 2009): 46–50; Paul Glader, "Corporate News: GE's Immelt to Cite Lessons Learned," *The Wall Street Journal*, December 15, 2009; Shital Vakhariya and Menaka Rao, "Innovate for Growth: Immelt's Strategy for GE," *Journal of Operations Management* 8, no. 3–4 (August–November 2009): 86–92; and General Electric Web site, www.ge.com/products_services/index.html (accessed August 10, 2010).

40. This discussion and the following examples are from Ben Worthen, Cari Tuna, and Justin Scheck, "Companies More Prone to Go Vertical," *The Wall Street Journal*, November 30, 2009; and Jacqueline Doherty, "At Pepsi, the Glass Is Half Full," *Barron's* (November 30, 2009): 24–25.

41. The service company example is from Thomas Catan and Brent Kendall, "The New Antitrust Era," *The Wall Street Journal*, December 21, 2011, B1.

42. Michael E. Porter, "The Five Competitive Forces That Shape Strategy," *Harvard Business Review* (January 2008): 79–93; Michael E. Porter, *Competitive Strategy* (New York: Free Press, 1980), pp. 36–46; Danny Miller, "Relating Porter's Business Strategies to Environment and Structure: Analysis and Performance Implementations," *Academy of Management Journal* 31 (1988): 280–308; and Michael E. Porter, "From Competitive Advantage to Corporate Strategy," *Harvard Business Review* (May–June 1987): 43–59.

43. Jack Nicas, "A Stingy Spirit Lifts Airline's Profit," *The Wall Street Journal*, May 12, 2012, A1.

44. Bruce Einhorn, "Acer's Game-Changing PC Offensive," *BusinessWeek* (April 20, 2009): 65; Charmian Kok and Ting-I Tsai, "Acer Makes China Push from Taiwan; PC Maker's Chief Expects Best Gains in New Markets, Including Brazil, as Aims to Surpass H-P," *The Wall Street Journal*, April 1, 2010; and "Experience Will Propel Acer to Top of Smartphone Market by 2013," *Gulf News*, January 22, 2010.

45. Suzanne Kapner, "The Mighty Dollar," *Fortune* (April 27, 2009): 65–66.

46. "Building Wealth," Proamérica Bank Web site, https://www.proamericabank.com/en/index.asp (accessed July 31, 2012).

47. Joshua Rosenbaum, "Guitar Maker Looks for a New Key," *The Wall Street Journal*, February 11, 1998.

48. Nitin Nohria, William Joyce, and Bruce Roberson, "What Really Works," *Harvard Business Review* (July 2003): 43–52.

49. "Issue of the Week: J.C. Penney's No-Sales Misfire," *The Week* (July 6–13, 2012), 36; Brad Tuttle, "The Price Is Righter," *Time* (February 13, 2012), www.time.com/time/magazine/article/0,9171,2105961,00.html#ixzz2275GLNTv (accessed July 30, 2012); Dana Mattioli, "Penney's to Make Deeper Price Cuts," *The Wall Street Journal*, July 26, 2012, B1.

50. Brad Tuttle, "A Store Without a Checkout Counter? JCPenney Presses on with Retail Revolution," *Time* (July 20, 2012), http://moneyland.time.com/2012/07/20/a-store-without-a-checkout-counter-jcpenney-presses-on-with-retail-revolution/ (accessed July 30, 2012).

51. Kenichi Ohmae, "Managing in a Borderless World," *Harvard Business Review* (May–June 1990): 152–161.

52. Theodore Levitt, "The Globalization of Markets," *Harvard Business Review* (May–June 1983): 92–102.

53. Cesare Mainardi, Martin Salva, and Muir Sanderson, "Label of Origin: Made on Earth," *strategy + business*, Issue 15, Second Quarter, 1999, www.strategy-business.com/article/16620 (accessed August 10, 2010).

54. Joanne Lipman, "Marketers Turn Sour on Global Sales Pitch Harvard Guru Makes," *The Wall Street Journal*, May 12, 1988.

55. Annie Gasparro, "Domino's Sticks to Its Ways Abroad," *The Wall Street Journal*, April 17, 2012, B10.

56. Michael E. Porter, "Changing Patterns of International Competition," *California Management Review* 28 (Winter 1986): 40.

57. Laurie Burkitt, "Kraft Craves More of China's Snacks Market," *The Wall Street Journal*, May 30, 2012, B6.

58. Mohanbir Sawhney and Sumant Mandal, "What Kind of Global Organization Should You Build?" *Business 2.0* (May 2000): 213.

59. Based on Michael A. Hitt, R. Duane Ireland, and Robert E. Hoskisson, *Strategic Management: Competitiveness and Globalization* (St. Paul, MN: West, 1995), p. 238.

60. Anil K. Gupta and Vijay Govindarajan, "Converting Global Presence into Global Competitive Advantage," *Academy of Management Executive* 15, no. 2 (2001): 45–56.

61. Betsy McKay, "Coke Bets on Russia for Sales Even as Economy Falls Flat," *The Wall Street Journal*, January 28, 2009.

62. Quote from Gary Getz, Chris Jones, and Pierre Loewe, "Migration Management: An Approach for Improving Strategy Implementation," *Strategy & Leadership* 37, no. 6 (2009): 18–24.

63. Lawrence G. Hrebiniak, "Obstacles to Effective Strategy Implementation," *Organizational Dynamics* 35, no. 1 (2006): 12–31; Eric M. Olson, Stanley F. Slater, and G. Tomas M. Hult, "The Importance of Structure and Process to Strategy Implementation," *Business Horizons* 48 (2005): 47–54; L. J. Bourgeois III and David R. Brodwin, "Strategic Implementation: Five Approaches to an Elusive Phenomenon," *Strategic Management Journal* 5 (1984): 241–264; Anil K. Gupta and V. Govindarajan, "Business Unit Strategy, Managerial Characteristics, and Business Unit Effectiveness at Strategy Implementation," *Academy of Management Journal* (1984): 25–41; and Jeffrey G. Covin, Dennis P. Slevin, and Randall L. Schultz, "Implementing Strategic Missions: Effective Strategic, Structural, and Tactical

Choices," *Journal of Management Studies* 31, no. 4 (1994): 481–505.

64. Riaz Khadem, "Alignment and Follow-Up: Steps to Strategy Execution," *Journal of Business Strategy* 29, no. 6 (2008): 29–35; Stephen Bungay, "How to Make the Most of Your Company's Strategy," *Harvard Business Review* (January–February 2011): 132–140; and Olson, Slater, and Hult, "The Importance of Structure and Process to Strategy Implementation."

65. This discussion is based on Eric Beaudan, "Creative Execution," *Ivey Business Journal*, March–April 2010, www.iveybusinessjournal.com/article.asp?intArticle_ ID=891 (accessed March 26, 2010); Jay R. Galbraith and Robert K. Kazanjian, *Strategy Implementation: Structure, Systems and Process*, 2d ed. (St. Paul, MN: West, 1986); Victoria L. Crittenden and William F. Crittenden, "Building a Capable Organization: The Eight Levers of Strategy Implementation," *Business Horizons* 51 (2008): 301–309; Paul C. Nutt, "Selecting Tactics to Implement Strategic Plans," *Strategic Management Journal* 10 (1989): 145–161; and Lawrence G. Hrebiniak, *Making Strategy Work: Leading Effective Execution and Change* (Upper Saddle River, NJ: Wharton School Publishing/Pearson Education Inc., 2005).

66. Crittenden and Crittenden, "Building a Capable Organization."

67. This example is from Bingham, Eisenhardt, and Furr, "Which Strategy When?"

68. Based on survey results reported in Hrebiniak, "Obstacles to Effective Strategy Implementation."

69. Jessica Silver-Greenberg and Nelson D. Schwartz, "Discord at Key JPMorgan Unit Is Blamed in Bank's Huge Loss," *The New York Times*, May 20, 2012, A1.

70. Beaudan, "Creative Execution."

71. Tuttle, "The Price Is Righter."

72. Example reported in Stanley F. Slater, Eric M. Olson, and G. Tomas M. Hult, "Worried About Strategy Implementation? Don't Overlook Marketing's Role," *Business Horizons* 53 (2010): 469–479.

73. John Bussey, "The Anti-Kodak: How a U.S. Firm Innovates," *The Wall Street Journal*, January 13, 2012, B1.

74. Based on Ellen Goldman, Terrence Cahill, and Rubens Pessanha Filho, "Experiences That Develop the Ability to Think Strategically," *Journal of Healthcare Management* 54, no. 6 (November–December 2009): 403–417; and Noel B. Zabriskie and Alan B. Huellmantel, "Developing Strategic Thinking in Senior Management," *Long Range Planning*, 24 no. 6 (1991): 25–32.

75. Adapted from Richard L. Daft and Dorothy Marcic, *Understanding Management* (Mason, OH: South-Western, 2008), pp. 177–178.

3

PLANNING

Decision Making

Dennis Flaherty/Jupiter Images

Chapter Outline

Learning Outcomes

After studying this chapter, you should be able to:

1. Explain why decision making is an important component of good management.

2. Discuss the difference between programmed and nonprogrammed decisions and the decision characteristics of certainty and uncertainty.

3. Describe the ideal, rational model of decision making and the political model of decision making.

4. Explain the process by which managers actually make decisions in the real world.

5. Identify the six steps used in managerial decision making.

6. Describe four personal decision styles used by managers, and explain the biases that frequently cause managers to make bad decisions.

7. Identify and explain innovative techniques for decision making, including brainstorming, evidence-based management, and after-action reviews.

How Do You Make Decisions?

INSTRUCTIONS: Most of us make decisions automatically, without realizing that people have diverse decision-making behaviors, which they bring to management positions.[1] Think back to how you make decisions in your personal, student, or work life, especially where other people are involved. Please answer whether each of the following items is Mostly True or Mostly False for you.

	Mostly True	Mostly False
1. I like to decide quickly and move on to the next thing.	_____	_____
2. I would use my authority to make a decision if certain I am right.	_____	_____
3. I appreciate decisiveness.	_____	_____
4. There is usually one correct solution to a problem.	_____	_____
5. I identify everyone who needs to be involved in the decision.	_____	_____
6. I explicitly seek conflicting perspectives.	_____	_____
7. I use discussion strategies to reach a solution.	_____	_____
8. I look for different meanings when faced with a great deal of data.	_____	_____
9. I take time to reason things through and use systematic logic.	_____	_____

SCORING AND INTERPRETATION: All nine items in the list reflect appropriate decision-making behavior, but items 1–4 are more typical of new managers. Items 5–8 are typical of successful senior manager decision making. Item 9 is considered part of good decision making at all levels. If you checked Mostly True for three or four of items 1–4 and 9, consider yourself typical of a new manager. If you checked Mostly True for three or four of items 5–8 and 9, you are using behavior consistent with top managers. If you checked a similar number of both sets of items, your behavior is probably flexible and balanced.

New managers typically use a different decision behavior than seasoned executives. The decision behavior of a successful CEO may be almost the opposite of a first-level supervisor. The difference is due partly to the types of decisions and partly to learning what works at each level. New managers often start out with a more directive, decisive, command-oriented behavior to establish their standing and decisiveness and gradually move toward more openness, diversity of viewpoints, and interactions with others as they move up the hierarchy.

Solar energy is a great idea. U.S. President Barack Obama agrees, and when visiting the Solyndra plant in 2010, he proudly proclaimed that "companies like Solyndra are leading the way toward a brighter and more prosperous future." The solar panel manufacturing start-up had received a $535 million federal stimulus loan guarantee to help the United States gain dominance in solar technology while generating thousands of jobs. The problem, however, was that Solyndra's managers had made decisions based on faulty assumptions, and the company was losing money fast, with no likelihood of turning things around. Barely a year after Obama's visit, Solyndra declared bankruptcy, laid off more than 1,000 employees, and was raided by the Federal Bureau of Investigation (FBI) seeking evidence of possible fraud. Meanwhile, the Obama administration's flawed decision to back Solyndra could cost taxpayers a half billion dollars.[2]

Welcome to the world of managerial decision making. Managers often are referred to as *decision makers*, and every organization grows, prospers, or fails as a result of decisions made by its managers. Yet decision making, particularly in relation to complex problems,

1 INTRODUCTION
2 ENVIRONMENT
3 PLANNING
4 ORGANIZING
5 LEADING
6 CONTROLLING

is not always easy. Solyndra's executives based many of their decisions on the assumption that the price of silicon, a primary component in solar panels made by competitors, would remain high. Solyndra's innovative panels didn't use silicon, but the higher manufacturing costs meant the company had to charge a premium to make a profit. When the price of silicon dropped, competitors had a whopping advantage. As for the U.S. government's decision to invest in Solyndra, there are charges that administration officials failed to evaluate the risks properly and heed the troubling signs that the company was financially unstable.[3] Managers can sometimes make the wrong decision, even when their intentions are right. Managers frequently must make decisions amid ever-changing factors, unclear information, and conflicting points of view.

The business world is full of evidence of both good and bad decisions. YouTube was once referred to as "Google's Folly," but decisions made by the video platform's managers have more than justified the $1.65 billion that Google paid for it and turned YouTube into a highly admired company that is redefining the entertainment industry.[4] On the other hand, Microsoft's decision to purchase ad giant aQuantive for $6.3 billion hasn't turned out so well. Microsoft managers believed that aQuantive, at the time a thriving 2,600-employee company with rapidly growing sales and profits, would help the software giant be more competitive against Google and establish it as a leader in online advertising. But poor decision making regarding how to integrate aQuantive into the larger software company contributed to a disaster that required Microsoft to take a $6.2 billion writedown. Today, aQuantive is a shell of its former self. "From the initial decision to put aQuantive under the absolutely wrong Microsoft leadership—who had no knowledge or interest or skills in it . . . this acquisition had snafu written on it from day one," said a former aQuantive employee.[5]

Good decision making is a vital part of good management because decisions determine how the organization solves problems, allocates resources, and accomplishes its goals. This chapter describes decision making in detail. First, we examine decision characteristics. Then we look at decision-making models and the steps executives should take when making important decisions. The chapter also explores some biases that can cause managers to make bad decisions. Finally, we examine some specific techniques for innovative decision making in today's fast-changing environment.

Types of Decisions and Problems

A **decision** is a choice made from available alternatives. For example, an accounting manager's selection among Colin, Tasha, and Carlos for the position of junior auditor is a decision. Many people assume that making a choice is the major part of decision making, but it is only a part of it.

Decision making is the process of identifying problems and opportunities and then resolving them. Decision making involves effort both before and after the actual choice. Thus, the decision of whether to select Colin, Tasha, or Carlos requires the accounting manager to ascertain whether a new junior auditor is needed, determine the availability of potential job candidates, interview candidates to acquire necessary information, select one candidate, and follow up with the socialization of the new employee into the organization to ensure the decision's success.

Take a Moment

Go to the Ethical Dilemma for Chapter 9 on pages 300–301 that pertains to making nonprogrammed decisions.

PROGRAMMED AND NONPROGRAMMED DECISIONS

Management decisions typically fall into one of two categories: programmed and nonprogrammed. **Programmed decisions** involve situations that have occurred often enough to enable decision rules to be developed and applied in the future.[6] Programmed decisions are made in response to recurring organizational problems. The decision to reorder paper and other office supplies when inventories drop to a certain

Green Power

Revitalizing Small Farms

PepsiCo executives discovered for themselves that sustainability decisions can be observed and measured in the lives of individuals. Management's decision to launch a pilot project cutting the middleman from the supply chain for Sabritas, its Mexican line of snacks, by initiating direct purchase of corn from 300 small farmers in Mexico brought unimagined benefits.

The decision resulted in visible, measureable outcomes, including lower transportation costs and a stronger relationship with small farmers, who were able to develop pride and a businesslike approach to farming. The arrangement with PepsiCo gave farmers a financial edge in securing much-needed credit for purchasing equipment, fertilizer, and other necessities, resulting in higher crop yields. New levels of financial security also reduced the once-rampant and highly dangerous treks back and forth across the U.S. border that farmers made at great personal risk as they sought ways to support their families. Within three years, PepsiCo's pilot program was expanded to 850 farmers.

Source: Stephanie Strom, "For Pepsi, a Business Decision with Social Benefits," *The New York Times*, February 21, 2011, www.nytimes.com/2011/02/22/business/global/22pepsi.html?pagewanted=all (accessed August 2, 2012).

level is a programmed decision. Other programmed decisions concern the types of skills required to fill certain jobs, the reorder point for manufacturing inventory, and selection of freight routes for product deliveries. Once managers formulate decision rules, subordinates and others can make the decision, freeing managers for other tasks. For example, when staffing banquets, many hotels use a rule that specifies having one server per 30 guests for a sit-down function and one server per 20 guests for a buffet.[7]

Nonprogrammed decisions are made in response to situations that are unique, are poorly defined and largely unstructured, and have important consequences for the organization. Sprint Nextel's decision about carrying the iPhone is a good example of a nonprogrammed decision. Apple has power over wireless carriers right now and is requiring them to make long-term volume commitments. Sprint managers had to decide whether to agree to purchase at least 30.5 million iPhones over a period of four years at a cost of $20 billion or more—regardless of whether the company could find customers to buy them. For Sprint, the stakes were high. The company was losing customers and hadn't turned a profit for years. To sell that many iPhones, Sprint managers realized they would have to double their contract customers and commit all of them to purchasing iPhones. However, not carrying the iPhone might mean Sprint wouldn't stand a chance against other carriers like AT&T and Verizon. As one person said of Sprint's decision process, it was "a bet-the-company kind of thing." Managers eventually decided to go with the Apple contract.[8] Another good example of a nonprogrammed decision comes from Bremen Castings, a small family-owned foundry and machine shop in Bremen, Indiana.

▶▶▶ **Concept Connection**

Having filled in for Steve Jobs during three medical leaves, COO Tim Cook was ready and able to take the helm of Apple when Jobs had to step down shortly before his death in 2011. The choice of Cook as the new CEO was a **nonprogrammed decision** that had been made well in advance, giving Cook some time to prepare for a seamless transition to his new role. Since then, investors, employees, and customers alike seem impressed with his abilities and generally happy with his performance.

Brendan McDermid/Reuters

Innovative
Way

Bremen Castings Inc.

What do you do if you're about halfway into a $10 million expansion when the economy crashes, the stock market tumbles, and the United States is grappling with its first credit downgrade? You've already invested $5 million. If you continue with the expansion plan, it will require getting another $5 million bank loan right away.

That's the situation that J. B. Brown, president of Bremen Castings, discussed for four hours with his top managers in the midst of the largest expansion plan in the company's 72-year history. Should they halt the expansion and start cutting costs rather than spending more money? Would the increased capacity be worth the risk they were taking? The uncertainties were tremendous. The executive team reviewed order rates and relationships with customers and considered what-ifs: What would happen if Bremen's 15 largest customers cut their order rates by 30 to 40 percent, or if agricultural customers stopped picking cotton and corn, or if new Environmental Protection Agency (EPA) regulations created a decline in demand from trucking customers? "If we go out and spend another 3 or 4 million and that work is not there," Brown asked, "what are we going to do to capture more market share?"

The team also looked at the positive side of the slow economy. Casting companies in the United States, like Bremen, face tough competition from lower-cost Chinese producers, but the uncertain economy means some customers have turned back to smaller domestic suppliers who will fill small orders. Eventually, the team decided to go forward with the planned expansion. "If we don't, someone else will," said Brown. "Those are the chances you take in business."[9]

Many nonprogrammed decisions, such as the ones at Bremen Castings and Sprint Nextel, are related to strategic planning because uncertainty is great and decisions are complex. Decisions to acquire a company, build a new factory, develop a new product or service, enter a new geographical market, or relocate headquarters to another city are all nonprogrammed decisions.

FACING CERTAINTY AND UNCERTAINTY

One primary difference between programmed and nonprogrammed decisions relates to the degree of certainty or uncertainty that managers deal with in making the decision. In a perfect world, managers would have all the information necessary for making decisions. In reality, however, some things are unknowable; thus, some decisions will fail to solve the problem or attain the desired outcome. Managers try to obtain information about decision alternatives that will reduce decision uncertainty. Every decision situation can be organized on a scale according to the availability of information and the possibility of failure. The four positions on the scale are certainty, risk, uncertainty, and ambiguity, as illustrated in Exhibit 9.1. Whereas programmed decisions can be made in situations involving certainty, many situations that managers deal with every day involve at least some degree of uncertainty and require nonprogrammed decision making.

Certainty

Certainty means that all the information the decision maker needs is fully available.[10] Managers have information on operating conditions, resource costs, or constraints and each course of action and possible outcome. For example, if a company considers a $10,000 investment in new equipment that it knows for certain will yield $4,000 in cost savings per year over the next five years, managers can calculate a before-tax rate of return of about 40 percent. If managers compare this investment with one that will yield only $3,000 per year in cost savings, they can confidently select the 40 percent return. However, few decisions are certain in the real world. Most contain risk or uncertainty.

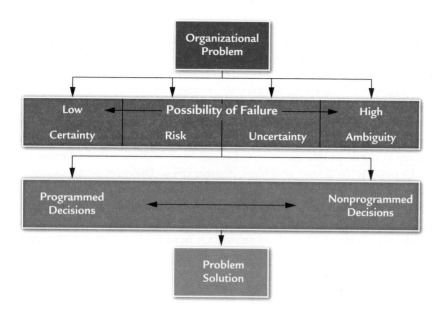

EXHIBIT   9.1

Conditions That Affect the
Possibility of Decision Failure

3

PLANNING

Risk

Risk means that a decision has clear-cut goals and that good information is available, but the future outcomes associated with each alternative are subject to some chance of loss or failure. However, enough information is available to estimate the probability of a successful outcome versus failure.[11] In some cases, managers use computerized statistical analysis to calculate the probabilities of success or failure for each alternative. At Boeing, managers had to decide whether to build a new version of the company's single-aisle 737 jet. They noted that European rival Airbus was getting a lot of orders for the redesigned A320, which included a more fuel-efficient engine, something Boeing's customers also wanted. Perhaps installing new engines on 737 jets was a better alternative than building a completely new plane, Boeing managers thought. They projected production costs for designing and building a new plane versus designing and installing new engines, calculated potential increases in fuel efficiency, considered whether new engines rather than a new plane would meet customer's needs, and looked at total operating costs. CEO James McNerney and other managers eventually decided to go with the new engines. McNerney said Boeing believed that new engines would yield a 10 to 12 percent fuel savings on 737 planes, while also enabling the company to maintain a cost advantage over the Airbus A320. It proved to be a good decision. In mid-2012, Boeing was on track to retake the lead from Airbus as the world's top producer of commercial airplanes.[12]

▶▶▶ **Concept Connection**

Uncertainty is a standard feature in the life of any farmer. Changing weather patterns and unexpected events, like the drought of 2012, can have devastating effects on crops that no amount of planning can prevent. Yet, despite these unforeseeable situations, farmers must make decisions and continue to operate based on assumptions and expectations.

Inga Spence/Alamy

Uncertainty

Uncertainty means that managers know which goals they wish to achieve, but information about alternatives and future events is incomplete. Factors that may affect a decision, such as price, production costs, volume, or future interest rates, are difficult to analyze and predict. Managers may have to make assumptions from which to forge the decision even though it will be wrong if the assumptions are incorrect. Former U.S. treasury secretary Robert Rubin defined uncertainty as a situation in which even a good decision might produce a bad outcome.[13] Managers face uncertainty every day. Many problems have no clear-cut solution, but managers rely on creativity, judgment, intuition, and experience to craft a response.

Consider the uncertainty faced by managers in the movie industry. The movie *Men in Black 3* cost $250 million to make and at least that much in marketing expenses. The movie managed to break even, but many films don't, which reflects the tremendous uncertainty in the industry. What do people want to see this summer? Will comic book heroes, vampires, or aliens be popular? Will animated films, disaster epics, classics, or romantic comedies attract larger audiences? The interests and preferences of moviegoers are extremely difficult to predict. Moreover, it is hard for managers to understand even after the fact what made a particular movie a hit. Was it because of the storyline, the actors in starring roles, the director, the release time? All of those things? Or none of them? Despite the uncertainty, managers in the big Hollywood studios make relatively good decisions overall, and one big hit can pay for a lot of flops.[14]

Ambiguity and Conflict

Ambiguity is by far the most difficult decision situation. Ambiguity means that the goals to be achieved or the problem to be solved is unclear, alternatives are difficult to define, and information about outcomes is unavailable.[15] Ambiguity is what students would feel if an instructor created student groups and told each group to complete a project, but gave the groups no topic, direction, or guidelines whatsoever. In some situations, managers involved in a decision create ambiguity because they see things differently and disagree about what they want. Managers in different departments often have different priorities and goals for the decision, which can lead to conflicts over decision alternatives.

A highly ambiguous situation can create what is sometimes called a *wicked decision problem*. Wicked decisions are associated with conflicts over goals and decision alternatives, rapidly changing circumstances, fuzzy information, unclear links among decision elements, and the inability to evaluate whether a proposed solution will work. For wicked problems, there often is no "right" answer.[16] Managers have a difficult time coming to grips with the issues and must conjure up reasonable scenarios in the absence of clear information. Consider the differing opinions regarding whether to blast a gap in the Birds Point levee as water levels on the Ohio River near the confluence with the Mississippi reached 60.97 feet. Some people believed strongly that the breach was necessary to prevent the town of Cairo, Illinois, from flooding and to relieve pressure on the overburdened system of levees protecting the entire region. Others questioned whether breaking the levee would have the intended result and said the one sure thing it would do would be to destroy about 90 homes and flood 130,000 acres of farmland in Missouri. Major-General Michael J. Walsh, head of the Mississippi Valley Division of the Army Corps of Engineers, had to consult with experts and consider varied opinions, as well as weigh the interests of people whose homes and farms in Missouri would be flooded against the safety of Cairo, a poverty-ridden town with a population of around 3,000. "These are people's homes, their livelihoods," said the chief of the corps' operations division. "We really don't want to do this." The situation was changing from minute to minute as flood waters continued to rise. Missouri's state attorney general even asked the U.S. Supreme court to overturn a decision that would allow the Corps to blast the levee. "There are still a lot of decision points as we move forward," Major-General Walsh said. "He'll still have to make the decision," said one person involved with the situation. Another said: "I don't figure it's going to do what they think it's going to do."[17]

Take **a** Moment

Managers make many decisions in situations that contain some ambiguity. How comfortable are you when dealing with ambiguity? Complete the New Manager Self-Test to find out.

New Manager Self-Test

Intolerance of Ambiguity

Instructions: Rate each statement below from 1–7, based on how strongly you disagree or agree with it. There are no right or wrong answers, so answer honestly to receive accurate feedback.

	Strongly Disagree 1	Moderately Disagree 2	Slightly Disagree 3	Neither Agree nor Disagree 4	Slightly Agree 5	Moderately Agree 6	Strongly Agree 7
1. An expert who doesn't come up with a definite answer probably doesn't know too much.							
2. I would like to live in a foreign country for a while.							
3. There is really no such thing as a problem that can't be solved.							
4. People who live their lives to a schedule probably miss most of the joy of living.							
5. A good job is one where what is done and how it is to be done are always clear.							
6. It is more fun to tackle a complicated problem than to solve a simple one.							
7. In the long run, it is possible to get more done by tackling small, simple problems rather than large and complicated ones.							
8. Often the most interesting and stimulating people are those who don't mind being different and original.							
9. What we are used to is always preferable to what is unfamiliar.							
10. People who insist upon a yes or no answer just don't know how complicated things really are.							
11. A person who leads an even, regular life in which few surprises or unexpected happenings arise really has a lot to be grateful for.							
12. Many of our most important decisions are based on insufficient information.							
13. I like parties where I know most of the people more than ones where all or most of the people are complete strangers.							
14. Teachers or supervisors who hand out vague assignments give one a chance to show initiative and originality.							
15. The sooner we all acquire similar values and ideals the better.							
16. A good teacher is one who makes you wonder about your way of looking at things.							

3

PLANNING

Scoring and Interpretation. Sum the odd-numbered statements, giving 7 points for each Strongly Agree, 6 points for each Moderately Agree, 5 points for each Slightly Agree, 4 points for Neither Agree nor Disagree, 3 points for Slightly Disagree, 2 points for Moderately Disagree, and 1 point for each Strongly Disagree. Reverse-score the even-numbered statements, giving 7 points for each Strongly Disagree through 1 point for each Strongly Agree.

These questions were originally designed to help identify students who would be comfortable with the ambiguity associated with the practice of medicine. Managers also must manage ambiguity in their decisions about rapid change, strategy, people, and social and political dynamics. Intolerance of ambiguity means that an individual tends to perceive novel, complex, and ambiguous situations as potentially threatening rather than as desirable. A high score means greater *intolerance* of ambiguity. A low score means that you tolerate ambiguity and likely see promise and potential in ambiguous situations. Managers make many decisions under conditions of some or much ambiguity, so learning to be comfortable with ambiguity is something to work toward as a manager. A group of New York psychology students had an average score of 50.9 on the above questions, New York evening students 53.0, nursing students 51.9, Far East medical students 44.6, and Midwestern medical students 45.2.

Source: "Intolerance of Ambiguity as a Personality Variable" by S. Budner. From the Journal of Personality (30), pp. 29–59. Copyright (1962) John Wiley & Sons. Reproduced with permission of John Wiley & Sons Inc.

Remember This

- Good decision making is a vital part of good management, but decision making is not easy.
- **Decision making** is the process of identifying problems and opportunities and then resolving them.
- A **decision** is a choice made from available alternatives.
- A **programmed decision** is one made in response to a situation that has occurred often enough to enable managers to develop decision rules that can be applied in the future.
- A **nonprogrammed decision** is one made in response to a situation that is unique, is poorly defined and largely unstructured, and has important consequences for the organization.
- Decisions differ according to the amount of certainty, risk, uncertainty, or ambiguity in the situation.
- **Certainty** is a situation in which all the information the decision maker needs is fully available.
- **Risk** means that a decision has clear-cut goals and good information is available, but the future outcomes associated with each alternative are subject to chance.
- **Uncertainty** occurs when managers know which goals they want to achieve, but information about alternatives and future events is incomplete.
- **Ambiguity** is a condition in which the goals to be achieved or the problem to be solved is unclear, alternatives are difficult to define, and information about outcomes is unavailable.
- Highly ambiguous circumstances can create a wicked decision problem, the most difficult decision situation that managers face.

Decision-Making Models

The approach that managers use to make decisions usually falls into one of three types—the classical model, the administrative model, or the political model. The choice of model depends on the manager's personal preference, whether the decision is programmed or nonprogrammed, and the degree of uncertainty associated with the decision.

THE IDEAL, RATIONAL MODEL

The **classical model** of decision making is based on rational economic assumptions and manager beliefs about what ideal decision making should be. This model has arisen within the management literature because managers are expected to make decisions that are economically sensible and in the organization's best economic interests. The four assumptions underlying this model are as follows:

- The decision maker operates to accomplish goals that are known and agreed on. Problems are precisely formulated and defined.
- The decision maker strives for conditions of certainty, gathering complete information. All alternatives and the potential results of each are calculated.
- Criteria for evaluating alternatives are known. The decision maker selects the alternative that will maximize the economic return to the organization.
- The decision maker is rational and uses logic to assign values, order preferences, evaluate alternatives, and make the decision that will maximize the attainment of organizational goals.

The classical model of decision making is considered to be **normative**, which means it defines how a decision maker *should* make decisions. It does not describe how managers actually make decisions so much as it provides guidelines on how to reach an ideal outcome for the organization. The ideal, rational approach of the classical model is often unattainable by real people in real organizations, but the model has value because it helps decision makers be more rational and not rely entirely on personal preference in making decisions. Indeed, a global survey by McKinsey & Company found that when managers incorporate thoughtful analysis into decision making, they get better results. Studying the responses of more than 2,000 executives regarding how their companies made a specific decision, McKinsey concluded that techniques such as detailed analysis, risk assessment, financial models, and considering comparable situations typically contribute to better financial and operational outcomes.[18]

The classical model is most useful when applied to programmed decisions and to decisions characterized by certainty or risk because relevant information is available and probabilities can be calculated. For example, new analytical software programs automate many programmed decisions, such as freezing the account of a customer who has failed to make payments, determining the cell phone service plan that is most appropriate for a particular customer, or sorting insurance claims so that cases are handled most efficiently.[19]

The growth of quantitative decision techniques that use computers has expanded the use of the classical approach. The New York City Police Department uses computerized mapping and analysis of arrest patterns, paydays, sporting events, concerts, rainfall, holidays, and other variables to predict likely "hot spots" and decide where to assign officers. Retailers like Target, Walmart, and Kohl's make decisions about what to stock and how to price it based on analysis of sales, economic and demographic data, and so forth.[20] Airlines use automated systems to optimize seat pricing, flight scheduling, and crew assignment decisions.

HOW MANAGERS ACTUALLY MAKE DECISIONS

Another approach to decision making, called the **administrative model**, is considered to be **descriptive**, meaning that it describes how managers actually make decisions in complex situations rather than dictating how they *should* make decisions according to a theoretical ideal. The administrative model recognizes the human and environmental limitations that affect the degree to which managers can pursue a rational decision-making process. In difficult situations, such as those characterized by nonprogrammed decisions, uncertainty, and ambiguity, managers are typically unable to make economically rational decisions even if they want to.[21]

Bounded Rationality and Satisficing

The administrative model of decision making is based on the work of Herbert A. Simon. Simon proposed two concepts that were instrumental in shaping the administrative model: bounded rationality and satisficing. **Bounded rationality** means that people have limits, or boundaries, on how rational they can be. Organizations are incredibly complex, and managers have the time and ability to process only a limited amount of information with which to make decisions.[22] Because managers do not have the time or cognitive ability to process complete information about complex decisions, they must satisfice. **Satisficing** means that decision makers choose the first solution alternative that satisfies minimal decision criteria. Rather than pursuing all alternatives to identify the single solution that will maximize economic returns, managers will opt for the first solution that appears to solve the problem, even if better solutions are presumed to exist. The decision maker cannot justify the time and expense of obtaining complete information.[23]

Managers sometimes generate alternatives for complex problems only until they find one that they believe will work. For example, Liz Claiborne managers hired designer Isaac Mizrahi and targeted younger consumers in an effort to revive the flagging Liz Claiborne brand, but sales and profits continued to decline. Faced with the failure of the new youth-oriented line, a 90 percent cutback in orders from Macy's, high unemployment, a weak economy, and other complex and multifaceted problems, managers weren't sure how to stem the years-long tide of losses and get the company back in the black. They satisficed with a quick decision to form a licensing agreement that will have Liz Claiborne clothing sold exclusively at JC Penney, which will handle all manufacturing and marketing for the brand.[24]

The administrative model relies on assumptions different from those of the classical model and focuses on organizational factors that influence individual decisions. According to the administrative model:

- Decision goals often are vague, conflicting, and lack consensus among managers. Managers often are unaware of problems or opportunities that exist in the organization.

- Rational procedures are not always used, and, when they are, they are confined to a simplistic view of the problem that does not capture the complexity of real organizational events.

- Managers' searches for alternatives are limited because of human, information, and resource constraints.

- Most managers settle for a satisficing rather than a maximizing solution, partly because they have limited information and partly because they have only vague criteria for what constitutes a maximizing solution.

Intuition

Another aspect of administrative decision making is intuition. **Intuition** represents a quick apprehension of a decision situation based on past experience but without conscious thought.[25] Intuitive decision making is not arbitrary or irrational because it is based on years of practice and hands-on experience. Movie mogul Harvey Weinstein, co-chairman of independent film production and distribution studio The Weinstein Company (TWC), has been in the movie business since he and his brother Bob founded Miramax in 1979. Many people told Weinstein he was crazy to even think about making a black-and-white silent film called *The Artist*, but Weinstein thought it would work.

Concept Connection ◀◀◀

James Leynse/Corbis

"Lots of people hear what I'm doing and think, 'That's a crazy idea!'" says Russell Simmons. The successful entrepreneur, who heads the New York–based media firm Rush Communications, has relied on his **intuition** to build a half-billion-dollar empire on one profitable "crazy idea" after another. It all began with his belief that he could go mainstream with the vibrant rap music he heard in African American neighborhoods. In 1983, he started the pioneering hip-hop Def Jam record label, launching the careers of Beastie Boys, LL Cool J, and Run-DMC, among others. He's since moved on to successful ventures in fashion, media, consumer products, and finance.

It did. The film earned TWC a Best Picture Oscar (among other awards) at the 2012 Academy Awards.[26] In today's fast-paced business environment, intuition plays an increasingly important role in decision making. Numerous studies have found that effective managers use a combination of rational analysis and intuition in making complex decisions under time pressure.[27]

Psychologists and neuroscientists have studied how people make good decisions using their intuition under extreme time pressure and uncertainty.[28] Good intuitive decision making is based on an ability to recognize patterns at lightning speed. When people have a depth of experience and knowledge in a particular area, the right decision often comes quickly and effortlessly as a recognition of information that has been largely forgotten by the conscious mind. For example, firefighters make decisions by recognizing what is typical or abnormal about a fire, based on their experience. This ability can also be seen among soldiers in Iraq, who have been responsible for stopping many roadside bomb attacks based on gut feelings. High-tech gear designed to detect improvised explosive devices, or IEDs, is merely a supplement rather than a replacement for the ability of the human brain to sense danger and act on it. Soldiers with experience in Iraq subconsciously know when something doesn't look or feel right. It might be a rock that wasn't there yesterday, a piece of concrete that looks too symmetrical, odd patterns of behavior, or just a different feeling of tension in the air.[29] Similarly, in the business world, managers continuously perceive and process information that they may not consciously be aware of, and their base of knowledge and experience helps them make decisions that may be characterized by uncertainty and ambiguity.

However, intuitive decisions don't always work out, and managers should take care to apply intuition under the right circumstances and in the right way, rather than considering it a magical technique for making all important decisions.[30] Managers may walk a fine line between two extremes: on the one hand, making arbitrary decisions without careful study, and on the other, relying obsessively on rational analysis. One is not better than the other, and managers need to take a balanced approach by considering both rationality and intuition as important components of effective decision making.[31]

THE POLITICAL MODEL

The third model of decision making is useful for making nonprogrammed decisions when conditions are uncertain, information is limited, and there are manager conflicts about what goals to pursue or what course of action to take. Most organizational decisions involve many managers who are pursuing different goals, and they have to talk with one another to share information and reach an agreement. Managers often engage in coalition building for making complex organizational decisions.[32] A **coalition** is an informal alliance among managers who support a specific goal. *Coalition building* is the process of forming alliances among managers. In other words, a manager who supports a specific alternative, such as increasing the corporation's growth by acquiring another company, talks informally to other executives and tries to persuade them to support the decision. Without a coalition, a powerful individual or group could derail the decision-making process. Coalition building gives several managers an opportunity to contribute to decision making, enhancing their commitment to the alternative that is ultimately adopted. Results from the global survey by McKinsey & Company mentioned earlier suggest that informal coalition building is associated with faster implementation of decisions because managers have developed consensus about which action to pursue.[33]

Failing to build a coalition can allow conflict and disagreements to derail a decision, particularly if the opposition builds a powerful coalition of its own. Consider what happened when University of Virginia Rector Helen Dragas decided to force President Teresa Sullivan to resign.

Innovative Way

University of Virginia

The showdown between the first female president and the first female rector of the University of Virginia played out over a period of 18 tumultuous days in front of a cast of thousands. "Palace coup meets grassroots rebellion," one politics professor tweeted at the peak of the drama.

Teresa Sullivan was shocked when she was told in a meeting with rector Helen Dragas and vice rector Mark Kington that the board was unhappy with her performance as president of the University of Virginia after two years on the job, and they wanted her to resign. Presenting her with a separation agreement, Dragas informed Sullivan that they controlled 15 of the 16 board votes, so her departure was a foregone conclusion. How wrong she was. Dragas might have thought the board was on her side in the decision to oust Sullivan, but she hadn't anticipated the backlash that would come from faculty and students, deans, alumni, former board members, donors, politicians, and the community. Dragas apologized for the way the resignation had been handled and tried to shore up support for her decision, but it was too late.

After two weeks of turmoil, Mark Kington resigned as vice rector, and the governor of Virginia was threatening to fire the entire board if they didn't resolve the crisis. Six board members were pushing for Sullivan's reinstatement, five opposed it, and four votes were up for grabs. A week later, Dragas threw in the towel, stating that "It's time to bring the U-Va family back together." The vote to reinstate Sullivan was unanimous.[34]

Assuming she had the backing of the board, Helen Dragas failed to build an effective coalition to support her decision. Nor did she build a broader coalition of support with key players in the university community. Indeed, most board members might have supported her decision had there not been such an outcry from the entire university community. Managers always have to anticipate resistance, talk with people all across the organization, and make sure that their decisions will benefit the overall organization. The political model closely resembles the real environment in which most managers and decision makers operate. For example, interviews with CEOs in high-tech industries found that they strived to use some type of rational process in making decisions, but the way they actually decided things was through a complex interaction with other managers, subordinates, environmental factors, and organizational events.[35] Decisions are complex and involve many people, information is often ambiguous, and disagreement and conflict over problems and solutions are normal. The political model begins with four basic assumptions:

- Organizations are made up of groups with diverse interests, goals, and values. Managers disagree about problem priorities and may not understand or share the goals and interests of other managers.

- Information is ambiguous and incomplete. The attempt to be rational is limited by the complexity of many problems, as well as personal and organizational constraints.

- Managers do not have the time, resources, or mental capacity to identify all dimensions of the problem and process all relevant information. Managers talk to each other and exchange viewpoints to gather information and reduce ambiguity.

- Managers engage in the push and pull of debate to decide goals and discuss alternatives. Decisions are the result of bargaining and discussion among coalition members.

The key dimensions of the classical, administrative, and political models are listed in Exhibit 9.2. Research into decision-making procedures found rational, classical procedures to be associated with high performance for organizations in stable environments. However, administrative and political decision-making procedures and intuition have been associated with high performance in unstable environments in which decisions must be made rapidly and under more difficult conditions.[36]

Classical Model	Administrative Model	Political Model
Clear-cut problem and goals	Vague problem and goals	Pluralistic; conflicting goals
Condition of certainty	Condition of uncertainty	Condition of uncertainty or ambiguity
Full information about alternatives and their outcomes	Limited information about alternatives and their outcomes	Inconsistent viewpoints; ambiguous information
Rational choice by individual for maximizing outcomes	Satisficing choice for resolving problem using intuition	Bargaining and discussion among coalition members

EXHIBIT 9.2

Characteristics of Classical, Administrative, and Political Decision-Making Models

Remember This

- The ideal, rational approach to decision making, called the **classical model**, is based on the assumption that managers should make logical decisions that are economically sensible and in the organization's best economic interest.

- The classical model is **normative**, meaning that it defines how a manager *should* make logical decisions and provides guidelines for reaching an ideal outcome.

- Software programs based on the classical model are being applied to programmed decisions, such as how to schedule airline crews or how to process insurance claims most efficiently.

- The **administrative model** includes the concepts of *bounded rationality* and *satisficing* and describes how managers make decisions in situations that are characterized by uncertainty and ambiguity.

- The administrative model is **descriptive**, an approach that describes how managers actually make decisions, rather than how they should make decisions according to a theoretical model.

- **Bounded rationality** means that people have the time and cognitive ability to process only a limited amount of information on which to base decisions.

- **Satisficing** means choosing the first alternative that satisfies minimal decision criteria, regardless of whether better solutions are presumed to exist.

- **Intuition** is an aspect of administrative decision making that refers to a quick comprehension of a decision situation based on past experience but without conscious thought.

- Soldiers in Iraq have been known to detect roadside bombs using their intuition.

- The political model takes into consideration that many decisions require debate, discussion, and coalition building.

- A **coalition** is an informal alliance among managers who support a specific goal or solution.

Decision-Making Steps

Whether a decision is programmed or nonprogrammed and regardless of managers' choice of the classical, administrative, or political model of decision making, six steps typically are associated with effective decision processes. These steps are summarized in Exhibit 9.3.

RECOGNITION OF DECISION REQUIREMENT

Managers confront a decision requirement in the form of either a problem or an opportunity. A **problem** occurs when organizational accomplishment is less than established goals. Some aspect of performance is unsatisfactory. An **opportunity** exists when managers see potential accomplishment that exceeds specified current goals. Managers see the possibility of enhancing performance beyond current levels.

3

PLANNING

EXHIBIT 9.3

Six Steps in the Managerial
Decision-Making Process

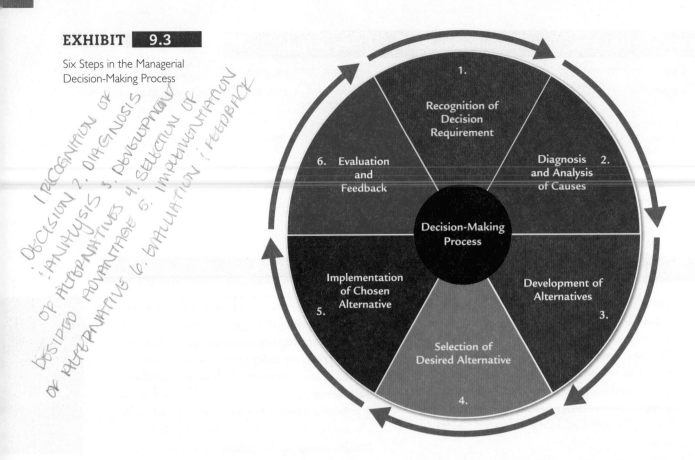

Awareness of a problem or opportunity is the first step in the decision-making sequence and requires surveillance of the internal and external environment for issues that merit executive attention.[37] This process resembles the military concept of gathering intelligence. Managers scan the world around them to determine whether the organization is satisfactorily progressing toward its goals.

Some information comes from periodic financial reports, performance reports, and other sources that are designed to discover problems before they become too serious. Managers also take advantage of informal sources. They talk to other managers, gather opinions on how things are going, and seek advice on which problems should be tackled or which opportunities embraced.[38] For example, the board of Hewlett-Packard fired Leo Apotheker after only 11 months as CEO because they heard from other managers that Apotheker did not seem to keep his team informed of plans, failed to rally the troops behind his efforts, and was unclear on strategic direction for the company.[39] Recognizing decision requirements is difficult because it often means integrating bits and pieces of information in novel ways.

DIAGNOSIS AND ANALYSIS OF CAUSES

Once a problem or opportunity comes to a manager's attention, the understanding of the situation should be refined. **Diagnosis** is the step in the decision-making process in which managers analyze underlying causal factors associated with the decision situation.

Many times, the real problem lies hidden behind the problem that managers *think* exists. By looking at a situation from different angles, managers can identify the true problem. In addition, they often discover opportunities they didn't realize were there.[40] Charles Kepner and Benjamin Tregoe, who conducted extensive studies of

> "It isn't that they can't see the solution. It's that they can't see the problem."
>
> — G. K. CHESTERTON, ENGLISH NOVELIST

manager decision making, recommend that managers ask a series of questions to specify underlying causes, including the following:

- What is the state of disequilibrium affecting us?
- When did it occur?
- Where did it occur?
- How did it occur?
- To whom did it occur?
- What is the urgency of the problem?
- What is the interconnectedness of events?
- What result came from which activity?[41]

Take a Moment

The Small Group Breakout on pages 291–292 will give you a chance to practice a new approach to decision making that focuses on desired outcomes rather than looking at the cause of problems.

Such questions help specify what actually happened and why. Diagnosing a problem can be thought of as peeling an onion layer by layer. Consultant Daniel Burrus tells of meeting with the CEO of a large accounting and professional services firm who said the company's biggest problem was the inability to hire enough qualified people to serve their global clients. As the two peeled the onion further, they got down to the real problem, which was not the lack of staff but inefficiency in internal collaboration and communication. The CEO discovered that he might actually be able to *reduce* staff with more effective and efficient systems.[42] Managers cannot solve problems if they don't know about them, or if they are addressing the wrong issues.

DEVELOPMENT OF ALTERNATIVES

The next stage is to generate possible alternative solutions that will respond to the needs of the situation and correct the underlying causes.

For a programmed decision, feasible alternatives are easy to identify and in fact usually are already available within the organization's rules and procedures. Nonprogrammed decisions, however, require developing new courses of action that will meet the company's needs. For decisions made under conditions of high uncertainty, managers may develop only one or two custom solutions that will satisfice for handling the problem. However, studies find that limiting the search for alternatives is a primary cause of decision failure in organizations.[43]

Decision alternatives can be thought of as tools for reducing the difference between the organization's current and desired performance. Smart managers tap into the knowledge of people throughout the organization for decision alternatives. At WGB Construction, a small homebuilder near Boston, managers ask everyone—from architects to deck builders—for input on how to solve a problem such as a decrease in sales. Similarly, when data storage company EMC was faced with a need to cut costs, managers used the company's social media platform to ask employees all across the organization for alternatives. The resulting decisions were better, and employees were more supportive because they had been involved in the process of identifying alternatives for the cuts.[44]

SELECTION OF THE DESIRED ALTERNATIVE

Once feasible alternatives are developed, one must be selected. In this stage, managers try to select the most promising of several alternative courses of action. The best alternative solution is one which best fits the overall goals and values of the organization and achieves the desired results using the fewest resources.[45] Managers want to select the choice with the least amount of risk and uncertainty. Because some risk is inherent for most nonprogrammed decisions, managers try to gauge prospects for success. They might rely on their intuition and experience to estimate whether a given course of action is likely to succeed. Basing choices on overall goals and values can also guide the selection of alternatives.

3

PLANNING

Concept Connection ◀◀◀

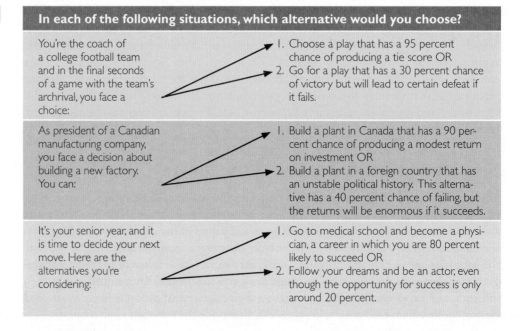

Courtesy of Red Door Interactive

Reid Carr, founder and CEO of San Diego-based Red Door Interactive, Inc., a firm that manages clients' online presence, involves his staff throughout the decision-making process. Carr believes that when **developing, selecting, and implementing alternatives**, managers should "decide slowly and collaboratively so that you have the best plan produced by those who are tasked with execution. Then, let them execute." Red Door's annual "Start, Stop, and Keep" survey is one way Carr gathers feedback. It asks employees to suggest which internal processes and practices should be introduced, continued, or discontinued.

Choosing among alternatives also depends on managers' personality factors and willingness to accept risk and uncertainty. **Risk propensity** is the willingness to undertake risk with the opportunity of gaining an increased payoff. At drug maker Novartis, for example, researchers want CEO Daniel L. Vasella to give the go-ahead for an experimental vaccine for Alzheimer's disease. The potential payoff is huge, but Vasella thinks the risks are too high. He prefers to focus research on smaller, narrowly defined groups of patients, often suffering from rare diseases that are well understood scientifically but that desperately need new drugs. For Vasella, investing in a drug for Alzheimer's before the disease is better understood is wasting time and money.[46] The level of risk that a manager is willing to accept will influence the analysis of costs and benefits to be derived from any decision. Consider the situations in Exhibit 9.4. In each situation, which alternative would you choose? A person with a low risk propensity would tend to take ensured moderate returns by going for a tie score, building a domestic plant, or pursuing a career as a physician. A risk taker would go for the victory, build a plant in a foreign country, or embark on an acting career.

IMPLEMENTATION OF THE CHOSEN ALTERNATIVE

The **implementation** stage involves the use of managerial, administrative, and persuasive abilities to ensure that the chosen alternative is carried out. This step is similar to the idea of strategy execution described in Chapter 8. The ultimate success of the chosen alternative depends on whether it can be translated into action.[47] Sometimes an alternative never

EXHIBIT 9.4

Decision Alternatives with Different Levels of Risk

In each of the following situations, which alternative would you choose?

You're the coach of a college football team and in the final seconds of a game with the team's archrival, you face a choice:	1. Choose a play that has a 95 percent chance of producing a tie score OR 2. Go for a play that has a 30 percent chance of victory but will lead to certain defeat if it fails.
As president of a Canadian manufacturing company, you face a decision about building a new factory. You can:	1. Build a plant in Canada that has a 90 percent chance of producing a modest return on investment OR 2. Build a plant in a foreign country that has an unstable political history. This alternative has a 40 percent chance of failing, but the returns will be enormous if it succeeds.
It's your senior year, and it is time to decide your next move. Here are the alternatives you're considering:	1. Go to medical school and become a physician, a career in which you are 80 percent likely to succeed OR 2. Follow your dreams and be an actor, even though the opportunity for success is only around 20 percent.

becomes reality because managers lack the resources or energy needed to make things happen. Implementation may require discussion with people affected by the decision. Communication, motivation, and leadership skills must be used to see that the decision is carried out. When employees see that managers follow up on their decisions by tracking implementation success, they are more committed to positive action.[48]

EVALUATION AND FEEDBACK

In the evaluation stage of the decision process, decision makers gather information that tells them how well the decision was implemented and whether it was effective in achieving its goals. Feedback is important because decision making is an ongoing process. Decision making is not completed when a manager or board of directors votes yes or no. Feedback provides decision makers with information that can precipitate a new decision cycle. The decision may fail, thus generating a new analysis of the problem, evaluation of alternatives, and selection of a new alternative. Many big problems are solved by trying several alternatives in sequence, each providing modest improvement. Feedback is the part of monitoring that assesses whether a new decision needs to be made.

To illustrate the overall decision-making process, including evaluation and feedback, consider the decision at *The New York Times* to begin a paid subscription plan for the newspaper's Web site.

Innovative Way

The New York Times

In March 2011, *The New York Times* took a giant strategic leap—it asked readers to begin paying for access to its journalism online. The decision wasn't made lightly. In fact, executives and senior editors had spent years studying the problem, analyzing various alternatives, and reaching an agreement to implement the new subscription plan.

Managers agreed on the issue: declining revenues. Analyzing the causes of this problem, they recognized that the economic recession had hit the newspaper's revenue hard, and that both print and online advertising had gone down since the recession began. However, another major cause was the continuing decline in print subscriptions. Why should people pay for a subscription when they could simply go to the *Times'* Web site and access the paper's high-quality journalism free of charge? Managers believed that some type of online subscription model was needed. Debate and discussion of various alternatives went on for months, both formally and informally. Eventually, a coalition of managers came together around the idea of a tiered subscription service that would allow Web site visitors to read 20 articles a month at no charge before being asked to select one of three subscription models at various price levels.

Evaluation and feedback began immediately and continues to this day. On the day the paper launched the subscription model, executives gathered with web developers around two long tables, "their heads buried in their laptops monitoring the launch," as one writer put it. The first subscriber signed up at practically the same moment the announcement was made. One year later, managers were surprised by the success of this decision. They had set a measure of 300,000 subscribers during the first year as a benchmark for success, and the total was actually around 390,000. Interestingly, at the same time, home delivery subscriptions of the print edition increased for the first time in five years, perhaps because some readers feared losing the paper edition altogether if they didn't support it. In addition, advertising revenues began to grow again as advertisers saw that the new digital subscription model was working.[49]

The decision at *The New York Times* to implement a digital subscription plan illustrates all the decision steps, and the process ultimately ended in success. However, digital subscriptions have slowed since the initial burst of activity, so managers continue to monitor the situation and consider if additional decisions need to be made.[50] Strategic decisions always contain some risk, but feedback and follow-up can help keep companies on track. When decisions don't work out so well, managers can learn from their mistakes—and sometimes turn problems into opportunities.

3

PLANNING

Remember This

- Managers face the need to make a decision when they either confront a problem or see an opportunity.
- A **problem** is a situation in which organizational accomplishments have failed to meet established goals.
- An **opportunity** is a situation in which managers see potential organizational accomplishments that exceed current goals.
- The decision-making process typically involves six steps: recognition of the need for a decision, diagnosing causes, developing alternatives, selecting an alternative,

implementing the alternative, and evaluating decision effectiveness.

- **Diagnosis** is the step in which managers analyze underlying causal factors associated with the decision situation.
- Selection of an alternative depends partly on managers' **risk propensity**, or their willingness to undertake risk with the opportunity of gaining an increased payoff.
- The **implementation** step involves using managerial, administrative, and persuasive abilities to translate the chosen alternative into action.

Personal Decision Framework

Imagine you were a manager at Google, *The New York Times*, an AMC movie theater, or the local public library. How would you go about making important decisions that might shape the future of your department or company? So far in this chapter, we have discussed a number of factors that affect how managers make decisions. For example, decisions may be programmed or nonprogrammed, situations are characterized by various levels of uncertainty, and managers may use the classical, administrative, or political model of decision making. In addition, the decision-making process follows six recognized steps.

However, not all managers go about making decisions in the same way. In fact, significant differences distinguish the ways in which individual managers may approach problems and make decisions concerning them. These differences can be explained by the concept of personal **decision styles**. Exhibit 9.5 illustrates the role of personal style in the decision-making process. Personal decision style refers to distinctions among people with respect to how they evaluate problems, generate alternatives, and make choices. Research has identified four major decision styles: directive, analytical, conceptual, and behavioral.[51]

1. The *directive style* is used by people who prefer simple, clear-cut solutions to problems. Managers who use this style often make decisions quickly because they do not like to deal with a lot of information and may consider only one or two alternatives. People who prefer the directive style generally are efficient and rational and prefer to rely on existing rules or procedures for making decisions.

2. Managers with an *analytical style* like to consider complex solutions based on as much data as they can gather. These individuals carefully consider alternatives and often base their decisions on objective, rational data from management control systems and other sources. They search for the best possible decision based on the information available.

3. People who tend toward a *conceptual style* also like to consider a broad amount of information. However, they are more socially oriented than those with an analytical style and like to talk to others about the problem and possible alternatives for solving it. Managers using a conceptual style consider many broad alternatives, rely on information from both people and systems, and like to solve problems creatively.

4. The *behavioral style* is often the style adopted by managers having a deep concern for others as individuals. Managers using this style like to talk to people one-on-one, understand their feelings about the problem, and consider the effect of a given decision on them. People with a behavioral style usually are concerned with the personal development of others and may make decisions that help others achieve their goals.

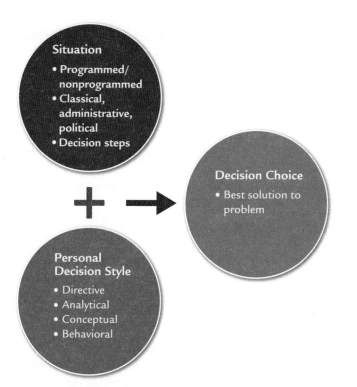

EXHIBIT   9.5

Personal Decision Framework

SOURCES: Based on A. J. Rowe, J. D. Boulgaides, and M. R. McGrath, *Managerial Decision Making* (Chicago: Science Research Associates, 1984); and Alan J. Rowe and Richard O. Mason, *Managing with Style: A Guide to Understanding, Assessing, and Improving Your Decision Making* (San Francisco: Jossey-Bass, 1987).

3

PLANNING

Many managers have a dominant decision style. For example, U. S. President Barack Obama's decision to increase troop strength in Afghanistan reflected his primarily conceptual style of decision making. The president held ten meetings with key military decision makers in a decision process that was called "intense, methodical, earnest, and at times deeply frustrating." Obama requested detailed reports, asked numerous questions, and showed an almost insatiable need for information. One participant described him as a cross "between a college professor and a gentle cross-examiner."[52]

However, managers frequently use several different styles or a combination of styles in making the varied decisions that they confront daily. A manager might use a directive style for determining which company to use for office supplies, yet shift to a more conceptual style when handling an interdepartmental conflict. The most effective managers are able to shift among styles as needed to meet the situation. Being aware of one's dominant decision style can help a manager avoid making critical mistakes when his or her usual style may be inappropriate to the problem at hand.

Take a Moment

To learn more about how you make decisions, go to the Experiential Exercise on page 291 that evaluates your personal decision style.

Remember This

- A manager's personal decision style influences how he or she makes decisions.
- **Decision styles** are differences among people with respect to how they perceive problems and make choices.
- Four major decision styles are directive, analytical, conceptual, and behavioral.

- President Barack Obama uses a primarily conceptual style of decision making.
- Most experienced managers use a variety of styles depending on the decision situation.

Why Do Managers Make Bad Decisions?

Managers are faced with a relentless demand for decisions, from solving minor problems to implementing major strategic changes. Even the best manager will make mistakes, but managers can increase their percentage of good decisions by understanding some of the factors that cause people to make bad ones. Most bad decisions are errors in judgment that originate in the human mind's limited capacity and in the natural biases managers display during decision making. Answer the questions in the Shoptalk box to learn how biases can affect decisions and choices. Are you aware of biases that cloud your judgment when you make decisions and solve problems? Awareness of the following six biases can help managers make more enlightened choices.[53]

1. **Being influenced by initial impressions.** When considering decisions, the mind often gives disproportionate weight to the first information it receives. These initial impressions, statistics, or estimates act as an anchor to our subsequent thoughts and judgments. Anchors can be as simple as a random comment by a colleague or a statistic read in a newspaper. Past events and trends also act as anchors. For example, in business, managers frequently look at the previous year's sales when estimating sales for the coming year. Giving too much weight to the past can lead to poor forecasts and misguided decisions.

2. **Justifying past decisions.** Many managers fall into the trap of making choices that justify their past decisions, even if those decisions no longer seem valid. Consider managers who invest tremendous time and energy into improving the performance of a problem employee whom they now realize should never have been hired in the first place. Another example is when a manager continues to pour money into a failing project, hoping to turn things around. One study of product development found that managers who initiate a new product are much more likely to continue funding it despite evidence that it is failing.[54] People don't like to make mistakes, so they continue to support a flawed decision in an effort to justify or correct the past.

3. **Seeing what you want to see.** People frequently look for information that supports their existing instinct or point of view and avoid information that contradicts it.

   This bias affects where managers look for information, as well as how they interpret the information they find. People tend to give too much weight to supporting information and too little to information that conflicts with their established viewpoints. For example, managers at Tokyo Electric Power Company (Tepco) have been accused of delaying for too long the decision to use seawater to cool nuclear reactors at Fukushima Daiichi following the 2011 Japan earthquake and tsunami. Tepco managers knew that seawater would destroy the reactors, so they gave greater weight to information that supported their decision to delay its use, emphasizing that they were "taking the safety of the whole plant into consideration" in judging the appropriate timing to use seawater in the cooldown efforts. Unfortunately, it took an explosion at the plant to convince managers that using seawater was essential to control the overheating of the reactors.[55]

Concept Connection ◀◀◀

Justin Sullivan/Getty Images News/Getty Images

By most accounts, Facebook's initial public offering (IPO) in 2012 was considered something of a flop, as it was shrouded in controversy and allegations of misconduct and wrongdoing. The IPO was just one in a series of missteps and mistakes by Facebook's leaders, including founder Mark Zuckerberg. Many critics attribute Zuckerberg's lapses in good judgment to his **overconfidence** and the fact that he surrounded himself with board members who didn't question his decisions perhaps as thoroughly as they should have.

Manager's *Shoptalk*

Do Biases Influence Your Decision Making?

All of us have biases, but most of us have a hard time seeing our own. What biases influence your decisions and solutions to problems? Answer the following questions to get an idea of the difficulties and mistakes that likely await you as a new manager.

1. A piece of paper is folded in half, in half again, etc. After 100 folds, how thick will it be? Take your best guess: _____. I am 90 percent sure that the correct answer lies between _____ and _____.

2. Which figure below is most different from the others?

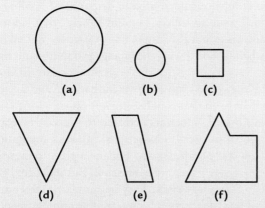

    (a)   (b)   (c)

    (d)   (e)   (f)

3. As owner and CEO of your company, you decided to invest $100 million to build pilotless drones that cannot be detected by enemy radar. When the project is 90 percent complete, a competing firm begins marketing a completed drone that cannot be detected by radar. In addition, their drone is much faster, smaller, cheaper, and more sophisticated than the drone that your company is developing. The question is: Should you invest the last 10 percent of the research funds to finish your drone? Check one of the following answers.

_____ No—There is no reason to continue spending money on the project.

_____ Yes—After investing $90 million, we might as well finish the project.

4. Give a quick (five-second) estimate of the following product without actually calculating:

$8 \times 7 \times 6 \times 5 \times 4 \times 3 \times 2 \times 1 = $ _____.

5. Robert is envious, stubborn, critical, impulsive, industrious, and intelligent. In general, how emotional do you think Robert is? (Circle one number.)

Not emotional   Extremely
at all   1 2 3 4 5 6 7 8 9   emotional

6. Which would you choose between the two alternatives below?

_____ Alternative A: A 50 percent chance of gaining $1,000.00

_____ Alternative B: A sure gain of $500.00

Which would you choose between the two alternatives below?

_____ Alternative C: A 50 percent chance of losing $1,000.00

_____ Alternative D: A sure loss of $500.00

After you have specified an answer to each problem, you will find the answers and a description of the potential related bias on page 292.

Sources: Questions 1 and 3–6 are from research studies reviewed in Scott Plous, *The Psychology of Judgment and Decision Making* (Philadelphia: Temple University Press, 1993); question 2 is based on an item in the *Creativity in Action Newsletter*, as reported in Arthur B. VanGundy, *Idea Power: Techniques & Resources to Unleash the Creativity in Your Organization* (New York: Amacom, 1992).

4. ***Perpetuating the status quo.*** Managers may base decisions on what has worked in the past and fail to explore new options, dig for additional information, or investigate new technologies. For example, General Motors (GM) stuck with its strategic decision to offer a multitude of brands long after there was clear evidence that trying to cover the whole range of the auto market was paving the way to disaster. The strategy started to fray in the 1970s with increased competition from Japanese automakers and spikes in oil prices. Yet, as late as February 2008, managers were saying that talk about killing brands was "not a thoughtful discussion." Only bankruptcy and a forced restructuring finally pushed managers to cut GM's brands from eight down to four.[56]

5. ***Being influenced by emotions.*** If you've ever made a decision when you were angry, upset, or even ecstatically happy, you might already know the danger of being influenced by emotions. A recent study of traders in London investment banks found that effective regulation of emotions was a characteristic of higher-performing traders. Lower-performing traders were less effective in managing and modulating their emotional responses.[57] Another finding is that doctors make less effective decisions when they feel emotions of like or dislike for a patient. If they like a patient, they are less likely to prescribe a painful procedure. If they feel dislike, they may blame the patient for the condition and provide less treatment.[58] Unfortunately, some managers let their emotions influence their decisions on a regular basis. There is some evidence that when people make poor decisions under the influence of strong emotions (such as firing off an angry e-mail message), they tend to continue to make poor decisions because it becomes part of the mind's blueprint for how to behave.[59] Managers make better decision when—to the extent possible—they take emotions out of the decision-making process.

6. ***Overconfidence.*** Most people overestimate their ability to predict uncertain outcomes. For example, when people are asked to define quantities about which they have little direct knowledge ("What was Target's 2011 revenue?" or "What was the market value of Facebook as of August 14, 2012?"), they overestimate their accuracy. Similarly, many managers have unrealistic expectations of their ability to understand the risks and make the right choice. Consider how overconfidence contributed to decisions at JPMorgan Chase's chief investment office, made by the so-called "London Whale," that led to a multibillion-dollar loss. All banks take risks, but JPMorgan was praised for not taking the kind of outsized risks that many banks took during the mortgage boom—and that contributed to the collapse of the U.S. economy. After the Wall Street crisis, JPMorgan's CEO, Jamie Dimon, was called "the world's most important banker," and his top executives were hailed as a management team that could seemingly do no wrong. The company's chief investment office in London, which was created to protect the bank from volatility caused by complex global financial transactions, gained a reputation for its trading prowess. The unit was a star performer and became a profit center for JPMorgan at a time when industry earnings were under pressure. But managers got overconfident of their ability to spot and manage risks. They began taking larger and larger gambles, including involvement in a highly complicated trading strategy involving derivatives—similar in some ways to the risks that led to the Wall Street crisis. The strategy backfired, eventually causing a loss of almost $6 billion, leading to the firing of several key executives, and damaging the reputation of both the bank and its CEO. Moreover, federal investigators were looking into potential fraud, suspecting that some traders improperly marked their trades to obscure the magnitude of the losses.[60]

Remember This

- Being aware of biases that cloud judgment helps managers avoid decision traps and make better decisions.
- Biases to watch out for include being influenced by initial impressions, trying to correct or justify past flawed decisions, seeing only what you want to see, perpetuating the status quo, being influenced by emotions, and being overconfident.

Innovative Decision Making

The ability to make fast, widely supported, high-quality decisions on a frequent basis is a critical skill in today's fast-moving organizations.[61] Considering that managers are under pressure to decide quickly and that biases creep in and cloud judgment, how do managers ever make good decisions? Some innovative techniques can help managers watch out for and avoid mistakes caused by cognitive biases. It is difficult for most managers to see their own biases, but they can build in mechanisms that neutralize or reduce bias-related decision errors at the organizational level.[62]

START WITH BRAINSTORMING

Brainstorming uses a face-to-face interactive group to spontaneously suggest a wide range of alternatives for decision making. The keys to effective brainstorming are that people can build on one another's ideas; all ideas are acceptable, no matter how crazy they seem; and criticism and evaluation are not allowed. The goal is to generate as many ideas as possible. Brainstorming has been found to be highly effective for quickly generating a wide range of alternate solutions to a problem, but it does have some drawbacks.[63] For one thing, people in a group often want to conform to what others are saying. Others may be concerned about pleasing the boss or impressing colleagues. In addition, many creative people simply have social inhibitions that limit their participation in a group session or make it difficult to come up with ideas in a group setting. In fact, one study found that when four people are asked to "brainstorm" individually, they typically come up with twice as many ideas as a group of four brainstorming together.

One recent approach, electronic brainstorming, takes advantage of the group approach while overcoming some disadvantages. **Electronic brainstorming**, sometimes called *brainwriting*, brings people together in an interactive group over a computer network.[64] One member writes an idea, another reads it and adds other ideas, and so on. Studies show that electronic brainstorming generates about 40 percent more ideas than individuals brainstorming alone, and 25 to 200 percent more ideas than regular brainstorming groups, depending on group size.[65] Why? Because the process is anonymous, the sky's the limit in terms of what people feel free to say. People can write down their ideas immediately, avoiding the possibility that a good idea might slip away while the person is waiting for a chance to speak in a face-to-face group. Social inhibitions and concerns are avoided, which typically allows for a broader range of participation. Another advantage is that electronic brainstorming can potentially be done with groups made up of employees from around the world, further increasing the diversity of alternatives.

USE HARD EVIDENCE

Using hard evidence can help take emotion out of the decision-making process, keep people from relying on faulty assumptions, and prevent managers from "seeing what they want to see," as described earlier. **Evidence-based decision making** means a commitment to make more informed and intelligent decisions based on the best available facts and evidence. It means being alert to potential biases and seeking and examining the evidence with rigor. Managers practice evidence-based decision making by being careful and thoughtful rather than carelessly relying on assumptions, past experience, rules of thumb, or intuition.[66] For example, the Educational Testing Service (ETS), which develops and administers tests such as the Scholastic Aptitude Test (SAT) and the Graduate Record Examination (GRE), created a task force to examine

▶▶▶ **Concept Connection**

Flying Colours/Jupiter images

Brainstorming has its share of critics. Some say that it prevents the quiet people from participating, and that a group can be too easily influenced by the emotions of some of the dominant players. In response, a number of brainstorming alternatives have been developed. In fact, some companies bring in certified trainers to teach employees how to use new methods such as the Six Thinking Hats, Lateral Thinking, Nominal Group Technique, Ideation, and more.

3

PLANNING

the company's decision-making processes for new products and services. The team found that many product decisions were made without clear information about intellectual property, cycle times, or even the expected market opportunities. The team then worked with managers to create a more systematic, evidence-based decision making process, including the use of forms that required specific metrics and information about each proposal and defined standards for what constituted strong evidence that the product or service would fit with ETS strategy and likely market demand.[67]

A recent study by Erik Brynjolfsson, an economist at the Sloan School of Management at MIT, provides hard evidence that organizational decisions can be improved with the use of evidence-based decision making. Brynjolfsson and his colleagues studied 179 large companies and found that the ones that have adopted data-driven decision making achieved productivity that was 5 to 6 percent higher than could be explained by any other factors.[68]

ENGAGE IN RIGOROUS DEBATE

An important key to better decision making is to encourage a rigorous debate of the issue at hand. Good managers recognize that constructive conflict based on divergent points of view can bring a problem into focus, clarify people's ideas, stimulate creative thinking, limit the role of bias, create a broader understanding of issues and alternatives, and improve decision quality.[69] Reed Hastings, CEO of Netflix, is trying to build rigorous debate into the decision-making process to avoid another calamity such as the one the company experienced following two successive unpopular decisions: to increase the price of the service, and to split Netflix into two separate businesses—one for Internet streaming and one for DVD rentals. Customers were furious, and they showed it by cancelling their Netflix memberships in droves. When Hastings had told a friend before the decision that he was thinking of splitting the business, the friend said, "That is awful. I don't want to deal with two accounts." But Hastings didn't listen. He admits now that he was guilty of overconfidence and being out of touch with customers' thinking. By using rigorous debate about major decisions, Hastings hopes to get Netflix back on the right track—gaining rather than losing customers.[70]

Stimulating rigorous debate can be done in several ways. One way is by ensuring that the group is diverse in terms of age and gender, functional area of expertise, hierarchical level, and experience with the business. Some groups assign a **devil's advocate**, who has the role of challenging the assumptions and assertions made by the group.[71] The devil's advocate may force the group to rethink its approach to the problem and avoid reaching premature conclusions. Jeffrey McKeever, CEO of MicroAge, often plays the devil's advocate, changing his position in the middle of a debate to ensure that other executives don't just go along with his opinions.[72]

Another approach is to have group members develop as many alternatives as they can as quickly as they can.[73] It allows the team to work with multiple alternatives and encourages people to advocate ideas they might not prefer, simply to encourage debate. Still another way to encourage constructive conflict is to use a technique called **point-counterpoint**, which breaks a decision-making group into two subgroups and assigns them different, often competing, responsibilities.[74] The groups then develop and exchange proposals and discuss and debate the various options until they arrive at a common set of understandings and recommendations.

AVOID GROUPTHINK

It is important for managers to remember that some disagreement and conflict is much healthier than blind agreement. Pressures for conformity exist in almost any group, and particularly when people in a group like one another, they tend to avoid anything that might create disharmony. **Groupthink** refers to the tendency of people in groups to suppress contrary opinions.[75] When people slip into groupthink, the desire for harmony outweighs concerns over decision quality. Group members emphasize maintaining unity rather than realistically challenging problems and alternatives. People censor their personal opinions and are reluctant to criticize the opinions of others.

Author and scholar Jerry Harvey coined the related term *Abilene paradox* to illustrate the hidden pressures for conformity that can exist in groups.[76] Harvey tells the story of how members of his extended family sat sweltering on the porch in 104-degree heat in a small town about 50 miles from Abilene, Texas. When someone suggested driving to a café in Abilene, everyone went along with the idea, even though the car was not air conditioned. Everyone was miserable and returned home exhausted and irritable. Later, each person admitted that they hadn't wanted to make the trip and thought it was a ridiculous idea. They only went because they thought the others wanted to go.

KNOW WHEN TO BAIL

In a fast-paced environment, good managers encourage risk taking and learning from mistakes, but they also aren't hesitant to pull the plug on something that isn't working. Walt Disney Company managers shut down production of the remake of *The Lone Ranger* with Johnny Depp because they considered the budget too high. Although production had begun and set construction was underway, the budget had increased out of line with what managers considered reasonable. CEO Bob Iger said the company would rather skip a project entirely than commit too many resources to a risky bet.[77] Unlike Disney managers involved with *The Lone Ranger* movie, however, research has found that managers and organizations often continue to invest time and money in a solution even when there is strong evidence that it is not appropriate. This tendency is referred to as **escalating commitment**. Managers might block or distort negative information because they don't want to be responsible for a bad decision, or they might simply refuse to accept that their solution is wrong.[78] A study in Europe verified that even highly successful managers often miss or ignore warning signals because they become committed to a decision and believe that if they persevere, it will pay off.[79] As companies face increasing competition, complexity, and change, it is important that managers don't get so attached to their own ideas that they're unwilling to recognize when to move on. According to Stanford University professor Robert Sutton, the key to successful creative decision making is to "fail early, fail often, and pull the plug early."[80]

> "The most dangerous thing is to be successful. You then think every decision is the right one."
>
> — WONG WAI MING, CFO OF LENOVO

DO A POSTMORTEM

To improve decision making, managers need to reflect and learn from every decision they make. When people review the results of their decisions, they learn valuable lessons for how to do things better in the future. A technique many companies have adopted from the U.S. Army to encourage examination of the evidence and continuous learning is the **after-action review**, a disciplined procedure whereby managers invest time to review the results of decisions on a regular basis and learn from them.[81] After implementation of any significant decision, managers meet to evaluate what worked, what didn't, and how to do things better. Many problems are solved by trial and error. For example, postmortem reviews of decisions regarding attacks from roadside bombs in Iraq led soldiers to suggest implementation of an overall counterinsurgency strategy rather than relying so much on technology.[82] Numerous business organizations have adopted some form of after-action review. A similar technique emphasized by Lenovo founder Liu Chuanzhi is called *fu pan*, which means "replaying the chess board." The idea is to review every move to improve the next one. Lenovo managers are trained to apply *fu pan* in everything from a small quick review of a workday incident to a full, in-depth review of a major decision.[83] When managers get prompt feedback on decisions through after action reviews, it gives them the chance to incorporate new information and greater understanding into their thinking and decision making.

PLANNING

3

Remember This

- Most decisions within organizations are made as part of a group, and whereas managers can't always see their own biases, they can build in mechanisms to prevent bias from influencing major decisions at the organizational level.

- **Brainstorming** is a technique that uses a face-to-face group to spontaneously suggest a broad range of alternatives for making a decision.

- **Electronic brainstorming** brings people together in an interactive group over a computer network, rather than meeting face to face.

- **Evidence-based decision making** is founded on a commitment to examining potential biases, seeking and examining evidence with rigor, and making informed and intelligent decisions based on the best available facts and evidence.

- A **devil's advocate** is a person who is assigned the role of challenging the assumptions and assertions made by the group to prevent premature consensus.

- A group decision-making technique that breaks people into subgroups and assigns them to express competing points of view regarding the decision is called **point-counterpoint**.

- **Groupthink** refers to the tendency of people in groups to suppress contrary opinions in a desire for harmony.

- **Escalating commitment** refers to continuing to invest time and money in a decision despite evidence that it is failing.

- A technique adopted from the U.S. Army, the **after-action review** is a disciplined procedure whereby managers review the results of decisions to evaluate what worked, what didn't, and how to do things better.

- Managers at Lenovo apply a technique called *fu pan*, which means "replaying the chess board," reviewing every move to improve the next one.

ch9: Discussion Questions

1. You are a busy partner in a legal firm, and an experienced administrative assistant complains of continued headaches, drowsiness, dry throat, and occasional spells of fatigue and flu. She tells you she believes that the air quality in the building is bad and would like something to be done. How would you respond?

2. Managers at Gap Inc., a once-popular retail chain, are reported to have made a series of decisions that hurt the company: they expanded so rapidly that the chain lost touch with customers; they tried to copy the successful approach of rivals rather than charting their own course; they cut quality to reduce costs; they shifted from one fashion approach to another as each failed to appeal to customers, and so on. What techniques would you recommend Gap managers use to improve the quality of their decisions?

3. Explain the difference between risk and ambiguity. How might decision making differ for a risky versus an ambiguous situation?

4. Analyze three decisions you made over the past six months. Which of these were programmed and which were nonprogrammed? Which model—the classical, administrative, or political—best describes the approach you took to making each decision?

5. What opportunities and potential problems are posed by the formation of more than one coalition within an organization, each one advocating a different direction or alternative? What steps can you take as a manager to make sure that dueling coalitions result in constructive discussion rather than dissension?

6. Can you think of a bad decision from your own school or work experience or from the recent business or political news that was made in an effort to correct or justify a past decision? As a new manager, how might you resist the urge to choose a decision alternative based on the idea that it might correct or validate a previous decision?

7. Experts advise that most catastrophes in organizations result from a series of small problems or mistakes. As a new, entry-level manager, how might you apply this understanding to help your organization avoid making major mistakes?

8. List some possible advantages and disadvantages to using computer technology for managerial decision making.

9. Can intuition and evidence-based decision making co-exist as valid approaches within an organization? How might managers combine their intuition with a rational, data-driven, evidence-based approach?

10. What do you think is your dominant decision style? Is your style compatible with group techniques such as brainstorming and engaging in rigorous debate? Discuss.

ch9: Apply Your Skills: Experiential Exercise

What's Your Personal Decision Style?[84]

Read each of the following questions and circle the answer that best describes you. Think about how you typically act in a work or school situation and mark the answer that first comes to mind. There are no right or wrong answers.

1. **In performing my job or class work, I look for**
   a. Practical results *(circled)*
   b. The best solution
   c. Creative approaches or ideas
   d. Good working conditions

2. **I enjoy jobs that**
   a. Are technical and well defined
   b. Have a lot of variety
   c. Allow me to be independent and creative *(circled)*
   d. Involve working closely with others

3. **The people I most enjoy working with are**
   a. Energetic and ambitious *(circled)*
   b. Capable and organized
   c. Open to new ideas
   d. Agreeable and trusting

4. **When I have a problem, I usually**
   a. Rely on what has worked in the past
   b. Apply careful analysis *(circled)*
   c. Consider a variety of creative approaches
   d. Seek consensus with others

5. **I am especially good at**
   a. Remembering dates and facts
   b. Solving complex problems
   c. Seeing many possible solutions *(circled)*
   d. Getting along with others

6. **When I don't have much time, I**
   a. Make decisions and act quickly
   b. Follow established plans or priorities
   c. Take my time and refuse to be pressured
   d. Ask others for guidance and support *(circled)*

7. **In social situations, I generally**
   a. Talk to others *(circled)*
   b. Think about what's being discussed
   c. Observe
   d. Listen to the conversation

8. **Other people consider me**
   a. Aggressive
   b. Disciplined
   c. Creative
   d. Supportive *(circled)*

9. **What I dislike most is**
   a. Not being in control
   b. Doing boring work *(circled)*
   c. Following rules
   d. Being rejected by others

10. **The decisions I make are usually**
    a. Direct and practical *(circled)*
    b. Systematic or abstract
    c. Broad and flexible
    d. Sensitive to others' needs

Scoring and Interpretation

These questions rate your personal decision style, as described in the text and listed in Exhibit 9.5.

Count the number of *a* answers. They provide your *directive* score.   4

Count the number of *b* answers for your *analytical* score.   2

The number of *c* answers is your *conceptual* score.   2

The number of *d* answers is your *behavioral* score.   2

What is your dominant decision style? Are you surprised, or does this result reflect the style that you thought you used most often?

ch9: Apply Your Skills: Small Group Breakout

A New Approach to Making Decisions[85]

Managers are typically effective at focusing on problems and diagnosing what is wrong and how to fix it when they have to make a decision. The typical questions managers might ask themselves include: What is the problem here? What is the cause of this problem? Why is this problem happening to me? What alternatives do I have? What is the best alternative? How do I implement this alternative?

There is a novel approach to decision-making, called *outcome-directed thinking*, that some managers have learned to use. It focuses on future outcomes and possibilities rather than on the causes of the problem. People tend to feel more positive emotions, have more creative ideas, and experience more optimism about solving a problem when they focus on desired future outcomes rather than on who or what caused the problem.

Step 1. Think of a problem you have in your life right now, in which something is not what you would like it to be. It could be any problem you are having at school, home, or work that you would like to solve. Summarize the problem below in a few words:

_____

_____

_____

_____

Step 2. Now write brief answers to the following questions:

A. What outcome do I really want with respect to this problem? (Your answer equals your desired result about the problem.)

_____

_____

_____

_____

B. How will I know when I have achieved this future outcome? (What will I see, hear, and feel?)

_____

_____

_____

_____

C. What resources do I need to pursue this future outcome?

_____

_____

_____

_____

D. What is the first step I can take to achieve this outcome?

_____

_____

_____

_____

Step 3. In a group of three to five students, take turns sharing your answers to the above four questions. In addition, share what you are feeling about your desired outcome for the problem. For example, do you feel that you have created the beginning of a solution that you can implement? In addition, share whether your thinking is more creative and effective by focusing on achieving a desired outcome rather than on the cause of the problem.

ch9: Answers to Questions in Manager's Shoptalk

1. The answer is unbelievably huge: roughly 800,000,000,000,000 times the distance between the Earth and the sun. Your mind was likely anchored in the thinness of a sheet of paper, thereby leading you to dramatically underestimate the effect of doubling the thickness 100 times. Initial mental anchoring to a low or high point leads to frequent incorrect solutions. How certain did you feel about your answer? This is an example of *overconfidence*, a major cause of manager mistakes.

2. Every figure is different in some way. Figure (a) has the greatest area, (b) has the least area, (c) is the only square, (d) is the only three-sided figure, (e) is most narrow and lopsided, and (f) is least symmetrical and five-sided. Did you stop after finding one correct answer? *Failure to go beyond initial impressions and dig below the surface* often prevents managers from understanding what the real problem is or identifying the correct or best solution.

3. If you checked "yes," you felt the desire to continue investing in a previous decision even when it was failing, which is called *escalating commitment*. This is a mistake many managers make because they are *emotionally attached* to the previous decision, even one as hopeless as this inadequate drone.

4. The median estimate from students is 2,250. When the numbers are given in reverse order starting with 1×2, etc., the median estimate is 512. The correct answer is 40,320. The *order in which information is presented* makes a difference to a person's solution, and acting quickly produces an answer that is far from correct.

5. When judging people, early information has more impact than later information, called the *primacy effect*. Reversing the word sequence so that *intelligent* and *industrious* come first creates a more favorable impression. Respondents rate Robert more or less emotional depending on the order of the descriptive words. Were you guilty of rating Robert as more emotional because of being *influenced by initial impressions*?

6. Although the options are numerically equivalent, most people choose alternatives B and C. People hate losing more than they enjoy winning, and hence about 80 percent choose a sure small gain (B), and 70 percent will take more risk in the hope of avoiding a loss (C). *Taking emotions out of the process* typically leads to better decisions.

ch9: Endnotes

1. See Stephen J. Sauer, "Why Bossy Is Better for Rookie Managers," *Harvard Business Review* (May 2012): 30; and Kenneth R. Brousseau et al., "The Seasoned Executive's Decision Making Style," *Harvard Business Review* (February 2006): 110–121, for a discussion of how decision-making behavior evolves as managers progress in their careers.

2. Eric Lipton and John M. Broder, "In Rush to Assist a Solar Company, U.S. Missed Warning Signs," *The New York Times*, September 23, 2011, A1.

3. *Ibid.*

4. Danielle Sacks, "Blown Away," *Fast Company* (February 2011): 58–65, 104.

5. John Cook, "After the Writedown: How Microsoft Squandered Its $6.3B Buy of Ad Giant aQuantive," *GeekWire*, July 12, 2012, www.geekwire.com/2012/writedown-microsoft-squandered-62b-purchase-ad-giant-aquantive/ (accessed August 2, 2012).

6. Herbert A. Simon, *The New Science of Management Decision* (Englewood Cliffs, NJ: Prentice Hall, 1977), p. 47.

7. Paul J. H. Schoemaker and J. Edward Russo, "A Pyramid of Decision Approaches," *California Management Review* (Fall, 1993): 9–31.

8. Joann S. Lublin and Spencer E. Ante, "Inside Sprint's Bet on iPhone," *The Wall Street Journal*, October 4, 2011, A1.

9. Kris Maher, "At Indiana Machine Shop, Tough Calls Amid Turmoil," *The Wall Street Journal*, August 10, 2011, B1.

10. Samuel Eilon, "Structuring Unstructured Decisions," *Omega* 13 (1985): 369–377; and Max H. Bazerman, *Judgment in Managerial Decision Making* (New York: Wiley, 1986).

11. James G. March and Zur Shapira, "Managerial Perspectives on Risk and Risk Taking," *Management Science* 33 (1987): 1404–1418; and Inga Skromme Baird and Howard Thomas, "Toward a Contingency Model of Strategic Risk Taking," *Academy of Management Review* 10 (1985): 230–243.

12. Christopher Drew, "Improved Sales Help Boeing Beat Forecasts," *The New York Times*, July 28, 2011, B7; and Christopher Drew, "Deliveries Up, Boeing Beats Forecasts of Analysts," *The New York Times*, July 26, 2012, B3.

13. Reported in David Leonhardt, "This Fed Chief May Yet Get a Honeymoon," *The New York Times*, August 23, 2006.

14. Adam Davidson, "When You Wish Upon 'Ishtar': How Does the Film Industry Actually Make Money?" *The New York Times Magazine* (July 1, 2012): 16–17.

15. Michael Masuch and Perry LaPotin, "Beyond Garbage Cans: An AI Model of Organizational Choice," *Administrative Science Quarterly* 34 (1989): 38–67; and Richard L. Daft and Robert H. Lengel, "Organizational Information Requirements, Media Richness and Structural Design," *Management Science* 32 (1986): 554–571.

16. Peter C. Cairo, David L. Dotlich, and Stephen H. Rhinesmith, "Embracing Ambiguity," *The Conference Board Review* (Summer 2009): 56–61; John C. Camillus, "Strategy as a Wicked Problem," *Harvard Business Review* (May 2008): 98–106; and Richard O. Mason and Ian I. Mitroff, *Challenging Strategic Planning Assumptions* (New York: Wiley Interscience, 1981).

17. Malcolm Gay, "Preparations Advance in Plan to Breach a Levee in Missouri as a Storm Brews," *The New York Times*, May 2, 2011, A19; and Malcolm Gay, "Levee Breach Moves One Step Closer," *The New York Times*, May 1, 2011, A31.

18. "How Companies Make Good Decisions: McKinsey Global Survey Results," *The McKinsey Quarterly*, January 2009, www.mckinseyquarterly.com (accessed February 3, 2009).

19. Thomas H. Davenport and Jeanne G. Harris, "Automated Decision Making Comes of Age," *MIT Sloan Management Review* (Summer 2005): 83–89; and Stacie McCullough, "On the Front Lines," *CIO* (October 15, 1999): 78–81.

20. These examples are from Steve Lohr, "The Age of Big Data," *The New York Times*, February 12, 2012, SR1.

21. Herbert A. Simon, *The New Science of Management Decision* (New York: Harper & Row, 1960), pp. 5–6; and Amitai Etzioni, "Humble Decision Making," *Harvard Business Review* (July–August 1989): 122–126.

22. James G. March and Herbert A. Simon, *Organizations* (New York: Wiley, 1958).

23. Herbert A. Simon, *Models of Man* (New York: Wiley, 1957), pp. 196–205; and Herbert A. Simon, *Administrative Behavior*, 2d ed. (New York: Free Press, 1957).

24. Rachel Dodes, "Targeting Younger Buyers, Liz Claiborne Hits a Snag," *The Wall Street Journal*, August 16, 2010, A1.

25. Weston H. Agor, "The Logic of Intuition: How Top Executives Make Important Decisions," *Organizational Dynamics* 14 (Winter 1986): 5–18; and Herbert A. Simon, "Making Management Decisions: The Role of Intuition and Emotion," *Academy of Management Executive* 1 (1987): 57–64. For a recent review of research, see Erik Dane and Michael G. Pratt, "Exploring Intuition and Its Role in Managerial Decision Making," *Academy of Management Review* 32, no. 1 (2007): 33–54.

26. Harvey Weinstein, as told to Diane Brady, "Etc.: Hard Choices," *Bloomberg Businessweek* (January 30–February 5, 2012): 84.

27. Jaana Woiceshyn, "Lessons from 'Good Minds': How CEOs Use Intuition, Analysis, and Guiding Principles

to Make Strategic Decisions," *Long-Range Planning* 42 (2009): 298–319; Ann Hensman and Eugene Sadler-Smith, "Intuitive Decision Making in Banking and Finance," *European Management Journal* 29 (2011): 51–66; Eugene Sadler-Smith and Erella Shefy, "The Intuitive Executive: Understanding and Applying 'Gut Feel' in Decision-Making," *The Academy of Management Executive* 18, no. 4 (November 2004): 76–91.

28. See Gary Klein, *Intuition at Work: Why Developing Your Gut Instincts Will Make You Better at What You Do* (New York: Doubleday, 2002); Kurt Matzler, Franz Bailom, and Todd A. Mooradian, "Intuitive Decision Making," *MIT Sloan Management Review* 49, no. 1 (Fall 2007): 13–15; Malcolm Gladwell, *Blink: The Power of Thinking Without Thinking* (New York: Little Brown, 2005); and Sharon Begley, "Follow Your Intuition: The Unconscious You May Be the Wiser Half," *The Wall Street Journal*, August 30, 2002.

29. Benedict Carey, "Hunches Prove to Be Valuable Assets in Battle," *The New York Times*, July 28, 2009.

30. C. Chet Miller and R. Duane Ireland, "Intuition in Strategic Decision Making: Friend or Foe in the Fast-Paced 21st Century?" *Academy of Management Executive* 19, no. 1 (2005): 19–30; and Eric Bonabeau, "Don't Trust Your Gut," *Harvard Business Review* (May 2003): 116ff.

31. Sadler-Smith and Shefy, "The Intuitive Executive"; Simon, "Making Management Decisions"; and Ann Langley, "Between 'Paralysis by Analysis' and 'Extinction by Instinct,'" *Sloan Management Review* (Spring 1995): 63–76.

32. This discussion is based on Stephen Friedman and James K. Sebenius, "Organizational Transformation: The Quiet Role of Coalitional Leadership," *Ivey Business Journal* (January–February 2009): 1ff; Gerald R. Ferris, Darren C. Treadway, Pamela L. Perrewé, Robyn L. Brouer, Ceasar Douglas, and Sean Lux, "Political Skill in Organizations," *Journal of Management* (June 2007): 290–320; and William B. Stevenson, Jon L. Pierce, and Lyman W. Porter, "The Concept of 'Coalition' in Organization Theory and Research," *Academy of Management Review* 10 (1985): 256–268.

33. "How Companies Make Good Decisions."

34. Paul Schwartzman et al., "U-Va Upheaval: 18 Days of Leadership Crisis," *The Washington Post*, June 30, 2012, www.washingtonpost.com/local/education/u-va-upheaval-18-days-of-leadership-crisis/2012/06/30/gJQAVXEgEW_story.html (accessed August 6, 2012).

35. George T. Doran and Jack Gunn, "Decision Making in High-Tech Firms: Perspectives of Three Executives," *Business Horizons* (November–December 2002): 7–16.

36. James W. Fredrickson, "Effects of Decision Motive and Organizational Performance Level on Strategic Decision Processes," *Academy of Management Journal* 28 (1985): 821–843; James W. Fredrickson, "The Comprehensiveness of Strategic Decision Processes: Extension,

Observations, Future Directions," *Academy of Management Journal* 27 (1984): 445–466; James W. Dean, Jr., and Mark P. Sharfman, "Procedural Rationality in the Strategic Decision-Making Process," *Journal of Management Studies* 30, no. 4 (July 1993): 587–610; Nandini Rajagopalan, Abdul M. A. Rasheed, and Deepak K. Datta, "Strategic Decision Processes: Critical Review and Future Directions," *Journal of Management* 19, no. 2 (1993): 349–384; and Paul J. H. Schoemaker, "Strategic Decisions in Organizations: Rational and Behavioral Views," *Journal of Management Studies* 30, no. 1 (January 1993): 107–129.

37. Marjorie A. Lyles and Howard Thomas, "Strategic Problem Formulation: Biases and Assumptions Embedded in Alternative Decision-Making Models," *Journal of Management Studies* 25 (1988): 131–145; and Susan E. Jackson and Jane E. Dutton, "Discerning Threats and Opportunities," *Administrative Science Quarterly* 33 (1988): 370–387.

38. Richard L. Daft, Juhani Sormumen, and Don Parks, "Chief Executive Scanning, Environmental Characteristics, and Company Performance: An Empirical Study" (unpublished manuscript, Texas A&M University, 1988).

39. Ben Worthen, Justin Scheck, and Joann S. Lublin, "H-P Defends Hasty Whitman Hire," *The Wall Street Journal*, September 23, 2011, http://online.wsj.com/article/SB10001424053111903703604576586753827390510.html (accessed August 6, 2012).

40. Daniel Burrus and John David Mann, "Whatever Your Problem . . . That's Not Likely to Be Your Real Problem," *Leadership Excellence* (February 2011): 7–8.

41. C. Kepner and B. Tregoe, *The Rational Manager* (New York: McGraw-Hill, 1965).

42. This image and example is from Burrus and Mann, "Whatever Your Problem."

43. Paul C. Nutt, "Expanding the Search for Alternatives During Strategic Decision Making," *Academy of Management Executive* 18, no. 4 (2004): 13–28; and P. C. Nutt, "Surprising But True: Half the Decisions in Organizations Fail," *Academy of Management Executive* 13, no. 4 (1999): 75–90.

44. These examples are from Thomas H. Davenport, "The Wisdom of Your In-House Crowd," *Harvard Business Review* (May 2012): 40.

45. Peter Mayer, "A Surprisingly Simple Way to Make Better Decisions," *Executive Female* (March–April 1995): 13–14; and Ralph L. Keeney, "Creativity in Decision Making with Value-Focused Thinking," *Sloan Management Review* (Summer 1994): 33–41.

46. Kerry Capell, "Novartis: Radically Remaking Its Drug Business," *BusinessWeek* (June 22, 2009): 30–35.

47. Mark McNeilly, "Gathering Information for Strategic Decisions, Routinely," *Strategy & Leadership* 30, no. 5 (2002): 29–34.

48. *Ibid.*

49. Joe Pompeo, "A Year into the *Times*' Digital Subscription Program, Analysts and Insiders See Surprising Success, and More Challenges to Come," *Capital New York Website*, March 19, 2012, www.capitalnewyork .com/article/media/2012/03/5509293/year-times-digital-subscription-program-analysts-and-insiders-see-surp (accessed August 3, 2012); Jeremy W. Peters, "The Times's Online Pay Model Was Years in the Making," *The New York Times* (March 20, 2011), www.nytimes.com/2011/03/21/business/media/21times.html?pagewanted=all (accessed September 27, 2011); and J. W. Peters, "New York Times is Set to Begin Charging for Web Access; Chairman Concedes Plan is Risky But Says It's an 'Investment in Our Future,'" *International Herald Tribune* (March 18, 2011), 15.

50. Pompeo, "A Year into the *Times*' Digital Subscription Program."

51. Based on A. J. Rowe, J. D. Boulgaides, and M. R. McGrath, *Managerial Decision Making* (Chicago: Science Research Associates, 1984); and Alan J. Rowe and Richard O. Mason, *Managing with Style: A Guide to Understanding, Assessing, and Improving Your Decision Making* (San Francisco: Jossey-Bass, 1987).

52. Peter Baker, "How Obama's Afghanistan War Plan Came to Be," *International Herald Tribune*, December 7, 2009; and Ron Walters, "Afghanistan: The Big Decision," *The Washington Informer*, December 10–16, 2009.

53. This section is based on John S. Hammond, Ralph L. Keeney, and Howard Raiffa, *Smart Choices: A Practical Guide to Making Better Decisions* (Boston: Harvard Business School Press, 1999); Max H. Bazerman and Dolly Chugh, "Decisions Without Blinders," *Harvard Business Review* (January 2006): 88–97; J. S. Hammond, R. L. Keeney, and H. Raiffa, "The Hidden Traps in Decision Making," *Harvard Business Review* (September–October 1998): 47–58; Oren Harari, "The Thomas Lawson Syndrome," *Management Review* (February 1994): 58–61; Dan Ariely, "Q&A: Why Good CIOs Make Bad Decisions," *CIO* (May 1, 2003): 83–87; Leigh Buchanan, "How to Take Risks in a Time of Anxiety," *Inc.* (May 2003): 76–81; and Max H. Bazerman, *Judgment in Managerial Decision Making*, 5th ed. (New York: John Wiley & Sons, 2002).

54. J. B. Schmidt and R. J. Calantone, "Escalation of Commitment During New Product Development," *Journal of the Academy of Marketing Science* 30, no. 2 (2002): 103–118.

55. Norihiko Shirouzu, Phred Dvorak, Yuka Hayashi, and Andrew Morse, "Bid to 'Protect Assets' Slowed Reactor Fight," *The Wall Street Journal*, March 19, 2011, http://online.wsj.com/article/SB10001424052748704608504576207912642629904.html (accessed August 6, 2012).

56. John D. Stoll, Kevin Helliker, and Neil E. Boudette, "A Saga of Decline and Denial," *The Wall Street Journal*, June 2, 2009.

57. Mark Fenton-O'Creevy et al., "Thinking, Feeling, and Deciding: The Influence of Emotions on the Decision Making and Performance of Traders," *Journal of Organizational Behavior* 32 (2011): 1044–1061.

58. Example from Jerome Groopman, *How Doctors Think* (New York: Houghton Mifflin, 2007).

59. Dan Ariely, "The Long-Term Effects of Short-Term Emotions," *Harvard Business Review* (January–February 2010): 38.

60. Jessica Silver-Greenberg, "New Fraud Inquiry as JPMorgan's Loss Mounts," *The New York Times*, July 13, 2012, http://dealbook.nytimes.com/2012/07/13/jpmorgan-says-traders-obscured-losses-in-first-quarter/ (accessed August 7, 2012); Ben Protess et al., "In JPMorgan Chase Trading Bet, Its Confidence Yields to Loss," *The New York Times*, May 11, 2012, http://dealbook.nytimes.com/2012/05/11/in-jpmorgan-chase-trading-bet-its-confidence-yields-to-loss/ (accessed May 15, 2012); Peter Eavis and Susanne Craig, "The Bet That Blew Up for JPMorgan Chase," *The New York Times*, May 11, 2012, http://dealbook.nytimes.com/2012/05/11/the-bet-that-blew-up-for-jpmorgan-chase/ (accessed May 15, 2012); and Jessica Silver-Greenberg and Nelson D. Schwartz, "Red Flags Said to Go Unheeded by Bosses at JPMorgan," *The New York Times*, May 14, 2012, http://dealbook.nytimes.com/2012/05/14/warnings-said-to-go-unheeded-by-chase-bosses/ (accessed May 15, 2012).

61. Kathleen M. Eisenhardt, "Strategy as Strategic Decision Making," *Sloan Management Review* (Spring 1999): 65–72.

62. Daniel Kahneman, Dan Lovallo, and Olivier Sibony, "Before You Make That Big Decision," *Harvard Business Review* (June 2011): 50–60.

63. Josh Hyatt, "Where the Best—and Worst—Ideas Come From" (a brief synopsis of "Idea Generation and the Quality of the Best Idea," by Karen Girotra, Christian Terwiesch, and Karl T. Ulrich), *MIT Sloan Management Review* (Summer 2008): 11–12; and Robert C. Litchfield, "Brainstorming Reconsidered: A Goal-Based View," *Academy of Management Review* 33, no. 3 (2008): 649–668.

64. R. B. Gallupe et al., "Blocking Electronic Brainstorms," *Journal of Applied Psychology* 79 (1994): 77–86; R. B. Gallupe and W. H. Cooper, "Brainstorming Electronically," *Sloan Management Review* (Fall 1993): 27–36; and Alison Stein Wellner, "A Perfect Brainstorm," *Inc.* (October 2003): 31–35.

65. Wellner, "A Perfect Brainstorm"; Gallupe and Cooper, "Brainstorming Electronically."

66. This section is based on Jeffrey Pfeffer and Robert I. Sutton, "Evidence-Based Management," *Harvard*

Business Review (January 2006), 62–74; Rosemary Stewart, *Evidence-based Decision Making* (Radcliffe Publishing, 2002); and Joshua Klayman, Richard P. Larrick, and Chip Heath, "Organizational Repairs," *Across the Board* (February 2000), 26–31.

67. Thomas H. Davenport, "Make Better Decisions," *Harvard Business Review* (November 2009), 117–123.

68. Study by Erik Brynjolfsson, Lorin Hitt, and Heekyung Kim; results reported in Steve Lohr, "The Age of Big Data," *The New York Times*, February 12, 2012, SR1.

69. Sydney Finkelstein, "Think Again: Good Leaders, Bad Decisions," *Leadership Excellence* (June 2009): 7; "Flaws in Strategic Decision Making: McKinsey Global Survey Results," *The McKinsey Quarterly*, January 2009, www.mckinsey.com; Michael A. Roberto, "Making Difficult Decisions in Turbulent Times," *Ivey Business Journal* (May–June 2003): 1–7; Eisenhardt, "Strategy As Strategic Decision Making"; and David A. Garvin and Michael A. Roberto, "What You Don't Know About Making Decisions," *Harvard Business Review* (September 2001): 108–116.

70. Nick Wingfield and Brian Stelter, "A Juggernaut Stumbles," *The New York Times*, October 25, 2011, B1.

71. David M. Schweiger and William R. Sandberg, "The Utilization of Individual Capabilities in Group Approaches to Strategic Decision Making," *Strategic Management Journal* 10 (1989): 31–43; "Avoiding Disasters," sidebar in Paul B. Carroll and Chunka Mui, "7 Ways to Fail Big," *Harvard Business Review* (September 2008): 82–91; and "The Devil's Advocate," *Small Business Report* (December 1987): 38–41.

72. Doran and Gunn, "Decision Making in High-Tech Firms."

73. Eisenhardt, "Strategy As Strategic Decision Making."

74. Garvin and Roberto, "What You Don't Know About Making Decisions."

75. Irving L. Janis, *Groupthink: Psychological Studies of Policy Decisions and Fiascoes*, 2d ed. (Boston: Houghton Mifflin, 1982).

76. Jerry B. Harvey, "The Abilene Paradox: The Management of Agreement," *Organizational Dynamics* (Summer 1988): 17–43.

77. Ethan Smith, "Disney Hobbles 'Lone Ranger,'" *The Wall Street Journal*, August 15, 2011, B1.

78. S. Trevis Certo, Brian L. Connelly, and Laszlo Tihanyi, "Managers and Their Not-So-Rational Decisions," *Business Horizons* 51 (2008): 113–119.

79. Hans Wissema, "Driving Through Red Lights; How Warning Signals Are Missed or Ignored," *Long Range Planning* 35 (2002): 521–539.

80. *Ibid.*

81. Thomas E. Ricks, "Army Devises System to Decide What Does, Does Not, Work," *The Wall Street Journal*, May 23, 1997, A1; David W. Cannon and Jeffrey McCollum, "Army Medical Department Lessons Learned Program Marks 25th Anniversary," *Military Medicine* (November 2011): 1212–1214.

82. Peter Eisler, Blake Morrison, and Tom Vanden Brook, "Strategy That's Making Iraq Safer Was Snubbed for Years," *USA Today*, December 19, 2007.

83. Chuck Salter, "Lenovo: Protect and Attack," *Fast Company* (December 2011–January 2012): 116–121, 154–155.

84. Adapted from Rowe and Mason, *Managing with Style*, pp. 40–41.

85. This approach to decision making was developed by Robert P. Bostrom and Victoria K. Clawson of Bostrom and Associates, Columbia, Missouri, and this exercise is based on a write-up appearing in *Inside USAA*, the company newsletter of USAA (September 11, 1996), pp. 8–10; and Victoria K. Clawson and Robert P. Bostrom, "Research-Driven Facilitation Training for Computer-Supported Environments," *Group Decision and Negotiation* 5 (1996): 7–29.

ch7: Apply Your Skills: Ethical Dilemma

Inspire Learning Corporation*

When the idea first occurred to her, it seemed like such a win-win situation. Now she wasn't so sure.

Marge Brygay was a hardworking sales rep for Inspire Learning Corporation, a company intent on becoming the top educational software provider in five years. That newly adopted strategic goal translated into an ambitious, million-dollar sales target for each of Inspire's sales reps. At the beginning of the fiscal year, her share of the sales department's operational goal seemed entirely reasonable to Marge. She believed in Inspire's products. The company had developed innovative, highly regarded math, language, science, and social studies programs for the K–12 market. What set the software apart was a foundation in truly cutting-edge research. Marge had seen for herself how Inspire programs could engage whole classrooms of normally unmotivated kids; the significant rise in test scores on those increasingly important standardized tests bore out her subjective impressions.

But now, just days before the end of the year, Marge's sales were $1,000 short of her million-dollar goal. The sale that would have put her comfortably over the top fell through due to last-minute cuts in one large school system's budget. At first, she was nearly overwhelmed with frustration, but then it occurred to her that if she contributed $1,000 to Central High, the inner-city high school in her territory probably most in need of what she had for sale, they could purchase the software and put her over the top.

Her scheme would certainly benefit Central High students. Achieving her sales goal would make Inspire happy, and it wouldn't do her any harm, either professionally or financially. Making the goal would earn her a $10,000 bonus check that would come in handy when the time came to write out that first tuition check for her oldest child, who had just been accepted to a well-known, private university.

Initially, it seemed like the perfect solution all the way around. The more she thought about it, however, the more it didn't quite sit well with her conscience. Time was running out. She needed to decide what to do.

What Would You Do?

1. Donate the $1,000 to Central High, and consider the $10,000 bonus a good return on your investment.

2. Accept the fact that you didn't quite make your sales goal this year. Figure out ways to work smarter next year to increase the odds of achieving your target.

3. Don't make the donation, but investigate whether any other ways are available to help Central High raise the funds that would allow them to purchase the much-needed educational software.

*Based on Shel Horowitz, "Should Mary Buy Her Own Bonus?" *Business Ethics* (Summer 2005): 34.

ch7: Apply Your Skills: Case for Critical Analysis

Central City Museum

The recently completed new building to house the exhibits and staff of the Central City Museum was located adjacent to the campus of a private university. The new building was financed by the generosity of local donors. The university provided the land and would cover the annual operating expenses with the understanding that the museum would provide a resource for student education. The new governing board would be made up of key donors, as well as selected university administrators and faculty members.

The planning committee of the governing board hired two business students to interview various stakeholders about the future direction of the museum in its new relationship with the university. These interviews were conducted in person, and the interviewees seemed uniformly interested and eager to help. The major questions pertained to the future mission and goals of the museum. Some excerpts from the interviews are listed here:

A major donor: *I think the museum should be a major community resource. My wife and I gave money for the new building with the expectation that the museum would promote visits from the public schools in the area, and particularly serve the inner-city children who don't have access to art exhibits. We don't want the museum to be snobbish or elitist. The focus should definitely be local.*

A university administrator: *The important thing is to have lively contemporary exhibits that will attract both university students and community adults and provide new insight and dialogue about current events. We can bring attention to the museum by having an occasional controversial exhibit, such as on Islamic art, and exhibits that appeal to Hispanics and African-Americans. This approach would entail bringing in traveling exhibitions from major museums, which would save the administrative costs and overhead of producing our own exhibits.*

Head of the art history department: *The key thing is that the museum will not have the artistic resources or the financial resources to serve the community at large. We have a wonderful opportunity to integrate the museum with the academic faculty and make it a teaching institution. It can be a major resource for both undergraduate and graduate students in art education and art history. We can also work with engineering students, architecture students, and liberal arts students. This is a unique opportunity that will distinguish our art history department's teaching mission from others in the country.*

A faculty member in the art history department:
The best use of the museum's relationship with the university is to concentrate on training Ph.D.-level students in art history and to support scholarly research. I strongly urge the museum to focus on graduate education, which would increase the stature of the university nationally. Graduate students would be involved in the design of exhibits that would fit their research. Trying to make the museum popular on campus or in the community will waste our limited resources. Our Ph.D. graduates will be sought after by art history departments throughout the country.

The reason you have been given this information from the interviews is that you have been invited to interview for the position of museum director. The previous director retired with the understanding that a new director would

be hired upon the completion of fundraising and construction of the new building. You are thinking about what you would do if you took the job.

Questions

1. What goal or mission for the Central City Museum do you personally prefer? As director, would you try to implement your preferred direction? Explain.

2. How would you resolve the underlying conflicts among key stakeholders about museum direction and goals? What actions would you take?

3. Review the Manager's Shoptalk on page 211. Do you think that building a coalition and working out stakeholder differences in goal preferences is an important part of a manager's job? Why?

ch7: On the Job Video Cases

On the Job: Modern Shed: Managerial Planning and Goal Setting

Questions

1. What level of planning and goal setting does marketer Scott Pearl perform for Modern Shed?

2. Do Scott Pearl's goals meet the criteria of effective goal setting as discussed in the chapter? Explain.

3. What are some of the ways in which Scott Pearl's plans and goals benefit Modern Shed as an organization? Are there potential downsides to such planning?

ch8: Apply Your Skills: Ethical Dilemma

The Spitzer Group*

Irving Silberstein, marketing director for the Spitzer Group, a growing regional marketing and corporate communications firm, was hard at work on an exciting project. He was designing Spitzer's first word-of-mouth campaign for an important client, a manufacturer of beauty products.

In a matter of just a few years, word-of-mouth advertising campaigns morphed from a small fringe specialty to a mainstream marketing technique embraced by no less than consumer products giant Procter & Gamble (P&G). The basic idea was simple, really. You harnessed the power of existing social networks to sell your products and services. The place to start, Irving knew, was to take a close look at how P&G's in-house unit, Vocalpoint, conducted its highly successful campaigns, both for its own products and those of its clients.

Because women were key purchasers of P&G consumer products, Vocalpoint focused on recruiting mothers with extensive social networks, participants known internally by the somewhat awkward term *connectors*. The Vocalpoint Web page took care to emphasize that participants were members of an "exclusive" community of moms

who exerted significant influence on P&G and other major companies. Vocalpoint not only sent the women new product samples and solicited their opinions, but it also carefully tailored its pitch to the group's interests and preoccupations so the women would want to tell their friends about a product. For example, it described a new dishwashing foam that was so much fun to use, kids would actually volunteer to clean up the kitchen (music to any mother's ears). P&G then furnished the mothers with coupons to hand out if they wished. It was all voluntary, P&G pointed out. According to a company press release issued shortly before Vocalpoint went national in early 2006, members "are never obligated to do or say anything."

One of the things Vocalpoint members weren't obligated to say, Irving knew, was that the women were essentially unpaid participants in a P&G-sponsored marketing program. When asked about the policy, Vocalpoint CEO Steve Reed replied, "We have a deeply held belief you don't tell the consumer what to say." However, skeptical observers speculated that what the company really feared was that the women's credibility might be affected adversely if their Vocalpoint affiliation were known. Nondisclosure really amounted to lying for financial gain, Vocalpoint's critics argued, and furthermore, the whole campaign shamelessly exploited personal relationships for commercial purposes. Others thought the critics were making mountains out of molehills. P&G wasn't forbidding participants from disclosing their ties to Vocalpoint and P&G. And the fact that they weren't paid meant the women had no vested interest in endorsing the products.

So, as Irving designs the word-of-mouth campaign for his agency's client, just how far should he emulate the company that even its detractors acknowledge is a master of the technique?

*Based on Robert Berner, "I Sold It Through the Grapevine," *BusinessWeek* (May 29, 2006): 32–34; "Savvy Moms Share Maternal Instincts; Vocalpoint Offers Online Moms the Opportunity to be a Valuable Resource to Their Communities," *Business Wire* (December 6, 2005); and Steve Hall, "Word of Mouth Marketing: To Tell or Not to Tell," *AdRants.com*, May 2006, www.adrants.com/2006/05/word-of-mouth-marketing-to-tell-or-not-to.php (accessed August 23, 2010).

What Would You Do?

1. Don't require Spitzer "connectors" to reveal their affiliation with the corporate word-of-mouth marketing campaign. They don't have to recommend a product they don't believe in.

2. Require that Spitzer participants reveal their ties to the corporate marketing program right up front before they make a recommendation.

3. Instruct Spitzer participants to reveal their participation in the corporate marketing program only if directly asked by the person they are talking to about the client's products.

ch8: Apply Your Skills: Case for Critical Analysis

Costco: A Different Path*

In 2010, Costco's reputation for rock-bottom pricing and razor-thin profit margins helped the company maintain its position as the nation's fourth-largest retailer and the number one membership warehouse retailer, with 572 stores (425 in the United States), 142,000 employees, and 55 million members. Sales reached $76 billion, up 9.1 percent, reflecting, in part, a unique corporate culture that doesn't just pay lip service to the value of its employees, but maintains a reputation for honoring that value.

CEO James Sinegal believes the secret to Costco's success lies in the many ways the company overturns conventional wisdom. Despite Wall Street criticism, the company is devoted to a well-compensated workforce and scoffs at the notion of sacrificing the well-being of its employees for the sake of profits. Hourly wages of $17 smash those of competitors ($10–$11.50 per hour). Costco's competitors attempt to improve profits and shareholder earnings by keeping wages and benefits low. As a result, Costco enjoys the reputation for a loyal, highly productive workforce, and store openings attract thousands of quality applicants.

Sinegal is a no-nonsense CEO whose annual salary ($550,000) is a fraction of the traditional pay for large corporate executives and dramatizes an organizational culture that attempts to minimize disparity between management and workers. Luxury corporate offices are out of the question. It is the "in the trenches together" mind-set that defines Costco's corporate culture, contributing to a level of mutual support, teamwork, empowerment, and rapid response that can be activated for confronting any situation. A dramatic example occurred when employees instantly created a Costco emergency brigade, armed with forklifts and fire extinguishers, whose members organized themselves and rushed to offer first aid and rescue trapped passengers following the wreck of a commuter train behind a California warehouse store.

Whether attracting employees or customers, the need for public relations or advertising is nonexistent at Costco. Sinegal told a reporter for ABC News that the company doesn't spend a dime on advertising, with over 140,000 enthusiastic employee ambassadors spreading the word about Costco to friends and neighbors.

Equal care has been given to organizational design. Sinegal's belief in a "flat, fast, and flexible" organization encourages delegation of great authority to local warehouse managers who have the freedom and authority to make quick, independent decisions that suit the local needs of customers and employees. Moreover, Costco's new store location efforts seek "fit" between the organization and the community that it serves. Typical suburban locations emphasize the bulk shopping needs of families and small businesses, and Costco has extended its own private label, Kirkland Signature. The private label provides additional savings of up to 20 percent off of products produced by top manufacturers, such as tires made by Michelin specifically for the Kirkland label.

The rapid expansion from having one store in Seattle to becoming America's warehouse club leader and global retailer has come with its share of growing pains, as the organization attempts to adapt to its various environments. In the face of rapid growth, Costco management has come up against a myriad of new problems ranging from complaints of a lack of notification for management job openings to persistent complaints of a glass ceiling, providing few opportunities for the advancement of women within the organization. In response, the company has instituted online job postings, automated recruiting, the use of an outside vendor for hiring, and a recommitment to equity in promotion.

International issues are often more complex and often run up against local needs and perceptions. For example, efforts to expand into Cuernavaca, Mexico, were viewed from the company perspective as a win-win situation, opening a new market and also providing jobs and high-quality, low-priced items for area shoppers. When the site of a dilapidated casino became available, Costco moved quickly, but suddenly found itself facing charges of cultural insensitivity in Mexico. Accusations in Cuernavaca that Costco was going to build a parking lot on land with significant artistic and national heritage led to negotiations under which the company set aside millions of dollars to preserve the landscape, restore murals, and work alongside city planners and representatives of the Mexican Institute of Fine Arts and Literature in the construction of a new, state-of-the-art cultural center and museum.

Indications are bright for Costco's future, but questions loom on the horizon. Everyone—from Wall Street pundits to customers, shareholders, and employees—wonders how the organization might change after Sinegal steps down. Will future leaders be willing to maintain the modest levels of compensation for top management and maintain the

company's above-average wages and benefits for employees? And how will increased globalization alter the strong corporate culture?

Questions

1. Have you shopped at a Costco store? How do you think a Costco store compares to Sam's Club, Target, or Walmart stores? What do you value most when selecting a low-priced store at which to shop?

2. With respect to competitive strategy, identify and evaluate Costco's target customers, its core competence, and how it builds synergy and delivers value.

3. Would you rate Costco's competitive strategy as pursuing differentiation, cost-leadership, focus, or some combination? Why?

*Based on Richard L. Daft, "Costco Wholesale Corporation, Parts One–Six," *Management*, 8th ed. (Mason, OH: South-Western, 2008). *Table of Contents, Item 7—Management's Discussion and Analysis of Financial Conditions, Costco 2010 Annual Report*; Wayne F. Cascio, "The High Cost of Low Wages," *Harvard Business Review* (December 2006); and Alan B. Goldberg and Bill Ritter, "Costco CEO Finds Pro-Worker Means Profitability," *ABC News 20/20*, August 2, 2006.

ch8: On the Job Video Cases

On the Job: Theo Chocolate:
Strategy Formulation and Execution

Questions

1. Evaluate Theo's new strategy in light of the company's strengths, weaknesses, opportunities, and threats.

2. Using the BCG matrix, explain Theo's decision to offer a classic line of chocolate bars after having limited success with Fantasy Flavor chocolates.

3. Which of the three competitive strategies—differentiation, cost leadership, or focus—do you think is right for Theo Chocolate? Explain.

ch9: Apply Your Skills: Ethical Dilemma

The No-Show Consultant*

Jeffrey Moses was facing one of the toughest decisions of his short career as a manager with International Consulting. Andrew Carpenter, one of his best consultants, was clearly in trouble, and his problems were affecting his work. International Consulting designs, installs, and implements complex back-office software systems for companies all over the world. About half the consultants work out of the main office, while the rest, including Carpenter, work primarily from home.

This Monday morning, Moses had gotten an irate call from a major New York client saying Carpenter never showed up at the company's headquarters, where the client had been expecting his new computer system to go live for the first time. In calling around to other customers on the East Coast trying to locate the missing consultant, Moses heard other stories. Carpenter had also missed a few other appointments—all on Monday mornings—but no one had felt the need to report it because he had called to reschedule. In addition, he practically came to blows with an employee who challenged him about the capabilities of the new

system, and he inexplicably walked out of one customer's office in the middle of the day, without a word to anyone. Another client reported that the last time he saw Carpenter, he appeared to have a serious hangover. Most of the clients liked Carpenter, but they were concerned that his behavior was increasingly erratic. One client suggested that she would prefer to work with someone else. As for the major New York customer, he preferred that Andrew rather than a new consultant finish the project, but he also demanded that International eat half the $250,000 consultant's fee.

After Moses finally located Carpenter by calling his next-door neighbor, Carpenter confessed that he'd had a "lost weekend" and been too drunk to get on the plane. He then told Moses that his wife had left and taken their two-year-old son with her. He admitted that he had been drinking a little more than usual lately, but insisted that he was getting himself under control and promised no more problems. "I'm really not an alcoholic or anything," he said. "I've just been upset about Brenda leaving, and I let it get out of hand this weekend." Moses told Carpenter that if he would get to New York and complete the project, all would be forgiven.

Now, however, he wondered whether he should really just let things slide. Moses talked to Carpenter's team leader about the situation and was told that the leader was aware of his recent problems but thought everything would smooth itself over. "Consultants with his knowledge, level of skill, and willingness to travel are hard to find. He's well liked among all the customers; he'll get his act together." However, when Moses discussed the problem with Carolyn Walter, vice president of operations, she argued that Carpenter should be dismissed. "You're under no obligation to keep him just because you said you would," she pointed out. "This was a major screw-up, and it's perfectly legal to fire someone for absenteeism. Your calls to customers should make it clear to you that this situation was not a onetime thing. Get rid of him now before things get worse. If you think eating half that $250,000 fee hurts now, just think what could happen if this behavior continues."

What Would You Do?

1. Give Carpenter a month's notice and terminate. He's known as a good consultant, so he probably won't have any trouble finding a new job, and you'll avoid any further problems associated with his emotional difficulties and his possible alcohol problem.

2. Let it slide. Missing the New York appointment is Carpenter's first big mistake. He says he is getting things under control, and you believe that he should be given a chance to get himself back on track.

3. Let Carpenter know that you care about what he's going through, but insist that he take a short paid leave and get counseling to deal with his emotional difficulties and evaluate the seriousness of his problems with alcohol. If the alcohol abuse continues, require him to attend a treatment program or find another job.

*Based on information in Jeffrey L. Seglin, "The Savior Complex," *Inc.* (February 1999): 67–69; and Nora Johnson, "'He's Been Beating Me,' She Confided," *Business Ethics* (Summer 2001): 21.

ch9: Apply Your Skills: Case for Critical Analysis

The Office

Krista Acklen was the "golden girl" of metropolitan government in a large Midwestern city. The top graduate of a local high school, she studied in France and interned at *Vogue* in Paris before returning to the States to get an MBA, and she landed a position with a top New York PR firm. She knew *everyone*, and chatting with or "doing lunch" with the rich and famous was a normal day for Acklen.

The only child of a single mom, Acklen dropped it all and willingly returned to her Midwestern hometown when her mother's health declined suddenly. She had barely settled in and established home care for her mother when the mayor's office contacted her with a job proposal. Would Acklen consider a position developing and directing a public arts program for the city? She enthusiastically accepted the job. With her winning connections, drive, and abilities, she quickly expanded her mission to develop a range of arts programs. Donations and grant money poured into programs under her established nonprofit organization developed to support city parks. Headquarters for Acklen and her staff was a comfortable unused third-floor space in the city library that used to hold books and magazines that were now stored digitally.

Then John Mitchell, director of parks and recreation, summoned her to a meeting "to learn of a decision I have made that will affect your group." Acklen was curious to find out what was going on. Knowing that budget factors recently forced reduction in staff and office space throughout city government, and aware of the importance of dealing carefully with public opinion, as well as the feelings of employees and other stakeholders, Acklen felt that she was prepared for any decision Mitchell might have reached.

She tried to get comfortable in the chair across from Mitchell, who seemed ill at ease. Avoiding small talk, Mitchell said that he intentionally did not discuss the decision in advance because he believed Acklen would object.

He would not accept her objections anyway, he indicated, so the decision was final.

"What is the decision?" asked Acklen.

"The mayor wants half of your group's office space for the Greenways project," Mitchell replied, "and I see no alternative except for you to agree. The mayor's idea makes sense, and you must go along."

Acklen felt fury rising in her chest as she stared at Mitchell while thinking, "This people-pleasing, brown-nosing jerk. He will do anything to win the mayor's favor."

The Greenways project, directed by Lisa Todd, had developed a number of beautiful areas throughout the city. In recent years, Greenways had received the bulk of new money and attention from the federal government, and Todd's staff had grown with the additional funding and development projects.

As Acklen regained her composure, she shot back at Mitchell, "Not consulting me on this is unacceptable. I should be part of any decision affecting my staff and program. I could have helped plan a solution that worked for everyone." Mitchell started to speak, but Acklen cut him off. "You have a responsibility to my group as well as to the mayor. I think you are giving us the shaft as an easy way to please her."

The two argued a while longer, but Mitchell wouldn't budge. Finally, Acklen said, "John, since this was your decision, you should be the one to tell my people. You better come over soon before the word gets out."

"No," Mitchell said, "you are their immediate boss. You have to tell them. That's your job. Where is your team spirit, anyway?"

Acklen returned to her office, seething, and vented about the problem to Joanne Franklin, her most senior employee. "Oh no," Joanne moaned. "We really need all this space. Our program is growing, too."

Acklen agreed, but she explained Mitchell's support of the suggestion from the mayor's office to make additional office space available to Lisa Todd and her staff. Joanne started brainstorming. "I suppose we could pair up in the offices."

Acklen shook her head. "We *are* team players. But John Mitchell and the mayor need to know that this was not handled in a way that shows respect for our employees." After a pause, she continued, "I'm too frazzled to think about it anymore today. Let's talk about this tomorrow."

Questions

1. What mistakes do you think John Mitchell made with the way he solved the problem of limited office space? Explain.

2. What approach would you have used if you were Mitchell? Why?

3. What are Krista Acklen's options for responding to Mitchell's decision? What should she do now? Why?

ch9: On the Job Video Cases

On the Job: Plant Fantasies: Managerial Decision Making

Questions

1. Did Plant Fantasies owner Teresa Carleo follow the rational decision-making process to launch Plant Fantasies? Explain.

2. List an example of a programmed decision at Plant Fantasies. Identify a nonprogrammed decision at Plant Fantasies.

3. How might managers at Plant Fantasies conduct the final evaluation stage of the decision-making process when installing a new garden for a client?

pt3: Integrative Case

Companies Form Strategic Partnership to Build America's Natural Gas Highway

Consumers face a series of important questions when shopping for a new vehicle: Electric or hybrid? Regular or diesel? Powerful or fuel-efficient? Sporty or economical? Yet for eco-minded consumers who seek the ultimate in green motoring, the decision to purchase a vehicle often comes down to one simple question: Where do I fill it up?

Where to refuel is a perplexing issue for buyers of alternative-fuel vehicles. This is because cutting-edge green vehicles lack a nationwide fueling infrastructure. The United States has more than 100,000 standard gas stations, yet few are equipped to fuel vehicles that run on electricity, natural gas, or biofuel. For most consumers, that's a deal breaker.

Despite the push for cleaner autos, today's car buyers find themselves in a Catch-22: an ecologically responsible vehicle might fit in with their needs and desires, but if there is no place to fill up, they can't drive it, so why consider buying one? A similar dilemma exists for fleet purchasers, automakers, and gas station chains: why purchase or even manufacture alternative-fuel vehicles if there aren't any filling stations? On the other hand, why build filling stations if no one is purchasing or making alternative-fuel vehicles?

Fortunately for consumers and the environment, Clean Energy Fuels Corp. and Navistar International have a plan to solve this chicken-and-egg dilemma. In 2012, the California alternative fuels provider and the Illinois semi-trailer truck giant announced a strategic partnership to build America's Natural Gas Highway, a first-of-its-kind network of natural gas fueling stations across the United States. Slated for completion by the end of 2013, America's Natural Gas Highway will feature 150 liquefied natural gas (LNG) filling stations in major metropolitan areas across the country—San Diego, Los Angeles, and Las Vegas out west; Houston, San Antonio, and Dallas in the Texas Triangle; New York in the east; and major cities in the Midwest and South. Well-placed stations on in-between routes will tie the whole network together, resulting in a coast-to-coast refueling infrastructure for natural gas vehicles.

Top-level planners behind America's Natural Gas Highway say their goal is to offer transport companies a package deal made up of eco-friendly fleets, inexpensive fuel, and reliable fueling stations. "Navistar and Clean Energy have come up with a breakthrough program that offers customers a quicker payback on their investment, plus added fuel cost savings from day one of operation," says Navistar CEO Dan Ustian. "Together our companies will demonstrate how a natural-gas-integrated vehicle offering the right distribution and fueling solution can be integrated into a fleet's operations to reduce costs and drive efficiencies."

For a natural gas highway to work, effective collaboration must occur between a truck maker, a fuel supplier, a truck stop chain, and a natural gas driller. Navistar and Clean Energy have the first two bases covered: Navistar will sell its best-in-class LNG truck fleets to shippers, along with a mandatory five-year fuel-purchase contract through Clean Energy. News releases indicate that two other companies are included in the plan. Pilot Flying J Travel Centers, the largest network of truck and travel stops, is providing service locations where trucks can refuel. Likewise, Chesapeake Energy, the No. 2 natural gas driller in the United States, is investing $150 million towards the initial rollout. So Navistar sells natural gas trucks to shippers, Clean Energy supplies the fuel, Pilot Flying J provides the fueling stations, and Chesapeake drills natural gas and provides investment capital.

The plan sounds good on paper, but can it work? Clean Energy CEO Andrew Littlefair says America's Natural Gas Highway is already well underway. "Clean Energy has already engaged over 100 shippers, private fleets, and for-hire carriers that have shared their operations to qualify for the economic opportunity of operating natural gas trucks. This has helped us in turn plan the first phase of the natural gas fueling highway," Littlefair says. Clean Energy's chief marketing guru, Jim Harger, adds that the financial advantages of the plan are such that transport businesses simply can't refuse. "You get the same lease cost of a diesel truck and get fuel savings too," Harger says.

There are many good reasons to think that America's Natural Gas Highway will succeed. However, executives at Navistar and Clean Energy say their plan will work because natural gas is the energy of the future and requires no government subsidies. "We remain committed to provide natural gas fuel for transportation because it has genuinely proven to be the cleaner, cheaper, domestic alternative fuel choice," says Andrew Littlefair. Navistar's chief agrees, adding that natural gas is both economically sustainable and good for the environment.

"The program will allow the industry to transition to natural gas-powered vehicles without relying on government handouts," Ustian says. "This is going to work far differently than any other program in this field for alternative fuels. It can stand on its own and stand very tall, and that's why it's going to be successful."

Integrative Case Questions

1. Why do businesses form strategic partnerships? Does the creation of America's Natural Gas Highway require such a partnership? Why or why not?

2. What opportunities in the external environment may have led Navistar and Clean Energy to formulate their plan for America's Natural Gas Highway?

3. What threats in the external environment could cause this comprehensive natural gas strategy to fail? What can managers do to help ensure that the plan is executed successfully?

Sources: Based on Clean Energy Fuels Corp., *America's Natural Gas Highway: The Clean Energy Solution* (Seal Beach, CA: Clean Energy, 2012), http://cleanenergyfuels.com/pdf/CE-OS.ANGH.011212 .ff.pdf (accessed July 10, 2012); John Stodder, "Natural Gas Vehicles Face Chicken-and-Egg Syndrome," *The Daily Reporter*, May 9, 2012, http://dailyreporter.com/2012/05/09/natural-gas-vehicles-face-chicken-and-egg-syndrome/ (accessed July 10, 2012); "Navistar International and Clean Energy Fuels Team on Natural Gas Trucks," *Fleets & Fuels*, February 2, 2012, www.fleetsandfuels.com/fuels/ngvs/2012/02/navistar-clean-energy-team-on-natural-gas-trucks-2012/ (accessed July 10, 2012); James Menzies, "Navistar Partnership with Clean Energy Takes Sting out of Cost of NG-Powered Trucks," *Truck News*, February 3, 2012, www.trucknews.com/news/navistar-partnership-with-clean-energy-takes-sting-out-of-cost-of-ng-powered-trucks/1000876051/ (accessed July 12, 2012); Dave Hurst, "Clean Energy Fuels and Navistar Agreement: More than Marketing Hype?" Pike Research, May 30, 2012, www.pikeresearch.com/blog/clean-energy-fuels-and-navistar-agreement-more-than-marketing-hype (accessed July 12, 2012); Clean Energy Fuels, "Clean Energy Unveils Backbone Network for America's Natural Gas Highway," press release, January 12, 2012, www.businesswire.com/news/home/20120112005432/en/Clean-Energy-Unveils-Backbone-Network-America's-Natural (accessed July 10, 2012); "Clean Energy Unveils Network Plan for Natural Gas Highway," Trucker News Service, January 16, 2012, www.thetrucker.com/News/Stories/2012/1/16/CleanEnergyunveilsnetworkplanfornaturalgashighway.aspx (accessed July 12, 2012).

Designing Adaptive Organizations

Fuse/Jupiter Images

Learning Outcomes

After studying this chapter, you should be able to:

1. Discuss the fundamental characteristics of organizing, including concepts such as work specialization, chain of command, span of management, and centralization versus decentralization.

2. Describe functional and divisional approaches to structure.

3. Explain the matrix approach to structure and its application to both domestic and international organizations.

4. Describe the contemporary team and virtual network structures and why they are being adopted by organizations.

5. Explain why organizations need coordination across departments and hierarchical levels, and describe mechanisms for achieving coordination.

6. Identify how structure can be used to achieve an organization's strategic goals.

7. Define production technology and explain how it influences organization structure.

1 INTRODUCTION

2 ENVIRONMENT

3 PLANNING

4 ORGANIZING

5 LEADING

6 CONTROLLING

What Are Your Leadership Beliefs?[1]

http:
See It
Online
www.

INSTRUCTIONS: The fit between a new manager and the organization is often based on personal beliefs about the role of leaders. Things work best when organization design matches a new manager's beliefs about his or her leadership role.

Think about the extent to which each statement reflects your beliefs about a leader's role in an organization. Mark as Mostly True the four statements that are *most* true for you, and mark as Mostly False the four that are *least* true for you.

	Mostly True	Mostly False
1. A leader should take charge of the group or organization.	_____	_____
2. The major tasks of a leader are to make and communicate decisions.	_____	_____
3. Group and organization members should be loyal to designated leaders.	_____	_____
4. The responsibility for taking risks lies with the leaders.	_____	_____
5. Leaders should foster discussions among members about the future.	_____	_____
6. Successful leaders make everyone's learning their highest priority.	_____	_____
7. An organization needs to be always changing the way it does things to adapt to a changing world.	_____	_____
8. Everyone in an organization should be responsible for accomplishing organizational goals.	_____	_____

SCORING AND INTERPRETATION: Each question pertains to one of two subscales of *leadership beliefs*. Questions 1–4 reflect *position-based* leadership beliefs. This is the belief that the most competent and loyal people are placed in positions of leadership where they assume responsibility and authority for the group or organization. Questions 5–8 reflect *nonhierarchical* leadership beliefs. This belief is that the group or organization faces a complex system of adaptive challenges, and leaders see their job as facilitating the flow of information among members and their full engagement to respond to those challenges. The subscale for which you checked more items Mostly True may reveal your personal beliefs about position-based versus nonhierarchical leadership.

Position-based beliefs typically work for managers in a traditional vertical hierarchy or mechanistic organization. Nonhierarchical beliefs typically work for managers engaged with horizontal organizing or organic organizations, such as managing teams, projects, and networks.

Valve Software Corporation, which makes some of the most popular video and digital games in the world, has more than 300 employees, provides free food and massage rooms, and offers on-site laundry service. But it is what the company *doesn't* have that's really interesting: no bosses. Valve's unique organization structure caused a minor media blitz after someone posted the employee handbook online in the spring of 2012, but Valve has been functioning smoothly without bosses since it was founded in 1996. Founders Gabe Newell and Mike Harrington, former Microsoft employees, wanted to create a flat, fast organization that allowed employees maximum flexibility to be creative. The company prizes "fast and flexible" so much that desks are on wheels. Employees recruit colleagues to work on a project they think is worthwhile, and people wheel their desks around to form team work areas as they choose. It sounds like a dream for employees, but many people don't adapt to the "no structure structure" and leave for more traditional jobs.[2]

Could you work in a company with no bosses, no permanent offices, and no clearly defined structure? Valve is unusual, but many companies are flattening their hierarchies and cutting out layers of management to improve efficiency and be more flexible. Some people thrive in less hierarchical organizations, whereas others have difficulty without a clearly defined vertical structure. New managers in particular are typically more comfortable and more effective working in an organization system that is compatible with their leadership beliefs.

In your career as a manager, you will have to understand and learn to work within a variety of structural configurations. All organizations wrestle with the question of structural design, and reorganization often is necessary to reflect a new strategy, changing market conditions, or innovative technology. In recent years, many companies have realigned departmental groupings, chains of command, and horizontal coordination mechanisms to attain new strategic goals or to cope with a turbulent environment. Managers at Hachette Filipacchi Media U.S., which owns magazines such as *Elle* and *Woman's Day*, created brand officer positions to increase horizontal coordination across departments and make sure everyone from editorial to event marketing is in the information loop. Michael Dell created a separate division at his company that will focus specifically on products such as mobile phones and other portable devices, the fastest-growing part of the computer industry. At Sony, executives added a new position of chief information security officer (CISO) to the hierarchy after hackers accessed millions of customer files on the supposedly secure Sony network. The company had to shut down the PlayStation Network temporarily to figure out what went wrong, leading to lost revenue, investigation expenses, and the loss of customer loyalty and goodwill. The newly created position of CISO, said a Sony spokesman, "will keep a dynamic focus on the latest security threats and advanced defenses . . . to uphold our unwavering commitment to protect our customers' data."[3] Each of these organizations is using fundamental concepts of organizing.

Organizing is the deployment of organizational resources to achieve strategic goals. The deployment of resources is reflected in the organization's division of labor into specific departments and jobs, formal lines of authority, and mechanisms for coordinating diverse organization tasks.

Organizing is important because it follows strategy—the topic of Part 3 of this book. Strategy defines *what* to do; organizing defines *how* to do it. Structure is a powerful tool for reaching strategic goals, and a strategy's success often is determined by its fit with organizational structure. Part 4 of this book explains the variety of organizing principles and concepts used by managers. This chapter covers fundamental concepts that apply to all organizations and departments, including organizing the vertical structure and using mechanisms for horizontal coordination. Chapter 11 discusses how organizations can be structured to facilitate innovation and change. Chapters 12 and 13 consider how to use human resources to the best advantage within the organization's structure.

Organizing the Vertical Structure

The organizing process leads to the creation of organization structure, which defines how tasks are divided and resources deployed. **Organization structure** is defined as (1) the set of formal tasks assigned to individuals and departments; (2) formal reporting relationships, including lines of authority, decision responsibility, number of hierarchical levels, and span of managers' control; and (3) the design of systems to ensure effective coordination of employees across departments.[4] Ensuring coordination across departments is just as critical as defining the departments to begin with. Without effective coordination systems, no structure is complete.

The set of formal tasks and formal reporting relationships provides a framework for vertical control of the organization. The characteristics of vertical structure are portrayed in the **organization chart**, which is the visual representation of an organization's structure.

A sample organization chart for a water bottling plant is illustrated in Exhibit 10.1. The plant has four major departments—accounting, human resources, production, and

EXHIBIT 10.1

Organization Chart for a
Water Bottling Plant

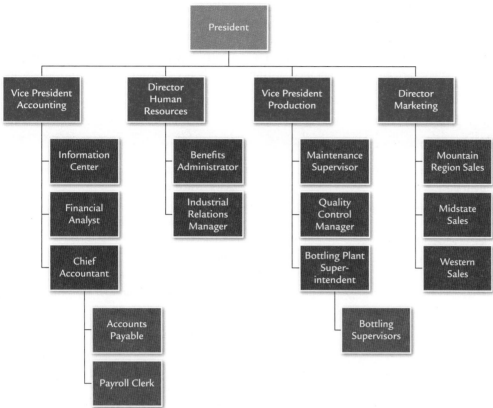

marketing. The organization chart delineates the chain of command, indicates departmental tasks and how they fit together, and provides order and logic for the organization. Every employee has an appointed task, line of authority, and decision responsibility. The following sections discuss several important features of vertical structure in more detail.

WORK SPECIALIZATION

Organizations perform a wide variety of tasks. A fundamental principle is that work can be performed more efficiently if employees are allowed to specialize.[5] **Work specialization**, sometimes called *division of labor*, is the degree to which organizational tasks are subdivided into separate jobs. Work specialization in Exhibit 10.1 is illustrated by the separation of production tasks into bottling, quality control, and maintenance. Employees within each department perform only the tasks relevant to their specialized function. When organizations face new strategic issues, managers often create new positions or departments to deal with them, just as Sony created a new position of chief information security officer (CISO), described earlier in the chapter. Many corporations have created a new position for chief diversity officer because of the importance today of creating an environment where minorities and women can flourish. Even the position of chief information officer (CIO) was practically unheard of even a decade ago, but almost every government agency, nonprofit organization, and business firm has a CIO today. In 2009, President Barack Obama appointed Vivek Kundra as the first CIO for the U.S. government.[6]

When work specialization is extensive, employees specialize in a single task. Jobs tend to be small, but they can be performed efficiently. Work specialization is readily visible on an automobile assembly line, where each employee performs the same task over and over again. It would not be efficient to have a single employee build the entire automobile, or even perform a large number of unrelated jobs.

4

ORGANIZING

Despite the apparent advantages of specialization, many organizations are moving away from this principle. With too much specialization, employees are isolated and do only a single, boring job. In addition, too much specialization creates separation and hinders the coordination that is essential for organizations to be effective. Many companies are implementing teams and other mechanisms that enhance coordination and provide greater challenge for employees.

Remember This

- Managers in every organization face the question about how to organize for maximum efficiency and effectiveness.
- **Organizing** refers to the deployment of organizational resources to achieve strategic goals.
- Sony created a new position of chief information security officer (CISO) after hackers accessed customer data on the company's computer network.
- **Organization structure** is defined as the framework in which the organization defines how tasks are divided, resources are deployed, and departments are coordinated.

- An **organization chart** is the visual representation of an organization's structure.
- Fundamental characteristics of vertical organization structure include work specialization, chain of command, span of management, and centralization and decentralization.
- **Work specialization**, sometimes called *division of labor*, is the degree to which organizational tasks are subdivided into individual jobs.

CHAIN OF COMMAND

The **chain of command** is an unbroken line of authority that links all employees in an organization and shows who reports to whom. It is associated with two underlying principles. *Unity of command* means that each employee is held accountable to only one supervisor. The *scalar principle* refers to a clearly defined line of authority in the organization that includes all employees. Authority and responsibility for different tasks should be distinct. All individuals in the organization should know to whom they report as well as the successive management levels all the way to the top. For example, at Sony, the new CISO reports to the chief information officer, who reports to the chief transformation officer, who in turn reports to the CEO.[7] In Exhibit 10.1, the payroll clerk reports to the chief accountant, who in turn reports to the vice president, who in turn reports to the company president.

Concept Connection ◀◀◀

AP Photo/ M.Lakshman

Cognizant Technology Solutions Corporation, a U.S.-based outsourcing firm, has an unusual **chain of command** referred to as "two in a box." Originally, project managers supervised company staff in India while living in the United States, where most customers were located. Because spanning that many time zones was difficult, chief operating officer Francisco D'Souza (now CEO, pictured second from right) implemented a solution: assign two managers to each project—one in India and one at the client's site. Each is equally responsible for the project's success. The model works because it enhances the company's customer responsiveness, even though it violates the principle of **unity of command**.

Authority, Responsibility, and Delegation

The chain of command illustrates the authority structure of the organization. **Authority** is the formal and legitimate right of a manager to make decisions, issue orders, and allocate resources to achieve organizationally desired outcomes. Authority is distinguished by three characteristics:[8]

1. *Authority is vested in organizational positions, not people.* Managers have authority because of the positions they hold, and other people in the same positions would have the same authority.

2. *Authority flows down the vertical hierarchy.* Positions at the top of the hierarchy are vested with more formal authority than are positions at the bottom.

3. *Authority is accepted by subordinates.* Although authority flows from the top down, subordinates comply because they believe that managers have a legitimate right to issue orders. The *acceptance theory of authority* argues that a manager has authority only if subordinates choose to accept his or her commands. If subordinates refuse to obey because the order is outside their zone of acceptance, a manager's authority disappears.[9]

Responsibility is the flip side of the authority coin. **Responsibility** is the duty to perform the task or activity as assigned. Typically, managers are assigned authority commensurate with responsibility. When managers have responsibility for task outcomes but little authority, the job is possible but difficult. They rely on persuasion and luck. When managers have authority exceeding responsibility, they may become tyrants, using authority to achieve frivolous outcomes.[10]

Accountability is the mechanism through which authority and responsibility are brought into alignment. **Accountability** means that the people with authority and responsibility are subject to reporting and justifying task outcomes to those above them in the chain of command.[11] For organizations to function well, everyone needs to know what they are accountable for and accept the responsibility and authority for performing it. At Apple, the late Steve Jobs instituted an accountability mindset throughout the organization. The term *DRI*, meaning "directly responsible individual," typically appears on meeting agendas and so forth, so that everyone knows who is responsible for what.[12]

Another important concept related to authority is delegation.[13] **Delegation** is the process managers use to transfer authority and responsibility to positions below them in the hierarchy. Most organizations today encourage managers to delegate authority to the lowest possible level to provide maximum flexibility to meet customer needs and adapt to shifts in the environment. Consider how top managers at Meetup.com revived the company by pushing authority and responsibility down to the front lines.

"I think the most difficult transition for anybody from being a worker bee to a manager is this issue of delegation. What do you give up? How can you have the team do what you would do yourself without you doing it?"

— TACHI YAMADA, PRESIDENT OF THE BILL & MELINDA GATES FOUNDATION'S GLOBAL HEALTH PROGRAM

4

ORGANIZING

Innovative Way

Meetup.com

Meetup.com is the company known for organizing Howard Dean's presidential campaign in 2004. As an organization that helps other people create organizations, Meetup has been instrumental in setting up local groups for everything from protests to gardening clubs. When Meetup.com went through a period of rapid expansion, top executives implemented a command-and-control structure as a way to regulate and monitor performance. The company even had a "review board" that worked with managers to oversee what employees could and could not do. The trouble was, "productivity went through the floor," says chief technology officer Greg Whalin. One day, a senior manager pulled CEO Scott Heiferman into a conference room and showed him a list of complaints, including *We aren't a creative company*, and, *I hate the organization chart.*

Heiferman decided to go in the opposite direction and push authority and responsibility down to his employees. Now, Meetup's employees have almost total freedom to select the projects they work on and how and when they accomplish them. With the authority and responsibility for setting priorities and making decisions, employee creativity soared. In addition, many people began working harder than ever before. "We got more done in six weeks than in six months last year," said Heiferman.[14]

New Manager Self-Test

Delegation

Instructions: How do you share tasks with others at school or work, such as when performing group assignments or club activities? Answer whether each of the following statements is Mostly True or Mostly False for you.

		Mostly True	Mostly False
1.	I completely trust other people to do good work.	_____	_____
2.	I give assignments by patiently explaining the rationale and desired outcomes.	_____	_____
3.	I genuinely believe that others can do a job as well as I can.	_____	_____
4.	I leave people alone after I delegate a task to them.	_____	_____
5.	I am better at managing the work of others than actually doing it.	_____	_____
6.	I often end up doing tasks myself.	_____	_____
7.	I get upset when someone doesn't do the task correctly.	_____	_____
8.	I really enjoy doing task details to get them just right.	_____	_____
9.	I try to do the work better than anyone else.	_____	_____
10.	I set very high standards for myself.	_____	_____

Scoring and Interpretation: The questions above represent two related aspects of delegating work—delegation and perfectionism. Give yourself one point for each Mostly True answer:

Delegation, sum questions 1–5: _____

Perfectionism, sum questions 6–10: _____

Delegation and perfectionism are opposite sides of the same coin. Your score for delegation reflects your attitude toward entrusting others with work for which you are responsible. Your score for perfectionism indicates your desire to be in personal control, which prevents delegation. Perfectionists want to do everything themselves so it is just exactly the way they want it. A lower score for delegation (0–2) and a higher score for perfectionism (4–5) probably means that delegation of authority will not come easily for you. When managers cannot delegate tasks to individuals and teams, an organization will struggle to decentralize authority and engage people in coordination. How does your delegation score compare to your perfectionism score? What would you need to change about yourself to be a better delegator?

Take a Moment

As a manager, how effective will you be at delegating? Get an idea by completing the New Manager Self-Test above.

As illustrated by this example, delegating decision making to lower-level managers and employees can be highly motivating and improve speed, flexibility, and creativity. However, many managers find delegation difficult. When managers can't delegate, they undermine the role of their subordinates and prevent people from doing their jobs effectively.

Line and Staff Authority

An important distinction in many organizations is between line authority and staff authority, reflecting whether managers work in line or staff departments in the organization's structure. *Line departments* perform tasks that reflect the organization's primary goal and mission. In a software company, line departments make and sell the product. In an Internet-based company, line departments would be those that develop and

Green **Power**

A New Department

SAP created its first-ever chief sustainability officer position in 2009, and Peter Graf, formerly a computer scientist, leads a global team that oversees sustainability initiatives. To change SAP, Graf and his team focused on the top of the hierarchy, educating SAP's board of directors as their first target. Regular e-mails and newsletters to board members defined terminology and answered questions (such as, "What does 'offset' mean in regard to sustainability?"). In addition, Graf and his team reminded board members of incidents within SAP's own corporate history, such as the decision by a major German customer to stop ordering SAP software because SAP had no sustainability code of conduct.

By the time SAP's board held its next official meeting, members were fully engaged in adopting sustainability policies, speaking with an informed, unified voice as they assisted the new department's efforts to change the sustainability thinking of employees, suppliers, and customers.

Source: Michael S. Hopkins, "How SAP Made the Business Case for Sustainability," *MIT Sloan Management Review* 52, no. 1 (Fall 2010): 69–72.

manage online offerings and sales. *Staff departments* include all those that provide specialized skills in support of line departments. Staff departments have an advisory relationship with line departments and typically include marketing, labor relations, research, accounting, and human resources.

Line authority means that people in management positions have formal authority to direct and control immediate subordinates. **Staff authority** is narrower and includes the right to advise, recommend, and counsel in the staff specialists' area of expertise. Staff authority is a communication relationship; staff specialists advise managers in technical areas. For example, the finance department of a manufacturing firm would have staff authority to coordinate with line departments about which accounting forms to use to facilitate equipment purchases and standardize payroll services. BP's new safety department, created in the wake of the 2010 BP-Transocean Deepwater Horizon oil rig explosion in the Gulf of Mexico that killed 11 crew members and set off an environmental disaster, advises managers in line departments regarding risk management, agreements with contractors, and other safety-related issues. Safety staff specialists are embedded throughout the company, including on exploration projects and in refineries. Unlike many staff specialists, BP's safety unit has broad power to challenge line managers' decisions if it considers them too risky.[15]

To understand the importance of the chain of command and clear lines of authority, responsibility, and delegation, consider the Deepwater Horizon oil rig explosion. Activities were so loosely organized that no one seemed to know who was in charge or what their level of authority and responsibility was. When the explosion occurred, confusion reigned. Twenty-three-year-old Andrea Fleytas issued a mayday (distress signal) over the radio when she realized no one else had done so, but she was chastised for overstepping her authority. One manager says he didn't call for help because he wasn't sure he had authorization to do so. Still another said he tried to call to shore but was told that the order needed to come from someone else. Crew members knew the emergency shutdown needed to be triggered, but there was confusion over who had the authority to give the OK. As fire spread, several minutes passed before people got directions to evacuate. Again, an alarmed Fleytas turned on the public address system and announced that the crew was abandoning the rig. "The scene was very chaotic," said worker Carlos Ramos. "There was no chain of command. Nobody in charge." In the aftermath of the explosion and oil spill, several federal agencies are also on the hot seat because of loose oversight and confusion over responsibility that led to delays and disagreements that prolonged the suffering of local communities.[16]

4

ORGANIZING

Take a Moment

Go to the Ethical Dilemma for Chapter 10 on page 442 that pertains to issues of authority, responsibility, and delegation.

SPAN OF MANAGEMENT

The **span of management** is the number of employees reporting to a supervisor. Sometimes called the *span of control*, this characteristic of structure determines how closely a supervisor can monitor subordinates. Traditional views of organization design recommended a span of management of about 7 to 10 subordinates per manager. However, many lean organizations today have spans of management as high as 30, 40, and even higher. At PepsiCo, Inc.'s Gamesa cookie operation in Mexico, for instance, employees are trained to keep production running smoothly and are rewarded for quality, teamwork, and productivity. Teams are so productive and efficient that Gamesa factories operate with around 56 subordinates per manager.[17] Research over the past 40 or so years shows that span of management varies widely and that several factors influence the span.[18] Generally, when supervisors must be closely involved with subordinates, the span should be small, and when supervisors need little involvement with subordinates, it can be large. The following list describes the factors that are associated with less supervisor involvement and thus larger spans of control:

- Work performed by subordinates is stable and routine.
- Subordinates perform similar work tasks.
- Subordinates are concentrated in a single location.
- Subordinates are highly trained and need little direction in performing tasks.
- Rules and procedures defining task activities are available.
- Support systems and personnel are available for the manager.
- Little time is required in nonsupervisory activities, such as coordination with other departments or planning.
- Managers' personal preferences and styles favor a large span.

The average span of control used in an organization determines whether the structure is tall or flat. A **tall structure** has an overall narrow span and more hierarchical levels. A **flat structure** has a wide span, is horizontally dispersed, and has fewer hierarchical levels.

Having too many hierarchical levels and narrow spans of control is a common structural problem for organizations. In a survey conducted for The Conference Board, 72 percent of managers surveyed said they believed their organizations had too many levels of management.[19] The result may be that routine decisions are made too high in the organization, which pulls higher-level executives away from important, long-range strategic issues and limits the creativity, innovativeness, and accountability of lower-level managers.[20] The trend in recent years has been toward wider spans of control as a way to facilitate delegation.[21] One recent study found that the span of management for CEOs has doubled over the past two decades, rising from about 5 to around 10 managers reporting directly to the top executive, with the span of management for those managers also increasing. At the same time, the types of positions in the top team are shifting, with the position of chief operating officer (COO) declining and positions such as CIO or chief marketing officer being added to the top team.[22] Exhibit 10.2 illustrates how an international metals company was reorganized. The multilevel set of managers shown in panel *a* was replaced with 10 operating managers and 9 staff specialists reporting directly to the CEO, as shown in panel *b*. The CEO welcomed this wide span of 19 management subordinates because it fit his style, his management team was top quality and needed little supervision, and they were all located on the same floor of an office building.

CENTRALIZATION AND DECENTRALIZATION

Centralization and decentralization pertain to the hierarchical level at which decisions are made. **Centralization** means that decision authority is located near the top of the organization. With **decentralization**, decision authority is pushed downward to lower organization

EXHIBIT 10.2   Reorganization to Increase Span of Management for President of an International Metals Company

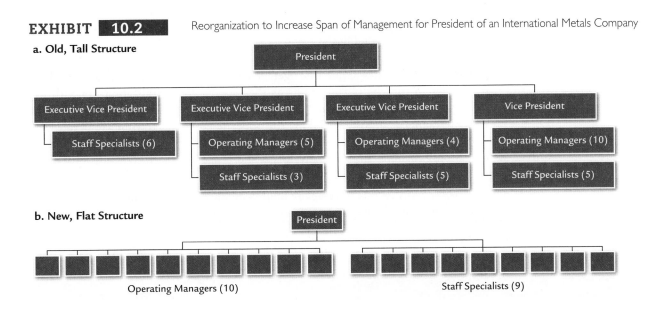

a. Old, Tall Structure

b. New, Flat Structure

levels. Organizations may have to experiment to find the correct hierarchical level at which to make decisions. For example, most large school systems are highly centralized. However, a study by William Ouchi found that three large urban school systems that shifted to a decentralized structure, giving school principals and teachers more control over staffing, scheduling, and teaching methods and materials, performed better and more efficiently than centralized systems of similar size.[23] Government leaders in Great Britain hope the same thing will happen when they decentralize the country's National Health Service (NHS). The system is undergoing the most radical restructuring since it was founded in 1948, with a key part of the plan to shift control of the multibillion annual health care budget to doctors at the local level. Leaders believe decentralization will cut costs, simplify and streamline procedures, and reduce inefficiency by "putting power in the hands of patients and clinicians."[24]

In the United States and Canada, the trend over the past 30 years has been toward greater decentralization of organizations. Decentralization is believed to relieve the burden on top managers, make greater use of employees' skills and abilities, ensure that decisions are made close to the action by well-informed people, and permit more rapid response to external changes. Stanley McChrystal, former commander of U.S. and NATO forces in Afghanistan, once said, "I learned . . . that any complex task is best approached by flattening hierarchies. It gets everybody feeling like they're in the inner circle, so that they develop a sense of ownership."[25] Nearly a decade of fighting a complex, decentralized enemy has pushed the U.S. armed forces to decentralize as well. The U.S. Army recently implemented its Starfish Program to train leaders to think, act, and operate in a decentralized fashion. The program is based on ideas in Ori Brafman and Rod Beckstrom's book *The Starfish and the Spider*, which makes the case that decentralized "starfish" are less vulnerable to attack than centralized "spiders."[26]

However, not every organization should decentralize all decisions. Within many companies, there is often a "tug of war between centralization and decentralization" as top executives want to centralize some operations to eliminate duplication, while business division managers want to maintain decentralized control.[27] Managers should diagnose the organizational situation and select the decision-making level that will best meet the organization's needs. Factors that typically influence centralization versus decentralization are as follows:

- *Greater change and uncertainty in the environment are usually associated with decentralization.* A good example of how decentralization can help cope with rapid change and uncertainty occurred following Hurricane Katrina. Mississippi Power restored power in just 12 days, thanks largely to a decentralized management system that empowered people at the electrical substations to make rapid, on-the-spot decisions.[28]

- *The amount of centralization or decentralization should fit the firm's strategy.* Top executives at the Walt Disney Company adopt a decentralization approach when they buy small creative companies such as Pixar Animation Studios and Marvel Entertainment. Disney CEO Bob Iger believes in allowing the managers of these companies to run the organizations as they see fit. Decentralization fits with the strategy of allowing creative units to respond quickly and innovatively to changes in the entertainment industry.[29] Taking the opposite approach, to compete better with Kohl's and Macy's, managers at JCPenney centralized product planning and buying operations, enabling the company to get more fashionable merchandise to stores quickly and at lower prices.[30]

- *In times of crisis or risk of company failure, authority may be centralized at the top.* When Honda could not get agreement among divisions about new car models, President Nobuhiko Kawamoto made the decision himself.[31]

Remember This

- The **chain of command** is an unbroken line of authority that links all individuals in the organization and specifies who reports to whom.
- **Authority** is the formal and legitimate right of a manager to make decisions, issue orders, and allocate resources to achieve outcomes desired by the organization.
- **Responsibility** is the flip side of the authority coin; it refers to the duty to perform the task or activity that one has been assigned.
- **Accountability** means that people with authority and responsibility are subject to reporting and justifying task outcomes to those above them in the chain of command.
- When managers transfer authority and responsibility to positions below them in the hierarchy, it is called **delegation**.
- Managers may have **line authority**, which refers to the formal power to direct and control immediate

- subordinates, or **staff authority**, which refers to the right to advise, counsel, and recommend in the manager's area of expertise.
- **Span of management**, sometimes called *span of control*, refers to the number of employees reporting to a supervisor.
- A **tall structure** is characterized by an overall narrow span of management and a relatively large number of hierarchical levels.
- A **flat structure** is characterized by an overall broad span of management and relatively few hierarchical levels.
- The trend is toward broader spans of management and greater decentralization.
- **Decentralization** means that decision authority is pushed down to lower organization levels.
- **Centralization** means that decision authority is located near top organization levels.

Departmentalization

Another fundamental characteristic of organization structure is **departmentalization**, which is the basis for grouping positions into departments and departments into the total organization. Managers make choices about how to use the chain of command to group people together to perform their work. Five approaches to structural design reflect different uses of the chain of command in departmentalization, as illustrated in Exhibit 10.3. The functional, divisional, and matrix are traditional approaches that rely on the chain of command to define departmental groupings and reporting relationships along the hierarchy. Two innovative approaches are the use of teams and virtual networks, which have emerged to meet changing organizational needs in a turbulent global environment.

The basic difference among structures illustrated in Exhibit 10.3 is the way in which employees are departmentalized and to whom they report.[32] Each structural approach is described in detail in the following sections.

EXHIBIT 10.3   Five Approaches to Structural Design

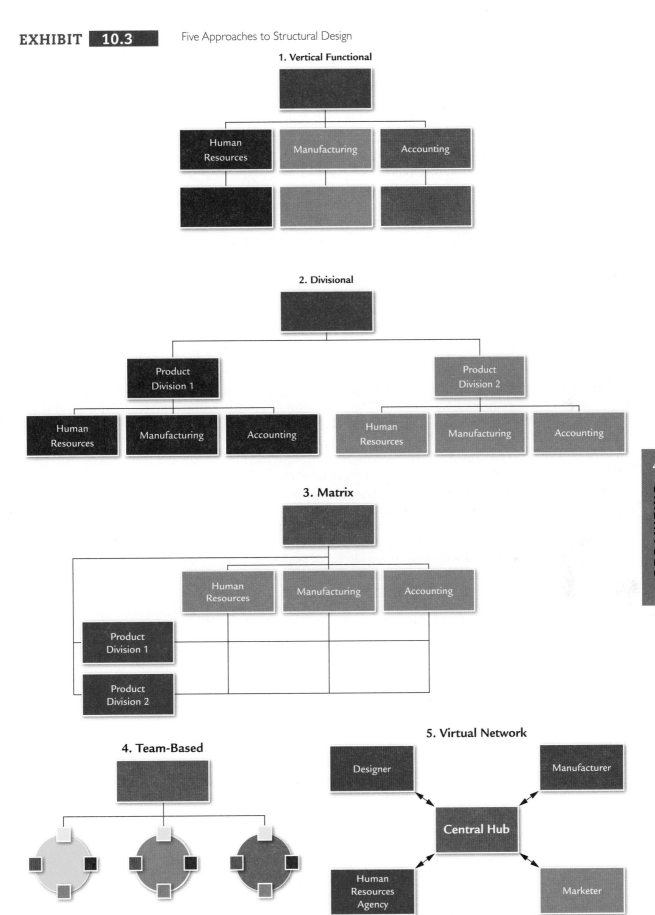

4

ORGANIZING

VERTICAL FUNCTIONAL APPROACH

What It Is

In a **functional structure**, also called a *U-form (unitary structure)*, activities are grouped together by common function from the bottom to the top of the organization.[33] The functional structure groups positions into departments based on similar skills, expertise, work activities, and resource use. A functional structure can be thought of as departmentalization by organizational resources because each type of functional activity—accounting, human resources, engineering, and manufacturing—represents specific resources for performing the organization's task. People, facilities, and other resources representing a common function are grouped into a single department. One example is Blue Bell Creameries, which relies on in-depth expertise in its various functional departments to produce high-quality ice cream for a limited regional market. The quality control department, for example, tests all incoming ingredients and ensures that only the best go into Blue Bell's ice cream. Quality inspectors also test outgoing products and, because of their years of experience, can detect the slightest deviation from expected quality. Blue Bell also has functional departments such as sales, production, maintenance, distribution, research and development, and finance.[34]

How It Works

Refer to Exhibit 10.1 on page 307 for an example of a functional structure. The major departments under the president are groupings of similar expertise and resources, such as accounting, human resources, production, and marketing. Each of the functional departments is concerned with the organization as a whole. The marketing department is responsible for all sales and marketing, for example, and the accounting department handles financial issues for the entire company.

The functional structure is a strong vertical design. Information flows up and down the vertical hierarchy, and the chain of command converges at the top of the organization. In a functional structure, people within a department communicate primarily with others in the same department to coordinate work and accomplish tasks or implement decisions that are passed down the hierarchy. Managers and employees are compatible because of similar training and expertise. Typically, rules and procedures govern the duties and responsibilities of each employee, and employees at lower hierarchical levels accept the right of those higher in the hierarchy to make decisions and issue orders.

Functional Advantages and Disadvantages

Grouping employees by common task permits economies of scale and efficient resource use. For example, at American Airlines, all information technology people work in the same large department. They have the expertise and skills to handle almost any issue related to information technology for the organization. Large, functionally based departments enhance the development of in-depth skills because people work on a variety of related problems and are associated with other experts within their own department. Because the chain of command converges at the top, the functional structure also offers a way to centralize decision making and provide unified direction from top managers. The primary disadvantages reflect barriers that exist across departments. Because people are separated into distinct departments, communication and coordination across functions are often poor, causing a slow response to environmental changes. Innovation and change require involvement of several departments. Another problem is that decisions involving more than one department may pile up at the top of the organization and be delayed.

DIVISIONAL APPROACH

What It Is

In contrast to the functional approach, in which people are grouped by common skills and resources, the **divisional structure** occurs when departments are grouped together based on similar organizational outputs. With a divisional structure, also called an *M-form (multidivisional)* or a *decentralized form*, separate divisions can be organized with responsibility for individual products, services, product groups, major projects or programs, divisions, businesses, or profit centers.[35] The divisional structure is also sometimes called a *product structure, program structure,* or *self-contained unit structure*. Each of these terms means essentially the same thing: Diverse departments are brought together to produce a single organizational output, whether it is a product, a program, or service to a single customer.

Most large corporations have separate divisions that perform different tasks, use different technologies, or serve different customers. When a huge organization produces products for different markets, the divisional structure works because each division is an autonomous business. For example, Walmart uses divisions for Wal-Mart Stores, Sam's Club (U.S.), and International Stores. Each of these large divisions is further subdivided into smaller geographical divisions to better serve customers in different regions.[36]

▶▶▶ **Concept Connection**

A maker of products used for the prevention, diagnosis, and treatment of diseases, the health science company Nordion Inc. recently split into two new business units: one called Targeted Therapies and the other Specialty Isotopes. Nordion's CEO Steve West explained that the new **divisional structure** is strategically designed to "take into account the unique product life cycles and the needs of our customers in each of our businesses." Based in Ottawa, Ontario, Canada, Nordion does business in 60 countries around the world.

How It Works

Functional and divisional structures are illustrated in Exhibit 10.4. In a divisional structure, divisions are created as self-contained units, with separate functional departments for each division. For example, in Exhibit 10.4, each functional department resource needed to produce the product is assigned to each division. Whereas in a functional structure, all R&D engineers are grouped together and work on all products, in a divisional structure, separate R&D departments are created within each division. Each department is smaller and focuses on a single product line or customer segment. Departments are duplicated across product lines.

4

ORGANIZING

EXHIBIT 10.4 Functional versus Divisional Structures

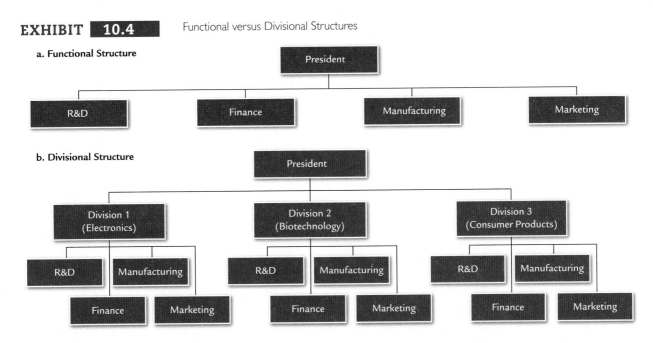

a. Functional Structure

President
- R&D
- Finance
- Manufacturing
- Marketing

b. Divisional Structure

President
- Division 1 (Electronics)
  - R&D
  - Manufacturing
  - Finance
  - Marketing
- Division 2 (Biotechnology)
  - R&D
  - Manufacturing
  - Finance
  - Marketing
- Division 3 (Consumer Products)
  - R&D
  - Manufacturing
  - Finance
  - Marketing

EXHIBIT   10.5   Geographic-Based Global Organization Structure

```
                           ┌─────────────────────────┐
                           │ Chief Executive Officer │
                           └────────────┬────────────┘
                                        │
                              ┌─────────┴─────────┐
                              │  Corporate Staff  │
                              └─────────┬─────────┘
          ┌─────────────────┬──────────┴──────────┬─────────────────┐
 ┌────────┴────────┐ ┌──────┴──────┐     ┌────────┴────────┐ ┌──────┴──────┐
 │  Western U.S.   │ │ Eastern U.S.│     │ Latin American  │ │    Asian    │
 │    Division     │ │   Division  │     │    Division     │ │   Division  │
 └─────────────────┘ └─────────────┘     └─────────────────┘ └─────────────┘
```

The primary difference between divisional and functional structures is that in a divisional structure, the chain of command from each function converges lower in the hierarchy. In a divisional structure, differences of opinion among R&D, marketing, manufacturing, and finance would be resolved at the divisional level rather than by the president. Thus, the divisional structure encourages decentralization. Decision making is pushed down at least one level in the hierarchy, freeing the president and other top managers for strategic planning.

Geographic- or Customer-Based Divisions

An alternative for assigning divisional responsibility is to group company activities by geographic region or customer group. For example, the Internal Revenue Service (IRS) shifted to a structure focused on four distinct taxpayer (customer) groups: individuals, small businesses, corporations, and nonprofit or government agencies.[37] A global geographic structure is illustrated in Exhibit 10.5. In a geographic-based structure, all functions in a specific country or region report to the same division manager. The structure focuses company activities on local market conditions. Competitive advantage may come from the production or sale of a product or service adapted to a given country or region. Walt Disney Company CEO Bob Iger reorganized the Disney Channel into geographic divisions because what appeals to people in different countries varies. Studio executives in Burbank, California, were miffed at the reorganization, but it has paid off. Iger learned that the Number 1 program on Italy's Disney Channel was one he had never heard of—"Il Mondo di Patty," an inexpensive, telenovela-style show about an Argentine girl. "It's important that Disney's products are presented in ways that are culturally relevant," Iger said about the geographic reorganization.[38] Large nonprofit organizations such as the National Council of YMCAs, Habitat for Humanity International, and the Girl Scouts of the USA also frequently use a type of geographical structure, with a central headquarters and semi-autonomous local units.[39]

Divisional Advantages and Disadvantages

By dividing employees and resources along divisional lines, the organization will be flexible and responsive to change because each unit is small and tuned in to its environment. By having employees working on a single product line, the concern for customers' needs is high. Coordination across functional departments is better because employees are grouped together in a single location and committed to one product line. Great coordination exists within divisions; however, coordination *across* divisions is often poor. Problems occurred at Hewlett-Packard (HP), for example, when autonomous divisions went in opposite directions. The software produced in one division did not fit the hardware produced in another. Thus, the divisional structure was realigned to establish adequate coordination across divisions. Another major disadvantage is duplication of resources and the high cost of running separate divisions. Instead of a single research department in which all research people use a single facility, each division may have its own research facility. The organization loses efficiency and economies of scale. In addition, the small size of departments within each division may result in a lack of technical specialization, expertise, and training.

MATRIX APPROACH

What It Is

The **matrix approach** combines aspects of both functional and divisional structures simultaneously, in the same part of the organization. The matrix structure evolved as a way to improve horizontal coordination and information sharing.[40] One unique feature of the matrix is that it has dual lines of authority. In Exhibit 10.6, the functional hierarchy of authority runs vertically, and the divisional hierarchy of authority runs horizontally. The vertical structure provides traditional control within functional departments, and the horizontal structure provides coordination across departments. The U.S. operation of Starbucks, for example, uses geographic divisions for Western/Pacific, Northwest/Mountain, Southeast/Plains, and Northeast/Atlantic. Functional departments including finance, marketing, and so forth are centralized and operate as their own vertical units, as well as supporting the horizontal divisions.[41] The matrix structure therefore supports a formal chain of command for both functional (vertical) and divisional (horizontal) relationships. As a result of this dual structure, some employees actually report to two supervisors simultaneously.

How It Works

The dual lines of authority make the matrix unique. To see how the matrix works, consider the global matrix structure illustrated in Exhibit 10.7. The two lines of authority are

EXHIBIT 10.6 Dual-Authority Structure in a Matrix Organization

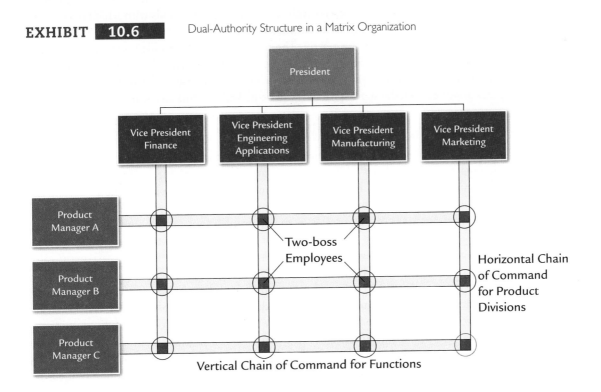

EXHIBIT 10.7   Global Matrix Structure

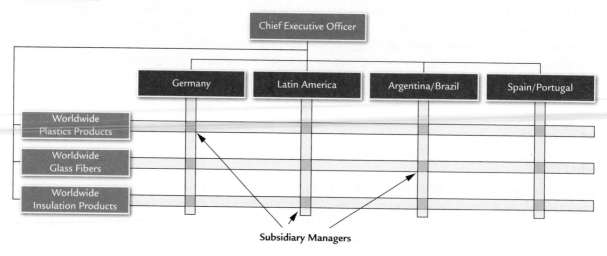

geographic and product. The geographic boss in Germany coordinates all subsidiaries in Germany, and the plastics products boss coordinates the manufacturing and sale of plastics products around the world. Managers of local subsidiary companies in Germany would report to two superiors, both the country boss and the product boss. The dual authority structure violates the unity-of-command concept described earlier in this chapter, but that is necessary to give equal emphasis to both functional and divisional lines of authority. Dual lines of authority can be confusing, but after managers learn to use this structure, the matrix provides excellent coordination simultaneously for each geographic region and each product line.

The success of the matrix structure depends on the abilities of people in key matrix roles. **Two-boss employees**, those who report to two supervisors simultaneously, must resolve conflicting demands from the matrix bosses. They must work with senior managers to reach joint decisions. They need excellent human relations skills with which to confront managers and resolve conflicts. The **matrix boss** is the product or functional boss, who is responsible for one side of the matrix. The top leader is responsible for the entire matrix. The **top leader** oversees both the product and functional chains of command. His or her responsibility is to maintain a power balance between the two sides of the matrix. If disputes arise between them, the problem will be kicked upstairs to the top leader.

Matrix Advantages and Disadvantages

The matrix can be highly effective in a complex, rapidly changing environment in which the organization needs to be flexible, innovative, and adaptable.[42] The conflict and frequent meetings generated by the matrix allow new issues to be raised and resolved. The matrix structure makes efficient use of human resources because specialists can be transferred from one division to another. A major problem with the matrix is the confusion and frustration caused by the dual chain of command.[43] Matrix bosses and two-boss employees have difficulty with the dual reporting relationships. The matrix structure also can generate high conflict because it pits divisional against functional goals in a domestic structure, or product line versus country goals in a global structure. Rivalry between the two sides of the matrix can be exceedingly difficult for two-boss employees to manage. This problem leads to the third disadvantage: time lost to meetings and discussions devoted to resolving this conflict. Often the matrix structure leads to more discussion than action because different goals and points of view are being addressed. Managers may spend a great deal of time coordinating meetings and assignments, which takes time away from core work activities.

Remember This

- **Departmentalization** is the basis for grouping individual positions into departments and departments into the total organization.
- Three traditional approaches to departmentalization are functional, divisional, and matrix.
- A **functional structure** groups employees into departments based on similar skills, tasks, and use of resources.
- The **divisional structure** groups employees and departments based on similar organizational outputs (products or services), such that each division has a mix of functional skills and tasks.
- An alternative approach to divisional structure is to group employees and departments based on geographic region or customer group.

- The Disney Channel is structured into geographic divisions to better address the interests of children and teens in different parts of the world.
- The **matrix approach** uses both functional and divisional chains of command simultaneously, in the same part of the organization.
- In a matrix structure, some employees, called **two-boss employees**, report to two supervisors simultaneously.
- A **matrix boss** is a functional or product supervisor responsible for one side of the matrix.
- In a matrix structure, the **top leader** oversees both the product and the functional chains of command and is responsible for the entire matrix.
- Each approach to departmentalization has distinct advantages and disadvantages.

TEAM APPROACH

What It Is

Probably the most widespread trend in departmentalization in recent years has been the implementation of team concepts. The vertical chain of command is a powerful means of control, but passing all decisions up the hierarchy takes too long and keeps responsibility at the top. The team approach gives managers a way to delegate authority, push responsibility to lower levels, and be more flexible and responsive in a complex and competitive global environment. Chapter 18 will discuss teams in detail.

How It Works

One approach to using teams in organizations is through **cross-functional teams**, which consist of employees from various functional departments who are responsible to meet as a team and resolve mutual problems. For example, at Total Attorneys, a Chicago-based company that provides software and services to small law firms, CEO Ed Scanlan realized that the functional structure, which broke projects down into sequential stages that moved from one department to another, was slowing things down so much that clients' needs had sometimes changed by the time the product was completed. He solved the problem by creating small, cross-functional teams to increase horizontal coordination. Now, designers, coders, and quality-assurance testers work closely together on each project.[44] Cross-functional teams can provide needed horizontal coordination to complement an existing divisional or functional structure. A frequent use of cross-functional teams is for change projects, such as new product or service innovation. Team members typically still report to their functional departments, but they also report to the team, one member of whom may be the leader.

The second approach is to use **permanent teams**, groups of employees who are organized in a way similar to a formal department. Each team brings together employees from all functional areas focused on a specific task or project, such as parts supply and logistics for an automobile plant. Emphasis is on horizontal communication and information sharing because representatives from all functions are coordinating their work and skills to complete a specific organizational task. Authority is pushed down to lower levels, and front-line employees are often given the freedom to make decisions and take action on their

4 ORGANIZING

Concept Connection ◄◄◄

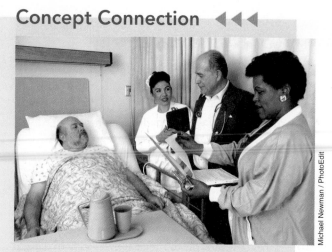

Michael Newman / PhotoEdit

Hospitals and other health care providers face a great need for **coordination** because medical care needs to be integrated. For instance, collaborative care, like this **cross-functional team** of a nurse, doctor, and dietitian, helps patients with chronic illnesses require fewer emergency department visits. Rush University Medical Center in Chicago started its Virtual Integrated Practice (VIP) project to give physicians in private practice access to teams of physicians, dieticians, pharmacists, and social workers. VIP replicates the collaboration that can occur in a hospital setting by enabling members to share information via e-mail, phone, and fax.

own. Team members may share or rotate team leadership. With a **team-based structure**, the entire organization is made up of horizontal teams that coordinate their work and work directly with customers to accomplish the organization's goals. At Whole Foods Market, a team structure is considered a major contributor to the company's success. Each Whole Foods store is made up of eight or so self-directed teams that oversee departments such as fresh produce, prepared foods, dairy, or checkout. Teams are responsible for all key operating decisions, such as product selection, pricing, ordering, hiring, and in-store promotions, and they are accountable for their performance.[45]

Team Advantages and Disadvantages

The team approach breaks down barriers across departments and improves coordination and cooperation. Team members know one another's problems and compromise rather than blindly pursue their own goals. The team concept also enables the organization to adapt more quickly to customer requests and environmental changes and speeds decision making because decisions need not go to the top of the hierarchy for approval. Another big advantage is the morale boost. Employees are typically enthusiastic about their involvement in bigger projects rather than narrow departmental tasks. At video games company Ubisoft, for example, each studio is set up so that teams of employees and managers work collaboratively to develop new games. Employees don't make a lot of money, but they're motivated by the freedom they have to propose new ideas and put them into action.[46]

Yet the team approach has disadvantages as well. Employees may be enthusiastic about team participation, but they may also experience conflicts and dual loyalties. A cross-functional team may make different work demands on members than do their department managers, and members who participate in more than one team must resolve these conflicts. A large amount of time is devoted to meetings, thus increasing coordination time. Unless the organization truly needs teams to coordinate complex projects and adapt to the environment, it will lose production efficiency with them. Finally, the team approach may cause too much decentralization. Senior department managers who traditionally made decisions might feel left out when a team moves ahead on its own. Team members often do not see the big picture of the corporation and may make decisions that are good for their group but bad for the organization as a whole.

VIRTUAL NETWORK APPROACH

What It Is

The most recent approach to departmentalization extends the idea of horizontal coordination and collaboration beyond the boundaries of the organization. In a variety of industries, vertically integrated, hierarchical organizations are giving way to loosely interconnected groups of companies with permeable boundaries.[47] *Outsourcing*, which means farming out certain activities, such as manufacturing or credit processing, has become a significant trend. British retailer J. Sainsbury, for example, lets Accenture handle its entire information technology department. Ohio State University plans to outsource its parking system. And the City of Manwood, California, decided to outsource everything from street maintenance to policing and public safety. The budget for the police department used to be nearly $8 million. Now the city pays about half that to the Los Angeles

County Sheriff's Department and residents say service has improved.[48] The pharmaceuticals company Pfizer is using an innovative approach that lets some employees pass off certain parts of their jobs to an outsourcing firm in India with a click of a button. Rather than shifting entire functions to contractors, this "personal outsourcing" approach allows people to shift only certain tedious and time-consuming tasks to be handled by the outsourcing partner while they focus on higher-value work.[49]

Some organizations take this networking approach to the extreme to create an innovative structure. The **virtual network structure** means that the firm subcontracts most of its major functions to separate companies and coordinates their activities from a small headquarters organization.[50] Philip Rosedale runs LoveMachine from his home and coffee shops around San Francisco. LoveMachine makes software that lets employees send Twitter-like messages to say "Thank you," or "Great job!" When the message is sent, everyone in the company gets a copy, which builds morale, and the basic software is free to companies that want to use it. LoveMachine has no full-time development staff but instead works with a network of freelancers who bid on jobs such as creating new features, fixing glitches, and so forth. Rosedale also contracts out payroll and other administrative tasks.[51] How would you feel about working as a freelance employee for a virtual company? The Shoptalk describes some pros and cons of "never having to go to the office."

▶ ▶ ▶ **Concept Connection**

William Wang, founder of Vizio, Inc., produces competitively priced LCD and plasma televisions using the **virtual network approach**. Wang keeps costs down by running a lean operation, outsourcing manufacturing, research and development, and technical support. Vizio televisions are priced about 50 percent lower than most brands. The network approach has paid off. After only seven years in business, the company surpassed Sony in 2010 to become the second best-selling brand in the United States.

AP Photo/Chris Carlson

How It Works

The organization may be viewed as a central hub surrounded by a network of outside specialists, sometimes spread all over the world, as illustrated in Exhibit 10.8. Rather than

EXHIBIT 10.8 Network Approach to Departmentalization

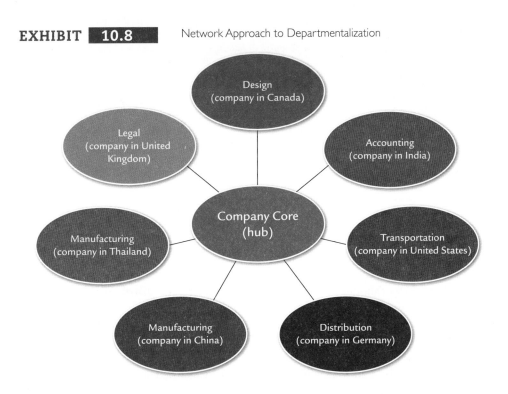

Manager's *Shoptalk*

Would You Like to Work in Your Pajamas?

There are about 34 million Americans who work from home at least part of the time, and millions more in other countries. Some of those people are freelancers, or "solopreneurs," who enter into outsourcing contracts to perform services for companies around the world. Escaping the 9-to-5 office grind sounds like a dream to many people, but working solo has its down side. Most people who are accustomed to working in an office go through a bumpy transition when they switch to working virtually. Here are just a few of the good and bad things about working on your own.

Pro: You can be more productive. Many people find they can get more done working from home. For one thing, you might gain a couple of extra hours a day that you used to spend commuting. When reporters, editors, designers, and the numerous other professionals who put together *Inc.* magazine experimented with putting out an issue by working entirely outside the office, most of them found that they accomplished more work in an environment where they could focus for long stretches of time without distractions.

Con: It's all up to you to make it work. It takes discipline, self-management, and organization skills to make sure you complete all the jobs you've agreed to do. Some people can't resist funny Web sites, the television, the kids and pets, or the refrigerator long enough to actually get any work done. These types typically don't do well working from home and need the structure of an office to keep them motivated and productive. On the other hand, some people find that they work *too much* and have to learn to set boundaries. "My work-life balance sucks," said Matt Trifiro, who directs the virtual company 1000 Markets from his home.

Pro: You can set your own schedule and define your own work. If you want to sleep in and work later in the day, fine. If you want to take a three-hour lunch break, there's no one telling you that you can't. You can choose your own projects and organize the activities and tasks the way it makes sense to you rather than having someone else dictating how to do things. You can choose the companies you want to work for—anywhere in the world.

Con: Lack of recognition and feedback can create self-doubt, stress, and frustration. Lack of recognition is a common complaint among virtual workers. In addition, it's often hard to assess what your client really thinks of you and your performance. A lot of virtual solopreneurs don't get regular feedback, which can lead to self-doubt—and the solitary nature of the work doesn't help. "I was spending all day in my tiny apartment, not talking to anyone," said one virtual worker. Many people counteract the isolation of virtual work by taking their laptop to a coffee shop or spending some time at a "co-working center," where they can rent an office space on a daily basis.

And Finally . . . A blog on the ThereItIs Web site offered a lighthearted look at some of the pros and cons of virtual work: You never again have to worry about a bad hair day or spend an hour getting dressed for work. But you just might miss the chance to "power dress" once in a while.

Sources: Based on Max Chafkin, "The Office Is Dead. Long Live the Office: The Case, and the Plan, for the Virtual Company," *Inc.* (April 2010): 62–73; Laurie Sheppard, "Challenges to Working Virtually," *Creating at Will* Web site, 2011, http://creatingatwill.com/challenges-to-working-virtually/ (accessed August 17, 2012); Sara Fletcher, "5 Challenges of Working from Home," *RecruitingBlogs*, August 14, 2012, www.recruitingblogs.com/profiles/blogs/5-challenges-of-working-from-home (accessed August 16, 2012); and "Perks and Challenges of Virtual Work," *ThereItIs.com*, http://blog.thereitis.com/post/22640167629/challenges-of-virtual-work (accessed August 17, 2012).

being housed under one roof, services such as accounting, design, manufacturing, and distribution are outsourced to separate organizations that are connected electronically to the central office.[52] Networked computer systems, collaborative software, and the Internet enable organizations to exchange data and information so rapidly and smoothly that a loosely connected network of suppliers, manufacturers, assemblers, and distributors can look and act like one seamless company.

The idea behind networks is that a company can concentrate on what it does best and contract out other activities to companies with distinctive competence in those specific areas, which enables a company to do more with less.[53] The "heart-healthy" food company Smart Balance has been able to innovate and expand rapidly by using a virtual network approach.

Smart Balance has about 67 employees, but nearly 400 people are working for the company. Smart Balance started by making a buttery spread and now has a line of spreads, all-natural peanut butter, nutrient-enhanced milk, cheese, sour cream, popcorn, and other products. Managers credit the virtual network approach for helping the company innovate and expand rapidly.

Smart Balance keeps product development and marketing in-house but uses contractors to do just about everything else, including manufacturing, distribution, sales, information technology services, and research and testing. The way the company got into the milk business shows how the network structure increases speed and flexibility. Peter Dray, vice president of product development, was able to get the help he needed to perfect the product from contractors. Outside scientists and research and development consultants worked on the formula. The company contracted with a dairy processor to do tests and trial production runs. An outside laboratory assessed nutritional claims and another company managed consumer taste tests.

Each morning, full-time employees and virtual workers exchange a flurry of e-mail messages and phone calls to update each other on what took place the day before and what needs to happen today. Executives spend much of their time managing relationships. Twice a year, they hold all-company meetings that include permanent staff and contractors. Information is shared widely, and managers make a point of recognizing the contributions of contractors to the company's success, which helps create a sense of unity and commitment.[54]

With a network structure such as that used at Smart Balance, it is difficult to answer the question "Where is the organization?" in traditional terms. The different organizational parts are drawn together contractually and coordinated electronically, creating a new form of organization. Much like building blocks, parts of the network can be added or taken away to meet changing needs.[55]

A similar approach to networking is called the **modular approach**, in which a manufacturing company uses outside suppliers to provide entire chunks of a product, which are then assembled into a final product by a handful of workers. The modular approach hands off responsibility for engineering and production of entire sections of a product, such as a Volkswagen automobile or a Boeing airplane, to outside suppliers. Suppliers design a module, making some of the parts themselves and subcontracting others. Parts for the Boeing 787 Dreamliner jet, for example, came from 135 companies in two dozen countries.[56] These modules are delivered right to the assembly line, where a handful of employees bolt them together into a finished vehicle.

Virtual Network Advantages and Disadvantages

The biggest advantages to a virtual network approach are flexibility and competitiveness on a global scale. The extreme flexibility of a network approach is illustrated by recent antigovernment protests and the overthrow of leaders in Tunisia and Egypt, for instance.[57] A far-flung collection of groups that share a similar mission and goals but are free to act on their own joined together to mastermind the "Arab Spring" uprisings, much in the same way terrorist groups have masterminded attacks against the United States and other countries. "Attack any single part of it, and the rest carries on largely untouched," wrote one journalist about the terrorist network. "It cannot be decapitated, because the insurgency, for the most part, has no head."[58]

Similarly, today's business organizations can benefit from a flexible network approach that lets them shift resources and respond quickly. A network organization can draw on resources and expertise worldwide to achieve the best quality and price and can sell its products and services worldwide. Flexibility comes from the ability to hire whatever services are needed and to change a few months later without constraints from owning plants, equipment, and facilities. The organization can redefine itself continually to fit new product and market opportunities. This structure is perhaps the leanest of all organization forms because little supervision is required. Large teams of staff specialists and administrators are not needed. A network organization may have only two or three levels of hierarchy, compared with ten or more in traditional organizations.[59]

One of the major disadvantages is lack of hands-on control.[60] Managers do not have all operations under one roof and must rely on contracts, coordination, negotiation, and electronic linkages to hold things together. Each partner in the network necessarily acts in its own self-interest. The weak and ambiguous boundaries create higher uncertainty and greater demands on managers for defining shared goals, managing relationships, keeping people focused and motivated, and coordinating activities so that everything functions as intended. Consider, for instance, that production of Boeing's 787 Dreamliner fell two years behind schedule because the "modules" from various contractors that were supposed to be snapped together didn't always fit.[61] Customer service and loyalty can also suffer if outsourcing partners fail to perform as expected.[62] The reputation of United Airlines was severely damaged when the employee assigned by an outsourcing contractor to supervise an unaccompanied 10-year-old at Chicago's busy O'Hare Airport didn't show up. The story made the national news when United's own employees failed to respond appropriately and the parents couldn't locate their missing child for nearly an hour.[63] Finally, in this type of organization, employee loyalty can weaken. Employees might feel they can be replaced by contract services. A cohesive corporate culture is less likely to develop, and turnover tends to be higher because emotional commitment between organization and employee is fragile.

Exhibit 10.9 summarizes the major advantages and disadvantages of each type of structure we have discussed.

EXHIBIT 10.9   Structural Advantages and Disadvantages

Structural Approach	Advantages	Disadvantages
Functional	Efficient use of resources; economies of scale In-depth skill specialization and development Top manager direction and control	Poor communication across functional departments Slow response to external changes; lagging innovation Decisions concentrated at top of hierarchy, creating delay
Divisional	Fast response, flexibility in unstable environment Fosters concern for customer needs Excellent coordination across functional departments	Duplication of resources across divisions Less technical depth and specialization Poor coordination across divisions
Matrix	More efficient use of resources than single hierarchy Flexibility, adaptability to changing environment Interdisciplinary cooperation, expertise available to all divisions	Frustration and confusion from dual chain of command High conflict between two sides of the matrix Many meetings, more discussion than action
Team	Reduced barriers among departments, increased compromise Shorter response time, quicker decisions Better morale, enthusiasm from employee involvement	Dual loyalties and conflict Time and resources spent on meetings Unplanned decentralization
Virtual network	Can draw on expertise worldwide Highly flexible and responsive Reduced overhead costs	Lack of control; weak boundaries Greater demands on managers Weaker employee loyalty

Remember This

- Popular contemporary approaches to departmentalization include team and virtual network structures.
- A **cross-functional team** is a group of employees from various functional departments that meet as a team to resolve mutual problems.
- Total Attorneys uses cross-functional teams to improve coordination on software and services projects for small law firm clients.
- A **permanent team** is a group of employees from all functional areas permanently assigned to focus on a specific task or activity.
- A **team-based structure** is one in which the entire organization is made up of horizontal teams that

coordinate their activities and work directly with customers to accomplish organizational goals.
- Whole Foods Market uses a team-based structure.
- With a **virtual network structure**, the organization subcontracts most of its major functions to separate companies and coordinates their activities from a small headquarters organization.
- The **modular approach** is one in which a manufacturing company uses outside suppliers to provide large chunks of a product such as an automobile, which are then assembled into a final product by a few employees.
- Both the team and the network approach have distinct advantages and disadvantages.

Organizing for Horizontal Coordination

One reason for the growing use of teams and networks is that many managers recognize the limits of traditional vertical organization structures in a fast-shifting environment. In general, the trend is toward breaking down barriers between departments, and many companies are moving toward horizontal structures based on work processes rather than departmental functions.[64] However, regardless of the type of structure, every organization needs mechanisms for horizontal integration and coordination. The structure of an organization is not complete without designing the horizontal as well as the vertical dimensions of structure.[65]

THE NEED FOR COORDINATION

As organizations grow and evolve, two things happen. First, new positions and departments are added to deal with factors in the external environment or with new strategic needs, as described earlier in the chapter. As companies add positions and departments to meet changing needs, they grow more complex, with hundreds of positions and departments performing incredibly diverse activities.

Second, senior managers have to find a way to tie all these departments together. The formal chain of command and the supervision it provides is effective, but it is not enough. The organization needs systems to process information and enable communication among people in different departments and at different levels. **Coordination** refers to the managerial task of adjusting and synchronizing the diverse activities among different individuals and departments. **Collaboration** means a joint effort between people from two or more departments to produce outcomes that meet a common goal or shared purpose and that are typically greater than what any of the individuals or departments could achieve working alone.[66] To understand the value of collaboration, consider the 2011 U.S. mission to raid Osama bin Laden's compound in Pakistan. The raid could not have succeeded without close collaboration between the Central Intelligence Agency (CIA) and the U.S. military. There has traditionally been little interaction between the nation's intelligence officers and its military officers, but the war on terrorism has changed that mindset. During planning for the bin Laden mission, military officers spent every day for months

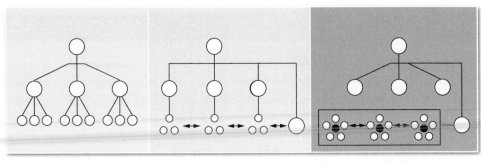

Traditional Vertical
Structure

Cross-Functional Teams and
Project Managers

Reengineering to
Horizontal Teams

working closely with the CIA team in a remote, secure facility on the CIA campus. "This is the kind of thing that, in the past, people who watched movies thought was possible, but no one in the government thought was possible," one official later said of the collaborative mission.[67]

Collaboration and coordination within business organizations is just as important. Without coordination, a company's left hand will not act in concert with the right hand, causing problems and conflicts. Coordination is required regardless of whether the organization has a functional, divisional, or team structure. Employees identify with their immediate department or team, taking its interest to heart, and they may not want to compromise and collaborate with other units for the good of the organization as a whole. The dangers of poor coordination are reflected in recent quality and safety issues with Toyota vehicles and the inadequate initial response by top managers. A panel investigating the situation pinpointed lack of information sharing and poor communication and collaboration across different units as one distinct problem.[68]

The problem is amplified in the international arena because organizational units are differentiated not only by goals and work activities, but also by geographical distance, time differences, cultural values, and perhaps language. Toyota, for instance, is a huge organization with divisions all over the world. How can managers ensure that needed coordination and collaboration will take place in their company, both domestically and globally? Coordination is the outcome of information and cooperation. Managers can design systems and structures to promote horizontal coordination and collaboration.

Exhibit 10.10 illustrates the evolution of organizational structures, with a growing emphasis on horizontal coordination. Although the vertical functional structure is effective in stable environments, it does not provide the horizontal coordination needed in times of rapid change. Innovations such as cross-functional teams, task forces, and project managers work within the vertical structure but provide a means to increase horizontal communication and cooperation. The next stage involves reengineering to structure the organization into teams working on horizontal processes. **Reengineering** refers to the radical redesign of business processes to achieve dramatic improvements in cost, quality, service, and speed. Because the focus of reengineering is on horizontal workflows rather than function, reengineering generally leads to a shift away from a strong vertical structure to one emphasizing stronger horizontal coordination. The vertical hierarchy is flattened, with perhaps only a few senior executives in traditional support functions such as finance and human resources.

TASK FORCES, TEAMS, AND PROJECT MANAGEMENT

A **task force** is a temporary team or committee designed to solve a problem involving several departments.[69] Task force members represent their departments and share information that enables coordination. For example, at Irving Medical Center, a unit of Kaiser Permanente in California, a task force made up of operating room nurses, surgeons, technicians, housekeeping staff, and others came together to streamline the procedure for performing total-hip and knee-joint replacements, the hospital's costliest and most time-consuming surgeries. The resulting combination of enhanced coordination and reallocated resources meant that the number of these surgeries that could be performed increased from one or two a day up to four a day. Better coordination freed up 188 hours of operating room time a year, reflecting a significant cost savings.[70] In addition to creating task forces, companies also set up *cross-functional teams,* such as the ones at Total Attorneys described earlier. A cross-functional team furthers horizontal coordination because participants from several departments meet regularly to solve ongoing problems of common interest.[71] This team is similar to a task force except that it works with continuing rather than temporary problems and might exist for several years. Team members think in terms of working together for the good of the whole rather than just for their own department.

Companies also use project managers to increase coordination. A **project manager** is a person who is responsible for coordinating the activities of several departments for the completion of a specific project.[72] Project managers might also have titles such as product manager, integrator, program manager, or process owner. The distinctive feature of the project manager position is that the person is not a member of one of the departments being coordinated. Project managers are located outside the departments and have responsibility for coordinating several departments to achieve desired project outcomes. At General Mills, for example, a manager is assigned to each product line, such as Cheerios, Bisquick, and Hamburger Helper. Product managers set budget goals, marketing targets, and strategies and obtain the cooperation from advertising, production, and sales personnel needed for implementing product strategy.

In some organizations, project managers are included on the organization chart, as illustrated in Exhibit 10.11. The project manager is drawn to one side of the chart to

4

ORGANIZING

EXHIBIT 10.11 Example of Project Manager Relationships to Other Departments

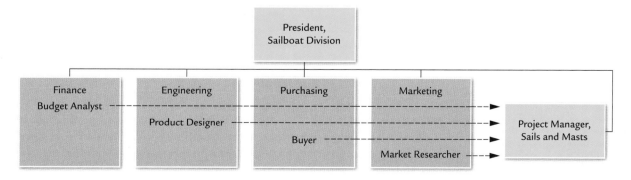

indicate authority over the project but not over the people assigned to it. The *dashed lines* to the project manager indicate responsibility for coordination and communication with assigned team members, but department managers retain line authority over functional employees.

RELATIONAL COORDINATION

The highest level of horizontal coordination is relational coordination. **Relational coordination** refers to "frequent, timely, problem-solving communication carried out through [employee] relationships of shared goals, shared knowledge, and mutual respect."[73] Relational coordination isn't a structural device or mechanism such as a project manager, but rather is part of the very fabric and culture of the organization. In an organization with a high level of relational coordination, people share information freely across departmental boundaries, and people interact on a continuous basis to share knowledge and solve problems. Coordination is carried out through a web of ongoing positive relationships rather than because of formal coordination roles or mechanisms.[74] Employees coordinate directly with each other across units.

To build relational coordination into the fabric of the organization, managers invest in training people in the skills needed to interact with one another and resolve cross-departmental conflicts based on shared goals rather than emphasizing goals of their separate departments. People are given freedom from strict work rules so they have the flexibility to interact and contribute wherever they are needed, and rewards are based on team efforts and accomplishments. Front-line supervisors typically have smaller spans of control so they can develop close working relationships with subordinates and coach and mentor employees. Southwest Airlines provides a good illustration.

Innovative Way

Southwest Airlines

Airlines face many challenges, but one that they face hundreds of times on a daily basis is getting airplanes loaded and off the ground safely and on time. Flight departure is a highly complex process. It involves numerous employees from various departments—such as ticket agents, pilots, flight attendants, baggage handlers, gate agents, mechanics, ramp agents, fuel attendants, and so forth—performing multiple tasks within a limited time period, under uncertain and ever-changing conditions. If all these groups aren't tightly coordinated, a successful on-time departure is difficult to achieve.

Southwest Airlines has the shortest turnaround time in the business, partly because managers promote relational coordination to achieve superior on-time performance and a high level of customer satisfaction. In any airline, there can be serious disagreements among employees about who is to blame when a flight is delayed, so Southwest managers created what they call *team delay*. Rather than searching for who is to blame when something goes wrong, the team delay is used to point out problems in coordination between various groups. The emphasis on the team focuses everyone on their shared goals of on-time departure, accurate baggage handling, and customer satisfaction. Because delay becomes a team problem, people are motivated to work closely together and coordinate their activities rather than looking out for themselves and trying to avoid or shift blame. Supervisors work closely with employees, but their role is less "being the boss" as it is facilitating learning and helping people do their jobs. Southwest uses a small supervisory span of control—about one supervisor for every eight or nine front-line employees—so that supervisors have the time to coach and assist employees, who are viewed as internal customers.[75]

By using practices that facilitate relational coordination, managers ensure that all the departments involved in flight departure are tightly coordinated. When relational coordination is high, people share information and coordinate their activities without having to have bosses or formal mechanisms telling them to do so.

Remember This

- In addition to the vertical structure, every organization needs mechanisms for horizontal integration and coordination.
- **Coordination** refers to the managerial task of adjusting and synchronizing the diverse activities among different individuals and departments.
- **Collaboration** means a joint effort between people from two or more departments to produce outcomes that meet a common goal or shared purpose.
- The successful U.S. mission to raid Osama bin Laden's compound in Pakistan was a result of collaboration between the nation's intelligence officers and its military officers.
- As organizations grow, they add new positions, departments, and hierarchical levels, which leads to greater coordination problems.
- Ways to increase horizontal coordination include task forces, teams, project managers, and relational coordination.

- A **task force** is a temporary team or committee formed to solve a specific short-term problem involving several departments.
- A **project manager** is a person responsible for coordinating the activities of several departments for the completion of a specific project.
- Companies often shift to a more horizontal approach after going through **reengineering**, which refers to the radical redesign of business processes to achieve dramatic improvements in cost, quality, service, and speed.
- **Relational coordination** refers to frequent horizontal coordination and communication carried out through ongoing relationships of shared goals, shared knowledge, and mutual respect.
- Southwest Airlines achieves the shortest turnaround time in the airline industry because managers foster relational coordination among the varied people and departments involved in the flight departure process.

Factors Shaping Structure

Vertical hierarchies continue to thrive because they provide important benefits for organizations. Some degree of vertical hierarchy is often needed to organize a large number of people effectively to accomplish complex tasks within a coherent framework. Without a vertical structure, people in a large, global firm wouldn't know what to do. However, in today's environment, an organization's vertical structure often needs to be balanced with strong horizontal mechanisms to achieve peak performance.[76]

How do managers know whether to design a structure that emphasizes the formal, vertical hierarchy or one with an emphasis on horizontal communication and collaboration? The answer lies in the organization's strategic goals and the nature of its technology. Exhibit 10.12 illustrates that forces affecting organization structure come from both outside and inside the organization. External strategic needs, such as environmental conditions, strategic direction, and organizational goals, create top-down pressure for designing the organization in such a way as to fit the environment and accomplish strategic goals. Structural decisions also take into consideration pressures from the bottom up—that is, from the technology and work processes that are performed to produce the organization's products and services.

STRUCTURE FOLLOWS STRATEGY

Studies demonstrate that business performance is strongly influenced by how well the company's structure is aligned with its strategic intent and the needs of the environment, so managers strive to pick strategies and structures that are congruent.[77] In Chapter 8, we discussed several strategies that business firms can adopt. Two strategies proposed by Michael E. Porter are

"The organizations that are most likely to survive are those that can balance themselves on the edge of chaos—and between the forces of change and the forces of stability."

— CHRISTIAN GIBBONS, DIRECTOR, BUSINESS AND INDUSTRY AFFAIRS, NEW ECONOMY PROJECT

4

ORGANIZING

EXHIBIT **10.12**   Factors Affecting Organization Structure

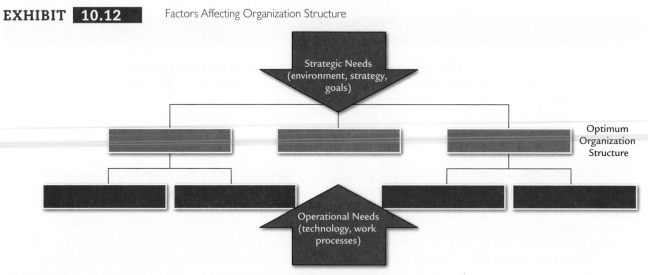

SOURCE: Based on David A. Nadler and Michael L. Tushman, with Mark B. Nadler, *Competing by Design: The Power of Organizational Architecture* (New York: Oxford University Press, 1997), p. 54.

Take ⓐ Moment

Go to the Experiential Exercise on pages 336–337 that pertains to organic versus mechanistic structure.

differentiation and cost leadership.[78] With a differentiation strategy, the organization attempts to develop innovative products unique to the market. With a cost leadership strategy, the organization strives for internal efficiency.

Typically, strategic goals of cost efficiency occur in more stable environments, while goals of innovation and flexibility occur in more uncertain environments. The terms *mechanistic* and *organic* can be used to explain structural responses to strategy and the environment.[79] Goals of efficiency and a stable environment are associated with a mechanistic system. This type of organization typically has a rigid, vertical, centralized structure, with most decisions made at the top. The organization is highly specialized and characterized by rules, procedures, and a clear hierarchy of authority. With goals of innovation and a rapidly changing environment, however, the organization tends to be much looser, free-flowing, and adaptive, using an organic system. The structure is more horizontal, and decision-making authority is decentralized. People at lower levels have more responsibility and authority for solving problems, enabling the organization to be more fluid and adaptable to changes.[80]

Exhibit 10.13 shows a simplified continuum that illustrates how different structural approaches are associated with strategy and the environment. The pure functional structure is appropriate for achieving internal efficiency goals in a stable environment. The vertical functional structure uses task specialization and a strict chain of command to gain

EXHIBIT **10.13**   Relationship of Structural Approach to Strategy and the Environment

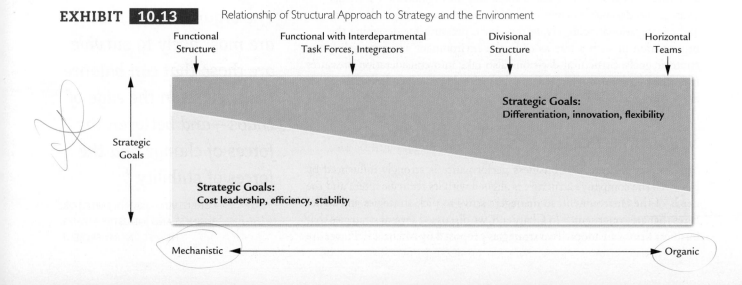

efficient use of scarce resources, but it does not enable the organization to be flexible or innovative. In contrast, horizontal teams are appropriate when the primary goal is innovation and the organization needs flexibility to cope with an uncertain environment. Each team is small, is able to be responsive, and has the people and resources necessary for performing its task. The flexible horizontal structure enables organizations to differentiate themselves and respond quickly to the demands of a shifting environment but at the expense of efficient resource use.

Exhibit 10.13 also illustrates how other forms of structure represent intermediate steps on the organization's path to efficiency or innovation. The functional structure with cross-functional teams and project managers provides greater coordination and flexibility than the pure functional structure. The divisional structure promotes differentiation because each division can focus on specific products and customers, although divisions tend to be larger and less flexible than small teams. Exhibit 10.13 does not include all possible structures, but it illustrates how structures can be used to facilitate the organization's strategic goals.

Take a Moment

The Small Group Breakout on page 337 will give you a chance to practice organizing to meet strategic needs.

Remember This

- Contingency factors of strategic goals, environment, and technology influence the correct structural approach.
- A mechanistic, vertical structure is appropriate for a cost leadership strategy, which typically occurs in a stable environment.

- An organic, horizontal approach is needed for a differentiation strategy and when the organization needs flexibility to cope with an uncertain environment.

STRUCTURE FITS THE TECHNOLOGY

Technology includes the knowledge, tools, techniques, and activities used to transform organizational inputs into outputs.[81] Technology includes machinery, employee skills, and work procedures. A useful way to think about technology is as "production activities." The production activities may be to produce Web site content, steel castings, television programs, or computer software. Technologies vary between manufacturing and service organizations.

Woodward's Manufacturing Technology

The most influential research into the relationship between manufacturing technology and organization structure was conducted by Joan Woodward, a British industrial sociologist.[82] She gathered data from 100 British firms to determine whether basic structural characteristics, such as administrative overhead, span of control, and centralization were different across firms. She found that manufacturing firms could be categorized according to three basic types of production technology:

Small-batch and unit production. **Small-batch production** firms produce goods in batches of one or a few products designed to customer specification. This technology also is used to make large, one-of-a-kind products, such as computer-controlled machines. Small-batch manufacturing is close to traditional skilled-craft work, because human beings are a large part of the process. Examples of items produced through small-batch manufacturing include custom clothing, special-order machine tools, space capsules, satellites, and submarines.

Large-batch and mass production. **Mass production** technology is distinguished by standardized production runs. A large volume of products is produced, and all customers receive the same product. Standard products go into inventory for sale as customers need them. This technology makes greater use of machines than does small-batch production. Machines are designed to do most of the physical work, and employees complement the machinery. Examples of mass production are automobile assembly lines and the large-batch techniques used to produce tobacco products and textiles.

Continuous process production. In **continuous process production**, the entire workflow is mechanized in a sophisticated and complex form of production technology. Because the process runs continuously, it has no starting and stopping. Human operators are not part of actual production because machinery does all the work. Human operators simply read dials, fix machines that break down, and manage the production process. Examples of continuous process technologies are chemical plants, distilleries, petroleum refineries, and nuclear power plants.

The difference among the three manufacturing technologies is called **technical complexity**. Technical complexity is the degree to which machinery is involved in the production to the exclusion of people. With a complex technology, employees are hardly needed except to monitor the machines.

The structural characteristics associated with each type of manufacturing technology are illustrated in Exhibit 10.14. Note that centralization is high for mass production technology and low for small-batch and continuous process. Unlike small-batch and continuous process production, standardized mass-production machinery requires centralized decision making and well-defined rules and procedures. The administrative ratio and the percentage of indirect labor required also increase with technological complexity. Because the production process is nonroutine, closer supervision is needed. More indirect labor in the form of maintenance people is required because of the machinery's complexity; thus, the indirect/direct labor ratio is high. Span of control for first-line supervisors is greatest for mass production. On an assembly line, jobs are so routinized that a supervisor can handle an average of 48 employees. The number of employees per supervisor in small-batch and continuous process production is lower because closer supervision is needed. Overall, small-batch and continuous process firms have somewhat loose, flexible structures (organic), and mass production firms have tight vertical structures (mechanistic).

Woodward found that the relationship between structure and technology was directly related to company performance. Low-performing firms tended to deviate from the preferred structural form, often adopting a structure appropriate for another type of technology. High-performing organizations had characteristics similar to those listed in Exhibit 10.14.

EXHIBIT 10.14

Relationship Between Manufacturing Technology and Organization Structure

	Manufacturing Technology		
	Small Batch	**Mass Production**	**Continuous Process**
Technical Complexity of Production Technology	Low	Medium	High
Structural Characteristics:			
Centralization	Low	High	Low
Top administrator ratio	Low	Medium	High
Indirect/direct labor ratio	1/9	1/4	1/1
Supervisor span of control	23	48	15
Communication:			
Written (vertical)	Low	High	Low
Verbal (horizontal)	High	Low	High
Overall Structure	Organic	Mechanistic	Organic

SOURCE: Based on Joan Woodward, *Industrial Organizations: Theory and Practice* (London: Oxford University Press, 1965).

Service Technology

Examples of service organizations include consulting companies, law firms, brokerage houses, airlines, hotels, advertising companies, amusement parks, and educational organizations. In addition, service technology characterizes many departments in large corporations, even manufacturing firms. In a manufacturing company such as Ford Motor Company, the legal, human resources, finance, and market research departments all provide service. Thus, the structure and design of these departments reflect their own service technology rather than the manufacturing plant's technology. **Service technology** can be defined as follows:

Intangible output. The output of a service firm is intangible. Services are perishable and, unlike physical products, cannot be stored in inventory. The service is either consumed immediately or lost forever. Manufactured products are produced at one point in time and can be stored until sold at another time.

Direct contact with customers. Employees and customers interact directly to provide and purchase the service. Production and consumption are simultaneous. Service firm employees have direct contact with customers. In a manufacturing firm, technical employees are separated from customers, and hence no direct interactions occur.[83]

One distinct feature of service technology that directly influences structure is the need for employees to be close to the customer.[84] Structural characteristics are similar to those for continuous manufacturing technology, shown in Exhibit 10.14. Service firms tend to be flexible, informal, and decentralized. Horizontal communication is high because employees must share information and resources to serve customers and solve problems. Services also are dispersed; hence each unit is often small and located geographically close to customers. For example, banks, hotels, fast-food franchises, and doctors' offices disperse their facilities into regional and local offices to provide faster and better service to customers.

Some services can be broken down into explicit steps, so that employees can follow set rules and procedures. An interesting example comes from India, where Dr. Devi Shetty runs a hospital that performs open heart surgery for about 10 percent of the cost charged by hospitals in the United States, without reduced quality, by applying standardized operating procedures and principles of mass production. His approach is in line with a trend toward *lean services* that looks at how to design service work to improve both quality and efficiency. "In healthcare, you can't do one thing and reduce the price," Dr. Shetty says. "We have to do 1,000 small things."[85] When services can be standardized, a tight centralized structure can be effective, but service firms in general tend to be more organic, flexible, and decentralized.

Remember This

- Types of technologies include manufacturing and service.
- **Small-batch production** is a type of manufacturing technology that involves the production of goods in batches of one or a few products designed to customer specification.
- **Mass production** is characterized by long production runs to manufacture a large volume of products with the same specifications.
- **Continuous process production** involves mechanization of the entire workflow and nonstop production, such as in chemical plants or petroleum refineries.
- Small batch and continuous process technologies are associated with a more flexible horizontal structure,

whereas a tighter vertical structure is appropriate for mass production.
- Manufacturing technologies differ in terms of **technical complexity**, which refers to the degree to which complex machinery is involved in the production process to the exclusion of people.
- **Service technology** is characterized by intangible outputs and direct contact between employees and customers.
- Examples of service firms include banks, hotels, and fast-food restaurants.
- Service technologies tend to have more flexible horizontal structures.

ch10: Discussion Questions

1. Sandra Holt, manager of Electronics Assembly, asked Hector Cruz, her senior technician, to handle things in the department while Sandra worked on the budget. She needed peace and quiet for at least a week to complete her figures. After ten days, Sandra discovered that Hector had hired a senior secretary, not realizing that Sandra had promised interviews for the position to two other people. Evaluate Sandra's approach to delegation.

2. How does relational coordination differ from teams and task forces? Do you think relational coordination seems more valuable for a service technology or a manufacturing technology? Explain your answer.

3. An organizational consultant was heard to say, "Some aspect of functional structure appears in every organization." Do you agree? Explain.

4. Some people argue that the matrix structure should be adopted only as a last resort because the dual chains of command can create more problems than they solve. Discuss. Do you agree or disagree? Why?

5. What is the virtual network approach to structure? Is the use of authority and responsibility different compared to other forms of departmentalization? Explain.

6. The Hay Group published a report that some managers have personalities suited to horizontal relationships, such as project management, that achieve results with little formal authority. Other managers are more suited to operating roles with much formal authority in a vertical structure. What type of structure—functional, matrix, team, or virtual network—do you believe your personality would best fit into? Which structure would be the most challenging for you? Give your reasons.

7. Describe the primary differences between manufacturing and service technology. How do these differences influence the type of structure that will be most effective?

8. Experts say that organizations are becoming increasingly decentralized, with authority, decision-making responsibility, and accountability being pushed farther down into the organization. How will this trend affect what will be asked of you as a new manager?

9. The chapter suggested that structure should be designed to fit strategy. Some theorists argue that strategy should be designed to fit the organization's structure. With which theory do you agree? Explain.

10. Would you expect the structure of a company such as Facebook that operates almost entirely online to differ from the structure of a bricks-and-mortar company such as AT&T that uses the Internet for some things, such as customer service and business-to-business transactions? Why or why not?

ch10: Apply Your Skills: Experiential Exercise

Organic Versus Mechanistic Organization Structure

Interview an employee at your university, such as a department head or secretary. Have the employee answer the following 13 questions about his or her job and organizational conditions. Then answer the same set of questions for a job you have held.

Disagree Strongly ① ② ③ ④ ⑤ Agree Strongly

1. Your work would be considered routine.
   1   2   3   4   5

2. A clearly known way is established to do the major tasks you encounter.
   1   2   3   4   5

3. Your work has high variety and frequent exceptions.
   1   2   3   4   5

4. Communications from above consist of information and advice rather than instructions and directions.
   1   2   3   4   5

5. You have the support of peers and your supervisor to do your job well.
   1   2   3   4   5

6. You seldom exchange ideas or information with people doing other kinds of jobs.
   1   2   3   4   5

7. Decisions relevant to your work are made above you and passed down.
   1   2   3   4   5

8. People at your level frequently have to figure out for themselves what their tasks are for each day.
   1   2   3   4   5

9. Lines of authority are clear and precisely defined.
   1   2   3   4   5

10. Leadership tends to be democratic rather than autocratic in style.
    1   2   3   4   5

11. Job descriptions are written and up to date for each job.
    1   2   3   4   5

12. People understand each other's jobs and often do different tasks.
    1   2   3   4   5

13. A manual of policies and procedures is available to use when a problem arises.
    1   2   3   4   5

Scoring and Interpretation

To obtain the total score, subtract the scores for questions 1, 2, 6, 7, 9, 11, and 13 from the number 6 and add up the adjusted scores.

Total Score, Employee: _____

Total Score, You: _____

Compare the total score for a place you have worked to the score of the university employee you interviewed. A total score of 52 or above suggests that you or the other respondent is working in an organic organization. The score reflects a loose, flexible structure that is often associated with uncertain environments and small-batch or service technology. People working in this structure feel empowered. Many organizations today are moving in the direction of flexible structures and empowerment.

A score of 26 or below suggests a mechanistic structure. This structure uses traditional control and functional specialization, which often occurs in a certain environment, a stable organization, and routine or mass-production technology. People in this structure may feel controlled and constrained.

Discuss the pros and cons of organic versus mechanistic structure. Does the structure of the employee you interviewed fit the nature of the organization's environment, strategic goals, and technology? How about the structure for your own workplace? How might you redesign the structure to make the work organization more effective?

ch10: Apply Your Skills: Small Group Breakout

Family Business

Step 1. In groups of three to five students, assume that you are a consulting team to a family business. The family has used an inheritance to acquire a medium-sized pharmaceutical company. Last year, sales were down 10 percent from the previous year. Indeed, business has declined over the past three years, even though the pharmaceutical industry has been growing. The family that acquired the business seeks your help.

Step 2. Your task as a group is to rank the priority of the departmental functions in the order of importance for assigning additional resources to improve business in the future.

Step 3. Individually, rank the following ten functions in order of importance, and make a note of your reasons:

Distribution

Manufacturing

Market research

New-product development

Human resources

Product promotion

Quality assurance

Sales

Legal and governmental affairs

Office of the comptroller

Step 4. As a group, discuss the order of importance for the ten functions, sharing your reasons for how functional priority should relate to the company's strategic needs.

Step 5. How does the group's reasoning and ranking differ from your original thinking?

Step 6. What did you learn about organization structure and design from this exercise?

ch10: Endnotes

1. This questionnaire is based on Richard M. Wielkiewicz, "The Leadership Attitudes and Beliefs Scale: An Instrument for Evaluating College Students' Thinking About Leadership and Organizations," *Journal of College Student Development* 41 (May–June 2000): 335–346.

2. Claire Suddath, "Why There Are No Bosses at Valve," *Bloomberg Businessweek*, April 27, 2012, www.businessweek.com/articles/2012-04-27/why-there-are-no-bosses-at-valve (accessed August 10, 2012); Rachel Emma Silverman, "Who's the Boss? There Isn't One," *The Wall Street Journal*, June 20, 2012, B1; and Alex Hern, "Valve Software: Free Marketer's Dream, or Nightmare?" *New Statesman*, August 3, 2012, www.newstatesman.com/blogs/economics/2012/08/valve-software-free-marketeers-dream-or-nightmare (accessed August 10, 2012).

3. Russell Adams, "Hachette to Break Through 'Silos' As It Restructures Women's Magazines," *The Wall Street Journal*, March 2, 2009; Justin Scheck, "Dell Reorganizes, Creating New Mobile Device Division," *The Wall Street Journal*, December 5, 2009, B6; and Sony example from John Bussey, "Has Time Come for More CIOs to Start Reporting to the Top?" *The Wall Street Journal*, May 17, 2011, http://online.wsj.com/article/SB10001424052748704281504576327510720752684.html (accessed August 14, 2012).

4. John Child, *Organization: A Guide to Problems and Practice*, 2d ed. (London: Harper & Row, 1984).

5. Adam Smith, *The Wealth of Nations* (New York: Modern Library, 1937).

6. Leslie Kwoh, "Firms Hail New Chiefs (of Diversity)," *The Wall Street Journal* (January 5, 2012), http://online

.wsj.com/article/SB10001424052970203899504577 129261732884578.html (accessed August 13, 2012); Brian Knowlton, "White House Names First Chief Information Officer," *The New York Times*, March 5, 2009, http://thecaucus.blogs.nytimes.com/2009/ 03/05/white-house-names-first-chief-information-officer/ (accessed August 13, 2012).

7. Bussey, "Has Time Come for More CIOs to Start Reporting to the Top?"

8. This discussion is based on A. J. Grimes, "Authority, Power, Influence, and Social Control: A Theoretical Synthesis," *Academy of Management Review* 3 (1978): 724–735; and W. Graham Astley and Paramjit S. Sachdeva, "Structural Sources of Intraorganizational Power: A Theoretical Synthesis," *Academy of Management Review* 9 (1984): 104–113.

9. C. I. Barnard, *The Functions of the Executive* (Cambridge, MA: Harvard University Press, 1938).

10. Thomas A. Stewart, "CEOs See Clout Shifting," *Fortune* (November 6, 1989): 66.

11. Michael G. O'Loughlin, "What Is Bureaucratic Accountability and How Can We Measure It?" *Administration & Society* 22, no. 3 (November 1990): 275–302; and Brian Dive, "When Is an Organization Too Flat?" *Across the Board* (July–August 2003): 20–23.

12. Adam Lashinsky, "Inside Apple," *Fortune* (May 23, 2011): 125–134.

13. Carrie R. Leana, "Predictors and Consequences of Delegation," *Academy of Management Journal* 29 (1986): 754–774.

14. Chris Taylor, "Democracy Works," *Fortune Small Business* (May 2009): 40; and Heather Green, "How Meetup Tore Up the Rule Book," *BusinessWeek* (June 16, 2008): 88–89.

15. Clifford Krauss and Julia Werdigier, "BP's New Chief, Not Formally in the Role, Is Already Realigning Senior Managers," *The New York Times*, September 30, 2010, B3; and Guy Chazan, "BP's New Chief Puts Emphasis on Safety," *The Wall Street Journal*, September 29, 2010, http:// online.wsj.com/article/SB10001424052748704116004575521394170919842.html (accessed August 14, 2012).

16. Ian Urbina, "In Gulf, It Was Unclear Who Was in Charge of Oil Rig," *The New York Times*, June 5, 2010; and Douglas A. Blackmon et al., "There Was 'Nobody in Charge,'" *The Wall Street Journal*, May 27, 2010.

17. George Anders, "Overseeing More Employees—With Fewer Managers" (Theory & Practice column), *The Wall Street Journal*, March 24, 2008.

18. Barbara Davison, "Management Span of Control: How Wide Is Too Wide?" *Journal of Business Strategy* 24, no. 4 (2003): 22–29; Paul D. Collins and Frank Hull, "Technology and Span of Control: Woodward Revisited," *Journal of Management Studies* 23 (March 1986): 143–164; David D. Van Fleet and Arthur G. Bedeian, "A History of the Span of Management," *Academy of*

Management Review 2 (1977): 356–372; and C. W. Barkdull, "Span of Control—A Method of Evaluation," *Michigan Business Review* 15 (May 1963): 25–32.

19. Reported in Brian Dive, "Hierarchies for Flow and Profit," *Strategy + Business*, August 26, 2008, www.strategy-business.com/article/08315 (accessed May 25, 2010).

20. Dive, "Hierarchies for Flow and Profit"; and Gary Neilson, Bruce A. Pasternack, and Decio Mendes, "The Four Bases of Organizational DNA," *Strategy + Business*, Issue 33 (December 10, 2003): 48–57.

21. Anders, "Overseeing More Employees"; Barbara Davison, "Management Span of Control"; Brian Dive, "When Is an Organization Too Flat?"; Brian Dumaine, "What the Leaders of Tomorrow See," *Fortune* (July 3, 1989): 48–62; and Raghuram G. Rajan and Julie Wulf, "The Flattening Firm: Evidence from Panel Data on the Changing Nature of Corporate Hierarchies," working paper, reported in Caroline Ellis, "The Flattening Corporation," *MIT Sloan Management Review* (Summer 2003): 5.

22. Gary L. Neilson and Julie Wulf, "How Many Direct Reports?" *Harvard Business Review* (April 2012): 112–119; and Bussey, "Has Time Come for More CIOs to Start Reporting to the Top?"

23. William G. Ouchi, "Power to the Principals: Decentralization in Three Large School Districts," *Organization Science* 17, no. 2 (March–April 2006): 298–307.

24. Sarah Lyall, "Britain Plans to Decentralize Health Care," *The New York Times*, July 24, 2010, www.nytimes.com/ 2010/07/25/world/europe/25britain.html?pagewanted= all (accessed August 14, 2012).

25. Quoted in Robert D. Kaplan, "Man Versus Afghanistan," *The Atlantic* (April 2010): 60–71.

26. Gen. Martin E. Dempsey, "The Army's Starfish Program and an Emphasis on Decentralization," Official Army Web site, April 26, 2010, www.army.mil/-news/2010/ 04/26/37979-the-armys-starfish-program-and-an-emphasis-on-decentralization/ (accessed August 30, 2010); and Bruce E. DeFeyter, "The Lion, the Starfish, and the Spider: Hitting Terrorists Where It Hurts," *Special Warfare* (March–April 2010): 26; Ori Brafman and Rod Beckstrom, *The Starfish and the Spider: The Unstoppable Power of Leaderless Organizations* (New York: Portfolio/Penguin 2006).

27. Andrew Campbell, Sven Kunisch, and Günter Müller-Stewens, "To Centralize or Not to Centralize?" *McKinsey Quarterly*, June 2011, www.mckinseyquarterly .com/To_centralize_or_not_to_centralize_2815 (accessed August 14, 2012).

28. Dennis Cauchon, "The Little Company That Could," *USA Today*, October 9, 2005, www.usatoday.com/ money/companies/management/2005-10-09-mississippi- power-usat_x.htm.

29. Jennifer Reingold, "The Fun King," *Fortune* (May 21, 2012): 166–174.

30. Penney example reported in Ann Zimmerman, "Home Depot Learns to Go Local," *The Wall Street Journal*, October 7, 2008.

31. Clay Chandler and Paul Ingrassia, "Just As U.S. Firms Try Japanese Management, Honda Is Centralizing," *The Wall Street Journal*, April 11, 1991.

32. The following discussion of structural alternatives draws from Jay R. Galbraith, *Designing Complex Organizations* (Reading, MA: Addison-Wesley, 1973); Jay R. Galbraith, *Organization Design* (Reading, MA: Addison-Wesley, 1977); Jay R. Galbraith, *Designing Dynamic Organizations* (New York: AMACOM, 2002); Robert Duncan, "What Is the Right Organization Structure?" *Organizational Dynamics* (Winter 1979): 59–80; N. Anand and Richard L. Daft, "What Is the Right Organization Design?" *Organizational Dynamics* 36, no. 4 (2007): 329–344; and J. McCann and Jay R. Galbraith, "Interdepartmental Relations," in *Handbook of Organizational Design*, ed. P. Nystrom and W. Starbuck (New York: Oxford University Press, 1981), pp. 60–84.

33. Raymond E. Miles et al., "Designing Organizations to Meet 21st-Century Opportunities and Challenges," *Organizational Dynamics* 39, no. 2 (2010): 93–103.

34. Based on the story of Blue Bell Creameries in Richard L. Daft, *Organization Theory and Design*, 9th ed. (Mason, OH: South-Western, 2007), p. 103.

35. R. E. Miles et al., "Designing Organizations to Meet 21st Century Opportunities and Challenges."

36. Jaimelynn Hitt, "The Organizational Structure of Starbucks, Unilever, and Wal-Mart," http://voices .yahoo.com/the-organizational-structure-starbucks-unilever-1495147.html (accessed August 15, 2012); Mae Anderson, "Wal-Mart Reorganizes U.S. Operations to Help Spur Growth," *USA Today*, January 28, 2010, www.usatoday.com/money/industries/retail/ 2010-01-28-walmart-reorganization_N.htm (accessed August 15, 2012); and "Walmart," *TheOfficialBoard.com*, www.theofficialboard.com/org-chart/wal-mart-stores (accessed August 15, 2012).

37. Eliza Newlin Carney, "Calm in the Storm," *Government Executive* (October 2003): 57–63; and the Internal Revenue Service Web site, www.irs.gov (accessed April 20, 2004).

38. Brooks Barnes, "Is Disney's Chief Having a Cinderella Moment?" *The New York Times*, April 11, 2010, BU1.

39. Maisie O'Flanagan and Lynn K. Taliento, "Nonprofits: Ensuring That Bigger Is Better," *McKinsey Quarterly*, no. 2 (2004): 112ff.

40. The discussion of matrix structure is based on S. H. Appelbaum, D. Nadeau, and M. Cyr, "Performance Evaluation in a Matrix Organization: A Case Study," *Industrial and Commercial Training* 40, no. 5 (2008): 236–241; T. Sy and S. Cote, "Emotional Intelligence: A Key Ability to Succeed in the Matrix Organization," *Journal of Management Development* 23, no. 5 (2004):

439; L. R. Burns, "Matrix Management in Hospitals: Testing Theories of Matrix Structure and Development," *Administrative Science Quarterly* 34 (1989): 349–368; Carol Hymowitz, "Managers Suddenly Have to Answer to a Crowd of Bosses," *The Wall Street Journal*, August 12, 2003; and Stanley M. Davis and Paul R. Lawrence, *Matrix* (Reading, MA: Addison-Wesley, 1977).

41. Howard Schultz, "Starbucks Makes Organizational Changes to Enhance Customer Experience," February 11, 2008, http://news.starbucks.com/article_display .cfm?article_id=66 (accessed August 15, 2012).

42. Robert C. Ford and W. Alan Randolph, "Cross-Functional Structures: A Review and Integration of Matrix Organization and Project Management," *Journal of Management* 18, no. 2 (1992): 267–294; and Thomas Sy and Laura Sue D'Annunzio, "Challenges and Strategies of Matrix Organizations: Top-Level and Mid-Level Managers' Perspectives," *Human Resources Planning* 28, no. 1 (2005): 39–48.

43. These disadvantages are based on Sy and D'Annunzio, "Challenges and Strategies of Matrix Organizations"; and Michael Goold and Andrew Campbell, "Making Matrix Structures Work: Creating Clarity on Unit Roles and Responsibilities," *European Management Journal* 21, no. 3 (June 2003): 351–363.

44. Darren Dahl, "Strategy: Managing Fast, Flexible, and Full of Team Spirit," *Inc.* (May 2009): 95–97.

45. Gary Hamel, "Break Free," *Fortune* (October 1, 2007): 119–126, excerpted from Gary Hamel, *The Future of Management* (Boston: Harvard Business School Press, 2007); and Nick Paumgarten, "Food Fighter: The Whole Foods CEO vs. His Customers" (Profiles column), *The New Yorker* (January 4, 2010): 36.

46. Geoff Keighley, "Massively Multinational Player," *Business 2.0* (September 2005): 64–66.

47. Melissa A. Schilling and H. Kevin Steensma, "The Use of Modular Organizational Forms: An Industry-Level Analysis," *Academy of Management Journal* 44, no. 6 (December 2001): 1149–1169.

48. Bob Sechler, "Colleges Shedding Non-Core Operations," *The Wall Street Journal*, April 2, 2012, A6; David Streitfeld, "A City Outsources Everything. California's Sky Doesn't Fall," *The New York Times*, July 20, 2010, A1.

49. Jena McGregor, "The Chore Goes Offshore," *Business-Week* (March 23 & 30, 2009): 50–51.

50. Raymond E. Miles and Charles C. Snow, "The New Network Firm: A Spherical Structure Built on a Human Investment Philosophy," *Organizational Dynamics* (Spring 1995): 5–18; and Raymond E. Miles et al., "Organizing in the Knowledge Age: Anticipating the Cellular Form," *Academy of Management Executive* 11, no. 4 (1997): 7–24.

51. Darren Dahl, "Want a Job? Let the Bidding Begin; A Radical Take on the Virtual Company," *Inc.* (March 2011), 93–96.

4

ORGANIZING

52. Raymond E. Miles and Charles C. Snow, "Organizations: New Concepts for New Forms," *California Management Review* 28 (Spring 1986): 62–73; and John W. Wilson and Judith H. Dobrzynski, "And Now, the Post-Industrial Corporation," *BusinessWeek* (March 3, 1986): 64–74.

53. N. Anand, "Modular, Virtual, and Hollow Forms of Organization Design," working paper, London Business School (2000); Don Tapscott, "Rethinking Strategy in a Networked World," *Strategy + Business*, Issue 24 (Third Quarter 2001): 34–41.

54. Joann S. Lublin, "Smart Balance Keeps Tight Focus on Creativity" (Theory & Practice column), *The Wall Street Journal*, June 8, 2009; and Rebecca Reisner, "A Smart Balance of Staff and Contractors," *BusinessWeek Online*, June 16, 2009, www.businessweek.com/managing/content/jun2009/ca20090616_217232.htm (accessed April 30, 2010).

55. Gregory G. Dess et al., "The New Corporate Architecture," *Academy of Management Executive* 9, no. 3 (1995): 7–20.

56. Harry Hurt III, "The Pain of Change at Boeing," *The New York Times*, November 20, 2011, www.nytimes.com/2010/11/21/business/21shelf.html (accessed August 15, 2012).

57. Charles Levinson and Margaret Coker, "The Secret Rally That Sparked an Uprising; Cairo Protest Organizers Describe Ruses Used to Gain Foothold Against Police," *The Wall Street Journal Online*, February 11, 2011, http://online.wsj.com/article/SB10001424052748704132204576135882356532702.html (accessed August 16, 2012).

58. Dexter Filkins, "Profusion of Rebel Groups Helps Them Survive in Iraq," *The New York Times*, December 2, 2005, www.nytimes.com/2005/12/02/international/middleeast/02insurgency.html (accessed August 30, 2010).

59. Raymond E. Miles, "Adapting to Technology and Competition: A New Industrial Relations System for the Twenty-First Century," *California Management Review* (Winter 1989): 9–28; and Miles and Snow, "The New Network Firm."

60. These disadvantages are based on Cecily A. Raiborn, Janet B. Butler, and Marc F. Massoud, "Outsourcing Support Functions: Identifying and Managing the Good, the Bad, and the Ugly," *Business Horizons* 52 (2009): 347–356; Dess et al., "The New Corporate Architecture"; Anand and Daft, "What Is the Right Organization Design?"; Henry W. Chesbrough and David J. Teece, "Organizing for Innovation: When Is Virtual Virtuous?" *The Innovative Entrepreneur* (August 2002): 127–134; N. Anand, "Modular, Virtual, and Hollow Forms of Organization Design"; and M. Lynne Markus, Brook Manville, and Carole E. Agres, "What Makes a Virtual Organization Work?" *Sloan Management Review* (Fall 2000): 13–26.

61. Hurt, "The Pain of Change at Boeing."

62. Steven Pearlstein, "Lifeguard's Ordeal Is Parable about Outsourcing," *The Washington Post*, July 14, 2012, www.washingtonpost.com/business/lifeguards-ordeal-is-parable-about-outsourcing/2012/07/13/gJQAN6TtkW_story.html (accessed August 16, 2012).

63. Bob Sutton, "United Airlines Lost My Friends' 10-Year-Old Daughter and Didn't Care," *Bob Sutton Work Matters Blog*, http://bobsutton.typepad.com/my_weblog/2012/08/united-airlines-lost-my-friends-10-year-old-daughter-and-didnt-care.html (accessed August 16, 2012).

64. Laurie P. O'Leary, "Curing the Monday Blues: A U.S. Navy Guide for Structuring Cross-Functional Teams," *National Productivity Review* (Spring 1996): 43–51; and Alan Hurwitz, "Organizational Structures for the 'New World Order,'" *Business Horizons* (May–June 1996): 5–14.

65. Jay Galbraith, Diane Downey, and Amy Kates, "Processes and Lateral Capability," *Designing Dynamic Organizations* (New York: AMACOM, 2002) Chapter 4.

66. Thomas Kayser, "Six Ingredients for Collaborative Partnerships," *Leader to Leader* (Summer 2011): 48–54.

67. Siobhan Gorman and Julian E. Barnes, "Spy, Military Ties Aided bin Laden Raid," *The Wall Street Journal*, May 23, 2011, http://online.wsj.com/article/SB10001424052748704083904576334160172068344.html (accessed May 23, 2011).

68. "Panel Says Toyota Failed to Listen to Outsiders," *USA Today*, May 23, 2011, http://content.usatoday.com/communities/driveon/post/2011/05/toyota-panel-calls-for-single-us-chief-paying-heed-to-criticism/1 (accessed August 16, 2012).

69. William J. Altier, "Task Forces: An Effective Management Tool," *Management Review* (February 1987): 52–57.

70. Example from Paul Adler and Laurence Prusak, "Building a Collaborative Enterprise," *Harvard Business Review* (July–August 2011): 95–101.

71. Henry Mintzberg, *The Structure of Organizations* (Englewood Cliffs, NJ: Prentice Hall, 1979).

72. Paul R. Lawrence and Jay W. Lorsch, "New Managerial Job: The Integrator," *Harvard Business Review* (November–December 1967): 142–151; and Ronald N. Ashkenas and Suzanne C. Francis, "Integration Managers: Special Leaders for Special Times," *Harvard Business Review* (November–December 2000): 108–116.

73. Jody Hoffer Gittell, *The Southwest Airlines Way: Using the Power of Relationships to Achieve High Performance* (New York: McGraw-Hill, 2003).

74. This discussion is based on Jody Hoffer Gittell, "Coordinating Mechanisms in Care Provider Groups: Relational Coordination as a Mediator and Input Uncertainty as a Moderator of Performance Effects," *Management Science* 48, no 11 (November 2002), 1408–1426; J. H. Gittell, "The Power of Relationships,"

Sloan Management Review (Winter 2004),16–17; and J. H. Gittell, *The Southwest Airlines Way.*

75. Jody Hoffer Gittell, "Paradox of Coordination and Control," *California Management Review* 42, no 3 (Spring 2000): 101–117.

76. Claudio Feser, "Long Live Bureaucracy," *Leader to Leader* (Summer 2012): 57–65; and Harold J. Leavitt, "Why Hierarchies Thrive," *Harvard Business Review* (March 2003): 96–102, discuss the benefits and problems of vertical hierarchies. See Timothy Galpin, Rod Hilpirt, and Bruce Evans, "The Connected Enterprise: Beyond Division of Labor," *Journal of Business Strategy* 28, no. 2 (2007): 38–47, for a discussion of the advantages of horizontal over vertical designs.

77. Eric M. Olson, Stanley F. Slater, and G. Tomas M. Hult, "The Importance of Structure and Process to Strategy Implementation," *Business Horizons* 48 (2005): 47–54; and Dale E. Zand, "Strategic Renewal: How an Organization Realigned Structure with Strategy," *Strategy & Leadership* 37, no. 3 (2009): 23–28.

78. Michael E. Porter, *Competitive Strategy* (New York: Free Press, 1980), pp. 36–46.

79. Tom Burns and G. M. Stalker, *The Management of Innovation* (London: Tavistock, 1961).

80. John A. Coutright, Gail T. Fairhurst, and L. Edna Rogers, "Interaction Patterns in Organic and Mechanistic Systems," *Academy of Management Journal* 32 (1989): 773–802.

81. For more on technology and structure, see Denise M. Rousseau and Robert A. Cooke, "Technology and Structure: The Concrete, Abstract, and Activity Systems of Organizations," *Journal of Management* 10 (1984): 345–361; Charles Perrow, "A Framework for the Comparative Analysis of Organizations," *American Sociological Review* 32 (1967): 194–208; and Denise M. Rousseau, "Assessment of Technology in Organizations: Closed versus Open Systems Approaches," *Academy of Management Review* 4 (1979): 531–542.

82. Joan Woodward, *Industrial Organizations: Theory and Practice* (London: Oxford University Press, 1965); and Joan Woodward, *Management and Technology* (London: Her Majesty's Stationery Office, 1958).

83. Peter K. Mills and Thomas Kurk, "A Preliminary Investigation into the Influence of Customer-Firm Interface on Information Processing and Task Activity in Service Organizations," *Journal of Management* 12 (1986): 91–104; Peter K. Mills and Dennis J. Moberg, "Perspectives on the Technology of Service Operations," *Academy of Management Review* 7 (1982): 467–478; and Roger W. Schmenner, "How Can Service Businesses Survive and Prosper?" *Sloan Management Review* 27 (Spring 1986): 21–32.

84. Richard B. Chase and David A. Tansik, "The Customer Contact Model for Organization Design," *Management Science* 29 (1983): 1037–1050; and Gregory B. Northcraft and Richard B. Chase, "Managing Service Demand at the Point of Delivery," *Academy of Management Review* 10 (1985): 66–75.

85. Geeta Anand, "The Henry Ford of Heart Surgery," *The Wall Street Journal*, November 25, 2009, A16.

4

ORGANIZING

Change and Innovation

Fuse/Jupiter Images

Learning Outcomes

After studying this chapter, you should be able to:

1. Define organizational change and explain the forces driving innovation and change in today's organizations.

2. Identify the three innovation strategies that managers implement for changing products and technologies.

3. Explain the value of creativity, a bottom-up approach, internal contests, idea incubators, idea champions, and new-venture teams for innovation.

4. Describe the horizontal linkage model and how it contributes to successful product and service innovations.

5. Explain open innovation and how it is being used by today's organizations.

6. Discuss why changes in people and culture are critical to any change process.

7. Define organization development (OD) and large group interventions.

8. Explain the OD stages of unfreezing, changing, and refreezing.

9. Identify sources of resistance to change and describe the implementation tactics that managers can use to overcome resistance.

1
INTRODUCTION

2
ENVIRONMENT

3
PLANNING

4
ORGANIZING

5
LEADING

6
CONTROLLING

© Alan Bailey/Sexto Sol/Getty Images

Are You Innovative?[1]

INSTRUCTIONS: Think about your current life. Indicate whether each item below is Mostly True or Mostly False for you.

	Mostly True	Mostly False
1. I am always seeking new ways to do things.	_____	_____
2. I consider myself creative and original in my thinking and behavior.	_____	_____
3. I rarely trust new gadgets until I see whether they work for people around me.	_____	_____
4. In a group or at work, I am often skeptical of new ideas.	_____	_____
5. I typically buy new foods, gear, and other innovations before other people.	_____	_____
6. I like to spend time trying new things.	_____	_____
7. My behavior influences others to try new things.	_____	_____
8. Among my coworkers, I will be among the first to try out a new idea or method.	_____	_____

SCORING AND INTERPRETATION: *Personal innovativeness* reflects the awareness of the need to innovate and a readiness to try new things. Innovativeness is also thought of as the degree to which a person adopts innovations earlier than other people in the peer group. Innovativeness is considered a positive characteristic for people in many companies where individuals and organizations are faced with a constant need to change.

To compute your score on the Personal Innovativeness scale, add the number of Mostly True answers to items 1, 2, 5, 6, 7, and 8 above and the Mostly False answers to items 3 and 4 to get your score. A score of 6–8 indicates that you are very innovative and likely are one of the first people to adopt changes. A score of 4–5 would suggest that you are average or slightly above average in innovativeness compared to others. A score of 0–3 means that you might prefer the tried and true and hence are not excited about new ideas or innovations. As a new manager, a high score suggests you will emphasize innovation and change. A low score suggests you may prefer stability and established methods.

Have you ever dreamed of designing vehicles, weapons, or other equipment for the U.S. military? You might get a chance. The Defense Advanced Research Projects Agency (DARPA) believes that by opening up innovation to a range of participants—including small businesses, academic research labs, corporations, and individual engineers—it can tap more brainpower than with the traditional defense contractor approach, while also saving time and money. The first step in this new model is a competition to see if volunteers can come up with a design for a new amphibious vehicle to replace the 1970s-era one the Marines are now using. Military leaders—and U.S. taxpayers—can hope that the competition produces a design that can be manufactured in a timely and cost-efficient way. In 2011, the military canceled its contract on a project for a new amphibious vehicle led by General Dynamics Corporation because it concluded it would be too expensive—after spending more than $3 billion on development.[2]

The military is similar to organizations in all industries in searching for any innovation edge they can find. Companies might still be struggling through a tough economy, but smart managers know they can't let innovation take a back seat. Winning companies are continually innovating in both large and small ways. Hidden Valley Foods, owned by Clorox Company, came out with a thicker, creamier version of its popular Hidden Valley

Ranch dressing and is marketing it as "the new ketchup," hoping to get bottles on restaurant tables everywhere.[3] Apple once again produced a groundbreaking innovation with the launch of communications technology Siri, prompting Amazon and Google to buy technologies to provide their own similar services.[4]

If organizations don't change and innovate successfully, they die. Consider that only a small number of large companies reach the age of 40, according to a recent study of more than 6 million firms. The ones that survive are ruthless about innovation and change.[5] Every organization sometimes faces the need to change swiftly and dramatically to cope with a changing environment. Consider General Motors (GM). After sinking into bankruptcy and having to be bailed out by the U.S. government just a few years ago, GM amazingly regained its position as the world's largest automaker by implementing a combination of management, structure, strategy, culture, and product changes.[6]

In this chapter, we look at how organizations can be designed to respond to the environment through internal change and development. First, we look at two key aspects of change in organizations: introducing new products and technologies, and changing people and culture. Then we examine how managers implement change, including overcoming resistance.

Innovation and the Changing Workplace

Organizational change is defined as the adoption of a new idea or behavior by an organization.[7] Sometimes change and innovation are spurred by forces outside the organization, such as when a powerful customer demands annual price cuts, when a key supplier goes out of business, or when new government regulations go into effect. In China, for example, organizations are under pressure from the government to increase wages to help workers cope with rising food costs.[8] Managers in all types of organizations in the United States are facing a need for change to be in line with provisions of the new Patient Protection and Affordable Care Act (a health care law passed in March 2010), which was upheld by the Supreme Court as constitutional in 2012. Insurance companies will no longer be able to deny coverage based on preexisting conditions. Small businesses will be required to provide health insurance for employees or pay penalties. State governments are evaluating options for expanding Medicaid coverage or creating new insurance exchanges where people can purchase affordable coverage. Health care providers are entering into partnerships with each other and with insurance providers to stave off financial pressures that may result from mandates and price controls.[9]

These types of outside forces compel managers to look for greater efficiencies in operations and other changes to keep their organizations profitable. Other times, managers within the company want to initiate major changes, such as forming employee-participation teams, introducing new products, or instituting new training systems, but they don't know how to make the changes successful.

Disruptive innovation is becoming a goal for companies that want to remain competitive on a global basis. **Disruptive innovation** refers to innovations in products, services, or processes that radically change an industry's rules of the game for producers and consumers. DVDs all but wiped out the videotape industry, and now streaming video is threatening the same fate for DVDs. Digital cameras appear to be eliminating the photographic film industry. A company called Square developed a credit card reader that plugs into a smartphone. This is a disruptive innovation in the trillion-dollar financial services system for credit card payments. Square enabled millions of small businesses that couldn't afford the transaction fees charged by financial companies to begin accepting credit cards.[10] Many disruptive innovations come from small entrepreneurial firms like Square, founded by Twitter inventor Jack Dorsey. Some observers think companies in emerging markets such as China and India will produce a great percentage of such innovations in the coming years.[11]

In addition, Western firms are increasingly using an approach referred to as *trickle-up innovation* or *reverse innovation*. Rather than innovating in affluent countries and transferring products to emerging markets, companies such as General Electric (GE), John Deere, Nestlé, Procter & Gamble (P&G), and Xerox are creating innovative low-cost products for emerging markets and then quickly and inexpensively repackaging them for sale in developed countries. GE Healthcare's team in China created a portable ultrasound machine that sold for less than 15 percent of the cost of the company's high-end machines. GE now sells the product around the world, and it grew to a $278 million global product line within six years. John Deere developed a high-quality, low-cost tractor for farmers in India that is increasingly in demand in the United States among farmers reeling from the recession.[12]

However, change—especially major change—is not easy, and many organizations struggle with changing successfully. In some cases, employees don't have the desire or motivation to come up with new ideas, or their ideas never get heard by managers who could put them into practice. In other cases, managers learn about good ideas but have trouble getting cooperation from employees for implementation. Successful change requires that organizations be capable of both creating and implementing ideas, which means the organization must learn to be *ambidextrous*.

An **ambidextrous approach** means incorporating structures and processes that are appropriate for both the creative impulse and for the systematic implementation of innovations. For example, a loose, flexible structure and greater employee freedom are excellent for the creation and initiation of ideas; however, these same conditions often make it difficult to implement a change because employees are less likely to comply. With an ambidextrous approach, managers encourage flexibility and freedom to innovate and propose new ideas with creative departments and other mechanisms we will discuss in this chapter, but they use a more rigid, centralized, and standardized approach for implementing innovations.[13] For example, Mike Lawrie, CEO of the London-based software company Misys, created a separate unit for Misys Open Source Solutions, a venture aimed at creating a potentially disruptive technology in the health care industry. Lawrie wanted creative people to have the time and resources they needed to work on new software that holds the promise of seamless data exchange among hospitals, physicians, insurers, and others involved in the health care system. Implementation of new ideas, where routine and precision is important, occurs within the regular organization.[14]

▶ ▶ ▶ **Concept Connection**

Blue Images/Corbis

Technological advances in smartphones have paved the way for mobile credit card readers from providers such as Square, Intuit GoPayment, and Merchant Anywhere. This **disruptive innovation** has been a major step forward for small business owners, allowing them to accept credit card payments on the fly and with minimal transaction fees. The mobile readers are especially useful for merchants who sell their wares in outdoor environments, such as flea markets, arts and crafts fairs, and farmer's markets.

4

ORGANIZING

Remember This

- Every organization must change and innovate to survive.
- **Organizational change** is defined as the adoption of a new idea or behavior by an organization.
- **Disruptive innovation** refers to innovations in products, services, or processes that radically change competition in an industry, such as the advent of streaming video or e-books.
- An **ambidextrous approach** means incorporating structures and processes that are appropriate for both the creative impulse and the systematic implementation of innovations.

Changing *Things:* New Products and Technologies

Organizations must embrace many types of change. One vital area of innovation is the introduction of new products and technologies. A **product change** is a change in the organization's product or service outputs. Product and service innovation is the primary way in which organizations adapt to changes in markets, technology, and competition.[15] Examples of new products include the Amazon Kindle Fire; Frigidaire's Double Oven Range, which fits two ovens in the space of a standard 30-inch appliance; and the Yonanas countertop blender, which transforms frozen bananas into an ice-cream–like treat.[16] HBO Go, the first comprehensive mobile television service, is an example of a service innovation, as is the launch of online programs for undergraduate and graduate education. Southern New Hampshire University (SNHU) zoomed to number 12 on *Fast Company's* list of the world's 50 most innovative companies due to managers' creative reinvention of online education. SNHU president Paul LeBlanc hired the former CEO of an online customer relationship company to retool the college's operations in the style of Zappos.com, to provide exceptional customer service. And he didn't stop there. "We want to create the business model that blows up our current business model, because if we don't, someone else will," LeBlanc said.[17]

Product and service changes are related to changes in the technology of the organization. A **technology change** is a change in the organization's production process—how the organization does its work. Technology changes are designed to make the production of a product or service more efficient. Hammond's Candies saves hundreds of thousands of dollars a year by implementing technology changes suggested by employees. One example was tweaking a machine gear that reduced the number of employees needed on an assembly line from five to four. Another idea was a new way to package candy canes that would protect them from getting broken while en route to stores.[18] Other examples of technology change include the introduction of efficiency-boosting winglets on aircraft at Southwest Airlines, the adoption of automatic mail-sorting machines by the U.S. Postal Service, and the use of biosimulation software to run virtual tests on new drugs at Johnson & Johnson pharmaceutical research and development.

Three critical innovation strategies for changing products and technologies are illustrated in Exhibit 11.1.[19] The first strategy, *exploration*, involves designing the organization to encourage creativity and the initiation of new ideas. The strategy of *cooperation* refers to creating

Green Power

Building a Better Mouse . . .

We all have them: old laptops stuffed into closets, computer monitors, hard drives, and printers crammed into the corners of the garage. And who can forget the mouse (five of them, actually, still attached to cords) jammed into a drawer? In a world focused on sustainability, the challenge for managers in the electronics industry is how to change and innovate when the large outer casings for our products *won't go away*. **Fujitsu** broke this barrier by developing a keyboard made from renewable materials. A year later, using organic materials as a substitute for plastic, the company unveiled a mouse casing that was 100 percent biodegradable. Now, the race is on. Fujitsu's innovations offer a visionary promise that one day, all our electronic devices will be part of the sustainability revolution.

Source: Staff writers, "Fujitsu Unveils 'World's First' Biodegradable Mouse," *Business Green*, January 25, 2011, www.businessgreen.com/bg/news/1939343/fujitsu-unveils-worlds-biodegradable-mouse (accessed January 25, 2011).

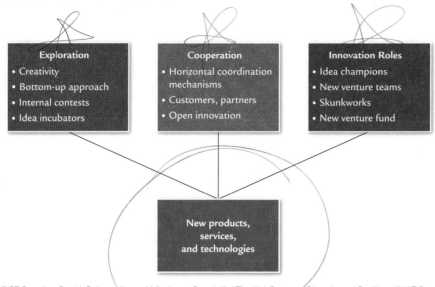

SOURCE: Based on Patrick Reinmoeller and Nicole van Baardwijk, "The Link Between Diversity and Resilience," *MIT Sloan Management Review* (Summer 2005): 61–65.

EXHIBIT 11.1

Three Innovation Strategies for New Products and Technologies

conditions and systems to facilitate internal and external coordination and knowledge sharing. Finally, *innovation roles* means that managers put in place processes and structures to ensure that new ideas are carried forward for acceptance and implementation.

EXPLORATION

Exploration is the stage where ideas for new products and technologies are born. Managers design the organization for exploration by establishing conditions that encourage creativity and allow new ideas to spring forth. **Creativity** refers to the generation of novel ideas that might meet perceived needs or respond to opportunities for the organization.[20] People noted for their creativity include Edwin Land, who invented the Polaroid camera, and Swiss engineer George de Mestral, who created Velcro after noticing the tiny hooks on some burrs caught on his wool socks. These people saw unique and creative opportunities in familiar situations.

Characteristics of highly creative people are illustrated in the left column of Exhibit 11.2. Creative people often are known for originality, open-mindedness, curiosity, a focused approach to problem solving, persistence, a relaxed and playful attitude, and receptiveness to new ideas.[21] Creativity can also be designed into organizations. Most companies want more creative employees and often seek to hire creative individuals. However, the individual is only part of the story, and each of us has some potential for creativity. Managers are responsible for creating a work environment that allows creativity to flourish.[22]

The characteristics of creative organizations correspond to those of individuals, as illustrated in the right column of

Take a Moment

Assess your creativity by completing the New Manager Self-Test on page 348.

4

ORGANIZING

▶ ▶ ▶ **Concept Connection**

Innovative companies such as Intuit want everyone to be coming up with new ideas continually. Managers encourage **creativity** during the **exploration phase** by embracing failure as readily as they do success. "I've had my share of really bad ideas," founder Scott Cook, pictured here with former CEO Steve Bennett, admits. Yet failure can have hidden possibilities. Sticky notes, such as those shown here on Intuit's board, were invented at 3M Corporation based on a failed product—a not-very-sticky adhesive that resulted from a chemist's attempts to create a superglue. Post-it Notes became one of the best-selling office products ever.

New Manager  Self-Test

Assess Your Creativity

Instructions: In the list below, check each adjective that you believe accurately describes your personality. Be very honest with yourself. Check all the words that fit your personality.

1. affected___	11. honest___	21. original___
2. capable___	12. humorous___	22. reflective___
3. cautious___	13. individualistic___	23. resourceful___
4. clever___	14. informal___	24. self-confident___
5. commonplace___	15. insightful___	25. sexy___
6. confident___	16. intelligent___	26. snobbish___
7. conservative___	17. interests narrow___	27. sincere___
8. conventional___	18. interests wide___	28. submissive___
9. egotistical___	19. inventive___	29. suspicious___
10. dissatisfied___	20. mannerly___	30. unconventional___

Scoring and Interpretation: Add one point for checking each of the following words: 2, 4, 6, 9, 12, 13, 14, 15, 16, 18, 19, 21, 22, 23, 24, 25, 26, and 30. Subtract one point for checking each of the following words: 1, 3, 5, 7, 8, 10, 11, 17, 20, 27, 28, and 29. Score = _____. The highest possible score is +18; the lowest possible score is −12.

Innovation starts with creativity. Your score on this questionnaire reflects your creativity for solving problems and finding novel solutions. The average score for a set of 256 males on this creativity scale was 3.57, and for 126 females was 4.4. A group of 45 male research scientists and a group of 530 male psychology graduate students both had average scores of 6.0, and 124 male architects received an average score of 5.3. A group of 335 female psychology students had an average score of 3.34. If you have a score above 5.0, your personality would be considered above average in creativity. To what extent do you think your score reflects your true creativity? Compare your score to others in your class. Which adjectives were more important for your score compared to other students?

Source: Harrison G. Clough, "A Creative Personality Scale for the Adjective Check List," *Journal of Personality and Social Psychology* 37, no. 8 (1979): 1398–1405.

Exhibit 11.2. Creative organizations are loosely structured. People find themselves in a situation of ambiguity, assignments are vague, territories overlap, tasks are loosely defined, and much work is done by teams. Managers in creative companies embrace risk and experimentation. They involve employees in a varied range of projects, so that people are not stuck in the rhythm of routine jobs, and they drive out the fear of making mistakes that can inhibit creative thinking.[23] Research shows that successful innovations are often accompanied by a high rate of failure. SurePayroll, a payroll-services company, gives out an annual "Best New Mistake" cash award to keep people taking creative risks. Similarly, Grey

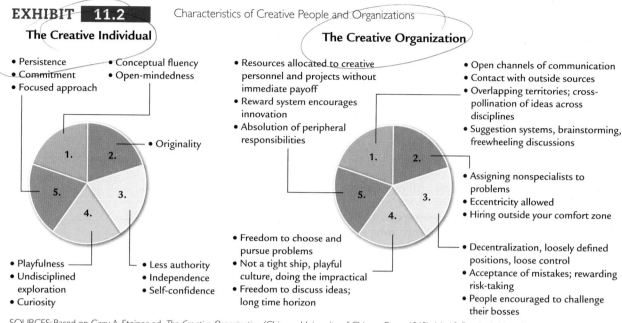

EXHIBIT 11.2 Characteristics of Creative People and Organizations

The Creative Individual

- Persistence
- Commitment
- Focused approach

- Conceptual fluency
- Open-mindedness

- Originality

1. 2. 3. 4. 5.

- Playfulness
- Undisciplined exploration
- Curiosity

- Less authority
- Independence
- Self-confidence

The Creative Organization

- Resources allocated to creative personnel and projects without immediate payoff
- Reward system encourages innovation
- Absolution of peripheral responsibilities

- Open channels of communication
- Contact with outside sources
- Overlapping territories; cross-pollination of ideas across disciplines
- Suggestion systems, brainstorming, freewheeling discussions

1. 2. 3. 4. 5.

- Assigning nonspecialists to problems
- Eccentricity allowed
- Hiring outside your comfort zone

- Freedom to choose and pursue problems
- Not a tight ship, playful culture, doing the impractical
- Freedom to discuss ideas; long time horizon

- Decentralization, loosely defined positions, loose control
- Acceptance of mistakes; rewarding risk-taking
- People encouraged to challenge their bosses

SOURCES: Based on Gary A. Steiner, ed., *The Creative Organization* (Chicago: University of Chicago Press, 1965): 16–18; Rosabeth Moss Kanter, "The Middle Manager as Innovator," *Harvard Business Review* (July–August 1982): 104–105; James Brian Quinn, "Managing Innovation: Controlled Chaos," *Harvard Business Review* (May–June 1985): 73–84; Robert I. Sutton, "The Weird Rules of Creativity," *Harvard Business Review* (September 2001): 94–103; and Bridget Finn, "Playbook: Brainstorming for Better Brainstorming," *Business* 2.0 (April 2005), 109–114.

New York, an advertising agency, awards an annual "Heroic Failure" trophy.[24] Creative organizations are those that have an internal culture of playfulness, freedom, challenge, and grass-roots participation.[25] Exhibit 11.3 shows the world's top ten innovative companies from the 2012 list in *Fast Company*.

Innovative companies use a **bottom-up approach,** which means encouraging the flow of ideas from lower levels and making sure they get heard and acted upon by top executives.[26] At Intuit, managers sponsor Design for Delight (D4D) forums, typically attended by more than 1,000 employees. Two employees who had been at Intuit for only a few months came up with the idea of an online social network for the D4D initiative. In the first year, the network generated 32 ideas that made it to market.[27] Japanese pharmaceutical firm Eisai Company encourages a bottom-up flow of ideas with innovation community forums that focus on specific health-care-related issues. One idea now on the market in Japan is technology for dispensing medications in a jellylike substance that Alzheimer's patients

Rank	Company	Reason
1	Apple	Creating markets others have to compete in
2	Facebook	Ever-widening platform for people to share information
3	Google	Transforming from search to a diversified Web power
4	Amazon	Constantly transforming itself
5	Square	Reinventing the process of making and taking credit payments
6	Twitter	Strengthening global dialogue
7	The Occupy Movement	Challenging the political, financial, and social establishment
8	Tencent	Advancing China's Internet boom
9	Life Technologies	Products that speed up genetic sequencing
10	SolarCity	Being a full-service provider of new solar technology

EXHIBIT 11.3

The World's Most Innovative Companies 2012

SOURCE: "The World's 50 Most Innovative Companies," *Fast Company* (March 2012): 70–149.

Manager's *Shoptalk*

Use Six Thinking Hats for Better Ideas

A technique that can promote broader thinking is called the *six thinking hats,* which was developed by Edward de Bono. The model encourages people in a group to combine negative and critical thinking with positive and creative thinking. Participants either literally or figuratively wear a hat to represent a distinct perspective. The wearing of the hats helps individuals step out of their comfort zone and generate creative ideas in a risk-free way. The six hats technique can transform a typical nonproductive meeting into a highly creative problem-solving endeavor.

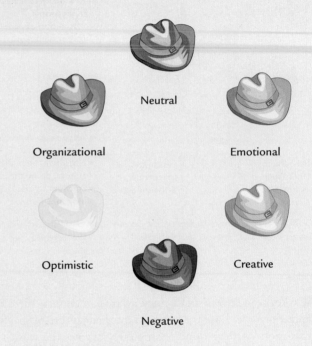

Neutral

Organizational

Emotional

Optimistic

Creative

Negative

The Six Hats

- *White Hat:* This thinking hat is neutral and concerned with just the objective facts, figures, and information pertaining to a problem.

- *Red Hat:* This hat allows an emotional response to the subject. It is a perspective based on feelings, intuitions, instincts, and hunches.

- *Green Hat:* The green hat is the one that generates new ideas, possibilities, alternatives, and unique solutions for better problem solving.

- *Black Hat:* This is the negative, pessimistic, and critical hat that focuses on why a suggestion will *not* work. When people wear this hat, they point out the flaws and false assumptions in an idea.

- *Yellow Hat:* The yellow hat is the opposite of the black hat. It is optimistic and focuses on the values and benefits of an idea. Its focus is on what *will* work.

- *Blue Hat:* This hat is concerned with group facilitation. The group leader typically assumes the blue hat role, although any member can wear the blue hat from time to time.

Using the Technique

To apply the six hats technique, schedule a specific time during a creative problem-solving meeting when every person in the group wears the same color of hat—that is, takes the same perspective. A time is set aside when everyone uses rational, fact-based thinking (white hat), emotional thinking (red hat), creative thinking (green hat), and so forth. The result is that each perspective (hat) is heard in sequence, and negative views or arguments do not overwhelm creativity. Everyone together has a time to think of good ideas, as well as a time for finding weak points.

Source: Based on Edward de Bono, *Serious Creativity: Using the Power of Lateral Thinking to Create New Ideas* (New York: HarperBusiness, 1992).

can swallow easily.[28] This chapter's Shoptalk describes a fun technique some companies use to get people to come up with creative ideas for solving specific problems.

Some companies also use internal *innovation contests.* Mike Hall, CEO of Borrego Solar Systems, holds "innovation challenge" contests on the company intranet to get his shy, introverted engineers to speak up with their ideas for improving the business. Employees vote on their favorites, and the winner takes home a cash prize. One idea that was quickly implemented was using software that enables sales and engineering teams to collaborate.[29] Managers at the accounting and consulting firm PricewaterhouseCoopers challenged the stereotype that accountants are boring and unimaginative by sponsoring an *American Idol*–style contest to spur employees to come up with creative ideas.

"We have an average age of 27, but we have roots in tax and assurance," said PricewaterhouseCoopers (PwC) U.S. chairman Bob Moritz. "So how do you make this place feel like a Google or a Facebook? A place that feels leading edge?"

Like other companies, PwC has felt the sting of increased competition and a shaky global economy. Harnessing the creativity of all employees in the search for profitable ideas seemed not only like a good thing to do, but like a business imperative. Mitra Best, PwC's "innovation leader" and a fan of *American Idol*, took ideas from that show, plus ideas from the videogame world of live chats and online discussions, to create PowerPitch, a fun, collaborative competition that would connect and inspire 30,000 PwC employees. Employees loved it. The competition, structured in three stages over a nine-month period, was open to any U.S. employee below the partner level. Each contestant had to recruit a team and pitch either a new service or a radical rethinking of an existing service that could be worth $100 million in revenue. The winning team would get a $100,000 prize, plus the chance to help implement the new idea.

Nearly 800 proposals were pitched at Round One, and by the time of the grand finale, nearly 60 percent of people in the firm had participated in one way or another—direct participation, voting, comments and suggestions, and so forth. The five finalist teams were flown to PwC headquarters in New York to present their proposals and answer questions from judges in a packed corporate auditorium. Offices around the country held viewing parties, watching the competition via live Webcast. The winning team, led by 25-year-old financial services associate Zachary Capozzi, proposed creating a sophisticated data-mining practice within PwC that uses the sort of analytics that Netflix uses to predict which movies customers are interested in. For clients who don't have that capability in-house, the service can be invaluable—and it can be a source of new clients and a big new revenue stream for PwC.[30]

Just as important as creating ideas is turning them into action. Sadly, research indicates that, on average, a U.S. employee's ideas are implemented only once every six years.[31] "There's nothing worse for morale than when employees feel like their ideas go nowhere," says Larry Bennett, a professor of entrepreneurship.[32] At PricewaterhouseCoopers, all of the final ideas were assigned to a senior "champion," who will help the teams further develop and implement their proposals. Other ideas from the top 20 semifinalists were assigned to an idea incubator group. An **idea incubator** is a mechanism that provides a safe harbor where ideas from employees throughout the company can be developed without interference from company bureaucracy or politics.[33]

Take a Moment

Go to the Experiential Exercise on pages 367–368 that pertains to creativity in organizations.

4

ORGANIZING

Remember This

- A **product change** is a change in the organization's products or services, such as the Whirlpool two-oven range or the Amazon Kindle Fire.
- **Technology change** refers to a change in production processes—how the organization does its work.
- *Exploration* involves designing the organization to encourage creativity and the initiation of new ideas.
- **Creativity** is the generation of novel ideas that may meet perceived needs or respond to opportunities for the organization.

- PricewaterhouseCoopers applied a **bottom-up approach**, using an *American Idol-style* contest to encourage employee ideas for new services at the giant accounting and consulting firm.
- An **idea incubator** is an organizational program that provides a safe harbor where employees can generate and develop ideas without interference from company bureaucracy or politics.

COOPERATION

Another important aspect of innovation is providing mechanisms for both internal and external cooperation. Ideas for product and technology innovations typically originate at lower levels of the organization and need to flow horizontally across departments. In addition, people and organizations outside the firm can be rich sources of innovative ideas. Lack of innovation is widely recognized as one of the biggest problems facing today's businesses. Consider that 72 percent of top executives surveyed by *Business Week* and the Boston Consulting Group reported that innovation is a top priority, yet almost half said they are dissatisfied with their results in that area.[34] Thus, many companies are undergoing a transformation in the way they find and use new ideas, focusing on improving both internal and external coordination and cooperation.

Internal Coordination

Successful innovation requires expertise from several departments simultaneously, and failed innovation is often the result of failed cooperation.[35] Sony, once the epitome of Japanese business and innovation success, is literally fighting to stay alive because the company hasn't had a hit product in years and hasn't turned a profit since 2008. To be sure, Sony was battered by one after another disruptive new technology or unexpected competitor, but the biggest problem was that managers were unable to fight back because of poor cooperation within the organization. The company had the technology to create a music player like the iPod long before Apple came out with it (co-founder Akio Morita actually envisioned such a device in the 1980s), but divisions couldn't cooperate to bring the idea to fruition. Today, some top executives complain about managers who refuse to share information or work with other divisions. Consequently, the company makes a lot of different gadgets that overlap and cannibalize one another and offers disjointed services for different products rather than an integrated common platform to deliver music, movies, and games.[36] "Innovation is a team sport," says Drew Boyd, a businessman who speaks about innovation to other companies.[37]

Companies that successfully innovate usually have the following characteristics:

- People in research and marketing actively work with customers to understand their needs and develop solutions.
- Technical specialists are aware of recent developments and make effective use of new technology.
- A shared new product development process that is advocated and supported by top management cuts across organizational functions and units.
- Members from key departments—research, manufacturing, marketing—cooperate in the development of the new product or service.
- Each project is guided by a core cross-functional team from beginning to end.[38]

One approach to successful innovation is called the **horizontal linkage model**, which is illustrated in the center circle of Exhibit 11.4.[39] The model shows that the research, manufacturing, and sales and marketing departments within an organization simultaneously contribute to new products and technologies. People from these departments meet frequently in teams and task forces to share ideas and solve problems. Research people inform marketing of new technical developments to learn whether they will be useful to customers. Marketing people pass customer complaints to research to use in the design of new products and to manufacturing people to develop new ideas for improving production speed and quality. Manufacturing informs other departments whether a product idea can be manufactured within cost limits. Throughout the process, development teams keep in close touch with customers. A study by McKinsey found that 80 percent of successful innovators periodically test and validate customer preferences during development of new products and services.[40] Unfortunately, "new products can take on a life of their own within an organization, becoming so hyped that there's no turning back," wrote Joan Schneider

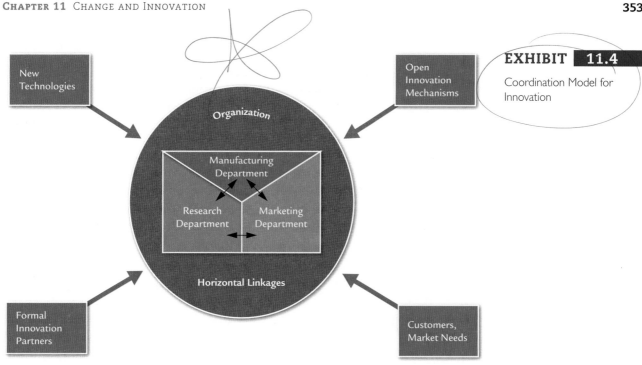

EXHIBIT 11.4

Coordination Model for Innovation

and Julie Hall, coauthors of *The New Launch Plan: 152 Tips, Tactics, and Trends from the Most Memorable New Products.* This is likely what happened with Coca-Cola's failed introduction of "New Coke" in the mid-1980s and its more recent launch of Coke C2, a failed product aimed at 20- to 40-year old men that promised half the calories and carbs but all the taste of original Coke. The product development team became so committed to the new product that it failed to look objectively at marketing data.[41]

The horizontal linkage model is increasingly important in a high-pressure business environment that requires rapidly developing and commercializing products and services. Speed is a pivotal strategic weapon in today's global marketplace.[42] This kind of teamwork is similar to a rugby match, wherein players run together, passing the ball back and forth as they move downfield.[43] Corning used a horizontal linkage model to create a new product for the mobile phone industry.

4

ORGANIZING

Innovative Way

Corning Inc.

Plastic screens on cell phones are easily scratched and broken, which gave a small team in Corning's specialty materials division an idea: What if they could find a way to make mobile screens out of a super-strong but flexible glass that the company had originally attempted (unsuccessfully) to sell for automobile windshields in the 1960s? Just producing an experimental batch to gauge customer interest would cost as much as $300,000, but managers took the risk because the project had a strong idea champion.

Once the test run was completed and potential customers expressed excitement, managers had to move quickly. Corning took the project from concept to commercial success in an amazingly short period of time. One reason is that the company had both the right culture and the right systems. Corning divisions and departments know that top managers expect, support, and reward collaboration on promising new product launches. Innovation at Corning is managed not by lone inventors or small teams in silos, but rather by multidisciplinary groups all across the organization. The company has two units—the Corporate Technology Council and the Growth and Strategy Council—that are charged with overseeing the innovation process and making sure departments effectively cooperate in new product development efforts that are sanctioned by management. Thus, employees from R&D, manufacturing, and sales quickly agreed to serve on the team developing the new glass product.

By 2010, Corning's cell phone glass, called Gorilla Glass, was used on more than three dozen mobile phones as well as some laptops and other devices. Gorilla Glass is projected to be a $500 million business by 2015.[44]

Concept Connection ◀◀◀

Innovation often requires **internal coordination** because it takes the combined expertise of a number of different team players, each with their own areas of specialization, to come up with a single creative, yet realistic, solution. In architecture, for example, projects are often designed by teams of people. One may be a specialist in structural engineering, another may focus on the plumbing and electrical systems, while yet others are concerned about the look of the interior and exterior of the structure. Working together, they ensure that all aspects of an innovative design will work together to meet the needs of the customer.

> "*Successful innovation requires rich cross-pollination both inside and outside the organization.*"
>
> — BRUCE BROWN AND SCOTT D. ANTHONY,
> IN "HOW P&G TRIPLED ITS INNOVATION
> SUCCESS RATE"

By using a horizontal linkage model for new product development, Corning has been highly effective in rapidly taking products from idea to success in the marketplace. Famous innovation failures—such as Microsoft's Zune music player and the U.S. Mint's Susan B. Anthony dollar, perhaps the most unpopular coin in American history—usually violate the horizontal linkage model.

External Coordination

Exhibit 11.4 also illustrates that organizations look outside their boundaries to find and develop new ideas. Engineers and researchers stay aware of new technological developments. Marketing personnel pay attention to shifting market conditions and customer needs. Some organizations build formal strategic partnerships such as alliances and joint ventures to improve innovation success.

Successful companies often include customers, strategic partners, suppliers, and other outsiders directly in the product and service development process. One of the hottest trends is *open innovation*.[45] In the past, most businesses generated their own ideas in-house and then developed, manufactured, marketed, and distributed them, which is a closed innovation approach. Today, however, forward-looking companies are trying a different method. **Open innovation** means extending the search for and commercialization of new ideas beyond the boundaries of the organization and even beyond the boundaries of the industry, sharing knowledge and resources with other organizations and individuals outside the firm.

For example, game maker Rovio extended the commercialization of the Angry Birds brand into books, movies, and toys by letting outsiders license the popular gaming app.[46] Some of the best-selling products from consumer products company Procter & Gamble, including the Swiffer SweeperVac, Olay Regenerist, and Mr. Clean Magic Eraser, were developed in whole or in part by someone outside the firm.[47] Even Apple, which has always been famously "closed" in many ways, has found a way to tap into the power of open innovation. For example, although the company sets guidelines and technological constraints, it allows anyone to create and market mobile applications for the iPhone in exchange for a small share of the revenue generated by the apps. Apple generates around $75 million in revenue a month through its App Store.[48]

The Internet has made it possible for companies to tap into ideas from around the world and let hundreds of thousands of people contribute to the innovation process, which is why some approaches to open innovation are referred to as *crowdsourcing*. Fiat introduced the first crowdsourced car, the Mio, in 2010. The automaker launched a Web site asking people to think about what the car of the future should be like, and more than 17,000 people around the world submitted ideas.[49] Oscar de la Renta has a "digital inspiration board" on the Internet, where anyone can upload images for new designs to inspire the next fashion collection. Goldcorp, a Canadian gold mining firm, asked people to examine its geologic data over the Web and submit proposals for locations to find more gold. With

StockLite/Shutterstock.com

a prize to the top 25 finalists of $500,000, the company received more than 475,000 tips and solutions, which confirmed many suspected deposits and identified some new ones.[50]

Crowdsourcing is also being used to gather creative ideas for solving social problems. After the devastating earthquake in Haiti, for example, relief workers trying to dispatch health care workers and supplies had 400 street addresses that might be clinics. They asked for help over the Internet in "geotagging" the addresses (putting coordinates on a map), and nearly all 400 were mapped within 24 hours. Having people physically check addresses might have taken weeks. Similarly, following the earthquake and tsunami in Japan, crowdsourced maps gave local relief workers a better picture of the situation and helped them set priorities for distribution of food, shelter, and sanitation services.[51]

Remember This

- Successful product and service innovation depends on cooperation, both within the organization and with customers and others outside the organization.

- Using a **horizontal linkage model** means that several departments, such as marketing, research, and manufacturing, work closely together to develop new products.

- Some companies, such as Procter & Gamble and Rovio, creator of the Angry Birds game, extend the search for

and commercialization of innovative ideas beyond the boundaries of the organization—a process called **open innovation.**

- *Crowdsourcing*, an open innovation approach used by Fiat, Oscar de la Renta, and many other companies, taps into ideas from around the world and lets thousands or hundreds of thousands of people participate in the innovation process, usually via the Internet.

INNOVATION ROLES

The third aspect of product and technology innovation is creating structural mechanisms to make sure new ideas are carried forward, accepted, and implemented. Managers can directly influence whether entrepreneurship flourishes in the organization by expressing support of entrepreneurial activities, giving employees a degree of autonomy, and rewarding learning and risk-taking.[52] One important factor is fostering idea champions. The formal definition of an **idea champion** is a person who sees the need for and champions productive change within the organization.

Remember: Change does not occur by itself. Personal energy and effort are required to promote a new idea successfully. When Texas Instruments studied 50 of its new-product introductions, a surprising fact emerged: Without exception, every new product that failed lacked a zealous champion. In contrast, most of the new products that succeeded had a champion. Managers made an immediate decision: No new product would be approved unless someone championed it. Similarly, at SRI International, a contract research and development firm, managers use the saying "No champion, no product, no exception."[53] Research confirms that successful new ideas are generally those that are backed by someone who believes in the idea wholeheartedly and is determined to convince others of its value.[54] Recall how the winning proposals at PricewaterhouseCoopers innovation contest were all assigned to a senior champion so they didn't get lost in the everyday shuffle.

Sometimes a new idea is rejected by top managers, but champions are passionately committed to a new idea or product despite rejection by others. For example, Robert Vincent was fired twice by two different division managers at a semiconductor company. Both times, he convinced the president and chairman of the board to reinstate him to continue working on his idea for an airbag sensor that measures acceleration and deceleration. He couldn't get approval for research funding, so Vincent pushed to finish another project in half the time and used the savings to support the new product development.[55]

Championing an idea successfully requires roles in organizations, as illustrated in Exhibit 11.5. Sometimes a single person may play two or more of these roles, but successful

4

ORGANIZING

EXHIBIT 11.5

Four Roles in Organizational Change

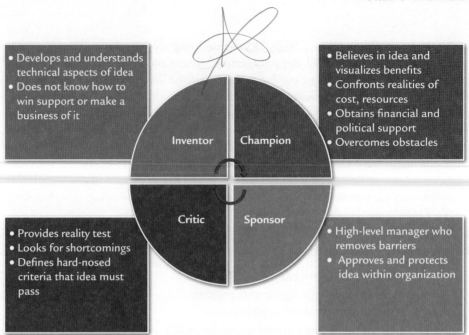

- Develops and understands technical aspects of idea
- Does not know how to win support or make a business of it

Inventor

Champion

- Believes in idea and visualizes benefits
- Confronts realities of cost, resources
- Obtains financial and political support
- Overcomes obstacles

Critic

Sponsor

- Provides reality test
- Looks for shortcomings
- Defines hard-nosed criteria that idea must pass

- High-level manager who removes barriers
- Approves and protects idea within organization

SOURCES: Based on Harold L. Angle and Andrew H. Van de Ven, "Suggestions for Managing the Innovation Journey," in *Research in the Management of Innovation: The Minnesota Studies*, ed. A. H. Van de Ven, H. L. Angle, and Marshall Scott Poole (Cambridge, MA: Ballinger/Harper & Row, 1989); and Jay R. Galbraith, "Designing the Innovating Organization," *Organizational Dynamics* (Winter 1982): 5–25.

innovation in most companies involves the interplay of different people, each adopting one role. The *inventor* comes up with a new idea and understands its technical value but has neither the ability nor the interest to promote it for acceptance within the organization. The *champion* believes in the idea, confronts the organizational realities of costs and benefits, and gains the political and financial support needed to bring it to reality. The *sponsor* is a high-level manager who approves the idea, protects the idea, and removes major organizational barriers to acceptance. The *critic* counterbalances the zeal of the champion by challenging the concept and providing a reality test against hard-nosed criteria. The critic prevents people in the other roles from adopting a bad idea.[56]

Another way to facilitate entrepreneurship is through a **new-venture team**. A new-venture team is a unit separate from the rest of the organization that is responsible for developing and initiating a major innovation.[57] New-venture teams give free rein to members' creativity because their separate facilities and location unleash people from the restrictions imposed by organizational rules and procedures. These teams typically are small, loosely structured, and flexible, reflecting the characteristics of creative organizations described in Exhibit 11.2. One good example is Nestlé's Nespresso venture, which developed a line of high-quality coffees packaged in individual capsules for use in specially designed coffee machines. The team found itself hampered by the large company's rules, structures, and regulations. In addition, the project faced resistance from managers who feared the new premium line would hurt the existing Nescafé brand. Top managers moved the Nespresso business outside the existing structure so it could thrive with an entrepreneurial culture and promote innovative ideas.[58] Procter & Gamble has established several new-business-creation groups that search for and develop breakthrough ideas that cross multiple businesses and divisions. These teams are partly responsible for a dramatic increase in P&G's innovation success rate.[59]

One variation of a new-venture team is called a **skunkworks**.[60] A skunkworks is a separate small, informal, highly autonomous, and often secretive group that focuses on breakthrough ideas for a business. The original skunkworks, which still exists, was created by Lockheed Martin more than 50 years ago. The essence of a skunkworks is that highly talented people are given the time and freedom to let creativity reign.[61] Consider the clandestine Google X lab, which was so hush-hush until *The New York Times* wrote about it that even many of Google's employees didn't know it existed. Google X is a top-secret lab in an undisclosed location where engineers are working on shoot-for-the-moon ideas like driverless cars, space elevators that can collect information from or haul things into space, and robots that can attend a conference for you while you stay at the office.[62] Similarly, at GM, the location of the skunkworks facility known as Studio X is kept secret even from the automaker's top executives.[63]

A related idea is the **new-venture fund**, which provides resources from which individuals and groups can draw to develop new ideas, products, or businesses. At Pitney Bowes, for example, the New Business Opportunity (NBO) program provides funding for teams to explore potentially lucrative but unproven ideas. The NBO program is intended to generate a pipeline of new businesses for the mail and document management services company. Similarly, Royal Dutch Shell puts 10 percent of its R&D budget into the GameChanger program, which provides seed money for innovation projects that are highly ambitious, radical, or long-term and would get lost in the larger product development system.[64] With these programs, the support and assistance of senior managers are often just as important as the funding.[65]

Take a Moment

Go to the Ethical Dilemma for Chapter 11 on pages 443–444 that pertains to structural change.

Remember This

- To increase innovation, managers develop an internal culture, philosophy, and structure that encourage entrepreneurial activity.
- An **idea champion** is a person who sees the need for change and is passionately committed to making it happen.
- One structural mechanism that promotes entrepreneurship is the **new-venture team**, which is a unit separate from the mainstream organization that is responsible for initiating and developing innovations.

- A variation of the new-venture team is a **skunkworks**, a separate informal, highly autonomous, and often secretive group that focuses on breakthrough ideas.
- The top-secret Google X lab is an example of a skunkworks.
- A **new-venture fund** provides financial resources from which individuals or teams can draw to develop new ideas, products, or businesses.

4

ORGANIZING

Changing People and Culture

All successful changes involve changes in people and culture as well. Changes in people and culture pertain to how employees think—changes in mind-set. **People change** concerns just a few employees, such as sending a handful of middle managers to a training course to improve their leadership skills. **Culture change** pertains to the organization as a whole, such as when the Internal Revenue Service (IRS) shifted its basic mind-set from an organization focused on collection and compliance to one dedicated to informing, educating, and serving customers (taxpayers).[66] Large-scale culture change is not easy. Indeed, managers routinely report that changing people and culture is their most difficult job.[67] New top managers at GM, for instance, have gotten praise for pulling the company back from bankruptcy and achieving impressive financial results, but even CEO Dan Akerson admits that in terms of changing the bureaucratic, tradition-bound culture, they are at only about 25 percent of where they want to be. One of Akerson's goals has been to get more women into top jobs, partly because he believes they can lead the radical culture change GM needs. Today, 4 of the company's 12 directors are female, a woman heads global product development, and some of the company's biggest plants are run by women.[68] Two specific tools that can smooth the culture change process are training and development programs and organization development (OD).

[handwritten margin note: RETRAIN]

[handwritten margin note: CHANGING ENTIRE COMPANY]

TRAINING AND DEVELOPMENT

Training is one of the most frequently used approaches to changing people's mind-sets. A company might offer training programs to large blocks of employees on subjects such as teamwork, diversity, emotional intelligence, quality circles, communication skills, or participative management.

Successful companies want to provide training and development opportunities for everyone, but they might particularly emphasize training and development for managers, with the idea that the behavior and attitudes of managers will influence people throughout the organization and lead to culture change. A number of Silicon Valley companies, including Intel and Advanced Micro Devices (AMD), regularly send managers to the Growth and Leadership Center (GLC), where they learn to use emotional intelligence to build better relationships. Nick Kepler, director of technology development at AMD, was surprised to learn how his emotionless approach to work was intimidating people and destroying the rapport needed to shift to a culture based on collaborative teamwork.[69]

ORGANIZATION DEVELOPMENT

Organization development (OD) is a planned, systematic process of change that uses behavioral science knowledge and techniques to improve an organization's health and effectiveness through its ability to adapt to the environment, improve internal relationships, and increase learning and problem-solving capabilities.[70] OD focuses on the human and social aspects of the organization and works to change attitudes and relationships among employees, helping to strengthen the organization's capacity for adaptation and renewal.[71]

OD can help managers address at least three types of current problems:[72]

Mergers/acquisitions. The disappointing financial results of many mergers and acquisitions are caused by the failure of executives to determine whether the administrative style and corporate culture of the two companies fit. Executives may concentrate on potential synergies in technology, products, marketing, and control systems but fail to recognize that two firms may have widely different values, beliefs, and practices. These differences create stress and anxiety for employees, and these negative emotions affect future performance. Cultural differences should be evaluated during the acquisition process, and OD experts can be used to smooth the integration of two firms.

Organizational decline/revitalization. Organizations undergoing a period of decline and revitalization experience a variety of problems, including a low level of trust, lack of innovation, high turnover, and high levels of conflict and stress. The period of transition requires opposite behaviors, including confronting stress, creating open communication, and fostering creative innovation to emerge with high levels of productivity. OD techniques can contribute greatly to cultural revitalization by managing conflicts, fostering commitment, and facilitating communication.

Conflict management. Conflict can occur at any time and place within a healthy organization. For example, a product team for the introduction of a new software package was formed at a computer company. Made up of strong-willed individuals, the team made little progress because members could not agree on project goals. At a manufacturing firm, salespeople promised delivery dates to customers that were in conflict with shop supervisor priorities for assembling customer orders. In a publishing company, two managers disliked each other intensely. They argued at meetings, lobbied politically against each other, and hurt the achievement of both departments. Organization development efforts can help resolve these kinds of conflicts, as well as conflicts that are related to growing diversity and the global nature of today's organizations.

Organization development can be used to solve the types of problems just described and many others. However, to be truly valuable to companies and employees, organization development practitioners go beyond looking at ways to settle specific problems. Instead, they become involved in broader issues that contribute to improving organizational life, such as encouraging a sense of community, pushing for an organizational climate of openness and trust, and making sure the company provides employees with opportunities for personal growth and development.[73] One recent study looked at the results of an OD project in a large metropolitan sheriff's department that was plagued by extremely high turnover, low morale, ineffective leadership, and internal conflicts. OD consultants used a variety of activities over a period of four years to solve the crisis threatening the department. It was a long, and sometimes difficult, process, but the study not only found that the OD interventions had highly beneficial results but the positive impact lasted over a period of 30 years to the present day.[74]

▶▶▶ **Concept Connection**

Spencer Platt/Getty Images News/Getty Images

Google managers rely on **survey feedback** to make sure they're providing the environment and benefits employees value. But Google doesn't stop there. In addition to the annual survey, managers solicit feedback on an ongoing basis through various innovative **organization development** tools. One example is the TGIF (Thank Goodness It's Friday) meeting held each week. Managers share the latest news, and employees ask questions and offer opinions about matters ranging from product decisions to human resource policies. Those unable to attend in person can participate online.

OD Activities

OD consultants use a variety of specialized techniques to help meet OD goals. Three of the most popular and effective are the following:

- *Team-building activities.* **Team building** enhances the cohesiveness and success of organizational groups and teams. For example, a series of OD exercises can be used with members of cross-departmental teams to help them learn to act and function as a team. An OD expert can work with team members to increase their communication skills, facilitate their ability to confront one another, and help them accept common goals.

- *Survey-feedback activities.* **Survey feedback** begins with a questionnaire distributed to employees on values, climate, participation, leadership, and group cohesion within their organization. After the survey is completed, an OD consultant meets with groups of employees to provide feedback about their responses and the problems identified. Employees are engaged in problem solving based on the data.

- *Large-group interventions.* In recent years, the need for bringing about fundamental organizational change in today's complex, fast-changing world prompted a growing interest in applications of OD techniques to large group settings.[75] The **large-group intervention** approach brings together participants from all parts of the organization—often including key stakeholders from outside the organization as well—to discuss problems or opportunities and plan for change. A large-group intervention might involve 50 to 500 people and last several days. The idea is to include everyone who has a stake in the change, gather perspectives from all parts of the system, and enable people to create a collective future through sustained, guided dialogue.

Large-group interventions are one of the most popular and fastest-growing OD activities and reflect a significant shift in the approach to organizational change from earlier OD concepts and approaches.[76] Exhibit 11.6 lists the primary differences between the traditional OD model and the large-scale intervention model of organizational change.[77]

4

ORGANIZING

EXHIBIT 11.6

OD Approaches to Culture Change

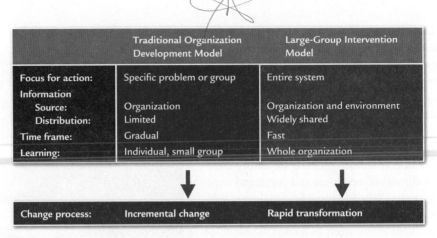

	Traditional Organization Development Model	Large-Group Intervention Model
Focus for action:	Specific problem or group	Entire system
Information Source:	Organization	Organization and environment
Distribution:	Limited	Widely shared
Time frame:	Gradual	Fast
Learning:	Individual, small group	Whole organization
Change process:	Incremental change	Rapid transformation

SOURCE: Adapted from Barbara Benedict Bunker and Billie T. Alban, "Conclusion: What Makes Large Group Interventions Effective?" *Journal of Applied Behavioral Science* 28, no. 4 (December 1992): 579–591.

In the newer approach, the focus is on the entire system, which takes into account the organization's interaction with its environment. The sources of information for discussion are expanded to include customers, suppliers, community members, and even competitors, and this information is shared widely so that everyone has the same picture of the organization and its environment. The acceleration of change when the entire system is involved can be remarkable. In addition, learning occurs across all parts of the organization simultaneously, rather than in individuals, small groups, or business units. The result is that the large-group approach offers greater possibilities for fundamental, radical transformation of the entire culture, whereas the traditional approach creates incremental change in a few individuals or small groups at a time.

Remember This

- Often, a manager's toughest job is changing people and culture.
- **People change** refers to a change in the attitudes and behaviors of a few employees.
- **Culture change** is a major shift in the norms, values, and mindset of the entire organization.
- **Organization development (OD)** is a planned, systematic process of change that uses behavioral science techniques to improve an organization's health and effectiveness through its ability to cope with environmental changes, improve internal relationships, and increase learning and problem-solving capabilities.
- OD can help managers with the task of blending corporate cultures following mergers and acquisitions, as well as with many other people-related problems.

- **Team building** is an OD intervention that enhances cohesiveness by helping groups of people learn to work together as a team.
- With **survey feedback**, OD change agents survey employees to gather their opinions regarding corporate values, leadership, participation, cohesiveness, and other aspects of the organization, then meet with small groups to share the results and brainstorm solutions to problems identified by the results.
- **Large-group intervention** is an OD approach that brings together people from different parts of the organization (and often including outside stakeholders) to discuss problems or opportunities and plan for change.

 OD Steps

OD experts acknowledge that changes in corporate culture and human behavior are tough to accomplish and require major effort. The theory underlying OD proposes three distinct stages for achieving behavioral and attitudinal change: (1) unfreezing, (2) changing, and (3) refreezing.[78]

The first stage, **unfreezing**, makes people throughout the organization aware of problems and the need for change. This stage creates the motivation for people to change their attitudes and behaviors. Unfreezing may begin when managers present information that shows discrepancies between desired behaviors or performance and the current state of affairs. In addition, managers need to establish a sense of urgency to unfreeze people and create an openness and willingness to change. The unfreezing stage is often associated with *diagnosis*, which uses an outside expert called a *change agent*. The **change agent** is an OD specialist who performs a systematic diagnosis of the organization and identifies work-related problems. He or she gathers and analyzes data through personal interviews, questionnaires, and observations of meetings. The diagnosis helps determine the extent of organizational problems and helps unfreeze managers by making them aware of problems in their behavior.

The second stage, **changing**, occurs when individuals experiment with new behavior and learn new skills to be used in the workplace. This process is sometimes known as *intervention*, during which the change agent implements a specific plan for training managers and employees. The changing stage might involve a number of specific steps.[79] For example, managers put together a coalition of people with the will and power to guide the change, create a vision for change that everyone can believe in, and widely communicate the vision and plans for change throughout the company. In addition, successful change involves using emotion as well as logic to persuade people and empowering employees to act on the plan and accomplish the desired changes.

The third stage, **refreezing**, occurs when individuals acquire new attitudes or values and are rewarded for them by the organization. The impact of new behaviors is evaluated and reinforced. The change agent supplies new data that show positive changes in performance. Managers may provide updated data to employees that demonstrate positive changes in individual and organizational performance. Top executives celebrate successes and reward positive behavioral changes. At this stage, changes are institutionalized in the organizational culture, so that employees begin to view the changes as a normal, integral part of how the organization operates. Employees may also participate in refresher courses to maintain and reinforce the new behaviors.

The process of unfreezing-changing-refreezing can be illustrated by efforts of managers at ENSR to create a high-performance, employee-focused culture.

Innovative Way
ENSR

When top executives at ENSR began hearing that high employee turnover was hurting the company's relationships with clients, they knew something had to be done. ENSR is a full-service environmental services firm with around 3,000 employees in 90 locations around the world. Long-term relationships with clients are the key to ENSR's success.

To attack the turnover problem, managers embarked on a process of changing the culture. To make people aware of the need for change (unfreezing), ENSR's president and CEO traveled with the senior vice president of human resources to the largest 50 or so of ENSR's global locations. They held town-hall-style meetings with employees and leadership workshops with ENSR managers. The *changing* stage included training. Surveys were conducted to find out what employees considered their primary needs. For example, supervisors were trained in how to help lower-performing employees improve their performance and how to provide greater challenge and rewards to employees who showed high potential for leadership.

Within a few years, new behaviors became the norm. Turnover dropped from 22 percent to only 9 percent, one of the lowest rates in the industry, and employees were recognized and rewarded for meeting high individual and collective goals (refreezing). ENSR continues to attract high-quality employees to fill job openings, which helps to keep the high-performance culture alive.[80]

4

ORGANIZING

Remember This

- OD practitioners recommend a three-stage approach for changing people's attitudes and behavior.
- **Unfreezing** is the stage in which people are made aware of problems and the need for change.
- Unfreezing requires diagnosing problems, which uses a **change agent**—an OD specialist who contracts with an organization to help managers facilitate change.

- **Changing** is the "intervention" stage of OD, when change agents teach people new behaviors and skills and guide them in using them in the workplace.
- At the **refreezing** stage, people have incorporated new values, attitudes, and behaviors into their everyday work and the changes become institutionalized in the culture.

Implementing Change

The final step to be managed in the change process is *implementation*. A new, creative idea will not benefit the organization until it is in place and being used fully. One frustration for managers is that employees often seem to resist change for no apparent reason. To manage the implementation process effectively, managers should be aware of the reasons people resist change and use techniques to enlist employee cooperation.

NEED FOR CHANGE   STAY INNOVATIVE / TO COMPETE

Many people are not willing to change unless they perceive a problem or a crisis. A crisis or strong need for change lowers resistance. The shifting relationship between GM and the United Auto Workers (UAW) provides a good example. GM managers' efforts to build a more collaborative relationship typically met with resistance from UAW leaders until bankruptcy proved the urgent need for working more closely together.[81] Sometimes, though, there is no obvious crisis. Many organizational problems are subtle, so managers have to recognize and then make others aware of the need for change.[82] A **need for change** is a disparity between existing and desired performance levels.

RESISTANCE TO CHANGE

Getting others to understand the need for change is the first step in implementation. Yet most changes will encounter some degree of resistance. Idea champions often discover that other employees are unenthusiastic about their new ideas. Members of a new-venture group may be surprised when managers in the regular organization do not support or approve their innovations. Managers and employees not involved in an innovation often seem to prefer the status quo. People resist change for several reasons, and understanding them can help managers implement change more effectively.

Self-Interest

People typically resist a change they believe conflicts with their self-interests. A proposed change in job design, structure, or technology may increase employees' workload, for example, or cause a real or perceived loss of power, prestige, pay, or benefits. *The fear of personal loss is perhaps the biggest obstacle to organizational change.*[83] Consider what is happening at Anheuser-Busch, which was acquired by the Belgian company InBev. The lavish executive suites at Anheuser-Busch headquarters have been demolished in favor of an open floor plan that has staff members and executives working side by side. Managers accustomed to flying first class or on company planes are now required to fly coach. It has become a competition to get a company-provided smartphone, as InBev has dramatically cut the number it will provide for employees. Free beer is a thing of the past, and complimentary tickets to sporting events are few and far between. Once the envy of others in the industry because of their lavish perks, Anheuser-Busch employees are resisting the new managers' wide-ranging changes because they feel they are losing both financially and in terms of status.[84]

Lack of Understanding and Trust

Employees often distrust the intentions behind a change or do not understand the intended purpose of a change. If previous working relationships with an idea champion have been negative, resistance may occur. When CareFusion Corporation was spun off as a subsidiary of Cardinal Health, CEO David L. Schlotterbeck and other top executives wanted to implement new values of collaboration and teamwork, but lower-level managers were initially suspicious of their intentions. Only when they saw that top leaders were fully committed to the values and honored them in their own behavior did others begin to support the changes.[85]

Uncertainty | FEAR

Uncertainty is the lack of information about future events. It represents a fear of the unknown. Uncertainty is especially threatening for employees who have a low tolerance for change and fear anything out of the ordinary. They do not know how a change will affect them and worry about whether they will be able to meet the demands of a new procedure or technology.[86] For example, employees at one mail-order company resisted the introduction of teams because they were comfortable with their working environment and uncertain about how the implementation of teams would alter it. People had developed good collaborative working relationships informally and they didn't see the need for being forced to work in teams.

Different Assessments and Goals

Another reason for resistance to change is that people who will be affected by a change or innovation may assess the situation differently from an idea champion or new-venture group. Critics frequently voice legitimate disagreements over the proposed benefits of a change. Managers in each department pursue different goals, and an innovation may detract from performance and goal achievement for some departments. For example, if marketing gets the new product it wants for customers, the cost of manufacturing may increase, and the manufacturing superintendent thus will resist. Apple executives are currently encountering this type of resistance. In August 2010, Apple became the largest U.S. corporation in terms of market valuation. But executives are currently under pressure for change because of poor working conditions in overseas supplier factories. More than half of the suppliers recently audited were found to have violated aspects of Apple's code of conduct and some have broken laws. However, there is conflict within the company because although top executives want to improve conditions, some managers argue that a radical overhaul will derail crucial supplier relationships and slow innovation and the delivery of new products.[87]

These reasons for resistance are legitimate in the eyes of employees affected by the change. Managers should not ignore resistance but instead diagnose the reasons and design strategies to gain acceptance by users.[88] Strategies for overcoming resistance to change typically involve two approaches: the analysis of resistance through the force-field technique and the use of selective implementation tactics to overcome resistance.

> *"Change hurts. It makes people insecure, confused, and angry. People want things to be the same as they've always been, because that makes life easier. But, if you're a leader, you can't let your people hang on to the past."*
>
> — RICHARD MARCINKO, FORMER U.S. NAVY SEAL, AUTHOR, AND CHAIRMAN OF RED CELL INTERNATIONAL CORPORATION

4

ORGANIZING

Take a Moment

The Small Group Breakout on page 368 will give you an idea of how difficult it can sometimes be for people to change.

HOT TOPIC

EXHIBIT 11.7 Using Force-Field Analysis to Change from Traditional to Just-in-Time Inventory System

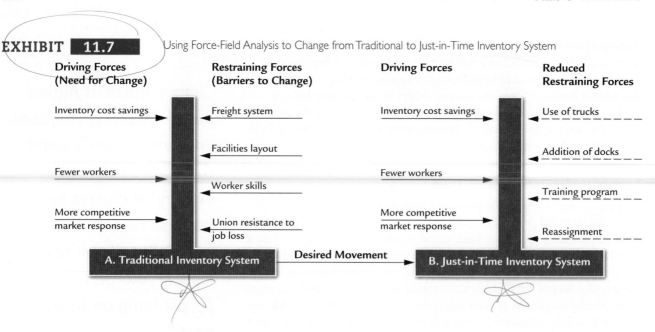

FORCE-FIELD ANALYSIS

Force-field analysis grew from the work of Kurt Lewin, who proposed that change was a result of the competition between *driving* and *restraining forces*.[89] Driving forces can be thought of as problems or opportunities that provide motivation for change within the organization. Restraining forces are the various barriers to change, such as a lack of resources, resistance from middle managers, or inadequate employee skills. When a change is introduced, managers should analyze both the forces that drive change (problems and opportunities) and the forces that resist it (barriers to change). By selectively removing forces that restrain change, the driving forces will be strong enough to enable implementation, as illustrated by the move from A to B in Exhibit 11.7. As barriers are reduced or removed, behavior will shift to incorporate the desired changes.

Just-in-time (JIT) inventory control systems schedule materials to arrive at a company just as they are needed on the production line. In an Ohio manufacturing company, management's analysis showed that the driving forces (opportunities) associated with the implementation of JIT were (1) the large cost savings from reduced inventories, (2) savings from needing fewer workers to handle the inventory, and (3) a quicker, more competitive market response for the company. Restraining forces (barriers) that managers discovered were (1) a freight system that was too slow to deliver inventory on time, (2) a facility layout that emphasized inventory maintenance over new deliveries, (3) worker skills that were inappropriate for handling rapid inventory deployment, and (4) union resistance to loss of jobs. The driving forces were not sufficient to overcome the restraining forces.

To shift the behavior to JIT, managers attacked the barriers. An analysis of the freight system showed that delivery by truck provided the flexibility and quickness needed to schedule inventory arrival at a specific time each day. The problem with facility layout was met by adding four new loading docks. Inappropriate worker skills were attacked with a training program to instruct workers in JIT methods and in assembling products with uninspected parts. Union resistance was overcome by agreeing to reassign workers no longer needed for maintaining inventory to jobs in another plant. With the restraining forces reduced, the driving forces were sufficient to allow the JIT system to be implemented.

IMPLEMENTATION TACTICS

The other approach to managing implementation is to adopt specific tactics to overcome resistance. Researchers have studied various methods for dealing with resistance to change. The following five tactics, summarized in Exhibit 11.8, have proven successful.[90]

EXHIBIT 11.8

Tactics for Overcoming
Resistance to Change

Approach	When to Use
Communication, education	• Change is technical. • Users need accurate information and analysis to understand change.
Participation	• Users need to feel involved. • Design requires information from others. • Users have power to resist.
Negotiation	• Group has power over implementation. • Group will lose out in the change.
Coercion	• A crisis exists. • Initiators clearly have power. • Other implementation techniques have failed.
Top management support	• Change involves multiple departments or reallocation of resources. • Users doubt legitimacy of change.

SOURCE: Based on J. P. Kotter and L. A. Schlesinger, "Choosing Strategies for Change," *Harvard Business Review* 57 (March–April 1979): 106–114.

Communication and Education

Communication and *education* are used when solid information about the change is needed by users and others who may resist implementation. Gina Raimondo, the state treasurer of Rhode Island, spent most of a year traveling all across the state to educate the public, union leaders, and legislators about the need for a radical overhaul of the state's pension system. "I would talk to social workers or social-service agencies who . . . would ask, 'Why should I care about pensions?' And I said, 'Because if you don't, your whatever it is, homeless shelter, is going to lose X thousand dollars of funding,'" she said. Raimondo "conducted a long, relentless, public-education campaign" because she believed reform was essential to keep the state from going broke.[91] Within organizations, education can be especially important when the change involves new technical knowledge or users are unfamiliar with the idea. Managers should also remember that implementing change requires speaking to people's hearts (touching their feelings) as well as to their minds (communicating facts). Emotion is a key component in persuading and influencing others. People are much more likely to change their behavior when they both understand the rational reasons for doing so and see a picture of change that influences their feelings.[92]

Participation

Participation involves users and potential resisters in designing the change. This approach is time consuming, but it pays off because users understand and become committed to the change. At Learning Point Associates, which needed to change dramatically to meet new challenges, the change team drew up a comprehensive road map for transformation but had trouble getting the support of most managers. The managers argued that they hadn't been consulted about the plans and didn't feel compelled to participate in implementing them.[93] Research studies have shown that proactively engaging front-line employees in up-front planning and decision making about changes that affect their work results in much smoother implementation.[94] Participation also helps managers determine potential problems and understand the differences in perceptions of change among employees.

Negotiation

Negotiation is a more formal means of achieving cooperation. *Negotiation* uses formal bargaining to win acceptance and approval of a desired change. For example, if the marketing department fears losing power if a new management structure is implemented, top

Concept Connection ◀◀◀

In the wake of the 2008 global economic crisis, many people felt that Wall Street and other financial institutions around the world were primarily responsible for the poor state of the world's economy. Motivated by a desire to change the way global financial systems operate, people took to the streets in protests like Occupy Wall Street, Occupy London, and many more. Their goal was to **educate** the public through **communication**, and to encourage **participation** in the change process.

managers may negotiate with marketing to reach a resolution. Companies that have strong unions frequently must formally negotiate change with the unions. The change may become part of the union contract reflecting the agreement of both parties.

Coercion

Coercion means that managers use formal power to force employees to change. Resisters are told to accept the change or lose rewards (or even their jobs). In most cases, this approach should not be used because employees feel like victims, are angry at change managers, and may even sabotage the changes. However, coercion may be necessary in crisis situations when a rapid response is urgent. For example, at the struggling Chrysler Group, some insiders say new CEO Sergio Marchionne "injected an element of fear into [Chrysler's] ranks" to get people to change. Several top managers were reassigned or terminated because they wouldn't go along with Marchionne's changes for returning Chrysler to profitability after it emerged from bankruptcy protection.[95]

Top Management Support

One survey found that 80 percent of companies that are successful innovators have top executives who frequently reinforce the importance of innovation both verbally and symbolically.[96] The visible support of top management helps overcome resistance. For instance, one of the primary correlates of the success of new business ventures is the strong support of top managers, which gives the project legitimacy.[97] *Top management support* symbolizes to all employees that the change is important for the organization. Top management support is especially important when a change involves multiple departments or when resources are being reallocated among departments. Without top management support, changes can get bogged down in squabbling among departments or contradictory orders from lower-level managers.

Managers can soften resistance and facilitate change and innovation by using smart techniques. By communicating with employees, providing training, and closely involving employees in the change process, managers can smooth implementation. In addition, change agents should never underestimate the importance of top management support for any change effort to succeed.

Remember This

- A **need for change** is a disparity between actual and desired performance.
- When managers see a need, they want to make changes to fill it, but they may be frustrated because employees seem to resist change for no apparent reason.
- Many people aren't willing to change unless they perceive a crisis.
- There are many legitimate reasons why people resist change, such as self-interest, uncertainty, or lack of trust.

- **Force-field analysis** is a technique for determining which forces drive a proposed change and which forces restrain it.
- Driving forces are problems or opportunities that provide motivation to change. Restraining forces are barriers such as a lack of resources or inadequate employee skills.
- The support of top executives is crucial to the successful implementation of a change. In addition, managers use a variety of techniques to smooth the implementation process.

ch11: Discussion Questions

1. Times of shared crisis, such as the September 11, 2001, terrorist attack on the World Trade Center or the devastation from Hurricane Sandy in 2012, can induce many companies that have been bitter rivals to put their competitive spirit aside and focus on cooperation and courtesy. Do you believe this type of change will be a lasting one? Discuss.

2. A manager of an international chemical company said that few new products in her company were successful. What would you advise the manager to do to help increase the company's success rate?

3. As a manager, how would you deal with resistance to change when you suspect employees' fears of job loss are well founded?

4. If you were a manager responsible for floor cleaning products at a consumer products company, how might you apply crowdsourcing to identify a new product that would meet customer needs?

5. To tap into the experience of battle-tested soldiers, the U.S. Army recently began encouraging personnel from all ranks to go online and collaboratively rewrite some of the Army's field manuals in a Wikipedia-like fashion. When the rank and file showed little interest, one retired colonel suggested top leaders should make soldiers participate. Does coercion seem like a good way to implement this type of change? Discuss.

6. Analyze the driving and restraining forces of a change you would like to make in your life. Do you believe understanding force-field analysis can help you more effectively implement a significant change in your own behavior?

7. Which role or roles—the inventor, champion, sponsor, or critic—would you most like to play in the innovation process? Why do you think idea champions are so essential to the initiation of change? Could they be equally important for implementation?

8. You are a manager, and you believe the expense reimbursement system for salespeople is far too slow, taking weeks instead of days. How would you go about convincing other managers that this problem needs to be addressed?

9. Do the underlying values of organization development differ from assumptions associated with other types of change? Discuss.

10. What do you see as the major advantages and disadvantages of a company moving to open innovation?

ch11: Apply Your Skills: Experiential Exercise

Is Your Company Creative?[98]

An effective way to assess the creative climate of an organization for which you have worked is to fill out the following questionnaire. Answer each question based on your work experience in that firm. Discuss the results with members of your group, and talk about whether changing the firm along the dimensions in the questions would make it more creative.

Instructions: Answer each of the following questions using the five-point scale (*Note:* No rating of 4 is used):

⓪ We never do this.
① We rarely do this.
② We sometimes do this.
③ We frequently do this.
⑤ We always do this.

1. We are encouraged to seek help anywhere inside or outside the organization with new ideas for our work unit.
   0 1 2 3 5

2. Assistance is provided to develop ideas into proposals for management review.
   0 1 2 3 5

3. Our performance reviews encourage risky, creative efforts, ideas, and actions.
   0 1 2 3 5

4. We are encouraged to fill our minds with new information by attending professional meetings and trade fairs, visiting customers, and so on.
   0 1 2 3 5

5. Our meetings are designed to allow people to freewheel, brainstorm, and generate ideas.
   0 1 2 3 5

6. All members contribute ideas during meetings.
   0 1 2 3 5

7. Meetings often involve much spontaneity and humor.
   0 1 2 3 5

8. We discuss how company structure and our actions help or spoil creativity within our work unit.
   0 1 2 3 5

9. During meetings, the chair is rotated among members.
   0 1 2 3 5

10. Everyone in the work unit receives training in creativity techniques and maintaining a creative climate.
   0 1 2 3 5

Scoring and Interpretation

Add your total score for all ten questions: _____

To measure how effectively your organization fosters creativity, use the following scale:

Highly effective: 35–50, Moderately effective: 20–34, Moderately ineffective: 10–19, Ineffective: 0–9

---

ch11: Apply Your Skills: Small Group Breakout

Are You Ready to Implement Personal Change?[99]

Step 1. Think about a specific behavior change—for example, stop smoking, schedule regular exercise, learn a new skill, adopt a healthier diet, drop a bad habit—you have considered making in your life. With that specific behavior or habit in mind, carefully answer each item below as Mostly True or Mostly False for you.

	Mostly True	Mostly False
1. To be honest, my problem is not so bad that it needs changing.	_____	_____
2. The behavior may be a fault, but it is nothing that I really need to change.	_____	_____
3. I am aware of the issue, but I am fine with it.	_____	_____
4. I have been thinking that I would like to change that behavior.	_____	_____
5. I wish I knew more about how to solve that problem.	_____	_____
6. I would like to understand that behavior better to start changing it.	_____	_____
7. I am actually doing something about it right now.	_____	_____
8. I am really starting to change, but I am not there yet.	_____	_____
9. I am in the process of changing, but I want to be more consistent.	_____	_____
10. I have already completed the change and I do not plan to backslide.	_____	_____
11. The change has become part of my day, and I notice if I do not stay with it.	_____	_____
12. The new behavior is now a part of my life and I do not think about it anymore.	_____	_____

Step 2. Scoring and Interpretation: The items above pertain to a person's stage of readiness to implement a personal change. Each of the four stages is measured by three questions in the scale. Give yourself one point for each item marked Mostly True.

    I.   Pre-contemplation: Items 1, 2, 3.   Score _____
    II. Contemplation: Items 4, 5, 6.   Score _____
    III. Action: Items 7, 8, 9.   Score _____
    IV. Maintenance: Items 10, 11, 12.   Score _____

You will probably find that you have a higher score for one of the stages, which means you are in that stage for your specific change. If you have the same score for two adjacent stages, then you are probably transitioning from one stage to the next. What does your score imply about your likelihood of success in making the change?

Step 3. In groups of three to five students, take turns describing your desired change and the meaning of the stage you are in. Compare notes and discuss progress on each person's change.

Step 4. Discuss the answers to the following questions as a group:

How likely is it that you will implement your desired change successfully? Why? To implement a personal change, how important is it to feel a strong need for change? Can you identify driving and restraining forces for the personal changes in your group? Which implementation tactics from this chapter would help your group members make the change? Why do you think so?

---

ch11: Endnotes

1. Based on H. Thomas Hurt, Katherine Joseph, and Chester D. Cook, "Scales for the Measurement of Innovativeness," *Human Communication Research* 4, no. 1 (1977): 58–65; and John E. Ettlie and Robert D. O'Keefe, "Innovative Attitudes, Values, and Intentions in Organizations," *Journal of Management Studies* 19, no. 2 (1982): 163–182.

2. James R. Hagerty, "Tapping Crowds for Military Design," *The Wall Street Journal*, August 16, 2012, A3.

3. Sarah Nassauer, "Marketing Decoder—The New 'Ketchup,'" *The Wall Street Journal*, April 5, 2012, D3.

4. "01: Apple, For Walking the Talk," in "The World's 50 Most Innovative Companies," *Fast Company* (March 2012): p. 81.

5. Study by Charles I. Stubbart and Michael B. Knight, reported in Spencer E. Ante, "Avoiding Innovation's Terrible Toll," *The Wall Street Journal*, January 7, 2012, http://online.wsj.com/article/SB1000142405297020433130457714498024749346.html (accessed August 21, 2012).

6. Alex Taylor III, "The New GM: A Report Card," *Fortune* (September 5, 2011): 38–46.

7. Richard L. Daft, "Bureaucratic vs. Nonbureaucratic Structure in the Process of Innovation and Change," in *Perspectives in Organizational Sociology: Theory and Research*, ed. Samuel B. Bacharach (Greenwich, CT: JAI Press, 1982), pp. 129–166.

8. Keith Bracsher, "Newest Export out of China: Inflation Fears," *The New York Times*, April 16, 2004, www.nytimes.com/2004/04/16/business/newest-export-out-of-china-inflation-fears.html?scp=1&sq=Newest+Export+Out+of+China%3A+Inflation+Fears&st=nyt (accessed August 30, 2010).

9. Richard Wolf, Brad Heath, and Chuck Raasch, "How Health Care Law Survived, And What's Next," *USA Today*, June 29, 2012, www.usatoday.com/NEWS/usaedition/2012-06-29-still2_CV_U.htm (accessed August 21, 2012).

10. "05: Square, For Making Magic Out of the Mercantile," in "The World's 50 Most Innovative Companies," *Fast Company* (March 2012): pp. 83–85, 146.

11. David W. Norton and B. Joseph Pine II, "Unique Experiences: Disruptive Innovations Offer Customers More 'Time Well Spent,'" *Strategy & Leadership* 37, no. 6 (2009): 4; and "The Power to Disrupt," *The Economist* (April 17, 2010): 16.

12. Jeffrey R. Immelt, Vijay Govindarajan, and Chris Trimble, "How GE Is Disrupting Itself," *Harvard Business Review* (October 2009): 3–11; and Navi Radjou, "Polycentric Innovation: A New Mandate for Multinationals," *The Wall Street Journal Online*, November 9, 2009, http://online.wsj.com/article/SB125774328035737917.html (accessed November 13, 2009).

13. For more information on the ambidextrous approach, see R. Duncan, "The Ambidextrous Organization: Designing Dual Structures for Innovation," in R. H. Killman, L. R. Pondy, and D. Sleven, eds., *The Management of Organization* (New York: North Holland), pp. 167–188; S. Raisch et al., "Organizational Ambidexterity: Balancing Exploitation and Exploration for Sustained Performance," *Organization Science* 20, no. 4 (July–August 2009): 685–695; C. Brooke Dobni, "The Innovation Blueprint," *Business Horizons* (2006): 329–339; Sebastian Raisch and Julian Birkinshaw, "Organizational Ambidexterity: Antecedents, Outcomes, and Moderators," *Journal of Management* 34, no 3 (June 2008): 375–409; Charles A. O'Reilly III and Michael L. Tushman, "The Ambidextrous Organization," *Harvard Business Review* (April 2004): 74–81; Duane Ireland and Justin W. Webb, "Crossing the Great Divide of Strategic Entrepreneurship: Transitioning Between Exploration and Exploitation," *Business Horizons* 52 (2009): 469–479; and Sebastian Raisch, "Balanced Structures: Designing Organizations for Profitable Growth," *Long Range Planning* 41 (2008): 483–508.

14. Michael L. Tushman, Wendy K. Smith, and Andy Binns, "The Ambidextrous CEO," *Harvard Business Review* (June 2011): 74–80.

15. Glenn Rifkin, "Competing Through Innovation: The Case of Broderbund," *Strategy + Business* 11 (Second Quarter 1998): 48–58; and Deborah Dougherty and Cynthia Hardy, "Sustained Product Innovation in Large, Mature Organizations: Overcoming Innovation-to-Organization Problems," *Academy of Management Journal* 39, no. 5 (1996): 1120–1153.

16. "2012 Good Housekeeping VIP (Very Innovative Products) Awards," www.goodhousekeeping.com/product-reviews/innovative-products-awards-2012#slide-1 (accessed August 21, 2012).

17. Anya Kamenetz, "12: Southern New Hampshire University, for Relentlessly Reinventing Higher Ed, Online and Off," in "The World's Most Innovative Companies," pp. 94–96.

18. Teri Evans, "Entrepreneurs Seek to Elicit Workers' Ideas—Contests with Cash Prizes and Other Rewards Stimulate Innovation in Hard Times," *The Wall Street Journal*, December 22, 2009.

19. Adapted from Patrick Reinmoeller and Nicole van Baardwijk, "The Link Between Diversity and Resilience," *MIT Sloan Management Review* (Summer 2005): 61–65.

20. Teresa M. Amabile, "Motivating Creativity in Organizations: On Doing What You Love and Loving What You Do," *California Management Review* 40, no. 1 (Fall 1997): 39–58; Brian Leavy, "Creativity: The New Imperative," *Journal of General Management* 28, no. 1 (Autumn 2002): 70–85; and Timothy A. Matherly and Ronald E. Goldsmith, "The Two Faces of Creativity," *Business Horizons* (September–October 1985): 8.

21. Gordon Vessels, "The Creative Process: An Open-Systems Conceptualization," *Journal of Creative Behavior* 16 (1982): 185–196.

22. Robert J. Sternberg, Linda A. O'Hara, and Todd I. Lubart, "Creativity as Investment," *California Management Review* 40, no. 1 (Fall 1997): 8–21; Amabile, "Motivating Creativity in Organizations"; Leavy, "Creativity: The New Imperative"; and Ken Lizotte, "A Creative State of Mind," *Management Review* (May 1998): 15–17.

4

ORGANIZING

23. James Brian Quinn, "Managing Innovation: Controlled Chaos," *Harvard Business Review* 63 (May–June 1985): 73–84; Howard H. Stevenson and David E. Gumpert, "The Heart of Entrepreneurship," *Harvard Business Review* 63 (March–April 1985): 85–94; Marsha Sinetar, "Entrepreneurs, Chaos, and Creativity—Can Creative People Really Survive Large Company Structure?" *Sloan Management Review* 6 (Winter 1985): 57–62; Constantine Andriopoulos, "Six Paradoxes in Managing Creativity: An Embracing Act," *Long Range Planning* 36 (2003): 375–388; and Michael Laff, "Roots of Innovation," *T&D* (July 2009): 35–39.

24. The research studies and examples are reported in Sue Shellenbarger, "Better Ideas Through Failure," *The Wall Street Journal*, September 27, 2011, D1.

25. Cynthia Browne, "Jest for Success," *Moonbeams* (August 1989): 3–5; and Rosabeth Moss Kanter, *The Change Masters* (New York: Simon and Schuster, 1983).

26. J. C. Spender and Bruce Strong, "Who Has Innovative Ideas? Employees." *The Wall Street Journal* (August 23, 2010), R5; and Rachel Emma Silverman, "How to Be Like Apple," *The Wall Street Journal* (August 29, 2011), http://online.wsj.com/article/SB1000142405311 1904009304576532842667854706.html (accessed September 16, 2011).

27. Roger L. Martin, "The Innovation Catalysts," *Harvard Business Review* (June 2011): 82–87.

28. Spender and Strong, "Who Has Innovative Ideas?"

29. Darren Dahl, "Technology: Pipe Up, People! Rounding Up Staff Ideas," *Inc.* (February 2010): 80–81.

30. Alison Overholt, "American Idol: Accounting Edition," *Fortune* (October 17, 2011): 100–106.

31. Reported in Rachel Emma Silverman, "For Bright Ideas, Ask the Staff," *The Wall Street Journal*, October 17, 2011, B7.

32. Dahl, "Technology: Pipe Up, People!"

33. Sherry Eng, "Hatching Schemes," *The Industry Standard* (November 27–December 4, 2000): 174–175.

34. Jena McGregor et al., "The World's Most Innovative Companies," *BusinessWeek* (April 24, 2006): 62ff.

35. James I. Cash, Jr., Michael J. Earl, and Robert Morison, "Teaming up to Crack Innovation and Enterprise Integration," *Harvard Business Review* (November 2008): 90–100; Barry Jaruzelski, Kevin Dehoff, and Rakesh Bordia, "Money Isn't Everything," *Strategy + Business*, no. 41 (December 5, 2005): 54–67; William L. Shanklin and John K. Ryans, Jr., "Organizing for High-Tech Marketing," *Harvard Business Review* 62 (November–December 1984): 164–171; Arnold O. Putnam, "A Redesign for Engineering," *Harvard Business Review* 63 (May–June 1985): 139–144; and Joan Schneider and Julie Hall, "Why Most Product Launches Fail," *Harvard Business Review* (April 2011): 21–23.

36. Hiroko Tabuchi, "How the Parade Passed Sony By," *The New York Times*, April 15, 2012, BU1.

37. Quoted in Janet Rae-DuPree, "Teamwork, the True Mother of Invention," *The New York Times*, December 7, 2008.

38. Based on Gloria Barczak and Kenneth B. Kahn, "Identifying New Product Development Best Practice," *Business Horizons* 55 (2012): 293–305; Andrew H. Van de Ven, "Central Problems in the Management of Innovation," *Management Science* 32 (1986): 590–607; Richard L. Daft, *Organization Theory and Design* (Mason, OH: SouthWestern 2010), pp. 424–425; and Science Policy Research Unit, University of Sussex, *Success and Failure in Industrial Innovation* (London: Centre for the Study of Industrial Innovation, 1972).

39. Based on Daft, *Organization Theory and Design*; and Lee Norris Miller, "Debugging Dysfunctional Development," *Industrial Management* (November–December 2011): 10–15.

40. Mike Gordon et al., "The Path to Successful New Products," *McKinsey Quarterly* (January 2010) www .mckinseyquarterly.com/The_path_to_successful_new_products_2489 (accessed February 10, 2012).

41. Reported in Schneide and Hall, "Why Most Product Launches Fail."

42. Erik Brynjolfsson and Michael Schrage, "The New, Faster Face of Innovation," *The Wall Street Journal Online*, August 17, 2009, http://online.wsj.com/article/SB 10001424052970204830304574130820184260340 .html (accessed August 21, 2009).

43. Brian Dumaine, "How Managers Can Succeed Through Speed," *Fortune* (February 13, 1989): 54–59; and George Stalk, Jr., "Time—The Next Source of Competitive Advantage," *Harvard Business Review* (July–August 1988): 41–51.

44. William J. Holstein, "Five Gates to Innovation," *Strategy + Business* (March 1, 2010), www.strategy-business.com/article/00021?gko=0bd39 (accessed September 16, 2011).

45. This discussion of open innovation is based on Henry Chesbrough, "The Era of Open Innovation," *MIT Sloan Management Review* (Spring 2003): 35–41; Ulrich Lichtenthaler, "Open Innovation: Past Research, Current Debates, and Future Directions," *Academy of Management Perspectives* (February 2011): 75–92; Julian Birkinshaw and Susan A. Hill, "Corporate Venturing Units: Vehicles for Strategic Success in the New Europe," *Organizational Dynamics* 34, no. 3 (2005): 247–257; Amy Muller and Liisa Välikangas, "Extending the Boundary of Corporate Innovation," *Strategy & Leadership* 30, no. 3 (2002): 4–9; Navi Radjou, "Networked Innovation Drives Profits," *Industrial Management* (January–February 2005): 14–21; and Henry Chesbrough, "The Logic of Open Innovation: Managing Intellectual Property," *California Management Review* 45, no. 3 (Spring 2003): 33–58.

46. Amy Muller, Nate Hutchins, and Miguel Cardoso Pinto, "Applying Open Innovation Where Your

Company Needs It Most," *Strategy & Leadership* 40, no. 2 (2012): 35–42.

47. A. G. Lafley and Ram Charan, *The Game Changer: How You Can Drive Revenue and Profit Growth with Innovation* (New York: Crown Business, 2008); Larry Huston and Nabil Sakkab, "Connect and Develop; Inside Procter & Gamble's New Model for Innovation," *Harvard Business Review* (March 2006): 58–66; and G. Gil Cloyd, "P&G's Secret: Innovating Innovation," *Industry Week* (December 2004): 26–34.

48. Farhad Manjoo, "Apple Nation," *Fortune* (July–August 2010): 68–112; and Jorge Rufat-Latre, Amy Muller, and Dave Jones, "Delivering on the Promise of Open Innovation," *Strategy & Leadership* 38, no. 6 (2010): 23–28.

49. Reported in Muller, Hutchins, and Cardoso Pinto., "Applying Open Innovation."

50. Elizabeth Holmes, "Before the Dresses, the Ideas; Oscar de la Renta Invites Fans to Submit Visual Inspiration for Next Collection," *The Wall Street Journal*, February 14, 2012, http://online.wsj.com/article/SB100014240529702048833045772214615607 20548.html (accessed February 17, 2012); and Sang M. Lee, David L. Olson, and Silvana Trimi, "Innovative Collaboration for Value Creation," *Organizational Dynamics* 41 (2012): 7–12.

51. Steve Lohr, "Online Mapping Shows Potential to Transform Relief Efforts," *The New York Times*, March 28, 2011, www.nytimes.com/2011/03/28/business/28map.html?_r=1 (accessed August 22, 2012); and Tina Rosenberg, "Crowdsourcing a Better World," *The New York Times*, March 28, 2011, http://opinionator.blogs.nytimes.com/2011/03/28/crowdsourcing-a-better-world/ (accessed March 29, 2011).

52. Daniel T. Holt, Matthew W. Rutherford, and Gretchen R. Clohessy, "Corporate Entrepreneurship: An Empirical Look at Individual Characteristics, Context, and Process," *Journal of Leadership and Organizational Studies* 13, no. 4 (2007): 40–54.

53. Curtis R. Carlson and William W. Wilmot, *Innovation: The Five Disciplines for Creating What Customers Want* (New York: Crown Business, 2006).

54. Robert I. Sutton, "The Weird Rules of Creativity," *Harvard Business Review* (September 2001): 94–103; and Julian Birkinshaw and Michael Mol, "How Management Innovation Happens," *MIT Sloan Management Review* (Summer 2006): 81–88.

55. Jane M. Howell, "The Right Stuff: Identifying and Developing Effective Champions of Innovation," *Academy of Management Executive* 19, no. 2 (2005): 108–119.

56. Harold L. Angle and Andrew H. Van de Ven, "Suggestions for Managing the Innovation Journey," in *Research in the Management of Innovation: The Minnesota Studies*, ed. A. H. Van de Ven, H. L. Angle, and Marshall Scott Poole (Cambridge, MA: Ballinger/Harper & Row, 1989).

57. C. K. Bart, "New Venture Units: Use Them Wisely to Manage Innovation," *Sloan Management Review* (Summer 1988): 35–43; Michael Tushman and David Nadler, "Organizing for Innovation," *California Management Review* 28 (Spring 1986): 74–92; Peter F. Drucker, *Innovation and Entrepreneurship* (New York: Harper & Row, 1985); and Henry W. Chesbrough, "Making Sense of Corporate Venture Capital," *Harvard Business Review* 80, no. 3 (March 2002): 90–99.

58. Raisch, "Balanced Structures."

59. Bruce B. Brown and Scott D. Anthony, "How P&G Tripled Its Innovation Success Rate," *Harvard Business Review* (June 2011): 64–72.

60. Christopher Hoenig, "Skunk Works Secrets," *CIO* (July 1, 2000): 74–76; and Tom Peters and Nancy Austin, *A Passion for Excellence: The Leadership Difference* (New York: Random House, 1985).

61. Hoenig, "Skunk Works Secrets."

62. Claire Cain Miller and Nick Bilton, "Google's Lab of Wildest Dreams," *The New York Times*, November 13, 2011, www.nytimes.com/2011/11/14/technology/at-google-x-a-top-secret-lab-dreaming-up-the-future.html?pagewanted=all (accessed November 14, 2011).

63. Taylor, "The New GM."

64. David Dobson, "Integrated Innovation at Pitney Bowes," *Strategy + Business Online*, October 26, 2009, www.strategy-business.com/article/09404b?gko=f9661 (accessed December 30, 2009); and Cash et al., "Teaming up to Crack Innovation and Enterprise Integration."

65. Robert C. Wolcott and Michael J. Lippitz, "The Four Models of Corporate Entrepreneurship," *MIT Sloan Management Review* (Fall 2007): 75–82.

66. E. H. Schein, "Organizational Culture," *American Psychologist* 45 (February 1990): 109–119; Eliza Newlin Carney, "Calm in the Storm," *Government Executive* (October 2003): 57–63.

67. Rosabeth Moss Kanter, "Execution: The Un-Idea," sidebar in Art Kleiner, "Our 10 Most Enduring Ideas," *Strategy + Business*, no. 41 (December 12, 2005): 36–41.

68. Alan Murray, "Women in a Man's World: Dan Akerson of General Motors on Changing a Male-Dominated Culture," *The Wall Street Journal*, May 7, 2012, B11; and Alex Taylor III, "The New GM: A Report Card," *Fortune* (September 5, 2011): 38–46.

69. Michelle Conlin, "Tough Love for Techie Souls," *BusinessWeek* (November 29, 1999): 164–170.

70. M. Sashkin and W. W. Burke, "Organization Development in the 1980s," *General Management* 13 (1987): 393–417; and Richard Beckhard, "What Is Organization Development?" in *Organization Development and Transformation: Managing Effective Change*, ed. Wendell L. French, Cecil H. Bell, Jr., and Robert A. Zawacki (Burr Ridge, IL: Irwin McGraw-Hill, 2000), pp. 16–19.

71. Wendell L. French and Cecil H. Bell, Jr., "A History of Organization Development," in French, Bell, and Zawacki, *Organization Development and*

4

ORGANIZING

Transformation, pp. 20–42; and Christopher G. Worley and Ann E. Feyerherm, "Reflections on the Future of Organization Development," *The Journal of Applied Behavioral Science* 39, no. 1 (March 2003): 97–115.

72. Paul F. Buller, "For Successful Strategic Change: Blend OD Practices with Strategic Management," *Organizational Dynamics* (Winter 1988): 42–55; Robert M. Fulmer and Roderick Gilkey, "Blending Corporate Families: Management and Organization Development in a Postmerger Environment," *The Academy of Management Executive* 2 (1988): 275–283; and Worley and Feyerherm, "Reflections on the Future of Organization Development."

73. W. Warner Burke, "The New Agenda for Organization Development," *Organizational Dynamics* (Summer 1997): 7–19.

74. R. Wayne Bass et al., "Sustainable Change in the Public Sector: The Longitudinal Benefits of Organization Development," *The Journal of Applied Behavioral Science* 46, no. 4 (2010): 436–472.

75. This discussion is based on Kathleen D. Dannemiller and Robert W. Jacobs, "Changing the Way Organizations Change: A Revolution of Common Sense," *The Journal of Applied Behavioral Science* 28, no. 4 (December 1992): 480–498; and Barbara Benedict Bunker and Billie T. Alban, "Conclusion: What Makes Large Group Interventions Effective?" *The Journal of Applied Behavioral Science* 28, no. 4 (December 1992): 570–591.

76. For a recent review of the literature related to large group interventions, see Christopher G. Worley, Susan A. Mohrman, and Jennifer A. Nevitt, "Large Group Interventions: An Empirical Study of Their Composition, Process, and Outcomes," *The Journal of Applied Behavioral Science* 47, no. 4 (2011): 404–431.

77. Bunker and Alban, "Conclusion: What Makes Large Group Interventions Effective?"

78. Kurt Lewin, "Frontiers in Group Dynamics: Concepts, Method, and Reality in Social Science," *Human Relations* 1 (1947): 5–41; and E. F. Huse and T. G. Cummings, *Organization Development and Change*, 3d ed. (St. Paul, MN: West, 1985).

79. Based on John Kotter's eight-step model of planned change, which is described in John P. Kotter, *Leading Change* (Boston: Harvard Business School Press, 1996), pp. 20–25, and John Kotter, "Leading Change: Why Transformation Efforts Fail," *Harvard Business Review* (March–April, 1995): 59–67.

80. Based on Bob Kelleher, "Employee Engagement Carries ENSR Through Organizational Challenges and Economic Turmoil," *Global Business and Organizational Excellence* 28, no. 3 (March–April 2009): 6–19.

81. Paul Ingrassia, "GM Gets a Second Chance," *The Wall Street Journal Europe*, July 10, 2009; and "Ford to Seek Same No-Strike Vow from UAW as GM and Chrysler Obtained," *National Post*, June 18, 2009.

82. Kotter, *Leading Change*, pp. 20–25; and "Leading Change: Why Transformation Efforts Fail."

83. J. P. Kotter and L. A. Schlesinger, "Choosing Strategies for Change," *Harvard Business Review* 57 (March–April 1979): 106–114.

84. David Kesmodel and Suzanne Vranica, "Unease Brewing at Anheuser as New Owners Slash Costs," *The Wall Street Journal*, April 29, 2009.

85. Joann S. Lublin, "Theory & Practice: Firm Offers Blueprint for Makeover in a Spinoff," *The Wall Street Journal*, June 29, 2009.

86. G. Zaltman and Robert B. Duncan, *Strategies for Planned Change* (New York: Wiley Interscience, 1977).

87. E. S. Browning, Steven Russolillo, and Jessica Vascellaro, "Apple Now Biggest-Ever U.S. Company," *The Wall Street Journal Europe*, August 22, 2012, 24; and Charles Duhigg and David Barboza, "In China, Human Costs Are Built Into an iPad," *The New York Times*, January 25, 2012, www.nytimes.com/2012/01/26/business/ieconomy-apples-ipad-and-the-human-costs-for-workers-in-china.html?pagewanted=all (accessed January 26, 2012).

88. Dorothy Leonard-Barton and Isabelle Deschamps, "Managerial Influence in the Implementation of New Technology," *Management Science* 34 (1988): 1252–1265.

89. Kurt Lewin, *Field Theory in Social Science: Selected Theoretical Papers* (New York: Harper & Brothers, 1951).

90. Paul C. Nutt, "Tactics of Implementation," *Academy of Management Journal* 29 (1986): 230–261; Kotter and Schlesinger, "Choosing Strategies for Change"; R. L. Daft and S. Becker, *Innovation in Organizations: Innovation Adoption in School Organizations* (New York: Elsevier, 1978); and R. Beckhard, *Organization Development: Strategies and Models* (Reading, MA: Addison-Wesley, 1969).

91. Allysia Finley, "The Democrat Who Took On the Unions," *The Wall Street Journal*, March 24, 2012, A13.

92. Gerard H. Seijts and Grace O'Farrell, "Engage the Heart: Appealing to the Emotions Facilitates Change," *Ivey Business Journal* (January–February 2003): 1–5; John P. Kotter and Dan S. Cohen, *The Heart of Change: Real-Life Stories of How People Change Their Organizations* (Boston: Harvard Business School Press, 2002); and Shaul Fox and Yair Amichai Hamburger, "The Power of Emotional Appeals in Promoting Organizational Change Programs," *Academy of Management Executive* 15, no. 4 (2001): 84–95.

93. Gina Burkhardt and Diane Gerard, "People: The Lever for Changing the Business Model at Learning Point Associates," *Journal of Organizational Excellence* (Autumn 2006): 31–43.

94. Henry Hornstein, "Using a Change Management Approach to Implement IT Programs," *Ivey Business Journal* (January–February 2008); Philip H. Mirvis, Amy L. Sales, and Edward J. Hackett, "The

Implementation and Adoption of New Technology in Organizations: The Impact on Work, People, and Culture," *Human Resource Management* 30 (Spring 1991): 113–139; Arthur E. Wallach, "System Changes Begin in the Training Department," *Personnel Journal* 58 (1979): 846–848, 872; and Paul R. Lawrence, "How to Deal with Resistance to Change," *Harvard Business Review* 47 (January–February 1969): 4–12, 166–176.

95. Kate Linebaugh and Jeff Bennett, "Marchionne Upends Chrysler's Ways: CEO Decries Detroit's 'Fanatical' Focus on Market Share," *The Wall Street Journal*, January 12, 2010.

96. Strategos survey results, reported in Pierre Loewe and Jennifer Dominiquini, "Overcoming the Barriers to Effective Innovation," *Strategy & Leadership* 34, no. 1 (2006): 24–31.

97. Donald F. Kuratko, Jeffrey G. Covin, and Robert P. Garrett, "Corporate Venturing: Insights from Actual Performance," *Business Horizons* 52 (2009): 459–467.

98. Adapted from Edward Glassman, *Creativity Handbook: Idea Triggers and Sparks That Work* (Chapel Hill, NC: LCS Press, 1990).

99. Based on Eileen A. McConnaughy, James O. Prochaska, and Wayne F. Velicer, "Stages of Change in Psychotherapy: Measurement and Sample Profiles," *Psychotherapy: Theory, Research, and Practice* 20, no. 3 (1983): 368–375.

4

ORGANIZING

Human Resource Management

Fuse/Jupiter Images

Learning Outcomes

After studying this chapter, you should be able to:

1. Explain the strategic role of human resource management.

2. Describe federal legislation and societal trends that influence human resource management.

3. Explain what the changing social contract between organizations and employees means for workers and human resource managers.

4. Show how organizations determine their future staffing needs through human resource planning.

5. Describe the tools that managers use to recruit and select employees.

6. Describe how organizations develop an effective workforce through training and performance appraisal.

7. Explain how organizations maintain a workforce through the administration of wages and salaries, benefits, and terminations.

1 INTRODUCTION
2 ENVIRONMENT
3 PLANNING
4 ORGANIZING
5 LEADING
6 CONTROLLING

Getting the Right People on the Bus[1]

http:
See It
Online
www.

INSTRUCTIONS: As a new manager, how much emphasis will you give to getting the right people on your team? Find out by answering the following questions based on your expectations and beliefs for handling the people part of your management job. Please answer whether each item is Mostly True or Mostly False for you.

	Mostly True	Mostly False
1. I will readily fire someone who isn't working out for the interests of the organization.	____	____
2. Selecting the right people for a winning business team is as important to me as it is to a winning sports team.	____	____
3. I expect to spend 40 percent to 60 percent of my management time on issues such as recruiting, developing, and placing people.	____	____
4. I will paint a realistic picture of negative job aspects that will help scare off the wrong people for the job.	____	____
5. My priority as a manager is first to hire the right people, second to put people in the right positions, and third to decide strategy and vision.	____	____
6. With the right people on my team, problems of motivation and supervision will largely go away.	____	____
7. I expect that hiring the right people is a lengthy and arduous process.	____	____
8. I view firing people as helping them find the place where they belong to find fulfillment.	____	____

SCORING AND INTERPRETATION: Most new managers are shocked at the large amount of time, effort, and skill required to recruit, place, and retain the right people. In recent years, the importance of "getting the right people on the bus" has been described in popular business books such as *Good to Great* and *Execution*. The right people can make an organization great; the wrong people can be catastrophic.

Give yourself 1 point for each item you marked as Mostly True. If you scored 4 or less, you may be in for a shock as a new manager. People issues will take up most of your time, and if you don't handle people correctly, your effectiveness will suffer. You should learn how to get the right people on the bus and how to get the wrong people off the bus. The faster you learn these lessons, the better a new manager you will be. A score of 5 or more suggests that you have the right understanding and expectations for becoming a manager and dealing with people on the bus.

Imagine enjoying yourself at a corporate dinner to welcome the new CEO when terrorists storm the hotel. That's what happened at the Taj Mahal Palace hotel in Mumbai (Taj Mumbai) at the end of a dinner hosted by Hindustan Lever. The Taj Mumbai banquet staff, led by 24-year-old Mallika Jagad, quickly recognized something was wrong and swung into action, locking the doors and turning off the lights. As the group huddled in the banquet room overnight, staff constantly went around offering water and calming the guests. The next morning, a fire broke out, forcing the group to climb out the windows. Again, the staff calmly evacuated all the guests first. "It was my responsibility," said Jagad. "I may have been the youngest person in the room, but I was still doing my job." Elsewhere in the hotel, similar acts of heroism were going on. At least 11 Taj Mumbai employees died while helping guests escape. The Taj Mumbai staff gave customer service a whole new meaning that night. There were no policy manuals

or procedures specifying how employees should behave in such a crisis situation. The actions of the staff were a result of unique hiring, training, and incentive systems that create a culture in which employees always put guests first, even if it means risking their own lives.[2]

Smart managers know that employees *are* the company—if they don't perform well, the company doesn't stand a chance of succeeding. Employees in most organizations don't have to risk their lives as the Taj Mumbai staff did, but all organizations need people who are willing and able to do what needs to be done to serve the interests of the organization and its customers. Hiring and keeping high-quality employees with the right set of skills is one of the most urgent concerns for today's organizations.[3] Employees give a company its primary source of competitive advantage, so even in an economic downturn, good managers make talent management a top priority. The term **human resource management (HRM)** refers to the design and application of formal systems in an organization to ensure the effective and efficient use of human talent to accomplish organizational goals.[4] This includes activities undertaken to attract, develop, and maintain an effective workforce. Managers have to find the right people, place them in positions where they can be most effective, and develop them so they contribute to company success.

HRM has shed its old "personnel" image and gained recognition as a vital player in corporate strategy.[5] "Many organizations are looking for their HR leader to be able to understand in great detail the business and the challenges of the business," says Fran Luisi of Charleston Partners, a search firm that specializes in human resource (HR) managers.[6] The growing clout of the HR function is reflected in the fact that current and former HR managers are increasingly being sought to fill board seats as outside directors at other companies. Hot-button issues such as executive compensation, changing government regulations, and the frequency of mergers and acquisitions make HRM a critical skill for both business and nonprofit organizations.[7]

All managers need to be skilled in the basics of HRM. With today's flatter organizations, managers throughout the organization play an active role in recruiting and selecting the right employees, developing effective training programs, designing appropriate compensation systems, or creating effective performance appraisal procedures.

The Strategic Role of HRM Is to Drive Organizational Performance

A survey of more than 1,700 CEOs around the world found that *human capital* was cited as the top factor in maintaining competitive success, which reflects the critical role of managing talent. **Human capital** refers to the economic value of the combined knowledge, experience, skills, and capabilities of employees.[8] Exhibit 12.1 shows the top three factors cited by CEOs in the survey. Human capital ranked far higher than assets such as technology, physical resources, and access to raw materials.[9]

EXHIBIT 12.1

Top Three Factors for Maintaining Competitive Success

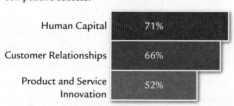

Percentage of CEOs reporting these factors as important for competitive success:

Human Capital 71%
Customer Relationships 66%
Product and Service Innovation 52%

SOURCE: "Leading through Connections: The IBM 2012 Chief Executive Officer Study," reported in Eric Lesser and Carl Hoffman, "Workforce Analytics: Making the Most of a Critical Asset," *Ivey Business Journal* (July–August 2012), www.iveybusinessjournal.com/topics/strategy/workforce-analytics-making-the-most-of-a-critical-asset (accessed August 27, 2012).

THE STRATEGIC APPROACH

The best HR departments not only support strategic objectives, but also actively pursue an ongoing, integrated plan for furthering the organization's performance.[10] Research has found that effective human resource management and the alignment of HR strategies with the organization's strategic direction has a positive impact on performance, including higher employee productivity and stronger financial results.[11]

Macy's HR department has implemented new systems to improve customer service and support the chain's growth strategy. All new sales associates attend a three-and-a-half hour training program, called "Magic Selling," that focuses on how associates can make more comfortable and natural connections with shoppers. Previously, training for new hires was limited to a 90-minute video, but Mary Martin, vice president of learning and development, knew a fresh approach was needed to revive the retailer's service reputation and drive the 3 percent growth in annual sales that top executives set as a goal.[12]

The strategic approach to HRM recognizes three key elements. First, all managers are involved in managing human resources. Second, employees are viewed as assets. No strategy can be implemented effectively without the right people to put it into action. Employees, not buildings and machinery, give a company its competitive edge. Third, HRM is a matching process, integrating the organization's strategy and goals with the correct approach to managing human capital.[13] Some current strategic issues of particular concern to managers include the following:

- Hiring the right people to become more competitive on a global basis

- Hiring the right people for improving quality, innovation, and customer service

- Knowing the right people to retain after mergers, acquisitions, or downsizing

- Hiring the right people to apply new information technology for e-business

All of these strategic decisions determine a company's need for skills and employees.

This chapter examines the three primary goals of HRM, as illustrated in Exhibit 12.2. HRM activities and goals do not take place inside a vacuum, but within the context of

Take a Moment

Go to the Experiential Exercise on page 404 that pertains to your potential for strategic human resource management.

> *"If each of us hires people who are smaller than we are, we shall become a company of dwarfs. But if each of us hires people who are bigger than we are, we shall become a company of giants."*
>
> — DAVID OGILVY (1911–1999), FOUNDER OF OGILVY & MATHER ADVERTISING AGENCY

4

ORGANIZING

EXHIBIT 12.2

Strategic Human Resource Management

Find the Right People
- HRM planning
- Job analysis
- Forecasting
- Recruiting
- Selecting

Company Strategy

Maintain an Effective Workforce
- Wages and salary
- Benefits
- Labor relations
- Terminations

Manage Talent
- Training
- Development
- Appraisal

Concept Connection ◄◄◄

Dick Blume/Syracuse Newspapers/The Image Works

Lowe's 215,000 employees help customers with remodeling, building, and gardening ideas at its 1,575 stores. They cut lumber, blinds, pipe, and chains; thread pipes; assemble items; provide computer project design and landscape garden design; match paint colors; teach how-to clinics; and offer many other services. Managers know that providing superior customer service depends on **human capital**, so they invest in finding the best people and helping them develop and apply their combined knowledge, skills, experience, and talent.

issues and factors affecting the entire organization, such as globalization, changing technology, the need for rapid innovation, quick shifts in markets and the external environment, societal trends, government regulations, and changes in the organization's culture, structure, strategy, and goals.

The three broad HRM activities outlined in Exhibit 12.2 are to find the right people, manage talent so that people achieve their potential, and maintain the workforce over the long term.[14]

BUILDING HUMAN CAPITAL TO DRIVE PERFORMANCE

Today, more than ever, strategic decisions are related to human resource considerations. In many companies, especially those that rely more on employee information, creativity, knowledge, and service rather than on production machinery, success depends on the ability to manage human capital, as described earlier.[15] To build human capital, HRM develops strategies for finding the best people, enhancing their skills and knowledge with training programs and opportunities for personal and professional development, and providing compensation and benefits that support the sharing of knowledge and appropriately reward people for their contributions to the organization.[16]

The importance of human capital for business results is illustrated in Exhibit 12.3. The exhibit shows a portion of a framework developed by Accenture and used by software and services company SAP. SAP needed a way to evaluate and revise its human capital processes to shift to a new strategy that called for stronger customer focus and greater individual employee accountability. The idea is to show how investments in human capital

The 'You' in Sustainability

"You are our sustainability edge!" is the new slogan to bring employees on board for sustainability. **HSBC** carried employee involvement to a new level by promoting individual projects and action plans through its Climate Champions Program. HSBC paved the way by partnering with powerful environmental organizations, including the Smithsonian Institution, Earthwatch, and the Climate Group. Participants must go through an application process for a 12-month residential program. Working alongside Earthwatch scientists, HSBC employees complete climate-related

business projects, gaining skills and developing methods that can be transferred to the workplace. HSBC's Climate Champions program has ignited employee curiosity and excitement. The program tells participants, "You have a voice in sustainability. You *own* this project. *You* are our sustainability edge."

Source: Matthew Gitsham, "Experiential Learning for Leadership and Sustainability at IBM and HSBC," *The Journal of Management Development* 31, no. 3 (2012): 298–307.

EXHIBIT 12.3

The Role and Value of Human Capital Investments

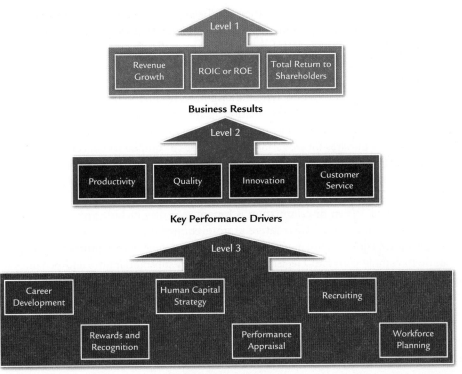

Business Results

Key Performance Drivers

Human Capital Processes

SOURCE: Adapted from Susan Cantrell et al., "Measuring the Value of Human Capital Investments: The SAP Case," *Strategy & Leadership* 34, no. 2 (2006): 43–52. Copyright 2006 by Emerald Group Publishing Limited. Reproduced with permission.

4

ORGANIZING

contribute to stronger organizational performance and better financial results. The framework begins at the bottom (level 3) by assessing internal processes such as workforce planning, career development, performance appraisal, and so forth. Managers use these activities to increase human capital capabilities that drive higher performance in key areas such as innovation or customer service (level 2). Improvements in key performance areas, in turn, lead to improved business results (level 1).[17]

Remember This

- **Human resource management (HRM)** refers to the design and application of formal systems to ensure the effective and efficient use of human talent to accomplish organizational goals.
- HRM includes activities undertaken to attract, select, develop, and maintain an effective workforce.
- HR managers are vital players in corporate strategy because no strategy can be effective without the right people to put it into action.

- **Human capital** refers to the economic value of the combined knowledge, experience, skills, and capabilities of employees.
- Retailer Macy's implemented new training programs to improve customer service and support a strategic goal of growing sales by 3 percent.

The Impact of Federal Legislation on HRM

Managing human resources effectively is a complex challenge for managers. For one thing, the legal and regulatory environment is constantly changing, and HR managers have to stay on top of issues that might have legal consequences. It is critically important that managers know and apply a variety of federal laws that have been passed to ensure equal employment opportunity (EEO). Some of the most significant legislation and executive orders are summarized in Exhibit 12.4. The point of the laws is to stop discriminatory practices that are unfair to specific groups and to define enforcement agencies for these laws. EEO legislation attempts to balance the pay given to men and women; provide employment opportunities without regard to race, religion, national origin, and gender; ensure fair treatment for employees of all ages; and avoid discrimination against disabled individuals.

The Equal Employment Opportunity Commission (EEOC) created by the Civil Rights Act of 1964 initiates investigations in response to complaints concerning discrimination. **Discrimination** occurs when hiring and promotion decisions are made based on criteria that are not job-relevant; for example, refusing to hire a black applicant for a job he is qualified to fill and paying a woman a lower wage than a man for the same work are discriminatory acts. When discrimination is found, remedies include providing back pay and taking affirmative action. **Affirmative action** requires that an employer take positive steps to guarantee equal employment opportunities for people within protected groups.

Failure to comply with EEO legislation can result in substantial fines and penalties for employers. Suits for discriminatory practices can cover a broad range of employee complaints. One issue of growing concern is *sexual harassment*, which is also a violation of Title VII of the Civil Rights Act. The EEOC guidelines specify that behavior such as unwelcome

EXHIBIT 12.4   Major Federal Laws Related to Human Resource Management

Federal Law	Year	Provisions
Equal Opportunity/ Discrimination Laws		
Civil Rights Act	1991	Provides for possible compensatory and punitive damages plus traditional back pay for cases of intentional discrimination brought under Title VII of the 1964 Civil Rights Act. Shifts the burden of proof to the employer.
Americans with Disabilities Act	1990	Prohibits discrimination against qualified individuals by employers on the basis of disability and demands that "reasonable accommodations" be provided for the disabled to allow performance of duties.
Vocational Rehabilitation Act	1973	Prohibits discrimination based on physical or mental disability and requires that employees be informed about affirmative action plans.
Age Discrimination in Employment Act (ADEA)	1967 (amended 1978, 1986)	Prohibits age discrimination and restricts mandatory retirement.
Civil Rights Act, Title VII	1964	Prohibits discrimination in employment on the basis of race, religion, color, sex, or national origin.
Compensation/ Benefits Laws		
Health Insurance Portability Accountability Act (HIPPA)	1996	Allows employees to switch health insurance plans when changing jobs and get the new coverage regardless of preexisting health conditions; prohibits group plans from dropping a sick employee.
Family and Medical Leave Act	1993	Requires employers to provide up to 12 weeks unpaid leave for childbirth, adoption, or family emergencies.
Equal Pay Act	1963	Prohibits sex differences in pay for substantially equal work.
Health/Safety Laws		
Patient Protection and Affordable Care Act	2010	Imposes a fee on firms with 50 or more employees if the government subsidizes their employees' health care coverage.
Consolidated Omnibus Budget Reconciliation Act (COBRA)	1985	Requires continued health insurance coverage (paid by employee) following termination.
Occupational Safety and Health Act (OSHA)	1970	Establishes mandatory safety and health standards in organizations.

advances, requests for sexual favors, and other verbal and physical conduct of a sexual nature becomes sexual harassment when submission to the conduct is tied to continued employment or advancement or when the behavior creates an intimidating, hostile, or offensive work environment.[18] Changes in the workplace have brought about shifts in the types of complaints being seen. Complaints of sexual harassment by men against both male and female bosses, for example, increased about 5 percent between 1997 and 2010. In addition, there are fewer complaints related to blatant harassment and more related to bosses who make sexually charged comments and send inappropriate e-mail or text messages.[19] Sexual harassment will be discussed in more detail in Chapter 13.

Exhibit 12.4 also lists major federal laws related to compensation and benefits and health and safety issues. This is only a sampling of the federal laws that HR managers must know and understand. In addition, many states and municipalities have their own laws that relate to HR issues. California, for example, requires that companies with 50 or more employees provide sexual harassment training for all employees every two years.[20] The scope of HR legislation is increasing at federal, state, and municipal levels. In addition, social and technological changes bring new legal challenges. The National Labor Relations Board (NLRB) recently filed suit on behalf of Dawnmarie Souza, who was fired because of a comment she made on Facebook—the NLRB's first, but likely not last, case involving a firing related to social media.[21]

Take a Moment

Are you suited to work as a human resources manager, which often requires following routine procedures and keeping detailed records to document compliance with federal laws and regulations? Complete the New Manager Self-Test on page 382 to get an idea of your natural orientation toward systematic recordkeeping.

Remember This

- HR managers have to understand and apply a variety of federal laws that prohibit discrimination, establish safety standards, or require organizations to provide certain benefits.
- **Discrimination** means making hiring and promotion decisions based on criteria that are not job-relevant.
- **Affirmative action** requires that employers take positive steps to guarantee equal employment opportunities for people within protected groups.
- The National Labor Relations Board (NLRB) recently filed suit on behalf of an employee who was fired because of a comment she made on a social networking site.

4

ORGANIZING

The Changing Nature of Careers

Another current issue is the changing nature of careers and a shift in the relationship between employers and employees.

THE CHANGING SOCIAL CONTRACT

In the old social contract between organization and employee, the employee could contribute ability, education, loyalty, and commitment and expect in return that the company would provide wages and benefits, work, advancement, and training throughout the employee's working life. But volatile changes in the environment have disrupted this contract. Consider the following list found on a bulletin board at a company undergoing major restructuring:

- We can't promise you how long we'll be in business.
- We can't promise you that we won't be acquired.
- We can't promise that there'll be room for promotion.
- We can't promise that your job will exist when you reach retirement age.
- We can't promise that the money will be available for your pension.
- We can't expect your undying loyalty, and we aren't even sure we want it.[22]

New Manager  Self-Test

What Is Your Focus?

Instructions: Think about your underlying motivations when doing tasks on a typical day at school or work. Respond to each statement below based on whether it is Mostly True or Mostly False for you. There are no right or wrong answers, so answer honestly to receive accurate feedback.

	Mostly True	Mostly False
1. I feel a sense of relief when I do well on a project or exam.	_____	_____
2. I focus on getting the details of my work done correctly.	_____	_____
3. I feel it is very important to carry out obligations placed on me.	_____	_____
4. I always try to make my work as accurate and error-free as possible.	_____	_____
5. For me, it is important not to do things wrong.	_____	_____
6. I think about and focus mostly on achieving positive outcomes in my life.	_____	_____
7. I like to finish a lot of work in a short amount of time.	_____	_____
8. I frequently imagine how I will achieve my hopes and aspirations.	_____	_____
9. I feel a sense of joy when I do well on a project or exam.	_____	_____
10. I am typically oriented toward accomplishing things mostly for my growth and satisfaction.	_____	_____

Scoring and Interpretation: These questions represent two types of mental regulatory focus during your work and school life, called *promotion* and *prevention*. Give yourself one point for each Mostly True answer.

1. Prevention Focus, sum points for questions 1–5: _____

2. Promotion Focus, sum points for questions 6–10: _____

3. Regulatory Focus Score (subtract the Promotion score from the Prevention score) = _____

Regulatory focus differentiates between internal motivation for promotion versus prevention. *Promotion* means a mental focus on winning desired outcomes and success whereas *prevention* is a focus on avoiding difficulties and failure. If your regulatory focus score is negative, you are likely a promotion-oriented person who is motivated toward positive outcomes and winning and who pursues goals to satisfy your hopes and wishes. If your score is positive, you are likely a prevention-oriented person more focused on preventing losing rather than on winning, and seeking to avoid failure and mistakes and meeting obligations and commitments. A positive score (prevention) may be associated with success in an HR department, which involves routine procedures and legal recordkeeping. A negative score (promotion) would more likely be associated with work in sales and marketing departments.

Sources: Based on J. Craig Wallace, Paul D. Johnson, and M. Lance Frazier, "An Examination of the Factorial, Construct, and Predictive Validity and Utility of the Regulatory Focus at Work Scale," *Journal of Organizational Behavior* 30 (2009): 805–831; Bernhard Fellner, Marianne Holler, and Erich Kirchler, "Regulatory Focus Scale (RFS): Development of a Scale to Record Dispositional Regulatory Focus," *Swiss Journal of Psychology* 66, no. 2 (2007): 109–116; and Penelope Lockwood, "Motivation by Positive or Negative Role Models: Regulatory Focus Determines Who Will Best Inspire Us," *Journal of Personal and Social Psychology* 83, no. 4 (2002): 854–864.

The recent economic downturn has accelerated the erosion of the old social contract. Two mainstays for many companies until recently—employer-subsidized retirement benefits and employer-paid health insurance—are in serious decline. One survey found that the number of employers offering health-care benefits declined from 69 percent in 2000 to 60 percent in 2009, at the height of the recession. As for retirement benefits, only about 20 percent of employees are covered by traditional pension plans today, and during the recession, many companies suspended their contributions to employee 401(k) plans. Moreover, many organizations that cut benefits say they don't intend to restore them.[23]

These changes and the list in the previous paragraph reflect a primarily negative view of the new employer-employee relationship, but there are positive aspects as well. While the shift has been difficult for workers from the baby boom generation, many young people don't have any desire to stay with one company throughout their careers. They like the expectation of responsibility and mobility embedded in the new social contract. Everyone is expected to be a self-motivated worker who is continuously acquiring new skills and demonstrating value to the organization. Workplace expert Lynda Gratton says building trust is more important than loyalty today, when "serial career monogamy" is the order for many young employees, who are continually evaluating whether their work is meaningful and challenging and fits with their lives. [24]

Exhibit 12.5 lists some elements of the new social contract. The new contract is based on the concept of employability rather than lifetime employment. Individuals are responsible for developing their own skills and abilities, understanding their employer's business needs, and demonstrating their value to the organization. The employer, in turn, invests in creative training and development opportunities so that people will be more employable when the company no longer needs their services. This means offering challenging work assignments, opportunities to participate in decision making, and access to information and resources. In addition, an important challenge for HRM is revising performance evaluation, compensation, and other practices to be compatible with the new social contract. For example, with the tough economy in recent years, companies have had to lay off thousands of experienced employees. Many organizations, including KPMG, IBM, Microsoft, and Lockheed Martin, have set up "alumni social networks" so that people who have to be let go can keep in touch with colleagues and the industry. Alumni social networks benefit the company by keeping managers in touch with qualified workers who might be recruited back when needed, and they benefit former employees by giving them access to information, contacts, and job leads that they might otherwise not have.[25]

The new social contract can benefit both employees and organizations. However, some companies take the new approach as an excuse to treat people as economic factors to be used when needed and then let go. This attitude hurts morale, employee commitment, and organizational performance. Studies in both the United States and China, for example, have found lower employee and firm performance and decreased commitment in companies where the interaction between employer and employee is treated as an economic exchange rather than a genuine human and social relationship.[26]

	New Contract	Old Contract
Employee	• Employability; personal responsibility • Partner in business improvement • Learning; skill development	• Job security • A cog in the machine • Knowing
Employer	• Creative development opportunities • Lateral career moves; incentive compensation • Challenging assignments • Information and resources; decision-making authority	• Standard training programs • Traditional compensation package • Routine jobs • Limited information

EXHIBIT 12.5

The Changing Social Contract

SOURCES: Based on Louisa Wah, "The New Workplace Paradox," *Management Review* (January 1998): 7; and Douglas T. Hall and Jonathan E. Moss, "The New Protean Career Contract: Helping Organizations and Employees Adapt," *Organizational Dynamics* (Winter 1998): 22–37.

4

ORGANIZING

INNOVATIONS IN **HRM**

The field of HRM is constantly changing. Some important HRM issues today are branding the company as an employer of choice, addressing the needs of temporary employees and part-time workers, and acknowledging growing employee demands for a work-life balance.

Branding the Company as an Employer of Choice

You might think with the high unemployment rate, companies wouldn't be worried about recruiting good people. But managers are finding that the most skilled and knowledgeable employees are in short supply and high demand.[27] Both small and large companies in a variety of industries are using employer branding to attract desirable job candidates. An **employer brand** is similar to a product brand except that rather than promoting a specific product, its aim is to make the organization seem like a highly desirable place to work. Employer-branding campaigns are like marketing campaigns to "sell" the company and attract the best job candidates. At Risk Management Solutions (RMS), HR executive Amelia Merrill used employer branding after she discovered that few people in Silicon Valley where the firm is based had a clue what RMS was. To attract the kind of high-quality technology professionals that RMS needed, Merrill's team began selling the company in the same way its salespeople sold its services. One step was to rent San Francisco's popular "Bacon Bacon" food truck for a day and set up at a local cloud-computing exposition. Merrill says branding is having a slow but sure effect on recruiting efforts, as people in the information technology industry become more familiar with the company name.[28] However, many large, well-known companies, including PepsiCo, General Electric (GE), Nokia, AT&T, and Credit Suisse Group, are also using employer branding as companies fight for talent.[29]

Using Temporary and Part-Time Employees

Contingent workers are becoming a larger part of the workforce in both the United States and Europe. **Contingent workers** are people who work for an organization, but not on a permanent or full-time basis.[30] In a 2012 survey by Workforce Management, nearly 44 percent of respondents said that they are using more or significantly more contingent workers, including temporary employees, contractors, and independent consultants, than they were a decade ago.[31] Although many of these people are "involuntary" temporary or part-time workers who lost jobs during the recession, other people like the option of working for different companies for short periods of time. For organizations, the primary goal is to access specialized skills for specific projects, enabling the company to maintain flexibility and keep costs low.

Although in the past, most temporary workers were in clerical and manufacturing positions, in recent years demand has grown for contingent professionals, such as accountants and financial analysts, interim managers, information technology specialists, product managers, and lawyers. Sometimes called *supertemps*, these are people who are highly skilled and choose to pursue independent careers. Supertemps often do mission-critical work. Ed Trevasani, who loves the freedom and flexibility of contingent work, has served as interim CEO for an international firm, developed a mergers and acquisitions strategy for a global manufacturer, and led the IT selection process for a major insurance company.[32]

Concept Connection ◀◀◀

In recent years, smart employers have come to appreciate the importance of employees' **work-life balance**. To attract the best candidates and keep the best employees happy, employers have to set human resource policies that help employees achieve that kind of balance. For example, many working parents value a policy known as **flexible scheduling**. Flexible scheduling allows employees to set their own work hours (within reason) and to work from home when necessary, both of which make caring for young children while working full time a little more manageable.

Ariel Skelley/Corbic

Promoting Work-Life Balance

Initiatives that enable people to lead a balanced life are a critical part of many organizations' retention strategies. Particularly today, when some companies can't afford pay raises for valued employees, managers are offering people more flexible scheduling or more control over their assignments as rewards. About 24 percent of companies surveyed by the Society for Human Resource Management report having a formal work-life balance policy, and 52 percent report having an informal policy.[33] One approach is to let employees work part of the time from home or another remote location.

Telecommuting means using computers and telecommunications equipment to do work without going to an office. More than 90 percent of employees surveyed by Cisco Systems say they work from home at least one day a week. Cisco was the lead sponsor of the 2012 National Telework Week, organized by Telework Exchange, a public-private partnership devoted to promoting telecommuting, especially in the federal government.[34] President Barack Obama signed the controversial federal Telework Enhancement Act into law on December 9, 2010, requiring all federal agencies to establish telecommuting policies. Critics say the requirement will cost taxpayers money, while supporters argue the opposite. The Patent and Trademark Office reports that it has saved $11 million in office space since the agency began allowing workers to telecommute in 1997.[35] Other forms of *flexible scheduling* are also important in today's workplace, and 53 percent of companies surveyed offer some form of flextime, including telecommuting, compressed workweeks, job sharing, schedule adjustment, and so forth.[36]

Many companies have implemented broad work-life balance initiatives in response to the shift in expectations among young employees.[37] Generation Y (Gen-Y) workers, or Millennials, are a fast-growing segment of the workforce. Typically, Gen-Y employees work smart and work hard on the job, but they refuse to let work be their whole life. Unlike their parents, who placed a high priority on career, Gen-Y workers expect their jobs to accommodate their personal lives.[38]

Remember This

- The new *social contract* between employers and employees is based on the notion of employability and personal responsibility rather than lifelong employment by an organization.
- An **employer brand** is similar to a product brand except that it promotes the organization as a great place to work, rather than promoting a specific product or service.
- **Contingent workers** are people who work for an organization, but not on a permanent or full-time basis, including temporary placements, independent contractors, freelancers, and part-time employees.
- **Telecommuting** means using computers and telecommunications equipment to perform work from home or another remote location.
- The U.S. Telework Enhancement Act, signed into law on December 9, 2010, requires all federal agencies to establish telecommuting policies.

Finding the Right People

Now let's turn to the three broad goals of HRM: finding, developing, and maintaining an effective workforce. The first step in finding the right people is human resource planning, in which managers or HRM professionals predict the need for new employees based on the types of vacancies that exist, as illustrated in Exhibit 12.6. The second step is to use recruiting procedures to communicate with potential applicants. The third step is to select from the applicants those persons believed to be the best potential contributors to the organization. Finally, the new employee is welcomed into the organization.

EXHIBIT 12.6   Attracting an Effective Workforce

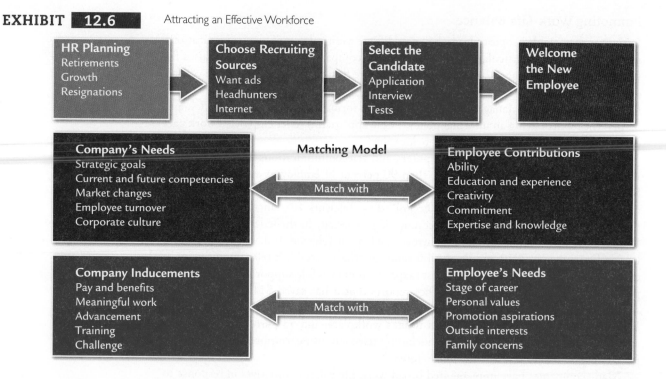

Underlying the organization's effort to attract employees is a matching model. With the **matching model**, the organization and the individual attempt to match the needs, interests, and values that they offer each other.[39] For example, a small software developer might require long hours from creative, technically skilled employees. In return, it can offer freedom from bureaucracy, tolerance of idiosyncrasies, and potentially high pay. A large manufacturer can offer employment security and stability, but it might have more rules and regulations and require greater skills for "getting approval from the higher-ups." The individual who would thrive working for the software developer might feel stymied and unhappy working for a large manufacturer. Both the company and the employee are interested in finding a good match.

HUMAN RESOURCE PLANNING

Human resource planning is the forecasting of HR needs and the projected matching of individuals with expected vacancies. Human resource planning begins with several big picture questions:

- What new technologies are emerging, and how will these affect the work system?
- What is the volume of the business likely to be in the next five to ten years?
- What is the turnover rate, and how much, if any, is avoidable?

The responses to these questions are used to formulate specific questions pertaining to HR activities, such as the following:

- What types of engineers will we need and how many?
- How many administrative personnel will we need to support the additional engineers?
- Can we use temporary, part-time, or virtual workers to handle some tasks?[40]

By anticipating future HR needs, the organization can prepare itself to meet competitive challenges more effectively than organizations that react to problems only as they arise.

RECRUITING

Recruiting is defined as "activities or practices that define the characteristics of applicants to whom selection procedures are ultimately applied."[41] Today, recruiting is sometimes referred to as *talent acquisition* to reflect the importance of the human factor in the organization's success.[42]

Although we frequently think of campus recruiting as a typical recruiting activity, many organizations use *internal recruiting*, or *promote-from-within* policies, to fill their high-level positions.[43] Internal recruiting has two major advantages: It is less costly than an external search, and it generates higher employee commitment, development, and satisfaction because it offers opportunities for career advancement to employees rather than outsiders. Frequently, however, *external recruiting*—recruiting newcomers from outside the organization—is advantageous. Applicants are provided by a variety of outside sources, including advertising, state employment services, online recruiting services, private employment agencies (headhunters), job fairs, and employee referrals.

Assessing Jobs

Basic building blocks of HRM include job analysis, job descriptions, and job specifications. **Job analysis** is a systematic process of gathering and interpreting information about the essential duties, tasks, and responsibilities of a job, as well as about the context within which the job is performed.[44] To perform job analysis, managers or specialists ask about work activities and work flow, the degree of supervision given and received in the job, knowledge and skills needed, performance standards, working conditions, and so forth. The manager then prepares a written **job description**, which is a clear and concise summary of the specific tasks, duties, and responsibilities, and **job specification**, which outlines the knowledge, skills, education, physical abilities, and other characteristics needed to perform the job adequately.

Job analysis helps organizations recruit the right kind of people and match them to appropriate jobs. For example, to enhance internal recruiting, Sara Lee Corporation identified six functional areas and 24 significant skills that it wants its finance executives to develop, as illustrated in Exhibit 12.7. Managers are tracked on their development and moved into other positions to help them acquire the needed skills.[45]

Realistic Job Previews

Job analysis also enhances recruiting effectiveness by enabling the creation of **realistic job previews**. A realistic job preview (RJP) gives applicants all pertinent and realistic information—positive and negative—about the job and the organization.[46] RJPs contribute to greater employee satisfaction and lower turnover because they facilitate matching individuals, jobs, and organizations. Individuals have a better basis on which to determine their suitability to the organization and "self-select" into or out of positions based on full information.

Social Media

Today, much recruiting is done via the Internet and social media sites such as LinkedIn, Facebook, and Meetup.[47] In a 2012 survey

▶▶▶ **Concept Connection**

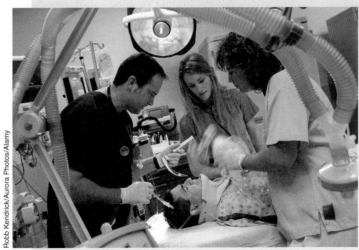

Robb Kendrick/Aurora Photos/Alamy

For people just entering the medical field, working in a hospital's emergency room where you can save lives every day may sound exciting and meaningful, but not everyone is cut out to deal with the hectic pace of a typical ER. That's why this hospital asks job applicants to work a shift or two as part of a **realistic job preview**. The trial run allows both the applicant and the hospital's staff to determine whether the job candidate is a good fit for this challenging work environment.

4

ORGANIZING

EXHIBIT **12.7**

Sara Lee's Required Skills for
Finance Executives

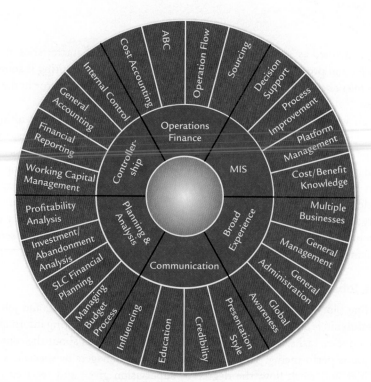

of global HR executives, 46 percent reported using social media to find good candidates.
Companies in China have become particularly adept at using this approach because traditional online recruiting boards attract far too many unqualified candidates to make them
valuable. So, managers turn to social media such as Weibo, a Twitter-like messaging service,
to build a community of potential candidates. Deloitte Touche Tohmatsu's China division
has a Weibo career page that has 48,500 followers; some keep in close touch with the company, developing relationships that can be beneficial to both sides. China's Lenovo Group
reports finding 70 good candidates during a three-month recruiting surge in 2012 via social media, including LinkedIn, Weibo, and Tianji, a Chinese professional social networking
site.[48] Companies still use other online recruiting methods, such as posting job openings
on company Web sites and searching commercial recruiting sites, but the trend is toward
more targeted online recruiting. Rather than using online job boards, for example, Science
Applications International Corporation now searches for qualified candidates on professional social networks before it ever posts a job opening.[49]

Internships

Another popular use of social media is to find people to serve as either paid or unpaid
interns at the organization. An **internship** is an arrangement whereby an intern, usually a
high school or college student, exchanges free or low-cost labor for the opportunity to explore whether a particular career is appealing or to gain valuable work experience in a particular field.[50] Companies are increasingly viewing internships as a valuable recruiting tool
because they provide a way to "test-drive" a potential employee, as well as allow the intern to
evaluate whether the job and the company make a good fit. The old image of the intern as
the "gopher" who makes coffee and photocopies has given way to the budding professional
who performs meaningful tasks and learns valuable skills. Interns aren't always offered a
job with the company, but one career development expert says internships are more closely
tied to permanent hiring today than ever before.[51] Media and online entertainment company IGN takes an innovative approach to recruiting via internships.

"Flipping burgers to scrape together enough cash to buy *Portal 2*? Blow our minds while you're here and we'll hire you." That was the recruitment ad for IGN's first Code Foo challenge—a no-résumés-allowed program designed to find exceptional "hackers," the term IGN's director of engineering prefers when referring to computer programmers and coders. "For serious engineers who really care about their craft, it's a good thing to be a hacker," Tony Ford says.

Applicants to the Code Foo challenge complete an online application in which they submit a statement of passion for IGN and answer questions that test their coding ability. For the 2011 challenge, 75,000 people viewed the application, 104 applied, and 30 were selected to participate. Only half of those had college degrees in a technical field, and some didn't have degrees at all. Once they are accepted, the Code Fooers spend six weeks working at IGN, getting paid a small amount while learning coding languages and working on real engineering projects. According to IGN president Roy Behat, the six weeks is for "teaching them something to see if we could get them to a level where we might actually want to hire them." Adam Passey, for example, spent his summer coding unique features for a hub for mobile games. IGN's engineers were impressed, and Passey was offered a job.

In fact, although Bahat hoped the Code Foo experiment would lead to one or two good hires, the company actually extended job offers to eight people. The success of the challenge convinced managers to hold it again for 2012. As the market for programmers and coders grows more competitive, it's a "guerilla recruitment strategy" that is paying off.[52]

Remember This

- Finding the right people starts with **human resource planning**, which refers to the forecasting of human resource needs and the projected matching of individuals with anticipated job vacancies.

- The **matching model** is a human resources approach in which the organization and the individual attempt to match each other's needs, interests, and values.

- **Recruiting** refers to activities or practices that define the desired characteristics of applicants for specific jobs.

- Many of today's organizations use social media, including Twitter, Weibo, LinkedIn, Tianji, and Facebook, for recruiting.

- **Job analysis** is the systematic process of gathering and interpreting information about the essential duties, tasks, and responsibilities of a job.

- Managers prepare a **job description** for each open position, which is a concise summary of the specific tasks and responsibilities of that job.

- A **job specification** outlines the knowledge, skills, education, physical abilities, and other characteristics needed to perform a specific job adequately.

- Managers use **realistic job previews** in recruiting to give applicants all pertinent and realistic information, both positive and negative, about a job and the organization.

- Internships are an increasingly popular approach to recruiting because they provide a way to "test-drive" a potential employee.

- An **internship** is an arrangement whereby an intern, usually a high school or college student, exchanges his or her services for the opportunity to gain work experience and see whether a particular career is appealing.

4

ORGANIZING

SELECTING

In the **selection** process, employers assess applicants' characteristics in an attempt to determine the "fit" between the job and applicant characteristics. The most frequently used selection devices are the application form, interview, employment test, and assessment center. In general, the greater the skill requirements and work demands of an open position, the greater the number and variety of selection tools the organization will use.[53]

Application Form

The **application form** is used to collect information about the applicant's education, previous job experience, and other background characteristics. Research shows that biographical information inventories can validly predict future job success.[54]

One pitfall to be avoided is the inclusion of questions that are irrelevant to job success. In line with EEO guidelines, the application form should not ask questions that will create an adverse impact on protected groups unless the questions are clearly related to the job.[55] For example, employers should not ask whether the applicant rents or owns his or her own home because (1) an applicant's response might adversely affect his or her chances at the job, (2) minorities and women may be less likely to own a home, and (3) home ownership is probably unrelated to job performance. By contrast, passing the CPA exam is relevant to job performance in a CPA firm; thus, it is appropriate to ask whether an applicant for employment has passed the CPA exam, even if only one-half of all female or minority applicants have done so, versus nine-tenths of white male applicants.

Interview

Some type of *interview* is used as a selection technique in almost every job category in nearly every organization. It is another area where the organization can get into legal trouble if the interviewer asks questions that violate EEO guidelines. Exhibit 12.8 lists some examples of appropriate and inappropriate interview questions.

There is some evidence that the typical interview is not generally a good predictor of job performance. One estimate is that conventional interviews have a 0.2 correlation with predicting a successful hire.[56] Managers can improve their interviewing skills, and candidates can improve their chances of having a successful interview, by understanding some dos and don'ts related to the interview, as outlined in the Shoptalk.

Managers use a variety of interview approaches to get a more reliable picture of a candidate's suitability for the job. **Structured interviews** use a set of standardized questions that

EXHIBIT 12.8 Employment Applications and Interviews: What Can You Ask?

Category	Okay to Ask	Inappropriate or Illegal to Ask
National origin	• The applicant's name • If applicant has ever worked under a different name	• The origin of applicant's name • Applicant's ancestry/ethnicity
Race	• Nothing	• Race or color of skin
Disabilities	• Whether applicant has any disabilities that might inhibit performance of job	• If applicant has any physical or mental defects • If applicant has ever filed a workers' compensation claim
Age	• If applicant is over 18	• Applicant's age • When applicant graduated from high school
Religion	• Nothing	• Applicant's religious affiliation • What religious holidays applicant observes
Criminal record	• If applicant has ever been convicted of a crime	• If applicant has ever been arrested
Marital/family status	• Nothing	• Marital status, number of children or planned children • Childcare arrangements
Education and experience	• Where applicant went to school • Prior work experience	• When applicant graduated • Hobbies
Citizenship	• If applicant has a legal right to work in the United States	• If applicant is a citizen of another country

SOURCES: Based on "Appropriate and Inappropriate Interview Questions," in George Bohlander, Scott Snell, and Arthur Sherman, *Managing Human Resources*, 12th ed. (Cincinnati, OH: South-Western, 2001), 207; and "Guidelines to Lawful and Unlawful Preemployment Inquiries," Appendix E, in Robert L. Mathis and John H. Jackson, *Human Resource Management*, 2nd ed. (Cincinnati, OH: South-Western, 2002), 189–190.

Manager's *Shoptalk*

Ace the Interview

Many of us have experienced job interviews where everything seems to be going well, but then, things take a drastic turn for the worse. Here are some thoughts that can help you ace your next interview—and improve your interviewing skills as a manager.

The Big Three Questions

No matter what questions you are asked in an interview, you can be more effective if you remember there are really only three essential things the hiring manager and company want to know:

- **Can you do the job?** The company wants to know your strengths, not just in terms of technical skills, but also your leadership, teamwork, and interpersonal strengths. Can you not only handle the tasks and activities of the job exceptionally well, but also interact effectively with your colleagues and contribute to a positive organizational atmosphere?

- **Will you love the job?** Organizations want people who bring enthusiasm and positive energy with them into the workplace every day. The hiring manager wants to be convinced that you're excited about the particular position you're interviewing for, as well as the overall industry, and that you'll thrive on embracing the challenges associated with the job.

- **Can we tolerate working with you?** Believing you'll be a good fit with the culture is a huge part of the equation when most managers are deciding among job candidates. At LivingSocial, every job candidate is interviewed by a member of the "culture police," a team of people who have a knack for spotting what works and doesn't work with the company's culture. No one gets hired unless the culture police give the okay.

Killer Interview Strategies

- **Do your research.** To answer the Big Three Questions, you have to understand the job you're applying for, know something about the overall industry the company operates in, and have some feeling for the organizational culture. Learn all you can. Find out how the company is structured and managed by looking at its Web site. Tap into your social networking connections, see if there are videos on YouTube, read stories in blogs, and so forth.

- **Turn questions into conversations.** If you've done your research, you'll be able to converse with the interviewer on a peer-to-peer level. If asked, for example, how you would restructure a division, you might politely say something like: "Do you mind if I ask you a couple of questions first? I know there's a plant in Greece. Has the business been affected by the country's economic troubles?" Also, think of a few stories and examples ahead of time that illustrate your skills and strengths, show off your commitment and motivation, and demonstrate how you will fit with the organization. Use them judiciously when you get the chance.

- **Think the way they do.** Again, if you've done your research, you should have some idea of the issues and problems the company faces and the type of questions you might be asked. A company such as Zappos.com will interview in a different way from a company like General Electric (GE). Imagine that you were a manager with the company, and think up 10 or so questions that *you* would ask a candidate.

Sources: George Brandt, "Top Executive Recruiters Agree There Are Only Three True Job Interview Questions," *Forbes*, April 27, 2011, www.forbes.com/sites/georgebradt/2011/04/27/top-executive-recruiters-agree-there-are-only-three-key-job-interview-questions/ (accessed August 29, 2012); Jennifer Alsever, "How to Get a Job: Show, Don't Tell," *Fortune* (March 19, 2012): 29–31; and LivingSocial example from Darren Dahl, "Hiring: You Get a Job, and You, and You . . . How to Staff Up in a Hurry," *Inc.* (November 2010): 128–129.

4

ORGANIZING

are asked of every applicant so comparisons can easily be made. These may include *biographical interviews*, which ask about the person's previous life and work experiences; *behavioral interviews*, which ask people to describe how they have performed a certain task or handled a particular problem; and *situational interviews*, which require people to describe how they might handle a hypothetical situation. With a **nondirective interview**, the interviewer asks broad, open-ended questions and permits the applicant to talk freely, with minimal interruption. Nondirective interviews may bring to light information, attitudes, and behavioral characteristics that might be concealed when answering structured questions.

Some organizations put candidates through a series of interviews, each one conducted by a different person and each one probing a different aspect of the candidate. Others use **panel interviews**, in which the candidate meets with several interviewers who take turns asking questions.[57] In addition, some firms are using offbeat approaches, sometimes referred to as *extreme interviewing*, to test job candidates' ability to handle problems, cope with change, think on their feet, and work well with others. Danielle Bemoras found herself in a joint interview with a rival candidate when she applied for a job with SceneTap, a digital nightlife guide. Rather than trying to upstage her competitor, Bemoras was respectful and helpful, an approach that won her an internship, followed by a full-time job offer.[58] To test candidates' creativity, a recruiter at one marketing firm told interviewees to "just entertain me for five minutes."[59]

Employment Test

Employment tests may include cognitive ability tests, physical ability tests, personality inventories, and other assessments. *Cognitive ability tests* measure an applicant's thinking, reasoning, verbal, and mathematical abilities. *Physical ability tests* that measure qualities such as strength, energy, and endurance may be used for jobs such as delivery drivers who must lift heavy packages, electric line workers who must climb ladders and carry equipment, and other positions that involve physical tasks. It is essential that these tests only assess cognitive and physical skills that are job related to avoid violating laws against discrimination.

Many companies also use various types of *personality tests* to assess such characteristics as openness to learning, agreeableness, conscientiousness, creativity, and emotional stability.

Concept Connection ◀◀◀

In addition, companies look for personality characteristics that match the needs of the particular job so there is a good fit. One company found that people who score high in traits such as assertiveness and extroversion typically make good salespeople, so they looked for those traits in testing candidates for new positions.[60] By one estimate, 80 percent of mid-sized and large companies use personality and ability tests for either pre-employment screening or new-employee orientation.[61] Another unusual type of test, called a *brain teaser*, is being used by companies that put a premium on innovativeness and problem solving. The answers aren't as important as how the applicant goes about solving the problem. See how you do answering the brain teasers in Exhibit 12.9.

Employment tests range from personality profiles to proficiency testing in specific skills required for a position. For a 911 operator position, an applicant should expect to take tests such as data entry for speed and accuracy, 911 address checking, 911 grid map reading and direction accuracy, 911 memorization, customer service assessment, and a personal characteristics profile. Here, Rick Bias, 911 communications director for Morgan County, Missouri, oversees operations in the Public Service Answer Point Area.

Assessment Center

First developed by psychologists at AT&T, assessment centers are typically used to select individuals for managerial and professional careers. **Assessment centers** present a series of managerial situations to groups of applicants over a two- or three-day period. One technique is the *in-basket simulation*, which requires the applicant to play the role of

EXHIBIT 12.9

Try Your Hand at Some
Interview Brain Teasers

How would you answer the following questions in a job interview?

1. How would you fit a stack of pennies as high as the Empire State Building in one room?
2. Why are manhole covers round?
3. How much should you charge to wash all the windows in Seattle?
4. You're shrunk and trapped in a blender that will turn on in 60 seconds. What do you do?
5. A man pushed his car to a hotel and lost his fortune. What happened?

Answers: There might be many solutions to these questions. Here are some that interviewers consider good answers:

1. The Empire State Building has about 110 floors. To fit the stack into one room, break it into a hundred shorter, floor-to-ceiling stacks.
2. A square cover might fall into its hole. If you hold a square manhole cover vertically and turn it a little, it will fall easily into the hole. In contrast, a round cover with a slight recess in the center can never fall in, no matter how it is held.
3. Assuming 10,000 city blocks, 600 windows per block, five minutes per window, and a rate of $20 per hour, about $10 million.
4. Use the measurement marks on the side of the container to climb out.
5. This is an oddball question more than a brain teaser, but one good answer would be: The man was playing Monopoly.

SOURCES: Similar questions are used at companies such as Microsoft, Google, and eBay. Reported in William Poundstone, "The Google Cheat Sheet," *Bloomberg Businessweek* (January 9–January 15, 2012): 79; Michael Kaplan, "Job Interview Brainteasers," *Business 2.0* (September 2007): 35–37; and William Poundstone, "Impossible Questions," *Across the Board* (September–October 2003): 44–48.

a manager who must decide how to respond to ten memos in his or her in-basket within a two-hour period. Panels of two or three trained judges observe the applicant's decisions and assess the extent to which they reflect interpersonal, communication, and problem-solving skills. At one Michigan auto parts plant, applicants for plant manager go through four-hour "day-in-the-life" simulations in which they have to juggle memos, phone calls, and employee or job problems.[62]

Some organizations use this technique for front line employees as well by administering **work sample tests**, which require an applicant to complete simulated tasks that are a part of the desired job. Google, for instance, has applicants for positions as coders write code during the interview. There is evidence that the use of work sample tests provides a better prediction of job performance than the usual job interview.[63] A communications firm in the United Kingdom asked candidates for the position of customer assistant to participate in simulated exercises with customers to assess their listening skills, customer sensitivity, and ability to cope under pressure.[64]

Online Checks

The Internet gives recruiters and hiring managers a new way to search for a candidate's criminal record, credit history, and other indications of honesty, integrity, and stability.[65] Moreover, many companies want to see what a candidate has to say about him or herself on blogs and social networking sites to gauge whether the person would be a good fit with the organization. A survey by Microsoft found that 75 percent of U.S. recruiters and HR professionals say their bosses require them to research job candidates online, and another survey found that 37 percent specifically investigate candidates' social media profiles. Nearly half say provocative or inappropriate photographs have caused them not to hire a candidate. For example, Miranda Shaw, a manager at a leading consulting firm, rejected a candidate she had previously been impressed with after she discovered photographs of him drinking and "smokin' blunts" with fraternity brothers on the Facebook page of one of his "friends" who hadn't enabled privacy settings.[66] Other recent college graduates looking for jobs have found doors closed to them because of risqué or teasing photos or vivid comments about drinking, drug use, or sexual exploits.[67]

4

ORGANIZING

Online checks aren't going away, but this is a murky and complex area for companies. Maryland became the first state to make it illegal for employers to ask job candidates for their social media passwords, and other states are considering similar laws. Using social networking as a background check without disclosing the investigation to the candidate can also open organizations to lawsuits. Moreover, because an online search often reveals information such as race, gender, sexual orientation, and so forth, HR managers have to be sure that this information isn't used in a way that could be construed as discriminatory. A new type of organization has emerged that helps companies perform online screening of job candidates in a way that ensures that no legal and ethical boundaries are crossed.[68]

Remember This

- **Selection** is the process of assessing the skills, abilities, and other attributes of applicants in an attempt to determine the fit between the job and each applicant's characteristics.
- The **application form** is a selection device that collects information about the applicant's education, previous work experience, and other background characteristics.
- A **structured interview** uses a set of standardized questions that are asked of every applicant so comparisons can be made easily.
- In a **nondirective interview**, the interviewer asks broad, open-ended questions and permits the applicant to talk freely with minimal interruption, in an attempt to bring to light information, attitudes, and behavioral characteristics that might be concealed when answering structured questions.
- A **panel interview** is an interview in which the candidate meets with several interviewers who take turns asking questions.

- Some companies are using offbeat approaches, called *extreme interviewing*, to test job candidates' ability to handle problems, cope with change, and work well with others.
- **Employment tests** assess candidates on various factors considered important for the job to be performed and include cognitive ability tests, physical ability tests, and personality tests.
- An **assessment center** is used to select individuals with high managerial potential based on their performance on a series of simulated managerial tasks.
- Managers may administer **work sample tests** to applicants for frontline positions to evaluate their performance in completing simulated tasks that are a part of the job.
- One way in which HR managers gauge an applicant's suitability for an open position is by checking what the applicant says on social media sites.
- Maryland was the first state to pass a law making it illegal to ask job applicants for their social networking passwords.

Managing Talent

Following selection, the next goal of HRM is to develop employees into an effective workforce. Key development activities include training and performance appraisal.

TRAINING AND DEVELOPMENT

Training and development programs represent a planned effort by an organization to facilitate employees' learning of job-related skills and behaviors.[69] *Training* magazine's most recent "Industry Report" shows that organizations spent some $59.7 billion on formal training programs in 2011, an increase of 13 percent over the previous year.[70] Exhibit 12.10 shows some frequently used types and methods of training. Training conducted by a "stand-and-deliver" instructor in a classroom remains the most popular method of training. Interestingly, this method of training, representing 41.6 percent of training hours reported, increased significantly from the 27.7 percent reported in 2010. Online training methods and delivering training via social media and mobile devices have declined, although mandatory and compliance training is frequently provided via these methods.

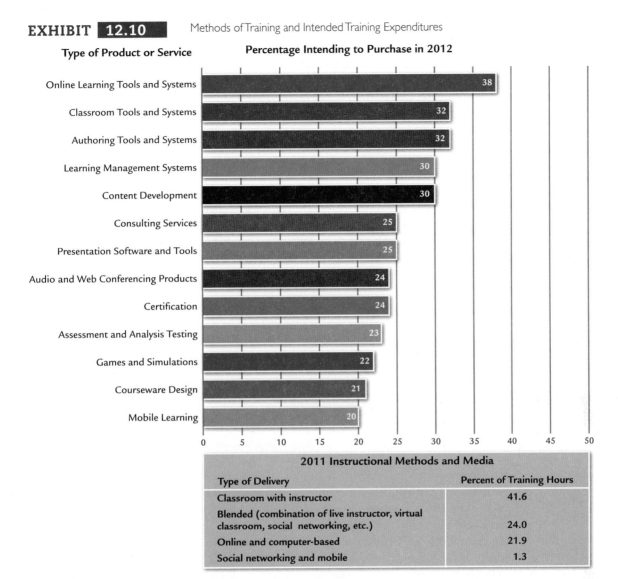

EXHIBIT 12.10   Methods of Training and Intended Training Expenditures

Type of Product or Service

Percentage Intending to Purchase in 2012

Type of Product or Service	Percentage
Online Learning Tools and Systems	38
Classroom Tools and Systems	32
Authoring Tools and Systems	32
Learning Management Systems	30
Content Development	30
Consulting Services	25
Presentation Software and Tools	25
Audio and Web Conferencing Products	24
Certification	24
Assessment and Analysis Testing	23
Games and Simulations	22
Courseware Design	21
Mobile Learning	20

2011 Instructional Methods and Media

Type of Delivery	Percent of Training Hours
Classroom with instructor	41.6
Blended (combination of live instructor, virtual classroom, social networking, etc.)	24.0
Online and computer-based	21.9
Social networking and mobile	1.3

SOURCES: "2011 Training Industry Report," *Training* (November–December 2011): 22–35.

The Bureau of Ocean Energy Management, Regulation, and Enforcement is struggling to revamp training programs after the 2010 BP-Transocean Deepwater Horizon disaster called attention to the outmoded way in which safety inspections of oil field operations were handled. The agency hired a formal training director to develop programs for training current and new inspectors in evaluating critical safety equipment (such as the blowout preventers that failed at Deepwater), as well as monitoring compliance with all environmental and workplace safety plans required by new government regulations.[71]

Development is sometimes distinguished from the general term training. Training is typically used to refer to teaching people how to perform tasks related to their present jobs, while development means teaching people broader skills that are not only useful in their present jobs but also prepare them for greater responsibilities in future jobs. At farming equipment manufacturer Deere, rising managers get coaching from influential board members, for example, to develop their leadership skills.[72] GE has adopted a new approach to developing managers due to changes in the global competitive environment.

Take a Moment

Go to the Small Group Breakout on pages 404–405 that pertains to the desired manager competencies at IBM.

4 ORGANIZING

GE has long been known for moving its executives around to different divisions every few years so that they gain a broad understanding of the company and develop general management skills. In recent years, though, a new philosophy has taken hold. Rather than moving people around, CEO Jeff Immelt wants to leave them where they are, in the belief that gaining a deeper understanding of the products and customers of a specific unit will help win more sales. "The world is so complex," says Susan Peters, leader of executive development at GE. "We need people who are pretty deep."

Putting greater emphasis on expertise in a particular business is aligned with Immelt's strategy to streamline the company. Immelt believes having managers who gain specialized expertise in a business area can help divisions better create products to meet customer needs, as well as develop the deep customer relationships needed to sell them.

To understand the changing philosophy, consider John Krenicki, the leader of GE Energy, the company's biggest industrial unit. Before being moved into that position seven years ago, Krenicki held management positions in the chemicals and materials, lighting, superabrasives, transportation, plastics, and advanced materials divisions. David Joyce, in contrast to Krenicki, has spent his entire career within the GE Aviation unit. Thomas Horton, CEO of AMR Corporation (American Airlines), one of the division's biggest customers, says the expertise of Joyce is a big part of AMR's positive relationship with GE. Horton was in Beijing when a critical question came up about an engine maintenance issue. He called Joyce at a late hour back in the United States, and Joyce was able to explain the issue in detail. "He's a good partner," says Horton.[73]

On-the-Job Training

The most common type of training is on-the-job training. In **on-the-job training (OJT)**, an experienced employee is asked to take a new employee "under his or her wing" and show the newcomer how to perform job duties. OJT has many advantages, such as few out-of-pocket costs for training facilities, materials, or instructor fees and easy transfer of learning back to the job. When implemented well, OJT is considered the fastest and most effective means of facilitating learning in the workplace.[74] At the Taj Mumbai, the hotel described in the chapter opening example, all employees go through an amazing 18 months of training, which includes both classroom and on-the-job training, to learn to be "customer ambassadors."[75] One type of OJT involves moving people to various types of jobs within the organization, where they work with experienced employees to learn different tasks. This *cross-training* may place an employee in a new position for as short a time as a few hours or for as long as a year, enabling the individual to develop new skills and giving the organization greater flexibility.

Social Learning

As shown in Exhibit 12.10, many companies report plans to purchase products and services for online and mobile learning in 2012. This reflects an awareness of the importance of social learning, particularly for younger employees. **Social learning** basically means learning informally from others by using social media tools, including mobile technologies, social networking, wikis and blogs, virtual games, and so forth.[76] A simple example might be an employee who asks a question on a blog or in a tweet, seeking advice from colleagues about a process or task. The majority of organizational learning occurs through informal rather than formal channels, so managers are supporting the use of social media technology for learning in day-to-day work. These tools allow people to share information, access knowledge, find resources, and collaborate in a natural way. An IBM survey found that high-performing organizations are 57 percent more likely than other companies to provide employees with collaborative and social media tools.[77]

Corporate Universities

Another popular approach to training and development is the corporate university. A **corporate university** is an in-house training and education facility that offers broad-based learning opportunities for employees—and frequently for customers, suppliers, and strategic partners as well—throughout their careers.[78] One well-known corporate university is Hamburger University, McDonald's worldwide training center. The institution is so well respected that its curriculum is recognized by the American Council on Education, so employees can actually earn college credits. Whereas all management training used to be held in the United States, there are now seven locations of Hamburger U. around the world, including São Paulo, Shanghai, Munich, and Mumbai.[79] Numerous other companies, including FedEx, GE, Intel, Harley-Davidson, Procter & Gamble (P&G), and Capital One, use corporate universities to build human capital.[80]

Nuclear energy company Westinghouse Electric recently invested "tens of millions" of dollars into a corporate university, according to director of talent management Jim Ice, to train current and new employees. Because there hasn't been much nuclear plant construction in the U.S. since the 1979 Three Mile Island disaster, the company has had to hire people with little or no experience in the nuclear industry and recognized a need for better training.[81]

Promotion from Within

Another way to further employee development is through promotion from within, which helps companies retain and develop valuable people. Promotions provide more challenging assignments, prescribe new responsibilities, and help employees grow by expanding and developing their abilities. The Peebles Hydro Hotel in Scotland is passionate about promoting from within as a way to retain good people and give them opportunities for growth. A maid has been promoted to head housekeeper, a wine waitress to restaurant head, and a student worker to deputy manager. The hotel also provides ongoing training in all areas. These techniques, combined with a commitment to job flexibility, helped the hotel retain high-quality workers at a time when others in the tourism and hospitality industry were suffering from a shortage of skilled labor. Staff members with 10, 15, or even 20 years of service aren't uncommon at Hydro.[82]

PERFORMANCE APPRAISAL

Performance appraisal refers to observing and assessing employee performance, recording the assessment, and providing feedback to the employee. During performance appraisal, skillful managers give feedback and praise concerning the acceptable elements of the employee's performance. They also describe performance areas that need improvement. One of the biggest corporate talent management mistakes, according to management expert Ram Charan, is the failure to provide candid performance assessments that focus on development needs.[83] When employees get this feedback, they can use it to improve their performance. Unfortunately, only three in ten employees in a recent survey believe their companies' performance review system actually helps to improve performance, indicating a need for improved methods of appraisal and feedback.[84]

Generally, HRM professionals concentrate on two things to make performance appraisal a positive force in their organizations: (1) the accurate assessment of performance through the development and application of assessment systems such as rating scales, and (2) training managers to effectively use the performance appraisal interview, so managers can provide feedback that will reinforce good performance and motivate employee development. Current thinking is that performance appraisal should be ongoing, not something that is done once a year as part of a consideration of raises.

4

ORGANIZING

Assessing Performance Accurately

Jobs are multidimensional, and performance thus may be multidimensional as well. A recent trend in performance appraisal is called **360-degree feedback**, a process that uses multiple raters, including self-rating, as a way to increase awareness of strengths and weaknesses and guide employee development. Members of the appraisal group may include supervisors, coworkers, and customers, as well as the individual, thus providing a holistic view of the employee's performance.[85] Some companies use social networking style systems to make 360-degree performance feedback a dynamic, ongoing process. One software program from Rypple, for example, lets people post short Twitter-style questions about their performance of a particular task and get feedback from managers, peers, or anyone else the user selects. Another system from Accenture has employees post photos, status updates, and two or three weekly goals that can be viewed, followed, and assessed by colleagues.[86]

Another alternative performance-evaluation method is the *performance review ranking system*.[87] This method is increasingly controversial because it essentially evaluates employees by pitting them against one another. As most commonly used, these systems rank employees according to their relative performance: 20 percent would be placed in the top group of performers; 70 percent have to be ranked in the middle; and 10 percent are ranked at the bottom. The bottom tier are given a set period of time to improve their performance, and if they don't improve, they are fired. The idea behind the forced ranking of employees is that everyone will be motivated to improve performance.

The advantages of a performance ranking system are that it (1) forces reluctant managers to make difficult decisions and identify the best and worst performers; and (2) creates and sustains a high performance culture in which people continuously improve. The disadvantages are that the system (1) may increase cutthroat competition among employees; (2) discourages collaboration and teamwork; and (3) potentially harms morale.[88] Many companies have dropped the ranking system or modified it so that it doesn't insist on quotas for underperformers. A study by the Institute for Corporate Productivity found that only 14 percent of companies surveyed reported using a strict performance ranking system in 2010, down from 42 percent a year earlier.[89]

Performance Evaluation Errors

Although we would like to believe that every manager assesses employees' performance in a careful and bias-free manner, researchers have identified several rating problems.[90] One of the most dangerous is **stereotyping**, which occurs when a rater places an employee into a class or category based on one or a few traits or characteristics—for example, stereotyping an older worker as slower and more difficult to train. Another rating error is the **halo effect**, in which a manager gives an employee the same rating on all dimensions, even if his or her performance is good on some dimensions and poor on others.

One approach to overcome performance evaluation errors is to use a behavior-based rating technique, such as the behaviorally anchored rating scale. The **behaviorally anchored rating scale (BARS)** is developed from critical incidents pertaining to job performance. Each job performance scale is anchored with specific behavioral statements that describe varying degrees of performance. By relating employee performance to specific incidents, raters can more accurately evaluate an employee's performance.[91]

Exhibit 12.11 illustrates the BARS method for evaluating a production line supervisor. The production supervisor's job can be broken down into several dimensions, such as equipment maintenance, employee training, or work scheduling. A BARS should be developed for each dimension. The dimension in Exhibit 12.11 is work scheduling. Good performance is represented by a 4 or 5 on the scale, and unacceptable performance by a 1 or 2. If a production supervisor's job has eight dimensions, the total performance evaluation will be the sum of the scores for each of eight scales.

EXHIBIT **12.11**   Example of a Behaviorally Anchored Rating Scale

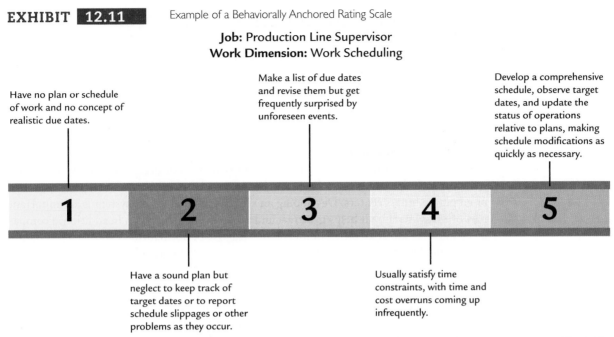

Job: Production Line Supervisor
Work Dimension: Work Scheduling

Have no plan or schedule of work and no concept of realistic due dates.

Make a list of due dates and revise them but get frequently surprised by unforeseen events.

Develop a comprehensive schedule, observe target dates, and update the status of operations relative to plans, making schedule modifications as quickly as necessary.

1 2 3 4 5

Have a sound plan but neglect to keep track of target dates or to report schedule slippages or other problems as they occur.

Usually satisfy time constraints, with time and cost overruns coming up infrequently.

SOURCES: Based on J. P. Campbell et al., "The Development and Evaluation of Behaviorally Based Rating Scales," *Journal of Applied Psychology* 57 (1973): 15–22; and Francine Alexander, "Performance Appraisals," *Small Business Reports* (March 1989): 20–29.

Remember This

- Training typically refers to teaching people skills needed in their current job, whereas development refers to teaching people broader career skills.
- The most common method of training is **on-the-job-training (OJT)**, in which an experienced employee is asked to teach a new employee how to perform job duties.
- **Social learning** refers to using social media tools to network and learn informally.
- A **corporate university** is an in-house training and development facility that offers broad-based learning opportunities for employees.
- McDonald's Hamburger University has seven management training centers around the world, including one in Shanghai and one in São Paulo.
- **Performance appraisal** is the process of observing and evaluating an employee's performance, recording the assessment, and providing feedback.
- A recent trend is **360-degree feedback**, which uses multiple raters, including self-rating, to appraise employee performance and guide development.

- Performance review ranking systems are increasingly being criticized because they tend to pit employees against one another rather than promoting cooperation and teamwork.
- **Stereotyping** is a performance evaluation error that occurs when a manager places an employee into a class or category based on one or a few traits or characteristics.
- The **halo effect** occurs when a manager gives an employee the same rating on all dimensions of the job, even though performance may be good on some dimensions and poor on others.
- One way to overcome evaluation errors is to use a **behaviorally anchored rating scale (BARS)**, which is a performance evaluation technique that relates an employee's performance to specific job-related incidents.

4

ORGANIZING

Maintaining an Effective Workforce

Now we turn to the topic of how managers and HRM professionals maintain a workforce that has been recruited and developed. Maintenance of the current workforce involves compensation, wage and salary systems, benefits, and (occasionally) termination.

COMPENSATION

The term **compensation** refers to (1) all monetary payments and (2) all goods or commodities used in lieu of money to reward employees.[92] An organization's compensation structure includes wages and salaries and benefits such as health insurance, paid vacations, or employee fitness centers. Developing an effective compensation system is an important part of HRM because it helps to attract and retain talented workers. In addition, a company's compensation system has an impact on strategic performance.[93] HR managers design the pay and benefits systems to fit company strategy and to provide compensation equity.

Wage and Salary Systems

Ideally, management's strategy for the organization should be a critical determinant of the features and operations of the pay system.[94] For example, managers may have the goal of maintaining or improving profitability or market share by stimulating employee performance. Thus, they should design and use a merit pay system rather than a system based on other criteria such as seniority. At retailer Macy's, for example, the board increased the sales component of bonuses for senior executives to encourage sales growth. In addition, if Macy's sales increase above the company plan, top executives can earn higher bonuses.[95]

The most common approach to employee compensation is *job-based pay*, which means linking compensation to the specific tasks an employee performs. However, these systems present several problems. For one thing, job-based pay may fail to reward the type of learning behavior needed for the organization to adapt and survive in a turbulent environment. In addition, these systems reinforce an emphasis on organizational hierarchy and centralized decision making and control, which are inconsistent with the growing emphasis on employee participation and increased responsibility.[96]

Skill-based pay systems are increasingly popular in both large and small companies, including Sherwin-Williams, Au Bon Pain, and Quaker Oats. Employees with higher skill levels receive higher pay than those with lower skill levels. At Quaker Oats pet food plant in Topeka, Kansas, for example, employees might start at something like $9.75 per hour but reach a top hourly rate of $15.50 when they master a series of skills.[97] Also called *competency-based pay*, skill-based pay systems encourage people to develop their skills and competencies, thus making them more valuable to the organization, as well as more employable if they leave their current jobs.

Compensation Equity

Whether the organization uses job-based pay or skill-based pay, good managers strive to maintain a sense of fairness and equity within the pay structure and thereby fortify employee morale. **Job evaluation** refers to the process of determining the value or worth of jobs within an organization through an examination of job content. Job evaluation techniques enable managers to compare similar and dissimilar jobs and to determine internally equitable pay rates—that is, pay rates that employees believe are fair compared with those for other jobs in the organization.

Organizations also want to make sure their pay rates are fair compared to other companies. HR managers may obtain **wage and salary surveys** that show what other organizations pay incumbents in jobs that match a sample of "key" jobs selected by the organization. These surveys are available from a number of sources, including the U.S. Bureau of Labor Statistics National Compensation Survey.

Pay-for-Performance

Many of today's organizations develop compensation plans based on a *pay-for-performance standard* to raise productivity and cut labor costs in a competitive global environment. **Pay-for-performance**, also called *incentive pay*, means tying at least part of compensation to employee effort and performance, whether it be through merit-based pay, bonuses, team incentives, or various gain-sharing or profit-sharing plans. With pay-for-performance, incentives are aligned with the behaviors needed to help the organization achieve its strategic goals. Employees have an incentive to make the company more efficient and profitable because if goals are not met, no bonuses are paid.

However, recent years have shown the potential dangers of misdirected pay-for-performance plans. Alan Blinder, Princeton professor of economics and public affairs, points out that a fundamental cause of the 2008–2009 financial crisis in the United States was the "perverse go-for-broke incentives" that rewarded people for taking excessive risks with other people's money.[98] During the financial meltdown, it became clear that people at every level of the financial system were getting rewarded for short-term performance—if things went wrong down the line, it was someone else's problem. Then it all came crashing down. Managers can take care to create pay-for-performance plans that align with the long-term interests of the organization, shareholders, and the broader society.

BENEFITS

An effective compensation package requires more than money. Although salary is an important component, benefits are equally important.

Organizations are required by law to provide some benefits, such as Social Security, unemployment compensation, and workers' compensation. Other types of benefits, such as health insurance, vacations, and things such as on-site daycare or educational reimbursements are not required by law but are provided by organizations to maintain an effective workforce. The benefits packages provided by large companies attempt to meet the needs of all employees.

Some companies, particularly in the technology industry where skilled employees are hard to find, offer extremely generous benefit packages. SAS Institute, for example, provides (among other benefits): 90 percent coverage of health insurance premiums; free health care at an onsite medical clinic; an onsite fitness center; unlimited sick days; three weeks annual vacation for entry-level employees; onsite child care; and a work-life center offering services ranging from parenting classes to elder care.[99] However, during the recent recession, many employers cut benefits not required by law, and most say that they don't plan to restore them to pre-recession levels. "Those days are gone. Benefits across the board are no longer sacred cows," says Tim Prichard, head of BridgeStreet Consulting, a benefits administration consulting firm.[100] Although new U.S. legislation requires that every American have minimal health insurance coverage by 2014, employer-sponsored plans are getting skimpier, more expensive, and less available.[101] HR managers are studying the law and advising executives on their responsibilities and options so the organization can be compliant and avoid penalties.

RIGHTSIZING THE ORGANIZATION

In some cases, organizations have more people than they need and have to let some employees go. **Rightsizing** refers to reducing the company's workforce intentionally to the point where the number of employees is deemed to be right for the company's current situation. Also called *downsizing*, planned reductions in the size of the workforce are a reality for many of today's companies. Although many companies have begun hiring workers again after major layoffs in 2009 and 2010, the unemployment rate in the United States was still hovering at around 7.8 percent in October 2012.[102]

Concept Connection ◀◀◀

Brad Swonetz/Redux

As the term *rightsizing* implies, the goal is to make the company stronger and more competitive by aligning the size of the workforce with the company's current needs. However, some researchers have found that massive cuts often fail to achieve the intended benefits and in some cases significantly harm the organization.[103] Unless HRM departments effectively and humanely manage the rightsizing process, layoffs can lead to decreased morale and performance. Managers can smooth the process by regularly communicating with employees and providing them with as much information as possible, providing assistance to workers who will lose their jobs, and using training and development to help address the emotional needs of remaining employees and enable them to cope with new or additional responsibilities.[104]

> "I have a hard time looking myself in the mirror if I keep someone around who can't do the job. It is not fair to the other employees, and it certainly is not fair to my customers."
>
> — JAY GOLTZ, ENTREPRENEUR AND BUSINESS SPEAKER

TERMINATION

Despite the best efforts of line managers and HRM professionals, the organization will lose employees. Some will retire, others will depart voluntarily for other jobs, and still others will be forced out through mergers and cutbacks or for poor performance.

The value of termination for maintaining an effective workforce is twofold. First, employees who are poor performers can be dismissed. Productive employees often resent disruptive, low-performing employees who are allowed to stay with the company and receive pay and benefits comparable to theirs. Second, managers can use exit interviews as a valuable HR tool, regardless of whether the employee leaves voluntarily or is forced out. An **exit interview** is an interview conducted with departing employees to determine why they are leaving the company. The value of the exit interview is to provide an inexpensive way to learn about pockets of dissatisfaction within the organization and hence find ways to reduce future turnover.[105] As John Donahoe, president and CEO of eBay, put it, "when people are leaving, they're often in a very reflective state and . . . they're also just stunningly direct, because it's like they have nothing to lose." One thing Donahoe learned from conducting exit interviews at eBay was that mid-level executives were unclear about their responsibility and authority, so he reorganized to clarify lines of decision-making responsibility and authority.[106] The oil services giant Schlumberger includes an exit interview as part of a full-scale investigation of every departure, with the results posted online so managers all around the company can get insight into problems.[107]

However, in some cases, employees who leave voluntarily are reluctant to air uncomfortable complaints or discuss their real reasons for leaving. Companies such as T-Mobile, Campbell Soup, and Conair found that having people complete an online exit questionnaire yields more open and honest information. When people have negative things to say about managers or the company, the online format is a chance to speak their mind without having to do it in a face-to-face meeting.[108]

Take a Moment

Go to the Ethical Dilemma for Chapter 12 on page 445 that pertains to termination of employees for poor performance.

Remember This

- **Compensation** refers to all monetary payments and all nonmonetary goods or benefits used to reward employees.
- Managers strive to maintain fairness and equity in the pay system.
- **Job evaluation** is the process of determining the value of jobs within an organization through an examination of job content.
- **Wage and salary surveys** show what other organizations pay incumbents in jobs that match a sample of key jobs selected by the organization.
- **Pay-for-performance**, also called *incentive pay*, means tying at least a portion of compensation to employee effort and performance.
- Benefits make up a large portion of labor costs in the United States.

- During the recession, many organizations have cut benefits that are not required by law.
- **Rightsizing**, also called *downsizing*, refers to reducing the company's workforce intentionally to the point where the number of employees is deemed right for the company's current situation.
- If not managed effectively and humanely, rightsizing can lead to decreased morale and performance.
- An **exit interview** is an interview conducted with departing employees to determine reasons for their departure and learn about potential problems in the organization.
- Campbell Soup Company lets people complete an online exit questionnaire so they can express their complaints or ideas freely, without having to talk face to face with a manager.

ch12: Discussion Questions

1. Assume that it is the year 2025. In your company, central planning has given way to frontline decision making, and bureaucracy has given way to teamwork. Shop floor workers use handheld devices and robots. A labor shortage currently affects many job openings, and the few applicants you do attract lack skills to work in teams, make their own production decisions, or use sophisticated technology. As vice president of HRM since 2010, what should you have done to prepare for this situation?

2. Is it wise for managers to evaluate a candidate's postings on social networking sites such as Facebook as grounds for rejection before even interviewing a promising candidate? What might be some ethical and legal issues managers should consider? Discuss.

3. What does it mean to say that HRM plays a strategic role in driving organizational performance? Consider recruiting, training, performance appraisal, and compensation strategies as part of your answer.

4. Which selection criteria (personal interview, employment test, assessment center) do you think would be most valuable for predicting effective job performance for a college professor? For an assembly-line worker in a manufacturing plant? Discuss.

5. If you were asked to advise a private company about its EEO responsibilities, what two points would you emphasize as most important?

6. As HR manager for a small company that makes computer games and software, what are some steps that you might take to create an employer brand?

7. One HR manager recently got a thank-you note on her iPhone that said "Thx 4 the Iview! Wud♥ to wrk 4 u!!!☺" The manager had liked the candidate's interview, but after getting the note, she put him in the reject pile. Do you think it was fair for the manager to reject the candidate so automatically? Should "text-speak" be considered acceptable workplace communication? Discuss.

8. If you are in charge of training and development, which training option or options—such as OJT, cross-training, and classroom—would you be likely to choose for your company's production line manager? A customer service representative? An entry-level accountant?

9. As a manager, how would you draw up a telecommuting contract with a new employee? Include considerations such as job description, compensation and benefits, performance measures, training, and grounds for dismissal.

10. How would you go about deciding whether to use a job-based, skills-based, or pay-for-performance compensation plan for employees in a textile manufacturing plant? For waitstaff in a restaurant? For salespeople in an insurance company?

ch12: Apply Your Skills: Experiential Exercise

Do You Want to Be an HR Manager?[109]

The following questions are based on a Human Resources Capability Model developed by the Australian Public Service (APS) Commission for HR managers who work in government agencies. People who work with HR managers complete a 72-item questionnaire assessing a range of expectations for the HR manager. The results are given to the manager, who then works to improve low scores. These questions give a glimpse of the expectations for APS HR managers. Please think about how strongly you are attracted to the requirement below.

① —Not attracted at all

② —Not very attracted

③ —Moderately attracted

④ —Very attracted

⑤ —Extremely attracted

Bringing HR to the Business

1. Has a detailed knowledge of current HR approaches, tools, and technology.
   1   2   3   4   5

2. Understands the human behavior triggers that affect or improve organizational performance.
   1   2   3   4   5

Connecting HR with the Business

3. Maintains knowledge of the business through frequent interaction with people in the workplace.
   1   2   3   4   5

4. Presents strong business cases for HR initiatives.
   1   2   3   4   5

Partnering with the Business

5. Establishes and maintains good relationships across the organization.
   1   2   3   4   5

6. Guides the top executive and line managers in actively managing people issues.
   1   2   3   4   5

Achieving High-Quality Business Results

7. Applies business acumen to HR decisions.
   1   2   3   4   5

8. Monitors HR initiatives continuously to maintain consistency with business outcomes.
   1   2   3   4   5

Bringing Ideas to the Business

9. Looks continually for ways to enhance or create new HR methods to achieve business outcomes.
   1   2   3   4   5

10. Critically evaluates and explores alternatives to the way things are done.
    1   2   3   4   5

Scoring and Interpretation

Correct answers are not the point of the preceding questions. The five subscales (Bringing HR to the Business, Partnering with Business, etc.) represent elements of the HR Capability Model that APS HR managers are expected to master. Any questions for which you receive a 4 or 5 would be strong areas for you. If you averaged 4 or higher for most of the five capabilities, you may want to consider a career in HR. If you aspire to become an HR manager, it would be good to study the entire model at the Web site www.apsc.gov.au/publications01/hrmodel.htm.

ch12: Apply Your Skills: Small Group Breakout

Management Competencies[110]

Step 1. An important responsibility of the HR department at many companies is to develop a list of managerial competencies and then to provide training to help managers improve on those competencies. The list below includes desired manager competencies from IBM. Make notes to the right of each competency describing the management behaviors you think would be covered.

* Collaborative influence _____

_____

* Developing IBM people and communities _____

_____

* Earning trust _____

_____

* Embracing challenge _____

_____

* Enabling growth _____

_____

* Passion for IBM's future _____

_____

- Strategic risk taking _____
_____

- Thinking horizontal_____
_____

Step 2. In groups of three to five students, compare, discuss, and agree upon the expected behaviors for each competency. One student be the recorder and be prepared to report the behaviors to the class.

Step 3. After agreeing upon competency behaviors, each student should take a turn stating the competencies they believe will be easiest and hardest for them to master.

Step 4. Why do you think IBM arrived at this set of competencies? How do you think it might differ from management or leadership competencies for other companies?

Step 5. Outside of class, go online and look up information on IBM's competencies. (Search for "IBM Leadership Competencies.") Are the competencies defined as you expected? Look up competencies for another company as well. Why do you think HR departments in these companies put so much energy into developing a list of desired manager competencies?

ch12: Endnotes

1. Based on ideas presented in Jim Collins, *Good to Great: Why Some Companies Make the Leap . . . and Others Don't* (New York: Harper Business, 2001).

2. Rohit Deshpandé and Anjali Raina, "The Ordinary Heroes of the Taj," *Harvard Business Review* (December 2011): 119–123.

3. Results of a McKinsey Consulting survey, reported in Leigh Branham, "Planning to Become an Employer of Choice," *Journal of Organizational Excellence* (Summer 2005): 57–68.

4. Robert L. Mathis and John H. Jackson, *Human Resource Management: Essential Perspectives*, 2d ed. (Cincinnati, OH: South-Western Publishing, 2002), p. 1.

5. See James C. Wimbush, "Spotlight on Human Resource Management," *Business Horizons* 48 (2005): 463–467; Jonathan Tompkins, "Strategic Human Resources Management in Government: Unresolved Issues," *Public Personnel Management* (Spring 2002): 95–110; Noel M. Tichy, Charles J. Fombrun, and Mary Anne Devanna, "Strategic Human Resource Management," *Sloan Management Review* 23 (Winter 1982): 47–61; Cynthia A. Lengnick-Hall and Mark L. Lengnick-Hall, "Strategic Human Resources Management: A Review of the Literature and a Proposed Typology," *Academy of Management Review* 13 (July 1988): 454–470; Eugene B. McGregor, *Strategic Management of Human Knowledge, Skills, and Abilities* (San Francisco: Jossey-Bass, 1991).

6. Quoted in Erin White, "HR Departments Get New Star Power at Some Firms; Business Executives Now Tapped to Lead as Job Is Rethought" (Theory & Practice column), *The Wall Street Journal*, June 23, 2008.

7. Joann S. Lublin, "HR Executives Suddenly Get Hot" (Theory & Practice column), *The Wall Street Journal*, December 14, 2009.

8. This definition is based on George Bohlander, Scott Snell, and Arthur Sherman, *Managing Human Resources*, 12th ed. (Cincinnati, OH: South-Western, 2001), pp. 13–15.

9. "Leading through Connections: The IBM 2012 Chief Executive Officer Study," reported in Eric Lesser and Carl Hoffman, "Workforce Analytics: Making the Most of a Critical Asset," *Ivey Business Journal* (July–August 2012), www.iveybusinessjournal.com/topics/strategy/workforce-analytics-making-the-most-of-a-critical-asset (accessed August 27, 2012).

10. P. Wright, G. McMahan, and A. McWilliams, "Human Resources and Sustained Competitive Advantage: A Resource-Based Perspective," *International Journal of Human Resource Management* 5 (1994): 301–326; Tompkins, "Strategic Human Resource Management in Government."

11. Liza Castro Christiansen and Malcolm Higgs, "How the Alignment of Business Strategy and HR Strategy Can Impact Performance," *Journal of General Management* 33, no. 4 (Summer 2008): 13–33; Seema Sanghi, "Building Competencies," *Industrial Management* (May–June 2009): 14–17; B. Becker and M. Huselid, "High Performance Work Systems and Firm Performance: A Synthesis of Research and Managerial Implications," *Research in Personnel and Human Resources Management* 16 (1998): 53–101; S. Ramlall, "Measuring Human Resource Management's Effectiveness in Improving Performance," *Human Resource Planning* 26 (2003): 51; Mark A. Huselid, Susan E. Jackson, and Randall S. Schuler, "Technical and Strategic Human Resource Management Effectiveness as Determinants of Firm Performance," *Academy of Management Journal* 40, no. 1 (1997): 171–188; and John T. Delaney and Mark A. Huselid, "The Impact of Human Resource Management Practices on Perceptions of Organizational Performance," *Academy of Management Journal* 39, no. 4 (1996): 949–969.

12. Rachel Dodes, "Managing & Careers: At Macy's, a Makeover on Service," *The Wall Street Journal*, April 11, 2011, B10.

13. James N. Baron and David M. Kreps, "Consistent Human Resource Practices," *California Management Review* 41, no. 3 (Spring 1999): 29–53.

4

ORGANIZING

14. Cynthia D. Fisher, "Current and Recurrent Challenges in HRM," *Journal of Management* 15 (1989): 157–180.

15. Floyd Kemske, "HR 2008: A Forecast Based on Our Exclusive Study," *Workforce* (January 1998): 46–60.

16. This discussion is based in part on George Bohlander, Scott Snell, and Arthur Sherman, *Managing Human Resources*, 12th ed. (Cincinnati, OH: South-Western, 2001), pp. 13–15; and Harry Scarbrough, "Recipe for Success," *People Management* (January 23, 2003): 22–25.

17. Susan Cantrell et al., "Measuring the Value of Human Capital Investments: The SAP Case," *Strategy & Leadership* 34, no. 2 (2006): 43–52.

18. Section 1604.1 of the EEOC Guidelines based on the Civil Rights Act of 1964, Title VII.

19. Reported in Jeff Green, "The Silencing of Sexual Harassment," *Bloomberg BusinessWeek* (November 21–November 27, 2011): 27–28.

20. *Ibid.*

21. Melanie Trottman, "For Angry Employees, Legal Cover for Rants," *The Wall Street Journal*, December 2, 2011, http://online.wsj.com/article/SB1000142405297 0203710704577049822809710332.html (accessed August 27, 2012).

22. Reported in D. T. Hall and P. H. Mirvis, "The New Protean Career: Psychological Success and the Path with a Heart," in D. T. Hall & Associates, *The Career is Dead—Long Live the Career: A Relational Approach to Careers* (San Francisco: Jossey-Bass, 1995), pp. 15–45.

23. Phred Dvorak and Scott Thurm, "Slump Prods Firms to Seek New Compact with Workers," *The Wall Street Journal*, October 20, 2009.

24. Lynda Gratton, as reported in Phyllis Korkki, "The Shifting Definition of Worker Loyalty," *The New York Times*, April 23, 2011, www.nytimes.com/2011/04/24/jobs/24search.html (accessed August 27, 2012).

25. Stephen Baker, "You're Fired—But Stay in Touch," *BusinessWeek* (May 4, 2009): 54–55.

26. A. S. Tsui et al., "Alternative Approaches to the Employee-Organization Relationship: Does Investment in Employees Pay Off?" *Academy of Management Journal* 40 (1997): 1089–1121; D. Wang et al., "Employment Relationships and Firm Performance: Evidence from an Emerging Economy," *Journal of Organizational Behavior* 24 (2003): 511–535.

27. This discussion is based on Joe Light, "In Hiring, Firms Shine Images," *The Wall Street Journal*, May 16, 2011, B9; and Lauren Weber, "On the Hunt for Tech Hires," *The Wall Street Journal*, April 11, 2012, B6.

28. Weber, "On the Hunt for Tech Hires."

29. Weber, "On the Hunt"; and Light, "In Hiring, Firms Shine Images."

30. This discussion is based on Jody Greenstone Miller and Matt Miller, "The Best Executive and Professional Jobs May No Longer Be Full-Time Gigs," *Harvard Business Review* (May 2012): 51–62; Peter Coy, Michelle Conlin, and Moira Herbst, "The Disposable Worker," *Bloomberg BusinessWeek* (January 18, 2010): 33–39; Lauren Weber, "Adeco Expects Temps Are Here to Stay as Hiring Revives," *The Wall Street Journal*, December 12, 2011, http://online.wsj.com/article/SB1000142405297 0204319004577086871681893212.html (accessed August 29, 2012); Motoko Rich, "Weighing Costs, Companies Favor Temporary Help," *The New York Times*, December 19, 2010, www.nytimes.com/2010/12/20/business/economy/20temp.html?pagewanted=all (accessed December 20, 2010); and Thomas Frank, "TSA Struggles to Reduce Persistent Turnover," *USA Today*, February 25, 2008.

31. "Workforce Survey: In the Company of Contingents," *Workforce Management*, August 6, 2012, www.workforce.com/article/20120806/NEWS02/120809957 (accessed August 27, 2012).

32. Jody Greenstone Miller and Matt Miller, "The Best Executive and Professional Jobs May No Longer Be Full-Time Gigs."

33. "SHRM Survey Findings: Work-Life Balance Policies," Society for Human Resource Management, July 12, 2012, downloaded at www.shrm.org/Research/SurveyFindings/Articles/Pages/WorkLifeBalance.aspx (accessed August 29, 2012).

34. Meg McSherry Breslin, "Teleworking Has Come a Long Way for Workers," *Workforce Management*, March 4, 2012, www.workforce.com/article/20120304/NEWS02/120309988/teleworking-has-come-a-long-way-for-workers (accessed August 27, 2012).

35. Bill Leonard, "President Signs Federal Employee Telework Legislation," *Society for Human Resource Management*, December 10, 2010, www.shrm.org/hrdisciplines/staffingmanagement/articles/pages/federaltelework.aspx (accessed August 29, 2012).

36. Reported in *2012 Employee Benefits: The Employee Benefits Landscape in a Recovering Economy, A Research Report by the Society for Human Resource Management*, Society for Human Resource Management and Colonial Life, June 22, 2012, www.shrm.org/Research/SurveyFindings/Articles/Documents/2012_EmpBenefits_Report.pdf (accessed August 29, 2012).

37. John Challenger, "There Is No Future for the Workplace," *Public Management* (February 1999): 20–23; Susan Caminiti, "Work-Life," *Fortune* (September 19, 2005): S1–S17.

38. Stephanie Armour, "Generation Y: They've Arrived at Work with a New Attitude," *USA Today*, November 6, 2005, www.usatoday.com/money/workplace/2005-11-06-gen-y _x.htm (accessed November 6, 2005); Ellyn Spragins, "The Talent Pool," *FSB* (October 2005): 92–101; and Caminiti, "Work-Life."

39. James G. March and Herbert A. Simon, *Organizations* (New York: Wiley, 1958).

40. Dennis J. Kravetz, *The Human Resources Revolution* (San Francisco: Jossey-Bass, 1989).

41. J. W. Boudreau and S. L. Rynes, "Role of Recruitment in Staffing Utility Analysis," *Journal of Applied Psychology* 70 (1985): 354–366.

42. Megan Santosus, "The Human Capital Factor," *CFO-IT* (Fall 2005): 26–27.

43. Brian Dumaine, "The New Art of Hiring Smart," *Fortune* (August 17, 1987): 78–81.

44. This discussion is based on Mathis and Jackson, *Human Resource Management*, chapter 4, pp. 49–60.

45. Victoria Griffith, "When Only Internal Expertise Will Do," *CFO* (October 1998): 95–96, 102.

46. J. P. Wanous, *Organizational Entry* (Reading, MA: Addison-Wesley, 1980).

47. Juro Osawa and Paul Mozur, "In China, Recruiting Gets Social," *The Wall Street Journal*, August 1, 2012, B4; Joe Light, "Recruiters Rethink Online Playbook," *The Wall Street Journal*, January 18, 2011, http://online.wsj.com/article/SB1000142405274870430740457608049261385 8846.html (accessed January 19, 2011); and Joe Walker, "PwC Pays for Priority: New Recruiting Tool for College Students Give Accounting Firm Top Billing," *The Wall Street Journal*, October 4, 2010 http://online.wsj.com/article/SB1000142405274870402930457552664129469 9972.html (accessed October 9, 2010).

48. Osawa and Mozur, "In China, Recruiting Gets Social."

49. Light, "Recruiters Rethink Online Playbook."

50. Based on "United Nations New York Headquarters Internship Programme," www.un.org/depts/OHRM/sds/internsh/index.htm (accessed August 29, 2012); and Phyllis Korkki, "The Internship as Inside Track," *The New York Times*, March 25, 2011, www.nytimes.com/2011/03/27/jobs/27searches.html (accessed March 27, 2011).

51. Trudy Steinfeld, as reported in Korrki, "The Internship as Inside Track."

52. "Silicon Valley's New Hiring Strategy," *Fast Company*, October 20, 2011, www.fastcompany.com/1784737/silicon-valleys-new-hiring-strategy (accessed August 29, 2012); and Andrea Siedsma, "Alternative Recruiting Strategies Employed by Companies Vying for Top Tech Talent," *Workforce Management*, May 18, 2012, www.workforce.com/article/20120518/NEWS02/120519953/alternative-recruiting-strategies-employed-by-companies-vying-for-top (accessed August 27, 2012).

53. Wimbush, "Spotlight on Human Resource Management."

54. Paul W. Thayer, "Somethings Old, Somethings New," *Personnel Psychology* 30, no. 4 (Winter 1977): 513–524.

55. J. Ledvinka, *Federal Regulation of Personnel and Human Resource Management* (Boston: Kent, 1982); and *Civil Rights Act*, Title VII, Section 2000e *et seq.*, U. S. Code 42 (1964).

56. Reported in Stephanie Clifford, "The New Science of Hiring," *Inc.* (August 2006): 90–98.

57. Bohlander, Snell, and Sherman, *Managing Human Resources*, p. 202.

58. Tiffany Hsu, "Job Interviewing, To the Extreme," *The Los Angeles Times*, February 19, 2012, http://articles.latimes.com/2012/feb/19/business/la-fi-extreme-interviewing-20120219 (accessed February 19, 2012).

59. *Ibid.*

60. Susan Greco, "Sales & Marketing: He Can Close, but How Is His Interpersonal Sensitivity: Testing Sales Recruits," *Inc.* (March 2009): 96–98.

61. Reported in Toddi Gutner, "Applicants' Personalities Put to the Test," *The Wall Street Journal*, August 26, 2008.

62. Erin White, "Walking a Mile in Another's Shoes—Employers Champion Tests of Job Candidates to Gauge Skills at 'Real World' Tasks" (Theory & Practice column), *The Wall Street Journal*, January 16, 2006.

63. Reported in William Poundstone, "How to Ace a Google Interview," *The Wall Street Journal*, December 24, 2011, http://online.wsj.com/article/SB10001424052 970204552304577112522982505222.html (accessed December 24, 2011).

64. Mike Thatcher, "'Front-line' Staff Selected by Assessment Center," *Personnel Management* (November 1993): 83.

65. Jim Rendon, "Ten Things Human Resources Won't Tell You," *The Wall Street Journal Online*, April 19, 2010, http://online.wsj .com/article/SB1000142405270230 349130457518802380137932 4 .html?KEYWORDS =ten+things+human+resources+won%27t +tell+you (accessed April 19, 2010).

66. Reported in "Should You Check Facebook Before Hiring?" *The Washington Post*, January 22, 2011, www .washingtonpost.com/wp-dyn/content/article/2011/01/22/AR2011012203193.html (accessed January 23, 2011); and CareerBuilder survey results reported in "Survey: 37% Use Social Media to Check Candidates," *Workforce Management*, April 18, 2012, www .workforce.com/article/20120418/NEWS01/120419964 (accessed June 19, 2012).

67. Alan Finder, "For Some, Online Persona Undermines a Résumé," *The New York Times*, June 11, 2006.

68. William P. Smith and Deborah L. Kidder, "You've Been Tagged! (Then Again, Maybe Not): Employers and Facebook," *Business Horizons* 53 (2010): 491–499; and Lisa Quast, "Recruiting Reinvented: How Companies are Using Social Media in the Hiring Process," *Forbes*, May 21, 2012, www.forbes.com/sites/lisaquast/2012/05/21/recruiting-reinvented-how-companies-are-using-social-media-in-the-hiring-process/ (accessed August 29, 2012).

69. Bernard Keys and Joseph Wolfe, "Management Education and Development: Current Issues and Emerging Trends," *Journal of Management* 14 (1988): 205–229.

70. "2011 Training Industry Report," *Training* (November–December 2011): 22–35.

71. Leslie Eaton, "U.S. News: Drilling Regulator Struggles to Add Inspectors," *The Wall Street Journal*, April 20, 2011, A6.

4

ORGANIZING

72. "How Do Great Companies Groom Talent?" *Fortune* (November 21, 2011): 166.

73. Kate Linebaugh, "The New GE Way: Go Deep, Not Wide," *The Wall Street Journal*, March 7, 2012, B1.

74. William J. Rothwell and H. C. Kazanas, *Improving On-the-Job Training: How to Establish and Operate a Comprehensive OJT Program* (San Francisco: Jossey-Bass, 1994).

75. Deshpandé and Raina, "The Ordinary Heroes of the Taj."

76. Matt Allen and Jennifer Naughton, "Social Learning: A Call to Action for Learning Professionals," *T+D* (August 2011): 50–55.

77. Reported in Margaret Schweer et al., "Building a Well-Networked Organization," *MIT Sloan Management Review* (Winter 2012): 35–42.

78. Jeanne C. Meister, "The Brave New World of Corporate Education," *The Chronicle of Higher Education* (February 9, 2001): B10; and Meryl Davids Landau, "Corporate Universities Crack Open Their Doors," *The Journal of Business Strategy* (May–June 2000): 18–23.

79. Janet Wiscombe, "McDonald's Corp." *Workforce Management* (November 2010): 38–40.

80. Meister, "The Brave New World of Corporate Education"; Edward E. Gordon, "Bridging the Gap," *Training* (September 2003): 30; and John Byrne, "The Search for the Young and Gifted," *BusinessWeek* (October 4, 1999): 108–116.

81. Lauren Weber, "Managing & Careers: Fine-Tuning the Perfect Employee," *The Wall Street Journal*, December 5, 2011, B9.

82. Jim Dow, "Spa Attraction," *People Management* (May 29, 2003): 34–35.

83. "Talent Tutor: Ram Charan's List of Biggest Corporate Talent-Management Mistakes," sidebar in Joann S. Lublin, "Managing & Careers—Boss Talk; Ram Charan: Message to CEOs: Do More to Keep Your Key Employees," *The Wall Street Journal*, December 27, 2010, B5.

84. Survey by HR consulting firm Watson Wyatt, reported in Kelley Holland, "Performance Reviews: Many Need Improvement," *The New York Times*, September 10, 2006.

85. Kyle Couch, "Talent Management: Build on Four Key Components," *Leadership Excellence* (February 2012): 18; Walter W. Tornow, "Editor's Note: Introduction to Special Issue on 360-Degree Feedback," *Human Resource Management* 32, no. 2–3 (Summer–Fall 1993): 211–219; and Brian O'Reilly, "360 Feedback Can Change Your Life," *Fortune* (October 17, 1994): 93–100.

86. Jena McGregor, "Job Review in 140 Keystrokes," *BusinessWeek* (March 23 & 30, 2009): 58.

87. This discussion is based on Dick Grote, "Forced Ranking: Behind the Scenes," *Across the Board* (November–December 2002): 40–45; Matthew Boyle, "Performance Reviews: Perilous Curves Ahead," *Fortune* (May 28, 2001): 187–188; Carol Hymowitz, "Ranking Systems Gain Popularity but Have Many Staffers Riled," *The Wall Street Journal*, May 15, 2001; and Kris Frieswick, "Truth and Consequences," *CFO* (June 2001): 56–63."

88. "Forced Ranking (Forced Distribution)," *HR Management Web site*, www.humanresources.hrvinet.com/forced-ranking-forced-distribution/ (accessed January 21, 2012).

89. Leslie Kwoh, "'Rank and Yank' Retains Vocal Fans," *The Wall Street Journal*, January 31, 2012.

90. V. R. Buzzotta, "Improve Your Performance Appraisals," *Management Review* (August 1988): 40–43; and H. J. Bernardin and R. W. Beatty, *Performance Appraisal: Assessing Human Behavior at Work* (Boston: Kent, 1984).

91. Bernardin and Beatty, *Performance Appraisal.*

92. Richard I. Henderson, *Compensation Management: Rewarding Performance*, 4th ed. (Reston, VA: Reston, 1985).

93. L. R. Gomez-Mejia, "Structure and Process Diversification, Compensation Strategy, and Firm Performance," *Strategic Management Journal* 13 (1992): 381–397; and E. Montemayor, "Congruence between Pay Policy and Competitive Strategy in High-Performing Firms," *Journal of Management* 22, no. 6 (1996): 889–908.

94. Renée F. Broderick and George T. Milkovich, "Pay Planning, Organization Strategy, Structure and 'Fit': A Prescriptive Model of Pay," paper presented at the 45th Annual Meeting of the Academy of Management, San Diego (August 1985).

95. Rachel Dodes and Dana Mattioli, "Theory & Practice: Retailers Try On New Sales Tactics," *The Wall Street Journal*, April 19, 2010, B9.

96. E. F. Lawler, III, *Strategic Pay: Aligning Organizational Strategies and Pay Systems* (San Francisco: Jossey-Bass, 1990); and R. J. Greene, "Person-Focused Pay: Should It Replace Job-Based Pay?" *Compensation and Benefits Management* 9, no. 4 (1993): 46–55.

97. L. Wiener, "No New Skills? No Raise," *U.S. News and World Report* (October 26, 1992): 78.

98. Alan S. Blinder, "Crazy Compensation and the Crisis," *The Wall Street Journal*, May 28, 2009.

99. Janet Wiscombe, "SAS," *Workforce Management* (October 2010): 36–38.

100. Joe Walker, "Even with a Recovery, Job Perks May Not Return," *The Wall Street Journal Online*, April 5, 2010, http://online.wsj.com/article/SB1000142405270 23040174045751658854181296256.html (accessed April 10, 2010).

101. Diane Stafford, "Health Plans to Take Some Hits Under New Insurance Reforms," *Buffalo News*, May 30, 2010; John C. Goodman, "Goodbye, Employer-Sponsored Insurance," *The Wall Street Journal*, May 21, 2010, A13.

102. U.S. Department of Labor, reported in Peter Whoriskey and Neil Irwin, "Job Growth,

Unemployment Rate Rose in October as Workers Re-entered Labor Force," *The Washington Post*, November 2, 2012, http://www.washingtonpost.com/business/economy/job-growth-and-unemployment-rate-rise-in-october-as-workers-reenter-labor-force/2012/11/02/d4e425c2-24e7-11e2-ba29-238a6ac36a08_story.html (accessed November 26, 2012).

103. James R. Morris, Wayne F. Cascio, and Clifford Young, "Downsizing After All These Years: Questions and Answers About Who Did It, How Many Did It, and Who Benefited from It," *Organizational Dynamics* (Winter 1999): 78–86; William McKinley, Carol M. Sanchez, and Allen G. Schick, "Organizational Downsizing: Constraining, Cloning, Learning," *Academy of Management Executive* 9, no. 3 (1995): 32–42; and Brett C. Luthans and Steven M. Sommer, "The Impact of Downsizing on Workplace Attitudes," *Group and Organization Management* 2, no. 1 (1999): 46–70.

104. Effective downsizing techniques are discussed in detail in Bob Nelson, "The Care of the Un-Downsized," *Training and Development* (April 1997): 40–43; Shari Caudron, "Teaching Downsizing Survivors How to Thrive," *Personnel Journal* (January 1996): 38; Joel Brockner, "Managing the Effects of Layoffs

on Survivors," *California Management Review* (Winter 1992): 9–28; and Kim S. Cameron, "Strategies for Successful Organizational Downsizing," *Human Resource Management* 33, no. 2 (Summer 1994): 189–211.

105. Scott Westcott, "Goodbye and Good Luck," *Inc.* (April 2006): 40–42.

106. Adam Bryant, "There's No Need to Bat .900," (Corner Office column, an interview with John Donahoe), *The New York Times*, April 5, 2009.

107. Nanette Byrnes, "Star Search," *BusinessWeek* (October 10, 2005): 68–78.

108. Mike Brewster, "No Exit," *Fast Company* (April 2005): 93.

109. Based on "Human Resources Capability Model," Australian Public Service (APS) Commission, Australian Government, www.apsc.gov.au/publications01/hrmodel.htm (accessed September 13, 2010).

110. Based on Linda Tischler, "IBM's Management Makeover," *Fast Company*, November 1, 2004, www.fastcompany.com/51673/ibms-management-makeover (accessed November 26, 2012); and www.zurich.ibm.com/employment/environment.html (accessed September 13, 2010).

part 4 : chapter 13

Meeting the Challenge of Diversity

Fuse/Jupiter Images

Chapter Outline

Do You Know Your Biases?

Diversity in the Workplace
Diversity in Corporate America
Diversity on a Global Scale

Managing Diversity
Diversity and Inclusion
Diversity of Perspective
Dividends of Workplace Diversity

Factors Shaping Personal Bias
Workplace Prejudice, Discrimination, and Stereotypes

New Manager Self-Test: Valuing Workplace Diversity

Ethnocentrism

Factors Affecting Women's Careers
The Glass Ceiling
Opt-Out Trend
The Female Advantage

Achieving Cultural Competence

Diversity Initiatives and Programs
Enhancing Structures and Policies
Expanding Recruitment Efforts
Establishing Mentor Relationships
Increasing Awareness of Sexual Harassment
Using Multicultural Teams
Encouraging Employee Affinity Groups

Learning Outcomes

After studying this chapter, you should be able to:

1. Appreciate the pervasive demographic changes occurring in the domestic and global workforces and how corporations are responding.

2. Understand how the definition of diversity has grown to recognize a broad spectrum of differences among employees, the importance of fostering a sense of inclusion, and the dividends of a diverse workforce.

3. Recognize the complex attitudes, opinions, and issues that people bring to the workplace, including prejudice, discrimination, stereotypes, and ethnocentrism.

4. Recognize the factors that affect women's opportunities, including the glass ceiling, the opt-out trend, and the female advantage.

5. Explain the five steps in developing cultural competence in the workplace.

6. Describe how diversity initiatives and training programs help create a climate that values diversity.

7. Understand how multicultural teams and employee affinity groups help organizations respond to the rapidly changing and complex workplace.

Do You Know Your Biases?[1]

INSTRUCTIONS: As a new manager, your day-to-day behavior will send signals about your biases and values. Some personal biases are active and well known to yourself and others. Other biases are more subtle, and the following questions may provide some hints about where you are biased and don't know it. Please answer whether each item is Mostly True or Mostly False for you.

	Mostly True	Mostly False
1. I prefer to be in work teams with people who think like me.	_____	_____
2. I have avoided talking about culture differences with people I met from different cultures because I didn't want to say the wrong thing.	_____	_____
3. I have jumped to a conclusion without first hearing all sides of a story.	_____	_____
4. The first thing I notice about people is the physical characteristics that make them different from the norm.	_____	_____
5. Before I hire someone, I have a picture in mind of what they should look like.	_____	_____
6. I typically ignore movies, magazines, and TV programs that are targeted toward groups and values that are different from mine.	_____	_____
7. When someone makes a bigoted remark or joke, I don't confront him or her about it.	_____	_____
8. I prefer to not discuss sensitive topics such as race, age, gender, sexuality, or religion at work.	_____	_____
9. There are people I like but would feel uncomfortable inviting to be with my family or close friends.	_____	_____

SCORING AND INTERPRETATION: Give yourself one point for each item you marked as Mostly True. The ideal score is zero, but few people reach the ideal. Each question reflects an element of "passive bias," which can cause people different from you to feel ignored or disrespected by you. Passive bias may be more insidious than active discrimination because it excludes people from opportunities for expression and interaction. If you scored 5 or more, you should take a careful look at how you think and act toward people different from yourself. The sooner you learn to actively include diverse views and people, the better a new manager you will be.

Texas Instruments does a good job recruiting women engineers right out of college—20 to 24 percent of the electrical engineers it hires are female. But there are few women in executive management positions. To help fill the pipeline to the corner office with women, Texas Instruments grooms them for positions of higher responsibility through initiatives like the Women's P&L Initiative, which puts women in positions where they will get "profit-and-loss" experience. Managers identify star women performers and prepare them for line-management roles with training in leadership traits and skills. In addition, aspiring managers are assigned to high-ranking mentors to develop skills needed for promotion. "We have to attract more of them into the jobs that lead to the highest levels," says CEO Richard K. Templeton.

Jennifer W. Christensen, a Chicago executive recruiter, knows why the Women's P&L Initiative is so important. Higher-level positions require profit-and-loss experience. "Men dominate profit-and-loss posts, in part because they ask for them, while women often wait

1 INTRODUCTION

2 ENVIRONMENT

3 PLANNING

4 ORGANIZING

5 LEADING

6 CONTROLLING

> "If we don't reflect the global nature of our business in our employees, how can we possibly hope to understand our customers? In the same way, we have to have a good balance of men and women. If we only have men building our products and services, how are we going to appeal to half the world's population?"
>
> — MARK PALMER-EDGECUMBE, GOOGLE'S HEAD OF DIVERSITY AND INCLUSION

for them to be offered," says Christensen. The company's initiative is paying off, leading to a 60 percent increase since 2009 in the number of women in profit-and-loss positions.[2]

Managers are discovering that it makes good business sense to support diversity programs like the Women's P&L Initiative. Not only are diversity programs the right thing to do ethically and culturally, but these initiatives also create new business opportunities. To capitalize on those opportunities, organizations recognize that workplaces need to reflect the diversity in the marketplace. "Our country's consumer base is so varied," says Shelley Willingham-Hinton, president of the National Organization for Diversity in Sales and Marketing. "I can't think of how a company can succeed without having that kind of diversity with their employees."[3] Forward-thinking managers agree and take steps to attract and retain a workforce that reflects the cultural diversity of the population. They take seriously the fact that there is a link between the diversity of the workforce and financial success in the marketplace. Exhibit 13.1 lists corporations that are considered leaders in diversity. They make diversity a top priority and actively pursue a corporate culture that values equality and reflects today's multicultural consumer base.

This chapter describes how the domestic and global workforce is becoming increasingly multicultural and how corporations are

EXHIBIT 13.1

Examples of Leaders in Corporate Diversity

Company	U.S. Employees	% Minority Employees
Baptist Health South Florida	12,249	73%
Four Seasons Hotels	11,729	67
The Methodist Hospital System	11,298	66
Kimpton Hotels & Restaurants	6,735	63
Marriott International	106,280	61
Qualcomm	12,520	55
Men's Wearhouse	14,548	53
Stew Leonard's	1,991	51
Scripps Health	11,847	48
Brocade Communications	3,112	48
Camden Property Trust	1,719	46
Genentech	11,464	45
Cisco	36,612	45
Children's Healthcare of Atlanta	6,521	44
Whole Foods Market	52,915	44
USAA	21,889	44
Darden Restaurants	167,537	42
CarMax	13,436	42
Nordstrom	49,447	41
Atlantic Health	7,418	41
Intel	42,694	40
Aflac	4,400	39%

SOURCE: "100 Best Companies to Work For, 2009; Top Companies: Most Diverse," http://money.cnn.com/magazines/fortune/bestcompanies/2011/minorities/ (accessed June 28, 2012).

responding to the challenges and opportunities this presents. We look at the myriad complex issues that face managers and employees in a diverse workplace, including prejudice, stereotypes, discrimination, and ethnocentrism. Factors that specifically affect women—the glass ceiling, the opt-out trend, and the female advantage—are also considered. After a review of the steps toward cultural competence, the chapter concludes by presenting an overview of initiatives taken by corporations to create an environment that welcomes and values a broad spectrum of diversity among its employees.

Diversity in the Workplace

When Brenda Thomson, the director of diversity and leadership education at the Las Vegas MGM Mirage, steps into one of the company's hotel lobbies, she closes her eyes and listens. "It's amazing all the different languages I can hear just standing in the lobbies of any of our hotels," she says. "Our guests come from all over the world, and it really makes us realize the importance of reflecting that diversity in our workplace."[4] The diversity Thomson sees in the lobbies of the MGM Mirage hotels is a small reflection of the cultural diversity in the larger domestic and global workplaces.

DIVERSITY IN CORPORATE AMERICA

Faced with fewer resources, a sputtering economy, and increased domestic and global competition, managers are searching for ways to set their organizations apart from the competition and create breakthrough innovations. One highly important tool for succeeding in a competitive environment is a diversified workforce. Managers who cultivate a diversified workforce have been shown to improve their organization's chances of success. Diverse teams that perform efficiently add value by combining individuals' strengths, making the whole greater than the sum of its parts.[5]

In the past, when managers thought of diversity, they focused on the "problems" associated with diversity, such as discrimination, bias, affirmative action, and tokenism.[6] Now managers recognize that the differences people bring to the workplace are valuable.[7] Rather than expecting all employees to adopt similar attitudes and values, managers are learning that these differences enable their companies to compete globally and tap into rich sources of new talent. Although diversity in North America has been a reality for some time, genuine efforts to accept and *manage* diverse people began only in recent years. Exhibit 13.2 lists some interesting milestones in the history of corporate diversity.

Diversity in corporate America has become a key topic in part because of the vast changes occurring in today's workplace. The following statistics illustrate how the workplace is changing and challenging frontline managers who are trying to build cohesive teams:

- *Unprecedented generational diversity.* Today's workforce is in a state of flux as a blend of four generations presents new management challenges, with people staying healthy and working longer not only in the United States, but in China, Brazil, Russia, and elsewhere.[8] Although most people from the World War II generation have retired, there are still some members in their late 60s, 70s, and even 80s in the workplace. In 2010, for example, this generation represented about 5 percent of the labor force in the United States, and nearly 7 percent in Canada. These employees, and the rapidly aging baby boomers, share a "corporate memory" that is invaluable to organizations, but as they stay in the workforce longer, there is little room for Generation X managers wanting to move up the hierarchy. As Gen-X workers move into middle age, they are struggling with reduced guarantees about their financial futures and job security. Meanwhile, Gen-Yers, sometimes called Millennials, are characterized as ambitious, lacking loyalty to one organization, and eager for quick success. Unlike different generations working together in the past, there are strong value differences among employees from different eras today.[9]

EXHIBIT   13.2

Milestones in the History
of Corporate Diversity

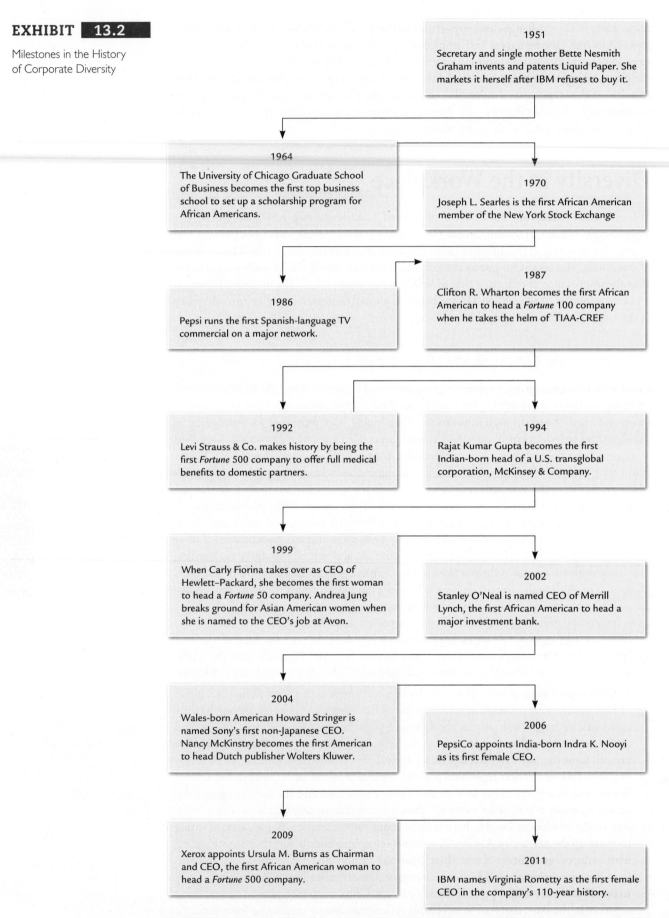

1951

Secretary and single mother Bette Nesmith Graham invents and patents Liquid Paper. She markets it herself after IBM refuses to buy it.

1964

The University of Chicago Graduate School of Business becomes the first top business school to set up a scholarship program for African Americans.

1970

Joseph L. Searles is the first African American member of the New York Stock Exchange

1986

Pepsi runs the first Spanish-language TV commercial on a major network.

1987

Clifton R. Wharton becomes the first African American to head a *Fortune* 100 company when he takes the helm of TIAA-CREF

1992

Levi Strauss & Co. makes history by being the first *Fortune* 500 company to offer full medical benefits to domestic partners.

1994

Rajat Kumar Gupta becomes the first Indian-born head of a U.S. transglobal corporation, McKinsey & Company.

1999

When Carly Fiorina takes over as CEO of Hewlett–Packard, she becomes the first woman to head a *Fortune* 50 company. Andrea Jung breaks ground for Asian American women when she is named to the CEO's job at Avon.

2002

Stanley O'Neal is named CEO of Merrill Lynch, the first African American to head a major investment bank.

2004

Wales-born American Howard Stringer is named Sony's first non-Japanese CEO. Nancy McKinstry becomes the first American to head Dutch publisher Wolters Kluwer.

2006

PepsiCo appoints India-born Indra K. Nooyi as its first female CEO.

2009

Xerox appoints Ursula M. Burns as Chairman and CEO, the first African American woman to head a *Fortune* 500 company.

2011

IBM names Virginia Rometty as the first female CEO in the company's 110-year history.

SOURCES: "Spotlight on Diversity," special advertising section, *MBA Jungle* (March–April 2003): 58–61; and Xerox corporate Web site, www.news.xerox.com.

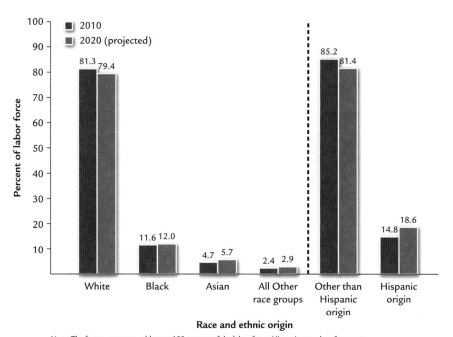

EXHIBIT 　13.3

Projected Changes in U.S.
Labor Force, 2010 to 2020

Note: The four race groups add up to 100 percent of the labor force. Hispanics may be of any race.

SOURCE: "Chart 2. Percent of Labor Force by Race and Ethnic Origin," in "Occupational Outlook Handbook, 2011–12 Edition, BLS Division of Industry Employment Projections," U. S. Department of Labor, Bureau of Labor Statistics, www.bls.gov/ooh/about/projections-overview.htm#laborforce (accessed June 29, 2012).

- *Aging workers.* Baby boomers continue to affect the workplace as this massive group of workers progresses through its life stages. A baby boomer turns 60 every seven seconds, continuously bumping up the average age of the workforce. While the number of workers between 25 and 45 years old is expected to decline from 66.9 percent to 63.7 percent by 2020, the number of boomers age 55 years and older will leap from 19.5 percent to 25.2 in the same period.[10]

- *Increased diversity.* Today's workplace is becoming more diverse as the number of foreign-born workers increases. Foreign-born workers make up 16 percent of the U.S. workforce and are most likely employed in service industries, such as food preparation, cleaning, and maintenance. Of the total number of foreign-born workers, nearly half are Hispanic and 23 percent are Asian.[11] Looking ahead, the number of Hispanic employees will grow the most, increasing 18.6 percent by 2020.[12] Exhibit 13.3 shows the projected changes in employment among different racial and ethnic groups in the United States.

- *Growth in women workers.* Today, women outnumber men in the workplace, and their numbers are projected to grow slightly faster, at 7.4 percent compared to 6.3 percent for men. The good news is that nearly 73 percent of *Fortune 500* companies now have at least one female executive officer, but women comprise just 14 percent of executive officers, according to Catalyst, a leading advocacy group for women.[13] To accelerate their progress, many corporations have initiated coaching and training programs that prepare women for senior-level positions.

These trends underscore the complex nature of today's workforce and the potential pitfalls managers face as they lead diverse teams toward common goals. While many managers recognize the value of multicultural diversity, some simply haven't kept pace with these demographic trends. In fact, as diversity has increased, so have the number of discrimination complaints with the Equal Employment Opportunity Commission (EEOC), which investigates employee claims and sometimes brings lawsuits on behalf of workers. Claims rose nearly 100,000 in 2010, up 7 percent from the year before. One recent complaint is against Bass Pro Shops, accused of repeatedly refusing to

4

ORGANIZING

Take a Moment

As a manager, will you value the differences people bring to the workplace? Check your results on the questionnaire at the beginning of this chapter to see if your biases are creating a stumbling block in your ability to embrace diversity.

Concept Connection ◄◄◄

AP Photo/Stuart Ramson

Successful organizations seek a **diverse and inclusive workforce**. Indra Nooyi was named CEO of PepsiCo in 2006 after 12 years with the food and beverage giant, spending most of those years leading its global strategy. Both *Fortune* and *Forbes* magazines named the Indian-born executive one of the most powerful women in America. "I am not your normal, nondiverse CEO. I am everything that this company took forth in diversity and inclusion, and it has all come together with me," says Nooyi.

hire non-white workers as clerks, cashiers, or managers, and using discriminatory language to explain their reasons. Among other charges in the lawsuit is the allegation that a senior worker in Indiana was seen discarding employment applications, explaining that he could tell by the job-seekers' names that they were black. The suit also alleges that the general manager of a Houston store regularly referred to those of Hispanic origin as "Pedro" or "Mexican."[14]

DIVERSITY ON A GLOBAL SCALE

Managers across the globe wrestle with many of the same diversity challenges as U.S. managers, especially concerning the progression of women into upper management positions. Consider, for example, that in Italy, only 6 percent of the total number of corporate board members are women, 14 percent in Britain, and 2 percent in Germany and India. As mentioned before, 14 percent of all board members in the United States are women.[15] To boost the percentage of women on the corporate boards of European countries, the European Commission is studying whether to introduce quotas across the continent, similar to a recent law in Italy that requires Italian listed and state-owned companies to ensure that one-third of their board members are women by 2015. "We needed a shock to the system," said Alessia Mosca, a member of Parliament for the center-left Democratic Party, who coauthored Italy's new "pink quota" law. "The hope is that this will set off cultural change."[16]

Japanese companies have an even greater struggle to bridge the gender gap on corporate boards, where women make up just 1.2 percent of senior executives.[17] In fact, only 65 percent of college-educated Japanese women are employed, many of them in low-paid temp jobs, compared with 80 percent of women in the United States The reasons for the dearth of women in the Japanese workforce are complex. Part of it relates to tepid economic growth. But over two-thirds of Japanese women leave work after their first child is born, compared to just one-third of U.S. women, often because of insufficient childcare and societal expectations.[18]

Cultural norms, such as those that restrict the progression of women in Japan, are intangible, pervasive, and difficult to comprehend. However, it is imperative that managers learn to understand local cultures and deal with them effectively.[19]

Remember This

- A workforce that displays characteristics of today's diversified marketplace is an important tool for managers who are striving for success in a highly competitive business environment.
- The U.S. workforce is being transformed by a four-generation workforce, aging baby boomers, an increase in Hispanic and Asian workers, and an increasing number of women employees.

- The progression of women into executive positions continues to be slow in both U.S. and global corporations, but innovative companies are initiating programs to boost women's advancement into higher levels of responsibility.
- To succeed in the global marketplace, managers need to understand other cultures and deal with them effectively.

Diversity and Biodiversity

As children running up against differing opinions, our grandmothers reminded us, "It takes all kinds to make a world." The preservation of diverse plant and animal life forms also echoes Grandma's words. To promote biodiversity preservation, managers at beverage maker **Bean and Body** use proceeds from the sale of its healthy coffees to sponsor *The Bean and Body Protected Grounds Initiative*, which works in collaboration with The World Land Trust US to buy, protect, and preserve the most threatened areas of the world's rain forests, wetlands, and coastlines. The award-winning effort meets corporate goals to promote a healthy lifestyle, while taking intentional steps to promote ecological, economic, and social preservation. The Bean and Body initiative works to solve biodiversity problems by helping the farmers whose cultivation of coffee beans affects the environment through ground water runoff and incursions into rain forests.

Sources: Andrew J. Hoffman, "Climate Change as a Cultural and Behavioral Issue: Addressing Barriers and Implementing Solutions," *Organizational Dynamics* 39 (2010): 295–305; and Erin Legg, "Coffee Re-imagined: Bean and Body Emerge as Global Leaders," *Healthy New Age* Web site, July 2010, www.healthynewage.com/blog/bean-and-body-wins-award/ (accessed August 1, 2012).

Managing Diversity

Managers who want to boost performance and jumpstart innovation agree that diverse teams produce the best results. In one survey of 32 department heads and executives, 84 percent stated that they prefer heterogeneous teams because they lead to multiple viewpoints and more prolific ideas.[20] The following sections describe the characteristics of a diverse workforce and the dividends of cultivating one.

Diversity and Inclusion

Diversity is defined as all the ways in which people differ.[21] Diversity wasn't always defined this broadly. Decades ago, many companies defined diversity in terms of race, gender, age, lifestyle, and disability. That focus helped create awareness, change mindsets, and create new opportunities for many. Today, companies are embracing a more inclusive definition of diversity that recognizes a spectrum of differences that influence how employees approach work, interact with each other, derive satisfaction from their work, and define who they are as people in the workplace.[22]

Exhibit 13.4 illustrates the difference between the traditional model and the inclusive model of diversity. The dimensions of diversity shown in the traditional model include inborn differences that are immediately observable and include race, gender, age, and physical ability. However, the inclusive model of diversity includes *all* of the ways in which employees differ, including aspects of diversity that can be acquired or changed throughout one's lifetime. These dimensions may have less impact than those included only in the traditional model, but they nevertheless affect a person's self-definition and worldview and the way the person is viewed by others. Many organizational leaders embrace this more inclusive definition of diversity. "Diversity has to be looked at in its broadest sense," said Wally Parker, former CEO of KeySpan Energy (now National Grid). "To me, it's all about recognizing, respecting, and supporting individuals regardless of what makes up that individuality. So, yes, that's race, gender and sexual orientation. But it's also introverted and extroverted, ethnic backgrounds, cultural upbringing, all those things."[23]

One of the challenges of managing a diverse workforce is creating an environment where all employees feel accepted as members of the team and where their unique talents

4

ORGANIZING

EXHIBIT 13.4   Traditional vs. Inclusive Models of Diversity

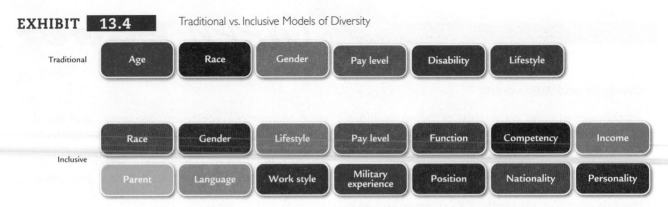

SOURCE: Based on Anthony Oshiotse and Richard O'Leary, "Corning Creates an Inclusive Culture to Drive Technology Innovation and Performance," *Global Business and Organizational Excellence* 26, no. 3 (March/April 2007): 7–21.

are appreciated. When managers create a feeling of inclusiveness, employees display more loyalty, cooperation, and trustworthiness. **Inclusion** is the degree to which an employee feels like an esteemed member of a group in which his or her uniqueness is highly appreciated. Inclusion creates a strong sense of belonging where all people can have their voices heard and appreciated.[24] Consider how a manager of a retail store embraced an employee's unique perspective with positive results. Hal, the manager, supervised an employee, Olivia, who was quiet and seemed to have few innovative ideas. But as Hal discussed marketing strategies for the store with Olivia, he was surprised to learn that she was a highly creative thinker, consistently interjecting novel ideas into the discussion. Over time, Hal realized that this seemingly quiet employee was one of the most creative marketing thinkers he had ever met, and together they created a very successful line of children's outerwear. Hal has become a strong supporter of inclusion and a champion for individuals who operate differently from the norm.[25]

In creating a culture of inclusion, managers may experience times of tension and discord as people with different backgrounds bring different opinions and ideas. Conflict, anxiety, and misunderstandings may increase. Embracing these differences and using them to improve company performance can be challenging. **Managing diversity**, a key management skill in today's global economy, means creating a climate in which the potential advantages of diversity for organizational or group performance are maximized, while the potential disadvantages are minimized.[26] The Manager's Shoptalk describes how managers can leverage differences to improve performance and strengthen corporate culture.

DIVERSITY OF PERSPECTIVE

You may have heard the expression that "great minds think alike." But when it comes to achieving breakthrough levels of innovation, the best minds are those that *don't* think alike. Successful managers understand the basic elements of successful teams, including competence, clear performance goals, shared vision, and a supportive work environment. You will learn more about managing successful teams in Chapter 18. But managers who cultivate a team with a "diversity of perspective" significantly increase the chance of creating hard-to-replicate competitive advantage. **Diversity of perspective** is achieved when a manager creates a heterogeneous team made up of individuals with diverse backgrounds and skill sets. By tapping into the strengths of diversity, teams are more likely to experience the following: higher efficiency, better quality, less duplication of effort among team members, and increased innovation and creativity.[27]

Take a Moment

In what ways do you feel unique from others you work or attend class with? Do these perceived differences affect your interpersonal relationships? Complete the Small Group Breakout on pages 436–437 to assess your personal diversity and gain insights about the factors that you believe set you apart from others.

Manager's *Shoptalk*

Change Your Frame

Managers who successfully manage diversity are well equipped to navigate the challenges of today's global economy. But some managers are skeptical of a "managing diversity" philosophy that imposes a requirement to recruit and blend together people of different ethnicities, cultures, and genders. (To assess your attitude toward diversity, complete the New Manager Self-Test on page 423) Instead of "managing diversity," leaders can embrace a new frame of reference that focuses on "leveraging differences" to build a stronger corporate culture and improve performance. The traditional frame of reference about imposing diversity ". . . originated from the Civil Rights era," said Dr. Rohini Anand, chief diversity officer at Sodexo. "This will never go away completely. However, diversity must go beyond this mentality."

The real value of diversity can only be achieved when managers focus on inviting and embracing the contributions from melding people of different backgrounds. Below are some reasons for adopting a "leveraging differences" mindset.

- **Greater collective intelligence.** A group of employees with a high collective intelligence learns quickly and thinks creatively. Its collective intelligence has little relationship to the average IQ of its members. Instead, collective intelligence is highest in groups whose members demonstrate social sensitivity, which refers to sensitivity to others' emotions. Groups with social sensitivity communicate effectively and encourage all members to express their ideas. Groups with the highest social sensitivity include both men and women. But the data show that the more women in a group, the better.

- **Greater creativity.** Instead of a narrow mindset that is blind to differences in a group,

managers can embrace the idea that people hold divergent perspectives and that there is something to be learned from each individual. Creativity is cultivated in environments where managers face the discomfort that can surface when group members disagree.

- **Broader perspectives.** Ideas that arise from less familiar places increase the breadth of information and knowledge to which people are normally exposed. Studies show that senior executives need a variety of perspectives, and they're much more likely to gain that if their organizations and management teams include people of different social and cultural backgrounds.

- **Preventing groupthink.** Many teams unconsciously seek to avoid conflict and place a priority on creating harmony. The term *groupthink* describes a faulty decision-making process by team members who are overly eager to agree with one another. Conforming to the consensus of the group restricts innovative thinking. A leveraging differences frame cultivates a decision-making environment that values divergent opinions and encourages healthy disagreements.

Sources: Glenn Llopis, "Diversity Management Is the Key to Growth: Make It Authentic," *Forbes*, June 13, 2011, www.forbes.com/sites/glennllopis/2011/06/13/diversity (accessed July 20, 2011); Martin Davidson, "The End of Diversity: How Leaders Make Differences Really Matter," *Executive Forum* (Spring 2012): 51–56; Peter Gwynne, "Group Intelligence, Teamwork, and Productivity," *Perspectives* (March–April, 2012): 7–8; Anita Woolley and Thomas Malone, "What Makes a Team Smarter? More Women," *Harvard Business Review* (June 2011): 32–33; and Natalie D. Brecher, "Diversity Delivers: Four Tips for Embracing Differences," *Journal of Property Management* (May–June 2012): 24.

What happens when employees are homogeneous and lack a diversity of perspective? A study conducted by Jonathan Haidt, a social psychologist at the University of Virginia, suggests that when a group is homogeneous, it can develop a tribe mentality, embracing only ideas that support its own values and ditching ideas that distort or threaten the group's norms. Haidt observed that nearly 80 percent of 1,000 psychologists attending a professional meeting identified themselves as "liberal." Haidt claims this dominate ideology creates a bias in thinking that leads to a hostile environment for non-liberals in the profession. He also observed that the small minority of psychologists who consider themselves "conservative" frequently hid their feelings from colleagues to avoid being shunned or ridiculed.[28] Haidt's study underscores how homogeneous groups may hinder innovative thinking and reject ideas from outsiders.

DIVIDENDS OF WORKPLACE DIVERSITY

Managers who build strong, diverse organizations reap numerous dividends as described here and shown in Exhibit 13.5.[29] The dividends of diversity include the following:

- **Better use of employee talent.** Companies with the best talent are the ones with the best competitive advantage. Attracting a diverse workforce is not enough; companies must also provide career opportunities and advancement for minorities and women to retain them.

- **Increased understanding of the marketplace.** A diverse workforce is better able to anticipate and respond to changing consumer needs. Ford Motor Company realized it could reach its business objectives only if it created a workforce that reflected the multicultural face of the country. So it assembled a workforce made up of 25 percent minorities (18.4 percent are African American) to foster a culture of inclusion, winning it a spot on *Black Enterprise's* "40 Best Companies for Diversity."[30]

- **Enhanced breadth of understanding in leadership positions.** Homogeneous top management teams tend to be myopic in their perspectives. According to Niall FitzGerald of Unilever, "It is important for any business operating in an increasingly complex and rapidly changing environment to deploy a broad range of talents. That provides a breadth of understanding of the world and environment and a fusion of the very best values and different perspectives which make up that world."[31]

- **Increased quality of team problem solving.** Teams with diverse backgrounds bring different perspectives to a discussion that result in more creative ideas and solutions.[32] Although a large percent of Ernst & Young's senior leadership is still male, the company is taking steps to create a more diverse leadership team because it's better for business. "We know you get better solutions when you put a diverse team at the table. People come from different backgrounds and they have different frames of reference. When you put these people together, you get the best solution for our clients," says Billie Williamson, director of flexibility and gender equity strategy at Ernst & Young.[33]

- **Reduced costs associated with high turnover, absenteeism, and lawsuits.** Companies that foster a diverse workforce reduce turnover, absenteeism, and the risk of lawsuits. Because family responsibilities contribute to turnover

Concept Connection ◀◀◀

Christopher J. Morris/Corbis News/Corbis

As part of its award-winning supplier diversity program, San Francisco–based Pacific Gas & Electric (PG&E) spent $1.6 billion in 2011, or 36 percent of its total procurement funds, on products and services from businesses owned by minorities, women, and service-disabled veterans. Because many of these suppliers are also PG&E customers, the utility's managers don't have to look far to find the **diversity dividend** PG&E reaps from this program.

EXHIBIT 13.5

Dividends of Workplace Diversity

- Better use of employee talent
- Increased understanding of the marketplace
- Enhanced breadth of understanding in leadership positions
- Increased quality of team problem solving
- Reduced costs associated with high turnover, absenteeism, and lawsuits

SOURCE: Gail Robinson and Kathleen Dechant, "Building a Business Case for Diversity," *Academy of Management Executive* 11, no. 3 (1997): 21–31.

and absenteeism, many companies now offer child-care and elder-care benefits, flexible work arrangements, telecommuting, and part-time employment to accommodate employee responsibilities at home. Discrimination lawsuits are also a costly side effect of a discriminatory work environment. A racial harassment suit against Lockheed Martin Corporation cost the company $2.5 million, the largest individual racial-discrimination payment obtained by the EEOC.[34]

The most successful organizations appreciate the importance of diversity and know that their biggest asset is their people. Organizations with diverse workforces are better prepared to anticipate strategic surprises, as the Central Intelligence Agency (CIA) discovered.

Innovative Way

Central Intelligence Agency (CIA)

Surprises always catch us off guard. When they happen, we ask ourselves, "Who would have seen that coming?" The surprise attacks in the United States by Islamic terrorists on September 11, 2001, left the nation stunned, especially the CIA officers who were responsible for gathering intelligence about terrorist activities and warning of possible threats. Why didn't the CIA, one of the most influential institutions of the last 60 years, predict these attacks? Why did they have such a hard time getting inside the heads of the Islamic terrorists who crafted a devastating attack on U.S. soil?

When an organization such as the CIA experiences a "strategic surprise"—an unexpected, game-changing event that throws it off course—the results can be devastating. To better anticipate strategic surprises, organizations need a diverse workforce, one that reflects the diversity in the communities they serve. The CIA's workforce has long been largely homogeneous in terms of race, gender, ethnicity, class, and culture. The majority of its agents and analysts have been a tight group of Caucasian, Protestant, liberal-arts-educated American males. Few have traveled abroad or learned to speak a foreign language. The results of this homogeneity are intelligence failures. Consider the Cuban missile crisis of the early 1960s, where CIA analysts dismissed key intelligence about the Cuban missile buildup because of racist attitudes about Cuban informants. Even up through September 11, 2001, Robert Gates, former CIA director and secretary of defense, claimed that the CIA was less and less willing to employ "people that are a little different, people who are eccentric, people who don't look good in a suit and tie, people who don't play well in the sandbox with others."[35]

Today's CIA, however, seems to be recognizing the value of a heterogeneous workforce. According to retired general David H. Petraeus, who resigned as CIA director in 2012, "Our key challenge now is to ensure that the CIA's extraordinarily gifted and dedicated workforce is contributing to its full potential. That means we must, at every level, be as inclusive as possible in our composition and in how we make decisions. Intelligence work is teamwork, and we have a duty, in our own teams, to reinforce each day the values of diversity, fairness, respect, and inclusion."[36]

4

ORGANIZING

Remember This

- **Diversity** is defined as all the ways in which employees differ.
- **Inclusion** is the degree to which an employee feels like an esteemed member of a group in which his or her uniqueness is highly appreciated.
- **Diversity of perspective** is achieved when a manager creates a heterogeneous team made up of individuals with diverse backgrounds and skill sets.
- **Managing diversity,** which means creating a climate in which the potential advantages of diversity for organizational performance are maximized while the potential disadvantages are minimized, is a key management skill today.
- Corporations that recruit and retain a diverse workforce reap numerous benefits, including improved team problem solving and increased understanding of the marketplace.
- The Central Intelligence Agency (CIA) is trying to recruit a more diverse workforce to improve intelligence gathering and team problem solving.

Factors Shaping Personal Bias

To reap the benefits of diversity described previously, organizations are seeking managers who will serve as catalysts in the workplace to reduce barriers and eliminate obstacles for women and minorities. To successfully manage a diverse workgroup and create a positive, productive environment for all employees, managers need to start with an understanding of the complex attitudes, opinions, and issues that already exist in the workplace or that employees bring into the workplace. These include several factors that shape personal bias: prejudice, discrimination, stereotypes, and ethnocentrism.

Take a Moment

What judgmental beliefs or attitudes do you have that influence your feelings about diversity in the workplace? Complete the New Manager Self-Test on page 423 to see how prepared you are to put stereotypes aside so you can manage effectively.

WORKPLACE PREJUDICE, DISCRIMINATION, AND STEREOTYPES

Prejudice is the tendency to view people who are different as being deficient. If someone acts out their prejudicial attitudes toward people who are the targets of their prejudice, **discrimination** has occurred.[37] Paying a woman less than a man for the same work is gender discrimination. Mistreating people because they have a different ethnicity is ethnic discrimination. Although blatant discrimination is not as widespread as in the past, bias in the workplace often shows up in subtle ways: a lack of choice assignments, the disregard by a subordinate of a minority manager's directions, or the ignoring of comments made by women and minorities at meetings. A survey by Korn Ferry International found that 59 percent of minority managers surveyed had observed a racially motivated double standard in the delegation of assignments.[38]

A major component of prejudice is **stereotypes**, rigid, exaggerated, irrational beliefs associated with a particular group of people.[39] To be successful managing diversity, managers need to eliminate harmful stereotypes from their thinking, shedding any biases that negatively affect the workplace. For example, old stereotypes often bubble up and block women's rise to higher-level positions. These silent but potent beliefs include the perception that women pose a greater risk in senior positions or that working mothers are unable to hold positions requiring extensive travel and stress. Stereotypes also may block the honest feedback women need for improving their performance. If a man makes a bad presentation, his male superiors might slap him on the back and say, "Buddy, what happened? You screwed up, man!" If a woman gives a bad presentation, she may never hear candid feedback. Instead, it may be spoken behind her back: "Wow! She really screwed up."[40]

Managers can learn to *value differences*, which means they recognize cultural differences and see these differences with an appreciative attitude. To facilitate this attitude, managers can learn about cultural patterns and typical beliefs of groups to help understand why people act the way they do. It helps to understand the difference between these two ways of thinking, most notably that stereotyping is a barrier to diversity but valuing cultural differences facilitates

Concept Connection ◀◀◀

Age discrimination has made a difficult situation even more trying for older workers looking for jobs in this economy. In March 2012, for instance, the average duration of unemployment for job seekers over age 55, such as Larry Visakowitz (pictured at a job fair for veterans), hovered around 55 weeks, over one full year. That's 16 weeks longer than the national average. **Stereotypes** that plague older job seekers include the beliefs that they are more expensive, harder to train, more likely to leave, and less productive, adaptable, and technologically adept.

Justin Sullivan/Getty Images News/Getty Images

New Manager  Self-Test

Valuing Workplace Diversity

Instructions: Circle all the words below that you associate with your personal response to the idea of workplace diversity.

Abnormal	Corrupt	Join	Reasonable
Accommodate	Criticize	Just	Retreat
Aggravation	Dislike	Listen	Right
Appreciative	Dispute	Necessary	Suitable
Assist	Dissatisfaction	Noble	Sympathetic
Baseless	Dread	Obstinate	Uneasy
Belittle	Eager	Oppose	Unfounded
Beneficial	Gratified	Optimistic	Valueless
Biased	Hostile	Partake	Welcoming
Committed	Impractical	Perplexed	
Comprehend	Irritation	Please	

Total Score A _____. Add 1 point for each of the following words circled: Beneficial, Just, Necessary, Noble, Reasonable, Right, Suitable. Subtract 1 point for each of the following words circled: Abnormal, Baseless, Biased, Corrupt, Impractical, Unfounded, Valueless.

Total Score B _____. Add 1 point for each of the following words circled: Appreciative, Committed, Eager, Gratified, Optimistic, Pleased, Sympathetic. Subtract 1 point for each of the following words circled: Aggravation, Dislike, Dissatisfaction, Dread, Irritation, Perplexed, Uneasy.

Total Score C _____. Add 1 point for each of the following words circled: Accommodate, Assist, Comprehend, Join, Listen, Partake, Welcoming. Subtract 1 point for each of the following words circled: Belittle, Criticize, Dispute, Hostile, Obstinate, Oppose, Retreat.

Scoring and Interpretation: Your scores on this questionnaire pertain to your attitudes toward workplace diversity, which are reflected in your personal diversity values. Your score for Part A pertains to your intellectual judgments toward workplace diversity, Part B pertains to your affective (emotional) reaction, and Part C to your behavioral response to diversity. If your scores are near zero, then your attitudes and values toward workplace diversity are neutral. Higher positive scores mean that you hold positive values toward diversity and will likely deal sympathetically with bias in the workplace. Higher negative scores mean you hold negative values toward diversity and may be ill prepared to deal with diversity issues that arise in your role as manager. What experiences have led to your diversity values? How do you think your values will contribute to a career in management for you?

Sources: Based on Kenneth P. De Meuse and Todd J. Hostager, "Developing an Instrument for Measuring Attitudes Toward and Perceptions of Workplace Diversity: An Initial Report," *Human Resource Development Quarterly* (Spring 2001): 33–51; and Alfred B. Heilbrun, "Measurement of Masculine and Feminine Sex Role Identities as Independent Dimensions," *Journal of Consulting and Clinical Psychology* 44 (1976): 183–190.

4

ORGANIZING

diversity. These two different ways of thinking are listed in Exhibit 13.6 and described below.[41]

- *Stereotypes are often based on folklore, media portrayals, and other unreliable sources of information.* In contrast, legitimate cultural differences are backed up by systematic research of real differences.

EXHIBIT **13.6**

Difference Between Stereotyping and Valuing Cultural
Differences

Stereotyping	Valuing Cultural Differences
Is based on false assumptions, anecdotal evidence, or impressions without any direct experience with a group	Is based on cultural differences verified by scientific research methods
Assigns negative traits to members of a group	Views cultural differences as positive or neutral
Assumes that all members of a group have the same characteristics	Does not assume that all individuals within a group have the same characteristics
Example: Suzuko Akoi is Asian, and is therefore not aggressive by white, male standards.	Example: As a group, Asians tend to be less aggressive than white, male Americans.

SOURCE: Adapted from Taylor Cox, Jr., and Ruby L. Beale, *Developing Competency to Manage Diversity: Readings Cases and Activities* (San Francisco: Berrett-Koehler Publishers, Inc., 1997).

- *Stereotypes contain negative connotations.* On the other hand, managers who value diversity view differences as potentially positive or neutral. For example, the observation that Asian males are typically less aggressive does not imply they are inferior or superior to white males—it simply means that there is a difference.

- *Stereotypes assume that all members of a group have the same characteristics.* Managers who value diversity recognize that individuals within a group of people may or may not share the same characteristics.[42]

Not only should managers rid themselves of stereotypical thinking, they should also recognize the stereotype threat that may jeopardize the performance of at-risk employees. **Stereotype threat** describes the psychological experience of a person who, when engaged in a task, is aware of a stereotype about his or her identity group that suggests he or she will not perform well on that task.[43] Suppose that you are a member of a minority group presenting complicated market research results to your management team and are anxious about making a good impression. Assume that some members of your audience have a negative stereotype about your identity group. As you ponder this, your anxiety skyrockets and your confidence is shaken. Understandably, your presentation suffers because you are distracted by worries and self-doubt as you invest energy in overcoming the stereotype. The feelings you are experiencing are called *stereotype threat.*

People most affected by stereotype threat are those we consider as disadvantaged in the workplace due to negative stereotypes—racial and ethnic minorities, members of lower socioeconomic classes, women, older people, gay and lesbian individuals, and people with disabilities. Although anxiety about performing a task may be normal, people with stereotype threat feel an extra scrutiny and worry that their failure will reflect not only on themselves as individuals but on the larger group to which they belong. As Beyoncé Knowles said, "It's like you have something to prove, and you don't want to mess it up and be a negative reflection on black women."[44]

ETHNOCENTRISM

Ethnocentrism is one roadblock for managers trying to recognize, welcome, and encourage differences among people so they can develop their unique talents and be effective organizational members. **Ethnocentrism** is the belief that one's own group and culture are inherently superior to other groups and cultures. Ethnocentrism makes it difficult to value diversity. Viewing one's own culture as the best culture is a natural tendency among most people. Moreover, the business world still tends to reflect the values, behaviors, and assumptions based on the experiences of a rather homogeneous, white, middle-class, male workforce. Indeed, most theories of management presume that workers share similar values, beliefs, motivations, and attitudes about work and life in general. These theories presume that one set of behaviors best helps an organization to be productive and effective and therefore should be adopted by all employees.[45]

Ethnocentric viewpoints and a standard set of cultural practices produce a **monoculture**, a culture that accepts only one way of doing things and one set of values and beliefs, which can cause problems for minority employees. People of color, women, gay people, the disabled, the elderly, and other diverse employees may feel undue pressure to conform, may be victims of stereotyping attitudes, and may be presumed deficient because they are different. White, heterosexual men, many of whom do not fit the notion of the "ideal" employee, may also feel uncomfortable with the monoculture and resent stereotypes that label white males as racists and sexists. Valuing diversity means ensuring that *all* people are given equal opportunities in the workplace.[46]

The goal for organizations seeking cultural diversity is pluralism rather than a monoculture and ethnorelativism rather than ethnocentrism. **Ethnorelativism** is the belief that groups and subcultures are inherently equal. **Pluralism** means that an organization accommodates several subcultures. Movement toward pluralism seeks to integrate fully into the organization the employees who otherwise would feel isolated and ignored. To promote pluralism in its Mountain View corporate headquarters, chefs at Google's corporate cafeteria ensure that its menu accommodates the different tastes of its ethnically diverse workforce.

Take a Moment

How tolerant are you of people who are different from you? Complete the Experiential Exercise on pages 435–436 to assess your tolerance for diversity.

Innovative Way

Google

Employees in Google's corporate headquarters come from all corners of the world, but they feel a little closer to home when they see familiar foods from their homeland on the cafeteria menu. With a goal of satisfying a diverse, ethnically varied palate, Google's first food guru and chef Charlie Ayers designed menus that reflected his eclectic tastes yet also met the needs of an increasingly diverse workforce. He created his own dishes, searched all types of restaurants for new recipes, and often got some of his best ideas from foreign-born employees. For example, a Filipino accountant offered a recipe for chicken *adobo*, a popular dish from her native country. Scattered around the Googleplex are cafés specializing in Southwestern, Italian, California-Mediterranean, and vegetarian cuisines. And because more and more Googlers originally hail from Asia, employees can find sushi at the Japanese-themed Pacific Café or Thai red curry beef at the East Meets West Café.

Google believes food can be a tool for supporting an inclusive workplace. The array of menu options gives people a chance to try new things and learn more about their coworkers. And Google knows that when people need a little comfort and familiarity, nothing takes the edge off of working in a foreign country like eating food that reminds you of home.[47]

4

ORGANIZING

Remember This

- The tendency to view people who are different as being deficient is called **prejudice**.
- **Discrimination** occurs when someone acts out their negative attitudes toward people who are the targets of their prejudice.
- A rigid, exaggerated, irrational belief associated with a particular group of people is called a **stereotype**.
- **Stereotype threat** occurs when a person who, when engaged in a task, is aware of a stereotype about his or her identity group suggesting that he or she will not perform well on that task.

- **Ethnocentrism** is the belief that one's own group is inherently superior to other groups.
- A culture that accepts only one way of doing things and one set of values and beliefs is called a **monoculture**.
- **Ethnorelativism** is the belief that groups and subcultures are inherently equal.
- **Pluralism** describes an environment in which the organization accommodates several subcultures, including employees who would otherwise feel isolated and ignored.

Factors Affecting Women's Careers

Progressive organizations realize the business advantage of hiring, retaining, and promoting women in the workplace. In fact, research shows that companies with several senior-level women outperform those without senior-level women both financially and organizationally. One survey of 58,000 employees in over 100 global companies revealed that companies with three or more women in top management are perceived to be more capable, have stronger leadership, and inspire higher employee motivation, among other important organizational characteristics.[48] However, there is evidence that women are stalling at the middle-management level. Women hold 53 percent of entry-level professional positions, but they hold only 37 percent of middle-management positions, 28 percent of vice-president and senior managerial roles, and 14 percent of executive positions.[49]

In addition, men as a group still have the benefit of higher wages and faster promotions. In the United States in 2009, for example, women employed full-time earned 80 cents for every dollar that men earned, compared to 79 cents in 2000.[50] Walmart, the world's largest retailer, struggled to rebound after seven women filed a class-action suit on behalf of all women working for the company in 2001. They complained of a general pattern of discrimination in pay and promotions. Six years before the lawsuit, a law firm found widespread gender disparities in pay and promotion at Walmart and Sam's Club stores and urged the company to take basic steps. In response to the report and the lawsuit, Walmart has taken steps to reduce the disparity occurring in the promotion and pay of women and men. In fact, Walmart has told its 50,000 managers to promote more women and minorities, with 15 percent of managers' bonuses tied to achieving diversity goals. Women now hold 46 percent of assistant store manager positions, up from 40 percent five years ago.[51]

Both the glass ceiling and the decision to "opt out" of a high-pressure career have an impact on women's advancement opportunities and pay. Yet women are sometimes favored in leadership roles for demonstrating behaviors and attitudes that help them succeed in the workplace, a factor called "the female advantage."

THE GLASS CEILING

For the first time in U.S. history, women hold a majority of the nation's jobs.[52] As they move up the career ladder, the numbers of men and women are comparable, with women holding 51 percent of all lower- and mid-level managerial and professional jobs.[53] But very few women break through the glass ceiling to reach senior management positions. In fact, only 3.6 percent of *Fortune* 500 companies have a woman CEO.[54] The **glass ceiling** is an invisible barrier that exists for women and minorities that limits their upward mobility in organizations. They can look up through the ceiling and see top management, but prevailing attitudes and stereotypes are invisible obstacles to their own advancement. This barrier also impedes the career progress of minorities. In particular, Asian managers bump up against the *bamboo ceiling*, a combination of cultural and organizational barriers that impede Asians' career progress. Today, while Asians are the most educated and

Concept Connection ◄ ◄ ◄

A number of studies conducted around the world in recent years confirm that weight discrimination adds to the **glass ceiling** effect for women. While overweight males are disproportionately represented among CEOs, overweight and obese women are underrepresented. Several years ago, ABC News sent a woman out to interview twice—once appearing to be an individual of normal weight and the second time in padded clothing to appear overweight. She received more job offers as a thin person despite the fact that she handed prospective employers a stronger résumé in her overweight incarnation.

Janet Kimber/The Image Bank/Getty Images

make up a good share of the entry-level workforce in certain industries, they make up only 1.5 percent of corporate board members in the United States.[55]

To break through the glass ceiling into senior management roles, top executives suggest female and minority managers follow this advice:

- **Gain profit-and-loss experience.** Women and minorities are often sidetracked into staff functions, such as human resources and administrative services, rather than line positions where they can gain profit-and-loss experience. For managers who want to be considered for top-level jobs, it is important to have experience in a line position with profit-and-loss responsibilities.[56]

- **Be assertive and ask for what you want.** Many Asian managers have found themselves stereotyped as "not top manager material" because they are too quiet and unassertive. Women in general are also uncomfortable asking for what they want, for fear of being perceived as too aggressive or too selfish. Sheryl Sandberg, Facebook's chief operating officer, argues that women "need to sit at the table." She said that 57 percent of men entering the workforce negotiate their salaries, but only 7 percent of women do likewise.[57] In addition, women and minorities need to build their case around things that matter most to their employer—principally, the impact on the bottom line.[58]

- **Be willing to take risks.** Jump in as a problem solver when an organization is in crisis, an opportunity known as the *glass cliff*. Jack Welch, former CEO of General Electric (GE), underscored this advice when he told a group of women executives, "To get ahead, raise your hand for line jobs and tough, risky assignments." When asked about her experience with the glass cliff, KeyCorp's CEO Beth Mooney said, "I have stepped up to many 'ugly' assignments that others didn't want."[59]

- **Highlight your achievements.** Women tend to downplay their accomplishments to avoid being judged as unfeminine. In addition, modest women and minorities from group-oriented cultures often will not ask for rewards for themselves, but they may ask for rewards for others. White males, on the other hand, typically self-promote their successes. To achieve recognition and credit for their successes, female and minority managers should highlight their achievements and promote their own accomplishments.[60]

- **Display confidence and credibility in your body language.** Women are champions in communicating warmth and empathy but fall short in communicating authority and power. Consultant Carol Kinsey Goman suggests that women who strive for leadership positions need to be aware of nonverbal messages that reduce their authority. Her advice includes avoiding the following actions: (1) head tilts when listening; (2) girlish behaviors such as biting a finger or twirling hair; (3) excessive smiling; (4) nodding too much; (5) delicate handshakes; and (6) flirting.[61]

> *"The most important factor in determining whether you will succeed isn't your gender, it's you. Be open to opportunity and take risks. In fact, take the worst, the messiest, the most challenging assignment you can find, and then take control."*
>
> — ANGELA BRALY, WELLPOINT CEO

OPT-OUT TREND

Some women never hit the glass ceiling because they choose to get off the fast track long before it comes into view. In recent years, an ongoing discussion concerns something referred to as the *opt-out trend*. In a survey of nearly 2,500 women and 653 men, 37 percent of highly qualified women report that they voluntarily left the workforce at some point in their careers, compared to only 24 percent of similarly qualified men.[62]

Quite a debate rages over the reasons for the larger number of women who drop out of mainstream careers. Opt-out proponents say women are deciding that corporate success isn't worth the price in terms of reduced family and personal time, greater stress, and negative health effects.[63] Anne-Marie Slaughter, a Princeton professor and top aide to Hillary Clinton, left her prestigious position to spend more time at home with a rebellious teenager. Unable to balance work and family with success, Slaughter challenged the concept that women can "have it all" in a controversial 2012 article in *The Atlantic*. In the article, Slaughter said today's workplace needs to adapt, and women who opt out have no need to apologize. "Women of my generation have clung to the feminist credo we were raised with . . . because we are determined not to drop the flag for the next generation," Ms. Slaughter wrote. "But when many members of the younger generation have stopped listening, on the grounds that glibly repeating 'you can have it all' is simply airbrushing reality, it is time to talk."[64]

One school of thought says that women don't want corporate power and status in the same way that men do, and clawing one's way up the corporate ladder has become less appealing. Yet critics argue that this view is just another way to blame women themselves for the dearth of female managers at higher levels.[65] Vanessa Castagna, for example, says she left JCPenney after decades with the company not because she wanted more family or personal time, but because she kept getting passed over for top jobs.[66] Although some women are voluntarily leaving the fast track, many more genuinely want to move up the corporate ladder but find their paths blocked. In a survey by Catalyst of executive women, 55 percent said they aspire to senior leadership levels.[67] In addition, a survey of 103 women voluntarily leaving executive jobs in *Fortune* 1000 companies found that corporate culture was cited as the number one reason for leaving.[68] The greatest disadvantages of women leaders stem largely from prejudicial attitudes and a heavily male-oriented corporate culture.[69] Some years ago, when Procter & Gamble (P&G) asked the female executives whom it considered "regretted losses" (that is, high performers that the company wanted to retain) why they left their jobs, the most common answer was that they didn't feel valued by the company.[70]

THE FEMALE ADVANTAGE

Some people think women might actually be better managers, partly because of a more collaborative, less hierarchical, relationship-oriented approach that is in tune with today's global and multicultural environment.[71] As attitudes and values change with changing generations, the qualities that women seem to possess naturally may lead to a gradual role reversal in organizations. For example, a stunning gender reversal is taking place in U.S. education, with girls taking over almost every leadership role from kindergarten to graduate school. In addition, women of all races and ethnic groups are outpacing men in earning bachelor's and master's degrees. In most higher-education institutions, women make up 58 percent of enrolled students.[72] Among 25- to 29-year-olds, 32 percent of women have college degrees, compared to 27 percent of men. Women are rapidly closing the M.D. and Ph.D. gap, and they make up about half of all U.S. law students, half of all undergraduate business majors, and about 30 percent of MBA candidates. Overall, women's participation in both the labor force and civic affairs has steadily increased since the mid-1950s, while men's participation has slowly but steadily declined.[73]

According to James Gabarino, an author and professor of human development at Cornell University, women are "better able to deliver in terms of what modern society requires of people—paying attention, abiding by rules, being verbally competent, and dealing with interpersonal relationships in offices."[74] His observation is supported by the fact that female managers are typically rated higher by subordinates on interpersonal skills, as well as on factors such as task behavior, communication, ability to motivate others, and goal accomplishment.[75] Recent research found a correlation between balanced gender composition in companies (that is, roughly equal male and female representation) and higher organizational performance. Moreover, a study by Catalyst indicates that organizations with the highest percentage of women in top management financially outperform, by about 35 percent, those with the lowest percentage of women in higher-level jobs.[76]

Remember This

- Companies that promote women to senior-level positions outperform those without women in these positions, both financially and organizationally.
- The **glass ceiling** is an invisible barrier that separates women and minorities from senior management positions.
- Proponents of the opt-out trend say some women choose to leave the workforce because they decide success isn't worth it in terms of reduced family and

- personal time, greater stress, and negative health effects.
- Critics say that opinion is just a way to blame women for the scarcity of female top managers and argue that organizations must change.
- Women are likely to be more collaborative, less hierarchical, and more relationship-oriented than men, qualities that prepare them to succeed in today's multicultural work environment.

Achieving Cultural Competence

A corporate culture, as discussed in Chapter 3, is defined by the values, beliefs, understandings, and norms shared by members of the organization. Although some corporate cultures foster diversity, many managers struggle to create a culture that values and nurtures the organization's diverse employees. Managers who have made strategic decisions to foster diversity need a plan that moves the corporate culture toward one that reduces obstacles for disadvantaged employees. A successful diversity plan leads to a workforce that demonstrates *cultural competence* in the long run. **Cultural competence** is the ability to interact effectively with people of different cultures.[77]

Exhibit 13.7 illustrates the five-step process for implementing a diversity plan.[78] These steps create cultural competence among employees by helping them better understand, communicate with, and successfully interact with diverse coworkers.

Step 1: Uncover diversity problems in the organization. Most doctors can't make a medical diagnosis without first examining the patient. Similarly, organizations cannot assess their progress toward cultural competence without first investigating where the culture is right now. A *cultural audit* is a tool that identifies problems or areas needing improvement in a corporation's culture. The cultural audit is completed by employees who answer the following types of questions: How do promotion rates compare? Is there pay disparity

EXHIBIT 13.7

Five Steps to Cultural Competence

SOURCE: Based on Ann M. Morrison, *The New Leaders: Guidelines on Leadership Diversity in America* (San Francisco: Jossey-Bass Publishers, 1992), p. 160.

between managers in the same pay grade? Does a glass ceiling limit the advancement of women and minorities? Answers to these questions help managers assess the cultural competence of the organization and focus their diversity efforts on specific problems.

Step 2: Strengthen top management commitment. The most important component of a successful diversity strategy is management commitment, leadership, and support.[79] Some of the ways that top managers demonstrate their support of diversity efforts are by allocating time and money to diversity activities, supporting the recommendations of problem-solving task forces, and communicating the commitment to diversity through speeches and vision and mission statements. Committed top managers also make diversity a priority by setting an example for others to follow.

Step 3: Choose solutions to fit a balanced strategy. The best solutions to diversity problems are those that address the organization's most pressing problems uncovered during Step 1. To be most effective, solutions should be presented in a balanced strategy and address three factors: education, enforcement, and exposure. *Education* may include new training programs that improve awareness and diversity skills. *Enforcement* means providing incentives for employees who demonstrate new behaviors and disciplinary action for those who violate diversity standards. A good example is Denny's restaurants. After facing discrimination lawsuits in the early 1990s, Denny's rebounded with a multifaceted diversity program that included 25 percent discretionary bonuses to all senior managers who significantly improved their record of hiring and promoting minority workers.[80] *Exposure* involves exposing traditional managers to nontraditional peers to help break down stereotypical beliefs. For example, a company might team a white male manager with a female African American manager.

Step 4: Demand results and revisit the goals. The simple rule "What doesn't get measured doesn't get done" applies to diversity efforts. Diversity performance should be measured by numerical goals to ensure solutions are being implemented successfully. Numerical goals demonstrate that diversity is tied to business objectives. Examples of numerical goals might include tracking the salaries, rates of promotion, and managerial positions for women and minorities. But these personnel statistics don't completely measure an organization's progress toward cultural competence. Other measures might include productivity and profitability tied to diversity efforts, employee opinions about their coworkers, and an assessment of the corporation's ability to provide a satisfying work environment for all employees.[81]

Step 5: Maintain momentum to change the culture. Success with any of the previous four steps is a powerful motivator for continuing diversity efforts. Corporations should use these successes as fuel to move forward and to provide leverage for more progress.

Remember This

- **Cultural competence** is the ability to interact effectively with people of different cultures.
- When a corporate culture embraces diversity and fosters an environment where all people thrive, the organization has achieved cultural competence.

- The five steps toward cultural competence include identifying diversity problems, strengthening top management commitment, choosing solutions, demanding results, and maintaining momentum.

Diversity Initiatives and Programs

In responding to a survey by the Society for Human Resource Management, 91 percent of companies said they believe that diversity initiatives and programs help maintain a competitive advantage. Some specific benefits they cited include improving employee morale, decreasing interpersonal conflict, facilitating progress in new markets, and increasing the organization's creativity.[82] As described in Step 3 of Exhibit 13.7, organizations can develop initiatives and programs that address their unique diversity problems.

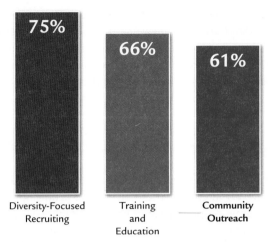

EXHIBIT 13.8

The Most Common Diversity
Initiatives: Percentage of
Fortune 1000 Respondents

SOURCE: Adapted from data in "Impact of Diversity Initiatives on the Bottom Line: A SHRM Survey of the *Fortune* 1000," pp. S12–S14, in *Fortune*, special advertising section, "Keeping Your Edge: Managing a Diverse Corporate Culture," produced in association with the Society for Human Resource Management, www.fortune.com/sections.

ENHANCING STRUCTURES AND POLICIES

Many policies within organizations originally were designed to fit the stereotypical male employee. Now leading companies are changing structures and policies to facilitate and support diversity. Most large organizations have formal policies against racial and gender discrimination, as well as structured grievance procedures and complaint review processes. Companies are also developing policies to support the recruitment and career advancement of diverse employees. Many have added a new senior management position called *chief diversity officer,* whose role is to create working environments where women and minorities can flourish. About 60 percent of *Fortune* 500 companies have chief diversity officers. Among them, 65 percent are women and 37 percent are African American.[83] Increasingly, organizations such as P&G, Ernst & Young, and Allstate Insurance are tying managers' bonuses and promotions to how well they diversify the workforce. Exhibit 13.8 illustrates some of the most common diversity initiatives.

IBM has a long history of notable and innovative policies for developing a richly diverse workforce.

Take a Moment

Read the Ethical Dilemma for Chapter 13 on pages 446–447 that pertains to accommodating the religious practices of employees. Think about how you would handle this challenging management situation.

4

ORGANIZING

Innovative Way

IBM

For years, many corporate leaders paid lip service to diversity, as reflected in the comments of one consumer goods executive: "Diversity is another way of saying affirmative action, and we are forced to support it in order to protect our brand in the trade and with consumers." Unfortunately, many executives still share this opinion.

IBM, however, considers diversity a time-sensitive business imperative. IBM's chief diversity officer Ron Glover believes that diversity must be an embedded mindset with common threads that touch all functional areas because diversity fuels innovation and business growth. "Innovation is about looking at complex problems and bringing new views to the table." Glover says. "Diversity has allowed IBM to be innovative and successful for 100 years and to work across lines of differences in 172 countries, amongst 427,000 employees."

IBM has a long history of supporting diversity efforts. The organization hired its first professional women, 25 college seniors working in systems services, in 1935. In 1943, it named its first female vice president. It instituted a three-month family leave policy in 1956, 37 years before it became required by law. In 2011, IBM hired its first female CEO, Virginia M. Rometty.[84]

IBM has one of the most diverse workforces in corporate America, and managers strongly encourage and support an inclusive culture. "IBM sees their ability to compete in today's marketplace, to approach new markets, and to make money as being tied to diversity," said Caroline Simard, vice president of research at the Anita Borg Institute for Women and Technology. "It really is a business imperative and not just a responsibility of HR"[85]

EXPANDING RECRUITMENT EFFORTS

For many organizations, a new approach to recruitment means making better use of formal recruiting strategies, offering internship programs to give people opportunities, and developing creative ways to draw on previously unused labor markets. Nationwide's Scholars Program brings in Hispanic and African American college students for a three-year program that includes summer internships and yearlong mentoring.[86] Marathon Petroleum created a six-point recruiting strategy to increase diversity, including (1) recruiting corporate-wide and cross-functionally, (2) building relationships with first- and second-tiered schools to recruit minority students, (3) offering internships for racial and ethnic minorities, (4) offering minority scholarships, (5) establishing informal mentoring programs, and (6) forming affiliations with minority organizations.[87]

ESTABLISHING MENTOR RELATIONSHIPS

The successful advancement of diverse employees means that organizations must find ways to eliminate the glass ceiling. One of the most successful structures to accomplish this goal is the mentoring relationship. A **mentor** is a higher-ranking organizational member who is committed to providing upward mobility and support to a protégé's professional career.[88] Mentoring provides minorities and women with direct training and inside information on the norms and expectations of the organization. A mentor also acts as a friend or counselor, enabling the employee to feel more confident and capable.

One researcher who studied the career progress of high-potential minorities found that those who advance the most all share one characteristic—a strong mentor or network of mentors who nurtured their professional development.[89] However, research also indicates that minorities, as well as women, are much less likely than white men to develop mentoring relationships.[90] Women and minorities might not seek mentors because they feel that job competency should be enough to succeed, or they might feel uncomfortable seeking out a mentor when most of the senior executives are white males. Women might fear that initiating a mentoring relationship could be misunderstood as a romantic

Concept Connection ◀◀◀

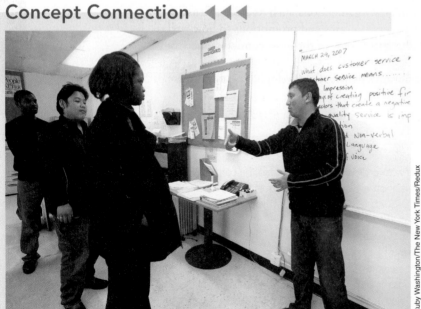

Ruby Washington/The New York Times/Redux

A counselor for CAMBA, a social services group in New York City, directs a role-playing session during a course to help immigrants apply for jobs at Whole Foods Market. The grocer helped CAMBA develop the course to support its **diversity recruiting goals**. The classes include instruction on organic foods, customer service, and tours of Whole Foods Markets.

overture, whereas male mentors may think of women as mothers, wives, or sisters rather than as potential executives. Cross-race mentoring relationships sometimes leave both parties uncomfortable, but the mentoring of minority employees must often be across race because of the low number of minorities in upper-level positions. The few minorities and women who have reached the upper ranks often are overwhelmed with mentoring requests from people like themselves, and they may feel uncomfortable in highly visible minority-minority or female-female mentoring relationships, which isolate them from the white male status quo.

The solution is for organizations to overcome some of the barriers to mentor relationships between white males and minorities. When organizations can institutionalize the value of white males actively seeking women and minority protégés, the benefits will mean that women and minorities will be steered into pivotal jobs and positions critical to advancement. Mentoring programs also are consistent with the Civil Rights Act of 1991, which requires the diversification of middle and upper management.

INCREASING AWARENESS OF SEXUAL HARASSMENT

Although psychological closeness between men and women in the workplace may be a positive experience, sexual harassment is not. Sexual harassment is illegal. As a form of sexual discrimination, sexual harassment in the workplace is a violation of Title VII of the 1964 Civil Rights Act. Sexual harassment in the classroom is a violation of Title VIII of the Education Amendment of 1972. Many companies offer sexual harassment awareness programs that create awareness of what defines sexual harassment and the legal ramifications of violations. The following list categorizes various forms of sexual harassment as defined by one university:

- *Generalized.* This form involves sexual remarks and actions that are not intended to lead to sexual activity but that are directed toward a coworker based solely on gender and reflect on the entire group.

- *Inappropriate/offensive.* Though not sexually threatening, the behavior causes discomfort in a coworker, whose reaction in avoiding the harasser may limit his or her freedom and ability to function in the workplace.

- *Solicitation with promise of reward.* This action treads a fine line as an attempt to "purchase" sex, with the potential for criminal prosecution.

- *Coercion with threat of punishment.* The harasser coerces a coworker into sexual activity by using the threat of power (through recommendations, grades, promotions, and so on) to jeopardize the victim's career.

- *Sexual crimes and misdemeanors.* The highest level of sexual harassment, these acts would, if reported to the police, be considered felonies or misdemeanors.[91]

USING MULTICULTURAL TEAMS

Companies have long known that putting together teams made up of members from different functional areas results in better problem solving and decision making. Now, they are recognizing that **multicultural teams**—teams made up of members from diverse national, racial, ethnic, and cultural backgrounds—provide even greater potential for enhanced creativity, innovation, and value in today's global marketplace.[92] Research indicates that diverse teams generate more and better alternatives to problems and produce more creative solutions than homogeneous teams.[93] A team made up of people with different perspectives, backgrounds, and cultural values creates a healthy mix of ideas and leads to greater creativity and better decisions.

4

ORGANIZING

Despite their many advantages,[94] multicultural teams are more difficult to manage because of the increased potential for miscommunication and misunderstanding. Multicultural teams typically have more difficulty learning to communicate and work together smoothly, but with effective cross-cultural training and good management, teams can learn to work well together.[95] One management team videotaped its meetings so members could see how their body language reflects cultural differences. An American manager remarked, "I couldn't believe how even my physical movements dominated the table, while Ron [a Filipino American] . . . actually worked his way off-camera within the first five minutes."[96]

ENCOURAGING EMPLOYEE AFFINITY GROUPS

Employee affinity groups are based on social identity, such as gender or race, and are organized by employees to focus on concerns of employees from that group.[97] Affinity groups pursue a variety of activities, such as meetings to educate top managers, mentoring programs, networking events, training sessions and skills seminars, minority intern programs, and community volunteer activities. These activities give people a chance to meet, interact with, and develop social and professional ties to others throughout the organization, which may include key decision makers. Affinity groups are a powerful way to reduce social isolation for women and minorities, help these employees be more effective, and enable members to achieve greater career advancement. A recent study confirms that affinity groups can be important tools for helping organizations retain managerial-level minority employees.[98] For example, when she was a senior vice president at Best Buy, Julie Gilbert launched a women's leadership forum, known as WOLF, to get more women involved in solving core business problems and to pull frontline employees into the top ranks. As a result of these "WOLF packs," recruitment of female regional sales managers increased 100 percent over the previous year, and turnover among women managers dropped almost 10 percentage points.[99]

An important characteristic of affinity groups is that they are created informally by employees, not the organization, and membership is voluntary. Affinity groups for minorities who have faced barriers to advancement in organizations, including African Americans, Hispanics, American Indians, Asian Americans, women, gays and lesbians, and disabled employees, show tremendous growth. Even managers who once thought of these as "gripe groups" are now seeing them as essential to organizational success because they help to retain minority employees, enhance diversity efforts, and spark new ideas that can benefit the organization.[100] At Kraft Foods, affinity groups are considered critical to the success of multicultural teams because they build awareness and acceptance of cultural differences and help people feel more comfortable working together.[101] In general, female and minority employees who participate in an affinity group feel more pride about their work and are more optimistic about their careers than those who do not have the support of a group.[102]

Concept Connection ◀◀◀

Stockbyte/Photos.com

Caterpillar's commitment to diversity and to the development of leaders from diverse backgrounds is supported by the number of affinity groups within the company. Employees are invited to participate in **support networks and affinity groups** for African Americans, Chinese, Asian Indians, Koreans, and Latinos, as well as young professionals, women, armed forces veterans, experienced professionals, and gay, lesbian, bisexual, and transgendered employees.

Remember This

- Many organizations have added a new senior management position called *chief diversity officer*, whose role is to spearhead diversity efforts and cultivate working environments that help women and minorities flourish.

- A **mentor** is a higher-ranking senior member of the organization who is committed to providing upward mobility and support to a protégé's professional career.

- To eliminate sexual harassment, companies may offer sexual harassment awareness programs that define harassment and the legal ramifications of harassment.

- **Multicultural teams** are made up of members from diverse national, racial, ethnic, and cultural backgrounds.

- **Employee affinity groups** are based on social identity, such as gender or race, and are organized by employees to focus on concerns of employees from that group.

ch13: Discussion Questions

1. What specific strategies might a manager employ to create a work environment that fosters inclusion?

2. Evaluate your own personal experiences with people from other cultural backgrounds. How well do you think those experiences have prepared you to understand the unique needs and dilemmas of a diverse workforce?

3. Until Sheryl Sandberg was promoted to chief operating officer of Facebook in 2012, its board was composed of only men. Yet a majority of Facebook's 845 million users are women. Given this demographic, explain how Facebook might benefit from increasing the presence of women on its corporate board.

4. Describe employees who are most vulnerable to stereotype threat. Why is it important for managers to understand that some employees may experience stereotype threat?

5. How might employee affinity groups contribute to the advancement of women and minorities to higher-level positions in an organization?

6. What is the first step in creating a culturally competent culture? What does this first step reveal?

7. What are the glass ceiling and bamboo ceiling, and why do you think they have proven to be such barriers to women and minorities?

8. Why do you think a large number of women are *opting out* of corporate management? Discuss whether this trend is likely to continue over the next ten years.

9. Describe how a diversity of perspective boosts creativity and innovation in the workplace. Why do managers consider a diversity of perspective a competitive advantage?

10. How might organizations strike a balance between respecting and meeting the needs of a diverse workforce and shaping a high-performance corporate culture where shared values contribute to the accomplishment of strategic goals?

ch13: Apply Your Skills: Experiential Exercise

How Tolerant Are You?[103]

For each of the following questions, circle the answer that best describes you.

1. Most of your friends:
   a. Are very similar to you
   b. Are very different from you and from each other
   c. Are like you in some respects but different in others

2. When someone does something you disapprove of, you:
   a. Break off the relationship
   b. Tell how you feel but keep in touch
   c. Tell yourself it matters little and behave as you always have

3. Which virtue is most important to you?
   a. Kindness
   b. Objectivity
   c. Obedience

4. When it comes to beliefs, you:
   a. Do all you can to make others see things the same way you do
   b. Advance your point of view actively, but stop short of argument
   c. Keep your feelings to yourself

5. Would you hire a person who has had emotional problems?
   a. No

b. Yes, provided that the person shows evidence of complete recovery

c. Yes, if the person is suitable for the job

6. Do you voluntarily read material that supports views different from your own?
    a. Never
    b. Sometimes
    c. Often

7. You react to old people with:
    a. Patience
    b. Annoyance
    c. Sometimes *a*, sometimes *b*

8. Do you agree with the statement, "What is right and wrong depends upon the time, place, and circumstance"?
    a. Strongly agree
    b. Agree to a point
    c. Strongly disagree

9. Would you marry someone from a different race?
    a. Yes
    b. No
    c. Probably not

10. If someone in your family were homosexual, you would:
    a. View this as a problem and try to change the person to a heterosexual orientation
    b. Accept the person as a homosexual with no change in feelings or treatment
    c. Avoid or reject the person

11. You react to little children with:
    a. Patience
    b. Annoyance
    c. Sometimes *a*, sometimes *b*

12. Other people's personal habits annoy you:
    a. Often
    b. Not at all
    c. Only if extreme

13. If you stay in a household run differently from yours (cleanliness, manners, meals, and other customs), you:
    a. Adapt readily
    b. Quickly become uncomfortable and irritated
    c. Adjust for a while, but not for long

14. Which statement do you agree with most?
    a. We should avoid judging others because no one can fully understand the motives of another person
    b. People are responsible for their actions and have to accept the consequences
    c. Both motives and actions are important when considering questions of right and wrong

Scoring and Interpretation

Circle your score for each of the answers and total the scores:

1. a = 4; b = 0; c = 2
2. a = 4; b = 2; c = 0
3. a = 0; b = 2; c = 4
4. a = 4; b = 2; c = 0
5. a = 4; b = 2; c = 0
6. a = 4; b = 2; c = 0
7. a = 0; b = 4; c = 2
8. a = 0; b = 2; c = 4
9. a = 0; b = 4; c = 2
10. a = 2; b = 0; c = 4
11. a = 0; b = 4; c = 2
12. a = 4; b = 0; c = 2
13. a = 0; b = 4; c = 2
14. a = 0; b = 4; c = 2

Total Score

0–14: If you score 14 or below, you are a very tolerant person, and dealing with diversity comes easily to you.

15–28: You are basically a tolerant person, and others think of you that way. In general, diversity presents few problems for you; you may be broad-minded in some areas and have less tolerant ideas in other areas of life, such as attitudes toward older people or male-female social roles.

29–42: You are less tolerant than most people and should work on developing greater tolerance of people different from you. Your low tolerance level could affect your business or personal relationships.

43–56: You have a very low tolerance for diversity. The only people you are likely to respect are those with beliefs similar to your own. You reflect a level of intolerance that could cause difficulties in today's multicultural business environment.

---

ch13: Apply Your Skills: Small Group Breakout

Personal Diversity

Each of us feels different in many ways from the average behavior or expectations that other people seem to value. This reflects our own feelings of diversity. The differences you feel compared to others could be about your physical characteristics (height, age, skin color), or they could reflect a difference in your thinking style, feelings, personality, or

behavior, especially when you feel different from what other people expect or what you perceive are the social norms. Make a list of six ways you feel different from others:

1. _____

2. _____

3. _____

4. _____

5. _____

6. _____

Now answer the following questions with respect to your perceived diversity.

What are your feelings about being different?

_____

_____

_____

Which elements of diversity are you proud of? Why?

_____

_____

_____

What element would you like to change so you would be less diverse? Why?

_____

_____

How do your differences contribute to a student team or work organization?

_____

_____

_____

_____

In a group of three to five students sitting in a circle, each person takes a turn to describe the answers to these questions. Then other students take turns providing feedback to the person about what perceived differences mean to them. Each student takes a turn reporting answers to the previous questions and then receiving feedback from other group members on the perceptions and impacts of those differences.

Here are additional questions to discuss in the group: What did you learn about perceived diversity and interpersonal relations? What does it mean when our differences appear larger to ourselves than they appear to others? How does personal diversity affect team or organizational performance? (Answers can be written on the board.)

4

ORGANIZING

ch13: Endnotes

1. Based on Lawrence Otis Graham, *Proversity: Getting Past Face Values and Finding the Soul of People* (New York: John Wiley & Sons, 1997).

2. Joann S. Lublin, "TI Battles a Gender Gap in Job Experience," *The Wall Street Journal*, June 13, 2012, B10.

3. Quoted in Susan Caminiti, "The Diversity Factor," *Fortune* (October 19, 2007): 95–105.

4. Caminiti, "The Diversity Factor."

5. Yair Holtzman and Johan Anderberg, "Diversify Your Teams and Collaborate: Because Great Minds Don't Think Alike," *Journal of Management Development* 30, no. 1 (2011): 75–92.

6. Lynn M. Shore et al., "Inclusion and Diversity in Work Groups: A Review and Model for Future Research," *Journal of Management* 37, no. 4 (July 2011): 1262–1289.

7. Taylor H. Cox, "Managing Cultural Diversity: Implications for Organizational Competitiveness," *Academy of Management Executive* 5, no. 3 (1991): 45–56; and Faye Rice, "How to Make Diversity Pay," *Fortune* (August 8, 1994): 78–86.

8. Rawn Shah, "Working with Five Generations in the Workplace," *Forbes.com*, April 20, 2011, www.forbes.com/sites/rawnshah/2011/04/20/working-with-five-generations-in-the-workplace/ (accessed August 9, 2012); and Jeanne Meister and Karie Willyerd, *The 2020 Workplace* (New York: HarperCollins 2010).

9. "Generations in the Workplace in the United States and Canada," Catalyst.org, May 2012, www.catalyst.org/publication/434/generations-in-the-workplace-in-the-united-states-canada (accessed August 9, 2012); Lisa Beyer, Samuel Greengard, Susan G. Hauser, and Todd Henneman, "Workforce 90th Anniversary: Workforce Management Looks Back at Workplace History," *Workforce.com*, July 2, 2012, www.workforce.com/article/20120702/WORKFORCE90/120629967/1066/newsletter01 (accessed August 9, 2012); and Shah, "Working with Five Generations in the Workplace."

10. Occupational Outlook Handbook, *Bureau of Labor Statistics*, www.bls.gov/ooh/about/projections-overview.htm#laborforce (accessed June 29, 2012).

11. "Foreign-Born Workers and Labor Force Characteristics: 2011," *United States Labor Department Bureau of Labor Statistics*, www.bls.gov/news.release/pdf/forbrn.pdf (accessed June 29, 2012).

12. Occupational Outlook Handbook, *Bureau of Labor Statistics*, www.bls.gov/ooh/about/projections-overview.htm#laborforce (accessed June 29, 2012).

13. Joann S. Lublin and Kelly Eggers, "More Women Are Primed to Land CEO Roles," *The Wall Street Journal Online*, April 30, 2012, http://online.wsj.com/article/SB10001424052702303990604577368344256435440.html (accessed June 29, 2012).

14. Ann Zimmerman, "U.S. Charges Bass Pro Shops with Racial Bias," *The Wall Street Journal*, September 22, 2011, B1, B2.

15. Giada Zampano, "Italy to Push Pink Quotas," *The Wall Street Journal Online*, June 5, 2012, https://www.google.com/search?sourceid=navclient&aq=0&oq=italy+to+push&ie=UTF-8&rlz=1T4ADRA_enUS426US427&q=italy+to+push+'pink+quotes'&gs_upl=0l0l0l4406lllllllllll0&aqi=g4&pbx=1 (accessed July 2, 2012); Katrin Bennhold, "Women Nudged out of German Workforce," *The New York Times Online*, June 28, 2011, www.nytimes.com/2011/06/29/world/europe/29iht-FFgermany29.html?pagewanted=all.

16. Zampano, "Italy to Push Pink Quotas."

17. Mariko Sanchanta, "Japan's Women Reach Job Milestones," *The Wall Street Journal*, July 14, 2010, A15.

18. Hiroka Tabuchi, "Leading in 3-D TV, Breaking Japan's Glass Ceiling," *The New York Times Online*, January 17, 2011, www.nytimes.com/2011/01/18/business/global/18screen.html?pagewanted=all (accessed July 3, 2012).

19. Richard L. Daft, *The Leadership Experience* (Cincinnati, OH: Cengage Learning, 2008), p. 340.

20. Holtzman and Anderberg, "Diversify Your Teams and Collaborate.'"

21. Michael L. Wheeler, "Diversity: Business Rationale and Strategies," *The Conference Board*, Report No. 1130-95-RR, 1995, p. 25.

22. Anthony Oshiotse and Richard O'Leary, "Corning Creates an Inclusive Culture to Drive Technology Innovation and Performance," Wiley InterScience, *Global Business and Organizational Excellence* 26, no. 3 (March/April 2007): 7–21.

23. "When CEOs Drive Diversity, Everybody Wins," *Chief Executive*, July 2005, www.chiefexecutive.net/ME2/dirmod.asp?sid=&nm=&type=Publishing&mod=Publications%3A%3AArticle&mid=8F3A702742184 1978F18BE895F87F791&tier=4&id=201D3B11B9 D4419893E78DDA4B7ACDC8 (accessed September 21, 2010).

24. Shore et al., "Inclusion and Diversity in Work Groups."

25. Martin N. Davidson, "The End of Diversity: How Leaders Make Differences Really Matter," *Leader to Leader* (Spring 2012): 51–55.

26. Taylor Cox, Jr., and Ruby L. Beale, *Developing Competency to Manage Diversity* (San Francisco: Berrett-Koehler Publishers, Inc., 1997), p. 2.

27. Holtzman and Anderberg, "Diversify Your Teams and Collaborate.'"

28. Reported in John Tierney, "Social Scientist Sees Bias Within," *The New York Times Online*, www.nytimes.com/2011/02/08/science/08tier.html (accessed July 5, 2012).

29. Gail Robinson and Kathleen Dechant, "Building a Business Case for Diversity," *Academy of Management Executive* 11, no. 3 (1997): 21–31.

30. Sonie Alleyne and Nicole Marie Richardson, "The 40 Best Companies for Diversity," *Black Enterprise* 36, no. 12 (July 2006): 15.

31. Robinson and Dechant, "Building a Business Case for Diversity."

32. *Ibid*.

33. Quoted in Carol Hymowitz, "Coaching Men on Mentoring Women Is Ernst & Young Partner's Mission," *The Wall Street Journal Online*, June 14, 2007, http://online.wsj.com/article/SB118167178575132768 search.html (accessed July 9, 2007).

34. Kris Maher, "Lockheed Settles Racial-Discrimination Suit," *The Wall Street Journal*, January 3, 2008.

35. Frederick E. Allen, "Lack of Diversity Paralyzed the CIA. It Can Cripple Your Organization Too," *Forbes*, April 26, 2012, www.forbes.com/sites/frederickallen/2012/04/26/lack-of-diversity-paralyzed-the-cia-it-can-cripple-your-organization-too/ (accessed July 19, 2012).

36. CIA Web site, https://www.cia.gov/careers/diversity/directors-diversity-commitment.html (accessed July 19, 2012).

37. Norma Carr-Ruffino, *Managing Diversity: People Skills for a Multicultural Workplace* (Tucson, AZ: Thomson Executive Press, 1996), p. 92.

38. Reported in Roy Harris, "The Illusion of Inclusion," *CFO* (May 2001): 42–50.

39. Carr-Ruffino, *Managing Diversity*, pp. 98–99.

40. Based on an interview with PepsiCo chairman and CEO Indra Nooyi, in Rebecca Blumenstein, "View from the Top," *The Wall Street Journal*, April 11, 2011, R9.

41. Cox and Beale, "Developing Competency to Manage Diversity," p. 79.

42. *Ibid*, pp. 80–81.

43. Loriann Roberson and Carol T. Kulik, "Stereotype Threat at Work," *Academy of Management Perspectives* 21, no. 2 (May 2007): 25–27.

44. *Ibid.*, 26.

45. Robert Doktor, Rosalie Tung, and Mary Ann von Glinow, "Future Directions for Management Theory Development," *Academy of Management Review* 16 (1991): 362–365; and Mary Munter, "Cross-Cultural Communication for Managers," *Business Horizons* (May–June 1993): 69–78.

46. Renee Blank and Sandra Slipp, "The White Male: An Endangered Species?" *Management Review* (September 1994): 27–32; Michael S. Kimmel, "What Do Men Want?" *Harvard Business Review* (November–December 1993): 50–63; and Sharon Nelton, "Nurturing Diversity," *Nation's Business* (June 1995): 25–27.

47. Jim Carlton, "Dig In," *The Wall Street Journal*, November 14, 2005; Tony DiRomualdo, "Is Google's Cafeteria a Competitive Weapon?" *Wisconsin Technology Network*, August 30, 2005, http://wistechnology.com/article .php?id=2190 (accessed August 31, 2005); and Marc Ramirez, "Tray Chic: At Work, Cool Cafeterias, Imaginative Menus," *The Seattle Times*, November 21, 2005, http://seattletimes.nwsource.com/html/living/ 2002634266_cafés21.html?pageid=display-in-thenews .module&pageregion=itnbody (accessed November 22, 2005).

48. Georges Desvaux, Sandrine Devillard-Hoellinger, and Mary C. Meaney, "A Business Case for Women," *The McKinsey Quarterly: The Online Journal of McKinsey & Co.*, September 2008, www.mckinseyquarterly.com/ A_business_case_for_women_2192 (accessed June 17, 2010).

49. Joanna Barsh and Lareina Yee, "Changing Companies' Minds About Women," *McKinsey Quarterly Online*, September, 2011, www.mckinsey.com/careers/women/ ~/media/Reports/Women/Changing_companies_ minds_about_women.ashx (accessed June 29, 2012).

50. Jena McGregor, "Why the Pay Gap Persists," *The Washington Post*, September 28, 2010, www .washingtonpost.com/wp-dyn/content/article/2010/09/ 28/AR2010092806188.html (accessed July 9, 2012).

51. Steven Greenhouse, "Report Warned Wal-Mart of Risks Before Bias Suit," *The New York Times*, June 3, 2010, www.nytimes.com/2010/06/04/ business/04lawsuit.html (accessed June 4, 2010).

52. Hanna Rosin, "The End of Men," *The Atlantic*, July/ August 2010, www.theatlantic.com/magazine/print/ 2010/07/the-end-of-men/8135/ (accessed July 9, 2012).

53. Jenny M. Hoobler, Grace Lemmon, and Sandy J. Wayne, "Women's Underrepresentation in Upper Management: New Insights on a Persistent Problem," *Organizational Dynamics* 40 (2011): 151–156.

54. John Bussey, "How Women Can Get Ahead: Advice from Female CEOs," *The Wall Street Journal Online*, May 18, 2012, http://online.wsj.com/article/SB1000 1424052702303879604577410520511235252.html (accessed July 8, 2012).

55. Jane Hyun, "Leadership Principles for Capitalizing on Culturally Diverse Teams: The Bamboo Ceiling Revisited," *Leader to Leader* (Spring 2012): 14–19.

56. Hoobler, Lemmon, and Wayne, "Women's Underrepresentation in Upper Management,"

57. Ken Auletta, "A Woman's Place," *The New Yorker*, (July 11 and 18, 2011): 55–63.

58. Peggy Klaus, "Don't Fret. Just Ask for What You Need," *The New York Times*, July 9, 2011, www.nytimes.com/ 2011/07/10/jobs/10pre.html (accessed July 8, 2012).

59. Bussey, "How Women Can Get Ahead: Advice from Female CEOs."

60. Marie-Helene Budworth and Sara L. Mann, "Becoming a Leader: The Challenge of Modesty for Women," *Journal of Management Development* 29, no. 2 (2010): 177–186.

61. Carol Kinsey Goman, "Body Language," *Leadership Excellence* (August, 2010): 9.

62. Sylvia Ann Hewlett and Carolyn Buck Luce, "Off-Ramps and On-Ramps: Keeping Talented Women on the Road to Success," *Harvard Business Review* (March 2005): 43–54.

63. Lisa Belkin, "The Opt-Out Revolution," *The New York Times Magazine* (October 26, 2002): 43–47, 58.

64. Jodi Kantor, "Elite Women Put a New Spin on an Old Debate," *The New York Times*, June 21, 2012, www. nytimes.com/2012/06/22/us/elite-women-put-a-new-spin-on-work-life-debate.html (accessed July 9, 2012); Anne-Marie Slaughter, "Why Women Still Can't Have It All," *The Atlantic*, July–August 2012, www.theatlantic .com/magazine/archive/2012/07/why-women-still-cant-have-it-all/309020/ (accessed October 15, 2012).

65. C. J. Prince, "Media Myths: The Truth About the Opt-Out Hype," *NAFE Magazine* (Second Quarter 2004): 14–18; Patricia Sellers, "Power: Do Women Really Want It?" *Fortune* (October 13, 2003): 80–100.

66. Jia Lynn Yang, "Goodbye to All That," *Fortune* (November 14, 2005): 169–170.

67. Sheila Wellington, Marcia Brumit Kropf, and Paulette R. Gerkovich, "What's Holding Women Back?" *Harvard Business Review* (June 2003): 18–19.

68. The Leader's Edge/Executive Women Research 2002 survey, reported in "Why Women Leave," *Executive Female* (Summer 2003): 4.

69. Barbara Reinhold, "Smashing Glass Ceilings: Why Women Still Find It Tough to Advance to the Executive Suite," *Journal of Organizational Excellence* (Summer 2005): 43–55; Jory Des Jardins, "I Am Woman (I Think)," *Fast Company* (May 2005): 25–26; and Alice H. Eagly and Linda L. Carli, "The Female Leadership Advantage: An Evaluation of the Evidence," *The Leadership Quarterly* 14 (2003): 807–834.

70. Claudia H. Deutsch, "Behind the Exodus of Executive Women: Boredom," *USA Today*, May 2, 2005.

71. Eagly and Carli, "The Female Leadership Advantage"; Reinhold, "Smashing Glass Ceilings"; Sally Helgesen, *The Female Advantage: Women's Ways of Leadership* (New York: Doubleday Currency, 1990); Rochelle Sharpe, "As Leaders, Women Rule: New Studies Find that Female Managers Outshine Their Male Counterparts in Almost Every Measure," *BusinessWeek* (November 20, 2000): 5ff; and Del Jones, "2003: Year

4

ORGANIZING

of the Woman Among the *Fortune 500?*" *USAToday*, December 30, 2003.

72. Tamar Lewin, "At Colleges, Women Are Leaving Men in the Dust," *The New York Times Online*, July 9, 2006, www.nytimes.com/2006/07/09/education/09college .html ?_r=1&scp=1&sq=at%20 colleges, %20women% 20are%20leaving% 20men%20in%20the%20 dust&st= cse&oref=slogin (accessed March 13, 2008).

73. Michelle Conlin, "The New Gender Gap," *BusinessWeek* (May 26, 2003): 74–82.

74. Quoted in Conlin, "The New Gender Gap."

75. Kathryn M. Bartol, David C. Martin, and Julie A. Kromkowski, "Leadership and the Glass Ceiling: Gender and Ethnic Group Influences on Leader Behaviors at Middle and Executive Managerial Levels," *The Journal of Leadership and Organizational Studies* 9, no. 3 (2003): 8–19; Bernard M. Bass and Bruce J. Avolio, "Shatter the Glass Ceiling: Women May Make Better Managers," *Human Resource Management* 33, no. 4 (Winter 1994): 549–560; and Sharpe, "As Leaders, Women Rule."

76. Dwight D. Frink et al., "Gender Demography and Organization Performance: A Two-Study Investigation with Convergence," *Group & Organization Management* 28, no. 1 (March 2003): 127–147; Catalyst research project cited in Reinhold, "Smashing Glass Ceilings."

77. Mercedes Martin and Billy Vaughn, "Cultural Competence: The Nuts & Bolts of Diversity & Inclusion," *Diversity Officer Magazine*, October 25, 2010, http://diversityofficermagazine.com/uncategorized/ cultural-competence-the-nuts-bolts-of-diversity-inclusion/ (accessed October 15, 2012).

78. Ann M. Morrison, *The New Leaders: Guidelines on Leadership Diversity in America* (San Francisco: Jossey-Bass Publishers, 1992), p. 235.

79. Wheeler, "Diversity: Business Rationale and Strategies."

80. Alleyne and Richardson, "The 40 Best Companies for Diversity," 100.

81. Morrison, *The New Leaders*.

82. "Impact of Diversity Initiatives on the Bottom Line: A SHRM Survey of the *Fortune* 1000," in "Keeping Your Edge: Managing a Diverse Corporate Culture," special advertising section produced in association with the Society for Human Resource Management, *Fortune* (June 3, 2001): S12–S14.

83. Leslie Kwoh, "Firms Hail New Chiefs (of Diversity)," *The Wall Street Journal Online*, January 5, 2012, http://online.wsj.com/article/SB1000142405297020 38995045771292617328845 78.html (accessed July 9, 2012).

84. Glenn Llopis, "Diversity Management Is the Key to Growth: Make It Authentic," *Forbes*, June 13, 2011, www.forbes.com/sites/glennllopis/2011/06/13/ diversity (accessed July 20, 2011); and Claire Cain

Miller, "For Incoming I.B.M. Chief, Self-Confidence Is Rewarded," *The New York Times*, October 27, 2011, www.nytimes.com/2011/10/28/business/for-incoming-ibm-chief-self-confidence-rewarded.html (accessed July 20, 2012).

85. Miller, "For Incoming I.B.M. Chief, Self-Confidence Is Rewarded."

86. Annie Finnigan, "Different Strokes," *Working Woman* (April 2001): 42–48.

87. "Diversity in an Affiliated Company," cited in Vanessa J. Weaver, "Winning with Diversity," *BusinessWeek* (September 10, 2001).

88. Melanie Trottman, "A Helping Hand," *The Wall Street Journal*, November 14, 2005; B. Ragins, "Barriers to Mentoring: The Female Manager's Dilemma," *Human Relations* 42, no. 1 (1989): 1–22; and Belle Rose Ragins, Bickley Townsend, and Mary Mattis, "Gender Gap in the Executive Suite: CEOs and Female Executives Report on Breaking the Glass Ceiling," *Academy of Management Executive* 12, no. 1 (1998): 28–42.

89. David A. Thomas, "The Truth About Mentoring Minorities—Race Matters," *Harvard Business Review* (April 2001): 99–107.

90. Mary Zey, "A Mentor for All," *Personnel Journal* (January 1988): 46–51.

91. "Sexual Harassment: Vanderbilt University Policy" (Nashville, TN: Vanderbilt University, 1993).

92. Joseph J. Distefano and Martha L. Maznevski, "Creating Value with Diverse Teams in Global Management," *Organizational Dynamics* 29, no. 1 (Summer 2000): 45–63; and Finnigan, "Different Strokes."

93. W. E. Watson, K. Kumar, and L. K. Michaelsen, "Cultural Diversity's Impact on Interaction Process and Performance: Comparing Homogeneous and Diverse Task Groups," *Academy of Management Journal* 36 (1993): 590–602; Robinson and Dechant, "Building a Business Case for Diversity"; and D. A. Thomas and R. J. Ely, "Making Differences Matter: A New Paradigm for Managing Diversity," *Harvard Business Review* (September–October 1996): 79–90.

94. See Distefano and Maznevski, "Creating Value with Diverse Teams" for a discussion of the advantages of multicultural teams.

95. Watson, Kumar, and Michaelsen, "Cultural Diversity's Impact on Interaction Process and Performance."

96. Distefano and Maznevski, "Creating Value with Diverse Teams."

97. This definition and discussion is based on Raymond A. Friedman, "Employee Network Groups: Self-Help Strategy for Women and Minorities," *Performance Improvement Quarterly* 12, no. 1 (1999): 148–163.

98. Raymond A. Friedman and Brooks Holtom, "The Effects of Network Groups on Minority Employee Turnover Intentions," *Human Resource Management* 41, no. 4 (Winter 2002): 405–421.

99. Diane Brady and Jena McGregor, "What Works in Women's Networks," *BusinessWeek* (June 18, 2007): 58.

100. Elizabeth Wasserman, "A Race for Profits," *MBA Jungle* (March–April 2003): 40–41.

101. Finnigan, "Different Strokes."

102. Raymond A. Friedman, Melinda Kane, and Daniel B. Cornfield, "Social Support and Career Optimism: Examining the Effectiveness of Network Groups among Black Managers," *Human Relations* 51, no. 9 (1998): 1155–1177.

103. Adapted from the Tolerance Scale by Maria Heiselman, Naomi Miller, and Bob Schlorman, Northern Kentucky University, 1982. In George Manning, Kent Curtis, and Steve McMillen, *Building Community: The Human Side of Work* (Cincinnati, OH: Thomson Executive Press, 1996), pp. 272–277.

4

ORGANIZING

ch10: Apply Your Skills: Ethical Dilemma

A Matter of Delegation*

Tom Harrington loved his job as an assistant quality-control officer for Rockingham Toys. After six months of unemployment, he was anxious to make a good impression on his boss, Frank Golopolus. One of his responsibilities was ensuring that new product lines met federal safety guidelines. Rockingham had made several manufacturing changes over the past year. Golopolus and the rest of the quality-control team had been working 60-hour weeks to troubleshoot the new production process.

Harrington was aware of numerous changes in product safety guidelines that he knew would affect the new Rockingham toys. Golopolus was also aware of the guidelines, but he was taking no action to implement them. Harrington wasn't sure whether his boss expected him to implement the new procedures. The ultimate responsibility was his boss's, and Harrington was concerned about moving ahead on his own. To cover for his boss, he continued to avoid the questions he received from the factory floor, but he was beginning

to wonder whether Rockingham would have time to make changes with the Christmas season rapidly approaching.

Harrington felt loyalty to Golopolus for giving him a job and didn't want to alienate him by interfering. However, he was beginning to worry what might happen if he didn't act. Rockingham had a fine product safety reputation and was rarely challenged on matters of quality. Should he question Golopolus about implementing the new safety guidelines?

What Would You Do?

1. Prepare a memo to Golopolus, summarizing the new safety guidelines that affect the Rockingham product line and requesting his authorization for implementation.

2. Mind your own business. Golopolus hasn't said anything about the new guidelines, and you don't want to overstep your authority. You've been unemployed and need this job.

3. Send copies of the reports anonymously to the operations manager, who is Golopolus's boss.

*Based on Doug Wallace, "The Man Who Knew Too Much," *Business Ethics* 2 (March–April 1993): 7–8.

ch10: Apply Your Skills: Case for Critical Analysis

Abraham's Grocery

The first Abraham's Grocery Store was started in 1967 by Bill Abraham and his sister Doris. They used a small inheritance to start a small grocery store in a suburb of Atlanta, Georgia, and it was immediately successful. The location was good, and both Bill and Doris had winning personalities and a "serve the customer" attitude. Abraham's rapidly growing number of customers enjoyed an abundance of good meats and produce, for which Abraham's became well known.

By 2007, Abraham's had over 200 stores. Company headquarters moved to downtown Atlanta to supervise stores throughout the southeastern United States. There were four regional managers responsible for about 50 stores each. Within each region, there were four districts of 12 to 13 stores each.

Because the stores specialized in excellent meats and produce, there was a separate meat department manager, grocery department manager, and produce department manager within each store. The grocery department manager also served as the store manager, but this person did not have direct authority over the meat department or the produce department. The store meat department manager reported directly to a district meat manager specialist, and the store produce department manager reported directly to a district produce manager specialist. The store manager (who is also the grocery department manager) reported directly to a district store supervisor. This direct line of

authority for each store department provided excellent quality control over the meat, produce, and grocery departments within individual stores.

However, there was growing dissatisfaction within the stores. The turnover of store managers was high, mostly because they had no control over the meat and produce departments within their stores. Coordination within stores was terrible, such as when a store manager decided to promote a sale on Coke products as a loss leader. Hundreds of cartons of Coke were brought into the store for the big sale, but the meat and produce department managers would not give up floor space to display Coke cartons. The frustrated store manager insisted that this was no way to run a business and quit on the spot. Many stores experienced conflict rather than cooperation among the meat, produce, and store managers because each was very protective of their separate responsibilities.

Doris Abraham asked a consultant for advice. The consultant recommended a reorganization within each store so that the meat, grocery, and produce departments would all report to the store manager. The store manager thus would have complete control over store activities and would be responsible for coordinating across the meat, produce, and grocery departments. The meat department manager in each store would report to the store manager and would also have a dashed-line relationship (communication, coordination) with the district meat specialist. Likewise, each store produce department manager would have a dashed-line relationship with the district produce specialist. The store manager would report directly to the district store supervisor. The district meat and produce specialists would visit individual stores periodically to provide advice and help the store department heads to ensure top quality in the meat, produce, and grocery areas.

The consultant was enthusiastic about the proposed structure. Store managers would have more freedom and responsibility. By assigning responsibility for all store departments to the store manager, the new structure would encourage coordination within stores and give managers the ability to adapt to local tastes and customer needs. The dashed-line relationships would ensure excellent meat, grocery, and produce departments across all stores.

Questions

1. Based on the information available in the case, sketch a picture of the original structure within an Abraham's store and the store managers' relationship with district specialist managers. What type of structure is this? Explain.

2. Based on the information available in the case, sketch a picture of the consultant's recommended structure within the store and the relationship of store department managers with district specialist managers. What type of structure is this? Explain.

3. What are some of the advantages and disadvantages you see for the two types of structures? Which structure do you think will work best for Abraham's? Why?

ch10: On the Job Video Cases

On the Job: Modern Shed: Designing Adaptive Organizations

Questions

1. Which of the five approaches to structural design is used at Modern Shed, and how are the company's departments organized and coordinated?

2. What are the advantages and disadvantages of Modern Shed's organizational structure?

3. How did Ryan Smith determine whether his company needed a mechanistic structure with a formal vertical hierarchy or an organic one involving free-flowing partnerships?

ch11: Apply Your Skills: Ethical Dilemma

Crowdsourcing*

Last year, when Ai-Lan Nguyen told her friend Greg Barnwell that Off the Hook Tees, based in Asheville, North Carolina, was going to experiment with crowdsourcing, he warned her she wouldn't like the results. Now, as she was about to walk into a meeting to decide whether to adopt this new business model, she was afraid her friend had been right.

Crowdsourcing uses the Internet to invite anyone, professionals and amateurs alike, to perform tasks such as product design that employees usually perform. In exchange, contributors receive recognition—but little or no pay. Ai-Lan, as vice president of operations for Off the Hook, a company specializing in witty T-shirts aimed at young adults, upheld the values of founder Chris Woodhouse, who, like Ai-Lan, was a graphic artist. Before he sold the company, the founder always insisted that T-shirts be well designed by top-notch graphic artists to make sure each screen print was a work of art. Those graphic artists reported to Ai-Lan.

During the past 18 months, Off the Hook's sales stagnated for the first time in its history. The crowdsourcing experiment was the latest in a series of attempts to jump-start sales growth. Last spring, Off the Hook issued its first open

call for T-shirt designs and then posted the entries on the Web so people could vote for their favorites. The top five vote-getters were handed over to the in-house designers, who tweaked the submissions until they met the company's usual quality standards.

When CEO Rob Taylor first announced the company's foray into crowdsourcing, Ai-Lan found herself reassuring the designers that their positions were not in jeopardy. Now Ai-Lan was all but certain she would have to go back on her word. Not only had the crowdsourced tees sold well, but Rob had put a handful of winning designs directly into production, bypassing the design department altogether. Customers didn't notice the difference.

Ai-Lan concluded that Rob was ready to adopt some form of the Web-based crowdsourcing because it made T-shirt design more responsive to consumer desires. Practically speaking, it reduced the uncertainty that surrounded new designs, and it dramatically lowered costs. The people who won the competitions were delighted with the exposure it gave them.

However, when Ai-Lan looked at the crowdsourced shirts with her graphic artist's eye, she felt that the designs were competent, but none achieved the aesthetic standards attained by her in-house designers. Crowdsourcing essentially replaced training and expertise with public opinion. That made the artist in her uncomfortable.

More distressing, it was beginning to look as if Greg had been right when he'd told her that his working definition of crowdsourcing was "a billion amateurs want your job." It was easy to see that if Off the Hook adopted crowdsourcing, she would be handing out pink slips to most of her design people, longtime employees whose work she admired. "Sure, crowdsourcing costs the company less, but what about the human cost?" Greg asked.

What future course should Ai-Lan argue for at the meeting? And what personal decisions did she face if Off the Hook decided to put the crowd completely in charge when it came to T-shirt design?

*Based on Paul Boutin, "Crowdsourcing: Consumers As Creators," *BusinessWeek Online*, July 13, 2006, www.businessweek.com/innovate/content/jul2006/id20060713_755844.htm (accessed August 30, 2010); Jeff Howe, "The Rise of Crowdsourcing," *Wired*, June 2006, www.wired.com/wired/archive/14.06/crowds.html (accessed August 30, 2010); and Jeff Howe, Crowdsourcing blog, www.crowdsourcing.com (accessed August 30, 2010).

What Would You Do?

1. Go to the meeting and argue for abandoning crowdsourcing for now in favor of maintaining the artistic integrity and values that Off the Hook has always stood for.

2. Accept the reality that because Off the Hook's CEO Rob Taylor strongly favors crowdsourcing, it's a fait accompli. Be a team player and help work out the details of the new design approach. Prepare to lay off graphic designers as needed.

3. Accept the fact that converting Off the Hook to a crowdsourcing business model is inevitable, but because it violates your own personal values, start looking for a new job elsewhere.

ch11: Apply Your Skills: Case for Critical Analysis

Cleaver's Sausage House

Allison Elam, Vice President of Operations for Cleaver's Sausage House, a maker of fine sausages in Minnesota, was stunned. She felt numb. Just 30 minutes ago, she had been happy and excited about the upcoming meeting to decide whether to launch the new MRP (material requirements planning) software system her department had been planning. Now the meeting was over and Cleaver's executive committee had not agreed to launch the system.

She thought the go/no-go decision would be just a formality. But David Martin, CFO, expressed a doubt about implementing the system, and things went downhill from there. "I *so* thought he was on board," Elam hissed to herself. Other senior staff then pushed back hard. They warned that the change could be a costly disaster. The vice president of sales doubted whether the MRP system could provide the solid sales forecasts that Cleaver needed. He called MRP "just big corporate BS." He also feared it would result in shortages of raw materials. The director of logistics, Susan Frisch, warned about problems that had erupted at one of her previous employers when a similar system was installed. She related a horror story about customers not getting orders and trucks leaving the plant half-full. Her final comment was, "We are successful. Why upset the apple cart?"

Cleaver CEO Jayden Anderson hired Elam to take the position vacated by his ailing brother Stefan, who died in late 2009. Elam has been on the job for ten months, spending much of her time working alone on the MRP project. Stefan had purchased the MRP software prior to his illness. It had sat unused since its purchase. She sometimes wondered if Stefan would have found implementation easier had he lived to see it through. Elam was a veteran of big companies such as Heinz and Coca-Cola. Anderson wanted an outsider like Elam to bring in new technology to help operations get to the next level. Elam had worked with successful MRP systems and assured Anderson that the new system would overhaul procurement, production, and shipping, and would impose much needed discipline on operations. She estimated her system would increase annual cash flow by $600,000 and save up to $200,000 annually by reducing wasted material. This was serious money for a company with 350 employees.

Elam wondered if the real problem was that implementing the MRP idea would require a radical overhaul of every facet of Cleaver's operations. Making the system work would require at least 25 Cleaver managers and employees to change how they did their jobs. Still angry, Elam thought to herself, *What are the VPs and department heads so scared of?*

Prior to the executive committee meeting, Elam had encountered plenty of obstacles. She was unable to get data from several people to create a mockup of how the system would work. Some key managers or their direct reports came late to the first and second meetings or simply skipped them. She complained about the lack of cooperation to the CEO. It was obvious to Elam that the topic was not a priority for the other VPs and department heads. Anderson's response was to suggest forming a cross-departmental task force to help her. Elam told him, "I believe in this technology and I will get it done. A task force will just slow me down."

Allison Elam was a pleasant, reserved individual who did not like conflict. She had been mentally unprepared for the executive committee's no-go decision, and she shuddered at the thought that the MRP system might not be adopted at all! She decided to sleep on it for a night or two and then plan a course of action to get this system implemented for Cleaver's benefit and for her own conscience.

Questions

1. What do you think are the reasons for people's resistance to the MRP implementation? Explain.

2. What is the value of the task force idea suggested by the CEO as a way to facilitate implementation? Explain.

3. Which implementation tactics do you think Elam should follow? Why?

ch11: On the Job Video Cases

On the Job: Holden Outerwear: Managing Change and Innovation

Questions

1. Identify the type of change that Holden's leaders are managing on a daily basis.

2. Is Holden's creative approach to outerwear an example of disruptive innovation? Why or why not?

3. What resistance has Holden encountered while introducing innovative garment designs?

ch12: Apply Your Skills: Ethical Dilemma

A Conflict of Responsibilities

As director of human resources, Tess Danville was asked to negotiate a severance deal with Terry Winston, the Midwest regional sales manager for Cyn-Com Systems. Winston's problems with drugs and alcohol had become severe enough to require his dismissal. His customers were devoted to him, but top management was reluctant to continue gambling on his reliability. Lives depended on his work as the salesperson and installer of Cyn-Com's respiratory diagnostic technology. Winston had been warned twice to clean up his act but had never succeeded. Only his unique blend of technical knowledge and high-powered sales ability had saved him before.

Now the vice president of sales asked Danville to offer Winston the option of resigning rather than being fired if he would sign a noncompete agreement and agree to go into rehabilitation. Cyn-Com would also extend a guarantee of confidentiality on the abuse issue and a good work reference as thanks for the millions of dollars of business that Winston had brought to Cyn-Com. Winston agreed to take the deal. After his departure, a series of near disasters was uncovered as a result of Winston's mismanagement. Some of his maneuvers to cover up his mistakes bordered on fraud.

Today, Danville received a message to call the HR director at a cardiopulmonary technology company to give a personal reference on Terry Winston. From the area code, Danville could see that he was not in violation of the noncompete agreement. She had also heard that Winston had completed a 30-day treatment program as promised. Danville knew she was expected to honor the confidentiality agreement, but she also knew that if his shady dealings had been discovered before his departure, he would have been fired without any agreement. Now she was being asked to give Winston a reference for another medical sales position.

What Would You Do?

1. Honor the agreement, trusting that Winston's rehabilitation is complete on all levels and that he is now ready for a responsible position. Give a good recommendation.

2. Contact the vice president of sales and ask him to release you from the agreement or to give the reference himself. After all, he's the one who made the agreement. You don't want to lie.

3. Without mentioning specifics, give Winston such an unenthusiastic reference that you hope the other HR director can read between the lines and believe that Winston will be a poor choice.

ch12: Apply Your Skills: Case for Critical Analysis

The Right Way with Employees?

As a senior manager for a global player in automobile production and sales, Kirby Ellis had joined thousands of fellow employees in the excitement surrounding production of the company's new hybrid vehicles.

But barely two years into production, embarrassing component shortages, delivery delays, and a recall of the first models had a ripple effect, presenting the company with mounting concerns. In the confusion, many customers canceled orders and turned to competitors for purchase of the eco-friendly vehicles. Ellis's company was facing a financial downturn.

With three decades of service to the company, Kirby led a contingent of managers intent upon keeping together as much of the company and as many employees as possible.

"We know there will be some necessary cuts," Kirby admitted. "But this company has a long history of sticking by its people. Our first priority should be internal streamlining of how we do things and making sure we have the right people on board."

Many managers liked what they heard from Kirby. He was well respected and had an unequaled reputation for his leadership and collaborative skills and his ability to work with managers, as well as line workers on the factory floors. People marveled at the number of individuals he knew on a personal level throughout the company.

Drew Cunningham influenced a second contingent within the management group. A brash go-getter with a reputation for *fixing* companies in crisis, Cunningham proposed across-the-board cuts in employees in order to implement a solution as quickly as possible. He proposed the immediate creation of a forced ranking system in order to identify and get rid of lower-ranking employees.

Kirby raised his hand and rose to his feet in objection. "So we're going to create a system to *fire* . . ."

"I didn't say *fire* . . ."

"OK, *cut* our own hard-working people? It sounds like some lame government commission," Kirby said. "We've got bright people. This thing simply got worse faster than we thought. We can work with the people we have in setting up more efficient workflow, establishing reasonable deadlines to increase output and . . ."

"Kirby, these are not the days of knowing everyone in the plant," Drew said. "You're not throwing out your wife's uncle Harry. We are taking a serious look at what we do, how we do it, and streamlining everything by keeping the right people in the organization and cutting the rest."

Questions

1. What kind of employee social contract is assumed by Kirby and Cunningham? Explain.

2. If you were an HR manager at the company, which view would you support? Why?

3. HR departments hire and develop human capital to serve the organization's strategy and drive performance. Which approach—Kirby's or Cunningham's—is more likely to have a greater positive impact on performance? Discuss.

ch12: On the Job Video Cases

http:
See It
Online
www.

On the Job: Barcelona Restaurant Group: Managing Human Resources

Questions

1. List the three main activities of HRM and identify which activity is examined at length in the video.

2. Of the various steps in Barcelona's employee selection process, the job interview is the briefest. Do you

agree with the company's approach to interviewing? Why or why not?

3. Identify Barcelona's three-stage process for matching job applicants with its organizational objectives, and explain how each stage reveals the fit between job applicants and the needs of the restaurant.

ch13: Apply Your Skills: Ethical Dilemma

Sunset Prayers*

Frank Piechowski, plant manager for a Minnesota North Woods Appliance Corporation refrigerator plant, just received his instructions from the vice president for manufacturing. He was to hire 40 more temporary workers through Twin Cities Staffing, the local labor agency that North Woods used. Frank already knew from past experience that most, if not all, of the new hires available to work the assembly line would be Muslim Somali refugees, people who had immigrated to Minnesota from their war-torn native country en masse over the past 15 years.

North Woods, like all appliance manufacturers, was trying to survive in a highly competitive, mature industry.

Appliance companies were competing mainly on price. The entrance of large chains such as Best Buy and Home Depot only intensified the price wars, not to mention that consumers could easily do comparison shopping before leaving home by logging on to the Internet. The pressure to keep production costs low was considerable.

That's where the Somali workers came in. In an effort to keep labor costs low, North Woods was relying more and more on temporary workers rather than increasing the ranks of permanent employees. Frank was quite pleased with the Somalis already at work on the assembly line. Although few in number, they were responsible, hard-working, and willing to work for the wages that he could afford to pay.

It was the first time this son of Polish immigrants had ever come into contact with Muslims, but so far, it had gone well. Frank had established a good working relationship with the Somalis' spokesperson, Halima Adan, who explained that unlike most Western faiths, Islamic religious practices were inextricably woven into everyday life. So together, they worked out ways to accommodate Muslim customs. Frank authorized changes in the plant's cafeteria menu so the Somali workers had more options that conformed to their dietary restrictions, and he allowed women to wear traditional clothing, so long as they weren't violating safety standards.

After learning that the Somalis would need to perform at least some of the ceremonial washing and prayers they were required to do five times a day during work hours, the plant manager set aside a quiet, clean room where they could observe their 15-minute rituals during their breaks and at sunset. The Maghrib sunset prayers that second shift workers had to perform were disruptive to a smooth workflow. Compared to their midday and afternoon rituals, the Muslim faithful had considerably less leeway as to when they said the sunset prayers, and of course, the sun set at a slightly different time each day. But so far, they'd all coped.

But what was he going to do about the sunset prayers with an influx of 40 Somali workers that would dramatically increase the number of people who would need to leave the line to pray? Was it time to modify his policy? He knew that Title VII of the Civil Right Act required that he make "reasonable" accommodations to his employees' religious practices unless doing so would impose an "undue hardship" on the employer. Had he reached the point where the accommodations that Halima Adan would probably request crossed the line from reasonable to unreasonable? But if he changed his policy, did he risk alienating his workforce?

What Would You Do?

1. Continue the current policy that leaves it up to the Muslim workers as to when they leave the assembly line to perform their sunset rituals.

2. Try to hire the fewest possible Muslim workers so the work line will be efficient on second shift.

3. Ask the Muslim workers to delay their sunset prayers until a regularly scheduled break occurs, pointing out that North Woods is primarily a place of business, not a house of worship.

*Based on Rob Johnson, "30 Muslim Workers Fired for Praying on Job at Dell," *The Tennessean*, March 10, 2005; Anayat Durrani, "Religious Accommodation for Muslim Employees," *Workforce.com*, www.workforce.com/archive/feature/religious-accommodation-muslimemployees/index.php (accessed September 21, 2010); "Questions and Answers About Employer Responsibilities Concerning the Employment of Muslims, Arabs, South Asians, and Sikhs," The U. S. Equal Employment Opportunity Commission, www.eeoc.gov/facts/backlash-employer.html (accessed September 20, 2010); and "2006 Household Appliance Industry Outlook," U. S. Department of Commerce, International Trade Administration, www.ita.doc.gov/td/ocg/outlook06_appliances.pdf (accessed September 21, 2010).

ch13: Apply Your Skills: Case for Critical Analysis

True To Myself

Ethney Gentry was thrilled to have infiltrated the ultimate "good old boy" network, landing a job with a mid-size, Tulsa-based oil company. Armed with solid credentials and what she considered the strengths of female leadership—listening, collaboration, consensus building, and organization—she looked forward to her first meeting with the company's first female manager, Alexis Bale, who was about to retire.

Alexis offered a firm, almost painful, handshake and a cup of coffee.

"I've been looking forward to meeting you, Alexis," Ethney said.

"It's Alex."

"Oh, I didn't know." Ethney took a sip of piping hot coffee with a sudden vague feeling of discomfort. The first moments of this much-anticipated meeting seemed awkward and somewhat strained.

"I'll be honest with you," Alex said as she walked around and sat in the oversized chair behind her desk. "You're here for the same reason I was here. When our founder, Champ Luman, died 12 years ago, his three middle-aged daughters, referred to throughout the company as *the girls*, became major shareholders. They pushed hard

for the inclusion of a woman in management. That *was* me. Now it's you."

Ethney tried to show no reaction as she set her cup on the desk. "Are you implying that I was selected over more qualified male candidates?"

"No. I was not on the selection team. I've seen your résumé and you are an excellent addition to the organization. But qualifications aside, you and I fulfill, shall we say—the 'diversity' requirements for an otherwise all-male club."

Ethney could not believe the undisguised cynicism of the woman across the desk. She was torn between a desire to get up and march out of the office and a desire to stay and hear the entire lecture. She decided to take the high road. "My understanding was that you have been very successful here," she said.

"I suppose so." Alex gazed up at the numerous photographs showing oil rigs scattered across the Oklahoma plains. "I learned to play the game," she said somewhat wistfully. Then she suddenly turned and looked at Ethney. "I'm not trying to intimidate you. But I think that coming in, you should understand some things."

"Such as?"

"Such as . . . don't be too eager with your ideas or opinions. When I started, I intended to jump right in and contribute. The men resented it. I was considered a 'pushy broad,' as one *gentleman* told me to my face. The reaction to me was harsh. They may have been stuck with me, but these guys could marginalize me; make sure I didn't count, and make sure I knew it."

"What did you do?"

"I stewed awhile and finally tried the opposite tactic. I jumped up to get coffee for everyone. I sought the *wise counsel* of their opinions before daring to make a suggestion in meetings. I played the female image that was in their minds. I felt like an idiot. I kowtowed till I thought I would throw up."

"How did they react?"

"I was no longer marginalized. But I wasn't respected either. I had quietly stepped back and accepted *my place*."

"Why didn't you just quit?"

"Because I knew that's exactly what they wanted me to do. And I'm just mean enough and stubborn enough not to give them what they wanted."

Ethney took a deep breath and shook her head. "This sounds like *Mad Men* in the 1950s. I can't believe men in management act like this."

"Uh-huh. It may be a little better now, but they are still throwbacks to *Mad Men*."

"So how did you develop this reputation for success if you went from being ignored to being a doormat?"

"Have you met Bill Ledson?"

Ethney nodded, took a sip of coffee and leaned forward, waiting to hear the secret of success.

"At an industry meeting in Houston, his wife, Margaret, got drunk, cornered me, and drawled, 'Listen, Honey. I've been around oil men all my life. My daddy and his daddy were oil men. You're going to have to wise up and take the plunge—become one of the boys. It's the only way you'll ever be accepted.' She reminded me that I'm on *their* turf. Margaret told me, 'Honey, as a wife and hostess for this crowd, I've talked more football than you can imagine. I hate football. I hang on for the commercials. But they don't know that. Bill doesn't know that. Me and God—we're the only ones who know that. Trust me,' she said. 'These guys do get down to some serious business, but not until they grouse about how Oklahoma State was robbed of its chance to play LSU for the national championship.'"

"Isn't that trivializing the men in this company?" Ethney asked.

Alex shrugged. "It worked. I became Alex, and I became one of the guys. And, over time, I came to be treated with grudging respect, and promotions followed. I held the room spellbound for 15 minutes at the last board meeting with my theory that Texas A&M joined the Southeastern Conference in order to up their chances for better bowls because the BCS favors the SEC. Later, when I submitted my ideas for improving coordination of teams in the oil fields, they thought it was *brilliant!* I'm one of them!"

Etheny nodded, somewhat impressed.

"Take my advice. Change your name. Ethney is too girly. What's your middle name?"

"Madison."

"Be Madison." Alex walked Ethney to the door and shook her hand. The meeting was over.

As the door closed behind her, Ethney's feelings about what she had just heard ranged from bewilderment to anger to depression.

She sold out. All of these women sold out. They can't even be who they are. I am an experienced, educated, qualified, capable woman. I don't want to be Madison, Ethney thought confidently and pushed the elevator button.

The elevator opened and she stepped inside. *What have I gotten myself into?*

Questions

1. If you were Ethney, how would you try to conduct yourself at the oil company? Would you act differently from your normal personality? Do you think your approach would be successful? Why?

2. What other strategies might Ethney adopt to work with the oil company men as an active member of the team? What are the pros and cons of each strategy?

3. What does it mean to be "true to yourself"? Is being true to yourself more important than achieving personal career success in a male-dominated company? Is it okay to *enable* the continuation of an "unhealthy" work environment for women? Why do you think the way you do about this?

ch13: On the Job Video Cases

On the Job: Mitchell Gold + Bob Williams: Managing Diversity

Questions

1. What are advantages and disadvantages of diversity at Mitchell Gold + Bob Williams?

2. Which belief is championed at MG+BW: ethnocentrism or ethnorelativism?

3. How might a commitment to diversity at MG+BW help managers with globalization?

pt4:   Integrative Case

Westport Innovations: A Look Under the Hood of the Clean Auto Revolution

Despite transportation's many benefits, the idea of a clean-burning automobile has been largely unimaginable due to the car engine's link to petroleum-based gas. But with the recent introduction of natural-gas engines, the car has begun one of the biggest evolutions in its history. Not since Ford introduced the Model T has an innovation promised to transform so thoroughly the automotive industry and the carbon footprint it leaves behind.

The greening of modern transportation can be traced in part to Dr. Philip Hill, a mechanical engineering professor at the University of British Columbia (UBC). In the 1980s, Hill became interested in clean energy and began a quest to improve the internal combustion engine. With an eye toward clean technology, Hill and a group of graduate students conducted experiments to see if diesel engines could run on natural gas, a clean-burning fuel that produces fewer emissions than petroleum-based gas. Hill wanted to preserve the diesel engine's astounding torque, but he envisioned a future where high-powered engines didn't leave behind smog or dirty exhaust. "Though the diesel engine was a wonderful machine, it really needed cleaning up as far as emissions goes," Hill says, thinking back on his early research. Hill's breakthrough came in the form of High-Pressure Direct Injection (HPDI), a new fuel injector system in which a tiny amount of diesel fuel sprays through one injector needle to ignite natural gas in another, which leads to combustion. Hill's patented duel-injector system was so ingenious that now virtually any diesel engine can be converted to run on natural gas—with no loss of horsepower.

Hill's invention might have stalled there if it hadn't found a use in the marketplace. But in 1995, UBC tapped businessman David R. Demers to commercialize Hill's HPDI system, and Westport Innovations Inc. was born. Since that time, HPDI technology has found its way under the hoods of trucking fleets, heavy machinery, and consumer vehicles around the world. From Kenworth and Peterbilt to Volvo and Ford, top automotive brands are adopting Westport natural-gas engines for cars, trucks, and industrial vehicles. According to founder and CEO Demers, Westport's emergence as the global leader in natural gas engines is owed to Hill's system. "The initial research conducted by Hill and his team at UBC was the genesis of our company's leadership in developing and commercializing low-emissions, environmentally friendly engine

systems," Demers says. "Westporters continue to draw inspiration from Dr. Hill's design and technical brilliance."

How did Westport Innovations grow from a start-up to a global leader of the green automotive revolution? With Hill's HPDI technology as a principal strategic asset, Demers resolved to bring natural-gas engines to various gasoline-based automotive sectors. In 2001, Westport and diesel engine giant Cummins Inc. formed a joint venture to introduce HPDI technology to the trucking market. With Hill's injector system and Cummins's heavy-duty engine blocks, Cummins Westport Inc. has succeeded in manufacturing over 34,000 natural gas engines for high-powered buses and semi-trailer trucks. The success of the venture led Demers to establish Westport's first business unit, Westport HD, which specializes in liquefied natural gas (LNG) systems for heavy-duty Class 8 trucks—eighteen-wheel road warriors manufactured by companies like Kenworth and Peterbilt. In 2007, Demers launched a joint venture with Italy's OMVL SpA and began producing light-duty engines for consumer vehicles, including the Volvo V70 station wagon and Ford F-250 pickup. Westport acquired OMVL in 2010, and a new light-duty division was established—Westport LD. The creation of Westport LD opened the door for Westport to build natural-gas engines for General Motors (GM). Most recently, in 2012, Westport and equipment manufacturer Caterpillar formed a partnership to make natural gas engines for mining vehicles, locomotives, and off-road machines. These changes to Westport's structure have positioned the company to dominate multiple markets for years to come.

Why are automakers and equipment manufacturers suddenly snatching up natural-gas engines? According to Hill, market forces are at work. "For a decade, emissions was a primary driving motive for alternative fuels for diesels," says Hill. "But economic factors are a huge driving force right now, particularly with the abundance of shale gas reserves being discovered, and the economic advantages of domestically produced fuels." As Hill notes, shale gas discoveries in the United States have boosted domestic supply, driving down methane prices to approximately half the cost of diesel. The change is leading businesses and industries to switch to natural gas. If the trend continues, the Westport brand could become as recognizable as Navistar, Ford, or Mopar.

As for Hill, the UBC professor and 2011 Manning Innovation Award recipient says helping transportation

http:
See It
Online
www.

go green has been humbling. "I feel grateful for being able to play a small part in the beginning of what's turned out to be a fascinating venture," he says. "It has been an eye-opener to me how people of wonderful talents can come together, trust each other, and work cooperatively, not worrying about who gets the credit, but just being focused on the job and getting it done."

Integrative Case Questions

1. What type of change and innovation is taking place at Westport Innovations Inc.? Which innovation strategies helped turn Hill's research ideas into successful new products?

2. Which structural design approach are managers using to organize and grow Westport Innovations Inc.?

3. In what way has Westport's organization structure followed its business strategy?

Sources: Based on University-Industry Liaison Office, "Dr. Phil Hill Wins Manning Award for Innovation," the University of British Columbia, November 2, 2011, www.uilo.ubc.ca/uilo/dr-phil-hill-wins-manning-award-innovation (accessed July 2, 2012); "2011 Encana Principal Award Winner Dr. Philip G. Hill: High-Pressure Direct Injection (HPDI) of Natural Gas into Diesel Engines," Ernest C. Manning Awards Foundation, Online Video, www.manningawards.ca/awards/winners/2011-principal-award-hill.shtml (accessed July 2, 2012); Daniel Ferry, "Westport & Caterpillar: Natural Gas is Taking Over the World," Motley Fool, June 5, 2012, http://beta.fool.com/catominor/2012/06/05/westport-caterpillar-natural-gas-taking-over-world/5399/ (accessed July 1, 2012); Westport Corporate Web site, "Westport History," www.westport.com/corporate/history (accessed July 1, 2012); "Could British Columbia Become the Next Cleantech Mecca?" *Cantech Letter,* August 2, 2011, www.cantechletter.com/2011/08/tech-sparks-could-bc-become-the-next-cleantech-mecca (accessed July 1, 2012); and Glenn Rogers, "Boone Pickens Is Right: Natural Gas Is the Future," *Seeking Alpha,* June 21, 2012, http://seekingalpha.com/article/675311-boone-pickens-is-right-natural-gas-is-the-future-at-least-for-now-buy-westport-innovations (accessed July 1, 2012).

Dynamics of Behavior in Organizations

Pavel Filatov/Alamy

Learning Outcomes

After studying this chapter, you should be able to:

1. Explain why understanding yourself is essential for being a good manager, and describe two methods for enhancing self-awareness.

2. Define attitudes and discuss the importance of work-related attitudes.

3. Describe the perception process and explain perceptual distortions.

4. Define major personality traits and describe how personality can influence workplace attitudes and behaviors.

5. Identify positive and negative emotions and describe how emotions affect behavior.

6. Define the four components of emotional intelligence and explain why they are important for today's managers.

7. Outline a step-by-step system for managing yourself and your time.

8. Explain the difference between challenge stress and threat stress.

9. Identify ways individuals and organizations can manage stress to improve employee health, satisfaction, and productivity.

Are You Self-Confident?

INSTRUCTIONS: Self-confidence is the foundation for many important behaviors of a new manager. To learn something about your level of self-confidence, answer the following questions. Please answer whether each item is Mostly True or Mostly False for you.

	Mostly True	Mostly False
1. I have lots of confidence in my decisions.	_____	_____
2. I would like to change some things about myself.	_____	_____
3. I am satisfied with my appearance and personality.	_____	_____
4. I would be nervous about meeting important people.	_____	_____
5. I come across as a positive person.	_____	_____
6. I sometimes think of myself as a failure.	_____	_____
7. I am able to do things as well as most people.	_____	_____
8. I find it difficult to believe nice things someone says about me.	_____	_____

SCORING AND INTERPRETATION: Many good things come from self-confidence. How self-confident are you? Give yourself one point for each *odd-numbered* item above marked as Mostly True and one point for each *even-numbered* item marked Mostly False. If you scored 3 or less, your self-confidence may not be very high. You might want to practice new behavior in problematic areas to develop greater confidence. A score of 6 or above suggests a high level of self-confidence and a solid foundation on which to begin your career as a new manager.

If a new manager lacks self-confidence, he or she is more likely to avoid difficult decisions and confrontations and may tend to overcontrol subordinates, which is called *micromanaging*. A lack of self-confidence also leads to less sharing of information and less time hiring and developing capable people. Self-confident managers, by contrast, can more easily delegate responsibility, take risks, give credit to others, confront problems, and assert themselves for the good of their team.

IBM's first female CEO, Virginia M. Rometty, says she learned an important lesson early in her career. Rometty was offered a big job but she felt that she didn't have enough experience. So, she told the recruiter she needed time to think it over. Later, Rometty's husband asked her, "Do you think a man would have ever answered that question that way?" The lesson that Rometty learned, she says, was that "you have to be very confident, even though you're so self-critical inside about what it is you may or may not know." Managers can accomplish significant results—and advance in their careers—only when they have the self-confidence to take risks and push beyond their comfort zones. Rometty spent 30 years at IBM, rising through the ranks until being named CEO in 2011.[1]

Naturally, when people take risks, they sometimes fail, but many people who have accomplished great outcomes give credit to their previous failures for driving them to succeed. Consider billionaire author J. K. Rowling, whose first *Harry Potter* book was rejected by 12 publishers before Bloomsbury bought it for the equivalent of $4,000. In her commencement speech to the 2008 graduating class at Harvard University, Rowling recounted how setbacks and rejection had not discouraged her, but simply made her stronger.[2] Unlike J. K. Rowling and Virginia Rometti, there are many talented individuals who experience one defeat or discouragement and never try again.[3]

1 INTRODUCTION

2 ENVIRONMENT

3 PLANNING

4 ORGANIZING

5 LEADING

6 CONTROLLING

http: See It Online www.

What makes the difference? Psychologists suggest it comes down to a characteristic called *self-efficacy*. It is one of the many ways in which individuals differ, along with their personality traits, attitudes, emotions, and values. **Self-efficacy** is an individual's strong belief that he or she can accomplish a specific task or outcome successfully.[4] Self-efficacy is one dimension of **self-confidence**, which refers to general assurance in one's own ideas, judgment, and capabilities. Personality traits, attitudes, emotions, and characteristics such as self-confidence and self-efficacy influence how people behave, including how they handle work situations and relate to others.

Understanding Yourself and Others

Having insight into why people behave the way they do is a part of good management. People bring their individual differences to work each day, and these differences influence how they interpret assignments, whether they like to be told what to do, how they handle challenges, and how they interact with others. By increasing their understanding of individual differences, as described throughout this chapter, managers can learn how to get the best out of each employee and more effectively lead people through workplace challenges. However, the first requirement for being a good manager is understanding oneself. Managers' characteristics and behavior can profoundly affect the workplace and influence employee motivation, morale, and job performance.

THE VALUE AND DIFFICULTY OF KNOWING YOURSELF

A survey of 75 members of the Stanford Graduate School of Business's Advisory Council revealed the nearly unanimous answer to a question about the most important capability for leaders to develop: self-awareness.[5] **Self-awareness** means being aware of the internal aspects of one's nature, such as personality traits, beliefs, emotions, attitudes, and perceptions, and appreciating how your patterns affect other people. Most management experts agree that a primary characteristic of effective leaders is that they know who they are and what they stand for.[6] When managers deeply understand themselves, they remain grounded and constant. People know what to expect from them. As one employee put it, ". . . it's like they have a stick down through the center of them that's rooted in the ground."[7]

Yet developing self-awareness is easier said than done. Consider Charlotte Beers, former chairwoman and CEO of Ogilvy & Mather Worldwide, who now conducts seminars for women leaders. When Beers first became a management supervisor, she considered herself to be a friendly, approachable, easygoing leader. She was shocked when a friend told her that one of her colleagues described her management style as "menacing." That comment was devastating to Beers because it was the exact opposite of the way she thought of herself.[8]

Many of us, like Charlotte Beers, might be surprised to find out what others honestly think about us. Most of us don't take the time to think about who we really are or the effect our patterns of thought and behavior have on others. To be a good manager, such self-reflection is essential.

> "Nothing's more helpful than finding out how others see you. . . . It's like doing consumer research."
>
> — CHARLOTTE BEERS, FORMER CHAIRWOMAN AND CEO OF OGILVY & MATHER WORLDWIDE

ENHANCING YOUR SELF-AWARENESS

There are a number of ways people can increase their understanding of themselves. Two important approaches to enhancing self-awareness, as shown in Exhibit 14.1, are soliciting feedback from others and using self-assessments.

EXHIBIT 14.1

Two Keys to Self-Awareness

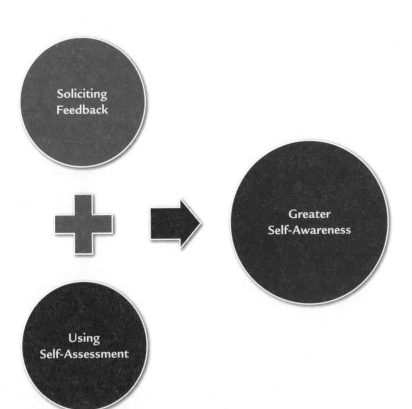

Soliciting Feedback

Just as we use a mirror in the mornings to shave or fix our hair, we can use other people as a mirror to see ourselves more clearly.[9] A manager might consider himself to be patient and understanding, but his employees may see that he is easily irritated and unsympathetic. Doug Rauch, retired president of Trader Joe's, recognized his micromanaging was hurting the company when a brave senior buyer pulled him aside and said "You're driving us crazy. You've got to back off." Rauch went to the team and admitted his problem, told them he was a "recovering controlaholic," and said he "needed them to give me regular feedback" so he didn't fall off the wagon.[10] When we go through life without feedback, we're like the balding man who sweeps thin strands of hair across his scalp and thinks no one notices. Seeking feedback to enhance self-awareness can improve performance and job satisfaction for both managers and employees.[11] We all have illusions about ourselves, so we need help from others to get a clear picture of who we are.

Self-Assessment

Another highly valuable way to increase self-awareness is *self-assessment*, which uses self-inquiry and reflection to gain insights into oneself from the results of scores on self-assessment instruments such as those throughout this text. By completing these assessments as honestly as possible, you can analyze your scores and increase your understanding of various aspects of yourself. Self-assessment also means regularly reflecting on our thoughts and feelings. Introspection—reflecting on our experiences, examining the effects of our actions and behavior, looking at the consequences for ourselves and others, and asking, "What can I learn?" is a valuable use of time that too many managers overlook. Some people keep a journal, meditate, or just sit quietly and think through their day.[12] Landon Donovan used both feedback and introspection to increase his understanding of himself and improve his life and relationships, as described in the following example.

Innovative Way

**Landon Donovan,
U.S. Soccer Player**

In the world of soccer, Landon Donovan holds the all-time record for both U.S. goals scored and assists. Currently playing with the Los Angeles Galaxy, Donovan's contract expires at the end of the 2013 season and he admits he hasn't decided if he will continue to play. What? Retiring at the height of his career?

"Why wouldn't I [consider retiring]?" he asks. "When I was younger, I . . . wanted to score all the time, I wanted to be famous. I wanted to be popular. I wanted to make money. I wanted to do all of those things, but at the end of it all, those things don't do a lot for you." Landon Donovan has been on a years-long journey of exploration—learning who he is and what matters to him. The journey began after he played so poorly in the 2006 World Cup that the United States was eliminated in the first round. Donovan went the entire calendar year without scoring a goal. Four years later, he became a national icon during the 2010 World Cup, and was named the most valuable player in Major League Soccer.

What happened? "I've been on a long journey for the last four years," Donovan said, revealing that he had been attending therapy sessions and spending long hours in introspective conversations with family and friends. Referring to himself at the time of the 2006 competition, Donovan said he was "someone completely unfamiliar." He went on to explain: "Most people don't want to spend time digging deep and finding out why you are the way you are. But I do want to, and I want to embrace it. I want to find the good pieces and leave the bad pieces behind."[13]

Whether Donovan will continue to play soccer or not, one thing seems certain: he will do whatever seems right for his life, without feeling that he has to prove anything to anyone else. Not everyone wants to engage in therapy, as Landon Donovan did, but forms of introspection and feedback can help each of us benefit by learning more about ourselves. When a manager understands him or herself, the manager is better able to understand and interact effectively with others.

Remember This

- Individual differences among people, including personality traits, attitudes, emotions, and characteristics such as self-confidence and self-efficacy influence how people relate to others and behave at work.
- **Self-efficacy** is an individual's strong belief that he or she can successfully accomplish a specific task or outcome.
- J. K. Rowling demonstrated self-efficacy with her belief that she could publish her first book about Harry Potter despite repeated rejections.
- Self-efficacy is related to **self-confidence**, which means general assurance in one's own ideas, judgment, and capabilities.

- Understanding oneself is essential for being a good manager, but self-awareness is not easy to achieve. **Self-awareness** means being conscious of the internal aspects of one's nature, such as personality traits, beliefs, emotions, attitudes, and perceptions, and appreciating how your patterns affect other people.
- Two valuable ways to enhance self-awareness are soliciting feedback and self-assessment, including introspection.
- Soccer player Landon Donovan spent many hours in introspective conversations with family and friends to increase his understanding of himself.

Attitudes

Most students have probably heard the expression that someone "has an attitude problem," which means some consistent quality about the person affects his or her behavior in a negative way. An employee with an attitude problem might be hard to get along with, might constantly gripe and cause problems, and might persistently resist new ideas. We all seem to know intuitively what an attitude is, but we do not consciously think about how strongly attitudes affect our behavior. Defined formally, an **attitude** is an evaluation—either positive or negative—that predisposes a person to act in a certain way. Understanding attitudes is important to managers because attitudes determine how people perceive the work environment, interact with others, and behave on the job. Emerging research is revealing the importance of positive attitudes to both individual and organizational success. For example, studies have found that the characteristic most common to top executives is an optimistic attitude. People rise to the top because they have the ability to see opportunities where others see problems and can instill in others a sense of hope and possibility for the future.[14] Managers strive to develop and reinforce positive attitudes among all employees, because happy, positive people are healthier, more effective, and more productive.[15]

HIGH-PERFORMANCE WORK ATTITUDES

The attitudes of most interest to managers are those related to work, especially attitudes that influence how well people perform on the job. Two attitudes that might relate to high performance are satisfaction with one's job and commitment to the organization.

Job Satisfaction

A positive attitude toward one's job is called **job satisfaction**, which reflects the degree to which a person finds fulfillment in his or her job. In general, people experience this attitude when their work matches their needs and interests, when working conditions and rewards (such as pay) are satisfactory, when they like their coworkers, and when they have positive relationships with supervisors. You can take the quiz in Exhibit 14.2 to better understand some of the factors that contribute to job satisfaction.

▶▶▶ Concept Connection

JetBlue founder David Neeleman illustrates the **positive attitude** and **optimism** that are common traits of successful leaders. Neeleman was shocked when JetBlue's board of directors removed him as CEO after the widely reported stranding of 131,000 passengers during an ice storm in February 2007. In 2008, Neeleman launched a new low-cost carrier, Azul (Portuguese for *blue*), in Brazil. "Every time a door closes, another one opens up," Neeleman says. So far, Neeleman's optimism is paying off. Azul had 2.2 million passengers in its first year, shattering the previous record for an airline start-up—held by JetBlue.

EXHIBIT 14.2 Rate Your Job Satisfaction

Instructions: Think of a job—either a current or previous job—that was important to you, and then answer the following questions with respect to how satisfied you were with that job. Please answer the six questions with a number 1–5 that reflects the extent of your satisfaction.

1 = Very dissatisfied	3 = Neutral	5 = Very satisfied
2 = Dissatisfied	4 = Satisfied	

	1	2	3	4	5
1. Overall, how satisfied are you with your job?	1	②	3	4	5
2. How satisfied are you with the opportunities to learn new things?	1	②	3	4	⑤
3. How satisfied are you with your boss?	1	2	③	④	5
4. How satisfied are you with the people in your work group?	1	2	③	4	5
5. How satisfied are you with the amount of pay you receive?	1	2	③	4	5
6. How satisfied are you with the advancement you are making in the organization?	①	2	3	4	5

Scoring and Interpretation: Add up your responses to the six questions to obtain your total score: _18_. The questions represent various aspects of satisfaction that an employee may experience on a job. If your score is 24 or above, you probably feel satisfied with the job. If your score is 12 or below, you probably do not feel satisfied. What is your level of performance in your job, and is your performance related to your level of satisfaction?

SOURCES: These questions were adapted from Daniel R. Denison, *Corporate Culture and Organizational Effectiveness* (New York: John Wiley, 1990); and John D. Cook et al., *The Experience of Work: A Compendium and Review of 249 Measures and Their Use* (San Diego, CA: Academic Press, 1981).

5

LEADING

Green Power

Make It Meaningful

The success of a sustainability program often depends on the ability of managers to engage employees. Canada's **LoyaltyOne** management team believes the secret to employee satisfaction lies in doing small things that transform employee thinking and behavior over time. LoyaltyOne's sustainability efforts, including regular town hall meetings, annual environmental fairs, contests, and giveaways, create a participatory culture of fun as the organization moves to fulfill its sustainability goals. Employees are encouraged to build initiatives based on their own concerns. LoyaltyOne provided people with take-home meters to measure their personal power usage, which had greater impact on individual social responsibility than

any lecture or position paper. Recognized in 2011 as one of the Best Employers in Canada, LoyaltyOne successfully injects challenge, empowerment, creativity, fun, and "making a difference" into the workplace sustainability experience of each employee.

Sources: "Environmental Sustainability and Top Talents," *Cool Choices*, August 4, 2011, www.coolchoicesnetwork.org/2011/08/04/ environmental-sustainability-and-top-talents/ (accessed August 1, 2012); and Derek Wong, "Top Talents Attracted to Socially Responsible Companies," *Environmental Leaders: Environmental and Energy Management News*, July 11, 2011, http://www.environmentalleader. com/2011/07/11/top-talents-attracted-to-socially-responsible-companies (accessed August 1, 2012).

Many managers believe job satisfaction is important because they think satisfied employees will do better work. In fact, research shows that the link between satisfaction and performance is generally small and is influenced by other factors.[16] For example, the importance of satisfaction varies according to the amount of control the employee has; an employee doing routine tasks may produce about the same output no matter how he or she feels about the job. Managers of today's knowledge workers, however, often rely on job satisfaction to keep motivation and enthusiasm high. They can't afford to lose talented, highly skilled employees. Regrettably, a 2009 survey by the Conference Board found that only 45 percent of U.S. employees say they are satisfied at work, the lowest satisfaction level in the survey's history.[17]

Managers create the environment that determines whether employees have positive or negative attitudes toward their jobs.[18] A related attitude is organizational commitment.

Concept Connection ◀◀◀

Just how has the recession affected **job satisfaction**? Polls conducted in the United States, such as the Gallup-Healthways Well-Being Index, have shown minor fluctuations in job satisfaction, but the degree of satisfaction generally ranges between 85 and 90 percent. Some economic pundits say that many U.S. employees, like this automobile assembly plant worker, are reluctant to complain and remain thankful for their jobs, given that the unemployment rate reached a peak of 10 percent in 2010 and has remained fairly high ever since.

Organizational Commitment

Organizational commitment refers to an employee's loyalty to and engagement with the organization. An employee with a high degree of organizational commitment is likely to say *we* when talking about the company. Such a person likes being a part of the organization and tries to contribute to its success. People who are committed to the organization practice **organizational citizenship**, which refers to the tendency of people to help one another and put in extra effort that goes beyond job requirements to contribute to the organization's success. An employee demonstrates organizational citizenship by being helpful to coworkers and customers, doing extra work when necessary, and looking for ways to improve products and procedures. Organizational citizenship is illustrated by an incident at the A. W. Chesterton Company, a manufacturer of mechanical seals and pumps. When two Chesterton pumps that supply water on Navy ship *USS John F. Kennedy* failed on a Saturday night just before the ship's scheduled departure, the team that produces the seals swung into action. Two members worked through the night to make new seals and deliver them to be installed before the ship left port.[19]

Results of a Towers Perrin study of more than 360,000 employees from 40 companies around the world indicate that companies with highly committed employees perform better.[20] Alarmingly, though, another recent survey suggests that commitment levels around the world are relatively low. Only one-fifth of the respondents were categorized as fully engaged; that is, reflecting a high level of commitment. In the United States, the percentage classified as fully engaged was 29 percent, compared to 54 percent in Mexico, 37 in percent in Brazil, and 36 percent in India. Countries where employees reflect similar or lower levels of commitment than the United States include Canada at 23 percent, Spain at 19 percent, Germany at 17 percent, China at 16 percent, the United Kingdom at 14 percent, France at 12 percent, and Japan at only 3 percent.[21]

Trust in management decisions and integrity is one important component of organizational commitment.[22] Unfortunately, in recent years, many employees in the United States have lost that trust. Only 20 percent of people surveyed by Leadership IQ, a leadership training organization, said they strongly trust their top management, with 36 percent reporting a moderate trust level, and 44 percent saying they either do not trust or strongly distrust their bosses.[23] In addition, the survey confirms that trust relates to organizational commitment. According to the study, about 32 percent of an employee's desire to stay with a company or leave depends on trust in management. Sadly, most of us don't need a poll to tell us that the level of trust in business and government leaders is dismal. From the Enron debacle to the scads of Wall Street managers and traders rewarded for unethical behavior with large bonuses, there are numerous reasons why people mistrust organizational leadership.

Managers can promote stronger organizational commitment by being honest and trustworthy in their business dealings, keeping employees informed, giving them a say in decisions, providing the necessary training and other resources that enable them to succeed, treating them fairly, and offering rewards that they value. "People in leadership positions simply have not done a good job of earning trust," says Doug Harward, president of Training Industry, Inc. "Employees have a right to expect that their managers are trustworthy and that they will create stable organizations. Too many of our leaders have violated that trust."[24]

CONFLICTS AMONG ATTITUDES

Sometimes a person may discover that his or her attitudes conflict with one another or are not reflected in behavior. For example, a person's high level of organizational commitment might conflict with a commitment to family members. If employees routinely work evenings and weekends, their long hours and dedication to the job might conflict with their belief that family ties are important. This conflict can create a state of **cognitive dissonance**, a psychological discomfort that occurs when individuals recognize inconsistencies in their own attitudes and behaviors.[25] The theory of cognitive dissonance, developed by social psychologist Leon Festinger in the 1950s, says that people want to behave in accordance with their attitudes and usually will take corrective action to alleviate the dissonance and achieve balance.

In the case of working overtime, people who can control their hours might restructure responsibilities so that they have time for both work and family. In contrast, those who are unable to restructure workloads might develop an unfavorable attitude toward the employer, reducing their organizational commitment. They might resolve their dissonance by saying they would like to spend more time with their kids, but their unreasonable employer demands that they work too many hours.

Remember This

- An **attitude** is a cognitive and affective evaluation that predisposes a person to act in a certain way.
- A positive attitude toward one's job is called **job satisfaction**.
- Surveys suggest that job satisfaction levels are at an all-time low.
- **Organizational commitment** refers to loyalty to and engagement with one's work organization.

- **Organizational citizenship** refers to work behavior that goes beyond job requirements and contributes as needed to the organization's success.
- A survey found that 32 percent of an employee's desire to stay with a company or leave depends on the employee's trust in management.
- **Cognitive dissonance** is a psychological discomfort that occurs when two attitudes or an attitude and a behavior conflict.

Perception

Another critical aspect of understanding behavior is perception. **Perception** is the cognitive process that people use to make sense out of the environment by selecting, organizing, and interpreting information from the environment. Because of individual differences in attitudes, personality, values, interests, and so forth, people often "see" the same thing in different ways. A class that is boring to one student might be fascinating to another. One student might perceive an assignment to be challenging and stimulating, whereas another might find it a silly waste of time.

We can think of perception as a step-by-step process, as shown in Exhibit 14.3. First, we observe information (sensory data) from the environment through our senses: taste, smell, hearing, sight, and touch. Next, our mind screens the data and will select only the items we will process further. Third, we organize the selected data into meaningful patterns for interpretation and response. Most differences in perception among people at work are related to how they select and organize sensory data. You can experience differences in perceptual organization by looking at the visuals in Exhibit 14.4. What do you see in part *a* of Exhibit 14.4? Most people see this as a dog, but others see only a series of unrelated ink blots. Some people will see the figure in part *b* as a beautiful young woman while others will see an old one. Now look at part *c*. How many blocks do you see—six or seven? Some people have to turn the figure upside down before they can see seven blocks. These visuals illustrate how complex perception is.

Of particular concern in the work environment are **perceptual distortions**, errors in perceptual judgment that arise from inaccuracies in any part of the perception process. One common perceptual error is **stereotyping**, the tendency to assign an individual to a group or broad category (e.g., female, black, elderly; or male, white, disabled) and then to attribute widely held generalizations about the group to the individual. Thus, someone

EXHIBIT 14.3

The Perception Process

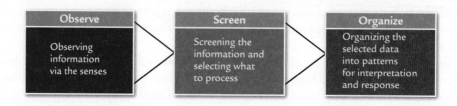

EXHIBIT 14.4   Perception—What Do You See?

a. Do you see the dog?   **b.** Old woman or young woman?   **c.** How many blocks?

meets a new colleague, sees he is in a wheelchair, assigns him to the category "physically disabled," and attributes to this colleague generalizations that she believes about people with disabilities, which may include a belief that he is less able than other coworkers. However, the person's inability to walk should not be seen as indicative of lesser abilities in other areas. Stereotyping prevents people from truly knowing those they classify in this way. In addition, negative stereotypes prevent talented people from advancing in an organization and fully contributing their talents to the organization's success.

The **halo effect** occurs when the perceiver develops an overall impression of a person or situation based on one characteristic, either favorable or unfavorable. In other words, a halo blinds the perceiver to other characteristics that should be used in generating a more complete assessment. The halo effect can play a significant role in performance appraisal, as we discussed in Chapter 12. For example, a person with an outstanding attendance record may be assessed as responsible, industrious, and highly productive; another person with less-than-average attendance may be assessed as a poor performer. Either assessment may be true, but it is the manager's job to be sure that the assessment is based on complete information about all job-related characteristics, not just his or her preferences for good attendance. How accurate is your perception? Answering the questions in Exhibit 14.5 will give you an idea of whether you allow perceptual distortions to cloud your judgment.

EXHIBIT 14.5   How Accurate Is Your Perception?

Instructions: Think about a job that you have held or a project that you have worked on in class or a volunteer organization. With respect to data or information coming to you, rate whether each statement below is Mostly True or Mostly False for you.

	Mostly True	Mostly False
1. I look for inconsistencies and seek explanations for them.	_____	_____
2. I generate multiple explanations for available information.	_____	_____
3. I check for omissions, distortions, or exaggerations in available information.	_____	_____
4. I make it a point to distinguish facts from opinions.	_____	_____
5. I stay conscious of my own style of approaching problems and how this might affect the way I process information.	_____	_____
6. I am well aware of my own biases and values that influence the way I see people.	_____	_____

Scoring and Interpretation: Your total score is the number of Mostly True answers to all six questions. A score of 5 or 6 suggests that you are conscious of and make attempts to remove distortions from your perception. A score of 3 or 4 indicates that you make solid effort, and a score of 1 or 2 suggests that you take perception for granted. Look at any individual items where you have marked Mostly False to get an idea of where you might have perceptual weaknesses. What can you do to improve your perception?

SOURCE: Adapted from Patricia M. Fandt, *Management Skills: Practice and Experience* (Minneapolis, MN: West Publishing, 1994), pp. 210–211.

- **Perception** is the cognitive process that people use to make sense out of the environment by selecting, organizing, and interpreting information.
- People often see the same thing in different ways.
- **Perceptual distortions** are errors in perceptual judgment that result from inaccuracies in any part of the perception process.

- **Stereotyping** refers to the tendency to assign an individual to a group or broad category and then attribute generalizations about the group to the individual.
- The **halo effect** occurs when a perceiver develops an overall impression of a person or situation based on one characteristic, either favorable or unfavorable.

Attributions

Among the assessments that people make as part of the perception process are attributions.[26] **Attributions** are judgments about what caused a person's behavior—something about the person or something about the situation. People make attributions as an attempt to understand why others behave as they do. An *internal attribution* says characteristics of the person led to the behavior. ("Susan missed the deadline because she's careless and lazy.") An *external attribution* says something about the situation caused the person's behavior. ("Susan missed the deadline because she couldn't get the information she needed in a timely manner.") Understanding attributions is important because attributions influence how a manager will handle a situation. In the case of the missed deadline, a manager who blames it on the employee's personality will view Susan as the problem and might give her unfavorable performance reviews and less attention and support. In contrast, a manager who blames the behavior on the situation might try to prevent such situations in the future, such as by improving horizontal communication mechanisms so people get the information they need in a timely way.

People often have biases that they apply when making attributions. When evaluating others, we tend to underestimate the influence of external factors and overestimate the influence of internal factors. This tendency is called the **fundamental attribution error**. Consider the case of someone being promoted to CEO. Employees, outsiders, and the media generally focus on the characteristics of the person that allowed him or her to achieve the promotion. In reality, however, the selection of that person might have been heavily influenced by external factors, such as business conditions creating a need for someone with a strong financial or marketing background at that particular time.

Another bias that distorts attributions involves attributions we make about our own behavior. People tend to overestimate the contribution of internal factors to their successes and overestimate the contribution of external factors to their failures. This tendency, called

- **Attributions** are judgments about what caused a person's behavior—either characteristics of the person or of the situation.
- An internal attribution says characteristics of the individual caused the person to behave in a certain way, whereas an external attribution places the cause on aspects of the situation.

- The **fundamental attribution error** is a tendency to underestimate the influence of external factors on another person's behavior and to overestimate the influence of internal factors.
- The **self-serving bias** is the tendency to overestimate the contribution of internal factors to one's successes and the contribution of external factors to one's failures.

the **self-serving bias**, means people give themselves too much credit for what they do well and give external forces too much blame when they fail. Thus, if your manager says you don't communicate well enough, and you think your manager doesn't listen well enough, the truth may actually lie somewhere in between.

Personality and Behavior

In recent years, many employers have shown heightened interest in matching people's personalities to the needs of the job and the organization. An individual's **personality** is the set of characteristics that underlie a relatively stable pattern of behavior in response to ideas, objects, or people in the environment. Interestingly, although 71 percent of HR professionals surveyed say person-
ality tests can be useful for predicting job-
related behavior and organizational fit, the use of such tests has actually declined in recent years. Only 18 percent reported that their companies use personality tests in hiring and promotion decisions. Part of the reason is that more companies are relying on social media to assess candidates based on what they have to say and show about themselves.[27]

PERSONALITY TRAITS

In common use, people think of personal-
ity in terms of traits, the fairly consistent characteristics that a person exhibits. Re-
searchers investigated whether any traits stand up to scientific scrutiny. Although investigators examined thousands of traits over the years, their findings fit into five general dimensions that describe personality. These dimensions, often called the "Big
Five" personality factors, are illustrated in Exhibit 14.6.[28] Each factor may contain a wide range of specific traits. The **Big Five personality factors** describe an individual's extroversion, agreeableness, conscientiousness, emotional stability, and openness to experience:

▶ ▶ ▶ **Concept Connection**

Marriott carefully screens candidates for critical customer service positions, such as this reservations and front desk clerk at a Cleveland, Ohio, Marriott Residence Inn. One important way that managers determine whether people have the "right stuff" is through **personality testing**. During the application process, candidates answer a series of questions about their beliefs, attitudes, work habits, and how they might handle situations, enabling Marriott to identify people with interests and motivations that are compatible with company values. As managers re-evaluate Marriott's mission and goals, the test evolves. Some fear that personality tests have too much influence, determining not just who gets hired, but who gets an interview in the first place.

1. *Extroversion.* The degree to which a person is outgoing, sociable, assertive, and comfortable with interpersonal relationships. INTROVERT IS OPPOSITE.

2. *Agreeableness.* The degree to which a person is able to get along with others by being good-natured, likable, cooperative, forgiving, understanding, and trusting.

3. *Conscientiousness.* The degree to which a person is focused on a few goals, thus behaving in ways that are responsible, dependable, persistent, and achievement-oriented.

4. *Emotional stability.* The degree to which a person is calm, enthusiastic, and self-
confident, rather than tense, depressed, moody, or insecure.

5. *Openness to experience.* The degree to which a person has a broad range of interests and is imaginative, creative, artistically sensitive, and willing to consider new ideas.

As illustrated in the exhibit, these factors represent a continuum. That is, a person may have a low, moderate, or high degree of each quality. Answer the questions in Exhibit 14.6 to see where you fall on the Big Five scale for each of the factors. Having a moderate-to-high

EXHIBIT 14.6 The Big Five Personality Factors

Each individual's collection of personality traits is different; it is what makes us unique. But, although each *collection* of traits varies, we all share many common traits. The following phrases describe various traits and behaviors. Rate how accurately each statement describes you, based on a scale of 1 to 5, with 1 being very inaccurate and 5 very accurate. Describe yourself as you are now, not as you wish to be. There are no right or wrong answers.

1 2 3 4 5
Very Inaccurate   Very Accurate

Extroversion
I am usually the life of the party.	1	2	3	4	5
I feel comfortable around people.	1	2	3	4	5
I am talkative.	1	2	3	4	5

Agreeableness
I am kind and sympathetic.	1	2	3	4	5
I have a good word for everyone.	1	2	3	4	5
I never insult people.	1	2	3	4	5

Conscientiousness
I am systematic and efficient.	1	2	3	4	5
I pay attention to details.	1	2	3	4	5
I am always prepared for class.	1	2	3	4	5

Neuroticism (Low Emotional Stability)
I often feel critical of myself.	1	2	3	4	5
I often envy others.	1	2	3	4	5
I am temperamental.	1	2	3	4	5

Openness to New Experiences
I am imaginative.	1	2	3	4	5
I prefer to vote for liberal political candidates.	1	2	3	4	5
I really like art.	1	2	3	4	5

Which are your most prominent traits? For fun and discussion, compare your responses with those of classmates.

degree of each of the Big Five personality factors is considered desirable for a wide range of employees, but this isn't always a key to success. For example, having an outgoing, sociable personality (extroversion) is considered desirable for managers, but many successful leaders, including Bill Gates, Hillary Clinton, Charles Schwab, and Steven Spielberg, are introverts, people who become drained by social encounters and need time alone to reflect and recharge their batteries. One study found that 4 in 10 top executives test out to be introverts.[29] Primerica Inc., the large insurance and financial products company based in Duluth, Georgia, succeeds by having both an introvert and an extrovert leading the company.

Innovative Way

Primerica Inc.

Primerica is considered one of the best-managed companies in the insurance and financial products industry. Part of that success may come from having both an introvert and an extrovert as CEO. No, it's not a split personality. Since 2000, Primerica has been led by co-CEOs Richard Williams and John Addison. The partnership works because the two have very different—yet complementary—personalities and skill sets.

"Rick would walk out of his way to not be in the spotlight," Addison says of his co-leader. "And if I see one on stage, I'll walk toward it." That statement was proven true at the company's biannual conference. As the two walked onstage to thunderous applause, Williams smiled and waved and quickly rushed to join his wife and investors in the front row of the audience, while Addison entertained and informed the 40,000-person crowd from the spotlight on stage.

Williams doesn't mind letting Addison have the spotlight; he prefers working behind the scenes and being the "analytical, financial, make-the-trains-run-on-time person." He's happy to let Addison be the outgoing, intuitive, motivational half of the duo. "I could never do John's job," Williams says, "and John wouldn't want to do my job."

Having co-CEOs isn't always successful for organizations, but it's been a magic formula for Primerica. Having two people with the right personalities who can both put their egos aside and work for the benefit of the organization has kept the company buzzing.[30]

Manager's Shoptalk

The Rise of the Introverted Manager

In today's world of open offices and collaborative work arrangements, being an introverted manager is a challenge, especially in the United States and other cultures that reward people for being outgoing and sociable. Yet experts are beginning to tout the virtues of the introverted manager, as well as offer tips for how introverts can make sure they don't get lost amid the gregarious leaders around them.

The Upside of Being an Introvert

Some benefits of an introverted personality include:

- **More cautious and deliberate.** Introverts tend to make more thoughtful decisions. They can become excited by opportunities and potential rewards, but they seem to have a keener awareness of risks than do extroverts, which can help to prevent train wrecks such as those that felled Bear Stearns and Lehmann Brothers.

- **Greater ability to listen and take suggestions.** We've all been charmed by charismatic, talkative people who are "working the room" while the introverts are huddled in a corner. Yet, when people are talking, they have a hard time listening. Adam M. Grant, who studies this subject, says introverted managers can be better bosses in dynamic and unpredictable environments because of their ability to listen, empathize with others, and empower employees to think for themselves.

- **More creative.** The most stunningly innovative people in many fields are introverts. Why? Because creativity thrives on solitude. "Without great solitude, no serious work is possible," Picasso said. Steve Jobs was the extrovert behind Apple, but the company would never have come into being without the hard work put in by introverted co-founder Steve Wozniak, who spent long hours working alone to create the company's first computer. "Most inventors and engineers I've met are like me . . . they live in their heads," Wozniak said.

Succeeding as an Introverted Manager

Introverted managers can get overlooked, particularly in large organizations. In addition, introverts are often, although not always, shy, which makes it harder for them to feel comfortable in the role of a manager.

- **Stretch your personality.** If you want something badly enough, you can stretch the limits of a naturally introverted personality. Consider Richard Branson, who says his flamboyant public persona, such as dressing up in silly costumes to publicize the Virgin Group, bears little resemblance to his innate personality. "I was a shy and retiring individual who couldn't make speeches and get out there," Branson says of himself prior to founding Virgin. "I had to train myself into becoming more of an extrovert" in order to promote the new company.

- **Let people know who you are.** Introverts like Richard Branson may be able to act more extroverted when they need to, but they will always need quiet time to reflect, process, and recharge their energies. This tendency to need time alone can be misinterpreted. Douglas Conant, who led Campbell Soup Company for years as a shy, introverted leader, says he'd give a little talk to new employees and colleagues right off the bat so they didn't think he was aloof and uninterested in them. "The more transparent I became, the more engaged people became," he says.

- **Mix with people, speak up, and get out there.** If you want to be a manager, and particularly if you want to advance to higher levels, there is no denying that you need to push yourself to get out there and connect with people both within and outside the organization. You will have to speak up at meetings, make presentations, and be more sociable and outgoing at conferences and other professional events. You can behave in more extroverted ways when you need to. Just remember to find alone time to recharge your batteries.

Sources: Based on Adam M. Grant, Francesca Gino, and David A. Hoffmann, "The Hidden Advantages of Quiet Bosses," *Harvard Business Review* (December 2010): 28; Susan Cain, "The Rise of the New Groupthink," *The New York Times*, January 15, 2012, SR-1; Bryan Walsh, "The Upside of Being an Introvert (and Why Extroverts Are Overrated)," *Time* (February 6, 2012): 40–45; "How Introverts Can Be Leaders—The Expert: Doug Conant," *Fortune* (May 21, 2012): 56; Joann S. Lublin, "Introverted Execs Find Ways to Shine," *The Wall Street Journal Asia*, April 18, 2011, 31; Jack and Suzy Welch, "The Welchway: Release Your Inner Extrovert," *BusinessWeek* (December 8, 2008): 92; and Richard Branson example from Ginka Toegel and Jean-Louis Barsoux, "How to Become a Better Leader," *MIT Sloan Management Review* (Spring 2012): 51–60.

5

LEADING

Rick Williams is glad to have someone else to do most of the outgoing, meet-and-greet, front-of-the-crowd activities associated with being a top executive. But what about introverted managers who don't have a co-leader? Every manager (including Williams) has to be able to put him or herself out there among the employees, customers, shareholders, and public to some extent. This chapter's Shoptalk describes some benefits of the introverted personality for managers, and offers some tips for introverted managers on how to shine despite their lack of natural gregariousness.

Although the quality of extroversion is not as significant as is often presumed, traits of agreeableness seem to be particularly important in today's collaborative organizations. Studies show that people who score high on agreeableness are more likely to get jobs and keep them than are less agreeable people.[31] Although there is also some evidence that people who are *overly* agreeable tend to be promoted less often, the days are over when a hard-driving manager can run roughshod over others to earn a promotion. Executive search firm Korn/Ferry International examined data from millions of manager profiles and found that the most successful executives today are team-oriented leaders who gather information and work collaboratively with many different people.[32] Recent research also suggests that traits of conscientiousness are more important than those of extroversion for effective leadership. A study at the Stanford Graduate School of Business found a link between how guilty people feel when they make serious mistakes and how well they perform as leaders. Guilt can be a positive emotion for a leader because it is associated with a heightened sense of responsibility to others, something that certainly could have benefited leaders involved in the recent mortgage and financial crisis![33]

ATTITUDES AND BEHAVIORS INFLUENCED BY PERSONALITY

An individual's personality influences his or her work-related attitudes and behaviors. As a new manager, you will have to manage people with a wide variety of personality characteristics. Four areas related to personality that are of particular interest to managers are locus of control, authoritarianism, Machiavellianism, and problem-solving styles.

Concept Connection ◀ ◀ ◀

Teach for America sends recent college graduates to teach for two years in low-income schools throughout the United States. What does Teach for America look for when reviewing approximately 45,000 applications for only about 5,000 positions? Founder and CEO Wendy Kopp says a high **internal locus of control** is at the top of her list. Those are the candidates who, when faced with a challenge, respond with optimism and resolve. Says Kopp, "They have the instinct to figure out what they can control and to own it, rather than to blame everyone else in the system."

Locus of Control

Individuals differ in terms of what they tend to accredit as the cause of their success or failure. **Locus of control** refers to how people perceive the cause of life events—whether they place the primary responsibility within themselves or on outside forces.[34] Some people believe that their own actions strongly influence what happens to them. They feel in control of their own fate. These individuals have a high *internal* locus of control. Other people believe that events in their lives occur because of chance, luck, or outside people and events. They feel more like pawns of their fate. These individuals have a high *external* locus of control.

Research on locus of control shows real differences in behavior across a wide range of settings. People with an internal locus of control are easier to motivate because they believe the rewards are the result of their behavior. They are better able to handle complex

MBI_Images/iStockphoto.com

EXHIBIT **14.7**   Measuring Locus of Control

Your Locus of Control

Instructions: For each of these 10 questions, indicate the extent to which you agree or disagree using the following scale:

1 = Strongly disagree	4 = Neither disagree nor agree	7 = Strongly agree
2 = Disagree	5 = Slightly agree	
3 = Slightly disagree	6 = Agree	

1. When I get what I want, it is usually because I worked hard for it.	1	2	3	4	5	6	(7)
2. When I make plans, I am almost certain to make them work.	1	2	3	4	(5)	6	7
3. I prefer games involving some luck over games requiring pure skill.	1	2	(3)	4	5	6	7
4. I can learn almost anything if I set my mind to it.	1	2	3	(4)	5	6	7
5. My major accomplishments are entirely due to my hard work and ability.	1	2	3	4	5	6	(7)
6. I usually don't set goals because I have a hard time following through on them.	1	2	3	4	(5)	6	7
7. Competition discourages excellence.	1	2	(3)	4	5	6	7
8. Often people get ahead just by being lucky.	1	2	(3)	4	5	6	7
9. On any sort of exam or competition, I like to know how well I do relative to everyone else.	1	2	3	4	(5)	6	7
10. It's pointless to keep working on something that's too difficult for me.	1	2	3	4	5	(6)	7

Scoring and Interpretation

To determine your score, reverse the values you selected for questions 3, 6, 7, 8, and 10 (1 = 7, 2 = 6, 3 = 5, 4 = 4, 5 = 3, 6 = 2, 7 = 1). For example, if you strongly disagree with the statement in question 3, you would have given it a value of 1. Change this value to a 7. Reverse the scores in a similar manner for questions 6, 7, 8, and 10. Now add the point values for all ten questions together. Your score _____

Researchers using this questionnaire in a study of college students found a mean of 51.8 for men and 52.2 for women, with a standard deviation of 6 for each. The higher your score on this questionnaire, the more you tend to believe that you are generally responsible for what happens to you; in other words, higher scores are associated with internal locus of control. Low scores are associated with external locus of control. Scoring low indicates that you tend to believe that forces beyond your control, such as powerful other people, fate, or chance, are responsible for what happens to you.

SOURCES: Adapted from J. M. Burger, *Personality: Theory and Research* (Belmont, CA: Wadsworth, 1986), pp. 400–401, cited in D. Hellriegel, J. W. Slocum, Jr., and R. W. Woodman, *Organizational Behavior,* 6th ed. (St. Paul, MN: West, 1992), pp. 97–100. Original source: D. L. Paulhus, "Sphere-Specific Measures of Perceived Control," *Journal of Personality and Social Psychology,* 44, no. 6 (1983): 1253–1265.

information and problem solving, are more achievement-oriented, but are also more independent and therefore more difficult to manage. By contrast, people with an external locus of control are harder to motivate, less involved in their jobs, and more likely to blame others when faced with a poor performance evaluation, but they are also more compliant and conforming and, therefore, easier to manage.[35]

Do you believe luck plays an important role in your life, or do you feel that you control your own fate? To find out more about your locus of control, read the instructions and complete the questionnaire in Exhibit 14.7.

Authoritarianism

Authoritarianism is the belief that power and status differences should exist within the organization.[36] Individuals high in authoritarianism tend to be concerned with power and toughness, obey recognized authority above them, stick to conventional values, critically judge others, and oppose the use of subjective feelings. The degree to which managers possess authoritarianism will influence how they wield and share power. The degree to which employees possess authoritarianism will influence how they react to their managers. If a manager and employees differ in their degree of authoritarianism, the manager may have difficulty leading effectively. The trend toward empowerment and shifts in expectations among younger employees for more equitable relationships contribute to a decline in strict authoritarianism in many organizations.

5

LEADING

Machiavellianism

Another personality dimension that is helpful in understanding work behavior is **Machiavellianism**, which is characterized by the acquisition of power and the manipulation of other people for purely personal gain. Machiavellianism is named after Niccolò Machiavelli, a sixteenth-century author who wrote *The Prince*, a book for noblemen of the day on how to acquire and use power.[37] Psychologists developed instruments to measure a person's Machiavellianism (Mach) orientation.[38] Research shows that high Machs are predisposed to being pragmatic, capable of lying to achieve personal goals, more likely to win in win-lose situations, and more likely to persuade than be persuaded.[39]

Different situations may require people who demonstrate one or the other type of behavior. In loosely structured situations, high Machs actively take control, while low Machs accept the direction given by others. Low Machs thrive in highly structured situations, while high Machs perform in a detached, disinterested way. High Machs are particularly good in jobs that require bargaining skills or that involve substantial rewards for winning.[40]

Remember This

- **Personality** is the set of characteristics that underlie a relatively stable pattern of behavior in response to ideas, objects, or people in the environment.
- Primerica Inc., a large insurance and financial products company, is led by co-CEOs who have different, yet complementary, personalities.
- The **Big Five personality factors** are dimensions that describe an individual's extroversion, agreeableness, conscientiousness, emotional stability, and openness to experience.
- **Locus of control** defines whether an individual places the primary responsibility for his successes and failures within himself or on outside forces.
- **Authoritarianism** is the belief that power and status differences should exist within an organization.
- A person high in authoritarianism is typically concerned with power and status, obeys established authority, and sticks to conventional values.
- **Machiavellianism** refers to a tendency to direct one's behavior toward the acquisition of power and the manipulation of other people for personal gain.

PROBLEM-SOLVING STYLES AND THE MYERS-BRIGGS TYPE INDICATOR

Managers also need to realize that individuals solve problems and make decisions in different ways. One approach to understanding problem-solving styles grew out of the work of psychologist Carl Jung. Jung believed differences resulted from our preferences in how we go about gathering and evaluating information.[41] According to Jung, gathering information and evaluating information are separate activities. People gather information either by *sensation* or *intuition*, but not by both simultaneously. Sensation-type people would rather work with known facts and hard data and prefer routine and order in gathering information. Intuitive-type people would rather look for possibilities than work with facts and prefer solving new problems and using abstract concepts.

Evaluating information involves making judgments about the information a person has gathered. People evaluate information by *thinking* or *feeling*. These represent the extremes in orientation. Thinking-type individuals base their judgments on impersonal

> "Each of us is meant to have a character all our own, to be what no other can exactly be, and do what no other can exactly do."
>
> — WILLIAM ELLERY CHANNING (1780–1842), AMERICAN WRITER AND CLERGYMAN

EXHIBIT 14.8 Four Problem-Solving Styles

Personal Style	Action Tendencies	Likely Occupations
Sensation-Thinking	• Emphasizes details, facts, certainty • Is a decisive, applied thinker • Focuses on short-term, realistic goals • Develops rules and regulations for judging performance	• Accounting • Production • Computer programming • Market research • Engineering
Intuitive-Thinking	• Prefers dealing with theoretical or technical problems • Is a creative, progressive, perceptive thinker • Focuses on possibilities using impersonal analysis • Is able to consider a number of options and problems simultaneously	• Systems design • Systems analysis • Law • Middle/top management • Teaching business, economics
Sensation-Feeling	• Shows concern for current, real-life human problems • Is pragmatic, analytical, methodical, and conscientious • Emphasizes detailed facts about people rather than tasks • Focuses on structuring organizations for the benefit of people	• Directing supervisor • Counseling • Negotiating • Selling • Interviewing
Intuitive-Feeling	• Avoids specifics • Is charismatic, participative, people oriented, and helpful • Focuses on general views, broad themes, and feelings • Decentralizes decision making, develops few rules and regulations	• Public relations • Advertising • Human Resources • Politics • Customer service

analysis, using reason and logic rather than personal values or emotional aspects of the situation. Feeling-type individuals base their judgments more on personal feelings such as harmony and tend to make decisions that result in approval from others.

According to Jung, only one of the four functions—sensation, intuition, thinking, or feeling—is dominant in an individual. However, the dominant function usually is backed up by one of the functions from the other set of paired opposites. Exhibit 14.8 shows the four problem-solving styles that result from these matchups, as well as occupations that people with each style tend to prefer.

Two additional sets of paired opposites not directly related to problem solving are *introversion-extroversion* and *judging-perceiving*. Introverts gain energy by focusing on personal thoughts and feelings, whereas extroverts gain energy from being around others and interacting with others. On the judging versus perceiving dimension, people with a judging preference like certainty and closure and tend to make decisions quickly based on available data. Perceiving people, on the other hand, enjoy ambiguity, dislike deadlines, and may change their minds several times as they gather large amounts of data and information to make decisions.

A widely used test that measures how people differ on all four of Jung's sets of paired opposites is the **Myers-Briggs Type Indicator (MBTI)** assessment. The MBTI™ assessment measures a person's preferences for introversion versus extroversion, sensation versus intuition, thinking versus feeling, and judging versus perceiving. The various combinations of these four preferences result in 16 unique personality types.

Each of the 16 different personality types can have positive and negative consequences for behavior. Based on the limited research that has been done, the two preferences that seem to be most strongly associated with effective management in a variety of organizations and industries are thinking and judging.[42] However, people with other preferences can also be good managers. One advantage of understanding your natural preferences is to maximize your innate strengths and abilities and minimize your weaknesses. John Bearden became a better manager because of what he learned from the MBTI assessment, as described in the following example.

Take a Moment

Go to the Experiential Exercise on pages 482–484 that pertains to evaluating your personality type.

5

LEADING

When John Bearden sold his real estate business in Canada, he decided to return to his hometown of Nashville, Tennessee, to reflect on his career and decide what was next. During this time of introspection, Bearden realized that he had often gotten to the finish line "dragging people with him." He recalled when a consultant had told him, *"John, you have so much potential, but you're running over everybody . . . you turn people off."* Bearden decided that now was the time to learn what made him tick.

Before restarting his career, Bearden completed the MBTI assessment and learned that he had a "field marshal" (ENTJ) leadership style (see the chart at the end of the Experiential Exercise on pages 483–484 that describes the 16 MBTI types in detail). Individuals with this style are dynamic and self-confident and display essential leadership qualities of vision, drive, and decisiveness. However, they can also be impatient, insensitive, overbearing, and hasty in their judgments. Bearden said the MBTI was a "quantum leap" in his understanding of his strengths and weaknesses. When he took the job as chief executive of GMAC Home Services, he began consciously refining his leadership style, making a determined effort to give more consideration to hard data and listen more carefully to colleagues' opinions. Bearden put himself to the test at a national convention. "In the past, I would have gotten very much involved, interjecting my own position very early on and probably biasing the process," he said. "But here I found myself quite content to allow their positions to be articulated and argued with creative tension. All I did was sit and absorb. It was a very satisfying process."[43]

Some organizations use the MBTI assessment to help put people in the right jobs—where they will be happiest and make their best contribution to the organization. In one survey, 89 of the *Fortune* 100 companies reported that they have used the test in hiring and promotion decisions.[44] Other companies have used the MBTI to help employees better understand themselves and improve their interactions with others. For example, the MBTI assessment was a central feature of a program at Hallmark Cards designed to give managers greater self-awareness and insight into how their patterns of thought and behavior affect employees.[45]

Remember This

- Four problem-solving styles are sensation-thinking, intuitive-thinking, sensation-feeling, and intuitive-feeling.
- The **Myers-Briggs Type Indicator (MBTI)** assessment measures a person's preferences for introversion versus extroversion, sensation versus intuition, thinking versus feeling, and judging versus perceiving.
- Hallmark Cards used the MBTI assessment to increase managers' self-awareness and enable them to understand how their patterns of behavior affect others.

Emotions

Managers might like to think people come to work and conduct their jobs in a logical and rational manner, leaving their emotions at home or tucked safely in the car until it's time to go home for the day. Yet people cannot be separated from their emotions, and organizations suffer when managers fail to pay attention to how employees' emotions affect productivity and the work environment.[46] Managers can increase their effectiveness by understanding positive and negative emotions and developing emotional intelligence.

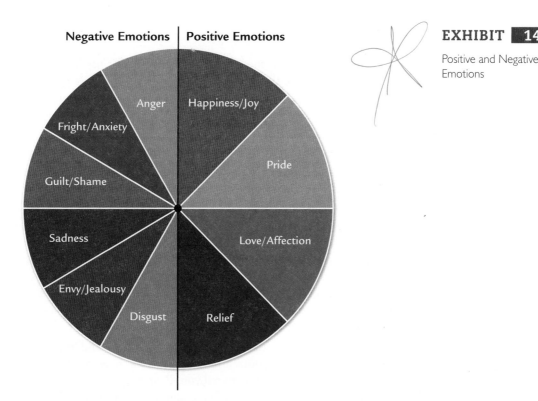

EXHIBIT 14.9

Positive and Negative
Emotions

POSITIVE AND NEGATIVE EMOTIONS

Although the term is somewhat difficult to define in a precise way, an **emotion** can be thought of as a mental state that arises spontaneously within a person based on interaction with the environment rather than through conscious effort and is often accompanied by physiological changes or sensations. People can experience a wide range of emotions at work, such as happiness, anger, fear, or relief, and these affect their workplace attitudes and behaviors. Researchers have been attempting to understand emotions for thousands of years, and scientific debate continues about how to categorize emotions.[47] One model that is useful for managers, shown in Exhibit 14.9, distinguishes the major positive and negative emotions. Negative emotions are sparked when a person becomes frustrated in trying to achieve his or her goals, while positive emotions are triggered when people are on track toward achieving goals.

Thus, emotions can be understood as being determined by whether people are getting their needs and goals met. An employee who fails to get a pay raise or is reprimanded by a supervisor would likely experience negative emotions such as sadness, anger, or anxiety, whereas a person who gets a promotion would experience feelings of pride and happiness. Managers can influence whether people experience primarily positive or negative emotions at work. For one thing, the emotional state of the manager influences the entire team or department. Most of us realize that we can "catch" emotions from others. If we're around someone who is happy and enthusiastic, the positive emotions rub off on us. On the other hand, someone who is sad and angry can bring us down. This *emotional contagion*[48] means that managers who express positive emotions such as happiness, enthusiasm, and appreciation trigger positive emotions in employees. Research suggests that nearly all human beings are subject to emotional contagion and will automatically and unconsciously start feeling and displaying the same emotions as those around them.[49]

Good managers pay attention to people's emotions, because positive emotions are typically linked to higher productivity and greater effectiveness. A *Gallup Management Journal* survey found that managers, especially front line supervisors, have a lot to do with whether employees have positive or negative emotions associated with their work lives.[50]

5

LEADING

EMOTIONAL INTELLIGENCE

In recent years, research in the area of *emotional intelligence* has shown that managers who are in touch with their own feelings and the feelings of others can enhance employee and organizational performance. Emotional intelligence includes four basic components:[51]

- *Self-awareness.* The basis for all the other components; being aware of what you are feeling. People who are in touch with their feelings are better able to guide their own lives and actions. A high degree of self-awareness means you can accurately assess your own strengths and limitations and have a healthy sense of self-confidence.

- *Self-management.* The ability to control disruptive or harmful emotions and balance one's moods so that worry, anxiety, fear, or anger do not cloud thinking and get in the way of what needs to be done. People who are skilled at self-management remain optimistic and hopeful despite setbacks and obstacles. This ability is crucial for pursuing long-term goals. MetLife found that applicants who failed the regular sales aptitude test but scored high on optimism made 21 percent more sales in their first year and 57 percent more in their second year than those who passed the sales test but scored high on pessimism.[52]

- *Social awareness.* The ability to understand others and practice *empathy*, which means being able to put yourself in someone else's shoes, to recognize what others are feeling without them needing to tell you. People with social awareness are capable of understanding divergent points of view and interacting effectively with many different types of people.

- *Relationship management.* The ability to connect to others, build positive relationships, respond to the emotions of others, and influence others. People with relationship management skills know how to listen and communicate clearly, and they treat others with compassion and respect.

Studies show a positive relationship between job performance and a high emotional intelligence quotient (EQ) in a variety of jobs. Numerous organizations, including the U.S. Air Force and Canada Life, use EQ tests to measure things such as self-awareness, ability to empathize, and capacity to build positive relationships.[53] Altera Corporation uses "empathy coaches" to help its salespeople develop greater social awareness and see things from their customers' point of view.[54] A high EQ seems to be particularly important for jobs such as sales that require a high degree of social interaction. It is also critical for managers, who are responsible for influencing others and building positive attitudes and relationships in the organization.

Managers with low emotional intelligence can undermine employee morale and harm the organization. Consider that 44 percent of people surveyed by the Employment Law Alliance say they have worked for a manager that they considered an abusive bully.[55] Growing concerns over workplace bullying have prompted enlightened companies to take action that helps managers develop greater emotional intelligence, such as by honing their self-awareness and empathy and enhancing their self-management skills. One form of bullying is sexual harassment, as discussed in previous chapters. Sexual harassment or abuse is a deadly reflection of low emotional intelligence that can destroy careers, as well as the lives of the victims. Even in countries where people often turn a blind or accepting eye to powerful politicians and businessmen engaging in extramarital dalliances, sexual abuse isn't tolerated. Former International Monetary Fund (IMF) leader Dominique Strauss-Kahn was likely on his way to the French presidency before he was arrested in New York and charged with the sexual assault of a hotel housekeeper, with further allegations from women in France later coming to light.[56]

Take a Moment

Complete the New Manager Self-Test to assess your level of positive emotional expression. You might also want to refer back to the questionnaire related to self-confidence at the beginning of this chapter. Self-confidence strongly influences a new manager's emotional intelligence.

HOT TOPIC

New Manager Self-Test

Expressed Emotions

Instructions: Think about the feelings you express to others during your interactions with people during a typical week of school or work activities. Rate each item below based on whether you typically express that emotion often, sometimes, or rarely during a typical week. There are no right or wrong answers, so answer honestly to receive accurate feedback.

	Often	Sometimes	Rarely
1. Enthusiastic			
2. Interested			
3. Inspired			
4. Energetic			
5. Proud			
6. Attentive			
7. Grateful			
8. Amused			
9. Hopeful			
10. Caring			

Scoring and Interpretation: Sum items 1–10, giving 3 points for each Often, 2 points for each Sometimes, and 1 point for each Rarely. Total = _____. In fulfilling their roles, managers are often required to display positive emotions in their relationships with employees and customers. Sometimes a manager may display an emotion without really feeling it, called *surface acting*. *Deep acting* is when managers generate the actual emotion that needs to be displayed as part of the job. If you have a high score, it probably means you display authentic positive emotion. If you have a lower score, can you display positive emotions when needed by pretending to feel the emotion or by generating the appropriate emotion from within? Frequent surface acting is related to stress, and frequent deep acting is related

to the perceived quality of emotion expression and with job satisfaction. Compare your score with others in your class. Can you express emotions on demand? Do you think emotional expression is related to the self-management aspect of emotional intelligence?

Sources: Based on David Watson, Lee Anna Clark, and Auke Tellegen, "Development and Validation of Brief Measures of Positive and Negative Affect: The PANAS Scales," *Journal of Personality and Social Psychology* 54, no. 6 (1988): 1063–1070; Celeste M. Brotheridge and Raymond T. Lee, "Development and Validation of the Emotional Labour Scale," *Journal of Occupational and Organizational Psychology* 76 (2003): 365–379; and Alicia A. Grandey, "When 'The Show Must Go On': Surface Acting and Deep Acting as Determinants of Emotional Exhaustion and Peer-Rated Service Delivery," *Academy of Management Journal* 46, no. 1 (2003): 86–96.

5

LEADING

Remember This

- An **emotion** is a mental state that arises spontaneously rather than through conscious effort and is often accompanied by physiological changes.
- People experience both positive emotions of happiness, pride, love, and relief, as well as negative emotions of anger, anxiety, sadness, envy, and disgust.
- The concept of *emotional contagion* suggests that people can catch emotions from those around them, so good managers try to express positive emotions at work.
- Emotional intelligence includes the components of self-awareness, self-management, social awareness, and relationship management.

Managing Yourself

Now let's turn to another topic every manager needs to know—time management. We introduced the topic of time management in Chapter 1, and that chapter's Manager's Shoptalk outlined some specific time management tips. In this chapter, we talk about a broader self-management system that people can apply to gain control over their hectic schedules. **Self-management** is the ability to engage in self-regulating thoughts and behavior to accomplish all your tasks and handle difficult or challenging situations. Yet all of us have patterns of habit and behavior that may make it hard to manage ourselves toward more efficient behavior. Even the best managers can sometimes find themselves feeling overwhelmed. Many people get stuck and can't take action when they have too much on their minds or too many competing demands on their time. One approach for "getting a grip" when you have too much to do and can't seem to get any of it done is to apply a bottom-up strategy that starts by analyzing the details of what you are actually doing right now, and then building a system to manage all your activities.

BASIC PRINCIPLES FOR SELF-MANAGEMENT

Three basic principles define how to manage your many big and small commitments effectively so that you can get them accomplished:[57]

- *Clarity of mind.* The first principle is that, if you're carrying too much around in your head, your mind can't be clear. If your mind isn't clear, you can't focus. If you can't focus, you can't get anything done. Thus, anything you consider unfinished needs to be placed in some kind of trusted system *outside* of your head.
- *Clarity of objectives.* Second, you have to be clear about exactly what you need to do and decide the steps to take toward accomplishing it.
- *An organized system.* Third, once you've decided the actions you need to take, you need to keep reminders in a well-organized system.

By building a self-management approach based on these three principles—clarity of mind, clarity of objectives, and a system of organized reminders—you can get unstuck and make measurable progress toward achieving all the things you need to do.

A STEP-BY-STEP GUIDE FOR MANAGING YOUR TIME

Many people don't realize they waste at least an hour of a typical workday simply because they are unorganized.[58] You can gain better control of your life and the many things you have to do by mastering some simple but powerful steps.[59] Exhibit 14.10 summarizes these five steps, and each is described below.

1. **Empty your head.** In order to clear your mind, you first have to see all the many things weighing on it. The first step, therefore, is to write down on separate scraps of paper all the activities, duties, tasks, or commitments that are demanding part of your attention. The idea is to get everything out of your head and down on paper.

   To organize all this "stuff," combine similar items into various "buckets." There are numerous tools that can serve as your buckets, including computer and wireless devices for electronic note-taking; physical in-baskets for holding mail, memos, and phone slips; notebooks or legal pads for writing down things to do; or digital recorders for recording things you need to remember. Keep a notepad or handheld device with you so that you can add new projects or commitments at any time and get them out of your head. Remember to keep the number of buckets to a minimum; otherwise, you'll still feel scattered and overwhelmed.

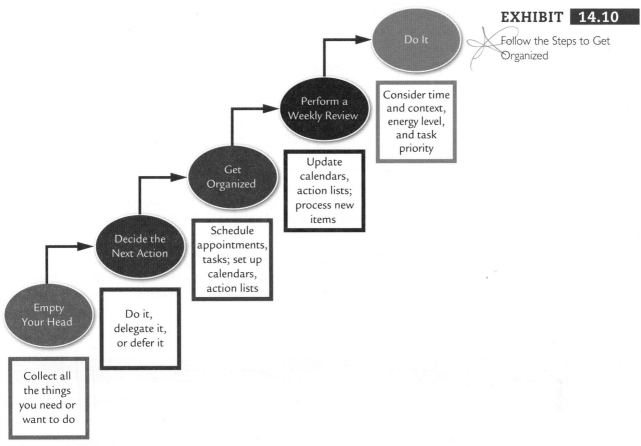

EXHIBIT 14.10

Follow the Steps to Get Organized

SOURCE: Based on David Allen, *Getting Things Done: The Art of Stress-Free Productivity* (New York: Viking, 2001).

2. **Decide the next action.** For each item in your buckets, decide the real, specific, physical action that you need to take next. If you have a team meeting on Friday to discuss a class project, your next action might be to draft thoughts and ideas that you want to share with the team. Then, you have three options:

   - *Do it.* Follow the two-minute rule: If something can be done in less than two minutes, do it now. In some cases, you'll find items in your bucket that require no action and are of no importance. These should be trashed immediately. For items that are of potential use in the future, file in a system for reference material.

   - *Delegate it.* Ask yourself if you're the right person to handle a task. If something can be done as well by someone else, delegate it.

   - *Defer it.* If something will take longer than two minutes but cannot be delegated to someone else, you'll have to defer it. These things go into an incubation or tickler file, such as an organized "To Do" list, which you will review regularly and perhaps schedule a specific time for their completion.

3. **Get organized.** The third step is to organize all the items you've deferred. At this stage, schedule any appointments you identified as "next actions" and record these on whatever calendar you check daily. Also record on your calendar any items that have to be done on a specific day or time. You can assign yourself a specific date in the future to perform certain tasks that are in your incubation or tickler file.

   For all other items, keep a list of "Next Actions," either on paper on in a portable device that you will have with you at all times so that you can take action when and where you have the time to do so. This can be either on a single list or in categories.

5

LEADING

4. **Perform a weekly review.** Once a week, review your complete Next Actions list and your calendar for the coming week. Scan the entire list of outstanding projects and actions needed so that you can make efficient choices about using your time. This weekly review is critical because it keeps your mind from taking back the job of trying to hold and remember everything. The weekly review is also the time to "put your house in order" by collecting, processing, and organizing new items. Thus, during the weekly review, you'll take four actions: (1) collect and process all the new stuff; (2) review your entire system; (3) revise your lists; and (4) get clear, up to date, and complete about what needs to be done next.

5. **Now do it.** Once you have collected, processed, organized, and reviewed your current commitments, you'll have a better sense of what needs to be done, enabling you to make better choices about how to use your time. Your intuition and your understanding of yourself can help you in deciding what to do when.

This approach to self-management can help you get a handle on all the various things you have to do and approach them in a systematic way with a clear mind. If you follow it, you'll find yourself getting more accomplished with less stress—and with fewer things falling between the cracks. Refer to the time management tips in the Chapter 1 Shoptalk. You can pick and choose the techniques that work for you and combine them with the overall self-management approach.

Remember This

- **Self-management** is the ability to engage in self-regulating thoughts and behavior to accomplish all your tasks and handle difficult or challenging situations.
- Three basic principles for self-management are clarity of mind, clarity of objectives, and an organized system.

- One self-management system is based on five steps: Empty your head; decide the next action; get organized; perform a weekly review; then do what needs to be done.

Stress and Stress Management

No matter how organized you are, as a manager you will likely experience stress—your own and that of others—at some time in your career. Formally defined, **stress** is an individual's physiological and emotional response to external stimuli that place physical or psychological demands on the individual and create uncertainty and lack of personal control when important outcomes are at stake.[60] These stimuli, called *stressors*, produce some combination of frustration (the inability to achieve a goal, such as the inability to meet a deadline because of inadequate resources) and anxiety (such as the fear of being disciplined for not meeting deadlines).

In recent years, financial worries and massive job cuts have upped the stress level in almost every organization. Managers have found themselves dealing with a workforce that is frightened, nervous, and unsure about the future.[61] The number of employees who are irritable, insulting, or discourteous has grown as people cope with the stress of job uncertainty, overwhelming debt, tighter access to credit, and increased workloads due to downsizing. In a recent survey, nearly half of U.S. workers responding reported experiencing yelling and verbal abuse on the job, and another study found that 2 to 3 percent of people admit to pushing, slapping, or hitting someone at work.[62] In addition, the stress caused by economic worries is contributing to health problems such as ulcers, severe depression, and heart attacks.[63]

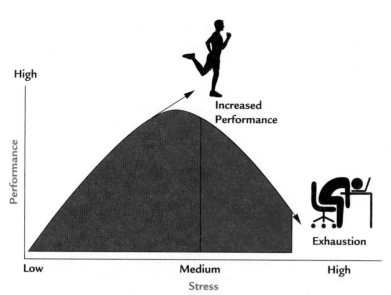

EXHIBIT 14.11

The Yerkes-Dodson Stress Curve

SOURCE: Based on an exhibit by Emeran A. Mayer, M.D., UCLA Center for Neurobiology of Stress.

CHALLENGE STRESS AND THREAT STRESS

Stress isn't always negative. Without a certain amount of stress, we would be complacent and accomplish little. Psychologists have long noted this "dual face of stress," and make a distinction between *challenge stress* and *threat stress*. Challenge stress fires you up, whereas threat stress burns you out.[64] As originally proposed by two Harvard researchers, Robert Yerkes and John Dodson, and illustrated in Exhibit 14.11, stress up to a certain point challenges you and increases your focus, alertness, efficiency, and productivity.[65] After that point, however, things go downhill quickly and stress compromises your job performance, your relationships, and even your health. Another interesting finding is that too much stress inhibits learning and flexibility.[66]

The point at which things tip over from challenge stress (good) to threat stress (bad) may vary with each individual. Most of us can easily tell when we've gone over the top of the stress curve. We stop feeling productive; experience emotions of anxiety, fear, depression, or anger; are easily irritated; and may have trouble making decisions. Many people also have physical symptoms, such as headaches, insomnia, or stomach problems. In the United States, an estimated 1 million people each day don't show up for work because of stress.[67] Similarly, a survey in the United Kingdom found that 68 percent of nonmanual workers and 42 percent of manual workers reported missing work because of stress-related illness.[68] Just as big a problem for organizations as absenteeism is *presenteeism*, which refers to people who go to work but are too stressed and distracted to be productive.[69]

TYPE A AND TYPE B BEHAVIOR

Researchers observed that some people seem to be more vulnerable than others to the ill effects of stress. From studies of stress-related heart disease, they categorized people as having behavior patterns called Type A and Type B.[70] The **Type A behavior** pattern includes extreme competitiveness, impatience, aggressiveness, and devotion to work. David Sacks, founder and CEO of Yammer, for example, says he is "in a perpetual state of frustration over the product. I want it to be perfect and it's not." He adds, "I think about work constantly, I wish I had an On/Off switch."[71] In contrast, people with a **Type B behavior** pattern exhibit less of these behaviors. They consequently experience less conflict with other people and a more balanced, relaxed lifestyle. Type A people tend to experience more stress-related illness than Type B people.

Most Type A individuals, like David Sacks, are high-energy people and may seek positions of power and responsibility. By pacing themselves and learning control and intelligent use of their natural high-energy tendencies, Type A individuals can be powerful forces for innovation and leadership within their organizations. However, many Type A personalities cause stress-related problems for themselves, and sometimes for those around them. At Yammer, Sacks has consciously changed some of his behaviors so his impatience doesn't cause stress for others. Type B individuals typically live with less stress unless they are in high-stress situations. A number of factors can cause stress in the workplace, even for people who are not naturally prone to high stress.

CAUSES OF WORK STRESS

Workplace stress has been skyrocketing worldwide for some years. The number of people in the United States who reported that work is a significant source of stress soared to 69 percent in 2009, and 41 percent say they typically feel stressed or tense during their workday.[72] Surveys in Canada consistently cite work as the top source of stress for people in that country. In India, growing numbers of young software professionals and call-center workers are falling prey to depression, anxiety, and other mental illnesses because of increasing workplace stress.[73] And the long hours and stressful conditions that have led to suicides among contract manufacturing workers in China have prompted managers at technology firms such as Apple, IBM, Hewlett-Packard, and Toshiba to do some serious soul-searching.[74] "Work conditions can cause mental illness," says psychologist Rodney L. Lowman. "If we put healthy, well-adjusted people in the right foxhole with guns blaring at them, the likelihood of them experiencing depression and anxiety is very high."[75]

Take a Moment

Go to the Ethical Dilemma for Chapter 14 on page 616 that pertains to organizational sources of stress.

Managers can better cope with their own stress and establish ways for the organization to help employees cope if they understand the conditions that tend to produce work stress. Unethical environments and unsafe working conditions such as those at some contract manufacturers are, of course, major stressors. In terms of more typical everyday work stressors, one approach is to think about stress caused by the demands of job tasks and stress caused by interpersonal pressures and conflicts.

- *Task demands* are stressors arising from the tasks required of a person holding a particular job. Some kinds of decisions are inherently stressful: those made under time pressure, those that have serious consequences, and those that must be made with incomplete information. For example, emergency room doctors are under tremendous stress as a result of the task demands of their jobs. They regularly have to make quick decisions based on limited information that may determine whether a patient lives or dies. Jobs in which people have to deal with irate customers can also be highly stressful. Turnover among customer service employees can be as high as 300 percent a year in some industries.[76] Almost all jobs, especially those of managers, have some level of stress associated with task demands. Task demands also sometimes cause stress because of **role ambiguity**, which means that people are unclear about what task behaviors are expected of them. In a 2012 survey by the American Psychological Association, 35 percent of respondents cited unclear job expectations as a cause of their workplace stress.[77]

- *Interpersonal demands* are stressors associated with relationships in the organization. Although in some cases interpersonal relationships can alleviate stress, they also can be a source of stress when the group puts pressure on an individual or when conflicts arise between individuals. Managers can resolve many conflicts using techniques that will be discussed in Chapter 18. **Role conflict** occurs when an individual perceives incompatible demands from others. Managers often feel role conflict because the demands of their superiors conflict with those of the employees in their department. They may be expected to support employees and provide them with opportunities to experiment and be creative, while at the same time, top executives are demanding a consistent level of output that leaves little time for creativity and experimentation.

INNOVATIVE RESPONSES TO STRESS MANAGEMENT

Organizations that want to challenge their employees and stay competitive will never be stress-free, but healthy workplaces promote the physical and emotional well-being of their employees. Managers have direct control over many of the things that cause people stress, including their own behavior. Exhibit 14.12 lists some of the top things managers do to cause excessive and unnecessary stress.

What You Can Do to Combat Stress

Scientist and stress researcher Hans Selye said, "It's not stress that kills us, it is our reaction to it." A variety of techniques can help individuals avoid or manage the harmful effects of stress.

- **Seek and destroy key sources of stress.** A recent study found that the most beneficial stress management competency is *prevention*.[78] None of us can eliminate all the potential sources of stress from our lives, but we can avoid some of them and manage others. Take some time each day to identify stressors in your life and find ways to eliminate or reduce them. Being well organized, planning ahead, and using the various time management techniques we've discussed in this chapter, such as emptying your head of all the pressures weighing on you, are highly effective ways to manage and prevent stress.

- **Find meaning and support.** You are much more likely to experience ill effects of stress if you're working in a job that has no meaning for you and if you feel alone in life without social support. The *buffering hypothesis* says that a perceived high degree of social support from family and friends protects one from the potentially adverse effects of stressful events.[79] That is, if you feel you have a lot of support, you're less susceptible to the negative effects of bad stress.

- **Meditate and manage your energy.** Meditation is a way to both prevent and alleviate harmful stress responses. Some people meditate every morning or evening as a routine practice. Others find that short breaks to meditate for a few minutes several times a day

▶ ▶ ▶ **Concept Connection**

Many companies help employees **manage stress** by offering discounts to local gyms, although a fairly recent workplace trend enables employees to work out while they work. Treadmill desks have shelves where employees can park their laptops and plug in their mobile phones so they can review documents, do online research, and hold meetings as they rack up the miles. Employees who've made use of these multitasking opportunities report they have more energy, feel less stressed, and have lost weight thanks to the treadmill desks.

EXHIBIT 14.12 How Managers Create Stress for Employees

Working for a bad boss is a major cause of workplace stress. Here are some things that bad bosses do to create stress for their subordinates:

1. Impose unreasonable demands and overwhelming workloads.
2. Don't let people have a say in how they do their work.
3. Create perpetual doubt about how well employees are performing.
4. Refuse to get involved in conflicts between employees; let them work it out.
5. Fail to give people credit for their contributions and achievements.
6. Keep people guessing about what is expected of them.
7. Bully and harass people to keep them on their toes.
8. Don't allow people to form a community; tell them work isn't a social club.

SOURCES: Based on "Getting the Least from Your Staff," sidebar in Don Mills, "Running on High Octane or Burning out Big Time?" *National Post*, April 8, 2006; Donna Callea, "Workers Feeling the Burn: Employee Burnout a New Challenge to Productivity, Morale, Experts Say," *News Journal*, March 27, 2006; and Joe Humphreys, "Stress Will Be Main Cause of Workplace Illness by 2020," *Irish Times*, July 27, 2005.

are just as effective.[80] Anytime during the day when you're feeling overwhelmed, you can close your eyes, focus on an image or a phrase that you find calming, and breathe deeply. Meditation can be an important part of an overall healthy lifestyle, such as eating right, getting enough rest, and exercising regularly, that helps you better cope with stress.

- **Find work-life balance.** The final technique for managing stress is to balance work with other interests and activities. Many organizations offer options to help people lead more balanced lives. But you, as an individual, are also responsible for finding work-life balance. A survey by the Society for Human Resource Management found that 70 percent of employees surveyed say they work beyond scheduled time and on weekends, but more than half of those admit that it is because of *self-imposed pressure*. People who live balanced lives typically accomplish more than those who push themselves.

What Managers and Organizations Can Do

Helping employees manage stress can sometimes be as simple as encouraging people to take regular breaks and vacations. Consider that more than a third of U.S. employees surveyed by the Families and Work Institute don't take their full allotment of vacation time.[81] Here are some proactive approaches managers can take to combat the growing stress level in today's workplace:

- **Create a psychologically healthy workplace.** The number one way to lessen employee stress is to create a healthy corporate culture that makes people feel valued.[82] This includes making sure that people don't have unreasonable workloads, providing opportunities for growth and advancement, and offering suitable salaries and benefits. It also means setting an example for employees to live balanced lives. Paul English, co-founder and chief technology officer of travel search engine Kayak, says Kayak's philosophy is to "work really hard for 40 to 45 hours a week, but we believe in people having strong personal lives."[83] English sometimes takes his children on business trips so they can have new experiences together. At night, he reads murder mysteries or books about global health rather than reading about business or technology.

- **Provide wellness programs and training.** Wellness programs that offer access to nutrition counseling and exercise facilities can be highly beneficial in helping people cope with stressful jobs. A worldwide study of wellness programs conducted by the Canadian government found that for each dollar spent, the company gets from $1.95 to $3.75 return payback from benefits.[84] Training programs and conferences can help people identify stressors and teach them coping mechanisms.

- **Train managers in stress intervention.** Training managers to recognize warning signs of stress overload is critical. Manager intervention is a growing trend in enlightened companies. At Boston Consulting Group, for instance, the boss steps in if he or she sees someone working too hard or displaying signs of excessive stress. Mark Ostermann says, "It was a great feeling [to have the boss provide support]. I didn't have to complain to anyone. They were proactive in contacting me."[85]

- **Make sure people get to have some fun at work.** Particularly for jobs that have a high degree of task-related stress, allowing people to blow off steam by having fun can make all the difference in the stress level. At one Tampa-based software company help desk, Zane Bond is the "go-to guy for angry callers," but the stress doesn't get to him. One reason is that he loves solving problems. Another is that he has fun with his team members, breaking out the foam-dart guns and launching into battle with the soundtrack from *Top Gun* playing in the background.[86]

Managers should always remember that employees are *human* resources with human needs. By acknowledging the personal aspects of employees' lives, these various initiatives communicate that managers and the organization care about employees. In addition, managers' attitudes make a tremendous difference in whether employees are stressed out and unhappy or relaxed, energetic, and productive.

Remember This

- **Stress** is a physiological and emotional response to stimuli that place physical or psychological demands on an individual and create uncertainty and lack of personal control when important outcomes are at stake.
- Stress can sometimes be a positive force, but too much stress is harmful to individuals and the organizations where they work.
- The behavior pattern referred to as **Type A behavior** is characterized by extreme competitiveness, impatience, aggressiveness, and devotion to work.
- **Type B behavior** is a behavior pattern that reflects few of the Type A characteristics and includes a more balanced, relaxed approach to life.
- Type A managers can be powerful forces for innovation and change, but they can also create high stress for themselves and others.

- Work stress can be caused by both task demands and interpersonal demands.
- **Role ambiguity** refers to uncertainty about what behaviors are expected of a person in a particular role.
- **Role conflict** refers to incompatible demands of different roles, such as the demands of a manager's superiors conflicting with those of the manager's subordinates.
- Managers have direct control over many of the things that cause stress for employees.
- Individuals can apply a variety of techniques to alleviate the ill effects of stress, and managers can implement initiatives in the workplace to help solve the problem of skyrocketing workplace stress.

ch14: Discussion Questions

1. Why is self-awareness important for being a good manager? Can you think of some specific negative consequences that might result from a manager with low self-awareness?

2. As a manager, how might you deal with an employee who is always displaying negative emotions that affect the rest of the team? How might you use an understanding of attributions and emotional contagion to help you decide what to do?

3. In what ways might attitudes influence the behavior of employees who are faced with learning an entirely new set of computer-related skills to retain their jobs at a manufacturing facility?

4. The chapter suggests that optimism is an important characteristic for a manager, yet some employees complain that optimistic managers cause them significant stress because they expect their subordinates to meet unreasonable goals or expectations. How might an employee deal with a perpetually optimistic manager?

5. How might a manager apply an understanding of perception to communicate more effectively with subordinates?

6. Surveys by the Conference Board show that job satisfaction has declined from 61 percent of people surveyed in 1987 to 45 percent in 2009, and one workplace analyst has said a high level of dissatisfaction is "the new normal." What are some factors that might explain this decline in satisfaction levels? Do you think it is possible for managers to reverse the trend? Discuss.

7. Which of the four components of emotional intelligence do you consider most important to an effective manager in today's world? Why?

8. How might understanding whether an employee has an internal or an external locus of control help a manager better communicate with, motivate, and lead the employee?

9. How do you think a system for self-management such as the five-step system described in this chapter could benefit you as a student? What parts of the system seem particularly useful to you? Explain.

10. Why do you think workplace stress is skyrocketing? Do you think it is a trend that will continue? Explain the reasons for your answer. Do you think it is the responsibility of managers and organizations to help employees manage stress? Why or why not?

ch14: Apply Your Skills: Experiential Exercise

Personality Assessment: Jung's Typology[87]

For each of the following items, circle either *a* or *b*. In some cases, both *a* and *b* may apply to you. You should decide which is more like you, even if it is only slightly more true.

1. I would rather:
   a. Solve a new and complicated problem
   b. Work on something that I have done before

2. I like to:
   a. Work alone in a quiet place
   b. Be where "the action" is

3. I want a boss who:
   a. Establishes and applies criteria in decisions
   b. Considers individual needs and makes exceptions

4. When I work on a project, I:
   a. Like to finish it and get some closure
   b. Often leave it open for possible change

5. When making a decision, the most important considerations are:
   a. Rational thoughts, ideas, and data
   b. People's feelings and values

6. On a project, I tend to:
   a. Think it over and over before deciding how to proceed
   b. Start working on it right away, thinking about it as I go along

7. When working on a project, I prefer to:
   a. Maintain as much control as possible
   b. Explore various options

8. In my work, I prefer to:
   a. Work on several projects at a time, and learn as much as possible about each one
   b. Have one project that is challenging and keeps me busy

9. I often:
   a. Make lists and plans whenever I start something and may hate to alter my plans significantly
   b. Avoid plans and just let things progress as I work on them

10. When discussing a problem with colleagues, it is easy for me:
    a. To see "the big picture"
    b. To grasp the specifics of the situation

11. When the phone rings in my office or at home, I usually:
    a. Consider it an interruption
    b. Don't mind answering it

12. The word that describes me better is:
    a. Analytical
    b. Empathetic

13. When I am working on an assignment, I tend to:
    a. Work steadily and consistently
    b. Work in bursts of energy with "down time" in between

14. When I listen to someone talk on a subject, I usually try to:
    a. Relate it to my own experience and see whether it fits
    b. Assess and analyze the message

15. When I come up with new ideas, I generally:
    a. "Go for it"
    b. Like to contemplate the ideas some more

16. When working on a project, I prefer to:
    a. Narrow the scope so it is clearly defined
    b. Broaden the scope to include related aspects

17. When I read something, I usually:
    a. Confine my thoughts to what is written there
    b. Read between the lines and relate the words to other ideas

18. When I have to make a decision in a hurry, I often:
    a. Feel uncomfortable and wish I had more information
    b. Am able to do so with available data

19. In a meeting, I tend to:
    a. Continue formulating my ideas as I talk about them
    b. Speak out only after I have carefully thought the issue through

20. In work, I prefer spending a great deal of time on issues of:
    a. Ideas
    b. People

21. In meetings, I am most often annoyed with people who:
    a. Come up with many sketchy ideas
    b. Lengthen the meeting with many practical details

22. I tend to be:
    a. A morning person
    b. A night owl

23. My style in preparing for a meeting is:
    a. To be willing to go in and be responsive
    b. To be fully prepared and sketch an outline of the meeting

24. In meetings, I would prefer for people to:
    a. Display a fuller range of emotions
    b. Be more task-oriented

25. I would rather work for an organization where:
    a. My job was intellectually stimulating
    b. I was committed to its goals and mission

26. On weekends, I tend to:
    a. Plan what I will do
    b. Just see what happens and decide as I go along

27. I am more:
    a. Outgoing
    b. Contemplative

28. I would rather work for a boss who is:
    a. Full of new ideas
    b. Practical

In the following, choose the word in each pair that appeals to you more:

29. a. Social   b. Theoretical
30. a. Ingenuity   b. Practicality
31. a. Organized   b. Adaptable
32. a. Active   b. Concentration

Scoring and Interpretation

Count one point for each of the following items that you circled in the inventory.

Score for I (Introversion)	Score for E (Extroversion)	Score for S (Sensing)	Score for N (Intuition)
2a	2b	1b	1a
6a	6b	10b	10a
11a	11b	13a	13b
15b	15a	16a	16b
19b	19a	17a	17b
22a	22b	21a	21b
27b	27a	28b	28a
32b	32a	30b	30a

Totals _____   _____   _____   _____

Circle the one with more points: Circle the one with more points:

I or E   S or N

(If tied on I/E, don't count #11)   (If tied on S/N, don't count #16)

Score for T (Thinking)	Score for F (Feeling)	Score for J (Judging)	Score for P (Perceiving)
3a	3b	4a	4b
5a	5b	7a	7b
12a	12b	8b	8a
14b	14a	9a	9b
20a	20b	18b	18a
24b	24a	23b	23a
25a	25b	26a	26b
29b	29a	31a	31b

Totals _____   _____   _____   _____

Circle the one with more points: Circle the one with more points:

T or F   J or P

(If tied on T/F, don't count #24)   (If tied on J/P, don't count #23)

Your Score Is: I or E _____ S or N _____ T or F _____ J or P _____

Your type is _____ (example: INTJ; ESFP; etc.)

Characteristics Frequently Associated with Each Type

The scores above measure variables similar to the Myers-Briggs Type Indicator (MBTI) assessment, based on the work of psychologist Carl Jung. The MBTI assessment, which was described in the chapter text, identifies four dimensions and 16 different "types." The dominant characteristics associated with each type are shown in the chart on the following page. Remember that no one is a pure type; however, each individual has preferences for introversion versus extroversion, sensing versus intuition, thinking versus feeling, and judging versus perceiving. Read the description

5

LEADING

of your type as determined by your scores in the survey. Do you believe the description fits your personality?

Characteristics associated with each type

ISTJ: Organizer, trustworthy, responsible, good trustee or inspector.

ISFJ: Quiet, conscientious, devoted, handles detail, good conservator.

INFJ: Perseveres, inspirational, quiet caring for others, good counselor.

INTJ: Independent thinker, skeptical, theory, competence, good scientist.

ISTP: Cool, observant, easy-going, good craftsperson.

ISFP: Warm, sensitive, team player, avoids conflict, good artist.

INFP: Idealistic, strong values, likes learning, good at noble service.

INTP: Designer, logical, conceptual, likes challenges, good architect.

ESTP: Spontaneous, gregarious, good at problem solving and promoting.

ESFP: Sociable, generous, makes things fun, good as entertainer.

ENFP: Imaginative, enthusiastic, starts projects, good champion.

ENTP: Resourceful, stimulating, dislikes routine, tests limits, good inventor.

ESTJ: Order, structure, practical, good administrator or supervisor.

ESFJ: People skills, harmonizer, popular, does things for people, good host.

ENFJ: Charismatic, persuasive, fluent presenter, sociable, active, good teacher.

ENTJ: Visionary planner, takes charge, hearty speaker, natural leader.

ch14: Apply Your Skills: Small Group Breakout

Personality Role Play[88]

Step 1. Read the following background information: You are the new distribution manager for French Grains Bakery. Five drivers report to you that deliver French Grains baked goods to grocery stores in the metropolitan area. The drivers are expected to complete the Delivery Report to keep track of actual deliveries and any changes that occur. The Delivery Report is a key element in inventory control and provides the data for French Grains' invoicing of grocery stores. Errors become excessive when drivers fail to complete the report each day, especially when store managers request additional or different breads and baked goods when the driver arrives. As a result, French Grains may not be paid for several loaves of bread a day for each mistake in the Delivery Report. The result is lost revenue and poor inventory control.

One of the drivers accounts for about 60 percent of the errors in the Delivery Reports. This driver is a nice person and is generally reliable, but he is sometimes late for work. His major problem is that he falls behind in his paperwork. A second driver accounts for about 30 percent of the errors, and a third driver for about 10 percent of the errors. The other two drivers turn in virtually error-free Delivery Reports.

Step 2. Divide into groups of four to six students. As a group, discuss why you think one driver makes so many mistakes. Then, one person volunteer to play the role of the new distribution manager and another person play the role of the driver who accounts for 60 percent of the errors in the delivery reports.

Step 3. The new distribution manager should act the role as if his or her personality is high on "thinking" and low on "feeling," or as if he or she is high on "authoritarianism." You have called the driver into your office to talk to him about doing a more complete and accurate job with the Delivery Report. Make some notes about how you will go about correcting this problem as a thinking-oriented or authoritarian leader. Exactly what will you say, and how will you get the driver to listen and change his behavior?

Step 4. Now, start the role play between the distribution manager and the driver. Other group members act as observers.

Step 5. After the role play is completed, the observers give feedback on what worked and did not work with respect to the thinking or authoritarian personality style of giving feedback. How effective was it?

Step 6. Repeat steps 3 through 5 with other students volunteering to be the distribution manager and driver. This time the manager should act as if his or her personality is strongly "feeling" or non-authoritarian. Was this personality style more or less effective for correcting the problem?

Step 7. The instructor can ask students to volunteer to play the role of the distribution manager and the driver in front of the class. Different students might take turns playing the role of distribution manager, emphasizing a different personality trait each time. The instructor can ask other students for feedback on the leader's effectiveness and about which approach seems more effective for correcting this situation and why.

ch14: Endnotes

1. Claire Cain Miller and Quentin Hardy, "For Incoming I.B.M. Chief, Self-Confidence Is Rewarded," *The New York Times*, October 27, 2011, www.nytimes .com/2011/10/28/business/for-incoming-ibm-chief-self-confidence-rewarded.html (accessed October 28, 2011).

2. "There's Life (and a Living) after Rejection," *The Independent on Sunday*, January 6, 2008; Amy Ellis Nutt, "Harry Potter's Disappearing Act," *Newhouse News Service* (April 23, 2007): 1; and Tom Muha, "Achieving Happiness: Setbacks Can Make Us Stronger," *The Capital*, May 31, 2009.

3. Muha, "Achieving Happiness"; and Melinda Beck, "If at First You Don't Succeed, You're in Excellent Company," *The Wall Street Journal*, April 29, 2008.

4. M. E. Gist, "Self-Efficacy: Implications for Organizational Behavior and Human Resource Management," *Academy of Management Review* (July 1987): 47; and Arthur Bandura, "Self-efficacy," in V. S. Ramachaudran, ed., *Encyclopedia of Human Behavior*, vol. 4 (New York: Academic Press, 1994): pp. 71–81.

5. Reported in William W. George et al., "Discovering Your Authentic Leadership," *Harvard Business Review* (February 2007): 129–138.

6. Bill George, "Leadership Skills: It Starts with Self-Awareness," *Leadership Excellence* (June 2011): 13; Tricia Bisoux, "What Makes Leaders Great" (interviews with leadership experts), *BizEd* (September–October 2005): 40–45; Warren Bennis, *Why Leaders Can't Lead* (San Francisco: Jossey-Bass, 1989); Daniel Goleman, "What Makes a Leader?" *Harvard Business Review* (November–December 1998): 93ff; and Richard E. Boyatzis, *The Competent Manager: A Model for Effective Performance* (New York: Wiley, 1982).

7. Employee quoted in Stratford Sherman, "How Tomorrow's Best Leaders Are Learning Their Stuff," *Fortune* (November 27, 1995): 90–102.

8. Charlotte Beers, interviewed by Adam Bryant, "The Best Scorecard Is the One You Keep for Yourself," *The New York Times*, March 31, 2012, www.nytimes. com/2012/04/01/business/charlotte-beers-on-the-importance-of-self-assessment.html?pagewanted=all (accessed April 1, 2012).

9. Thanks to Scott Williams, "Self-Awareness and Personal Development," *LeaderLetter* Web site, for this image, www.wright.edu/~scott.williams/LeaderLetter/ selfawareness.htm (accessed August 21, 2007).

10. Doug Rauch, "Failure Chronicles: 'You're Driving Us Crazy. You've Got to Back Off,'" *Harvard Business Review* (April 2011): 56.

11. C. Fletcher and C. Baldry, "A Study of Individual Differences and Self-Awareness in the Context of Multi-Source Feedback," *Journal of Occupational and Organizational Behavior* 73, no. 3 (2000): 303–319.

12. George, "Leadership Skills"; and Beers, "The Best Scorecard Is the One You Keep for Yourself."

13. Alex Labidou, "Landon Donovan Admits He Could Retire Following the 2013 Season," *Goal.com*, August 14, 2012, www.goal.com/en-us/news/66/united-states/ 2012/08/14/3305930/landon-donovan-admits-he-could-retire-following-the-2013 (accessed September 3, 2012); Paul Chant, "Is This Guy Mutts Nuts . . . Or a Dog of Awe? Answer June 12, D-Day for Donovan," *The People* (May 30, 2010): 7; Jere Longman, "Donovan Pushes Ahead, Looking Inside," *The New York Times*, May 19, 2010; Nancy Armour, "Top U.S. Soccer Star Finds Peace," *Journal-Gazette*, June 25, 2010; and Des Kelly, "Donovan's Late Show Is a Tear-Jerker as Clinton Joins Party," *Daily Mail*, June 24, 2010.

14. Reported in Del Jones, "Optimism Puts Rose-Colored Tint in Glasses of Top Execs; Or Do They Just Have a Feeble Grip on Reality?" *USA Today*, December 15, 2005.

15. Jerry Krueger and Emily Killham, "At Work, Feeling Good Matters," *Gallup Management Journal*, December 8, 2005, http://gmj.gallup.com/content/20311/work-feeling-good-matters.aspx (accessed September 17, 2010).

16. M. T. Iaffaldano and P. M. Muchinsky, "Job Satisfaction and Job Performance: A Meta-Analysis," *Psychological Bulletin* (March 1985): 251–273; C. Ostroff, "The Relationship Between Satisfaction, Attitudes, and Performance: An Organizational-Level Analysis," *Journal of Applied Psychology* (December 1992): 963–974; and M. M. Petty, G. W. McGee, and J. W. Cavender, "A Meta-Analysis of the Relationship between Individual Job Satisfaction and Individual Performance," *Academy of Management Review* (October 1984): 712–721.

17. Conference Board survey, reported in "Job Satisfaction in U.S. Hits All-Time Low," *News for You* (February 17, 2010): 4.

18. Tony Schwartz, "The Greatest Sources of Satisfaction in the Workplace Are Internal and Emotional," *Fast Company* (November 2000): 398–402.

19. William C. Symonds, "Where Paternalism Equals Good Business," *BusinessWeek* (July 20, 1998): 16E4, 16E6.

20. Towers Perrin survey reported in "Employee Engagement," TowersWatson.com www.towersperrin.com/ tp/showhtml .jsp?url=global/service-areas/research-and-surveys/employee-research/ee-engagement .htm&country=global (accessed September 17, 2010).

21. "Closing the Engagement Gap: A Road Map for Driving Superior Business Performance," *Towers Perrin Global Workforce Study 2007–2008*, www.towersperrin.com/ tp/getwebcachedoc?webc=HRS/USA/2008/200803/

5

LEADING

GWS _Global_Report20072008_31208 .pdf (accessed September 20, 2010).

22. W. Chan Kin and Renée Mauborgne, "Fair Process: Managing in the Knowledge Economy," *Harvard Business Review* (January 2003): 127–136.

23. Leadership IQ survey, reported in "Many Employees Don't Trust Their Boss," *Machine Design* (September 2007): 2.

24. Quoted in Paul Harris, "Leadership: Role Models Earn Trust and Profits," *T&D* (March 2010): 47.

25. For a discussion of cognitive dissonance theory, see Leon A. Festinger, *Theory of Cognitive Dissonance* (Stanford, CA: Stanford University Press, 1957).

26. This is a very brief introduction to the subject of attributions and their role in organizations. For a recent overview of the research on attributional theory and a special issue devoted to the topic, see Marie Dasborough, Paul Harvey, and Mark J. Martinko, "An Introduction to Attributional Influences in Organizations," *Group & Organization Management* 36, no. 4 (2011): 419–426.

27. "Poll: Most Organizations Don't Use Personality Tests," *HRMagazine* 57, no. 2 (February 2012): 88; and Stephen T. Watson, "Job Hunting in the Virtual Age: Recruiters Can Be Overwhelmed by the Flood of Resumes," *Buffalo News*, August 19, 2012, D1.

28. See J. M. Digman, "Personality Structure: Emergence of the Five-Factor Model," *Annual Review of Psychology* 41 (1990): 417–440; M. R. Barrick and M. K. Mount, "Autonomy As a Moderator of the Relationships between the Big Five Personality Dimensions and Job Performance," *Journal of Applied Psychology* (February 1993): 111–118; and J. S. Wiggins and A. L. Pincus, "Personality: Structure and Assessment," *Annual Review of Psychology* 43 (1992): 473–504.

29. Del Jones, "Not All Successful CEOs Are Extroverts," *USA Today*, June 6, 2006, www.usatoday.com/money/companies/management/2006-06-06-shy-ceo-usat_x .htm (accessed September 20, 2010).

30. Todd Henneman, "For Some Companies, Two Heads Are Better than One," *Workforce*, November 16, 2011, www.workforce.com/apps/pbcs.dll/article?AID=/20111116/NEWS02/111119975&template= (accessed November 23, 2011); "Banking and Finance Companies: A.M. Best Affirms Ratings of Primerica, Inc. and Its Subsidiaries," *Investment Weekly News* (July 7, 2012): 129.

31. Reported in Daisy Grewal, "When Nice Guys Finish First," *Scientific American Mind* (July–August 2012): 62–65.

32. Reported in Christopher Palmeri, "Putting Managers to the Test," *BusinessWeek* (November 20, 2006): 82.

33. Research reported in J. J. McCorvey, "Research Corner: Feeling Guilty? Good. Why Guilt Makes You a Better Leader," *Inc.* (July–August 2012): 26; and Rachel Emma Silverman, "Plagued by Guilt? You May Be Management Material," *The Wall Street Journal*, May

29, 2012, http://blogs.wsj.com/atwork/2012/05/29/plagued-by-guilt-you-may-be-management-material/ (accessed June 3, 2012).

34. Julian B. Rotter, "Generalized Expectancies for Internal versus External Control of Reinforcement," *Psychological Monographs* 80, no. 609 (1966); and J. B. Rotter, "Internal Versus External Control of Reinforcement: A Case History," *American Psychologist* 45, no. 4 (April 1990):489–493.

35. See P. E. Spector, "Behavior in Organizations as a Function of Employee's Locus of Control," *Psychological Bulletin* (May 1982): 482–497.

36. T. W. Adorno et al., *The Authoritarian Personality* (New York: Harper & Row, 1950).

37. Niccolò Machiavelli, *The Prince*, trans. George Bull (Middlesex: Penguin, 1961).

38. Richard Christie and Florence Geis, *Studies in Machiavellianism* (New York: Academic Press, 1970).

39. R. G. Vleeming, "Machiavellianism: A Preliminary Review," *Psychological Reports* (February 1979): 295–310.

40. Christie and Geis, *Studies in Machiavellianism*.

41. Carl Jung, *Psychological Types* (London: Routledge and Kegan Paul, 1923).

42. Mary H. McCaulley, "Research on the MBTI and Leadership: Taking the Critical First Step," keynote address, The Myers-Briggs Type Indicator and Leadership: An International Research Conference (January 12–14, 1994).

43. Coeli Carr, "Redesigning the Management Psyche," *The New York Times*, May 26, 2002, Section 3, p. 14.

44. Reported in Lisa Takeuchi Cullen, "SATs for J-O-B-S," *Time* (April 3, 2006): 89.

45. Jennifer Overbo, "Using Myers-Briggs Personality Type to Create a Culture Adapted to the New Century," *T+D* (February 2010): 70–72.

46. Michael Kinsman, "Businesses Can Suffer If Workers' Emotions Not Dealt With" (an interview with Mel Fugate), *The San Diego Union-Tribune*, December 17, 2006; and Mel Fugate, Angelo J. Kinicki, and Gregory E. Prussia, "Employee Coping with Organizational Change: An Examination of Alternative Theoretical Perspectives and Models," *Personnel Psychology* 61, no. 1 (Spring 2008): 1–36.

47. "Emotion," *The Free Dictionary*, www.thefreedictionary .com/Emotions (accessed June 15, 2010); and "Motivation and Emotion," *Psychology 101* (AllPsych Online), http://allpsych.com/psychology101/emotion .html (accessed June 15, 2010).

48. E. Hatfield, J. T. Cacioppo, and R. L. Rapson, *Emotional Contagion* (New York: Cambridge University Press, 1994).

49. Reported in Robert I. Sutton, "Are You Being a Jerk? Again?" *BusinessWeek* (August 25, 2008): 52.

50. Krueger and Killham, "At Work, Feeling Good Matters."

51. Daniel Goleman, "Leadership That Gets Results," *Harvard Business Review* (March–April 2000): 79–90; and Daniel Goleman, *Emotional Intelligence: Why*

It Can Matter More Than IQ (New York: Bantam Books, 1995).

52. Alan Farnham, "Are You Smart Enough to Keep Your Job?" *Fortune* (January 15, 1996): 34–47.

53. Hendrie Weisinger, *Emotional Intelligence at Work* (San Francisco: Jossey-Bass, 2000); D. C. McClelland, "Identifying Competencies with Behavioral-Event Interviews," *Psychological Science* (Spring 1999): 331–339; Goleman, "Leadership That Gets Results"; D. Goleman, *Working with Emotional Intelligence* (New York: Bantam Books, 1999); and Lorie Parch, "Testing . . . 1,2,3," *Working Woman* (October 1997): 74–78.

54. Cliff Edwards, "Death of a Pushy Salesman," *Business-Week* (July 3, 2006): 108–109.

55. Reported in Cari Tuna, "Lawyers and Employers Take the Fight to 'Workplace Bullies'" (Theory & Practice column), *The Wall Street Journal*, August 4, 2008.

56. Anne-Elisabeth Moutet, "Dominique Strauss-Kahn: A Frenchman Sunk by a Sex Scandal?" *The Telegraph*, May 16, 2011, www.telegraph.co.uk/news/worldnews/europe/france/8515714/Dominique-Strauss-Kahn-A-Frenchman-sunk-by-a-sex-scandal.html (accessed August 26, 2012).

57. This section on self-management is based heavily on David Allen, *Getting Things Done: The Art of Stress-Free Productivity* (New York: Viking Penguin, 2001).

58. Reported in "One of These Days," *The Wall Street Journal*, March 11, 1997, A1.

59. Based on Allen, *Getting Things Done*; and Francis Heylighen and Clément Vidal, "Getting Things Done: The Science Behind Stress-Free Productivity, *Long Range Planning* 41 (2008): 585–605.

60. T. A. Beehr and R. S. Bhagat, *Human Stress and Cognition in Organizations: An Integrated Perspective* (New York: Wiley, 1985); and Bruce Cryer, Rollin McCraty, and Doc Childre, "Pull the Plug on Stress," *Harvard Business Review* (July 2003): 102–107.

61. Anita Bruzzese, "Wall Street Woes, Election Add to Workplace Stress," *Gannett News Service* (September 29, 2008).

62. "Desk Rage Rising," *Office Solutions* (January 2009): 9; and Carol Hymowitz, "Bosses Have to Learn How to Confront Troubled Employees," *The Wall Street Journal*, April 23, 2007.

63. Jeannine Aversa, "Stress over Debt Taking Toll on Health," *USA Today*, June 9, 2008, www.usatoday.com/news/health/2008-06-09-debt-stress_N.htm (accessed June 10, 2008).

64. Discussed in Alice Park, "The Two Faces of Anxiety," *Time* (December 5, 2011): 54–65; and Melinda Beck, "Anxiety Can Bring Out the Best," *The Wall Street Journal*, June 18, 2012, http://online.wsj.com/article/SB10001424052702303836404577474451463041994.html (accessed June 20, 2012).

65. "Are You Working Too Hard? A Conversation with Mind-Body Researcher Herbert Benson," *Harvard Business Review* (November 2005): 53-58; and R. M. Yerkes and J. D. Dodson, "The Relation of Strength of Stimulus to Rapidity of Habit-Formation. *Journal of Comparative Neurology and Psychology* 18 (1908): 459–482.

66. Mathias V. Schmidt and Lars Schwabe, "Splintered by Stress," *Scientific American Mind* (September-October 2011): 22–29.

67. Reported in Brian Nadel, "The Price of Pressure," special advertising feature, *Fortune* (December 11, 2006): 143–146.

68. Health and Safety Authority survey, reported in Joe Humphreys, "Stress Will Be Main Cause of Workplace Illness by 2020," *Irish Times*, July 27, 2005.

69. Don Mills, "Running on High Octane or Burning out Big Time? Stress Flunkies," *National Post*, April 8, 2006.

70. M. Friedman and R. Rosenman, *Type A Behavior and Your Heart* (New York: Knopf, 1974).

71. David Sacks, "The Way I Work: Yammer," *Inc.* (November 2011): 123–124.

72. American Psychological Association, *Stress in America 2009*, APA.org, 2009, www.apa.org/news/press/releases/stress-exec-summary.pdf (accessed September 5, 2012).

73. Mills, "Running on High Octane or Burning out Big Time?"; Vani Doraisamy, "Young Techies Swell the Ranks of the Depressed," *The Hindu*, October 11, 2005.

74. Charles Duhigg and David Barboza, "In China, Human Costs Are Built Into an iPad," *The New York Times*, January 25, 2012, www.nytimes.com/2012/01/26/business/ieconomy-apples-ipad-and-the-human-costs-for-workers-in-china.html?pagewanted=all (accessed January 26, 2012); and Nick Wingfield and Charles Duhigg, "Apple Asks Outside Groups to Inspect Factories," *The New York Times*, February 13, 2012, http://bits.blogs.nytimes.com/2012/02/13/apple-announces-independent-factory-inspections/ (accessed February 13, 2012).

75. Quoted in Elizabeth Bernstein, "When a Co-Worker Is Stressed Out," *The Wall Street Journal*, August 26, 2008.

76. Reported in Sue Shellenbarger, "Health & Fitness: How to Keep Your Cool in Angry Times," *The Wall Street Journal Asia*, September 27, 2010, 11.

77. "APA Survey Finds Feeling Valued at Work Linked to Well-Being and Performance," American Psychological Association, March 12, 2012, www.apa.org/news/press/releases/2012/03/well-being.aspx (accessed September 5, 2012).

78. Robert Epstein, "Fight the Frazzled Mind," *Scientific American Mind* (September–October 2011): 30–35.

79. Sheldon Cohen and Thomas Ashby Wills, "Stress, Social Support, and the Buffering Hypothesis," *Psychological Bulletin* 85, no. 2 (1985): 310–357.

80. Eilene Zimmerman, "When Stress Flirts with Burnout," *The New York Times*, January 17, 2010; and Joanna Barsh, J. Mogelof, and C. Webb, "How Centered Leaders Achieve Extraordinary Results," *The McKinsey*

Quarterly, October 2010, www.mckinseyquarterly.com/ How_centered_leaders_achieve_extraordinary_results_ 2678 (accessed January 16, 2011).

81. Rosabeth Moss Kanter, "Balancing Work and Life," *Knight-Ridder Tribune News Service,* April 8, 2005.

82. "APA Survey Finds Feeling Valued at Work Linked to Well-Being and Performance."

83. "The Way I Work: Paul English, Kayak," *Inc.* (February 2010): 98–101.

84. Donalee Moulton, "Buckling Under the Pressure," *OH & S Canada* 19, no. 8 (December 2003): 36.

85. Jenna Goudreau, "Dispatches from the War on Stress," *BusinessWeek* (August 6, 2007): 74–75.

86. Shellenbarger, "Health & Fitness: How to Keep Your Cool in Angry Times."

87. From Dorothy Marcic, *Organizational Behavior,* 4th ed. (Mason, OH: South-Western, Cengage Learning, 1995). Reproduced by permission.

88. Based on K. J. Keleman, J. E. Garcia, and K. J. Lovelace, *Management Incidents: Role Plays for Management Development* (Dubuque, IA: Kendall-Hunt Publishing Company, 1990): 69–72.

Leadership

Pavel Filatov/Alamy

Learning Outcomes

After studying this chapter, you should be able to:

1. Define leadership and explain its importance for organizations.

2. Describe how leadership is changing in today's organizations, including Level 5 leadership, servant leadership, and authentic leadership.

3. Discuss how women's style of leading is typically different from men's.

4. Identify personal characteristics associated with effective leaders.

5. Define task-oriented behavior and people-oriented behavior and explain how these categories are used to evaluate and adapt leadership style.

6. Describe the situational model of leadership and its application to subordinate participation.

7. Discuss how leadership fits the organizational situation and how organizational characteristics can substitute for leadership behaviors.

8. Describe transformational leadership and when it should be used.

9. Explain how followership is related to effective leadership.

10. Identify sources of leader power and the tactics that leaders use to influence others.

What's Your Personal Style?

INSTRUCTIONS: Ideas about effective leadership change over time. To understand your approach to leadership, think about your personal style toward others or toward a student group to which you belong, and then answer each item below as Mostly True or Mostly False for you.

	Mostly True	Mostly False
1. I am a modest, unassuming person.	_____	_____
2. When a part of a group, I am more concerned about how the group does than how I do.	_____	_____
3. I prefer to lead with quiet modesty rather than personal assertiveness.	_____	_____
4. I feel personally responsible if the team does poorly.	_____	_____
5. I act with quiet determination.	_____	_____
6. I resolve to do whatever needs doing to produce the best result for the group.	_____	_____
7. I am proactive to help the group succeed.	_____	_____
8. I facilitate high standards for my group's performance.	_____	_____

SCORING AND INTERPRETATION: A recent view of leadership called Level 5 leadership says that the most successful leaders have two prominent qualities: humility and will. Give 1 point for each item marked Mostly True.

Humility: Items 1, 2, 3, 4
Will: Items 5, 6, 7, 8

"Humility" means a quiet, modest, self-effacing manner. A humble person puts group or organizational success ahead of personal success. "Will" means a quiet but fierce resolve to stay the course to achieve the group's desired outcome and to help the group succeed. The traits of humility and will are opposite the traditional idea of leadership as loud and self-centered. If you scored 3 or 4 on either humility or will, you are on track to Level 5 leadership, which says that ordinary people often make excellent leaders.

Mike Tomlin has coached the Pittsburgh Steelers to two Super Bowl wins in four seasons, but he won't be heard spouting off about his coaching prowess. In fact, Tomlin speaks only sparingly, and when he does, it is mostly about the abilities and dedication of his players. Tomlin says he learned to "lead through service" from Tony Dungy, former coach of the Indianapolis Colts and the first African American coach to win a Super Bowl. "Every day when I go to work ..." says Tomlin, "I think about the things I can do to make my men successful. I learned that from him...." Tomlin is confident and unapologetic about his desire to win Super Bowls (he says the two wins are "about two Super Bowls short of my vision"). But his ambition is not for himself, but for the team. "We've got a really good football team—guys who are not only talented, but are selfless in work," says Tomlin.[1]

Being selfless and having a "servant's mentality" are not phrases often thought about in terms of powerful leaders, but Mike Tomlin illustrates a new kind of leader for today's collaborative world—a leader who quietly builds strong teams and organizations rather than touting his or her own abilities and accomplishments. In the previous chapter, we explored differences in attitudes and personality that affect behavior. Some of the most important attitudes for the organization's success are those of its leaders because leader attitudes and

1 INTRODUCTION
2 ENVIRONMENT
3 PLANNING
4 ORGANIZING
5 LEADING
6 CONTROLLING

Concept Connection ◄◄◄

Chris Zane, founder and owner of Zane's Cycles in Branford, Connecticut, is an expert at turning first-time customers into lifetime customers. In fact, he wrote the book on it—*Reinventing the Wheel.* The book is a reflection of his enduring **goal**, which is to provide the ultimate shopping experience that makes customers feel great about his products and services. Zane actually started his business at age 16 with a $23,000 loan from his grandfather. Under his **leadership**, Zane's Cycles now posts about $21 million in annual sales.

behaviors play a critical role in shaping employee attitudes and performance. In this chapter, we define leadership and explore how managers develop leadership qualities. We look at some important leadership approaches for contemporary organizations, as well as examine trait, behavioral, and contingency theories of leadership effectiveness, discuss charismatic and transformational leadership, explore the role of followership, and consider how leaders use power and influence to get things done. Chapters 16 through 18 will look in detail at many of the functions of leadership, including employee motivation, communication, and encouraging teamwork.

The Nature of Leadership

In most situations, a team, military unit, department, or volunteer group is only as good as its leader. Yet there are as many variations among leaders as there are among other individuals, and many different styles of leadership can be effective.

So, what does it mean to be a leader? Among all the ideas and writings about leadership, three aspects stand out—people, influence, and goals. Leadership occurs among people, involves the use of influence, and is used to attain goals.[2] *Influence* means that the relationship among people is not passive. Moreover, influence is designed to achieve some end or goal. Thus, **leadership** as defined here is the ability to influence people toward the attainment of goals. This definition captures the idea that leaders are involved with other people in the achievement of goals. Leadership is reciprocal, occurring *among* people.[3] Leadership is a "people" activity, distinct from administrative paperwork or problem-solving activities.

Remember This

- The attitudes and behaviors of leaders shape the conditions that determine how well employees can do their jobs; thus, leaders play a tremendous role in the organization's success.

- **Leadership** is the ability to influence people toward the attainment of organizational goals.
- Many different styles of leadership can be effective.

Contemporary Leadership

The concept of leadership evolves as the needs of organizations change. That is, the environmental context in which leadership is practiced influences which approach might be most effective, as well as what kinds of leaders are most admired by society. The technology, economic conditions, labor conditions, and social and cultural mores of the times all play a role. A significant influence on leadership styles in recent years is the turbulence and uncertainty of the environment. Ethical and economic difficulties, corporate governance concerns, globalization, changes in technology, new ways of working, shifting employee expectations, and significant social transitions have contributed to a shift in how we think about and practice leadership. Four approaches that are in tune with leadership for today's turbulent times are Level 5 leadership, servant leadership, authentic leadership, and interactive leadership, which has been associated with women's style of leading.

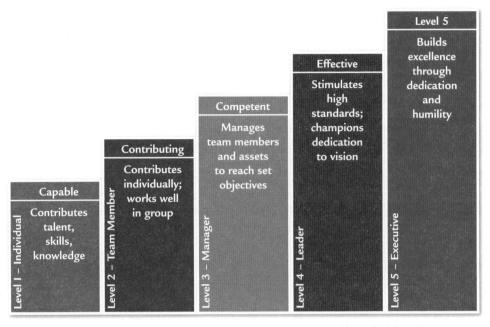

SOURCE: Based on Jim Collins, *Good to Great: Why Some Companies Make the Leap . . . and Others Don't* (New York: HarperCollins, 2001), p. 20.

EXHIBIT 15.1

Level 5 Hierarchy

LEVEL 5 LEADERSHIP

A study conducted by Jim Collins and his research associates identified the critical importance of what Collins calls *Level 5 leadership* in transforming companies from merely good to truly great organizations.[4] As described in his book *Good to Great: Why Some Companies Make the Leap . . . and Others Don't*, Level 5 leadership refers to the highest level in a hierarchy of manager capabilities, as illustrated in Exhibit 15.1.

As reflected in the exhibit, a key characteristic of Level 5 leaders is an almost complete lack of ego (humility) coupled with a fierce resolve to do what is best for the organization (will). **Humility** means being unpretentious and modest rather than arrogant and prideful. In contrast to the view of great leaders as larger-than-life personalities with strong egos and big ambitions, Level 5 leaders often seem shy and self-effacing. Although they accept full responsibility for mistakes, poor results, or failures, Level 5 leaders give credit for successes to other people. Level 5 leaders build organizations based on solid values that go far beyond just making money, with an unwavering resolve to do whatever is needed to make the company successful over the long term.[5]

One leader who demonstrates Level 5 leadership qualities is Qi Lu of Microsoft.

Innovative Way

Qi Lu, Microsoft

Qi Lu grew up in a rural village in China with no electricity or running water. Today, he is president of Microsoft's Online Services division. How did he get there? Not from personal ambition, say former colleagues at Yahoo!. "He shunned the limelight," said Tim Cadogan, now CEO of OpenX, "but he was considered one of the stars."

Lu rose through the ranks at Yahoo!, and he got the job at Microsoft based not on aggressiveness and pursuit of personal advancement, but rather because of his sheer intellectual abilities and his commitment to go above and beyond the call of duty to accomplish organizational goals. Lu feels a strong sense of duty and loyalty, pouring his heart and soul into the mission rather than spending his energies promoting himself. On his last day of work at Yahoo!, a problem came up with a database. Rather than leaving the problem for others, Lu worked side by side with his former employees to try to fix it. He finally left at midnight, when his network access was automatically cut off.[6]

5

LEADING

Level 5 leaders like Qi Lu are extremely ambitious for their companies rather than for themselves. As another example, consider Darwin Smith, CEO of Kimberly-Clark from 1971–1991. Over those 20 years, Smith transformed Kimberly-Clark from a stodgy paper company with falling stock prices into the leading consumer paper products company in the world. The company generated cumulative stock returns that were 4.1 times greater than those of the general market. Yet few people have ever heard of Smith. He shunned the spotlight and was never featured in splashy articles in *Fortune* magazine or *The Wall Street Journal*. He was ambitious for the company, not for himself.[7]

This attitude becomes highly evident in the area of succession planning. Level 5 leaders develop a solid corps of leaders throughout the organization, so that when they leave, the company can continue to thrive and grow even stronger. Egocentric leaders, by contrast, often set their successors up for failure because it will be a testament to their own greatness if the company doesn't perform well without them. Rather than building an organization around "a genius with a thousand helpers," Level 5 leaders want everyone to develop to their fullest potential.

SERVANT LEADERSHIP

When Jack Welch, longtime CEO of General Electric (GE), speaks to MBA students, he reminds them that "any time you are managing people, your job is not about you, it's about them. It starts out about you as . . . an individual in a company," Welch says. "But once you get a leadership job, it moves very quickly to being about them."[8] Some leaders operate from the assumption that work exists for the development of the worker as much as the worker exists to do the work.[9] The concept of servant leadership, first described by Robert Greenleaf in 1970, has gained renewed interest in recent years as companies recover from ethical scandals and compete to attract and retain the best human talent.[10]

A **servant leader** transcends self-interest to serve others, the organization, and society.[11] Marilyn Nelson, CEO of the Carlson Companies (Radisson Hotels, TGI Fridays, Regent Seven Seas Cruises), says being a true leader means you "have to subordinate your own emotions, your own desires, even make decisions on behalf of the whole that might conflict with what you would do on an individual basis."[12] A stunning example of this occurred in the spring of 2009 when a U.S.-flagged cargo ship, the *Maersk Alabama*, was seized and raided by Somali pirates. Captain Richard Phillips ordered crew members of the unarmed ship not to fight and gave himself up as a hostage to free the ship and crew. Contrast his behavior with that of *Costa Concordia* captain Francesco Schettino, who allegedly abandoned his ship while passengers were still aboard after the luxury cruise liner hit a rock and sank off the coast of Italy, killing at least 30 people. Schettino has been charged with manslaughter, shipwreck, and abandoning ship.[13]

In organizations, servant leaders operate on two levels: for the fulfillment of their subordinates' goals and needs and for the realization of the larger purpose or mission of their organization. Servant leaders give things away—power, ideas, information, recognition, credit for accomplishments, even money. Servant leaders often work in the nonprofit world because it offers a natural way to apply their leadership drive and skills to serve others. But servant leaders also succeed in business. Fred Keller has built a $250 million plastics manufacturing company, Cascade Engineering, by continuously asking one question: *What good can we do?* Keller started the business 40 years ago with six employees. Today, it has 1,000 employees in 15 business divisions. Keller has made social responsibility a cornerstone of the business. The company offers jobs to welfare recipients. Keller has also donated large amounts to various philanthropic causes, both as an individual and through Cascade.[14]

AUTHENTIC LEADERSHIP

Another popular concept in leadership today is the idea of **authentic leadership**, which refers to individuals who know and understand themselves, who espouse and

HOT TOPIC

Take a Moment

What did your score on the "What's Your Personal Style?" questions at the beginning of this chapter say about your humility? Go to the Ethical Dilemma for Chapter 15 on pages 617–618 that pertains to leadership for turbulent times.

act consistent with higher-order ethical values, and who empower and inspire others with their openness and authenticity.[15] To be authentic means being *real*, staying true to one's values and beliefs, and acting based on one's true self rather than emulating what others do. Authentic leaders inspire trust and commitment because they respect diverse viewpoints, encourage collaboration, and help others learn, grow, and develop as leaders.

Exhibit 15.2 outlines the key characteristics of authentic leaders, and each is discussed below.[16]

- *Authentic leaders pursue their purpose with passion.* Leaders who lead without a purpose can fall prey to greed and the desires of the ego. When leaders demonstrate a high level of passion and commitment to a purpose, they inspire commitment from followers.
- *Authentic leaders practice solid values.* Authentic leaders have values that are shaped by their personal beliefs, and they stay true to them even under pressure. People come to know what the leader stands for, which inspires trust.
- *Authentic leaders lead with their hearts as well as their heads.* All leaders sometimes have to make tough choices, but authentic leaders maintain a compassion for others as well as the courage to make difficult decisions.
- *Authentic leaders establish connected relationships.* Authentic leaders build positive and enduring relationships, which makes followers want to do their best. In addition, authentic leaders surround themselves with good people and work to help others grow and develop.
- *Authentic leaders demonstrate self-discipline.* A high degree of self-control and self-discipline keeps leaders from taking excessive or unethical risks that could harm others and the organization. When authentic leaders make mistakes, they openly admit them.

A leader who demonstrates many of the characteristics of authentic leadership is Mike Krzyzewski, coach of the Duke University Blue Devils and the most winning coach ever in men's college basketball. For Krzyzewski, almost everything in leadership depends on one

> *"True leadership is a fire in the mind. . . . It is a strength of purpose and belief in a cause that reaches out to others, touches their hearts, and makes them eager to follow."*
>
> — ROBERT M. GATES, FORMER U.S. SECRETARY OF DEFENSE

EXHIBIT 15.2   Components of Authentic Leadership

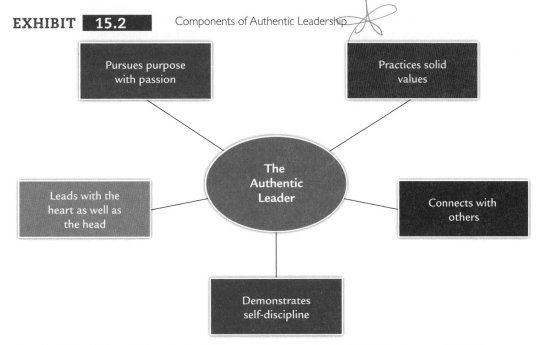

SOURCE: Based on Bill George, *Authentic Leadership: Rediscovering the Secrets to Lasting Value* (San Francisco: Jossey-Bass, 2003).

5

LEADING

Concept Connection ◄◄◄

The 2008 financial collapse put Debra Cafaro's leadership skills to the test. The CEO of Ventas Inc. saw the housing crisis approaching and insisted the Louisville-based healthcare real estate investment trust build cash reserves. Although she wanted to project calmness and certainty when the economic downturn hit, Cafaro says that "in order to be authentic, I also had to acknowledge, 'I'm scared, too.'" Throughout the crisis, Cafaro operated as an **interactive leader**, one who, in her words, makes sure "we're working together, collaborating—marching in the same direction." She succeeded. Ventas not only survived the recession but is flourishing.

Jin Lee/Bloomberg/Getty Images

element: personal relationships. When he recruits a player, Krzyzewski tells him, "We're developing a relationship here, and if you're not interested, tell me sooner rather than later." He emphasizes teamwork rather than individual performers, fosters a family feeling among players, and says he coaches "by feel." He builds such strong positive relationships among players that they communicate constantly and effortlessly on the court, sometimes without saying a word. Leading a basketball team, Krzyzewski believes, is just like leading a business, a military unit, a school, a volunteer group, or anything else: "You gotta get through all their layers and get right into their hearts."[17]

GENDER DIFFERENCES

Some of the general characteristics associated with Level 5 leaders and authentic leaders are also hallmarks of interactive leadership, which has been found to be associated with female leaders. **Interactive leadership** means that the leader favors a consensual and collaborative process, and influence derives from relationships rather than position power and formal authority.[18]

Although both men and women can practice interactive leadership, research indicates that women's style of leadership is typically different from that of most men and is particularly suited to today's organizations.[19] Using data from actual performance evaluations, one study found that when rated by peers, subordinates, and bosses, female managers scored significantly higher than men on abilities such as motivating others, fostering communication, and listening.[20] Another study of leaders and their followers in businesses, universities, and government agencies found that women were rated higher on social and emotional skills, which are crucial for interactive leadership.[21] Indeed, a recent review of more than 7,000 360-degree performance evaluations discovered that women outshone men in almost every leadership dimension measured, even some considered typically masculine qualities, such as driving for results. The exception was that women were typically rated lower on developing a strategic perspective, which some researchers believe hinders female managers' career advancement despite their exceptional ratings on other leadership dimensions.[22] Exhibit 15.3 shows results for five of the 16 dimensions measured by the study.

One good example of an interactive leader is Cindy Szadokierski, who started as a reservations agent for United Airlines and today is vice president in charge of operations for United's largest hub at O'Hare International Airport. As she oversees 4,000 employees and 600 flights a day, her favorite times are the weekly afternoon walkabouts on the O'Hare ramp and the weekly morning strolls through the terminal, where she can connect with employees and customers. Pete McDonald, chief operating officer of United's parent, UAL Corporation, says there were serious operations problems at O'Hare, so they put "the most communicative person" in the job. Szadokierski's approach to leadership is more collaborative than command and control.[23]

Men can be interactive leaders as well, as illustrated by the example of Pat McGovern, founder and chairman of IDG, a technology publishing and research firm that owns magazines such as *CIO*, *PC World*, and *Computerworld*. McGovern believes that having personal contact with employees and letting them know they're appreciated is a primary responsibility of leaders.[24] The characteristics associated with interactive leadership are emerging as valuable qualities for both male and female leaders in today's workplace. Values associated with interactive leadership include personal humility, inclusion, relationship building, and caring.

Leadership Ability	Who Does It Best?
Develops Others	(Women rated higher)
Drives for Results	(Women rated higher)
Inspires and Motivates Others	(Women rated higher)
Innovates	(Women and men rated about equally)
Builds Relationships	(Women rated higher)
Technical or Professional Expertise	(Women and men rated about equally)

EXHIBIT 15.3

Gender Differences in Leadership Behaviors

SOURCE: Data from Zenger Folkman, Inc., reported in Jack Zenger and Joseph Folkman, "Are Women Better Leaders than Men?" HBR Blog Network, *Harvard Business Review*, March 15, 2012, http://blogs.hbr.org/cs/2012/03/a_study_in_leadership_women_do.html (accessed September 12, 2012).

Remember This

- A significant influence on leadership styles in recent years is the turbulence and uncertainty of the environment.
- One effective approach in today's environment is Level 5 leadership, which is characterized by an almost complete lack of ego (humility), coupled with a fierce resolve to do what is best for the organization (will).
- **Humility** means being unpretentious and modest rather than arrogant and prideful.
- A **servant leader** is a leader who serves others by working to fulfill followers' needs and goals, as well as to achieve the organization's larger mission.
- **Authentic leadership** refers to leadership by individuals who know and understand themselves,

who espouse and act consistent with higher-order ethical values, and who empower and inspire others with their openness and authenticity.
- Women leaders typically score significantly higher than men on abilities such as motivating others, building relationships, and developing others—skills that are based on humility and authenticity and are particularly suited to today's organizations.
- **Interactive leadership** is a leadership style characterized by values such as inclusion, collaboration, relationship building, and caring.
- Although interactive leadership is associated with women's style of leading, both men and women can be effective interactive leaders.

From Management to Leadership

Hundreds of books and articles have been written in recent years about the differences between management and leadership. Good management is essential in organizations, yet managers have to be leaders too, because distinctive qualities are associated with management and leadership that provide different strengths for the organization. A good way to

EXHIBIT 15.4

Leader and Manager Qualities

SOURCES: Based on "What Is the Difference Between Management and Leadership?" *The Wall Street Journal Online*, http://guides.wsj.com/management/developing-a-leadership-style/what-is-the-difference-between-management-and-leadership (accessed June 28, 2009); and Genevieve Capowski, "Anatomy of a Leader: Where Are the Leaders of Tomorrow?" *Management Review* (March 1994): 12.

think of the distinction between management and leadership is that management organizes the production and supply of fish to people, whereas leadership teaches and motivates people to fish. Organizations need both types of skills.[25]

As shown in Exhibit 15.4, management and leadership reflect two different sets of qualities and skills that frequently overlap within a single individual. A person might have more of one set of qualities than the other, but ideally, a manager develops a balance of both manager and leader qualities.[26] A primary distinction between management and leadership is that management promotes stability and order within the existing organizational structure and systems. This ensures that suppliers are paid, customers invoiced, products and services produced on time, and so forth. Leadership, on the other hand, promotes vision and change. Leadership means questioning the status quo and being willing to take reasonable risks so that outdated, unproductive, or socially irresponsible norms can be replaced to meet new challenges.

Consider how Alan Mulally has applied both management and leadership to revive Ford Motor Company. Ford was losing $83 million a day in 2008. Three years later, in 2011, the company had a net profit of $20 billion. Ford was the only one of the Big Three automakers that didn't accept a bailout from the U.S. government. Mulally needed excellent management skills to root out operating inefficiencies, cut costs, streamline the structure, and improve quality. Yet the turnaround of Ford also depended on consummate leadership. Mulally inspired people with a vision of saving a storied American company—and transforming it to meet the challenges of the twenty-first century. He shifted the culture from one of ego-driven infighting to one of cooperation, accountability, and commitment. And he motivated thousands of employees to embrace change and execute the vision and strategy. Mulally ate in the company cafeteria rather than the executive dining room so that he could talk with people at all levels of the company, occasionally popped into meetings to offer encouragement and support, and personally answered e-mails from employees.[27]

Leadership cannot replace management; it should be in addition to management. Good management is needed to help the organization meet current commitments, while good leadership is needed to move the organization into the future. Leadership's power comes from being built on the foundation of a well-managed organization.

Remember This

- Leadership and management reflect two different sets of qualities and skills that provide different benefits for the organization.
- Management promotes stability and efficient organizing to meet current commitments, whereas leadership often inspires engagement and organizational change to meet new conditions.
- Both leadership and management are important to organizations, and people can learn to be good leaders as well as good managers.
- Alan Mulally applied both skilled management and good leadership in his turnaround of Ford Motor Company.

Leadership Traits

Early efforts to understand leadership success focused on the leader's traits. **Traits** are the distinguishing personal characteristics of a leader, such as intelligence, honesty, self-confidence, and even appearance. The early research looked at leaders who had achieved a level of greatness, and hence was referred to as the "Great Man" approach. The idea was relatively simple: Find out what made these people great and select future leaders who already exhibited the same traits or could be trained to develop them. Generally, early research found only a weak relationship between personal traits and leader success.[28]

In recent years, interest in examining leadership traits has reemerged. In addition to personality traits, physical, social, and work-related characteristics of leaders have been studied.[29] Exhibit 15.5 summarizes the physical, social, and personal leadership characteristics that have received the greatest research support. However, these characteristics do not stand alone. The appropriateness of a trait or set of traits depends on the leadership situation.

Effective leaders typically possess varied traits, and no single leader can have a complete set of characteristics that is appropriate for handling any problem, challenge, or opportunity that comes along. In addition, traits that are typically considered positive can sometimes have negative consequences, and traits sometimes considered negative can have positive consequences. For example, optimism is a highly desirable trait for a leader. As described in the previous chapter, studies

> "*The good news: these [leadership] traits are not genetic. It's not as if you have to be tall or left-handed. These qualities are developed through attitude, habit, and discipline—factors that are within your control.*"
>
> — ADAM BRYANT, SENIOR EDITOR FOR FEATURES AT *THE NEW YORK TIMES*, IN THE "CORNER OFFICE" COLUMN

5

LEADING

EXHIBIT 15.5   Personal Characteristics of Leaders

Physical Characteristics	Personality	Work-Related Characteristics
Energy	Self-confidence	Achievement drive, desire to excel
Physical stamina	Honesty and integrity	Conscientiousness in pursuit of goals
	Optimism	Persistence against obstacles, tenacity
	Desire to lead	
	Independence	
Intelligence and Ability	**Social Characteristics**	**Social Background**
Intelligence, cognitive ability	Sociability, interpersonal skills	Education
Knowledge	Cooperativeness	Mobility
Judgment, decisiveness	Ability to enlist cooperation	
	Tact, diplomacy	

SOURCES: Based on Bernard M. Bass, *Bass & Stogdill's Handbook of Leadership: Theory, Research, and Managerial Applications,* 3d ed. (New York: The Free Press, 1990), pp. 80–81; and S. A. Kirkpatrick and E. A. Locke, "Leadership: Do Traits Matter?" *Academy of Management Executive* 5, no. 2 (1991): 48–60.

have shown that optimism is the single characteristic most common to top executives.[30] Leaders need to be able to see possibilities where others see problems and instill in others a sense of hope for a better future. However, optimism can also lull leaders into laziness and overconfidence, causing them to miss danger signals and underestimate risks. The 2007–2008 crisis in the financial services industry can be blamed partly on leaders who grew overconfident and led their organizations astray. Optimism has to be paired with "reality testing" and conscientiousness, another trait common to successful leaders, as shown in the exhibit.[31]

Therefore, rather than just understanding their *traits*, the best leaders recognize and hone their *strengths*.[32] **Strengths** are natural talents and abilities that have been supported and reinforced with learned knowledge and skills and provide each individual with his or her best tools for accomplishment and satisfaction.[33] Every manager has a limited capacity; those who become good leaders are the ones who tap into their key strengths that can make a difference. Effective leadership isn't about having the "right" traits, but rather about finding the strengths that one can best exemplify and apply as a leader.

Remember This

- **Traits** are distinguishing personal characteristics, such as intelligence, self-confidence, energy, and independence.

- **Strengths** are natural talents and abilities that have been supported and reinforced with learned knowledge and skills.

Behavioral Approaches

The inability to define effective leadership based solely on traits led to an interest in looking at the behavior of leaders and how it might contribute to leadership success or failure. Two basic leadership behaviors identified as important for leadership are attention to tasks and attention to people.

TASK VERSUS PEOPLE (MGMT-BY-OBJECTIVE)

Two types of behavior that have been identified as applicable to effective leadership in a variety of situations and time periods are *task-oriented behavior* and *people-oriented behavior*.[34] Although they are not the only important leadership behaviors, concern for tasks and concern for people must be shown at some reasonable level. Thus, many approaches to understanding leadership use these *metacategories*, or broadly defined behavior categories, as a basis for study and comparison.

Important early research programs on leadership were conducted at The Ohio State University and the University of Michigan.[35] Ohio State researchers identified two major behaviors they called consideration and initiating structure. **Consideration** falls in the category of people-oriented behavior and is the extent to which the leader is mindful of subordinates, respects their ideas and feelings, and establishes mutual trust. **Initiating structure** is the degree of task behavior; that is, the extent to which the leader is task oriented and directs subordinate work activities toward goal attainment. Studies suggest that effective leaders may be high on consideration and low on initiating structure or low on consideration and high on initiating structure, depending on the situation.[36]

Research at the University of Michigan at about the same time also considered task- and people-oriented behaviors by comparing the behavior of effective and ineffective supervisors.[37] The most effective supervisors were those who established high performance goals and displayed supportive behavior toward subordinates.

Take a Moment

As a new manager, realize that both task-oriented behavior and people-oriented behavior are important, although some situations call for a greater degree of one over the other. Go to the Experiential Exercise on pages 519–520 to measure your degree of task orientation and people orientation.

These were referred to as *employee-centered leaders*. The less-effective leaders were called *job-centered leaders*; these leaders tended to be less concerned with goal achievement and human needs in favor of meeting schedules, keeping costs low, and achieving production efficiency.

THE LEADERSHIP GRID

Building on the work of the Ohio State and Michigan studies, Blake and Mouton of the University of Texas proposed a two-dimensional theory called the Managerial Grid®, which was later restated by Blake and McCanse as the **Leadership Grid®**.[38] The model and five of its major management styles are depicted in Exhibit 15.6. Each axis on the grid is a nine-point scale, with 1 meaning low concern and 9 meaning high concern.

Team management (9, 9) often is considered the most effective style and is recommended for leaders because organization members work together to accomplish tasks. *Country club management* (1, 9) occurs when primary emphasis is given to people rather than to work outputs. *Authority-compliance management* (9, 1) occurs when efficiency in operations is the dominant orientation. *Middle-of-the-road management* (5, 5) reflects a moderate amount of concern for both people and production. *Impoverished management* (1, 1) means the absence of a management philosophy; managers exert little effort toward interpersonal relationships or work accomplishment.

▶▶▶ **Concept Connection**

ZUMA Press/Newscom

How has Clarence Otis, Jr.'s leadership style changed since he became CEO of Darden Restaurants? His experience has driven home the importance of **team management**. Otis has found "it's less and less about getting the work done, and more and more about building the team." His team includes 180,000 employees working in the U.S.'s largest full-service restaurant operation. Darden's new headquarters was designed to facilitate teamwork among its brands—especially Olive Garden, Red Lobster, and Longhorn Steakhouse—by bringing approximately 1,500 executives and support staff previously scattered in separate buildings under one roof for the first time.

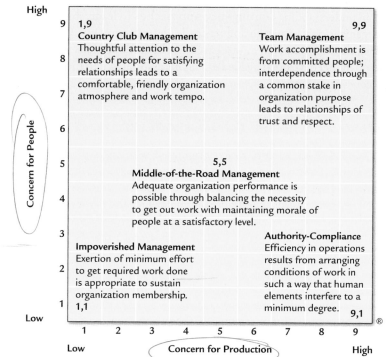

EXHIBIT 15.6

The Leadership Grid Figure

5

LEADING

SOURCE: The Leadership Grid figure, Paternalism figure, and Opportunism figure from Robert R. Blake and Anne Adams McCanse, *Leadership Dilemmas–Grid Solutions* (formerly the Managerial Grid by Robert R. Blake and Jane S. Mouton) (Houston: Gulf Publishing Company, 1991), Grid figure, p. 29; Paternalism figure, p. 30; Opportunism figure, p. 31. Copyright © 1991 by Blake and Mouton, and Scientific Methods, Inc. Reproduced by permission of the owners.

Remember This

- Two basic leadership behaviors identified as important for leadership are attention to tasks and attention to people.
- **Consideration** is the term used by researchers at The Ohio State University to describe the extent to which a leader is sensitive to subordinates, respects their ideas and feelings, and establishes mutual trust.
- **Initiating structure** is the term that describes the extent to which a leader is task oriented and directs subordinates' work activities toward goal accomplishment.
- Researchers at the University of Michigan used the terms *employee-centered leaders* and *job-centered leaders* to describe the same two basic leadership behaviors.
- The **Leadership Grid** is a two-dimensional leadership model that measures the leader's concern for people and concern for production to categorize the leader in one of five different leadership styles.

Contingency Approaches

Steven Sinofsky leads a team of Microsoft software engineers working on the next generation of Windows operating system software. At Apple, Bertrand Serlet is leading a team to try to make sure the new Macintosh operating system is better. Although they hold the same type of job, Sinofsky and Serlet are widely different in their approaches to leadership. Sinofsky is a meticulous planner and likes to run a tight ship. "Under Sinofsky," one engineer said, "you plan and you stick to the plan." Serlet, on the other hand, prefers things to be a little chaotic. He isn't a stickler for rules and procedures, emphasizing a more flexible, laid-back style. A programmer who has worked under both leaders compared Sinofsky's style to that of a martial marching band, while Serlet's was compared to an improvisational jazz group.[39]

How can two people with widely different styles both be effective leaders? The answer lies in understanding **contingency approaches** to leadership, which explore how the organizational situation influences leader effectiveness. Contingency approaches include the situational model based on the work of Hersey and Blanchard, the leadership model developed by Fiedler and his associates, and the substitutes-for-leadership concept.

Take a Moment

As a new manager, will you emphasize a task-oriented or a people-oriented leadership style? To find out, complete the New Manager Self-Test on page 503.

THE SITUATIONAL MODEL OF LEADERSHIP

The **situational model** of leadership, which originated with Hersey and Blanchard, is an interesting extension of the behavioral theories summarized in the leadership grid (see Exhibit 15.6). This approach focuses a great deal of attention on the characteristics of followers in determining appropriate leadership behavior. The point of the situational model is that subordinates vary in readiness, which is determined by the degree of willingness and ability a subordinate demonstrates while performing a specific task. *Willingness* refers to a combination of confidence, commitment, and motivation, and a follower may be high or low on any of the three variables. *Ability* refers to the amount of knowledge, experience, and demonstrated skill a subordinate brings to the task. Effective leaders adapt their style according to the readiness level of the people they are managing. People low in readiness—because of little ability or training or insecurity—need a different leadership style than those who are high in readiness and have good ability, skills, confidence, and willingness to work.[40]

According to the situational model, a leader can adopt one of four leadership styles, as shown in Exhibit 15.7. The *directing style* is a highly dictating style and involves giving explicit directions about how tasks should be accomplished. The *coaching style* is one

New Manager Self-Test

Task versus People Orientation

Instructions: Responding to the statements below can help you diagnose your approach to dealing with others when you are in a leadership role. If you have been a leader at work with people reporting to you, think back to that experience. Or you can think about how you usually behave as a formal or informal leader in a group to get an assignment completed. Please answer honestly about how frequently you display each behavior.

	Mostly True	Mostly False
1. I intentionally try to make people's work on the job more pleasant.	X	
2. I focus more on execution than on being pleasant with people.	X	
3. I go out of my way to help others.		
4. I personally hold people accountable for their performance.	X	
5. I work hard to maintain a friendly atmosphere on the team.	X	
6. I clearly tell people what I expect of them.	X	
7. I think a lot about people's personal welfare.		X
8. I check up on people to know how they are doing.		X
9. I am concerned more with relationships than with results.		X
10. I assign people to specific roles and tasks.		

11. I focus more on being pleasant with people than on execution of tasks. ____ X

12. I am concerned more with results than with peoples' feelings. X ____

Scoring and Interpretation: Give yourself 2 points for each Mostly True and 1 point for each Mostly False.

People Orientation: Sum your points for the odd-numbered questions: _____.

Task Orientation: Sum your points for the even-numbered questions: _____.

Your *People Orientation* score reveals your orientation toward people and relationships as described in the chapter. A score of 10 or higher suggests that you may be "high" on people behavior. A score of 9 or below suggests that you may be "low" on people orientation. Your *Task Orientation* score reveals your orientation toward tasks and outcomes. A score of 10 or higher suggests that you may be "high" on task-oriented behavior. A score of 9 or below suggests that you may be "low" on task orientation.

What is your primary leadership orientation? Which of the following best represents your leadership style (check one)? Look at Exhibit 15.7 on the following page to see the quadrant in which you fit.

_____ Low Task, Low People = Entrusting style

_____ Low Task, High People = Supporting style

_____ High Task, Low People = Directing style

_____ High Task, High People = Coaching style

Does your quadrant seem correct based on your experience? Compare your scores to other students'.

5

LEADING

EXHIBIT 15.7

The Situational Model of Leadership

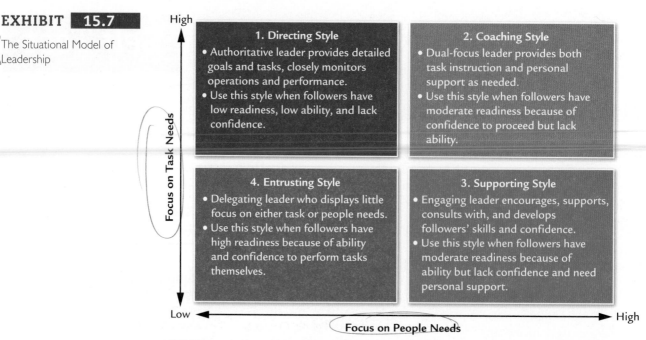

SOURCE: Based on Gary Yukl, Angela Gordon, and Tom Taber, "A Hierarchical Taxonomy of Leadership Behavior: Integrating a Half Century of Behavior Research," *Journal of Leadership and Organization Studies* 9, no. 1 (2002): 15–32, and Paul Hersey, Kenneth Blanchard, and Dewey Johnson, *Management of Organizational Behavior: Utilizing Human Resources,* 7th ed. (Upper Saddle River, NJ: Prentice Hall, 1996).

where the leader explains decisions and gives subordinates a chance to ask questions and gain clarity and understanding about work tasks. The *supporting style* is one where the leader shares ideas with subordinates, gives them a chance to participate, and facilitates decision making. The fourth style, the *entrusting style*, provides little direction and little support because the leader turns over responsibility for decisions and their implementation to subordinates.

Exhibit 15.7 summarizes the situational relationship between leader style and follower readiness. The directing style has the highest probability of successfully influencing low readiness followers who are unable or unwilling—because of poor ability and skills, little experience, or insecurity—to take responsibility for their own task behavior. The leader is specific, directing people exactly what to do, how to do it, and when. The coaching and supporting styles work for followers at moderate readiness levels. For example, followers might lack some education and experience for the job but have high confidence, interest, and willingness to learn. As shown in the exhibit, the coaching style is effective in this situation because it involves giving direction but also includes seeking input from others and clarifying tasks rather than simply instructing that they be performed. When followers have the necessary skills and experience but are somewhat insecure in their abilities or lack high willingness, the supporting style enables the leader to guide followers' development and act as a resource for advice and assistance. When followers demonstrate high readiness, that is, they have high levels of education, experience, and readiness to accept responsibility for their own task behavior, the entrusting style can effectively be used. Because of the high readiness level of followers, the leader can delegate responsibility for decisions and their implementation to subordinates who have the skills, abilities, and positive attitudes to follow through. The leader provides a general goal and sufficient authority to do the task as followers see fit.

To apply the situational model, the leader diagnoses the readiness level of followers and adopts the appropriate style—directing, coaching, supporting, or entrusting. For example, Jo Newton, an impulse import category leadership manager at Mars' Slough office near London, uses primarily a supporting style. Most members of Newton's team are at moderate to high readiness levels, so Newton advises them of the results the company wants and then steps back, providing guidance and support as needed. "I like people to come up with their own way of doing things. . . .," she says. "I like to support people as opposed to directing them to do things."[41] A leader taking over a new team of inexperienced or uncertain members would likely have to provide more direction with either a directing or coaching style. On the other hand, Warren Buffett uses a primarily entrusting style. The 80-year-old CEO of Berkshire Hathaway is considered one of the world's best managers, but he isn't closely involved in the day-to-day management of all the businesses Berkshire owns. He trusts the managers of the various units, who are highly skilled professionals able and willing to take responsibility for their own task behavior.[42] An entrusting leader style is not always appropriate, but all managers need to be able to delegate some tasks and decisions for the organization to work smoothly. The Shoptalk discusses techniques for effective delegation.

FIEDLER'S CONTINGENCY THEORY

Whereas the situational model focused on the characteristics of followers, Fiedler and his associates looked at some other elements of the organizational situation to assess when one leadership style is more effective than another.[43] The starting point for Fiedler's theory is the extent to which the leader's style is task oriented or relationship (people) oriented. Fiedler considered a person's leadership style to be relatively fixed and difficult to change; therefore, the basic idea is to match the leader's style with the situation most favorable for his or her effectiveness. By diagnosing leadership style and the organizational situation, the correct fit can be arranged.

Situation: Favorable or Unfavorable?

The suitability of a person's leadership style is determined by whether the situation is favorable or unfavorable to the leader. The favorability of a leadership situation can be analyzed in terms of three elements: the quality of relationships between leader and followers, the degree of task structure, and the extent to which the leader has formal authority over followers.[44]

A situation would be considered *highly favorable* to the leader when leader-member relationships are positive, tasks are highly structured, and the leader has formal authority over followers. In this situation, followers trust, respect, and have confidence in the leader. The group's tasks are clearly defined, involve specific procedures, and have clear, explicit goals. In addition, the leader has formal authority to direct and evaluate followers, along with the power to reward or punish. A situation would be considered *highly unfavorable* to the leader when leader-member relationships are poor, tasks are highly unstructured, and the leader has little formal authority. In a highly unfavorable situation, followers have little respect for or confidence and trust in the leader. Tasks are vague and ill-defined and lack clear-cut procedures and guidelines. The leader has little formal authority to direct subordinates and does not have the power to issue rewards or punishments.

▶▶▶ **Concept Connection**

"Let's get going. Let's do something, let's move, and let's not be constrained by something that has happened in the past." That's how Edward Whitacre, Jr., transitional CEO and chairman of General Motors (GM), described his leadership style. In the wake of the 2008 economic crisis and federal bailout, he faced a tough situation trying to restore the newly reorganized company's profitability so it could end government ownership. Whitacre used a **task-oriented style**, demanding quality and efficiency improvements and setting high standards. By the end of his brief tenure in 2010, GM had returned to profitability, paid back loans to U.S. and Canadian governments ahead of schedule, and begun the process of returning to private ownership.

Matching Leader Style to the Situation

When Fiedler examined the relationships among leadership style and situational favorability, he found the pattern shown in Exhibit 15.8. Task-oriented leaders are more effective when the situation is either highly favorable or highly unfavorable. Relationship-oriented leaders are more effective in situations of moderate favorability.

Manager's Shoptalk

How to Delegate

Sometimes, managers cling too tightly to their decision making and task responsibilities. Failure to delegate occurs for a number of reasons: Managers are most comfortable making familiar decisions; they feel they will lose personal status by delegating tasks; they believe they can do a better job themselves; or they have an aversion to risk—they will not take a chance on delegating because performance responsibility ultimately rests with them.

Yet delegating tasks and decision making offers an organization many advantages. Decisions are made at the right level, lower-level employees are motivated, and employees have the opportunity to develop decision-making skills. The following approach can help you delegate more effectively as a manager:

- **Delegate the whole task.** A manager should delegate an entire task to one person rather than dividing it among several people. This type of delegation gives the individual complete responsibility and increases his or her initiative while giving the manager some control over the results.

- **Select the right person.** Not all employees have the same capabilities and degree of motivation. Managers must match talent to task if delegation is to be effective. They should identify subordinates who made independent decisions in the past and show a desire for more responsibility.

- **Ensure that authority equals responsibility.** Merely assigning a task is not effective delegation. Managers often load subordinates with increased responsibility but do not extend their decision-making range. In addition to having responsibility for completing a task, the worker must be given the authority to make decisions about how best to do the job.

- **Give thorough instruction.** Successful delegation includes information on what, when, why, where, who, and how. The subordinate must clearly understand the task and the expected results. It is a good idea to write down all provisions discussed, including required resources and when and how the results will be reported.

- **Maintain feedback.** Feedback means keeping open lines of communication with the subordinate to answer questions and provide advice, but without exerting too much control. Open lines of communication make it easier to trust subordinates. Feedback keeps the subordinate on the right track.

- **Evaluate and reward performance.** Once the task is completed, the manager should evaluate results, not methods. When results do not meet expectations, the manager must assess the consequences. When they do meet expectations, the manager should reward employees for a job well done with praise, financial rewards when appropriate, and delegation of future assignments.

Are You a Positive Delegator?

Do you help or hinder the decentralization process? If you answer yes to more than three of the following questions, you may have a problem delegating:

- I tend to be a perfectionist.
- My boss expects me to know all the details of my job.
- I don't have the time to explain clearly and concisely how a task should be accomplished.
- I often end up doing tasks myself.
- My subordinates typically are not as committed as I am.
- I get upset when other people don't do the task right.
- I really enjoy doing the details of my job to the best of my ability.
- I like to be in control of task outcomes.

Sources: Thomas R. Horton, "Delegation and Team Building: No Solo Acts Please," *Management Review* (September 1992): 58–61; Andrew E. Schwartz, "The Why, What, and to Whom of Delegation," *Management Solutions* (June 1987): 31–38; "Delegation," *Small Business Report* (June 1986): 38–43; and Russell Wild, "Clone Yourself," *Working Woman* (May 2000): 79–80.

EXHIBIT **15.8** How Leader Style Fits the Situation

High
Performance
Low

Task-oriented leader

Relationship-oriented leader

| Situation Very Favorable to Leader | Situation Intermediately Favorable to Leader | Situation Very Unfavorable to Leader |

SOURCE: Based on Fred E. Fiedler, "The Effects of Leadership Training and Experience: A Contingency Model Interpretation," *Administrative Science Quarterly* 17 (1972): 455.

The task-oriented leader excels in the favorable situation because everyone gets along, the task is clear, and the leader has power; all that is needed is for someone to lead the charge and provide direction. Similarly, if the situation is highly unfavorable to the leader, a great deal of structure and task direction is needed. A strong leader will define task structure and establish strong authority. Because leader-member relations are poor anyway, a strong task orientation will make no difference in the leader's popularity. **Sergio Marchionne has used strong task-oriented leadership in an unfavorable situation at Chrysler.**

Innovative Way

Sergio Marchionne, Chrysler Group LLC

The fate of the smallest of the Big Three U.S. automakers rests in the hands of Italian-born Sergio Marchionne, who rescued Fiat from the brink of collapse a few years ago with his close attention to detail. Marchionne is a strong, task-oriented leader. Rather than settling into the top-floor executive suite at Chrysler's Auburn Hills, Michigan, headquarters, Marchionne chose an office in the fourth-floor engineering center. He carries six smartphones and keeps tabs on the smallest details, down to a faulty door handle on the new Dodge Charger. "If you really want to run the business," he says, "you need to get involved at this level."

Marchionne came into a highly unfavorable situation at Chrysler. Like GM, Chyrsler had to be rescued by a federal bailout several years ago, and Marchionne took charge just after the company emerged from bankruptcy and Fiat assumed part ownership. Sales were slumping, Chrysler's image was tarnished, morale and motivation were low, costs were high, and operational problems plagued the company. Marchionne became known at Fiat for working long hours 7 days a week, and he told his top executives at Chrysler to plan on doing the same for the foreseeable future. He meets with managers regularly and gives them specific orders for what he wants to see accomplished. Managers who were committed to staying stuck in the old way of doing things were fired.

Marchionne's task-oriented leadership is having a positive effect. Chrysler's auto sales are improving dramatically and operational problems have been brought under control. In addition, Marchionne's hard-hitting approach has brought a refreshing energy into the organization, giving employees a greater sense of hope and motivation.[45]

Sergio Marchionne's tough, task-oriented approach is suitable for the difficult situation at Chrysler. Researchers at the University of Chicago who looked at CEOs in turnaround situations—where companies typically have high debt loads and a need to improve results in a hurry—found that tough-minded, task-focused characteristics such as analytical skills, a focus on efficiency, and setting high standards were more valuable leader qualities than were relationship skills such as good communication, listening, and teamwork.[46]

5
LEADING

The relationship-oriented leader performs better in situations of intermediate favorability because human relations skills are important in achieving high group performance. In these situations, the leader may be moderately well liked, have some power, and supervise jobs that contain some ambiguity. A leader with good interpersonal skills can create a positive group atmosphere that will improve relationships, clarify task structure, and establish position power.

A leader, then, needs to know two things to use Fiedler's contingency theory. First, the leader should know whether he or she has a relationship- or task-oriented style. Second, the leader should diagnose the situation and determine whether leader-member relations, task structure, and position power are favorable or unfavorable.

Fiedler believed fitting leader style to the situation can yield big dividends in profits and efficiency.[47] On the other hand, the model has also been criticized.[48] For one thing, some researchers have challenged the idea that leaders cannot adjust their styles as situational characteristics change. Despite criticisms, Fiedler's model has continued to influence leadership studies. Fiedler's research called attention to the importance of finding the correct fit between leadership style and situation.

SITUATIONAL SUBSTITUTES FOR LEADERSHIP

The contingency leadership approaches considered so far focus on the leader's style, the subordinates' nature, and the situation's characteristics. The final contingency approach suggests that situational variables can be so powerful that they actually substitute for or neutralize the need for leadership.[49] This approach outlines those organizational settings in which a leadership style is unimportant or unnecessary.

Exhibit 15.9 shows the situational variables that tend to substitute for or neutralize leadership characteristics. A **substitute for leadership** makes the leadership style unnecessary or redundant. For example, highly professional subordinates who know how to do their tasks do not need a leader who initiates structure for them and tells them what to do. A **neutralizer** counteracts the leadership style and prevents the leader from displaying certain behaviors. For example, if a leader has absolutely no position power or is physically removed from subordinates, the leader's ability to give directions to subordinates is greatly reduced.

Situational variables in Exhibit 15.9 include characteristics of the group, the task, and the organization itself. When followers are highly professional and experienced, both leadership styles are less important. People do not need much direction or consideration. With

EXHIBIT 15.9   Substitutes and Neutralizers for Leadership

Variable		Task-Oriented Leadership	People-Oriented Leadership
Organizational variables	Group cohesiveness	Substitutes for	Substitutes for
	Formalization	Substitutes for	No effect on
	Inflexibility	Neutralizes	No effect on
	Low position power	Neutralizes	Neutralizes
	Physical separation	Neutralizes	Neutralizes
Task characteristics	Highly structured task	Substitutes for	No effect on
	Automatic feedback	Substitutes for	No effect on
	Intrinsic satisfaction	No effect on	Substitutes for
Group characteristics	Professionalism	Substitutes for	Substitutes for
	Training/experience	Substitutes for	No effect on

2/23

respect to task characteristics, highly structured tasks substitute for a task-oriented style, and a satisfying task substitutes for a people-oriented style. With respect to the organization itself, group cohesiveness substitutes for both leader styles. Formalized rules and procedures substitute for leader task orientation. Physical separation of leader and subordinate neutralizes both leadership styles.

The value of the situations described in Exhibit 15.9 is that they help leaders avoid leadership overkill. Leaders should adopt a style with which to complement the organizational situation. Consider the work situation for bank tellers. A bank teller performs highly structured tasks, follows clearly written rules and procedures, and has little flexibility in terms of how to do the work. The head teller should not adopt a task-oriented style because the organization already provides structure and direction. The head teller should concentrate on a people-oriented style to provide a more pleasant work environment. In other organizations, if group cohesiveness or intrinsic satisfaction meets employees' social needs, the leader is free to concentrate on task-oriented behaviors. The leader can adopt a style complementary to the organizational situation to ensure that both task needs and people needs of the work group will be met.

Remember This

- A **contingency approach** is a model of leadership that describes the relationship between leadership styles and specific situations.
- One contingency approach is the **situational model**, which links the leader's behavioral style with the readiness level of followers.
- In general, a task-oriented leader style fits a low-readiness follower, and a relationship leader style fits a higher-readiness follower.
- In Fiedler's contingency theory, the suitability of a leader's style is determined by whether the situation is considered favorable or unfavorable to the leader.

- Task-oriented leaders are considered to perform better in either highly favorable or highly unfavorable situations.
- Relationship-oriented leaders are considered to perform better in situations of intermediate favorability.
- A **substitute for leadership** is a situational variable that makes a leadership style redundant or unnecessary.
- A **neutralizer** is a situational variable that counteracts a leadership style and prevents the leader from displaying certain behaviors.

Charismatic and Transformational Leadership

Research has also looked at how leadership can inspire and motivate people beyond their normal levels of performance. Some leadership approaches are more effective than others for bringing about high levels of commitment and enthusiasm. Two types with a substantial impact are charismatic and transformational.

CHARISMATIC LEADERSHIP

Charisma has been referred to as "a fire that ignites followers' energy and commitment, producing results above and beyond the call of duty."[50] The **charismatic leader** has the ability to inspire and motivate people to do more than they would normally do, despite obstacles and personal sacrifice. Followers are willing to put aside their own interests for the sake of the team, department, or organization. The impact of charismatic leaders normally comes from (1) stating a lofty vision of an imagined future that employees identify with, (2) displaying an ability to understand and empathize with followers, and (3) empowering and trusting subordinates to accomplish results.[51] Charismatic leaders tend to be less predictable because they create an atmosphere of change, and they may be obsessed by visionary ideas that excite, stimulate, and drive other people to work hard. One of the best known charismatic leaders in the business world in recent years was Apple co-founder and CEO Steve Jobs.

Innovative Way

Steve Jobs, Apple

Steve Jobs was a legend long before he died in October 2011. His creativity and obsession with innovative product design, combined with the force of his personality, made Apple what it is today. Since his death, managers have been reading books and articles that describe his leadership style to try to tap into some of the Steve Jobs magic. Part of that magic relied on Jobs's charisma.

Jobs commanded a rock-star-like following. The tale of how he dropped out of college, cofounded Apple, got fired from his own company, returned years later to save it, and then transformed it by creating a whole new business with the iPod and iPhone is the stuff of legend. Jobs provided the pizzazz for Apple employees, business partners, and the public. His charismatic personality played an important role in persuading media companies to make their content available on Apple products. "When Steve talks, people listen," a Harvard Business School professor said a few months before Jobs's death. His passion and commitment inspired and motivated millions of employees and customers. However, his quick, unpredictable temper, driven, willful personality, impatience and relentless demands, and hypercritical attitude sometimes undermined performance.

Jobs challenged and inspired teams to reach beyond the possible, yet he could easily dismiss a promising idea or effort as "a piece of crap," contributing to disillusionment and the loss of potential. Despite this, many people—even some he mistreated—admired and respected (some have even said *worshiped*) Steve Jobs. They tell their "Steve-Jobs-yelled-in-my-face" stories with pride. His energizing personality and his refusal to "sell out" made people want to be around him and want to be *like* him. Indeed, one magazine article commented that the amazing staff loyalty he inspired turned Apple into "Steve Jobs with a thousand lives."[52]

As the example of Steve Jobs illustrates, there can be both positive and negative aspects of charisma. Other charismatic leaders include Mother Teresa, David Koresh, Sam Walton, Alexander the Great, Oprah Winfrey, Martin Luther King, Jr., and Osama bin Laden. Charisma can be used for positive outcomes that benefit the group, but it can also be used for self-serving purposes that lead to the deception, manipulation, and exploitation of others. When charismatic leaders respond to organizational problems in terms of the needs of the entire group rather than their own emotional needs, they can have a powerful, positive influence on organizational performance.[53] At Apple, Steve Jobs's personal identity was so closely aligned with his company that serving Apple and serving his own emotional needs were likely one and the same! As with the Level 5 and authentic leadership approaches that we discussed earlier in the chapter, *humility* typically plays an important part in distinguishing whether a charismatic leader will work to benefit primarily the larger organization or use his or her gifts for ego-building and personal gain.[54]

Charismatic leaders are skilled in the art of *visionary leadership*. A **vision** is an attractive, ideal future that is credible yet not readily attainable. Vision is an important component of both charismatic and transformational leadership. Visionary leaders speak to the hearts of employees, letting them be part of something bigger than themselves. Where others see obstacles or failures, they see possibility and hope.

Charismatic leaders typically have a strong vision for the future, almost an obsession, and they can motivate others to help realize it.[55] These leaders have an emotional impact on subordinates because they strongly believe in the vision and can communicate it to others in a way that makes the vision real, personal, and meaningful.

In the Hands of a Matador

It was, by any standard, a bold move. Taking the leadership reins in 2004 as CEO and president of Spain-based **Acciona**, one of Europe's most profitable real estate and construction businesses, José Manuel Entrecanales envisioned a future in which businesses would balance economic gain with environmental standards. Entrecanales convinced his board to address climate change and promote renewable energy development. The company wasted no time making a public announcement of its long-term sustainability plans and undertaking new strategies led by a Sustainability Committee. Over the next six years, Acciona managers made investments in sustainability including wind generators. By

2009, Acciona had risen to third in the world in wind energy production. In less than a decade, Acciona has established a green reputation, and it was the leadership of Entrecanales, with the precise timing and calculated moves of a great matador, that envisioned the new spheres of action.

Sources: Daniel Arenas, Jeremie Fosse, and Matthew Murphy, "Acciona: a Process of Transformation Towards Sustainability," in *The Journal of Management Development* 30, no. 10 (2011): 1027–1048; and Patricia McCormick, "A Brave Matador Explains the Bullfight," *Sports Illustrated*, March 11, 1963, http://sportsillustrated.cnn.com/vault/article/magazine/MAG1074594/2/index.htm (accessed August 4, 2012).

TRANSFORMATIONAL VERSUS TRANSACTIONAL LEADERSHIP

Transformational leaders are similar to charismatic leaders, but they are distinguished by their special ability to bring about innovation and change by recognizing followers' needs and concerns, providing meaning, challenging people to look at old problems in new ways, and acting as role models for the new values and behaviors. Transformational leaders inspire followers not just to believe in the leader personally, but to believe in their own potential to imagine and create a better future for the organization. Transformational leaders create significant change in both followers and the organization.[56]

Transformational leadership can be better understood in comparison to *transactional leadership*.[57] **Transactional leaders** clarify the role and task requirements of subordinates, initiate structure, provide appropriate rewards, and try to be considerate and meet the social needs of subordinates. The transactional leader's ability to satisfy subordinates may improve productivity. Transactional leaders excel at management functions. They are hardworking, tolerant, and fair minded. They take pride in keeping things running smoothly and efficiently. Transactional leaders often stress the impersonal aspects of performance, such as plans, schedules, and budgets. They have a sense of commitment to the organization and conform to organizational norms and values. Transactional leadership is important to all organizations, but leading change requires a different approach.

Transformational leaders have the ability to lead changes in the organization's mission, strategy, structure, and culture, as well as to promote innovation in products and technologies. Transformational leaders do not rely solely on tangible rules and incentives to control specific transactions with followers. They focus on intangible qualities such as vision, shared values, and ideas to build relationships, give larger meaning to diverse activities, and find common ground to enlist followers in the change process.[58] For example, Michelle Rhee, former chancellor of the District of Columbia public schools, acted as a transformational leader to revamp one of the most expensive, worst-performing school systems in the country. She attacked the dysfunctional culture that rewarded teachers for seniority rather than performance, revised systems and structures to slash bureaucracy, held school principals accountable for improving student performance, and focused people on a mission of putting the best interests of students first. Rhee quickly cut numerous administrative positions, fired teachers and principals who didn't meet performance standards, and closed

[handwritten margin note: BRING ABOUT CHANGES AND INNOVATION.]

[handwritten margin note: CLARIFY WHAT SUBORDINATES ROLES ARE.]

[margin tab: 5 LEADING]

underperforming schools. New procedures handsomely reward high-performing teachers, give principals more control over hiring, promoting, and firing, and new evaluation procedures put people on alert that low performance and complacency won't be tolerated. Rhee's transformational leadership brought new energy and movement to a long-stagnant system.[59]

Studies show that transformational leadership has a positive impact on follower development and follower performance.[60] Moreover, transformational leadership skills can be learned and are not ingrained personality characteristics. However, some personality traits may make it easier for a leader to display transformational leadership behaviors. For example, studies of transformational leadership have found that the trait of agreeableness, as discussed in the previous chapter, is often associated with transformational leaders.[61] In addition, transformational leaders are typically emotionally stable and positively engaged with the world around them, and they have a strong ability to recognize and understand others' emotions.[62] These characteristics are not surprising, considering that these leaders accomplish change by building networks of positive relationships.

Remember This

- A **charismatic leader** is a leader who has the ability to inspire and motivate people to transcend their expected performance, even to the point of personal sacrifice.
- Both charismatic and transformational leaders provide followers with an inspiring **vision**, an attractive, ideal future that is credible yet not readily attainable.

- A **transformational leader** is distinguished by a special ability to bring about innovation and change by creating an inspiring vision, shaping values, building relationships, and providing meaning for followers.
- A **transactional leader** clarifies subordinates' roles and task requirements, initiates structure, provides rewards, and displays consideration for followers.

Followership

No discussion of leadership is complete without a consideration of followership. Leadership matters, but without effective followers no organization can survive. People have different expectations of what constitutes a good follower versus a good leader, as illustrated by the results of studies asking people to rank the desired characteristics of leaders and followers. The top five qualities desired in each are as follows:[63]

Leader	Follower
Honest	Honest
Competent	Competent
Forward-looking	Dependable
Inspiring	Cooperative
Intelligent	Loyal

There may be some differences, but overall, many of the qualities that define a good follower are the same qualities as those possessed by a good leader. Leaders can develop an understanding of their followers and create the conditions that help them be most effective.[64]

One model of followership is illustrated in Exhibit 15.10. Robert E. Kelley conducted extensive interviews with managers and their subordinates and came up with five *follower styles*, which are categorized according to two dimensions, as shown in the exhibit.[65]

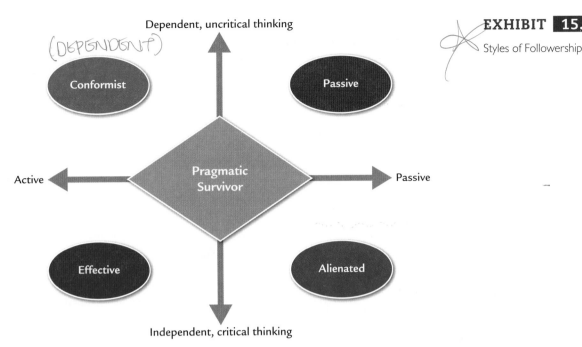

EXHIBIT 15.10

Styles of Followership

SOURCE: Based on Robert E. Kelley, *The Power of Followership* (New York: Doubleday, 1992).

The first dimension is the quality of independent, **critical thinking** versus dependent, **uncritical thinking**. Independent critical thinkers are mindful of the effects of their own and others' behavior on achieving organizational goals. They can weigh the impact of their boss's and their own decisions and offer constructive criticism, creativity, and innovation. Conversely, a dependent, uncritical thinker does not consider possibilities beyond what he or she is told, does not contribute to the cultivation of the organization, and accepts the supervisor's ideas without thinking.

The second dimension of follower style is active versus passive behavior. An active follower participates fully in the organization, engages in behavior that is beyond the limits of the job, demonstrates a sense of ownership, and initiates problem solving and decision making. A passive follower, by contrast, is characterized by a need for constant supervision and prodding by superiors. Passivity is often regarded as laziness; a passive person does nothing that is not required and avoids added responsibility.

The extent to which an individual is active or passive and is an independent, critical thinker or a dependent, uncritical thinker determines whether the person will be an alienated follower, a passive follower, a conformist, a pragmatic survivor, or an effective follower, as illustrated in Exhibit 15.10:

- The **alienated follower** is a passive, yet independent, critical thinker. Alienated employees are often effective followers who have experienced setbacks and obstacles, perhaps promises broken by their superiors. Thus, they are capable, but they focus exclusively on the shortcomings of their boss. Often cynical, alienated followers are able to think independently, but they do not participate in developing solutions to the problems or deficiencies that they see. These people waste valuable time complaining about their boss without offering constructive feedback.

- The **conformist** participates actively in a relationship with the boss but doesn't use critical thinking skills. In other words, a conformist typically carries out any and all orders, regardless of the nature of the request. The conformist participates willingly, but without considering the consequences of what he or she is being asked to do—even at the risk of contributing to a harmful endeavor. A conformist is concerned only with avoiding conflict. This follower style might reflect an individual's overdependent attitude toward authority, yet it can also result from rigid rules and authoritarian environments that create a culture of conformity.

- The **pragmatic survivor** has qualities of all four extremes—depending on which style fits with the prevalent situation. This type of person uses whatever style best benefits his or her own position and minimizes risk. Pragmatic survivors often emerge when an organization is going through desperate times, and individuals find themselves doing whatever is needed to get through the difficulty. Within any given company, some 25 to 35 percent of people tend to be pragmatic survivors, avoiding risks and fostering the status quo.[66]

- The **passive follower** exhibits neither critical, independent thinking nor active participation. Being passive and uncritical, these people show neither initiative nor a sense of responsibility. Their activity is limited to what they are told to do, and they accomplish things only with a great deal of supervision. Passive followers leave the thinking to the boss. Often, this style is the result of a micromanaging boss who encourages passive behavior. People learn that to show initiative, accept responsibility, or think creatively is not rewarded, and may even be punished by the boss, so they grow increasingly passive.

- The **effective follower** is both a critical, independent thinker and active in the organization. Effective followers behave the same toward everyone, regardless of their position in the organization. They develop an equitable relationship with their leaders and do not try to avoid risk or conflict. These people are capable of self-management, they discern strengths and weaknesses in themselves and their bosses, they are committed to something bigger than themselves, and they work toward competency, solutions, and positive impact.

Consider the effective followership of the night janitor at FAVI, a French copper-alloy foundry. While the janitor was cleaning one night, the phone rang, and she answered it to discover that an important visitor to the company had been delayed and was now waiting at the airport without the promised ride to his hotel. (FAVI's CEO had left the airport when the visitor didn't arrive as expected.) What did the janitor do? She simply took the keys to one of the company cars, drove 90 minutes to pick up the visitor and deliver him to his hotel, then went back to finish the cleaning that she had stopped three hours earlier.[67] Effective followers recognize that they have power in their relationships with superiors; thus, they have the courage to manage upward, to initiate change, and to put themselves at risk or in conflict with the boss if they believe that it serves the best interest of the team or organization.

Remember This

- Leaders can accomplish nothing without effective followers.
- **Critical thinking** means thinking independently and being mindful of the effect of one's behavior on achieving goals.
- **Uncritical thinking** means failing to consider the possibilities beyond what one is told, accepting others' ideas without thinking.
- An **effective follower** is a critical, independent thinker who actively participates in the organization.

- An **alienated follower** is a person who is an independent, critical thinker but is passive in the organization.
- A **conformist** is a follower who participates actively in the organization but does not use critical thinking skills.
- A **passive follower** is one who exhibits neither critical independent thinking nor active participation.
- A follower who has qualities of all four follower styles, depending on which fits the prevalent situation, is called a **pragmatic survivor**.

Power and Influence

Both followers and leaders use power and influence to get things done in organizations. Sometimes the terms *power* and *influence* are used synonymously, but there are distinctions between the two. **Power** is the potential ability to influence the behavior of others.[68] **Influence** is the effect that a person's actions have on the attitudes, values, beliefs, or behavior of others. Whereas power is the capacity to cause a change in a person, influence may be thought of as the degree of actual change.

Most discussions of power include five types that are available to leaders,[69] and these can be categorized as either *hard power* or *soft power*. Hard power is power that stems largely from a person's position of authority and includes legitimate, reward, and coercive power. Soft power includes expert power and referent power, which are based on personal characteristics and interpersonal relationships more than on a position of authority.

POSITION POWER (COMES FROM JOB)

The traditional manager's power comes from the organization (hard power). The manager's position gives him or her the power to reward or punish subordinates to influence their behavior. Legitimate power, reward power, and coercive power are all forms of position power used by managers to change employee behavior.

POWER HAS BEEN DELEGATED.

Legitimate Power

Power coming from a formal management position in an organization and the authority granted to it is called **legitimate power**. Once a person has been selected as a supervisor, most employees understand that they are obligated to follow his or her direction with respect to work activities. Subordinates accept this source of power as legitimate, which is why they comply.

Reward Power

Another kind of power, **reward power**, stems from the authority to bestow rewards on other people. Managers may have access to formal rewards, such as pay increases or promotions. They also have at their disposal rewards such as praise, attention, and recognition. Managers can use rewards to influence subordinates' behavior.

Coercive Power

The opposite of reward power is **coercive power**. It refers to the authority to punish or recommend punishment. Managers have coercive power when they have the right to fire or demote employees, criticize them, or withhold pay increases. If an employee does not perform as expected, the manager has the coercive power to reprimand him, put a negative letter in his file, deny him a raise, and hurt his chances for a promotion.

PERSONAL POWER (KNOWLEDGE/EXPERTISE)

Effective leaders don't rely solely on the hard power of their formal position to influence others. Jeff Immelt, CEO of GE, considers himself a failure if he exercises his formal authority more than seven or eight times a year. The rest of the time, he is using softer means to persuade and influence others and to resolve conflicting ideas and opinions.[70] In contrast to the external sources of position power, personal power most often comes from internal sources, such as an individual's special knowledge or personal characteristics. Personal power is the primary tool of the leader, and it is becoming increasingly important as more businesses are run by teams of workers who are less tolerant of authoritarian management.[71] Two types of personal power are expert power and referent power.

5

LEADING

Concept Connection ◀◀◀

"In business," says Daniel Amos, Aflac chairman and CEO, "you should treat your employees like they can vote." The insurance company that Amos heads has been named to *Fortune's* "100 Best Companies to Work For in America" for 10 consecutive years. Amos (pictured here with the Aflac duck) influences employees using a combination of **reward power** and **referent power.** "You kind of try to kiss the babies and shake the hands and tell 'em you appreciate 'em and would like them to support you. You can do it like a dictator, but I'm not sure very many of them in the long run are successful."

Michael A. Schwarz

Expert Power

Power resulting from a person's special knowledge or skill regarding the tasks being performed is referred to as **expert power.** When someone is a true expert, others go along with recommendations because of his or her superior knowledge. Followers as well as leaders can possess expert power. For example, some managers lead teams in which members have expertise that the leader lacks. Some leaders at top management levels may lack expert power because subordinates know more about technical details than they do.

Referent Power

Referent power comes from an individual's personal characteristics that command others' identification, respect, and admiration so they wish to emulate that individual. Referent power does not depend on a formal title or position. When employees admire a supervisor because of the way that she deals with them, the influence is based on referent power. Referent power is most visible in the area of charismatic leadership. In social and religious movements, we often see charismatic leaders who emerge and gain a tremendous following based solely on their personal power.

OTHER SOURCES OF POWER

There are additional sources of power that are not linked to a particular person or position, but rather to the role an individual plays in the overall functioning of the organization. These important sources include personal effort, relationships with others, and information.

Personal Effort

People who show initiative, work beyond what is expected of them, take on undesirable but important projects, and show interest in learning about the organization and industry often gain power as a result. Stephen Holmes says he got his start toward the CEO's office at Wyndham Worldwide because of personal effort. As a young internal auditor at a private-equity firm in the early 1980s, Holmes was spending his evenings trying to learn a new spreadsheet program. Noted investor Henry Silverman noticed him night after night and, intrigued by the young auditor's efforts, stopped by to see what he was doing. Silverman asked Holmes to move with him to future companies, including Blackstone, HMS, and eventually Wyndham. "I was a kid," Holmes says, "[but he] put me into positions that no one else my age was getting to do."[72]

Network of Relationships

People who are enmeshed in a network of relationships have greater power. A leader or employee with many relationships knows what's going on in the organization and industry, whereas one who has few interpersonal connections is often in the dark about important activities or changes. Developing positive associations with superiors or other powerful people is a good way to gain power, but people with the greatest power are those who cultivate relationships with individuals at all levels, both inside and outside the organization.

Information

Information is a primary business resource, and people who have access to information and control over how and to whom it is distributed are typically powerful. To some extent, access to information is determined by a person's position in the organization. Top managers typically have access to more information than middle managers, who in turn have access to more information than lower-level supervisors or front-line employees.

Both leaders and followers can tap into these additional sources of power. Leaders succeed when they take the time to build relationships both inside and outside the organization and to talk informally about important projects and priorities. Jack Griffin was forced out as CEO of Time Inc., after less than six months on the job, largely because he failed to develop positive relationships. Griffin tried to use the hard power of his position to make needed changes at Time without building the soft power connections needed to implement the changes. Board members began to realize that Griffin had become so unpopular that the company was likely to lose valuable employees if he stayed on as CEO.[73]

INTERPERSONAL INFLUENCE TACTICS

Leaders often use a combination of influence strategies, and people who are perceived as having greater power and influence typically are those who use a wider variety of tactics. One survey of a few hundred leaders identified more than 4,000 different techniques that these people used to influence others.[74]

However, these tactics fall into basic categories that rely on understanding the principles that cause people to change their behavior and attitudes. Exhibit 15.11 lists six principles for asserting influence. Notice that most of these involve the use of personal power rather than relying solely on position power or the use of rewards and punishments.[75]

1. *Use rational persuasion.* The most frequently used influence strategy is to use facts, data, and logical argument to persuade others that a proposed idea, request, or decision is appropriate. Using rational persuasion can often be highly effective because most people have faith in facts and analysis.[76] Rational persuasion is most successful when a leader has technical knowledge and expertise related to the issue at hand (expert power), although referent power is also used. That is, in addition to facts and figures, people have to believe in the leader's credibility.

EXHIBIT 15.11

Six Interpersonal Influence Tactics for Leaders

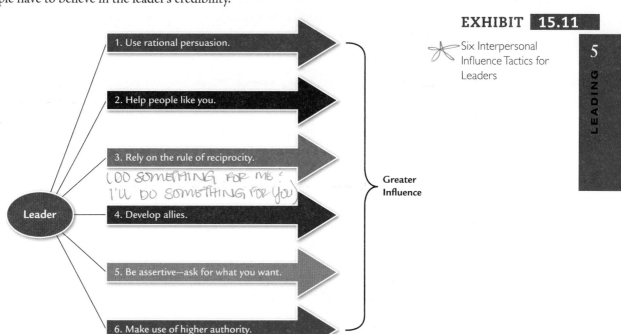

1. Use rational persuasion.
2. Help people like you.
3. Rely on the rule of reciprocity.
   (DO SOMETHING FOR ME? I'LL DO SOMETHING FOR YOU)
4. Develop allies.
5. Be assertive—ask for what you want.
6. Make use of higher authority.

Leader

Greater Influence

5

LEADING

2. *Help people like you.* People would rather say yes to someone they like than to someone they don't. Effective leaders strive to create goodwill and favorable impressions. When a leader shows consideration and respect, treats people fairly, and demonstrates trust in others, people are more likely to want to help and support the leader by doing what he or she asks. In addition, most people like a leader who makes them feel good about themselves, so leaders should never underestimate the power of praise.

3. *Rely on the rule of reciprocity.* Leaders can influence others through the exchange of benefits and favors. Leaders share what they have—whether it is time, resources, services, or emotional support. The feeling among people is nearly universal that others should be paid back for what they do, in one form or another. This unwritten "rule of reciprocity" means that leaders who do favors for others can expect that others will do favors for them in return.[77]

4. *Develop allies.* Effective leaders develop networks of allies—people who can help the leader accomplish his or her goals. Leaders talk with followers and others outside of formal meetings to understand their needs and concerns as well as to explain problems and describe the leader's point of view. They strive to reach a meeting of minds with others about the best approach to a problem or decision.[78]

5. *Ask for what you want.* Another way to influence others is to make a direct and personal request. Leaders have to be explicit about what they want, or they aren't likely to get it. An explicit proposal is sometimes accepted simply because others have no better alternative. Also, a clear proposal or alternative will often receive support if other options are less well defined.

6. *Make use of higher authority.* Sometimes to get things done leaders have to use their formal authority, as well as gain the support of people at higher levels to back them up. However, research has found that the key to successful use of formal authority is to be knowledgeable, credible, and trustworthy—that is, to demonstrate expert and referent power as well as legitimate power. Managers who become known for their expertise, who are honest and straightforward with others, and who inspire trust can exert greater influence than those who simply issue orders.[79]

Research indicates that people rate leaders as "more effective" when they are perceived to use a variety of influence tactics. But not all managers use influence in the same way. Studies have found that leaders in human resources, for example, tend to use softer, more subtle approaches such as building goodwill, using favors, and developing allies, whereas those in finance are inclined to use harder, more direct tactics such as formal authority and assertiveness.[80]

Remember This

- **Power** is the potential ability to influence the behavior of others.
- All leaders use power to influence people and accomplish organizational goals.
- **Influence** is the effect a person's actions have on the attitudes, values, beliefs, or behavior of others.
- **Legitimate power** is power that stems from a manager's formal position in an organization and the authority granted by that position.
- **Reward power** results from the authority to bestow rewards.
- **Coercive power** stems from the authority to punish or recommend punishment.

- **Expert power** is power that results from a leader's special knowledge or skill in the tasks performed by subordinates.
- **Referent power** results from characteristics that command subordinates' identification with, respect and admiration for, and desire to emulate the leader.
- Both leaders and followers can tap into other sources of power, including personal effort, networks of relationships, and access to or control over information.
- Leaders use a wide range of interpersonal influence tactics, and people who use a wider variety of tactics are typically perceived as having greater power.

ch15: Discussion Questions

1. Suggest some personal traits that you believe would be useful to a business leader today. Are these traits more valuable in some situations than in others? How do you think traits differ from strengths?

2. In a study asking what people wanted from leaders versus followers, people ranked *maturity* number 8 for followers, but number 15 for leaders. What might account for people wanting a higher maturity level from followers?

3. If a male manager changes his behaviors to incorporate elements of interactive leadership more common to female managers, can he still be an "authentic" leader? Discuss.

4. Suggest the sources of power that would be available to a leader of a student government organization. What sources of power may not be available? To be effective, should student leaders keep power to themselves or delegate power to other students?

5. What skills and abilities does a manager need to lead effectively in a virtual environment? Do you believe a leader with a consideration style or an initiating-structure style would be more successful as a virtual leader? Explain your answer.

6. What is transformational leadership? Give examples of organizational situations that would call for transformational, transactional, or charismatic leadership.

7. How does Level 5 leadership differ from the concept of servant leadership? Do you believe anyone has the potential to become a Level 5 leader? Discuss.

8. Why do you think so little attention is given to followership compared to leadership in organizations? Discuss how the role of an effective follower is similar to the role of a leader.

9. Do you think leadership is more important or less important in today's flatter, team-based organizations? Are some leadership styles better suited to such organizations as opposed to traditional hierarchical organizations? Explain.

10. Consider the leadership position of a senior partner in a law firm. What task, subordinate, and organizational factors might serve as substitutes for leadership in this situation?

ch15: Apply Your Skills: Experiential Exercise

What Is the Impact of Leadership?[81]

What are your beliefs and understandings about how top leaders influence organizational performance. To learn about your beliefs, please answer whether each item below is Mostly True or Mostly False based on your personal beliefs.

	Mostly True	Mostly False
1. The quality of leadership is the most important influence on the performance of an organization.	____	____
2. People in top-level leadership positions have the power to make or break an organization.	____	____
3. Most activities in an organization have little to do with the decisions or activities of the top leaders.	____	____
4. Even in a bad economy, a good leader can prevent a company from doing poorly.	____	____
5. A company cannot do well unless it has high quality leadership at the top.	____	____
6. High-quality versus low-quality leadership has a bigger impact on a firm's performance than does the business environment.	____	____
7. Poor organizational performance is often due to factors beyond the control of even the best leaders.	____	____
8. Eventually, bad leadership at the top will trigger poor organizational performance.	____	____
9. Leaders typically should not be held responsible for a firm's poor performance.	____	____

Interpretation: This scale is about the "romance" of leadership, which is the romantic view that leaders are very responsible for organizational performance, while ignoring other factors such as economic conditions. Company performance is difficult to control and is an outcome of complex forces. Attributing too much responsibility to leaders is a simplification shaped by our own mental construction more than by the reality and complexity of organizational performance. Top leaders are not heroes, but they are important as one of several key factors that can shape organizational performance.

Scoring: Give yourself 1 point for each item 1, 2, 4, 5, 6, and 8 marked as Mostly True and each item 3, 7, and 9 marked as Mostly False. A score of 7 or higher suggests a belief in the romance of leadership—that leaders have more control over performance outcomes than is actually the case. If you scored 3 or less, you may underestimate the impact of top leaders, a somewhat skeptical view. A score of 4 to 6 suggests a balanced view of leadership.

In Class: Sit with a student partner and explain your scores to each other. What are your beliefs about leadership? What is the basis for your beliefs? The instructor can ask for a show of hands concerning the number of high, medium, and low scores on the questionnaire. Discuss the following questions: Do you believe that presidents, top executives, and heads of nonprofit organizations act alone and hence are largely responsible for performance? What is the evidence for this belief? What other forces will affect an organization? What is a realistic view of top leader influence in a large organization?

ch15: Apply Your Skills: Small Group Breakout

Which Leadership Styles Are More Effective?

Step 1. Think about one situation in which a formal or informal leader was effective at motivating people, and another situation in which a leader was ineffective, perhaps demotivating people. When you have these situations firmly in mind, answer the following questions:

- What source or type of power was used by the effective leader? The ineffective leader?

- Did the effective leader emphasize a task-oriented or relationship-oriented style? Explain your rating. What about the ineffective leader?

- Did the effective leader come across as a humble person serving others or something larger than him- or herself, or did the leader seem ego-centered and self-serving? What about the ineffective leader?

Step 2. Divide into groups of three to five students. Compare your answers and look for patterns that distinguish effective from ineffective leaders across your group members' experiences. What patterns do you find?

Step 3. Each group member should describe the leadership situation, with respect to its "favorability" or "readiness of followers." What relationship do you observe between the leadership situations and the style that the leader used?

Step 4. Prepare to present your findings to the class and to participate in a discussion led by your instructor.

ch15: Endnotes

1. William C. Rhoden, "Steelers' Coach Takes a Quiet Route to Brilliance," *The New York Times*, February 6, 2011, SP.9.
2. Gary Yukl, "Managerial Leadership: A Review of Theory and Research," *Journal of Management* 15 (1989): 251–289.
3. James M. Kouzes and Barry Z. Posner, "The Credibility Factor: What Followers Expect from Their Leaders," *Management Review* (January 1990): 29–33.
4. Jim Collins, "Level 5 Leadership: The Triumph of Humility and Fierce Resolve," *Harvard Business Review* (January 2001): 67–76; Jim Collins, "Good to Great," *Fast Company* (October 2001): 90–104; A. J. Vogl, "Onward and Upward" (an interview with Jim Collins), *Across the Board* (September–October 2001): 29–34; and Jerry Useem, "Conquering Vertical Limits," *Fortune* (February 19, 2001): 84–96.
5. Jim Collins, "Enduring Greatness," *Leadership Excellence* (January 2011): 8.
6. Miguel Helft, "A Hired Gun for Microsoft, in Dogged Pursuit of Google," *The New York Times*, August 31, 2009, www.nytimes.com/2009/08/31/technology/internet/31search.html (accessed August 31, 2009).
7. Collins, "Level 5 Leadership."
8. Quoted in William J. Holstein, "The View's Still Great from the Corner Office," *The New York Times*, May 8, 2005.
9. Richard L. Daft and Robert H. Lengel, *Fusion Leadership: Unlocking the Subtle Forces That Change People and Organizations* (San Francisco: Berrett-Koehler, 1998).
10. Leigh Buchanan, "In Praise of Selflessness: Why the Best Leaders Are Servants," *Inc.* (May 2007): 33–35.
11. Robert K. Greenleaf, *Servant Leadership: A Journey into the Nature of Legitimate Power and Greatness* (Mahwah, NJ: Paulist Press, 1977).
12. "Not Her Father's Chief Executive" (an interview with Marilyn Carlson Nelson), *U.S. News & World Report* (October 30, 2006): 64–65.
13. "*Maersk Alabama* Crew Recalls Pirate Attack," *USA Today* (April 16, 2009), www.usatoday.com/news/nation/2009-04-16-pirates_N.htm (accessed April 30, 2009); Stacy Meichtry, Arian Campo-Flores, and Leslie Scism, "Cruise Company Blames Captain," *The Wall Street Journal*, January 17, 2012, http://online.wsj.com/article/SB10001424052970203735304577165290656739300.html (accessed January 20, 2012); and "Death Toll of Italy's Costa Concordia Wreck Rises to 30,"

Philippine Star, March 23, 2012, www.philstar.com/
article.aspx?articleid=790169&publicationsubcategoryid
=200 (accessed September 14, 2012).

14. Adam Bluestein, "Start a Company. Change the World."
Inc. (May 2011): 71–80.

15. Bill George et al., "Discovering Your Authentic Leadership," *Harvard Business Review* (February 2007):
129–138; and Bill George, *Authentic Leadership:
Rediscovering the Secrets to Lasting Value* (San Francisco:
Jossey-Bass, 2003). For a recent review of the literature
on authentic leadership, see William L. Gardner et al.,
"Authentic Leadership: A Review of the Literature and
Research Agenda," *The Leadership Quarterly* 22 (2011):
1120–1145.

16. George, *Authentic Leadership*; and Bill George, "Truly
Authentic Leadership," Special Report: America's Best
Leaders, *U.S. News & World Report*, October 22, 2006,
www.usnews.com/usnews/news/articles/061022/
30authentic.htm (accessed October 5, 2010).

17. Michael Sokolove, "Follow Me," *The New York Times
Magazine* (February 2006): 96; and Jena McGregor,
"Coach K's Leadership ABCs," *The Washington Post*,
November 17, 2011, www.washingtonpost.com/blogs/
post-leadership/post/coach-ks-leadership-abcs/2011/04/
01/gIQAkIpPUN_blog.html (accessed September 12,
2012).

18. Judy B. Rosener, *America's Competitive Secret: Utilizing
Women as a Management Strategy* (New York: Oxford
University Press, 1995), pp. 129–135.

19. Alice H. Eagly and Linda L. Carli, "The Female Leader-
ship Advantage: An Evaluation of the Evidence," *The
Leadership Quarterly* 14 (2003): 807–834; Rosener,
America's Competitive Secret; Judy B. Rosener, "Ways
Women Lead," *Harvard Business Review* (November–
December 1990): 119–125; Sally Helgesen, *The Female
Advantage: Women's Ways of Leadership* (New York:
Currency/Doubleday, 1990); Bernard M. Bass and
Bruce J. Avolio, "Shatter the Glass Ceiling: Women May
Make Better Managers," *Human Resource Management*
33, no. 4 (Winter 1994): 549–560; and Carol Kinsey
Goman, "What Men Can Learn from Women about
Leadership in the 21st Century," *The Washington Post*,
August 10, 2011, www.washingtonpost.com/national/
on-leadership/what-men-can-learn-from-women-
about-leadership/2011/08/10/gIQA4J9n6I_story.html
(accessed September 12, 2012).

20. Rochelle Sharpe, "As Leaders, Women Rule," *Business-
Week* (November 20, 2000): 75–84.

21. Kevin S. Groves, "Gender Differences in Social and
Emotional Skills and Charismatic Leadership,"
Journal of Leadership and Organizational Studies 11,
no. 3 (2005): 30ff.

22. Jack Zenger and Joseph Folkman, "Are Women Better
Leaders Than Men?" HBR Blog Network, *Harvard
Business Review*, March 15, 2012, http://blogs.hbr.org/
cs/2012/03/a_study_in_leadership_women_do.html
(accessed September 12, 2012); and Herminia Ibarra

and Otilia Obodaru, "Women and the Vision Thing,"
Harvard Business Review (January 2009): 62–70.

23. Susan Carey, "More Women Take Flight in Airline
Operations," *The Wall Street Journal*, August 14, 2007,
B1; and Ann Therese Palmer, "Teacher Learns All About
Airline; United VP Began as Reservations Clerk, Rose
Through Ranks," *Chicago Tribune*, December 24, 2006, 3.

24. Leigh Buchanan, "Pat McGovern . . . For Knowing the
Power of Respect," segment in "25 Entrepreneurs We
Love," *Inc.* (April 2004): 110–147.

25. This analogy is from Gordon P. Rabey, "Leadership
Is Response: A Paper for Discussion," *Industrial and
Commercial Training* 42, no. 2 (2010): 87–92.

26. This discussion is based on Philip A. Dover and Udo
Dierk, "The Ambidextrous Organization: Integrating Managers, Entrepreneurs, and Leaders," *Journal of
Business Strategy* 31, no. 5 (2010): 49–58; Gary Yukl
and Richard Lepsinger, "Why Integrating the Leading
and Managing Roles Is Essential for Organizational
Effectiveness," *Organizational Dynamics* 34, no. 4
(2005): 361–375; and Henry Mintzberg, *Managing*
(San Francisco: Berrett-Kohler Publishers, 2009).

27. Nancy F. Koehn, "The Driver in Ford's Amazing Race,"
The New York Times, April 1, 2012, BU.1.

28. G. A. Yukl, *Leadership in Organizations* (Englewood
Cliffs, NJ: Prentice Hall, 1981); and S. C. Kohs and
K. W. Irle, "Prophesying Army Promotion," *Journal of
Applied Psychology* 4 (1920): 73–87.

29. R. Albanese and D. D. Van Fleet, *Organizational
Behavior: A Managerial Viewpoint* (Hinsdale, IL: The
Dryden Press, 1983); and S. A. Kirkpatrick and E. A.
Locke, "Leadership: Do Traits Matter?" *Academy of
Management Executive* 5, no. 2 (1991): 48–60.

30. A summary of various studies and surveys is reported
in Del Jones, "Optimism Puts Rose-Colored Tint in
Glasses of Top Execs," *USA Today*, December 15, 2005.

31. Annie Murphy Paul, "The Uses and Abuses of
Optimism (and Pessimism)," *Psychology Today*
(November–December 2011): 56–63.

32. Tom Rath and Barry Conchie, *Strengths Based Leader-
ship* (Gallup Press, 2009); Marcus Buckingham and
Donald O. Clifton, *Now, Discover Your Strengths*
(New York: The Free Press, 2001), p. 12.

33. Buckingham and Clifton, *Now, Discover Your Strengths*.

34. Gary Yukl, Angela Gordon, and Tom Taber, "A Hierarchical Taxonomy of Leadership Behavior: Integrating a
Half Century of Behavior Research," *Journal of Leadership and Organizational Studies* 9, no. 1 (2002): 13–32.

35. C. A. Schriesheim and B. J. Bird, "Contributions of the
Ohio State Studies to the Field of Leadership," *Journal
of Management* 5 (1979): 135–145; C. L. Shartle, "Early
Years of the Ohio State University Leadership Studies,"
Journal of Management 5 (1979): 126–134; and R. Lik-
ert, "From Production- and Employee-Centeredness to
Systems 1–4," *Journal of Management* 5 (1979): 147–156.

36. P. C. Nystrom, "Managers and the High-High Leader
Myth," *Academy of Management Journal* 21 (1978):

5

LEADING

325–331; and L. L. Larson, J. G. Hunt, and Richard N. Osborn, "The Great High-High Leader Behavior Myth: A Lesson from Occam's Razor," *Academy of Management Journal* 19 (1976): 628–641.

37. R. Likert, "From Production- and Employee-Centeredness to Systems 1–4."

38. Robert R. Blake and Jane S. Mouton, *The Managerial Grid III* (Houston, TX: Gulf, 1985).

39. John Markoff, "Competing as Software Goes to Web," *The New York Times*, June 5, 2007, C1, C5.

40. This discussion is based on Paul Hersey and Ken Blanchard, "Revisiting the Life-Cycle Theory of Leadership," in "Great Ideas Revisited," *Training & Development* (January 1996): 42–47; Kenneth H. Blanchard and Paul Hersey, "Life-Cycle Theory of Leadership," in "Great Ideas Revisited," *Training & Development* (January 1996): 42–47; Paul Hersey, "Situational Leaders: Use the Model in Your Work," *Leadership Excellence* (February 2009): 12; and Paul Hersey and Kenneth H. Blanchard, *Management of Organizational Behavior: Utilizing Human Resources*, 4th ed. (Englewood Cliffs, NJ: Prentice Hall, 1982). The concept of *readiness* comes from Hersey, "Situational Leaders."

41. Jennifer Robison, "Many Paths to Engagement: How Very Different Management Styles Get the Same Great Results at Mars Incorporated," *Gallup Management Journal*, January 10, 2008, http://gmj.gallup.com/content/103513/Many-Paths-Engagement.aspx (accessed July 31, 2010).

42. Andrew Ross Sorkin, "Warren Buffett, Delegator in Chief," *The New York Times*, www.nytimes.com/2011/04/24/weekinreview/24buffett.html (accessed September 14, 2012).

43. Fred E. Fiedler, "Assumed Similarity Measures as Predictors of Team Effectiveness," *Journal of Abnormal and Social Psychology* 49 (1954): 381–388; F. E. Fiedler, *Leader Attitudes and Group Effectiveness* (Urbana, IL: University of Illinois Press, 1958); and F. E. Fiedler, *A Theory of Leadership Effectiveness* (New York: McGraw-Hill, 1967).

44. Fred E. Fiedler and M. M. Chemers, *Leadership and Effective Management* (Glenview, IL: Scott, Foresman, 1974).

45. Neal E. Boudette, "Fiat CEO Sets New Tone at Chrysler," *The Wall Street Journal*, June 21, 2009, http://online.wsj.com/article/SB124537403628329989.html (accessed September 14, 2012); Jeff Bennett and Neal E. Boudette, "Boss Sweats Details of Chrysler Revival," *The Wall Street Journal*, January 31, 2011, A1; and Kate Linebaugh and Jeff Bennett, "Marchionne Upends Chrysler's Ways," *The Wall Street Journal*, January 12, 2010, http://online.wsj.com/article/SB10001424052748703652104574652364158366106.html (accessed September 14, 2012).

46. Reported in George Anders, "Theory & Practice: Tough CEOs Often Most Successful, a Study Finds," *The Wall Street Journal*, November 19, 2007.

47. Fred E. Fiedler, "Engineer the Job to Fit the Manager," *Harvard Business Review* 43 (1965): 115–122; and F. E. Fiedler, M. M. Chemers, and L. Mahar, *Improving Leadership Effectiveness: The Leader Match Concept* (New York: Wiley, 1976).

48. R. Singh, "Leadership Style and Reward Allocation: Does Least Preferred Coworker Scale Measure Tasks and Relation Orientation?" *Organizational Behavior and Human Performance* 27 (1983): 178–197; and D. Hosking, "A Critical Evaluation of Fiedler's Contingency Hypotheses," *Progress in Applied Psychology* 1 (1981): 103–154.

49. S. Kerr and J. M. Jermier, "Substitutes for Leadership: Their Meaning and Measurement," *Organizational Behavior and Human Performance* 22 (1978): 375–403; and Jon P. Howell and Peter W. Dorfman, "Leadership and Substitutes for Leadership among Professional and Nonprofessional Workers," *Journal of Applied Behavioral Science* 22 (1986): 29–46.

50. Katherine J. Klein and Robert J. House, "On Fire: Charismatic Leadership and Levels of Analysis," *Leadership Quarterly* 6, no. 2 (1995): 183–198.

51. Jay A. Conger and Rabindra N. Kanungo, "Toward a Behavioral Theory of Charismatic Leadership in Organizational Settings," *Academy of Management Review* 12 (1987): 637–647; Jaepil Choi, "A Motivational Theory of Charismatic Leadership: Envisioning, Empathy, and Empowerment," *Journal of Leadership and Organizational Studies* 13, no. 1 (2006): 24ff; and William L. Gardner and Bruce J. Avolio, "The Charismatic Relationship: A Dramaturgical Perspective," *Academy of Management Review* 23, no. 1 (1998): 32–58.

52. Jon Katzenbach, "The Steve Jobs Way," *Strategy + Business* (Summer 2012), www.strategy-business.com/article/00109?gko=d331b (accessed June 11, 2012); Steve Moore, "Not Bad for a Hippie Dropout," *Management Today* (March 2009): 27; Connie Guglielmo, "What Makes Steve Jobs Run?" *National Post* (May 17, 2008), FW–8; "Editorial: Apple—and U.S.—Need Steve Jobs," *McClatchy-Tribune Business News* (January 18, 2009); Leslie Kwoh and Emma Silverman, "Bio as Bible: Managers Imitate Steve Jobs," *The Wall Street Journal* (March 31, 2012), B1; and Miguel Helft and Claire Cain Miller, "A Deep Bench of Leadership at Apple," *The New York Times*, January 17, 2011, www.nytimes.com/2011/01/18/technology/18cook.html?_r=0 (accessed January 18, 2011).

53. Robert J. House and Jane M. Howell, "Personality and Charismatic Leadership," *Leadership Quarterly* 3, no. 2 (1992): 81–108; and Jennifer O'Connor et al., "Charismatic Leaders and Destructiveness: A Historiometric Study," *Leadership Quarterly* 6, no. 4 (1995): 529–555.

54. Rob Nielsen, Jennifer A. Marrone, and Holly S. Slay, "A New Look at Humility: Exploring the Humility Concept and Its Role in Socialized Charismatic Leadership," *Journal of Leadership and Organizational Studies* 17, no. 1 (February 2010): 33–44.

55. Robert J. House, "Research Contrasting the Behavior and Effects of Reputed Charismatic vs. Reputed

Non-Charismatic Leaders," paper presented as part of a symposium, "Charismatic Leadership: Theory and Evidence," Academy of Management, San Diego, 1985.

56. Bernard M. Bass, "Theory of Transformational Leadership Redux," *Leadership Quarterly* 6, no. 4 (1995): 463–478; Noel M. Tichy and Mary Anne Devanna, *The Transformational Leader* (New York: John Wiley & Sons, 1986); James C. Sarros, Brian K. Cooper, and Joseph C. Santora, "Building a Climate for Innovation Through Transformational Leadership and Organizational Culture," *Journal of Leadership and Organizational Studies* 15, no. 2 (November 2008): 145–158; and P. D. Harms and Marcus Crede, "Emotional Intelligence and Transformational and Transactional Leadership: A Meta-Analysis," *Journal of Leadership and Organizational Studies* 17, no. 1 (February 2010): 5–17.

57. The terms *transactional* and *transformational* come from James M. Burns, *Leadership* (New York: Harper & Row, 1978); and Bernard M. Bass, "Leadership: Good, Better, Best," *Organizational Dynamics* 13 (Winter 1985): 26–40.

58. Daft and Lengel, *Fusion Leadership*.

59. Michelle Rhee and Adrian Fenty, "Review—The Education Manifesto—Michelle Rhee and Adrian Fenty on What They Learned While Pushing to Reform D.C.'s Failing Public Schools," *The Wall Street Journal*, October 30, 2010, C1; Jeff Chu, "The Iron Chancellor," *Fast Company* (September 2008): 112–143; Amanda Ripley, "Can She Save Our Schools?" *Time* (December 8, 2008): 36–44; and William McGurn, "Giving Lousy Teachers the Boot; Michelle Rhee Does the Once Unthinkable in Washington," *The Wall Street Journal*, July 27, 2010.

60. Gang Wang et al., "Transformational Leadership and Performance Across Criteria and Levels: A Meta-Analytic Review of 25 Years of Research," *Group & Organization Management* 36, no. 2 (2011): 223–270; Taly Dvir et al., "Impact of Transformational Leadership on Follower Development and Performance: A Field Experiment," *Academy of Management Journal* 45, no. 4 (2002): 735–744.

61. Robert S. Rubin, David C. Munz, and William H. Bommer, "Leading from Within: The Effects of Emotion Recognition and Personality on Transformational Leadership Behavior," *Academy of Management Journal* 48, no. 5 (2005): 845–858; and Timothy A. Judge and Joyce E. Bono, "Five-Factor Model of Personality and Transformational Leadership," *Journal of Applied Psychology* 85, no. 5 (October 2000): 751ff.

62. Rubin, Munz, and Bommer, "Leading from Within."

63. Augustine O. Agho, "Perspectives of Senior-Level Executives on Effective Followership and Leadership," *Journal of Leadership and Organizational Studies* 16, no. 2 (November 2009): 159–166; and James M. Kouzes and Barry Z. Posner, *The Leadership Challenge: How to Get Extraordinary Things Done in Organizations* (San Francisco: Jossey-Bass, 1990).

64. Barbara Kellerman, "What Every Leader Needs to Know About Followers," *Harvard Business Review* (December 2007): 84–91.

65. Robert E. Kelley, *The Power of Followership* (New York: Doubleday, 1992).

66. *Ibid.*, 117–118.

67. Vignette recounted in Isaac Getz, "Liberating Leadership: How the Initiative-Freeing Radical Organizational Form Has Been Successfully Adopted," *California Management Review* (Summer 2009): 32–58.

68. Henry Mintzberg, *Power In and Around Organizations* (Englewood Cliffs, NJ: Prentice Hall, 1983); and Jeffrey Pfeffer, *Power in Organizations* (Marshfield, MA: Pitman, 1981).

69. John R. P. French, Jr., and Bertram Raven, "The Bases of Social Power," in D. Cartwright and A. F. Zander, eds., *Group Dynamics* (Evanston, IL: Row Peterson, 1960), pp. 607–623.

70. Reported in Vadim Liberman, "Mario Moussa Wants You to Win Your Next Argument" (Questioning Authority column), *Conference Board Review* (November–December 2007): 25–26.

71. Jay A. Conger, "The Necessary Art of Persuasion," *Harvard Business Review* (May–June 1998): 84–95.

72. Roger Yu, "Co-Workers Praise Wyndham CEO's Welcoming Demeanor," *USA Today*, November 22, 2010, www.usatoday.com/money/companies/management/profile/2010-11-22-wyndhamceo22_ST_N.htm (accessed September 14, 2012).

73. Jeremy W. Peters, "Time Inc. Chief Executive Jack Griffin Out," *The New York Times*, February 17, 2011, http://mediadecoder.blogs.nytimes.com/2011/02/17/time-inc-chief-executive-jack-griffin-out/ (accessed February 18, 2011).

74. D. Kipnis et al., "Patterns of Managerial Influence: Shotgun Managers, Tacticians, and Politicians," *Organizational Dynamics* (Winter 1984): 58–67.

75. These tactics are based on Kipnis et al., "Patterns of Managerial Influence"; and Robert B. Cialdini, "Harnessing the Science of Persuasion," *Harvard Business Review* (October 2001): 72–79.

76. Kipnis et al., "Patterns of Managerial Influence"; and Jeffrey Pfeffer, *Managing with Power: Politics and Influence in Organizations* (Boston: Harvard Business School Press, 1992), Chapter 13.

77. *Ibid.*

78. V. Dallas Merrell, *Huddling: The Informal Way to Management Success* (New York: AMACOM, 1979).

79. Robert B. Cialdini, *Influence: Science and Practice*, 4th ed. (Boston: Pearson Allyn & Bacon, 2000).

80. Harvey G. Enns and Dean B. McFarlin, "When Executives Influence Peers, Does Function Matter?" *Human Resource Management* 4, no. 2 (Summer 2003): 125–142.

81. Adapted from Birgit Schyns, James R. Meindl, and Marcel A. Croon, "The Romance of Leadership Scale: Cross-Cultural Testing and Refinement," *Leadership* 3, no. 1 (2007): 29–46.

5

LEADING

Motivation

Pavel Filatov/Alamy

Learning Outcomes

After studying this chapter, you should be able to:

1. Define *motivation* and explain the difference between intrinsic and extrinsic rewards.

2. Identify and describe content theories of motivation based on employee needs.

3. Identify and explain process theories of motivation.

4. Describe the reinforcement perspective and social learning theory and how they can be used to motivate employees.

5. Discuss major approaches to job design and how job design influences motivation.

6. Describe how managers build a thriving workforce for a high-performing organization.

7. Explain how empowerment heightens employee motivation.

8. Identify three elements of employee engagement and describe some ways that managers can create a work environment that promotes engagement.

Are You Engaged or Disengaged?[1]

INSTRUCTIONS: The term *employee engagement* is popular in the corporate world. To learn what engagement means, answer the following questions twice—(1) once for a course that you both enjoyed and performed well in, and (2) a second time for a course that you did not enjoy and performed poorly in. Please mark a "1" to indicate whether each item is Mostly True or Mostly False for the course you enjoyed and performed well in. Please mark a "2" to indicate whether each item is Mostly True or Mostly False for the course you did not enjoy and performed poorly in.

	Mostly True	Mostly False
1. I made sure to study on a regular basis.	_____	_____
2. I put forth effort.	_____	_____
3. I found ways to make the course material relevant to my life.	_____	_____
4. I found ways to make the course interesting to me.	_____	_____
5. I raised my hand in class.	_____	_____
6. I had fun in class.	_____	_____
7. I participated actively in small-group discussions.	_____	_____
8. I helped fellow students.	_____	_____

SCORING AND INTERPRETATION: Engagement means that people involve and express themselves in their work, going beyond the minimum effort required. Engagement typically has a positive relationship with both personal satisfaction and performance. If this relationship was true for your classes, the number of "1s" in the Mostly True column will be higher than the number of "2s." You might expect a score of 6 or higher for a course in which you were engaged, and possibly 3 or lower if you were disengaged.

The challenge for a new manager is to learn to engage subordinates in the same way that your instructors in your favorite classes were able to engage you. Teaching is similar to managing. What techniques did your instructors use to engage students? Which techniques can you use to engage people when you become a new manager?

W hen Joie de Vivre Hospitality took over the Hotel Carlton in San Francisco, most employees were just putting in their hours until quitting time. Annual turnover was around 50 percent (about average for the hotel industry), but employees showed no energy and enthusiasm for serving guests. Joie de Vivre managers knew it didn't have to be that way. Hervé Blondel, the new Hotel Carlton general manager, decided to treat employees like partners. He started by finding out what they needed in order to do their jobs better and feel a sense of joy in their work lives. For Theophilus McKinney, who oversaw the front desk, it was working evenings instead of days, rearranging the phones so they were easier to answer, and being allowed to wear the funky shoes he preferred. For Anita Lum and her colleagues in housekeeping, it was simply having new vacuum cleaners that did what they were supposed to do. The previous management had refused to replace the aging vacuums, but Blondel bought a new one for each member of the housekeeping staff, and the company now replaces them every year. Blondel also gives people more leeway in serving guests and encourages them to participate in decisions that directly affect their

1 INTRODUCTION
2 ENVIRONMENT
3 PLANNING
4 ORGANIZING
5 LEADING
6 CONTROLLING

jobs. Within a few years, annual turnover was down to less than 10 percent, and customer satisfaction had dramatically improved. "It seems that this company cares about us . . .," says Lum. Front-desk worker Emelie Dela Cruz adds that "we're all just happier."[2]

Managers in other companies are discovering that creating an environment where people feel valued and feel that they are making an important contribution is one key to high employee motivation, which is an essential ingredient for organizational success. Most people begin a new job with energy and enthusiasm, but employees can lose their drive if managers fail in their role as motivators. Yet motivation is a challenge for many managers because motivation arises from within employees and may differ for each person. Some people are motivated primarily by money, others are motivated to perform well because managers make them feel appreciated for doing a good job, and still others find their primary motivation in the challenge of solving complex problems or making a contribution to society. With such diverse motivations among individuals, how do managers find the right way to motivate people toward common organizational goals?

This chapter reviews several approaches to employee motivation. First, we define motivation and the types of rewards that managers use. Then, we examine several models that describe the employee needs and processes associated with motivation. We also look at the use of reinforcement for motivation, explain social learning theory, and examine how job design—changing the structure of the work itself—can affect employee satisfaction and productivity. Finally, we discuss the trend of empowerment and look at how managers imbue work with a sense of meaning by fostering employee engagement.

The Concept of Motivation

Most of us get up in the morning, go to school or work, and behave in ways that are predictably our own. We respond to our environment and the people in it with little thought as to why we work hard, enjoy certain classes, or find some recreational activities so much fun. Yet all these behaviors are motivated by something. **Motivation** refers to the forces either within or external to a person that arouse enthusiasm and persistence to pursue a certain course of action. Employee motivation affects productivity, and part of a manager's job is to channel motivation toward the accomplishment of organizational goals.[3]

INDIVIDUAL NEEDS AND MOTIVATION

A simple model of human motivation is illustrated in Exhibit 16.1. People have *needs*—such as for recognition, achievement, or monetary gain—that translate into an internal tension that motivates specific behaviors with which to fulfill various needs. To the extent that the behavior is successful, the person is rewarded because the need is satisfied. The reward also informs the person that the behavior was appropriate and can be used again in the future.

Managers who understand the motives that compel people to initiate, alter, or continue a desired behavior are more successful as motivators. Exhibit 16.2 illustrates four categories of motives based on two criteria. The vertical dimension contrasts intrinsic versus extrinsic rewards. **Intrinsic rewards** are the satisfactions a person receives in the process

EXHIBIT 16.1   A Simple Model of Motivation

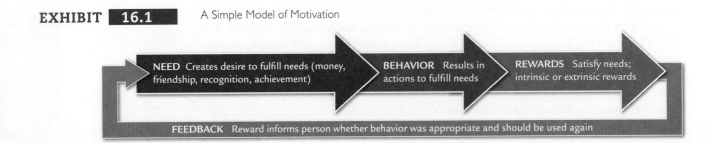

NEED Creates desire to fulfill needs (money, friendship, recognition, achievement) → BEHAVIOR Results in actions to fulfill needs → REWARDS Satisfy needs; intrinsic or extrinsic rewards

FEEDBACK Reward informs person whether behavior was appropriate and should be used again

of performing a particular action. The completion of a complex task may bestow a pleasant feeling of accomplishment, or solving a problem that benefits others may fulfill a personal mission. For example, employees at Salesforce.com, which provides cloud computing services to organizations such as Bank of America, Cisco, Google, and the Japanese government, are motivated by being on the "cutting edge" of reinventing how companies handle ordinary but critical tasks like sales, customer relations, and internal communications.[4] **Extrinsic rewards** are given by another person, typically a manager, and include promotions, praise, and pay increases. They originate externally, as a result of pleasing others. At the Alta Gracia factory in the Dominican Republic, owned by Knights Apparel, employees are motivated by the extrinsic reward of high pay because they need money to support their families and can't make nearly as much anywhere else.[5]

▶▶▶ **Concept Connection**

Photo Courtesy of The Container Store

The Container Store has the motto that one great person equals three good people. Here, an Elfa storage system designer works with a couple to design a custom storage plan. Getting hired is quite competitive at this retailer, which has been on *Fortune* magazine's list of 100 Best Companies to Work for in America year after year since 2000. Employees get **intrinsic rewards** from knowing that they were selected to work for this winning company. The Container Store also puts its money where its motto is—providing the **extrinsic rewards** of higher-than-average retail pay and other benefits.

The horizontal dimension of Exhibit 16.2 contrasts behaviors that are driven by fear or pain versus those driven by growth or pleasure. The four quadrants represent four differing approaches for motivating people.

Quadrants 1 and 2 are both negative approaches to motivating. Quadrant 1 uses negative, extrinsic methods, such as threats or punishments, to get people to perform as desired. Quadrant 2 methods attempt to motivate people by tapping into their self-doubts or anxieties. For example, a manager might motivate people to work hard by emphasizing the weak economy and high unemployment rate. Quadrant 1 and 2 methods can indeed be effective, as fear is a powerful motivator.[6] However, using fear to motivate people in organizations almost always has negative consequences for employee development and long-term performance. This chapter's Shoptalk takes a lighthearted approach by looking at some negative techniques that kill employee motivation and happiness.

EXHIBIT 16.2   Four Categories of Motives Managers Can Use

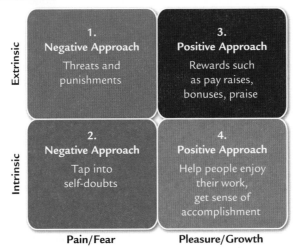

	Pain/Fear	Pleasure/Growth
Extrinsic	**1.** Negative Approach — Threats and punishments	**3.** Positive Approach — Rewards such as pay raises, bonuses, praise
Intrinsic	**2.** Negative Approach — Tap into self-doubts	**4.** Positive Approach — Help people enjoy their work, get sense of accomplishment

SOURCE: Based on Bruce H. Jackson, "Influence Behavior; Become a Master Motivator," *Leadership Excellence* (April 2010): 14.

5

LEADING

Manager's *Shoptalk*

How to Utterly Destroy Motivation

Many managers unknowingly demolish positive emotions in the workplace. Destroying people's positive feelings about themselves and their work is a sure way to kill motivation. Managers use a variety of techniques that make people miserable at work. If you've ever had a manager who used any of these, you know how it feels. Keep that in mind when you become a practicing manager.

- **Never allow people to feel a sense of pride or accomplishment.** In a recent study, one of the top *demotivators* reported by employees was constant setbacks. *Setbacks* are instances where people are blocked or stalled in doing their most important work or unable to make a meaningful contribution. One head of product development moved people on and off projects so often that they never experienced a sense of accomplishment. Motivation level? Zero.

- **Set such grandiose and vague goals that people don't know what they mean or have any idea how to achieve them.** There is nothing wrong with challenging goals. In fact, they can be highly motivating. But some managers set goals that have little relevance to employees, that are so extreme as to seem unattainable, or that are so vague that they have no meaning.

- **Pass up every opportunity to say "thank you."** No one likes to feel appreciated, after all, right?

Smart managers know *that's* not true! Sincerely thanking people for their efforts can provide a tremendous motivational boost, especially when times have been tough. In response to a McKinsey survey, 67 percent of people cited praise from an immediate supervisor as an effective motivator. It ranked higher than any other incentive on the list, including pay raises and cash bonuses.

- **Make sure people don't have any fun.** When people have fun at work, they want to be there. Managers influence whether people develop positive relationships and are able to have moments of levity and joy during their workday. Without some light moments, work is a hard slog every day. No wonder people just want to stay home.

Sources: Based on Teresa Amabile and Steven Kramer, "How to Completely, Utterly Destroy an Employee's Work Life," *The Washington Post*, March 6, 2012, www.washingtonpost.com/national/on-leadership/how-to-completely-utterly-destroy-an-employees-work-life/2012/03/05/gIQAxU3iuR_story.html (accessed March 8, 2012); T. Amabile and S. Kramer, "How Leaders Kill Meaning at Work," *McKinsey Quarterly*, January 2012, www.mckinseyquarterly.com/How_leaders_kill_meaning_at_work_2910 (accessed February 10, 2012); Martin Dewhurst, Matthew Guthridge, and Elizabeth Mohr, "Motivating People: Getting Beyond Money," *McKinsey Quarterly*, Issue 1 (2010): 12–15; and Regina M. Clark, "Are We Having Fun Yet? Creating a Motivating Work Environment," *Industrial and Commercial Training* 41, no. 1 (2009): 43–46.

Quadrants 3 and 4 are positive motivational approaches. Quadrant 3 methods attempt to influence behavior by using extrinsic rewards that create pleasure. At Hilcorp Energy, for example, managers offered employees the chance to earn a bonus of $50,000 each if they help the organization meet its growth goal.[7] This positive motivational approach is useful but limited. External rewards are important, but they can lose their power as motivational tools over time. The most effective managers also emphasize Quadrant 4 techniques that tap into deep-seated employee energy and commitment by helping people get intrinsic rewards from their work. For example, Chip Conley, CEO of Joie de Vivre, encourages managers of hotel housekeeping staff to "focus on the impact they're making rather than just the task of cleaning the toilet."[8]

Take a Moment

As a new manager, remember that people will be more engaged when they do things they really like. To reinforce this understanding, refer back to your answers on the questionnaire at the beginning of this chapter.

MANAGERS AS MOTIVATORS

Studies have found that high employee motivation goes hand in hand with high organizational performance and profits.[9] It is the responsibility of managers to find the right combination of motivational techniques and rewards to satisfy employees' needs and simultaneously encourage high work performance. Some ideas about motivation, referred to as *content theories*, stress the analysis of underlying human needs and how managers can satisfy needs in the workplace. *Process theories* concern the thought processes that influence behavior. They focus on how people seek rewards in work circumstances. *Reinforcement* and *social learning theories* focus on employee learning of desired work behaviors. In Exhibit 16.1, content theories focus on the concepts in the first box, process theories on those in the second, and reinforcement and social learning theories on those in the third.

Remember This

- **Motivation** is the arousal of enthusiasm and persistence to pursue a certain course of action.
- All behaviors are motivated by something, such as the desire to fulfill needs for money, recognition, friendship, or a sense of accomplishment.
- **Intrinsic rewards** are the satisfactions that a person receives in the process of performing a particular action.
- **Extrinsic rewards** are given by another person, such as a manager, and include pay increases, promotions, and praise.

- People can be driven to act by fear, but good managers avoid the use of fear tactics to motivate people because this approach damages employee commitment and performance in the long run.
- In addition to providing appropriate extrinsic rewards, effective managers try to help people achieve intrinsic rewards from their work.

Content Perspectives on Motivation

Content theories emphasize the needs that motivate people. At any point in time, people have a variety of needs. These needs translate into an internal drive that motivates specific behaviors in an attempt to fulfill the needs. In other words, our needs are like a hidden catalog of the things that we want and will work to get. To the extent that managers understand employees' needs, they can design reward systems to meet them and direct employees' energies and priorities toward attaining organizational goals.

THE HIERARCHY OF NEEDS

Probably the most famous content theory was developed by Abraham Maslow.[10] Maslow's **hierarchy of needs theory** proposes that people are motivated by multiple needs and that these needs exist in a hierarchical order, as illustrated in Exhibit 16.3. Maslow identified five general types of motivating needs in order of ascendance:

1. *Physiological needs.* These most basic human physical needs include food, water, and oxygen. In the organizational setting, they are reflected in the needs for adequate heat, air, and base salary to ensure survival.

2. *Safety needs.* These needs include a safe and secure physical and emotional environment and freedom from threats—that is, for freedom from violence and for an orderly society. In the workplace, safety needs reflect the needs for safe jobs, fringe benefits, and job security. Because of the weak economy and high unemployment in recent years, safety needs have taken priority for many people. A recent job satisfaction survey indicated that job security was the most important element of job satisfaction, with good benefits being second most important.[11] When managers at Burgerville, a regional restaurant chain based in Vancouver, Washington, began paying at least 90 percent of health insurance premiums for hourly employees who worked at least 20 hours a week, turnover plunged, employees began working harder to get more hours (which are assigned based on performance), service improved, and sales increased.[12]

EXHIBIT 16.3   Maslow's Hierarchy of Needs

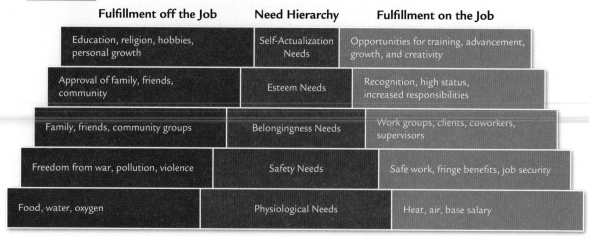

3. **Belongingness needs.** These needs reflect the desire to be accepted by one's peers, have friendships, be part of a group, and be loved. In the organization, these needs influence the desire for good relationships with coworkers, participation in a work group, and a positive relationship with supervisors. PortionPac Chemical, a maker of cleaning fluids in Chicago, has exceptionally low turnover because people feel a sense of belonging. Most of the employees have worked together for more than a decade, and people treat one another like family, which contributes to a high level of motivation.[13]

4. **Esteem needs.** These needs relate to the desire for a positive self-image and to receive attention, recognition, and appreciation from others. Within organizations, esteem needs reflect a motivation for recognition, an increase in responsibility, high status, and credit for contributions to the organization. One example comes from Intuit, where Jennifer Lepird spent weeks working long, grueling hours on a big acquisition deal. After the deal closed, Lepird was delighted to get a thank-you note from her manager, along with a small gift certificate, because it met her need to feel appreciated. "The fact that somebody took the time to recognize the effort made the long hours just melt away," she says.[14]

5. **Self-actualization needs.** These needs include the need for self-fulfillment, which is the highest need category. They concern developing one's full potential, increasing one's competence, and becoming a better person. Self-actualization needs can be met in the organization by providing people with opportunities to grow, be creative, and acquire training for challenging assignments and advancement.

According to Maslow's theory, low-order needs take priority—they must be satisfied before higher-order needs are activated. The needs are satisfied in sequence: Physiological needs come before safety needs, safety needs before social needs, and so on. A person desiring physical safety will devote his or her efforts to securing a safer environment and will not be concerned with esteem needs or self-actualization needs. Once a need is satisfied, it declines in importance and the next higher need is activated.

A study of employees in the manufacturing department of a major health-care company in the United Kingdom provides some support for Maslow's theory. Most line workers said they worked at the company primarily because of the good pay, benefits, and job security. Thus, employees' lower-level physiological and safety needs were being met. When questioned about their motivation, employees indicated the importance of positive social relationships with both peers and supervisors (belongingness needs) and a desire for greater respect and recognition from management (esteem needs).[15]

Take a Moment

As a new manager, recognize that some people are motivated primarily to satisfy lower-level physiological and safety needs, while others want to satisfy higher-level needs. Learn which lower- and higher-level needs motivate you by completing the Experiential Exercise on pages 550–551.

ERG THEORY

Clayton Alderfer proposed a modification of Maslow's theory in an effort to simplify it and respond to criticisms of its lack of empirical verification.[16] His **ERG theory** identified three categories of needs:

1. *Existence needs.* The needs for physical well-being
2. *Relatedness needs.* The needs for satisfactory relationships with others
3. *Growth needs.* The needs that focus on the development of human potential and the desire for personal growth and increased competence

The ERG model and Maslow's needs hierarchy are similar because both are in hierarchical form and presume that individuals move up the hierarchy one step at a time. However, Alderfer reduced the number of need categories to three and proposed that movement up the hierarchy is more complex, reflecting a **frustration-regression principle**; namely, that failure to meet a high-order need may trigger a regression to an already fulfilled lower-order need. Thus, a worker who cannot fulfill a need for personal growth may revert to a lower-order need and redirect his or her efforts toward making a lot of money. The ERG model therefore is less rigid than Maslow's needs hierarchy, suggesting that individuals may move down as well as up the hierarchy, depending on their ability to satisfy needs. Needs hierarchy theories explain why organizations find ways to recognize employees, encourage their participation in decision making, and give them opportunities to make significant contributions to the organization and society.

Many companies are finding that creating a humane work environment that allows people to achieve a balance between work and personal life is also a great high-level motivator.

▶ ▶ ▶ **Concept Connection**

Najlah Feanny/Corbis

Gen Yers, who according to their managers report for work with self-esteem to spare, often proceed directly from **existence needs** to **growth needs**. Once they're satisfied they're receiving fair pay, what younger employees want most is training. In fact, recent studies found that respondents chose training from a list of benefits three times more often than a cash bonus. There's a practical reason for this interest in personal growth. Gen Yers know they need to acquire skills that will make them attractive job candidates. Unlike many of their elders, they don't expect to work for a single employer throughout their careers.

Employees in low-wage hourly jobs don't often get white-collar perks, but some managers are trying a fresh and unlikely approach—letting hourly workers do some jobs at home, set their own schedules, or otherwise have more control over their work lives.

At Johnson Storage & Moving, based in Centennial, Colorado, and operating in five states, administrative workers, call center staff, and dispatchers have been able to work remotely or to work hours of their own choosing for 16 years. Among the employees taking advantage of the flexible policy, there has been almost no turnover in that time span. Movers and warehouse employees, of course, can't work from home, but company president Jim Johnson gives them as much control as possible over their start and end times, which has significantly reduced no-shows, tardiness, and turnover.

Managers in other companies are also giving manual workers more flexibility. Turck Inc., a manufacturer of automation equipment in Plymouth, Minnesota, is evaluating a plan to let people do some jobs from home. "We have a lot of products where literally you just need to sit there and put a label on," says production supervisor Dee Comeau. "Honestly, it can be done anywhere." Kaiser Permanente and Marriott International have both implemented a variety of innovative policies, such as offering people control over their start and end times and providing paid time off in short increments so an employee doesn't have to take a full day off for a doctor's appointment, for example. At Kaiser Permanente, employee surveys show rising levels of commitment and engagement since the flex programs began.[17]

Innovative Way

Johnson Storage & Moving

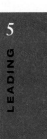

5

LEADING

Some companies go even further with job flexibility. At J. A. Coulter & Associates, an insurance and investment advisory firm in New Richmond, Wisconsin, employees can come and go as they please, without telling anyone where they are going or why, so long as they get their jobs done. Shannon Mehls, who works as an assistant to one of Coulter's senior investment advisors, says employees now feel like "mini entrepreneurs," managing their own schedules and focusing on results instead of just putting in 40 hours and getting a paycheck.[18] Although not all managers would be comfortable working in an environment where employees come and go as they please, there is some evidence that people who have greater control over their work schedules are significantly less likely to suffer job burnout and are more highly committed to their employers.[19]

In the recent economic downturn, some companies found flexible options a great way to cut payroll costs while retaining and motivating valued employees. Accounting firm KPMG tried a program called Flexible Futures, which offered employees in its British operations several options: (1) go to a four-day workweek and take a 20 percent pay cut; (2) choose a mini-sabbatical at 30 percent base pay; (3) opt for both of these; or (4) stay with their current employment arrangement. Over 80 percent of employees chose one of the flexible options. Other companies have implemented similar programs with great success.[20]

A TWO-FACTOR APPROACH TO MOTIVATION

Frederick Herzberg developed another popular theory of motivation called the *two-factor theory*.[21] Herzberg interviewed hundreds of workers about times when they were highly motivated to work and other times when they were dissatisfied and unmotivated. His findings suggested that the work characteristics associated with dissatisfaction were quite different from those pertaining to satisfaction, which prompted the notion that two factors influence work motivation.

The two-factor theory is illustrated in Exhibit 16.4. The center of the scale is neutral, meaning that workers are neither satisfied nor dissatisfied. Herzberg believed that two entirely separate dimensions contribute to an employee's behavior at work. The first, called

EXHIBIT 16.4

Herzberg's Two-Factor Theory

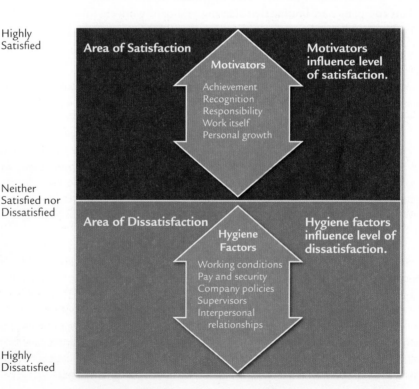

hygiene factors, involves the presence or absence of job dissatisfiers, such as working conditions, pay, company policies, and interpersonal relationships. When hygiene factors are poor, work is dissatisfying. However, good hygiene factors simply remove the dissatisfaction; they do not in themselves cause people to become highly satisfied and motivated in their work.

The second set of factors does influence job satisfaction. **Motivators** focus on high-level needs and include achievement, recognition, responsibility, and opportunity for growth. Herzberg believed that when motivators are absent, workers are neutral toward work, but when motivators are present, workers are highly motivated and satisfied. Thus, hygiene factors and motivators represent two distinct factors that influence motivation. Hygiene factors work only in the area of dissatisfaction. Unsafe working conditions or a noisy work environment will cause people to be dissatisfied, but their correction will not lead to a high level of motivation and satisfaction. Motivators such as challenge, responsibility, and recognition must be in place before employees will be highly motivated to excel at their work.

There is a growing realization among managers of the importance of employee recognition, perhaps because tough economic conditions have made it more difficult for them to reward people with large pay increases. The Globoforce 2012 Mood Tracker survey found that employee recognition programs are on the rise. Moreover, 82 percent of employees say that being recognized for their contributions motivates them, and 78 percent say that they would work harder if their efforts were better recognized and appreciated.[22]

The implication of the two-factor theory for managers is clear. On one hand, providing hygiene factors will eliminate employee dissatisfaction but will not motivate workers to high achievement levels. On the other hand, recognition, challenge, and opportunities for personal growth are powerful motivators and will promote high satisfaction and performance. The manager's role is to remove dissatisfiers—that is, to provide hygiene factors sufficient to meet basic needs—and then to use motivators to meet higher-level needs and propel employees toward greater achievement and satisfaction.

ACQUIRED NEEDS

The *acquired needs theory*, developed by David McClelland, proposes that certain types of needs are acquired during the individual's lifetime. In other words, people are not born with these needs but may learn them through their life experiences.[23] The three needs most frequently studied are these:

- *Need for achievement.* The desire to accomplish something difficult, attain a high standard of success, master complex tasks, and surpass others

- *Need for affiliation.* The desire to form close personal relationships, avoid conflict, and establish warm friendships

- *Need for power.* The desire to influence or control others, be responsible for others, and have authority over others

Early life experiences typically determine whether people acquire these needs. If children are encouraged to do things for themselves and receive reinforcement, they will acquire a need to achieve. If they are reinforced for forming warm human relationships, they will develop a need for affiliation. If they get satisfaction from controlling others, they will acquire a need for power.

For more than 20 years, McClelland studied human needs and their implications for management. People with a high need for *achievement* are frequently entrepreneurs. People who have a high need for *affiliation* are successful integrators, whose job is to coordinate the work of several departments in an organization. Integrators include brand managers and project managers who must have excellent people skills. A high need for *power* often is associated with successful attainment of top levels in the organizational hierarchy.[24]

New Manager Self-Test

Need for Achievement, Affiliation, and Power

Instructions: This questionnaire asks you to describe situations that you like. For each item below, give the number "3" to the phrase that best describes you, "2" to the item that is next best, and "1" for the item that is least like you.

1. _____ a. I like to do my best in whatever I undertake.

_____ b. I like to form new friendships.

_____ c. I like to tell other people how to do their jobs.

2. _____ a. I like to be able to say that I have done a difficult job well.

_____ b. I like to have strong attachments with my friends.

_____ c. I like to take on responsibilities and obligations.

3. _____ a. I like to accomplish tasks that require skill and effort.

_____ b. I like to share things with my friends.

_____ c. I like to be called upon to settle arguments and disputes between others.

4. _____ a. I like to be successful in things I undertake.

_____ b. I like to do things for my friends.

_____ c. I like to be able to persuade others to do what I want to do.

5. _____ a. I like to seek satisfaction from accomplishing a difficult task.

_____ b. I like to meet new people.

_____ c. I like to be regarded by others as a leader.

6. _____ a. I would like to be a recognized authority in my career field.

_____ b. I like to participate in groups in which the members have warm and friendly feelings toward one another.

_____ c. When with a group, I like to make the decisions about what we are going to do.

7. _____ a. I like to confront the difficult challenges of the job.

_____ b. I like to make as many friends as I can.

_____ c. I would like to be a powerful executive or politician.

Scoring and Interpretation: Compute your scores as follows:

Need for achievement = 1a + 2a + 3a + 4a + 5a + 6a + 7a = _____

Need for affiliation = 1b + 2b + 3b + 4b + 5b + 6b + 7b = _____

Need for power = 1c + 2c + 3c + 4c + 5c + 6c + 7c = _____

David McClelland's research found that some human needs are learned during early life experiences, and the three that he studied are personal need for achievement, affiliation, and power. *Achievement* means the need to excel. *Affiliation* means the need for harmonious relationships. *Power* means the need to direct and influence others. One of the three needs is typically stronger than the others in most people. The higher your score on a need, the stronger it is and the more it will guide your behavior. What do the relative strengths of the three needs mean to you? If you can align your career to use and satisfy your stronger needs, you are more likely to be successful.

Sources: Based on Joel B. Bennett, "Power and Influence as Distinct Personality Traits: Development and Validation of a Psychometric Measure," *Journal of Research in Personality* 22 (1988): 361–394; Yongmei Liu, Jun Liu, and Longzeng Wu, "Are You Willing and Able? Roles of Motivation, Power, and Politics in Career Growth," *Journal of Management* 36, no. 6 (2010): 1432–1460.

For example, McClelland studied managers at AT&T for 16 years and found that those with a high need for power were more likely to follow a path of continued promotion over time. More than half of the employees at the top levels had a high need for power. In contrast, managers with a high need for achievement but a low need for power tended to peak earlier in their careers and at a lower level. The reason is that achievement needs can be met through the task itself, but power needs can be met only by ascending to a level at which a person has power over others.

In summary, content theories focus on people's underlying needs and label those particular needs that motivate behavior. The hierarchy of needs theory, the ERG theory, the two-factor theory, and the acquired needs theory all help managers understand what motivates people. In this way, managers can design work to meet needs and hence elicit appropriate and successful work behaviors.

Take a Moment

Do you have a greater need for achievement, affiliation, or power? Complete the New Manager Self-Test on page 534 to learn more about which needs motivate you.

Remember This

- **Content theories** emphasize the needs that motivate people.
- The most well-known content theory is Maslow's **hierarchy of needs theory**, which proposes that people are motivated by five categories of needs—physiological, safety, belongingness, esteem, and self-actualization—that exist in a hierarchical order.
- **ERG theory** is a modification of the needs hierarchy and proposes three categories of needs: existence, relatedness, and growth.
- The **frustration-regression principle** is the idea that failure to meet a high-order need may cause a regression to an already satisfied lower-order need; thus, people may move down as well as up the needs hierarchy.
- Giving people more control over their work schedules and opportunities to contribute ideas are two ways that managers meet people's higher-level needs.

- Johnson Storage & Moving lets hourly administrative personnel work remotely or work hours of their own choosing and gives movers and warehouse workers control over their start and end times.
- One element of Herzberg's two-factor theory, **hygiene factors**, focuses on lower-level needs and involves the presence or absence of job dissatisfiers, including working conditions, pay, and company policies.
- Herzberg's second factor, **motivators**, influences job satisfaction based on fulfilling higher-level needs such as achievement, recognition, responsibility, and opportunities for personal growth.
- The *acquired needs theory* proposes that certain types of needs, including the need for achievement, need for affiliation, and need for power, are acquired during an individual's lifetime of experiences.

Process Perspectives on Motivation

Process theories explain how people select behavioral actions to meet their needs and determine whether their choices were successful. Important perspectives in this area include goal-setting, equity theory, and expectancy theory.

GOAL SETTING

Recall from Chapter 7 our discussion of the importance and purposes of goals. Numerous studies have shown that specific, challenging targets significantly enhance people's motivation and performance levels.[25] You have probably noticed in your own life that you are more motivated when you have a specific goal, such as making an A on a final exam, losing 10 pounds before spring break, or earning enough money during the summer to buy a used car.

EXHIBIT **16.5**

Criteria for Motivational Goals

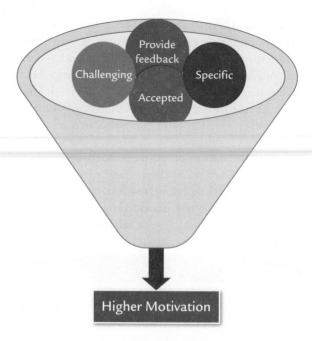

Goal-setting theory, described by Edwin Locke and Gary Latham, proposes that managers can increase motivation and enhance performance by setting specific, challenging goals, and then helping people track their progress toward goal achievement by providing timely feedback. Exhibit 16.5 illustrates key components of goal-setting theory.[26]

- *Goal specificity* refers to the degree to which goals are concrete and unambiguous. Specific goals such as "Visit one new customer each day," or "Sell $1,000 worth of merchandise a week" are more motivating than vague goals such as "Keep in touch with new customers" or "Increase merchandise sales." For example, a lack of clear, specific goals is cited as a major cause of the failure of pay-for-performance incentive plans in many organizations.[27] Vague goals can be frustrating for employees.

- In terms of *goal difficulty*, hard goals are more motivating than easy ones. Easy goals provide little challenge for employees and don't require them to increase their output. Highly ambitious but achievable goals ask people to stretch their abilities and provide a basis for greater feelings of accomplishment and personal effectiveness. A study in Germany found that, over a three-year period, only employees who perceived their goals as difficult reported increases in positive emotions and feelings of job satisfaction and success.[28]

- *Goal acceptance* means that employees have to "buy into" the goals and be committed to them. Having people participate in setting goals is a good way to increase acceptance and commitment.

- Finally, the component of *feedback* means that people get information about how well they are doing in progressing toward goal achievement. It is important for managers to provide performance feedback on a regular, ongoing basis. However, self-feedback, where people are able to monitor their own progress toward a goal, has been found to be an even stronger motivator than external feedback.[29]

Why does goal setting increase motivation? For one thing, it enables people to focus their energies in the right direction. People know what to work toward, so they can direct their efforts toward the most important activities to accomplish the goals. Goals also energize behavior because people feel compelled to develop plans and strategies

> "If you look at the modern workplace, I would say it's one of the most feedback-deprived places in American civilization."
>
> — DANIEL PINK, JOURNALIST AND AUTHOR OF *DRIVE: THE SURPRISING TRUTH ABOUT WHAT MOTIVATES US*

that keep them focused on achieving the target. Specific, difficult goals provide a challenge and encourage people to put forth high levels of effort. In addition, when goals are achieved, pride and satisfaction increase, contributing to higher motivation and morale.[30] The following example illustrates the motivational power of goal setting.

When Advanced Circuits of Aurora, Colorado, was having trouble with frequent stops and restarts on its production line, costing the company about $50,000 a month, former CEO Ron Huston came up with a plan. He bought a junk car, placed it in the parking lot, and told employees they could take a sledgehammer to the car every day the production line didn't have a restart. Employees set a goal of flattening the car in 90 days. Everybody had fun, and they met the 90-day goal by solving production line problems, which was the whole point of the exercise for Huston.

Huston realized how motivating it could be for people to have a clear, specific goal, especially if achieving it was fun. He began setting goals for other aspects of the business and rewarding people when the goals were met. "He sets up goals that are really hard, and then defines exactly what it will take to reach them," said technical support employee Kami Lichtenberg. Just as importantly, Huston steered performance toward goals and kept people energized by giving everyone ongoing numerical feedback about every aspect of the business. People began checking the data throughout the day to track their progress toward goals. "The more goals we get, the better it is for us," said employee Barb Frevert.[31]

Recent research points to the importance of *making progress toward goals* as a key to motivation. The **making progress principle** is the idea that the single most important factor that can boost motivation, positive emotions, and perceptions during a workday is making progress toward meaningful goals.[32] Providing feedback on how well people are progressing and giving them a way to track their progress toward goals, as Ron Huston did at Advanced Circuits, provides a renewable energy that fuels motivation. Sometimes managers underestimate the importance of the continuous feedback aspect of goal setting and achievement. Knowing that they are making everyday progress (even only small steps) can make all the difference in how motivated people feel to continue pursuing a goal.

EQUITY THEORY

Equity theory focuses on individuals' perceptions of how fairly they are treated compared with others. Developed by J. Stacy Adams, equity theory proposes that people are motivated to seek social equity in the rewards that they receive for performance.[33]

According to equity theory, if people perceive their compensation as equal to what others receive for similar contributions, they will believe that their treatment is fair and equitable. People evaluate equity by a ratio of inputs to outcomes. Inputs to a job include education, experience, effort, and ability. Outcomes from a job include pay, recognition, benefits, and promotions. The input-to-outcome ratio may be compared to another

▶▶▶ Concept Connection

Alyson Aliano

At Computerized Facility Integration (CFI), **clear, specific goals** enhance employee motivation and commitment. CFI's turnover is 4 percent, dramatically lower than the industry average of 30 percent. Every employee—from clerical help to senior management—receives a monthly bonus for meeting established targets. "It varies by role, of course, but we clearly state what everyone should be achieving, and we reward people accordingly," says founder and CEO Robert Verdun. "One of the big advantages of this bonus system is that it obliges us to keep communicating." The company, based in Southfield, Michigan, installs and services technology systems in office buildings and factories.

person in the work group or to a perceived group average. A state of **equity** exists whenever the ratio of one person's outcomes to inputs equals the ratio of another's outcomes to inputs.

Inequity occurs when the input-to-outcome ratios are out of balance, such as when a new, inexperienced employee receives the same salary as a person with a high level of education or experience. Interestingly, perceived inequity also occurs in the other direction. Thus, if an employee discovers that he or she is making more money than other people who contribute the same inputs to the company, the employee may feel the need to correct the inequity by working harder or getting more education. Scientific studies indicate that the human brain seems programmed to dislike inequity, even when we benefit from it. Moreover, people get less satisfaction from money they receive without having to earn it than they do from money they work to receive.[34] Perceived inequity creates tensions within individuals that motivate them to bring equity into balance.[35]

The most common methods for reducing a perceived inequity are these:

- *Change work effort.* A person may choose to increase or decrease his or her inputs to the organization. Individuals who believe that they are underpaid may reduce their level of effort or increase their absenteeism. Overpaid people may increase effort on the job.

- *Change outcomes.* A person may change his or her outcomes. An underpaid person may request a salary increase or a bigger office. A union may try to improve wages and working conditions to be consistent with a comparable union whose members make more money.

- *Change perceptions.* Research suggests that people may change perceptions of equity if they are unable to change inputs or outcomes. They may increase the status attached to their jobs artificially or distort others' perceived rewards to bring equity into balance.

- *Leave the job.* People who feel inequitably treated may decide to leave their jobs rather than suffer the inequity of being underpaid or overpaid. In their new jobs, they expect to find a more favorable balance of rewards.

The implication of equity theory for managers is that employees indeed evaluate the perceived equity of their rewards compared to others'. Many big law firms are reducing the compensation of 10 to 30 percent of their partners each year in order to free up money to hire and reward "star performers," rejecting the traditional practice of paying partners relatively similar amounts. The change fits with the strategy of rewarding people who generate more business, but it is having a damaging effect on the morale and motivation of other partners, who perceive the new compensation scheme as inequitable.[36] Inequitable pay puts pressure on employees that is sometimes almost too great to bear. They attempt to change their work habits, try to change the system, or leave the job.[37]

EXPECTANCY THEORY

Expectancy theory suggests that motivation depends on individuals' expectations about their ability to perform tasks and receive desired rewards. Expectancy theory is associated with the work of Victor Vroom, although a number of scholars have made contributions in this area.[38]

Expectancy theory is concerned not with identifying types of needs, but with the thinking process that individuals use to achieve rewards. For example, one interesting study of expectancy theory looked at patrol officer drug arrests in the midwestern United States. The research found that officers who produced the most drug arrests were more likely to have perceived that such arrests were a management priority and were rewarded by their organization, received specialized training to hone their skills related to drug interdiction, and perceived that they had sufficient time and resources to investigate suspected drug activity properly.[39]

EXHIBIT 16.6 Major Elements of Expectancy Theory

```
┌─────────────────────────┐                                    ┌─────────────────────────┐
│ E ▶ P expectancy        │                                    │ Valance                 │
│ Probability that effort │                                    │ (value of outcomes)     │
│ will lead to desired    │                                    │                         │
│ performance             │                                    │                         │
└───────────┬─────────────┘                                    └───────────┬─────────────┘
            │                                                               │
            ▼                                                               ▼
┌──────────────┐          ┌──────────────┐                    ┌─────────────────────────┐
│              │          │              │                    │ Outcomes                │
│   Effort     │ ───────▶ │ Performance  │ ─────────────────▶ │ (Pay, recognition,      │
│              │          │              │                    │ other rewards)          │
└──────────────┘          └──────────────┘         ▲          └─────────────────────────┘
                                                    │
                                    ┌───────────────┴─────────────┐
                                    │ P ▶ O expectancy            │
                                    │ Probability that performance│
                                    │ will produce desired outcome│
                                    └─────────────────────────────┘
```

Expectancy theory is based on the relationship among the individual's *effort*, the individual's *performance*, and the desirability of *outcomes* associated with high performance. These elements and the relationships among them are illustrated in Exhibit 16.6. The keys to expectancy theory are the expectancies for the relationships among effort, performance, and the value of the outcomes to the individual.

E → P expectancy involves determining whether putting effort into a task will lead to high performance. For this expectancy to be high, the individual must have the ability, previous experience, and necessary equipment, tools, and opportunity to perform. Let's consider a simple sales example. If Paloma, a salesperson at the Diamond Gift Shop, believes that increased selling effort will lead to higher personal sales, we can say that she has a high E → P expectancy. However, if Paloma believes she has neither the ability nor the opportunity to achieve high performance, the expectancy will be low, and so will be her motivation.

P → O expectancy involves determining whether successful performance will lead to the desired outcome or reward. If the P → O expectancy is high, the individual will be more highly motivated. If the expectancy is that high performance will not produce the desired outcome, motivation will be lower. If Paloma believes that higher personal sales will lead to a pay increase, we can say that she has a high P → O expectancy. She might be aware that raises are coming up for consideration and talk with her supervisor or other employees to see if increased sales will help her earn a better raise. If not, she will be less motivated to work hard.

Valence is the value of outcomes, or attraction to outcomes, for the individual. If the outcomes that are available from high effort and good performance are not valued by employees, motivation will be low. Likewise, if outcomes have a high value, motivation will be higher. If Paloma places a high value on the pay raise, valence is high and she will have a high motivational force. On the other hand,

▶ ▶ ▶ **Concept Connection**

Richard Levine/Alamy

According to **expectancy theory**, a reward that effectively motivates one individual doesn't necessarily work for another. So how can employers create attractive rewards that motivate all their employees, especially when economic conditions necessitate cuts in salary and benefits budgets? Many managers are turning to gift cards. One advantage is that they can be issued in virtually any denomination. But even more importantly, many gift cards allow the recipient to tailor a reward to his or her individual preference. A person can choose to splurge on some small luxury or use the card for essentials such as groceries.

5

LEADING

if the money has low valence for Paloma, the overall motivational force will be low. For an employee to be highly motivated, all three factors in the expectancy model must be high.[40]

Expectancy theory attempts not to define specific types of needs or rewards, but only to establish that they exist and may be different for every individual. One employee might want to be promoted to a position of increased responsibility, and another might have high valence for good relationships with peers. Consequently, the first person will be motivated to work hard for a promotion and the second for the opportunity of a team position that will keep him or her associated with a group. Studies substantiate the idea that rewards need to be individualized to be motivating. A recent finding from the U.S. Department of Labor shows that the top reason people leave their jobs is because they "don't feel appreciated." Yet Gallup's analysis of 10,000 workgroups in 30 industries found that making people feel appreciated depends on finding the right kind of reward for each individual. Some people prefer tangible rewards such as bonuses, gifts, or luxury trips, while others place high value on words of appreciation and recognition. In addition, some want public recognition while others prefer to be quietly praised by someone they admire and respect.[41]

Remember This

- **Process theories**, including goal-setting theory, equity theory, and expectancy theory, explain how people select behaviors with which to meet their needs and determine whether their choices were successful.
- **Goal-setting theory** proposes that specific, challenging goals increase motivation and performance when the goals are accepted by subordinates and these subordinates receive feedback to indicate their progress toward goal achievement.
- The **making progress principle** is the idea that the single most important factor that can boost motivation, positive emotions, and perceptions during a workday is making progress toward meaningful goals.

- **Equity theory** focuses on individuals' perceptions of how fairly they are treated relative to others.
- A situation of **equity** exists when the ratio of one person's outcomes to inputs equals that of another's.
- **Expectancy theory** proposes that motivation depends on individuals' expectations about their ability to perform tasks and receive desired rewards.
- A person's **E → P expectancy** is the expectancy that putting effort into a given task will lead to high performance.
- **P → O expectancy** is the expectancy that high performance of a task will lead to the desired outcome.
- **Valence** is the value of outcomes (rewards) to the individual.

Reinforcement Perspective on Motivation

The reinforcement approach to employee motivation sidesteps the issues of employee needs and thinking processes described in the content and process theories. **Reinforcement theory** simply looks at the relationship between behavior and its consequences. It focuses on changing or modifying employees' on-the-job behavior through the appropriate use of immediate rewards and punishments.

DIRECT REINFORCEMENT

Behavior modification is the name given to the set of techniques by which reinforcement theory is used to modify human behavior.[42] The basic assumption underlying behavior modification is the **law of effect**, which states that behavior that is positively reinforced tends to be repeated, and behavior that is not reinforced tends not to be repeated. **Reinforcement** is defined as anything that causes a certain behavior to be repeated or inhibited. For example, Whole Foods gives employees a 30 percent discount on store purchases if they meet certain

EXHIBIT 16.7 Changing Behavior with Reinforcement

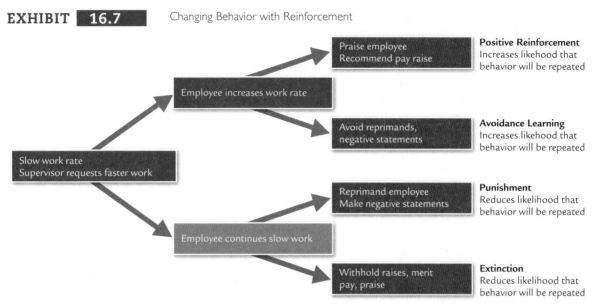

SOURCE: Based on Richard L. Daft and Richard M. Steers, *Organizations: A Micro/Macro Approach* (Glenview, IL: Scott, Foresman, 1986), p. 109.

criteria for healthy habits, such as maintaining low cholesterol and blood pressure or quitting smoking. With health insurance costs on the rise, many companies are searching for ways to reinforce behaviors that create healthier employees.[43] The four reinforcement tools are positive reinforcement, avoidance learning, punishment, and extinction, as summarized in Exhibit 16.7.

- **Positive reinforcement** is the administration of a pleasant and rewarding consequence following a desired behavior, such as praise for an employee who arrives on time or does a little extra work. Research shows that positive reinforcement does help motivate desired behaviors. Moreover, nonfinancial reinforcements such as positive feedback, social recognition, and attention are just as effective as financial incentives.[44] Studies of children indicate that those praised for trying hard and taking risks tend to enjoy challenges and find greater success over the long term. A study of employees at fast-food drive-thru windows found that performance feedback and supervisor recognition had a significant effect on increasing the incidence of "up-selling," or asking customers to increase their order.[45]

- **Avoidance learning** is the removal of an unpleasant consequence once a behavior is improved, thereby encouraging and strengthening the desired behavior. Avoidance learning is sometimes called *negative reinforcement*. The idea is that people will change a specific behavior to avoid the undesired result that the behavior provokes. As a simple example, a supervisor who constantly reminds or nags an employee who is goofing off on the factory floor and stops the nagging when the employee stops goofing off is applying avoidance learning.

- **Punishment** is the imposition of unpleasant outcomes on an employee. Punishment typically occurs following undesirable behavior. For example, a supervisor may berate an employee for performing a task incorrectly. The supervisor expects that the negative outcome will serve as a punishment and reduce the likelihood of the behavior recurring. The use of punishment in organizations is controversial and often criticized because it fails to indicate the correct behavior. However, almost all managers report that they find it necessary to occasionally impose forms of punishment ranging from verbal reprimands to employee suspensions or firings.[46]

- **Extinction** is the withholding of a positive reward. Whereas with punishment, the supervisor imposes an unpleasant outcome such as a reprimand, extinction involves withholding praise or other positive outcomes. With extinction, undesirable behavior is essentially ignored. The idea is that behavior that is not positively reinforced will gradually disappear. A *New York Times* reporter wrote a humorous article about how she learned to stop nagging and instead use reinforcement theory to shape her husband's behavior after studying how professionals train animals.[47] When her husband did something she liked, such as throw a dirty shirt in the hamper, she would use *positive reinforcement*, thanking him or giving him a hug and a kiss. Undesirable behaviors, such as throwing dirty clothes on the floor, on the other hand, were simply ignored, applying the principle of *extinction*.

SOCIAL LEARNING THEORY

Social learning theory is related to the reinforcement perspective, but it proposes that an individual's motivation can result not just from direct experience of rewards and punishments but also from the person's observations of other people's behavior.[48]

Vicarious learning, or *observational learning*, occurs when an individual sees others perform certain behaviors and get rewarded for them. Young children often learn to behave well in school because they see that well-behaved children get more positive attention from the teacher, for example. Managers can enhance an individual's motivation to perform desired behaviors by ensuring that the individual (1) has a chance to observe the desirable behaviors, (2) accurately perceives the behaviors, (3) remembers the behaviors, (4) has the necessary skills to perform the behaviors, and (5) sees that the behaviors are rewarded by the organization.[49] Recall the discussion from Chapter 12 of on-the-job training. Managers typically pair a new employee with someone who models the type of behavior that the organization wants. Managers also promote social learning by highlighting top performers' strengths and grooming them as examples for others.[50] A key to vicarious motivation, though, is to make sure the learner knows that the desired behaviors are rewarded.

Remember This

- **Reinforcement theory** is based on the relationship between a given behavior and its consequences.
- **Behavior modification** refers to the set of techniques by which reinforcement theory is used to modify human behavior.
- The **law of effect** asserts that positively reinforced behavior tends to be repeated, and unreinforced or negatively reinforced behavior tends to be inhibited.
- **Reinforcement** is anything that causes a certain behavior to be repeated or inhibited.
- **Positive reinforcement** is the administration of a pleasant and rewarding consequence following a desired behavior.
- Managers apply **avoidance learning**, called *negative reinforcement*, when they remove an unpleasant consequence once a behavior is improved.
- **Punishment** refers to the imposition of an unpleasant outcome following an undesirable behavior.
- **Extinction** refers to withholding positive rewards and essentially ignoring undesirable behavior.
- **Social learning theory** proposes that an individual's motivation can result not just from direct experience of rewards and punishments but also from thoughts, beliefs, and observations of other people's behavior.
- **Vicarious learning** occurs when an individual sees others perform certain behaviors and get rewarded for them.

Job Design for Motivation

A *job* in an organization is a unit of work that a single employee is responsible for performing. A job could include writing tickets for parking violators in New York City, performing MRIs at Salt Lake Regional Medical Center, or doing long-range planning for the A&E television network. Jobs are an important consideration for motivation because performing their components may provide rewards that meet employees' needs. Managers need to know what aspects of a job provide motivation as well as how to compensate for routine tasks that have little inherent satisfaction. **Job design** is the application of motivational theories to the structure of work for improving productivity and satisfaction.

JOB ENRICHMENT

Recall from Chapter 2 the principles of scientific management, in which tasks are designed to be simple, repetitive, and standardized. This contributes to efficiency, but simplified jobs aren't typically effective as a motivational technique because they can be boring and routine. Thus, managers in many companies are redesigning simplified jobs into jobs that provide greater variety and satisfaction. One technique, called *job rotation*, is to move employees systematically from one job to another to provide variety and stimulation. Another approach is to combine a series of small tasks into one new, broader job so that people perform a variety of activities, which is referred to as *job enlargement*.

Andy Sacks/Jupiter Images

In the past, an employee might have been assigned to complete just one step in the overall assembly of a new vehicle, car after car after car. A second worker would do the next step, and so forth. In manufacturing plants where **job enrichment** is practiced, however, one employee might be asked to complete a whole series of steps in the assembly process. Not only does the variety make the work more interesting and engaging, it also helps the employee feel more responsible and invested in his or her work.

Overall, the trend is toward **job enrichment**, which means incorporating high-level motivators into the work, including responsibility, recognition, and opportunities for growth, learning, and achievement. In an enriched job, employees have control over the resources necessary for performing tasks, make decisions on how to do the work, experience personal growth, and set their own work pace. Research shows that when jobs are designed to be controlled more by employees than by managers, people typically feel a greater sense of involvement, commitment, and motivation, which in turn contributes to higher morale, lower turnover, and stronger organizational performance.[51]

JOB CHARACTERISTICS MODEL

One significant approach to job design is the job characteristics model developed by Richard Hackman and Greg Oldham.[52] Hackman and Oldham's research concerned **work redesign**, which is defined as altering jobs to increase both the quality of employees' work experience and their productivity. Hackman and Oldham's research into the design of hundreds of jobs yielded the **job characteristics model**, which is illustrated in Exhibit 16.8. The model consists of three major parts: core job dimensions, critical psychological states, and employee growth-need strength.

Core Job Dimensions

Hackman and Oldham identified five dimensions that determine a job's motivational potential:

- *Skill variety.* This is the number of diverse activities that compose a job and the number of skills used to perform it. A routine, repetitious assembly-line job is low in variety, whereas an applied research position that involves working on new problems every day is high in variety.

5

LEADING

EXHIBIT 16.8 The Job Characteristics Model

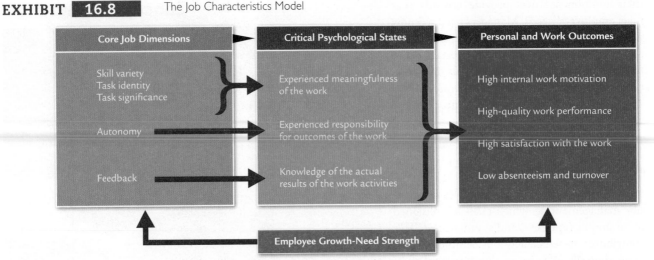

SOURCE: Adapted from J. Richard Hackman and G. R. Oldman, "Motivation Through the Design of Work: Test of a Theory," *Organizational Behavior and Human Performance* 16 (1976): 256.

- *Task identity.* This is the degree to which an employee performs a total job with a recognizable beginning and ending. A chef who prepares an entire meal has more task identity than a worker on a cafeteria line who ladles mashed potatoes.
- *Task significance.* This is the degree to which the job is perceived as important and having an impact on the company or consumers. People who distribute penicillin and other medical supplies during times of emergencies would feel they have significant jobs.
- *Autonomy.* This is the degree to which the worker has freedom, discretion, and self-determination in planning and carrying out tasks. A house painter can determine how to paint the house; a paint sprayer on an assembly line has little autonomy.
- *Feedback.* This is the extent to which doing the job provides feedback to the employee about his or her performance. Jobs vary in their ability to let workers see the outcomes of their efforts. A football coach knows whether the team won or lost, but a basic research scientist may have to wait years to learn whether a research project was successful.

The job characteristics model says that the more these five core characteristics can be designed into the job, the more the employees will be motivated and the higher will be the employees' performance, quality of work, and satisfaction.

Critical Psychological States

The model posits that core job dimensions are more rewarding when individuals experience three psychological states in response to job design. In Exhibit 16.8, skill variety, task identity, and task significance tend to influence the employee's psychological state of *experienced meaningfulness of work*. The work itself is satisfying and provides intrinsic rewards for the worker. The job characteristic of autonomy influences the worker's *experienced responsibility*. The job characteristic of feedback provides the worker with *knowledge of actual results*. The employee thus knows how he or she is doing and can change work performance to increase desired outcomes.

Personal and Work Outcomes

The impact of the five job characteristics on the psychological states of experienced meaningfulness, responsibility, and knowledge of actual results leads to the personal and work outcomes of high work motivation, high work performance, high satisfaction, and low absenteeism and turnover.

Employee Growth-Need Strength

The final component of the job characteristics model is called *employee growth-need strength*, which means that people have different needs for growth and development. If a person wants to satisfy low-level needs, such as safety and belongingness, the job characteristics model has less effect. When a person has a high need for growth and development, including the desire for personal challenge, achievement, and challenging work, the model is especially effective. People with a high need to grow and expand their abilities respond favorably to the application of the model and to improvements in core job dimensions.

One interesting finding concerns the cross-cultural differences in the impact of job characteristics. Intrinsic factors such as autonomy, challenge, achievement, and recognition can be highly motivating in countries such as the United States. However, they may contribute little to motivation and satisfaction in a country such as Nigeria and might even lead to *demotivation*. A recent study indicates that the link between intrinsic characteristics and job motivation and satisfaction is weaker in economically disadvantaged countries with poor governmental social welfare systems, as well as in countries that value high power distance, as defined in Chapter 4.[53] Thus, the job characteristics model would be expected to be less effective in these countries.

Remember This

- Jobs are an important consideration for motivation because performing their components may provide intrinsic rewards that meet employees' needs.
- **Job design** refers to applying motivational theories to the structure of work to improve motivation, productivity, and satisfaction.
- Most companies are moving away from simplified jobs and are using job rotation, job enlargement, and job enrichment to provide employees with greater variety, stimulation, and satisfaction.
- **Job enrichment** refers to incorporating high-level motivators, such as achievement, recognition, and opportunities for growth, into the work.
- **Work redesign** means altering jobs to increase both the quality of employees' work experience and their productivity.
- The **job characteristics model** is a model of job design that considers core job dimensions, individuals' critical psychological states, and employee growth-need strength.

Innovative Ideas for Motivating

Organizations are increasingly using various types of incentive compensation as a way to motivate employees to higher levels of performance. For example, when Elise Lelon, owner of the leadership-consulting firm The You Business, couldn't give pay raises because of budget pressures, she created a generous lump-sum bonus program tied to the amount of revenue that employees generated for the firm. "It gets their juices flowing and it helps the business grow," Lelon says.[54] Exhibit 16.9 summarizes several popular methods of incentive pay.

Variable compensation and forms of "at risk" pay such as bonus plans are key motivational tools that are becoming more common than fixed salaries at many companies. However, unless they are carefully designed, incentive plans can backfire, as evidenced by problems in the mortgage and finance industries, where some people resorted to overly aggressive and even unethical behavior to earn huge bonuses. Numerous companies, including financial firms such as Morgan Stanley, Credit Suisse, and Goldman Sachs, as well as other organizations such as Home Depot, Verizon, and Aflac, are revising compensation plans to make sure that incentives reward the desired behaviors.[55] Unfortunately, many managers are still encouraging the wrong kinds of behavior by rewarding people who behave unethically to get more business, signaling to employees that profits are more important than

Take a Moment

Go to the Ethical Dilemma for Chapter 16 on pages 619–620 that pertains to the use of incentive compensation as a motivational tool.

LEADING 5

EXHIBIT 16.9 New Motivational Compensation Programs

Program	Purpose
Pay for performance	Rewards individual employees in proportion to their performance contributions. Also called *merit pay.*
Gain sharing	Rewards all employees and managers within a business unit when predetermined performance targets are met. Encourages teamwork.
Employee stock ownership plan (ESOP)	Gives employees part ownership of the organization, enabling them to share in improved profit performance.
Lump-sum bonuses	Rewards employees with a one-time cash payment based on performance.
Pay for knowledge	Links employee salary with the number of task skills acquired. Workers are motivated to learn the skills for many jobs, thus increasing company flexibility and efficiency.
Flexible work schedule	*Flextime* allows workers to set their own hours. *Job sharing* allows two or more part-time workers to jointly cover one job. *Telecommuting,* sometimes called *flex-place,* allows employees to work from home or an alternative workplace.
Team-based compensation	Rewards employees for behavior and activities that benefit the team, such as cooperation, listening, and empowering others.
Lifestyle awards	Rewards employees for meeting ambitious goals with luxury items, such as high-definition televisions, tickets to big-name sporting events, and exotic travel.

integrity. The 2011 National Business Ethics Survey from the Ethics Resource Center indicates that 45 percent of people have witnessed ethical misconduct at work, and 13 percent say they have felt pressure to bend the rules or even break the law to earn rewards—an *increase* of 5 percentage points from 2010.[56]

Incentive programs can be effective if they are used appropriately and combined with motivational ideas that also provide people with intrinsic rewards and meet higher-level needs. The most effective motivational programs typically involve much more than money or other external rewards in order to create an environment in which people thrive.

BUILDING A THRIVING WORKFORCE

Recent research examining what creates a consistently high-performing organization has focused on the importance of an environment in which people can thrive. A **thriving workforce** is one in which people are not just satisfied and productive but also engaged in creating the future—their own and that of the organization.[57] Two components of thriving individuals are *vitality* and *learning.* A thriving employee is one who feels alive, energized, and passionate about what he or she is doing. The individual has a sense that his or her work has purpose and meaning. In addition, a thriving employee is one who is learning and growing, developing new knowledge, skills, and abilities that can be applied now and in the future.

Managers promote thriving by applying many of the motivational techniques described throughout this chapter, such as meeting higher-level needs, helping people get intrinsic rewards from their work, and providing regular feedback on performance and progress. Two specific approaches to building a thriving workforce are empowering employees and creating an environment that promotes employee engagement.

EMPOWERING PEOPLE TO MEET HIGHER NEEDS

One significant way that managers can meet higher motivational needs is to shift power down from the top of the organization and share it with employees to enable them to achieve goals. **Empowerment** is power sharing, the delegation of power and authority to subordinates in an organization.[58] Increasing employee power heightens motivation for task accomplishment because people improve their own effectiveness, choosing how to do a task and using their creativity.[59] Empowering employees involves giving them four elements that enable them to act more freely to accomplish their jobs: information, knowledge, power, and rewards.[60]

1. *Employees receive information about company performance.* In companies where employees are fully empowered, all employees have access to all financial and operational information.

2. *Employees have knowledge and skills to contribute to company goals.* Companies use training programs and other development tools to help people acquire the knowledge and skills that they need to contribute to organizational performance.

3. *Employees have the power to make substantive decisions.* Empowered employees have the authority to influence work procedures and organizational performance directly, such as through quality circles or self-directed work teams.

4. *Employees are rewarded based on company performance.* Organizations that empower workers often reward them based on the results shown in the company's bottom line. Organizations may also use other motivational compensation programs described in Exhibit 16.9 to tie employee efforts to company performance.

The following example from Hilcorp Energy illustrates the four elements of empowerment.

> *"I think a lot of times it's not money that's the primary motivation factor; it's the passion for your job and the professional and personal satisfaction that you get out of doing what you do that motivates you."*
>
> — MARTIN YAN, CHINESE CHEF, AUTHOR, AND HOST OF COOKING SHOWS INCLUDING *YAN CAN COOK* AND *MARTIN YAN'S CHINA*

Innovative Way

Hilcorp Energy

Hilcorp Energy, based in Houston, Texas, is the nation's fourth-largest private producer of onshore crude oil and natural gas. But Hilcorp is different from most energy companies. Hilcorp takes over holes abandoned by the big energy companies—and produces about 25 million barrels of oil and gas a year from them. "It's rewarding to be the one responsible for squeezing those last drops of energy out of a formation," said a Hilcorp senior geologist. "I'm proud to be part of that."

Hilcorp is different from most other energy companies in its approach to managing people, too. Hilcorp was started by three guys with nothing but a telephone in 1989 and has grown to more than 600 employees (called associates). Managers attribute the company's success to the people on the front lines. Jack Stack, founder of SRC Holdings, said of Hilcorp: "I don't know any other company that puts as much time and money into training its people in how to run their company through the practices of open-book management."

Open-book management means that all associates have access to all financial and operating information. Because managers put decision-making power in the hands of people on the front lines, those people need to have full information to make good choices. "You want to know how we're doing? How your slice of the pie is performing? We share the good news and the bad," said a senior financial analyst. "We owe that to every employee whose work generates the numbers we report."

Associates at Hilcorp are always interested in how well the company is doing because they are rewarded based on company performance. Managers share both the risks and the rewards. Associates can earn bonuses of up to 60 percent of their annual salaries based on meeting performance goals. In addition, they can choose to purchase an economic stake in one of Hilcorp's reclamation projects. At Hilcorp, employees truly do feel like owners. "Since we pull together, not competing against each other, and we all have skin in the game, it's amazing what we can accomplish," said founder Jeff Hildebrand.[61]

At some companies, such as Hilcorp Energy, empowerment means giving employees almost complete freedom and power to make decisions and exercise initiative and imagination. However, organizations empower workers to varying degrees, from a situation where managers encourage employee ideas but retain final authority for decisions to a condition of full empowerment such as that at Hilcorp. Research shows that empowerment typically increases employee satisfaction, motivation, and productivity.[62]

5

LEADING

GIVING MEANING TO WORK THROUGH ENGAGEMENT

Employee **engagement** means that people enjoy their jobs and are satisfied with their work conditions, contribute enthusiastically to meeting team and organizational goals, and feel a sense of belonging and commitment to the organization. Fully engaged employees care deeply about the organization and actively seek ways to serve the mission.[63]

How do managers engage employees? Exhibit 16.10 illustrates the three elements that create employee engagement: a sense of meaningfulness, a sense of connection, and a sense of growth.[64] When managers organize the workplace in such a way as to create these feelings, employee engagement grows, leading to high motivation and high organizational performance.

- *People feel that they are working toward something of importance.* When employees have a chance to accomplish something that provides real value, they feel a sense of *meaningfulness*. Good managers help people understand the purpose of their work, which contributes to feelings of pride and dignity. Kenexa, the leading human resources services company in the United States (recently purchased by IBM), uses psychologists and other scientists to study what motivates employees. One finding is that turnover is significantly lower among people who feel pride in their company and its mission than among those who don't.[65]

- *People feel connected to the company, to one another, and to their managers.* In a survey asking people what factors contribute to their engagement, 79 percent of people said "good relationships with coworkers" drove engagement to a high or very high extent. Even more, 91 percent, pointed to good relationships with their immediate supervisor as highly important.[66] It is the behavior of managers that makes the biggest difference in whether or not people feel engaged at work.[67] Managers promote engagement when they listen to employees, genuinely care about their concerns, and help them develop positive relationships with colleagues.

- *People have the chance to learn, grow, and advance.* To be fully engaged, people need not only to feel that they are competent to handle what is asked of them, but also that they have the chance to learn and expand their potential. Good managers help employees understand their own unique set of talents, skills, interests, attitudes, and needs; put people in jobs where they can make their best contribution and receive intrinsic rewards every day; and make sure people have what they need to perform well. In addition, they give people the chance to work on challenging projects, participate in high-quality training and learning programs, and provide opportunities for advancement within the organization.

Studies have identified a correlation between employee engagement and company performance, including less turnover, greater profitability, and stronger employee and customer loyalty, as illustrated in the exhibit.[68] Alarmingly, recent surveys reflect low levels

EXHIBIT 16.10

Employee Engagement Model

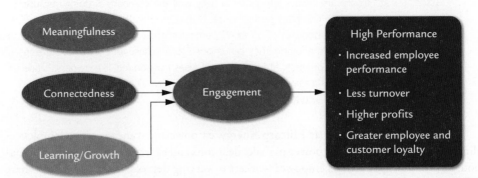

SOURCE: Based on Fig. 1, "Integrative Model of Employee Engagement," in J. Lee Whittington and Timothy J. Galpin, "The Engagement Factor: Building a High-Commitment Organization in a Low-Commitment World," *Journal of Business Strategy* 32, no. 5 (2010): 14–24.

of engagement among U.S. workers. Gallup's most recent available survey showed that 52 percent of American workers reported that they were not engaged, and 19 percent reported being *actively disengaged*.[69] Active disengagement means that people are actively undermining their organization's success.

Managers can use strategies to facilitate engagement and improve performance. Morrison Management Specialists, which provides food, nutrition, and dining services to the health care and senior living industries, found a way to engage employees who often perform menial jobs.

Innovative Way

Morrison Management Specialists

Several years ago, executives at Morrison Management Specialists, which has 14,000 employees in 450 locations, decided to make employee engagement a top priority. They started by making sure that everyone understood the company's mission statement and five core values of trust, teamwork, customer focus, learning, and profit. The company's Web site address and ending for corporate e-mail addresses is *iammorrison.com*, which reinforces that every employee *is* the company.

Each year, top executives present an update of the company's direction and accomplishments to managers, who in turn hold conversations with people throughout the organization to disseminate information about where the company stands and where it wants to go. Training sessions for hourly associates are organized under the title "Our Great Partnership" and strive to help people see how their everyday jobs tie in with the larger mission. A "People First" recognition program gives employees a chance to recognize one another for exceptional service. The company builds connections in other ways, too, such as monthly meetings that give managers and employees a chance to discuss issues on a personal level.[70]

Sometimes, even simple changes in how managers treat employees can make all the difference. Nate Carrasco, a 26-year-old employee at an auto parts store, agrees. "Most of the time, [managers] only listen to what their bosses are saying. They need to come down to the employee level more and see what actually goes on, versus what their paperwork tells them."[71]

Remember This

- Variable compensation and "at risk" pay have become key motivational tools, although these practices have been criticized in recent years for rewarding the wrong types of behavior.
- Employee empowerment and engagement are recent motivational trends that focus less on extrinsic rewards and more on creating a work environment that enables people to achieve intrinsic rewards and meet higher-level needs.
- A **thriving workforce** is one in which people are satisfied, productive, and engaged in creating the future for themselves and their organization.
- Two components of thriving employees are vitality and learning, which managers can promote through empowering people and creating the conditions for employee engagement.
- **Empowerment** is the delegation of power and authority to subordinates in an organization.

- Empowering employees involves giving them information, knowledge, power, and rewards.
- Employee engagement has been one of the hottest topics in management in recent years.
- **Engagement** is an emotional and mental state in which employees enjoy their work, contribute enthusiastically to meeting goals, and feel a sense of belonging and commitment to the organization.
- Managers create an environment that promotes engagement by providing employees with a sense of meaning, a sense of connection, and a sense of competence and growth.
- The behavior of managers is the biggest factor in determining whether people feel motivated and engaged at work.

5

LEADING

ch16:　Discussion Questions

1. Why do you think *making progress* ranks as the most important factor contributing to motivation according to a recent study? How can managers provide a sense of progress for employees working on long-range projects that might not show results for months or even years?

2. One small company recognizes an employee of the month, who is given a parking spot next to the president's space near the front door. What theories would explain the positive motivation associated with this policy?

3. Assume that you are a front-line manager at a call center. Try to come up with a specific motivational idea that fits in each of the four quadrants in Exhibit 16.2: Positive Extrinsic; Positive Intrinsic; Negative Extrinsic; Negative Intrinsic.

4. In response to security threats in today's world, the U.S. government federalized airport security workers. Many argued that simply making screeners federal workers would not solve the root problem: bored, low-paid, and poorly trained security workers have little motivation to be vigilant. How might these employees be motivated to provide the security that travel threats now demand?

5. Using Hackman and Oldham's core job dimensions, compare and contrast the jobs of these two state employees: (1) Jared, who spends much of his time researching and debating energy policy to make

recommendations that will eventually be presented to the state legislature and (2) Anise, who spends her days planting and caring for the flower gardens and grounds surrounding the state capitol building.

6. If an experienced executive assistant discovered that she made the same amount of money as a newly hired janitor, how do you think she would react? What inputs and outcomes might she evaluate to make this comparison?

7. A survey of teachers found that two of the most important rewards were the belief that their work was important and a feeling of accomplishment. According to Maslow's theory, what needs do these rewards meet?

8. The teachers in question 7 also reported that pay and benefits were poor, yet they continue to teach. Use Herzberg's two-factor theory to explain this finding.

9. How does empowerment provide the two conditions (vitality and learning) for a thriving workforce that are described in the chapter? Do you see any ways in which a manager's empowerment efforts might contribute to demotivation among employees? Discuss.

10. Gallup's 2011 survey shows that highly educated workers are significantly less likely to be engaged than are those with a high school diploma or less. What might be some reasons for this lower level of engagement among more-educated employees?

ch16:　Apply Your Skills: Experiential Exercise

What Motivates You?[72]

Indicate how important each characteristic is to you. Answer according to your feelings about the most recent job you had or about the job you currently hold. Circle the number on the scale that represents your feeling—1 (very unimportant) to 7 (very important).

1. The feeling of self-esteem a person gets from being in that job
   1　2　3　4　5　6　7

2. The opportunity for personal growth and development in that job
   1　2　3　4　5　6　7

3. The prestige of the job inside the company (i.e., regard received from others in the company)
   1　2　3　4　5　6　7

4. The opportunity for independent thought and action in that job
   1　2　3　4　5　6　7

5. The feeling of security in that job
   1　2　3　4　5　6　7

6. The feeling of self-fulfillment a person gets from being in that position (i.e., the feeling of being able

to use one's own unique capabilities, realizing one's potential)
   1　2　3　4　5　6　7

7. The prestige of the job outside the company (i.e., the regard received from others not in the company)
   1　2　3　4　5　6　7

8. The feeling of worthwhile accomplishment in that job
   1　2　3　4　5　6　7

9. The opportunity in that job to give help to other people
   1　2　3　4　5　6　7

10. The opportunity in that job for participation in the setting of goals
    1　2　3　4　5　6　7

11. The opportunity in that job for participation in the determination of methods and procedures
    1　2　3　4　5　6　7

12. The authority connected with the job
    1　2　3　4　5　6　7

13. The opportunity to develop close friendships in the job
    1　2　3　4　5　6　7

Scoring and Interpretation

Score the exercise as follows to determine what motivates you:

Rating for question 5 = _____.

Divide by 1 = _____ security.

Rating for questions 9 and 13 = _____.

Divide by 2 = _____ social.

Rating for questions 1, 3, and 7 = _____.

Divide by 3 = _____ esteem.

Rating for questions 4, 10, 11, and 12 = _____.

Divide by 4 = _____ autonomy.

Rating for questions 2, 6, and 8 = _____.

Divide by 3 = _____ self-actualization.

Your instructor has national norm scores for presidents, vice presidents, and upper-middle-level, lower-middle-level, and lower-level managers with which you can compare your mean importance scores. How do your scores compare with the scores of managers working in organizations?

ch16: Apply Your Skills: Small Group Breakout

Should, Need, Like, Love

Step 1. Divide into groups of three to five students. Individually write down answers to the following four instructions.

1. Think of a school or work task that you felt an obligation to complete, but that you did not want to do. Write the task here:

   _____

   _____

2. Think of a school or work task that you did only because you needed an extrinsic benefit, such as money or course credit. Write the task here:

   _____

   _____

3. Think of a school or work task that you do because you like it—it is enjoyable for you. Write that task here:

   _____

   _____

4. Think of a school or work task that you love to do— one in which you become completely absorbed and

from which you feel deep satisfaction when finished. Write the task here:

_____

_____

Step 2. Reflect on those four tasks and what they mean to you. Rate how highly motivated (high, medium, low) you were to perform each of the four tasks. Then rate how much mental effort (high, medium, low) was required for you to complete each of the four tasks.

Step 3. Compare your ratings with other members of your team. What is the correlation between doing a task because you Should-Need-Like-Love, your level of motivation, and the amount of mental effort required to complete the task? Develop conclusions from your analysis to present to the class.

Step 4. Discuss in your group: Are you more highly motivated when engaged in tasks that you like or love versus tasks you should do or need to do? Why? Does this corroborate any motivation theory in the chapter? How can you increase the number of "like" and "love" tasks in your life? How might you reduce the number of "should" and "need" tasks? When you become a manager, will you want to increase the number of "like" and "love" tasks for your employees? How might you do so?

ch16: Endnotes

1. Questions based on Mitchell M. Handelsman et al., "A Measure of College Student Course Engagement," *Journal of Educational Research* 98 (January/ February 2005): 184–191.
2. Phred Dvorak, "Hotelier Finds Happiness Keeps Staff Checked In; Focus on Morale Boosts Joie de Vivre's Grades from Workers, Guests," *The Wall Street Journal*, December 17, 2007, B3.
3. Richard M. Steers and Lyman W. Porter, eds., *Motivation and Work Behavior*, 3d ed. (New York: McGraw-Hill, 1983); Don Hellriegel, John W. Slocum, Jr., and Richard

W. Woodman, *Organizational Behavior*, 7th ed. (St. Paul, MN: West, 1995), p. 170; and Jerry L. Gray and Frederick A. Starke, *Organizational Behavior: Concepts and Applications*, 4th ed. (New York: Macmillan, 1988), pp. 104–105.
4. David A. Kaplan, "Salesforce's Happy Workforce," *Fortune* (February 6, 2012): 100–112.
5. Steven Greenhouse, "A Factory Defies Stereotypes, But Can It Thrive?" *The New York Times*, July 18, 2010, BU1.
6. Ashley Halsey III, "Fines Lower Drivers' Use of Cellphones," *The Washington Post*, July 10, 2011,

5

LEADING

www.washingtonpost.com/local/fines-lower-drivers-use-of-cellphones/2011/07/08/gIQAMvX67H_story.html (accessed July 11, 2011).

7. Jack Stack, "Hilcorp Energy Shares the Wealth," *The New York Times*, July 6, 2010, http://boss.blogs.nytimes.com/2010/07/06/hilcorp-energy-shares-the-wealth/ (accessed July 7, 2010).

8. Dvorak, "Hotelier Finds Happiness Keeps Staff Checked In."

9. See Linda Grant, "Happy Workers, High Returns," *Fortune* (January 12, 1998): 81; Elizabeth J. Hawk and Garrett J. Sheridan, "The Right Stuff," *Management Review* (June 1999): 43–48; Michael West and Malcolm Patterson, "Profitable Personnel," *People Management* (January 8, 1998): 28–31; Anne Fisher, "Why Passion Pays," *FSB* (September 2002): 58; and Curt Coffman and Gabriel Gonzalez-Molina, *Follow This Path: How the World's Great Organizations Drive Growth by Unleashing Human Potential* (New York: Warner Books, 2002).

10. Abraham F. Maslow, "A Theory of Human Motivation," *Psychological Review* 50 (1943): 370–396.

11. Barbara Bowes, "More than Money: Make Your Employees Feel Secure, Satisfied in Job," *Winnipeg Free Press*, July 24, 2010, I.1.

12. Sarah E. Needleman, "Burger Chain's Health-Care Recipe," *The Wall Street Journal*, August 31, 2009.

13. Leigh Buchanan, "The Un-Factory," *Inc.* (June 2010): 62–67.

14. Telis Demos, "The Way We Work: Motivate Without Spending Millions," *Fortune* (April 12, 2010): 37–38.

15. Sarah Pass, "On the Line," *People Management* (September 15, 2005): 38.

16. Clayton Alderfer, *Existence, Relatedness, and Growth* (New York: Free Press, 1972).

17. Rachel Emma Silverman, "For Manual Jobs, White-Collar Perks," *The Wall Street Journal*, October 3, 2011, B8.

18. Scott Westcott, "Beyond Flextime; Trashing the Work Week," *Inc.* (August 2008): 30–31.

19. Studies and surveys reported in Karol Rose, "Work-Life Effectiveness," special advertising section, *Fortune* (September 29, 2003): S1–S17.

20. Sylvia Ann Hewlett, "Making Flex Time a Win-Win," *The New York Times*, December 19, 2009.

21. Frederick Herzberg, "One More Time: How Do You Motivate Employees?" *Harvard Business Review* (January 2003): 87–96.

22. "Workforce Mood*Tracker* Spring 2012 Report: The Growing Influence of Employee Recognition," (Southborough, MA: Globoforce, 2012), www.workforce.com/assets/PDF/WF80532710.PDF (accessed September 18, 2012).

23. David C. McClelland, *Human Motivation* (Glenview, IL: Scott, Foresman, 1985).

24. David C. McClelland, "The Two Faces of Power," in *Organizational Psychology*, ed. D. A. Colb, I. M. Rubin, and J. M. McIntyre (Englewood Cliffs, NJ: Prentice Hall, 1971), pp. 73–86.

25. See Gary P. Latham and Edwin A. Locke, "Enhancing the Benefits and Overcoming the Pitfalls of Goal Setting," *Organizational Dynamics* 35, no. 4 (2006): 332–338; Edwin A. Locke and Gary P. Latham, "Building a Practically Useful Theory of Goal Setting and Task Motivation: A 35-Year Odyssey," *The American Psychologist* 57, no. 9 (September 2002): 705ff; Gary P. Latham and Edwin A. Locke, "Self-Regulation Through Goal Setting," *Organizational Behavior and Human Decision Processes* 50, no. 2 (December 1991): 212–247; G. P. Latham and G. H. Seijts, "The Effects of Proximal and Distal Goals on Performance of a Moderately Complex Task," *Journal of Organizational Behavior* 20, no. 4 (1999): 421–428; P. C. Early, T. Connolly, and G. Ekegren, "Goals, Strategy Development, and Task Performance: Some Limits on the Efficacy of Goal Setting," *Journal of Applied Psychology* 74 (1989): 24–33; E. A. Locke, "Toward a Theory of Task Motivation and Incentives," *Organizational Behavior and Human Performance* 3 (1968): 157–189; Gerard H. Seijts, Ree M. Meertens, and Gerjo Kok, "The Effects of Task Importance and Publicness on the Relation Between Goal Difficulty and Performance," *Canadian Journal of Behavioural Science* 29, no. 1 (1997): 54ff. See Gerard H. Seijts and Gary P. Latham, "Knowing When to Set Learning versus Performance Goals," *Organizational Dynamics* 41 (2012): 1–6, for a discussion of the importance of learning goals versus performance goals in turbulent environments.

26. Locke and Latham, "Building a Practically Useful Theory of Goal Setting and Task Motivation."

27. Edwin A. Locke, "Linking Goals to Monetary Incentives," *Academy of Management Executive* 18, no. 4 (2005): 130–133.

28. Latham and Locke, "Enhancing the Benefits and Overcoming the Pitfalls of Goal Setting."

29. J. M. Ivanecevich and J. T. McMahon, "The Effects of Goal Setting, External Feedback, and Self-Generated Feedback on Outcome Variables: A Field Experiment," *Academy of Management Journal* 25, no. 2 (June 1982): 359–372; G. P. Latham and E. A. Locke, "Self-Regulation through Goal Setting," *Organizational Behavior and Human Decision Processes* 50, no. 2 (1991): 212–247.

30. Gary P. Latham, "The Motivational Benefits of Goal-Setting," *Academy of Management Executive* 18, no. 4 (2004): 126–129.

31. Julie Sloane, "The Number Cruncher," in Ellyn Spragins, "The Best Bosses," *Fortune Small Business* (October 2004): 39–57; and Maggie Rauch, "Great Expectations," *Incentive* (December 2004): 18–19.

32. This definition and discussion is based on Teresa M. Amabile and Steven J. Kramer, "The Power of Small Wins," *Harvard Business Review* (May 2011): 71–80; and Teresa M. Amabile and Steven J. Kramer, "What Really Motivates Workers: Understanding the Power of

Progress," *Harvard Business Review* (January–February 2010): 44–45.

33. J. Stacy Adams, "Injustice in Social Exchange," in *Advances in Experimental Social Psychology*, 2d ed., ed. L. Berkowitz (New York: Academic Press, 1965); and J. Stacy Adams, "Toward an Understanding of Inequity," *Journal of Abnormal and Social Psychology* (November 1963): 422–436.

34. Elizabeth Weise, "Our Brains Dislike Inequality, Even When It's In Our Favor," *USA Today*, February 25, 2010, http://content.usatoday.com/communities/ sciencefair/post/2010/02/our-brains-dont-like- inequality-even-when-its-in-our-favor/1 (accessed March 21, 2011); Daniel Yee, "Brain Prefers Working over Money for Nothing," *Cincinnati Post*, May 14, 2004.

35. Ray V. Montagno, "The Effects of Comparison to Others and Primary Experience on Responses to Task Design," *Academy of Management Journal* 28 (1985): 491–498; and Robert P. Vecchio, "Predicting Worker Performance in Inequitable Settings," *Academy of Management Review* 7 (1982): 103–110.

36. Nathan Koppel and Vanessa O'Connell, "Pay Gap Widens at Big Law Firms as Partners Chase Star Attorneys," *The Wall Street Journal*, February 8, 2011, http://online.wsj.com/article/SB10001424052748704 570104576124232780067002.html (accessed February 8, 2011).

37. James E. Martin and Melanie M. Peterson, "Two-Tier Wage Structures: Implications for Equity Theory," *Academy of Management Journal* 30 (1987): 297–315.

38. Victor H. Vroom, *Work and Motivation* (New York: Wiley, 1964); B. S. Gorgopoulos, G. M. Mahoney, and N. Jones, "A Path-Goal Approach to Productivity," *Journal of Applied Psychology* 41 (1957): 345–353; and E. E. Lawler III, *Pay and Organizational Effectiveness: A Psychological View* (New York: McGraw-Hill, 1981).

39. Richard R. Johnson, "Explaining Patrol Officer Drug Arrest Activity Through Expectancy Theory," *Policing* 32, no. 1 (2009): 6ff.

40. Richard L. Daft and Richard M. Steers, *Organizations: A Micro/Macro Approach* (Glenview, IL: Scott, Foresman, 1986).

41. Studies reported in Tom Rath, "The Best Way to Recognize Employees," *Gallup Management Journal* (December 9, 2004): 1–5; and Erin White, "Theory & Practice: Praise from Peers Goes a Long Way— Recognition Programs Help Companies Retain Workers as Pay Raises Get Smaller," *The Wall Street Journal*, December 19, 2005.

42. Alexander D. Stajkovic and Fred Luthans, "A Meta-Analysis of the Effects of Organizational Behavior Modification on Task Performance, 1975–95," *Academy of Management Journal* (October 1997): 1122–1149; H. Richlin, *Modern Behaviorism* (San Francisco: Freeman, 1970); and B. F. Skinner, *Science and Human Behavior* (New York: Macmillan, 1953).

43. "100 Best Companies to Work For: Whole Foods Market," *Fortune* (May 23, 2011): 30; "Employees Earn Cash for Exercising More," *The Wall Street Journal*, June 2, 2010, D3.

44. Stajkovic and Luthans, "A Meta-Analysis of the Effects of Organizational Behavior Modification on Task Performance, 1975–95," and Fred Luthans and Alexander D. Stajkovic, "Reinforce for Performance: The Need to Go Beyond Pay and Even Rewards," *Academy of Management Executive* 13, no. 2 (1999): 49–57.

45. Michael Alison Chandler, "In Schools, Self-Esteem Boosting Is Losing Favor to Rigor, Finer-Tuned Praise," *The Washington Post*, January 15, 2012, www .washingtonpost.com/local/education/in-schools- self-esteem-boosting-is-losing-favor-to-rigor-finer- tuned-praise/2012/01/11/gIQAXFnF1P_story.html (accessed January 16, 2012); and Daryl W. Wiesman, "The Effects of Performance Feedback and Social Reinforcement on Up-Selling at Fast-Food Restaurants," *Journal of Organizational Behavior Management* 26, no. 4 (2006): 1–18.

46. Kenneth D. Butterfield and Linda Klebe Treviño, "Punishment from the Manager's Perspective: A Grounded Investigation and Inductive Model," *Academy of Management Journal* 39, no. 6 (December 1996): 1479–1512; and Andrea Casey, "Voices from the Firing Line: Managers Discuss Punishment in the Workplace," *Academy of Management Executive* 11, no. 3 (1997): 93–94.

47. Amy Sutherland, "What Shamu Taught Me About a Happy Marriage," *The New York Times*, June 25, 2006, www.nytimes .com/2006/06/25/fashion/25love .html ?ex=1175659200&en=4c3d257c4d16e70d&ei=5070 (accessed April 2, 2007).

48. Arthur Bandura, *Social Learning Theory* (Englewood Cliffs, NJ: Prentice Hall, 1977); and T. R. V. Davis and F. Luthans, "A Social Learning Approach to Organizational Behavior," *Academy of Management Review* 5 (1980): 281–290.

49. Bandura, *Social Learning Theory*; and Davis and Luthans, "A Social Learning Approach to Organizational Behavior."

50. Ilya Pozin, "The Takeaway: Three Things That Motivate Employees More Than Money," *Inc.* (February 2012): 6.

51. Christine M. Riordan, Robert J. Vandenberg, and Hettie A. Richardson, "Employee Involvement Climate and Organizational Effectiveness," *Human Resource Management* 44, no. 4 (Winter 2005): 471–488.

52. J. Richard Hackman and Greg R. Oldham, *Work Redesign* (Reading, MA: Addison-Wesley, 1980); and J. Richard Hackman and Greg Oldham, "Motivation Through the Design of Work: Test of a Theory," *Organizational Behavior and Human Performance* 16 (1976): 250–279.

53. Xu Huang and Evert Van de Vliert, "Where Intrinsic Job Satisfaction Fails to Work: National Moderators of Intrinsic Motivation," *Journal of Organizational Behavior* 24 (2003): 157–179.

5

LEADING

54. Sarah E. Needleman, "Business Owners Try to Motivate Employees; As Recession Lingers, Managers Hold Meetings and Change Hiring Practices to Alleviate Workers' Stress," *The Wall Street Journal*, January 14, 2010.

55. Aaron Lucchetti, "Morgan Stanley to Overhaul Pay Plan," *The Wall Street Journal*, December 29, 2009; Graham Bowley, "Credit Suisse Overhauls Compensation," *The New York Times*, October 21, 2009; Liam Pleven and Susanne Craig, "Deal Fees Under Fire Amid Mortgage Crisis; Guaranteed Rewards of Bankers, Middlemen Are in the Spotlight," *The Wall Street Journal*, January 17, 2008; Phred Dvorak, "Companies Seek Shareholder Input on Pay Practices," *The Wall Street Journal*, April 6, 2009; and Carol Hymowitz, "Pay Gap Fuels Worker Woes," *The Wall Street Journal*, April 28, 2008.

56. Reported in Sarah Fister Gale, "Keeping Your Nose Clean: A Look at Ethics in the Workplace," *Workforce .com*, September 6, 2012, www.workforce.com/article/ 20120906/NEWS02/120909987/keeping-your-nose-clean-a-look-at-ethics-in-the-workplace (accessed September 24, 2012).

57. This section is based on Gretchen Spreitzer and Christine Porath, "Creating Sustainable Performance," *Harvard Business Review* (January–February 2012): 92–99; and Gretchen Spreitzer, Christine L. Porath, and Cristina B. Gibson, "Toward Human Sustainability: How to Enable More Thriving at Work," *Organizational Dynamics* 41 (2012): 155–162.

58. Edwin P. Hollander and Lynn R. Offermann, "Power and Leadership in Organizations," *American Psychologist* 45 (February 1990): 179–189.

59. Jay A. Conger and Rabindra N. Kanungo, "The Empowerment Process: Integrating Theory and Practice," *Academy of Management Review* 13 (1988): 471–482.

60. David E. Bowen and Edward E. Lawler III, "The Empowerment of Service Workers: What, Why, How, and When," *Sloan Management Review* (Spring 1992): 31–39; and Ray W. Coye and James A. Belohav, "An Exploratory Analysis of Employee Participation," *Group and Organization Management* 20, no. 1 (March 1995): 4–17.

61. Stack, "Hilcorp Energy Shares the Wealth."

62. Golnaz Sadri, "Empowerment for the Bottom Line," *Industrial Management* (May–June 2011): 8–13; and Robert C. Ford and Myron D. Fottler, "Empowerment: A Matter of Degree," *Academy of Management Executive* 9, no. 3 (1995): 21–31.

63. This definition is based on Mercer Human Resource Consulting's Employee Engagement Model, as described in Paul Sanchez and Dan McCauley, "Measuring and Managing Engagement in a Cross-Cultural Workforce: New Insights for Global Companies," *Global Business and Organizational Excellence* (November–December 2006): 41–50.

64. This section is based on Maureen Soyars and Justin Brusino, "Essentials of Engagement: Contributions, Connections, Growth," *T&D* (March 2009): 62–65; Kenneth W. Thomas, "The Four Intrinsic Rewards That Drive Employee Engagement," *Ivey Business Journal*, November–December 2009, www.iveybusinessjournal .com/article.asp?intArticle_id=867 (accessed November 24, 2009); and Cristina de Mello e Souza Wildermuth and Patrick David Pauken, "A Perfect Match: Decoding Employee Engagement—Part II: Engaging Jobs and Individuals," *Industrial and Commercial Training* 40, no. 4 (2008): 206–210.

65. Kate Rockwood, "The Employee Whisperer," *Fast Company* (November 2008): 72–73.

66. Soyars and Brusino, "Essentials of Engagement."

67. Theresa M. Welbourne, "Employee Engagement: Beyond the Fad and into the Executive Suite," *Leader to Leader* (Spring 2007): 45–51.

68. See J. K. Harter, F. L. Schmidt, and T. L. Hayes, "Business-Unit-Level Relationship Between Employee Satisfaction, Employee Engagement, and Business Outcomes: A Meta-Analysis," *Journal of Applied Psychology* 87, no. 2 (2002): 268–279; Coffman and Gonzalez, *Follow This Path*; M. Buckingham and C. Coffman, *First, Break All the Rules: What the World's Greatest Managers Do Differently* (New York: Simon & Schuster, 1999); A. M. Saks, "Antecedents and Consequences of Employee Engagement," *Journal of Managerial Psychology* 21, no. 7 (2006): 600–619; and Nikki Blacksmith and Jim Harter, "Majority of American Workers Not Engaged in Their Jobs," *Gallup.com*, October 28, 2011, www.gallup.com/ poll/150383/majority-american-workers-not-engaged-jobs.aspx (accessed September 24, 2012).

69. Reported in Blacksmith and Harter, "Majority of American Workers Not Engaged in Their Jobs."

70. This example is from Soyars and Brusino, "Essentials of Engagement."

71. Rockwood, "The Employee Whisperer"; and quote from "Americans' Job Satisfaction Falls to Record Low," *USA Today*, January 5, 2010.

72. Lyman W. Porter, *Organizational Patterns of Managerial Job Attitudes* (New York: American Foundation for Management Research, 1964), pp. 17, 19. Used with permission.

Communication

Pavel Filatov/Alamy

Learning Outcomes

After studying this chapter, you should be able to:

1. Explain why communication is essential for effective management, and describe the model of communication.

2. Describe how an open communication climate and the choice of a communication channel influence the quality of communication.

3. Understand how communicating with candor, asking questions, listening, and nonverbal communication affect communication between a manager and employee.

4. Explain the difference between formal and informal organizational communications.

5. Appreciate the role of personal communication channels, including the grapevine, in enhancing organizational communication.

6. Recognize the manager's role in using social media to improve organizational communication.

7. Explain strategies for managing communication during a crisis.

1

INTRODUCTION

2

ENVIRONMENT

3

PLANNING

4

ORGANIZING

5

LEADING

6

CONTROLLING

Are You Building a Personal Network?

INSTRUCTIONS: How much effort do you put into developing connections with other people? Personal networks may help a new manager in the workplace. To learn something about your networking skills, answer the questions below. Please indicate whether each item is Mostly True or Mostly False for you in school or at work.

	Mostly True	Mostly False
1. I learn early on about changes going on in the organization and how they might affect me or my position.	_____	_____
2. I network as much to help other people solve problems as to help myself.	_____	_____
3. I am fascinated by other people and what they do.	_____	_____
4. I frequently use lunches to meet and network with new people.	_____	_____
5. I regularly participate in charitable causes.	_____	_____
6. I maintain a list of friends and colleagues to whom I send holiday greeting cards.	_____	_____
7. I maintain contact with people from previous organizations and school groups.	_____	_____
8. I actively give information to subordinates, peers, and my boss.	_____	_____

SCORING AND INTERPRETATION: Give yourself one point for each item marked as Mostly True. A score of 6 or higher suggests active networking and a solid foundation on which to begin your career as a new manager. When you create a personal network, you become well connected to get things done through a variety of relationships. Having sources of information and support helps a new manager gain career traction. If you scored 3 or less, you may want to focus more on building relationships if you are serious about a career as a manager. People with active networks tend to be more effective managers and have broader impact on the organization.

Nick Chen loved his job as a software engineer designing programs for mobile phones. The work was rewarding, the pay was good, and the working conditions were excellent. "The best part of being a software engineer," said Nick, "is working with a team of professionals who are excited about finding the next breakthrough in mobile technology." Nick's team had recently designed a chipset that would revolutionize the way people communicate with their mobile phones. Nick's managers recognized his contributions with a year-end bonus, so he was feeling confident about his future with the company. However, Nick had become eager for more responsibility, so he began looking for a management position. During his one-hour commute to work every morning, he used LinkedIn to strengthen his professional network and explore job openings in the mobile technology industry. His efforts paid off. One morning while updating his profile, Nick got a message from a former colleague who had recently taken a position at Qualcomm in San Diego. She recommended that Nick apply for a new position as product manager for the Android smartphone. Eager to learn more, Nick started following Qualcomm as one of the company's 54,000 LinkedIn followers. He learned Qualcomm had earned a strong reputation as a great place to work and had been named to *Fortune* magazine's list of "100 Best Companies to Work For" 14 years in a row. Nick quickly updated his resume and applied for the position.[1]

Personal networking, enhanced through social and professional networking sites like LinkedIn, is an important skill for managers because it enables them to get things done more smoothly and rapidly than they could do in isolation. Networking builds social, work, and career relationships that facilitate mutual benefit. How do managers build a personal network that includes a broad range of professional and social relationships? One key is to know how to communicate effectively. In fact, communication is a vital factor in every aspect of the manager's job.

The most successful organizations are the ones whose managers keep the lines of communication open. They have the courage to talk about what employees want to hear and explain difficult decisions, especially during tough economic times. In fact, one study shows that companies with highly effective communication had 47 percent higher total returns to shareholders between 2004 and 2009, compared to companies with less effective communication practices.[2]

Not only does effective communication lead to better bottom-line results, but also much of a manager's time is spent communicating. Managers spend at least 80 percent of every working day in direct communication with others. In other words, 48 minutes of every hour is spent in meetings, on the telephone, communicating online, or talking informally while walking around. The other 20 percent of a typical manager's time is spent doing desk work, most of which is also communication in the form of reading and writing.[3]

This chapter explains why managers should make effective communication a priority. First, we examine communication as a crucial part of the manager's job and describe a model of the communication process. Next, we consider how the interpersonal aspects of communication, including open communication climates, communication channels, persuasion, communicating with candor, asking questions, and listening, affect managers' ability to communicate. Then, we look at the organization as a whole and consider formal upward, downward, and horizontal communications, as well as personal networks and informal communications. Finally, we describe the manager's role in using social media to enhance organizational communication and developing strategies to manage crisis communication.

Communication Is the Manager's Job

Exhibit 17.1 illustrates the crucial role of managers as communication champions. Managers gather important information from both inside and outside the organization and then distribute appropriate information to others who need it. Managers' communication is *purpose-directed* in that it directs everyone's attention toward the vision, values, and desired goals of the team or organization and influences people to act in a way to achieve the goals. Managers facilitate *strategic conversations* by using open communication, actively listening to others, asking questions, and using feedback for learning and change. **Strategic conversation** refers to people talking across boundaries and hierarchical levels about the team or organization's vision, critical strategic themes, and the values that help achieve important goals.[4]

Managers use different *methods* to communicate, depending on the purpose of the communication and the audience. Social media is one method that is growing in popularity. In fact, 65 percent of managers surveyed say that they expect to use social media more next year to communicate with employees.[5] When Red Robin Gourmet Burgers introduced its new line of Tavern Burgers, top executives decided to use an internal social network to communicate the recipe and cooking methods to company managers. Instead of mailing out spiral-bound books, Red Robin successfully used social media as a method to train managers and encourage freewheeling discussions and feedback.[6]

WHAT IS COMMUNICATION?

Most of us think of spoken or written language when we think about communication, but words are only a small part of human communication. Managers are observed carefully by employees, so it's important to remember that everything a manager does and says will communicate something. In addition, communication is a two-way street that includes asking questions, seeking feedback, paying attention to nonverbal communication of others, and listening actively. **Communication** is the process by which information is exchanged and understood by two or more people, usually with the intent to influence or motivate behavior.

Surveys of managers show that they consider communication their most critical skill and one of their top responsibilities.[7] Most managers reveal, however, that they need to improve their communication effectiveness. Fewer than half of responding managers bother to tailor their messages to employees, customers, or suppliers. Even fewer seek feedback from employees or customers because they fear hearing bad news. Without

▶▶▶ **Concept Connection**

Roger Coulam/Alamy

Michael Newcombe has climbed the corporate ladder of the prestigious Four Seasons Hotel chain successfully due to his exceptional management capabilities, including his **communication skills**. Newcombe firmly believes in routinely talking with all his workers at all levels in order to understand their changing needs and to prevent problems before they occur. His personal interest in every employee also makes them feel valued and invested in the organization.

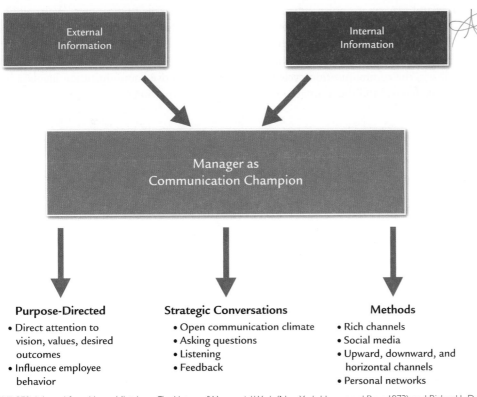

EXHIBIT 17.1

The Manager as Communication Champion

External Information → **Manager as Communication Champion** ← **Internal Information**

Purpose-Directed
- Direct attention to vision, values, desired outcomes
- Influence employee behavior

Strategic Conversations
- Open communication climate
- Asking questions
- Listening
- Feedback

Methods
- Rich channels
- Social media
- Upward, downward, and horizontal channels
- Personal networks

SOURCES: Adapted from Henry Mintzberg, *The Nature of Managerial Work* (New York: Harper and Row, 1973); and Richard L. Daft, *The Leadership Experience*, 3d ed. (Cincinnati, OH: South-Western, 2005), p. 346.

5

LEADING

feedback, though, managers can't respond adequately to problems or opportunities, and their plans and decisions may be out of alignment with employee perceptions and interests.[8]

A MODEL OF COMMUNICATION

Being a good communicator starts with appreciating how complex communication is and understanding the key elements of the communication process, as illustrated in Exhibit 17.2 and described in the following text.

Many people think communication is simple and natural. After all, we communicate every day without even thinking about it. In reality, though, human communication is quite complex and fraught with opportunities for misunderstanding. Communication is not just sending information, but sharing information in a planned way. A manager who has the ability to deliver rousing speeches or write brilliant commentary, but who doesn't know how to listen, is not an effective communicator. Honoring this distinction between *sharing* and *proclaiming* is crucial for successful management.

Knowing what communication entails helps you appreciate the complexity of it. As shown in Exhibit 17.2, a manager who wants to communicate with an employee **encodes** a thought or idea by selecting symbols (such as words) with which to compose a message. The **message** is the tangible formulation of the thought or idea sent to the employee, and the **channel** is the medium by which the message is sent. The channel might be a telephone call, an e-mail message, a formal report, or a face-to-face conversation. The employee **decodes** the symbols to interpret the meaning of the message. **Feedback** occurs when the employee responds to a manager's communication with a return message. As illustrated in the exhibit, the nature of effective communication is cyclical, in that a sender and receiver may exchange messages several times to achieve a mutual understanding.

Encoding and decoding sometimes can cause communication errors. Have you heard someone say, "But that's not what I meant!" or wasted time and energy on misunderstood instructions? Individual differences, knowledge, values, attitudes, and background act as filters and may create "noise" when translating from symbols to meanings. We've all likely experienced communication breakdowns because people can misinterpret a message easily. Feedback enables a manager to determine whether the employee correctly interpreted the message. The potential for communication errors is why feedback is so important. Without feedback, the communication cycle is incomplete. Effective communication involves both the transference and the mutual understanding of information.[9]

EXHIBIT 17.2

A Model of Communication

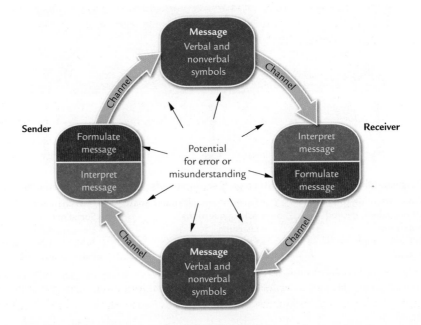

Communicating Among People

Many top managers admit their performance as communication champions likely fell short during the worst of the recent economic crisis as they spent more time trying to make sure the financial status of their companies remained sound. Yet, as soon as the worst was over, Quicken Loans CEO Bill Emerson got back out among Quicken's 3,000 employees to reinforce his commitment to open communication. Emerson holds two-hour lunch meetings with groups of 15 employees at a time. He fills them in on what is happening with the company and the mortgage industry, asks about their problems and concerns, and solicits ideas and opinions about how the company operates. Emerson depended heavily on middle- and lower-level managers for maintaining a strong communication climate while he wrestled with business problems, but he knows that his visible commitment is essential to keep effective organizational conversations going.[10]

To achieve the best possible outcome, managers must understand how factors such as open communication climates, communication channels, the ability to persuade, communicating with candor, asking questions, listening, and nonverbal behavior all work to enhance or detract from communication. Managers should also consider how gender affects communication. The Shoptalk explores how gender differences influence the effectiveness of communication between men and women.

OPEN COMMUNICATION CLIMATE

A survey of U.S. employees reveals that people genuinely want open and honest communication from their managers, including the bad news as well as the good.[11] This created a dilemma for Tom Szaky, CEO of TerraCycle, a waste-recycling business, because he was hesitant to share bad news with his employees. He didn't want them worrying about something that didn't affect their jobs and becoming distracted and unproductive. "The problem with hiding information," Szaky said, "was that when challenges came up, I felt pretty much alone on them, and the staff was left guessing what was happening. Predictably, the lack of information fueled rumors and damaged morale." Today, Szaky encourages transparency and promotes open, honest communication. Employees see everything in great detail, even the bad news. This new climate has fostered a feeling of ownership and trust. It also brings issues to the forefront faster than ever before.[12]

Open communication means sharing all types of information throughout the organization, across functional and hierarchical boundaries. People throughout the organization

Manager's Shoptalk

Gender Differences in Communication

To improve the effectiveness of workplace communication, managers should be aware of various factors that influence how people communicate. One important consideration is gender roles, the learned behaviors associated with being male or female. Deborah Tannen, author of *You Just Don't Understand: Women and Men in Conversation*, has spent three decades studying gender differences in communication. Grasping the following different communication styles of men and women can help managers maximize every employee's talents and encourage both men and women to contribute more fully to the organization.

- **Purposes of conversations.** Men's conversations tend to focus on hierarchy—competition for relative power. To men, talk is primarily a means to preserve independence and negotiate and maintain status in a hierarchy. Men tend to use verbal language to exhibit knowledge and skill, such as by telling stories, joking, or passing on information. For most women, although certainly not all, conversation is primarily a language of rapport, a way to establish connections and negotiate relationships. Women use their unique conversational style to show involvement, connection, and participation, such as by seeking similarities and matching experiences with others.

- **Decision-making styles.** When women make decisions, they tend to process and think of options out loud. Men process internally until they come up with a solution. Men can sometimes misunderstand women's verbal brainstorming and assume a woman is seeking approval rather than just thinking aloud.

- **Success in collaborative environments.** A report from McKinsey & Company, "Leadership Through

the Crisis and After," notes that the kinds of behaviors that executives say will help their companies through the economic crisis are most often practiced by female managers. Women typically score higher than men on abilities such as motivating others, fostering communication, and listening, abilities that are more important than ever when organizations are going through tough times.

- **Interpretation of nonverbal messages.** About 70 percent of communication occurs nonverbally, but men and women interpret nonverbal communication differently. Women believe that good listening skills involve making eye contact and demonstrating understanding by nodding. To men, listening can take place with minimum eye contact and almost no nonverbal feedback. Further, when a man nods, it means he agrees. When a woman nods, it communicates that she is listening. Women tend to be better at interpreting nonverbal communication. They are able to assess coalitions and alliances just by noting who is making eye contact during critical points in a meeting.

Interestingly, some male managers may be shifting to a more female-oriented communication style in today's challenging economic environment because women's approach to leadership and communication may be more suited to inspiring employees and helping people pull together toward goals during difficult times.

Sources: Based on Deborah Tannen, "He Said, She Said," *Scientific American Mind* (May–June 2010): 55–59; and Carol Kinsey Goman, "Men and Women and Workplace Communication," *Business Analyst Times*, May 26, 2009, www.batimes.com/articles/men-and-women-and-workplace-communication.html (accessed September 20, 2012).

need to see the big picture, understand the decisions that managers make, and know how their work contributes to the success of the company. Particularly in times of change, if people don't hear what's happening from managers, they rely on rumors and will often assume the worst.[13] In an open communication environment, people know where they stand and what rules they need to play by. Open communication helps people accept, understand, and commit to goals. People can see how their actions interact with and affect others in the organization. When people have access to complete information, they are more likely to come up with creative solutions to problems and make decisions that are good for the company.

Unfortunately, when the employees in the survey mentioned above were asked to evaluate how well their managers were doing in providing open and honest communication, the average score on a scale of zero to 100 was 69.[14] Managers can build an open communication climate by breaking down conventional hierarchical and department boundaries that may be barriers to communication. They can take care to communicate honestly with subordinates, keep people posted when things change in either a positive or negative direction, and help people see the financial impact of their decisions and actions.[15]

To achieve the advantages of open communication, managers should use the type of communication network that maximizes employee performance and job satisfaction. Research into employee communication has focused on two characteristics of effective communication: the extent to which team communications are centralized and the nature of the team's task.[16] The relationship between these characteristics is illustrated in Exhibit 17.3. In a **centralized network**, team members must communicate through one individual to solve problems or make decisions. Centralized communication can be effective for large teams because it limits the number of people involved in decision making. The result is a faster decision that involves fewer people.[17] In a **decentralized network**, individuals can communicate freely with other team members. Members process information equally among themselves until all agree on a decision.[18] Decentralized communication is best for complex, difficult work environments where teams need a free flow of communication in all directions.[19]

▶▶▶ **Concept Connection**

Research has shown that a culture of **open communication** offers many benefits to an organization and its employees, including higher productivity, better decision making, and lower turnover rates. Experts say that, even in the largest organizations, face-to-face communication is still the best means of being open and honest. Staff meetings or larger "town hall" meetings like this one emphasize the importance of the information being shared, more so than any form of written communication, such as e-mail.

COMMUNICATION CHANNELS

Managers have a choice of many channels through which to communicate. A manager may discuss a problem face to face, make a telephone call, use text messaging, send an e-mail, write a memo or letter, or post an entry to a company blog, depending on the nature of the message. Research has attempted to explain how managers select communication channels to enhance communication effectiveness.[20] One approach to selecting an effective communication channel is to interpret the emotions of the person who will be receiving the message and then select the channel that will result in the best outcome. Scientists have shown that managers can understand how a person is feeling by studying important clues: facial expressions, gestures, body posture, and tone of voice. A smirk, a furrowed brow, or sagging body posture are strong indicators of a person's emotions.[21]

EXHIBIT 17.3 Communication Networks

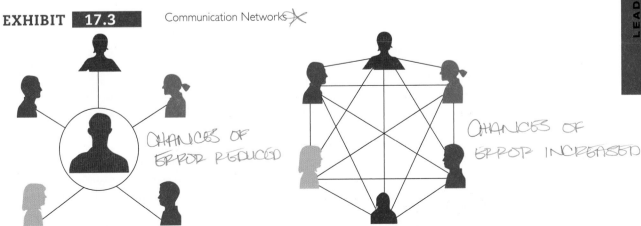

Centralized Network

CHANCES OF ERROR REDUCED

Decentralized Network

CHANCES OF ERROR INCREASED

SOURCE: Joel Spolsky, "A Little Less Conversation," *Inc.* (February 2010): 28–29. Copyright 2010 by Mansueto Ventures LLC. Reproduced with permission of Mansueto Ventures LLC.

Another factor that shapes a manager's selection of a communication channel is the type and amount of information to be communicated. Research has shown that channels differ in their capacity to convey data. Just as a pipeline's physical characteristics limit the kind and amount of liquid that can be pumped through it, a communication channel's physical characteristics limit the kind and amount of information that can be conveyed through it. The channels available to managers can be classified into a hierarchy based on information richness.

The Hierarchy of Channel Richness

Channel richness is the amount of information that can be transmitted during a communication episode. The hierarchy of channel richness is illustrated in Exhibit 17.4. The capacity of an information channel is influenced by three characteristics: (1) the ability to handle multiple cues simultaneously; (2) the ability to facilitate rapid, two-way feedback; and (3) the ability to establish a personal focus for the communication. Face-to-face discussion is the richest medium because it permits direct experience, multiple information cues, immediate feedback, and personal focus. Because of its richness, it is the best channel when communicating to people who are exhibiting strong emotions, such as anxiety, fear, or defensiveness. Face-to-face discussions facilitate the assimilation of broad cues and deep, emotional understanding of the situation. Telephone conversations are next in the richness hierarchy. Although eye contact, posture, and other body language cues are missing, the human voice still can carry a tremendous amount of emotional information.

Electronic communication, such e-mail, instant messaging, and text messaging, is increasingly being used for messages that were once handled face to face or by telephone. However, in a survey by researchers at The Ohio State University, most respondents said they preferred the telephone or face-to-face conversation for communicating difficult news, giving advice, or expressing affection.[22] Because e-mail messages lack both visual and verbal cues and don't allow for interaction and feedback, messages can sometimes be misunderstood. Using e-mail to discuss disputes, for example, can lead to an escalation rather than a resolution of conflict.[23] Too often, managers use e-mail or text messaging to avoid the emotional discomfort of a real-time conversation, hiding behind their computers to send rebukes or criticisms that they would never deliver in person. "Because we can't see their hurt, it doesn't matter as much," says business consultant Margie Warrell. She advises managers to never use e-mail in the following circumstances:

When you are angry. As our anger increases, so does our inability to communicate effectively. Wait at least two hours to cool off before sending an e-mail message. Then you will be more able to choose the most constructive way to convey that you are upset.

EXHIBIT 17.4

A Continuum of Channel Richness

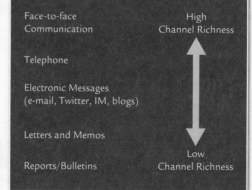

✦ ***When your message may be misunderstood.*** Meet in person with someone who may be defensive about certain issues. A face-to-face conversation ensures that the other person hears your message in the most positive way.

✦ ***When you are cancelling or apologizing.*** To cancel an engagement, pick up the phone and call instead of e-mailing to demonstrate that you care about the relationship. When an apology is called for, meet in person so you can ask and receive forgiveness, which goes a long way toward restoring a damaged relationship.

✦ ***When you are rebuking or criticizing.*** While it is never easy to deliver negative feedback, it is better to communicate rebukes or criticisms in person so you can read visual cues and address any issues the other person might raise. [24]

Still lower on the hierarchy of channel richness are written letters and memos. Written communication can be personally focused, but it conveys only the cues written on paper and is slower to provide feedback. Impersonal written media, including flyers, bulletins, and standard computer reports, are the lowest in richness. These channels are not focused on a single receiver, use limited information cues, and do not permit feedback.

> *"Electric communication will never be a substitute for the face of someone who with their soul encourages another person to be brave and true."*
>
> — CHARLES DICKENS (1812–1870), ENGLISH NOVELIST

Selecting the Appropriate Channel

It is important for managers to understand that each communication channel has advantages and disadvantages and that each can be an effective means of communication in the appropriate circumstances. [25] Channel selection depends on whether the message is routine or nonroutine. *Nonroutine messages* typically are ambiguous, concern novel events, and involve great potential for misunderstanding. They often are characterized by time pressure and surprise. Managers can communicate nonroutine messages effectively by selecting rich channels. *Routine* messages are simple and straightforward. They convey data or statistics or simply put into words what managers already agree on and understand. Routine messages can be efficiently communicated through a channel lower in richness, such as a memo, e-mail, text message, or Twitter. Written communications should be used when the communication is official and a permanent record is required. [26]

The key is to select a channel to fit the message. During a major acquisition, one firm decided to send top executives to all major work sites of the acquired company, where most of the workers met the managers in person, heard about their plans for the company, and had a chance to ask questions. The results were well worth the time and expense of the personal face-to-face meetings because the acquired workforce saw their new managers as understanding, open, and willing to listen. [27] Communicating their nonroutine message about the acquisition in person prevented damaging rumors and misunderstandings. The choice of a communication channel can also convey a symbolic meaning to the receiver; in a sense, the medium becomes the message. The firm's decision to communicate face to face with the acquired workforce signaled to employees that managers cared about them as individuals.

COMMUNICATING TO PERSUADE AND INFLUENCE OTHERS

Communication is not just for conveying information, but also to persuade and influence people. Although communication skills have always been important to managers, the ability to persuade and influence others is even more critical today. The command-and-control mindset of managers telling workers what to do and how to do it is gone. Key points for practicing the art of persuasion include the following: [28]

✦ **Establish credibility.** A manager's credibility is based on knowledge, expertise, and interpersonal skills. By demonstrating a consistent ability to make well-informed, sound decisions, managers inspire employees to have stronger confidence in the manager's leadership abilities.

Build goals on common ground. To be persuasive, managers should describe the benefits that employees will experience by embracing a new policy or fulfilling a request. An example is the manager who wanted to persuade fast food franchisees to support new pricing discounts desired by headquarters. The manager didn't just explain that headquarters wanted the policies implemented; he cited research showing that the revised pricing would increase franchisees' profits.[29] When the franchisees saw how they would benefit personally, they were eager to adopt the new policies. If a manager can't find common advantages, this is typically a good signal that goals and plans need to be adjusted.

 Connect emotionally. The most effective managers learn to understand others' emotions and adjust their approach to match the audience's ability to receive their message. In addition, by looking at how people have interpreted and responded to past events, a manager can get a better grasp on how they might react to new ideas and proposals that the manager wants them to adopt.

Use multiple media to send important messages. When managers send the same message using different media, they move their projects forward faster and more smoothly. By saying the same thing twice, they add more weight to the message and keep their issues at the top of the employee's mind. For example, one manager explained a request to an employee in person. He immediately composed a follow-up e-mail to the same employee that summarized the request in writing.[30]

To persuade and influence, managers have to communicate frequently and easily with others. Yet some people find interpersonal communication experiences unrewarding or difficult and thus tend to avoid situations where communication is required. The term **communication apprehension** describes this avoidance behavior and is defined as "an individual's level of fear or anxiety associated with either real or anticipated communication." With training and practice, managers can overcome their communication apprehension and become more effective communicators.

Becoming an effective communicator may require you to overcome your fears and anxiety when communicating. Go to the Experiential Exercise on pages 581–582 to assess your communication apprehension in a variety of communication settings.

COMMUNICATING WITH CANDOR

To influence and persuade, managers also have to be frank and straightforward about what they want and need from others. Communicating with candor means being direct, honest, and clear about what employees need to do to meet objectives, while also expressing respect for others and not making people feel slighted, controlled, or exploited. Unfortunately, communicating with candor is a problem for many managers. Jack Welch, speaker, author, and former CEO of General Electric (GE), says that when he asks groups of managers how many of them have received candid performance appraisals, only about 10 percent of people raise their hands. When he asks how many have given candid appraisals to their employees, the results aren't much better.[31]

Communicating with candor is a confident, positive approach that lets others know exactly where you stand and what you're asking of them. The appropriate use of candid communication acknowledges the other person's perspective and opinion, yet is very specific about what the manager wants and why. Some valuable techniques for communicating with candor include:[32]

 Use "I statements." To communicate with candor, you should keep the focus on the specific perception you have, how it makes you feel, and the effect it is having on you, rather than accusing or blaming the other person. Suppose that you share office space with a sloppy colleague. Rather than saying, "You drive me crazy by leaving food wrappers scattered all over the place," you might say, "I'm finding it really hard to get our work done with all this clutter on the work table."

 Stick to facts rather than judgments. Don't tell your colleague that she's a disgusting slob; just let her know that the clutter she's leaving on the table is interfering with your ability to do your work.

New Manager Self-Test

Candor

Instructions: Respond to the statements below based on how you speak to others during personal or work conversations. Answer whether each statement is Mostly True or Mostly False for you. There are no right or wrong answers, so answer honestly.

	Mostly True	Mostly False
1. I try to be courteous and respectful of people's feelings.	_____	_____
2. I say exactly what I think to people.	_____	_____
3. I never hesitate to upset someone by telling the truth.	_____	_____
4. I like to be strictly candid about what I say.	_____	_____
5. I am very straightforward when giving feedback.	_____	_____
6. I present evidence for my opinions.	_____	_____
7. I am an extremely frank communicator.	_____	_____
8. I would not deliberately say something that would hurt someone's feelings.	_____	_____

Scoring and Interpretation: Give yourself one point for each Mostly True answer to items 2–7, plus one point for each Mostly False answer to items 1 and 8. Total score: _____.

Your score reflects the level of candor with which you communicate. Many people have a hard time giving straightforward opinions and feedback because they don't want to hurt a person's feelings nor do they want people to dislike them. Hence, the sharing of honest observations is limited. A score of 6–8 on this scale suggests that you may have a habit of candor, which will add to your managerial effectiveness. A score of 1–3 may mean that you have a hard time speaking your mind and you may want to practice to improve your candor.

 Be clear, specific, and direct in your requests. Say "I'd like for you to keep the work table clean because we both have to use it to get our jobs done," rather than "Why don't you clean up the mess you leave around here?"

Communicating with candor is an important part of creating an open communication climate. When managers communicate with candor, they encourage others to do the same. In an organization where candid communication is the norm, everything works faster and better.[33] When everyone feels free to open up and speak frankly, more people get involved in organizational conversations, which leads to more ideas and faster learning. In addition, candor means that ideas get debated, adapted, and acted upon more quickly. Candid communication leads to genuine ongoing conversations and limits common problems such as meaningless meetings, workplace incivility, or rancorous silence.

Carol Bartz, former CEO of Yahoo! and Autodesk, has always been a straight talker. She believes that if a person has an opinion, they should state it, which allows others to either try to change the opinion, to agree with it, or to agree to disagree. "Agreeing is easy" she said. "Disagreeing takes more guts." At Autodesk, Bartz noticed that a successful senior-level woman was wearing inappropriate clothing at work. Her attire was distracting, and she was not being taken seriously. Bartz called her in and frankly stated, "You're not getting the respect you deserve. Go to Nordstrom and get a personal shopper. Just say, 'I'm a senior businessperson and need help dressing

5

LEADING

Take a Moment

Take the New Manager Self-Test above to see if you typically communicate with candor.

like one.'" The employee returned with a professional wardrobe, and her credibility within the workplace improved considerably.[34]

ASKING QUESTIONS

The traditional top-down, command-and-control approach to organizational communication is no longer viable in today's global, technologically sophisticated workplace. This traditional model is giving way to a more dynamic form of communication that is characterized by *organizational conversations*, which involve a give-and-take exchange of information.[35] To have successful organizational conversations, managers need to learn to ask questions. Most managers do 80 percent telling and 20 percent asking, while it should be the other way around. Asking questions can benefit both managers and employees in numerous ways.[36]

Asking questions builds trust and openness between managers and employees. Managers who ask questions encourage their employees to share ideas and offer feedback. Duke Energy's president and CEO, James E. Rogers, holds listening sessions with groups of 90–100 employees, where he asks questions and offers responses. By engaging with employees in a format that resembles ordinary person-to-person conversation, Rogers is developing a culture built on trust and authenticity.[37]

Asking questions builds critical thinking skills. In one survey, 99 percent of top managers said critical thinking skills at all levels are crucial to the success of their organizations.[38] Asking questions stimulates critical, independent thinking, encourages people to use their creativity, and leads to deeper, more lasting learning.

Questions stimulate the mind and give people a chance to make a difference. When a manager asks a question of someone, it puts the individual on alert in a way that making a statement does not. People have to think in order to respond to a question. If a plant foreman says, "We have to increase production to fill this order," workers can listen to him or not and try to speed things up or continue working as they have been. If, instead, the foreman asks employees, "What can we do to make sure we fill this order on time?" people can't ignore him; they have to start looking for solutions. Thus, asking questions gets people to accept responsibility for solving their own problems.

Asking questions is an important dimension of the organizational conversation. Consider how Cisco Systems uses powerful technology and instant connectivity to facilitate fluid and open conversations among managers and employees.

Innovative Way
Cisco Systems

Organizational conversations occur when managers talk *with* employees, not just *to* them. To transform its organizational communication into a two-way conversation between managers and employees, Cisco successfully implemented several innovative strategies that include state-of-the-art technology.

First, Cisco uses its own next-generation video conferencing, called Telepresence, to facilitate interactive communication. Telepresence is a three-screen communication system that simulates in-person meetings by beaming video feeds between locations. Telepresence allows for a natural dialogue among people, no matter the time, place, or type of computer system. Participants appear life-size and can look one another in the eye. Randy Pond, Cisco's executive vice president of operations, processes, and systems, thinks that this type of interaction offers the benefit of the "whole" conversation.

In addition, Cisco CEO John Chambers keeps in touch with employees using other communication technologies, including social media. Chambers records a video blog about once a month to deliver brief, improvisational messages. These messages allow him to speak to employees directly and informally without a script. Chambers and his team have made it interactive by inviting reactions and responses by video or text messages.[39]

LISTENING

Of all the competencies critical to successful managerial communication, listening is at the top of the list. Yet listening seems to be a rare skill among managers, and the inability to listen is one of the key reasons that managers fail. In fact, a startling 67 percent of new managers fail within 18 months because they don't listen.[40]

Listening involves the skill of grasping both facts and feelings to interpret a message's genuine meaning. Only then can the manager provide the appropriate response. Listening requires attention, energy, and skill. Although about 75 percent of effective communication is listening, most people spend only 30 to 40 percent of their time listening, which leads to many communication errors.[41] One of the secrets of highly successful salespeople is that they spend 60 to 70 percent of a sales call letting the customer talk.[42] However, listening involves much more than just not talking. Many people do not know how to listen effectively. They concentrate on formulating what they are going to say next rather than on what is being said to them. Our listening efficiency, as measured by the amount of material understood and remembered by subjects 48 hours after listening to a 10-minute message, is, on average, no better than 25 percent.[43]

Most managers now recognize that important information flows from the bottom up, not the top down, and managers had better be tuned in.[44] Some organizations use innovative techniques for finding out what's on employees' and customers' minds. Intuit, for example, instituted an annual employee survey that gives managers an opportunity to listen to employees' feelings on a range of company practices. Then, during the year, managers are encouraged to meet with subordinates to gather more feedback. Since instituting these listening strategies, turnover at Intuit has dropped from 24 percent to 12 percent. "Employees know that we are serious about asking for their feedback, and we listen and do something about it," said former CEO Stephen Bennett.[45]

Managers are also tapping into the interactive nature of blogs to stay in touch with employees and customers. *Blogs*, running Web logs that allow people to post opinions, ideas, and information, provide a low-cost, always-fresh, real-time link between organizations and customers, employees, the media, and investors.[46] One estimate is that 16 percent of *Fortune* 500 companies use blogs to keep in touch with stakeholders.[47] Blogs give managers another way to get valuable feedback. Done correctly, listening is a vital link in the communication process, shown in the model of communication in Exhibit 17.2.

What constitutes good listening? Exhibit 17.5 gives ten keys to effective listening and illustrates a number of ways to distinguish a bad listener from a good listener. A good listener finds areas of interest, is flexible, works hard at listening, and uses thought speed to mentally summarize, weigh, and anticipate what the speaker says. Good listening means shifting from thinking about self to empathizing with the other person, which requires a high degree of emotional intelligence, as described in Chapter 14.

NONVERBAL COMMUNICATION

Managers should be aware that their body language—facial expressions, gestures, touch, and use of space—can communicate a range of messages, from enthusiasm, warmth, and confidence to arrogance, indifference, and displeasure.[48] **Nonverbal communication** refers to messages sent through human actions and behavior rather than through words.[49] Managers are watched, and their behavior, appearance, actions, and attitudes are symbolic of what they value and expect of others.

▶▶▶ **Concept Connection**

Artiga Photo/Comet/Corbis

Messages are conveyed not only by what is said, but by how it is said and the facial expressions and body language of the people involved. Face-to-face communication is the richest **communication channel** because it facilitates these **nonverbal cues** and allows for immediate feedback. Important issues should be discussed face to face.

EXHIBIT 17.5 Ten Keys to Effective Listening

Keys to Effective Listening	Poor Listener	Good Listener
1. Listen actively.	Is passive, laid back	Asks questions, paraphrases what is said
2. Find areas of interest.	Tunes out dry subjects	Looks for new learning
3. Resist distractions.	Is easily distracted; answers phone or sends text messages	Gives full attention, fights distractions, maintains concentration
4. Capitalize on the fact that thought is faster.	Tends to daydream	Mentally summarizes; weighs the evidence
5. Be responsive.	Avoids eye contact; is minimally involved	Nods and shows interest
6. Judge content, not delivery.	Tunes out if delivery is poor	Judges content; skips over delivery errors
7. Avoid premature judgment.	Has preconceptions	Does not judge until comprehension is complete
8. Listen for ideas.	Listens for facts	Listens to central themes
9. Work at listening.	Shows no energy; forgets what the speaker says	Works hard; exhibits active body state and eye contact
10. Exercise one's mind.	Resists difficult material in favor of light, recreational material	Uses heavier material as exercise for the mind

SOURCES: Adapted from Diann Daniel, "Seven Deadly Sins of (Not) Listening," *CIO*, September 7, 2004, www.cio.com/article/134801/Seven_Deadly_Sins_of_Not_Listening_ (accessed December 7, 2012; Sherman K. Okum, "How to Be a Better Listener," *Nation's Business* (August 1975): 62; and Philip Morgan and Kent Baker, "Building a Professional Image: Improving Listening Behavior," *Supervisory Management* (November 1985): 34–38.

Most of us have heard the saying "Actions speak louder than words." Indeed, we communicate without words all the time, whether we realize it or not. Most managers are astonished to learn that words themselves carry little meaning. A significant portion of the shared understanding from communication comes from the nonverbal messages of facial expression, voice, mannerisms, posture, and dress. Consider the following example. During an interview about Facebook's new privacy policy with reporters from *The Wall Street Journal*, Mark Zuckerberg, Facebook's 26-year old chief executive, sweated profusely and appeared shaken. As he defended the company's policy, so much sweat was dripping from his forehead that the interviewer suggested he take off his hoodie. While his verbal responses provided plausible explanations for the new privacy policy, Zuckerberg's nonverbal cues suggested that he was unprepared and lacked confidence in the new direction.[50]

Nonverbal communication occurs mostly face to face. One researcher found three sources of communication cues during face-to-face communication: the *verbal*, which are the actual spoken words; the *vocal*, which include the pitch, tone, and timbre of a person's voice; and *facial expressions*. According to this study, the relative weights of these three factors in message interpretation are as follows: verbal impact, 7 percent; vocal impact, 38 percent; and facial impact, 55 percent.[51] To some extent, we are all natural *face readers*, but at the same time, facial expressions can be misinterpreted, suggesting that managers need to ask questions to make sure they're getting the right message. Managers can hone their skills at reading facial expressions and improve their ability to connect with and influence followers. Studies indicate that managers who seem responsive to the unspoken emotions of employees are more effective and successful in the workplace.[52]

Managers should take care to align their facial expressions and body language to support an intended message. When nonverbal signals contradict a manager's words, people become confused and may discount what is being said and believe the body language instead.[53] One manager who was a master at using body language to convey credibility and confidence was Steve Jobs of Apple. When he unveiled Apple's new cloud service, iCloud, in June 2011, Jobs fully faced the audience, made eye contact, kept his movements relaxed and natural, and stood tall. Through his body language, he communicated credibility, commitment, and honesty.[54]

Remember This

- **Open communication** means sharing all types of information throughout the organization and across functional and hierarchical boundaries.
- A **centralized network** is a communication structure in which team members communicate through a single individual to solve problems or make decisions.
- A **decentralized network** is a communication structure in which team members freely communicate with one another and arrive at decisions together.
- **Channel richness** is the amount of information that can be transmitted during a communication episode.
- Although communication skills have always been important to managers, the ability to persuade and influence others is even more critical today.

- **Communication apprehension** is an individual's level of fear or anxiety associated with interpersonal communication.
- Communicating with candor means being direct, honest, and clear about what employees need to do to meet objectives, while also expressing respect for others and not making people feel slighted, controlled, or exploited.
- To encourage a give-and-take exchange of information between managers and employees, managers need to learn to ask questions.
- **Listening** involves the skill of grasping both facts and feelings to interpret a message's genuine meaning.
- **Nonverbal communication** means communicating through actions, gestures, facial expressions, and behavior rather than through words.

Organizational Communication

Another aspect of management communication concerns the organization as a whole. Organization-wide communications typically flow in three directions—downward, upward, and horizontally. Managers are responsible for establishing and maintaining formal channels of communication in these three directions. Managers also use informal channels, which means that they get out of their offices and mingle with employees.

FORMAL COMMUNICATION CHANNELS

Formal communication channels are those that flow within the chain of command or task responsibility defined by the organization. The three formal channels and the types of information conveyed in each are illustrated in Exhibit 17.6.[55] Downward and upward communications are the primary forms of communication used in most traditional, vertically

EXHIBIT 17.6 Downward, Upward, and Horizontal Communication in Organizations

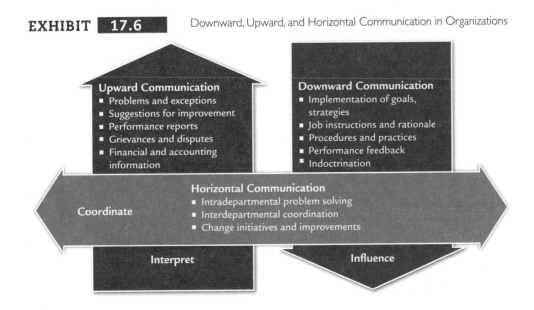

Upward Communication
- Problems and exceptions
- Suggestions for improvement
- Performance reports
- Grievances and disputes
- Financial and accounting information

Downward Communication
- Implementation of goals, strategies
- Job instructions and rationale
- Procedures and practices
- Performance feedback
- Indoctrination

Horizontal Communication
- Intradepartmental problem solving
- Interdepartmental coordination
- Change initiatives and improvements

Coordinate

Interpret

Influence

Concept Connection ◀◀◀

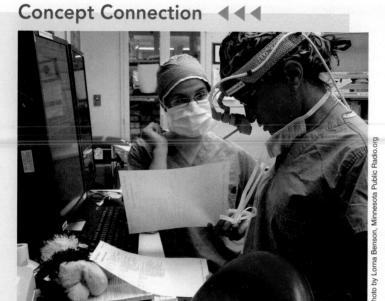

Photo by Lorna Benson, Minnesota Public Radio.org

When the Mayo Clinic formulated a strategic plan for the world-famous medical center in 2007, the communications department experimented with a new way to facilitate **upward and downward communications**. They created "Let's Talk," an internal blog that allowed managers to use videos and blog posts to explain the plan. The clinic's employees found the blog to be so useful that it continues to be used years later as an ongoing, open communication channel. The Mayo Clinic has since added numerous external blogs to facilitate greater **horizontal communication** with customers and other stakeholders as well.

organized companies. However, many of today's organizations emphasize horizontal communication, with people continuously sharing information across departments and levels.

Electronic communication methods such as e-mail and instant messaging have made it easier than ever for information to flow in all directions. For example, the U.S. Army has used technology to rapidly transmit communications about weather conditions and the latest intelligence on the insurgency to lieutenants in the field in Afghanistan and Iraq. Similarly, the U.S. Navy uses instant messaging to communicate within ships, across Navy divisions, and even back to the Pentagon in Washington. "Instant messaging has allowed us to keep our crew members on the same page at the same time," says Lt. Cmdr. Mike Houston, who oversees the navy's communications program. "Lives are at stake in real time, and we're seeing a new level of communication and readiness."[56]

Downward Communication

The most familiar and obvious flow of formal communication, **downward communication**, refers to the messages and information sent from top management to subordinates in a downward direction. Managers can communicate downward to employees in many ways. Some of the most common are through speeches, videos, blogs, podcasts, and company intranets.

It is impossible for managers to communicate with employees about everything that goes on in the organization, so they have to make choices about the important information to communicate.[57] Unfortunately, many U.S. managers could do a better job of effective downward communication. The results of one survey show that employees want open and honest communication about both the good and the bad aspects of the organization's performance. But when asked to rate their company's communication effectiveness on a scale of 0 to 100, the survey respondents' score averaged 69. In addition, a study of 1,500 managers, mostly at first and second management levels, found that 84 percent of these leaders perceive communication as one of their most important tasks, yet only 38 percent believe they have adequate communication skills.[58]

Managers can do a better job of downward communication by focusing on specific areas that require regular communication. Downward communication usually encompasses these five topics:

- **Goals and strategies.** Communicating new strategies and goals provides information about specific targets and expected behaviors. It gives direction for lower levels of the organization. *Example:* "The new quality campaign is for real. We must improve product quality if we are to survive."

- **Job instructions and rationale.** These directives indicate how to do a specific task and how the job relates to other organizational activities. For high-priority or time-sensitive issues, some managers use Twitter as a preferred channel of downward communication. With a limit of 140 characters, reading and replying to a "tweet" is a lot faster than other forms of communication.[59] *Example of a Twitter message:* "Brand managers from Adele will attend our presentation at the Chicago trade show on October 24. We'll meet Friday at 9 A.M. to outline the presentation."

- *Procedures and practices.* These messages define the organization's policies, rules, regulations, benefits, and structural arrangements. *Example:* "After your first 90 days of employment, you are eligible to enroll in our company-sponsored savings plan."

- *Performance feedback.* These messages appraise how well individuals and departments are doing their jobs. *Example:* "Joe, your work on the computer network has greatly improved the efficiency of our ordering process."

- *Indoctrination.* These messages are designed to motivate employees to adopt the company's mission and cultural values and to participate in special ceremonies, such as picnics and United Way campaigns. *Example:* "The company thinks of its employees as family and would like to invite everyone to attend the annual picnic and fair on March 3."

A major problem with downward communication is *drop-off*, the distortion or loss of message content. Although formal communications are a powerful way to reach all employees, much information gets lost—25 percent or so each time a message is passed from one person to the next. In addition, the message can be distorted if it travels a great distance from its originating source to the ultimate receiver. A tragic example is the following historical case.

> A reporter was present at a hamlet burned down by the U.S. Army 1st Air Cavalry Division in 1967. Investigations showed that the order from the division headquarters to the brigade was: "On no occasion must hamlets be burned down."
> The brigade radioed the battalion: "Do not burn down any hamlets unless you are absolutely convinced that the Viet Cong are in them."
> The battalion radioed the infantry company at the scene: "If you think there are any Viet Cong in the hamlet, burn it down."
> The company commander ordered his troops: "Burn down that hamlet."[60]

Information drop-off cannot be avoided completely, but the techniques described in the previous sections can reduce it substantially. Using the right communication channel, consistency between verbal and nonverbal messages, and active listening can maintain communication accuracy as it moves down the organization.

Upward Communication

Formal **upward communication** includes messages that flow from the lower to the higher levels of the organization's hierarchy. Most organizations take pains to build in healthy channels for upward communication. Employees need to air grievances, report progress, and provide feedback on management initiatives. Coupling a healthy flow of upward and downward communication ensures that the communication circuit between managers and employees is complete.[61] Five types of information communicated upward are the following:

- *Problems and exceptions.* These messages describe serious problems with and exceptions to routine performance to make senior managers aware of difficulties. *Example:* "The Web site went down at 2:00 A.M., and our engineers are currently working to resolve the problem."

- *Suggestions for improvement.* These messages are ideas for improving task-related procedures to increase quality or efficiency. *Example:* "I think we should eliminate step 2 in the audit procedure because it takes a lot of time and produces no results."

- *Performance reports.* These messages include periodic reports that inform management how individuals and departments are performing. *Example:* "We completed the audit report for Smith & Smith on schedule but are one week behind on the Jackson report."

- *Grievances and disputes.* These messages are employee complaints and conflicts that travel up the hierarchy for a hearing and possible resolution. *Example:* "After the

5

LEADING

reorganization of my district, I am working excessively long hours. I have lost any semblance of a work/life balance."

- *Financial and accounting information.* These messages pertain to costs, accounts receivable, sales volume, anticipated profits, return on investment, and other matters of interest to senior managers. *Example:* "Costs are 2 percent over budget, but sales are 10 percent ahead of target, so the profit picture for the third quarter is excellent."

Take a Moment

You can polish your professional listening skills by completing the Small Group Breakout on page 582.

Smart managers make a serious effort to facilitate upward communication. For example, Mike Hall, CEO of Borrego Solar Systems, found an effective way to encourage his introverted engineers to speak up and submit ideas for improving the business. To get his staff to offer feedback and suggestions, Hall organized an internal contest he called the Innovation Challenge. All employees were encouraged to submit ideas about improving the business using the company intranet. Once all of the ideas were submitted, employees voted for their favorite idea, and the winner won $500 in cash. Nearly all of Borrego's employees participated in the contest. "We've been able to generate a lot of great ideas by tapping everyone's brains," Hall says.[62]

Horizontal Communication   LATERAL COMMUNICATION

Horizontal communication is the lateral or diagonal exchange of messages among peers or coworkers. It may occur within or across departments. The purpose of horizontal communication is not only to inform but also to request support and coordinate activities. Horizontal communication falls into one of three categories:

- *Intradepartmental problem solving.* These messages take place among members of the same department and concern task accomplishment. *Example:* "Kelly, can you help us figure out how to complete this medical expense report form?"
- *Interdepartmental coordination.* Interdepartmental messages facilitate the accomplishment of joint projects or tasks. *Example:* "Michael, please ask your team to edit the IBM report using Google Docs by Monday morning."
- *Change initiatives and improvements.* These messages are designed to share information among teams and departments that can help the organization change, grow, and improve. *Example:* "We are streamlining the company travel procedures and would like to discuss them with your department."

Recall from Chapter 10 that many organizations build in horizontal communications in the form of task forces, committees, or even a matrix or horizontal structure to encourage coordination. At Chicago's Northwestern Memorial Hospital, two doctors created a horizontal task force to reduce the incidence of hospital-borne infections. The infection epidemic that kills nearly 100,000 people a year is growing worse worldwide, but Northwestern reversed the trend by breaking down communication barriers. Infectious-disease specialists Lance Peterson and Gary Noskin launched a regular Monday morning meeting involving doctors and nurses, lab technicians, pharmacists, computer technicians, admissions representatives, and even the maintenance staff. The enhanced communication paid off. Over a three-year period, Northwestern's rate of hospital-borne infections plunged 22 percent and was roughly half the national average.[63]

PERSONAL COMMUNICATION CHANNELS

Personal communication channels exist outside the formally authorized channels. These informal communications coexist with formal channels but may skip hierarchical levels, cutting across vertical chains of command to connect virtually anyone in the organization. In most organizations, these informal channels are the primary way that information spreads and work gets accomplished. Three important types of personal communication channels are *personal networks*, the *grapevine*, and *written communication*.

Developing Personal Communication Networks

Personal networking refers to the acquisition and cultivation of personal relationships that cross departmental, hierarchical, and even organizational boundaries.[64] Successful managers consciously develop personal communication networks and encourage others to do so. In a communication network, people share information across boundaries and reach out to anyone who can further the goals of the team and organization. Exhibit 17.7 illustrates a communication network. Some people are central to the network while others play only a peripheral role. The key is that relationships are built across functional and hierarchical boundaries.

The value of personal networks for managers is that people who have more contacts have greater influence in the organization and get more accomplished. For example, in Exhibit 17.7, Sharon has a well-developed personal communication network, sharing information and assistance with many people across the marketing, manufacturing, and engineering departments. Contrast Sharon's contacts with those of Mike or Jasmine, who are on the periphery of the network. Who do you think is likely to have greater access to resources and more influence in the organization? Here are a few tips from one expert networker for building a personal communication network:[65]

- **Build it before you need it.** Smart managers don't wait until they need something to start building a network of personal relationships—by then, it's too late. Instead, they show genuine interest in others and develop honest connections.

- **Never eat lunch alone.** People who excel at networking make an effort to be visible and connect with as many people as possible. Master networkers keep their social as well as business conference and event calendars full.

- **Make it win-win.** Successful networking isn't just about getting what *you* want; it's also about making sure that other people in the network get what *they* want.

- **Focus on diversity.** The broader your base of contacts, the broader your range of influence. Build connections with people from as many different areas of interest as possible (both within and outside the organization).

Most of us know from personal experience that "who you know" sometimes counts for more than what you know. By cultivating a broad network of contacts, managers can extend their influence significantly and accomplish greater results.

EXHIBIT 17.7   An Organizational Communication Network

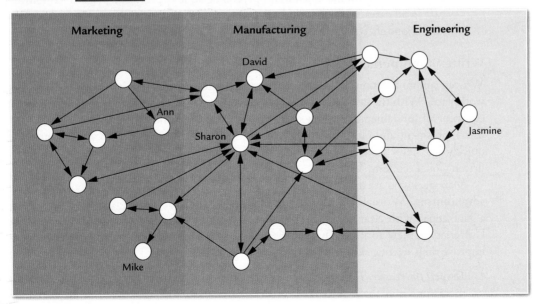

The Grapevine

Because 90 percent of employees engage in gossip, every manager eventually will have to contend with its effects in the workplace.[66] Although the word *gossip* has a negative connotation, it may actually be good for a company, especially during times of significant organizational change, such as layoffs or downsizing. In fact, gossip can be an invaluable tool for managers. Gossip provides an efficient channel to communicate information because it will move more rapidly than through a formal channel. Another advantage of gossip is that managers who tap into the gossip network may find it a useful "early warning system" that helps them learn about internal situations or events that might need their attention. Plus, gossip is one way employees relieve feelings of tension and anxiety, especially during periods of change. Another benefit is that gossip may give marginalized employees an opportunity to have a voice within the organization.[67]

Gossip typically travels along the **grapevine**, an informal, person-to-person communication network that is not officially sanctioned by the organization.[68] The grapevine links employees in all directions, ranging from the CEO through middle management, support staff, and line employees. The grapevine will always exist in an organization, but it can become a dominant force when formal channels are closed. In such cases, the grapevine is actually a service because the information that it provides helps makes sense of an unclear or uncertain situation. Employees use grapevine rumors to fill in information gaps and clarify management decisions. One estimate is that as much as 70 percent of all communication in a firm is carried through its grapevine.[69] The grapevine tends to be more active during periods of change, excitement, anxiety, and sagging economic conditions. For example, a survey by professional employment services firm Randstad found that about half of all employees reported first hearing of major company changes through the grapevine.[70]

Surprising aspects of the grapevine are its accuracy and its relevance to the organization. About 80 percent of grapevine communications pertain to business-related topics rather than personal gossip. Moreover, from 70 to 90 percent of the details passed through a grapevine are accurate.[71] Many managers would like the grapevine to be destroyed because they consider its rumors to be untrue, malicious, and harmful, which typically is not the case. Managers should be aware that almost five of every six important messages are carried to some extent by the grapevine rather than through official channels. In a survey of 22,000 shift workers in varied industries, 55 percent said they get most of their information via the grapevine.[72] Smart managers understand the company's grapevine. "If a leader has his ear to the ground, gossip can be a way for him to get a sense of what his employees are thinking or feeling," says Mitch Kusy, an organizational consultant, psychologist, and professor at Antioch University.[73] In all cases, but particularly in times of crisis, executives need to manage communications effectively so that the grapevine is not the only source of information.[74]

Written Communication

Written communication skills are becoming increasingly important in today's collaborative workplace. "With the fast pace of today's electronic communications, one might think that the value of fundamental writing skills has diminished in the workplace," said Joseph M. Tucci, president and CEO of EMC Corporation. "Actually, the need to write clearly and quickly has never been more important than in today's highly competitive, technology-driven global economy."[75]

Managers who are unable to communicate in writing will limit their opportunities for advancement. "Writing is both a 'marker' of high-skill, high-wage, professional work and a 'gatekeeper' with clear equity implications," says Bob Kerrey, president of New School University in New York and chair of the National Commission on Writing. Managers can improve their writing skills by following these guidelines:[76]

- *Respect the reader.* The reader's time is valuable; don't waste it with a rambling, confusing memo or e-mail that has to be read several times to try to make sense of it. Pay attention

Take a Moment

As a new manager, it is essential to build and nurture a personal communication network. Refer to the questionnaire at the beginning of the chapter to determine the effectiveness of your networking skills.

to your grammar and spelling. Sloppy writing indicates that you think your time is more important than that of your readers. You'll lose their interest—and their respect.

- *Know your point and get to it.* What is the key piece of information that you want the reader to remember? Many people just sit and write, without clarifying in their own mind what it is they're trying to say. To write effectively, know what your central point is and write to support it.

- *Write clearly rather than impressively.* Don't use pretentious or inflated language, and avoid jargon. The goal of good writing for business is to be understood the first time through. State your message as simply and as clearly as possible.

- *Get a second opinion.* When the communication is highly important, such as a formal memo to the department or organization, ask someone you consider to be a good writer to read it before you send it. Don't be too proud to take their advice. In all cases, read and revise the memo or e-mail a second and third time before you hit the send button.

A former manager of communication services at consulting firm Arthur D. Little Inc. has estimated that around 30 percent of all business memos and e-mails are written simply to get clarification about an earlier written communication that didn't make sense to the reader.[77] By following the guidelines above, you can get your message across the first time.

Remember This

- A communication channel that flows within the chain of command is called a **formal communication channel**.
- **Downward communication** refers to messages sent from top management down to subordinates; **upward communication** includes messages that flow from the lower to the higher levels in the organization's hierarchy.
- **Horizontal communication** is the lateral or diagonal exchange of messages among peers or coworkers and includes team communication.
- **Personal communication channels** exist outside formally authorized channels and include personal networks, the grapevine, and written communication.
- **Personal networking** refers to the acquisition and cultivation of personal relationships that cross departmental, hierarchical, and even organizational boundaries.
- The **grapevine** carries workplace gossip, a dominant force in organization communication when formal channels are not functioning effectively.

Workplace Communication

Two additional aspects of effective manager communication are using social media to improve internal and external communication and developing strategies for managing crisis communication.

Social Media

Social media is a group of Internet-based applications that allow the creation and exchange of user-generated content. Social media covers a broad number of applications including wikis, blogs, micro-blogs (e.g., Twitter and China's Weibo), content communities (e.g., YouTube), social networking sites (e.g., Facebook), and virtual social networks (e.g., Social Life).[78] Social media is reinventing how people in organizations communicate. Dr. Pepper, for example, uses social media to listen to its customers by building an 8.5 million-strong fan base on Facebook. These loyal followers who "like" the soft drink help the brand hone its marketing message. The company sends out two messages daily on its Facebook fan page and then monitors the fans' reactions. Using tools from Facebook, Dr. Pepper measures how many times a message is viewed, how many times it is shared

Concept Connection ◀◀◀

Home decor retailer Pottery Barn has been acknowledged as a leader in the use of **social media** for **listening to and communicating with customers**. The organization has representatives dedicated to monitoring the company Facebook page, for example, so that customer questions and complaints are addressed right away—often within minutes of the initial posting. Pottery Barn also follows the current etiquette for social media by focusing on sharing information rather than seizing the opportunity to "hard-sell" its products.

AP Photo/Pottery Barn, Eric Piasecki, Brad Knipstein

with other Facebook users, and what responses it gets. These data help managers adjust their brand messaging. "We mine data to understand what is appreciated, and what is not," says Robert Stone, director of interactive media services for Dr. Pepper Snapple Group Inc. "It helps us shape what we are."[79]

Companies also use social media to build teams that solve problems faster, share information better among their employees and partners, and respond to customer ideas for new product designs. In fact, big business is embracing social media in a big way. Forrester Research says that sales of software to run corporate social networks will grow 61 percent a year and be a $6.4 billion business by 2016.[80] So far, social media hasn't boosted U.S. productivity significantly, but economists such as MIT's Erik Brynjolfsson say that it takes about five years for a new technology to show its full impact on companies that use it. Social media has been used for only two or three years in most companies, largely for communicating with customers and enhancing employee collaboration.[81]

Listening to Customers

Managers in many organizations, from small entrepreneurial firms and nonprofit agencies to huge corporations, are experimenting with using social media to listen to customers. One organization that has implemented a clearly thought-out social media strategy is Dell's computer division. Through its IdeaStorm site, Dell has received 17,000 ideas for new or improved products and has adopted nearly 500, including backlit keyboards that are better for working on airplanes. Dell also promotes its own new product ideas on IdeaStorm and requests customer feedback before moving forward with product development. After posting an idea related to a specialty laptop, customers posted 83 ideas for refinements to the machine, more feedback than Dell would receive from traditional focus groups.[82]

Communicating to Customers

Managers also use social media to communicate corporate news quickly to customers. Domino's relied on the popularity of online communities to calm jittery customers after a damaging prank video showing two employees defacing pizzas and sandwiches was uploaded to YouTube. Domino's managers chose to respond with a viral video of their own. The company president apologized and thanked the online community for bringing the issue to his attention. He announced that the wrongdoers would be prosecuted and outlined the steps that Domino's was taking to ensure that the episode would never happen again. By engaging in an online conversation about the crisis, Domino's demonstrated concern for its customers and squelched further rumors and fears.[83]

Connecting Employees

Using social media can enable people to connect with one another easily across organizational and geographical boundaries based on professional relationships, shared interests, problems, or other criteria. **Social networking**, both through public sites and corporate networks, offers peer-to-peer communication channels where employees

> **"Don't think of social media as just another checkbox on your list of things to do. . . . It's not just about putting information out there, but listening and engaging in conversation."**
>
> — LASANDRA BRILL, SENIOR MANAGER OF GLOBAL SOCIAL MEDIA, CISCO

interact in an online community, sharing personal and professional information and photos, producing and sharing all sorts of ideas and opinions. Social networks designed for business use, such as Yammer and Chatter, increase productivity by making it easier for employees to share their knowledge. 7-Eleven, a Dallas-based convenience store, has 2,000 employees who use Yammer to help the company's field consultants and franchisees share their knowledge and learn best practices from one another. A local franchisee might post a picture of a display that worked particularly well in one location, for instance, so that others can see it and try the same approach in their own stores.[84] SuperValu tapped into social networks to build a virtual network of executives and store managers.

Innovative Way

SuperValu

Supermarket chains are struggling to compete against big rivals like Target and Walmart, as well as the dollar chains that lure customers with lower prices. Conventional grocery stores now account for 51 percent of grocery sales, down from 66 percent in 2000. For these stores operating in a complex, competitive environment, improved employee communication and collaboration is paramount. Social media is one tool that SuperValu has applied effectively.

SuperValu is a grocery giant with stores in 48 states, from Shaw's in Massachusetts to Albertsons in California. Because the company has been created through a series of acquisitions, most of the managers are spread across different divisions and don't know one another. Hoping to improve communication and build a sense of shared culture, Wayne Shurts, chief information officer, decided to install Yammer for the company's 15,000 associates. Yammer brings Facebook-like functionality into the office. Employees post queries and comments to internal conversation threads, where coworkers can offer feedback and solutions. Content can be shared and searched, so the same issues don't keep resurfacing. Managers also can organize themselves into virtual groups to talk about specific challenges.

For example, managers from different divisions at SuperValu joined a virtual group to discuss their shared problem of the best way to run stores in college towns. Another group of 153 managers banded together to talk about running stores in beach communities, where business is seasonal. These virtual groups allow managers with shared interests to collaborate and share solutions without incurring the expense of meeting together in one location.[85]

CRISIS COMMUNICATION

A manager's skill at communicating becomes even more crucial during times of rapid change, uncertainty, or crisis. Over the past few years, the sheer number and scope of crises have made communication a more demanding job for managers. Consider the importance of communication in the success of Robert Dudley, appointed as CEO for BP in the midst of the 2010 oil spill crisis in the Gulf of Mexico. Dudley faced the massive task of helping BP survive the greatest environmental disaster in history, caused when a rig drilling a well for BP exploded, killing 11 workers and making hundreds of millions of gallons of oil spew into the Gulf. Dudley entered his new role facing a myriad of challenges, all requiring superior communication skills: restoring trust among communities and the public, dealing with the costs and legal consequences of the oil spill, repairing damaged relationships with federal and state authorities, bolstering morale among BP employees, and winning back investors. His ability to communicate confidence, concern, and stability were critically important. "I can't think of any new chief executive of an oil company stepping into a more complicated situation," said Daniel Yergin, chairman of IHS Cambridge Energy Research Associates. "BP is going to be in a rebuilding mode, and the aftermath of the spill will go on for a long time."[86]

As a manager, your ability to communicate effectively during a crisis will determine how effectively the organization survives the upheaval. Consider the mistakes made by the luxury cruise ship captain who ran his ship aground in January 2012, causing a disaster that claimed 32 lives. The *Costa Concordia* ran aground and capsized off the coast of the Tuscan island of Giglio after Captain Francesco Schettino allegedly took it off course as part of a stunt. Schettino is accused of manslaughter and abandoning the ship before all

5

LEADING

passengers had been evacuated. Schettino is said to have contributed to the crisis by failing to respond for 45 minutes after the crew told him that the ship was flooding and its motors were dead. He issued the "abandon ship order" nearly an hour after the ship had run aground—too late to save many lives. Schettino also failed to step forward, accept responsibility, and explain what happened during the days following the disaster.[87]

Four primary skills for managers to follow when communicating in a crisis are outlined next. As you read them, consider how (in)effective Captain Schettino was in communicating during and after the cruise ship crisis.[88]

- *Stay calm, listen hard.* Good crisis communicators don't allow themselves to be overwhelmed by the situation. Calmness and listening become more important than ever. Managers also learn to tailor their communications to reflect hope and optimism as they acknowledge current difficulties.

- *Be visible.* Many managers underestimate just how important their presence is during a crisis.[89] A manager's job is to step out immediately, both to reassure employees and respond to public concerns. Face-to-face communication with employees is crucial for letting people know that managers care about them and what they're going through.

- *Get the awful truth out.*[90] Effective managers gather as much information as they can, do their best to determine the facts, and tell the truth to employees and the public as soon as possible. Getting the truth out quickly prevents harmful rumors and misunderstandings.

- *Communicate a vision for the future.* People need to feel that they have something to work for and look forward to. Moments of crisis present opportunities for managers to communicate a vision of a better future and unite people toward common goals.

Remember This

- **Social media** is a group of Internet-based applications that allow the creation and exchange of user-generated content.
- **Social networking** sites offer peer-to-peer communication channels where employees interact in an online community, sharing personal and professional information, ideas, and opinions.
- During a communication crisis, a manager should stay calm and listen carefully, reassure employees and the public, tell the truth, and communicate a vision for the future.

ch17: Discussion Questions

1. What are the characteristics of an open communication climate? Describe the organizational benefits of managers cultivating an open communication climate.

2. Describe the elements of the communication model in Exhibit 17.2. Give an example of each part of the model as it exists in the classroom during communication between teacher and students.

3. Lana Lowery, a regional manager for a 100-person inside sales staff, notices that the team's best performer is struggling. Her sales are down 20 percent from a year ago, and she frequently arrives late for work, looking upset. Lowery needs to find out why her performance is suffering. What advice would you give Lowery for communicating with this employee? Which communication channel should she use? What would be the relative importance of candor, listening, and asking questions? Explain.

4. What are the characteristics of an effective listener? How would you rate yourself on those characteristics?

5. Some senior managers believe they should rely on written information and computer reports because these yield more accurate data than do face-to-face communications. Do you agree? Why or why not?

6. During times of significant organizational change, such as downsizing and layoffs, the grapevine becomes more active as anxious employees share organizational news and rumors. As a manager, what communication strategies would you employ during a time of uncertainty in the workplace? What are the advantages and disadvantages of gossip during a time of uncertainty?

7. Assume that you manage a small online business that sells herbal supplements. Without your knowledge, a disgruntled employee has posted damaging

information about your company in the company's blog, including false information about dangerous ingredients in your best-selling supplement. What specific steps would you take to minimize the impact of this crisis?

8. If you were asked to design a training program to help managers become better communicators, what would you include in the program?

9. Suppose that you manage an employee who is spending too much time using social media at work. The result is that he has missed three important deadlines in one week. You are planning a face-to-face conversation to address this performance problem and your goal is to communicate with candor. Using "I statements" as described in this chapter, how would you begin this conversation?

10. Describe specific ways that an organization might use social media to communicate with customers. How about with employees?

ch17: Apply Your Skills: Experiential Exercise

Personal Assessment of Communication Apprehension[91]

The following questions are about your feelings toward communication with other people. Indicate the degree to which each statement applies to you by marking (5) Strongly agree, (4) Agree, (3) Undecided, (2) Disagree, or (1) Strongly disagree. There are no right or wrong answers. Many of the statements are similar to other statements. Do not be concerned about their similarities. Work quickly, and just record your first impressions.

Disagree Strongly ① ② ③ ④ ⑤ **Agree Strongly**

1. When talking in a small group of acquaintances, I am tense and nervous.

   1   2   3   4   5

2. When presenting a talk to a group of strangers, I am tense and nervous.

   1   2   3   4   5

3. When conversing with a friend or colleague, I am calm and relaxed.

   1   2   3   4   5

4. When talking in a large meeting of acquaintances, I am calm and relaxed.

   1   2   3   4   5

5. When presenting a talk to a group of friends or colleagues, I am tense and nervous.

   1   2   3   4   5

6. When conversing with an acquaintance or colleague, I am calm and relaxed.

   1   2   3   4   5

7. When talking in a large meeting of strangers, I am tense and nervous.

   1   2   3   4   5

8. When talking in a small group of strangers, I am tense and nervous.

   1   2   3   4   5

9. When talking in a small group of friends and colleagues, I am calm and relaxed.

   1   2   3   4   5

10. When presenting a talk to a group of acquaintances, I am calm and relaxed.

    1   2   3   4   5

11. When I am conversing with a stranger, I am calm and relaxed.

    1   2   3   4   5

12. When talking in a large meeting of friends, I am tense and nervous.

    1   2   3   4   5

13. When presenting a talk to a group of strangers, I am calm and relaxed.

    1   2   3   4   5

14. When conversing with a friend or colleague, I am tense and nervous.

    1   2   3   4   5

15. When talking in a large meeting of acquaintances, I am tense and nervous.

    1   2   3   4   5

16. When talking in a small group of acquaintances, I am calm and relaxed.

    1   2   3   4   5

17. When talking in a small group of strangers, I am calm and relaxed.

    1   2   3   4   5

18. When presenting a talk to a group of friends, I am calm and relaxed.

    1   2   3   4   5

19. When conversing with an acquaintance or colleague, I am tense and nervous.

    1   2   3   4   5

20. When talking in a large meeting of strangers, I am calm and relaxed.

    1   2   3   4   5

21. When presenting a talk to a group of acquaintances, I am tense and nervous.

    1   2   3   4   5

22. When conversing with a stranger, I am tense and nervous.

    1   2   3   4   5

23. When talking in a large meeting of friends or colleagues, I am calm and relaxed.

    1   2   3   4   5

24. When talking in a small group of friends or colleagues, I am tense and nervous.

    1   2   3   4   5

Scoring and Interpretation

This questionnaire permits computation of four subscores and one total score. Subscores relate to communication apprehension in four common situations—public speaking, meetings, group discussions, and interpersonal conversations. To compute your scores, add or subtract your scores for each item as indicated next.

Subscore/Scoring Formula: For each subscore, start with 18 points. Then add the scores for the plus (+) items and subtract the scores for the minus (−) items.

Public Speaking

18 + scores for items 2, 5, and 21; − scores for items 10, 13, and 18. Score = _____

Meetings

18 + scores for items 7, 12, and 15; − scores for items 4, 20, and 23. Score = _____

Group Discussions

18 + scores for items 1, 8, and 24; − scores for items 9, 16, and 17. Score = _____

Interpersonal Conversations

18 + scores for items 14, 19, and 22; − scores for items 3, 6, and 11. Score = _____

Total Score

Sum the four subscores for Total Score _____

This personal assessment provides an indication of how much apprehension (fear or anxiety) you feel in a variety of communication settings. Total scores may range from 24 to 120. Scores above 72 indicate that you are more apprehensive about communication than the average person. Scores above 85 indicate a high level of communication apprehension. Scores below 59 indicate a low level of apprehension. These extreme scores (below 59 and above 85) are generally outside the norm. They suggest that the degree of apprehension you may experience in any given situation may not be associated with a realistic response to that communication situation.

Scores on the subscales can range from a low of 6 to a high of 30. Any score above 18 indicates some degree of apprehension. For example, if you score above 18 for the public speaking context, you are like the overwhelming majority of people.

To be an effective communication champion, you should work to overcome communication anxiety. The interpersonal conversations create the least apprehension for most people, followed by group discussions, larger meetings, and then public speaking. Compare your scores with another student. What aspect of communication creates the most apprehension for you? How do you plan to improve it?

ch17: Apply Your Skills: Small Group Breakout

Listen Like A Pro

The fastest way to become a great listener is to act like a professional listener, such as a clinical psychologist. Therapists drop the need to interrupt or to express their own point of view in order to concentrate on the client's point of view. The therapist focuses intently and listens totally, drawing out information rather than thinking about a response.

Step 1. Divide into groups of four students. Within this group, each student selects one partner. Sit face to face with your partner, at a comfortable distance, and hold a steady gaze into your partner's left eye (not the nose or face, but the left eye)—use a soft gaze, not a hard stare.

Step 2. After you are comfortable with the eye contact, one partner should tell of an annoying experience over the last few days. The listener should maintain eye contact and can use facial expression, but should say nothing—just gaze into the pupil of the left eye. When the talker has finished, the partners should trade roles, with the previous listener now telling about an annoying experience and the new listener maintaining eye contact but not speaking.

Step 3. Discuss in your group how it felt to maintain eye contact and to not make any verbal response to what your partner was saying.

Step 4. Select a new partner in your group, and follow the same procedure, with the speaker talking about the same annoyance. The only change is that the listener is to paraphrase what the speaker said after the speaker is finished. If the paraphrase is incorrect, the speaker can repeat the annoyance, and the listener can paraphrase a second time to be more accurate.

Step 5. Discuss in your group how it felt to maintain eye contact and to paraphrase what was said. How did paraphrasing affect your ability to concentrate on what the speaker was saying?

Step 6. Select another partner in your group, and follow the same procedure; only this time, instead of paraphrasing at the end, the listener is to ask five questions during the speaker's story. Each partner takes a turn as speaker and listener.

Step 7. Discuss in your group how it felt to ask questions. How did the questions affect your concentration on what the speaker was saying? In addition, discuss in your group the relative importance of each technique (eye contact, paraphrasing, and asking questions) for helping you maintain focus and listen like a professional. Your instructor may facilitate a class discussion about which listening techniques are more effective in various listening situations.

ch17: Endnotes

1. Careercast.com Web site, www.careercast.com/jobs-rated/10-best-jobs-2012 (accessed September 21, 2012); George Anders, "LinkedIn's Edge: The 7 Habits of a Well-Run Social Network," *Forbes*, August 3, 2012, www.forbes.com/sites/georgeanders/2012/08/03/linkedins-edge-the-7-habits-of-a-well-run-social-network/ (accessed September 3, 2012); CNNmoney.com Web site, http://money.cnn.com/magazines/fortune/best-companies/2012/full_list/.

2. "Capitalizing on Effective Communication: How Courage, Innovation, and Discipline Drive Business Results in Challenging Times," Communication ROI Study Report by Watson, Wyatt, Worldwide, 2009/2010, www.towerswatson.com/assets/pdf/670/Capitalizing%20on%20Effective%20Communication.pdf (accessed September 5, 2012).

3. Henry Mintzberg, *The Nature of Managerial Work* (New York: Harper & Row, 1973).

4. Phillip G. Clampitt, Laurey Berk, and M. Lee Williams, "Leaders as Strategic Communicators," *Ivey Business Journal* (May–June 2002): 51–55.

5. Communication ROI Study Report.

6. Tim Mullaney, "Social Media Is Reinventing How Business Is Done," *USA Today*, August 31, 2012, www.usatoday.com/money/economy/story/2012-05-14/social-media-economy-companies/55029088/1 (accessed September 5, 2012).

7. Eric Berkman, "Skills," *CIO* (March 1, 2002): 78-82; Louise van der Does and Stephen J. Caldeira, "Effective Leaders Champion Communication Skills," *Nation's Restaurant News* (March 27, 2006): 20; and Byron Reimus, "Ready, Aim, Communicate," *Management Review* (July 1996).

8. Reimus, "Ready, Aim, Communicate"; and Dennis Tourish, "Critical Upward Communication: Ten Commandments for Improving Strategy and Decision Making," *Long Range Planning* 38 (2005): 485–503.

9. Bernard M. Bass, *Bass & Stogdill's Handbook of Leadership*, 3d ed. (New York: The Free Press, 1990).

10. Dana Mattioli, "As Crisis Eases, CEOs Give Staff Some TLC," *The Wall Street Journal*, April 5, 2010, http://online.wsj.com/article/SB10001424052702303450704575159850647117086.html (accessed September 21, 2012).

11. Reported in van der Does and Caldeira, "Effective Leaders Champion Communication Skills."

12. Tom Szaky, "How Much Information Do You Share With Employees?" *The New York Times*, September 8, 2011, http://boss.blogs.nytimes.com/author/tom-szaky/page/2/ (accessed September 5, 2012).

13. Quint Studer, "Case for Transparency," *Leadership Excellence*, (April 2010): 19.

14. Van der Does and Caldeira, "Effective Leaders Champion Communication Skills."

15. Studer, "Case for Transparency."

16. E. M. Rogers and R. A. Rogers, *Communication in Organizations* (New York: Free Press, 1976); and A. Bavelas and D. Barrett, "An Experimental Approach to Organization Communication," *Personnel* 27 (1951): 366–371.

17. Joel Spolsky, "A Little Less Conversation," *Inc.* (February, 2010): 28–29.

18. This discussion is based on Richard L. Daft and Richard M. Steers, *Organizations: A Micro/Macro Approach* (New York: Harper Collins, 1986).

19. Richard L. Daft and Norman B. Macintosh, "A Tentative Exploration into the Amount and Equivocality of Information Processing in Organizational Work Units," *Administrative Science Quarterly* 26 (1981): 207–224.

20. Robert H. Lengel and Richard L. Daft, "The Selection of Communication Media as an Executive Skill," *Academy of Management Executive* 2 (August 1988): 225–232; Richard L. Daft and Robert H. Lengel, "Organizational Information Requirements, Media Richness, and Structural Design," *Managerial Science* 32 (May 1986): 554–572; and Jane Webster and Linda Klebe Treviño, "Rational and Social Theories as Complementary Explanations of Communication Media Choices: Two Policy-Capturing Studies," *Academy of Management Journal* 38, no. 6 (1995): 1544–1572.

21. Janina Seubert and Christina Regenbogen, "I Know How You Feel," *Scientific American Mind* (March/April 2012): 54–58.

22. Research reported in "E-mail Can't Mimic Phone Calls," *Johnson City Press*, September 17, 2000.

23. Raymond E. Friedman and Steven C. Currall, "E-Mail Escalation: Dispute Exacerbating Elements of Electronic Communication," http://papers.ssrn.com/sol3/papers.cfm?abstract_id=459429 (accessed September 21, 2010); Lauren Keller Johnson, "Does E-Mail Escalate Conflict?" *MIT Sloan Management Review* (Fall 2002): 14–15; and Alison Stein Wellner, "Lost in Translation," *Inc. Magazine* (September 2005): 37–38.

24. Margie Warrell, "Hiding Behind E-mail? Four Times You Should Never Use E-mail," *Forbes*, www.forbes.com/sites/margiewarrell/2012/08/27/do-you-hide-behind-email/ (accessed September 10, 2012).

25. Ronald E. Rice, "Task Analyzability, Use of New Media, and Effectiveness: A Multi-Site Exploration of Media Richness," *Organizational Science* 3, no. 4 (November 1992): 475–500; and M. Lynne Markus, "Electronic Mail as the Medium of Managerial Choice," *Organizational Science* 5, no. 4 (November 1994): 502–527.

26. Richard L. Daft, Robert H. Lengel, and Linda Klebe Treviño, "Message Equivocality, Media Selection and Manager Performance: Implication for Information Systems," *MIS Quarterly* 11 (1987): 355–368.

27. Mary Young and James E. Post, "Managing to Communicate, Communicating to Manage: How Leading Companies Communicate with Employees," *Organizational Dynamics* (Summer 1993): 31–43.

28. This section is based heavily on Jay A. Conger, "The Necessary Art of Persuasion," *Harvard Business Review* (May–June 1998): 84–95.

5

LEADING

29. Conger, "The Necessary Art of Persuasion."

30. Tsedal Neeley and Paul Leonardi, "Effective Managers Say the Same Thing Twice (and More)," *Harvard Business Review* (May 2011): 38–39.

31. This discussion is based in part on Jack Welch with Suzy Welch, *Winning* (New York: HarperBusiness, 2005), Chapter 2.

32. These are based on E. Raudsepp, "Are You Properly Assertive?" *Supervision* (June 1992); and M. J. Smith, *When I Say No, I Feel Guilty* (New York: Bantam Books, 1975).

33. Based on Welch, *Winning*, Chapter 2.

34. Carol Bartz, "Speak Your Mind," *BusinessWeek*, www .businessweek.com/articles/2012-04-12/how-to-speak-your-mind-carol-bartz#r=auth-s (accessed September 12, 2012).

35. Boris Groysberg and Michael Slind, "Leadership Is a Conversation," *Harvard Business Review* (June 2012): 75–84.

36. Many of these benefits are based on "The Power of Questions," *Leader to Leader* (Spring 2005): 59–60; Quinn Spitzer and Ron Evans, "The New Business Leader: Socrates with a Baton," *Strategy & Leadership* (September–October 1997): 32–38; and Gary B. Cohen, "Just Ask Leadership: Why Great Managers Always Ask the Right Questions," *Ivey Business Journal*, July–August 2010, www.iveybusinessjournal.com/topics/leadership/just-ask-leadership-why-great-managers-always-ask-the-right-questions (accessed March 7, 2011).

37. Groysberg and Slind, "Leadership Is a C888888onversation."

38. Reported in Spitzer and Evans, "The New Business Leader: Socrates with a Baton."

39. Groysberg and Slind, "Leadership Is a Conversation."

40. Kevin Cashman, "Powerful Pause: Listening Is Leadership," *Leadership Excellence* (January 2012): 5.

41. M. P. Nichols, *The Lost Art of Listening* (New York: Guilford Publishing, 1995).

42. "Benchmarking the Sales Function," a report based on a study of 100 salespeople from small, medium, and large businesses, conducted by the Ron Volper Group, White Plains, New York, as reported in "Nine Habits of Highly Effective Salespeople," *Inc.com*, June 1, 1997, www.inc.com/articles/1997/06/12054.html (accessed September 23, 2010).

43. Gerald M. Goldhaber, *Organizational Communication*, 4th ed. (Dubuque, IA: Brown, 1980), p. 189.

44. C. Glenn Pearce, "Doing Something About Your Listening Ability," *Supervisory Management* (March 1989): 29–34; and Tom Peters, "Learning to Listen," *Hyatt Magazine* (Spring 1988): 16–21.

45. Kelley Holland, "Under New Management; The Silent May Have Something to Say," *The New York Times*, November 5, 2006.

46. Debbie Weil, *The Corporate Blogging Book* (New York: Penguin Group, 2006), p. 3.

47. *Fortune 500 Business Blogging Wiki*, www.socialtext .net/bizblogs/index.cgi (accessed July 26, 2010).

48. Carol Kinsey Goman, "Body Language: Mastering the Silent Language of Leadership" (The Leadership Playlist column), *The Washington Post Online*, July 17, 2009, http://views.washingtonpost.com/leadership/leadership_playlist/2009/07/body-language-mastering-the-silent-language-of-leadership.html (accessed July 17, 2009).

49. I. Thomas Sheppard, "Silent Signals," *Supervisory Management* (March 1986): 31–33.

50. Carmine Gallo, "How to Stay Cool in the Hot Seat," *BusinessWeek*, June 22, 2010, www.businessweek.com/print/smallbiz/content/jun2010/sb20100622_820980 .htm (accessed July 28, 2010).

51. Albert Mehrabian, *Silent Messages* (Belmont, CA: Wadsworth, 1971); and Albert Mehrabian, "Communicating Without Words," *Psychology Today* (September 1968): 53–55.

52. Meridith Levinson, "How to Be a Mind Reader," *CIO* (December 1, 2004): 72–76; Mac Fulfer, "Non-verbal Communication: How to Read What's Plain as the Nose . . . ," *Journal of Organizational Excellence* (Spring 2001): 19–27; and Paul Ekman, *Emotions Revealed: Recognizing Faces and Feelings to Improve Communication and Emotional Life* (New York: Time Books, 2003).

53. Goman, "Body Language: Mastering the Silent Language of Leadership."

54. *Ibid.*

55. Daft and Steers, *Organizations*; and Daniel Katz and Robert Kahn, *The Social Psychology of Organizations*, 2d ed. (New York: Wiley, 1978).

56. Greg Jaffe, "Tug of War: In the New Military, Technology May Alter Chain of Command," *The Wall Street Journal*, March 30, 2001; and Aaron Pressman, "Business Gets the Message," *The Industry Standard* (February 26, 2001): 58–59.

57. Phillip G. Clampitt, Robert J. DeKoch, and Thomas Cashman, "A Strategy for Communicating about Uncertainty," *Academy of Management Executive* 14, no. 4 (2000): 41–57.

58. Reported in van der Does and Caldeira, "Effective Leaders Champion Communication Skills."

59. Alexandra Samuel, "Better Leadership Through Social Media," *The Wall Street Journal*, http://online.wsj.com/article/SB10001424052970203753704577255531558 650636.html (accessed September 12, 2012).

60. Story recounted in J. G. Miller, "Living Systems: The Organization," *Behavioral Science* 17 (1972): 69.

61. Michael J. Glauser, "Upward Information Flow in Organizations: Review and Conceptual Analysis," *Human Relations* 37 (1984): 613–643; and "Upward/Downward Communication: Critical Information Channels," *Small Business Report* (October 1985): 85–88.

62. Darren Dahl, "Pipe Up People! Rounding Up Staff," *Inc.* (February 2010): 80–81.

63. Thomas Petzinger, "A Hospital Applies Teamwork to Thwart an Insidious Enemy," *The Wall Street Journal*, May 8, 1998.

64. This discussion of informal networks is based on Rob Cross, Nitin Nohria, and Andrew Parker, "Six Myths About Informal Networks," *MIT Sloan Management*

Review (Spring 2002): 67–75; and Rob Cross and Laurence Prusak, "The People Who Make Organizations Go—or Stop," *Harvard Business Review* (June 2002): 105–112.

65. Tahl Raz, "The 10 Secrets of a Master Networker," *Inc.* (January 2003).

66. Travis J. Grosser et al., "Hearing It Through the Grapevine: Positive and Negative Workplace Gossip," *Organizational Dynamics* 41 (2012): 52–61.

67. Grant Michelson, Ad van Iterson, and Kathryn Waddington, "Gossip in Organizations: Contexts, Consequences, and Controversies," *Group & Organizational Management* 35, no. 4 (2010): 371–390.

68. Keith Davis and John W. Newstrom, *Human Behavior at Work: Organizational Behavior*, 7th ed. (New York: McGraw-Hill, 1985).

69. Suzanne M. Crampton, John W. Hodge, and Jitendra M. Mishra, "The Informal Communication Network: Factors Influencing Grapevine Activity," *Public Personnel Management* 27, no. 4 (Winter 1998): 569–584.

70. Survey results reported in Jared Sandberg, "Ruthless Rumors and the Managers Who Enable Them," *The Wall Street Journal*, October 29, 2003.

71. Donald B. Simmons, "The Nature of the Organizational Grapevine," *Supervisory Management* (November 1985): 39–42; and Davis and Newstrom, *Human Behavior at Work*.

72. Barbara Ettorre, "Hellooo. Anybody Listening?" *Management Review* (November 1997): 9.

73. Eilene Zimmerman, "Gossip Is Information by Another Name," *The New York Times*, February 3, 2008, www.nytimes.com/2008/02/03/jobs/03career.html?scp=1&sq=Gossip%20Is%20Information%20by%20Another%20Name&st=cse (accessed February 3, 2008).

74. Lisa A. Burke and Jessica Morris Wise, "The Effective Care, Handling, and Pruning of the Office Grapevine," *Business Horizons* (May–June 2003): 71–74; "They Hear It Through the Grapevine," cited in Michael Warshaw, "The Good Guy's Guide to Office Politics," *Fast Company* (April–May 1998): 157–178; and Carol Hildebrand, "Mapping the Invisible Workplace," *CIO Enterprise*, section 2 (July 15, 1998): 18–20.

75. The National Commission on Writing, "Writing Skills Necessary for Employment, Says Big Business," September 14, 2004, www.writingcommission.org/pr/writing_for_employ.html (accessed April 8, 2008).

76. Based on Michael Fitzgerald, "How to Write a Memorable Memo," *CIO* (October 15, 2005): 85–87; and Jonathan Hershberg, "It's Not Just What You Say," *Training* (May 2005): 50.

77. Mary Anne Donovan, "E-Mail Exposes the Literacy Gap," *Workforce* (November 2002): 15.

78. Andreas M. Kaplan and Michael Haenlein, "Social Media: Back to the Roots and Back to the Future," *Journal of Systems and Information Technology* 14, no. 2 (2012): 101–104.

79. Geoffrey A. Fowler, "Are You Talking to Me?" *The Wall Street Journal*, April 25, 2011, http://online.wsj.com/article/SB10001424052748704116404576263083970961862.html (accessed September 18, 2012).

80. Mullaney, "Social Media Is Reinventing How Business Is Done."

81. *Ibid.*

82. *Ibid.*

83. Richard S. Levick, "Domino's Discovers Social Media," *BusinessWeek*, April 21, 2009, www.businessweek.com/print/managing/content/apr2009/ca20090421_555468.htm (accessed April 21, 2009).

84. Shayndi Raice, "Social Networking Heads to the Office," *The Wall Street Journal*, http://online.wsj.com/article/SB10001424052702304459804577285354046601614.html (accessed September 18, 2012).

85. "Supervalu Ousts Chief Executive," *The New York Times*, July 30, 2012, www.nytimes.com/2012/07/31/business/supervalu-grocery-chain-ousts-chief-executive.html?_r=0 (accessed July 30, 2012).

86. Julia Werdigier and Jad Mouawad, "Road to New Confidence at BP Runs Through U.S.," *The New York Times*, July 26, 2010, www.nytimes.com/2010/07/27/business/27dudley.html?_r=1&sq=BP%20Hayward&st=cse&adxnnl=1&scp=7&adxnnlx=1280315332-P6V 5i9wUaL40EYFeOSH52w (accessed July 27, 2010).

87. Stacy Meichtry, Arian Camp-Flores, and Leslie Scism, "Cruise Company Blames Captain," *The Wall Street Journal*, January 17, 2012, http://online.wsj.com/article/SB10001424052970203735304577165290656739300.html (accessed September 19, 2012).

88. This section is based on Leslie Wayne and Leslie Kaufman, "Leadership, Put to a New Test," *The New York Times*, September 16, 2001; Ian I. Mitroff, "Crisis Leadership," *Executive Excellence* (August 2001): 19; Jerry Useem, "What It Takes," *Fortune* (November 12, 2001): 126–132; Andy Bowen, "Crisis Procedures That Stand the Test of Time," *Public Relations Tactics* (August 2001): 16; and Matthew Boyle, "Nothing Really Matters," *Fortune* (October 15, 2001): 261–264.

89. Stephen Bernhut, "Leadership, with Michael Useem" (interview), *Ivey Business Journal* (January–February 2002): 42–43.

90. Mitroff, "Crisis Leadership."

91. J. C. McCroskey, "Measures of Communication-Bound Anxiety," *Speech Monographs* 37 (1970): 269–277; J. C. McCroskey and V. P. Richmond, "Validity of the PRCA as an Index of Oral Communication Apprehension," *Communication Monographs* 45 (1978): 192–203; J. C. McCroskey and V. P. Richmond, "The Impact of Communication Apprehension on Individuals in Organizations," *Communication Quarterly* 27 (1979): 55–61; and J. C. McCroskey, *An Introduction to Rhetorical Communication* (Englewood Cliffs, NJ: Prentice Hall, 1982).

Teamwork

Pavel Filatov/Alamy

Learning Outcomes

After studying this chapter, you should be able to:

1. Identify the types of teams in organizations.

2. Explain contributions that teams make and how managers can make teams more effective.

3. Discuss some of the problems and challenges of teamwork.

4. Identify roles within teams and the type of role that you could play to help a team be effective.

5. Explain the general stages of team development.

6. Identify ways in which team size and diversity of membership affect team performance.

7. Explain the concepts of team cohesiveness and team norms and their relationship to team performance.

8. Understand the causes of conflict within and among teams, and how to reduce conflict.

9. Describe the different characteristics and consequences of task conflict versus relationship conflict.

How Do You Like to Work?[1]

INSTRUCTIONS: Your approach to your job or schoolwork may indicate whether you thrive on a team. Answer the questions below about your work preferences. Please answer whether each item below is Mostly True or Mostly False for you.

	Mostly True	Mostly False
1. I prefer to work on a team rather than do individual tasks.	_____	_____
2. Given a choice, I try to work by myself rather than face the hassles of group work.	_____	_____
3. I enjoy the personal interaction when working with others.	_____	_____
4. I prefer to do my own work and let others do theirs.	_____	_____
5. I get more satisfaction from a group victory than an individual victory.	_____	_____
6. Teamwork is not worthwhile when people do not do their share.	_____	_____
7. I feel good when I work with others, even when we disagree.	_____	_____
8. I prefer to rely on myself rather than others to do an assignment.	_____	_____

SCORING AND INTERPRETATION: Give yourself one point for each odd-numbered item you marked Mostly True and one point for each even-numbered item you marked Mostly False. As a new manager, you will both be part of a team and work alone. These items measure your preference for group work. Teamwork can be both frustrating and motivating. If you scored 2 or fewer, you definitely prefer individual work. A score of 7 or above suggests that you prefer working in teams. A score of 3 to 6 indicates comfort working alone and in a team. A new manager needs to do both.

Managers at Boeing knew it was a good problem to have—demand for the company's 737 jetliner was soaring. But they had to find a way to keep pace with the demand without jeopardizing Boeing's future with a rapid expansion of factories and operating costs. How to produce more aircraft without expanding became the driving question at Boeing—and cross-functional teams provided the innovative answers. One team made up of engineers, mechanics, and other employees came up with a new process for assembling the hydraulic tubes that go into the landing gear wheel-well of the 737. The new process saves about 30 hours of mechanics' time (and a lot of money) on each system. Another team redesigned the workspace so that four engines rather than three could be produced at a time. Boeing has about 1,300 of these "innovation teams" across its commercial jet programs. Each team of 7 to 10 workers typically focuses on a specific part of a jet; teams meet each week to work on problems or come up with new processes. Overall, Boeing's teams have come up with ideas that have boosted 737 output to 35 jets a month, up from 31, and the goal is to be producing 42 a month by 2014.[2]

Many people get their first management experience in a team setting, and you probably will sometimes have to work in a team as a new manager. Many companies, like Boeing, have discovered that teams have real advantages, but it can be tough to work in a team. You may have already experienced the challenges of teamwork as a student, where you've had to give up some of your independence and rely on the team to perform well in order to earn a good grade.

Good teams can produce amazing results, but teams aren't always successful. In a survey of manufacturing organizations, about 80 percent of respondents reported using some kind of teams, but only 14 percent of those companies rated their teaming efforts as highly effective. Just over half of the respondents said their efforts were only "somewhat effective," and 15 percent considered their efforts not effective at all.[3]

This chapter focuses on teams and their applications within organizations. We define what a team is, look at the contributions that teams can make, and define various types of teams. Then we discuss the dilemma of teamwork and present a model of work team effectiveness, explore the stages of team development, and examine how characteristics such as size, cohesiveness, diversity, and norms influence team effectiveness. The chapter also looks at the roles that individuals play on teams, discusses techniques for managing team conflict, and describes how negotiation can facilitate cooperation and teamwork. Teams are a central aspect of organizational life, and the ability to manage them is a vital component of manager and organization success.

The Value of Teams

Why aren't organizations just collections of individuals going their own way and doing their own thing? Clearly, teamwork provides benefits or companies wouldn't continue to use this structural mechanism. One illustration of the value of teamwork comes from the military, where forward surgical teams made up of U.S. Navy surgeons, nurses, anesthesiologists, and technicians operated for the first time ever in combat during Operation Iraqi Freedom. These teams were scattered over Iraq and were able to move to new locations and be set up within an hour. With a goal of saving the lives of the 15 to 20 percent of wounded soldiers and civilians who die unless they receive critical care within 24 hours, members of these teams smoothly coordinated their activities to accomplish a critical shared mission.[4]

Although their missions might not involve life or death, all organizations are made up of various individuals and groups that have to work together and coordinate their activities to accomplish objectives. Much work in organizations is *interdependent*, which means that individuals and departments rely on other individuals and departments for information or resources to accomplish their work. When tasks are highly interdependent, a team can be the best approach to ensuring the level of coordination, information sharing, and exchange of materials necessary for successful task accomplishment.

The Team's the Thing

Managers at **Subaru Indiana Automotive** (SIA) put the company's desire to reduce, reuse, and recycle waste squarely on the line with television ads boasting "zero-landfill." SIA was not hedging, maintaining that "zero means zero," and managers placed confidence in every member of every team in every manufacturing process to hit the target. And the teams proved to be up to the challenge. For example, shop floor initiatives within the stamping unit led to partnering agreements with suppliers for more precise steel sheeting that reduced 100 pounds of steel per vehicle. Teams initiated efforts to use plant water-flow to drive mini-hydraulic electric generators,

and the company's Green Payback Curve recycled a variety of waste products. Assembly-line lights were turned down during breaks and shift changes to decrease the company's carbon footprint. Respect for and confidence in its teams has made SIA a recognized leader of sustainability in manufacturing.

Sources: Brad Kenney, "The Zero Effect: How to Green Your Facility," *Industry Week* (July 2008): 36–41; and Dean M. Schroeder and Alan G. Robinson, "Green Is Free: Creating Sustainable Competitive Advantage Through Green Excellence," *Organizational Dynamics* 39, no. 4 (2010): 345–352.

WHAT IS A TEAM?

A **team** is a unit of two or more people who interact and coordinate their work to accomplish a common goal to which they are committed and hold themselves mutually accountable.[5] The definition of a team has four components. First, two or more people are required. Second, people in a team have regular interaction. People who do not interact (for example, when standing in line at a lunch counter or riding in an elevator) do not compose a team. Third, people in a team share a performance goal, whether it is to design a new smartphone, build an engine, or complete a class project. Fourth, people in a team are committed to the goal and hold themselves mutually accountable for performance. Although a *team* is a *group* of people, these two terms are not interchangeable. An employer, a teacher, or a coach can put together a group of people and never build a team. The team concept implies a sense of shared mission and collective responsibility. Exhibit 18.1 lists the primary differences between groups and teams.

> *"Individual commitment to a group effort—that is what makes a team work, a company work, a society work, a civilization work."*
>
> — VINCE LOMBARDI (1913–1970), NFL FOOTBALL COACH

CONTRIBUTIONS OF TEAMS

Effective teams can provide many advantages in organizations, as illustrated in Exhibit 18.2. These contributions of teams lead to stronger competitive advantage and higher overall organizational performance.

- **Creativity and innovation:** Because teams include people with diverse skills, strengths, experiences, and perspectives, they contribute to a higher level of creativity and innovation in the organization.[6] One factor that has been overlooked in the success of Apple, for instance, is that Steve Jobs built a top management team of superb technologists, marketers, designers, and others who kept the company's innovative juices flowing. Most of Jobs's top management team worked with him for a decade or more.[7]

- **Improved quality:** One criterion for organizational effectiveness is whether products and services meet customer requirements for quality. Perhaps nowhere is this more essential than in health care. The days when a lone physician could master all the skills, keep all the information in his or her head, and manage everything required to treat a patient are long gone. Organizations that provide the highest quality of patient care are those in which teams of closely coordinated professionals provide an integrated system of care.[8]

EXHIBIT 18.1   Differences Between Groups and Teams

Group	Team
• Has a designated strong leader	• Shares or rotates leadership roles
• Holds individuals accountable	• Holds team members accountable to each other
• Sets identical purpose for group and organization	• Sets specific team vision or purpose
• Has individual work products	• Has collective work products
• Runs efficient meetings	• Runs meetings that encourage open-ended discussion and problem solving
• Measures effectiveness indirectly by influence on business (such as financial performance)	• Measures effectiveness directly by assessing collective work
• Discusses, decides, and delegates work to individuals	• Discusses, decides, and shares work

SOURCE: Adapted from Jon R. Katzenbach and Douglas K. Smith, "The Discipline of Teams," *Harvard Business Review* (March–April 1995): 111–120.

5

LEADING

EXHIBIT 18.2

Five Contributions Teams Make

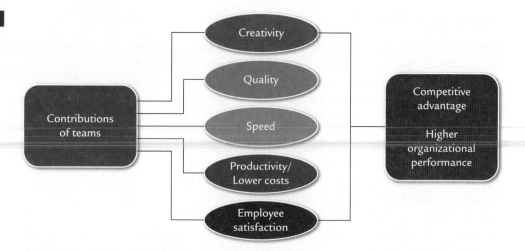

Concept Connection ◀◀◀

In recent years, hundreds of hospitals have been forming palliative care **teams** to address the unique needs of patients with terminal illnesses. These teams consist of doctors, nurses, social workers, and various types of spiritual advisors, who work together to treat each patient holistically—physically, mentally, emotionally, and spiritually. Dr. Diane Meier, a leader in the palliative care trend, notes, "Patients [typically] see a different person for every single part of their body or every problem. The patient as a whole person gets lost." Hospitals are adopting these teams because they **improve the quality** of care provided to patients just when they need it most.

- **Speed of response:** Tightly integrated teams can maneuver incredibly fast. Apple again provides an example. Apple's close-knit team has changed pricing as late as 48 hours before the launch of a new product, which would be inconceivable at most companies.[9] In addition, teams can speed product development (as we discussed in Chapter 10), respond more quickly to changing customer needs, and solve cross-departmental problems more quickly.

- **Higher productivity and lower costs:** Effective teams can unleash enormous energy from employees. **Social facilitation** refers to the tendency for the presence of others to enhance one's performance. Simply being around others has an energizing effect.[10] In addition, the blend of perspectives enables creative ideas to percolate. As described in the opening example, teams at Boeing have come up with numerous ideas that help them build planes faster and at lower cost.

- **Enhanced motivation and satisfaction:** As described in Chapter 16, people have needs for belongingness and affiliation. Working in teams can meet these needs and create greater camaraderie across the organization. Teams also reduce boredom, increase people's feelings of dignity and self-worth, and give people a chance to develop new skills. Individuals who work in an effective team cope better with stress, enjoy their jobs more, and have a higher level of motivation and commitment to the organization.

TYPES OF TEAMS

Organizations use many types of teams to achieve the advantages discussed in the previous section. Two common types of teams in organizations are functional and cross-functional, as illustrated in Exhibit 18.3. Organizations also use self-managed teams to increase employee participation.

EXHIBIT 18.3   Functional and Cross-Functional Teams in an Organization

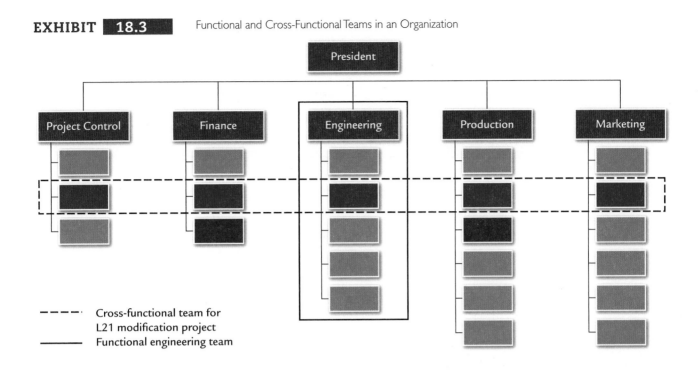

- - - - - Cross-functional team for
L21 modification project
———— Functional engineering team

Functional Teams

A **functional team** is composed of a manager and his or her subordinates in the formal chain of command. Sometimes called a *command team*, the functional team in some cases may include three or four levels of hierarchy within a functional department. Typically, the team includes a single department in an organization. A financial analysis department, a quality control department, an engineering department, and a human resource department are all functional teams. Each is created by the organization to attain specific goals through members' joint activities and interactions.

Cross-Functional Teams

A **cross-functional team** is composed of employees from about the same hierarchical level, but from different areas of expertise. One type of cross-functional team is a *task force*, which is a group of employees from different departments formed to deal with a specific activity and existing only until the task is completed. Georgetown Preparatory School used a task force to develop a flu preparedness plan some years ago, and was one of the few schools that was ready when the H1N1 (swine flu) outbreak hit in the winter of 2009. To share knowledge and responsibility all across the school community, leaders put together a task force made up of teachers, coaches, administrators, support staff, parents, and outside consultants. The result was FluPrep, a plan that makes everyone aware of what they can do individually and collectively to combat seasonal influenza, as well as to learn about and prepare for other, more deadly health threats.[11]

Another type of cross-functional team, the **special-purpose team**, is created outside the formal organization structure to undertake a project of special importance or creativity.[12] Sometimes called a *project team*, a special-purpose team still is part of the formal organization structure, but members perceive themselves as a separate entity. Special-purpose teams are often created for developing a new product or service. In 2008, Ford Motor Company created a special-purpose team to solve a problem that could determine whether the organization survived the turmoil in the automotive industry.

Innovative Way

Ford Motor Company

The Big Three U.S. automakers [General Motors (GM), Chrysler, and Ford] weren't the only organizations in the auto industry on the brink of bankruptcy by the fall of 2008. Most of their suppliers were also struggling to stay alive, and some had already gone out of business. Managers at Ford knew that without parts, nothing else they did to save the company would matter.

Tony Brown, Ford's vice president of global purchasing, suggested creating a special-purpose team to monitor parts manufacturers, prevent supply chain disruptions, and speed up Ford's plan to narrow its base of suppliers. CEO Alan Mulally quickly agreed, and Project Quark (named after the family dog in the movie *Honey, I Shrunk the Kids*) came into being. The team included people from all of Ford's divisions and functional departments— manufacturing, human resources, engineering, finance, information technology, legal, and others.

Time was of the essence, so the team started out in high gear—meeting every day, sometimes gathering before 7:00 a.m. and working late into the night, and providing regular reports to the CEO every Thursday. The team's meeting room walls were covered with printouts listing each supplier, the specific parts it provided, its financial condition, the plants it supported, and its other customers. A risk profile was created for each supplier, and the team narrowed the list down to 850 critical suppliers that Ford wanted to keep. Making sure that these companies survived was Project Quark's top priority.

The team and managers knew that Ford couldn't save the global supply base on its own, so they began reaching out to other automakers. GM wasn't interested (perhaps because its managers had even bigger problems to worry about), but Toyota and Honda quickly jumped on board, realizing that the web of interconnected suppliers was in danger of collapsing. In some cases, the three companies agreed to share the costs of keeping a particular supplier in business.[13]

This special-purpose team played a critical role in helping Ford prevent a supply breakdown—and ultimately in helping Alan Mulally and other managers revive the company. The Project Quark team illustrates many of the advantages of teams discussed earlier, particularly creativity and speed.

Concept Connection ◀◀◀

At Lucasfilm Ltd., teams form around projects. To facilitate these **self-managed teams**, the company responsible for the *Star Wars* and *Indiana Jones* franchises moved its formerly separate divisions to a campus in the Presidio of San Francisco. An easily reconfigurable work environment encourages the sharing of ideas and technology between the visual effects division Industrial Light & Magic and LucasArts, the video game company. Project teams also work on visual effects for other films, such as the visual effects for the *Transformers* and the *Pirates of the Caribbean* franchises. In this photo, producer Julio Torres reviews work on the LucasArts video game *Star Wars: The Force Unleashed*.

Self-Managed Teams

The third common type of team used in organizations is designed to increase the participation of workers in decision making and the conduct of their jobs, with the goal of improving performance. **Self-managed teams** typically consist of 5 to 20 multiskilled workers who rotate jobs to produce an entire product or service or at least one complete aspect or portion of a product or service (e.g., engine assembly or insurance claim processing). The central idea is that the teams themselves, rather than managers or supervisors, take responsibility for their work, make decisions, monitor their own performance, and alter their work behavior as needed to solve problems, meet goals, and adapt to changing conditions.[14] At the Chicago-based software firm 37signals, for example, customer service is run by a self-managed team that handles everything associated with providing service and support. The role of team leader rotates each week. Customer service, support, and satisfaction have improved since the company started using a self-managed team. "We've measured the difference, and we know it works," says co-founder Jason Fried. Today, 37signals is run almost entirely by self-managed teams.[15]

Self-managed teams are permanent teams that typically include the following elements:

- The team includes employees with several skills and functions, and the combined skills are sufficient to perform a major organizational task. For example, in a manufacturing plant, a team may include members from the foundry, machining, grinding, fabrication, and sales departments, with members cross-trained to perform one another's jobs. The team eliminates barriers among departments, enabling excellent coordination to produce a product or service.

- The team is given access to resources such as information, equipment, machinery, and supplies needed to perform the complete task.

- The team is empowered with decision-making authority, which means that members have the freedom to select new members, solve problems, spend money, monitor results, and plan for the future. Self-managed teams can enable employees to feel challenged, find their work meaningful, and develop a stronger sense of identity with the organization.

Remember This

- A **team** is a unit of two or more people who interact and coordinate their work to accomplish a goal to which they are committed and hold themselves mutually accountable.

- Organizations as diverse as Ford Motor Company, Apple, and the U.S. Navy use teams to perform tasks that are highly interdependent and require a high level of coordination.

- Teams provide distinct advantages in the areas of innovation, quality, speed, productivity, and employee satisfaction.

- **Social facilitation** is the tendency for the presence of other people to influence an individual's motivation and performance.

- A **functional team** is composed of a manager and his or her subordinates in the formal chain of command.

- A **cross-functional team** is made up of employees from about the same hierarchical level but from different areas of expertise.

- Cross-functional teams include task forces and special purpose teams.

- A task force is a group of employees from different departments who deal with a specific activity and exist as a team only until the task is completed.

- A **special-purpose team** is a team created outside the formal structure to undertake a project of special importance, such as developing a new product.

- A **self-managed team** consists of multiskilled employees who rotate jobs to produce an entire product or service, often led by an elected team member.

- Self-managed teams take responsibility for their work, make decisions, monitor their own performance, and alter their work behavior as needed to solve problems and meet goals.

The Dilemma of Teams

When David Ferrucci was trying to recruit scientists to participate on a team at IBM to build a computer smart enough to beat grand champions at the game of *Jeopardy*, he learned firsthand that teamwork presents a dilemma for many people. To be sure, building "Watson" was an unusual project, and its results would be put to the test in a televised "human versus machine" competition. If it failed, it would be a public fiasco that would hurt the credibility of everyone involved. And if it succeeded, the hero would be the team, not any individual team member. Many of the scientists that Ferrucci approached preferred to work on their individual projects, where the success would be theirs alone. Eventually, he pulled together a core team of people willing to take the risk. "It was a proud moment, frankly, just to have the courage as a team to move forward," Ferrucci says.[16] In organizations all over the world, some people love the idea of teamwork, others hate it, and many people have both positive and negative emotions about being part of a team. There are three primary reasons teams present a dilemma for many people:

- *We have to give up our independence.* When people become part of a team, their success depends on the team's success; therefore, they must depend on how well other people perform, not just on their own individual initiative and actions. Most people are comfortable with the idea of making sacrifices to achieve their own individual success, yet teamwork demands that they make sacrifices for *group* success.[17] The idea is that each person should put the team first, even if it hurts the individual at times. Many employees, particularly in individualistic cultures such as the United States, have a hard time appreciating and accepting that concept. A recent study suggests that Americans have become increasingly focused on the individual over the group since 1960, reflecting "a sea change in American culture toward more individualism."[18] Some cultures, such as Japan, have had greater success with teams because traditional Japanese culture values the group over the individual.

- *We have to put up with free riders.* Teams are sometimes made up of people who have different work ethics. The term **free rider** refers to a team member who attains benefits from team membership but does not actively participate in and contribute to the team's work. You might have experienced this frustration in a student project team, where one member put little effort into the group project but benefited from the hard work of others when grades were handed out. Free riding is sometimes called *social loafing* because some members do not exert equal effort.[19]

- *Teams are sometimes dysfunctional.* Some companies have had great success with teams, but there are also numerous examples of how teams in organizations fail spectacularly.[20] "The best groups will be better than their individual members, and the worst groups will be worse than the worst individual," says organizational psychologist Robert Sutton.[21] A great deal of research and team experience over the past few decades has produced significant insights into what causes teams to succeed or fail. The evidence shows that the way teams are managed plays the most critical role in determining how well they function.[22] Exhibit 18.4 lists five dysfunctions that are common in teams and describes the contrasting desirable characteristics that effective team leaders develop.

Take a Moment

The Small Group Breakout on page 612 gives you a chance to evaluate and discuss various team member behaviors.

EXHIBIT 18.4

Five Common Dysfunctions of Teams

Dysfunction	Effective Team Characteristics
Lack of trust—People don't feel safe to reveal mistakes, share concerns, or express ideas.	**Trust**—Members trust one another on a deep emotional level; feel comfortable being vulnerable with one another.
Fear of conflict—People go along with others for the sake of harmony; don't express conflicting opinions.	**Healthy conflict**—Members feel comfortable disagreeing and challenging one another in the interest of finding the best solution.
Lack of commitment—If people are afraid to express their true opinions, it's difficult to gain their true commitment to decisions.	**Commitment**—Because all ideas are put on the table, people can achieve genuine buy-in around important goals and decisions.
Avoidance of accountability—People don't accept responsibility for outcomes; engage in finger-pointing when things go wrong.	**Accountability**—Members hold one another accountable rather than relying on managers as the source of accountability.
Inattention to results—Members put personal ambition or the needs of their individual departments ahead of collective results.	**Results orientation**—Individual members set aside personal agendas; focus on what's best for the team. Collective results define success.

SOURCES: Based on Patrick Lencioni, *The Five Dysfunctions of a Team* (New York: John Wiley & Sons, 2002); and P. Lencioni, "Dissolve Dysfunction: Begin Building Your Dream Team," *Leadership Excellence* (October 2009): 20.

Remember This

- Teams present a dilemma for most people because individual success depends on how well others perform, there are common dysfunctions that afflict teams, and there is a potential for free riders.

- A **free rider** is a person who benefits from team membership but does not make a proportionate contribution to the team's work.
- Five common dysfunctions of teams are lack of trust, fear of conflict, lack of commitment, avoidance of accountability, and inattention to results.

Model of Team Effectiveness

Smoothly functioning teams don't just happen. Stanford sociologist Elizabeth Cohen studied group work among young schoolchildren and found that only when teachers took the time to define roles, establish norms, and set goals did the groups function effectively as a team.[23] In organizations, effective teams are built by managers who take specific actions to help people come together and perform well as a team. The Shoptalk examines the role of the team leader in creating an effective team.

Some of the factors associated with team effectiveness are illustrated in Exhibit 18.5. Work team effectiveness is based on three outcomes—productive output, personal satisfaction, and the capacity to adapt and learn.[24] *Satisfaction* pertains to the team's ability to meet the personal needs of its members and hence maintain their membership and commitment. *Productive output* pertains to performance and the quality and quantity of task outputs as defined by team goals. *Capacity to adapt and learn* refers to the ability of teams to bring greater knowledge and skills to job tasks and enhance the potential of the organization to respond to new threats or opportunities in the environment.

The model of team effectiveness in Exhibit 18.5 provides a structure for this chapter. The factors that influence team effectiveness begin with the organizational context.[25] The organizational context in which the team operates is described in other chapters and includes such matters as overall leadership, strategy, environment, culture, and systems for controlling and rewarding employees. Within that context, managers define teams. Important team characteristics are the type of team, the team structure, and team composition. Managers must decide when to create permanent self-managed teams and when to use a temporary task force or special-purpose team. The diversity of the team in terms of

EXHIBIT 18.5 Work Team Effectiveness Model

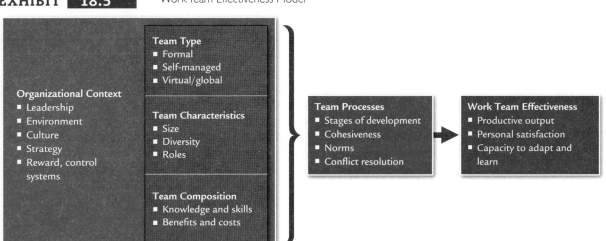

5

LEADING

Manager's *Shoptalk*

How to Be a Great Team Leader

Perhaps no single factor plays a greater role in determining team effectiveness than the team leader. Teams fail when leaders try to manage them in traditional command-and-control fashion. There are four specific ways in which leaders contribute to team success:

- **Rally people around a compelling purpose.** It is the leader's responsibility to articulate a clear, compelling purpose, one of the key elements of effective teams. This ensures that everyone is moving in the same direction rather than floundering around, wondering why the team was created and where it's supposed to be going. Effective leaders also establish clear goals and timelines.

- **Share control to spur commitment and motivation.** Overly controlling leaders sabotage team effectiveness. Good team leaders share power, information, control, and genuine responsibility. When Todd Conger became a team leader at Morton International, he felt the impulse to jump in as soon as the project started falling behind schedule. But the more work he did, the less work seemed to be accomplished—and the less motivated team members became. Conger's "helping" was actually hurting the team because they interpreted it as criticism and felt no control over their work. Sharing power and control requires that the leader have faith that team members will make good decisions, even if those decisions might not be the ones that the leader would make.

- **Clarify norms and expectations.** Leaders should define roles and expectations clearly from the start so that everyone knows what they should be doing and what they can expect from their teammates. Team members who are confused about their roles will be unproductive, which will spark resentment from other members. Sometimes a leader might need to meet with each team member individually to make sure that each person understands and accepts his or her obligations.

- **Admit ignorance.** Often, people appointed to lead teams find that they don't know nearly as much as their teammates know. Good team leaders aren't afraid to admit their ignorance and ask for help. This serves as a *fallibility model* that lets people know that lack of knowledge, problems, concerns, and mistakes can be discussed openly without fear of appearing incompetent. Although it's hard for many managers to believe, admitting ignorance and being willing to learn from others can earn the respect of team members faster than almost any other behavior.

Sources: Based on J. Richard Hackman, *Leading Teams: Setting the Stage for Great Performances* (Boston, MA: Harvard Business School Press, 2002); Lee G. Bolman and Terrence E. Deal, "What Makes a Team Work?" *Organizational Dynamics* (August 1992): 34–44; Amy Edmondson, Richard Bohmer, and Gary Pisano, "Speeding up Team Learning," *Harvard Business Review* (October 2001): 125–132; Jeanne M. Wilson, Jill George, and Richard S. Wellings, with William C. Byham, *Leadership Trapeze: Strategies for Leadership in Team-Based Organizations* (San Francisco: Jossey-Bass, 1994); Sarah Fister Gale, "The Turn Around Artist," *PM Network* (October 2007): 28–35; and Eric Matson, "Congratulations, You're Promoted (Now What?)," *Fast Company* (June-July 1997): 116–130.

Take a Moment

Go to the Experiential Exercise on page 611 that pertains to effective versus ineffective teams.

task-related knowledge and skills can have a tremendous impact on team processes and effectiveness. In addition, diversity in terms of gender and race affect a team's performance.[26] Team size and roles also are important.

These team characteristics influence processes that are internal to the team, which, in turn, affect output, satisfaction, and the team's contribution to organizational adaptability. Good team leaders understand and manage stages of team development, cohesiveness, norms, and conflict to build an effective team. These processes are influenced by team and organizational characteristics and by the ability of members and leaders to direct these processes in a positive manner.

Virtual Teams

An exciting new approach to teamwork has resulted from advances in information technology, shifting employee expectations, and the globalization of business. A **virtual team** is a group made up of geographically or organizationally dispersed members who are linked primarily through advanced information and telecommunications technologies.[27]

A 2010 survey of employees at multinational corporations found that 80 percent of respondents belong to virtual teams.[28] In a virtual team, members use groupware, e-mail, instant messaging, telephone and text messaging, wikis and blogs, videoconferencing, and other technology tools to collaborate and perform their work, although they also might meet face to face at times. Although some virtual teams are made up of only organizational members, virtual teams often include contingent workers, members of partner organizations, customers, suppliers, consultants, or other outsiders. Many virtual teams are also global teams. A **global team** is a cross-border team made up of members of different nationalities whose activities span multiple countries.[29]

One of the primary advantages of virtual teams is the ability to assemble the most talented group of people to complete a complex project, solve a particular problem, or exploit a specific strategic opportunity. The diverse mix of people can fuel creativity and innovation. On a practical level, organizations can save employees time and cut travel expenses when people meet in virtual rather than physical space. IBM reported that it saved more than $50 million in travel-related expenses in 2007 by using virtual teams.[30]

▶ ▶ ▶ **Concept Connection**

To update Lotus Symphony, a package of PC software applications, IBM assigned the project to teams in Beijing, China; Austin, Texas; Raleigh, North Carolina; and Böblingen, Germany. Leading the project, the Beijing group—shown here with Michael Karasick (center), who runs the Beijing lab, and lead developer Yue Ma (right)—navigated the **global team** through the programming challenges. To help bridge the distance gap, IBM uses Beehive, a corporate social network similar to Facebook, where employees create profiles, list their interests, and post photos.

Mark Leong/Redux

However, virtual teams also present unique challenges. Exhibit 18.6 lists some critical areas that managers should address when leading virtual teams. Each of these areas is discussed in more detail in the following list:[31]

- _**Using technology to build trust and relationships is crucial for effective virtual teamwork.**_ Leaders first select people who have the right mix of technical, interpersonal, and communication skills to work in a virtual environment, and then make sure that they have opportunities to know one another and establish trusting relationships. Encouraging online social networking, where people can share photos and personal biographies, is one key to virtual team success. One study suggests that higher levels of

EXHIBIT 18.6   What Effective Virtual Team Leaders Do

Practice	How It's Done
Use technology to build relationships	• Bring attention to and appreciate diverse skills and opinions • Use technology to enhance communication and trust • Ensure timely responses online • Manage online socialization
Shape culture through technology	• Create a psychologically safe virtual culture • Share members' special experience/strengths • Engage members from cultures where they may be hesitant to share ideas
Monitor progress and rewards	• Scrutinize electronic communication patterns • Post targets and scorecards in virtual work space • Reward people through online ceremonies, recognition

SOURCES: Based on Table 1, "Practices of Effective Virtual Team Leaders," in Arvind Malhotra, Ann Majchrzak, and Benson Rosen, "Leading Virtual Teams," _Academy of Management Perspectives_ 21, no. 1 (February 2007): 60–69; and Table 2, " 'Best Practices' Solutions for Overcoming Barriers to Knowledge Sharing in Virtual Teams," in Benson Rosen, Stacie Furst, and Richard Blackburn, "Overcoming Barriers to Knowledge Sharing in Virtual Teams," _Organizational Dynamics_ 36, no. 3 (2007): 259–273.

5

LEADING

online communication increase team cohesiveness and trust.[32] Leaders also build trust by making everyone's roles, responsibilities, and authority clear from the beginning, by shaping norms of full disclosure and respectful interaction, and by providing a way for everyone to stay up to date. In a study of which technologies make virtual teams successful, researchers found that round-the-clock virtual work spaces, where team members can access the latest versions of files, keep track of deadlines and timelines, monitor one another's progress, and carry on discussions between formal meetings, got top marks.[33]

- *Shaping culture through technology reinforces productive norms.* This involves creating a virtual environment in which people feel safe to express concerns, admit mistakes, share ideas, acknowledge fears, or ask for help. Leaders reinforce a norm of sharing all forms of knowledge, and they encourage people to express "off-the-wall" ideas and ask for help when it's needed. Team leaders set the example by their own behavior. Leaders also make sure that they bring diversity issues into the open and educate members early on regarding possible cultural differences that could cause communication problems or misunderstandings in a virtual environment.

- *Monitoring progress and rewarding members keep the team progressing toward goals.* Leaders stay on top of the project's development and make sure that everyone knows how the team is progressing toward meeting its goals. Posting targets, measurements, and milestones in the virtual workspace can make progress explicit. Leaders also provide regular feedback, and they reward both individual and team accomplishments through avenues such as virtual award ceremonies and recognition at virtual meetings. They are liberal with praise and congratulations, but criticism or reprimands are handled individually, rather than in the virtual presence of the team.

As the use of virtual teams grows, there is growing understanding of what makes them successful. Some experts suggest that managers solicit volunteers as much as possible for virtual teams, and interviews with virtual team members and leaders support the idea that members who truly want to work as a virtual team are more effective.[34] At Nokia, many of its virtual teams consist of people who volunteered for the task.

Innovative Way
Nokia

In a study of 52 virtual teams in 15 leading multinational companies, London Business School researchers found that Nokia's teams were among the most effective, even though they were made up of people working in several different countries, across time zones and cultures. What makes Nokia's teams so successful?

Nokia managers are careful to select people who have a collaborative mind-set, and they form many teams with volunteers who are highly committed to the task or project. The company also tries to make sure that some members of a team have worked together before, providing a base for trusting relationships. Making the best use of technology is critical. In addition to a virtual work space that team members can access 24 hours a day, Nokia provides an online resource where virtual workers are encouraged to post photos and share personal information. With the inability of members to get to know each another being one of the biggest barriers to effective virtual teamwork, encouraging and supporting social networking has paid off for Nokia.[35]

Global teams such as the ones at Nokia present even greater challenges for team leaders, who have to bridge gaps of time, distance, and culture. Different cultural attitudes can affect work pacing, team communications, decision making, the perception of deadlines, and other issues, and provide rich soil for misunderstandings and conflict. No wonder when the executive council of *CIO* magazine asked global chief information officers (CIOs) to rank their greatest challenges, managing virtual global teams ranked as the most pressing issue.[36]

- A **virtual team** is a team made up of members who are geographically or organizationally dispersed, rarely meet face to face, and interact to accomplish their work primarily using advanced information and telecommunications technologies.

- A **global team** is a group made up of employees who come from different countries and whose activities span multiple countries.

- Virtual teams provide many advantages, but they also present new challenges for leaders, who must learn to build trusting relationships in a virtual environment.

Team Characteristics

After deciding the type of team to use, the next issue of concern to managers is designing the team for greatest effectiveness. Team characteristics of particular concern are size, diversity, and member roles.

SIZE

More than 30 years ago, psychologist Ivan Steiner examined what happened each time the size of a team increased, and he proposed that a team's performance and productivity peaked when it had about five members—a quite small number. He found that adding members beyond five caused a decrease in motivation, an increase in coordination problems, and a general decline in performance.[37] Since then, numerous studies have found that smaller teams perform better, although most researchers say that it's impossible to specify an optimal team size. One investigation of team size based on data from 58 software development teams found that the best-performing teams ranged in size from three to six members.[38]

Teams need to be large enough to incorporate the diverse skills needed to complete a task, enable members to express good and bad feelings, and aggressively solve problems. However, they also should be small enough to permit members to feel an intimate part of the team and to communicate effectively and efficiently. The ability of people to identify with the team is an important determinant of high performance.[39] At Amazon.com, CEO Jeff Bezos established a "two-pizza rule." If a team gets so large that members can't be fed with two pizzas, it should be split into smaller teams.[40] In general, as a team increases in size, it becomes harder for each member to interact with and influence the others. Subgroups often form in larger teams, and conflicts among them can occur. Turnover and absenteeism are higher because members feel less like an important part of the team.[41] Although the Internet and advanced technologies are enabling larger groups of people to work more effectively in virtual teams, studies show that members of smaller virtual teams participate more actively, are more committed to the team, are more focused on team goals, and have higher levels of rapport than larger virtual teams.[42]

DIVERSITY

Because teams require a variety of skills, knowledge, and experience, it seems likely that heterogeneous teams would be more effective than homogeneous ones. In general, research supports this idea, showing that diverse teams produce more innovative solutions to problems.[43] Diversity in terms of functional area and skills, thinking styles, and personal characteristics is often a source of creativity. In addition, diversity may contribute to a healthy level of disagreement that leads to better decision making.

Research studies have confirmed that both functional diversity and demographic diversity can have a positive impact on work team performance.[44] For example, recent research

Concept Connection ◄◄◄

The U.S. women's gymnastics team excelled in the 2012 London Olympics, and team captain Aly Raisman (second from left) succeeded in her role as their **socioemotional** leader. In the initial round of competition, teammate Jordyn Wieber did not perform as well as expected and failed to qualify for the all-around final, which left the entire team stunned and anxious. Raisman needed to draw upon all her leadership skills to **encourage**, **harmonize**, and **reduce tension** among the group. The team emerged victorious, winning the team gold medal.

suggests that gender diversity, particularly with more women on a team, leads to better performance.[45] Ethnic, national, and racial diversity sometimes can hinder team interaction and performance in the short term, but with effective leadership, the problems fade over time.[46]

MEMBER ROLES

For a team to be successful over the long run, it must be structured so as to both maintain its members' social well-being and accomplish its task. To understand the importance of members fulfilling various roles on a team, consider the 33 miners who were trapped underground after a copper mine collapsed in San José, Chile, in August 2010. With little food, scant water, dusty conditions, and frayed nerves, the situation could have led to chaos. However, the miners organized into several teams in charge of critical activities such as communication with rescue workers, the transport of supplies from above ground, rationing and distribution of food, managing health concerns, and securing the mine to prevent further collapses.

Some team members were clearly focused on helping the trapped miners meet their needs for physical survival; some focused on helping people coordinate their activities; and still others focused on the group's psychological and social needs, helping people maintain hope and a sense of solidarity as the ordeal stretched to a harrowing 69 days. Experts agree that teamwork and leadership were key to the miners' survival.[47]

In successful teams, the requirements for task performance and social satisfaction are met by the emergence of two types of roles: task specialist and socioemotional.[48]

People who play a **task specialist role** spend time and energy helping the team reach its goal. They often display the following behaviors:

- *Initiate ideas.* Propose new solutions to team problems
- *Give opinions.* Offer judgments on task solutions; give candid feedback on others' suggestions
- *Seek information.* Ask for task-relevant facts
- *Summarize.* Relate various ideas to the problem at hand; pull ideas together into a brief overview
- *Energize.* Stimulate the team into action when interest drops[49]

People who adopt a **socioemotional role** support team members' emotional needs and help strengthen the social entity. They display the following behaviors:

Take a Moment

Complete the New Manager Self-Test on page 601 to see how you contribute as a team member.

- *Encourage.* Are warm and receptive to others' ideas; praise and encourage others to draw forth their contributions
- *Harmonize.* Reconcile group conflicts; help disagreeing parties reach agreement
- *Reduce tension.* Tell jokes or diffuse emotions in other ways when the group atmosphere is tense
- *Follow.* Go along with the team; agree to other team members' ideas
- *Compromise.* Will shift own opinions to maintain team harmony[50]

New Manager Self-Test

Are You a Contributing Team Member?

Instructions: Think about how you have behaved as a member of a specific student or work team. Respond to the statements below based on how you typically behaved on that team.

	Mostly True	Mostly False
1. I engaged the team in clarifying plans and deadlines.	_____	_____
2. I suggested corrective actions to improve performance.	_____	_____
3. I kept the discussion focused on relevant items.	_____	_____
4. I came to meetings well prepared.	_____	_____
5. I was consistently on time to meetings.	_____	_____
6. I followed through on promises and commitments.	_____	_____
7. I was a focused, active listener.	_____	_____
8. I verbalized my insights and recommendations.	_____	_____
9. I provided constructive feedback to others.	_____	_____
10. I did not shy away from disputes.	_____	_____
11. I knew when to stop pushing for my own position.	_____	_____
12. I intervened constructively when conflicts arose.	_____	_____
13. I showed team members appreciation and support.	_____	_____
14. I celebrated the accomplishments of others.	_____	_____
15. I praised people for a job well done.	_____	_____

Scoring and Interpretation: These questions pertain to your contributions as a team member, which are important to the success of any type of formal team and especially to self-managed teams.

Give yourself one point for each Mostly True answer.

Total score: _____.

Generally, if you score 11 or higher, you are considered a contributing team member. A score of 5 or lower suggests that you should be contributing more to the team.

You also can assess the specific ways in which you contributed most or least to the team.

1. Meeting the team's performance needs; one point for each Mostly True answer to questions 1–3: _____

2. Taking personal responsibility for own participation; one point for each Mostly True answer to questions 4–6: _____

3. Facilitating team communication; one point for each Mostly True answer to questions 7–9: _____

4. Managing healthy conflict among members; one point for each Mostly True answer to questions 10–12: _____

5. Meeting socioemotional needs of team members; one point for each Mostly True answer to questions 13–15: _____

A score of 3 in any of the above categories suggests a high contribution on that dimension. A score of 0 or 1 suggests a low contribution. An effective team must have someone performing each of the five parts, but no single member is expected to perform all parts. Indeed, if you scored well on most questions, you were likely playing a leadership role on the team.

There are five types of contributions that someone on a team must make, including performance management or focus on accomplishing the team's tasks (1–3), displaying personal responsibility (4–6), facilitating quality team communication (7–9), managing conflict among team members (10–12), and meeting the social needs of members (13–15). How do you feel about your contributions to the team? In what ways do you take the initiative to be an effective member? What might you do to be more effective?

5

LEADING

Teams with mostly socioemotional roles can be satisfying, but they also can be unproductive. At the other extreme, a team made up primarily of task specialists will tend to have a singular concern for task accomplishment. This team will be effective for a short period of time but will not be satisfying for members over the long run. Effective teams have people in both task specialist and socioemotional roles. A well-balanced team will do best over the long term because it will be personally satisfying for team members, as well as permit the accomplishment of team tasks.

Remember This

- Issues of particular concern to managers for team effectiveness are selecting the right type of team for the task, balancing the team's size and diversity, and ensuring that both task and social needs are met.
- Small teams are typically more productive and more satisfying to their members than are large teams.
- Jeff Bezos established a "two-pizza rule" at Amazon .com: If a team gets so large that members can't be fed with two pizzas, it is split into smaller teams.

- The **task specialist role** is a team role in which an individual devotes personal time and energy to helping the team accomplish its activities and reach its goal.
- The **socioemotional role** is a team role in which an individual provides support for team members' emotional needs and helps strengthen social unity.

Team Processes

Now we turn our attention to internal team processes. Team processes pertain to those dynamics that change over time and can be influenced by team leaders. In this section, we discuss stages of development, cohesiveness, and norms. The fourth type of team process, conflict, will be covered in the next section.

STAGES OF TEAM DEVELOPMENT

After a team has been created, it develops by passing through distinct stages. New teams are different from mature teams. Recall a time when you were a member of a new team, such as a fraternity or sorority pledge class, a committee, or a small team formed to do a class assignment. Over time, the team changed. In the beginning, team members had to get to know one another, establish roles and norms, divide the labor, and clarify the team's task. In this way, each member became part of a smoothly operating team. The challenge for leaders is to understand the stages of development and take action that will lead to smooth functioning.

Research findings suggest that team development is not random, but evolves over definitive stages. One useful model for describing these stages is shown in Exhibit 18.7. Each stage confronts team leaders and members with unique problems and challenges.[51]

Forming

The **forming** stage of development is a period of orientation and getting acquainted. Members break the ice and test one another for friendship possibilities and task orientation. Uncertainty is high during this stage, and members usually accept whatever power or authority is offered by either formal or informal leaders. During this initial stage, members are concerned about things such as "What is expected of me?" "What behavior is acceptable?" and "Will I fit in?" During the forming stage, the team leader should provide time for

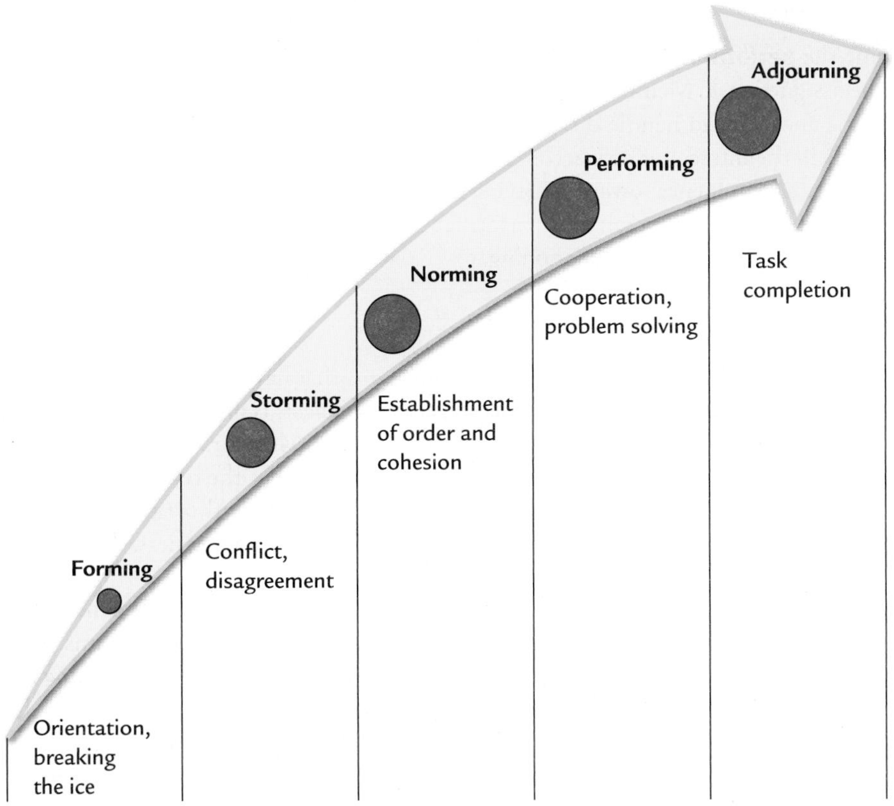

EXHIBIT **18.7**

Five Stages of Team
Development

SOURCES: Based on the stages of small group development in Bruce W. Tuckman, "Developmental Sequence in Small Groups," *Psychological Bulletin* 63 (1965): 384–399; and B. W. Tuckman and M. A. Jensen, "Stages of Small Group Development Revisited," *Group and Organizational Studies* 2 (1977): 419–427.

members to get acquainted with one another and encourage them to engage in informal social discussions.

Storming

During the **storming** stage, individual personalities emerge. People become more assertive in clarifying their roles and what is expected of them. This stage is marked by conflict and disagreement. People may disagree over their perceptions of the team's goals or how to achieve them. Members may jockey for position, and coalitions or subgroups based on common interests may form. Unless teams can successfully move beyond this stage, they may get bogged down and never achieve high performance. Think of the Miami Heat basketball team, which had trouble getting a team loaded with superstar players with disparate personalities to "gel and excel." The team started coming together and show signs of solidarity only when it became clear that they couldn't win unless they did. "When it's raw, when you don't get along, that's when there's the most opportunity for growth," said head coach Erik Spoelstra.[52] During the storming stage, the team leader should encourage participation by each team member. Members should propose ideas, disagree with one another, and work through the uncertainties and conflicting perceptions about team tasks and goals.

Norming

During the **norming** stage, conflict is resolved, and team harmony and unity emerge. Consensus develops on who has the power, who the leaders are, and what members' roles are. Members come to accept and understand one another. Differences are resolved, and members develop a sense of team cohesion. During the norming stage, the team leader should emphasize unity within the team and help to clarify team norms and values.

Performing

During the **performing** stage, the major emphasis is on problem solving and accomplishing the assigned task. Members are committed to the team's mission. They are coordinated with one another and handle disagreements in a mature way. They confront and resolve problems in the interest of task accomplishment. They interact frequently and direct their discussions and influence toward achieving team goals. During this stage, the leader should concentrate on managing high task performance. Both socioemotional and task specialist roles contribute to the team's functioning.

Adjourning

The **adjourning** stage occurs in committees and teams that have a limited task to perform and are disbanded afterward. During this stage, the emphasis is on wrapping up and gearing down. Task performance is no longer a top priority. Members may feel heightened emotionality, strong cohesiveness, and depression or regret over the team's disbanding. At this point, the leader may wish to signify the team's disbanding with a ritual or ceremony, perhaps giving out plaques and awards to signify closure and completeness.

These five stages typically occur in sequence, but in teams that are under time pressure, they may occur quite rapidly. The stages may also be accelerated for virtual teams. For example, at a large consumer goods company with a virtual team of engineers working in the United States and India, leaders started the project with a couple of days of team building to help the team move rapidly through the forming and storming stages.

Innovative Way

Spring Company

When top executives at Spring Company decided to move some aspects of supply chain process development to one of the company's Indian facilities, one of their key concerns was making sure that the engineers in the United States and the ones in India came together quickly around a shared mission and a focus on key performance goals, putting the success of the team ahead of individual interests.

To take the team to the performing stage as quickly as possible, leaders and consultants held a series of team-building activities during which team members together created a shared vision, developed specific team norms and agreements, built virtual relationships, and clarified roles and responsibilities. Cultural education and exercises on virtual communication were also a part of the process. By the end of the team-building activities, members were laughing together and eager to get on with their work. A follow-up by Webinar and phone found that the team was on track toward meeting its goals; moreover, everyone was still having a good time working together.[53]

TEAM COHESIVENESS

Another important aspect of the team process is cohesiveness. **Team cohesiveness** is defined as the extent to which members are attracted to the team and motivated to remain in it.[54] Members of highly cohesive teams are committed to team activities, attend meetings, and are happy when the team succeeds. Members of less cohesive teams are less concerned about the team's welfare. High cohesiveness is normally considered an attractive feature of teams.

Determinants of Team Cohesiveness

Several characteristics of team structure and context influence cohesiveness. First is *team interaction*. When team members have frequent contact, they get to know one another, consider themselves a unit, and become more committed to the team.[55] Second is the concept of *shared goals*. If team members agree on purpose and direction, they will be more cohesive. Third is *personal attraction to the team*, meaning that members have similar attitudes and values and enjoy being together.

Two factors in the team's context also influence cohesiveness. The first is the *presence of competition*. When a team is in moderate competition with other teams, its cohesiveness increases as it strives to win. Finally, *team success* and the favorable evaluation of the team by outsiders add to cohesiveness. When a team succeeds in its task and others in the organization recognize the success, members feel good, and their commitment to the team will be high.

Consequences of Team Cohesiveness

The outcome of team cohesiveness can fall into two categories—morale and productivity. As a general rule, morale is higher in cohesive teams because of increased communication among members, a friendly team climate, maintenance of membership because of commitment to the team, loyalty, and member participation in team decisions and activities. High cohesiveness has almost uniformly good effects on the satisfaction and morale of team members.[56]

With respect to the productivity of the team as a whole, research findings suggest that teams in which members share strong feelings of connectedness and generally positive interactions tend to perform better.[57] Thus, a friendly, positive team environment contributes to productivity, as well as member satisfaction. Other research, however, indicates that the degree of productivity in cohesive teams may depend on the relationship between management and the work team. One study surveyed more than 200 work teams and correlated job performance with their cohesiveness.[58] Highly cohesive teams were more productive when team members felt management support and less productive when they sensed management hostility and negativism.

TEAM NORMS

A **team norm** is an informal standard of conduct that is shared by team members and guides their behavior.[59] Norms are valuable because they provide a frame of reference for what is expected and acceptable.

Norms begin to develop in the first interactions among members of a new team. Exhibit 18.8 illustrates four common ways in which norms develop.[60] Sometimes the first

EXHIBIT 18.8   Four Ways Team Norms Develop

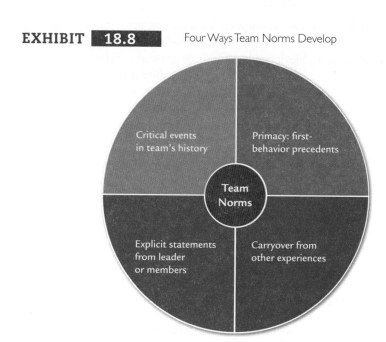

behaviors that occur in a team set a precedent. For example, at one company, a team leader began his first meeting by raising an issue and then "leading" team members until he got the solution he wanted. The pattern became ingrained so quickly into an unproductive team norm that members dubbed meetings the "Guess What I Think" game.[61] Other influences on team norms include critical events in the team's history, as well as behaviors, attitudes, and norms that members bring with them from outside the team.

Team leaders play an important role in shaping norms that will help the team be effective. For example, research shows that when leaders have high expectations for collaborative problem solving, teams develop strong collaborative norms.[62] Making explicit statements about desired team behaviors is a powerful way that leaders influence norms. When he was CEO of Ameritech, Bill Weiss established a norm of cooperation and mutual support among his top leadership team by telling them bluntly that if he caught anyone trying to undermine the others, the guilty party would be fired.[63]

Remember This

- The **forming** stage of team development is a period of orientation and getting acquainted.
- **Storming** is the stage of team development in which individual personalities and roles emerge, along with resulting conflicts.
- **Norming** refers to the stage of development in which conflicts are resolved and team harmony and unity emerge.
- The **performing** stage is the stage in which members focus on problem solving and accomplishing the team's assigned task.
- **Adjourning** is the stage during which members of temporary teams prepare for the team's disbanding.
- **Team cohesiveness** refers to the extent to which team members are attracted to the team and motivated to remain a part of it.
- Morale is almost always higher in cohesive teams, and cohesiveness can also contribute to higher productivity.
- A **team norm** is an informal standard of conduct that is shared by team members and guides their behavior.

Managing Team Conflict

The final characteristic of team process is conflict. Conflict can arise among members within a team or between one team and another. **Conflict** refers to antagonistic interaction in which one party attempts to block the intentions or goals of another.[64] Whenever people work together in teams, some conflict is inevitable. Bringing conflicts into the open and effectively resolving them is one of the team leader's most challenging, yet most important, jobs. Effective conflict management has a positive impact on team cohesiveness and performance.[65]

"In great teams, conflict becomes productive. The free flow of ideas and feelings is critical for creative thinking, for discovering new solutions no one individual would have come to on his own."

— PETER SENGE, AUTHOR OF *THE FIFTH DISCIPLINE: THE ART AND PRACTICE OF THE LEARNING ORGANIZATION*

TYPES OF CONFLICT

Two basic types of conflict that occur in teams are task conflict and relationship conflict.[66] **Task conflict** refers to disagreements among people about the goals to be achieved or the content of the tasks to be performed. Two shop foremen might disagree over whether to replace a valve, or let it run despite the unusual noise that it is making. Or two members of a top management team might disagree about whether to acquire a company or enter into a joint venture as a way to expand globally. **Relationship conflict** refers to interpersonal incompatibility that creates tension and personal animosity among people. For example, in one team at a company that manufactures and sells upscale children's furniture, team members found their differing perspectives and working styles to be a significant source of conflict during crunch times. Members who needed peace and quiet were irked at those who wanted music playing in the background. Compulsively neat members found it almost impossible to work with those who liked working among stacks of clutter.[67]

In general, research suggests that task conflict can be beneficial because it leads to better decision making and problem solving. On the other hand, relationship conflict is typically associated with negative consequences for team effectiveness.[68] One study of top management teams, for example, found that task conflict was associated with higher decision quality, greater commitment, and more decision acceptance, while the presence of relationship conflict significantly reduced those same outcomes.[69]

BALANCING CONFLICT AND COOPERATION

There is evidence that mild conflict can be beneficial to teams.[70] A healthy level of conflict helps to prevent *groupthink*, as discussed in Chapter 9, in which people are so committed to a cohesive team that they are reluctant to express contrary opinions. When people in work teams go along simply for the sake of harmony, problems typically result. Thus, a degree of conflict leads to better decision making because multiple viewpoints are expressed.

However, conflict that is too strong, that is focused on personal rather than work issues, or that is not managed appropriately can be damaging to the team's morale and productivity. Too much conflict can be destructive, tear relationships apart, and interfere with the healthy exchange of ideas and information.[71] Team leaders have to find the right balance between conflict and cooperation, as illustrated in Exhibit 18.9. Too little conflict can decrease team performance because the team doesn't benefit from a mix of opinions and ideas—even disagreements—that might lead to better solutions or prevent the team from making mistakes. At the other end of the spectrum, too much conflict outweighs the team's cooperative efforts and leads to a decrease in employee satisfaction and commitment, hurting team performance. A moderate amount of conflict that is managed appropriately typically results in the highest levels of team performance.

Take a Moment

Go to the Ethical Dilemma for Chapter 18 on pages 623–624 that pertains to team cohesiveness and conflict.

EXHIBIT 18.9 Balancing Conflict and Cooperation

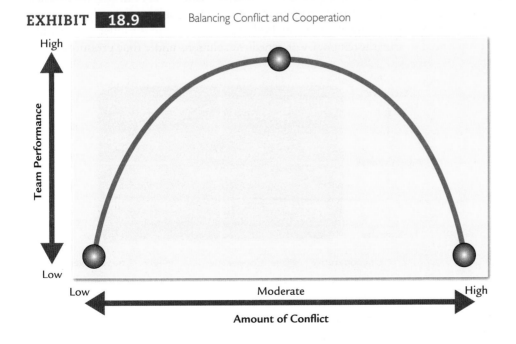

CAUSES OF CONFLICT

Several factors can lead to conflict:[72] One of the primary causes of conflict is competition over resources, such as money, information, or supplies. When individuals or teams must compete for scarce or declining resources, conflict is almost inevitable. In addition, conflict often occurs simply because people are pursuing differing goals. Goal differences are natural in organizations. Individual salespeople's targets may put them in conflict with one another or with the sales manager. Moreover, the sales department's goals might conflict with those of manufacturing, and so forth.

Conflict may also arise from communication breakdowns. Poor communication can occur in any team, but virtual and global teams are particularly prone to communication breakdowns. In one virtual team developing a custom polymer for a Japanese manufacturer, the marketing team member in the United States was frustrated by a Japanese team member's failure to provide her with the manufacturer's marketing strategy. The Japanese team member, in turn, thought that her teammate was overbearing and unsupportive. She knew that the manufacturer hadn't yet developed a clear marketing strategy, and that pushing for more information could damage the relationship by causing the customer to "lose face."[73] Trust issues can be a major source of conflict in virtual teams if members feel that they are being left out of important communication interactions.[74] In addition, the lack of nonverbal cues in virtual interactions leads to more misunderstandings.

STYLES TO HANDLE CONFLICT

Teams as well as individuals develop specific styles for dealing with conflict, based on the desire to satisfy their own concern versus the other party's concern. A model that describes five styles of handling conflict is in Exhibit 18.10. The two major dimensions are the extent to which an individual is assertive versus cooperative in his or her approach to conflict.[75]

- The *dominating style* (my way) reflects assertiveness to get one's own way and should be used when quick, decisive action is vital on important issues or unpopular actions, such as during emergencies or urgent cost cutting.

- The *avoiding style* (no way) reflects neither assertiveness nor cooperativeness. It is appropriate when an issue is trivial, when there is no chance of winning, when a delay to gather more information is needed, or when a disruption would be costly.

- The *compromising style* (halfway) reflects a moderate amount of both assertiveness and cooperativeness. It is appropriate when the goals on both sides are equally important, when opponents have equal power and both sides want to split the difference, or when people need to arrive at temporary or expedient solutions under time pressure.

EXHIBIT **18.10**

A Model of Styles to Handle Conflict

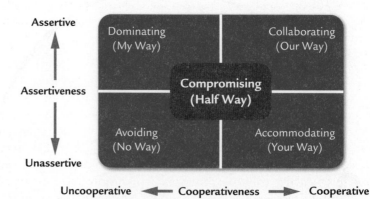

SOURCES: Adapted from Kenneth Thomas, "Conflict and Conflict Management," in *Handbook of Industrial and Organizational Behavior*, ed. M. D. Dunnette (New York: John Wiley, 1976), p. 900; and Nan Peck, "Conflict 101: Styles of Fighting," North Virginia Community College Web site, September 20, 2005, www.nvcc.edu/home/npeck/conflicthome/conflict/Conflict101/conflictstyles.htm (accessed April 13, 2011).

- The *accommodating style* (your way) reflects a high degree of cooperativeness, which works best when people realize that they are wrong, when an issue is more important to others than to oneself, when building social credits for use in later discussions, and when maintaining harmony is especially important.

- The *collaborating style* (our way) reflects a high degree of both assertiveness and cooperativeness. The collaborating style enables both parties to win, although it may require substantial bargaining and negotiation. The collaborating style is important when both sets of concerns are too important to be compromised, when insights from different people need to be merged into an overall solution, and when the commitment of both sides is needed for a consensus.

▶ ▶ ▶ **Concept Connection**

Just who's running the Large Hadron Collider (LHC) project, an international $6 billion particle accelerator designed to simulate the universe's birth by producing high-energy proton collisions? The answer: everyone. Built at CERN, the European particle laboratory near Geneva, LHC involves 10,000 scientists and engineers working in hundreds of institutions. Because participants recognize that they need everyone's cooperation to succeed, they've adopted a **collaborative style of handling conflicts**. Each research group is a democratic collective; those collectives appoint members to negotiate with other groups. "The top guy," notes CERN's "top guy," Director-General Rolf-Dieter Heuer, "can only convince the other guys to do what he wants them to do."

AP Photo/Keystone, Laurent Gillieron

An example of the collaborating style comes from the 2008 Summer Olympics in Beijing. When building the Beijing National Aquatics Center (typically called the "Water Cube"), two architectural firms—one Chinese and the other Australian—developed designs that were totally different. Although this created some tension, instead of fighting for their own ideas, the two sides came up with a totally new concept that excited everyone. The resulting award-winning building is spectacular.[76] Each of the five styles is appropriate in certain cases, and effective team members and leaders vary their style to fit the specific situation.

NEGOTIATION

One distinctive type of conflict management is **negotiation**, whereby people engage in give-and-take discussions and consider various alternatives to reach a joint decision that is acceptable to both parties. Negotiation is used when a conflict is formalized, such as between a union and management.

Types of Negotiation

Conflicting parties may embark on negotiation from different perspectives and with different intentions, reflecting either an *integrative* approach or a *distributive* approach. **Integrative negotiation** is based on a win-win assumption, in that all parties want to come up with a creative solution that can benefit both sides. Rather than viewing the conflict as a win-lose situation, people look at the issues from multiple angles, consider trade-offs, and try to "expand the pie" rather than divide it. With integrative negotiation, conflicts are managed through cooperation and compromise, which fosters trust and positive long-term relationships. **Distributive negotiation**, on the other hand, assumes that the size of the "pie" is fixed, and each party attempts to get as much of it as they can. One side wants to win, which means the other side must lose. With this win-lose approach, distributive negotiation is competitive and adversarial, rather than collaborative, and does not typically lead to positive long-term relationships.[77]

Most experts emphasize the value of integrative negotiation for today's collaborative business environment. That is, the key to effectiveness is to see negotiation not as a zero-sum game, but as a process for reaching a creative solution that benefits everyone.[78]

Rules for Reaching a Win-Win Solution

Achieving a win-win solution through integrative negotiation is based on four key strategies:[79]

- *Separate the people from the problem.* For successful integrative negotiation, people stay focused on the problem and the source of conflict, rather than attacking or attempting to discredit each other.

- *Focus on interests, not current demands.* Demands are what each person wants from the negotiation, whereas interests represent the "why" behind the demands. Consider two sisters arguing over the last orange in the fruit bowl. Each insisted she should get the orange and refused to give up (demands). If one sister had asked the other *why* she wanted the orange (interests), the sisters would have discovered that one wanted to eat it, and the other wanted the peel to use for a project. By focusing on interests, the sisters would be able to arrive at a solution that gave each what she wanted.[80] *Demands* create yes-or-no obstacles to effective negotiation, whereas *interests* present problems that can be solved creatively.

- *Listen and ask questions.* A good strategy for most negotiations is to listen and ask questions. You can learn more about your opponent's position, their constraints, and their needs by being quiet or asking questions. Smart negotiators want to learn the other side's constraints so that they can help overcome them. Don't dismiss the opposing party's limitation as unreasonable or think "That's their problem." You can take it on as your own problem and try to come up with a solution for your opponent so that you can get closer to an agreement.

- *Insist that results be based on objective standards.* Each party in a negotiation has its own interests and naturally would like to maximize its outcomes. Successful negotiation requires focusing on objective criteria and maintaining standards of fairness rather than using subjective judgments about the best solution.

Remember This

- **Conflict** refers to antagonistic interaction in which one party attempts to block the intentions or goals of another.
- Some conflict, particularly task conflict, can be beneficial to teams.
- **Task conflict** is conflict that results from disagreements about the goals to be achieved or the content of the tasks to be performed.
- **Relationship conflict** results from interpersonal incompatibility that creates tension and personal animosity among people.
- Causes of conflict include competition over resources, goal differences, and communication breakdowns.
- Teams and individuals use a variety of styles for dealing with conflict, including the dominating style, the

avoiding style, the compromising style, the accommodating style, and the collaborating style, and each can be effective under certain circumstances.

- **Negotiation** is a conflict management strategy whereby people engage in give-and-take discussions and consider various alternatives to reach a joint decision that is acceptable to both parties.
- **Integrative negotiation** is a collaborative approach that is based on a win-win assumption, whereby the parties want to come up with a creative solution that benefits both sides of the conflict.
- **Distributive negotiation** is a competitive and adversarial approach in which each party strives to get as much as it can, usually at the expense of the other party.

ch18: Discussion Questions

1. One company had 40 percent of its workers and 20 percent of its managers resign during the first year after reorganizing into teams. What might account for this dramatic turnover? How might managers ensure a smooth transition to teams?

2. Have you experienced any of the five contributions of teams shown in Exhibit 18.2 with a team you have participated in? Describe your experience and why you think the team was able to make that specific contribution.

3. Suppose that you are the leader of a team that has just been created to develop a new registration process at your college or university. How can you use an understanding of the stages of team development to improve your team's effectiveness?

4. Imagine yourself as a potential member of a team responsible for designing a new package for a breakfast cereal. Do you think interpersonal skills would be equally important if the team is organized face to face versus a virtual team? Why or why not? Might different types of interpersonal skills be required for the two types of teams? Be specific.

5. If you were the leader of a special-purpose team developing a new computer game and conflicts arose related to power and status differences among team members, what would you do? How might you use the various conflict-resolution techniques described in the chapter?

6. Experts say that for teams to function well, members have to get to know one another in some depth. What specifically would you do to facilitate this in a colocated team? What about in a global virtual team?

7. Think of your favorite sports team, or observe a sports team at your university. Can you identify which members seem to play task specialist roles and who might play a socioemotional role? What behaviors did you observe for each type of role?

8. Some people argue that the presence of an outside threat correlates with a high degree of team cohesion. Would you agree or disagree? Explain your answer.

9. Discuss how the dilemmas of teamwork might be intensified in a virtual team. What dilemmas do you encounter when you have to do class assignments as part of a team? Discuss.

10. If you were the leader of a newly formed team, what might you do to make sure that the team developed norms of high performance?

ch18: Apply Your Skills: Experiential Exercise

This and That: Best Team—Worst Team[81]

Think of two teams of which you were a member—the best and the worst in terms of personal satisfaction and team performance. These teams could come from any area in your experience—for example, athletic team, student club, class team, work team, project team, church committee, or volunteer organization. List here the specific behaviors of the teams that made them the best and worst for you.

Best team behaviors: _____

_____

Worst team behaviors: _____

_____

In class: (1) Sit in a small group of three to five students. Each student tells the brief story of his or her best and worst team experiences. (2) After all stories are heard, one team member writes on a flipchart (or blackboard) two headings—"More of This" and "Less of That." Under "This," write team member suggestions for positive behaviors that make for effective teamwork. Under "That," write team member suggestions for negative behaviors that prevent effective teamwork. (3) After brainstorming items, each group condenses each list to five key behaviors that the group considers most important. (4) After the lists are finalized, students can walk around the classroom and review all lists. (5) Discuss answers to the following questions, either in your group or as a class.

1. What is the most important behavior for This and for That?

2. What factors influence the presence of This or That behaviors on a team?

3. What personal changes would you need to make as a team member to demonstrate more of This?

4. What personal changes would you need to make as a team member to demonstrate less of That?

5. How might a team leader be able to attain more of This on a team and less of That?

5

LEADING

ch18: Apply Your Skills: Small Group Breakout

Team Feedback Exercise

Step 1. Divide into groups of three to four students. Think back to recent experiences working in a team, either at work or school. Write down your answers to the following questions.

What behaviors by other team members did you most appreciate?

_____

_____

What behaviors of other team members did you least appreciate?

_____

_____

What do you think the team members appreciated about you?

_____

_____

What actions of yours might the team members have appreciated least?

_____

_____

Step 2. Take turns sharing your answers with other members of your group. Make notes about common themes for answers to each of the above questions. What is the single most important theme for each of these answers?

Step 3. What are the implications of these answers for you as a member of a future team? How might you change your behavior to make a larger contribution to a team?

ch18: Endnotes

1. Based on Eric M. Stark, Jason D. Shaw, and Michelle K. Duffy, "Preference for Group Work, Winning Orientation, and Social Loafing Behavior in Groups," *Group & Organization Management* 32, no. 6 (December 2007): 699–723.

2. David Kesmodel, "Boeing Teams Speed Up 737 Output," *The Wall Street Journal Online*, February 7, 2012, http://online.wsj.com/article/SB100014240529702034369045771552040349077744.html (accessed September 25, 2012).

3. Industry Week/Manufacturing Performance Institute's Census of Manufacturers for 2004, reported in Traci Purdum, "Teaming, Take 2," *Industry Week* (May 2005): 41–43.

4. "'Golden Hour' Crucial Time for Surgeons on Front Line," *Johnson City Press*, April 1, 2003.

5. Carl E. Larson and Frank M. J. LaFasto, *TeamWork* (Newbury Park, CA: Sage, 1989); J. R. Katzenbach and D. K. Smith, *The Wisdom of Teams* (Boston, MA: Harvard Business School Press, 1993); and Dawn R. Utley and Stephanie E. Brown, "Establishing Characteristic Differences Between Team and Working Group Behaviors," *Institute of Industrial Engineers Annual Conference Proceedings* (2010): 1–6.

6. Some of the advantages in this section are discussed in "The Rewards of Teaming" sidebar in Amy C. Edmondson, "Teamwork on the Fly," *Harvard Business Review* (April 2012): 72–80.

7. Geoff Colvin, "First: Team Players Trump All-Stars," *Fortune* (May 21, 2012): 46–47.

8. See the excellent discussion in Atul Gawande, "Cowboys and Pit Crews," 2011 Harvard Medical School commencement address, *The New Yorker* (May 26, 2011), www.newyorker.com/online/blogs/newsdesk/2011/05/atul-gawande-harvard-medical-school-commencement-address.html (accessed September 26, 2012).

9. Colvin, "First: Team Players Trump All-Stars."

10. R. B. Zajonc, "Social Facilitation," *Science* 145 (1969): 269–274.

11. Margaret Frazier, "Flu Prep," *The Wall Street Journal*, March 25–26, 2006, A8.

12. Susanne G. Scott and Walter O. Einstein, "Strategic Performance Appraisal in Team-Based Organizations: One Size Does Not Fit All," *Academy of Management Executive* 15, no. 2 (2001): 107–116.

13. Bryce G. Hoffman, "Inside Ford's Fight to Avoid Disaster," *The Wall Street Journal*, March 9, 2012, B1.

14. The discussion of self-managed teams is based on Ruth Wageman, "Critical Success Factors for Creating Superb Self-Managing Teams," *Organizational Dynamics* (Summer 1997): 49–61; James H. Shonk, *Team-Based Organizations* (Homewood, IL: Business One Irwin, 1992); and Thomas Owens, "The Self-Managing Work Team," *Small Business Report* (February 1991): 53–65.

15. Jason Fried, "Get Real: When the Only Way Up is Out," *Inc.* (April 2011): 35–36.

16. David A. Ferrucci, "Building the Team That Built Watson," *The New York Times*, January 7, 2012, www.nytimes.com/2012/01/08/jobs/building-the-watson-team-of-scientists.html?_r=0 (accessed October 1, 2012).

17. Study by G. Clotaire Rapaille, reported in Karen Bernowski, "What Makes American Teams Tick?" *Quality Progress* 28, no. 1 (January 1995): 39–42.

18. Study by Jean Twenge and colleagues, reported in Sharon Jayson, "What's on Americans' Minds? Increasingly, 'Me,'" *USA Today*, July 10, 2012, http://usatoday30.usatoday.com/LIFE/usaedition/2012-07-11-Individualism--Twenge----_ST_U.htm (accessed October 2, 2012).

19. Avan Jassawalla, Hemant Sashittal, and Avinash Malshe, "Students' Perceptions of Social Loafing: Its Antecedents and Consequences in Undergraduate Business Classroom Teams," *Academy of Management Learning and Education* 8, no. 1 (2009): 42–54; and Robert Albanese and David D. Van Fleet, "Rational Behavior in Groups: The Free-Riding Tendency," *Academy of Management Review* 10 (1985): 244–255.

20. See David H. Freedman, "The Idiocy of Crowds" ("What's Next" column), *Inc.* (September 2006): 61–62.

21. Quoted in Jason Zweig, "The Intelligent Investor: How Group Decisions End Up Wrong-Footed," *The Wall Street Journal*, April 25, 2009.

22. "Why Some Teams Succeed (and So Many Don't)," *Harvard Management Update* (October 2006): 3–4; Frederick P. Morgeson, D. Scott DeRue, and Elizabeth P. Karam, "Leadership in Teams: A Functional Approach to Understanding Leadership Structure and Processes," *Journal of Management* 36, no. 1 (January 2010): 5–39; and Patrick Lencioni, "Dissolve Dysfunction: Begin Building Your Dream Team," *Leadership Excellence* (October 2009): 20.

23. Reported in Jerry Useem, "What's That Spell? Teamwork!" *Fortune* (June 12, 2006): 65–66.

24. Eric Sundstrom, Kenneth P. DeMeuse, and David Futtrell, "Work Teams," *American Psychologist* 45 (February 1990): 120–133; María Isabel Delgado Piña, Ana María Romero Martínez, and Luis Gómez Martínez, "Teams in Organizations: A Review on Team Effectiveness," *Team Performance Management* 14, no. 1–2 (2008): 7–21; and Morgeson, DeRue, and Karam, "Leadership in Teams."

25. Deborah L. Gladstein, "Groups in Context: A Model of Task Group Effectiveness," *Administrative Science Quarterly* 29 (1984): 499–517. For an overview of research on team effectiveness, see John Mathieu et al., "Team Effectiveness 1997–2007: A Review of Recent Advancements and a Glimpse into the Future," *Journal of Management* 34, no. 3 (June 2008): 410–476.

26. Sujin K. Horwitz and Irwin B. Horwitz, "The Effects of Team Diversity on Team Outcomes: A Meta-Analytic Review of Team Demography," *Journal of Management* 33, no. 6 (December 2007): 987–1015; and Dora C. Lau and J. Keith Murnighan, "Demographic Diversity and Faultlines: The Compositional Dynamics of Organizational Groups," *Academy of Management Review* 23, no. 2 (1998): 325–340.

27. The discussion of virtual teams is based on Phillip L. Hunsaker and Johanna S. Hunsaker, "Virtual Teams: A Leader's Guide," *Team Performance Management* 14, no. 1–2 (2008): 86ff; Chris Kimble, "Building Effective Virtual Teams: How to Overcome the Problems of Trust and Identity in Virtual Teams," *Global Business and Organizational Excellence* (January–February 2011): 6–15; Wayne F. Cascio and Stan Shurygailo, "E-Leadership and Virtual Teams," *Organizational Dynamics* 31, no. 4 (2002): 362–376; Anthony M. Townsend, Samuel M. DeMarie, and Anthony R. Hendrickson, "Virtual Teams: Technology and the Workplace of the Future," *Academy of Management Executive* 12, no. 3 (August 1998): 17–29; and Deborah L. Duarte and Nancy Tennant Snyder, *Mastering Virtual Teams* (San Francisco: Jossey-Bass, 1999).

28. Survey by RW3CultureWizard, reported in Golnaz Sadri and John Condia, "Managing the Virtual World," *Industrial Management* (January–February 2012): 21–25.

29. Vijay Govindarajan and Anil K. Gupta, "Building an Effective Global Business Team," *MIT Sloan Management Review* 42, no. 4 (Summer 2001): 63–71.

30. Jessica Lipnack and Jeffrey Stamps, "Virtual Teams: The New Way to Work," *Strategy & Leadership* (January–February 1999): 14–19; and Sadri and Condia, "Managing the Virtual World."

31. This discussion is based on Arvind Malhotra, Ann Majchrzak, and Benson Rosen, "Leading Virtual Teams," *Academy of Management Perspectives* 21, no. 1 (February 2007): 60–69; Benson Rosen, Stacie Furst, and Richard Blackburn, "Overcoming Barriers to Knowledge Sharing in Virtual Teams," *Organizational Dynamics* 36, no. 3 (2007): 259–273; Marshall Goldsmith, "Crossing the Cultural Chasm; Keeping Communication Clear and Consistent with Team Members from Other Countries Isn't Easy, Says Author Maya Hu-Chan," *BusinessWeek Online*, May 31, 2007, www.businessweek.com/careers/content/may2007/ca20070530_521679.htm (accessed August 24, 2007); and Bradley L. Kirkman et al., "Five Challenges to Virtual Team Success: Lessons from Sabre, Inc.," *Academy of Management Executive* 16, no. 3 (2002): 67–79.

32. Darl G. Kolb, Greg Prussia, and Joline Francoeur, "Connectivity and Leadership: The Influence of Online Activity on Closeness and Effectiveness," *Journal of Leadership and Organizational Studies* 15, no. 4 (May 2009): 342–352.

33. Ann Majchrzak et al., "Can Absence Make a Team Grow Stronger?" *Harvard Business Review* 82, no. 5 (May 2004): 131.

34. Lynda Gratton, "Working Together . . . When Apart," *The Wall Street Journal*, June 18, 2007; and Kirkman et al., "Five Challenges to Virtual Team Success."

35. Pete Engardio, "A Guide for Multinationals: One of the Greatest Challenges for a Multinational Is Learning

How to Build a Productive Global Team," *BusinessWeek* (August 20, 2007): 48–51; and Gratton, "Working Together . . . When Apart."

36. Reported in Richard Pastore, "Global Team Management: It's a Small World After All," *CIO*, January 23, 2008, www.cio.com/article/174750/Global_Team_Management_It_s_a_Small_World_After_All (accessed May 20, 2008).

37. Reported in Jia Lynn Yang, "The Power of Number 4.6," part of a special series, "Secrets of Greatness: Teamwork," *Fortune* (June 12, 2006): 122.

38. Martin Hoegl, "Smaller Teams–Better Teamwork: How to Keep Project Teams Small," *Business Horizons* 48 (2005): 209–214.

39. Stephanie T. Solansky, "Team Identification: A Determining Factor of Performance," *Journal of Managerial Psychology* 26, no. 3 (2011): 247–258.

40. Reported in Yang, "The Power of Number 4.6."

41. For research findings on group size, see Erin Bradner, Gloria Mark, and Tammie D. Hertel, "Team Size and Technology Fit: Participation, Awareness, and Rapport in Distributed Teams," *IEEE Transactions on Professional Communication* 48, no. 1 (March 2005): 68–77; M. E. Shaw, *Group Dynamics*, 3d ed. (New York: McGraw-Hill, 1981); G. Manners, "Another Look at Group Size, Group Problem-Solving, and Member Consensus," *Academy of Management Journal* 18 (1975): 715–724; and Martin Hoegl, "Smaller Teams— Better Teamwork."

42. Bradner, Mark, and Hertel, "Team Size and Technology Fit: Participation, Awareness, and Rapport in Distributed Teams"; Sadri and Condia, "Managing the Virtual World."

43. Warren E. Watson, Kamalesh Kumar, and Larry K. Michaelsen, "Cultural Diversity's Impact on Interaction Process and Performance: Comparing Homogeneous and Diverse Task Groups," *Academy of Management Journal* 36 (1993): 590–602; Gail Robinson and Kathleen Dechant, "Building a Business Case for Diversity," *Academy of Management Executive* 11, no. 3 (1997): 21–31; and David A. Thomas and Robin J. Ely, "Making Differences Matter: A New Paradigm for Managing Diversity," *Harvard Business Review* (September–October 1996): 79–90.

44. D. van Knippenberg and M. C. Schippers, "Work Group Diversity," *Annual Review of Psychology* 58 (2007): 515–541; J. N. Cummings, "Work Groups: Structural Diversity and Knowledge Sharing in a Global Organization," *Management Science* 50, no, 3 (2004): 352–364; J. Stuart Bunderson and Kathleen M. Sutcliffe, "Comparing Alternative Conceptualizations of Functional Diversity in Management Teams: Process and Performance Effects," *Academy of Management Journal* 45, no. 5 (2002): 875–893; and Marc Orlitzky and John D. Benjamin, "The Effects of Sex Composition on Small Group Performance in a Business School Case Competition,"

Academy of Management Learning and Education 2, no. 2 (2003): 128–138.

45. Anita Woolley and Thomas Malone, "Defend Your Research: What Makes a Team Smarter? More Women," *Harvard Business Review* (June 2011), http://hbr.org/2011/06/defend-your-research-what-makes-a-team-smarter-more-women/ar/1 (accessed October 1, 2012).

46. Watson et al. "Cultural Diversity's Impact on Interaction Process and Performance"; and D. C. Hambrick et al., "When Groups Consist of Multiple Nationalities: Towards a New Understanding of the Implications," *Organization Studies* 19, no. 2 (1998): 181–205.

47. Matt Moffett, "Trapped Miners Kept Focus, Shared Tuna—Foiled Escape, Bid to Organize Marked First Two Weeks Underground in Chile," *The Wall Street Journal*, August 25, 2010; and "Lessons on Leadership and Teamwork—From 700 Meters Below the Earth's Surface," Universia Knowledge @ Wharton, September 22, 2010, www.wharton.universia.net/index.cfm?fa=viewArticle&id=1943&language=english (accessed September 29, 2010).

48. R. M. Belbin, *Team Roles at Work* (Oxford, UK: Butterworth Heinemann, 1983); Tony Manning, R. Parker, and G. Pogson, "A Revised Model of Team Roles and Some Research Findings," *Industrial and Commercial Training* 38, no. 6 (2006): 287–296; George Prince, "Recognizing Genuine Teamwork," *Supervisory Management* (April 1989): 25–36; K. D. Benne and P. Sheats, "Functional Roles of Group Members," *Journal of Social Issues* 4 (1948): 41–49; and R. F. Bales, *SYMOLOG Case Study Kit* (New York: Free Press, 1980).

49. Robert A. Baron, *Behavior in Organizations*, 2d ed. (Boston: Allyn & Bacon, 1986).

50. *Ibid.*

51. Bruce W. Tuckman and Mary Ann C. Jensen, "Stages of Small-Group Development Revisited," *Group and Organizational Studies* 2 (1977): 419–427; and Bruce W. Tuckman, "Developmental Sequences in Small Groups," *Psychological Bulletin* 63 (1965): 384–399. See also Linda N. Jewell and H. Joseph Reitz, *Group Effectiveness in Organizations* (Glenview, IL: Scott Foresman, 1981).

52. Chuck Salter, "The World's Greatest Chemistry Experiment," *Fast Company* (May 2011): 81–85, 128–130.

53. This is based on a true story of an anonymous company reported in Vicki Fuller Hudson, "From Divided to Ignited to United," *Industrial Management* (May–June 2010): 17–20.

54. Shaw, *Group Dynamics*.

55. Daniel C. Feldman and Hugh J. Arnold, *Managing Individual and Group Behavior in Organizations* (New York: McGraw-Hill, 1983).

56. Amanuel G. Tekleab, Narda R. Quigley, and Paul E. Tesluk, "A Longitudinal Study of Team Conflict, Conflict

Management, Cohesion, and Team Effectiveness," *Group & Organization Management* 34, no. 2 (April 2009): 170–205; Dorwin Cartwright and Alvin Zander, *Group Dynamics: Research and Theory*, 3d ed. (New York: Harper & Row, 1968); and Elliot Aronson, *The Social Animal* (San Francisco: W. H. Freeman, 1976).

57. Vishal K. Gupta, Rui Huang, and Suman Niranjan, "A Longitudinal Examination of the Relationship Between Team Leadership and Performance," *Journal of Leadership and Organizational Studies* 17, no. 4 (2010): 335–350; and Marcial Losada and Emily Heaphy, "The Role of Positivity and Connectivity in the Performance of Business Teams," *American Behavioral Scientist* 47, no. 6 (February 2004): 740–765.

58. Stanley E. Seashore, *Group Cohesiveness in the Industrial Work Group* (Ann Arbor, MI: Institute for Social Research, 1954).

59. J. Richard Hackman, "Group Influences on Individuals," in *Handbook of Industrial and Organizational Psychology*, ed. M. Dunnette (Chicago: Rand McNally, 1976).

60. These are based on Daniel C. Feldman, "The Development and Enforcement of Group Norms," *Academy of Management Review* 9 (1984): 47–53.

61. Jeanne M. Wilson et al., *Leadership Trapeze: Strategies for Leadership in Team-Based Organizations* (San Francisco: Jossey-Bass, 1994), p. 12.

62. Simon Taggar and Robert Ellis, "The Role of Leaders in Shaping Formal Team Norms," *The Leadership Quarterly* 18 (2007): 105–120.

63. Geoffrey Colvin, "Why Dream Teams Fail," *Fortune* (June 12, 2006): 87–92.

64. Stephen P. Robbins, *Managing Organizational Conflict: A Nontraditional Approach* (Englewood Cliffs, NJ: Prentice Hall, 1974).

65. Tekleab, Quigley, and Tesluk, "A Longitudinal Study of Team Conflict, Conflict Management, Cohesion, and Team Effectiveness."

66. Based on K. A. Jehn, "A Multimethod Examination of the Benefits and Determinants of Intragroup Conflict," *Administrative Science Quarterly* 40 (1995): 256–282; and K. A. Jehn, "A Qualitative Analysis of Conflict Types and Dimensions in Organizational Groups," *Administrative Science Quarterly* 42 (1997): 530–557.

67. Linda A. Hill, "A Note for Analyzing Work Groups," *Harvard Business School Cases*, August 28, 1995; revised April 3, 1998, Product # 9-496-026, ordered at http://hbr.org/search/linda+a+hill/4294934969/.

68. A. Amason, "Distinguishing the Effects of Functional and Dysfunctional Conflict on Strategic Decision Making: Resolving a Paradox for Top Management Teams," *Academy of Management Journal* 39, no. 1 (1996): 123–148; Jehn, "A Multimethod Examination of the Benefits and Determinants of Intragroup Conflict"; and K. A. Jehn and E. A. Mannix, "The Dynamic Nature of Conflict: A Longitudinal Study of Intragroup Conflict and Group Performance," *Academy of Management Journal* 44 (2001): 238–251.

69. Amason, "Distinguishing the Effects of Functional and Dysfunctional Conflict on Strategic Decision Making."

70. Dean Tjosvold et al., "Conflict Values and Team Relationships: Conflict's Contribution to Team Effectiveness and Citizenship in China," *Journal of Organizational Behavior* 24 (2003): 69–88; C. De Dreu and E. Van de Vliert, *Using Conflict in Organizations* (Beverly Hills, CA: Sage, 1997); and Kathleen M. Eisenhardt, Jean L. Kahwajy, and L. J. Bourgeois III, "Conflict and Strategic Choice: How Top Management Teams Disagree," *California Management Review* 39, no. 2 (Winter 1997): 42–62.

71. Kenneth G. Koehler, "Effective Team Management," *Small Business Report* (July 19, 1989): 14–16; and Dean Tjosvold, "Making Conflict Productive," *Personnel Administrator* 29 (June 1984): 121.

72. This discussion is based in part on Richard L. Daft, *Organization Theory and Design* (St. Paul, MN: West, 1992), Chapter 13; and Paul M. Terry, "Conflict Management," *Journal of Leadership Studies* 3, no. 2 (1996): 3–21.

73. Edmondson, "Teamwork on the Fly."

74. Yuhyung Shin, "Conflict Resolution in Virtual Teams," *Organizational Dynamics* 34, no. 4 (2005): 331–345.

75. This discussion is based on K. W. Thomas, "Towards Multidimensional Values in Teaching: The Example of Conflict Behaviors," *Academy of Management Review* 2 (1977): 487.

76. Edmondson, "Teamwork on the Fly."

77. "Negotiation Types," The Negotiation Experts, June 9, 2010, www.negotiations.com/articles/negotiation-types/ (accessed September 28, 2010).

78. Rob Walker, "Take It or Leave It: The Only Guide to Negotiating You Will Ever Need," *Inc.* (August 2003): 75–82.

79. Based on Roger Fisher and William Ury, *Getting to Yes: Negotiating Agreement Without Giving In* (New York: Penguin, 1983); Walker, "Take It or Leave It"; Robb Mandelbaum, "How to Negotiate Effectively," *Inc.*, November 1, 2010, www.inc.com/magazine/20101101/how-to-negotiate-effectively.html (accessed April 12, 2011); and Deepak Malhotra and Max H. Bazerman, "Investigative Negotiation," *Harvard Business Review* (September 2007): 72–78.

80. This familiar story has been reported in many publications, including "The Six Best Questions to Ask Your Customers," Marketing and Distribution Company Limited, www.madisco.bz/articles/The%20Six%20Best%20Questions%20to%20Ask%20Your%20Customers.pdf (accessed September 28, 2010).

81. Based on James W. Kinneer, "This and That: Improving Team Performance," in *The 1997 Annual: Volume 2, Consulting* (San Francisco: Pfeiffer, 1997), pp. 55–58.

5

LEADING

ch14: Apply Your Skills: Ethical Dilemma

Should I Fudge the Numbers?*

Sara MacIntosh recently joined MicroPhone, a large tele-communications company, to take over the implementation of a massive customer service training project. The program was created by Kristin Cole, head of human resources and Sara's new boss. According to the grapevine, Kristin was hoping this project alone would give her the "star quality" she needed to earn a coveted promotion. Industry competition was heating up, and MicroPhone's strategy called for being the best at customer service, which meant having the most highly trained people in the industry, especially those who worked directly with customers. Kristin's new training program called for an average of one full week of intense customer service training for each of 3,000 people and had a price tag of about $40 million.

Kristin put together a team of overworked staffers to develop the training program, but now she needed someone well qualified and dedicated to manage and implement the project. Sara, with eight years of experience, a long list of accomplishments, and advanced degrees in finance and organizational behavior, seemed perfect for the job. However, during a thorough review of the proposal, Sara discovered some assumptions built into the formulas that raised red flags. She approached Dan Sotal, the team's coordinator, about her concerns, but the more Dan tried to explain how the financial projections were derived, the more Sara realized that Kristin's proposal was seriously flawed. No matter how she tried to work them out, the most that could be squeezed out of the $40 million budget was 20 hours of training per person, not the 40 hours everyone expected for such a high price tag.

Sara knew that, although the proposal had been largely developed before she came on board, it would bear her signature. As she carefully described the problems with the proposal to Kristin and outlined the potentially devastating consequences, Kristin impatiently tapped her pencil. Finally, she stood up, leaned forward, and interrupted Sara, quietly saying, "Sara, make the numbers work so that it adds up to 40 hours and stays within the $40 million budget."

Sara glanced up and replied, "I don't think it can be done unless we either change the number of employees who are to be trained or the cost figure...."

Kristin's smile froze on her face as she again interrupted. "I don't think you understand what I'm saying. We have too much at stake here. *Make the previous numbers work.*" Stunned, Sara belatedly began to realize that Kristin was ordering her to fudge the numbers. She felt an anxiety attack coming on as she wondered what she should do.

What Would You Do?

1. Make the previous numbers work. Kristin and the entire team have put massive amounts of time into the project, and they all expect you to be a team player. You don't want to let them down. Besides, this project is a great opportunity for you in a highly visible position.

2. Stick to your principles and refuse to fudge the numbers. Tell Kristin you will work overtime to help develop an alternate proposal that stays within the budget by providing more training to employees who work directly with customers and fewer training hours for those who don't have direct customer contact.

3. Go to the team and tell them what you've been asked to do. If they refuse to support you, threaten to reveal the true numbers to the CEO and board members.

*Adapted from Doug Wallace, "Fudge the Numbers or Leave," *Business Ethics* (May–June 1996): 58–59. Copyright © 1996 by New Mountain Media LLC. Reproduced with permission of New Mountain Media LLC.

ch14: Apply Your Skills: Case for Critical Analysis

A Nice Manager

Chisum Industries' management promotion process was a benchmark for providing lateral moves as well as promotion to the next level within the company. With offices, plants, and warehouses located in seven Texas cities, opportunities for the best and brightest at Chisum were extensive for middle management employees. The process invited candidates to explore their goals, strengths, and weaknesses, and to recount real-life scenarios and accomplishments. The selection team also visited the work sites of candidates for on-the-job observations and talks with fellow workers before bringing the final candidates to Dallas for interviews. The process offered personal insight and growth opportunities to all candidates for promotion. In March, 2011, top management, including Marcus Chisum, Karl Jacobson,

Mitch Ivey, Wayne Hughes, and Barbara Kennedy, were midway through a meeting to consider which of four middle management candidates to promote to the top position in the San Antonio office.

Marcus: "Who do we have next?"

Barbara: "Harry Creighton."

Scanning the group, Marcus sees a few nods and a shrug.

Marcus: "Feedback?"

Karl and Wayne, simultaneously: "Great guy."

Karl: "We all know that Harry came into a situation in which that particular location was suffering a drop in performance. Morale was low, and there were rumors of lay-offs. He came in and calmed employee fears and has done a good job of raising performance levels."

Wayne: "He has a great relationship with employees. As we went around and talked to people, it was obvious that he has developed a level of trust and a vision that workers buy into."

Barbara: "The word that kept coming up among the workers was 'nice.'"

As was his habit during meetings, Mitch leaned back in his chair, tapping his pencil on the table. Initially annoyed by the habit, the team had gotten used to the sound over time.

Marcus: "Mitch, your initial reaction to his name was a shrug. What are you thinking?"

Mitch: "Just wondering if *nice* is what we're looking for here."

The remark was met with laughter.

Mitch: "Tell me, how does a manager achieve an across-the-board reputation as a *nice* guy? I've worked for and with a number of managers during my life. I respected them, thought many of them were fair and up-front in their treatment of us, thought some were jerks who should be canned . . ."

Marcus: "I hope I don't fall into that last category." (Laughter)

Mitch: "I don't recall any consensus about a manager being *nice*."

Karl: "Several people mentioned that Harry always has their back."

Barbara: "I got the impression that Harry covers for them."

Marcus: "Meaning what?"

Wayne: "Meaning, giving them some slack when it comes to things like overlooking their weaknesses, a little sloppiness with deadlines or taking time off."

Barbara: "Several mentioned that he's always willing to . . . let me look at my notes . . . *'Always willing to step in and help out.'* The phrase came up more than a few times and when I pressed them, they didn't elaborate. But I wondered . . .'"

Karl: ". . . Is he managing or taking on some of their responsibilities?"

Barbara: "Exactly."

Mitch: "It's bothering me that he comes across as the parent who does his kid's project for the science fair."

Wayne: "I don't think it's that bad, but when you look at him in comparison with the other candidates, it makes me question whether he can take on the tough part of top management. There is nothing distinctive about him or his style."

Karl: "There's no *edge* here. No sense of boundaries. Does he want to manage employees or be popular with them? Can he say 'No' and mean it?"

Barbara: "Does Harry have the capability to walk that fine line that separates leaders; that distinguishes respect versus popularity or encouragement and support over *stepping in and helping out?*"

Marcus: "So, we see some good things about Harry. He has a lot of potential. But we also see that he has not yet reached a level where we can entrust him with this top management position. Our task here then, is to move on with the selection process, but over the next weeks I would like for us to consider ways to help Harry reach that potential for future opportunities."

Questions

1. What does *nice* mean to you? Is being considered nice a good trait for managers to have or the kiss of death?

2. Is *nice* related to any concepts in the chapter, such as agreeableness, conscientiousness, or emotional intelligence? Discuss.

3. If Harry is passed over for promotion, what feedback and advice should he be given about how to improve his management skills for possible future promotion?

ch14: On the Job Video Cases

On the Job: Mitchell Gold + Bob Williams: Understanding Individual Behavior

Questions

1. In the video, vice president Dan Gauthreaux says, "I think you can learn from any job you do and try to make the best of it." What does this statement say about Gauthreaux's personality and self-awareness?

2. How did Kim Clay's organizational citizenship behavior lead to the creation of a new computer help desk at MG+BW?

3. What role did management play in fostering Kim Clay's high organizational commitment? In what ways does this commitment benefit the organization?

http:
See It
Online
www.

ch15: Apply Your Skills: Ethical Dilemma

Too Much of a Good Thing?

Not long ago, Jessica Armstrong, vice president of administration for Delaware Valley Chemical Inc., a New Jersey–based multinational company, made a point of stopping by department head Darius Harris's office and lavishly praising him for his volunteer work with an after-school program for disadvantaged children in a nearby urban neighborhood. Now she was about to summon him to her office so she could take him to task for his dedication to the same volunteer work.

It was Carolyn Clark, Harris's secretary, who'd alerted her to the problem. "Darius told the community center he'd take responsibility for a fund-raising mass mailing. And then he asked me to edit the letter he'd drafted, make all the copies, stuff the envelopes, and get it into the mail—most of this on my own time," she reported, still obviously indignant. "When I told him, 'I'm sorry, but that's not my job,' he looked me straight in the eye and asked when I'd like to schedule my upcoming performance appraisal."

Several of Harris's subordinates also volunteered with the program. After chatting with them, Armstrong concluded most were volunteering out of a desire to stay on the boss's good side. It was time to talk to Harris.

"Oh, come on," responded Harris impatiently when Armstrong confronted him. "Yes, I asked for her help as a personal favor to me. But I only brought up the appraisal because I was going out of town, and we needed to set some time aside to do the evaluation." Harris went on to talk about how important working for the after-school program was to him personally. "I grew up in that neighborhood, and if it hadn't been for the people at the center, I wouldn't be here today," he said. Besides, even if he had pressured employees to help out—and he wasn't saying he had—didn't all the emphasis the company was putting on employee volunteerism make it okay to use employees' time and company resources?

After Harris left, Armstrong thought about the conversation. There was no question that Delaware Valley actively encouraged employee volunteerism—and not just because it was the right thing to do. The chemical company had suffered a couple of unfortunate accidental spills in its recent past that caused environmental damage and sparked community anger.

Volunteering had the potential to help employees acquire new skills, create a sense of camaraderie, and play a role in recruiting and retaining talented people. But most of all, it gave a badly needed boost to the company's public image. Recently, Delaware Valley took every opportunity to publicize its employees' extracurricular community work on its Web site and in company publications. And the company created the annual Delaware Prize, which granted cash awards ranging from $1,000 to $5,000 to outstanding volunteers.

So now that Armstrong had talked with everyone concerned, just what was she going to do about the dispute between Darius Harris and Carolyn Clark?

What Would You Do?

1. Tell Carolyn Clark that employee volunteerism is important to the company and that while her performance evaluation will not be affected by her decision, she should consider helping Harris because it is an opportunity to help a worthy community project.

2. Tell Darius Harris that the employee volunteer program is just that: a volunteer program. Even though the company sees volunteerism as an important piece of its campaign to repair its tarnished image, employees must be free to choose whether to volunteer. He should not ask for the help of his direct employees with the after-school program.

3. Discipline Darius Harris for coercing his subordinates to spend their own time on his volunteer work at the community after-school program. This action will send a signal that coercing employees is a clear violation of leadership authority.

ch15: Apply Your Skills: Case for Critical Analysis

"What's Wrong With the Team?"

What's wrong with the team? What's wrong with the team? Nichole Dyer's words repeated over and over in Henry Rankin's head as he boarded the plane from Los Angeles to Chicago.

Rankin is responsible for the technical implementation of the new customer relationship management (CRM) software being installed for western and eastern sales offices in both cities. The software is badly needed to improve follow-up sales for his company, Reflex Systems. Reflex sells exercise equipment to high schools and colleges, as well as to small to midsize businesses for recreation centers, through a national force of 310 salespeople. The company's low prices have won a lot of sales; however, follow-up service is uneven and the new CRM system promises to resolve those problems with historical data, inquiries, reminders, and updates going to sales reps daily. The CEO of Reflex has ordered the CRM system installed with all possible haste.

Rankin pulled a yellow pad and pen from the side pocket of his carry-on bag and tossed it in the seat beside the window, stashed the bag in the overhead compartment, and sat down as other passengers filed past. In an effort to shut out his thoughts, he closed his eyes and concentrated on the muffled voices and low whooshing sound of the air

vents. He wrote *What's wrong with the team* three times and began drawing arrows to circles bearing the names of his team members: Barry Livingston and Max Wojohowski in L.A., and Bob Finley, Lynne Johnston, and Sally Phillips in Chicago.

He marked through Sally's name. She had jumped ship recently, taking her less-than-stellar but still-much-needed talents with her to another company. It was on a previous L.A.-to-Chicago flight that Sally had pumped him for feedback on her future with Reflex. She had informed him that she had another job offer. She admitted it was less money, but she was feeling under pressure as a member of the team and she wanted more "quality of life." Rankin told Sally bluntly that her technical expertise, on which he placed top importance, was slightly below her peers, so future promotion was less likely despite her impressive people and team skills.

He wrote "quality of life," circled it, and then crossed it out and wrote "what the hell?" *Why should she get quality of life?* he mused. *I've barely seen my wife and kids since this project started.* Rankin's team was under a great deal of pressure, and he had needed Sally to stick it out. He told her so, but the plane had barely touched down when she went directly to the office and quit, leaving the team shorthanded and too close to deadline to add another body.

What's wrong with the team? Rankin furiously scribbled as his thoughts raced:

(1) *The deadline is ridiculously short.* Dyer had scheduled a ten-week completion deadline for the new CRM software, including installation and training for both cities. He suddenly stopped writing and drew a rider and horse, then returned to his list.

(2) *I feel like some frazzled pony-express rider running back and forth across the country, trying to develop, build, set-up and work the kinks out of a new system that everyone at Reflex is eager to see NOW.*

He was interrupted by the flight attendant. "Would you care for a drink, sir?"

"Yes. Make it a scotch and water. And be light on the water."

Rankin took his drink and continued to write.

(3) *Thank God for L.A.* From the outset, Barry and Max had worked feverishly while avoiding the whining and complaining that seemed to overwhelm members of the Chicago team. The atmosphere was different. Although the project moved forward, meeting deadlines, there appeared to be less stress. The L.A. guys focused tirelessly on work, with no families to consider, alternating intense work with joking around. *Those are my kind of people,* he thought.

(4) *But there is Chicago,* he wrote. Earlier in the day, Sam Matheny from sales had e-mailed, then called, Rankin to tell him the two remaining members of the Chicago team appeared to be alternating between bickering and avoiding one another. Apparently this had been going on for some time. *What's with that?* Rankin wondered. *And why did Sam know and I didn't?* So that morning, before his flight, Rankin had to make time to call and text both Finley and Johnston. Finley admitted he had overreacted to Johnston.

"Look, man. I'm tired and stressed out," Finley said. "We've been working nonstop. My wife is not happy."

"Just get along until this project is completed," Rankin ordered.

"When will *that* be?" Finley asked before hanging up.

Rankin thought about Dyer's persistent complaints to him that the team appeared to have a lack of passion, and she admonished him to "get your people to understand the urgency of this project." Her complaints only added to his own stress level. He had long considered himself the frontrunner for Dyer's job when she retired in two years. But had his team ruined that opportunity? The sense of urgency could be measured now in the level of stress and the long hours that they had all endured. He admitted his team members were unenthusiastic, but they seemed committed.

Rankin wondered, *Is it too late to turn around and restore the level of teamwork?* He tore off the sheet from the pad, crumpled it in his hand, and stared out the window.

Questions

1. How would you characterize Rankin's leadership style? What approach do you think is correct for this situation? Why?

2. What would you do now if you were Rankin? How might you awaken more enthusiasm in your team for completing this project on time? Suggest specific steps.

3. How would you suggest that Rankin modify his leadership style if he wants to succeed Dyer in two years? Be specific.

---

ch15: On the Job Video Cases

On the Job: Camp Bow Wow: Leadership

Questions

1. Does Camp Bow Wow CEO Heidi Ganahl possess qualities associated with contemporary leadership?

2. In what way is Ganahl's leadership charismatic and visionary? Give examples.

3. Where does Ganahl's leadership fall on the Leadership Grid discussed in the chapter and illustrated in Exhibit 15.6? Explain.

---

ch16: Apply Your Skills: Ethical Dilemma

To Renege or Not to Renege?*

Federico Garcia, vice president of sales for *Puget Sound Building Materials,* a company based in Tacoma, Washington, wasn't all that surprised by what company president Michael Otto and CFO James Wilson had to say during their meeting that morning.

Last year, launching a major expansion made sense to everyone at Puget, a well-established company that provided building materials as well as manufacturing and installation services to residential builders in the Washington and Oregon markets. Puget looked at the record new housing starts and decided it was time to move into the California and Arizona markets, especially concentrating on San Diego and Phoenix, two of the hottest housing markets in the country. Federico carefully hired promising new sales representatives and offered them hefty bonuses if they reached the goals set for the new territory over the following 12 months. All the representatives had performed well, and three of them had exceeded Puget's goal—and then some. The incentive system he'd put in place had worked well. The sales reps were expecting handsome bonuses for their hard work.

Early on, however, it became all too clear that Puget had seriously underestimated the time that it would take them to build new business relationships and the costs associated with the expansion, a mistake that was already eating into profit margins. Even more distressing were the most recent figures for new housing starts, which were heading in the wrong direction. As Michael said, "Granted, it's too early to tell if this is just a pause or the start of a real long-term downturn. But I'm worried. If things get worse, Puget could be in real trouble."

James looked at Federico and said, "Our lawyers built enough contingency clauses into the sales reps' contracts that we're not really obligated to pay those bonuses you promised. What would you think about not paying them?" Federico turned to the president, who said, "Why don't you think about it, and get back to us with a recommendation?"

Federico felt torn. On the one hand, he knew the CFO was correct. Puget wasn't, strictly speaking, under any legal obligation to pay out the bonuses, and the eroding profit margins were a genuine cause for concern. The

president clearly did not want to pay the bonuses. But Federico had created a first-rate sales force that had done exactly what he'd asked them to do. He prided himself on being a man of his word, someone others could trust. Could he go back on his promises?

What Would You Do?

1. Recommend to the president that a meeting be arranged with the sales representatives entitled to a bonus and tell them that their checks were going to be delayed until Puget's financial picture clarified. The sales reps would be told that the company had a legal right to delay payment and that it may not be able to pay the bonuses if its financial situation continues to deteriorate.

2. Recommend a meeting with the sales representatives entitled to a bonus and tell them the company's deteriorating financial situation triggers one of the contingency clauses in their contract so that the company won't be issuing their bonus checks. Puget will just have to deal with the negative impact on sales rep motivation.

3. Recommend strongly to the president that Puget pay the bonuses as promised. The legal contracts and financial situation don't matter. Be prepared to resign if the bonuses are not paid as you promised. Your word and a motivated sales team mean everything to you.

*Based on Doug Wallace, "The Company Simply Refused to Pay," *Business Ethics* (March–April 2000): 18; and Adam Shell, "Over-heated Housing Market Is Cooling," *USA Today*, November 2, 2005, www.usatoday.com/money/economy/housing/2005-11-01-real-estateusat_x.htm.

ch16: Apply Your Skills: Case for Critical Analysis

Lauren's Balancing Act

DeMarco's Department Store manager Lauren Brewster's "Wow" moment came when she observed a Chicago restaurant staff's gushing treatment of an international celebrity.

"Everyone dreams of that kind of star treatment," Lauren told her assistant, Jack Klein. "Think about it. People brag about their bank or the local bar where 'everybody knows your name,' or enjoy showing off a favorite restaurant where the hostess always remembers their favorite table."

DeMarco's, like other upscale department stores, suffered the double whammy of a slumping economy and increased competition from discount retailers and online shopping. How could the store, the "box," compete, retain its old customers, and build a strong future customer base?

"We've always known that it's all about customer service," Lauren said. "But what's so great about grabbing a giant plastic shopping cart and slogging through some giant warehouse in your shorts and flip-flops, and then joining the herd at the checkout? That is not a shopping *experience*."

"And what *isn't* great about being treated like Oprah from the moment you hit the door until the sales associate swipes your card and hands over something lovely that you just purchased?" Jack asked.

Lauren's idea was that store customers receive that personal, upscale, "you're somebody special here" treatment at DeMarco's. Sales associates would raise their own professional level, regard customers as worthy of personalized service, and build their own clientele. As added incentive, the entire DeMarco's sales team was changed over from hourly pay to straight commission. "Your pay is built through your own initiative and individualized service that makes customers return to you again and again," Lauren instructed the sales force at the outset of the experiment. The idea intrigued Corporate, which approved a two-year experiment.

As expected, the new plan created a minor exodus among those who wanted the assurance of a "regular paycheck." But as the program moved through its first year, both store and corporate management was pleased with the overall results. Marketing pushed the new image of elite, personalized customer service, and phrases such as "Katherine at DeMarco's helped me select this outfit," or "Damien always lets me know when something new arrives at DeMarco's that he thinks is perfect for me" became the typical boast of savvy shoppers.

Now, two years into the experiment, Corporate urged Lauren to submit a full assessment of the program as a potential model for implementation throughout the department store chain. Sales numbers vouched for the overall success, particularly over the last two quarters of the second year. Certain associates, including Katherine Knowles in designer dresses and Damien Fotopolous in women's shoes, showed significant gains as a result of straight commissions, and sales associates and customers responded favorably overall, urging a continuation of the program. Reliance on commissions inspired these and other sales associates to treat their individual department as if it were their own small business, becoming experts on nuances of merchandise, exploring designs and trends, finding ways to promote their expertise, and building an impressive number of loyal customers.

The satisfaction level of customers was apparent in the numbers—not only sales numbers, but in repeat business, customer referrals to friends, and customer comment cards, all of which had been tracked since the beginning of the program.

The down side of the experiment was that while some associates soared, others either veered toward an aggressive, pushy sales style or became intimidated by coworkers and teetered, monthly, on the verge of being replaced because they weren't making sales. The once-proud tradition of cooperation among sales staff was, in many instances, being eaten away by relentless competition. Work assignments away from the sales floor were resented. In addition, the managers and sales associates of certain departments, such as women's accessories, complained of lower wages because,

as one sales associate pointed out, "My commission on a $50 belt is nothing compared to Katherine's commission on a $2,800 designer dress." Resentment was mounting among those who witnessed the extravagant wages of a few.

"If we change this program, if we keep straight commission for some and return to hourly pay for others, how does that fit with our new image?" Lauren said to Jack. "How does it deal with the difference in pay scale? How does it assure us that the attitudes of our sales team and the culture of this store will not return to what we were before—just another store?"

Questions

1. What do you see as the advantages and disadvantages of the incentive system that DeMarco's is using for sales associates? What impact do you think it is having on the DeMarco's culture? Explain.

2. Do you think the complaints of lower-paid sales associates are legitimate? Why? How do you suggest Lauren respond to these complaints, such as the gripe that the system offers few opportunities for large commissions in some departments?

3. Have the successes of sales associates such as Katherine or Damien created a situation in which loyalty to customers is stronger than loyalty to the store? For example, if a successful associate leaves DeMarco's, might the customer leave also?

ch16: On the Job Video Cases

On the Job: Urban Escapes: Motivating Employees

Questions

1. Which needs in Maslow's hierarchy are most important to the employees who work for Urban Escapes, and how can managers use this information to develop a highly motivated workforce?

2. According to equity theory, how might an Urban Escapes guide react if he or she feels underpaid or unappreciated?

3. What outcomes or rewards possess high valence for managers and guides who work at Urban Escapes?

ch17: Apply Your Skills: Ethical Dilemma

On Trial*

When Werner and Thompson, a Los Angeles business and financial management firm, offered Iranian-born Firoz Bahmania a position as an accountant assistant one spring day in 2007, Bahmani felt a sense of genuine relief, but his relief was short-lived.

With his degree in accounting from a top-notch American university, he knew he was more than a little overqualified for the job. But time after time, he'd been rejected for suitable positions. His language difficulties were the reason most often given for his unsuccessful candidacy. Although the young man had grown up speaking both Farsi

and French in his native land, he'd begun to pick up English only shortly before his arrival in the United States a few years ago. Impressed by his educational credentials and his quiet, courtly manner, managing partner Beatrice Werner overlooked his heavy accent and actively recruited him for the position, the only one available at the time. During his interview, she assured him that he would advance in time.

It was clear to Beatrice that Firoz was committed to succeeding at all costs. But it soon also became apparent that Firoz and his immediate supervisor, Cathy Putnam, were at odds. Cathy was a seasoned account manager who had just transferred to Los Angeles from the New York office.

Saddled with an enormous workload, she let Firoz know right from the start, speaking in her rapid-fire Brooklyn accent, that he'd need to get up to speed as quickly as possible.

Shortly before Cathy was to give Firoz his three-month probationary review, she came to Beatrice, expressed her frustration with Firoz's performance, and suggested that he be let go. "His bank reconciliations and financial report preparations are first-rate," Cathy admitted, "but his communication skills leave a lot to be desired. In the first place, I simply don't have the time to keep repeating the same directions over and over again when I'm trying to teach him his responsibilities. Then there's the fact that public contact is part of his written job description. Typically, he puts off making phone calls to dispute credit card charges or ask a client's staff for the information he needs. When he does finally pick up the phone . . . well, let's just say I've had more than one client mention how hard it is to understand what he's trying to say. Some of them are getting pretty exasperated."

"You know, some firms feel it's their corporate responsibility to help foreign-born employees learn English," Beatrice began. "Maybe we should help him find an English-as-a-second-language course and pay for it."

"With all due respect, I don't think that's our job," Cathy replied, with barely concealed irritation. "If you come to the United States, you should learn our language. That's what my mom's parents did when they came over from Italy. They certainly didn't expect anyone to hold their hands. Besides," she added, almost inaudibly, "Firoz's lucky we let him into this country."

Beatrice had mixed feelings. On one hand, she recognized that Werner and Thompson had every right to expect someone in Firoz's position to be capable of carrying out his public contact duties. Perhaps she had made a mistake in hiring him. But as the daughter of German immigrants herself, she knew firsthand both how daunting language and cultural barriers could be and that they could be overcome in time. Perhaps in part because of her family background, she had a passionate commitment to the firm's stated goals of creating a diverse workforce and a caring, supportive culture. Besides, she felt a personal sense of obligation to help a hard-working, promising employee realize his potential. What will she advise Cathy to do now that Firoz's probationary period is drawing to a close?

What Would You Do?

1. Agree with Cathy Putnam. Despite your personal feelings, accept that Firoz Bahmani is not capable of carrying out the accountant assistant's responsibilities. Make the break now, and give him his notice on the grounds that he cannot carry out one of the key stated job requirements. Advise him that a position that primarily involves paperwork would be a better fit for him.

2. Place Firoz with a more sympathetic account manager who is open to finding ways to help him improve his English and has the time to help him develop his assertiveness and telephone skills. Send Cathy Putnam to diversity awareness training.

3. Create a new position at the firm that will allow Firoz to do the reports and reconciliations for several account managers, freeing the account assistants to concentrate on public contact work. Make it clear that he will have little chance of future promotion unless his English improves markedly.

*Mary Gillis, "Iranian Americans," *Multicultural America*, www.everyculture.com/multi/Ha-La/Iranian-Americans.html (accessed September 19, 2006); and Charlene Marmer Solomon, "Managing Today's Immigrants," *Personnel Journal* 72, no. 3 (February 1993): 56–65.

ch17: Apply Your Skills: Case for Critical Analysis

E-mail Adventure

The toy industry is highly competitive and can be as cutthroat as any pirate adventure. *Yo-ho-ho!* Snooping, corporate espionage, and efforts to keep emerging ideas under wraps are all part of life in the toy industry. A certain level of managerial paranoia is expected. But when the private e-mail of an industry CEO was discovered and began making the rounds, it unleashed a firestorm and brought disastrous results on company morale, unwanted media attention, and public embarrassment.

Howard Tannenbaum is the long-time CEO of a major toy company. Over the past few years, his company worked to develop a new product line, called Brainchild, that all concerned believed would be a blockbuster. The passion of Tannenbaum, the new line of toys was so top-secret that portions of the line were created and produced, piecemeal, among the various divisions. In the beginning, it was all very hush-hush. But as the line moved closer to completion and the expected Christmas season launch date more than a year away, press and industry rumors gained momentum.

At 8:00 A.M. on a June morning, Barry Paine, Tannenbaum's attorney and longtime friend and confidante, arrived at his office, opened his e-mail and saw a flagged message from Howard:

Barry:

We have a disaster in the making here. Looks like I'm going to have to come down hard on all of my managers. Somebody will go—perhaps several people before this situation is over. They're obviously getting EXTREMELY slack on design security. I won't say now how I discovered the breach or what was stolen with regard to the new product designs, but suffice it to say that at this point, EVERYONE is suspect. Needless to say, I am FURIOUS! When I find out who it is—and it could be anyone—believe me, heads will roll!!! I'll call you later this morning. WE NEED TO MEET. Thanks for letting me vent. Now, I can compose the REAL e-mail to managers.

Howard

Later that same morning, managers throughout the company received the following:

TO ALL MANAGERS:

We have a situation here in which product design information on the new line, information that should have been under the HIGHEST SECURITY, has been breached. Let me make it clear that each of you is responsible for investigating your division and finding the source of the leak. Please be thorough in your investigation and be TOTALLY HONEST with me in presenting your findings in this matter. Someone will pay for this. THIS IS TOP PRIORITY!

Howard Tannenbaum, CEO

Many recipients of the e-mail felt personally attacked and threatened. Before day's end, e-mail, phone calls, and rumors were flying. By the following day, Tannenbaum felt pressured into trying to defuse the anger by issuing a second, apologetic, e-mail. However, events were already spiraling out of hand, as somehow the contents of the original e-mail to Barry Paine began circulating throughout management and beyond—to employees and at least one member of the press, who dubbed the debacle *Toy-Gate*. The perception of a CEO and a company out of control increased and the stock price took a minor hit.

"The first e-mail left me stunned," one long-time manager said. "But when I saw the e-mail to Paine about how Howard *really* felt and the level of contempt he showed for all of us, making us *all* appear incompetent and dishonest—that, for me, is the last straw. Even if I stay, it has destroyed the relationship with Howard forever."

Now Tannenbaum sat, head in hands, in Paine's office. "Barry, I was simply trying to find the truth."

Paine walked over to a bookshelf and pulled an old, well-used volume. "Do you remember your Sophocles from school, Howard? In one Greek tragedy, Oedipus the King and his persistent search for truth in the murder of his predecessor, King Laius, followed a path that abandoned reason and led to his own undoing. My friend, in your case, it's not the search for truth, but it's the path you take—what you say, how you say it, and to whom you say it—that is important."

"OK—what do you think I should do next?"

Questions

1. What is the underlying communication mistake in this case? Why do you think Howard Tannenbaum sent those e-mails?

2. How do you think Tannenbaum should have communicated his concerns about the information link? Why?

3. What should Tannenbaum do now to try to recover from the negative impact of his e-mails? Suggest specific steps.

ch17: On the Job Video Cases

On the Job: Plant Fantasies: Managing Communication

Questions

1. Using the concept of channel richness, explain why leaders at Plant Fantasies place a high value on face-to-face communication.

2. What influence might gender have on the communication styles of Teresa Carleo and Steve Martucci? Give examples.

3. Which of the three types of formal organizational communication would you expect to originate from Teresa Carleo and Steve Martucci, and why?

http:
See It
Online
www.

ch18: Apply Your Skills: Ethical Dilemma

One for All and All for One?*

Melinda Asbel watched as three of her classmates filed out of the conference room. Then she turned back to the large wooden table and faced her fellow members (a student and three faculty members) of the university's judiciary committee.

The three students—Joe Eastridge, Brad Hamil, and Lisa Baghetti—had just concluded their appeal against a plagiarism conviction stemming from a group project for an international marketing course. Melinda, who happened to be in the class with the students on trial, remembered the day that the professor, Hank Zierden, had asked Joe, Brad, and Lisa, along with the group's leader, Paul Colgan, to stay after class. She happened to walk by the classroom a half hour later to see four glum students emerge. Even though Paul had a chagrined expression on his face, Joe was the one who looked completely shattered. It didn't take long for word to spread along the ever-active grapevine that Paul had admitted to plagiarizing his part of the group paper.

At the hearing, the students recounted how they'd quickly and unanimously settled on Paul to lead the group. He was by far the most able student among them, someone who managed to maintain a stellar GPA even while handling a full course load and holding down a part-time job. After the group worked together for weeks analyzing the problem and devising a marketing plan, Paul assigned a section of the final paper to each member. With the pressure of all those end-of-the-semester deadlines bearing down on them, everyone was delighted when Paul volunteered to write the company and industry background, the section that typically took the most time to produce. Paul gathered in everyone's contributions, assembled them into a paper, and handed the final draft to the other members. They each gave it a quick read. They liked what they saw and thought they had a good chance for an A.

Unfortunately, as Paul readily admitted when Professor Zierden confronted them, he had pulled the section that he'd contributed directly off the Internet. Pointing out the written policy that he had distributed at the beginning of the semester, which stated that each group member was equally responsible for the final product, the professor gave all four students a zero for the project. The group project and presentation counted for 30 percent of the course grade.

Joe, Brad, and Lisa maintained that they were completely unaware that Paul had cheated. "It just never occurred to us Paul would ever need to cheat," Brad said. They were innocent bystanders, the students argued. Why should they be penalized? Besides, the consequences weren't going to fall on each of them equally. Although Paul was suffering the embarrassment of public exposure, the failing group project grade would only put a dent in his solid GPA. Joe, on the other hand, was already on academic probation. A zero probably meant he wouldn't make the 2.5 GPA that he needed to stay in the business program.

At least one of the faculty members of the judiciary committee supported Professor Zierden's actions. "We're assigning more and more group projects because increasingly that's the way these students are going to find themselves working when they get real jobs in the real world," he

said. "And the fact of the matter is that if someone obtains information illegally while on the job, it's going to put the whole corporation at risk for being sued, or worse."

Even though she could see merit to both sides, Melinda was going to have to choose. If you were Melinda, how would you vote?

What Would You Do?

1. Vote to exonerate the three group project members who didn't cheat. You're convinced that they had no reason to suspect Paul Colgan of dishonesty. Exonerating them is the right thing to do.

2. Vote in support of Hank Zierden's decision to hold each individual member accountable for the entire project. The professor clearly stated his policy at the beginning of the semester, and the students should have been more vigilant. The committee should not undercut a professor's explicit policy.

3. Vote to reduce each of the three students' penalties. Instead of a zero, each student will receive only half of the possible total points for the project, which would be an F. You're still holding students responsible for the group project, but not imposing catastrophic punishment. This compromise both undercuts the professor's policy and punishes "innocent" team members to some extent, but not as severely.

*Based on Ellen R. Stapleton, "College to Expand Policy on Plagiarism," *The Ithacan Online*, April 12, 2001, www.ithaca.edu/ithacan/articles/0104/12/news/0college_to_e.htm (accessed April 12, 2001).

ch18: Apply Your Skills: Case for Critical Analysis

Are We a Team?

Hi. My name is Jenny McConnell. I am the newly appointed CIO of a medium-sized technology company. Our company recruits top graduates from schools of business and engineering. Talent, intellect, creativity—it's all there. If you lined up this crowd for a group photo, credentials in hand, the "wow" factor would be there.

Our company is spread over a dozen states, mostly in the Northwest. The talent pool is amazing across the board, both in information technology (IT) and the rest of the company. But when the CEO hired me, he said that we are performing nowhere near our potential. On the surface, the company is doing fine. But we should be a *Fortune* 500 organization. With this much talent, we should be growing at a much faster rate. The CEO also said that I was inheriting "a super team with disappointing performance." His task for me was to pull the IT stars into a cohesive team that would meet company needs for new IT systems and services much faster and more effectively.

Without making our superstars feel that they were being critiqued and second-guessed, or indicating "there's a real problem here," I wanted to gather as much information and feedback as possible from the 14 team members (regional CIOs and department heads) who report to me.

I held one-on-one meetings in order to give a voice to each person, allowing each individual to provide an honest assessment of the team as well as areas for improvement and a vision for the future of team efforts.

I was surprised by the consistency of remarks and opinions. For example, a picture emerged of the previous CIO, who was obviously awed by the talent level of team members. Comments such as, "Bob pretty much let us do what we wanted," and "Bob would start the meeting and then just fade into the background, as if he found us intimidating" were typical. The most disturbing comment, "Bob always agreed with *me*," was expressed by most of the team members at some point in our conversation. It was as if the regional heads believed that the CIO wanted them to succeed by doing as they thought best for themselves.

I queried members about the level of cooperation during meetings and uncovered areas of concern, including the complaint that others at the table were constantly checking their iPads and Blackberrys during meetings. One department head told me, "You could turn off the sound while watching one of our meetings and just by the body language and level of attention tell who is aligned with whom and who wishes the speaker would just shut up. It would be comical if it weren't so distressing."

Such remarks were indicative of a lack of trust and respect and a breakdown of genuine communication. One team member told me, "I recently encountered a problem that a department head from another region had successfully solved, but the information was never shared, so here I am reinventing the wheel and wasting valuable time." It was apparent that these so-called high performers were territorial, and that the "each division for itself" attitude was becoming a cultural norm, which, unchecked, was slowing our response to line departments and customers.

I was also struck by the similarity of the regional IT leaders in their backgrounds, comments, and attitudes, which presented a whole new dilemma: How do we create diversity, jump-start ideas, and reignite passion? This looks like a group of individualists who don't know how to play as a team. I don't want to diminish the individual talent, but I am concerned by the lack of cohesion. I need to find a way to help people think less about themselves and more about sharing work and information and achieving collective results for the good of the company.

Team building is an art, anchored by trust and communication, and committed to mutual success. What I'm seeing looks like team dysfunction to me. Now, I have to determine the steps necessary to build a cohesive, visionary team.

Questions

1. What type of team does the new CIO have? What do you see as the key problem with the team?

2. How do you think the team evolved to this low level of cooperation and cohesiveness?

3. What suggestions do you have for the CIO to help her turn this collection of individual regional and department heads into a top-performing team? Explain.

ch18: On the Job Video Cases

On the Job: Holden Outerware: Leading Teams

Questions

1. Is design manager Nikki Brush part of a group, or part of a team? Explain the difference.

2. What type of team did Nikki Brush participate in when she was a freelancer? What type of team does she participate in as a full-time employee at Holden?

3. What are potential disadvantages of these teams for Holden's apparel designers? What can managers do to help avoid these downsides?

pt5: Integrative Case

Range Resources: Leading Ethically, Communicating Openly

"Natural gas has been a godsend to this area. It has helped farmers see a return on all the hard work they have put into their land just to keep it," says Bev Romanetti, a Pennsylvania cattle farmer. "I have found that Range Resources wants to be responsible; they want to do the right things, they want to protect our environment, and they want to do right by us," remarks Albie Rinehart, a retired schoolteacher from Greene County, Pennsylvania. "I personally know a lot of the people who work for Range Resources—it's like dealing with your neighbors," states Buzz Meddings, a firefighter from Washington County, Pennsylvania.

Citizens of rural Pennsylvania are the people most affected by natural gas exploration in the eastern region of the United States. They are farmers, firefighters, teachers, single moms, restaurant owners, and volunteers. They are hardy. They are the salt of the earth. More important, they are the face of natural gas development in the Keystone State, and they provide the voices through which Texas-based energy company Range Resources communicates its message of good corporate citizenship to the public. At the company's public outreach site, MyRangeResources.com, everyday people offer video testimonials about the economic and social benefits that Range brings to local communities, whether in terms of jobs, new development, or concern for the natural environment. The site, which functions as part of Range's communications strategy, is an information clearinghouse for all things related to natural gas exploration.

Since discovering the second-largest natural gas field in the world in 2004, Range has used open communication to build trust among the stakeholders most affected by the development of natural gas resources. While natural gas is recognized as a clean energy solution to America's energy needs, citizens still want to know that natural gas exploration is safe for communities and good for the environment.

As explained at MyRangeResources.com, Range makes safety a central component of its natural gas production. To extract methane from rock formations deep down in the Earth, engineers guide a 5-inch-diameter drill straight down more than a mile and then turn it horizontally to penetrate shale rock thousands of feet in all directions. This horizontal drilling method is a groundbreaking advancement that allows drillers to capture far more methane than the old vertical-only method, which requires many more wells to get a fraction of the output. Once Range's drill arrives at its destination 6,500 feet below the Earth's surface, electric charges produce cracks in the rock from which methane gas escapes. To enlarge these fractures for maximum gas recovery, millions of gallons of water and sand are pumped to the area under extreme pressure, expanding the cracks and freeing even more gas to flow back up to the well head at the surface. For environmental safety, Range houses its drill in a 24-inch-diameter casing comprised of five layers of steel and concrete, isolating the entire production process from contact with surrounding land and water.

In its desire to leave as small an environmental footprint as possible, Range has pioneered a way to recycle the millions of gallons of water used in the drilling process. "One thing we've done from an environmental point of view is we now recycle 100 percent of our water in our development areas in Pennsylvania. In fact, we're recycling nearly all of our fluid, which is a real breakthrough for the industry," says Jeffrey Ventura, president and CEO of Range Resources. "Back when we began that process, a lot of people felt that it couldn't be done, that it was physically impossible. Lo and behold, not only did we do it successfully, but now we're doing it large-scale." Ventura, the leader credited with Range's decision to explore the Marcellus Shale gas formation in Pennsylvania, says water recycling is a major innovation in natural gas production. "Just like the Marcellus Shale was a breakthrough," Ventura says, "on the environmental side, water recycling was a real breakthrough."

To keep stakeholders informed about safety, Range has also led the industry in the disclosure of core production processes, especially the use of liquids for drilling and fracturing. "In the middle of 2010, there was a lot of concern nationwide about what's in frack fluid, and Range was the first company in the industry to say exactly what's in our frack fluid," Ventura says. "We post it on our website and we supply it to the state for every Marcellus Shale well that we're drilling. It's 99.9 percent water, and the 0.1 percent are common everyday household chemicals." Range's open communication with the public has earned the respect of environmental groups and also the U.S. Environmental Protection Agency (EPA), which in 2012 announced that natural gas production was safe for drinking water at its test site in Dimock Township, Pennsylvania.

Safety, open communication, and leadership—these are the qualities that have made Range Resources a vanguard of America's natural gas boom and a pioneer of sustainable energy development. "I'm proud of what our technical team has done on the environmental side and the communications side," says Ventura of his company's contribution to America's clean energy future.

Integrative Case Questions

1. Range Resources CEO Jeffrey Ventura emphasizes public safety, environmental concern, and open communication with stakeholders. Which of the four contemporary leadership approaches do you think best describes Ventura? Explain.

2. Managers at Range Resources use communication to develop a climate of trust and openness. Why is this especially important for energy companies, and what specific actions can managers take to enhance this communication approach?

3. How might Range's leadership, communication, and values affect employees' organizational commitment? Explain.

Sources: Based on My Range Resources Video Interview Series, Range Resources, www.myrangeresources.com (accessed July 20, 2012); Jeffrey Ventura (President and Chief Executive Officer of Range Resources), interview by Rodney Waller, "Range Up Close: Range's Technical Team," Range Resources corporate site, 2010, online video, www.rangeresources.com/Media-Center/Featured-Stories.aspx (accessed July 20, 2012); Jack Z. Smith, "New CEO Taking Helm as Range Continues Push into Marcellus," *Star-Telegram*, December 17, 2011, www.star-telegram.com/2011/12/17/3601200/new-ceo-taking-helm-as-range-continues.html (accessed July 19, 2012); Rick Stouffer, "Range Resources Recycles All Waste Water from Washington Drilling," *Pittsburgh Tribune-Review*, October 19, 2009, http://triblive.com/x/pittsburghtrib/business/s_648781.html (accessed July 20, 2012); Natural Gas Company Reveals Fracking Chemical Composition," NewsWorks, July 16, 2012, www.newsworks.org/index.php/local/healthscience/5361-natural-gas-company-reveals-fracking-chemical-composition (accessed July 19, 2012); Range Resources, "Hydraulic Fracturing: Marcellus," Range Resources corporate site, www.rangeresources.com/rangeresources/files/6f/6ff33c64-5acf-4270-95c7-9e991b963771.pdf (accessed July 19, 2012); Laura Legere, "EPA to Stop Dimock Water Deliveries," *Scranton Times-Tribune*, July 26, 2012, http://thetimes-tribune.com/news/gas-drilling/epa-to-stop-dimock-water-deliveries-1.1348393 (accessed July 26, 2012); Timothy Gardner, "Dimock, PA Water Deemed Safe By EPA," Reuters, May 11, 2012, www.huffingtonpost.com/2012/05/11/dimock-pa-water-safe-epa_n_1510035.html (accessed July 19, 2012).

part 6 : chapter 19

Quality and Performance

JLImages/Alamy

Learning Outcomes

After studying this chapter, you should be able to:

1. Define organizational control and explain why it is a key management function.

2. Explain the four steps in the control process.

3. Explain the benefits of using the balanced scorecard to track the performance and control of the organization.

4. Discuss the use of financial statements, financial analysis, and budgeting as management controls.

5. Contrast the hierarchical and decentralized methods of control.

6. Identify the benefits of open-book management.

7. Describe the concept of total quality management (TQM) and major TQM techniques, such as quality circles, benchmarking, Six Sigma principles, quality partnering, and continuous improvement.

8. Identify current trends in quality and financial control, including ISO 9000 and corporate governance, and discuss their impact on organizations.

© Alan Bailey/Sexto Sol/Getty Images

What Is Your Attitude Toward Organizational Regulation and Control?[1]

INSTRUCTIONS: Managers have to control people for organizations to survive, yet this control should be the right amount and type. Companies are often less democratic than the society of which they are a part. Honestly consider your beliefs about the regulation of other people and answer each item that follows as Mostly True or Mostly False.

	Mostly True	Mostly False
1. I believe people should be guided more by feelings and less by rules.	_____	_____
2. I think employees should be on time to work and to meetings.	_____	_____
3. I believe efficiency and speed are not as important as letting everyone have their say when making a decision.	_____	_____
4. I think employees should conform to company policies.	_____	_____
5. I let my significant other make the decision and have his or her way most of the time.	_____	_____
6. I like to tell other people what to do.	_____	_____
7. I am more patient with the least capable people.	_____	_____
8. I like to have things running "just so."	_____	_____

SCORING AND INTERPRETATION: Give yourself one point for each Mostly True answer to the odd-numbered questions and one point for each Mostly False answer to the even-numbered questions. A score of 6 or above suggests that you prefer decentralized control for other people in an organization. A score of 3 or less suggests a preference for more control and bureaucracy in a company. Enthusiastic new managers may exercise too much of their new control and get a negative backlash. However, too little control may mean less accountability and productivity. The challenge for new managers is to strike the right balance for the job and people involved.

G roupon is a popular online-coupon company that advertises and promotes discounted gift certificates for local and national companies. The company earns a percentage of the revenue generated from the featured discounts. For example, for a $10 purchase at a sandwich shop, Groupon might make $5 and give the rest to the merchant. When Groupon was founded in November 2008, few would have anticipated its stunning success. After just two years, *Forbes* reported that this technology startup was the world's fastest-growing company, on pace to make an astonishing $1 billion in sales. But in its first quarter as a public company, Groupon reported unsettling news to investors. Managers were unprepared to handle the high rate of returns during the 2011 holiday season, and as a result, they were forced to drive down reported fourth-quarter revenue by $14 million and earnings by about 3 percent. Sandra Peters, head of financial reporting policy for the CFA Institute, said, "It really demonstrates, for a [new public company], were they really ready to go? Did they have the financial systems? Did they have the processes and procedures in place?" Groupon grew so fast that its accounting and control systems were unable to keep up, creating havoc for managers and investors.[2]

As a manager, you will use a variety of measures to monitor performance and keep track of the organization's finances. Many of these measures will involve control issues,

1 INTRODUCTION

2 ENVIRONMENT

3 PLANNING

4 ORGANIZING

5 LEADING

6 CONTROLLING

Concept Connection ◄◄◄

David Zanzinger/Alamy

The state of California has deep concerns about paint solvents, concrete slurry, and other pollutants entering the water supply through work done at construction sites. Thus, the state government now offers training programs for contractors and others in the construction industry to learn how to improve **organizational control**. In addition to using filters that keep the water supply clean, effective control means ensuring that builders comply with new state regulations.

> *"Managing is like holding a dove in your hand. Squeeze too hard and you kill it, not hard enough and it flies away."*
>
> — TOMMY LASORDA, MAJOR LEAGUE BASEBALL PLAYER AND COACH, INDUCTED INTO THE NATIONAL BASEBALL HALL OF FAME IN 1997

including controlling work processes, regulating employee behavior, setting up basic systems for allocating financial resources, developing human resources, analyzing financial performance, and evaluating overall profitability.

This chapter introduces basic mechanisms for controlling the organization. We begin by defining organizational control and summarizing the four steps in the control process. Then we discuss the use of the balanced scorecard to measure performance and methods for controlling financial performance, including the use of budgets and financial statements. The next sections examine the changing philosophy of control, today's approach to total quality management (TQM), and trends such as International Organization for Standardization (ISO) certification and corporate governance.

The Meaning of Control

Before New York City buildings are demolished or renovated, licensed inspectors are required to inspect them for the presence of lead or asbestos. Both substances can cause severe, long-term health problems, including cancer. If either substance is found, it must be either removed or contained using an expensive and time-consuming process. Given the serious health risks associated with these two substances, you could assume that the inspection process would be carefully regulated and controlled. Yet, many law enforcement officials and industry experts say that New York City's inspection system is highly corrupt. As evidence, licensed safety inspector Saverio F. Todaro recently made a stunning confession in federal court. He revealed that although he had submitted clean asbestos and lead test results for over 200 buildings and apartments, he had not performed a single one of the tests. Although shocking, the Department of Environmental Protection (DEP) claims that these crimes occur frequently and easily because of a lack of controls. The DEP audits only a tiny fraction of the roughly 28,400 projects that inspectors like Todaro certify each year as safe. "We can always look for new ways to improve our process," said a spokesman for the mayor. "DEP is going to start increasing audits, which is the right step to ensure inspections are being completed properly."[3]

Organizational control refers to the systematic process of regulating organizational activities to make them consistent with the expectations established in plans, targets, and standards of performance. In a classic article on the control function, Douglas S. Sherwin summarizes the concept as follows: "The essence of control is action which adjusts operations to predetermined standards, and its basis is information in the hands of managers."[4] Thus, effectively controlling an organization requires information about performance standards and actual performance, as well as actions taken to correct any deviations from the standards.

Managers must decide what information is essential, how they will obtain that information, and how they can and should respond to it. Having the correct data is essential. Managers decide which standards, measurements, and metrics are needed to monitor and control the organization effectively and set up systems for obtaining that information. If a hospital, for example, carefully monitors and controls its health care services, patients should receive safe, high-quality health care. Unfortunately, medical mistakes happen, many of which go unreported. Without data that describe these mistakes, it's often difficult to correct common problems such as drug mix-ups, radiation overdoses, and surgical blunders. To generate more data about medical mishaps and make health care safer, federal officials are launching a program where consumers report medical mistakes and unsafe practices by doctors, hospitals, pharmacists, and others who provide treatment. This new source of information from consumers will provide valuable data that may explain why one-fourth of patients in hospitals experience "adverse events" during their stay. "Patients and their families are a potential gold mine of information," said Martin J. Hatlie, CEO of Project Patient Care. "They see things that busy health care workers don't see. Doctors and nurses are in and out. But relatives are there continuously with the patient. They often know how to fix problems that cause errors."[5] The Manager's Shoptalk describes an innovative reporting system for individuals, called *auto-analytics*, which can provide information that may lead to personal and professional growth.

Take a Moment

The Small Group Breakout on page 654 will give you a chance to practice developing a control system that includes rules to guide behavior and statistics for measuring performance.

Remember This

- Statistical measurement is an important part of achieving high performance.
- **Organizational control** is the systematic process through which managers regulate organizational

activities to meet planned goals and standards of performance.
- Most organizations measure and control performance using quantitative financial measures.

Feedback Control Model

A feedback control model helps managers meet strategic goals by monitoring and regulating an organization's activities and using feedback to determine whether performance meets established standards. Consider how FreshDirect, a premium online grocer in New York City, has used a feedback control model to improve the quality of its products and customer service. With more than 45,000 deliveries per week, FreshDirect is known for its farm-fresh produce, custom-butchered meat, seafood, and bakery-fresh pastries and breads. It may be surprising that this successful organization stumbled through a series of missteps during its early days. Although FreshDirect was very successful attracting first-time customers with coupons and incentives, the majority of these customers dropped the service after placing one or two orders because of poor customer service. "We broke too many eggs," said Richard S. Braddock, who became CEO in 2008. "We showed up with thawed ice cream. We bruised produce. We delivered late. We missed boxes." Braddock decided to take drastic action by creating a system of continuous feedback, a real-time database that would follow every step—and misstep—of each business day, so minor problems could be corrected before they erupted into big problems.[6] A four-step feedback control system that managers can use is described in the following section.

STEPS OF FEEDBACK CONTROL

Managers set up control systems that consist of the four key steps illustrated in Exhibit 19.1: establish standards, measure performance, compare performance to standards, and make corrections as necessary.

Establish Standards of Performance

Within the organization's overall strategic plan, managers define goals for organizational departments in specific, operational terms that include a *standard of performance* against

Manager's *Shoptalk*

Quantify Yourself

Imagine becoming better at your job and more satisfied with your life by tracking information that reveals exactly how you spend your day. For 22 years, entrepreneur and scientist Stephen Wolfram did just that. He mapped data about his time spent in meetings, e-mail usage, and the number of keystrokes he logged so that he could analyze how he spent his time. Wolfram was able to identify work habits that squelched his creativity and stymied his productivity. So he started planning changes that would help him become more productive and happier.

New devices such as computer software and smartphone apps help people gather and analyze data about what they do at work so they can use it to do their jobs better. This interest in self-awareness is part of a growing discipline called *auto-analytics*, which is the practice of voluntarily collecting and analyzing data about oneself in order to improve.

- **Tracking screen time** While it may be unsettling to have our managers watching what's on our computer screens, it's much more acceptable when we do the watching. New technology called *knowledge workload tracking* records how you use your computer, such as measuring how long you have an open window, how often you switch between windows, and how long you're idle. The software turns all the measurements into charts so that you can see where you're spending your time and how you can improve your productivity. One computer programmer thought his online chats were eating into his programming time, so he analyzed how much time he spent chatting during certain periods, and then looked at how much code he wrote during those times. Surprisingly, he found that talking online with colleagues actually *improved* his productivity.

- **Measuring cognitive tasks** Another set of tracking tools can help you gather data as you perform cognitive tasks, such as client research on your smartphone or statistical analysis in Excel. Although it is notoriously difficult to measure knowledge work, a tool such as MeetGrinder can measure the time and money spent doing any activity. Bob Evans, a Google engineer, used it to explore the relationship between his attention and productivity. "As engineers, we load up our heads with all these variables, the intellectual pieces of the systems we are building. If we get distracted, we lose that thread in our heads," he said. MeetGrinder revealed to him that he needs about four straight hours to get anything challenging done, so he tackles those projects when he has that kind of time, not on days that are interrupted with meetings and phone calls.

- **Improving health** Exercise, amount of sleep, and the stress levels of knowledge workers have been shown to affect productivity, creativity, and job performance. Employees can choose from a variety of mobile apps and wearable sensors that collect valuable data about their physical health. Sacha Chua wanted to better understand how her sleep schedule affected her professional priorities, so she monitored her bedtimes, wake-up times, and amount of sleep over several weeks using a tracker called Sleep On It. She changed her routine and started waking up at 5:40 A.M. instead of 8:30 A.M. She gave up late-night activities like browsing the Web and started going to bed earlier. With these adjustments, she discovered that her work productivity soared. The data from Sleep On It gave Chua measurable information that allowed her to establish priorities on what really mattered to her.

Tools used for auto-analytics will continue to become more sophisticated. The data that they reveal will provide the hard evidence we sometimes need to adjust the way we use our time and nurture our minds and bodies to have more success in work and life.

Sources: Based on H. James Wilson, "Employees, Measure Yourselves," *The Wall Street Journal*, April 2, 2012, http://online.wsj.com/article/SB100 01424052970204520204577249691204802060.html#articleTabs%3Darticle (accessed September 28, 2012); and H. James Wilson, "You, by the Numbers," *Harvard Business Review* (September, 2012): 2–5.

---

which to compare organizational activities. FreshDirect developed performance standards designed to strengthen customer service and build loyal customers. For example, managers introduced a rating system to measure the quality of its produce and seafood. Every morning, managers and buyers rank their products from one star (below average) to five (never better) and share that information with customers so they can simulate

EXHIBIT 19.1 Feedback Control Model

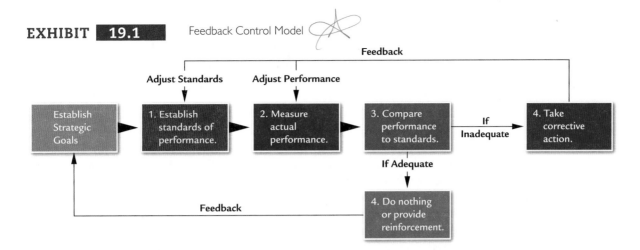

Feedback

Adjust Standards | Adjust Performance

Establish Strategic Goals → 1. Establish standards of performance. → 2. Measure actual performance. → 3. Compare performance to standards. → If Inadequate → 4. Take corrective action.

If Adequate →

4. Do nothing or provide reinforcement.

Feedback

the in-store shopping experience and decide what to purchase. Other standards of performance included tracking on-time deliveries and the number of errors per order.[7]

Tracking such measures as customer service, product quality, or order accuracy is an important supplement to traditional financial and operational performance measurement, but many companies have a hard time identifying and defining nonfinancial measurements. To evaluate and reward employees effectively for the achievement of standards, managers need clear standards that reflect activities that contribute to the organization's overall strategy in a significant way. Standards should be defined clearly and precisely so that employees know what they need to do and can determine whether their activities are on target.[8]

Measure Actual Performance

Most organizations prepare formal reports of quantitative performance measurements that managers review daily, weekly, or monthly. These measurements should be related to the standards set in the first step of the control process. For example, if sales growth is a target, the organization should have a means of gathering and reporting sales data. If the organization has identified appropriate measurements, regular review of these reports helps managers stay aware of whether the organization is doing what it should or not. FreshDirect has a warehouse on Long Island where workers are responsible for butchering, baking, and food preparation. Warehouse managers analyze numerous reports that track plant operations, including inventory levels, quality assurance, and freshness. Managers also monitor real-time data that show the popularity of certain products in specific delivery zones and time slots.[9]

Compare Performance to Standards

ARE WE GETTING WHAT WE WANT?

The third step in the control process is comparing actual activities to performance standards. When managers read computer reports or walk through the plant, they identify whether actual performance meets, exceeds, or falls short of standards. Typically,

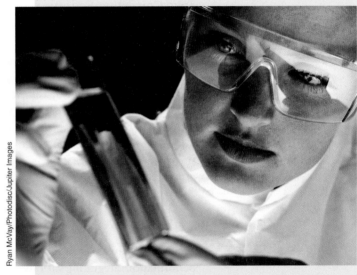

▶▶▶ **Concept Connection**

When it comes to pharmaceutical drugs, accuracy is essential—human lives are at stake. Researchers like this one follow precise procedures to ensure that test results are both objective and accurate and that the testing processes meet research objectives. Pharmaceutical firms establish **standards of performance** to measure research activities and results. For example, many companies set a standard for how many compounds should move forward at each stage of the drug development process.

Ryan McVay/Photodisc/Jupiter Images

6

CONTROLLING

performance reports simplify such comparisons by placing the performance standards for the reporting period alongside the actual performance for the same period and by computing the variance—that is, the difference between each actual amount and the associated standard. To correct the problems that most require attention, managers focus on variances.

When performance deviates from a standard, managers must interpret the deviation. They are expected to dig beneath the surface and find the cause of the problem. Assume that FreshDirect established a goal of increasing seafood sales by 10 percent during the month of July, but sales increased by only 8 percent. Managers must investigate the reasons behind the shortfall. They may discover that recent price increases for shrimp and three late shipments of salmon from Canada caused weaker sales during July, for instance. Managers should take an inquiring approach to deviations to gain a broad understanding of factors that influence performance. Effective management control involves subjective judgment and employee discussions, as well as objective analysis of performance data.

Take Corrective Action

Managers also determine what changes, if any, are needed. In 2008, FreshDirect was falling short of its revenue and cash goals, and customers were complaining about sold-out items, limited delivery options, and mistakes in orders. Sales were suffering, and 85 percent of customers placed only one or two orders before giving up on the company. The CEO chose to take corrective action by remaking the company with a focus on customer service. He dropped the company's obsession with luring in new customers with coupons and began focusing on building loyal customers. He upgraded the company's Web site and developed a database to profile customers and provide a customized online experience. Now, the Web site can analyze order patterns, remind customers of their favorite products, and suggest other items they might like.[10]

THE BALANCED SCORECARD

A current approach to organizational control is to take a balanced perspective of company performance, integrating various dimensions of control that focus on markets and customers, as well as employees and financials.[11] Managers recognize that relying exclusively on financial measures can result in short-term, dysfunctional behavior. Nonfinancial measures provide a healthy supplement to the traditional financial measures, and companies are investing significant sums in developing more balanced measurement systems as a result.[12] The **balanced scorecard** is a comprehensive management control system that balances traditional financial measures with operational measures relating to a company's critical success factors.[13]

A balanced scorecard contains four major perspectives, as illustrated in Exhibit 19.2: financial performance, customer service, internal business processes, and the organization's capacity for learning and growth.[14] Within these four areas, managers identify key performance metrics the organization will track.

- **Financial performance.** The *financial performance* perspective reflects a concern that the organization's activities contribute to improving short- and long-term financial performance. It includes traditional measures such as net income and return on investment.

- **Customer service.** *Customer service* indicators measure information such as how customers view the organization and customer retention and satisfaction. This data may be collected in many forms, including testimonials from customers describing superlative service or from customer surveys that explore important product or service attributes.[15]

EXHIBIT 19.2   The Balanced Scorecard

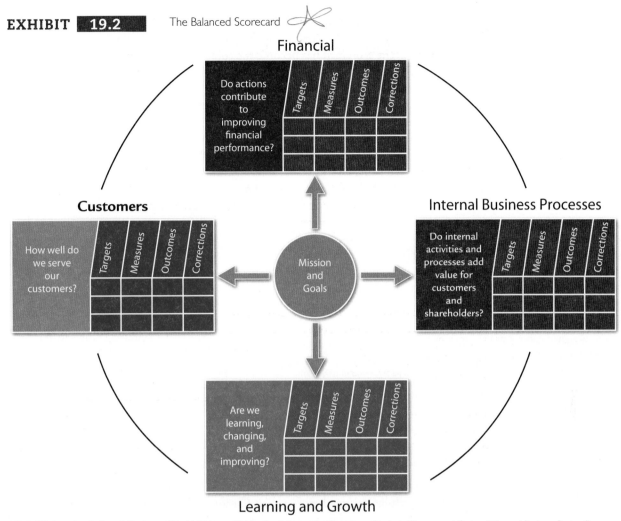

SOURCES: Based on Robert S. Kaplan and David P. Norton, "Using the Balanced Scorecard as a Strategic Management System," *Harvard Business Review* (January–February 1996): 75–85; and Chee W. Chow, Kamal M. Haddad, and James E. Williamson, "Applying the Balanced Scorecard to Small Companies," *Management Accounting* 79, no. 2 (August 1997): 21–27.

- **Internal business processes.** *Business process* indicators focus on production and operating statistics. For an airline, business process indicators may include on-time arrivals and adherence to safety guidelines. A recent event at Washington, D.C.'s Reagan National Airport reflected weak adherence to safety standards. When a lone air traffic controller at Reagan National Airport fell asleep while on duty and failed to respond to repeated radio transmissions, two pilots waiting to land jets carrying a total of 160 people decided to land without clearance, violating Federal Aviation Administration (FAA) safety regulations and damaging the reputations of both airlines involved, as well as the airport.[16]

- **Potential for learning and growth.** The final component of the balanced scorecard looks at the organization's *potential for learning and growth*, focusing on how well resources and human capital are being managed for the company's future. Metrics may include things such as employee retention and the introduction of new products. The components of the scorecard are designed in an integrative manner, as illustrated in Exhibit 19.2.

Managers record, analyze, and discuss these various metrics to determine how well the organization is achieving its strategic goals. The balanced scorecard is an effective tool for managing and improving performance, but only if it is clearly linked to a well-defined

6

CONTROLLING

organizational strategy and goals.[17] At its best, use of the scorecard cascades down from the top levels of the organization so that everyone becomes involved in thinking about and discussing strategy. The scorecard has become the core management control system for many organizations, including well-known organizations such as Bell Emergis (a division of Bell Canada), Exxon Mobil Corp., CIGNA (insurance), Hilton Hotels, and even some units of the U.S. federal government.[18] As with all management systems, the balanced scorecard is not right for every organization in every situation. The simplicity of the system causes some managers to underestimate the time and commitment that is needed for the approach to become a truly useful management control system. If managers implement the balanced scorecard using a *performance measurement* orientation rather than a *performance management* approach that links targets and measurements to corporate strategy, use of the scorecard can actually hinder or even decrease organizational performance.[19]

Remember This

- The feedback control model involves using feedback to determine whether performance meets established standards.
- Well-designed control systems include four key steps: establish standards, measure performance, compare performance to standards, and make corrections as necessary.

- A **balanced scorecard** is a comprehensive management control system that balances traditional financial measures with measures of customer service, internal business processes, and the organization's capacity for learning and growth.

Budgetary Control

Debbie Dusenberry was following her dream as a successful entrepreneur. She had opened a beautifully designed store called Curious Sofa and filled its expansive showroom with antiques, offbeat furniture, accessories, and gifts. She had a dedicated staff and sales reaching $800,000 per year. She had borrowed a lot of money and was planning to expand her inventory. Business was growing fast. But Dusenberry was typical of many small business owners who are long on drive and passion but short on financial experience. Caught up in the excitement of growing sales, she was unaware that excessive costs in staffing, inventory, and freight were hurting her profitability. She was operating without a budget and not keeping track of all her expenses. When sales dropped during the economic recession, the glaring weaknesses in her financial system were exposed. Scared and exasperated, Dusenberry began thinking about how she could save her business and realized she needed a new system that would help her monitor and manage her costs. Her first step was to create a budget.[20]

Budgetary control, one of the most commonly used methods of managerial control, is the process of setting targets for an organization's expenditures, monitoring results and comparing them to the budget, and making changes as needed. As a control device, budgets are reports that list planned and actual expenditures for cash, assets, raw materials, salaries, and other resources. In addition, budget reports usually list the variance between the budgeted and actual amounts for each item.

A budget is created for every division or department within an organization, no matter how small, as long as it performs a distinct project, program, or function. The fundamental unit of analysis for a budget control system is called a responsibility center. A **responsibility center** is defined as any organizational department or unit under the supervision of a single person who is responsible for its activity.[21] A three-person appliance sales office in Watertown, New York, is a responsibility center, as is a quality control department, a marketing department, and an entire refrigerator

Take a Moment

Go to the Experiential Exercise on page 654 that pertains to budgetary control.

manufacturing plant. The manager of each unit has budget responsibility. Top managers use budgets for the company as a whole, and middle managers traditionally focus on the budget performance of their department or division. Budgets that managers typically use include expense budgets, revenue budgets, cash budgets, and capital budgets.

EXPENSE BUDGET

An **expense budget** includes anticipated and actual expenses for each responsibility center and for the total organization. An expense budget may show all types of expenses, or it may focus on a particular category, such as materials or research and development expenses. When actual expenses exceed budgeted amounts, the difference signals the need for managers to identify possible problems and take corrective action if needed. The difference may arise from inefficiency, or expenses may be higher because the organization's sales are growing faster than anticipated. Conversely, expenses below budget may signal exceptional efficiency or possibly the failure to meet some other standards, such as a desired level of sales or quality of service. Either way, expense budgets help identify the need for further investigation but do not substitute for it.

REVENUE BUDGET

A **revenue budget** lists forecasted and actual revenues of the organization. In general, revenues below the budgeted amount signal a need to investigate the problem to see whether the organization can improve revenues. In contrast, revenues above budget would require determining whether the organization can obtain the necessary resources to meet the higher-than-expected demand for its products or services. Managers then formulate action plans to correct the budget variance.

CASH BUDGET

The **cash budget** estimates receipts and expenditures of money on a daily or weekly basis to ensure that an organization has sufficient cash to meet its obligations. The cash budget shows the level of funds flowing through the organization and the nature of cash disbursements. If the cash budget shows that the firm has more cash than necessary to meet short-term needs, the company can arrange to invest the excess to earn interest income. In contrast, if the cash budget shows a payroll expenditure of $20,000 coming at the end of the week but only $10,000 in the bank, the organization must borrow cash to meet the payroll.

CAPITAL BUDGET

The **capital budget** lists planned investments in major assets such as buildings, heavy machinery, or complex information technology systems, often involving expenditures over more than a year. Capital expenditures not only have a large impact on future expenses, but they also are investments designed to enhance profits. Therefore, a capital budget is necessary to plan the impact of these expenditures on cash flow and profitability. Controlling involves not only monitoring the amount of capital expenditures, but also evaluating whether the assumptions made about the return on the investments are holding true. Managers can evaluate whether continuing investment in particular projects is advisable, as well as whether their procedures for making capital expenditure decisions are adequate. Some companies, including Boeing, Merck, Shell, United Technologies, and Whirlpool, evaluate capital projects at several stages to determine whether they are still in line with the company's strategy.[22]

6

CONTROLLING

EXAMINE EACH EXPENSE EVERY YEAR.

ZERO-BASED BUDGET

Zero-based budgeting is an approach to planning and decision making that requires a complete justification for every line item in a budget, instead of carrying forward a prior budget and applying a percentage change. A zero-based budget begins with a starting point of $0, and every dollar added to the budget is reflected by an actual, documented need.[23] Shell, the oil and gas industry giant, implemented a zero-based budget to drive significant financial performance improvements. Facing unpredictable oil and gas demand and an uncertain global economy, CFO Gerard Paulides believed that a cost reduction strategy was as important to Shell's business as oil and gas production and hydrocarbon maturation. "We dove in deeply, stripping all business areas down to zero and then going back through the exercise of building them back up." Paulides and other executives looked at the minimum resources required to run each part of the business, which Paulides referred to as the *must-haves*. "All other activities are essentially discretionary and optional, or in the zero-based framework, *nice to have*," said Paulides.[24] This approach to budgeting helped Shell shave excessive and unnecessary costs from its yearly expenditures.

V.P. TELLS MIDDLE MGMT TO DETERMINE / EST. BUDGET

Budgeting is an important part of organizational planning and control. Many traditional companies use **top-down budgeting**, which means that the budgeted amounts for the coming year are literally imposed on middle- and lower-level managers.[25] These managers set departmental budget targets in accordance with overall company revenues and expenditures specified by top executives. Although the top-down process provides some advantages, the movement toward employee empowerment, participation, and learning means that many organizations are adopting **bottom-up budgeting**, a process in which lower-level managers anticipate their departments' resource needs and pass them up to top management for approval.[26] Companies of all kinds are increasingly involving line managers in the budgeting process. At the San Diego Zoo, scientists, animal keepers, and other line managers use software and templates to plan their department's budget needs because, as CFO Paula Brock says, "Nobody knows that side of the business better than they do."[27] Each of the 145 zoo departments also does a monthly budget close and reforecast so that resources can be redirected as needed to achieve goals within budget constraints. Thanks to the bottom-up process, for example, the zoo was able to redirect resources quickly to protect its valuable exotic bird collection from an outbreak of a highly infectious bird disease without significantly damaging the rest of the organization's budget.[28]

Remember This

- Budgetary control, one of the most commonly used forms of managerial control, is the process of setting targets for an organization's expenditures, monitoring results and comparing them to the budget, and making changes as needed.
- A **responsibility center** is any organizational department or unit under the supervision of a single person who is responsible for its activity.
- An **expense budget** outlines the anticipated and actual expenses for a responsibility center.
- A **revenue budget** lists forecasted and actual revenues of the organization.
- The **cash budget** estimates receipts and expenditures of money on a daily or weekly basis to ensure that an organization has sufficient cash to meet its obligations.

- A budget that plans and reports investments in major assets to be depreciated over several years is called a **capital budget**.
- **Zero-based budgeting** is an approach to planning and decision making that requires a complete justification for every line item in a budget, instead of carrying forward a prior budget and applying a percentage change.
- Many companies use **top-down budgeting**, which means that the budgeted amounts for the coming year are literally imposed on middle- and lower-level managers.
- On the other hand, **bottom-up budgeting** involves lower-level managers anticipating their department's budget needs and passing them up to top management for approval.

Financial Control

"Numbers run companies," claims Norm Brodsky, a veteran entrepreneur and writer for *Inc.* magazine.[29] In every organization, managers need to watch how well the organization is performing financially by watching the numbers. Not only do the numbers tell whether the organization is on sound financial footing, but they also can be useful indicators of other kinds of performance problems. For example, a sales decline may signal problems with products, customer service, or sales force effectiveness.

FINANCIAL STATEMENTS

Financial statements provide the basic information used for financial control of an organization. Two major financial statements—the balance sheet and the income statement—are the starting points for financial control.

Think of the balance sheet as a thermometer that provides a reading on the health of the business at the moment you take its temperature.[30] The **balance sheet** shows the firm's financial position with respect to assets and liabilities at a specific point in time. An example of a balance sheet is presented in Exhibit 19.3. The balance sheet provides three types of information: assets, liabilities, and owners' equity. *Assets* are what the company owns, and they include *current assets* (those that can be converted into cash in a short time period) and *fixed assets* (such as buildings and equipment that are long term in nature). *Liabilities* are the firm's debts, including both *current debt* (obligations that will be paid by the company in the near future) and *long-term debt* (obligations payable over a long period). *Owners' equity* is the difference between assets and liabilities and is the company's net worth in stock and retained earnings.

The **income statement**, sometimes called a *profit-and-loss statement* or *P&L* for short, summarizes the firm's financial performance for a given time interval, usually one year. A sample income statement is shown in Exhibit 19.4. Some organizations calculate the income statement at three-month intervals during the year to see whether they are on target for sales and profits. The income statement shows revenues coming into the organization from all sources and subtracts all expenses, including cost of goods sold, interest, taxes, and depreciation. The *bottom line* indicates the net income—profit or loss—for the given time period.

EXHIBIT 19.3   Balance Sheet   *(ASSETS)*   *HOW MUCH $ you HAVE; HOW much you OWE*

New Creations Landscaping
Consolidated Balance Sheet
December 31, 2015

Assets			Liabilities and Owners' Equity		
Current assets:			Current liabilities:		
Cash	$ 25,000		Accounts payable	$200,000	
Accounts receivable	75,000		Accrued expenses	20,000	
Inventory	500,000		Income taxes payable	30,000	
Total current assets		$ 600,000	Total current liabilities		$ 250,000
Fixed assets:			Long-term liabilities:		
Land	250,000		Mortgages payable	350,000	
Buildings and fixtures	1,000,000		Bonds outstanding	250,000	
			Total long-term liabilities		$ 600,000
Less depreciation	200,000		Owners' equity:		
Total fixed assets		$1,050,000	Common stock	540,000	
			Retained earnings	260,000	
			Total owners' equity		$ 800,000
Total assets		$1,650,000	Total liabilities and net worth		$1,650,000

6

CONTROLLING

EXHIBIT 19.4

Income Statement

HOW MUCH $ YOU BRING IN AND AFTER EXPENSES

New Creations Landscaping Income Statement For the Year Ended December 31, 2015		
Gross sales	$3,100,000	
Less sales returns	200,000	
Net sales		$2,900,000
Less expenses and cost of goods sold:		
Cost of goods sold	2,110,000	
Depreciation	60,000	
Sales expenses	200,000	
Administrative expenses	90,000	2,460,000
Operating profit		$ 440,000
Other income		$ 20,000
Gross income		$ 460,000
Less interest expense	80,000	
Income before taxes		380,000
Less taxes	165,000	
Net income		$ 215,000

(ABOUT 8% ROI)

During the economic recession, companies cut discretionary spending, such as travel expenses, to improve the bottom line, and managers are pushing to keep those expenses from creeping back up. If managers keep costs low where they can, they can spend scarce dollars on higher-priority areas, such as salary increases for staff or research and development. To avoid a cost creep in travel expenses, Deloitte reminds employees of company travel policies when managers see costs rising. Employees are discouraged from traveling to meetings that are expected to last less than eight hours and to use video and Web conferencing whenever possible as an alternative to travel.[31]

The following example describes how one successful franchise owner uses a financial control system to manage one of the most profitable 7-Eleven stores in Manhattan.

Innovative Way

7-Eleven

Norman Jemal, an enthusiastic and gregarious 7-Eleven franchise owner in Manhattan, loves crunching the numbers with field consultant Kunta Natapraya. Together, they study the sales data and profit margins for the thousands of snack foods that Jemal sells in his three profitable stores. Some claim that Jemal's success is due to the location of his stores on busy Manhattan streets. High vehicle and pedestrian traffic produce lots of potential customers. But Jemal's success also comes from his knack for analyzing financial data to spot the most profitable products in his inventory and maximizing profits through efficient ordering.

When faced with reordering decisions, Jemal uses 7-Eleven's proprietary Retail Information System (RIS), which helps him analyze sales and profitability data for each product in his inventory. For example, when corporate 7-Eleven announced it was rolling out a sugar-free Slurpee Lite and an empanada, Jemal needed to make room for both by eliminating an existing product. Using RIS, he studied the profitability of each snack product and discovered that the spicy beef patty was lagging in sales and profitability, so he slashed it from the stores' inventory to make room for the new products.

7-Eleven focuses on its core competence of figuring out what to sell to rushed customers and how to sell it to them. "Other franchises pitch their name," Jemal says. "7-Eleven, which I think has a great name, pitched their [RIS] system." That system is part of a carefully designed financial control model that also includes regular audits. A good audit performance will go a long way toward determining if 7-Eleven allows Jemal to open more stores. He says he'd like to open 20 more.[32]

FINANCIAL ANALYSIS: INTERPRETING THE NUMBERS

A manager needs to be able to evaluate financial reports that compare the organization's performance with earlier data or industry norms. These comparisons enable the manager

Liquidity Ratios		EXHIBIT **19.5**
Current ratio	Current assets/Current liabilities	
Quick ratio	Cash + accounts receivable/Current liabilities	Common Financial Ratios
Activity Ratios		
Inventory turnover	Total sales/Average inventory	
Conversion ratio	Purchase orders/Customer inquiries	
Profitability Ratios		
Profit margin on sales	Net income/Sales	
Gross margin	Gross income/Sales	
Return on assets (ROA)	Net income/Total assets	
Leverage Ratios		
Debt ratio	Total debt/Total assets	

to see whether the organization is improving and whether it is competitive with others in the industry. The most common financial analysis focuses on ratios, statistics that express the relationships between performance indicators such as profits and assets, sales, and inventory. Ratios are stated as a fraction or proportion; Exhibit 19.5 summarizes some financial ratios, which are measures of an organization's liquidity, activity, profitability, and leverage. These ratios are among the most common, but many measures are used. Managers decide which ratios reveal the most important relationships for their business.

Liquidity Ratios

The **liquidity ratio** indicates an organization's ability to meet its current debt obligations. For example, the *current ratio* (current assets divided by current liabilities) tells whether the company has sufficient assets to convert into cash to pay off its debts, if needed. If a hypothetical company, Oceanographics, Inc., has current assets of $600,000 and current liabilities of $250,000, the current ratio is 2.4, meaning it has sufficient funds to pay off immediate debts 2.4 times. This level for the current ratio is normally considered a satisfactory margin of safety. Another liquidity ratio is the *quick ratio*, which is typically expressed as cash plus accounts receivable divided by current liabilities. The quick ratio is a popular metric to pair with the current ratio to gauge liquidity. "If a business does not have decent liquidity, then one unexpected expense could severely hurt it," said Brad Schaefer, an analyst with Sageworks Inc., a financial information company.[33]

Activity Ratios

The **activity ratio** measures internal performance with respect to key activities defined by management. For example, *inventory turnover* is calculated by dividing total sales by average inventory. This ratio tells how many times the inventory is used up to meet the total sales figure. If inventory sits too long, money is wasted. Dell Inc. achieved a strategic advantage by minimizing its inventory costs. Dividing Dell's annual sales by its small inventory generates an inventory turnover rate of 35.7.[34]

Another type of activity ratio, the *conversion ratio*, is purchase orders divided by customer inquiries. This ratio is an indicator of a company's effectiveness in converting inquiries into sales. For example, if Cisco Systems moves from a 26.5 to a 28.2 percent conversion ratio, more of its inquiries are turned into sales, indicating better sales activity.

Profitability Ratios

Managers analyze a company's profits by studying **profitability ratios**, which state profits relative to a source of profits, such as sales or assets. When Alan Mulally became CEO of Ford Motor Company in 2008, he emphatically stressed the importance of profitability. At that time, Ford was a sick company, losing $83 million a day, and the stock price had plummeted to $1.01. Mulally initiated Ford's remarkable turnaround by fostering a new culture of accountability that emphasized the use of consistent metrics to gauge performance.

6

CONTROLLING

Concept Connection ◀◀◀

Can you imagine a world without milk? If milk's **profitability ratio** doesn't recover soon, dairy farmers may opt out of producing milk. Analysts say that milk is profitable only when its ratio is 3.0 or higher, but milk's ratio has been hovering around 2.0 in recent years. This is due to the high cost of feed for dairy cows, which is corn, and given that the drought of 2012 killed off a huge percentage of the corn crop, the price of corn is expected to remain high.

Mulally expected each department head to know and report how his or her department was performing. His emphasis on data-driven management permanently changed the culture at Ford. In 2010, Ford posted a profit of $6.6 billion, the most money the company had made in more than a decade.[35]

One important profitability ratio is the *profit margin on sales*, which is calculated as net income divided by sales. Similarly, *gross margin* is the gross (before-tax) profit divided by total sales. Another profitability measure is *return on assets (ROA)*, which is a percentage representing what a company earned from its assets, computed as net income divided by total assets. ROA is a valuable yardstick for comparing a company's ability to generate earnings with other investment opportunities. In basic terms, the company should be able to earn more by using its assets to operate the business than it could by putting the same investment in the bank.

Leverage Ratios

Leverage refers to funding activities with borrowed money. A company can use leverage to make its assets produce more than they could on their own. However, too much borrowing can put the organization at risk that it will be unable to keep up with repayment of its debt. Managers therefore track their *debt ratio*, or total debt divided by total assets, to make sure it does not exceed a level that they consider acceptable. Lenders may consider a company with a debt ratio above 1.0 to be a poor credit risk.

Remember This

- Financial statements provide the basic information used for financial control of an organization.
- The **balance sheet** shows the firm's financial position with respect to assets and liabilities at a specific point in time.
- The **income statement** summarizes the firm's financial performance for a given time interval.
- The most common financial analysis focuses on the use of ratios—statistics that express the relationships between

performance indicators such as profits and assets, sales, and inventory.
- The **liquidity ratio** indicates the organization's ability to meet its current debt obligations.
- The **activity ratio** measures the organization's internal performance with respect to key activities defined by management.
- The **profitability ratio** describes the firm's profits relative to a source of profits, such as sales or assets.

The Changing Philosophy of Control

Managers' approach to control is changing in many of today's organizations. In connection with the shift to employee participation and empowerment, many companies are adopting a *decentralized* rather than a *hierarchical* control process. Hierarchical control and decentralized control represent different philosophies of corporate culture, which was discussed in Chapter 3. Most organizations display some aspects of both hierarchical and decentralized control, but managers generally emphasize one or the other, depending on the organizational culture and their own beliefs about control.

(REGULATIONS) (CULTURE FUNDAMENTALS)

HIERARCHICAL VERSUS DECENTRALIZED APPROACHES

Hierarchical control involves monitoring and influencing employee behavior through extensive use of rules, policies, hierarchy of authority, written documentation, reward systems, and other formal mechanisms.[36] In contrast, decentralized control relies on cultural values, traditions, shared beliefs, and trust to foster compliance with organizational goals. Managers operate on the assumption that employees are trustworthy and willing to perform effectively without extensive rules and close supervision.

Exhibit 19.6 contrasts the use of hierarchical and decentralized methods of control. Hierarchical methods define explicit rules, policies, and procedures for employee behavior. Control relies on centralized authority, the formal hierarchy, and close personal supervision. Responsibility for quality control rests with quality control inspectors and supervisors rather than with employees. Job descriptions generally are specific and task related, and managers define minimal standards for acceptable employee performance. In exchange for meeting the standards, individual employees are given extrinsic rewards such as wages, benefits, and possibly promotions up the hierarchy. Employees rarely participate in the control process, with any participation being formalized through mechanisms such as grievance procedures. With hierarchical control, the organizational culture is somewhat rigid, and managers do not consider culture a useful means of controlling employees and the organization. Technology often is used to control the flow and pace of work or to monitor employees, such as by measuring the number of minutes employees spend on phone calls or how many keystrokes they make at the computer.

The hierarchical approach to control is strongly evident in many Japanese companies. Japanese culture reflects an obsession with rules and a penchant for bureaucracy that can excel at turning chaos to order. For example, after the devastating 2011 earthquake and tsunami, the Japanese efficiently organized evacuation centers for families who lost homes during the disaster. Self-governing committees managed these temporary shelters and laid out in painstaking detail the daily responsibilities of the residents. People were assigned specific tasks, including sorting the garbage, washing the bathrooms, and cleaning fresh-water tanks. "The Japanese people are the type to feel more reassured

EXHIBIT 19.6 — Hierarchical and Decentralized Methods of Control

	Hierarchical Control	Decentralized Control
Basic Assumptions	People are incapable of self-discipline and cannot be trusted. They need to be monitored and controlled closely.	People work best when they are fully committed to the organization.
Actions	Uses detailed rules and procedures; formal control systems. Uses top-down authority, formal hierarchy, position power, quality control inspectors. Relies on task-related job descriptions. Emphasizes extrinsic rewards (pay, benefits, status). Features rigid organizational culture; distrust of cultural norms as means of control.	Features limited use of rules; relies on values, group and self-control, selection, and socialization. Relies on flexible authority, flat structure, expert power; everyone monitors quality. Relies on results-based job descriptions; emphasizes goals to be achieved. Emphasizes extrinsic and intrinsic rewards (meaningful work, opportunities for growth). Features adaptive culture; culture recognized as means for uniting individual, team, and organizational goals for overall control.
Consequences	Employees follow instructions and do *just* what they are told. Employees feel a sense of indifference toward work. Employee absenteeism and turnover is high.	Employees take initiative and seek responsibility. Employees are actively engaged and committed to their work. Employee turnover is low.

SOURCES: Based on Naresh Khatri et al., "Medical Errors and Quality of Care: From Control to Commitment," *California Management Review* 48, no. 3 (Spring, 2006): 118; Richard E. Walton, "From Control to Commitment in the Workplace," *Harvard Business Review* (March–April 1985): 76–84; and Don Hellriegel, Susan E. Jackson, and John W. Slocum, Jr., *Management*, 8th ed. (Cincinnati, Ohio: South-Western, 1999), p. 663.

CONTROLLING

6

HOT TOPIC

the more rules are in place," said Shintara Goto, a tsunami survivor. This hierarchical method of managing the temporary evacuation centers helped survivors find routine and responsibility, which could play a big role in reducing the long-term psychological and physical toll of this natural disaster.[37]

Decentralized control is based on values and assumptions that are almost opposite to those of hierarchical control. Rules and procedures are used only when necessary. Managers rely instead on shared goals and values to control employee behavior. The organization places great emphasis on the selection and socialization of employees to ensure that workers have the appropriate values needed to influence behavior toward meeting company goals. No organization can control employees 100 percent of the time, and self-discipline and self-control are what keep workers performing their jobs up to standard. Empowerment of employees, effective socialization, and training all can contribute to internal standards that provide self-control.

With decentralized control, power is more dispersed and is based on knowledge and experience as much as position. The organizational structure is flat and horizontal, as discussed in Chapter 10, with flexible authority and teams of workers solving problems and making improvements. Everyone is involved in quality control on an ongoing basis. Job descriptions generally are results-based, with an emphasis more on the outcomes to be achieved than on the specific tasks to be performed. Managers use not only extrinsic rewards such as pay, but the intrinsic rewards of meaningful work and the opportunity to learn and grow. Technology is used to empower employees by giving them the information they need to make effective decisions, work together, and solve problems. People are rewarded for team and organizational success as well as their individual performance, and the emphasis is on equity among employees. Employees participate in a wide range of areas, including setting goals, determining standards of performance, governing quality, and designing control systems.

With decentralized control, the culture is adaptive, and managers recognize the importance of organizational culture for uniting individual, team, and organizational goals for greater overall control. Ideally, with decentralized control, employees will pool their areas of expertise to arrive at procedures that are better than managers could come up with working alone. Campbell Soup is using decentralized control by enlisting its workers to help squeeze efficiency out of its plants.

Innovative Way

Campbell Soup Company

Campbell Soup Company, which controls 60 percent of the U.S. soup market, is piling up profits by implementing cost-saving ideas suggested by its employees. At the plant in Maxton, North Carolina, factory workers huddle every morning with managers to find ways to save the company money. These employees, who live in an area with an 11.1 percent jobless rate, are part of a decentralized culture where both managers and workers share the company's goals and collaborate on ways to improve efficiency. The daily worker-manager huddles are about "getting everybody involved," says "Big John" Filmore, a 28-year plant veteran. "Instead of being told what to do, we get to tell people about our problems," he said.

When challenged to find efficiency in the new Swanson broth line, which processes 260 million pounds of raw ingredients per year, operators and mechanics devised a numbering system for each gasket to speed repairs of the processing equipment. They cut windows into the metal covers over conveyor belts so they could identify signs of wear. They color-coded valve handles to avoid confusion in settings. With employee-driven changes like these, Campbell says operating efficiency at the Maxton plant has climbed to 85 percent of what its managers say is the maximum possible, up from 75 percent three years ago. That pays off, as a 1 percent gain in plant efficiency adds $3 million to operating profits.

Campbell's latest challenge is reinventing how the company makes soup. In the past, each soup had its own recipe. Now many soups will share a common base, such as chicken broth, and will be adapted by adding different types of meats and vegetables. Employees at all levels of the organization will help plan and implement the new processes. "We have to collaborate at the highest levels of the organization right down to the plant floor," says Dave Biegger, Campbell's vice-president for North America supply chain.[38]

OPEN-BOOK MANAGEMENT

One important aspect of decentralized control in many organizations is open-book management. An organization that promotes information sharing and teamwork admits employees throughout the organization into the loop of financial control and responsibility to encourage active participation and commitment to goals. **Open-book management** allows employees to see for themselves—through charts, computer printouts, meetings, and so forth—the financial condition of the company. Second, open-book management shows the individual employee how his or her job fits into the big picture and affects the financial future of the organization. Finally, open-book management ties employee rewards to the company's overall success. With training in interpreting the financial data, employees can see the interdependence and importance of each function. If they are rewarded according to performance, they become motivated to take responsibility for their entire team or function, rather than merely their individual jobs.[39]

The goal of open-book management is to get every employee thinking and acting like a business owner. To get employees to think like owners, management provides them with the same information owners have: what money is coming in and where it is going. Open-book management helps employees appreciate why efficiency is important to the organization's success as well as their own. Laura Ortmann, who owns Ginger Bay Salon and Spa with her husband, discovered that her hairstylists and massage therapists became more motivated to reach their own performance goals once she trained them to understand the company's financial goals. Individual and company goals were recorded prominently on a scoreboard in the break room and listed each employee's daily sales results and whether

Country	2009 Opacity Score	2008 Opacity Score
Nigeria	55	57
Venezuela	48	48
Saudi Arabia	45	47
China	42	45
India	41	44
Indonesia	40	41
Russia	40	41
Mexico	37	37
Taiwan	32	34
South Korea	29	31
South Africa	24	26
Japan	25	25
United States	22	23
Canada	20	22
Germany	17	17
Ireland	15	16
Singapore	14	14
Hong Kong	12	12
Finland	9	9

EXHIBIT 19.7

International Opacity Index: Which Countries Have the Most Secretive Economies?

OPAQUE

The higher the opacity score, the more secretive the national economy, meaning that prevailing attitudes and standards discourage openness regarding financial results and other data.

SOURCE: Joel Kurtzman and Glenn Yago, "Opacity Index, 2009: Measuring Global Risks," published by Milken Institute (April 2009), www.kurtzmangroup.com/pdf/InstituteOpacityIndex_Apr8.pdf (accessed October 4, 2012).

goals were met. "Behavior changed overnight," said Ortmann. "No one wants their name next to a low number." By helping her employees see how their efforts affected the financial success of the company, Ortmann increased their motivation. "I love the numbers, and I love knowing how I'm doing," says nail technician Terri Kavanaugh.[40]

Managers in some countries have more trouble running an open-book company because prevailing attitudes and standards encourage confidentiality and even secrecy concerning financial results. Many businesspeople in countries such as China, Russia, and India, for example, are not accustomed to disclosing financial details publicly, which can present problems for multinational companies operating there.[41] Exhibit 19.7 lists a portion of a recent Opacity Index, which offers some indication of the degree to which various countries are open regarding economic matters. The higher the rating, the more opaque, or hidden, the economy of that country. In the partial index in Exhibit 19.7, Nigeria has the highest opacity rating at 57, and Finland the lowest at 9. The United States has an opacity rating of 23. In countries with higher ratings, financial figures are typically closely guarded, and managers may be discouraged from sharing information with employees and the public. Globalization is beginning to have an impact on economic opacity in various countries by encouraging a convergence toward global accounting standards that support more accurate collection, recording, and reporting of financial information. Thus, most countries have improved their ratings over the past few years. Indonesia, Singapore, and Ireland all show significant decreases in opacity since the 2005–2006 ratings, for example.

Remember This

- The philosophy of control has shifted to reflect changes in leadership methods.
- **Hierarchical control** involves monitoring and influencing employee behavior through extensive use of rules, policies, hierarchy of authority, written documentation, reward systems, and other formal mechanisms.
- With **decentralized control**, the organization fosters compliance with organizational goals through the use of organizational culture, group norms, and a focus on goals rather than rules and procedures.
- Campbell Soup uses decentralized control at its plant in Maxton, North Carolina, to encourage employees to cut costs and increase efficiency.
- **Open-book management** allows employees to see for themselves the financial condition of the organization and encourages them to think and act like business owners.

Total Quality Management

Another popular approach based on a decentralized control philosophy is **total quality management (TQM)**, an organizationwide effort to infuse quality into every activity in a company through continuous improvement. Managing quality is a concern for every organization. Ford, for example, vows that its new compact and subcompact vehicles will have substantially fewer problems during their first three months on the road than models from other automakers. According to Vice President of Global Quality Bennie Fowler, Ford will keep the number of quality problems (called "things gone wrong") at 800 problems per 1,000 vehicles, well below the industry average of around 1,500 problems per 1,000 vehicles. Problems include a range of customer complaints, from things customers just don't like to product features that fail or don't work properly. The company is working hard to regain customer confidence after lagging behind foreign competitors such as Toyota and Honda.[42] It hopes that an emphasis on TQM will recapture confidence by U.S. consumers.

TQM became attractive to U.S. managers in the 1980s because it had been implemented successfully by Japanese companies, such as Toyota, Canon, and Honda, which were gaining market share and an international reputation for high quality. The Japanese system was based on the work of such U.S. researchers and consultants as W. Edwards Deming, Joseph Juran, and Armand Feigenbaum, whose ideas attracted U.S. executives after the methods were tested overseas.[43] The TQM philosophy focuses on teamwork, increasing customer satisfaction, and lowering costs. Organizations implement TQM by encouraging managers and employees to collaborate across functions and departments, as well as with customers and suppliers, to identify areas for improvement, no matter how small. Each quality improvement is a step toward perfection and meeting a goal of zero defects. Quality control becomes part of the day-to-day business of every employee, rather than being assigned to specialized departments.

TQM Techniques

The implementation of TQM involves the use of many techniques, including quality circles, benchmarking, Six Sigma principles, quality partnering, and continuous improvement.

Quality Circles   *How do we improve quality?*

A **quality circle** is a group of 6 to 12 volunteer employees who meet regularly to discuss and solve problems affecting the quality of their work.[44] At a set time during the workweek, the members of the quality circle meet, identify problems, and try to find solutions. Circle members are free to collect data and take surveys. Many companies train people in team building, problem solving, and statistical quality control. The reason for using quality circles is to push decision making to an organization level at which recommendations can be made by the people who do the job and know it better than anyone else.

Benchmarking

Introduced by Xerox in 1979, benchmarking is now a major TQM component. **Benchmarking** is defined as "the continuous process of measuring products, services, and practices against the toughest competitors or those companies recognized as industry leaders to identify areas for improvement."[45] Organizations may also use benchmarking for generating new business ideas, assessing market demand, or identifying best practices within an industry. A five-step benchmarking process is shown in Exhibit 19.8.[46]

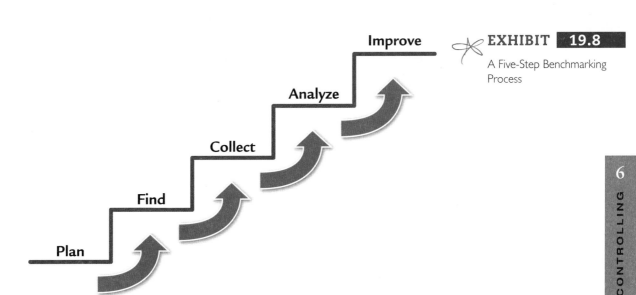

EXHIBIT 19.8

A Five-Step Benchmarking Process

SOURCE: Based on Deven Shah and Brian H. Kleiner, "Benchmarking for Quality," *Industrial Management* (March-April 2011): 22–25.

6

CONTROLLING

"*Quality is the result of a carefully constructed cultural environment. It has to be the fabric of the organization, not part of the fabric.*"

— PHILIP CROSBY (1926–2001), AMERICAN BUSINESSMAN AND QUALITY GURU

The first step involves planning the benchmarking study, which includes identifying the objectives of the study and the characteristics of a product or service that significantly influence customer satisfaction. The second step involves identifying the source of the information to be collected. For example, the sources of data for a Sherwin-Williams benchmarking study may include national independent lab studies or studies published in *Consumer Reports* magazine. Once the source of information is identified, data is then collected. Xerox collected information on the order fulfillment techniques of L. L. Bean, the Freeport, Maine, mail-order firm, and learned ways to reduce warehouse costs by 10 percent. The fourth step includes analyzing the benchmarking data that has been collected and recommending areas of improvement. The fifth step includes implementing recommendations and then monitoring them through continuous benchmarking.

Six Sigma IN PURSUIT OF EXCELLENCE

Six Sigma quality principles were first introduced by Motorola in the 1980s and were later popularized by General Electric (GE), where former CEO Jack Welch praised Six Sigma for quality and efficiency gains that saved the company billions of dollars. Based on the Greek letter *sigma*, which statisticians use to measure how far something deviates from perfection, **Six Sigma** is a highly ambitious quality standard that specifies a goal of no more than 3.4 defects per million parts. That essentially means being defect-free 99.9997 percent of the time.[47] However, Six Sigma has deviated from its precise definition to become a generic term for a quality-control approach that takes nothing for granted and emphasizes a disciplined and relentless pursuit of higher quality and lower costs. The discipline is based on a five-step methodology referred to as *DMAIC*, pronounced "deMay-ick" (standing for Define, Measure, Analyze, Improve, and Control), which provides a structured way for organizations to approach and solve problems.[48]

Effectively implementing Six Sigma requires a major commitment from top management because Six Sigma involves widespread change throughout the organization. At Honeywell, for example, all employees are expected to understand Six Sigma fundamentals. Six Sigma provides a common language among employees, complements efforts to remove fat from the organization, and supports efforts to "get it right the first time."

Green Power

The Honeybee Style

The honeybee is known for its hard work and wise use of natural resources, as well as for living in a cooperative, interconnected community. Likewise, Munich-based **BMW** recognizes that true sustainability involves the protection and wise use of not only the environment, but of every resource used to provide quality vehicles for consumers. Dating back to the 1970s, BMW's approach to sustainable growth can be seen throughout its well-controlled production process. Self-managed teams oversee rigorous quality control measurement of sustainability, building for BMW an A+ international sustainability rating. A total of 23 interconnected "honeybee" practices address everything from ethical behavior and social responsibility to quality and innovation. The results include the recycling of production waste and the reuse of scrap from BMW's new carbon-fiber car bodies.

Source: Gayle C. Avery and Harald Bergsteiner, "How BMW Successfully Practices Sustainable Leadership Principles," *Strategy & Leadership* 39, no. 6 (2011): 11–18.

99 Percent Amounts to:	Six Sigma Amounts to:
117,000 pieces of lost first-class mail per hour	1 piece of lost first-class mail every two hours
800,000 mishandled personal checks each day	3 mishandled checks each day
23,087 defective computers shipped each month	8 defective computers shipped each month
7.2 hours per month without electricity	9 seconds per month without electricity

EXHIBIT 19.9

The Importance of Quality Improvement Programs

SOURCE: Based on data from *Statistical Abstract of the United States*, U.S. Postal Service, as reported in Tracy Mayor, "Six Sigma Comes to IT: Targeting Perfection," *CIO* (December 1, 2003): 62–70.

Honeywell explains its dedication to Six Sigma and what it means to reach this high level of performance with these examples:

- If your water heater operated at Four Sigma (not Six), you would be without hot water for more than 54 hours each year. At Six Sigma, you would be without hot water for less than two minutes a year.
- If your cell phone operated at Four Sigma, you would be without service for more than four hours a month. At Six Sigma, it would be about nine seconds a month.
- A Four Sigma process will typically result in one defective package of product for every three truckloads shipped. A Six Sigma process means one defective package for every 5,350 truckloads.[49]

Exhibit 19.9 lists some additional statistics that illustrate why Six Sigma is important for both manufacturing and service organizations.

Quality Partnering

One of the drawbacks of a traditional quality control program is that people from the quality control department are often seen as "outsiders" to the business groups that they serve. Because they don't always have a strong knowledge of the processes that they are studying, their work may be viewed with suspicion or as an interruption to the normal work routine. The risk here is that quality control is seen as separate from everyday work. Another drawback of the traditional model is that quality control is usually conducted after a product is completed or a service delivered—the time when it's most expensive to make corrections.

A new approach called **quality partnering** involves assigning dedicated personnel within a particular functional area of the business. In this approach, the quality control personnel work alongside others within a functional area identifying opportunities for quality improvements throughout the work process. This integrated, partnering approach to quality makes it possible to detect and address defects early in the product life cycle, when they can be corrected most easily. Another advantage of this approach is that quality partners are viewed as "insiders" and peers who are readily accepted into the work group.[50]

Continuous Improvement

In North America, crash programs and designs traditionally have been the preferred method of innovation. Managers measure the expected benefits of a change and favor the ideas with the biggest payoffs. In contrast, Japanese companies have realized extraordinary success from making a series of mostly small improvements. This approach, called **continuous improvement**, or *kaizen*, is the implementation of a large number of small, incremental improvements in all areas of the organization on an ongoing basis. In a successful TQM program, all employees learn that they are expected to contribute by initiating changes in their own job activities. The basic philosophy is that improving things a little

Take a Moment

As a new manager, will you support TQM by taking personal responsibility for improving the tasks and activities that you work on? Complete the New Manager Self-Test on page 650 to get some feedback on your attitude toward continuous improvement.

New Manager Self-Test

Improvement Attitude

Instructions: Respond to each statement below based on how you think and act in a typical situation of work accomplishment at school or on the job. Mark whether each statement is Mostly True or Mostly False for you. There are no right or wrong answers, so answer honestly.

	Mostly True	Mostly False
1. I spend time developing new ways of approaching old problems.	_____	_____
2. So long as things are done correctly and efficiently, I prefer not to take on the hassle of changing them.	_____	_____
3. I believe the effort to improve something should be rewarded, even if the final outcome is disappointing.	_____	_____
4. A single change that improves things 30 percent is much better than 30 improvements of 1 percent each.	_____	_____
5. I frequently compliment other people on changes that they have made.	_____	_____
6. I let people know in a variety of ways that I like to be on my own to do my job efficiently.	_____	_____
7. I am typically involved in several improvement projects at one time.	_____	_____
8. I try to be a good listener and to be patient with what people say, except when it is a stupid idea.	_____	_____
9. I am frequently proposing unconventional techniques and ideas to improve things.	_____	_____
10. I usually do not take the risk of proposing an idea that might fail.	_____	_____

Scoring and Interpretation: Score one point for each Mostly True answer to the odd-numbered items and one point for each Mostly False answer to the even-numbered items. Total score _____

In organizations, continuous improvement in quality sometimes competes with managerial desires for production efficiency. Efficiency can be maximized by eliminating changes and quality improvements. Continuous improvement, however, is an attitude that productivity can always get better, and each employee can take responsibility to improve it. This attitude is appropriate for quality-conscious managers striving for continuous improvement. Introducing frequent small changes that may temporarily reduce efficiency is the best path to continuous improvement. A score of 7 or higher indicates that you may take personal responsibility for improving activities on which you work. A score of 3 or lower indicates that you may prefer stable and efficient work. A score of 4–6 suggests that you are balanced between efficiency and continuous improvement.

bit at a time, all the time, has the highest probability of success. Innovations can start simple, and employees can build on their success in this unending process.

TQM SUCCESS FACTORS

Despite its promise, TQM does not always work. A few firms have had disappointing results. In particular, Six Sigma principles might not be appropriate for all organizational

Positive Factors	Negative Factors
• Tasks make high skill demands on employees. • TQM serves to enrich jobs and motivate employees. • Problem-solving skills are improved for all employees. • Participation and teamwork are used to tackle significant problems. • Continuous improvement is a way of life.	• Management expectations are unrealistically high. • Middle managers are dissatisfied about loss of authority. • Workers are dissatisfied with other aspects of organizational life. • Union leaders are left out of quality-control discussions. • Managers wait for big, dramatic innovations.

EXHIBIT 19.10

Quality Program Success Factors

problems, and some companies have expended tremendous energy and resources for little payoff.[51] Many contingency factors (listed in Exhibit 19.10) can influence the success of a TQM program. For example, quality circles are most beneficial when employees have challenging jobs; participation in a quality circle can contribute to productivity because it enables employees to pool their knowledge and solve interesting problems. TQM also tends to be most successful when it enriches jobs and improves employee motivation. In addition, when participating in the TQM program improves workers' problem-solving skills, productivity is likely to increase. Finally, a TQM program has the greatest chance of success in a corporate culture that values quality and stresses continuous improvement.

Remember This

- **Total quality management (TQM)** is an organizationwide effort to infuse quality into every activity in a company through continuous improvement.
- The TQM philosophy focuses on teamwork, increasing customer satisfaction, and lowering costs.
- **Quality circles** offer one technique for implementing TQM and include a group of 6 to 12 volunteer employees who meet regularly to discuss and solve problems affecting the quality of their work.
- Another option for tracking quality is **benchmarking**, the continuous process of measuring products, services,

and practices against major competitors or industry leaders.
- **Six Sigma** is a quality control approach that emphasizes a relentless pursuit of higher quality and lower costs.
- **Quality partnering** involves assigning dedicated personnel within a particular functional area of the business to identify opportunities for improvement throughout the work process.
- **Continuous improvement**, or *kaizen*, is the implementation of a large number of small, incremental improvements in all areas of the organization on an ongoing basis.

Trends in Quality and Financial Control

Many companies are responding to changing economic realities and global competition by reassessing organizational management and processes—including control mechanisms. Two major trends are international quality standards and increased corporate governance.

INTERNATIONAL QUALITY STANDARDS

One impetus for TQM in the United States is the increasing significance of the global economy. Many countries have adopted a universal benchmark for quality management practices, **ISO 9000 standards**, which represent an international consensus of what constitutes effective quality management as outlined by the International Organization for Standardization (ISO).[52] Hundreds of thousands of organizations in 157 countries,

Concept Connection ◄◄◄

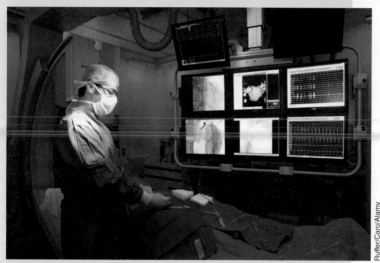

Ruffer/Caro/Alamy

In order to become **ISO 9000–certified**, companies have to work with an independent registrar that will audit the company's practices and procedures according to the certification guidelines. U.S.-based Heartlab, Inc., for example, worked with the International Organization for Standardization (ISO) in Geneva, Switzerland, to earn its certification. Heartlab makes medical information management systems that store data about heart patients.

including the United States, have been certified against ISO 9000 standards to demonstrate their commitment to quality. Europe continues to lead in the total number of certifications, but the greatest number of new certifications in recent years has been in the United States. One of the more interesting organizations to become ISO certified was the Phoenix, Arizona, police department's Records and Information Bureau. In today's environment, where the credibility of law enforcement agencies has been called into question, the bureau wanted to make a clear statement about its commitment to the high quality and accuracy of information provided to law enforcement personnel and the public.[53] ISO certification has become the recognized standard for evaluating and comparing companies on a global basis, and more U.S. companies are feeling the pressure to participate to remain competitive in international markets. In addition, many countries and companies require ISO certification before they will do business with an organization.

CORPORATE GOVERNANCE *GOVERN FAIRLY*

Many organizations have moved toward increased control from the top in terms of corporate governance. Traditionally defined as the ways in which an organization safeguards the interests of shareholders, the term **corporate governance** has been expanded to refer to the framework of systems, rules, and practices by which an organization ensures accountability, fairness, and transparency in its relationships with all stakeholders, including investors, employees, customers, and the general public.[54]

Concerns over corporate governance came to the forefront some years ago in light of the failure of top executives and corporate directors to provide adequate oversight and control at failed companies such as Enron, HealthSouth, Adelphia Communications, and WorldCom. In some cases, financial reporting systems were manipulated to produce false results and hide internal failures. In response, the U.S. government enacted the Sarbanes-Oxley Act of 2002, often referred to as SOX, which requires several types of reforms, including better internal monitoring to reduce the risk of fraud, certification of financial reports by top leaders, improved measures for external auditing, and enhanced public financial disclosure. The initial cost of implementing the SOX reforms may run as high as $5 million to $10 million for a small business once it has gone public. Private firms do not have to meet the same accounting and compliance regulations imposed by SOX. To ease the significant burden on small, emerging growth firms, the JOBS Act (an acronym for Jumpstart Our Business Startups) allows some small companies to avoid the internal control requirements of SOX and the associated costs for up to five years. The statute defines an eligible firm as one with less than $1 billion in annual gross revenue. The JOBS Act is a boon to small companies because it lowers the costs associated with outside auditor review requirements for internal controls.[55]

With the failure of large firms such as Lehman Brothers and Bear Stearns in 2008, corporate governance again became a hot topic. Lax oversight likely contributed both to

Take a Moment

As a new manager, find a balance between oversight and control on the one hand and mutual trust and respect on the other. Go to the Ethical Dilemma for Chapter 19 on page 658 that pertains to new workplace control issues.

HOT TOPIC

the failure of these firms and to a worldwide economic crisis. "I don't think there's any question that a dramatic failure of corporate governance was a central issue of the crisis," said Phil Angelides, chairman of the Financial Crisis Inquiry Commission appointed by the U.S. Congress. Global regulators from 27 countries recently imposed new rules and restraints on financial institutions designed to limit risk-taking and increase oversight.[56] In addition, the U.S. Securities and Exchange Commission (SEC) now requires that companies justify their board structure in proxy statements to ensure that boards are designed in a way to provide needed oversight of management actions.[57]

Remember This

- As global business expands, many companies have adopted a universal benchmark for quality management practices, including **ISO 9000 standards**, which represent an international consensus of what constitutes effective quality management as outlined by the International Organization for Standardization (ISO).

- Many organizations are moving toward increased control from the top in terms of **corporate governance**, which refers to the framework of systems, rules, and practices by which an organization ensures accountability, fairness, and transparency in the firm's relationships with stakeholders.

ch19: Discussion Questions

1. You have been hired to manage a 20-person staff for Nightlight Travels, a travel agency in Las Vegas. For five years, sales have been hammered by the global recession, and staff morale has plummeted as star employees have left for positions in more secure industries. Key customer relationships have been damaged by the sloppy and unprofessional work habits of the remaining staff members. Your first responsibility as new manager is to create next year's budget for all planned expenditures. But first you must decide if you will adopt a hierarchical approach or a decentralized approach to control. Which one would you choose, and why?

2. You're a manager who employs a participative control approach. You've concluded that corrective action is necessary to improve customer satisfaction, but first you need to convince your employees that the problem exists. What kind of evidence do you think employees will find more compelling: quantitative measurements or anecdotes from your interactions with customers? Explain your answer.

3. Describe the advantages of using a balanced scorecard to measure and control organizational performance. Suppose you created a balanced scorecard for Walmart. What specific customer service measures would you include?

4. In zero-based budgeting, every account starts at $0, and every dollar added to the budget is reflected by an actual, documented need. Identify the possible advantages of zero-based budgeting.

5. Most companies have policies that regulate employees' personal use of work computers during work hours. Some even monitor employee e-mails and track the Web sites that have been visited. Do you consider this type of surveillance an invasion of privacy? What are the advantages of restricting employee use of the Internet and e-mail at work?

6. Think of a class that you've taken in the past. What standards of performance did your professor establish? How was your actual performance measured? How was your performance compared to the standards? Do you think the standards and methods of measurement were fair? Were they appropriate to your assigned work? Why or why not?

7. Some critics argue that Six Sigma is a collection of superficial changes that often result in doing a superb job of building the wrong product or offering the wrong service. Do you agree or disagree? Explain.

8. What types of analysis can managers perform to help them diagnose a company's financial condition? How might a review of financial statements help managers diagnose other kinds of performance problems as well?

9. Why is benchmarking an important component of TQM programs? Do you believe a company could have a successful TQM program without using benchmarking?

10. What is ISO certification? Why would a global company like GE want ISO certification?

ch19: Apply Your Skills: Experiential Exercise

Is Your Budget in Control?

By the time you are in college, you are in charge of at least some of your own finances. How well you manage your personal budget may indicate how well you will manage your company's budget on the job. Respond to the following statements to evaluate your own budgeting habits. If the statement doesn't apply directly to you, respond the way you think you would behave in a similar situation.

1. I spend all my money as soon as I get it. Yes No

2. At the beginning of each week (or month, or term), I write down all my fixed expenses. Yes No

3. I never seem to have any money left over at the end of the week (or month). Yes No

4. I pay all my expenses, but I never seem to have any money left over for fun. Yes No

5. I am not putting any money away in savings right now; I'll wait until after I graduate from college. Yes No

6. I can't pay all my bills. Yes No

7. I have a credit card, but I pay the balance in full each month. Yes No

8. I take cash advances on my credit card. Yes No

9. I know how much I can spend on eating out, movies, and other entertainment each week. Yes No

10. I pay cash for everything. Yes No

11. When I buy something, I look for value and determine the best buy. Yes No

12. I lend money to friends whenever they ask, even if it leaves me short of cash. Yes No

13. I never borrow money from friends. Yes No

14. I am putting aside money each month to save for something that I really need. Yes No

Scoring and Interpretation:

Yes responses to statements 2, 9, 10, 13, and 14 point to the most disciplined budgeting habits; *Yes* responses to 4, 5, 7, and 11 reveal adequate budgeting habits; *Yes* responses to 1, 3, 6, 8, and 12 indicate the poorest budgeting habits. If you have answered honestly, chances are you'll have a combination of all three. Look to see where you can improve your budgeting behaviors.

ch19: Apply Your Skills: Small Group Breakout

Create a Group Control System

Step 1. Form into groups of three to five students. Each group will assume that another student group has been given an assignment of writing a major paper that will involve research by individual group members that will be integrated into the final paper. Each group member has to do his or her part.

Step 2. Your assignment is to develop a list of rules and identify some statistics by which to control the behavior of members in that group. Brainstorm and discuss potential rules to govern member behavior and consequences for breaking those rules.

Step 3. First, select the five rules you think are most important for governing group member behavior. Consider the following situations that rules might cover: arriving late for a meeting; missing a meeting; failing to complete a work assignment; disagreements about desired quality of work; how to resolve conflicts about paper content; differences in

participation, such as one person doing all the talking and someone else talking hardly at all; how to handle meetings that start late; the use of an agenda and handling deviations from the agenda; and any other situation that your group thinks a rule should cover.

Step 4. Now consider what statistics could be developed to measure the behavior and outcome of the group pertaining to those five rules. What kinds of things could be counted to understand how the group is performing and whether members are following the rules?

Step 5. Discuss the following questions: Why are rules important as a means of control? What are the advantages and disadvantages of having many rules (hierarchical control) versus few rules (decentralized control) for a student group? How can statistics help a group ensure appropriate behavior and a high-quality product?

Step 6. Be prepared to present your conclusions to the class.

ch19: Endnotes

1. Adapted from J. J. Ray, "Do Authoritarians Hold Authoritarian Attitudes?" *Human Relations* 29 (1976): 307–325.

2. Shayndi Raice and John Letzing, "Groupon Forced to Revise Results," *The Wall Street Journal*, March 31, 2012, http://online.wsj.com/article/SB10001424052702303

816504577313983768173826.html (accessed October 9, 2012); Adam Hartung, "Groupon Needs a New CEO – NOW!!" *Forbes*, August 15, 2012, www.forbes.com/sites/adamhartung/2012/08/15/groupon-needs-a-new-ceo-now/ (accessed October 9, 2012); Rolfe Winkler, "Groupon Gets Socked by Accounting," *The Wall Street Journal*, March 30, 2012, http://www.localeyesurgeon.com/groupon-gets-socked-by-accounting-wall-street-journal/ (accessed October 9, 2012).

3. Willaim K. Rashbau, "Inspector Says He Faked Data in New York Building Tests," *The New York Times*, April 26, 2010, www.nytimes.com/2010/04/27/nyregion/27inspect.html?pagewanted=all&_r=0 (accessed October 2, 2012).

4. Douglas S. Sherwin, "The Meaning of Control," *Dunn's Business Review* (January, 1956).

5. Robert Pear, "New System for Patients to Report Medical Mistakes," *The New York Times*, September 22, 2012, www.nytimes.com/2012/09/23/health/new-system-for-patients-to-report-medical-mistakes.html?_r=0 (accessed October 11, 2012).

6. Jessica Bruder, "Can FreshDirect Survive a Crisis and Reinvent Itself?" *The New York Times*, www.nytimes.com/2010/08/12/business/smallbusiness/12sbiz.html?pagewanted=all&_r=0 (accessed September 28, 2012).

7. *Ibid.*

8. Richard E. Crandall, "Keys to Better Performance Measurement," *Industrial Management* (January–February 2002): 19–24; Christopher D. Ittner and David F. Larcker, "Coming up Short on Nonfinancial Performance Measurement," *Harvard Business Review* (November 2003): 88–95.

9. Bruder, "Can FreshDirect Survive a Crisis and Reinvent Itself?"

10. *Ibid.*

11. This discussion is based on a review of the balanced scorecard in Richard L. Daft, *Organization Theory and Design*, 7th ed. (Cincinnati, OH: South-Western, 2001), pp. 300–301.

12. Andy Neely and Mohammed Al Najjar, "Management Learning Not Management Control: The True Role of Performance Measurement," *California Management Review* 48, no. 3 (Spring 2006): 101–114.

13. Robert Kaplan and David Norton, "The Balanced Scorecard: Measures That Drive Performance," *Harvard Business Review* (January–February 1992): 71–79; and Chee W. Chow, Kamal M. Haddad, and James E. Williamson, "Applying the Balanced Scorecard to Small Companies," *Management Accounting* 79, no. 2 (August 1997): 21–27.

14. Based on Kaplan and Norton, "The Balanced Scorecard"; Chow, Haddad, and Williamson, "Applying the Balanced Scorecard"; and Cathy Lazere, "All Together Now," *CFO* (February 1998): 28–36.

15. Karen S. Cravens, Elizabeth Goad Oliver, and Jea S. Stewart, "Can a Positive Approach to Performan Evaluation Help Accomplish Your Goals?" *Business Horizons* 53 (2010): 269–279.

16. Andy Pasztor, "Decisions by Pilots to Land Criticized, *The Wall Street Journal*, March 28, 2011, http://online.wsj.com/article/SB10001424052748703576204576227111819017454.html (accessed October 11, 2012).

17. Geert J. M. Braam and Edwin J. Nijssen, "Performance Effects of Using the Balanced Scorecard: A Note on the Dutch Experience," *Long Range Planning* 37 (2004): 335–349; Kaplan and Norton, "The Balanced Scorecard"; and Cam Scholey, "Strategy Maps: A Step-by-Step Guide to Measuring, Managing, and Communicating the Plan," *Journal of Business Strategy* 26, no. 3 (2005): 12–19.

18. Nils-Göran Olve et al., "Twelve Years Later: Understanding and Realizing the Value of Balanced Scorecards," *Ivey Business Journal Online*, May–June 2004, www.iveybusinessjournal .com/article.asp?intArticle_ID=487 (accessed October 4, 2010); Eric M. Olson and Stanley F. Slater, "The Balanced Scorecard, Competitive Strategy, and Performance," *Business Horizons* (May–June 2002): 11–16; Eric Berkman, "How to Use the Balanced Scorecard," *CIO* (May 15, 2002): 93–100; and Brigitte W. Schay et al., "Using Standardized Outcome Measures in the Federal Government," *Human Resource Management* 41, no. 3 (Fall 2002): 355–368.

19. Braam and Nijssen, "Performance Effects of Using the Balanced Scorecard."

20. Jay Goltz, "The Dusenberry Diary: When Passion Meets Math," *The New York Times*, June 23, 2009, http://boss.blogs.nytimes.com/2009/06/23/the-dusenberry-diary-when-passion-meets-math/ (accessed October 2, 2012).

21. Sumantra Ghoshal, *Strategic Control* (St. Paul, MN: West, 1986), Chapter 4; and Robert N. Anthony, John Dearden, and Norton M. Bedford, *Management Control Systems*, 5th ed. (Homewood, IL: Irwin, 1984).

22. John A. Boquist, Todd T. Milbourn, and Anjan V. Thakor, "How Do You Win the Capital Allocation Game?" *Sloan Management Review* (Winter 1998): 59–71.

23. Jason Gillikin, "What Is Zero-Based Budgeting and How Is It Used by an Organization?" *Houston Chronicle*, http://smallbusiness.chron.com/zerobased-budgeting-used-organization-22586.html (accessed October 3, 2012).

24. Gerard Paulides, "Resetting the Cost Structure at Shell," *Strategy + Business* 65 (Winter 2011): 1–4.

25. Anthony, Dearden, and Bedford, *Management Control Systems.*

26. Participation in budget setting is described in a number of studies, including Neil C. Churchill, "Budget Choice: Planning versus Control," *Harvard Business Review* (July–August 1984): 150–164; Peter Brownell, "Leadership Style, Budgetary Participation, and Managerial

Behavior," *Accounting Organizations and Society* 8 (1983): 307–321; and Paul J. Carruth and Thurrell O. McClandon, "How Supervisors React to 'Meeting the Budget' Pressure," *Management Accounting* 66 (November 1984): 50–54.

27. Tim Reason, "Budgeting in the Real World," *CFO* (July 2005): 43–48.

28. *Ibid.*

29. Norm Brodsky, "Balance-Sheet Blues," *Inc.* (October, 2011): 34.

30. This analogy is from Brodsky, "Balance-Sheet Blues."

31. Dana Mattioli, "CEOs Fight to Prevent Discretionary Spending from Creeping Back Up," *The Wall Street Journal*, January 1, 1998, http://online.wsj.com/article/SB10001424052748703609004575354901545566456.html (accessed December 11, 2012).

32. Willy Staley, "How 7-Eleven Plans to Put the Bodega Out of Business," *New York* (May 14, 2012): 38–41; 87–88.

33. Mary Ellen Biery, "Five Metrics You Should Know," *The Washington Post*, May 25, 2012, www.washingtonpost.com/blogs/on-small-business/post/5-financial-metrics-you-should-know/2012/05/25/gJQAuDSjpU_blog.html (accessed October 9, 2012).

34. Lawrence M. Fisher, "Inside Dell Computer Corporation: Managing Working Capital," *Strategy + Business* 10, (First Quarter 1998): 68–75; and Randy Myers, "Cash Crop: The 2000 Working Capital Survey," *CFO* (August 2000): 59–69.

35. Nancy F. Koehn, "The Driver in Ford's Amazing Race," *The New York Times*, March 31, 2012, www.nytimes.com/2012/04/01/business/american-icon-examines-fords-rebound-review.html?pagewanted=all&_r=0 (accessed September 28, 2012).

36. William G. Ouchi, "Markets, Bureaucracies, and Clans," *Administrative Science Quarterly* 25 (1980): 129–141; and B. R. Baligia and Alfred M. Jaeger, "Multinational Corporations: Control Systems and Delegation Issues," *Journal of International Business Studies* (Fall 1984): 25–40.

37. Daisuke Wakabayashi and Toko Sekiguchi, "Disaster in Japan: Evacuees Set Rules to Create Sense of Normalcy," *The Wall Street Journal*, http://online.wsj.com/article/SB10001424052748703784004576220382991112672.html (accessed October 3, 2012).

38. Craig Torres and Anthony Feld, "Campbell's Quest for Productivity," *Bloomberg BusinessWeek* (November 29–December 5, 2010): 15–16.

39. Perry Pascarella, "Open the Books to Unleash Your People," *Management Review* (May 1998): 58–60.

40. Leigh Buchanan, "Learning from the Best," *Inc.* (June 2010): 85–86.

41. Mel Mandell, "Accounting Challenges Overseas," *World Trade* (December 1, 2001): 48–50.

42. Matthew Dolan and Jeff Bennett, "Corporate News: Ford Vows to Build Higher-Quality Small Cars," *The Wall Street Journal*, August 12, 2008.

43. A. V. Feigenbaum, *Total Quality Control: Engineering and Management* (New York: McGraw-Hill, 1961); John Lorinc, "Dr. Deming's Traveling Quality Show," *Canadian Business* (September 1990): 38–42; Mary Walton, *The Deming Management Method* (New York: Dodd-Meade & Co., 1986); and J. M. Juran and Frank M. Gryna, eds., *Juran's Quality Control Handbook*, 4th ed. (New York: McGraw-Hill, 1988).

44. Edward E. Lawler III and Susan A. Mohrman, "Quality Circles After the Fad," *Harvard Business Review* (January–February 1985): 65–71; and Philip C. Thompson, *Quality Circles: How to Make Them Work in America* (New York: AMACOM, 1982).

45. D. J. Ford, "Benchmarking HRD," *Training & Development* (July 1993): 37–41.

46. Deven Shah and Brian H. Kleiner, "Benchmarking for Quality," *Industrial Management* (March/April, 2011): 22–25.

47. Tracy Mayor, "Six Sigma Comes to IT: Targeting Perfection," *CIO* (December 1, 2003): 62–70; Hal Plotkin, "Six Sigma: What It Is and How to Use It," *Harvard Management Update* (June 1999): 3–4; Tom Rancour and Mike McCracken, "Applying Six Sigma Methods for Breakthrough Safety Performance," *Professional Safety* 45, no. 10 (October 2000): 29–32; G. Hasek, "Merger Marries Quality Efforts," *Industry Week* (August 21, 2000): 89–92; and Lee Clifford, "Why You Can Safely Ignore Six Sigma," *Fortune* (January 22, 2001): 140.

48. Dick Smith and Jerry Blakeslee, "The New Strategic Six Sigma," *Training & Development* (September 2002): 45–52; Michael Hammer and Jeff Goding, "Putting Six Sigma in Perspective," *Quality* (October 2001): 58–62; and Mayor, "Six Sigma Comes to IT."

49. Jack Bouck, "Creating a Customer-Focused Culture: The Honeywell Experience," *Industrial Management*, (November/December, 2007): 11.

50. This discussion is based on Eileen Newman Rubin, "A Partnered Approach to QA Increases Efficiency Through Early Problem Detection," *Global Business and Organizational Excellence* (May–June 2012): 28–37.

51. Clifford, "Why You Can Safely Ignore Six Sigma"; and Hammer and Goding, "Putting Six Sigma in Perspective."

52. Syed Hasan Jaffrey, "ISO 9001 Made Easy," *Quality Progress* 37, no. 5 (May 2004): 104; Frank C. Barnes, "ISO 9000 Myth and Reality: A Reasonable Approach to ISO 9000," *SAM Advanced Management Journal* (Spring 1998): 23–30; and Thomas H. Stevenson and Frank C. Barnes, "Fourteen Years of ISO 9000: Impact, Criticisms, Costs, and Benefits," *Business Horizons* (May–June 2001): 45–51.

53. David Amari, Don James, and Cathy Marley, "ISO 9001 Takes On a New Role—Crime Fighter," *Quality Progress* 37, no. 5 (May 2004): 57ff.

54. "Corporate Governance," Business Dictionary Web site, www.businessdictionary.com/definition/corporate-governance.html (accessed September 16, 2010);

"Words to Understand: Corporate Governance Models," Gruppo Hera Italy Web site, http://eng.gruppohera.it/group/hera_ondemand/words _understand/page23.html (accessed September 16, 2010); and "Corporate Governance Issues in 2009," *The Corporate Eye*, March 10, 2009, www.corporate-eye .com/blog/2009/03/corporate-governance-issues-2009 (accessed September 16, 2010).

55. Peter J. Henning, "At Large and Small Companies, Internal Controls Matter," *The New York Times*, April 5, 2012, http://dealbook.nytimes.com/2012/04/05/at-large-and-small-companies-internal-controls-matter/ (accessed October 8, 2012).

56. Damian Paletta and David Enrich, "Banks Get New Restraints," *The Wall Street Journal*, September 13, 2010.

57. Joann S. Lublin, "Lead Directors Gain Clout to Counterbalance Strong CEOs," *The Wall Street Journal*, September 13, 2010.

ch19: Apply Your Skills: Ethical Dilemma

The Wages of Sin?*

Chris Dykstra, responsible for loss prevention at Westwind Electronics, took a deep breath before he launched into making his case for the changes that he was proposing to the company's shoplifting policy. He knew that convincing Ross Chenoweth was going to be a hard sell. Ross, the president and CEO, was the son of the founder of the local, still-family-owned consumer electronics chain based in Phoenix, Arizona. He'd inherited not only the company, but also his father's strict moral code.

"I think it's time to follow the lead of other stores," Chris began. He pointed out that most other retailers didn't bother calling the police and pressing charges unless the thief had shoplifted merchandise worth more than $50 to $100. In contrast, Westwind currently had the zero-tolerance policy toward theft that Ross's father had put in place when he started the business. Chris wanted to replace that policy with one that prosecuted only individuals between 18 and 65 who had stolen more than $20 worth of goods, and who had a previous history of theft at Westwind. In the case of first-time culprits under 18 or over 65, he argued for letting them off with a strict warning, regardless of the value of their ill-gotten goods. Repeat offenders would be arrested.

"Frankly, the local police are getting pretty tired of having to come to our stores every time a teenager sticks a CD in his jacket pocket," Chris pointed out. "And besides, we just can't afford the costs associated with prosecuting everyone." Every time he pressed charges against a shoplifter who'd made off with a $10 item, Westwind lost money. The company had to engage a lawyer and pay employees overtime for their court appearances. In addition, Chris was looking at hiring more security guards to keep up with the workload. Westwind was already in a losing battle at the moment with mass retailers who were competing all too successfully on price, so passing on the costs of its zero-tolerance policy to customers wasn't really an option. "Let's concentrate on catching dishonest employees

and those organized-theft rings. They're the ones who are really hurting us," Chris concluded.

There was a long pause after Chris finished his carefully prepared speech. Ross thought about his recently deceased father, both an astute businessman and a person for whom honesty was a key guiding principle. If he were sitting here today, he'd no doubt say that theft was theft, that setting a minimum was tantamount to saying that stealing was acceptable just as long as you don't steal too much. He looked at Chris. "You know, we've both got teenagers. Is this really a message you want to send out, especially to kids? You know as well as I do that there's nothing they like better than testing limits. It's almost an invitation to see if you can beat the system." But then Ross faltered as he found himself glancing at the latest financial figures on his desk—another in a string of quarterly losses. If Westwind went under, a lot of employees would be looking for another way to make a living. In his heart, he believed in his father's high moral standards, but he had to ask himself: Just how moral could Westwind afford to be?

What Would You Do?

1. Continue Westwind's zero-tolerance policy toward shoplifting. It's the right thing to do—and it will pay off in the end in higher profitability because the chain's reputation for being tough on crime will reduce overall losses from theft.

2. Adopt Chris Dykstra's proposed changes and show more leniency to first-time offenders. It is a more cost-effective approach to the problem than the current policy, plus it stays close to your father's original intent.

3. Adopt Chris Dykstra's proposed changes with an even higher limit than the proposed $20 amount (say, $50 or $100), but which is still less than the cost of prosecution. In addition, make sure the policy isn't publicized. That way, you'll reduce costs even more and still benefit from your reputation for prosecuting all shoplifters.

*Based on Michael Barbaro, "Some Leeway for the Small Shoplifter," *The New York Times*, July 13, 2006.

ch19: Apply Your Skills: Case for Critical Analysis

Five Stars

Cousins Jeri Lynn DeBose, Tish Hoover, and Josephine (Joey) Parks looked forward to meeting up during the Christmas holidays to compare notes on the results of mid-year teacher evaluations.

All were public school teachers in districts scattered over the state. In the pressured search for new levels of teacher accountability demanded by legislators, the state department of education joined 16 other states in implementing a new teacher evaluation system. The goal is to hold teachers accountable for student learning progress in the classroom. Under the guidance of the National Council for Teacher Quality, criteria varied by state, but in most cases, 40 percent of each teacher's accountability score would be based on the

principal's evaluation and ranking based on personal observation, 30 percent would be based on personal observation by a master teacher from outside the district, and the other 30 percent would be based on student test score gains. The state department of education would set a performance goal for each school district, and the principal would set a performance goal for each teacher. In preparation, the state conducted intensive training sessions for principals and designated master teachers who would conduct the evaluations based on four class observations per teacher. Officials use standardized achievement tests to derive value-added scores that measure student learning over the year.

Teacher ratings were 1–5, with 1 being the lowest and 5 representing near perfection. The publication of the first year's evaluations stirred interest and controversy, particularly among teachers who worried about the possible long-term effects on job retention and tenure.

Now, with the first-year evaluations in hand, the three cousins pored over their experiences. The three represented different types of school systems within the state. Jeri Lynn worked for a metropolitan system in the state capital. The system included many low-income students whose first language was not English, and several schools within the system were teetering on the brink of state takeover if improvement in student scores didn't materialize this school year. Tish worked in a county system dominated by upper-income residents, and Joey taught in the rural community in which all three grew up. The rural community had high unemployment, and a low percentage of graduates went on to college. As a result, the cousins came to the table with differing teaching experiences.

"The numbers are all over the place," Jeri Lynn remarked as she studied the pages.

"The whole system is flawed and they need to make changes," Joey said. "It's too subjective. The principal and master teacher observations are subjective because there are personal factors that affect a true outcome."

"Yeah, look at the numbers from your upper-income district," Jeri Lynn said to Tish. "How can 60 percent of the teachers score 5s?"

Tish chuckled. "Yeah, lucky us. Our schools are overflowing with children from wealthy families. These are the kids who will apply to Ivy League schools. I can tell you that the principals are going to avoid confrontation on all fronts. No principal is going to give any indication that their students are receiving an education that's less than perfect, and that means cramming the rankings with 5s. They claim a higher level of motivation for students and thus the selection of an elite team of educators. So with those pressures, I don't think we get personal feedback that is accurate."

"At the other end of the spectrum, we have my rural district," Joey said. "The big problem is that the principals know everyone and have longstanding relationships with everyone in the county, so I think scores are based on personal history. We could almost predict who would get high or low scores *before* the observations. For principals, it can go back as far as 'his daddy and my daddy hated each other in high school, and now I get to evaluate his daughter.'"

"I think that in many cases, principals feel pressure to align scores with state expectations. The state *expected* my district to have high scores and *expected* rural schools such as yours to be lower," Tish said.

"But isn't that partially offset by lower goals for the rural school districts?" responded Joey.

"The key to the accountability system is the principal in each school," Jeri Lynn suggested. "With several of the schools in Metro teetering on the edge of state takeover by the end of the year, we had lots of strict principals who wanted to hold our feet to the fire with lower scores."

"I thought the whole idea was to provide the teachers with feedback so that we would know the areas where we need improvement," Tish said.

"The principals were supposed to conduct two observations in the fall and two more in the spring," Jeri Lynn said. "I think that's asking too much of them when they already have so much on their plates. I think a lot of them are skimping on their visits. I know I only had one observation last semester, and I'm sure Mr. Talley just faked the second set of numbers. The master teachers make only two observations a year, which may be more objective but counts for less."

"I'm wondering, too, how a principal measures performance in a course area outside his area of expertise, such as math," Joey said. "If the guy has a phobia about math, anything the teacher says or does is going to look brilliant—thus a 5."

Tish and Jeri Lynn looked at each other and laughed. "Maybe we picked the wrong subjects," Tish said.

"My question is one of perception," Jeri Lynn said. "A large percentage of my students are ELL. That affects their scores. How do you measure a 3 in my situation against a 5 for Tish? At the end of the school year, little Carlos is thrilled that his reading in English has improved, but there's no Big Bang here. It's a slow steady improvement that may not actually show up in big strides for a couple of years."

"So the question is *how do they create a system that is fair?*" Tish asked.

"*And accurate,*" added Jeri Lynn.

Questions

1. What do you see as the major strengths and flaws in the feedback control system used in the schools in this scenario? What changes do you recommend to overcome the flaws?

2. Is a 1–5 grading system by principals and master teachers a valuable part of a feedback control system for teachers? Why?

3. How might the state control the accuracy of principals who are conducting teacher evaluations? Explain.

ch19: On the Job Video Cases

On the Job: Barcelona Restaurant Group: Managing Quality and Performance

Questions

1. How do managers at Barcelona control the company's financial performance?

2. What is the "balanced scorecard" approach to measuring corporate performance, and in what ways does Barcelona use this approach?

3. List the four steps of the feedback control model and describe an instance where Barcelona followed this process to improve its performance.

pt6:   Integrative Case

Range Resources Leads Great Shale Gas Rush Amidst Global Recession

When Range Resources began drilling a vertical test well between the towns of Westland and Hickory, Pennsylvania, in 2004, the Texas exploration-and-production (E&P) company had no idea what it would discover. The sedimentary layers of gray shale rock lying more than a mile beneath the Appalachian Basin had been thought to hold a modest 1.9 trillion cubic feet of natural gas. But when Range's Renz well No.1 instantly tapped a large methane reserve, the company's technical team realized that they were onto something big. As geological experts descended on the rocky area known as the Marcellus Formation, the public soon learned that the shale might contain as much as 516 trillion cubic feet of natural gas, making it one of the largest natural gas reserves in the world. The Great Shale Gas Rush had begun.

Since the drilling of the Renz well in 2004, leaders in industry and government have called the Marcellus discovery "a game changer" and a potential savior of the U.S. economy. Range Resources, with its 1.4 million acres of drilling territory in the region, is one of only a handful of exploration companies positioned to turn that hope into reality. In 2008, Range's technical teams extracted 30 million cubic feet of natural gas per day from the Marcellus Formation. By 2012, production had jumped to 400 million cubic feet of gas per day. Looking ahead, Range executives predict that crews could capture as much as 1 billion cubic feet of natural gas daily.

"Our technical team is one of the best in the industry," says Jeffrey Ventura, Range's president and CEO. "They not only discovered the Marcellus and ramped production up, but we were the first company to drill a horizontal Devonian shale well in Pennsylvania, which is the shale right on top of the Marcellus, and we were the first to drill a horizontal well in the Utica, which is below the Marcellus. So we have a great technical team and a great acreage position."

According to Range's top executives, the discovery of the Marcellus has led the company to adopt a ten-year growth outlook based on high production and a low-cost operating structure. "Our low-cost structure gives us a huge competitive advantage," says Roger Manny, Range's chief financial officer (CFO). "In the commodity business, all of us are selling our products for about the same price. So being able to do it at a lower cost really gives you a big edge." Manny adds that controlling costs improves Range's cash flow and gives the company discretionary cash to explore and drill more wells.

Range's financial managers have various tools to monitor performance and control costs. "Our balance sheet is the first element of that strategy," says Manny. "It's a simple balance sheet that consists of senior bank debt, ten-year subordinated notes, and common equity. So having a simple strong balance sheet is the core to our financial strategy." While financial statements help measure the company's financial health over time, a strong cash position helps the company battle turbulence in the economy. Because of the topsy-turvy nature of the global recession, Range manages its massive land acreage portfolio in a way that provides added liquidity—the ability to sell assets in a pinch to pay off debts. "Another feature of our financial strategy is having liquidity to absorb shocks in the market," Manny states.

At Range, keeping a lid on expenses is not just the job of company accountants—it's everyone's job. "Maintaining a low-cost structure is not so much what we do but who we are," Manny says. "It's part of our culture." Range encourages employees to make cost-cutting a part of their regular duties, and it rewards them with equity in the company. "Equity ownership creates a unique bond among employees and also between the employees and shareholders," says Manny, "because, after all, they themselves are shareholders." Range's CFO believes that companies perform best when everyone has skin in the game. "I think the fact that everybody owns equity in the company makes them more willing to be vigilant about costs. And that's a big contributor to the long-term cost performance of the company," Manny states.

Range's money management philosophy has paid off. Over the past ten years, Range Resources has been one of the top three performing E&P companies on the New York Stock Exchange (NYSE). In addition, the company has delivered nearly a decade of sequential annual growth with some of the lowest finding and development costs in the industry—all this during a global recession that has torpedoed top corporations. "Clearly, 2009 was one of the most difficult periods in time in terms of running a business in America," says Range executive chairman John Pinkerton, reflecting on the economic downturn. "A number of companies simply didn't make it, a lot of companies had to totally restructure their business, and other companies issued a lot of equity and diluted their shareholders. The good news is that none of that happened at Range; we ended that year with less debt than we started, and we didn't have to issue any equity to prop up our balance sheet."

"Most importantly," Pinkerton adds, "we've had terrific operating results. We drove up double-digit growth in production reserves. So the company came through a very challenging financial market in stronger shape than we began, and I think that really is going to set the tone for the next decade."

Ultimately, effective financial control frees Range to do what it does best: develop America's clean energy future. Says Pinkerton: "I think the most exciting thing when you look at Range going forward is some of the assets we have, in particular the Marcellus. It could be one of the largest gas fields in the United States and maybe the world. To be involved with that is fabulous, and it's going to help drive our growth."

Integrative Case Questions

1. Managers at Range Resources say that maintaining a low-cost structure is the job of every employee, and they make cost control part of the company culture. Is this indicative of a hierarchical or a decentralized philosophy of control? Explain.

2. What is liquidity, and how can Range's managers know if they have enough of it to keep the company's finances on track?

3. Short-term thinking can be disastrous for a business. What indications are there to show that financial managers at Range Resources take a long-term approach to financial performance and control?

Sources: Based on Christopher Helman, "Range Resources Is King of the Marcellus Shale," *Forbes*, July 22, 2010, www.forbes.com/forbes/2010/0809/companies-energy-range-resources-bp-gas-blowout-beneficiary.html (accessed July 14, 2012); Roger Manny (Executive Vice President and Chief Financial Officer of Range Resources), interview by Rodney Waller, "Range Up Close: Corporate Overview," Range Resources corporate site, 2010, online video, www.rangeresources.com/Media-Center/Videos/Corporate-Overview.aspx (accessed July 15, 2012); Jeffrey Ventura (President and Chief Executive Officer of Range Resources), interview by Rodney Waller, "Range Up Close: Competitive Advantage," Range Resources corporate site, 2010, online video, www.rangeresources.com/Media-Center/Featured-Stories.aspx (accessed July 15, 2012); John Pinkerton (Executive Chairman of Range Resources), interview by Rodney Waller, "Range Up Close: Corporate Overview," Range Resources corporate site, 2010, online video, www.rangeresources.com/Media-Center/Videos/Corporate-Overview.aspx (accessed July 15, 2012); Elwin Green, "Natural Gas Locked in the Marcellus Shale Has Companies Rushing to Cash in on Possibilities," *Pittsburgh Post-Gazette*, March 16, 2012, www.post-gazette.com/stories/business/news/natural-gas-locked-in-the-marcellus-shale-has-companies-rushing-to-cash-in-on-possibilities-370058/(accessed July 10, 2012); and Martin Neil Baily and Philip K. Verleger Jr, "Could Cheap Gas Save the Economy?" CNN Money, June 27, 2012, http://money.cnn.com/2012/06/27/news/economy/shale-gas/ (accessed July 15, 2012).

Managing the Value Chain, Information Technology, and E-Business

Which Side of Your Brain Do You Use?[1]

Instructions: The following questions ask you to describe your behavior. For each question, check the answer that best describes you.

1. I am usually running late for class or other appointments:

_____ **a.** Yes

_____ **b.** No

2. When taking a test, I prefer:

_____ **a.** Subjective questions (discussion or essay)

_____ **b.** Objective questions (multiple-choice)

3. When making decisions, I typically:

_____ **a.** Go with my gut—what feels right

_____ **b.** Weigh each option carefully

4. When solving a problem, I would more likely:

_____ **a.** Take a walk, mull things over, and then discuss

_____ **b.** Write down alternatives, prioritize them, and then pick the best

5. I consider time spent daydreaming as:

_____ **a.** A viable tool for planning my future

_____ **b.** A waste of time

6. To remember directions, I typically:

_____ **a.** Visualize the information

_____ **b.** Make notes

7. My work style is mostly:

_____ **a.** To juggle several things at once

_____ **b.** To concentrate on one task at a time until it is completed

8. My desk, work area, or laundry area are typically:

_____ **a.** Cluttered

_____ **b.** Neat and organized

Scoring and Interpretation: People have two thinking processes—one visual and intuitive, which is often referred to as *right-brained thinking*, and the other verbal and analytical, referred to as *left-brained thinking*. The thinking process that you prefer predisposes you to certain types of knowledge and information—visual charts and operations dashboards vs. written reports, intuitive suggestions vs. quantitative data—as effective input to your thinking and decision making.

Count the number of checked *a* items and *b* items. Each *a* represents right-brain processing, and each *b* represents left-brain processing. If you scored 6 or higher on either, you have a distinct processing style. If you checked less than 6 for either, you probably have a balanced style. New managers typically need left-brain processing to handle data and to justify decisions. At middle- and upper-management levels, right-brain processing enables visionary thinking and strategic insights.

The airline industry is brutal. Almost every day, there's a new report about an airline in trouble. European airlines reported a loss of $1.7 billion in the first quarter of 2012. With costs going up and revenue going down, Air Canada managers are considering filing for bankruptcy. In the United States, U.S. Airways, United, Northwest, and Delta all filed for bankruptcy protection within the space of a few years. Managers at AMR Corporation, the parent company of American Airlines and American Eagle, filed for bankruptcy protection in 2011 to reorganize and reduce costs. Labor unrest, flight delays and cancellations, skyrocketing fuel costs, emergency landings due to equipment malfunctions—the airlines just don't seem to stand a chance of making a profit.[2]

And then there's Southwest Airlines, which in 2012 recorded its thirty-ninth consecutive year of profitability. In an industry where profits are agonizingly tough to eke out, how has Southwest done it? The short answer: operational efficiency. Southwest keeps operations simple, so fewer things can go wrong. Southwest uses just one type of aircraft, the Boeing 737, whereas most airlines use ten or more types. That means Southwest has to train mechanics and keep parts in inventory for only one type of plane. If something goes wrong and a plane has to be swapped at the last minute, the fleet is totally interchangeable. Southwest has numerous other procedures that save time and contribute to operational efficiency. Even the decision not to charge passengers to check bags was based on operations considerations. "When you charge people to check bags, they try to carry more on," said Chris Wahlenmaier, vice president of ground operations. "That results in more bags being checked at the gate, right before departure. And that wastes time." Southwest managers know that "we only make money off our planes when they're in the air," as Wahlenmaier puts it.[3]

Managers in all types of organizations, from airlines to smartphone manufacturers to rock bands, have to be concerned with operational issues. Van Halen became infamous during the rock band's touring heyday for one unusual clause buried in its complex touring contract: a demand for a bowl of M&Ms backstage, with all the brown ones removed. What was the purpose of this unusual demand? It may look like just the unreasonable whim of spoiled celebrities, but really it was a way for the band to assess quickly whether stagehands were paying attention to operational issues. If lead singer David Lee Roth spotted a brown M&M, he would demand a line check of the entire production. "Guaranteed you're going to arrive at a technical error," he wrote in his autobiography. "Sometimes it would threaten to destroy the whole show."[4]

Today's managers rely on all types of data and information to spot problems and keep their business operations running smoothly. As suggested by the opening questionnaire, people gather and use information in different ways. Some people prefer written reports with lots of explicit data, while others like a visual presentation and a broad overview. Both styles are useful, and as managers grow in their abilities, they typically learn to use and appreciate a balanced approach.

This appendix describes techniques for the planning and control of manufacturing and service operations and the use of information technology in today's organizations. Chapter 19 described overall control concepts. This appendix will focus on the control of production operations and the use of information systems for management and control. First, we define operations management and supply chain management, consider specific operational design issues, such as facilities layout and the use of technology in the production system, and take a close look at inventory management. The second part of this appendix explores the application of information technology, including enterprise resource planning systems, Web 2.0 for knowledge management, and strategies for e-business.

The Organization as a Value Chain

In Chapter 1, we discussed the organization as a system used for transforming inputs into outputs. At the center of this transformation process is the

EXHIBIT   A.1   The Organization as a Value Chain

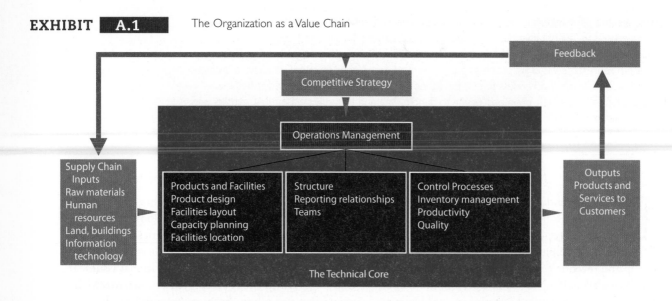

technical core, which is the heart of the organization's production of its product or service.[5] In a university, the technical core includes the academic activities of teaching and research. In an automobile company, the technical core includes the plants that manufacture automobiles.

As illustrated in Exhibit A.1, the organization can be thought of as a *value chain* that receives inputs from the environment, such as raw materials and other resources, and adds value by transforming them into products and services for customers. Inputs into the technical core typically include materials and equipment, human resources, land and buildings, and information. Outputs from the technical core are the goods and services produced by the organization and sold or provided to customers and clients. Operations strategy and control feedback shape the quality of outputs and the efficiency of operations within the technical core. The topic of operations management pertains to the day-to-day management of the technical core, as illustrated in Exhibit A.1, including acquiring inputs, transforming them, and distributing outputs. **Operations management** refers to using various tools and techniques to ensure that goods and services are delivered successfully to customers or clients. This involves bringing people, processes, raw materials, and technology together to create value. The importance of operations management becomes clear when one looks at critical situations where things go haywire. Consider the chaos that McDonald's managers faced after the 2011 earthquake and tsunami in Japan disrupted the supply of food to the company's 3,300 restaurants in that country. Agricultural regions were devastated and several of McDonald's processing plants and distribution centers were damaged, meaning that food had to be imported from the United States and parts of Asia. However, fuel shortages, delays at ports, and other logistics snafus created additional problems. About

three weeks after the earthquake, Simone Hoyle, vice president of supply chain for McDonald's Asia, Pacific, Middle East, and Africa region, said "We've been working around the clock to keep our restaurants stocked." Nevertheless, at that point, 88 McDonald's in Japan remained closed, and others were still on restricted menus.[6]

When managers must organize a project quickly to deliver a product or service on time, operations management can be particularly challenging. Yet, all managers deal with operations management issues every day. They have to consider the best location to manufacture products or provide services, how to most cost-effectively obtain raw materials and other resources, and how to produce products or services and get them delivered to customers efficiently.

SERVICE AND MANUFACTURING OPERATIONS

As the example of McDonald's illustrates, operations management applies to service organizations as well as manufacturing. The service sector has increased three times as fast as the manufacturing sector in the North American economy. More than half of all businesses in the United States are service organizations, and two-thirds of the U.S. workforce is employed in services such as hospitals, hotels and resorts, retail, financial services, information services, or telecommunications firms. Exhibit A.2 shows the differences between manufacturing and service organizations. **Manufacturing organizations** are those that produce physical goods, such as cars, e-readers, television sets, or smartphones. In contrast, **service organizations** produce nonphysical outputs, such as medical, educational, communication, or transportation services for customers. Doctors,

EXHIBIT   A.2   Differences Between Manufacturing and Service Organizations

Manufacturing Organizations	Service Organizations
Produce physical goods	Produce nonphysical outputs
Goods inventoried for later consumption	Simultaneous production and consumption
Quality measured directly	Quality perceived and difficult to measure
Standardized output	Customized output
Production process removed from consumer	Consumer participates in production process
Examples:	*Examples:*
Automobile manufacturers	Airlines
Steel companies	Hotels
Soft-drink companies	Hospitals

SOURCES: Based on Richard L. Daft, *Organization Theory and Design* (Cincinnati, OH: South-Western, 2005), p. 256; and Byron J. Finch and Richard L. Luebbe, *Operations Management* (Fort Worth, TX: Dryden Press, 1995), p. 50.

consultants, online auction companies, and the local barber all provide services. Services also include the sale of merchandise. Although merchandise is a physical good, the service company does not manufacture it but merely sells it as a service to the customer.

Services differ from manufactured products in two primary ways. First, the service customer is involved in the actual production process.[7] The patient actually visits the doctor to receive the service, and it's difficult to imagine a hairstylist providing services without direct customer contact. The same is true for airlines, restaurants, and banks. Second, manufactured goods can be placed in inventory, whereas service outputs, being intangible, cannot be stored. Manufactured products such as clothes, food, cars, or iPhones all can be put in warehouses and sold at a later date. However, a hairstylist cannot wash, cut, and style hair in advance and leave it on the shelf for the customer's arrival, nor can a doctor place examinations in inventory. The service must be created and provided for the customer exactly when he or she wants it.

There are also similarities between services and manufacturing. For instance, most manufacturing firms have substantial service components, and most service firms have some tangible elements that must be managed. An auto manufacturer has to provide both a well-made car and good customer service for warranty repairs. A fast-food restaurant has to provide top-notch service, but it also has to provide a high-quality product. Almost all organizations have a combination of

manufacturing and service components, and manufacturing and service firms face similar operational problems. First, each kind of organization is concerned with scheduling. A medical clinic must schedule appointments so that both doctors' and patients' time will be used efficiently. Second, both manufacturing and service organizations must obtain materials and supplies. Third, both types of organizations are concerned with quality and productivity. Because many operational problems are similar, operations management tools and techniques can be applied to service organizations as readily as they are to manufacturing operations.

SUPPLY CHAIN MANAGEMENT

Managers in both service and manufacturing organizations focus on managing the entire supply chain, coordinating the flow of materials, information, and other resources to maximize customer value. As defined in Chapter 2, **supply chain management** refers to managing the sequence of suppliers and purchasers, covering all stages of processing from obtaining raw materials to distributing finished goods to consumers. Supply chain management means managing all the activities that facilitate the satisfactory fulfillment of an order at the highest degree of customer satisfaction and the lowest possible cost.[8] The importance of supply chain management can be seen by looking at the "Supply Chain Top 25 for 2012" from Gartner, Inc., which reflects that organizations with excellent supply

EXHIBIT   A.3   An Integrated Supply Chain

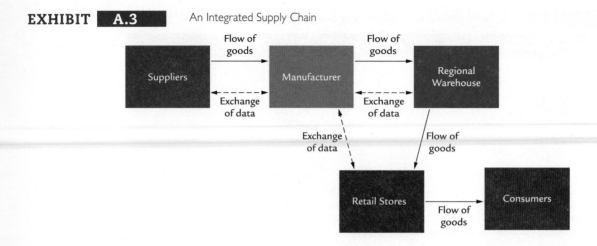

chain management are some of the most successful organizations in the world. Apple, for instance, was ranked the best-performing supply chain for the fifth year in a row. Other 2012 rankings include Amazon.com at No. 2, Procter & Gamble (P&G) at No. 5, Walmart at No. 9, Samsung at No. 13, and Nestlé at No. 18.[9]

Exhibit A.3 illustrates a simplified goods-producing supply chain, consisting of suppliers, manufacturers, distributors, retailers, and final consumers. The most recent advances in supply chain management involve using Internet technologies to achieve the right balance of low inventory levels and customer responsiveness. An e-supply chain creates a seamless, integrated link that stretches from customers to suppliers by establishing electronic linkages between the organization and these external partners for the sharing and exchange of data.[10] For example, in Exhibit A.3, a manufacturer would be electronically connected to suppliers, distributors, and retailers so that everyone along the supply chain has almost completely transparent information about sales, orders, shipments, and other data. A manufacturer such as P&G is linked to Walmart and knows how quickly products are selling and when a new shipment will be needed; suppliers know what materials and supplies are needed at P&G factories; and distributors know when final products are ready to be shipped.

Enterprise integration through the use of electronic linkages is creating a level of cooperation not previously imaginable for many organizations. Supplier relationships used to be based on an *arm's-length* approach, in which an organization spreads purchases among many suppliers and encourages them to compete with one another. With integration, more companies are opting for a *partnership* approach, which involves cultivating intimate relationships with a few carefully selected suppliers and collaborating closely to coordinate tasks that benefit both parties. Both Boeing and Airbus are taking a new approach to

supply chain management to speed the development and manufacture of new planes. To build the new A350, which is scheduled to be available to airlines in 2014, Airbus established electronic links with key suppliers so that they are constantly seeing updated digital blueprints. Frequent design changes immediately ripple through the entire supply chain, avoiding problems such as the one that occurred several years ago when Airbus was building the A380 superjumbo jetliner. The company still has bins overflowing with useless wiring from suppliers that was too short to be used.[11]

Integrating every company along the supply chain means a quicker response to end consumers by reducing the time it takes to move critical data through the information pipeline. An integrated supply chain enables managers at Spanish clothing manufacturer Inditex to have hot-selling items in its Zara retail stores within two days and to get new items from concept to store shelf within weeks, rather than the six months that it typically takes.[12]

Facilities Layout

Another important consideration for operations management is planning the facilities layout for producing goods or services. The four most common types of layout are process, product, cellular, and fixed-position, shown in Exhibit A.4.

PROCESS LAYOUT

Exhibit A.4(a) illustrates a **process layout** for an auto detail shop. This shop provides a variety of services. All the equipment and materials that relate to a similar function or service task—such as prepping the car and cleaning the engine, shampooing the trunk and interior, or washing,

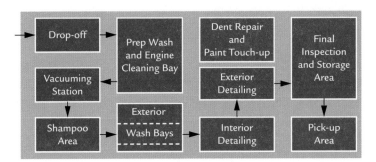

(a) Process Layout

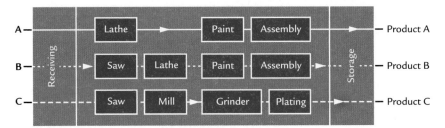

(b) Product Layout

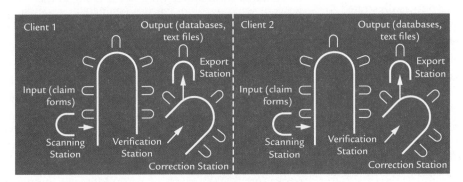

(c) Cellular Layout

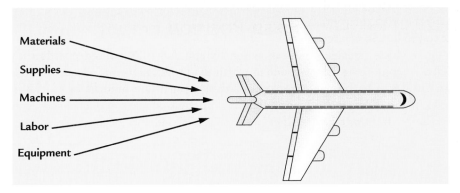

(d) Fixed-Position Layout

SOURCES: Based on J. T. Black, "Cellular Manufacturing Systems Reduce Setup Time, Make Small Lot Production Economical," *Industrial Engineering* (November 1983): 36–48; Richard J. Schonberger, "Plant Layout Becomes Product-Oriented with Cellular, Just-in-Time Production Concepts," *Industrial Engineering* (November 1983): 66–77; Keith Duplessie, "Designing a Detail Shop for Success," *ModernCarCare.com*, June 17, 2009, www.moderncarcare.com/articles/2009/06/designing-a-detail-shop-for-success .aspx (accessed September 15, 2010); and Rely Services Web site, www.relyservices.com/insurance-claims-processing-services .htm (accessed September 15, 2010).

APPENDIX

waxing, and polishing the paint—are grouped together.[13] Similarly, in a manufacturing firm, all machines that perform a similar function or task are grouped together. In a machine shop, the lathes are located in one section of the shop, the grinders in another section, the milling machines in another, and so forth.

The advantage of the process layout is that it has the potential for economies of scale and reduced costs. For example, having all painting done in one spray-painting area means that fewer machines and people are required to paint all products for the organization. In a bank, having all tellers located in one controlled area provides increased security. At Montefiore Medical Center in the Bronx, New York, rather than having specialized medical, surgical, cardiothoracic, and neurosurgical intensive care units (ICUs), Dr. Vladimir Kvetan combined them into a central critical-care department to increase efficiency and improve patient care. Kvetan, director of critical-care medicine, is continually thinking of ways to provide better care more efficiently, which means Montefiore rarely encounters the critical-care bottlenecks that many other large hospitals experience.[14]

One drawback to the process layout, as illustrated in Exhibit A.4 (a), is that the actual path a product or service takes can be long and complicated. For a full auto detail, the car needs several different services performed on it and thus must travel through many different areas before the entire process is complete.

PRODUCT LAYOUT

Exhibit A.4(b) illustrates a **product layout**—one in which machines and tasks are arranged according to the progressive steps in producing a single product. The automobile assembly line is a classic example because it produces a single product, starting from the raw materials to the finished output. Many fast-food restaurants use the product layout, with activities arranged in sequence to produce hamburgers or fried chicken, depending on the products available. For example, the founder of Taco Bell restaurants designed a wire basket with six slots for corn tortillas. After being dunked in boiling oil, the shells are placed on a sliding rack that passes trays of beef, lettuce, and cheese, the tacos taking shape much the same way a car does as it rolls along an assembly line. Other menu items are handled similarly. "If you have it laid out where it doesn't flow right, that means less order flow, less product, lower sales," says Mike Watson, executive vice president of WD Partners, a consulting firm that works with "QSR" (quick-serve restaurant) brands. "The most advanced operational thinking in the world is going on in the back of a QSR," Watson adds.[15]

The product layout is efficient when the organization produces or provides huge volumes of identical products or services, such as at Taco Bell. Note in Exhibit A.4 (b) that two lines have paint areas. This duplication of functions can be economical only if the volume is high enough to keep each paint area busy working on specialized products.

CELLULAR LAYOUT

Illustrated in Exhibit A.4(c) is an innovative layout, called **cellular layout**, based on group-technology principles. In a service firm that processes millions of insurance and institutional claims for organizations in the medical field, people and equipment are grouped into cells that perform all the tasks needed to serve a particular client, as shown in the exhibit.[16] Work flows from one station to another, such as from scanning to verification to correction. In a manufacturing plant, all machines dedicated to sequences of operations are grouped into cells, and materials flow from one station to another.[17] Grouping technology into cells provides some of the efficiencies of both process and product layouts. Even more important, the U-shaped cells in Exhibit A.4(c) offer efficiencies in material and tool handling and inventory movement. People and technology within the cluster can be allocated to whatever work needs doing in that cluster. Arranging employees in clusters facilitates teamwork and joint problem solving. Staffing flexibility is enhanced because people are cross-trained so that each worker can perform all the tasks, assisting coworkers as needed. Conmed, a maker of surgical devices, replaced its long assembly lines with U-shaped workstations where teams of employees build products to order. The assembly area for fluid-injection devices used in orthoscopic surgery once covered 3,300 square feet and had $93,000 worth of parts on hand. With the cellular layout, it takes up one-fifth of that space and stocks just $6,000 worth of parts. Moreover, output per worker increased 21 percent with the new system.[18]

FIXED-POSITION LAYOUT

As shown in Exhibit A.4(d), the **fixed-position layout** is one in which the product remains in one location and employees and equipment are brought to it. The fixed-position layout is used to create a product or service that is either large or one of a kind. Product examples include aircraft, ships, and buildings. The product cannot be moved from function to function or along an assembly line; rather, the people, materials, and machines all come to the fixed-position site for assembly and processing. London-based Imagination Ltd., Europe's largest independent design and communications agency, provides an interesting service example. The Imagination team was hired to stage a one-of-a-kind event at a historic London building for the launch of the *Harry Potter and the Prisoner of Azkaban* DVD.[19]

The fixed-position layout is not good for high volume, but it is often necessary for large, bulky products, custom orders, and special events like the launch of the *Harry Potter*

DVD. Many manufacturers are adapting the fixed-position layout to speed up production. Boeing now builds many of its planes on a type of moving assembly line, which has cut in half the time that it takes to assemble a single-aisle 737. Airbus uses assembly stations, moving the plane only from one major workstation to the next, with the idea that a glitch in one plane won't slow a whole production line.[20]

Technology Automation

A goal for many of today's operations managers is to find the right combination of technology and management to produce goods and services most efficiently. Let's look at three advances in manufacturing and service operations.

> "One machine can do the work of fifty ordinary men. No machine can do the work of one extraordinary man."
>
> — ELBERT HUBBARD, 19TH-CENTURY AMERICAN WRITER

RADIO-FREQUENCY IDENTIFICATION (RFID)

In August 2010, Walmart began putting tiny electronic tags on individual pieces of men's clothing, including jeans, underwear, and socks. The tags emit a weak radio signal that enables employees to know what sizes are missing on the shelf and what items are available in the stock room. The retailer plans to expand this use of *radio-frequency identification (RFID)* tags to all types of merchandise.[21] RFID tags can identify and track pallets of merchandise or individual items such as jeans, books, jugs of laundry detergent, automobiles, or even people. Until recently, most retailers had used RFID only to track pallets or cases of goods, and the move to individual items has raised concerns over potential invasions of privacy.

However, RFID has been used effectively for years. One of the best-known uses of RFID is OnStar, which is a satellite-based RFID system used in automobiles. RFID tags emit radio signals that can be read remotely by electronic readers and provide precise, real-time information about the location of specific items, whether

it be a Cadillac with a dead battery, a misplaced book in a bookstore, or a pallet of merchandise in a warehouse.[22] Although RFID is also used by manufacturing firms, the technology has revolutionized services. Dutch bookseller Selexyz tags every book on its shelves with RFID, which increases profits and cuts costs because taking inventory by hand is unnecessary, lost books can be found, and returns to publishers have decreased.[23] The potential of RFID for streamlining inventory management and cutting costs for retailers is enormous, which has prompted many companies to require that suppliers use the new technology.

Other service firms use RFID as well. New York's E-Z Pass and California's FasTrak both use RFID to speed cars through toll booths, for example.[24] The U.S. Department of Defense requires suppliers to use RFID on shipping pallets and cases, enabling the military to track shipments of combat-support goods and other items easily.[25] A recent application of RFID is for contactless payments, which means a shopper can wave an RFID-embedded debit card, credit card, or other device over a reader to pay for items without having to swipe a card or go through a cashier.[26] The technology might even ameliorate the age-old problem of lost luggage, which is maddening for passengers and costly for airlines. An RFID baggage-tagging system in use at the Las Vegas McCarran International Airport reduced lost luggage by about 20 percent, and bags that do go astray are located more quickly.[27]

DIGITAL MANUFACTURING SYSTEMS

Advanced technology has also revolutionized manufacturing. Most of today's factories use a variety of new technologies, including robots, numerically controlled machine tools, RFID, wireless technology, and computerized software for product design, engineering analysis, and remote control of machinery. A study found that manufacturers in the United States use more than six times the amount of information-processing equipment (computers, etc.) as they used 20 years ago.[28] The ultimate automated factories are referred to as **digital factories**.[29] Also called *computer-integrated manufacturing, flexible manufacturing systems, smart factories, advanced manufacturing technology,* or *agile manufacturing,* digital factories use computers to link together manufacturing components that previously stood alone. Thus, robots, machines, product design, and engineering analysis are coordinated by a single computer system.

The computer can instruct the machines to change parts, machining, and tools when a new product must be produced. Human operators make adjustments

APPENDIX

to the computer and not the production machinery it-self, dramatically cutting the time and expense of making changes. This approach is a breakthrough compared with the traditional assembly line in which a single line is restricted to a single product. With a digital manufacturing system, a single production line can be readily adapted to small batches of different products based on computer instructions. Consider the flexibility that Honda has achieved at its plant in East Liberty, Ohio. Considered the most flexible auto manufacturer in North America, the Honda plant can switch from making Civic compacts to making the longer, taller CRV crossover in as little as five minutes. Most of the company's vehicles are designed to be put together the same way, even if their parts are different. All that's needed to switch assembly from one type of vehicle to another is to put different "hands" on the robots to handle different parts. The ability to adjust inventory levels of different types of vehicles quickly has been a key strategic advantage for Honda in an era of volatile gasoline prices and shifting vehicle popularity.[30]

Digital manufacturing also enables **mass customization**, a process by which products are produced cost-effectively in high volume but are customized to meet individual needs.[31] A customer can order a Dell laptop with one of several hard drive capacities, processing chip speeds, and software packages, or a BMW automobile with the exact combination of features and components desired. About 60 percent of the cars BMW sells in Europe are built to order.[32]

LEAN THINKING

Starbucks Corporation recently hired a vice president of lean thinking, who has been traveling with a *lean team* around the world to work with employees to find ways to cut waste and improve customer service. Rival Dunkin' Donuts uses lean thinking techniques "everywhere from manufacturing to in-store organization and workflow," says Joe Scafido, chief creative and innovation officer at Dunkin' Brands.[33] **Lean thinking** basically means combining advanced technology and innovative management processes and using highly trained employees to solve problems, cut waste, improve the productivity, quality, and efficiency of products and services, and increase customer value.[34] At one Starbucks store that implemented lean methods, customer satisfaction improved from 56 percent to 76 percent within a couple of months.

Lean thinking is based on the principles of *lean manufacturing*, pioneered by Toyota. In fact, Japan Post, under pressure to cut a $191 million loss in operations, hired Toyota's Toshihiro Takahashi to help apply the famed Toyota Production System (TPS) to the collection, sorting, and delivery of mail. In all, Takahashi's team came up with 370

improvements and reduced the post office's person-hours by 20 percent. The waste reduction is expected to cut costs by around $350 million a year.[35] Technology plays a key role in lean manufacturing, but the heart of the process for both manufacturing and service organizations is not machines or technology, but people.[36] A lean system combines techniques, systems, and management philosophy, such as commitment to employee empowerment and a creative culture.

Besides installing the methodology for running an efficient assembly line, such as *just-in-time* shipments of supplies, managers must instill the necessary attitudes, such as concern for quality and a desire to innovate.[37] At E-Z GO of Augusta, Georgia, which manufactures golf cars for the top golf courses in America, implementation of a lean system involved four critical areas: process flow, or the physical aspects of production; material flow and inventory management; information flow; and culture and mindset changes. Employees received training in leadership and practical problem solving and were empowered to identify and address issues and drive continuous improvement throughout the plant. The full implementation of lean thinking led to a 200-percent increase in profits and systemwide improvements that helped E-Z GO earn the prestigious Shingo Prize for Operational Excellence.[38]

Inventory Management

Inventory is the goods the organization keeps on hand for use in the production process. Most organizations have three types of inventory: finished goods prior to shipment, work in process, and raw materials.

Finished-goods inventory includes items that have passed through the entire production process but have not been sold. This inventory is highly visible. The new cars parked in the storage lot of an automobile factory are finished-goods inventory, as are the hamburgers and French fries stacked under the heat lamps at a McDonald's restaurant. Finished-goods inventory is expensive because the organization has invested labor and other costs to make the finished product.

Work-in-process inventory includes the materials moving through the stages of the production process that are not completed products. Work-in-process inventory in an automobile plant includes engines, wheel and tire assemblies, and dashboards waiting to be installed. In a fast-food restaurant, the French fries in the fryer and hamburgers on the grill are work-in-process inventory.

Raw materials inventory includes the basic inputs to the organization's production process. This inventory is cheapest because the organization has not yet invested labor in it. Steel, wire, glass, and paint are the raw materials inventory for an auto plant, and meat patties, buns, and raw potatoes are the raw materials inventory in a fast-food restaurant.

The Importance of Inventory

Inventory management is vitally important to organizations because inventory sitting idly on the shop floor or in the warehouse costs money. Many years ago, a firm's wealth was measured by its inventory. Today, inventory is recognized as an unproductive asset in cost-conscious firms. One CEO went so far as to put it this way: "Inventory is evil." By trimming it, said Drew Greenblatt, CEO of Marlin Steel Wire, "you find a big pile of cash."[39]

Darden Restaurants recently automated its supply chain so that it buys only what its restaurants need when they need it.[40] Sealy, the world's top maker of mattresses, has cut raw materials inventory by 50 percent, down to 16 days' worth.[41] Managers at Acer Inc. are currently assessing the company's inventory policies because tough economic conditions in Europe have left large quantities of finished inventory, such as PCs and netbooks, sitting in warehouses and distribution centers. Inventory management is crucial for companies such as Acer because finished products sitting in warehouses depreciate quickly as new technology emerges.[42]

The Japanese analogy of rocks and water describes the current thinking about the importance of inventory.[43] As illustrated in Exhibit A.5, water is the inventory in the organization. The higher the water, the less managers have to worry about the rocks, which represent problems. In operations management, these problems apply to scheduling, facilities layout, or quality. When the water level goes down, managers see the rocks and must deal with them. When inventories are reduced, the problems of a poorly designed and managed operations process also are revealed and then must be solved. When inventory can be kept at an absolute minimum, operations management is considered excellent.

Just-in-Time Inventory

Just-in-time (JIT) inventory systems are designed to reduce the level of an organization's inventory and its associated costs, aiming to push to zero the amount of time that raw materials and finished products are sitting in the factory, being inspected, or in transit.[44] Sometimes these systems are referred to as *stockless systems*, *zero inventory systems*, or *kanban systems*. Each system centers on the concept that suppliers deliver materials only at the exact moment needed, thereby reducing raw material inventories to zero. Moreover, work-in-process inventories are kept to a minimum because goods are produced only as needed to service the next stage of production. Finished-goods inventories are minimized by matching them exactly to sales demand. JIT systems have tremendous advantages. Reduced inventory level frees productive capital for other company uses. In addition, JIT plays a crucial role in enhancing flexibility. A study of manufacturing firms in seven countries found that those that were performing better in terms of flexibility ranked JIT as one of their top two improvement initiatives, along with total quality management (TQM), as defined in Chapter 19.[45]

Recall the analogy of the rocks and the water. To reduce inventory levels to zero means that all management and coordination problems will surface and must be resolved. Scheduling must be scrupulously precise and logistics tightly coordinated. For example, follow the movement of a shipment of odometers and speedometers from a supplier in Winchester, Virginia, to the Nissan plant in Canton, Mississippi.

Thursday, 9 A.M.:	A truck arrives at the supplier. As workers load the parts, drivers check on-board computers for destination, route, and estimated time of arrival (ETA) data.
Friday, 3 A.M.:	The truck arrives at Canton, Mississippi, and approaches a switching yard two miles from the Nissan plant, parking in a

EXHIBIT A.5   Large Inventories Hide Operations Management Problems

SOURCES: Based on R. J. Schonberger, *Japanese Manufacturing Techniques: Nine Hidden Lessons in Simplicity* (New York: Free Press, 1982).

computer-assigned spot. The driver downloads arrival information from the onboard computer into the trucking company's mainframe, which relays the performance report directly to Nissan.

Friday, 12:50 P.M.: The trailer leaves the switching yard at a designated time and arrives at a predetermined receiving dock at the Nissan plant, where workers unload the parts and send them to the production line just in time.[46]

The coordination required by JIT demands that information be shared among everyone in the supply chain. Communication between only adjoining links in the supply chain is too slow. Rather, coordination requires a kind of information web in which members of the supply chain share information simultaneously with all other participants, often using Internet technologies and RFID.[47]

Many companies in South Africa are learning a whole new approach to doing business now that Walmart's acquisition of South African retail chain Massmart has been approved. Walmart is famous for its tightly coordinated, JIT procurement and distribution system. Johannesburg-based Foodcorp, one of South Africa's largest food companies, was one of the first suppliers chosen to learn the system at Walmart's Bentonville, Arkansas, headquarters. Tom Pienaar, group sales director for Foodcorp, says that Walmart's procurement and distribution system works "like a machine."[48]

Information Technology Has Transformed Management

Advanced information technology makes JIT inventory management work seamlessly, but it has also transformed management in many other ways. An organization's **information technology (IT)** consists of the hardware, software, telecommunications, database management, and other technologies that the company uses to store data and make them available in the form of information for organizational decision making. In general, information technology has positive implications for the practice of management.

BOUNDARIES DISSOLVE; COLLABORATION REIGNS

The hospitals of Partners HealthCare System, the largest hospital network in New England, are linked by an electronic medical records system with the offices of more than 4,000 physicians with admitting privileges. The system ties doctors, nurses, staff specialists, and others into a coordinated team to provide better care, avoid redundant tests, and prevent potentially conflicting prescriptions.[49] Via an Internet competition, PepsiCo let consumers decide which new flavor of Mountain Dew to stock permanently on store shelves. And at the EBC High School for Public Service in Brooklyn, New York, teams of students use blogs and wikis to collaborate and share information about human rights violations with one another and with people from around the world.[50]

Time, distance, and other boundaries between individuals, departments, and organizations are irrelevant in today's world. Collaboration is what it's all about. Information technology can connect people around the world for the sharing and exchange of information and ideas. As Pulitzer Prize–winning journalist and author Thomas L. Friedman put it, "Wherever you look today . . . hierarchies are being flattened and value is being created less and less within vertical silos and more and more through horizontal collaboration within companies, between companies, and among individuals."[51]

KNOWLEDGE MANAGEMENT AND WEB 2.0

Information technology plays a key role in managers' efforts to support and leverage organizational knowledge. **Knowledge management** refers to the efforts to systematically gather knowledge, organize it, make it widely available throughout the organization, and foster a culture of continuous learning and knowledge sharing.[52]

IT systems facilitate knowledge management by enabling organizations to collect, store, and analyze tremendous amount of data, as well as share information and knowledge all across the enterprise.[53] One IT application for knowledge management is the use of **business intelligence software** that analyzes data and extracts useful insights, patterns, and relationships that might be significant.[54] Managers can identify sets of products that particular market segments purchase, patterns of transactions that signal possible fraud, or patterns of product performance that may indicate defects. Another hot topic in corporate IT concerns **expert-locator systems** that identify and catalog experts in a searchable database so people can identify who has knowledge that they can use.[55] Consider the example of Converteam, a company with headquarters in the United Kingdom that maintains power generation and propulsion systems for hundreds of ships and oil exploration platforms around the world. Employees working in China, India, Brazil, the United States, and Norway can access an IT system that includes contact details for engineers working in various countries along with an expertise inventory. Engineers can contact one another directly regarding new products, challenges, and so forth, rather than having to go through headquarters.[56]

Many organizations use **groupware**, software that works on a computer network or via the Internet to link people or workgroups across a room or around the globe. The software enables managers or team members to communicate, share information, and work simultaneously on the same document, chart, or diagram and see changes and comments as they are made by others. Sometimes called *collaborative work systems*, groupware systems allow people to interact with one another in an electronic meeting space and at the same time take advantage of computer-based support data.

Many of today's companies also incorporate the use of new technologies collectively referred to as *Web 2.0* to support knowledge sharing. Web 2.0 encompasses a range of tools, the most commonly used being blogs, wikis, and social networks. A *blog* is a running Web log that allows an individual to post opinions and ideas. The simplicity and informality of blogs make them an easy and comfortable medium for people to communicate and share ideas. The microblogging service Twitter has become a phenomenon, used by organizations as diverse as FedEx, Newell Rubbermaid, and the National Football League (NFL).[57] A *wiki* is similar to a blog and uses software to create a Web site that allows people to create, share, and edit content through a browser-based interface. Rather than simply sharing opinions and ideas as with a blog, wikis are free-form, allowing people to edit what they find on the site and add content.[58] At Rosen Law, a law firm in Raleigh, North Carolina, managers moved all contracts, court orders, case files, and other documents to a secure wiki. If people see a better way to organize information, they go ahead and do it. Lawyers and paralegals, for instance, have different needs, so the two groups edited one another's entries until both were happy with certain categorizations.[59]

> ## "The qualities that make Twitter inane and half-baked are what make it so powerful."
>
> — JONATHAN ZITTRAIN, HARVARD LAW PROFESSOR AND INTERNET EXPERT

Social networking is an extension of blogs and wikis. Social networking sites provide an unprecedented peer-to-peer communication channel, where people interact in an online community, producing and sharing all sorts of information and opinions.[60] Because of the popularity of Facebook in people's personal lives, most employees are comfortable with the idea of "following" and communicating with their colleagues online. Using social networks enables employees to connect with one another across organizational and geographical boundaries based on professional relationships, shared interests, problems, or other criteria. Dallas-based 7-Eleven Inc. has thousands of field consultants using Yammer to share knowledge among themselves and with local franchise owners.[61] A Symantec salesman in Dubai created a group on the company's social network that exchanges sales tips from employees around the world.[62] The nature of social networking builds trust so that people are more likely to cooperate and share information.[63]

ENTERPRISE RESOURCE PLANNING SYSTEMS

Another key IT component for many companies is an approach to information management called enterprise resource planning. **Enterprise resource planning (ERP) systems** integrate and optimize all the various business processes across the entire firm.[64] An ERP system can collect, process, and provide information about an organization's entire enterprise, including orders, product design, production, purchasing, inventory, distribution, human resources, receipt of payments, and forecasting of future demand. Such a system links these areas of activity into a network, as illustrated in Exhibit A.6.

When a salesperson takes an order, the ERP system checks to see how the order affects inventory levels, scheduling, human resources, purchasing, and distribution. The system replicates organizational processes in software, guides employees through the processes step by step, and automates as many of them as possible. For example, the software can cut an accounts payable check automatically as soon as a clerk confirms that goods have been received in inventory, send an online purchase order immediately after a manager has authorized a purchase, or schedule production at the most appropriate plant after an order is received.[65] In addition, because the system integrates data about all aspects of operations, managers and employees at all levels can see how decisions and actions in one part of the organization affect other parts, using this information to make better decisions. More recently, ERP has incorporated tools for supply chain management, so that coordination across organizational boundaries with customers and suppliers is strengthened as well.[66] ERP systems can be expensive and difficult to implement, but when applied successfully, an ERP system can cut costs, shorten cycle time, enhance productivity, and improve relationships with customers and suppliers.

APPENDIX

EXHIBIT   A.6   Example of an ERP Network

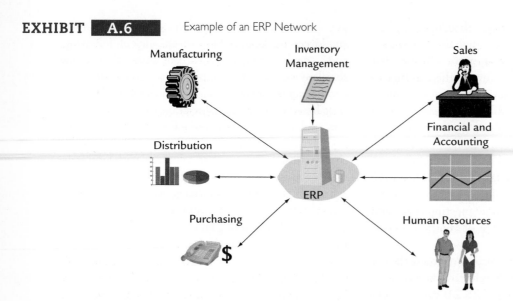

The Internet and E-Business

Managers in almost every organization have incorporated the Internet as part of their information technology strategies.[67] Business, government, military, and nonprofit organizations quickly realized the potential of the Internet for expanding their operations globally, improving business processes, reaching new customers or clients, and making the most of their resources. Intelligence officers for the U.S. military, for example, study live video feeds from drones and spy planes, visit social networking sites, and carry on conversations in chat rooms to track insurgents and relay warnings to soldiers in the field about roadside bombs and other dangers. The fluid connections enabled by the Internet help the military act more quickly and more effectively.[68] Dr. Pepper has built a Facebook fan base of 8.5 million people. Managers put out two messages a day on the company's fan page and then mine the data to see what people are thinking.[69] Greenpeace International used Facebook, Twitter, and YouTube to organize and conduct an online protest claiming food giant Nestlé purchases palm oil from companies that are destroying the Indonesian rain forest.[70] And numerous businesses advertise and sell products over the Internet. Exhibit A.7 shows one of the many products that Apple sells over the Internet and in retail stores. Most large organizations, and many small ones, are involved in some type of e-business. **E-business** can be defined as any business that takes place by digital processes over a computer network rather than in physical space. **E-commerce** is a more limited term that refers specifically to business exchanges or transactions that occur electronically. Today, e-commerce is transforming into *m-commerce*, which simply means the ability to conduct business transactions through a mobile device. The world has gone mobile. For many

EXHIBIT   A.7

Apple Sells Products in Retail Stores and via the Internet

AP Photo/Koji Sasahara

people, their cell phone is always within reach, and they use it for everything from ordering a pizza to accessing their bank accounts.[71] A study by ABI Research suggests that by 2015, shoppers around the world will spend about $119 billion on goods and services bought via their mobile phones.[72]

Some organizations, such as eBay, Amazon.com, Expedia, and Google, would not exist without the Internet. However, most traditional, established organizations, including General Electric (GE); the City of Madison, Wisconsin; Macy's; and the U.S. Postal Service, also make extensive use of the Internet, and we will focus on these types of organizations in the remainder of this section.

Exhibit A.8 illustrates the key components of e-business for two organizations, a manufacturing company and a retail chain. First, each organization operates an **intranet**, an internal communications system that uses the technology and standards of the Internet but is accessible only to people within the company. The next component is a system that allows the separate companies to share data and information. An **extranet** is an external communications system that uses the Internet and is shared by two or more organizations. With an extranet, each organization moves certain data outside its private intranet but makes the data available only to the other companies sharing the extranet. The final piece of the overall system is the Internet, which is accessible to the general public. Organizations make some information available to the public through their Web sites, which may include products or services offered for sale.

The first step toward a successful e-business for an established firm is for managers to determine why they need such a business to begin with.[73] Failure to align the e-business initiative with corporate strategy can lead to e-business failure. Two basic strategic approaches for traditional organizations setting up an Internet operation are illustrated in Exhibit A.9. Some companies embrace e-business primarily to expand into new markets and reach new customers. Others use e-business as a route to increased productivity and cost efficiency.

E-BUSINESS STRATEGY: MARKET EXPANSION

Using the Internet allows a company to establish direct links to customers and expand into new markets. For example, to increase sales for his family's wine business, Wine Library, Gary Vaynerchuk offered free shipping of online orders and promoted it three ways. A direct marketing mailing cost $15,000 and attracted 200 new customers. A billboard ad cost $7,500 and brought in 300 new customers. When Vaynerchuk tweeted the promotion on Twitter, it cost him nothing and attracted 1,800 new customers. Vaynerchuk also posts a daily Webcast that has won a wide following. He calls it "virtual handshaking, working the room."[74]

An Internet division enables the organization to provide access around the clock to a worldwide market. Despite the huge lead of Amazon.com in online sales of merchandise, traditional retailers have been big winners with a market expansion strategy. JCPenney was one of the first traditional retailers to launch a Web site, in 1994, and it now has one of the most productive online stores among mainstream retailers. The Web site

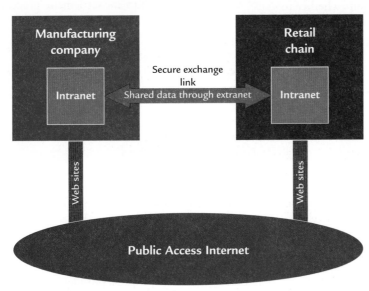

EXHIBIT **A.8**

The Key Components of E-Business for Two Traditional Organizations

SOURCES: Based on Jim Turcotte, Bob Silveri, and Tom Jobson, "Are You Ready for the E-Supply Chain?" *APICS—The Performance Advantage* (August 1998): 56–59.

APPENDIX

EXHIBIT **A.9**

Strategies for Engaging Clicks
with Bricks

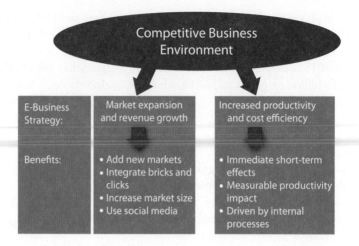

enabled the company to attract a younger customer base than those who typically shopped at JCPenney and find ways to lure them into bricks-and-mortar stores.[75] Most other retailers selling products online also use their Web sites to drive more traffic into stores. Getting people to the store gives staff a chance to push accessory items and increase sales. Interestingly, though, Walmart is testing a new concept as it strives to increase online sales: at a store near Chicago, shoppers can now pick up their Walmart.com purchases at the store's drive-through window.[76]

E-BUSINESS STRATEGY: INCREASING EFFICIENCY

With this approach, the e-business initiative is seen primarily as a way to improve the bottom line by increasing productivity and cutting costs. Managers at some companies are following tweets on Twitter to help them predict sales for the coming weeks and make decisions such as how many products to manufacture and ship, whether to increase store inventories, or whether to cut the price of certain items.[77] Managers at Wet Seal, a specialty clothing store selling mainly to teenage girls, uses the Internet to spot changing trends fast so that they can make better decisions about what to manufacture. A Web feature called

Outfitter allows users to put together their own outfits online; analyzing the 300,000 user-generated outfits gave managers an early lead on the trend toward wearing dressy tops with casual pants and jeans.[78] At Nibco, a manufacturer of piping products, 12 plants and distribution centers automatically share data on inventory and orders via the Internet, resulting in about 70 percent of orders being automated. The technology has helped Nibco trim its inventory by 13 percent, as well as respond more quickly to changes in orders from customers.[79]

Several studies attest to real and significant gains in productivity from e-business.[80] Even the smallest companies can realize gains. Rather than purchasing parts from a local supplier at premium rates, a small firm can access a worldwide market and find the best price, or negotiate better terms with the local supplier.[81] Service firms and government agencies can benefit too. In 2004, New York City became the first city to use the Internet to settle personal injury claims more efficiently by integrating the services of Cybersettle.com into its settlement process. Lawyers for both sides submit blind offers until a match is made. If an agreement can't be reached, the parties go back to face-to-face negotiations. Between 2004 and 2011, the city settled around 5,000 claims using Cybersettle, saving an estimated $94 million in settlement-related costs.[82]

Discussion Questions

1. What are the major differences between manufacturing and service organizations? Give examples of how each type might benefit from using Web 2.0 tools such as microblogging and social networks.

2. Boeing's 787 Dreamliner was seriously delayed because of slow deliveries from suppliers who were responsible for large chunks of the jet. Outsourcing has become an important aspect of supply chain management as companies strive to cut costs, yet the practice gives managers less

control, as at Boeing, and may decrease speed and flexibility. As an operations manager, how would you decide if a multinational supply chain is a better approach than trying to manufacture as much as possible in-house?

3. What type of production layout do you think would work best in a car dealership? What type might work best for an insurance company that provides customers with auto, home, health, and life insurance products? Discuss reasons for your answers.

4. What are the three types of inventory? Which type is most likely to be affected by the JIT inventory system? Explain.

5. Some companies are using both lean manufacturing and Six Sigma (discussed in Chapter 19) methods simultaneously to improve their operations. How do you think the two approaches might complement or conflict with each other? Explain.

6. Critics argue that RFID can potentially jeopardize consumer privacy by making it possible to link purchases to individuals or even to track the movement of individuals. Should this concern prevent companies from adopting RFID? Explain.

7. How might the organizers of an upcoming Olympics use an extranet to get all the elements of the event up and running on schedule?

8. Do you think it makes sense for a company such as Sears Holdings Corp., which has numerous shabby Sears and Kmart stores in need of makeovers, to focus resources on building the online business at the expense of its bricks-and-mortar business? Discuss.

9. The openness of wikis is both their strength and their weakness. As a business owner, why might you want to take advantage of this technology? How might you guard against potential problems, such as vulnerability to mistakes, pranks, self-serving posts, or cybervandalism?

Endnotes

1. Adapted from Carolyn Hopper, *Practicing Management Skills* (New York: Houghton Mifflin, 2003); and Jacquelyn Wonder and Priscilla Donovan, "Mind Openers," *Self* (March 1984).

2. Lida Mantzavinou, "The Airline Industry—In Serious Financial Trouble," *Public Service Europe*, June 15, 2012, www.publicserviceeurope.com/article/2082/the-airline-industry-in-serious-financial-trouble (accessed October 4, 2012); James Cowan, "Can Air Canada Be Saved?" *Canadian Business*, April 16, 2012, www.canadianbusiness.com/article/79337--can-air-canada-be-saved (accessed October 4, 2012); and Genevieve Shaw Brown, "American Airlines: Timeline of Troubles," *ABC News*, October 2, 2012, http://abcnews.go.com/blogs/lifestyle/2012/10/american-airlines-timeline-of-troubles/ (accessed October 4, 2012).

3. Seth Stevenson, "How Southwest Airlines Turns a Profit, Year After Year After Year," *Slate*, June 12, 2012, www.slate.com/articles/business/operations/2012/06/southwest_airlines_profitability_how_the_company_uses_operations_theory_to_fuel_its_success_.html (accessed October 4, 2012).

4. Dan Heath and Chip Heath, "The Telltale Brown M&M," *Fast Company* (March 2010): 36–38.

5. James D. Thompson, *Organizations in Action* (New York: McGraw-Hill, 1967).

6. Dana Mattioli and Julie Jargon, "McDonald's Boosts Imports to Japan Amid Supply-Chain Problems," *The Wall Street Journal*, March 31, 2011, http://online.wsj.com/article/SB10001424052748703806304576232902575855330.html (accessed October 4, 2012).

7. Based on Gregory B. Northcraft and Richard B. Chase, "Managing Service Demand at the Point of Delivery," *Academy of Management Review* 10 (1985): 66–75; and Richard B. Chase and David A. Tanski, "The Customer Contact Model for Organization Design," *Management Science* 29 (1983): 1037–1050.

8. Definition based on "Supply Chain Management," *BusinessDictionary .com*, www.businessdictionary.com/definition/supply-chain-management-SCM.html (accessed August 27, 2010); Thomas Wailgum, "Supply Chain Management Definition and Solutions," *CIO*, November 20, 2008, www.cio.com/article/40940/Supply_Chain_Management_Definition_and_Solutions (accessed August 27, 2010); and Steven A. Melnyk and David R. Denzler, *Operations Management: A Value-Driven Approach* (Burr Ridge, IL: Richard D. Irwin, 1996), p. 613.

9. "Gartner Announces Ranking of Its 2012 Supply Chain Top 25," Gartner press release, May 22, 2012, www.gartner.com/it/page.jsp?id=2023116 (accessed October 4, 2012).

10. Based on Jim Turcotte, Bob Silveri, and Tom Jobson, "Are You Ready for the E-Supply Chain?" *APICS—The Performance Advantage* (August 1998): 56–59.

11. Daniel Michaels, "Hit by Delays, Airbus Tries New Way of Building Planes," *The Wall Street Journal*, July 11, 2012, A1.

12. Kevin O'Marah, "The AMR Supply Chain Top 25 for 2010," AMR Research, June 2, 2010, www.gartner.com/DisplayDocument?ref=clientFriendlyUrl&id=1379613 (accessed August 27, 2010); and Cecilie Rohwedder and Keith Johnson, "Pace-Setting Zara Seeks More Speed to Fight Its Rising Cheap-Chic Rivals," *The Wall Street Journal*, February 20, 2008.

13. Based on ideas from Keith Duplessie, "Designing a Detail Shop for Success," *ModernCarCare.com*, June 17, 2009, www.modern carcare.com/articles/2009/06/designing-a-detail-shop-for-success.aspx (accessed September 15, 2010).

14. Melinda Beck, "Critical (Re)thinking: How ICUs Are Getting a Much-Needed Makeover," *The Wall Street Journal*, March 28, 2011, http://online.wsj.com/article/

SB10001424052748704132204576190632996146752
.html (accessed October 5, 2012).

15. Karl Taro Greenfeld, "Fast and Furious," *Bloomberg Business-week* (May 9–May 15, 2011): 64-69.

16. Based on the claims form processing method used by Rely Systems, www.relyservices.com /insurance-claims-processing-services. htm (accessed September 15, 2010).

17. Nancy Lea Hyer and Karen A. Brown, "Work Cells with Staying Power: Lessons for Process–Complete Operations," *California Management Review* 46, no. 1 (Fall 2003): 27–52.

18. Pete Engardio, "Lean and Mean Gets Extreme," *Business-Week* (March 23 & 30, 2009): 60–62.

19. Kelly Wardle, "One Enchanted Evening," *Special Events*, February 1, 2006, www.specialevents .com/corporate/ events_one _enchanted_evening_20060203 /index .html (accessed May 27, 2008).

20. Daniel Michaels and J. Lynn Lunsford, "Streamlined Plane Making," *The Wall Street Journal*, April 1, 2005.

21. Anne D'Innocenzio, "Wal-Mart Plan to Use Smart Tags Raises Privacy Concerns," *USA Today*, July 25, 2010, www .usatoday.com /money/industries/retail/2010-07-25-wal-mart-smart-tags_N.htm (accessed July 26, 2010).

22. Dean Elmuti and Michael Abebe, "RFID Reshapes the Global Supply Chain," *Industrial Management* (March–April 2005): 27–31; John Teresko, "Plant Strategies: Winning with Wireless," *Industry Week* (June 2003): 60–66; Meridith Levinson, "The RFID Imperative," *CIO* (December 1, 2003): 78–91; and Rob Bamforth, "Plenty of Life Ahead for RFID and NFC," *ZDNet*, December 2, 2009, http://www.zdnet.com/plenty-of-life-ahead-for-rfid-and-nfc-3040153140/ (accessed October 30, 2012).

23. Erick Schonfeld, "Tagged for Growth," *Business 2.0* (December 2006): 58–61.

24. Maryanne Murray Buechner, "Cracking the Code," *FSB: Fortune Small Business* (March 2004): 72–73.

25. Barnaby J. Feder, "Military to Urge Suppliers to Adopt Radio ID Tags," *The New York Times*, November 12, 2005.

26. Zach Dubinsky, "New Credit Cards Pose Security Problem," *CBC News*, June 2, 2010, www.cbc.ca/news/ technology/story/2010/05/31/f-rfid-credit-cards-security-concerns.html (accessed October 30, 2012).

27. Claire Swedberg, "Tagsys, ICM Airport Technics Market RFID Bag Tag to Airlines," *RFID Journal*, November 16, 2011, www.rfidjournal.com/article/view/8966/ (accessed October 30, 2012); and Scott McCartney, "The Middle Seat: A New Way to Prevent Lost Luggage," *The Wall Street Journal*, February 27, 2007.

28. Heritage Foundation statistic, based on data from the U.S. Department of Labor, Bureau of Labor Statistics, "Multifactor Productivity, 1987–2007," and reported in James Sherk, "Technology Explains Drop in Manufacturing Jobs," *Backgrounder* (October 12, 2010): 1–8.

29. This discussion is based on Jim Brown, "Leveraging the Digital Factory," *Industrial Management* (July–August 2009): 26–30; John Teresko, "Winning with Digital Manufacturing," *IndustryWeek* (July 2008): 45–47; Jack R. Meredith, "The

Strategic Advantages of the Factory of the Future," *California Management Review* 29 (Spring 1987): 27–41; and Althea Jones and Terry Webb, "Introducing Computer Integrated Manufacturing," *Journal of General Management* 12 (Summer 1987): 60–74.

30. Kate Linebaugh, "Honda's Flexible Plants Provide Edge; Company Can Rejigger Vehicle Output to Match Consumer Demand Faster than Its Rivals," *The Wall Street Journal*, September 23, 2008, B1.

31. B. Joseph Pine II, *Mass Customization: The New Frontier in Business Competition* (Boston, MA: Harvard Business School Press, 1999).

32. Erick Schonfeld, "The Customized, Digitized, Have-It-Your-Way Economy," *Fortune* (September 28, 1998): 115–124.

33. Julie Jargon, "Latest Starbucks Buzzword: 'Lean' Japanese Techniques," *The Wall Street Journal*, August 4, 2009.

34. Definition based on "Principles of Lean Thinking," National Research Council, July 2004, www.itc.mb.ca/downloads/ resources_by _topic/princ_lean%20thinking/Principleso-fLeanThinking RevD2004.pdf (accessed August 31, 2010); and "What Is Lean?" Lean Enterprise Institute, http://www .lean.org/Whatslean/ (accessed August 31, 2010).

35. Paul Migliorato, "Toyota Retools Japan," *Business 2.0* (August 2004): 39–41.

36. Peter Strozniak, "Toyota Alters Face of Production," *Industry Week* (August 13, 2001): 46–48; and Jeffrey K. Liker and James M. Morgan, "The Toyota Way in Services: The Case of Lean Product Development," *Academy of Management Perspectives* (May 2006): 5–20.

37. Art Kleiner, "Leaning Toward Utopia," *Strategy + Business*, no. 39 (Second Quarter 2005): 76–87; Fara Warner, "Think Lean," *Fast Company* (February 2002): 40, 42; Norihiko Shirouzu, "Gadget Inspector: Why Toyota Wins Such High Marks on Quality Surveys," *The Wall Street Journal*, March 15, 2001; and James P. Womack and Daniel T. Jones, *The Machine That Changed the World: The Story of Lean Production* (New York: HarperCollins, 1991).

38. Renée Stern, "Going Lean Drives Business Success at E-Z GO," *Global Business and Organizational Excellence* (March–April 2011): 15–24.

39. Paul Davidson, "Lean Manufacturing Helps Companies Survive Recession," *USA Today*, November 1, 2009.

40. Julie Jargon, "Corporate News: Eateries' New Way to Shop," *The Wall Street Journal*, April 1, 2011, B5.

41. Reported in Davidson, "Lean Manufacturing Helps Companies Survive Recession."

42. Loretta Chao and Lorraine Luk, "Acer Reassesses Inventory Policies," *The Wall Street Journal*, June 6, 2011, B5.

43. R. J. Schonberger, *Japanese Manufacturing Techniques: Nine Hidden Lessons in Simplicity* (New York: Free Press, 1982).

44. Luciana Beard and Stephen A. Butler, "Introducing JIT Manufacturing: It's Easier than You Think," *Business Horizons* (September–October 2000): 61–64.

45. Robert J. Vokurka, Rhonda R. Lummus, and Dennis Krumwiede, "Improving Manufacturing Flexibility: The

Enduring Value of JIT and TQM," *SAM Advanced Management Journal* (Winter 2007): 14–21.

46. Based on Ronald Henkoff, "Delivering the Goods," *Fortune* (November 28, 1994): 64–78.

47. Noel P. Greis and John D. Kasarda, "Enterprise Logistics in the Information Era," *California Management Review* 39, no. 4 (Summer 1997): 55–78; "Kanban: The Just-in-Time Japanese Inventory System," *Small Business Report* (February 1984): 69–71; and Richard C. Walleigh, "What's Your Excuse for Not Using JIT?" *Harvard Business Review* 64 (March–April 1986): 38–54.

48. Devon Maylie, "Africa Learns the Wal-Mart Way," *The Wall Street Journal*, September 7, 2012, B1.

49. Catherine Arnst, "Upsetting the Caste System," *BusinessWeek* (May 4, 2009): 36.

50. George Raine, "Sharing Wisdom; Brick-and-Mortar Shops Among Those Embracing Philosophy of Web 2.0," *San Francisco Chronicle*, July 20, 2008; and Liz Pape, "Blended Teaching & Learning," *School Administrator* (April 2010): 16–21.

51. Thomas L. Friedman, "It's a Flat World, After All," *The New York Times Magazine* (April 3, 2005): 32–37.

52. Based on Andrew Mayo, "Memory Bankers," *People Management* (January 22, 1998): 34–38; William Miller, "Building the Ultimate Resource," *Management Review* (January 1999): 42–45; and Todd Datz, "How to Speak Geek," *CIO Enterprise*, Section 2 (April 15, 1999): 46–52.

53. Thomas H. Davenport, Laurence Prusak, and Bruce Strong, "Business Insight (A Special Report): Organization; Putting Ideas to Work: Knowledge Management Can Make a Difference—But It Needs to Be More Pragmatic," *The Wall Street Journal*, March 10, 2008.

54. Meridith Levinson, "Business Intelligence: Not Just for Bosses Anymore," *CIO* (January 15, 2006): 82–88; and Alice Dragoon, "Business Intelligence Gets Smart," *CIO* (September 15, 2003): 84–91.

55. Dorit Nevo, Izak Benbasat, and Yair Wand, "Knowledge Management; Who Knows What?" *The Wall Street Journal*, October 26, 2009.

56. Mark Easterby-Smith and Irina Mikhailava, "Knowledge Management: In Perspective," *People Management* (June 2011): 34–37.

57. Shel Israel, "In Business, Early Birds Twitter Most Effectively," *Bloomberg Businessweek*, October 8, 2009, www.businessweek .com/managing/content/oct2009/ca2009106_370257.htm (accessed September 1, 2010).

58. Rob Koplowitz, "Building a Collaboration Strategy," *KM World* (November–December 2009): 14–15; and Cindy Waxer, "Workers of the World—Collaborate," *Fortune Small Business* (April 2005): 57–58.

59. Evelyn Nussenbaum, "Tech to Boost Teamwork," *Fortune Small Business* (February 2008): 51–54.

60. Andreas M. Kaplan and Michael Haenlein, "Users of the World, Unite! The Challenges and Opportunities of Social Media," *Business Horizons* 53 (2010): 59–68; and

61. Shayndi Raice, "Social Networking Heads to the Office," *The Wall Street Journal*, April 2, 2012, R6.

61. Raice, "Social Networking Heads to the Office."

62. Verne G. Kopytoff, "Companies Stay in the Loop by Using In-House Social Networks," *The New York Times*, June 27, 2011, B3.

63. Nevo, Benbasat, and Wand, "Who Knows What?"

64. This discussion is based on Judy Sweeney and Simon Jacobson, "ERP Breaks," *Industry Week* (January 2007): 11a–13a; and Vincent A. Mabert, Ashok Soni, and M. A. Venkataramanan, "Enterprise Resource Planning: Common Myths Versus Evolving Reality," *Business Horizons* (May–June 2001): 69–76.

65. Derek Slater, "What Is ERP?" *CIO Enterprise* (May 15, 1999): 86.

66. Raymond F. Zammuto et al., "Information Technology and the Changing Fabric of Organization," *Organization Science* 18, no. 5 (September–October 2007): 749–762.

67. Turcotte, Silveri, and Jobson, "Are You Ready for the E-Supply Chain?"

68. Christopher Drew, "Military Taps Social Networking Skills," *The New York Times*, June 7, 2010.

69. Geoffrey A. Fowler, "Leadership: Information Technology (A Special Report)—Are You Talking to Me?" *The Wall Street Journal*, April 25, 2011, R5.

70. Emily Steel, "Nestlé Takes a Beating on Social Media Sites; Greenpeace Coordinates Protests over Food Giant's Palm-Oil Purchases from Firm Alleged to Have Cut Down Rain Forest," *The Wall Street Journal*, March 29, 2010.

71. Stephanie Marcus, "Top 5 Mobile Commerce Trends for 2010," Mobile Trends Series, Mashable.com, July 22, 2010, http://mashable.com/2010/07/22/2010-mobile-commerce-trends/ (accessed August 25, 2011); and Julie Jargon, "Business Technology: Domino's IT Staff Delivers Slick Site, Ordering System," *The Wall Street Journal*, November 24, 2009, B5.

72. ABI Research study reported in Stephanie Marcus, "Top 5 Mobile Commerce Trends for 2010."

73. This discussion is based on Long W. Lam and L. Jean Harrison-Walker, "Toward an Objective-Based Typology of E-Business Models," *Business Horizons* (November–December 2003): 17–26; and Detmar Straub and Richard Klein, "E-Competitive Transformations," *Business Horizons* (May–June 2001): 3–12.

74. Jan M. Rosen, "Be It Twittering or Blogging, It's All About Marketing," *The New York Times* (March 12, 2009), www.nytimes.com/2009/03/12/business/smallbusiness/12social.ready.html (accessed March 12, 2009).

75. Robert Berner, "J. C. Penney Gets the Net," *BusinessWeek* (May 7, 2007): 70; and "JCPenney.com Celebrates 10th Anniversary of Online Shopping," *Business Wire* (November 8, 2004).

76. Nanette Byrnes, "More Clicks at the Bricks," *BusinessWeek* (December 17, 2007): 50–52; and Miguel Bustillo

and Geoffrey A. Fowler, "Wal-Mart Uses Its Stores to Get an Edge Online," *The Wall Street Journal*, December 15, 2009.

77. Huaxia Rui, Andrew Whinston, and Elizabeth Winkler, "Follow the Tweets," *The Wall Street Journal*, November 30, 2009.

78. Steve Lohr, "A Data Explosion Remakes Retailing," *The New York Times* (January 3, 2010), BU3.

79. "The Web Smart 50," *Business Week* (November 21, 2005): 82–112.

80. Jonathan L. Willis, "What Impact Will E-Commerce Have on the U.S. Economy?" *Economic Review—Federal Reserve Bank of Kansas City* 89, no. 2 (Second Quarter 2004): 53ff; and Timothy J. Mullaney with Heather Green, Michael Arndt, Robert D. Hof, and Linda Himelstein, "The E-Biz Surprise," *Business Week* (May 12, 2003): 60–68.

81. Straub and Klein, "E-Competitive Transformations."

82. "The Web Smart 50"; and "Cybersettle for Governments and Municipalities," Cybersettle.com Web site, www.cybersettle .com/pub/home/about/users/govt.aspx.http://www .cybersettle.com/pub/home/about/users/govt.aspx (accessed October 30, 2012).

Glossary

A

Accountability Means that people with authority and responsibility are subject to reporting and justifying task outcomes to those above them in the chain of command.

Achievement culture A results-oriented culture that values competitiveness, personal initiative, and achievement.

Activity ratio Measures the organization's internal performance with respect to key activities defined by management.

Adaptability culture Characterized by values that support the company's ability to interpret and translate signals from the environment into new behavior responses.

Adjourning The stage during which members of temporary teams prepare for the team's disbanding.

Administrative model A decision-making model that includes the concepts of *bounded rationality* and *satisficing* and describes how managers make decisions in situations that are characterized by uncertainty and ambiguity.

Administrative principles approach A subfield of the classical perspective that focuses on the total organization rather than the individual worker and delineates the management functions of planning, organizing, commanding, coordinating, and controlling.

Affirmative action Requires that employers take positive steps to guarantee equal employment opportunities for people within protected groups.

After-action review A disciplined procedure whereby managers review the results of decisions to evaluate what worked, what didn't, and how to do things better.

Alienated follower A person who is an independent, critical thinker but is passive in the organization.

Ambidextrous approach Incorporating structures and processes that are appropriate for both the creative impulse and the systematic implementation of innovations.

Ambiguity A condition in which the goals to be achieved or the problem to be solved is unclear, alternatives are difficult to define, and information about outcomes is unavailable.

Angel financing Occurs when a wealthy individual who believes in the idea for a start-up provides personal funds and advice to help the business get started.

Application form A selection device that collects information about the applicant's education, previous work experience, and other background characteristics.

Assessment center Used to select individuals with high managerial potential based on their performance on a series of simulated managerial tasks.

Attitude A cognitive and affective evaluation that predisposes a person to act in a certain way.

Attribution A judgment about what caused a person's behavior—either characteristics of the person or of the situation.

Authentic leadership Leadership by individuals who know and understand themselves, who espouse and act consistent with higher-order ethical values, and who empower and inspire others with their openness and authenticity.

Authoritarianism The belief that power and status differences should exist within an organization.

Authority The formal and legitimate right of a manager to make decisions, issue orders, and allocate resources to achieve outcomes desired by the organization.

Avoidance learning Removing an unpleasant consequence once a behavior is improved. Also called *negative reinforcement*.

B

Balanced scorecard A comprehensive management control system that balances traditional financial measures with measures of customer service, internal business processes, and the organization's capacity for learning and growth.

Balance sheet Shows the firm's financial position with respect to assets and liabilities at a specific point in time.

BCG matrix A concept developed by the Boston Consulting Group (BCG) that evaluates strategic business units with respect to two dimensions—business growth rate and market share—and classifies them as cash cows, stars, question marks, or dogs.

Behavioral sciences approach Draws from psychology, sociology, and other social sciences to develop theories about human behavior and interaction in an organizational setting.

Behaviorally anchored rating scale (BARS) A performance evaluation technique that relates an employee's performance to specific job-related incidents.

Behavior modification The set of techniques by which reinforcement theory is used to modify human behavior.

Benchmarking The continuous process of measuring products, services, and practices against major competitors or industry leaders.

Big Five personality factors Dimensions that describe an individual's extroversion, agreeableness, conscientiousness, emotional stability, and openness to experience.

Bottom of the pyramid (BOP) concept Proposes that corporations can alleviate poverty and other social ills, as well as make significant profits, by selling to the world's poor.

Bottom-up budgeting Involves lower-level managers anticipating their department's budget needs and passing them up to top management for approval.

Boundary-spanning roles Link to and coordinate the organization with key elements in the external environment.

Bounded rationality Means that people have the time and cognitive ability to process only a limited amount of information on which to base decisions.

Brainstorming A technique that uses a face-to-face group to spontaneously suggest a broad range of alternatives for making a decision.

Bureaucratic organizations approach Emphasizes management on an impersonal, rational basis through elements such as clearly defined authority and responsibility, formal recordkeeping, and separation of management and ownership.

Business incubator Helps start-up companies by connecting them with a range of experts and mentors who nurture them, thus increasing their likelihood of success.

Business intelligence software Software that analyzes data from multiple sources and extracts useful insights, patterns, and relationships that might be significant.

Business-level strategy Pertains to each business unit or product line within the organization.

Business plan A document specifying the details of the business.

C

Capital budget A budget that plans and reports investments in major assets to be depreciated over several years.

Cash budget A budget that estimates receipts and expenditures of money on a daily or weekly basis to ensure that an organization has sufficient cash to meet its obligations.

Cellular layout A facilities layout in which machines dedicated to sequences of production are grouped into cells in accordance with group-technology principles.

Centralization Means that decision authority is located near top organization levels.

Ceremony A planned activity at a special event.

Certainty A situation in which all the information the decision maker needs is fully available.

Chain of command An unbroken line of authority that links all individuals in the organization and specifies who reports to whom.

Change agent An organization development (OD) specialist who contracts with an organization to help managers facilitate change.

Changing The "intervention" stage of organization development (OD), when change agents teach people new behaviors and skills and guide them in using them in the workplace.

Channel The medium by which a message is sent, such as a phone call, blog, or text message.

Channel richness The amount of information that can be transmitted during a communication episode.

Charismatic leader A leader who has the ability to inspire and motivate people to transcend their expected performance, even to the point of personal sacrifice.

Chief ethics officer A manager who oversees all aspects of ethics and legal compliance.

Classical model A decision-making model based on the assumption that managers should make logical decisions that are economically sensible and in the organization's best economic interest.

Classical perspective Takes a rational, scientific approach to management and seeks to turn organizations into efficient operating machines.

Coalition An informal alliance among managers who support a specific goal or solution.

Code of ethics A formal statement of the organization's values regarding ethics and social responsibility.

Coercive power Power that stems from the authority to punish or recommend punishment.

Cognitive dissonance A psychological discomfort that occurs when two attitudes or an attitude and a behavior conflict.

Collaboration A joint effort between people from two or more departments to produce outcomes that meet a common goal or shared purpose.

Collectivism A preference for a tightly knit social framework in which individuals look after one another and organizations protect their members' interests.

Communication The process by which information is exchanged and understood by two or more people.

Compensation All monetary payments and all nonmonetary goods or benefits used to reward employees.

Compensatory justice Argues that individuals should be compensated for the cost of their injuries by the party responsible, and individuals should not be held responsible for matters over which they have no control.

Competitive advantage Refers to what sets the organization apart from others and provides it with a distinctive edge in the marketplace.

Competitors Organizations within the same industry or type of business that vie for the same set of customers.

Conceptual skill The cognitive ability to see the organization as a whole and the relationships among its parts.

Conflict Antagonistic interaction in which one party attempts to block the intentions or goals of another.

Conformist A follower who participates actively in the organization but does not use critical thinking skills.

Consideration Describes the extent to which a leader is sensitive to subordinates, respects their ideas and feelings, and establishes mutual trust.

Consistency culture Values and rewards a methodical, rational, orderly way of doing things.

Content theories Theories that emphasize the needs that motivate people.

Contingency approach A model of leadership that describes the relationship between leadership styles and specific situations.

Contingency planning Identifies important factors in the environment and defines a range of alternative responses to be taken in the case of emergencies, setbacks, or unexpected conditions.

Contingency view Tells managers that what works in one organizational situation might not work in others.

Contingent worker A person who works for an organization, but not on a permanent or full-time basis, including temporary placements, independent contractors, freelancers, and part-time employees.

Continuous improvement The implementation of a large number of small, incremental improvements in all areas of the organization on an ongoing basis. Also called *kaizen*.

Continuous process production Involves mechanization of the entire workflow and nonstop production, such as in chemical plants or petroleum refineries.

Controlling Is concerned with monitoring employees' activities, keeping the organization on track toward meeting its goals and making corrections as necessary.

Coordination The managerial task of adjusting and synchronizing the diverse activities among different individuals and departments.

Core competence Something that the organization does particularly well in comparison to others.

Corporate governance Refers to the framework of systems, rules, and practices by which an organization ensures accountability, fairness, and transparency in the firm's relationships with stakeholders.

Corporate-level strategy Pertains to the organization as a whole and the combination of business units and products that make it up.

Corporate social responsibility The obligation of organizational managers to make choices and take actions that will enhance the welfare and interests of society as well as the organization.

Corporate university An in-house training and development facility that offers broad-based learning opportunities for employees.

Corporation An artificial entity created by the state and existing apart from its owners.

Cost leadership strategy A strategy with which managers aggressively seek efficient facilities, cut costs, and use tight cost controls to be more efficient than others in the industry.

Creativity The generation of novel ideas that may meet perceived needs or respond to opportunities for the organization.

Critical thinking Thinking independently and being mindful of the effect of one's behavior on achieving goals.

Cross-functional team A group of employees from various functional departments that meet as a team to resolve mutual problems.

Crowdfunding A way of raising capital that involves getting small amounts of money from a large number of investors, usually using social media or the Internet.

Cultural competence The ability to interact effectively with people of different cultures.

Cultural leader Defines and articulates important values that are tied to a clear and compelling mission.

Culture The set of key values, beliefs, understandings, and norms shared by members of an organization.

Culture change A major shift in the norms, values, and mindset of an entire organization.

Customers Include people and organizations that acquire goods or services from the organization.

Customer relationship management (CRM) Systems that use information technology to keep in close touch with customers, collect and manage large amounts of customer data, and provide superior customer value.

D

Debt financing Involves borrowing money, such as from friends, family, or a bank, that has to be repaid at a later date in order to start a business.

Decentralization Means that decision authority is pushed down to lower organization levels.

Decentralized control A situation where the organization fosters compliance with organizational goals through the use of organizational culture, group norms, and a focus on goals rather than rules and procedures.

Decentralized planning An approach where top executives or planning experts work with managers in major divisions or departments to develop their own goals and plans.

Decision A choice made from available alternatives.

Decision making The process of identifying problems and opportunities and then resolving them.

Decision styles Differences among people with respect to how they perceive problems and make choices.

Decode To read symbols to interpret the meaning of a message.

Delegation When managers transfer authority and responsibility to positions below them in the hierarchy.

Departmentalization The basis for grouping individual positions into departments and departments into the total organization.

Descriptive An approach that describes how managers actually make decisions, rather than how they should make decisions according to a theoretical model.

Devil's advocate A person who is assigned the role of challenging the assumptions and assertions made by the group to prevent premature consensus.

Diagnosis The step in which managers analyze underlying causal factors associated with the decision situation.

Differentiation strategy A strategy with which managers seek to distinguish the organization's products and services from those of others in the industry.

Digital factories Factories that use advanced technology such as RFID, robots, and wireless technology and apply computers to link together manufacturing components that previously stood alone.

Direct investing A market entry strategy in which the organization is directly involved in managing its production facilities in a foreign country.

Discretionary responsibility A voluntary measure guided by the organization's desire to make social contributions not mandated by economics, laws, or ethics.

Discrimination (1) Making hiring and promotion decisions based on criteria that are not job-relevant. (2) When someone acts out their negative attitudes toward people who are the targets of their prejudice.

Disruptive innovation Innovations in products, services, or processes that radically change competition in an industry, such as the advent of streaming video or e-books.

Distributive justice Requires that different treatment of individuals not be based on arbitrary characteristics.

Distributive negotiation A competitive and adversarial approach in which each party strives to get as much as it can, usually at the expense of the other party.

Diversification The strategy of moving into new lines of business.

Diversity All the ways in which employees differ.

Diversity of perspective Achieved when a manager creates a heterogeneous team made up of individuals with diverse backgrounds and skill sets.

Divisional structure An organizational structure that groups employees and departments based on similar organizational outputs (products or services), such that each division has a mix of functional skills and tasks.

Downward communication Messages sent from top management down to subordinates.

E

E → P expectancy The expectancy that putting effort into a given task will lead to high performance.

E-business Any business that takes place by digital processes over a computer network rather than in physical space.

E-commerce Business exchanges or transactions that occur electronically.

Economic dimension Represents the general economic health of the country or region in which the organization operates.

Economic force Affects the availability, production, and distribution of a society's resources.

Effective follower A critical, independent thinker who actively participates in the organization.

Effectiveness The degree to which the organization achieves a stated goal.

Efficiency The amount of resources—raw materials, money, and people—used to produce a desired volume of output.

Electronic brainstorming Brainstorming that takes place in an interactive group over a computer network, rather than meeting face to face.

Emotion A mental state that arises spontaneously rather than through conscious effort and is often accompanied by physiological changes.

Employee affinity group A group based on social identity, such as gender or race, and organized by employees to focus on concerns of employees from that group.

Empowerment The delegation of power and authority to subordinates in an organization.

Encode To select symbols with which to compose a message.

Engagement An emotional and mental state in which employees enjoy their work, contribute enthusiastically to meeting goals, and feel a sense of belonging and commitment to the organization.

Enterprise resource planning (ERP) system A networked information system that collects, processes, and provides information about an organization's entire enterprise, from identification of customer needs and receipt of orders to distribution of products and receipt of payments.

Entrepreneur A person who recognizes a viable idea for a business product or service and carries it out by finding and assembling the necessary resources.

Entrepreneurship The process of initiating a business, organizing the necessary resources, and assuming the associated risks and rewards.

Equity When the ratio of one person's outcomes to inputs equals that of another's.

Equity financing Funds that are invested in exchange for ownership in the company.

Equity theory A theory that focuses on individuals' perceptions of how fairly they are treated relative to others.

ERG theory A modification of the needs hierarchy that proposes three categories of needs: existence, relatedness, and growth.

Escalating commitment Refers to continuing to invest time and money in a decision despite evidence that it is failing.

Ethical dilemma A situation in which all alternative choices or behaviors have potentially negative consequences.

Ethics The code of moral principles and values that governs the behaviors of a person or group with respect to what is right or wrong.

Ethics committee A group of executives (and sometimes lower-level employees as well) charged with overseeing company ethics by ruling on questionable issues and disciplining violators.

Ethnocentrism The natural tendency among people to regard their own culture as superior to others.

Ethnorelativism The belief that groups and cultures are inherently equal.

Euro A single European currency that has replaced the currencies of 16 member nations of the European Union (EU).

Evidence-based decision making A process founded on a commitment to examining potential biases, seeking and examining evidence with rigor, and making informed and intelligent decisions based on the best available facts and evidence.

Exit interview An interview conducted with departing employees to determine reasons for their departure and learn about potential problems in the organization.

Expectancy theory Proposes that motivation depends on individuals' expectations about their ability to perform tasks and receive desired rewards.

Expense budget A budget that outlines the anticipated and actual expenses for a responsibility center.

Expert-locator systems Computerized systems that identify and catalog experts in a searchable database so people can quickly identify who has knowledge they can use.

Expert power Power that results from a leader's special knowledge or skill in the tasks performed by subordinates.

Exporting A market entry strategy in which a company maintains production facilities within its home country and transfers products for sale in foreign countries.

Extinction Withholding positive rewards and essentially ignoring undesirable behavior.

Extranet An external communications system that uses the Internet and is shared by two or more organizations.

Extrinsic reward A reward given by another person, such as a manager, including pay increases, promotions, and praise.

F

Feedback Occurs when the receiver responds to the sender's communication with a return message.

Femininity A cultural preference for relationships, cooperation, group decision making, and quality of life.

Finished-goods inventory Inventory consisting of items that have passed through the complete production process but have yet to be sold.

First-line manager A manager who is at the first or second level of the hierarchy and is directly responsible for overseeing a group of production employees.

Fixed-position layout A facilities layout in which the product remains in one location and the required tasks and equipment are brought to it.

Flat structure An organizational structure characterized by an overall broad span of management and relatively few hierarchical levels.

Focus strategy A strategy where managers use either a differentiation or a cost leadership approach, but they concentrate on a specific regional market or buyer group.

Force-field analysis A technique for determining which forces drive a proposed change and which forces restrain it.

Forming The stage of team development involving a period of orientation and getting acquainted.

Franchising (1) A form of licensing in which a company provides its foreign franchisees with a complete package of materials and services. (2) An arrangement by which the owner of a product or service allows others to purchase the right to distribute a product or service with help from the owner.

Free rider A person who benefits from team membership but does not make a proportionate contribution to the team's work.

Frustration-regression principle Suggests that failure to meet a high-order need may cause a regression to an already satisfied lower-order need; thus, people may move down as well as up the needs hierarchy.

Functional-level strategy Pertains to the major functional departments within each business unit, such as manufacturing, marketing, and research and development.

Functional manager A manager responsible for a department that performs a single functional task, such as finance or marketing.

Functional structure An organizational structure in which activities are grouped together by common function from the bottom to the top of the organization.

Functional team A team composed of a manager and his or her subordinates in the formal chain of command.

Fundamental attribution error A tendency to underestimate the influence of external factors on another person's accomplishments and to overestimate the influence of internal factors.

G

General environment Indirectly influences all organizations within an industry and includes five dimensions.

General manager A manager responsible for several departments that perform different functions.

Glass ceiling An invisible barrier that separates women and minorities from senior management positions.

Globalization The extent to which trade and investments, information, ideas, and political cooperation flow between countries.

Globalization strategy A strategy where product design and advertising are standardized throughout the world.

Global mindset The ability to appreciate and influence individuals, groups, organizations, and systems that represent different social, cultural, political, institutional, intellectual, and psychological characteristics.

Global outsourcing Engaging in the international division of labor so as to obtain the cheapest sources of labor and supplies, regardless of country. Sometimes called *offshoring*.

Global team A group made up of employees who come from different countries and whose activities span multiple countries.

Goal A desired future state that the organization wants to realize.

Goal-setting theory A theory that proposes that specific, challenging goals increase motivation and performance when the goals are accepted by subordinates and these subordinates receive feedback to indicate their progress toward goal achievement.

Grapevine A system that carries workplace gossip, a dominant force in organization communication when formal channels are not functioning effectively.

Greenfield venture An investment in which a company builds a subsidiary from scratch in a foreign country.

Groupthink The tendency of people in groups to suppress contrary opinions in a desire for harmony.

Groupware Software that works on a computer network or the Internet to facilitate information sharing, collaborative work, and group decision making.

H

Halo effect Occurs when a manager gives an employee the same rating on all dimensions of the job, even though performance may be good on some dimensions and poor on others.

Hawthorne studies A series of research efforts that was important in shaping ideas concerning how managers should treat workers.

Hero A figure who exemplifies the deeds, character, and attributes of a strong culture.

Hierarchical control Involves monitoring and influencing employee behavior through the use of rules, policies, hierarchy of authority, written documentation, reward systems, and other formal mechanisms.

Hierarchy of needs theory A theory proposed by Abraham Maslow saying that people are motivated by five categories of needs—physiological, safety, belongingness, esteem, and self-actualization—that exist in a hierarchical order.

High-context culture A culture in which people use communication to build personal relationships.

High-performance culture Emphasizes both cultural values and business results.

Horizontal communication The lateral or diagonal exchange of messages among peers or coworkers and includes team communication.

Horizontal linkage model Means that several departments, such as marketing, research, and manufacturing, work closely together to develop new products.

Human capital The economic value of the combined knowledge, experience, skills, and capabilities of employees.

Humanistic perspective Emphasizes understanding human behavior, needs, and attitudes in the workplace.

Human relations movement Stresses the satisfaction of employees' basic needs as the key to increased productivity.

Human resource management (HRM) The design and application of formal systems to ensure the effective and efficient use of human talent to accomplish organizational goals.

Human resource planning The forecasting of human resource needs and the projected matching of individuals with anticipated job vacancies.

Human resources perspective Suggests that jobs should be designed to meet people's higher-level needs by allowing employees to use their full potential.

Human skill A manager's ability to work with and through other people and to work effectively as part of a group.

Humility Being unpretentious and modest rather than arrogant and prideful.

Hygiene factors Factors that focus on lower-level needs and consider the presence or absence of job dissatisfiers, including working conditions, pay, and company policies.

I

Idea champion A person who sees the need for change and is passionately committed to making it happen.

Idea incubator An organizational program that provides a safe harbor where employees can generate and develop ideas without interference from company bureaucracy or politics.

Implementation Involves using managerial, administrative, and persuasive abilities to translate a chosen decision alternative into action.

Inclusion The degree to which an employee feels like an esteemed member of a group in which his or her uniqueness is highly appreciated.

Income statement Summarizes the firm's financial performance for a given time interval.

Individualism A preference for a loosely knit social framework in which individuals are expected to take care of themselves.

Individualism approach A decision-making approach suggesting that actions are ethical when they promote the individual's best long-term interests, because with everyone pursuing self-interest, the greater good is ultimately served.

Influence The effect a person's actions have on the attitudes, values, beliefs, or behavior of others.

Information technology (IT) The hardware, software, telecommunications, database management, and other technologies used to store, process, and distribute information.

Infrastructure A country's physical facilities, such as highways, utilities, and airports, that support economic activities.

Initiating structure Describes the extent to which a leader is task oriented and directs subordinates' work activities toward goal accomplishment.

Integrative negotiation A collaborative approach that is based on a win-win assumption, whereby the parties want to come up with a creative solution that benefits both sides of the conflict.

Intelligence team A cross-functional group of people who work together to gain a deep understanding of a specific competitive issue and offer insight and recommendations for planning.

Interactive leadership A leadership style characterized by values such as inclusion, collaboration, relationship building, and caring.

Internal environment Includes elements within the organization's boundaries, such as employees, management, and corporate culture.

International dimension In the external environment, represents events originating in foreign countries, as well as opportunities for companies in other countries.

International management Managing business operations in more than one country.

Internship An arrangement whereby an intern, usually a high school or college student, exchanges his or her services for the opportunity to gain work experience and see whether a particular career is appealing.

Interorganizational partnership Reduces boundaries and increases collaboration with other organizations.

Intranet An internal communications system that uses the technology and standards of the Internet but is accessible only to people within the organization.

Intrinsic reward The satisfaction that a person receives in the process of performing a particular action.

Intuition An aspect of administrative decision making that refers to a quick comprehension of a decision situation based on past experience but without conscious thought.

Inventory The goods the organization keeps on hand for use in the production process up to the point of selling the final products to customers.

Involvement culture A culture that places high value on meeting the needs of employees and values cooperation and equality.

ISO 9000 standards Represent an international consensus of what constitutes effective quality management as outlined by the International Organization for Standardization (ISO).

J

Job analysis The systematic process of gathering and interpreting information about the essential duties, tasks, and responsibilities of a job.

Job characteristics model A model of job design that considers core job dimensions, individuals' critical psychological states, and employee growth-need strength.

Job description A concise summary of the specific tasks and responsibilities of a position.

Job design Refers to applying motivational theories to the structure of work to improve motivation, productivity, and satisfaction.

Job enrichment Incorporating high-level motivators, such as achievement, recognition, and opportunities for growth, into the work.

Job evaluation The process of determining the value of jobs within an organization through an examination of job content.

Job satisfaction A positive attitude toward one's job.

Job specification Outlines the knowledge, skills, education, physical abilities, and other characteristics needed to perform a specific job adequately.

Joint venture A strategic alliance or program by two or more organizations.

Justice approach Says that ethical decisions must be based on standards of equity, fairness, and impartiality.

Just-in-time (JIT) inventory system An inventory control system that schedules materials to arrive precisely when they are needed on a production line.

K

Knowledge management The process of systematically gather knowledge, making it widely available throughout the organization, and fostering a culture of learning.

L

Labor market The people available for hire by the organization.

Large-group intervention An organization development (OD) approach that brings together people from different parts of the organization (and often including outside stakeholders) to discuss problems or opportunities and plan for change.

Law of effect Asserts that positively reinforced behavior tends to be repeated, and unreinforced or negatively reinforced behavior tends to be inhibited.

Leadership The ability to influence people toward the attainment of organizational goals.

Leadership grid A two-dimensional leadership model that measures the leader's concern for people and concern for production to categorize the leader in one of five different leadership styles.

Leading Using influence to motivate employees to achieve the organization's goals.

Lean thinking Philosophy that combines advanced technology and innovative management processes and uses highly-trained employees to solve problems, cut waste, improve the productivity, quality, and efficiency of products and services, and increase customer value.

Legal-political dimension Includes government regulations at the local, state, and federal levels, as well as political activities designed to influence company behavior.

Legitimate power Power that stems from a manager's formal position in an organization and the authority granted by that position.

Licensing A strategy where a company in one country makes certain resources available to companies in other countries to participate in the production and sale of its products abroad.

Line authority The formal power to direct and control immediate subordinates.

Liquidity ratio Indicates the organization's ability to meet its current debt obligations.

Listening The skill of grasping both facts and feelings to interpret a message's genuine meaning.

Locus of control Defines whether an individual places the primary responsibility for his successes and failures within himself or on outside forces.

Long-term orientation Reflects a greater concern for the future and a high value on thrift and perseverance.

Low-context culture A culture where people use communication primarily to exchange facts and information.

M

Machiavellianism A tendency to direct one's behavior toward the acquisition of power and the manipulation of other people for personal gain.

Making progress principle The idea that the single most important factor that can boost motivation, positive emotions, and perceptions during a workday is making progress toward meaningful goals.

Management The attainment of organizational goals in an effective and efficient manner through planning, organizing, leading, and controlling organizational resources.

Management by means (MBM) An approach that focuses people on the methods and processes used to attain results, rather than on the results themselves.

Management by objectives (MBO) A method whereby managers and employees define goals for every department, project, and person and use them to monitor subsequent performance.

Management science Uses mathematics, statistical techniques, and computer technology to facilitate management decision making, particularly for complex problems. Also called the *quantitative perspective*.

Managing diversity Creating a climate in which the potential advantages of diversity for organizational performance are maximized while the potential disadvantages are minimized.

Manufacturing organization An organization that produces physical goods.

Market entry strategy A tactic that managers use to enter foreign markets.

Masculinity A cultural preference for achievement, heroism, assertiveness, work centrality, and material success.

Mass customization A process by which products are produced cost-effectively in high volume but are customized to meet individual customer desires.

Mass production Characterized by long production runs to manufacture a large volume of products with the same specifications.

Matching model A human resources approach in which the organization and the individual attempt to match each other's needs, interests, and values.

Matrix approach A structural approach that uses both functional and divisional chains of command simultaneously, in the same part of the organization.

Matrix boss A functional or product supervisor responsible for one side of the matrix.

Mentor A higher-ranking senior member of the organization who is committed to providing upward mobility and support to a protégé's professional career.

Merger When two or more organizations combine to become one.

Message The tangible formulation of an idea to be sent to the employee.

Middle manager A manager who works at the middle level of the organization and is responsible for a major division or department.

Mission An organization's purpose or reason for existence.

Mission statement A broadly stated definition of the organization's basic business scope and operations that distinguishes it from similar types of organizations.

Modular approach An approach in which a manufacturing company uses outside suppliers to provide large chunks of a product such as an automobile, which are then assembled into a final product by a few employees.

Monoculture A culture that accepts only one way of doing things and one set of values and beliefs.

Moral rights approach Holds that ethical decisions are those that best maintain the fundamental rights of the people affected by them.

Motivation The arousal of enthusiasm and persistence to pursue a certain course of action.

Motivators Influence job satisfaction based on fulfilling higher-level needs such as achievement, recognition, responsibility, and opportunities for personal growth.

Multicultural team A team that is made up of members from diverse national, racial, ethnic, and cultural backgrounds.

Multidomestic strategy Means that competition in each country is handled independently, and product design and advertising are modified to suit the specific needs of individual countries.

Multinational corporation (MNC) An organization that receives more than 25 percent of its total sales revenues from operations outside the parent company's home country and has a number of distinctive managerial characteristics.

Myers-Briggs Type Indicator (MBTI) An assessment that measures a person's preferences for introversion versus extroversion, sensation versus intuition, thinking versus feeling, and judging versus perceiving.

N

Natural dimension Includes all elements that occur naturally on Earth, including plants, animals, rocks, and natural resources such as air, water, and climate.

Need for change A disparity between actual and desired performance.

Need to achieve An individual characteristic meaning that a person is motivated to excel and will pick situations in which success is likely.

Negotiation A conflict management strategy whereby people engage in give-and-take discussions and consider various alternatives to reach a joint decision that is acceptable to both parties.

Neutralizer A situational variable that counteracts a leadership style and prevents the leader from displaying certain behaviors.

New-venture team A unit separate from the mainstream organization that is responsible for initiating and developing innovations.

Nondirective interview An interview where the interviewer asks broad, open-ended questions and permits the applicant to talk freely with minimal interruption, in an attempt to bring to light information, attitudes, and behavioral characteristics that might be concealed when answering structured questions.

Nonprogrammed decision A decision made in response to a situation that is unique, is poorly defined and largely unstructured, and has important consequences for the organization.

Nonverbal communication Communicating through actions, gestures, facial expressions, and behavior rather than through words.

Normative Means that it defines how a manager *should* make logical decisions and provides guidelines for reaching an ideal outcome.

Norming The stage of development in which conflicts are resolved and team harmony and unity emerge.

O

On-the-job-training (OJT) A process in which an experienced employee is asked to teach a new employee how to perform job duties.

Open-book management Allows employees to see for themselves the financial condition of the organization and encourages them to think and act like business owners.

Open communication Sharing all types of information throughout the organization and across functional and hierarchical boundaries.

Open innovation A process where people search for and commercialize innovative ideas beyond the boundaries of the organization.

Operational goal A specific, measurable result that is expected from departments, work groups, and individuals.

Operational plan Specifies the action steps toward achieving operational goals and supports tactical activities.

Operations management The field of management that uses various tools and techniques to ensure that goods and services are produced efficiently and delivered successfully to customers or clients.

Opportunity A situation in which managers see potential organizational accomplishments that exceed current goals.

Organization A social entity that is goal directed and deliberately structured.

Organizational change The adoption of a new idea or behavior by an organization.

Organizational citizenship Work behavior that goes beyond job requirements and contributes as needed to the organization's success.

Organizational commitment Loyalty to and engagement with one's work organization.

Organizational control The systematic process through which managers regulate organizational activities to meet planned goals and standards of performance.

Organizational ecosystem Includes organizations in all the sectors of the task and general environments that provide the resource and information transactions, flows, and linkages necessary for an organization to thrive.

Organizational environment Includes all elements existing outside the boundary of the organization that have the potential to affect the organization.

Organization chart A visual representation of an organization's structure.

Organization development (OD) A planned, systematic process of change that uses behavioral science techniques to improve an organization's health and effectiveness through its ability to cope with environmental changes, improve internal relationships, and increase learning and problem-solving capabilities.

Organization structure The framework in which an organization defines how tasks are divided, resources are deployed, and departments are coordinated.

Organizing The deployment of organizational resources to achieve strategic goals; involves assigning tasks, grouping tasks into departments, and allocating resources.

P

P → O expectancy The expectancy that high performance of a task will lead to the desired outcome.

Panel interview An interview in which the candidate meets with several interviewers who take turns asking questions.

Partnership An unincorporated business owned by two or more people.

Passive follower A person who exhibits neither critical independent thinking nor active participation.

Pay-for-performance Tying at least a portion of compensation to employee effort and performance. Also called *incentive pay*.

People change A change in the attitudes and behaviors of a few employees.

Perception The cognitive process that people use to make sense out of the environment by selecting, organizing, and interpreting information.

Perceptual distortion An error in perceptual judgment that results from inaccuracies in any part of the perception process.

Performance The organization's ability to attain its goals by using resources in an efficient and effective manner.

Performance appraisal The process of observing and evaluating an employee's performance, recording the assessment, and providing feedback.

Performing The stage of development in which team members focus on problem solving and accomplishing the team's assigned task.

Permanent team A group of employees from all functional areas permanently assigned to focus on a specific task or activity.

Personal communication channels Channels that exist outside formally authorized channels and connect people across boundaries for sharing information and accomplishing tasks.

Personality The set of characteristics that underlie a relatively stable pattern of behavior in response to ideas, objects, or people in the environment.

Personal networking The acquisition and cultivation of personal relationships that cross departmental, hierarchical, and even organizational boundaries.

Pivot To change the strategic direction of a business.

Plan A blueprint specifying the resource allocations, schedules, and other actions necessary for attaining goals.

Planning The management function concerned with defining goals for future performance and how to attain them.

Pluralism An environment in which the organization accommodates several subcultures, including employees who would otherwise feel isolated and ignored.

Political force Relates to the influence of political and legal institutions on people and organizations.

Political instability Events such as riots, revolutions, or government upheavals that can affect the operations of an international company.

Political risk A company's risk of loss of assets, earning power, or managerial control due to politically based events or actions by host governments.

Portfolio strategy Pertains to the mix of SBUs and product lines that fit together in a logical way to provide synergy and competitive advantage.

Positive reinforcement The administration of a pleasant and rewarding consequence following a desired behavior.

Power The potential ability to influence the behavior of others.

Power distance The degree to which people accept inequality in power among institutions, organizations, and people.

Practical approach A decision-making approach that sidesteps debates about what is right, good, or just, and bases decisions on the prevailing standards of the profession and the larger society.

Pragmatic survivor A follower who has qualities of all four follower styles, depending on which fits the prevalent situation.

Prejudice The tendency to view people who are different as being deficient.

Pressure group Works within the legal-political framework to influence companies to behave in socially responsible ways.

Problem A situation in which organizational accomplishments have failed to meet established goals.

Procedural justice Holds that rules should be clearly stated and consistently and impartially enforced.

Process layout A facilities layout in which machines that perform the same function are grouped together in one location.

Process theories A set of theories, including goal-setting theory, equity theory, and expectancy theory, which explains how people select behaviors with which to meet their needs and determine whether their choices were successful.

Product change A change in an organization's products or services, such as the Whirlpool two-oven range or the Amazon Kindle Fire.

Product layout A facilities layout in which machines and tasks are arranged according to the sequence of steps in the production of a single product.

Profitability ratio Describes the firm's profits relative to a source of profits, such as sales or assets.

Programmed decision A decision made in response to a situation that has occurred often enough to enable managers to develop decision rules that can be applied in the future.

Project manager A manager who is responsible for a specific work project that involves people from various functions and levels of the organization.

Punishment The imposition of an unpleasant outcome following an undesirable behavior.

Q

Quality circle A total quality management (TQM) technique that involves a group of 6 to 12 volunteer employees who meet regularly to discuss and solve problems affecting the quality of their work.

Quality partnering Involves assigning dedicated personnel within a particular functional area of the business to identify opportunities for quality improvements throughout the work process.

Quants Refers to financial managers and others who make decisions based primarily on complex quantitative analysis.

R

Raw materials inventory Inventory consisting of the basic inputs to the organization's production process.

Realistic job preview Gives applicants all pertinent and realistic information, both positive and negative, about a job and the organization.

Recruiting Activities or practices that define the desired characteristics of applicants for specific jobs. Sometimes called *talent acquisition*.

Reengineering The radical redesign of business processes to achieve dramatic improvements in cost, quality, service, and speed.

Referent power Power that results from characteristics that command subordinates' identification with, respect and admiration for, and desire to emulate the leader.

Refreezing The stage of organization development (OD) where people have incorporated new values, attitudes, and behaviors into their everyday work and the changes become institutionalized in the culture.

Reinforcement Anything that causes a certain behavior to be repeated or inhibited.

Reinforcement theory A theory based on the relationship between a given behavior and its consequences.

Related diversification Moving into a new business that is related to the corporation's existing business activities.

Relational coordination Frequent horizontal coordination and communication carried out through ongoing relationships of shared goals, shared knowledge, and mutual respect.

Relationship conflict Conflict that results from interpersonal incompatibility that creates tension and personal animosity among people.

Responsibility The duty to perform the task or activity that one has been assigned.

Responsibility center Any organizational department or unit under the supervision of a single person who is responsible for its activity.

Reward power Power that results from the authority to bestow rewards.

Revenue budget A budget that lists forecasted and actual revenues of the organization.

Rightsizing Reducing the company's workforce intentionally to the point where the number of employees is deemed right for the company's current situation. Also called *downsizing*.

Risk Means that a decision has clear-cut goals and good information is available, but the future outcomes associated with each alternative are subject to chance.

Risk propensity The willingness to undertake risk with the opportunity of gaining an increased payoff.

Role A set of expectations for one's behavior.

Role ambiguity Uncertainty about what behaviors are expected of a person in a particular role.

Role conflict Incompatible demands of different roles, such as the demands of a manager's superiors conflicting with those of the manager's subordinates.

S

Satisficing Refers to choosing the first alternative that satisfies minimal decision criteria, regardless of whether better solutions are presumed to exist.

Scenario building An approach where managers look at trends and discontinuities and imagine possible alternative futures to build a framework within which unexpected future events can be managed.

Scientific management A subfield of the classical perspective that emphasizes scientifically determined changes in management practices as the solution to improving labor productivity.

Selection The process of assessing the skills, abilities, and other attributes of applicants in an attempt to determine the fit between the job and each applicant's characteristics.

Self-awareness Being conscious of the internal aspects of one's nature, such as personality traits, beliefs, emotions, attitudes, and perceptions, and appreciating how your patterns affect other people.

Self-confidence General assurance in one's own ideas, judgment, and capabilities.

Self-efficacy An individual's strong belief that he or she can successfully accomplish a specific task or outcome.

Self-managed team A team that consists of multiskilled employees who rotate jobs to produce an entire product or service, often led by an elected team member.

Self-management The ability to engage in self-regulating thoughts and behavior to accomplish all your tasks and handle difficult or challenging situations.

Self-serving bias The tendency to overestimate the contribution of internal factors to one's successes and the contribution of external factors to one's failures.

Servant leader A leader who serves others by working to fulfill followers' needs and goals, as well as to achieve the organization's larger mission.

Service organization An organization that produces nonphysical outputs that require customer involvement and cannot be stored in inventory.

Service technology Characterized by intangible outputs and direct contact between employees and customers.

Short-term orientation Reflects a concern with the past and present and a high value on meeting current obligations.

Single-use plan A plan that is developed to achieve a set of goals that is unlikely to be repeated in the future.

Situational model A leadership model that links the leader's behavioral style with the readiness level of followers.

Six Sigma A quality control approach that emphasizes a relentless pursuit of higher quality and lower costs.

Skunkworks A separate informal, highly autonomous, and often secretive group that focuses on breakthrough ideas.

Slogan A phrase, such as Disney's "The happiest place on earth," that succinctly expresses a key corporate value.

Small-batch production A type of manufacturing technology that involves the production of goods in batches of one or a few products designed to customer specification.

Social entrepreneur An entrepreneurial leader who is committed to both good business and changing the world for the better.

Social forces Aspects of a society that guide and influence relationships among people, such as their values, needs, and standards of behavior.

Social learning Using social media tools to network and learn informally.

Social learning theory A theory that proposes that an individual's motivation can result not just from direct experience of rewards and punishments but also from thoughts, beliefs, and observations of other people's behavior.

Social media A group of Internet-based applications that allow the creation and exchange of user-generated content.

Social media programs Include online community pages, social media sites, microblogging platforms, and company online forums that enable managers to interact electronically with employees, customers, partners, and other stakeholders.

Social networking Using peer-to-peer communication channels to interact in an online community, sharing personal and professional information, ideas, and opinions.

Sociocultural dimension Includes demographic characteristics, norms, customs, and values of a population within which the organization operates.

Socioemotional role A team role in which an individual provides support for team members' emotional needs and helps strengthen social unity.

Sole proprietorship An unincorporated for-profit business owned by an individual.

Span of management The number of employees reporting to a supervisor. Sometimes called *span of control.*

Special-purpose team A team created outside the formal structure to undertake a project of special importance, such as developing a new product.

Staff authority The right to advise, counsel, and recommend in the manager's area of expertise.

Stakeholder Any group or person within or outside the organization that has some type of investment or interest in the organization's performance.

Stakeholder mapping A systematic way to identify the expectations, needs, importance, and relative power of various stakeholders.

Standing plan An ongoing plan used to provide guidance for tasks that occur repeatedly in the organization.

Stereotype A rigid, exaggerated, irrational belief associated with a particular group of people.

Stereotype threat Occurs when a person who, when engaged in a task, is aware of a stereotype about his or her identity group suggesting that he or she will not perform well on that task.

Stereotyping A performance evaluation error that occurs when a manager places an employee into a class or category based on one or a few traits or characteristics.

Story A narrative based on true events that is repeated frequently and shared among organizational employees.

Strategic business unit (SBU) A division of the organization that has a unique business, mission, product or service line, competitors, and markets relative to other units of the same organization.

Strategic conversation Dialogue across boundaries and hierarchical levels about the team or organization's vision, critical strategic themes, and the values that help achieve important goals.

Strategic goal A broad statement of where an organization wants to be in the future. Pertains to the organization as a whole rather than to specific divisions or departments.

Strategic issue An event or force that alters an organization's ability to achieve its goals.

Strategic management Refers to the set of decisions and actions used to formulate and implement strategies that will provide a competitively superior fit between an organization and its environment so as to achieve organizational goals.

Strategic plan Action steps by which an organization intends to attain strategic goals.

Strategy A plan of action that describes resource allocation and activities for dealing with the environment, achieving a competitive advantage, and attaining goals.

Strategy execution The stage of strategic management that involves the use of managerial and organizational tools to direct resources toward achieving strategic outcomes.

Strategy formulation The stage of strategic management that includes the planning and decision making that lead to the establishment of the organization's goals and a specific strategic plan.

Strategy map A visual representation of the key drivers of an organization's success, showing the cause-and-effect relationship among goals and plans.

Strengths Natural talents and abilities that have been supported and reinforced with learned knowledge and skills.

Stress A physiological and emotional response to stimuli that place physical or psychological demands on an individual and create uncertainty and lack of personal control when important outcomes are at stake.

Stretch goal A reasonable yet highly ambitious and compelling goal that energizes people and inspires excellence.

Structured interview An interview that uses a set of standardized questions that are asked of every applicant so comparisons can be made easily.

Substitute for leadership A situational variable that makes a leadership style redundant or unnecessary.

Subsystems Parts of a system that depend on one another for their functioning.

Suppliers Provide the raw materials the organization uses to produce its output.

Supply chain management Managing the sequence of suppliers and purchasers, covering all stages of processing from obtaining raw materials to distributing finished goods to consumers.

Survey feedback Where organization development (OD) change agents survey employees to gather their opinions regarding corporate values, leadership, participation, cohesiveness, and other aspects of the organization, then meet with small groups to share the results and brainstorm solutions to problems identified by the results.

Sustainability Economic development that generates wealth and meets the needs of the current population while preserving society and the environment for the needs of future generations.

SWOT analysis An audit or careful examination of *strengths, weaknesses, opportunities,* and *threats* that affect organizational performance.

Symbol An object, act, or event that conveys meaning to others.

Synergy A concept that says that the whole is greater than the sum of its parts.

System A set of interrelated parts that function as a whole to achieve a common purpose.

Systems thinking Looking not just at discrete parts of an organizational situation, but also at the continually changing interactions among the parts.

T

Tactical goal The outcome that major divisions and departments must achieve for an organization to reach its overall goals.

Tactical plan Designed to help execute major strategic plans and to accomplish a specific part of a company's strategy.

Tall structure An organizational structure characterized by an overall narrow span of management and a relatively large number of hierarchical levels.

Task conflict Conflict that results from disagreements about the goals to be achieved or the content of the tasks to be performed.

Task environment Includes the sectors that conduct day-to-day transactions with the organization and directly influence its basic operations and performance.

Task specialist role A team role in which an individual devotes personal time and energy to helping the team accomplish its activities and reach its goal.

Team A unit of two or more people who interact and coordinate their work to accomplish a goal to which they are committed and hold themselves mutually accountable.

Team-based structure A structure in which an entire organization is made up of horizontal teams that coordinate their activities and work directly with customers to accomplish organizational goals.

Team building An organization development (OD) intervention that enhances cohesiveness by helping groups of people learn to work together as a team.

Team cohesiveness The extent to which team members are attracted to the team and motivated to remain a part of it.

Team norm An informal standard of conduct that is shared by team members and guides their behavior.

Technical complexity The degree to which complex machinery is involved in the production process to the exclusion of people.

Technical core The heart of the organization's production of its product or service.

Technical skill The understanding of and proficiency in the performance of specific tasks.

Technological dimension In the general environment, includes scientific and technological advances in society.

Technology change A change in production processes—how an organization does its work.

Telecommuting Using computers and telecommunications equipment to perform work from home or another remote location.

360-degree feedback Uses multiple raters, including self-rating, to appraise employee performance and guide development.

Thriving workforce A workforce in which people are satisfied, productive, and engaged in creating the future for themselves and their organization.

Tolerance for ambiguity The psychological characteristic that allows a person to be untroubled by disorder and uncertainty.

Top-down budgeting Means that the budgeted amounts for the coming year

are literally imposed on middle- and lower-level managers.

Top leader In a matrix structure, the person who oversees both the product and the functional chains of command and is responsible for the entire matrix.

Top manager A manager who is at the top of the organizational hierarchy and is responsible for the entire organization.

Total quality management (TQM) Focuses on managing the total organization to deliver quality to customers.

Traits Distinguishing personal characteristics, such as intelligence, self-confidence, energy, and independence.

Transactional leader A leader who clarifies subordinates' roles and task requirements, initiates structure, provides rewards, and displays consideration for followers.

Transformational leader A leader distinguished by a special ability to bring about innovation and change by creating an inspiring vision, shaping values, building relationships, and providing meaning for followers.

Transnational strategy A strategy that combines global coordination to attain efficiency with local flexibility to meet needs in different countries.

Triple bottom line Refers to measuring the organization's financial performance, social performance, and environmental performance.

Two-boss employee In a matrix structure, a person who reports to two supervisors simultaneously.

Type A behavior Behavior characterized by extreme competitiveness, impatience, aggressiveness, and devotion to work.

Type B behavior A behavior pattern that reflects few of the Type A characteristics and includes a more balanced, relaxed approach to life.

U

Uncertainty Occurs when managers know which goals they want to achieve, but information about alternatives and future events is incomplete.

Uncertainty avoidance Characterized by people's intolerance for uncertainty and ambiguity and resulting support for beliefs that promise certainty and conformity.

Uncritical thinking Failing to consider the possibilities beyond what one is told, accepting others' ideas without thinking.

Unfreezing The stage of organization development (OD) in which people are made aware of problems and the need for change.

Unrelated diversification Refers to expanding into totally new lines of business.

Upward communication Messages that flow from the lower to the higher levels in the organization's hierarchy.

Utilitarian approach A method of ethical decision making saying that the ethical choice is the one that produces the greatest good for the greatest number.

V

Valence The value of outcomes (rewards) to the individual.

Venture capital firm A group of companies or individuals that invests money in new or expanding businesses for ownership and potential profits.

Vertical integration A strategy of expanding into businesses that either provide the supplies needed to make products or distribute and sell the company's products.

Vicarious learning Learning that occurs when an individual sees others perform certain behaviors and get rewarded for them.

Virtual network structure An organizational structure in which the organization subcontracts most of its major functions to separate companies and coordinates their activities from a small headquarters organization.

Virtual team A team made up of members who are geographically or organizationally dispersed, rarely meet face to face, and interact to accomplish their work primarily using advanced information and telecommunications technologies.

Vision An attractive, ideal future that is credible yet not readily attainable.

W

Wage and salary survey A survey that shows what other organizations pay incumbents in jobs that match a sample of key jobs selected by the organization.

Whistle-blowing The disclosure by employees of unethical, illegitimate, or illegal practices by an organization.

Wholly owned foreign affiliate A foreign subsidiary over which an organization has complete control.

Work-in-process inventory Inventory composed of the materials that still are moving through the stages of the production process.

Work redesign Altering jobs to increase both the quality of employees' work experience and their productivity.

Work sample test A test given to applicants for frontline positions to evaluate their performance in completing simulated tasks that are a part of the job.

Work specialization The degree to which organizational tasks are subdivided into individual jobs. Sometimes called *division of labor*.

Z

Zero-based budgeting An approach to planning and decision making that requires a complete justification for every line item in a budget, instead of carrying forward a prior budget and applying a percentage change.

Name Index

Company Index

Subject Index